AUSTRALIAN DICTIONARY
OF BIOGRAPHY

Editors

JOHN RITCHIE

DIANE LANGMORE

AUSTRALIAN DICTIONARY OF BIOGRAPHY

VOLUME 16 : 1940-1980

Pik - Z

General Editor
JOHN RITCHIE

Deputy General Editor
DI LANGMORE

MELBOURNE UNIVERSITY PRESS

MELBOURNE UNIVERSITY PRESS
(an imprint of Melbourne University Publishing)
PO Box 1167, Carlton, Victoria 3053, Australia
mup-info@unimelb.edu.au
www.mup.com.au

First published 2002

Text © Melbourne University Publishing 2002
Design and typography © Melbourne University Publishing 2002

Typeset by Syarikat Seng Teik Sdn. Bhd., Malaysia
Printed in Australia by Brown Prior Anderson

National Library of Australia Cataloguing-in-Publication entry

Australian dictionary of biography. Volume 16, 1940–1980,
   Pik–Z.
   ISBN 0 522 84236 4 (set).
   ISBN 0 522 84997 0.
   1. Australia—Biography—Dictionaries. 2. Australia—
   History—1945– —Biography. I. Ritchie, John, 1941–.
   II. Langmore, Diane.
920.094

PREFACE

Six hundred and seventy-three individuals with surnames from Pike to Zinnbauer are included in Volume 16 of the *Australian Dictionary of Biography*. Fittingly, the first entry in the volume is Douglas Pike, the project's founding editor. The last is Alfred Freund Zinnbauer, a Viennese-born pastor and one of many Europeans of Jewish origin whose escape from Nazism is chronicled in the present series of volumes. Between them is a host of men and women from all walks of life who died in the years from 1940 to 1980. The 673 entries have been written by 569 authors. It is the fourth and final volume for this period.

Incorporating the lives of some 2700 individuals, volumes 13 to 16 illustrate such topics as immigration, accelerating industrialism, urbanization and suburbanization, and war (World War II, Korea, Malaya and Vietnam). While other themes are also illuminated—material progress, increasing cultural maturity, conservative and radical politics, conflict and harmony, loss of isolation and innocence—the emphasis of the biographies is on the individuals. The entries throw light on the complexity of the human situation, and on the greatness and the littleness of moral response and actual behaviour which this can evoke. The subjects of Volume 16 range in lifespan from Peter Santo, an indentured labourer who arrived in Queensland from the New Hebrides in 1888 and died in 1966 aged about 105, to Catherine Warnes, a 19-year-old entertainer killed in Vietnam in 1969. Although the majority of men and women included in this volume flourished in the 1940-1980 period, a minority of the lives, such as those of John Shephard, a manufacturing engineer born in 1852, Isaac Selby, a writer born in 1859, or Isabella Bruce Reid, born in 1878 and reputed to be the world's first female veterinarian, reveal facets of Australian history long before 1940.

The two volumes of the 1788-1850 section of the *A.D.B.*, the four of the 1851-1890 section and the six of the 1891-1939 section were published between 1966 and 1990. Volumes 13, 14 and 15, the first three of the 1940-1980 section, were published in 1993, 1996 and 2000 respectively. Douglas Pike was general editor for volumes 1 to 5, Bede Nairn for volume 6, Nairn and Geoffrey Serle for volumes 7 to 10, Serle for volume 11, and John Ritchie for volumes 12 to 15. An index to volumes 1-12 was published in 1991, and the *A.D.B.* was produced on CD-ROM in 1996. The chronological division was designed to simplify production. 7211 entries have been included in volumes 1-12 (volumes 1-2, for 1788-1850, had 1116 entries; volumes 3-6, for 1851-1890, 2053; volumes 7-12, for 1891-1939, 4042). For the three sections between 1788 and 1939, the placing of each individual's name was determined by when he/she did his/her most important work (*floruit*). In contrast, the 1940-1980 section only includes individuals who died in this period. The 'date of death' principle will be maintained in future volumes. Work has begun on Volume 17, the first of two volumes covering the period 1981-1990.

The choice of subjects for inclusion in this volume required prolonged consultation. After quotas were estimated, working parties in each State, and the Armed Services and Commonwealth working parties, prepared provisional lists which were widely circulated and carefully amended. Many individuals were obviously significant and worthy of inclusion as leaders in politics, business, the armed services, the church, the professions, the arts and the labour movement. Some have been included as representatives of ethnic and social minorities, and of a wide range of occupations;

others have found a place as innovators, notorieties or eccentrics. A number had to be omitted through pressure of space or lack of material, and thereby joined the great mass whose members richly deserve a more honoured place, but thousands of these names, and information about them, have been gathered in the biographical register at the A.D.B.'s headquarters at the Australian National University.

Most authors were nominated by working parties. The burden of writing has been shared almost equally by the staff of universities and by a variety of other specialists.

The *A.D.B.* is a project based on consultation and co-operation. The Research School of Social Sciences at the A.N.U. has borne the cost of the headquarters staff, of much research and of occasional special contingencies, while other Australian universities have supported the project in numerous ways. The *A.D.B.*'s policies were initially determined by a national committee composed mainly of representatives from the departments of history in each Australian university. That committee's successor, the editorial board, has kept in touch with historians at many universities, and with working parties, librarians, archivists and other local experts, as well as with research assistants in each Australian capital city and correspondents abroad. With such varied support, the *A.D.B.* is truly a national project.

ACKNOWLEDGMENTS

The Australian Dictionary of Biography is a programme fully supported by the Research School of Social Sciences at the Australian National University. Special thanks are due to Professor Jill Roe for guidance as chair of the editorial board, and to Professor I. McAllister, director of the R.S.S.S., and Mrs Pauline Hore, formerly the school's business manager. Those who helped in planning the shape of the work have been mentioned in earlier volumes.

Within Australia the A.D.B. is indebted to many librarians and archivists, schools, colleges, universities, institutes, historical and genealogical societies, and numerous other organizations; to the National Library of Australia, the Australian War Memorial, the Commonwealth Scientific and Industrial Research Organization, the Australian Institute of Aboriginal and Torres Strait Islander Studies and the National Archives of Australia; to the archives and public records offices in the various States and Territories, and to registrars of probates and of the Supreme and Family courts, whose co-operation has solved many problems; to various town and shire clerks; to the Returned & Services League of Australia, the Australian Department of Defence and State education departments; to the Australian Broadcasting Corporation, the Australian Political Studies Association, the New South Wales College of Nursing, the Nurses Registration Board, the Pharmaceutical Society of Australia, the Marist Fathers, the Marist Sisters, the Missionaries of the Sacred Heart and St Paul's Library, the Religious Society of Friends, the Rosicrucian Order, Royal Prince Alfred Hospital, Royal Alexander Hospital for Children, Royal Hospital for Women, St Luke's Hospital, Potts Point, Tresillian Family Care Centres, Chartered Secretaries, Australia, the Sydney Cricket and Sports Ground Trust and the Australian Hereford Association, all in Sydney, and to the Aberdeen Angus Cattle Society, Armidale, New South Wales; to the Association of Sculptors, Victoria, the Australian Institute of Management and Public Administration, the Federal Institute of Accountants, the Royal Humane Society of Australasia, the St John Ambulance (Victoria), the Australian Red Cross, the Melbourne Club, the Australian Music Examinations Board, the Royal Victorian Institute for the Blind, the Austin and Repatriation Medical Centre, the B.H.P. archives, all in Melbourne, and the Great Western Race Club, Victoria; to the Australian College of Education, the Australian Institute of International Affairs, the Institution of Engineers, Australia, and the Australian Institute of Building, all in Canberra; to the Queensland Teachers' Union, Brisbane, and the Tully District Hospital, Queensland; to the Law Society of South Australia, Adelaide, the Historical Society of Katherine, Northern Territory, and the Queen Victoria Museum and Art Gallery, Launceston, Tasmania.

Warm thanks for the free gift of their time and talents are due to contributors, to members of the editorial board and to the working parties. For particular advice the A.D.B. owes much to Molly Angel, Bob Douglas, John Dowie, Justin Corfield, Bill Gammage, Helga Griffin, Ian Hancock, Ken Inglis, John Molony, Hank Nelson and F. B. Smith.

Essential assistance with birth, death and marriage certificates has been provided by the co-operation of registrars in New South Wales, Queensland, South Australia, Tasmania, Victoria, Western Australia, the Northern Territory and the Australian Capital Territory; by the General Register offices in London and Edinburgh; by the

ACKNOWLEDGMENTS

registrars-general in Papua New Guinea and Malaysia; by the Public Registry, Valetta, Malta; by the mayor of Chantilly, France; by the civil registration offices in The Hague; by the National State Archives, Belgium; by the consul-general for Poland in Sydney, and by the consul for Italy in Adelaide; by the Austrian, Belgian, Brazilian, Egyptian, Greek, Hungarian, Italian, Netherlands, Pakistan and Thai embassies, and the British, Indian, South African, and Zimbabwe high commissions, Canberra.

For other assistance overseas, thanks are due to Judith Farrington, London, William Murphy, Dublin, Betty Iggo, Edinburgh, and Roger Joslyn, New York; to the universities of Birmingham, Cambridge, Durham, Leeds, Liverpool, London, Manchester and Oxford, and to Jesus College, Christ's College, and Gonville and Caius College, Cambridge, and Oriel College, Oxford, England; to the universities of Aberdeen, Edinburgh and St Andrew's, Scotland; to the University of Aberystwyth, Wales, to the National University of Ireland, Dublin; to Technische Universität, Berlin, and Bayerische-Julius-Maximilian-Universität, Wurzburg, Germany; to the Graduate Institute of International Studies, Geneva; to Columbia University, New York, Harvard University, Cambridge, and Springfield College, Springfield, Massachusetts, Michigan Technological University, and the universities of Washington and Indiana, U.S.A.; and to the universities of Canterbury and Otago, New Zealand.

Gratitude is also due to Trinity College of Music, the Central St Martin's College of Art and Design, the Royal College of Physicians, the Royal College of Surgeons of England, the Royal Humane Society, the Royal Geographical Society, the Royal Anthropological Institute of Great Britain and Ireland, the Zoological Society of London, the Royal Philatelic Society, the Royal Institute of British Architects, the Institution of Civil Engineers, the Ministry of Defence, the Naval Historical Branch and the Air Historical Branch, R.A.F., all in London; to the Institute of Actuaries, Oxford, England; to the Secretariat of the Chapter of Orders, Copenhagen; to the Österreichisches Staatarchiv, Vienna; and to the New Zealand Defence Force, Wellington; to the staffs of the *Northern Territory Dictionary of Biography*, *Österreichisches Biographisches Lexikon*, Vienna, *Dictionary of Canadian Biography*, Toronto, and *Dictionary of New Zealand Biography*, Wellington, and to other individuals and institutions who have co-operated with the A.D.B.

The A.D.B. deeply regrets the deaths of such notable contributors as E. M. Andrews, J. M. Antill, H. W. Arndt, John Béchervaise, H. C. Bolton, D. F. Bourke, Donald Bradman, F. Brown, Graeme Bucknall, J. V. Byrnes, A. W. Campbell, Nancy Cato, R. J. K. Chapman, Brian Clerehan, Kay Daniels, R. A. Douglas, C. J. Duffy, Geoffrey Dutton, Ronald East, H. Vaughan Evans, Audrey Ferguson, R. A. Ferrall, Cedric Flower, G. J. Fraenkel, A. D. Garrison, K. E. Gill, C. J. M. Glover, L. Goldberg, John Griffith, R. M. Hague, Dorothy Helmrich, J. P. Holroyd, C. J. Horne, W. J. Hudson, John V. Hurley, J. Keith Jarrot, Lorna M. Jolly, John D. Keating, E. F. Kunz, P. N. Lamb, Godfrey Laurie, C. J. Lloyd, Judith Wright McKinney, Ian F. McLaren, J. F. McMahon, A. W. Martin, P. E. Maskell, Elyne Mitchell, Francis Robert Moulds, D. M. Myers, K. B. Noad, William N. Oats, Harold Perkins, O. H. K. Spate, G. T. Stilwell, Jacqueline Templeton, P. V. Vernon, D. F. Waterhouse, D. B. Webster, Peter Westcott, E. T. Williams, June C. Warrillow-Williams, Paul D. Wilson, A. T. Yarwood.

Grateful acknowledgment is due to the director and staff of Melbourne University Press, to Chris Coulthard-Clark, Gillian O'Loghlin, Sally O'Neill, Sue Graham-Taylor and Fay Woodhouse who worked for the A.D.B. while Volume 16 was being produced, and to Robert O'Neill and Ross Johnston for twenty-five years' and fifteen years' service respectively as section editors.

The A.D.B. expresses its deep appreciation of financial assistance from Mrs Caroline Simpson of Sydney and the Myer Foundation, Melbourne, which helped in the production of this volume.

WORKING PARTIES

Armed Services
Peter Burness, C. D. Clark, John Coates, Alec Hill, David Horner (chair), John McCarthy, Perditta McCarthy, Philip Mulcare, Anthony Staunton, Alan Stephens, D. Stevens, A. J. Sweeting.

Commonwealth
Nicholas Brown, David Carment, Patricia Clarke, Bill Gammage, Tom Griffiths (chair), Robert Hyslop, Graeme Powell, Libby Robin, John Thompson.

New South Wales
J. J. Carmody, C. Cunneen, R. Curnow, F. Farrell, S. Garton, Bridget Griffen-Foley, E. M. Goot, Warwick Hirst, Beverley Kingston (chair), J. K. McLaughlin, A. J. Moore, N. B. Nairn, Heather Radi, Jill Roe, Dagmar Schmidmaier, A. Ventress.

Queensland
Pat Buckridge (chair), M. D. Cross, Kay Ferres, Richard Fotheringham, M. W. French, Jennifer Harrison, I. F. Jobling, Lorna McDonald, Belinda McKay, Dawn May, Olivia Robinson, S. J. Routh, Joanne Scott, C. G. Sheehan.

South Australia
R. André, J. Bannon, Joyce Gibberd, R. M. Gibbs, P. A. Howell (chair), Helen Jones, J. H. Love, Judith Raftery, Jenny Tilby Stock, Patricia Stretton.

Tasmania
G. P. R. Chapman, Shirley Eldershaw, Margaret Glover, Elizabeth McLeod, S. Petrow, Anne Rand, O. M. Roe (chair), J. A. Taylor.

Victoria
J. Arnold, G. R. Browne, Mimi Colligan, B. J. Costar, Jim Davidson, D. Dunstan, F. J. Kendall, J. F. Lack (chair), P. Love, Janet McCalman, R. A. Murray, J. R. Poynter, Carolyn Rasmussen, J. D. Rickard, Judith Smart, F. Strahan.

Western Australia
Wendy Birman, D. Black, G. C. Bolton (chair), Michal Bosworth, Dorothy Erickson, Charles Fox, Sue Graham-Taylor, Jenny Gregory, Lenore Layman, John McIlwraith, Jenny Mills, Jill Milroy, C. Mulcahy, Jan Ryan, Tom Stannage.

AUTHORS

ABBOTT, Jacqueline:
Stokes, Sir H.
ADAIR, Daryl:
Scarfe.
ALLPORT, Carolyn:
Ryan, M.
ANDRÉ, Roger:
Symes, G.
ANDREWS, E. M.*:
Wells, Sir H.
ANGUS, Beverley M.:
Roberts, F. H.
ARMSTRONG, Judith:
Tritton.
ATCHISON, John:
Shand, D.
ATKINSON, Anne:
Yuen.
AUDLEY, R. M.:
Winsor.

BAIN, Jim:
Utz.
BANNON, J. C.:
Walsh, F.
BARKER, Heather:
Smith, A. V.
BARNETT, P. J.:
Stephenson.
BAUER, Gaston·
Wood, P.
BAXTER, Carol J.:
Sandford.
BEBBINGTON, Warren A.:
Prerauer.
BECERRA, Poppy Biazos:
Sodersten.
BELLIS, Clare:
Sneddon.
BENNET, Darryl:
Rogers, J.; Steele; Stevens, D.; Woodward.
BENNETT, J. M.:
Snelling; Street, Sir K.
BENNETT, Scott:
Townley.
BERESFORD, Quentin:
Wallwork.
BERSTEN, Ian J.:
Repin.
BERTOLA, Patrick:
Telfer, A.
BEST, Yeola:
Smith, C.
BETTISON, Margaret:
Spencer, G.

BIDDINGTON, Judith:
Sandes.
BIRMAN, Wendy:
Plowman, E.; Prevost; Robertson, A.
BLAAZER, D. P.:
Vanthoff.
BLACK, David:
Watts, A.
BLACKLEY, Leanne L.:
Quirk.
BLUNDELL, Valda J.:
Umbagai.
BOADLE, Donald:
Turnbull, Sir W.
BODDINGTON, Jennie:
Wilson, L.
BOLTON, G. C.:
Pilpel; Pollak; Prescott; Tomlinson; Uren.
BOLTON, H. C.*:
Shephard.
BONGIORNO, Frank:
Riley, F.; Rosevear.
BONNIN, Nancy:
Tullipan.
BOTT, Tony:
Stevens, G.; Stuckey.
BOXALL, Helen:
Rowe, F.
BOYCE, Peter:
Rossiter.
BOYLE, Janice:
Scully.
BOYLE, Michael:
Stevens, Sir J.
BRADBURY, Keith:
Sheldon, E. & E.; Simmonds, R.
BRANAGAN, D. F.:
Raggatt; Read; Watson, G.; Williams, G.
BRAZIER, Jan:
Walkom.
BREWARD, Ian:
Watson, A.
BRIDGE, Carl:
Skipper.
BRODRICK, Lloyd:
Tonkin; Weston, J.
BROOME, Richard:
Sands, D.; Wallis; Williams, M.
BROUGHTON, Lindsay:
Richmond.
BROWN, Elaine:
Russell, N.
BROWN, Malcolm:
Roberts, M.; Taylor, J.

BROWN, Nicholas:
  Till.
BROWN, Patricia:
  Samson.
BROWNE, Geoff:
  Spicer; Thompson, J. T.; Tipper, A.
BRUCE, Robin:
  White, M.
BUCKRIDGE, Patrick:
  Truebridge.
BUNDOCK, Anthea:
  Taylor, L.
BURNESS, Peter:
  Sykes.
BYGOTT, Ursula:
  Telfer, M.
BYRNE, Dianne:
  Rosenstengel.

CABLE, K. J.:
  Waldock.
CAIN, John:
  Smithers.
CALABY, Matthew:
  Thorpe, F. G.
CAMPION, Edmund:
  Rumble.
CANNON, Michael:
  Slater.
CAREY, Hilary M.:
  Reid, E.
CAREY, P. R.:
  Sherlock.
CARMAN-BROWN, Lesley:
  Robertson, T.
CARMODY, John:
  Prerauer; Richardson, P.
CARRIGAN, Belinda:
  Webb, A.
CASHMAN, R. I.:
  Squire; Szabados; Young, W.
CHAPMAN, Richard E.:
  Whitehouse.
CHARLTON, Peter:
  Richards, H.
CHUA, Cathy:
  Sullivan, M.
CLARK, Mary Ryllis
  Robertson, E.
CLARKE, Patricia:
  Woodger.
CLEMENT, Cathie:
  Quilty.
CLIFFORD, H. Trevor:
  White-Haney.
CLODE, Danielle:
  Wakefield.
CLOSE, Cecily:
  Thorpe, D.
CLUNE, David:
  Sheahan; Stewart, F. E.
COBCROFT, M. D.:
  Welch.

COHEN, Kay:
  Trout.
COLEMAN, Peter:
  Scorfield.
COLLINS PERSSE, Michael D. de B.:
  Slim.
COLLINS, Diane:
  Post; Sverjensky.
CONNELL, W. F.:
  Radford.
CONNOR, John:
  Winning, R.
CONNORS, Jane:
  Vernon.
CONSANDINE, Marion:
  Varley, G.
COOK, Margaret:
  Stewart, C.
COPPEL, Stephen:
  Spowers, E.; Syme, E.
COSGROVE, Betty:
  Streeten; Voss.
COSTAR, B. J.:
  Rylah; Warner.
COSTIGAN, Michael:
  Simonds.
COULTHARD-CLARK, C. D.:
  Pither; Pollard; Wrigley.
COWAN, Henry J.:
  Priddle.
CRAFTER, Greg:
  Taylor, D. I.
CRESWELL, C. C.:
  Waugh.
CROSS, Manfred:
  Schmella.
CROUCH, Bruce:
  Tully.
CUNNEEN, Chris:
  Spencer, F.; Wakehurst.
CURNOW, Greg:
  Vale, M. M.
CURNOW, Jill:
  Rennie.
CURNOW, Ross:
  Woolacott; Wurth.
CURTHOYS, Patricia:
  Vickery, E.

D'APRANO, Zelda:
  Williams, K.
DAMOUSI, Joy:
  Vasey, J.; Wearne.
DANAHER, P. A.:
  Symes, P.
DARLING, Elaine:
  Wilding.
DAVIDSON, Ron:
  Sleep.
DAVIES, Elizabeth:
  Tooth.
DAVISON, Graeme:
  Tipping.

GARTON, Stephen:
Swanton; Yeo.
GASCOIGNE, S. C. B.:
Rimmer.
GAYNOR, Andrea:
Rutherford.
GIBBERD, Joyce:
Rymill, S. & H.
GIBBS, R. M.:
Richardson, A.
GIBSON-WILDE, Dorothy:
Priestley, H.
GIFFORD, Peter:
Sayers; Shackleton.
GILL, J. C. H.*:
Veitch.
GILLESPIE, James:
White, J.
GLADSTONES, John:
Smart.
GOAD, Philip:
Seabrook, N.
GODDEN, Judith:
Zepps.
GOLDER, Hilary:
Stonham.
GOLDRICK, J. V. P.:
Waller, H.
GOLLAN, Anne:
Simmonds, K.
GOOT, Murray:
Rubensohn.
GORDON, Harry:
Stedman.
GORRELL, Julie:
Sawyer.
GORRELL, Richard:
Turner, W.
GOVOR, Elena:
Putilin.
GOWER, S. N.:
Ramsay, Sir A.
GOWERS, Richard:
Tipper, J.
GRAHAME, Rachel:
Sherrard; Stelzer.
GRANT, Donald:
Ronan.
GRAY, Geoffrey:
Riley, A.
GREEN, Guy:
Rowallan.
GREVILLE, P. J.:
Reinhold; Secombe.
GREY, Jeffrey:
Robertson, Sir H.
GRIFFEN-FOLEY, Bridget:
Prior; Watson, J. K.
GRIFFITHS, Tom:
Stretton.
GUEST, J. S.:
Trumble.

* deceased

HAINES, Gregory:
Sissons; Stanton.
HALDANE, Robert:
Salisbury.
HALE, Patricia:
Rowe, O.
HAMMETT, Jenny:
West, E.
HANCOCK, I. R.:
Ritchie, Sir T.
HARCOURT, G. C.:
Russell, E.
HARDY, J. S.:
Swanson.
HARFORD, Jane:
Swift, Sir B. & N.
HARLOW, Sue:
Zimin.
HARMSTORF, Ian:
Schulz.
HARPER, Marjorie:
Tucker, G.
HARPER, Melissa:
Waters, W.
HARRISON, Jennifer:
Pike, L.
HASKELL, Dennis:
Slessor.
HAZLEHURST, Cameron:
Whitlam.
HEAGNEY, Brenda:
Reye.
HEATHCOTE, R. L.:
Price.
HELSON, Peter:
Swan.
HENDERSON, P. G. F.:
Strutt.
HERMANN, Elfriede:
Yali.
HESELTINE, H. P.:
Webb, F.
HICKS, Neville:
Swift, Sir B. & N.
HILL, A. J.:
Rowell; Wootten.
HILL, M. R.:
Richardson, E.
HINDMARSH, Laurie:
Rickard.
HOGAN, Michael:
Robson, E.
HOLDEN, Colin:
Sambell.
HOLLAND, H. G.:
Ritchie, E.
HOLLAND, Robert A. B.:
Starr.
HOME, R. W.:
Roberts, J.; Rogers, J. S.
HOOKER, Claire:
Vickery, J.
HOOPER, Beverley:
Steinberg.

HOPLEY, J. B.:
Stevenson.
HORNE, Julia:
Quentin.
HORNER, David:
Shedden; Vasey, G.
HORNER, Jolyon:
Simpson, W.
HOWARD, Graham:
Stewart, M.
HOWARD, Keith D.:
Thornton, A.
HOWELL, P. A.:
Riddle, A. & D.; Smith, S. T.
HOWIE-WILLIS, Ian:
Willis.
HUDSON, David:
Walker, B.
HUGGONSON, David:
Stanley; Waters, D.
HUGHES, Jackson:
Whitelaw.
HUMPHREYS, L. R.:
Summerville; Wadham.
HUNT, Jane E.:
Weston, N.
HURLEY, Frank:
Stevens, J. H.
HURLEY, John V.*:
Upjohn.
HURST, Doug:
Wiggins.
HYSLOP, Robert:
Sinclair.

INDER, Stuart:
Tier.
INGLIS, K. S.:
Rivett.
IRVING, T. H.:
Plowman, Sir C.; Scott Griffiths.

JAMES, Neil:
Rogers, J. D.
JAMES, Stephen:
White, Sir A. & E.
JAMIESON, Suzanne:
Winter.
JEBB, Mary Anne:
Smith, D.; Umbagai.
JENKIN, John:
Wood, E.
JENNINGS, Reece:
Stott.
JENNINGS, Rosemary:
Provan.
JETSON, Tim:
Sherriff.
JOHNSON, Heather:
Young, J.
JOHNSTON, Mark:
Porter.

* deceased

JONES, Barry O.:
Wilson, A.
JONES, Helen:
Thomas, K.
JONES, Philip:
Strehlow.

KADIBA, John:
Webb, T.
KEATING, Gavin Michael:
Savige.
KELLY, Brian:
Simpson, R.
KELLY, Farley:
Wisewould.
KENDALL, F. J.:
Solly.
KENNY, Geoffrey:
Wilkinson, H. J.
KENT, Christopher J.:
Shillito.
KENT, Hilary:
Sutcliffe.
KERIN, Sitarani:
Vroland, A. & A.
KINGSLAND, Richard:
Ryland.
KINGSTON, Beverley:
Tearle; White, A.
KIRKPATRICK, Peter:
Thompson, J. J.
KIRKPATRICK, Rod:
Westacott.
KIRSOP, Wallace:
Thompson, F. W.
KISS, R.:
West, R.
KYLE, Nocline J.:
Robinson, J.

LACK, John:
Shepherd, A.; Siddons; Storey; Wang; Wilson, J.
LAMB, Tony:
Wilson, A.
LANGMORE, Diane:
Ryan, R. S.; Whitehead.
LATREILLE, Anne:
Stones.
LAVERTY, John:
Ringrose; Thatcher.
LAWRENCE, T. F. C.:
Upton.
LAWSON, Valerie:
Williamson, A.
LAWTON, Colin:
Stirling, K.
LAYMAN, Lenore:
Reid, Sir A.
LEE, David:
Shaw, Sir P.
LEVI, J. S.:
Sanger.

LINDSAY, Neville:
Watson, J. Alexander.
LINN, R. W.:
Stobie.
LITHGOW,Shirley:
Seton.
LLOYD, C. J.*:
Pratt; Rodgers.
LLOYD, Peter L.:
Veitch.
LONDEY, Peter:
Selby, A.
LONERAGAN, Jack F.:
Teakle.
LONG, Jeremy:
Raiwala.
LONGHURST, Robert I.:
Poulson; Small.
LOVE, J. H.:
Priestley, J.; Wilson, Sir T.
LOVE, Peter:
Stout.
LUDBROOK, Juliet:
Walton.
LUPTON, Roger:
Rowntree.

MCALLESTER, James C.:
Thomson, E.
MCBURNIE, Grant:
Wallace, V.
MCCALMAN, Janet:
Simpson, G.
MCCARTHY, Janice:
Sage.
MCCARTHY, John:
Scherf.
MCCARTHY, Louella:
Wolinski.
MCCARTHY, Perditta M.:
Shumack.
MCCAUGHEY, Davis:
Yarnold.
MCCONVILLE, Kieran:
Sparkes.
MCCORKINDALE, Shirley:
Stapleton.
MACDONALD, Graham:
Sands, J.
MCDONALD, Lorna:
Vallis, R. & E.
MCDONALD, Neil:
Wilmot.
MCGINNESS, Mark:
Tanner.
MCGRATH, Sophie:
Scollen; Vale, M.
MCILWRAITH, John:
Raine.
MCINTYRE, Darryl:
Winning, N.
MACINTYRE, Stuart:
Sharkey; Troy.
* deceased

MCKAY, Gary:
Scott.
MCLAUGHLIN, John Kennedy:
Walsh, Sir C.
MCLENNAN, N. T.:
Van de Velde.
MCMULLIN, Ross:
Ward, E.
MCPHERSON, Mary:
Riddell; Savage; Tierney.
MAGUIRE, Carmel:
Remington.
MAHER, Brian:
Thompson, J. C.
MAIN, A. R.:
Waring.
MANSFIELD, Joan:
Thom.
MARCUS, Julie:
Pink.
MARKEY, Ray:
Schreiber.
MARSDEN, Susan:
Ramsay, A. M.
MARTYR, Philippa:
Walsh, A.
MASSAM, Katharine:
Prendiville.
MAY, Dawn:
Sunners.
MENNIS, Mary R.:
Ross.
MERRETT, D. T.:
Wilson, E. J.
MERRILLEES, R. S.:
Stewart, J.
MESSENGER, Dally:
Whitta.
MILLER, David Philip:
Sutherland.
MILLIKEN, Robert:
Rabin; Roxon.
MILLS, Jenny:
Sandover; Stoate.
MOIR, R. J.:
Underwood.
MOLONY, John N.:
Seiffert.
MOORE, Andrew:
Prentice; Revell; Stokes, S.
MOORE, Clive R.:
Santo.
MOORE, Felicity St J.:
Vassilieff.
MORISON, Ian W.:
Rudduck; Stockdill.
MORONEY, Tim:
Rymer.
MORPHY, Howard:
Thomson, D.
MOULDS, Francis Robert*:
Semmens.
* deceased

xvi

MOYAL, Ann:
Witt.
MOYE, Ros:
Ramsden.
MULCAHY, Clement:
Teasdale.
MULLER, H. Konrad:
Wilhelm.
MURRAY, Maree:
Roughley; Whitley, G.
MURRAY, Robert:
Russell, R.; Thornton, E.; Wagstaff; Weeks.
MYER, Rod:
Smorgon.

NADEL, Dave:
Warne-Smith.
NAIRN, Bede:
Pike, D.
NASH, David:
Ward, M.
NELSON, H. N.:
Robinson, A.
NISSEN, Judith A.:
Willmore.
NOBBS, Raymond:
Vaughan.
NOBLE, Jennifer:
Wheller.
NORTHEY, R. E.:
van Otterloo.

O'BRIEN, Michael:
Walker, T.
O'BRIEN, Philippa:
Skinner.
O'CARRIGAN, Catherine:
Wilson, E.
O'CONNOR, T. M.:
Thompson, L.
O'DONNELL, Dan:
Zerner.
O'NEIL, Bernard:
Ward, L.
O'NEILL, Sally:
Sainthill.
OLIVER, Bobbie:
Schnaars.
OPPENHEIMER, Jillian:
Wright, P.
OPPENHEIMER, Melanie:
Robertson, P.
OSBORNE, Graeme:
Seyler.

PALMER, David:
Wills.
PARR, Peter:
Purdy.
PARSONS, George:
White, C.
PASH, J. H.:
West, R. A.

PATMORE, Greg:
Walker, C.
PATON, Simon:
Sparkes.
PEARCE, Barry:
Strachan; Thomas, L.
PEERS, Juliet:
Wentcher.
PEGGIE, Ian D.:
Tindale.
PEGRUM, Roger:
Whitley, C.
PELVIN, Richard:
Rankin, R.
PERKINS, John:
Rydge.
PERRY, Warren:
Wynter.
PERSSE, Jonathan W. de B.:
Riley, B.
PETTIT, G. E.:
Pinner.
PHILLIPS, Harry C. J.:
Watson, Sir H.
PITCHFORD, John:
Salter.
POMEROY, John:
Rawling.
POTTS, Annette:
Singh.
POULOS, Judy:
Smith, A. S.
POWELL, Graeme:
Strahan.
POWER, Rachel:
Rehfisch.
POYNTER, J. R.:
Ride; Wheure.
PRATTEN, Garth:
Torr.
PRENZLER, Tim:
Stuart.
PRESTON, A. N.:
Riordan.
PRIESTLEY, Susan:
Taylor, H.
PRING, Allan:
Tilley, C.
PROUST, Anthony:
Wunderly.
PUGLISI, A. (Len):
Roberts, C.
PURDY, John S.:
Steiner.

RADBOURNE, Jennifer:
Trundle.
RADFORD, Robin:
Robin.
RADI, Heather:
Roberts, F.; Street, J.; Swain.
RAE, Ian D.:
Raw.

RAFTERY, Judith:
Rankine; Woollacott.
RALPH, Neil:
Vickers.
RASMUSSEN, Carolyn:
Rubbo; Syme, K.; Tiegs.
RAY, Andrew J.:
Rodd, J.
RAYNER, Michelle:
Warnes.
REECE, Lesley:
Rees.
REFSHAUGE, Richard:
Syme, H.
REFSHAUGE, W. D.:
Thomson, E.
REGAN, Kerry:
Smith, C. I.
REID, Richard E.:
Taylor, H. B.
RENNIE, Sarah-Jane:
Tate.
REYNOLDS, Peter:
Sodersten.
RICHARDS, Mike:
Ryan, R. J.
RICHMOND, Mark:
Reichstein.
RICKARD, John:
White, Sir T.; White, V.
RILETT, Margaret*:
Zinnbauer, A. & H.
RITCHIE, John:
Plunkett, W.
RITCHIE, W.:
Shipp.
ROACH, John:
Roughley; Whitley, G.
ROBERTSON, N. R. G.:
Ross-Watt.
ROBERTSON, Peter:
Smerd.
ROBINSON, Suzanne:
Stirling, L.
ROUTH, S. J.:
Plunkett, T.; Scrymgeour.
RUTLAND, Suzanne D.:
Rabinovitch.
RUTLEDGE, Martha:
Reid, A. T.; Reid, M.; Shaw, C.; Stirling,
H. D.; Taylor, Sir A.; Ward, C.; Watts, M.
RYAN, Alan:
Warfe.
RYAN, Peter:
Turnbull, S.

SAUNDERS, Malcolm:
Rankin, G.
SCHREUDER, D. M.:
Roberts, Sir S.
SCHULZ, Liz:
Schulz.

* deceased

SCOBIE, Doug:
Wedgwood, Dame I.
SCOTT, Edmond:
Sunderland.
SCULLY, P. J.:
Spence.
SEAR, Martha:
Propsting.
SEAR, Tom:
Scarf.
SEARS, J. S.:
Rosenthal.
SEEAR, Lynne:
Rubin.
SELTH, P. A.:
Piper.
SHANAHAN, Martin:
Queale; Smith, Sir T.
SHARMAN, R. C.:
Warlow-Davies.
SHELLER, Simon:
Williams, Sir D.
SHERINGTON, G. E.:
Robson, L.
SHIRLEY, Graham:
Smith, F.
SIMPSON, Caroline:
Simpson, E.; Wyatt.
SINCLAIR, James:
Stewart, F. S.
SINFIELD, Peter:
Wagner.
SLEE, John:
Shand, J.
SMALLWOOD, Rosalind:
Simpson, H.
SMART, Judith:
Rapke; Skene.
SMITH, Anne:
Tucker, P.
SMITH, Helen:
Richards, J.
SMITH, Neil:
Tovell.
SMITH, Philippa Mein:
Scantlebury.
SMITH, Rowan:
Walsh, H.
SOMERVILLE, Ross:
Schramm.
SOUTER, Ngaire M.:
Ralston.
SPAULL, Andrew:
Vroland, A. & A.
SPEARRITT, Don:
Verco.
SPEARRITT, Peter:
Scott Waine; Sellheim.
SPECHT, Ray:
Wood, J.
SPEER, Albert:
Wright, E.
SPIERINGS, John:
Worrall.

xviii

SPROD, Dan:
Truchanas.
STARR, Graeme:
Spooner.
STAUNTON, Anthony:
Ranford; Wheatley.
STEINBERGER, Margaret:
Schroder.
STELL, Marion K.:
Wicks.
STEPHENS, Alan:
Truscott.
STEVENS, Catherine J.:
Spivakovsky.
STEVENSON, Rex:
Reed.
STOCK, Jenny Tilby:
Rudall.
STODDART, Brian:
Williamson, W.
STONE, Jonathan:
Shellshear; Stump.
STOREY, G. N. B.:
Reye.
STRAHAN, Frank:
Ricketson; Selby, I.; Watts, E.
STRANGIO, Paul:
Sheehan.
STRETTON, Hugh:
Rowe, A.
STURMA, Michael:
Robertson, J.
SUTTON, R.:
Plant; Simpson, N.
SWAIN, Shurlee:
Smith, S. G.
SWAN, Geoffrey:
Wathin.
SWEENEY, Kay:
Tilley, F.
SWEETING, A. J.:
Taylor, D. R.
SWIFT, Robert S.:
Willoughby.
SWINDEN, Greg:
Taylor, R.

TALENT, John A.:
Thomas, D.
TAPLIN, Harry:
Spowers, A.
TASSELL, Margaret:
Walker, W.
TATE, Audrey:
Rouse; Sear.
TAYLOR, Jack:
Rogers, J. N.
TAYLOR, Luke:
Yirawala.
TAYLOR, Robert I.:
Rose; Seddon.
TEALE, Ruth:
Roseby.

THOMAS, Daniel:
Tuckson.
THOMAS, David:
Waller, C.
THOMIS, Malcolm I.:
Watson, J. Andrew.
THORNHILL, John:
Woodbury.
THORNTON, Robert:
Veale.
THRELFALL, Neville:
Toliman.
TREGEAR, Peter John:
Seidel.
TREMBATH, Richard:
Smith, N.
TURNER, Ted:
Venning.

UHR, Janet:
Varley, A.
UHR, Michael:
Uhr.

VALENTINE, Barbara:
Smith, R.; Walker, W.
VENTRESS, Alan:
Thomas, B.

WAHLQUIST, Gil:
Tyrrell.
WALSH, G. P.:
Ronald; Schlunke; Sleigh.
WARHURST, John:
Ratcliffe; Webb, L.
WARREN, Alan:
Thyer.
WATERHOUSE, Michael:
Waterhouse.
WATERHOUSE, Richard:
Sellwood; Tancred.
WATERSON, D. B.:
Turner, I.; Walsh, E.
WATSON, Don:
Wilson, R.
WATSON, N.:
Sheean.
WATSON, Tom:
Wright, S.
WATTS, Peter:
Walling.
WEBB, Gwenda M.:
Skemp.
WEBB, Peter G.:
Skemp.
WEBBER, Peter:
Rembert.
WELD, H. A.:
Webb, Sir W.
WETHERELL, David:
Wedgwood, C.
WHEELER, Mark:
Taylor, G.

WHITE, Kate:
Williams, R.
WHITE, Margaret H.:
Schoenheimer.
WHITELAW, J.:
Simpson, C.
WHITTALL, Christopher:
Wylde.
WHITTON, William I.:
Russell, A.
WILLIAMS, Lynne:
Polglaze.
WILLIAMS, Paul D.:
Pizzey.
WILLIAMSON, Vicki:
Robertson, T.
WILSON, Blair:
Wilson, R.
WILSON, David:
Saville; Schaaf.
WILSON, Robert:
Wood, G.
WIMBORNE, Brian:
Shepherd, G.; Townsend, A. & H.

WINTER, Gillian:
Shepherd, C.
WIRTH, Hugh J.:
Reid, I.
WOOD, James:
Sturdee.
WOOD, Richard V.:
Richardson, M.
WOODHOUSE, Fay.
Sher.

YORK, Barry:
Scerri.
YOUNG, Jim:
Ryder.
YOUNG, John:
Scott Waine; Selleck.

ZEHNER, Robert:
Shaw, J.
ZONGOLLOWICZ, Bogumila:
Poninski.

A NOTE ON SOME PROCEDURES

Differences of opinion exist among our authors, readers and the editorial board as to whether certain information should normally be included—such as cause of death, burial or cremation details, and value of estate. In this volume our practices have been as follows:

Cause of death: usually included, except in the case of those aged over 70.

Burial/cremation: included when details available.

Value of estate: included where possible for categories such as businessmen, and if the amount is unusually high or low. In recent years, when the practice developed of distributing assets early to avoid estate and probate duties, the sum is not always meaningful; moreover, at times it is impossible to ascertain full details. Hence we have resorted to discretionary use.

Some other procedures require explanation:

Measurements: as the least unsatisfactory solution we have used imperial system measurements (as historically appropriate), followed by the metric equivalent in brackets.

Money: we have retained £ (for pounds) for references prior to 14 February 1966 (when the conversion rate was A£1 = A$2).

Religion: stated whenever information is available, but there is often no good evidence of actual practice, e.g. the information is confined to marriage and funeral rites.

[q.v.]: the particular volume is given for those included in volumes 1-15, but not for those in this volume. Note that the cross-reference [q.v.] now accompanies the names of all who have separate articles in the *A.D.B.* In volumes 1-6 it was not shown for royal visitors, governors, lieutenant-governors and those Colonial Office officials who were included.

Small capitals: used for relations and others when they are of substantial importance, though not included in their own right; these people are also q.v.'d.

Floruit and 'date of death': for the period 1788 to 1939, the placing of subjects in volumes 1 to 12 was determined by when they flourished; in contrast, volumes 13 to 16 (for the period 1940 to 1980) only include people who died in those years.

CORRIGENDA

Every effort is made to check every detail in every article, but a work of the *A.D.B.*'s size and complexity is bound to contain some errors.

Corrigenda have been published with each volume. A consolidated list, including corrections made after the publication of volume 12 (1990), forms part of the Index (1991). A list of corrigenda compiled since 2000 accompanies volume 16.

Only corrections are shown; additional information is not included; nor is any re-interpretation attempted. The exception to this procedure occurs when new details about parents, births, marriages and deaths become available.

Documented corrections are welcomed. Additional information, with sources, is also invited, and will be placed in the appropriate files for future use. In both cases, readers should write to:

The General Editor
Australian Dictionary of Biography
Research School of Social Sciences
Coombs Building, No 9
Australian National University
CANBERRA ACT 0200
Australia.

REFERENCES

The following and other standard works of reference have been widely used, though not usually acknowledged in individual biographies:

Australian Encyclopaedia, 1-2 (Syd, 1925), 1-10 (1958), 1-12 (1983)

Biographical registers for various Australian parliaments: (A. W. Martin & P. Wardle *and* H. Radi, P. Spearritt & E. Hinton *and* C. N. Connolly—New South Wales; D. Black & G. Bolton—Western Australia; K. Thomson & G. Serle *and* G. Browne—Victoria; D. B. Waterson *and* D. B. Waterson & J. Arnold—Queensland; H. Coxon, J. Playford & R. Reid—South Australia; S. & B. Bennett—Tasmania; and J. Rydon—Commonwealth)

O'M. Creagh and E. M. Humphris (eds), *The V.C. and D.S.O.: a complete record . . .* 1-3 (Lond, 1934)

Dictionary of National Biography (Lond, 1885-1990)

C. A. Hughes and B. D. Graham, *A Handbook of Australian Government and Politics 1890-1964* (Canb, 1968) and *1965-1974* (1977); *Voting for the Australian House of Representatives 1901-1964*, with corrigenda (Canb, 1975), *Queensland Legislative Assembly 1890-1964* (Canb, 1974), *New South Wales . . .* (1975), *Victoria . . .* (1975), and *South Australian, Western Australian and Tasmanian Lower Houses . . .* (1976), D. Black, *An Index to Parliamentary Candidates in Western Australian Elections 1890-1989* (Perth, 1989)

J. Thomas (ed), *South Australians 1836-1885*, 1-2 (Adel, 1990), J. Statton (ed), *Biographical Index of South Australians 1836-1885*, 1-4 (Adel, 1986)

F. Johns, *Johns's Notable Australians* (Melb, 1906), *Fred Johns's Annual* (Lond, 1914); *An Australian Biographical Dictionary* (Melb, 1934); P. Serle, *Dictionary of Australian Biography*, 1-2 (Syd, 1949); D. Carment et al (eds), *Northern Territory Dictionary of Biography*, 1 (Darwin, 1990), 2 (Darwin, 1992), 3 (Darwin, 1996); D. Horton (ed), *The Encyclopaedia of Aboriginal Australia*, 1-2 (Canb, 1994)

S. Sadie (ed), *The New Grove Dictionary of Music and Musicians*, 1-20 (Lond, 1980); W. Bebbington (ed), *The Oxford Companion to Australian Music* (Melb, 1997); P. Parsons (ed), *Companion to Theatre in Australia* (Syd, 1995)

W. Moore, *The Story of Australian Art*, 1-2 (Syd, 1934), (Syd, 1980); A. McCulloch, *Encyclopedia of Australian Art* (Lond, 1968), 1-2 (Melb, 1984), revised S. McCulloch (Syd, 1994)

E. M. Miller, *Australian Literature . . . to 1935* (Melb, 1940), extended to 1950 by F. T. Macartney (Syd, 1956); H. M. Green, *A History of Australian Literature*, 1-2 (Syd, 1961, 2nd edn 1971), revised by D. Green (Syd, 1984-85); W. H. Wilde, J. Hooton & B. Andrews, *The Oxford Companion to Australian Literature* (Melb, 1985), 2nd ed (1994)

Who's Who (Lond) and *Who's Who in Australia* (Syd, Melb), present and past edns

Jobson's Year Book of Public Companies (Syd, Melb), present and past edns

ABBREVIATIONS USED IN BIBLIOGRAPHIES

AAA	Amateur Athletic Association	Govt	Government
ABC	Australian Broadcasting Commission/Corporation	HA	House of Assembly
		Hist	History, Historical
ACT	Australian Capital Territory	Hob	Hobart
ADB	Australian Dictionary of Biography, Canb	HR	House of Representatives
		HSSA	Historical Society of South Australia
Adel	Adelaide		
ADFA	Australian Defence Force Academy, Canb	Inc	Incorporated
		Inst	Institute, Institution
Agr	Agriculture, Agricultural	intro	introduction, introduced by
AIF	Australian Imperial Force	*J*	*Journal*
AJCP	Australian Joint Copying Project	JCU	James Cook University of North Queensland, Townsville
ALP	Australian Labor Party		
ANU	Australian National University, Canb	L	Library
		LA	Legislative Assembly
ANUABL	ANU Archives of Business and Labour (Noel Butlin Archives Centre), Canb	LaTL	La Trobe Library, Melb
		Launc	Launceston
		LC	Legislative Council
ANZAAS	Australian and New Zealand Association for the Advancement of Science	Lond	London
		Mag	*Magazine*
		MDHC	Melbourne Diocesan Historical Commission (Catholic), Fitzroy
A'sia/n	Australasia/n		
Assn	Association	Melb	Melbourne
Aust	Australia/n	mf/s	microfilm/s
AWM	Australian War Memorial, Canb	*MJA*	*Medical Journal of Australia*
Bass L	Adolph Basser Library, Australian Academy of Science, Canb	ML	Mitchell Library, Syd
		Mort L	Mortlock Library of South Australiana
Bd	Board		
BHP	Broken Hill Proprietary Co. Ltd	ms/s	manuscript/s
bib	bibliography	mthly	monthly
biog	biography, biographical	NAA	National Archives of Australia
BL	J. S. Battye Library of West Australian History, Perth	nd	date of publication unknown
		NL	National Library of Australia, Canb
Brisb	Brisbane		
c	circa	no	number
CAE	College of Advanced Education	np	place of publication unknown
Canb	Canberra	NSW	New South Wales
cat	catalogue	NSWA	The Archives Authority of New South Wales (State Records NSW), Syd
CO	Colonial Office, London		
co	company		
C of E	Church of England	NT	Northern Territory
Com	Commission/er	NY	New York
comp	compiler	NZ	New Zealand
Corp	Corporation/s	OL	John Oxley Library, Brisb
CSIRO	Commonwealth Scientific and Industrial Research Organization	p, pp	page, pages
		pc	photocopy
ctc	committee	*PD*	*Parliamentary Debates*
Cwlth	Commonwealth	*PIM*	*Pacific Islands Monthly*
Dept	Department	PNG	Papua New Guinea
DNB	*Dictionary of National Biography*	*PP*	*Parliamentary Papers*
ed/s	editor/s	PRGSSA	*Proceedings of the Royal Geographical Society of Australasia (South Australian Branch)*
Edinb	Edinburgh		
edn	edition		
Eng	England	PRO	Public Record Office
Fr	Father (priest)	*Procs*	*Proceedings*
Geog	Geographical	pt/s	part/s

PTHRA	*Papers and Proceedings of the Tasmanian Historical Research Association*	Soc	Society
		SRSA	State Records of South Australia, Adel
pub	publication, publication number	supp	supplement
Q	*Quarterly*	Syd	Sydney
QA	Queensland State Archives, Brisb	TA	Tasmanian State Archives (Archives Office of Tasmania), Hob
Qld	Queensland		
RAHS	Royal Australian Historical Society (Syd)	Tas	Tasmania/n
		T&CJ	*Australian Town and Country Journal*
RG	Registrar General's Office		
RGS	Royal Geographical Society	*Trans*	*Transactions*
RHSQ	Royal Historical Society of Queensland (Brisb)	ts	typescript or transcript
		UK	United Kingdom
RHSV	Royal Historical Society of Victoria (Melb)	UNE	University of New England, Armidale
RMIT	Royal Melbourne Institute of Technology (RMIT University)	Univ	University
		UNSW	University of New South Wales
Roy	Royal	UPNG	University of Papua New Guinea
RWAHS	Royal Western Australian Historical Society (Perth)	US	United States of America
		v, vol	volume
1st S	First Session	*VHM(J)*	*Victorian Historical Magazine (Journal)*
2nd S	Second Session		
SA	South Australia/n	Vic	Victoria/n
Sel	Select	*V&P*	*Votes and Proceedings*
SLNSW	State Library of New South Wales	WA	Western Australia/n
		WAA	Western Australian State Archives (State Records Office of WA), Perth
SLSA	State Library of South Australia		
SLT	State Library of Tasmania		
SLV	State Library of Victoria		
SMH	*Sydney Morning Herald*	*	deceased

P

PIKE, DOUGLAS HENRY (1908-1974), station worker, clergyman, historian and editor, was born on 3 November 1908 at Tuhshan (Dushan), Kweichow (Guizhou), China, second of five children of Douglas Fowler Pike and his wife Louisa, née Boulter, Australian-born Baptist missionaries with the China Inland Mission. Young Douglas attended the Boys' Collegiate School, run by members of the mission at Chefoo (Yantai). He and his elder sister Allison accompanied their parents who took leave in Australia in 1924. Young Doug remained in Melbourne to complete his education. When her husband was killed by bandits in Kweichow in September 1929, Louisa continued her missionary work until her retirement in 1944.

While employed as a junior state school teacher in the Victorian Education Department, Pike studied (1925-26) at the University of Melbourne. In 1927, for family reasons, he went to New South Wales and took a job as a rouseabout on properties in the Cassilis-Merriwa district; he also worked as a shearer and as a surveyor's-assistant. For a time he managed a small religious printery in Sydney, but soon went back to the land and became a station overseer successively on several properties, including Collaroy. He valued the experiences of his country years and what they taught him about life and people. The qualities he later showed as teacher, raconteur and colleague, and his direct, but quietly determined manner, owed much to this period.

With a sense of vocation Pike returned to Melbourne in September 1938 and trained at the College of the Bible, Glen Iris, run by the Churches of Christ. In 1941 he became a minister. On 25 November that year he married Olive Gertrude, daughter of Rev. Thomas Hagger, a minister of the Churches of Christ, who conducted the service at his Camberwell home. In Adelaide from 1942, Pike served at Colonel Light Gardens, Edwardstown and Glenelg. Meanwhile, he enrolled at the University of Adelaide (B.A., 1948; M.A., 1951; D.Litt., 1957); he gained first-class honours in history and political science, and won the Tinline [q.v.6] scholarship. In 1948, with characteristic intellectual honesty, and without prospects, he resigned his ministry and became 'a parson who has found the doctrinal way too strait'. G. V. Portus [q.v.11] offered him a temporary lectureship in history at the university. Thus, at the age of almost 40, he began an academic career.

In 1949 Pike was appointed temporary lecturer at the University of Western Australia.

By late 1950 he was back in Adelaide as reader—a senior position for one so new to university teaching. Within the history and political science department he was effectively in charge of history until 1954, when Hugh Stretton arrived and history was made a separate department. Appointed to the chair of history at the University of Tasmania in 1960, Pike became foundation general editor of the *Australian Dictionary of Biography* on 31 January 1962. For almost two years he commuted between Hobart and Canberra, before settling in the national capital on 1 January 1964 as a professor in the Research School of Social Sciences, Australian National University.

A national dictionary of biography had been mooted in the 1950s and by 1961 a small staff had been engaged on preliminary work, but no firm plans had been made for its production. With energy and foresight, Pike set about organizing the project. He soon discovered that a general editor required the skills of a manager and the tact of a diplomat, as well as the qualities of a historian and biographer. Once again his years of country pioneering stood him in good stead. He needed his diverse range of experience as he consolidated the administrative structure, comprising section editors, national committee, editorial board and working parties, and began the task of producing the first two volumes—1116 entries, covering the years from 1788 to 1850. Volume 1 appeared in 1966 and Volume 2 in 1967.

By that time Pike had put into shape a complex and efficient production system. His natural courtesy and firm belief in the value of the *A.D.B.* had enabled him to obtain the co-operation of a variety of people: his office staff, who helped in administration, research and checking; senior academics, who assisted in the broad aspects of editing, the listing of entries and the allocation of authors; and many writers (about three hundred for each volume), from a range of occupations and locations. Nearly all of them, except the office staff, were unpaid. The principle of honorary national collaboration was firmly established. The history departments of every Australian university, local historical and genealogical societies, State and national libraries and archives, and many individuals throughout the continent were involved. Not the least of Pike's achievements was to gain the support of registrars of births, deaths and marriages, and of probates. He was warmly appreciative of all this willing help.

Volumes 1 and 2 established the scholarly base of the *A.D.B.*, and its social and

educational value. Pike's passion was concise-
ness, without the sacrifice of humanity and
style. He had developed a flair for lean prose
and acquired a distaste for adjectives and ad-
verbs; his style gave the volumes a sense of
unity and uniformity. He jested that, as there
were no adjectives in the psalms, there would
be none in the *A.D.B.* Of course, many of
them slipped through his net, but he was
always sadly aware of it. More than once he
claimed that, when he was a minister, he could
reduce his sermons to one sentence as he
stepped up to the pulpit. He did not overtly
expect his authors to do the same with their
articles, but often gave the impression that
he wanted something like it; a few of them
objected, but reconciliations were nearly
always reached. A number of authors failed
to produce the articles they had promised,
or scamped on the work required. Such instances did not 'induce cheerful resignation in
a fiercely dedicated man'. Even when articles
were written or substantially rewritten by Pike
or other members of his staff, he refused to
append his name (or theirs) to them. Each
volume won renown (as he might have put
it) for succinct restatement of what was well
known and much compact presentation of
what was new. This high repute was mainly
attributable to Pike's skill and industry, but he
never tired of acknowledging the teamwork
that went into the project.

Pike's sympathetic and effective teaching,
and his publications—especially *Paradise of
Dissent: South Australia 1829-1857* (London,
1957) and *Australia: The Quiet Continent*
(London, 1962)—had established him as one
of Australia's most distinguished historians.
His work on the *A.D.B.* revealed him as in-
comparably the country's best academic editor. He was quietly spoken, with a dry but
genial sense of humour, leavened by the wisdom that flowed from his innate generosity,
spacious experience and fertile memory; his
personal qualities complemented his erudition to enable him to grasp the total substance
of the *A.D.B.*, as well as the significance of
every article and its relationship to the whole.
He was conscious of the constraint to keep
volumes and articles within the allotted word
lengths, but was equally aware of the individuality of each author and the uniqueness of
each entry. As successive volumes appeared
in 1969 and 1972 they revealed how he had
mastered the complex task of harmonizing
concise biographical writing, virtually all of it
new, with the occasionally conflicting demands of contributors and publishers. The
Ernest Scott [q.v.11] prize in 1969 and the
Britannica Australia award in 1971 provided
appropriate recognition of his achievement.

Elected to the Australian Humanities Research Council in 1961, Pike served as its
treasurer in 1966. The council was reconstituted as the Australian Academy of the Humanities in 1969; he was a foundation fellow,
secretary (1971-72) and treasurer (1969-73).
He was appointed (1969) to the National Memorials Committee, a body established by the
Federal government to oversee memorials,
and to name suburbs and streets, in Canberra.

In 1973 there were signs that Pike's health
was deteriorating, at least partly from his intense editorial efforts. A smallish, neat man,
he was physically stronger than he looked. He
had made a good recovery from a heart attack
in the 1950s. His hobby was paving court-
yards and making stone walls, and he built
them to last. None the less, in his last decade
he scarcely relaxed. He made a short visit to
New Zealand after the completion of Volume 2
to secure further evidence in his long pursuit
of E. G. Wakefield [q.v.2], and he spent eight
months study leave in England as a Commonwealth fellow at St John's College, Cambridge, in 1969-70. Typically, he used the
latter trip to visit national dictionary teams in
Canada and South Africa, and to interview the
scattered surviving organizers of the *Dictionary of American Biography*. By the latter part
of 1973 he had Volume 5 substantially prepared. He was due to retire on 31 December,
but had been offered a visiting fellowship from
1 January 1974 to complete Volume 6, the last
of the 1851-1890 series. Douglas Pike suffered
a cerebral thrombosis on 11 November 1973
and was admitted to Canberra Hospital. He
died there on 19 May 1974 and was cremated
with Presbyterian forms; his wife and their
two sons survived him.

ANU Reporter, 28 June 1974; *Hist Studies*, 16, no
64, Apr 1975; *Canb Times*, 20 Mar 1969, 21 May
1974; ADB papers, 1272, Q31-12, 15 (ANUABL); information from Mrs M. Keeble, Hamilton, Vic, and Mr
A. Pike, Campbell, Canb; personal knowledge.

BEDE NAIRN

PIKE, LEONARD HENRY (1885-1961),
public servant and agent-general, was born on
8 August 1885 at Streatham, London, one of
eight children of Thomas Pike, bricklayer, and
his wife Jane, née Sims. Educated at Emanuel
School and Birkbeck College, Len acquired
some elementary legal training with Peters &
Bolton, solicitors. In 1901-02 he served with
the City of London Yeomanry (Roughriders)
in the South African war. He held a post with
another law firm in London before working
as a clerk (from 1907) for Stag Brewery. On
31 March 1910 he married Lucy Raymond at
Holy Trinity parish church, Wimbledon. They
migrated to Queensland next day.

Joining the Queensland Public Service in
June 1910, Pike worked in the Department of
Justice and served (from 1914) as an officer in

the Militia. On 1 April 1916 he enlisted in the Australian Imperial Force. While serving on the Western Front with the 3rd Divisional Ammunition Column, he was promoted lieutenant in March 1917. A dislocated elbow forced him to return to Brisbane where his A.I.F. appointment terminated in December. Back in the public service, he was official secretary to three successive premiers, E. G. Theodore, W. N. Gillies and William McCormack [qq.v.12,9,10]. He organized official visits to Queensland, including the 1927 tour of the Duke and Duchess of York. His wife and only child had died in 1919. At the Holy Cross Church, Wooloowin, on 10 February 1923 he married with Catholic rites Margaret Hutton, a 29-year-old nurse.

In June 1927 Pike was appointed official secretary to the Queensland agent-general's office, London. He acted as agent-general in 1929 and again from 1931. In July 1936 he was authorized to use the designation of agent-general in his correspondence, but he was not formally appointed to the position until 19 August 1943.

Commended for his negotiating skills, Pike had been involved (from 1928) with international conferences on sugar. As an adviser to the Australian sugar delegation, he attended the Imperial Economic Conference, held in Ottawa in 1932, and the Monetary and Economic Conference, held in London in 1933. He visited Natal in 1938 as a guest of the South African government and the local sugar industry, and represented (1937-52) Australia on the International Sugar Council, of which he was vice-chairman. Convinced of the importance of the sugar agreement negotiated between Britain and Australia during World War II, he continued to reject British proposals to pay higher prices for colonial sugar than Australian.

Pike represented the Returned Sailors' and Soldiers' (and Airmen's) Imperial League of Australia on the British Empire Service League from 1927. In 1931-51 he was the Australian Soccer Football Association's delegate to the council of the Football Association, London. He resigned as agent-general in 1951 because of ill health. Mrs Pike thought that successive Queensland Labor governments undervalued the position of agent-general and wryly observed that knighthoods were conferred on eleven other agents-general during her husband's term.

A proficient horseman, Pike was also a chorister, organist and newspaper columnist. He died on 24 March 1961 at Bexhill, Sussex, and was buried in the cemetery at Bexley Hill; his wife and their son and daughter survived him.

Courier-Mail, 12 Apr 1938, 29 Aug 1951, 25 Mar 1961; *Telegraph* (Brisb), 18 Aug 1950, 9 Jan 1953;

A/54046, Public Service Bd, file 2153 (QA); file 39, Qld Women's Hist Assn, Brisb.

JENNIFER HARRISON

PILPEL, JOSHUA (1891-1978), master printer, was born on 25 November 1891 at Safed, Palestine (Zefat, Israel), son of Russian-born parents Menacham Isaac Philphil, merchant, and his wife Chaya Brocha, née Gershon. Emigrating to Western Australia, Josh reached Fremantle in the *Yarra* in December 1911 and was employed almost immediately by Detmold Ltd (later Spicers & Detmold Ltd), wholesale stationers. By the time he was naturalized in 1922 he had Anglicized the spelling of his surname. He worked as a bookbinder with Detmold's before becoming a commission agent. At the Synagogue, Perth, on 26 December 1928 he married 24-year-old Rose Prowolski (known as Provost).

In 1927 Pilpel had opened his own printery in the rented loft of a hardware warehouse, off Murray Street, in Perth's central business district. Pilpel & Co. began on borrowed capital and small reserves, but, contrary to predictions, survived and flourished during the Depression. Contracts were secured from government departments and from a large section of the medical profession. A major client for many years was the University of Western Australia, for whom the firm printed everything from letterhead stationery to programmes for graduation ceremonies and the student newspaper, *Pelican*. Pilpel's also printed the junior certificate and Leaving certificate examination papers for more than twenty years, all the printing requirements of the State School Teachers' Union of Western Australia, and a number of periodicals, including *Magistrate* for the Justices' Association of Western Australia and *Fortitude* for the Civilian Maimed and Limbless Association.

Genial, rotund, and bald from early middle age, Pilpel presided over a family firm respected for its integrity. He enjoyed good relations with unions, staff and the trade. The two senior staff members, an intensely religious compositor and a rumbustious Irish-Australian linotype operator (who combined branch secretaryship of the Returned Sailors', Soldiers' and Airmen's Imperial League of Australia with emphatic socialist principles) agreed on little except loyalty to the firm.

Pilpel's recreation was bowls, until several years of declining eyesight—due to glaucoma—culminated in blindness in 1948. He later continued to astonish staff and visitors with his dexterity in the finer points of operating a paper-cutting guillotine. A diligent collector for Jewish charities for the destitute, he published his own monthly newspaper, *Westralian*

Judean (1929-55), and from 1972 printed the *Maccabean* (at cost) for the Western Australian Jewish Board of Deputies.

In 1954 the firm moved to premises in Stirling Street, custom-built by the architects Summerhayes & Associates and equipped with the latest technology. The doyen of Western Australia's printing trade, Pilpel died on 21 June 1978 at Royal Perth Hospital and was buried in Karrakatta cemetery; his wife, and their son and daughter survived him. In 2000 the family business, Pilpel Printing Co., flourished in Beaufort Street, specializing in colour printing, cheque encoding, bookwork and foiling. Next door an associate company, Print Finishing Line, provided folding, laminating and 'perfect' binding for Perth's major printing establishments.

Western Teacher, 14 July 1978; *Sunday Times* (Perth), 25 Dec 1977; naturalization file, A1/15, item 1922/6879 (NAA, Canb); PP302/1, item WA1483 (NAA, Perth); information from Mr R. Pilpel, Mount Lawley, Perth.   G. C. BOLTON

PINK, OLIVE MURIEL (1884-1975), artist, Aboriginal-rights activist, anthropologist and gardener, was born on 17 March 1884 in Hobart, elder surviving child of Robert Stuart Pink (d.1907), warehouseman, and his wife Eveline Fanny Margaret, née Kerr. Educated at Hobart Girls' High School, Olive studied art at the Hobart Technical School with the sculptor Benjamin Sheppard [q.v.11] before joining the staff as a teacher in 1909.

Some time after 1910 Pink moved with her mother and brother Eldon—first to Perth, where she gave private art lessons from her studio in St Georges Terrace, and then to Sydney, where she taught briefly in private girls' schools. The students loved her lessons, she said, but headmistresses found her independent spirit a problem. She also attended Julian Ashton's Sydney Art School, studying with Adrian Feint [qq.v.7,14]. In May 1915 her drafting skills gained her a position as a tracer in the New South Wales Department of Public Works. That month her 'very dear friend' Captain Harold Southern was killed at Gallipoli.

Employed by the New South Wales Government Railways and Tramways, Pink painted excursion posters and the like until she was retrenched during the Depression. In 1930 she embarked on a sketching tour of Central Australia and investigated the conditions in which Aboriginal people lived. Her interest in Aboriginal welfare had been sparked while visiting Daisy Bates [q.v.7] at her camp at Ooldea, South Australia, in 1926-27. These experiences were to shape her life. Encouraged by Professor R. W. Firth to study anthropology at the University of Sydney, she attended his lectures in 1932 and later those of A. P. Elkin

[q.v.14]. With Elkin's support, she received grants from the Australian National Research Council to visit the Northern Territory in 1933-36 and work among the eastern Arrernte of Alice Springs and the Warlpiri of the Tanami region. From her Arrernte research emerged two important papers which appeared in *Oceania* in 1933 and 1936; because her Warlpiri research relied on descriptions of secret rituals, that part of her work was never published. Her decision to lock away her research notes for fifty years infuriated Elkin and the A.N.R.C., and brought her anthropological career to an end.

Pink saw anthropology as a means of advancing the cause of Aborigines and aimed to secure land, mining and civil rights for them. She wanted to establish a 'secular sanctuary' for the Warlpiri, an area from which police, government and missions would be excluded in order to allow the Warlpiri to develop their own responses to colonization. T. G. H. Strehlow [q.v.] damned her lack of professional qualifications and thus assisted in having her prevented from visiting Aboriginal reserves and missions.

In 1938 Pink sought help from the Sheetmetal Workers' Union, Sydney. She provided information to its communist secretary Tom Wright which he used in his booklet, *New Deal for the Aborigines* (1939). Scrutinized by the Commonwealth Investigation Service and later the Australian Security Intelligence Organization, she was not found to be a threat.

With a small grant from Quaker benefactors and the S.W.U., Pink returned to Alice Springs in 1942 as an independent sociological investigator. To demonstrate the viability of the 'secular sanctuary', she applied for a grazing lease at Papinya in the Tanami region and, while waiting for it, settled at Thompsons Rockhole (Pirdi Pirdi) on the old Tanami Track. There she lived for four years, cared for by Warlpiri families, continuing her research and operating a ration depot funded by a tiny grant from the S.W.U. Her lease was finally granted in 1946, and she moved to Papinya with about thirty Warlpiri people. She began teaching the children English and dancing, introduced some gardening techniques, and described those few weeks as among the happiest ever. Increasing drought and the breakdown of her car brought the utopian venture to an end. Two young Warlpiri men beat her badly when she refused their demands for food. The rapidly worsening situation forced her to return to Alice Springs and the government eventually set up a base for the Warlpiri which became Yuendumu.

Pink lived in a corrugated-iron hut on Gregory Terrace. By this time her small inheritance had been spent on supporting her research and she had very little money. To survive, she sold fruit and flowers from her garden. She later worked as a cleaner in the court-house, where she also monitored cases in which Aboriginal defendants appeared. This arrangement proved uncongenial to magistrates and police alike. Pink formed a committee to obtain land for a museum. After this plan failed, she set up a small private display of her wildflower paintings and Aboriginal artefacts at one end of her hut. She charged for admission, but friends were not asked to pay and time-wasters were refused entry. The noise from the fire-station next door upset her, and quarrels led to court cases, a charge of assault, the burning of her hut, her eventual eviction, and the loss of her job at the court-house. She lived in a tent for some years before she was able to move to a small area of land which, with the help of the minister for territories (Sir) Paul Hasluck, was gazetted as a flora reserve in 1956. There she worked as honorary curator to establish a haven which is now named the Olive Pink Botanic Garden. She died on 6 July 1975 in Alice Springs Hospital and was buried in the local cemetery with the forms of the Society of Friends (Quakers).

Although Pink is remembered mainly for her Edwardian form of dress, her biting tongue and her isolated life on the flora reserve, she had achieved much: she pressed the government on a number of Aboriginal issues, contributed to anthropology by her understanding of Arrernte landownership, and ameliorated life for her Aboriginal friends. She was a passionate advocate for Aboriginal rights. It was her unwillingness to compromise which caused so much trouble to those whom she saw as doing wrong.

B. James, *No Man's Land* (Syd, 1989); D. Carment et al (eds), *Northern Territory Dictionary of Biography*, vol 1 (Darwin, 1990); J. Marcus, *A Passion for Truth* (Syd, 2001); *Mankind*, 17, no 3, 1987, p 185; ASIO file, A6126, item 19 (NAA, Canb); Elkin papers (Univ Syd Archives); Olive Pink collection, Inst of Aboriginal and Torres Strait Islander Studies, Canb.   JULIE MARCUS

PINNER, JOHN THOMAS (1888-1955), accountant and public servant, was born on 4 October 1888 in Melbourne, third child of Victorian-born parents William Edward Pinner, butcher, and his wife Jane, née Sloss. Educated at Rathdowne Street State School, Carlton, and Thomas Palmer's [q.v.11] University High School, John became a member of the Incorporated Institute of Accountants, Victoria. He practised and taught accountancy in Adelaide from 1911 before returning to Melbourne in 1913.

Enlisting in the Australian Imperial Force on 9 December 1915, Pinner was allotted to the Australian Army Pay Corps. When he was found to be unfit for active service he was transferred to the Militia in October 1916. He was commissioned in December, promoted captain in November 1918 and commended (1920) for his work in improving pay procedures. His appointment terminated in March 1921. At Scots Church, Melbourne, on 26 January 1918 he had married with Presbyterian forms Mancell Jeanott Drysdale, a dressmaker.

Pinner was appointed to the Commonwealth Public Service as an investigating officer in the taxation branch of the Treasury in February 1921. From 1922 he was chief accountant and a member of the Expropriation Board of New Guinea, which handled the disposal of German property seized in the Mandated Territory during World War I. Returning to Melbourne in 1925 as a clerk in the Treasury, he became assistant-accountant in the Federal Capital Commission in 1926 and moved to Canberra. Next year he was made the commission's internal auditor. 'J.T.' counted empty cement bags during construction of the Administrative Building and found that less cement was being used than stipulated in the contract, which was subsequently terminated. In 1928 he was appointed to the Public Service Board as an inspector. The recommendations in his report (1933) for savings in running Federal parliament proved contentious and were only partially implemented.

As senior inspector (from 1939), Pinner handled organizational problems that arose in departments involved in the war effort. In 1945 he became an assistant-commissioner on the board. He chaired a committee which reviewed the postwar structure and staffing of government departments: within six months in 1945-46 his committee produced a separate report on each of them. In January 1947 he was appointed a P.S.B. commissioner. Pinner worked hard to implement government policy and expected his subordinates to do the same. He helped to arrange a council of departments and public service associations, and to set up joint consultation on salary classifications. Five ft 8 ins (173 cm) tall, with grey eyes, he proved a hard, but courteous and fair negotiator. He wanted all avenues of the public service to be open to women. In 1951 he visited London to report on future economies at the Australian High Commission.

In 1953 Pinner was appointed O.B.E. He retired in November that year. An unassuming man of conservative habits, he audited the books of Canberra's Methodist and Presbyterian churches, and presided (1940-48) over the local branch of the Commonwealth Institute of Accountants. His favourite recreation was a game of billiards at home with friends. Survived by his wife and their two daughters, he died of hypertensive cerebrovascular disease on 17 May 1955 in his home at Deakin and was buried in Canberra cemetery.

G. E. Caiden, *Career Service* (Melb, 1965); *PD* (HR), 10 Nov 1933; *Public Administration* (Syd), Mar 1954; *Age* (Melb), 12 Nov 1953; *Bulletin*, 25 Nov 1953; *Canb Times*, 18 May 1955; Report . . . suggesting . . . economies in the administration of the Parliamentary Departments, June 1933, file 77/267 (HR, Canb); series CP23/3 and A11366 (NAA, Canb); Pinner papers (held by author).   G. E. PETTIT

PIPER, HAROLD BAYARD (1894-1953), judge and company director, was born on 26 April 1894 at Walkerville, Adelaide, third of eight children of Arthur William Piper [q.v.11], an English-born solicitor, and his wife Edner Elizabeth, née Counter, who was born in South Australia. Harold was educated at Prince Alfred College and at the University of Adelaide (LL.B., 1914) where he won a Stow [q.v.6] prize. After completing his articles in his father's firm, Bakewell, Stow & Piper, he was admitted to the Supreme Court as a solicitor and barrister on 8 June 1915. Thirteen days later he enlisted in the Australian Imperial Force. He served in Egypt and on the Western Front, and was discharged from the army on 4 June 1919, still with the rank of private.

Back in his father's firm, 'Bay' Piper developed a practice, mainly in commercial law. At the Flinders Street Baptist Church, Adelaide, on 7 June 1922 he married Dorothy Edna Smith. In 1922 he joined the Law Society of South Australia (councillor 1930, vice-president 1937-38) and in 1927 he became senior partner in Piper, Bakewell & Piper. A Freemason and a Congregationalist, he was sometime deacon at Stow [q.v.2] Memorial Church. He kept his interest in cricket, football, tennis and golf, and became a keen gardener.

Piper chaired royal commissions into the holding of lotteries to raise funds for charitable institutions in 1936 and into changes to betting laws in 1937. On 15 February 1938 he was appointed a judge of the Commonwealth Court of Conciliation and Arbitration, which necessitated his moving to Melbourne. He acted (1939 and 1942) as judge of the Supreme Court of the Australian Capital Territory. In 1939 he investigated the cause of several crashes of Royal Australian Air Force bombers.

On 31 July 1941 Piper succeeded Sir George Beeby [q.v.7] as chief judge of the Arbitration Court. From April 1942 to November 1944 he also chaired the Stevedoring Industry Commission. His excessive wartime workload led to health problems, initially with his heart and lungs, and then with his hearing. He took leave from the Arbitration Court in May 1946 and resigned in June 1947. Despite his lack of experience in industrial matters, he was widely respected for his honesty, sincerity and diligence, though he was 'not the strongest of judges'.

Active in the Australian Red Cross Society (chairman 1940-43, vice-president 1943-44 and honorary life member 1944), Piper was appointed an officer (1948) of the Order of St John of Jerusalem. He also served on the Victorian branch of the Boy Scouts' Association, the Braille Library of Victoria, the Lawn Tennis Association of Australia, the Victorian Society for Crippled Children and the Gowrie [q.v.9] scholarship trust fund. In his retirement he undertook some legal work for the National Bank of Australia and became a director of Broken Hill Proprietary Co. Ltd. Survived by his wife and their son, he died of cancer on 10 May 1953 at his Toorak home; having joined the Church of England, he was cremated with Anglican rites.

O. Foenander, *Studies in Australian Labour Law and Relations* (Melb, 1952); M. Perlman, *Judges in Industry* (Melb, 1954); R. W. Piper (comp), *The Abbotsham Pipers* (Adel, 1993); A2153, item Piper, H. B., A705, item 32/10/2387 (NAA, Canb); Piper papers (held by Mr D. Piper, Hawthorn, Melb).
                                                    P. A. SELTH

PITHER, ALFRED GEORGE (1908-1971), air force officer, was born on 16 October 1908 at Shepparton, Victoria, eldest of six children of James Luke Pither, farmer, and his wife Rosanna Amelia, née Fletcher, both Victorian born. Educated at the local agricultural high school, George served in the Militia before entering (1927) the Royal Military College, Duntroon, Federal Capital Territory, as one of the first cadets nominated by the Royal Australian Air Force. On graduating in 1930, he was commissioned in the R.A.A.F. as a pilot officer.

After completing flying training at Point Cook, Victoria, in December 1931, Pither spent the next five years engaged in flying and staff duties in various units. He had been a radio enthusiast since his schooldays and began to specialize in signals. Early in 1936 he was promoted flight lieutenant and sent to England to attend the Royal Air Force signals school. Returning to Victoria in September 1937, he was appointed to command the Signal Training School, Laverton. He found the S.T.S. in a 'parlous condition', and set about reorganizing and improving it before finally designing a school to be built at Point Cook. The move took place on 1 September 1939; Pither received the temporary rank of squadron leader that day.

In October 1939 Pither was posted to Air Force Headquarters, Melbourne, as a staff officer in the Directorate of Training, where he planned and administered the signals programme. In September 1940 he travelled to England to learn about the new and secret technology of radar; he also studied developments in this field in Canada and the United States of America. At Christ Church Cathedral, Vancouver, Canada, on 13 April 1941 he married Sydney-born Lillian Ruth Ball (d.1964) with Anglican rites. Back home in May, with the rank of wing commander, he resumed work in the Directorate of Signals. He established a chain of long-range radar stations throughout Australia and the Pacific. In March 1942 his section was expanded and he was made head of what became, in September 1943, the Directorate of Radar.

In October 1943 Pither was sent to England on exchange duty. He was posted to headquarters, Allied Expeditionary Air Force, and helped to plan the Normandy invasion. From July 1944 he served with No.80 Wing, R.A.F., in command of a radio-jamming unit set up on the south-east coast of England to counter German V-1 rockets. Crossing to France, his unit followed the allied forces into Belgium on a campaign to jam V-2 rockets.

Pither returned to Australia in December 1944 and resumed his post as director of radar. Following the Japanese surrender, he was appointed (October 1945) to a three-man Australian mission charged with examining the state of Japanese scientific development and investigating Australia's claims for reparations. He left Japan in February 1946 and in May became an R.A.A.F. member of the Australian delegation to the Commonwealth Defence Science Conference, held in England. Reaching Australia in July 1946, Pither was appointed to R.A.A.F. headquarters and given responsibility for guided missiles. In April 1947, as a temporary group captain, he helped in planning an Australian rocket-range. When it was decided to proceed with the project, he was appointed R.A.A.F. liaison officer. It was he who suggested naming the new establishment 'Woomera'. In May 1951 he was seconded to the Department of Supply and made range-superintendent. The next three years marked an important phase of atomic and guided-missile testing.

On reverting to duty with the R.A.A.F. in July 1954, Pither was posted to R.A.A.F. headquarters as director of telecommunications and radar. In 1956 he was appointed C.B.E. Placed in command of No.1 Aircraft Depot at Laverton in June 1959, he was officer commanding Laverton base headquarters in 1961-62. From January 1963 he was staff officer for telecommunication engineering at headquarters, Support Command, Melbourne, until he retired from the air force in February 1966 with the honorary rank of air commodore. At the Methodist Church, Camberwell, on 18 December 1964 he had married Ethel Constance Jones, née Wilton.

In his retirement Pither served as treasurer and councillor of the State branch of the Royal Flying Doctor Service of Australia. He kept fit, swam, skied and played golf, and dabbled in water-colours. Survived by his wife, and by the twin son and daughter of his first marriage, he died suddenly of coronary infarction on 2 July 1971 at Hawthorn and was cremated.

E. R. Hall, *A Saga of Achievement* (Melb, 1978); P. Morton, *Fire Across the Desert* (Canb, 1989); *Hist Records of Aust Science*, 12, no 4, 1999; information from Rev K. M. Pither, Ivanhoe, Melb, Mr R. A. V. Pither, Mt Eliza, and Mr R. V. Pither, Boundary Bend, Vic.   C. D. COULTHARD-CLARK

PITT, GEORGE HENRY (1891-1972), librarian, archivist and historian, was born on 21 January 1891 at Norwood, Adelaide, one of five children of James Pitt, jeweller, and his wife Annie, née Jeffrey. George attended Rose Park and Norwood public schools, won a public exhibition and proceeded to Prince Alfred College. Although he was not especially attracted to librarianship, he accepted the position of junior cataloguing clerk at the Public Library of South Australia in 1906. Told that he would be expected to undertake a university course, he enrolled at the University of Adelaide (B.A., 1920). To disguise the fact that he was only 15, he changed from short pants to long trousers before going to evening-classes, but, when his age became known, had to abandon his course temporarily.

Promoted to cataloguer in 1910 and senior cataloguer in 1918, Pitt published his *Alphabetical List of Serial Publications: Scientific, Technical and Historical* (1914). His application, accuracy and systematic skills equipped him for the demands of author-and-subject cataloguing and general indexing—two fields that were to play an important part in the future management of archives and libraries. At St Theodore's Anglican Church, Rose Park, on 8 December 1915 he married Ruby Calley, a tailoress; they were later to separate.

In 1917-18, as a preliminary step towards the establishment of the State archives in line with G. C. Henderson's [q.v.9] proposals (1915), Pitt listed South Australian records held in the Mitchell [q.v.5] Library, Sydney, and the Public Library of South Australia. His appointment as archivist in charge of the library's new archives department on 1 February 1919 was the first professional archival appointment in Australia. With one assistant he did some initial work in the library until, in 1920, an old government building off North Terrace was ready for the storage of records and use by readers. Because the little theoretical writing on archival management then available in English was not widely circulated, Pitt devised his own techniques which reflected some library practices familiar to him. While his methods did not obscure provenance, they were not primarily based on it, and, as the volume of records increased, his system of accession register-books and dictionary catalogue had to be modified. Some aspects of his archival administration foreshadowed later Australian practice, notably his successful advocacy of legislation in 1925 to regulate the disposal of public documents, and his control of records by series units.

As archivist, Pitt provided the kind of professional help that Henderson wanted for researchers, an achievement that owed much to Pitt's skill as a cataloguer and indexer. Recognizing the need for specialized indexing to complement the main catalogue, he compiled detailed indexes to shipping arrivals and passenger lists (1836-1900), the official files of the colonial secretary's office, and parliamentary papers. He also laid the foundation of a pictorial collection which included a systematic record of Adelaide's architectural development. It was all done on a modest budget and, for six years in the 1930s, without an assistant. He happily worked long hours. Although he later said that the creation of the archives department was a demanding task, he saw it as one of the two achievements of his professional life that pleased him most.

With archival services closed (from March 1942) and the records safely dispersed for fear of enemy bombing, in November 1943 Pitt was appointed librarian-in-charge of the planned Adelaide Lending Service and sent to observe practices in other States. Two years of delay followed. Then, in less than three months and helped by an enthusiastic young staff, he assembled, catalogued and made service arrangements for the stock of 11 000 books. Lending began on 19 March 1946. This was the other professional achievement that most pleased him.

On 17 March 1948 Pitt was appointed principal librarian. Soon after, he began a tour of libraries in Britain and the United States of America. He was impressed by some municipal library services and the interest in non-book materials; he was less impressed with library involvement in community work, particularly when he suspected fundamental cataloguing was neglected. In March 1949 he submitted a detailed plan for reorganization to the Libraries Board, the chief concern of which was the provision of adequate space for the library's expanding public services. When the government did nothing to overcome the problem, he had no alternative but to continue to reduce the stock of out-dated and non-South Australian material to make room for current needs. It was a measure he regretted, but, as with the disposal of some types of archival material in earlier years, he did not shirk decisions. His reorganization plan also

recommended the creation of a new dictionary catalogue (begun in 1950) for the reference library.

Pitt encouraged greater use of the library's many services, negotiated to set up professionally staffed libraries in government departments, and established a lending service for children. Lacking strong support from the Libraries Board and virtually any government interest, he was unable effectively to promote municipal public libraries, though he had at least provided the prototype with the Adelaide Lending Service. He served on the council of the Australian Institute of Librarians (1939-40 and 1947-48) and on its cataloguing and classification committee (1945-46). In 1963 he was made a fellow of the institute's successor, the Library Association of Australia.

He contributed to the history of his State by writing a chapter in *The Centenary History of South Australia* (1936), a monograph on *The Press in South Australia, 1836 to 1850* (1946), and articles in journals. Pitt lectured on Australian history to combined University of Adelaide-Workers' Educational Association classes. His research notes, compiled as archivist in answer to countless historical queries, were filed in the archives for public use. As principal librarian, his involvement in history was less direct but his interest remained, though his attempt to create a museum-collection of printed items illustrating South Australian life had to be abandoned.

His professional dedication inspired a younger generation of librarians, some of whom later took up senior positions in South Australia and elsewhere. Those who worked with him were expected to give of their best at all times. Pitt was a ready listener who acknowledged their contributions. He respected civilized values, recognized the case for promoting women to senior positions, opposed censorship, and had much common sense and humour. He displayed a somewhat old-fashioned courtesy in formal staff relations and throughout his career always had 'the honour to be' the board's 'Obedient Servant'. Reflecting on his work, he hoped that any criticism would relate to what he had done and not to what he had to leave undone. He retired in February 1955.

Of middle height and fair complexion, Pitt had a voice with a slightly reedy timbre. His pastimes included tennis, swimming, dancing, music and, above all, reading. He lived in modest rooms and accumulated few possessions—libraries contained all the books he wished to read. Pitt's passion for indexing was almost a way of life. His administrative commitments were laid out chronologically on small cards in a tray, and he made an author-index to his notes on the numerous books he read for pleasure. In retirement he several times travelled abroad. He had been raised in the Unitarian Church, but later became an agnostic. Survived by his daughter, he died on 4 April 1972 in North Adelaide and was cremated. His estate was sworn for probate at $157 524.

C. Bridge, *A Trunk Full of Books* (Adel, 1986); H. Bryan (ed), *ALIAS*, 3 vols (Syd, 1988-91); Libraries Bd of SA, Annual Report, *PP* (SA), no 54, 1948-56; *Archives and Manuscripts*, 4, no 7, 1972, p 2; *Aust Lib J*, May 1972, p 176; *Sth Australiana*, 11, no 2, 1972; G. L. Fischer, 'The South Australian Archives Department: its founders and contribution to South Australian historical studies', *J of Hist Soc of SA*, 13, 1985, p 5; *Advertiser* (Adel), 5, 8 Apr 1972; Pitt papers (Mort L); N. Adams, George Pitt (taped interview and ts, 1969, Mort L).   G. L. FISCHER

PIZZEY, JACK CHARLES ALLAN (1911-1968), schoolteacher and premier, was born on 2 February 1911 at Childers, Queensland, second child of John Thomas Pizzey, bookseller, and his second wife Ellen Elliott, née Brand, both Queensland born. Educated at Childers State, Maryborough Central Boys' and Bundaberg High schools, Jack became a pupil-teacher at Bundaberg South State School in 1927. He went on to teach at Childers and Leichhardt Street (Brisbane) State schools, at the former from 1932 and the latter from 1935. In his youth he played tennis and Rugby League football, but it was as a cricketer that he showed most potential, winning a place (1929-30) as a spin bowler in the Queensland Colts. In 1931 he was selected for the Sheffield Shield team to play Victoria, but the match was washed out. He was later a founding member (1959-68) of the Queensland Cricketers' Club. At the Presbyterian Church, Childers, on 27 March 1937 he married Mabel Audrey Kingston, a shop-assistant; they were to have two children.

Mobilized in the Militia as a gunner on 15 July 1940, Captain Pizzey transferred to the Australian Imperial Force on 30 September 1942. He served in Australia, mainly with the 5th Field Regiment in which he held the post of quartermaster (from January 1944). During this time he continued his studies at the University of Queensland (B.A., 1942; Dip.Ed., 1954). After his A.I.F. appointment ended on 25 January 1945, he returned to teaching, at Ayr High and Intermediate School. Appointed district organizer for the Board of Adult Education in 1946, he supervised the establishment of centres at Townsville and Maryborough.

In 1949 Pizzey resigned from the Department of Public Instruction to become manager of the Childers Cane Farmers' Co-Operative and secretary to the Isis District Cane Growers' Executive. The experience gained in representing sugar-farmers fired his ambition for a parliamentary career. In 1950 he won the safe Country Party seat of Isis in the Legislative Assembly. Made responsible for education matters on the Opposition front-bench, he gained a reputation as an 'analytical critic' and a 'hard debater'. Although he maintained 'friendly' relations with his political opponents, he frequently became 'red-faced' in debate.

Following the split in the Queensland branch of the Australian Labor Party in 1957, the conservative parties took office in August, for the first time in almost twenty-five years, under (Sir) Francis Nicklin [q.v.15]. Pizzey was elected deputy-leader of the Country Party and appointed minister for education, a post he held until January 1968; he also held the migration portfolio (1960-68), and had responsibility for Aboriginal and Island affairs (1962-68) and police (1962-68).

Pizzey focused his attention on secondary education, an area largely neglected by previous governments. He was convinced that secondary schooling should be available to all, rather than to the comparative few who passed the scholarship examination. That examination was abolished in 1962 and the minimum school leaving age was raised to 15 in 1964. Spending on education expanded significantly from £15 million in 1957-58 to £19 million in 1959-60. The number of high schools more than trebled, a university college was established (1961) at Townsville, and planning began for a second university in Brisbane. Pizzey came to be regarded as an 'enlightened' education minister. He even forged an unprecedented link between the Country Party and continuing education. The substantial advances made in the State's secondary education were his most important achievement. In 1962 the University of Queensland conferred on him an honorary LL.D.

Intervention in education matters did not always bring Pizzey praise. A dispute arose over whether the State's senior and junior certificate examinations should be set and marked by the University of Queensland or the Department of Education. Pizzey's Education Act (1964) gave increased authority to the department. Under pressure in 1966 from the Queensland Teachers' Union to ameliorate wage discrimination against female teachers and reduce classroom workloads, he inflamed the teachers by asserting that radicals had corrupted their union. Conflict over the employment of under-qualified teachers strained relations between the department and teaching staff. The situation so deteriorated that it led to Brisbane's first teachers' strike in 1968.

Less sympathetic than Nicklin towards issues of civil liberty, Pizzey proposed that the police should be given more powers.

When mass arrests occurred during anti-Vietnam War demonstrations in 1966-67, he was accused of making 'arbitrary use' of the Traffic Act to quell leftist protest. In the face of growing demands for cultural self-determination for Aborigines, he remained an ardent supporter of assimilation. He continued to represent sugar interests, and in May 1968 was appointed deputy-leader of the Australian mission to the international sugar conference, held in Geneva.

Nicklin retired on 17 January 1968, allowing the loyal Pizzey to succeed him as Country Party leader and premier. (Sir) Johannes Bjelke-Petersen was elected deputy-leader of the parliamentary party. The new premier's tasks as a leader were daunting, given the resolute style and long incumbency of his predecessor. Like Nicklin, and unlike Bjelke-Petersen, Pizzey maintained an amicable working relationship with his Liberal coalition partners, and more than once advocated an amalgamation of the two parties. Survived by his wife, and their daughter and son, he died suddenly of myocardial infarction on 31 July 1968 at Chermside, Brisbane. He was accorded a state funeral and was cremated with Anglican rites.

C. Lack (comp), *Three Decades of Queensland Political History, 1929-1960* (Brisb, 1962); R. Fitzgerald, *A History of Queensland from 1915 to the Early 1980s* (Brisb, 1984); A. Patience (ed), *The Bjelke-Petersen Premiership 1968-1983* (Melb, 1985); *PD* (Qld), vol 249, 1968, p 5; *Courier-Mail*, 1 Aug 1968, 19 Mar 1981.   PAUL D. WILLIAMS

PLANT, ERIC CLIVE PEGUS (1890-1950), army officer, was born on 23 April 1890 at Charters Towers, Queensland, fourth child of English-born parents Charles Frederic Plant, mining manager, and his wife Isabel Marion, née Pegus. E. H. T. Plant [q.v.5] was his uncle. Charles Plant later commanded the 3rd Queensland (Kennedy) Regiment. Educated at Brisbane Grammar School, Eric served in the cadets and gained a commission (March 1908) in the 9th Infantry (Moreton) Regiment. In December 1912 he joined the Administrative and Instructional Staff, Permanent Military Forces, as a lieutenant and was posted to Victoria. Next year he became adjutant of the 15th Light Horse Regiment. On 15 August 1914 he was transferred to the Australian Imperial Force and appointed junior aide-de-camp to Major General (Sir) William Bridges [q.v.7], commander of the 1st Division. They sailed for Egypt in October.

In March 1915 Plant was appointed assistant-adjutant, 9th Battalion. During the landing at Gallipoli on 25 April, he led some of the foremost troops possibly as far as Third ('Gun') Ridge before withdrawing to avoid being isolated. On the following day he was promoted captain. Wounded in the left hand on 3 June, he rejoined the battalion on 12 July. In September he was evacuated to Malta, and thence to England, suffering from enteric fever. After returning to Egypt, he was sent to the Western Front in March 1916 as brigade major, 6th Brigade. For his work at Fleurbaix, Rue Marle and Pozières, France, in March-August, he was awarded the Distinguished Service Order.

Following a bitter winter, Plant took part in the Bapaume operations in March-April 1917 and in the advance to the Hindenburg line. On 3 May, during the 2nd battle of Bullecourt, he reorganized 'broken' infantry and rallied stragglers while under heavy artillery fire; he won a Bar to his D.S.O. In July he was appointed to headquarters, 4th Australian Division. At St Margaret's parish church, Westminster, London, on 7 February 1918 he married Oona Hunter Brown. When the Armistice was announced he was seconded to the staff of the army's Repatriation and Demobilization Department. He was mentioned in dispatches five times in 1917-19, awarded the French Croix de Guerre and appointed O.B.E. in 1919, and promoted temporary lieutenant colonel in May 1920.

Plant came home to Australia in July and his A.I.F. appointment terminated on 10 September. On 1 October he was transferred to the Staff Corps with the rank of major. He attended the Staff College at Camberley, England, in 1921-22, held a staff post at Army Headquarters, Melbourne, as a brevet lieutenant colonel, and became an instructor at the Royal Military College, Duntroon, Federal Capital Territory, in January 1924. Sent on exchange to the War Office, London, in 1927, he returned to Australia and served on the staff of the 1st Cavalry Division (from 1929) and the 11th Mixed Brigade (from 1933). In March 1937 he was made director of military training, A.H.Q., with the brevet rank of colonel (from July); in October 1939 he was appointed commandant of the R.M.C., as a temporary brigadier.

On 1 July 1940 Plant was seconded to the A.I.F. and placed in command of the 24th Brigade, which sailed for the Middle East in December. From 5 March 1941 he commanded the A.I.F.'s Rear Echelon as a temporary major general. On 23 June he reverted to his former rank and took over the 25th Brigade. He led it during the final phase of the Syrian campaign in June-July and was once more mentioned in dispatches. Back in Australia, he headed (from January 1942) Western Command, again as a temporary major general. He took charge of the Victorian Lines of Communication Area in April 1942 and held the equivalent post in New South Wales from September 1943. On 6 August 1946 he was placed on the Retired List. He was appointed C.B. (1945) and an officer of the Order of St John of Jerusalem (1947).

Plant was a member of the United Service Institution of New South Wales and the United Service Club, Brisbane. Five ft 7¼ ins (171 cm) tall, he had a charming manner and dressed impeccably. Beginning as an ebullient junior leader at Gallipoli, he was inspired —as a seasoned soldier on the Western Front —by (Sir) John Gellibrand [q.v.8] and emerged as a hard-working, diplomatic, versatile and thoroughly professional officer with a flair for training and administration. Survived by his wife and their two sons, he died of cancer on 17 May 1950 at Bayview, Sydney, and was cremated. His elder son Harold served in the Royal Australian Air Force in World War II. Frank Crozier's portrait (1916) of Eric Plant is held by the R.M.C.

C. E. W. Bean, *The Story of Anzac*, 1, 2 (Syd, 1921, 1924) and *The A.I.F. in France, 1916-18* (Syd, 1929, 1933, 1937, 1942); N. K. Harvey, *From Anzac to the Hindenburg Line* (Brisb, 1941); J. E. Lee, *Duntroon* (Canb, 1952); G. Long, *Greece, Crete and Syria* (Canb, 1953); *Stand-To* (Canb), July 1950; *SMH*, 19 May 1950; information from Brig P. Pursey, Duntroon, Canb, and Sqn Ldr R. Cox, Narrabeen, Syd.

R. SUTTON

PLATE, CARL OLAF; *see* LEWERS

PLATE, MARGO; *see* LEWERS

PLAYFORD, MAXWELL ERNEST (1902-1943), metallurgical engineer, was born on 14 January 1902 at Norton Summit, South Australia, fourth of seven children of John Tomlinson Playford, orchardist, and his wife Rose Eliza, née Inglis, both South Australian born. Thomas Playford [q.v.11] was his grandfather and (Sir) Thomas Playford, premier (1938-65) of South Australia, was his first cousin. Educated at Norton Summit Public and Norwood High schools, Max studied mining and metallurgy at the University of Adelaide (B.E., 1925; M.E., 1928) and qualified as a fellow (1924) of the South Australian School of Mines and Industries.

During 1923 Playford worked at Port Pirie, and at Broken Hill, New South Wales. In 1924 he became a research metallurgist at the Mount Lyell Mining & Railway Co. Ltd, Queenstown, Tasmania. Promoted to mill superintendent in 1928, he redesigned and rebuilt the old, inefficient mill. It dramatically reduced the emission of sulphur dioxide. One bold innovation, the installation of an 8-ft (2.4 m) diameter ball mill, a giant for its time,

was regarded as an extraordinary achievement for a young man: it revealed his confidence, brilliance in research, determination in execution, qualities of leadership, and ability to win the trust of his superiors. On 28 March 1929 at Gormanston he married with Methodist forms Agnes Jessie Anderson, a 20-year-old teacher of art.

Playford was appointed plant superintendent at Great Boulder Pty Gold Mines Ltd, Kalgoorlie, Western Australia, in February 1934. Later that year he joined Wiluna Gold Mines Ltd as chief metallurgist. Because the arsenical ore at Wiluna was not amenable to the cyanide process (the common method of extracting gold), he built a smelter into which lead was added to collect the gold and silver, which were then easily separated. From March 1938 he was assistant general manager of Mount Morgan Ltd, Queensland, where he again improved metallurgical performance.

A fervent Baptist and regular churchgoer, Playford lived by the highest standards: he never swore, and was honest to a fault and studious in his disposition, yet he felt at ease with all manner of people. Tall and good-looking, with black, curly hair, he enjoyed gardening and photography, and loved mountaineering, bush-walking and children. He was a member (1934) of the Australasian Institute of Mining and Metallurgy and wrote numerous technical papers on metallurgical subjects.

In 1941, hoping to contribute more directly to the war effort, Playford joined the Commonwealth Department of Munitions. After working for the Directorate of Explosives Supply in Melbourne for a short time, he was sent to England and the United States of America to learn the latest methods of production. In Sydney, early in 1943, he was appointed manager of St Mary's Filling Factory, one of the largest munitions plants in Australia. Survived by his wife and their adopted daughter, he died of acute encephalomyelitis on 10 October that year in a private hospital in Sydney and was buried in the cemetery at Norton Summit. His estate was sworn for probate at £6988.

G. Blainey, *The Peaks of Lyell* (Melb, 1954); A'sian Inst of Mining and Metallurgy, *Procs*, Sept-Dec 1943, p xlii; *Advertiser* (Adel), 12 Oct 1943; information from Mr L. E. Fielding, Kew, Melb, Prof P. Howell, Flinders Univ, Mrs E. Playford, Sturt, Mrs J. H. Treloar, Linden Park, Adel, and Mrs M. Playford-Snarskis, Norton Summit, SA.

D. F. FAIRWEATHER

PLOWMAN, SIR CLAUDE (1895-1954), businessman and yachtsman, was born on 14 April 1895 in Hobart, eldest of three children of Thomas William Scudder, storekeeper, and

his wife Mary Isabel, née Crow. By 1899
Thomas Scudder had changed his surname to
Plowman. Claude was educated at Queen's
College and Hobart Technical School. During
World War I he served at sea as a marine engineer. After visiting the United States of
America to study the manufacture of radios,
he settled in Sydney where he worked as a
manufacturer's agent and (from 1926) as an
electrical engineer. On 9 July 1925 he married
Ruth Anna Hassell with Presbyterian forms at
Randwick. As chairman and managing director, he established in 1931 Airzone Ltd, which
built radios at Camperdown. At different
stages in World War II the factory produced
instruments for testing radar and electrical
communications, assembled grenades and
made asdic equipment.

Plowman's passion was sailing. In 1922 he
was a director and rear commodore of the
Sydney Amateur Sailing Club. He sailed *Sea
Rover* until about 1941. In 1929 he joined the
Royal Sydney Yacht Squadron. Although he
won several of the squadron's trophies in his 6-
metre, *Sjo-Ro*, he was best known for his successes with the cutter, *Morna*, which he
bought from (Sir) Frank Packer [q.v.15] about
1941. Built for Sir Alexander MacCormick
[q.v.10] in 1913, *Morna* was 64 ft (19.5 m) in
length, with an 85-ft (26 m) mast and a beam
of 13 ft (4 m). Her blue and gold racing flag
commemorated his wife's Swedish family
background. In World War II *Morna* carried
the Royal Australian Air Force roundel as a
sign that she was used to instruct members of
the Air Training Corps in seamanship. Plowman was deputy-commandant of the Sydney
Harbour Bomber Observers and helped to
set up a branch of the Royal Australian Naval
Auxiliary Patrol in Hobart. He also spent time
in England as an Australian Comforts Fund
commissioner.

As a senior member of the Royal Yacht
Club of Tasmania, Plowman was prominent in
the 1945 discussions that led to the establishment of the Sydney-Hobart Yacht Race. He
skippered *Morna* for three successive 'first
across the line' wins, beginning in 1946. In the
1948 race *Morna* carried a crew of sixteen (including a shipwright) in 'luxurious comfort',
as well as tools and materials for repairs, and
sufficient provisions for a month at sea. Plowman's attention to detail was legendary—
every member of the crew was given a typed
copy of his duties before and during the race.
After his 1948 win, he told the press that the
race should be held every two years, as it was
'a heavy cost' and 'a lot of people cannot spend
every Christmas away from home'. A 'stickler
for discipline', Plowman was accorded the deference due to a 'master of an ocean-going
liner'. Just a few hours after he crossed the
line on New Year's Eve 1948, for his third
Sydney-Hobart win, his knighthood (recom-

mended by the Tasmanian government) was
announced.

When his firm was taken over by Electricity
Meter & Allied Industries Ltd (later Email
Ltd) in 1946, Plowman remained as manager
of Airzone, which in the late 1940s had a large
factory at Silverwater. He was chairman of
Sealanes Pty Ltd and Silverwater Rubber Co.
Pty Ltd, and a director of Wondercakes Pty
Ltd and British Oil Engines (Australasia) Pty
Ltd. In 1953 he was vice-president of the
Employers' Federation of New South Wales.

Lady Plowman was a notable society hostess
and a patron of musicians and painters. Sunday cruises in *Morna* gave Plowman the
opportunity to offer lunch, as a 'polite and
gracious' host, to many foreign visitors. He belonged to the Australian, American National
and Elanora Country clubs, the Royal Sydney
and Australian golf clubs, and the Tasmanian
Club, Hobart. Plowman died of cancer on
5 September 1954 at his Darling Point home
and was cremated with Anglican rites; his
wife, and their son and daughter survived
him. *Morna*, renamed *Kurrewa IV* by the
Livingston brothers, was first across the line
in four more Sydney-Hobart races.

Email Ltd, *The Email Group-Australia* (Syd,
1956); P. R. Stephenson (comp), *Sydney Sails* (Syd,
1962); L. D'Alpuget, *Yachting in Australia* (Melb,
1980); Roy Syd Yacht Squadron, *Annual Report*,
1942; *SMH*, 26 June 1934, 4 Sept 1942, 9 Aug 1945,
1, 3 Jan 1949, 10 Feb 1951, 24 Oct 1953, 7 Sept 1954,
3 May 1955; *Examiner* (Launc), 1 Jan 1949; *Mercury* (Hob), 3 Jan 1949; PCS 1/39, item 79/9/48,
PCS 19/1, item 4/19 (TA); information from
Mr E. Bryden-Brown, Narrabeen, Mr V. Dibben,
Cremorne, Mr R. Hull, Annandale, Mrs J. Morris,
Edgecliff, Mr D. G. Robertson, Kirribilli, and Mr
D. Walker-Smith, Woollahra, Syd.   T. H. IRVING

PLOWMAN, ELSIE MAY (1905-1978),
hotelier, was born on 13 November 1905 at
Kalgoorlie, Western Australia, only daughter
of James Samuel Paxton, an English-born contractor, and his wife Elizabeth Josephine, née
McIntyre, who came from Victoria. Elsie was
sent to the Coolgardie convent school, where
she was reputedly reprimanded for ringing the
Angelus bell on Armistice Day, 1918. After her
family moved to Perth she attended Loreto
Convent, Claremont. In 1924 she gained a
diploma in book-keeping at Stott's Business
College. By 1921 her parents were managing
the Esplanade Hotel on the Swan River fore-
shore. That year, during a long-running strike
by the hotel's barmaids and caterers over
the employment of Chinese waiters, she witnessed a spirited clash between her mother
and the trade-union secretary Cecilia Shelley.

The Paxtons bought the hotel from N. W.
Harper [q.v.9] in 1927. Mrs Paxton, a stickler

for style and decorum, trained Elsie to run a good house modelled on the Menzies Hotel in Melbourne, where Elizabeth had been in service before her marriage. Comfort was paramount at the Esplanade. Fresh flower arrangements, and good quality crockery, silver and linen were mandatory; morning tea was served, guests' shoes were cleaned, and meals were provided for travellers. Disturbances were quelled with a look. At the district registrar's office, Perth, on 14 September 1937 Elsie married Reginald Plowman, a company director and a divorcee. Known as 'Peter', he served (1941-46) in the Royal Australian Naval Volunteer Reserve as a mine-disposal officer. The marriage was dissolved in 1948. Peter settled in Western Samoa, and was elected to the island's Legislative Assembly in 1954.

On 14 June 1957, following her brother Roy's death, Mrs Plowman became the hotel's sole licensee. As managing director of the Hotel Esplanade Pty Ltd, she worked closely with its chairman Geoffrey Arnott. A tall, imposing figure, well groomed and immaculately dressed, she provided a home away from home for prime ministers, ambassadors, musicians, dancers, actors, submarine commanders, financiers and golfers. Many became friends; some, like (Dame) Pattie and (Sir) Robert Menzies [q.v.15], were regular visitors. Elsie never drank in the public rooms, but in private proved a generous hostess and a discreet confidante. Her staff was loyal and gave long service. The cuisine was first rate: bubble and squeak (prepared by the Chinese chefs) and pavlova (a meringue cake made by Herbert Sachse and resembling its New Zealand counterpart) were *specialités de la maison*. The cellar was excellent.

If Elsie personified the Paxton family motto, *industria ditat* (industry enriches), she also liked to relax. She loved shopping at Georges Ltd in Melbourne; she usually backed outsiders at the races; and, after Mass at St Mary's Cathedral on Sunday evenings, she played poker for modest stakes. Her favourite charities were the St John of God Hospital, Subiaco, and the Little Sisters of the Poor. In July 1963 she won a much publicized case in the Supreme Court against the Perth City Council over a regulation requiring her to remove the hotel's verandah posts. She sold the hotel in 1969 and the building was demolished in 1972. Survived by one of her two sons, she died on 17 April 1978 in Perth and was buried with Catholic rites in Karrakatta cemetery.

West Australian, 19 Apr 1979; Plowman scrapbook and clippings held by, and information from, Mr W. Plowman, Manning, Perth; information from Mr P. Plowman, Crawley, Perth.

WENDY BIRMAN

PLUNKETT, THOMAS FLOOD (1877-1957), dairy-farmer and politician, was born on 19 December 1877 at Indooroopilly, Brisbane, fifth of eight children of THOMAS PLUNKETT (1840-1913), grazier, and his wife Maria, née Ryan. Thomas senior, son of John Plunkett and his wife Catherine, née Flood, was born in April 1840, probably at Arrigal, County Meath, Ireland. He arrived in Queensland in the *Fiery Star* in 1863 and took up a selection at Waterford. On 2 May 1866 at St Stephen's Catholic Church, Brisbane, he married Maria, an 18-year-old immigrant from Ireland.

In 1869 Plunkett bought a property on the Albert River near Tamborine; he engaged in dairy-farming, grazing and crop-growing, and also established a general store. A supporter of Sir Thomas McIlwraith [q.v.5], he won the seat of Albert in the Legislative Assembly in 1888 and held it until 1908, save for one term (1896-99). He advocated opening crown lands for closer settlement and backed co-operative initiatives by farmers. A member of the Colonists' Anti-Convention Bill League, he campaigned against Federation, fearing economic domination by New South Wales and Victoria. He wanted to exclude rural workers from general industrial awards, withdrew his support from the Kidston [q.v.9] government in 1907 and retired from parliament in the following year.

Plunkett had bought more land in the Logan area, and several of his children extended their family and business links in the district. He was described as 'tall, fair-bearded, and handsome, and a sort of unofficial governor of his neighbourhood'. Maria, who was cheerful, energetic and charitable, contributed to his influence. Survived by his wife, and their four daughters and four sons, Plunkett died on 2 September 1913 at Sandgate, Brisbane, and was buried in Tamborine cemetery.

His son Thomas Flood was educated at Tamborine State School and St Joseph's College, Gregory Terrace, Brisbane. A good sportsman, like his father, he represented his district in cricket and football. About 1898 he moved to a family property on the Albert River, at Kerry, near Beaudesert, and made it a leading dairy-farm. He was a founding director (1904) and chairman (1915-57) of the Logan & Albert Co-operative Dairy Co. Ltd; the latter post was to remain the linchpin of his career in the dairy industry. Active in the Farmers' Union and a number of local societies, he sat (1914-32) on the Beaudesert Shire Council. At St Mary's Catholic Church, Beaudesert, on 12 October 1915 he married Margaret Ellen Higgins ('Nan') Deerain, the daughter of a farmer.

Queensland's butter-production seasons complemented those in the southern States, though conditions were, in general, less benign. Representatives from the industry in

Queensland, including Plunkett and James Purcell [q.v.11], became national leaders in promoting co-operative pricing and exports. Plunkett was prominent on dairy-marketing committees (1915-21) and chairman (1921-23) of the Queensland-New South Wales Butter Pool Committee. Founding chairman (1925-48) and a member (until 1957) of the Australian Dairy Produce Board (which supervised exports), he visited Britain and Europe in 1935 to investigate marketing. He was also a member (1926-34) of the Australian Stabilisation Committee (which implemented Thomas Paterson's [q.v.11] scheme), and a founding director (1934) and chairman (1950-57) of its successor, the Commonwealth Dairy Produce Equalisation Committee Ltd. In addition, he chaired (1939-48) the Dairy Produce Control Committee, set up to deal with wartime contingencies.

In Queensland, where there was a long tradition of legislative support for agricultural co-operatives, Plunkett was a member (1925-57) of the Butter Marketing Board. He held the Legislative Assembly seat of Albert (1929-50) for the Country and Progressive National Party (Country Party from 1936) and, following a redistribution, that of Darlington (1950-57).

A forceful speaker for dairying interests, Plunkett was, again like his father, respected for his integrity, equanimity and good humour. He was considered to have 'made a great contribution to dairying . . . by treating every section of it with absolute fairness for the general good'. In 1957 he was appointed C.B.E. Survived by his wife, and their two daughters and three sons, he died on Christmas Eve 1957 in the Mater Misericordiae Hospital, South Brisbane, and was buried in Gleneagle cemetery, near Beaudesert. His former home was sold in 1960 and converted into Boys Town.

M. J. Fox (comp), *The History of Queensland, its People and Industries* (Adel, 1919); R. J. J. Twohill, *Epitome of Dairying Industry Organisations in Australia* (Syd, 1956); N. T. Drane and H. R. Edwards (eds), *The Australian Dairy Industry* (Melb, 1961); *Plunkett* (Tamborine, Qld, 1980, OL); *Queenslander*, 13 Sept 1913; *Qld Dairyfarmer*, 18 Jan 1958; Z. Abidin, The Origins and Development of the Queensland Country Party 1909-1932 (M.A. thesis, Univ Qld, 1958).   S. J. ROUTH

PLUNKETT, WILLIAM GEORGE (1910-1975), printer and aphorist, was born on 29 October 1910 at Herberton, Queensland, elder child of Queensland-born parents Samuel Joseph Wark, miner, and his wife Mary Honorah, née Doherty, both of whom died in 1912, within five weeks of each other. Raised in Sydney (from 1915) by his aunt Mary Plunkett (née Wark) and her husband James (d.1928), Bill attended Woollahra Public School and won a scholarship to Christian Brothers' College, Waverley, but left at the age of 14 to help to support the family. He served a five-year apprenticeship (from 1926) to a compositor and linotype operator at the Waverley Press Ltd. By 1934 Plunkett was the firm's foreman. At St Stephen's Anglican Church, Newtown, on 29 September that year he married Ruby Adell Brewer, a ledgerkeeper.

On 23 November 1943 Plunkett enlisted in the Royal Australian Air Force. He was then 5 ft 8 ins (173 cm) tall, with blue eyes and light brown hair. Serving in Australia as an aircrafthand and telephone-operator, he rose to leading aircraftsman before being discharged in Sydney on 26 March 1946. As printing production manager (from 1947) with W. Nevill & Co. Ltd, manufacturing stationers and publishers of the *Olympic Desk Calendar*, he began to collect literary quotations to provide the calendar's 'thought for the day'. Plunkett included a few pithy phrases of his own in 1961, and added more in the ensuing years. Many of his aphorisms were based on family incidents; others were drawn from conversations with colleagues at the Earlwood-Bardwell Park branch of the Returned Sailors', Soldiers' and Airmen's Imperial League of Australia, of which he was vice-president.

Jotted down on anything to hand—a packet of Tally-Ho cigarette papers, a newspaper, or even a toilet roll—and shaped into quotable form, Plunkett's maxims appeared in some 400 000 desk calendars each year, usually on Wednesdays, above the initials W.G.P. His words stood alongside quotations from the Bible, Shakespeare, Bacon, Milton, Pope and Coleridge. Most of his own epigrams were homely and didactic: 'One of the real secrets of happiness is to be content with what you have', 'A good deed, no matter how small, is worth more than the grandest good intention' and 'Husbands are like the fire on the hearth —likely to go out if unattended'. There was often a sardonic touch: 'Experience is a good school, but the fees come high', 'Travel may well broaden the mind, but it certainly narrows the bank account' and 'Many a self-made man worships his maker'. A number referred to women: 'Clothes that make the woman break the man', 'Lots of women aren't as young as they're painted' and 'For every girl with a curve there are several men with angles'.

Some desk-calendar readers thought that W.G.P. stood for 'Wednesday's Golden Proverb'. The relative few who knew the identity of the motto-maker dubbed Plunkett 'the man of a thousand sayings'. A quick-witted raconteur, he enjoyed a joke, a bet and a beer, but he could also be strict, pedantic and unyielding. He read avidly, habitually consulted the *Oxford English Dictionary*, usually carried a cryptic crossword puzzle in his pocket, and described himself as an 'ordinary bloke' who liked to 'play around with words'. Almost weekly, for fourteen years, he provided a touch of wisdom (or at least reflection) and moments of pleasure (or occasional irritation) for countless office workers. Survived by his wife, and their daughter and son, he died of cancer on 24 June 1975 at Royal Prince Alfred Hospital and was cremated. Australian desk calendars continue to quote him.

Tudor Bunch of Dates (Syd, 1997); *Collins Desk Calendar Refill* (Syd, 1998); *Corporate Express Top Hole Calendar Refill* (Syd, 1999); *Canb Times*, 11 June 1967; *SMH*, 13 Aug 1968, 25 June 1975, 26 Feb 1982; *Sun* (Syd), 8 July 1969; *National Times*, 4-9 Mar 1974; information from Mrs B. Rogers, North Ryde, Syd.   JOHN RITCHIE

POLGLAZE, MURIEL JEAN (1911-1978), economist, was born on 21 May 1911 at Ararat, Victoria, daughter of William Henry Polglaze, schoolteacher, and his wife Annie Murdison, née Talbett, both Victorian born. The family moved to Canterbury and Jean attended Melbourne Girls' High School. Professor (Sir) Douglas Copland [q.v.13] lived near the Polglazes and probably encouraged her to enter the University of Melbourne (B.Com., 1932; M.Com., 1936). After graduating, she remained in the faculty of commerce as Copland's research assistant. From 1933 she also worked as a tutor.

While holding (1934-35) a Kilmany scholarship for economic research, Miss Polglaze wrote a thesis on business profits in relation to changes in economic activity in Australia. In 1936 she was appointed temporary lecturer in economics. A newspaper article described her as 'modest', 'graceful' and 'golden-haired'. Awarded a Rockefeller Foundation fellowship, she visited (1937-38) universities in England, Sweden and the United States of America, 'studying the measurement and analysis of investment, and familiarizing herself with techniques that might be applied to Australian data'. She also studied the measurement of business cycles. In 1939 she returned to the University of Melbourne as lecturer in statistical method.

On Copland's recommendation, the Federal government established in 1940 a statistical section in the Department of Defence Co-ordination (later the Department of Defence) with Polglaze as part-time head. Her unit was responsible for analysing data provided by the departments of the Army, the Navy, Air, Munitions, and Aircraft Production with the aim of presenting to the War Cabinet, at regular intervals, a 'picture of the Australian war effort'. Working with minimum time and under difficult circumstances, she and her staff were required to produce infor-

mation that was accurate, concise and easily understood. For her services she was appointed M.B.E. (1952).

After World War II Polglaze resumed full-time teaching at the university and in 1946 was appointed senior lecturer in the new department of economics. In 1953 she was promoted to associate-professor. She taught several honours courses, but specialized in statistical method. 'Polly', as she came to be affectionately known, advised honours students on their careers and guided some of them in their choice of postgraduate study abroad. Her standard practice was to invite the best honours students to continue in the department as tutors while pursuing a master's degree part time. This course gave them the chance to find out whether they were suited to academic life.

In addition to lecturing and tutoring, Polglaze served as sub-dean of the faculty of economics and commerce and as acting-head of the department of economics. She sat on numerous university, faculty and departmental committees. A 'perfectionist' and 'at times a hard task-master', she had 'a pleasant personality and delightful sense of humour, which was not always readily recognized by those who did not know her well'. After five years of poor health, Polglaze retired on 31 March 1977. She died of ischaemic heart disease on 19 June 1978 at Box Hill and was cremated with Anglican rites.

Univ Melb, *Staff News*, 6, Aug 1978, p 91; *Economic Record*, 54, Dec 1978, p 406.
          LYNNE WILLIAMS

POLLAK, HANS (1885-1976), philologist, was born on 28 April 1885 in Vienna, son of Jewish parents Moriz Pollak and his wife Marie, née Pessl. Hans studied Scandinavian and comparative philology under Max Jellinek at the University of Vienna (D.Phil., 1908); his special field was the structure of the Gothic verb. In 1907 he was converted to Catholicism. Employed (1908-15) in the phonetic archives section of the Austrian Academy of Sciences, he visited Sweden in 1910, and was granted tenure in 1912. On 3 February 1910 at the Votivkirche, Vienna, he married Ella Johanna Löwith; they were to have one child before being divorced in 1912. While retaining part-time status (1915-26) in the academy, he taught in senior high schools.

Pollak was seconded (1916-18) as *lektor* to the University of Lund, Sweden, and had charge (1920-26) of German and Latin at the Bundesrealgymnasium, one of Vienna's leading schools. A consistent advocate of reform in the teaching of German, he published over thirty learned articles on aspects of philology.

In a civil ceremony in Vienna on 9 January 1926 he married Margaret Hamilton, daughter of Justice Theyre Weigall [q.v.12]. That year he was reappointed to the University of Lund, where he wrote and translated several works on the pedagogy of philology.

Returning to Vienna in 1934, Pollak resumed teaching until 1938 when, he remarkcd, 'I was ... suddenly retired by the Nazis in consideration of my Jewish blood'. Through his wife's connexions, he was able to migrate to Australia; he reached Sydney on 8 April 1939 in the *Aorangi*. In 1940 Professor Augustin Lodewyckx [q.v.10] appointed him part-time tutor in German at the University of Melbourne. Pollak took up a full-time post as assistant-lecturer in German at the University of Western Australia in 1941 and was to be promoted senior lecturer in 1949. In July 1944 he was naturalized. He built up a three-year undergraduate course in German and fostered teaching of the language in secondary schools. Students responded to the courtesy and enthusiasm of the greying scholar, whose slight stammer did not disguise the efficiency born of decades of teaching. Particularly interested in German Romantic writers, he founded (1949) the Western Australian branch of the Australian Goethe Society.

Retirement in 1951 from full-time teaching enabled Pollak to resume productivity in publication. In 1963 he encouraged the establishment of a newsletter in comparative education, to which he contributed. Six years later, at the age of 84, he gave a notable paper on concepts of time in language to the Australasian Universities Language and Literature Association, showing his awareness of contemporary developments in Aboriginal as well as European linguistics. In 1970 he was awarded a D.Litt. by the university. He published eleven more articles in the 1970s, mostly in the *Zeitschrift für Deutsche Philologie*.

Pollak was greatly respected as an exemplar of scholarly values retained and exercised into vigorous old age. He died on 24 April 1976 at Shenton Park and was buried in Karrakatta cemetery. His wife survived him; the son of his first marriage predeceased him. The Pollaks were a devoted couple whose cosmopolitan perspectives contributed, unobtrusively but valuably, to the provincial culture of Perth in the 1940s and 1950s.

F. Alexander, *Campus at Crawley* (Melb, 1963); *Comparative Education*, Nov 1963, May 1964; item 102/1, Univ WA Archives; naturalization file, PP302/1, item WA18210 (NAA, Perth); immigration file, A443, item 1952/15/4522 (NAA, Canb).

G. C. BOLTON

POLLARD, SIR REGINALD GEORGE (1903-1978), army officer, was born on 20 January 1903 at Bathurst, New South Wales, third son of Albert Edgar Pollard, an accountant from England, and his Australian-born wife Thalia Rebecca, née McLean. Educated at the local primary and high schools, Reg entered the Royal Military College, Duntroon, Federal Capital Territory, in 1921; he graduatcd in 1924 wlth the sword of honour for exemplary conduct and performance. In March 1925 he was allotted to the 51st Infantry Brigade. Four months later he was made adjutant and quartermaster of the 17th Battalion (Militia). At St Andrew's Anglican Church, Strathfield, Sydney, on 31 October that year he married Daisy Ethel Potter, a typiste.

In September 1927 Lieutenant Pollard sailed for India where he trained with British regiments. Returning to Sydney in November 1928, he served as adjutant and quartermaster of the 18th and then the 44th battalions (Militia) before being posted to Army Headquarters, Melbourne, in October 1936. He was sent to England in November 1938 to attend the Staff College, Camberley, for a two-year course. Due to the outbreak of World War II, he graduated early (September 1939) and was posted to the Australian High Commission, London, as assistant military liaison officer.

On 21 June 1940 Pollard was transferred to the Australian Imperial Force and promoted major. He was appointed brigade major, 25th Brigade, but on his arrival in the Middle East in March 1941 was detached to headquarters, 7th Division, in Libya. In June-July he commanded the 2nd/31st Battalion during the Syrian campaign and was mentioned in dispatches. Promoted lieutenant colonel in August, he raised and commanded the A.I.F. Junior Staff School.

Pollard was appointed temporary colonel on the A.I.F.'s staff in Ceylon in March 1942. Back in Australia in August, he joined the 6th Division's headquarters (as a general staff officer, 1st grade) and moved with it to Papua in September. He was temporarily attached to the 7th Division from November. For his work during operations (from December 1942 to January 1943) against the Japanese he was awarded the Distinguished Service Order. From January 1943 he trained with the 6th Division in Queensland until being posted in December as chief instructor of the senior wing of the Staff School (Australia), Duntroon. He was appointed to Allied Land Forces Headquarters in February 1945 as deputy director of military operations.

Between February and August 1946 Pollard commanded the Recruit Training Centre at Greta, New South Wales. Sent to England to study air support for land operations, he returned in February 1947 and became an instructor at the Royal Australian Air Force

School of Air Support (School of Land/Air Warfare from March 1948) at Laverton, Victoria. In January 1949 he was posted to A.H.Q. as director of personnel administration; next year he was given responsibility for handling a new national scheme of compulsory military service. After attending the 1951 course at the Imperial Defence College, London, he was appointed director of military operations and plans, and also chairman of the Joint Planning Committee. He accompanied R. G. (Baron) Casey [q.v.13], the minister for external affairs, to Honolulu in August 1952 for the inaugural meeting of the Australia New Zealand United States Council; he also attended the Commonwealth Prime Ministers' Conference in London as Australian military adviser. In March 1953 he was promoted temporary brigadier.

From July to November Pollard commanded the Australian army component of the British Commonwealth Forces, Korea. He was later deputy adjutant general at A.H.Q., Melbourne. Promoted temporary major general in September 1954, he became quartermaster general and third military member of the Military Board. In 1955 he was appointed C.B.E. He was transferred to Sydney in August 1957 as head of Eastern Command. In June 1959 he was promoted lieutenant general and appointed C.B. Five ft 7 ins (170 cm) tall, trim and neat-looking, he had a no-nonsense approach and a likeable manner. He was the embodiment of the professional Staff Corps officer. On 1 July 1960 he became chief of the General Staff. He was appointed K.B.E. in 1961. His term as C.G.S. coincided with a major reorganization of the army's Field Force into a 'pentropic' division, but he was personally ambivalent about this innovation.

Sir Reginald retired on 20 January 1963. He spent his time gardening and raising cattle on a small farm at Wesburn, Victoria, and (from 1974) on a property at Wyrallah, New South Wales, which he named Duntroon. In July 1965 he was appointed honorary colonel (colonel commandant 1968-71) of the Royal Australian Regiment. He visited troops in the Republic of Vietnam (South Vietnam) several times. In 1970 he was Australian secretary to Queen Elizabeth II during her Australian visit and was appointed K.C.V.O. that year. Survived by his wife and their two sons, he died on 9 March 1978 at Wyrallah and was cremated.

G. Long, *To Benghazi* (Canb, 1952); I. McNeill, *The Team* (Canb, 1984), and *To Long Tan* (Syd, 1993); C. D. Coulthard-Clark, *Duntroon* (Syd, 1986); D. M. Horner (ed), *Duty First* (Syd, 1990); *Sun News-Pictorial*, 3 Aug 1950, 13 Sept 1954; *Age* (Melb), 14 Sept 1954, 19-20 Jan 1963; information from Lt-Gen Sir Thomas Daly, Bellevue Hill, Syd, Lt-Col R. L. Pollard, Mount Tamborine, Qld, and Brig G. D. Solomon, Farrer, Canb.

C. D. COULTHARD-CLARK

PONINSKI, ALFRED EMERYK (1896-1968), diplomat and journalist, was born on 18 June 1896 at Koscielisko, Posen (Poznan) province, Poland, son of Count Adolf Poninski, landowner, and his wife Countess Zofia, née Hutten-Czapska. Alfred attended a *gymnasium* at Bromberg (Bydgoszcz), read law at the University of Berlin, and continued his historical and archival studies at Posen, and in Berlin, Brussels, Paris and Bucharest. In 1914 he began work as a journalist.

Count Alfred Poninski was appointed a press attaché at the Polish Legation in Berlin in October 1918 and spent 1919-20 in Warsaw as an assistant in the Ministry of Foreign Affairs. Exempted from military service because of an injury to his leg, he completed a course on diplomatic and consular practice. In 1921 in Warsaw he married Janina Nowodworska; they were to remain childless. From 1921 to 1933 he served in diplomatic posts successively in Brussels, Paris and Moscow. He published an article, 'Les Traditions de la Diplomatie Polonaise', in the *Revue d'Histoire Diplomatique* (1925), and a book, *La Question Polonaise depuis 1830 jusqu'à la Grande Guerre* (Paris, 1926).

Councillor (from 1935) of the Polish Legation (Embassy from 1938) in Bucharest, Poninski endeavoured to popularize Polish history and culture. Following the declaration of World War II, he witnessed the Polish government's escape to Romanian territory. He was minister plenipotentiary until the Romanian authorities closed the Polish consulates and embassy in November 1940. Based at the Polish Embassy in Ankara in 1941, he served as consul general at Istanbul, Turkey, next year. While Polish ambassador to China (1942-45), he was stationed at Chungking. He was appointed to the Légion d'honneur, the Order of the Star of the People's Republic of Romania and the Ordre de Leopold II.

After a short stay in India, Poninski and his wife reached Australia on 12 December 1946 in the *Massula*. He settled at Potts Point, Sydney, and became active in political and public affairs. President (1947-50) of the Polish Democratic Society, Sydney, he was a founding president (1950-51) of the Federal Council of Polish Associations in Australia. He was also involved in organizations designed to forge links with European immigrants: he was vice-president of the United Council of Migrants and of the New Australians' Cultural Association, and a council-member of the State division of the New Settlers' League of Australia, the Australian Council for International Social Service, and the Australian Institute of International Affairs which he assisted with translations and analyses of Russian-language documents. At the time of the (Petrov) royal commission into espionage (1954) he offered his services to the Federal government to translate Russian. He was naturalized on 14 July 1959.

In 1953 Poninski began to contribute regularly to *Tygodnik Katolicki* (*Tygodnik Polski* from 1965), Melbourne; from 1963 he was its chief commentator on world affairs. For many years he wrote a column dealing with world political events for *Wiadomości Polskie*, Sydney, in which he published (1967-68) a series of articles, 'Poland in the Second War'. He was also associated with the Catholic press in Sydney, including the *Catholic Weekly* and the monthly, *Vision*. Adam Nasielski, a colleague, found him 'brilliant, intelligent, unpretentious, forgiving and tactful, but not always patient'; Brunon Grzebyta criticized Poninski, but still admired 'his greatness and his perseverance in working for the Polish community'.

Survived by his wife, Poninski died on 25 March 1968 in Sydney and was buried with Catholic rites in Rookwood cemetery.

S. Loza, *Czy wiesz, kto to jest?* (Warsaw, 1938); T. G. Jackowski, *W walce o polskość* (Krakow, Poland, 1972); J. Drohojowski, *Wspomnienia dyplomatyczne* (Krakow, 1972); S. Schimitzek, *Drogi i bezdroza minionej epoki* (Warsaw, 1976); *Polski Slownik Biograficzny*, 27 (Warsaw, 1983); J. Szembek, *Diariusz wrzesień-grudzień, 1939* (Warsaw, 1989); *Tygodnik Polski*, no 19, 1968, p 2; ASIO file, A6119, item 349 (NAA, Canb).

BOGUMIŁA ZONGOLLOWICZ

PORT, LEO WEISER (1922-1978), businessman and lord mayor, was born on 7 September 1922 at Cracow, Poland, son of Aron Rappaport, poulterer, and his wife Leia, née Amsterdamer. In 1928 the family moved to Berlin, where Leo attended the Adass Yisroel Realgymnasium. They fled to Prague in 1939, and reached Sydney on 24 March in the *Viminale*. Leo attended Sydney Boys' High and Parramatta High schools, won a Commonwealth scholarship, and studied electrical and mechanical engineering at the University of Sydney (B.E., 1946). Like his father and brother, he adopted the surname, Port, and was naturalized in 1945. He joined Donoghue & Carter, consulting engineers, in 1947, and became a partner in 1953. His lift-control system received a merit award for Australian design in 1969.

At the Temple Emanuel, Woollahra, on 25 October 1950 Port had married Edith Bertha Lucas, a Berlin-born pharmacy student. They attended the North Shore Synagogue and became involved in the cultural life of Sydney's Jewish community. After moving to Elizabeth Bay in 1972, Leo walked to the Great Synagogue to attend Sabbath services. He was the Temple Emanuel's delegate (1951-66) to the New South Wales Jewish Board of Deputies, and was active in the Jewish National Fund, a Zionist organization dedicated to raising funds for Israel. For relaxation, he cycled, played golf, swam and skied.

Representing the Civic Reform Association of Sydney, Port was elected to the Sydney City Council in 1969 for Fitzroy Ward. He also served as a member (1969-74) of the State Planning Authority. The new Civic Reform majority was committed to raising the quality of city planning. Port's skill lay in his ability to listen, and to seize upon the expertise of some of the best urban theorists in the country. *The City of Sydney Strategic Plan* of 1971, produced by Port and fellow alderman Andrew Briger, gave expression to a broad philosophical framework for revitalizing inner Sydney and generated much-needed public debate in a city experiencing large-scale commercial development. Port received good publicity, as did the urban-design projects in which he delighted—the creation of Martin Place as a pedestrian mall, the greening of the streets and the opening up of Sydney Square. In 1974 he was appointed M.B.E.

Port accepted an invitation in 1970 to join the Australian Broadcasting Commission's popular television programme, 'The Inventors'; as a panellist he was genial, intelligent and urbane. A passion for excellence in design drove his enthusiasms within and beyond the council. His list of his life's achievements included not only the establishment of a broad strategic plan for city development, but also the design of some golf clubs that impressed the comedian Bob Hope when he visited Sydney.

In 1975 and 1976 Port was elected lord mayor by his fellow aldermen. Neville Wran's Labor government altered the electoral regulations in 1977 to favour a Labor vote, but Civic Reform was again returned, albeit with a reduced majority. The people elected Port lord mayor for a term of three years. After the Labor government failed to oust Civic Reform, elements of the press began to report less kindly on Port's activities and increasingly portrayed him as arrogant. Resident action groups, involved in the 'green bans' that the Australian Builders' Labourers' Federation was placing on high-rise developments, pointed to his firm's involvement in some of those projects. On the council he was under constant pressure from aldermen who accused him of being too closely associated with developers. Although he had resigned from some boards, he remained a director of Manufacturing Investments Ltd and W. G. Watson & Co. Pty Ltd.

On 26 August 1978 a lengthy article by Max Suich and Anne Summers was published in the *National Times*, detailing Port's pecuniary involvement with two finance companies.

(The companies were linked to Citibank N.A., which had acquired a large parcel of urban land when developers mortgaged to it had failed in the property crash of 1974). Survived by his wife, and their daughter and three sons, Port died that day of myocardial infarction and bacterial endocarditis in St Vincent's Hospital, Darlinghurst, and was buried in Rookwood cemetery. He had seen in 'one drab corner of Sydney after another' the possibility of something better. His estate was sworn for probate at $442 615. The Leo Port Park in Tel Aviv, Israel, is named after him.

SMH, 17 Oct 1969, 2 Jan 1974, 4 Mar, 28 Aug 1978, 9, 27 June 1979; *Sun-Herald* (Syd), 25 Aug 1974, 27 Aug 1978; *Age* (Melb), 1 Nov 1976; *National Times*, 26 Oct 1977, 2 Sept 1978; naturalization filc A435, item 1944/4/5536 (NAA, Canb); Syd City Council, *Procs*, 1969-78; Leo Port file, *and* items 2649/70, 983/77, Syd City Council Archives; information from Mrs E. Port, Woollahra, Syd.

SHIRLEY FITZGERALD

PORTEOUS, RICHARD SYDNEY (1896-1963), author, was born on 18 August 1896 at Toorak, Melbourne, second child of Richard Porteous, an Irish-born photographer, and his wife Lillie Alice, née Short, who came from Scotland. Educated at St Albans State School, Richard studied (1911-13) under Bernard Hall and Frederick McCubbin [qq.v.9,10] at the National Gallery schools, Melbourne. He worked as a jackeroo in the Riverina, New South Wales, before enlisting in the Australian Imperial Force on 18 November 1914. Allotted to the 8th Light Horse Regiment, he was mentioned in dispatches (1916) for his services in the Middle East. He was wounded in action on 1 December 1917 at El Burj, Palestine, admitted to hospital with malaria in November 1918, promoted squadron quartermaster sergeant in May 1919 and discharged from the army on 6 October in Melbourne.

After working as a commercial artist, Porteous returned to jackerooing. By early 1925 he was employed by the Barnard family at Coomooboolaroo station, near Duaringa, Queensland. He eventually rose to station manager and acquired a share in the property. On 9 December 1927 he married 20-year-old Marion MacLaren Paterson at St Andrew's Presbyterian Church, Rockhampton. She died in childbirth on 2 August 1930, leaving him with a daughter. At St Paul's Anglican Cathedral, Rockhampton, on 23 August 1932 he married Madge Elizabeth Archer (d.1957), a member of the Archer [qq.v.1,7] family of Gracemere. They were to have two daughters.

In 1937 Porteous left Coomooboolaroo. He started a charter fishing business at Eimeo and gained his master's ticket on 8 August 1938. When the United States of America entered World War II in 1941, the U.S. Army assembled a fleet of small ships to carry supplies to troops in Papua and New Guinea. Porteous signed on as second mate in the *Mongana* on 6 December 1942. His most important posting was as first mate in the *Kurimarau*, which operated out of Milne Bay. He was discharged from the small ships service due to ill health on 6 December 1943.

During the war Porteous began writing stories. Because of wartime censorship, he disguised them as letters to his wife Betty who sent them to the *Bulletin* for publication under the pseudonym 'Standby'. A well-educated woman, she was probably his earliest editor. The first two stories, 'Little Known of These Waters' and 'Once a Fisherman', appeared in print in February 1944. Porteous's collection of stories, also entitled *Little Known of These Waters* (Sydney, 1945), was published by Dymock's [q.v.8] Book Arcade. The stories were well-crafted, realistic narratives in the style popular in contemporary magazines and military publications. The best of them combined humour, character study and seafaring action; the worth of manly labour and the contribution of the Small Ships Fleet to the war were recurring themes.

Porteous settled at Mackay where he built a home in 1950. His worsening health necessitated regular visits to Greenslopes Repatriation Hospital, Brisbane. He received radium treatment for a skin condition caused by exposure to the sun in Palestine; the treatment damaged his left eye, which was surgically removed in 1946. Writing became his main interest. An active member of the Mackay Community Theatre, he wrote and directed a number of plays, including *The Girl from Singapore*. In 1947 Porteous's book *Sailing Orders*, which examined the pressures of war on the crew of a small ship, won second prize in the *Sydney Morning Herald*'s competition for the best novel of the war. His second collection of stories, *Close to the Wind*, was published in 1955 by Angus & Robertson [qq.v.7, 11] Ltd with assistance from the Commonwealth Literary Fund, and a third, *Salvage and Other Stories*, was published in London in 1963.

He also produced a trilogy for young readers—*Tambai Island* (Sydney, 1955), *The Tambai Treasure* (1958) and *The Silent Isles* (1963)—told from the viewpoint of an Australian boy, Ken Gellatly ('Squit'), who lived with his father, a planter, on an island near the Solomons. The series recalled Edwardian boys' adventure books, with their themes of stolen treasure and espionage, and their casts of foreign agents and criminals. The 'ripping yarn' suited Porteous well.

His pastoral sagas, *Brigalow* (1957) and *Cattleman* (1960), were serialized in the

Bulletin and the Brisbane *Courier-Mail* respectively. *Cattleman* won the *Courier-Mail*'s £1000 Centenary Novel Competition. These two books were much loved by readers in Central Queensland for their accurate depictions of station life and their celebration of a rural ethos. Significant in the history of Queensland writing, they also reflected the broader tradition of literary nationalism. The Mackay *Daily Mercury* observed that Porteous's work 'has been praised for the authentic ring of its locale—often the Australian bush or Australian waters'.

By 1960 'Skip' Porteous had written about 130 stories. Many of them were published in the *Bulletin* and other magazines, but not all of them were reprinted in later collections. He developed friendships with Douglas Stewart, the *Bulletin*'s literary editor, and with the writers David Rowbotham and T. A. G. Hungerford. It was only in the final years of his life, after the publication of *Cattleman*, that writing brought him a modest income.

On 31 January 1961 at St John's Anglican Cathedral, Brisbane, Porteous married Jessie Mary Boden, née Archer, a 53-year-old nursing sister and a widow. He died of cancer on 10 April 1963 at his Mackay home and was buried with Anglican rites in Mount Bassett cemetery; his wife survived him, as did the daughters of his previous marriages.

Bulletin, 9, 23 Feb 1944; R. Laurent, *Changing Horses* (Highfields, Qld, 2001); Porteous papers (held by Mr R. Laurent, Cabarlah, Qld).

ROBERT DIXON

PORTER, SELWYN HAVELOCK WATSON CRAIG (1905-1963), army officer and commissioner of police, was born on 23 February 1905 at Tintaldra, Victoria, son of Australian-born parents William Thomas Porter, inspector of stock, and his wife Minnie Weller, née Craig. Educated at Wangaratta High School, Selwyn joined the State Savings Bank of Victoria as a clerk and worked in Melbourne. He was commissioned lieutenant in the 58th Battalion, Militia, in 1924 and promoted major in 1936. Meanwhile, he studied (1934-39) commerce part time at the University of Melbourne. At the Presbyterian Church, Gardenvale, on 30 December 1936 he married Hilda Vera Mavis Drury, a typiste.

In October 1939 Porter was appointed to the Australian Imperial Force as second-in-command of the 2nd/5th Battalion, which was sent to the Middle East in April 1940. During the Libyan campaign he temporarily commanded the 2nd/6th Battalion in the advance beyond Derna and was mentioned in dispatches (1941). Promoted lieutenant colonel and transferred to the 2nd/31st Battalion in February 1941, he led the unit in Syria, where he showed conspicuous bravery and aggression. Although he was wounded in the thigh at Jezzine on 14 June, he remained on duty until ordered to hospital. He was awarded the Distinguished Service Order (1942). One member of his staff marvelled at his extraordinary concentration and grasp of the overall picture throughout the demanding campaign. Porter knew that it was 'a big trust' to be the 'guardian of the lives' of 800 men, and he grieved for the dead.

Known as 'Promissory Bill' because of his frequent promises, Porter was an imposing figure: 6 ft 2 ins (188 cm) tall, with a thrusting chin and a voice that could be terrifying, he inspired respect, confidence and admiration. After returning to Australia, he was posted to Port Moresby in March 1942 with the temporary rank of brigadier and placed in command of the 30th Brigade, the only Militia formation then serving outside Australia. Aware that his brigade had recently been assessed at the bottom of the scale in combat readiness, he introduced A.I.F. officers to improve discipline and training.

Following Japanese landings at Buna in July, Porter led his brigade—and in August-September the larger Maroubra Force—on the Kokoda Track. His judgement that some members of the exhausted 21st Brigade, A.I.F., were suffering 'general demoralization' caused resentment at the time and controversy later. In October he declared that his own 'chocos' had 'earned fame' by their deeds, but he was bitterly and perhaps unfairly critical of the training and spirit of two fresh Militia battalions which fought under his command at Sanananda in December. The static warfare in this area, where he also commanded A.I.F. and American troops, did not suit his dashing nature.

In September 1943 Porter was appointed chief instructor at the Land Headquarters Tactical School, Canungra, Queensland. In November he was given command of the 24th Brigade, which was stationed near Sattelberg, New Guinea. He felt 'marvellous to be back in the A.I.F. again with ... voluntary fighters'. His men rated him highly for the changes he made in administration and the way he conducted the successful Finschhafen campaign. In March 1945 he planned his brigade group's invasion of British North Borneo; his plan included the unprecedented tactic of landing artillery with the assaulting infantry. He was appointed C.B.E. (1947).

Porter returned to Melbourne in October 1945 and was placed on the Reserve of Officers in November. Joining the Myer [qq.v.10,15] Emporium's personnel department, he rose to be staff superintendent. He also continued to serve in the Citizen Military Forces, commanding the 6th Brigade (from

1948), and the 3rd Division (from 1950) as a temporary major general (substantive January 1951). In 1953-54 he was the C.M.F. member of the Military Board.

In 1954 Porter was appointed chief commissioner of the Victoria Police. Although the choice of an outsider was controversial and provoked an outcry from the police, he held the post from January 1955 until his death. He set out to improve the force's efficiency, discipline and standing in the community. His genuine concern for, and pride in, those he commanded—in war and peace—emerged repeatedly in his correspondence and public statements. He was 'not just big in frame, he was big in personality'. Porter was a member of Rotary, patron of the Essendon Football Club and assistant chief commissioner (from 1946) of the Victorian branch of the Boy Scouts' Association. Survived by his wife and their two sons, he died of a coronary occlusion on 9 October 1963 at Mentone and was cremated.

G. Long, *To Benghazi* (Canb, 1952) and *Greece, Crete and Syria* (Canb, 1953) and *The Final Campaigns* (Canb, 1963); R. Paull, *Retreat from Kokoda* (Melb, 1958); D. McCarthy, *South-West Pacific Area —First Year* (Canb, 1959); J. Laffin, *Forever Forward* (Syd, 1994); *Herald* (Melb), 6 July 1954; *Sun News-Pictorial*, 29 Aug 1961, 10 Oct 1963; *Age* (Melb), 10 Oct 1963; Porter papers (AWM); Bosher papers (LaTL).   MARK JOHNSTON

POST, JOSEPH MOZART (1906-1972), musician, was born on 10 April 1906 at Erskineville, Sydney, eldest child of native-born parents John Anthony Joseph Post, law clerk, and his wife Annie Theresa, née Schadel. He grew up in a home rich in the traditions of amateur music-making. His mother was a talented chorister, and his father an enthusiastic conductor much involved with church choirs and suburban musical societies. Joe was regarded as a child prodigy. From about the age of 8 he provided the piano accompaniment at his parents' musical gatherings. He attended the Christian Brothers' parish school at Waverley, won a scholarship, and was among the first students at the New South Wales State Conservatorium of Music, opened under Henri Verbrugghen [q.v.12] in March 1916. Post studied piano and oboe, acquiring enough proficiency on the latter instrument by the age of 15 to play with the New South Wales State Orchestra until it was disbanded in 1922. He then toured with theatre orchestras, visiting New Zealand in 1924 with one of J. C. Williamson [q.v.6] Ltd's musical-comedy companies.

By 1926 Post was teaching oboe and cor anglais at the conservatorium; later, he also offered tuition in piano. He graduated in 1927 with diplomas in performance and teaching (pianoforte). Despite such auspicious beginnings, he did not see his vocation as a teacher nor as an orchestral musician, but chose to build a career as a conductor. The elder Post gave his son extensive informal training in the conductor's art. Joseph always regarded his father as his most important mentor and severest critic.

After valuable experience conducting the conservatorium's chamber orchestra and the choir at St Brigid's Catholic Church, Coogee, Post seized an opportunity in 1932 to organize a 350-voice choir for the Imperial Opera Company (a touring Italian troupe) to perform in the Williamson Imperial Grand Opera Season. When the regular conductor became indisposed, Post conducted a performance of *Aida* at only a few hours notice, which led to regular conducting appearances with the company.

The establishment of the Australian Broadcasting Commission in 1932 introduced a powerful new force to the Australian music scene. Post astutely recognized the potential of radio and accepted an offer from the A.B.C. to form a wireless chorus in Sydney. He severed his connexion with the conservatorium, did some conducting with Sir Benjamin Fuller's [q.v.8] Royal Grand Opera Company and visited Europe in 1935. Returning to Australia, he moved to Melbourne. From 1936 to 1947 he worked for the A.B.C. as a conductor of the Victorian Symphony Orchestra and the city's A.B.C. wireless chorus.

Post was commissioned lieutenant and mobilized in the Australian Army Service Corps, Militia, on 24 August 1940. Transferred to the Australian Imperial Force in July 1942, he was promoted temporary major in the following month and made commandant of the transshipment centre at Terowie, South Australia, an important staging point on the overland supply route to Darwin. He relinquished command in February 1945 and was placed on the Reserve of Officers in March. At St Patrick's Cathedral, Melbourne, on 12 May 1943 he had married Nancye Lille Tucker, a 28-year-old stenographer.

After World War II Post continued as one of the A.B.C.'s chief conductors. From 1947 to 1957 he was associate-conductor with the Sydney Symphony Orchestra, a term that virtually coincided with (Sir) Eugene Goossens's [q.v.14] period in charge. Post made many guest appearances with A.B.C. orchestras across Australia. In 1950 he went to Britain on exchange with Charles Groves, conductor of the British Broadcasting Corporation's Northern Orchestra. At his début at the Royal Albert Hall, Post became the first Australian to conduct at a Promenade Concert; he included a piece by the Australian composer Clive Douglas [q.v.14]. He also conducted the Hallé and other British orchestras. At his final concert with the Northern Orchestra, crowds filled the hall and flowed outside.

Despite such successes, Post's career with the A.B.C. was marred by disappointment. In 1945 he had submitted a proposal to the A.B.C. to establish the Victorian Symphony Orchestra on a full-time basis, but he was twice overlooked for the position of principal conductor. He made no secret of his chagrin when he was not appointed director of music in 1957. Throughout his long tenure with the A.B.C., he never relinquished his involvement with his first love, opera. He was musical director (1947-54) of Gertrude Johnson's [q.v.14] National Theatre Movement and principal conductor (from 1949) for its opera. In addition, Post also conducted seasons with the New South Wales National Opera in Sydney, and joint seasons of the combined opera companies in 1952. Granted leave from the A.B.C., he was appointed musical director of the Australian Elizabethan Theatre Trust in 1955. He conducted the trust's first opera production, *The Marriage of Figaro*, in 1956, but resigned next year to return to the A.B.C. as assistant-director of music.

Heavier administrative responsibilities did not significantly curtail the number of Post's performances. In 1963 he established the Sydney Little Symphony Orchestra and conducted its début series of four concerts. He also continued his long association with school concerts. The advent of television broadcasting created new audiences for him. He made television appearances with the S.S.O. and conducted numerous operas on television. In 1962 he travelled to Europe and the United States of America to investigate methods of presenting music on television.

At a time when most Australian classical musicians depended on success abroad, Post built a public career in Australia. He and Sir Bernard Heinze represented the first generation of native-born conductors to rise to prominence under the A.B.C. Post conducted when an Australian was required to support visiting celebrity musicians. The role suited his talents admirably. He was proud of his efforts to promote 'Australian' composers, releasing recordings of Raymond Hanson's [q.v.14] *Concerto for Trumpet and Orchestra* (1948) and Robert Hughes's *Xanadu* (1954). Nor was he averse to the performance of 'new music', though his tastes could hardly be regarded as *avant garde*.

In 1966 Post was appointed O.B.E. That year he succeeded Heinze as director of the New South Wales State Conservatorium. He was its first diplomate to fill the position. Although reluctant to take the job, he put considerable effort into the conservatorium's opera school, but limited his wider involvement to consolidating initiatives begun by Heinze.

Post was a small, spry man with an alert demeanour and an acerbic tongue. He had many interests beyond the music world, being fond of sport (especially golf and lawn bowls), gardening (particularly cultivating camellias) and cooking. A passionate 'do-it-yourself' home handyman (who whittled his own batons from English birch), he had an intensely practical approach to life. Post preferred to talk about anything but music, and always insisted that his favourite composer was the one 'whose work I am playing at the moment'. Like many musicians, he had a strong sense of effort insufficiently rewarded. While he and his brothers John Verdi and Noel Schumann were propelled into careers as professional musicians, Joseph actively discouraged his only child Nola from any sort of musical training. Privately, he spoke of a vanquished desire to practise architecture.

Increasingly dogged by ill health, Post resigned from the conservatorium in late 1971 and moved to the Gold Coast, Queensland. He died of myocardial disease on 27 December 1972 at Broadbeach and was cremated; his wife and their daughter survived him. Although the family had Jewish connexions, Post had been raised in the Catholic faith and died devout in his atheism. He made an unrivalled contribution to the development of opera-conducting in Australia and was, in Roger Covell's words, the 'first Australian-born musician to excel in this genre'. As an orchestral conductor, he was judged a 'good all-round man': he was well-regarded for his enthusiasm, clarity and economy of gesture, but he was not associated with inspiring or challenging musicianship. None the less, his ability to take over conducting assignments at very short notice became legendary and was greeted with 'rave' reviews. Such was the case in 1955 when he substituted for Goossens at a day's notice to conduct Max Rostal in Bartók's *Violin Concerto*, a score with which Post was unfamiliar.

P. Sametz, *Play On!* (Syd, 1992); *ABC Weekly*, 28 Dec 1946, p 7, 27 Nov 1957, p 11; *Aust Musical News*, 2 Aug 1948, 1 Sept 1950; *Listener-In*, 11 Mar 1950; *Con Brio*, Mar 1973; *SMH*, 11 Apr 1927, 21 May 1932, 11 June 1966, 1 Jan 1973; *Daily Telegraph*, 19 Mar 1955; NSW State Conservatorium of Music Archives; tapes and documents, ABC archives (NAA, Syd); family information.

DIANE COLLINS

POTTS, ARNOLD WILLIAM (1896-1968), army officer and farmer, was born on 16 September 1896 on the Isle of Man, younger child of William Potts, schoolmaster, and his second wife Mary, née Matthew. In 1904 the family migrated to Perth. Educated at Cottesloe State School and (as a boarder) at Guildford

Grammar School, Arnold began work at Fairbridge [q.v.8] Farm School, Pinjarra.

On 18 January 1915 Potts enlisted in the Australian Imperial Force and was posted to the 16th Battalion. He served at Gallipoli from July and was promoted sergeant in October. Commissioned in January 1916, he was sent to the Western Front where he commanded the 4th Light Trench Mortar Battery as a captain. For his actions in August at Mouquet Farm and at German Strong-Point 54, on the Somme battlefield in France, he won the Military Cross. In February 1918 he rejoined the 16th Battalion. He was severely wounded at Vaire Wood, near Hamel, in July and evacuated to England in August. His A.I.F. appointment terminated in Western Australia on 9 March 1919. He had been mentioned in dispatches.

Although Potts was still classified as 20 per cent disabled, he went jackerooing on Boolaloo station, about 150 miles (240 km) southeast of Onslow. In 1920 he bought a property just west of Kojonup and called it Barrule after the twin peaks on the Isle of Man. At the chapel of his old school on 9 November 1926 he married Doreen Helena Wigglesworth with Anglican rites.

Potts joined the 25th Light Horse (Machine-Gun) Regiment in April 1939 and was appointed temporary major in December. He transferred to the A.I.F. on 1 May 1940 and was posted to the 2nd/16th Battalion which sailed for the Middle East in October. For his leadership during the Syrian campaign in June-July 1941 he was awarded the Distinguished Service Order and again mentioned in dispatches. In August he was placed in command of the 2nd/16th and promoted lieutenant colonel. Back in Australia, he was granted the temporary rank of brigadier and given command of the 21st Brigade on 6 April 1942.

The 21st Brigade was sent to Papua early in August and Potts was ordered to recapture the village of Kokoda from the Japanese. Reaching Alola on the Owen Stanley Range on 23 August, he took command of Maroubra Force (then comprising two beleaguered Militia battalions and some Papuan troops). Because of inadequate supplies, he could only take defensive action. When the Japanese attacked on the 26th, the timely arrival of leading elements of two battalions (2nd/14th and 2nd/16th) of his brigade enabled him to hold his ground. After four days of fighting, often hand-to-hand, at Isurava, he retreated along the Kokoda Track to Efogi, maintaining a tenacious rearguard action. On 5 September part of the 2nd/27th Battalion joined him at Mission Ridge (Brigade Hill). When his headquarters came under attack three days later, he withdrew his force to Menari on the 9th.

On 10 September 1942 Potts was instructed to report to headquarters, New Guinea Force, Port Moresby. He later rejoined his brigade which had been withdrawn to Sogeri to re-form. General Sir Thomas Blamey [q.v.13] criticized him, and notified him on 22 October that he was to be relieved of his command and sent to Darwin next day. 'Pottsy's' removal grieved him and angered many of his men. In a letter to his wife he wrote: 'the reason for my dismissal is political mostly. Heads were needed . . . and mine was one of them'.

Blamey was under intense pressure from the Australian government and General Douglas MacArthur [q.v.15] to bolster resistance in Papua. Lieutenant General (Sir) Edmund Herring, who succeeded (Sir) Sydney Rowell [q.v.] as commander of N.G.F., later claimed to have initiated Potts's replacement in the belief that he needed resting. None the less, Potts thought that the actions of the high command amounted to 'moral cowardice'. His superiors showed little understanding of the difficulties he had confronted and a lack of awareness of his valiant and inspiring leadership. Potts took over the 23rd Brigade in Darwin and led it on Bougainville from September 1944 until he left for Australia on 5 December 1945. He was twice mentioned in dispatches for his service in this campaign, but his deeds in Papua remained unrecognized.

Potts resumed farming at Barrule. In 1949 he stood unsuccessfully for the House of Representatives seat of Forrest as a Country Party candidate. He later became involved in numerous community organizations and was appointed O.B.E. (1960). After suffering two strokes in December 1964, he was confined to a wheelchair. Survived by his wife, and their son and two daughters, he died on New Year's Day 1968 at Kojonup and was cremated.

D. M. Horner, *Blamey* (Syd, 1998); B. Edgar, *Warrior of Kokoda* (Syd, 1999), and for bib.

W. J. EDGAR

POULSON, CRISTIAN (1890-1947), fisherman and resort operator, was born on 16 April 1890 at Logstor, near Ålborg, Denmark, son of Mel Poulson, architect, and his wife Laura, née Olsen. Arriving in Sydney on 28 September 1908 in the *Baralong*, Cris took various jobs in the city; he also worked as a fisherman and on Coodra Vale, A. B. Paterson's [q.v.11] property, near Wee Jasper. In 1916-17 he visited the United States of America. By 1918 he was a master fisherman at Byron Bay, New South Wales. Naturalized in 1920, he subsequently moved to Queensland. At St Saviour's Anglican Church, Gladstone, on 20 July 1923 he married 22-year-old Katherine Mary Lord; they were to have five children before being divorced in 1946.

Poulson was one of several entrepreneurs who entered the lucrative turtle-soup canning industry. In 1924 he established the Barrier Reef Trading Co. Ltd on North West Island. Transferring the business to Heron Island, he was a founding director of Gladstone Fisheries & Cold Stores Ltd in 1926. That year a party of tourists from Rockhampton paid him for a return trip to Heron Island, he used the money as a deposit on a launch. Turtle harvesting and processing was essentially seasonal work, concentrated in the summer months. As the number of turtles diminished, Poulson found that hosting parties of tourists in the turtle industry's off-season was more profitable than canning soup. In 1929 he applied to have Barrier Reef Trading wound up.

After Gladstone Fisheries failed to raise sufficient money to establish a tourist hostel in 1930, Poulson took over the project and opened a resort on Heron Island in 1932. Visitors came in his launch *Coralita*, walked through the shallows to shore, and slept in the galvanized-iron huts which had once housed turtle-factory workers. The main building served as a recreation hall. Mrs Martin Tait, the wife of a former factory-hand, did the cooking.

In 1936 Poulson acquired the lease of Heron Island. By 1943, when the island was declared a national park, tourist facilities included one large main building, forty cabins, a tennis court, water-storage facilities and a salt-water septic system. The end of World War II brought new prospects for tourism in Queensland. Poulson operated Barrier Reef tours. With Captain S. C. Middlemiss, he formed Barrier Reef Airways in 1946 to provide a weekly Catalina flying-boat service between Brisbane and Heron Island.

On 28 November 1947 Poulson disappeared at sea while returning to Heron Island from a visit to a friend's launch, moored offshore. His upturned dinghy was found about ten miles south of Gladstone; despite an extensive search, his body was never recovered. He was survived by his son and four daughters. Some of his children continued to operate the resort and to transport tourists to Heron Island from Gladstone. By 1960 a staff of thirty catered for up to 130 visitors at a time. P. & O. Australia Ltd acquired a controlling interest in the resort in 1973 and bought out the family business in 1980.

Great Barrier Reef Committee, *Report*, vol 4, pt 1 (Brisb, 1933); L. McDonald, *Gladstone* (Brisb, 1988); *Courier-Mail*, 1, 2 Dec 1947; *Gladstone Observer*, 3 Dec 1947; naturalization file, A1, item 1920/7192 (NAA, Canb).   ROBERT I. LONGHURST

POWER, STELLA (1896-1977), soprano, was born on 27 June 1896 at Richmond, Melbourne, and baptized Tertia Stella, fifth of six children of Edward John Power, customs officer, and his wife Annie Elizabeth, née O'Brien (d.1904). Stella probably attended the local convent school before becoming one of the first students to train under (Dame) Nellie Melba [q.v.10] at the Albert Street Conservatorium, East Melbourne. Her voice earned her the sobriquet, 'the Little Melba', from the diva herself: while guaranteeing a degree of prestige, the term led to unfair comparisons with the older singer. Power's professional appearances began with a recital in Melbourne in 1916. At St Mary's Catholic Church, North Sydney, on 30 July 1917 she married William Francis O'Rourke, a commercial traveller; their son Billy was born in 1920.

Later that year Power sailed for the United States of America where, early in 1918, she performed in concerts with the violinists Eugene Ysaye and Mischa Elman. As Melba's associate-artist she embarked on an extensive tour, during which Thomas A. Edison Inc. recorded her singing. Following recitals in Australia in 1918-19, she made her British début at the Royal Albert Hall on 23 November 1919 in a concert conducted by (Sir) Landon Ronald. She appeared on stage in Britain with the cellists Jean Gerardy and Lauri Kennedy (a fellow Australian), the tenor John McCormack, the pianist Willhelm Backhaus and the violinist Jan Kubelík, and she also sang before the King and Queen of Norway. Under the conductor (Sir) Adrian Boult, she performed works by (Sir) Arthur Bliss and other composers for recording by His Master's Voice.

In 1923 Power returned to Australia where she gave recitals and sang under contract to Union Theatres Ltd in picture-palaces. Back in the United States in 1926, she began a nine-year period as a featured singer in a series of popular revues staged by the entrepreneur John Murray Anderson, appearing with performers such as Roy Rogers and Mae West. Billy travelled with her. Home again in 1935, Stella lived with her brother Cyril in Melbourne. She travelled interstate as a concert recitalist, and as a radio performer for the Australian Broadcasting Commission. In 1935-36 she spent four months in New Zealand, touring stations operated by that country's broadcasting board. She made guest appearances on commercial radio in Australia, and in 1946 provided the voice of the mature Melba in the serial, 'Melba—The Life Story of a Great Australian'. Although she stopped singing professionally in the 1950s, she continued to teach in the 1960s.

Power's operatic performances were rare. In 1924 she had appeared on stage in *Carmen*, singing the part of Micaela. For A.B.C. broadcasts in the 1930s she sang the title role in *Martha* (opposite the Italian tenor Dino Borgioli) and the role of Norina in *Don Pasquale*. Her recordings reveal a fine and well-trained lyric coloratura voice, and provide evidence of the type of teaching she received from Melba and her collaborators. Survived by her son, she died on 16 January 1977 at Cheltenham, Melbourne, and was buried in the local cemetery.

Stella Power collection, Performing Arts Museum, Victorian Arts Centre, Melb.

PETER DUNBAR-HALL

PRATT, SYDNEY ERNEST (1887-1973), journalist and trade union leader, was born on 28 March 1887 at Paddington, Sydney, fourth child of William Rider Pratt, a journalist from Scotland, and his English-born wife Alice Virginia, née Phillips. Educated at Fort Street Model School, he joined the *Sydney Morning Herald* as a journalist. After working briefly in Melbourne, he transferred to Adelaide where he reported for the *Register* and then for the *Daily Herald*, a Labor newspaper. Syd was prominent in the movement to form a national organization of journalists that culminated in the foundation of the Australian Journalists' Association in 1910 and its registration as a Federal trade union in the following year. At the Congregational Church, East Melbourne, on 2 September 1912 he married Adelaide Susan Mary Martin, a milliner.

While honorary secretary of the A.J.A.'s South Australian district in 1911-19, Pratt helped to establish and develop the union's national headquarters in Melbourne; for this work he was awarded (1915) the association's gold honour badge. He was a member of the team that prepared the union's submission in proceedings—before (Sir) Isaac Isaacs [q.v.9] in the Commonwealth Court of Conciliation and Arbitration—which led to the first Federal award (1917) covering journalists. In 1919 he became general secretary of the A.J.A. and moved to Melbourne.

Pratt was an adroit conciliator, settling most disputes and concluding industrial agreements with newspaper proprietors by extensive negotiations. Three events stood out in his long industrial career. In 1927-28 he and the A.J.A.'s president Syd Deamer [q.v.13] successfully argued before (Sir) Robert Menzies [q.v.15], who had been appointed arbitrator, that all newspaper literary staff should be graded as journalists covered by industrial awards. Menzies' arbitration endorsed the principle, established by Isaacs in 1917, of equal pay for men and women in the profession. Elements of the journalists' grading system were to survive for more than seventy years. During the 1930s Pratt worked assiduously to prevent substantial cuts in newsroom jobs and to minimize wage reductions at a time of large-scale labour attrition. He adeptly guided the A.J.A. through the Depression, but later conceded that the pressures on the association in those years had 'nearly wrecked it'. In 1954-55 he directed a protracted and arduous industrial-award hearing which resulted in significant improvements in salary and conditions; it was one of the few occasions when he was forced into a court battle with proprietors.

Straightforward, meticulous and pleasant in approach, Pratt enlivened his advocacy with touches of colour and hyperbole. At one hearing he described the modern press photographer as a combination of 'mechanic, electrician, chemist and racing driver'. Menzies had claimed (1927) that, if all trade-union leaders were of Pratt's quality, 'there would be no strikes or industrial disputes'. In 1944 the A.J.A. made Pratt an honorary life member. He was appointed M.B.E. in 1951 and he retired in 1955. Survived by his wife and their two sons, he died on 21 May 1973 at Donvale and was cremated; his estate was sworn for probate at $20 272. The A.J.A. paid a pension to his widow for the remainder of her life. Pratt's son Mel also worked as a journalist.

C. J. Lloyd, *Profession: Journalist* (Syd, 1985); *Journalist*, June 1973; *Age* (Melb) and *SMH*, 22 May 1973; information from Mr B. Porter, Media, Entertainment and Arts Alliance, Syd.   C. J. LLOYD*

PREECE, COLIN THOMAS (1903-1979), winemaker, was born on 5 May 1903 at Alberton, Adelaide, sixth of seven children of South Australian-born parents Thomas Henry Preece, miller, and his wife Elizabeth, née Stanners. Young Colin attended Unley High School and planned to manage the family's flour mill at Tumby Bay, but, after taking the optional subject of oenology at Roseworthy Agricultural College (dux 1923), joined the technical staff of B. Seppelt [q.v.6] & Sons Ltd at the firm's winery in the Barossa Valley. He developed Seppelt's Extra Dry Solero sherry and learned the significance of liquid sulphur dioxide in making good wine. At St John's Lutheran Church, Tanunda, on 8 February 1928 he married Dorothea Rhoda Tümmel.

In 1932 Preece moved to Victoria as manager of Seppelt's vineyards and cellars at Great Western, near Ararat. Great Western had been successively owned by Joseph Best, Hans Irvine [qq.v.3,9] and Benno Seppelt. Relishing the role of master of the little community, he upheld the winery's traditions, maintained the underground cellar-storage 'drives' and continued the practice of naming wines after prominent individuals, including the State governors Baron Huntingfield in 1934 and

Sir Dallas Brooks [qq.v.9,13] in 1950, both of whom he entertained. In 1941-61 a continuous programme of expansion was required to keep pace with the rising demand for Great Western wines, especially the sparkling varieties.

The nearby St Ethels and Hockheim properties were acquired in 1945. New buildings were constructed, 340 acres (136 ha) of additional vineyards planted and 80 acres (32 ha) replanted. By 1961 the total area under grapes was more than 600 acres (243 ha). Great Western champagne and sparkling burgundy were long established lines. In 1953-55 Seppelt released Moyston claret, Chalambar burgundy, Arawatta riesling and Rhymney chablis —all new wines named after localities in the district. Sparkling wines from Great Western dominated Australian wine shows and won international awards. These wines, with individual special releases and even wines sold in bulk to merchants, made Preece's reputation.

Ranked with Maurice O'Shea [q.v.15] and Roger Warren [q.v.] as a great Australian winemaker, Preece influenced wine enthusiasts, makers and professionals. In sparkling wine he had no peer. Like O'Shea and Warren, he was an accomplished technician and a masterful blender. Again like them, he enjoyed the full backing of his company and drew on the skills of others. He was supported in the sparkling and table wine cellars by Harold Carr and Leo Hurley respectively.

Preece was of less than average height, with a round face and spectacles. An amiable man and a wine educator, he was a gregarious and generous host who welcomed visitors with treasures from his cellars. He was also a mainstay of the Ararat Wine and Food Society and president (1933-63) of the Great Western Race Club, whose annual meeting the company supported. In 1963 he retired on the grounds of ill health, but remained in the district and undertook consultancy work. His clients included Nathan & Wyeth Pty Ltd, which had a vineyard near Avoca, and Ross Shelmerdine, whom he assisted with his wine and tourism venture, Mitchelton, near Nagambie. Preece died on 7 December 1979 at Ararat and was buried in Great Western cemetery; his wife, and their son and daughter survived him.

L. R. Francis, *100 Years of Wine Making* (np, 1965); *Age* (Melb), 1 Jan 1980; D. Seabrook, Oration at Colin Preece commemoration banquet, 1981 (ms, held by Mr C. R. Preece, Ararat, Vic); information from Mr D. Crittenden, Melb, and Mr L. Hurley, Stawell, Vic.   DAVID DUNSTAN

PRENDIVILLE, REDMOND (1900-1968), Catholic archbishop, was born on 11 September 1900 at Wood, parish of Brosna,

County Kerry, Ireland, youngest of at least thirteen children of Garrett Prendiville, farmer, and his wife Hannah, née Sullivan. Educated at the local National school and at St Brendan's College, Killarney, Redmond began studies for the priesthood at the seminary of All Hallows College, Dublin, in September 1918, but was expelled for playing cards on the night before a retreat. He studied philosophy and history at University College, Dublin (B.A., 1922, National University of Ireland), and theology at St Peter's College, Wexford (1921-25). Selected for the Kerry Gaelic football team in 1924, he played in the all-Ireland final and was named 'man of the match'. He was ordained priest at St Kieran's College, Kilkenny, on 11 June 1925.

Arriving in Perth on 15 September 1925, Prendiville was appointed to the cathedral parish of St Mary's, with particular responsibility for the church of St Francis Xavier, East Perth, and the working-class area around it. Walking city and suburban streets to visit parishioners replaced football as his main exercise. His reputation for having a 'mighty memory' for names was established in these years. The Catholic Young Ladies' Club—a precursor of the Catholic Action movements of the 1940s and 1950s—doubled its membership under his direction. In 1929 Prendiville was appointed administrator of the cathedral parish. He brought the construction of the cathedral's new sanctuary and transept to a successful close, and managed the opening ceremonies with adroit tact. The old parish hall was converted into offices, and he adopted the strong administrative style that remained his trademark.

On 22 October 1933, after only eight years as a priest, Prendiville was consecrated titular archbishop of Cypsela and coadjutor archbishop of Perth, becoming, reputedly, the youngest archbishop in the Catholic world. The decision to appoint a 'local man' as coadjutor was a popular one, and one affirmed by Archbishop Clune [q.v.8]. The new archbishop undertook a busy programme of visitation, observing first-hand and for the first time the realities of life in isolated parishes, and gaining, he remarked in letters, a different appreciation of the activity and comfort of the cathedral presbytery. In 1935 he succeeded Clune as fifth bishop and second archbishop of Perth. He was named bishop assistant at the Papal throne and Count of the Holy Roman Empire in 1958, the year that he welcomed Monsignor (Cardinal) Joseph Cardijn, international founder of the Young Christian Workers, to Perth for the movement's Australian conference.

Between 1933 and 1968 the number of Catholics in Western Australia increased from 80 000 to over 213 000. Prendiville recruited priests who spoke European languages to minister to the spiritual needs of immigrants. He held that Catholics should be able to walk to Sunday Mass in under half an hour: during his episcopacy sixty-one new churches and chapels were built in the Perth archdiocese. Furthermore, by overseeing the construction of 240 new buildings and 54 separate projects to extend existing ones, he earned his title of 'the builder'. He was also responsible for setting up St Thomas More College at the University of Western Australia which was officially opened in 1957.

The archbishop's policy of financial 'self-help' in parishes galvanized the support of the increasingly affluent Catholic population in postwar Western Australia. Institutions were staffed and often separately funded by religious Orders, including the twenty-one new communities invited to Perth during his years in office. In the spirit of the Second Vatican Council (1962-63), he 'ceaselessly encouraged' a network of organizations of Catholic laity, both devotional and activist, and handed over responsibility to priests and people in the parishes. His episcopacy spanned the Depression, World War II, and a period of increasing social and cultural change, both in Australian Catholicism and beyond it. Under the motto, *da anima cetera tolle* ('nothing else matters except the salvation of souls'), he aimed for, and achieved, a strong institutional framework of specialist Catholic associations to expand traditional activities in the archdiocese.

Prendiville suffered two strokes in 1946 and was frequently admitted to hospital over the ensuing years. His public appearances had to accommodate a partial paralysis in one arm. He suffered an aortic lesion and died of a cerebrovascular accident on 28 June 1968 at St John of God Hospital, Subiaco; following a requiem Mass at St Mary's Cathedral, he was buried in Karrakatta cemetery.

J. T. McMahon, *College, Campus, Cloister* (Perth, 1969); D. F. Bourke, *The History of the Catholic Church in Western Australia* (Perth, 1979); *West Australian*, 29 June 1968; *West Australian Catholic Record*, 4 July 1968; Prendiville papers (Archdiocesan Catholic Archives, Perth); information from Sr Frances Stibi, Perth.

KATHARINE MASSAM

PRENTICE, JOHN MURDOCH (1886-1964), army officer and broadcaster, was born on 10 March 1886 at Buangor, Victoria, fourth child of John Prentice, a Scottish-born farmer, and his wife Mary, née Usher, late Sands, who came from Mauritius. John grew up in an unassuming country family. He claimed that he had matriculated at the University of Melbourne in 1906 and worked as an accountant, but he did neither. By 1912 he was a salesman, living at Moonee Ponds. He enlisted in the Australian Imperial Force on 20 May 1915 and served in Egypt; by May 1916 he was a staff sergeant, handling records at A.I.F. Headquarters, France. Commissioned in June 1917, he was posted to the 39th Battalion on the Western Front in July and promoted lieutenant in September. On 30 August 1918 he was severely wounded in the right arm and admitted to hospital. He sailed for Australia in November. After his A.I.F. appointment terminated on 6 March 1919, he worked at Army Headquarters, Melbourne. He was mentioned in dispatches (1918), awarded the Belgian Croix de Guerre and appointed to the Ordre de la Couronne (1919).

On 1 October 1919 Prentice rejoined the A.I.F. Eight days later he sailed from Sydney as adjutant in a transport which took German prisoners to Rotterdam, the Netherlands. Resigning his A.I.F. appointment in London on 20 April 1920, he returned to Australia via the United States of America. In the early 1920s he worked for the War Service Homes Commission in Hobart.

An influential figure in Sydney in the pioneering days of commercial radio, Prentice —as 'Uncle Jack'—hosted a programme for children from 1925 for Broadcasters Ltd's radio-station 2UW. He also presented grand operas and symphonies (without commercial breaks) and delivered foreign affairs and political commentaries, strident in their anti-communism, until the 1950s. Anti-communism became the centrepiece of his political life. His outlook was characterized by the extremist remedies popular with some of his generation. He wrote in 1931 that General Sir John Monash [q.v.10] was 'the one man in Australia . . . I could have accepted and gladly served under . . . as a DICTATOR'. In the late 1930s Prentice was a prominent appeaser.

The brief time Prentice had spent in the U.S.A. convinced him of the evils of prohibition, which he opposed in Sydney in the late 1920s. Keenly interested in astrology and the occult, he had attended meetings of theosophists in London, but grown suspicious of Annie Besant and Anglo-Indian theosophy. Back in Sydney, he criticized C. W. Leadbeater [q.v.10], took a prominent role in the split in the Theosophical Society in Australia and by 1938 presided over the Sydney branch of the Universal Brotherhood and Theosophical Society.

Prentice was called up on 7 September 1939 for intelligence duties in the Militia. Promoted major in July 1940, he was appointed general staff officer, 3rd grade, at Eastern Command, Sydney, in September; he became G.S.O.1 and temporary lieutenant colonel in February 1942. He served at Victoria Barracks, Paddington, and was placed on the Reserve of Officers in December 1946. On the one hand, he was an energetic spymaster who revelled in the hierarchies of military life and the status of his position, believing that such covert work —particularly on the home front—proved decisive in winning the war. On the other, he promoted an Australia First Movement internee to a sensitive position in ciphers. In 1946 he was a central, if unimpressive, witness in the treason case against the broadcaster Charles Cousens [q.v.13].

At the height of the Cold War Prentice wrote 'intelligence bulletins' for 'The Association', a proto-fascist auxiliary, and contributed to the magazine, *Man*, and the journal, *Reveille*. Apart from showing diligent research, his articles suggest ongoing connections with the intelligence services. In 1955 he gave evidence against A. J. Dalziel [q.v.13] at the (Petrov) royal commission on espionage. Prentice attended conferences of the Asian Peoples' Anti-Communist League in Manila (1956) and Saigon (1957). He was treated as a 'bosom friend' of President Syngman Rhee who awarded him the Korean medal for 'Education and Culture'.

Prentice was fraught with contradictions. He worked hard to disguise his humble origins beneath a 'colonel blimp' persona, wearing a bow-tie, speaking in a sing-song, cultivated accent, and exaggerating his educational qualifications. Bespectacled and podgy, he enjoyed a large circle of well-connected friends, but was malicious and self-absorbed, 'a curious mixture of a sincere, upright, likeable man—and a phoney'. Unmarried and possibly homosexual, he lived in his Lavender Bay flat with his sister, but was often accompanied by a young mercantile marine engineer, whom he invariably introduced as his son. After suffering from diabetes mellitus for years, Prentice died on 4 November 1964 at the Repatriation General Hospital, Concord. His body was delivered to the University of Sydney, according to his will, and later cremated with Anglican rites.

I. Chapman, *Tokyo Calling* (Syd, 1990); *Aust Intelligence Corps Bulletin*, 1, no 6, Dec 1957, p 27; A. Moore, 'Fascism Revived? The Association Stands Guard 1945-52', *Labour Hist*, no 74, May 1998, p 105; *SMH*, 2 May, 24 Aug, 14 Sept 1928, 26 Nov 1932, 1 3 Aug 1934, 7 Sept 1935, 26 June 1941, 20 Aug 1943, 30 Jan 1948, 11 Jan 1950, 3 May, 27 June, 16 Aug 1951, 15 Apr, 24 Aug, 15 Nov 1955; A6122/40, item 2, A367, item C94121, Honours, A462, item 829/1/99, A1838, items 1516/6/15 (NAA, Canb); J. M. Prentice letters (AWM); information from Mr B. Carlin, Belmore, Mr L. Cohen, Bondi, Mr N. McDonald, Willoughby, Syd, Mr N. McVicker, Mudgee, and Mrs E. Maslen, North Richmond, NSW.

ANDREW MOORE

PRERAUER, KURT (1901-1967), pianist, conductor and music critic, was born on 1 April 1901 at Landeshut (Kamienna Góra), Silesia, Germany (Poland), elder son of Felix Prerauer, shoe manufacturer, and his Viennese-born wife Gertrud, née Hammerschlag. Kurt attended the local *realgymnasium*. From a very early age he learned to play the piano and the violin; later he took up the organ. In 1921 he graduated in music from the University of Breslau (Wroclaw), where one of his professors was Max Schneider. He studied law (on his parents' insistence) and music (under Adolf Sandberger) at the University of Munich in 1921-23, and music at the Bavarian (State) Academy of Music. Subsequently, he was a private composition student of Professor Hugo Leichtentritt in Berlin.

After appointments as *solorépétiteur* (vocal coach) at the opera houses at Oldenburg (1923-24) and Essen (1924-25), Prerauer joined the staff of the Staatsoper (State Opera), Berlin, in 1925 as *solorépétiteur* and organist. From 1926 he was personal assistant to the principal conductor Leo Blech. Eventually he was appointed director of studies. He worked with such conductors as Wilhelm Furtwängler, Bruno Walter, and, notably, Erich Kleiber for the world première in 1925 of Berg's *Wozzeck*, and also took part in the symphony concerts of the Staatsoper. In 1932 he was soloist in the world première of Weinberger's *Passacaglia* for organ and orchestra.

Prerauer's coaching engagement at the Festival Theatre, Bayreuth, was cancelled in 1933 on the insistence of Winifred Wagner and on 30 June that year his Berlin appointment was terminated under Hitler's anti-Jewish laws. Colleagues provided him with glowing references. By the end of that year he was in Britain, after accompanying Florence Austral [q.v.7] on a recital tour of the Netherlands. He was contracted to the British Broadcasting Corporation as coach for (Sir) Adrian Boult's concert première of *Wozzeck* in London in March 1934; its music department 'unanimously agreed that much of the success of the singers' was due to his coaching.

Sir Benjamin Fuller [q.v.8] engaged him to assemble his ambitious Royal Grand Opera Company and to be one of its three conductors. Prerauer arrived in Melbourne in August 1934 and, after Sydney and Melbourne seasons, received permission to remain in Australia. He settled in Sydney, spelt his name Curt and was to be naturalized in 1938. The series of operas that he organized for the Australian Broadcasting Commission in 1935-36 was a stimulating mix, including *Boris Godunov*, *Fidelio*, *The Mastersingers of Nuremberg*, *The Rhinegold* and *Hansel and Gretel*, many of which he had to cut due to the exigencies of broadcasting schedules. He wrote for the earliest issues of the *A.B.C. Weekly*.

Prerauer developed a reputation as a composer, music critic, and teacher at the Alfred Hill [q.v.9] Academy of Music. In May 1938 he was appointed conductor of the Royal Philharmonic Society of Sydney. He proceeded to 'jolt that royal and ancient body out of its conservative ways' with Sydney's first attempt at an 'authentic' *Messiah*, and a Mass by Lassus—the 'masons among the members were outraged by this piece of popery'. The 'stormy season' ended with Prerauer's much-publicized resignation in February 1939 amid accusations of his 'dictatorship'. Enlisting in the Militia on 8 January 1942, he initially joined the 13th Garrison Battalion. From October that year he served at Port Kembla in the 2nd Employment Company until he was discharged from the army as medically unfit in December 1943.

At St Clement's Anglican Church, Mosman, on 7 December 1942 Prerauer had married Marea Victusya Wolkowsky. One of his pupils, she was a formidably talented soprano, twenty years his junior. In 1950 he returned to Europe as her accompanist and manager. He also presented illustrated lectures on Australian music. She had successes, including a London season (1953) at Covent Garden in *Wozzeck*, under Kleiber. The Prerauers' work in East Berlin ended when they had to flee hurriedly after Kleiber resigned (1955) from the Staatsoper in protest against political interference. 'It was', Prerauer later recalled, 'my second flight from there'. Following ten years in Europe, Curt and Marea returned to Sydney where, in 1960, he became music critic for the magazine *Nation*. He also worked as critic for the *Sun* newspaper, wrote for numerous overseas journals, including *Music Survey* (England), *Melos* (Germany) and the *Österreichische Musikzeitschrift* (Austria), and reported for Swiss radio and almost every important radio network in Germany.

Curt and 'Maria' Prerauer produced *Zeitgenossiche Australische Lyrik* (*Contemporary Australian Poetry*) (München, 1961), with English and German texts on facing pages. They also translated into German *Riders in the Chariot* (at Patrick White's request) and numerous plays (among them Ray Lawler's *Summer of the Seventeenth Doll* which had many performances in Germany and Austria).

As a critic, Prerauer drew on deep knowledge and experience, and insisted on the highest standards. His 'critical absolutism and his rigorous division of the elect and non-elect' often elicited hostility, which was occasionally warranted as he did not always avoid partiality. Intolerant of the insincere and the insubstantial, he dismissed many eminent British composers as 'mediocrities and bad imitators', and told one correspondent that he had 'founded the A.C.C.C.C.—the Australian Composers' Copy-cat Club'.

People often found Prerauer intimidating and arrogant, though some felt that his manner was a 'protective front'. In correspon-

dence (1963-64) with Peter Sculthorpe he mixed detailed technical advice on Sculthorpe's compositions with philosophical encouragement. Referring the young Tasmanian to the qualities of John Antill's *Corroboree*, he stressed that he should discover his *Australian* voice. He also reflected on 'what the "Australian idiom"—if it were ever to arise in music—ought to look like: great loneliness, the cruelty of the bush, the "horizontal grandeur" of Australia—comparable with the "vertical grandeur" of the European Alps'. He responded to diverse music: he admired Dene Barnett's approach to Bach, described Richard Meale's *Las Alborados* as 'a truly great work', and delighted in the iconoclastic creations of David Ahern.

Prerauer's commitment to Australia never wavered. He died of subarachnoid haemorrhage on 29 November 1967 in Royal North Shore Hospital and was cremated with Jewish rites. His wife survived him and, as 'Maria Prerauer', became a well-known novelist, journalist, editor and music critic.

A. Gyger, *Opera for the Antipodes* (Syd, 1990); P. Sametz, *Play On* (Syd, 1992); *ABC Weekly*, 2 Dec 1939; *SMH*, 20 Apr, 13 June, 16 Nov 1935, 6 June 1936, 16 Jan, 1 May 1937, 22, 25, 27, 28 Feb, 1, 4 Mar, 2 Aug 1939, 15 July 1940, 29 Apr 1944, 26 Oct 1946, 6 July, 25 Nov 1957, 12 Feb 1958, 10 Nov 1962, 26 Sept 1966, 27 Feb, 12 Sept 1967; *Sun-Herald* (Syd), 27 Dec 1959; *Nation* (Syd), 16 Dec 1967; James Murdoch papers (NL); residence and naturalization files, B13, item 1934/17409, A446/169, item 1958/44648 and SP368/1, item 7/44/14 (NAA); information from Berliner Staatsoper, Theater und Philharmonie der Stadt Essen, *and* Oldenburgisches Staatstheater, Germany, *and* British Broadcasting Corporation Written Archives Centre, Caversham, Berkshire, Eng, *and* Mrs M. Prerauer, Castle Cove, and Mrs E. Wagner, Wollstonecraft, Syd.

JOHN CARMODY
WARREN A. BEBBINGTON

PRESCOTT, SIR STANLEY LEWIS (1910-1978), university vice-chancellor, was born on 21 March 1910 at Tetbury, Gloucestershire, England, son of John Prescott, pharmacist, and his wife Jessie Mary, née Lamplugh. Stanley was educated at Tetbury Grammar School and at the Victoria University of Manchester (B.Sc., 1932; M.Sc., 1934) where he was Wild prizeman and sub-warden (1934) of Lancashire Independent College. In 1936 he was appointed professor of physiology at the Cheeloo (Shantung Christian) University, Tsinan, China. On 15 September 1937 in Hong Kong he married Monica Mary Job, a medical practitioner.

Following the carnage and disruption caused by the Japanese invasion of China, Prescott became hospital superintendent at

Tsinan late in 1938. He sent his wife and son to Sydney in 1941 and followed them four months later. Commissioned in the Royal Australian Air Force on 23 August 1941, he served as a junior intelligence officer. From 1943 to 1945, as squadron leader, he commanded No.1 Flying Personnel Research Unit, Melbourne, which was involved in aviation medicine.

In 1946 Prescott was appointed master of Ormond [q.v.5] College, University of Melbourne. He took office as vice-chancellor of the University of Western Australia on 1 April 1953 and presided over a period of unprecedented growth in students, staff, budgets and building. New faculties of medicine, architecture, and economics and commerce were created, and work on the (A. J.) Reid [q.v.] Library was commenced. Determined that the new buildings should harmonize with the Spanish-mission idiom of the university's pre-war core, he persuaded the town-planner Gordon Stephenson in 1958 to act as consultant architect for a revised master-plan. The result was probably Australia's most unified and aesthetically satisfying campus.

Tall, slim and prematurely grey-haired, Prescott looked the diplomat he was. He cultivated amicable relations with the university senate and an able, but combative, professorial board: 'Come, let's not get cross with one another', he would say. Maintaining strong ties with the business community and Rotary, he kept on good terms with leading politicians of both major parties and chaired (1962-64) the Australian Vice-Chancellors' Committee. His own university escaped much of the student radicalism of the late 1960s and early 1970s.

Wider recognition came with Prescott's appointments to the Commission of Enquiry (1957) on the University of Malaya, as chairman (1959) of the Nanyang University Commission, Singapore, as a Commonwealth consultant (1960-71) on the Inter-University Council for Higher Education Overseas and as a member (1967) of Sir Lawrence Jackson's committee on tertiary education in Western Australia.

Appointed O.B.E. in 1958 and knighted in 1965, Prescott suffered a heart attack and took early retirement in 1970. That year the university conferred on him an honorary LL.D. Sir Stanley continued to serve on the board of the Royal Perth Hospital, becoming deputy-chairman (1973) and chairman (1976), and sat on the planning board (1971-73) and senate (1973-76) of Murdoch University. When he visited China in 1975 he was welcomed as an outsider with authentic reminiscences of its pre-revolutionary past. He was stimulated by the experience and began work on a phonetic dictionary of the Mandarin language. Survived by his wife, and their two sons and two daughters, he died of cancer on 14 July 1978 in R.P.H. and was cremated with Anglican rites.

Prescott left the University of Western Australia thriving and well nourished. His leadership was perhaps underestimated because of his preference for operating through a quiet diplomacy at times verging on mandarin subtlety. It was easy to believe the story that he once concluded a testimonial: 'You will be fortunate indeed if you get Dr ... to work for you'.

F. Alexander, *Campus at Crawley* (Melb, 1963); G. C. Bolton and P. Joske, *History of the Royal Perth Hospital* (Perth, 1982); B. de Garis (ed), *Campus in the Community* (Perth, 1988); P. Crawford and M. Tonkinson, *The Missing Chapters* (Perth, 1988); *West Australian*, 17 July 1978; Univ WA Archives; information from Monica (Lady) Prescott, Shenton Park, Perth; personal knowledge.   G. C. BOLTON

PREVOST, MARIA CAROLINE VERONA (1895-1976), 'flapper', was born on Christmas Day 1895 in the schooner, *Sree Pas-Sair*, at Roebuck Bay, Western Australia, fourth of ten children of Francis Filomeno Rodriguez, a Spanish-born master pearler, and his wife Maude Gwenevere, née Miller, who came from South Australia. Frank had settled at Broome in the mid-1880s and by 1904 owned a fleet of fourteen luggers and a schooner. He also built (1905-06) and ran the Hotel Continental during the heyday of the local pearling industry. Verona's childhood, spent rollicking with her siblings in a rambling house at Claremont, Perth, was interspersed with sojourns at Broome, where she met her father's exotic acquaintances from different parts of the world. Educated at Loreto Convent, Claremont, 'Ronnie' (as she was known) enrolled in medicine at the University of Melbourne in 1914 but withdrew that year and returned to Perth when her father's pearling enterprise collapsed.

Miss Rodriguez's beauty was legendary. She had olive skin, large, dark, luminous eyes, black wavy hair, bow-shaped lips and glistening teeth. After a brief stint as a nanny, she married Frederick Charles Grave (d.1924) on 19 November 1917 at the district registrar's office, Perth; he was 32 years old and a prominent businessman who held the Western Australian franchise for Ford motorcars. Svelte, elegantly dressed, always well groomed, intelligent and witty, Ronnie became the toast of the town. Whether dancing the Charleston on top of a table, or driving her open sports car around Peppermint Grove, with a brilliant scarf flying in the wind, she was seen as personifying the era of Isadora Duncan and the 'flappers'.

Not yet 30, widowed, wealthy, at the height of her beauty and accustomed to travelling in style, Ronnie Grave soon grew restless in Perth. In the mid-1920s she enrolled her two daughters as boarders at Loreto Convent and left for Europe and America where she mingled on the fringes of high society with the rich, the famous and the notorious. Back in Perth, on 18 February 1928 at the Star of the Sea Catholic Church, Cottesloe, she married Benjamin Champion Prevost (d.1969), a wealthy wool-buyer; they were to have one child, a son. The Prevosts lived at Wilma Lodge, Peppermint Grove, before building a thoroughly modern mansion at Mosman Park in the late 1930s.

When her daughter Joan died following a car crash near Wangaratta, Victoria, in August 1940, the glitter went out of Prevost's life and she fell into a state of chronic depression. Despite the efforts of medical practitioners at home and abroad, melancholia persisted. Day after day she stared into space, her fingers incessantly tapping the arm of her chair. In 1974 she moved to London to be near her son. Survived by a daughter of her first marriage, and by the son of her second, she died on 8 May 1976 at Kensington and was cremated.

Northern Times, 16 Dec 1965; *West Australian*, 25 May 1976, 26 Jan 1977; information from Sr A. Carter, Loreto Convent, Nedlands, Ms J. Crommelin, Cottesloe, and Mr B. Prevost, Cottesloe, Perth.
WENDY BIRMAN

PRICE, SIR ARCHIBALD GRENFELL (1892-1977), geographer, historian and educationist, was born on 28 January 1892 in North Adelaide, second and only surviving son of South Australian-born parents Henry Archibald Price, banker and businessman, and his wife Elizabeth Jane, née Harris. The death of his father in 1895 led to a close and lasting relationship with his mother and to an important formative relationship with his uncle, Captain Walter Goalen, R.N., who took him exploring along the Fleurieu Peninsula. Archie was sent to the Queen's School, North Adelaide, and the Collegiate School of St Peter, but failed the entrance examination for the University of Adelaide. He was successfully coached for Magdalen College, Oxford (B.A. Hons, 1914; Dip.Ed., 1915; M.A., 1919), and represented Magdalen in cricket, tennis, hockey, lacrosse and rowing. In holidays he explored England with his mother. During 1914 he was a student-teacher at Sherbourne School, Dorset. That year he tried to enlist in the British Army, but was rejected because of poor eyesight.

Returning to Adelaide, Price again volunteered (for the Australian Imperial Force) and was again turned down. He joined the staff of St Peter's College in 1916, coached (1916-24) its athletic team and became a housemaster

(1921). On 20 January 1917 at the school chapel he married with Anglican rites Kitty Pauline Hayward, daughter of an Adelaide solicitor; she was to become his lifelong confidante and associate researcher. His first two books, *A Causal Geography of the World* (1918) and *South Australians and their Environment* (1921), were in part the product of his teaching experience. He was elected a fellow (1921) of the Royal Geographical Society, London. In 1925 he was appointed founding master of St Mark's College, University of Adelaide, a post he was to hold until 1957.

Wider recognition as a scholar came with his studies of the history and historical geography of European settlement in South Australia, *The Foundation and Settlement of South Australia 1829-1845* (1924) and *Founders & Pioneers of South Australia* (1929). The former received commendatory reviews in Britain and the latter helped to earn him (in 1932) the first doctorate of letters from the University of Adelaide. In his view, previous studies had paid insufficient attention to the economic and physical factors influencing South Australia's development; he also thought that early colonists had misunderstood the vagaries of a Mediterranean climate and adopted unsuitable methods of agricultural production. Both books remained standard references on the history of South Australia until the late 1950s and on its historical geography until the early 1970s. A member of the editorial board of *The Centenary History of South Australia* (1936), he contributed three chapters to that book and collaborated on a fourth. He wrote a history of Elder, Smith [qq.v.4,6] & Co. Ltd, *The First Hundred Years* (1940), *Australia Comes of Age* (Melbourne, 1945), and *A History of St Mark's College* (1968). *The Skies Remember* (Sydney, 1969) commemorated (Sir) Keith and (Sir) Ross Smith's [qq.v.11] flight from England to Australia.

Price's geographical interests broadened in the 1920s, partly through co-operation with the leading British geographer L. Dudley Stamp on a school text, *The World: a General Geography* (London, 1929). He contributed a paper to the Australasian Association for the Advancement of Science on South Australia's efforts to control the Murray River (1925) and published *The History and Problems of the Northern Territory* (1930). With a developing interest in the tropics, he travelled in Java, the Straits Settlements, Burma and Ceylon in 1929. He also served (1924-62) on and presided (1937-38) over the council of the South Australian branch of the Royal Geographical Society of Australasia.

In 1932 Price was granted a Rockefeller travelling fellowship to study 'the adaptation of white settlers to tropical conditions in the Caribbean'. Extensive travel in the United States of America gathering primary sources, and careful field investigations in the Caribbean itself, were combined with previous experience in Australia and Asia to enable him to produce *White Settlers in the Tropics* (New York, 1939). The book was a widely acclaimed, scholarly and generally optimistic appraisal of the successes and failures of European settlements in the wet tropics. He attributed the failures to administrative incompetence, inappropriate development policies, the ravages of disease and acceptance of inadequate living standards. The successes seemed to be the result of care in maintaining health and fitness by diet, exercise and physical work. He dismissed simplistic explanations based on racial characteristics as unproven and emphasized the need to control tropical diseases, an idea to which he was to return in *The Importance of Disease in History* (1964).

The theme of European exploration and settlement of diverse physical environments was a continuous thread throughout Price's research. His controversial essay, 'The Social Challenge'—in *Northern Australia: Task for a Nation* (Sydney, 1954)—advocated the purchase by Australia of Dutch New Guinea (Irian Jaya) as a buffer against encroachment from the embryonic nation Indonesia. In *The Challenge of New Guinea* (Sydney, 1965) he assessed Australian efforts in colonizing the Territory of Papua and New Guinea. His interest in the travels of James Cook and Sir Douglas Mawson [qq.v.1,10] led to his edited version of Cook's journals, *The Explorations of Captain James Cook in the Pacific* (New York, 1957), and *The Winning of Australian Antarctica* (Sydney, 1962), based on Mawson's papers. He also published *The Western Invasions of the Pacific and its Continents* (Oxford, 1963) and *Island Continent* (Sydney, 1972).

Historical research and experience in the Northern Territory had led Price to an interest in archaeology and a concern for Aboriginal Australians. Under the auspices of the R.G.S.A., he led (1938) an 'inconclusive' expedition to examine supposed remains of the explorer Ludwig Leichhardt [q.v.2]. In 1951-52 he encouraged students from St Mark's College to assist with the investigation of an Aboriginal archaeological site at Fromms Landing on the Murray River. His pamphlet, *What of our Aborigines?* (1944), revealed his knowledge of the mistreatment of Aborigines. *White Settlers and Native Peoples* (Melbourne, 1949) dealt with racial contacts between English-speaking White settlers and indigenous peoples in the United States, Canada, Australia and New Zealand, and gave a pessimistic view of past contacts and future relationships.

Price's life was intimately linked to education, initially as a teacher, then as an administrator, and finally through his connection with libraries at State and Commonwealth levels. He served on the council of St Peter's College (1933-72) and on that of the University of Adelaide (1925-62), where he was a part-time lecturer (1949-57) in geography and dean (1951-52) of the faculty of arts. Appointed by the South Australian government in 1936 to inquire into the State's library system, he wrote a report that led to the widening of public library services and he was a founding member (1940-72) of the Libraries Board of South Australia. Chairman (1953-71) of the advisory board of the Commonwealth Literary Fund, he anticipated in 1956 the implementation of the public lending rights scheme for authors. As chairman (1960-71) of the council of the National Library of Australia, he had the honour in 1970 of showing the new library building to Queen Elizabeth II. In 1956 he had helped to found, and for some years held various offices in, the Australian Humanities Research Council.

In the 1930s Price had been alarmed by inflation and the spread of communism. Responding to what he saw as militant socialism during the Depression, he was active in the formation of the Emergency Committee of South Australia and chaired its first meeting in April 1931 at St Mark's College. The committee supported strict monetary policies and was seen as 'an anti-socialist organisation' with links to the United Australia Party. In 1933 Price was appointed C.M.G. For six nights a week between October 1939 and May 1941 he gave a series of radio broadcasts on contemporary events, including commentaries on the ebb and flow of the fight against fascism. Revealingly, he had predicted dangers from Japanese expansionism as early as 1925. In 1941 he stood as the U.A.P. candidate at a by-election for the House of Representatives seat of Boothby. His election on 24 May enabled the Menzies [q.v.15] government to retain power for a few more months. The loss of his seat at the 1943 election was a personal relief, yet he valued the insights he had gained, and subsequently took advantage of the contacts he had made in Canberra.

Although he came from a conservative background, Price had a strong sense of justice for all. As a junior master he helped to form the South Australian Assistant Masters' Association which successfully negotiated for better pay and conditions. In later years he tried to persuade Federal politicians to improve conditions for Aborigines in the Northern Territory. Raised in an Anglican family, he maintained strong links with the Church of England throughout his life. He was a lay preacher, a church warden (1940-50) of St Peter's Cathedral and a member (1942-57) of the Adelaide synod; he represented (1945-52) the diocese at the general synod, and sat on the Leigh trust which managed property of the Church in Adelaide.

Price's broad-ranging intellect, and his experience and interpretation of a wide variety of physical environments and their modifications by human endeavours around the world, led to the recognition of his multi-faceted contribution to Australian society. He received the John Lewis [q.v.10] gold medal (1949) of the South Australian branch of the R.G.S.A. and the Redmond Barry [q.v.3] award (1973) of the Library Association of Australia. Knighted in 1963 for his services to education, he was made an honorary fellow of the American Geographical Society in 1973. Recognition had its rewards, but appears not to have affected the modesty of a man who described himself as 'a good second-class brain'. Not surprisingly, Archie was variously described by contemporaries as 'an all-rounder of an uncommon kind', as 'a Renaissance man ... at home in several fields of knowledge' and as one who 'possessed ... kindly wisdom'. His final years were troubled by a hip operation which was only partially successful, and he gave up most of his public engagements in 1972.

Of a 'Pickwickian appearance', Price had apparently limitless enthusiasm and humour. He was a gracious host, a correct but forceful committee-man, a supporter of colleagues and students, and a chain-smoker. His inspiration and zest were such that a former student likened working with him to 'being on the tail of a comet'. Well known in Canberra and a regular visitor to that city, he was acquainted with Arthur Calwell, Harold Holt [qq.v.13,14] and E. G. Whitlam. Menzies claimed him as 'a good friend' and professed to be an 'admirer'. Sir Grenfell retained, however, staunch ties to Adelaide, where he lived in the suburb of Gilberton. He belonged to the Adelaide, Commonwealth (in Canberra) and Australasian Pioneers' (in Sydney) clubs, and enjoyed fishing and shooting. Survived by his wife, and their daughter and two sons, he died on 20 July 1977 in North Adelaide and was cremated. His elder son Charles (b.1920) became a noted demographer.

F. Gale and G. H. Lawton (eds), *Settlement & Encounter* (Melb, 1969); C. Kerr, *Archie, the Biography of Sir Archibald Grenfell Price* (Melb, 1983); *Geographers: Biobibliographical Studies*, 6, 1982, p 90; Price papers (SLSA).

R. L. HEATHCOTE

PRIDDLE, RAYMOND ARTHUR (1913-1971), consulting engineer, was born on 8 January 1913 at Wagga Wagga, New South Wales, son of native-born parents Ernest William Wills Priddle, civil engineer, and his wife May Adeline, née Mawson. Ray attended Cumnock Public School, Fort Street Boys' High School, Sydney, and Bathurst High School. He studied civil engineering at the University of Sydney (B.E., 1934), graduating with first-class honours and the university medal. Awarded Blues for rifle-shooting by the university, the Australian Universities Sports Association and the Imperial Universities, he also represented his faculty in tennis and cricket. From his early schooldays Priddle was interested in amateur radio, and for some time he operated radio-station 2RA. At St Augustine's Anglican Church, Neutral Bay, on 15 June 1940 he married Margaret Anne Lawson, a stenographer.

After almost two years experience (with the Department of Main Roads in the Yass-Canberra area and Sydney Municipal Council) Priddle joined the staff of A. S. Macdonald & Wagner, consulting engineers. He became a partner in 1944; the firm was thereafter known as A. S. Macdonald, Wagner & Priddle. When the partnership was incorporated in 1971 Priddle was appointed chairman. Noted for his skill in co-operating with architects, he worked as structural consultant for many large buildings, including the Sydney Opera House.

Priddle was an excellent mathematician. He designed the structures of the Commonwealth Scientific and Industrial Research Organization's radio-telescope at Parkes, the University of Sydney's Mills Cross radio-telescope near Canberra, and the Stellar Interferometer at Narrabri. In 1968 he visited a number of the world's largest telescopes; later, in association with the university, he made models of several alternative designs of polar-axis struts. His last project, still incomplete at the time of his death, was the Anglo-Australian Observatory's 150-inch (381 cm) optical-telescope at Siding Spring, near Coonabarabran.

A committee-member (from 1946) of the Sydney division of the Institution of Engineers, Australia, Priddle was elected to the council in 1954. As president (1963) and treasurer (1965-71), he worked closely with his friend G. I. Davey [q.v.13]. Priddle was awarded the I.E.A.'s 1963 R. W. Chapman [q.v.7] medal for his paper on 'Load Distribution in Piled Bents'. He never once refused to serve on any of the institution's committees. Sometime president of the Association of Consulting Structural Engineers of New South Wales and the Wireless Institute of Australia, he was a fellow (1967-71) of the senate of the University of Sydney, and a member (1958-62) of the National Capital Planning Committee and of numerous subcommittees of the Standards Association of Australia.

Priddle belonged to the University Club, the Royal Sydney Yacht Squadron and the Rotary Club of Sydney. He also enjoyed playing golf. Survived by his wife, and their son and daughter, he died of a pulmonary embolism on 11 August 1971 at the Hornsby and District Hospital and was cremated. His estate was sworn for probate at $540 532. He was posthumously awarded the Peter Nicol Russell [q.v.6] medal for 1971 by the I.E.A.

A. H. Corbett, *The Institution of Engineers, Australia* (Syd, 1973); Inst of Engineers, Aust, *J*, Oct-Nov 1971, p 23, Dec 1971, p 15; *SMH*, 31 Mar, 30 July 1932, 20 May 1933, 28 Apr 1934, 7 Nov 1967, 21 Mar 1972.   HENRY J. COWAN

PRIESTLEY, HENRY THOMAS (1912-1979), engineer and university deputy-chancellor, was born on 16 February 1912 at Kangaroo Point, Brisbane, eldest of four children of English-born parents Henry James Priestley [q.v.11], professor of mathematics, and his wife Margery Hope, née Hewitt. Tom attended Toowong State and Brisbane Grammar schools. He won a scholarship to the University of Queensland (B.E., 1933), studied mechanical and electrical engineering, and graduated with first-class honours. On 11 April 1936 at St Stephen's Catholic Cathedral, Brisbane, he married Anne Walsh (d.1977), a 31-year-old cane-tester. That year he travelled to England where he probably worked for British Thomson-Houston Co. Ltd at Rugby, Warwickshire.

Returning to Australia in 1937, Priestley joined the City Electric Light Co. of Brisbane as assistant-engineer and later became district engineer at Nambour. In 1950 he accepted a post with the Electrolytic Zinc Co. of Australasia Ltd at Risdon, Tasmania. Back in Queensland, he was appointed engineer-manager of the Mackay City Council Electricity Department in 1954. He was manager of the Townsville Regional Electricity Board in 1956-69 and of the Capricornia Regional Electricity Board at Rockhampton in 1969-74.

An energetic man who was keen to improve the lot of country people, Priestley supervised installation of the single-wire, earth-return system of distribution in the Townsville region, making it viable to provide mains supply to far-flung properties and towns throughout western parts of the State. He introduced co-generation arrangements with sugar-mills which led to more effective use of electricity. The increase in generating capacity encouraged industrial development in North Queensland.

In the late 1950s Priestley had become convinced that North Queensland needed a university to provide tertiary education for young people who were unable to travel to Brisbane to attend the University of Queensland. A driving force behind the formation of the Townsville and District University Society in 1958, he helped to gather support for the establishment of a university at Townsville. He was president (from 1960) of the North Queensland University Association which raised money for residential accommodation for students, library facilities and scholarships. When the University of Queensland opened the University College of Townsville at Pimlico in 1961, there were colleges for men and women—funded by the efforts of Priestley and his colleagues—ready for occupation. He was chairman of the new university college's advisory committee (1961) and council (1962-70).

The college became the James Cook University of North Queensland in 1970. Priestley chaired its first council until the appointment of a chancellor, and then served as deputy-chancellor (1971-79). Despite heavy commitments, he continued his association with the Catholic Church, and maintained his interests in cricket and bush-walking. He was a fellow of the Institution of Electrical Engineers, London, the Institution of Engineers, Australia, and the Australian Institute of Management, and a member of the Johnsonian (in Brisbane), North Queensland (at Townsville), Rockhampton and Mackay clubs.

Priestley died suddenly of coronary apoplexy on 29 August 1979 at St Paul's College, James Cook University, and was buried in Belgian Gardens cemetery, Townsville. His son and two daughters survived him.

K. Willey, *The First Hundred Years* (Melb, 1968); Univ College of Townsville, *Year of 1961* (Townsville, Qld, 1981); J. Maguire, *Prologue: A history of the Catholic Church as seen from Townsville 1863-1983* (Toowoomba, Qld, 1990); C. Doran, *Partner in Progress* (Townsville, Qld, 1990); *Townsville Daily Bulletin*, 30 Oct 1979; information from Mr D. Pearse, Townsville, Mr B. Gibson-Wilde, Aitkenvale, Qld, Mrs S. McCarthy, Glen Waverley, Melb, and the late Mr F. McKay.   DOROTHY GIBSON-WILDE

PRIESTLEY, JOHN (1903-1964), Presbyterian minister, was born on 8 September 1903 at Yackandandah, Victoria, fifth child of Alexander Priestley, bootmaker, and his wife Maude Elinor, née Burgis, both Victorian born. Educated at Yackandandah State School, John worked (1918-23) as a telegraph messenger with the Postmaster-General's Department before preparing for the ministry at St Andrew's Theological Training College, Carlton, and the Theological Hall, Ormond [q.v.5] College, University of Melbourne. While studying, he served as a 'home missionary'—a layman in charge of a parish, supervised by a nearby minister. At St Paul's Presbyterian Church, Wangaratta, on 5 April 1933 he married Elvie Sabina Peipers.

Ordained on 27 April 1933, Priestley ministered to the parishes of Tarnagulla (1933-35),

Portland (1935-42) and Brunswick (1942-55). He was the convenor of the Victorian General Assembly's committees for the beneficiary fund (1944-49) and the maintenance of the ministry (1949-55).

In January 1956 Priestley became commissioner of the Presbyterian Church of South Australia. Among other duties, he advised and encouraged parishes and their ministers, supervised the establishment of new congregations and liaised with the Presbyterian Church of Victoria, which was then subsidizing its smaller neighbour. Defying the illness that eventually killed him, he drove himself relentlessly. Central to his work was his combination of American methods of 'stewardship' and lay evangelism. In this system, lay men and women visited people in their neighbourhood, urging fellow parishioners to pledge a proportion of their income to the Church, and inviting nominal Presbyterians to become fully committed members. Active participation by the laity brought new vigour to the Church. By 1960 there were more parishes and more full-time church workers than at any previous time. In 1959, at the invitation of the Presbyterian Church in Ireland, he had demonstrated his methods of stewardship and lay evangelism at a parish in Belfast.

Within the Presbyterian Church of South Australia, Priestley successfully strove for the payment of adequate salaries and allowances to ministers, the appointment of a full-time director of Christian education, and the completion of a revised code of Church law and procedure, of which his knowledge was legendary. He also promoted co-operation with other Protestant denominations in new housing areas. While holding to what he saw as the essentials of Presbyterianism, he was involved in preliminary moves towards the formation of the Uniting Church in Australia.

Lean and wiry, with a low, husky voice, Priestley gained respect and affection with his quiet but insistently persuasive manner, earthy humour, sympathetic concern for his fellows and total devotion to his ministry. Illness compelled him to resign as commissioner, and from most of the committees and boards on which he served, on 30 June 1961. Survived by his wife, their daughter, and three of their four sons, he died of emphysema and secondary heart disease on 21 December 1964 at his Glenunga home and was cremated. Although his methods have been modified, his influence is still felt in the Uniting Church.

Presbyterian Church of Vic, *Procs of the General Assembly*, 1925-32 and 1965 (Uniting Church Archives, Melb); Presbyterian Church of SA, *Minutes of the General Assembly*, 1954-70 (Mort L); *Advertiser* (Adel), 22 Dec 1964; information from Rev J. D. Bentley, Glengowrie, Adel.   J. H. LOVE

PRIOR, HENRY KENNETH (1893-1967), newspaper publisher, was born on 13 March 1893 at Broken Hill, New South Wales, third child of Australian-born parents Samuel Henry Prior [q.v.11], journalist, and his wife Alice May, née Marsh. The family moved to Sydney in 1903. Ken was educated at Sydney Boys' High School and joined the *Bulletin* in 1910. Commissioned lieutenant in the Australian Imperial Force on 20 October 1915, he served with the 51st Battery, 13th Field Artillery Brigade, in Egypt and France. Major Prior's A.I.F. appointment ended in Sydney in October 1919. By then he had accepted William Macleod's [q.v.10] invitation to manage the *Bulletin*. At the Church of Our Lady of the Sacred Heart, Randwick, on 1 October that year he married with Catholic rites Josephine Mary (Molly) Lawler, a nurse.

Overriding Macleod's objections, Prior launched the *Australian Woman's Mirror* in 1924 to keep the *Bulletin*'s presses busy. The weekly magazine relied on contributions from its readers, and proved popular and cheap to produce. Five ft 10 ins (178 cm) tall, handsome and blue eyed, Prior rolled up his sleeves and helped to wrap the *Mirror*'s fashion patterns for its subscribers. In 1927 Macleod sold his shares in the Bulletin Newspaper Co. Ltd to the Priors. When Samuel died in 1933, Ken became chairman and managing director. In 1932 the firm had joined with P. R. Stephensen and Norman Lindsay [qq.v.12,10] to found the short-lived Endeavour Press. Despite Endeavour's demise, Ken gave local authors a boost in 1934 by establishing the S. H. Prior memorial prize of £100 for the best book of the year.

Employees found Prior unassuming and cordial, if a little remote. He always agreed to a rise when asked, but it was never more than 10 shillings. Former members of his brigade, his lifelong friends, often found their way on to the *Bulletin*'s staff. Two of his sons worked at the *Bulletin*, and all three served in World War II. Prior generously provided for employees in the services. He was shattered when Molly died just days before Japan's surrender.

Although he was an exacting proofreader, Prior knew that his expertise lay in accountancy and printing. Editorial policy was never his strength and he had taken charge of a magazine that had lost its old *élan*. By the 1950s traditional columns endorsing the White Australia policy and denouncing communists and Jews made the *Bulletin* appear increasingly outdated in its stridency. Late in that decade the fifty-five shareholders of the Bulletin Newspaper Co. Pty Ltd received no dividends. Prior sold the company in October 1960 to Sir Frank Packer [q.v.15] for about £400 000, admitting: 'We have found it impossible for an independent newspaper to carry on in these times'.

From the 1930s Prior had been involved with King & Prior Pty Ltd, paper merchants; after retiring, he established the publishing firm, Prior Press Pty Ltd. He enjoyed playing golf and lawn bowls. Survived by his daughter and sons, he died on 5 August 1967 at his Mosman home and was cremated. His portrait by H. A. Hanke is held by the family,

D. Stewart, *Writers of the Bulletin* (Syd, 1977); P. Rolfe (ed), *The Journalistic Javelin* (Syd, 1979); C. Munro, *Wild Man of Letters* (Melb, 1984); *Newspaper News*, 1 July 1933; *Bulletin*, 14 June 1933, 1 Feb 1961, 2 Sept 1967; *SMH*, 11 Oct 1960, 7 Aug 1967; *Australian*, 7 Aug 1967; information from Mr K. J. Prior, Mosman, Syd.

BRIDGET GRIFFEN-FOLEY

PROBY, LAWRENCE SHERLOCK (1919-1969), soldier and businessman, was born on 20 July 1919 at Osborne, near Mornington, Victoria, second child of Harley Lawrence Proby, orchardist, and his wife Janet Agnes, née Sherlock, both Victorian born. Lawrence was raised in several Melbourne suburbs, and educated in turn at Bentleigh State and Brighton Technical schools until he was about 15 years old. By 1939 he was working as a storeman. Five ft 11½ ins (182 cm) tall, with blue eyes and brown hair, he was a good-looking young man, with a characteristically cheerful grin.

Mobilized in the Militia in April 1940, Proby was posted to the 58th (later the 58th/59th) Battalion. After attending officers' training school at Seymour, he was promoted sergeant and called up for full-time duty in October 1941. He was commissioned lieutenant on 2 February 1942 and transferred to the Australian Imperial Force on 28 July. At St Mark's Anglican Church, Casino, New South Wales, on 2 February 1943 he married Norma Dorothy Gorton, a draper's assistant. Thirty-four days later he embarked for New Guinea.

In June 1943 the raw 58th/59th Battalion joined the fight for Bobdubi Ridge, the key to the Japanese stronghold at Salamaua. The Australians gradually advanced until they encountered a horseshoe-shaped fortress on a site known as Old Vickers. It withstood repeated attacks. On 28 July four platoons of the 58th/59th were involved in a new assault, with Proby's platoon in the centre. The approach was along a ridge so narrow that only one man could advance at a time. 'Butch' Proby was first to penetrate the enemy's defences and directed his men in mopping up enemy strong-points. Dazed by an exploding grenade, he regained consciousness while receiving medical attention and rejoined the action, trailing yards of bandage. For his leadership and courage, which played a sig-

nificant part in the capture of the fortress, he was awarded the Military Cross.

Admitted to hospital, first with dengue fever and then with malaria, Proby returned to Queensland in August 1944. Within five months he was sent to Bougainville. During the push towards Buin, 'A' Company of the 58th/59th (with Proby in temporary command) was ordered on 29 June 1945 to assault Japanese positions on the east bank of the Mobiai River. Coming under intense fire from a heavy machine-gun, Proby charged the pillbox, killed its four crew and captured the weapon. Soon after, he leapt into the river —while under further fire—to rescue two wounded men. He then led a flanking attack which overwhelmed another post upriver, securing the high ground controlling the Buin Road. He won a bar to his M.C.

Proby came home to Australia in September 1945. He held a staff post in Melbourne before being placed on the Reserve of Officers on 18 January 1947. After working for a paper-manufacturing firm in the city, he ran a newsagency at Shepparton. A few years later he opened an office-equipment business in the town. Survived by his wife, and their daughter and two sons, he died of cardiac disease on 14 March 1969 in Melbourne and was buried in Shepparton cemetery with Methodist forms.

D. Dexter, *The New Guinea Offensives* (Canb, 1961); R. Mathews, *Militia Battalion at War* (Syd, 1961); G. Long, *The Final Campaigns* (Canb, 1963); information from Mrs N. Proby, Mooroopna, and Mrs H. Carroll, Orrvale, Vic.   P. L. EDGAR

PROPSTING, MARJORIE GERTRUDE ELEANOR (1905-1972), librarian and mayor, was born on 25 November 1905 at Waverley, Sydney, eldest child of New South Wales-born parents Henry Thomas Albert Bowman, monumental mason, and his wife Sophia, née Farmilo. Leaving North Sydney Girls' High School, Marjorie studied part time at the University of Sydney (B.A., 1928) on an exhibition scholarship while training (from 1925) as a librarian at the Public Library of New South Wales. She was employed as a library-assistant at Teachers' College, Sydney (1927-33), and at the Public Library (1933-36). On 24 February 1934 at St Stephen's Anglican Church, Chatswood, she married Henry Sherwin Propsting (d.1968), an engineer; they were to have a son and daughter.

Involved in numerous local organizations, Mrs Propsting worked (1951-72) at the library of the Sydney Kindergarten Training (Teachers') College, Waverley. She had become associated with Lane Cove Municipal Council in 1947 when appointed a citizen member of its town-planning committee. In October 1949 she was elected an alderman for East Ward, an office she was to hold for twenty-two years. Deputy-mayor in 1960, she was elected mayor of Lane Cove in December 1963. While the press grappled with what to call the new civic leader, she suggested that 'Marj' or 'Mrs Propsting' would do. 'I'm against these high-sounding titles', she said, 'Can you imagine coming out of the butcher's shop and being called Your Worship?' Highlights of her period in office included the construction of the Lane Cove Lower Town Hall (now demolished), the foundation of the Lane Cove Homes for the Aged Association, the provision of a women's rest centre, and a visit to the Territory of Papua and New Guinea in January 1965. A member of the council's finance and library committees, and a consumer representative on the New South Wales advisory bread industry committees (1965 and 1970), she helped to establish the Greenwich branch library, later named after her.

Propsting believed there should be more women in local government because they brought 'that necessary woman's point of view'. She was a founder (1952) of the Australian Local Government Women's Association, and president of both the New South Wales and Australian Capital Territory branch (1952-72) and the national board (1966-70). Although she believed that the association was necessary because 'men have a closed clique on many things', she did not call herself a feminist. In her view, women 'can get things done if only they'll use gentle persistence instead of militancy'. She was active in the National Council of Women of New South Wales, the National Council of Women of Australia and the League of Women Voters, and was also a justice of the peace. A member of the New South Wales executive of the Liberal Party, she unsuccessfully stood for preselection in several State elections. In 1970 she was appointed M.B.E.

Survived by her children, Propsting died of myocardial infarction on 2 April 1972 in Macksville hospital and was cremated. An energetic citizen and a devoted mother, she was remembered as a 'calm, sincere and unaffected' woman characterized by 'quiet dignity'.

A. V. Smith, *Women in Australian Parliaments and Local Governments, Past and Present* (Canb, 1975); *Shire and Municipal Record*, 28 Jan 1964, p 815; National Council of Women of Aust, *Q Bulletin*, Mar/Apr 1972, p 4; *SMH*, 11 May, 30 Oct 1965, 4 Apr 1972; Propsting papers (Lane Cove Municipal L); family information.   MARTHA SEAR

PROVAN, FRANCES BETTY (1911-1963), naval officer and businesswoman, was born

on 17 November 1911 at Spring Hill, Brisbane, second daughter of Queensland-born parents Donald McCallum Provan, bookseller, and his wife Frances Mary Walpole, née Boyd. Her mother was descended from the Walpole family in England. Frances was educated at Toowoomba, at the Glennie [q.v.4] Preparatory School, Fairholme Presbyterian Girls' College, and the Glennie Memorial School. Margaret Brown, the headmistress of G.M.S., stressed moral behaviour and told her pupils: 'Remember, you are a Glennie Girl, and there is nothing a Glennie Girl cannot do'. After Frances's father died during her final year at school, she worked in turn as a trainee-teacher, nurse and governess. About 1939 she moved to Sydney. Five ft 6½ ins (169 cm) tall, with brown hair, large brown eyes, a fair complexion and classical features, she was a smart, slightly built, well-groomed young woman—a 'darling' and 'tremendous fun' according to her younger sister.

Believing war to be imminent, Provan began training with the Women's Emergency Signalling Corps which had been founded in Sydney by Florence McKenzie. By 1941 the Royal Australian Navy needed more wireless telegraphists. The availability of women who had learned these skills in the W.E.S.C. led to a decision to recruit twelve female telegraphists as the initial members of Women's Royal Australian Naval Service. Enlisting as a telegraphist on 28 April 1941, Provan was given the official number WR/1 and posted to H.M.A.S. *Harman*, the communications station in Canberra. She and her colleagues relayed messages to the fleet and maintained contact with many wireless stations around the world. The number of female telegraphists increased rapidly, and women were recruited to serve in other branches of the navy. By 1945 there were 2590 Wrans working in shore establishments throughout Australia.

Promoted leading telegraphist (September 1941) and petty officer telegraphist (December 1942), Provan attended the first W.R.A.N.S. officers' training course at Flinders Naval Depot, Westernport, Victoria. She was appointed third officer on 15 February 1943 and returned to *Harman* in August. In June 1945 she was posted as officer-in-charge of the only draft of Wrans to serve in an operational zone, in Darwin: her standards of behaviour and appearance led her contingent to be referred to as 'Miss Provan's Academy for Young Ladies'. She served briefly at bases in New South Wales and Queensland before being demobilized from the navy in October 1946 in Melbourne.

Miss Provan travelled to England where she was employed by a meat-importing firm. In the late 1950s her ability and competence won her the post of manager of the London office of Jackson's United Meat Co. Pty Ltd, a business based at Footscray, Melbourne. In 1963 she returned to Melbourne, met the firm's Australian directors and flew to Brisbane, planning to visit her mother. She died suddenly of heart disease on 21 June that year in a taxi *en route* from Eagle Farm to Camp Hill and was cremated with Presbyterian forms.

M. Curtis-Otter, *W.R.A.N.S.* (Syd, 1975); A. Nelson, *A History of HMAS Harman and its People* (Canb, 1993); information from Mrs J. Parker, Warrawee, Syd.   ROSEMARY JENNINGS

PURDY, CECIL JOHN SEDDON (1906-1979), chess master and author, was born on 27 March 1906 at Port Said, Egypt, eldest of three children of English-born parents John Smith Purdy [q.v.11], medical practitioner, and his wife Emily, née Crake. The family moved to New Zealand (1907), Tasmania (1910) and Sydney (1913); while John was serving with the Australian Imperial Force during World War I, his wife and children lived in Hobart. After the war the Purdys settled in Sydney. Cecil was educated at Cranbrook School and the University of Sydney (B.A., 1930). He began teaching himself chess in 1922, won the New Zealand championship in 1924-25 and finished third in the Australian championship in 1926.

In 1929 Purdy started the *Australasian Chess Review* (1929-44), later entitled *Check* (1944-45) and *Chess World* (from 1946), which he published continuously until 1967. Financially, life was a constant struggle for him. Despite featuring numerous articles contributed by Lajos Steiner [q.v.] and others, the magazine was never a money-spinner. It did serve, however, as a means of advertising books and chess goods, the sale of which provided most of Purdy's income. The remainder came from newspaper columns, book royalties, prize-money and coaching. At St John's Anglican Church, Maroubra, on 15 June 1934 he married Anne (Nancy), daughter of Spencer Crakanthorp who had won two Australian championships.

Purdy competed in 139 over-the-board chess tournaments, 43 telegraphic matches and 14 other matches. Between 1923 and 1979 he played 1586 competitive games over-the-board, winning 69 per cent of them. His greatest skills lay in his remarkable grasp of the strategic principles of the game, as opposed to tactical skills. Such deep understanding proved invaluable to him in correspondence chess, and as a writer. He competed in two Australian Correspondence championships, winning both. Representing Australia in the first World Correspondence Chess Championship, he surprised the chess world by winning the tournament which ended in 1953. This achievement constituted a triumph, but his love of the excitement and tension of the cross-board game was such that he possibly gained equal satisfaction from his four victories in the Australian Chess Championship (1934-35, 1936-37, 1948-49 and 1951).

In addition to his Australian wins, Purdy was twice champion of New Zealand, and in 36 attempts won 7 New South Wales titles and was runner-up 8 times. He was granted the titles of international chess master (1951) and international grand master of correspondence play (1953) by the Fédération Internationale des Échecs. In 1960 he won the championship of the Pacific and South East Asia. He represented Australia at the Chess Olympiad (1970) at Siegan, West Germany, and captained the Australian team at the Chess Olympiad, held at Nice, France, in 1974.

Purdy's international reputation rested less on his postal and cross-board successes than on the writings in his books and in his monthly magazine—reputedly the only magazine in the world that set out to teach its readers how to play better chess. His books included *How Euwe Won* (1936), *The Return of Alekhine* (1937), *Among These Mates* (1939, under his pseudonym, 'Chielamangus'), *Chess Made Easy* (1942, with his friend and rival Gregory Koshnitsky), *Guide to Good Chess* (1950) and *How Fischer Won* (Brisbane, 1972). He was recognized as one of the world's top writers on chess.

Slender and of middle height, Purdy possessed energy and determination, evident not only in his competitive play, but also in his work for the advancement of chess. He was sometime president of the Correspondence Chess League of Australia, the New South Wales Chess Association and the Sydney University Chess Club; he also held various positions in the Australian Chess Federation and was a vice-president of the World Correspondence Chess Federation. A major contributor to the accurate codification of the laws of chess, he was appointed A.M. in 1976.

Purdy collapsed on 6 November 1979 while playing in a tournament at the Chess Centre of New South Wales and died that day in Sydney Hospital. Survived by his wife, and their daughter and son John who was twice Australian champion, he was cremated. Frank Hutchings, his son-in-law, co-authored *How Purdy Won* (1983), and John Hammond and Robert Jamieson edited *C. J. S. Purdy, his Life, his Games and his Writings* (1982); both books were based on material written by Purdy.

Chess World, Mar 1948, p 50, May 1951, p 92; *CCLA Record*, Aug 1953, p 2, Feb 1980, p 159; *Chess in Australia*, 14, Nov 1979, p 233; *Aust Chess Lore*,

1, 1982, p 74; *SMH*, 26 Jan 1976, 8, 11 Nov 1979; information from Mrs A. Purdy and Mr J. Purdy, Greenwich, and Mr F. Hutchings, Epping, Syd.

PETER PARR

PURVES, JAMES RICHARD WILLIAM (1903-1979), philatelist and lawyer, was born on 5 March 1903 at Fulham, London, only son of Australian-born parents James George Purves, solicitor, and his wife Sarah, née Green. J. L. Purves [q.v.5] was his grandfather. Bill was born while James and Sarah were visiting England. The family returned to Victoria when he was 4. Educated at Green Vale College, Willaura, and Geelong Church of England Grammar School, he won an exhibition in chemistry, prizes for poetry and a scholarship to Trinity College, University of Melbourne (LL.B., 1925; LL.M., 1937). On 2 May 1927 he was admitted to practice as a barrister and solicitor.

In 1942 he became a senior partner in Purves & Purves. At St John's Anglican Church, Toorak, on 14 February that year he married Patricia Constance Warford-Mein. Commissioned lieutenant, Citizen Military Forces, on 7 August 1940, he transferred to the Australian Imperial Force in August 1942 and was promoted captain in October. He performed ordnance duties in New Guinea in 1943-44 before being placed on the Reserve of Officers on 28 June 1944.

From his childhood Purves had been an avid collector of marbles, coins, birds' eggs and cigarette cards. Concentrating on stamps, he began to build up an outstanding collection from many countries. His set of Commonwealth of Australia stamps, described as 'the most complete of its kind in the world', won a gold medal at the 1928 International Philatelic Exhibition in Melbourne and was bought in 1930 by King George V, reputedly for £1925. Thereafter, Purves specialized in stamps of the Australian colonies and States (1901-13). His collection won medals in New York, Paris, Prague and Vienna, and championships in Melbourne and Sydney. A member of the (Royal) Philatelic Society of Victoria (president for eight terms between 1929 and 1975) and of the Royal Philatelic Society, London (fellow 1932, honorary life fellow 1969), he also belonged to the Collectors Club, New York.

The study of science at school had taught Purves habits of 'ordered inquiry' which were apparent in his 'meticulous research' into philately. In 1928-30 he edited the *Victorian (Australian) Philatelic Record*, to which he contributed numerous editorials and articles. He won the Royal Philatelic Society's Tapling medal (1938) for an essay on Fijian stamps and its Crawford medal (1954) for a monograph, *The Half-Lengths of Victoria* (London, 1953). His other books included *The Postal History of the Port Phillip District 1837-1851* (1950) and *The "Emblems" of Victoria 1857-63* (1957). The Philatelic Congress of Great Britain listed (1937) him on the roll of distinguished philatelists. By 1951 he had been a judge at international exhibitions in New York and London.

Purves was a member of the Melbourne Club, a notary public, solicitor to the Victoria Racing Club and a director (1952-76) of Thomas Cook & Son (Australasia) Pty Ltd. Short and slightly plump, he wore a moustache and dressed conservatively. He was a kindly man, with 'a remarkable memory', who loved music and had played A-grade cricket and golf off scratch. Survived by his wife, and their two daughters, he died on 13 May 1979 at his South Yarra home and was cremated. His collection of stamps filled 350 volumes and he was described as 'one of the world's three greatest philatelists'.

B. Rogers-Tillstone and F. B. Howard-White, *The Royal Philatelic Society, London, 1869-1969* (Lond, 1969); *Philately* (Boston, US, 1974); *People* (Syd), 26 Sept 1951, p 17; *Philately from Australia*, June 1979, p 30; Geelong C of E Grammar School, *Corian*, Sept-Oct 1980, p 99; *SMH*, 12 Mar 1930; *Australian*, 16-17 June 1979; information from Mrs C. Brain, Armadale, Melb.   BARBARA DAWSON

PUTILIN, SERGIJ VASILEVICH (THEODOSY) (1897-1980), Russian Orthodox archbishop, was born on 18 August 1897 at Voronezh, Central Russia, son of Vasilij Putilin, priest, and his wife Darija, née Putilina (no relation). Sergij graduated from the Voronezh Theological Seminary in 1918. Opposed to Communist ideology and the October 1917 revolution, he joined the White Russians and fought as a volunteer in southern Russia. His toes were frostbitten and later amputated. On 14 October 1921 he married Olga Posen, whom he had met while in hospital; they were to have two daughters Zoja and Ija.

Persuaded that it was too dangerous to be ordained in post-revolutionary Russia, Putilin worked as an accountant in several enterprises while living with his family at Taganrog, on the Sea of Azov. He was imprisoned by the secret police in 1931 and again from 1936 to 1940. During World War II the Putilins were deported to Germany as forced labour. Sergij toiled as a welder. Remaining in the Federal Republic of Germany after the war, he was ordained priest on 14 October 1948 at Wildflecken.

The Putilins emigrated to Western Australia in the *Anna Salen*, reaching Fremantle on 31 December 1950. Settled in Perth, he became priest for the Orthodox community, which consisted of displaced people of Russian, Ukrainian, Byelorussian and Latvian origin. A sympathetic, tolerant, eloquent and educated man, he promoted peace and harmony in his parish. He was an able administrator who organized the building of the Orthodox Church of St Peter and St Paul, Meltham. On 18 June 1959 he and his wife were naturalized.

After Olga died in 1968, Putilin made his monastic vows. He was consecrated on 30 November 1969 as bishop of Melbourne, taking the religious name of Theodosy. In the following year he was transferred to Sydney as bishop of Sydney and Australia-New Zealand (Russian Orthodox Church Outside of Russia). On 29 September 1971 he was enthroned as archbishop.

Theodosy took charge of the Russian Church in Australia in troubled times. A long-lasting conflict in the parish of the Cathedral of St Peter and St Paul, Sydney, had split the community. His firmness of principle, wisdom, kindness and ability to forgive helped him to resolve the situation. Archbishop Theodosy gave his attention to all things great and small. Remaining simple, approachable and just, he was involved in a variety of pastoral duties, such as the education of children, the care of the elderly, and fund-raising for victims of the Darwin cyclone (1974). He personally oversaw the construction of the Orthodox Church of St John the Baptist in Canberra, drawing the whole eparchy into support of the project. Survived by his daughters, he died on 13 August 1980 in his home at Croydon, Sydney, and was buried in Karrakatta cemetery, Perth. His sermons had been recorded and were published in Russian by Fr Michael Protopopov in *Archbishop Theodosy Putilin* (Melbourne, 1995).

Edinenie (*Unification*, Syd), 8 Feb, 22 Aug 1980; *SMH*, 14, 21 Aug 1980; naturalization files, series PP545/1, item 1969/13569, *and* series PP181/1, item 1958/10587 (NAA, Perth); information from Fr M. Protopopov, Keysborough, Melb.

ELENA GOVOR

Q

QUEALE, WILLIAM (1889-1951), manufacturer, was born on 15 September 1889 at Snowtown, South Australia, third of ten children of Thomas Queale, an Irish-born railway inspector, and his wife Mary Eleanor, née Jane, who came from England. William attended school at Burra before moving with the family to Adelaide in 1902. From an early age he was afflicted with a hearing defect, but he later claimed that it prevented him from being distracted and gave him greater powers of concentration. At the Adelaide Shorthand and Business Training Academy he achieved a shorthand speed of 150 words per minute. In 1905 he passed the State civil service examination with honours. He worked for a firm that imported porcelain and glassware from Germany and then for a small electrical business.

About 1908 Queale and a number of his brothers attempted to establish a farm near Pinnaroo, but a succession of droughts led to the venture's failure. Prevented by deafness from enlisting in the Australian Imperial Force, he went to New South Wales to take up the post of secretary of the Broken Hill Junction Lead Mining Co. In 1915 he became its general manager. On 19 September 1918 he married 20-year-old Dorothy Griffiths with Methodist forms in her father's house at Broken Hill.

Returning to Adelaide in 1924, Queale founded Mechanical Supplies Ltd (Mechanical Products Ltd from 1932), which sold engineering supplies and held agencies for imported appliances. In 1934 the firm was renamed Kelvinator Australia Ltd after he gained the distribution and manufacturing rights for Kelvinator electric refrigerators. He remained its managing director until 1951. In addition, he was chairman of River Murray Broadcasters Pty Ltd (1935-51), Hume Broadcasters Ltd (1930-51) and Power Plant Pty Ltd (1935-51).

Queale encouraged his employees to continue their education beyond school. A widely read man, he established a technical library at Kelvinator. With other businessmen, he persuaded the State Library of South Australia to set up (1942) a research service for industry and helped to raise funds for the project. He urged Kelvinator's senior staff to travel abroad to gain new ideas and see new technology. His company adopted a number of innovative practices, including a programme of technical training for employees and incentive schemes for workers.

Chairman (1931-33) of the Citizens' League of South Australia, Queale was also a member (1930-31) of the Emergency Committee of South Australia, an anti-socialist organization chaired by (Sir) Grenfell Price [q.v.]. In 1932 he was appointed Commonwealth representative on the South Australian Unemployment Council. He worked closely with both sides of politics to further the industrial development of the State.

Premier (Sir) Thomas Playford regarded Queale as one of South Australia's leading industrialists. Prime Minister (Sir) Robert Menzies [q.v.15] later described him as 'dogged'. Queale was president of the South Australian Chamber of Manufactures (1941-44) and of the Associated Chambers of Manufactures of Australia (1945). While usually working behind the scenes in matters involving governments, he took a more public role during World War II when his views were sought on topics ranging from taxation and manpower issues to postwar reconstruction. He emphasized the importance of scientific management and the need for better employee-employer relations. A founder (1941) of the South Australian branch of the Australian-American Co-operation Movement and subsequently vice-president of the Australian-American Association, he was vice-president (from 1940) and president (1951) of the Metal Industries Association, South Australia, and president of the Adelaide division of the Institute of Industrial Management (1944-51) and the Australian Institute of Management (1951).

Queale took delight in his family, and in simple pleasures such as tending his garden, outings in his motorcar, and summer holidays at Victor Harbor. He had a gift for telling imaginative children's stories. Survived by his wife, their three daughters and three of their four sons, he died of a cerebral haemorrhage on Christmas Day 1951 at his St Georges home and was cremated. His estate was sworn for probate at £78 896. The Australian Institute of Management named a library and an annual lecture after him.

J of Industry, Jan 1947, p 3; *News* (Adel), 26, 27 Dec 1951; *Advertiser* (Adel), 27 Dec 1951; information from Mrs E. Millar, St Georges, and Mr D. Queale, Beaumont, Adel.   MARTIN SHANAHAN

QUENTIN, CECIL ROBERT BURNETT (1917-1979), professor of drama and theatre director, was born on 3 August 1917 at Coulsdon, Surrey, England, and named John Burnett, third child of Lieutenant George Augustus Frederick Quentin, army officer and later inspector of schools in Egypt, and his wife Edith Florence, née Beazley. John's name was changed to Cecil Robert by the time he entered Lancing College, Sussex. Robert read English language and literature at St Edmund Hall, Oxford (B.A., M.A., 1945), worked in various theatrical enterprises and passed his final examinations in July 1939.

In 1940 Quentin joined the Royal Naval Volunteer Reserve. Commissioned on 6 December that year and promoted lieutenant in August 1942, he carried out intelligence duties at Cape Town, South Africa (from 1941), and in Sydney (in 1945). At St Mark's Anglican Church, Darling Point, on 8 September 1945 he married Shirley Medea Nichols, a 20-year-old radio actress; their marriage ended in divorce. He produced *The Importance of Being Ernest* at Bryant's [q.v.13] Playhouse and directed Eugene O'Neill's *Mourning Becomes Electra* at the Independent Theatre for (Dame) Doris Fitton before becoming stage director for J. C. Williamson [q.v.6] Ltd. After returning to England in 1947, he worked for the Old Vic Theatre Company, at Bristol (1947-49) and in London (1950-51), and as a freelance producer until he left in 1953 for the United States of America where he continued to be involved with theatre and lectured on drama at several universities.

In 1955 Hugh Hunt, the executive-director of the Australian Elizabethan Theatre Trust, appointed Quentin general manager of its opera company, which was to be established in Sydney and to tour the country. This ambitious project provided a strong base for local operatic talent. On 8 February 1957 at the registrar-general's office, Sydney, Quentin married Verna June Collis, a 26-year-old actress. He had no children by either marriage.

Helped by H. C. Coombs, chairman of the trust, and (Sir) Philip Baxter, vice-chancellor of the University of New South Wales, Quentin (as founding director in 1959-63) and Hunt established the National Institute of Dramatic Art at the U.N.S.W. to train professional actors and teach stage-skills. Quentin was also associate-professor in the school of English, which was to offer drama as an academic subject. A separate school of drama, with Quentin as professor and its first head, was established in 1966. His drama department attracted students and enhanced the university's reputation. He was also director of drama (1964-65) for the A.E.T.T.

Meanwhile, Quentin had helped to found several professional drama companies that encouraged mainstream theatre. In 1963 he and Thomas Brown, N.I.D.A.'s new director, established the Old Tote Theatre Company to specialize in the classics. The Old Tote was located in a renovated tin shed (next to the old totalizator building) in the university's grounds. Its first production, Chekhov's *The Cherry Orchard*, which was directed by Quentin, set a new standard for professional theatre in Sydney. He was involved in the short-lived 'Three Shilling Theatre' (1963) at the Palace Theatre, where patrons could eat their sandwiches during a forty-minute lunchtime performance. In 1966 Quentin and others established the Jane Street Theatre, a venue for new Australian plays: H. G. Kippax described its opening as 'the theatrical event of this Sydney year'.

Yet, there was disquiet. Quentin believed that theatre, one of life's great educators, was under threat from an entertainment industry catering to the 'lowest common denominators of public taste'. This belief informed many of his projects. He held that the academic study of drama was a means of acquiring knowledge and taste, and might help to create an informed audience; and he saw N.I.D.A. as a training-school which would provide Australian dramatic productions with high technical standards.

Quentin was associated with a number of organizations to promote Australian theatre: he was chairman of the United Nations Educational, Scientific and Cultural Organization's local committee for the arts, president of the Australian centre of the International Theatre Institute, deputy-chairman of N.I.D.A. and of Australian Theatre for Young People, and vice-president of the Professional Drama Council. In December 1977 he tried to rescue the finances of the Old Tote with his last production, Alan Ayckbourn's *The Norman Conquests*, but the company went into liquidation next year.

Following his retirement from the U.N.S.W. on 31 December 1977, Quentin settled at Robertson with his wife, their dog and eight cats, a move which reflected his reserved nature and quest for a quiet life. Survived by his wife, he died suddenly of myocardial infarction on 7 July 1979 at his home and was cremated.

C. Bachali, *Jane St Theatre* (Katoomba, NSW, 1998); Univ NSW, *Uniken*, no 19, 1977, p 3; Aust Centre-International Theatre Inst, *Newsletter*, Feb 1978; *Kino*, 48, 1994, p 22; *SMH*, 15 Dec 1945, 30 May 1963, 22 Nov 1966, 14 Apr 1973, 30 July 1976, 9 July 1979; *Sun-Herald* (Syd), 14 July 1963; *Nation* (Syd), 6 Sept 1969, p 12; BRF-Robert Quentin papers, personnel and leave files (Univ NSW Archives); H. de Berg, Robert Quentin (taped interview, NL); family information.   JULIA HORNE

QUILTY, THOMAS JOHN (1887-1979), pastoralist and bush poet, was born on 4 April 1887 at Normanton, Queensland, second of six children of Irish-born parents Thomas Quilty, carrier, and his wife Mary, née Griffin. His father worked at various times as a fencer, teamster, innkeeper and grazier. In 1891 he settled on a property at Croydon, in the Gulf country, and named it Oakland Park.

Young Tom received some schooling at home before boarding (1904-07) at Nudgee College, Brisbane. He then helped his father and brothers Patrick (b.1888) and Reginald (b.1894) to run Oakland Park and Euroka Springs, another station which the family had acquired north of Julia Creek. Robust and energetic, he honed his horsemanship by riding with a band of wild young stockmen known as the 'Forest Devils'. In 1909 his parents and two of his sisters moved to Sydney. Property investment there increased the family's wealth and, in 1917, Quilty & Sons bought Bedford Downs, near Halls Creek, Western Australia, for £34 000. Patrick managed that station while Tom managed Euroka Springs. At All Saints Church, Roma, on 30 April 1919 he married with Catholic rites Charlotte Lillian Laura Isis Byrne; they were to have four children by 1926.

The 1920s brought low prices for cattle, poor rainfall and personal problems. Quilty's marriage foundered when he became involved with Olive Marion Underwood (b.1908), daughter of a neighbouring station-owner. In 1937 he and Olive left Queensland to join Patrick, who by then owned Bradshaws Run, on the Victoria River, Northern Territory. Next year they bought the adjacent Coolibah station, as well as the Six Mile Hotel at Wyndham, Western Australia. Patrick died in 1938. Favoured in his brother's will, Tom lived at Coolibah with his family for most of the ensuing decade. After consolidating their pastoral holdings, they moved west in 1948 to Springvale station, south of Bedford Downs. Tom eventually divorced his wife in July 1964 and married Olive on 11 September that year at the district registrar's office, Halls Creek.

Quilty was an outstanding cattleman, an authority on northern Australia, a skilled 'poddy-dodger' and 'a bit of a menace' to his neighbours. Generous, but loath to give praise, he participated enthusiastically in outback social activities. He invested in the Kimberley Hotel at Halls Creek and donated money for a grandstand at the local racing club. To raise funds for the Royal Flying Doctor Service, he published a slim volume of verse, *The Drover's Cook* (Sydney, 1958). The poems dealt with station-life, drinking, personal relationships, and raising children of mixed blood at Springvale homestead. In 1966 he donated the Tom Quilty Gold Cup for an event that has become a national endurance-riding championship.

By 1974 the family held about 3 million acres (1 214 000 ha) in Western Australia and 1.5 million acres (607 000 ha) in the Northern Territory. Quilty was appointed O.B.E. (1976) for his services to primary industry. In 1978,

incapacitated by a number of strokes, he left Springvale with Olive to live at Oakland Farm near Capel, Western Australia. He died there on 24 November 1979 and was cremated; his wife and their two sons survived him, as did the two daughters and one of the two sons of his first marriage.

C. McAdam, *Boundary Lines* (Melb, 1995); E. E. Quilty, *Nothing Prepared Me!* (Caloundra, Qld, 1999); *West Australian*, 12 June 1976, 28 Nov 1979; *Qld Endurance Riders Assn Newsletter*, Dec-Jan 1991; family papers (held by Mrs E. Quilty, Caloundra, Qld); information from Mr B. Quilty, Glen Innes, NSW.   CATHIE CLEMENT

QUINN, JOHN PAUL (1919-1961), diplomat, was born on 26 February 1919 at Paddington, Sydney, elder child of Victorian-born parents Michael Joseph Quinn, telephone mechanic, and his wife Mary Josephine, née Nugent. Educated at Sydney Boys' High School, John showed an interest in mechanical and scientific things, as well as proficiency in German. He read languages at the University of Sydney (B.A., 1938), graduated with first-class honours in French and German, and won the university medal for French and a French government scholarship to the University of Paris.

Having studied at the Sorbonne, Quinn returned home in 1939 and was employed by the Australian Broadcasting Commission. In 1940 he joined the Department of External Affairs. Next year he travelled with Sir Frederic Eggleston [q.v.8] to Rangoon before moving to Singapore to take up his appointment as political secretary to the Australian official representative V. G. Bowden [q.v.13]. Hours before the British base surrendered to the Japanese on 15 February 1942, Bowden and his staff left the island in a motor launch. The party was captured, Bowden executed, and Quinn interned at Palembang, Netherlands East Indies. Despite his youth, he became one of the camp's most respected figures, especially for his work as a hospital orderly and in bridging differences between Dutch, British, Australian and Eurasian prisoners. Although he was released in 1945, his internment affected his health for the rest of his life.

In 1946 Quinn was placed in charge of the Department of External Affairs' Sydney office. While private secretary (1947-48) to Dr H. V. Evatt [q.v.14], he accompanied the minister on a visit to Japan. Posted in 1948 as first secretary (later counsellor and chargé d'affaires) to The Hague, he joined the Australian delegation to the third session of the General Assembly of the United Nations, held in Paris. At St George's Church, Charlotte Square, Edinburgh, on 2 August 1949 he married an

Australian, Josephine Margaret Paton, with the forms of the Church of Scotland. In May 1950 he was transferred to London as external affairs officer (counsellor); his subsequent assignments included Pretoria (acting high commissioner 1951-52) and Saigon (minister 1952-54).

Again in Canberra in 1954-60, Quinn served as head of the department's South and South-East Asian branch, and of the defence liaison branch, during a crucial period in the evolution of Australia's foreign policy. In 1957 he was appointed O.B.E. From November 1960 he was based in Cairo as minister (ambassador April 1961). He was killed on 12 September 1961 when the Air France jet on which he was travelling to Morocco crashed near Rabat, with no survivors; his remains were brought to Sydney and buried in Northern Suburbs cemetery. His wife and their two daughters survived him, as did their son John who entered the diplomatic service in 1979.

Highly regarded for his perceptiveness and professionalism, Quinn was remembered for his strength of character, gentle sense of humour, modesty and genuine interest in others. He was also noted for his skills as an amateur photographer, especially of children.

F. Horner et al, *John Paul Quinn* (priv pub, Canb, 1968); A. Watt, *Australian Diplomat* (Syd, 1972); A. Stirling, *On the Fringe of Diplomacy* (Melb, 1973); *SMH* and *The Times*, 14 Sept 1961.

MIKE FOGARTY

QUIRK, MARY LILLY MAY (1880-1952), politician, was born on 7 December 1880 at Coonamble, New South Wales, second child of Julius Franz Frederick Deal, a butcher who had been born at sea, and his Victorian-born wife Emma Margretta, née White. By 1890 Julius was a butcher at Balmain, Sydney. Educated at Rozelle Superior Public School, Mary began work as a domestic servant. At St Joseph's Catholic Church, Balmain, on 28 September 1898 she married John Kelly (d.1926), a 39-year-old widower from England; they were to have a son and three daughters. She later worked as a shop-assistant for Grace [q.v.9] Bros Ltd for four and a half years and joined the Shop Assistants' Union of New South Wales.

On 9 February 1927 at St Patrick's Catholic Church, Sydney, Mary Kelly married John Quirk, a 56-year-old widower. Balmain born, he worked in the local post office and held the Legislative Assembly seats of Rozelle (1917-20 and 1927-30) and Balmain (1920-27 and 1930-38) for Labor. Following John's death in December 1938, Mary won the by-election for his Balmain seat on 14 January 1939. Both the Quirks were strong supporters of J. T. Lang [q.v.9] in the 1930s and 'were indefatigable in the interests of their constituents'.

On Mrs Quirk's first day in the Legislative Assembly in February 1939 the 'galleries were crowded with women' who had come to see her sworn in. The first Labor woman—and only the second woman—to be elected to New South Wales parliament, she later remarked that a 'lot of people told me that I only got in on a sympathy vote . . . But at the next election they stood by me'. She supported the entry of more women to parliament, so long as they were 'women of mature experience' like herself; and she claimed to understand her male counterparts, even if she thought that men were often 'really nothing but overgrown babies'. In 1941 Quirk's supporters unsuccessfully urged (Sir) William McKell to appoint her to his new ministry. Known in the House as a 'fervent advocate for the rights of the housewife', she threatened (1946) that housewives would apply a boycott if bread and milk prices were increased. She was also 'a skilled and able fighter' for people in industrial districts. When feelings in the Legislative Assembly ran high, her presence tended to promote 'moderation and forbearance'.

After two ballots and an appeal to the Australian Labor Party's State executive about 'irregularities' during voting, Mrs Quirk lost pre-selection in May 1950 and was defeated by the A.L.P.-endorsed candidate when she stood as an Independent for Balmain in June. She became a director of the Sunshine Homes for children. Survived by her three daughters, she died on 4 March 1952 in Sydney Hospital and was buried in the Field of Mars cemetery beside her second husband. In her will she requested that 'Mary Quirk (Ex. M.L.A.)' be inscribed on her tombstone. On her death, the premier James McGirr [q.v.15] remarked that she had 'added a special dignity to our Parliament'.

M. Sawer and M. Simms, *A Woman's Place* (Syd, 1984); J. Haines, *Suffrage to Sufferance* (Syd, 1992); M. Reynolds, *The Last Bastion* (Syd, 1995); *PD* (NSW), 5 Mar 1952, p 5158; *SMH*, 23 Dec 1938, 23 Feb 1939, 8 Feb 1946, 13 May, 19 June 1950, 14 May 1951, 5 Mar 1952; *Sun* (Syd), 26 Mar 1950.

LEANNE L. BLACKLEY

R

RABIN, ZALMENAS ('ZELL') (1932-1966), journalist and newspaper editor, was born on 5 March 1932 at Kovno (Kaunas), Lithuania, elder child of Jewish parents Aleksandras Rabinavicius, pharmacist, and his wife Zeny (Sonia), née Berman. Fleeing from the threat of war, the family reached Sydney—where some of Sonia's relations lived—on 18 February 1939 in the *Orontes*. Aleksandras was not permitted to practise without retraining; he farmed at Blacktown before buying a small chemical business in central Sydney. In 1944 he was naturalized and Anglicized his name to Alexander Rabin.

At the age of 6 Zell spoke German, Lithuanian, Russian and Yiddish, but not English. He attended public schools at Mosman, Blacktown, Rose Bay and Randwick, and, eventually, Sydney Boys' High School. Excelling at sport, he moved to Brisbane to enrol at the University of Queensland (Dip.Phys.Ed., 1953) where he also studied commerce. With another student David Malouf, Rabin co-edited *Semper Floreat*, the student newspaper. Although they embarked on a running battle with the conservative *Courier-Mail*, Rabin surprised Malouf by accepting a cadetship with that newspaper when he graduated.

In 1954 Rabin returned to Sydney and joined the *Sun*, an evening tabloid owned by John Fairfax & Sons [qq.v.4,8] Pty Ltd. He rose quickly and in 1956 was sent to its New York bureau. Rabin wrote a weekly column, 'New York Diary', for the *Sun* and articles for the *Sydney Morning Herald*, interviewing, among others, Marilyn Monroe, Arthur Miller and former president Harry S. Truman. While in New York he married Barbara Lewis, an American; they were to be divorced in Mexico a year later. After moving to London in 1958, he returned to Australia in 1959, travelling via Africa, where he reported on nascent nationalist movements.

Late that year Rabin went back to New York as bureau chief for the *Daily Mirror*, a rival Sydney evening tabloid briefly controlled by Fairfax and bought by Rupert Murdoch in 1960. Rabin arranged a visit to Cuba for Murdoch and, in December 1961, an interview with President John F. Kennedy at the White House. Murdoch saw in Rabin the man to lead the assault on his rival Sydney publishers. Rabin embarked for Sydney in 1962 to edit the *Sunday Mirror*. On the way home he married Regina Janine Dombek, another American, on 21 March 1962 at the registrar-general's office, Nadi, Fiji. They later separated.

In 1963 Rabin became editor of the *Daily Mirror*. He insisted on, and obtained from Murdoch, complete control of the newspaper's editorial side, something which Murdoch rarely granted to subsequent editors. Under Rabin's dynamic leadership the *Mirror* flourished. He had a flair for bold headlines, and a sense for giving world stories as much display as a local scandal. Encouraging women, he also promoted young journalists, hiring Robert Hughes as art critic. The *Mirror* was the only metropolitan newspaper to oppose Australia's involvement in the Vietnam War. Ron Saw, a columnist on the paper, wrote of Rabin's approach: 'He brooded and snapped and crackled at everyone from copyboys to Rupert Murdoch'.

Rabin died of cancer on 13 November 1966 at the Prince of Wales Hospital, Randwick, and was buried with Jewish rites in Rookwood cemetery. The son of his second marriage survived him.

R. Brasch, *Australian Jews of Today* (Syd, 1977); G. Souter, *Company of Heralds* (Melb, 1981); G. Munster, *A Paper Prince* (Melb, 1987); *Daily Mirror* (Syd) and *Sun* (Syd), 14 Nov 1966; *SMH*, 15 Nov 1966; naturalization file, A435, item 1944/4/1953 (NAA, Canb); information from Mrs M. and Mr P. Goldman, Bondi, and Mr D. Malouf, Darling Point, Syd.
ROBERT MILLIKEN

RABINOVITCH, ABRAHAM ISAAC (1889-1964), businessman and property investor, was born on 5 November 1889 at Tiraspol, near Odessa, Russia, third of five children of Yacob Zvi Rabinovitch, a teacher of Hebrew, and his wife Lea, née Gitman (Goodman). Educated in a traditional school until the age of 13, Abraham began work as a crockery salesman. Within two years, with the help of a partner, he was buying fruit at Odessa and selling it as far away as Warsaw. He married his first cousin Chaya (Hake) Sara Gitman (d.1965) about 1910 and served for three years in the Imperial Russian army.

In 1914 Rabinovitch briefly visited his brother Zalic at Harbin, China, before reaching Australia on 2 February 1915 in the *Niko Maru*. Hake joined him in the following year. Reunited with his brother Nuchem in Brisbane, he struggled to make a living: he was first employed as a ship's painter, then at S. Hoffnung [q.v.4] & Co. Ltd and eventually as a furniture dealer. Meanwhile, Hake worked as a dressmaker. She had a number of miscarriages and remained childless.

In 1921 they moved to Sydney where they were naturalized on 12 November. Rabinovitch developed a successful army disposal store in Pitt Street, near Central Railway Station. He had an excellent eye for property and was able to build up a significant fortune by developing real estate at Bondi Junction. In 1928 he brought to Sydney his brother-in-law's son, Nicholas Goodman, then aged 14. He moved from his Bondi home to a large house at 5 Vivian Street, Bellevue Hill, in 1935. His property included the Bondi Pacific Hotel which was requisitioned (1942-46) for accommodation for armed services personnel.

Rabinovitch devoted himself to activities within the Jewish community and was unstinting in his endeavours to assist orthodox institutions. Honorary treasurer in the 1930s of the Central Synagogue, Woollahra, he played a major role in the controversial dismissal (1932) of Rabbi Gedaliah Kirsner. He also served on the Chevra Kadisha and supported the Zionist movement. During World War II he befriended Rabbi Hans Elchanan Blumenthal, one of the *Dunera* internees. On arriving in Sydney in 1942, Blumenthal was dismayed that there was no *mikvah* (ritual bath), nor Talmud Torah (Jewish school), and that the Central Synagogue had a mixed choir. With financial support from Rabinovitch, the first *mikvah* was opened in April that year at 117 Glenayr Avenue, Bondi Beach. Rabinovitch acquired the property next door, where the North Bondi Hebrew School and Kindergarten opened in September 1942 with Blumenthal as principal. Initially the school's treasurer (1942-43), he served as its president in 1943-64.

In June 1952 Rabinovitch bought (for £30 500) Mark Foy's [q.v.8] home at 112 Victoria Road, Bellevue Hill, as premises for the day school which was renamed Moriah War Memorial College. Additional classrooms were built on the Vivian Street side in 1959-60. The Foy home was demolished in 1963 and replaced by a double-storey block of classrooms. It was to be named after Rabinovitch in 1965.

Rabinovitch had founded the Adath Yisroel Congregation in 1942 and sponsored Rabbi Shmuel Bernath (from Budapest) as its minister in 1948. After a falling out with the Adath, he founded the Sydney Talmudical College (under Rabbi Gedaliah Herc) in 1955 and bought a property for it in Flood Street, Bondi. In February 1964 Rabinovitch endowed a second kindergarten for Moriah College, the Mount Zion Kindergarten.

In addition to helping many individuals —particularly newcomers—to establish themselves, Rabinovitch contributed to improvements in the supply of kosher meat and pushed for a more committed religious lifestyle. His vision, tenacity and generosity had led to the provision of a range of Jewish institutions in Sydney. Although he devoted energy and money to the causes he espoused,

problems arose with his leadership. He acted in a dictatorial manner, appointing his boards, arguing with them and putting pressure on those who did not agree with him to resign. Tensions between Rabinovitch and the New South Wales Jewish Board of Deputies led to the creation of a second Jewish day school, the King David School, in 1960. After his death the two schools amalgamated.

Survived by his wife, Rabinovitch died on 26 July 1964 at his Bellevue Hill home and was buried in Rookwood cemetery. His portrait by Joseph Wolinski is held by Moriah College, Queens Park, Bondi Junction.

E. Blumenthal, *Trials and Challenges* (Jerusalem, 1994); *Moriah News*, Dec 1953; *Syd Jewish News*, 31 July 1964; *Aust Jewish Times*, 23 Aug 1984; S. Caplan, The Jewish Day School Movement in New South Wales (M.Ed. thesis, Univ Syd, 1975); Moriah War Memorial College, Annual Reports *and* Minutes, 1945-64; North Bondi Jewish Day School and Kindergarten Assn, Minutes, 1942-53; Mikvah Cte, Minutes, 1942-43; naturalization file A/1, item 1921/19133 (NAA, Canb); B985, item N/4/145 (NAA, Melb); information from Mr N. Goodman, Bellevue Hill, Syd.

SUZANNE D. RUTLAND

RADFORD, WILLIAM CROPLEY (1913-1976), educationist, was born on 20 May 1913 at Crowlands, Victoria, second child of Henry William Radford, state schoolteacher, and his wife Daisy, née Cropley, both Victorian born. Bill attended Horsham High School and stayed on as a junior teacher. In 1932 he entered Melbourne Teachers' College and the University of Melbourne (B.A., 1935; Dip.Ed., 1936; M.A., 1937; M.Ed., 1939); he graduated with first-class honours in English and French, and won the Childers [q.v.3] prize.

After teaching at Bairnsdale High School in 1936-37, Radford was seconded to the Australian Council for Educational Research. With K. S. Cunningham [q.v.13] and G. A. McIntyre, he edited *Review of Education in Australia, 1938* (1939). He published *The Educational Needs of a Rural Community* (1939) in which he argued that schools should become 'cultural centres for their districts'. In 1940 he taught briefly at Preston Technical School and worked in the curriculum and research branch of the Victorian Education Department.

Commissioned in the Militia in January 1940, Radford transferred to the Australian Imperial Force on 1 July. At All Saints' Church, Kooyong, on 30 August that year he married with Anglican rites Dorothea Eyres Allen, a teacher. He sailed for the Middle East in November. For his staff-work with the 9th Divisional Artillery in May-October 1942, he was appointed M.B.E. (1943). In 1943-44 he served in New Guinea as a temporary major at headquarters, II Corps. He then joined the Australian Army Staff in Britain. Enrolling at the University of London (Ph.D., 1954), he wrote a thesis on the effects of a scheme to consolidate schools in a rural area of Australia. Back in Melbourne, he was placed on the Reserve of Officers on 5 March 1946.

That year Radford was appointed assistant-director of the A.C.E.R. He co-edited its *Review of Education in Australia 1940-48* (1950). His comprehensive study, *The Non-Government Schools of Australia*, appeared in 1953. Succeeding Cunningham as director of the A.C.E.R. in 1955, he oversaw the publication of the *Review . . . 1948-1954* (1956) which he had helped to prepare. In his introduction to the *Review . . . 1955-1962* (1964) he noted that Australian education had made 'steady and even spectacular progress' at a time when the secondary and tertiary sectors were expanding rapidly and parents were showing more interest in schools. None the less, he thought that much remained to be done to extend educational opportunities for poorer children, to improve equipment and facilities, to enhance the professional training of teachers, and to provide adequate research on schools' curricula and educational practices.

During the 1950s the A.C.E.R. increased its interest in the development of intelligence and aptitude tests. The signing of an agreement with Science Research Associates, Chicago, United States of America, in 1961 to print and market the firm's 'reading laboratories' in Australia emphasized the new direction the council was taking. Radford had to become much more of an entrepreneur, a role he cautiously adopted. His book, *A Field for Many Tillings* (1964), analysed educational research in Australia.

Radford lectured part time in the University of Melbourne's faculty of education. He was president (1969-71) and an honorary fellow (1976) of the Australian College of Education, and president (1974) of the Australian Association for Research in Education. The Queensland government appointed him (1969) to chair a committee whose report, *Public Examinations for Queensland Secondary School Students* (Brisbane, 1970), led to the abolition of external examinations in that State. He also served on P. H. Karmel's committee of inquiry into education in South Australia. A welcome chairman of committees, a popular speaker at conferences, and an informed and honest referee, Radford was one of the best known and most widely consulted educationists in Australia.

In 1972 Monash University conferred on Radford an honorary LL.D., and the Australian and New Zealand Association for the Advancement of Science awarded him its Mackie [q.v.10] medal. In 1976 he was appointed A.O. He was president (1960-61) of Melbourne

Legacy and a part-time member (1961-72) of the Australian Broadcasting Control Board. The reduction in the Commonwealth government's financial support for the A.C.E.R. in the mid-1970s distressed him. Sensitive and concerned, he suffered bouts of depression. He committed suicide by inhaling carbon monoxide gas on 25 November 1976 at his Balwyn home and was cremated. His wife, son and two daughters survived him.

W. F. Connell, *The Australian Council for Educational Research, 1930-1980* (Melb, 1980) and *Reshaping Australian Education 1960-1985* (Melb, 1993); *Education News*, 15, no 10, 1976, p 54; Melb Legacy, *Bulletin*, 7 Dec 1976.   W. F. CONNELL

'RAFFERTY, CHIPS'; *see* GOFFAGE

RAGGATT, SIR HAROLD GEORGE (1900-1968), geologist, was born on 25 January 1900 in North Sydney, second of five children of Percy Claude Raggatt, a native-born grocer, and his wife Martha Annie, née Barker, who came from Wales. Harold attended Gordon Public School where, through its headmaster 'Cocky' Fry, he gained a love of the English language. He proceeded to Sydney Technical High School and the University of Sydney (B.Sc., 1922; M.Sc., 1932; D.Sc., 1939). After completing the first year of his undergraduate degree, he enlisted in the Australian Imperial Force on 4 March 1918 and embarked for England seventeen days later. In February 1919 he joined the 13th Field Company, Engineers, which undertook reconstruction work in the Meuse Valley, France. He also helped to build the monument to the 4th Division at Bellenglise, near St Quentin.

Demobilized from the A.I.F. in Sydney on 28 September 1919, Raggatt resumed his university course. He initially found it difficult to study, but came under the influence of Sir Edgeworth David [q.v.8] and decided to pursue a career in geology. In mid-1922 he joined the team which conducted the Geological Survey of New South Wales; he became a keen publicist and in 1924-25 made radio broadcasts, beginning with a popular account of the geology of Sydney. At St Philip's Anglican Church, Sydney, on 19 January 1927 he married Edith Thora Hellmers, a schoolteacher who had been a fellow undergraduate.

Apart from two long periods of special leave, Raggatt remained with the survey until 1939. He worked mostly in the upper Hunter Valley and the central west, producing maps of considerable quality. Fired by a hope of locating oil reserves, he had spent his leave in 1925 with an exploration company in the Aitape district of the Mandated Territory of

New Guinea. For six months in 1934-35 he looked for oil in Western Australia, particularly in the Carnarvon Basin. Returning to New South Wales, he continued his search, while also examining various mineral deposits on which he published articles in learned journals.

In 1939 W. G. Woolnough [q.v.12] chose Raggatt—partly because of their mutual links with David—to succeed him as geological adviser to the Commonwealth government. Rejecting an offer to become involved in the search for oil in Timor, Raggatt was appointed in June 1940. He moved to Canberra where his post was transferred in 1941 from the Department of the Interior to the Department of Supply and Development. Gathering a small group of assistants, he began to compile a comprehensive inventory of available minerals, an important undertaking in view of the strategic need to ensure supplies during World War II. His title was changed to director, mineral resources survey. In 1945 he and the geophysicist J. M. Rayner were sent to North America to examine geological surveys and associated organizations. Their report led to the formation (1946) of the Bureau of Mineral Resources, Geology and Geophysics. Its head office was in Melbourne. Raggatt lived in that city until 1951.

The success of B.M.R. stemmed from Raggatt's astute leadership, from the support of his chief geologist N. H. Fisher, and from their young staff who were eager for mapping and field-work. It also reflected the extraordinary confidence in Australia's future that characterized many people in the immediate postwar period. On 16 July 1951 Raggatt was appointed secretary of the Department of National Development (which included B.M.R.). Based in Canberra, he was reluctant to lose contact with geological work, but realized that he had been given an opportunity to achieve greater national objectives. He was strongly supported by his minister R. G. (Baron) Casey [q.v.13] who made manpower and money available for the search for minerals.

Raggatt was associated with the Australian Atomic Energy Commission from its inception in 1953. He was also an enthusiastic member of the Snowy Mountains Council, the Coal Utilization Research Advisory Committee, the Australian Mineral Development Laboratories and the Australian Water Resources Council. In 1954 he was elected a fellow of the Australian Academy of Science. He belonged to the Royal and Linnean societies of New South Wales, the Geological Society of Australia, the Society of Economic Geologists and the American Association of Petroleum Geologists. Made an honorary member (1961) of the Australasian Institute of Mining and Metallurgy, he was its medallist in 1964. He was appointed C.B.E. in 1954 and knighted in 1963.

Despite the time demanded by his official duties, Raggatt contributed to the Australian code of stratigraphic nomenclature and kept abreast of developments in the study of the Sydney Basin. He believed that geologists should be literate, in addition to having a thorough grounding in the basic principles of their profession. Following his retirement in 1965, he assisted the United Nations Development Programme, visiting countries in Africa and Asia.

Raggatt completed *Mountains of Ore* (Melbourne, 1968) just before his death: the book summarized the development of mining in Australia and encompassed his own contribution. His belief that oil would be found in Australia survived several disappointments. He passed his enthusiasm on to other officials, and to politicians such as (Sir) William Spooner [q.v.], thereby ensuring the continuance of Federal government support. His sensitivity to the rights and responsibilities of the States enabled him to succeed in the delicate task of evolving a national policy for the development of Australia's mineral resources.

A man of firm convictions, Raggatt was generally well liked. He had a strong sense of justice and fair play, and was gifted with down-to-earth common sense. Rugged in build, with bright eyes, lively and alert, he retained his integrity, modesty and endless good humour, seen for example in his gentle amusement at the impact of his work on the world's stock exchanges. Sir Harold died of myocardial infarction on 2 November 1968 in his home at Hughes, Canberra, and was cremated with Presbyterian forms; his wife and their daughter survived him. The Raggatt Mountains in Enderby Land, Antarctica, are named after him.

R. Wilkinson, *Rocks to Riches* (Syd, 1996); *Records of the Aust Academy of Science*, 2, no 3, June 1972, p 62; *Age* (Melb), 3 Oct 1964; *Canb Times*, 1 Feb 1965; *SMH*, 4 Nov 1968; Raggatt papers (NL).

D. F. BRANAGAN

RAINE, MARY BERTHA (1877-1960), businesswoman and philanthropist, was born on 17 February 1877 at Lambeth, London, eldest of thirteen children of Charles Carter, fruiterer, and his wife Mary Bertha, née Appleyard. Mary and her sister Daisy arrived at Moreton Bay, Queensland, in the *Jumna* on 20 November 1900 with £100 between them. They worked as barmaids in Brisbane and Sydney before deciding in 1904 to return to London. Forced by Daisy's seasickness to disembark at Fremantle, Western Australia, they again found jobs as barmaids. Mary lived frugally and saved enough money to buy a property at Subiaco which she leased out. On 5 May 1905 at the district registrar's office, Perth, she married William Morris Thomas (d.1918), a 44-year-old civil servant; they later separated.

An astute businesswoman, Mrs Thomas acquired considerable assets in Perth during the 1920s property boom, including Gordon's Cafe and Hotel, William Street. She renamed it the Hotel Wentworth and used it as her headquarters. The Wentworth achieved notoriety in World War II as the shore accommodation of submarine crews from the United States Navy. When the hotel was declared 'off limits' due to fights between American and Australian servicemen, 'Ma' Thomas (as she was known to patrons) protested to the prime minister John Curtin [q.v.13], himself a Western Australian. The ban was lifted within a week. At St Andrew's Presbyterian Church, Perth, on 3 December 1943 Mary married Arnold ('Joe') Yeldham Raine, a 56-year-old farmer and grazier.

Mrs Raine's philanthropy was inspired by her husband, whom she made her business partner. In the mid-1950s he was asked for a substantial donation to launch a medical school at the University of Western Australia. The Raines' contribution was more modest than the organizers of the appeal expected. Joe promised additional funds, but suffered a cerebral haemorrhage and died in February 1957. He left his estate, sworn for probate at £153 906, to his wife. Grief-stricken, she gave her legacy to the university to establish what was later called the Arnold Yeldham and Mary Raine Medical Research Foundation. Her only proviso was that research should initially be undertaken into the causes of arteriosclerosis, the disease that had led to her husband's death. Some unorthodox decisions helped to launch the foundation, with the State and Federal governments agreeing to waive death duties on Raine's estate. The partnership between Mrs Raine and the university proved surprisingly successful. The university shared the management of her extensive property interests, in particular a number of hotels.

Mary Raine died on 3 February 1960 in Royal Perth Hospital and was buried with Anglican rites in Karrakatta cemetery. Childless, she left the bulk of her estate to the Raine Foundation. In all, she gave the foundation nearly £1 million. Although she directed that no building or monument should be dedicated to her or her husband, Raine Square, which includes the site of the Hotel Wentworth, was named after them.

C. Georgeff, *The Mary Raine Story* (Perth, 1984); Univ WA, *Uninews*, 5 Aug 1991; *Daily News* (Perth), 17 Mar 1986; *West Australian*, 3 June 1998; *Mosman Park-Cottesloe Post*, 20-21, 27-28 June 1998.

JOHN MCILWRAITH

RAIWALA, RAY (c.1907-1965), Aboriginal leader and soldier, was born about 1907 into the Miltjingi clan of the Glyde River area of Arnhem Land, Northern Territory. As a youth he made occasional visits to the Methodist mission station that was established in 1923 at nearby Milingimbi in the Crocodile Islands. The American anthropologist Lloyd Warner wrote a vivid account of how Raiwala (Raiola) successfully defended a friend from attack during a clan feud 'in the interior country' probably in the mid-1920s.

In February 1927 Raiwala was at Milingimbi during the Sunday-morning service when Rev. T. T. Webb [q.v.] was assaulted and James Robertson, a lay missionary, speared. He appeared as a crown witness at the trial of the three men who were charged, and each was sentenced to three years gaol. Two years later he was charged as the 'leading spirit' in the killing at the mission of a 'self-proclaimed medicine man' reputed to have used sorcery to cause the death of several people. Raiwala and three others were found guilty of murder by a Darwin jury in May 1930 and sentenced to death, but the sentences were commuted to imprisonment for life. The trial aroused official concern about the way in which the criminal-justice system dealt with Aborigines who felt morally obliged to wound or kill others. Proposals for a 'court of native affairs' were considered, and legislation was passed removing the mandatory death sentence and allowing consideration of 'native law and custom' in Aboriginal murder cases. The four men were released from Darwin Gaol and Labour Prison in February 1934.

Raiwala returned to Milingimbi, where he helped to build a new timber church. About this time he married Mary Burramullagalli; within eight years he had entered into two more tribal marriages. He met the anthropologist Donald Thomson [q.v.] who, from August 1935, used the mission as a base for his investigations (for the Commonwealth government) into the situation of the Aborigines of eastern Arnhem Land. Thomson recorded that Raiwala, a lightly built man of middle height, had a reputation as the 'greatest single-combat fighter in Arnhem Land', and engaged him as a guide and interpreter for his patrol from Milingimbi to Blue Mud Bay. He acknowledged that the 'success of this journey owed much to the faithfulness and devotion' of Raiwala: he was always cheerful and kept the others—who were ill at ease away from their own territory—in a happy mood by his manner. Raiwala accompanied Thomson on visits in his vessel the *St Nicholas* to Groote Eylandt and Roper River, and on an overland patrol up the Wilton River. When Thomson turned back to the Roper in December and left to make his first report to the government, Raiwala parted from him with 'real tears ... streaming down his face' and continued on foot to the north coast.

Thomson came back in June 1936 to find Raiwala waiting on board the *St Nicholas* in Darwin harbour. Together they made a long voyage, visiting communities in western Arnhem Land, and calling at Milingimbi and Yirrkala. Raiwala and his wife accompanied him on overland patrols to investigate killings in the Arnhem Bay area. From October 1936 to July 1937 Thomson was mostly based in Raiwala's country. Raiwala instructed him in the life and techniques of the goose-hunters of the seasonally flooded Arafura Swamp.

In September 1937 Thomson left Milingimbi for Melbourne. Less than five years later he returned as a flight lieutenant, Royal Australian Air Force, on secondment to the army to organize an Aboriginal guerrilla unit. Raiwala, his first recruit, enlisted in Darwin on 6 February 1942. They sailed east at once in the ketch *Aroetta* to make a reconnaissance of the Arnhem Land coast. Raiwala landed near the Blyth River and gathered young men from the Cape Stewart to Glyde River area. They formed No.1 Section of Thomson's 'Special Reconnaissance Unit', under 'Corporal' Raiwala's command. Two more sections were formed, comprising men from the Arnhem Bay and Caledon Bay areas. During March, Thomson trained them at Roper River for guerrilla fighting, reconnaissance and scouting. After moving to Katherine, they came back to the Roper. Raiwala led a patrol to choose a site for an outpost at the river's mouth and another overland around Blue Mud Bay. He rejoined Thomson at Trial Bay. Most of the men began to return to their communities, but Raiwala stayed with Thomson, making sea patrols in the *Aroetta*. He was discharged from the army on 7 May 1943 when the unit was disbanded.

Thomson later wrote that 'valuable service was rendered by Raiwala, whose loyalty never flagged and who carried on anti-Japanese propaganda in his language'. Raiwala had been his 'constant companion', and had 'set an example of loyalty and selfless devotion to duty'. In 1963 an application to the Department of the Army led to 'this fine soldier' receiving his war service medals.

Following World War II, Raiwala remained in touch with Milingimbi. Early in 1949 he inadvertently occasioned a lengthy search when a rumour reached the mission that he had been murdered. A patrol travelled on foot from Milingimbi to Mainoru station in the wet season, only to learn that Raiwala had reached Mainoru two months earlier. He had collapsed during a hard journey across waterless country and, had it not been for his wife's success in finding water, the couple would have perished.

Raiwala preferred living independently of the missions and spent the 1950s with his family at Lee Bros' timber-mill on the Cobourg Peninsula. In 1963 he and his first wife, then living at Bagot, Darwin, were accorded full citizenship status when their names were removed from the Northern Territory Administration's register of wards. He died on 21 February 1965 in Darwin and was buried at Rapid Creek; his three wives survived him, as did the son and daughter of his first marriage.

W. L. Warner, *A Black Civilization* (NY, 1937); E. Shepherdson, *Half a Century in Arnhem Land* (Adel, 1981); D. Thomson, *Donald Thomson in Arnhem Land* (Melb, 1983); *SMH*, 10 June 1963; A1, items 1933/6965 *and* 1936/327, A432, item 1933/1958 (NAA, Canb); F1, item 1946/677 (NAA, Darwin); AWM 54, item 741/5/9 (AWM); information from Mr J. Burinyila, Ramingining, NT.   JEREMY LONG

RALSTON, EDITH MARION (1894-1967), headmistress, was born on 21 June 1894 at Ashfield, Sydney, eldest of three children of John Thompson Ralston, a native-born solicitor, and his wife Henrietta Marrianne, née Orr, who came from Ireland. Four months after Edith's birth, John was severely injured in a steam-train collision at Redfern station in which eleven passengers were killed. To avoid trains in future, the Ralstons moved to Neutral Bay whence transport to the city was by horse-drawn bus and paddle-steamer. Edith attended W. G. Doyle's College for Girls, Neutral Bay, and Woodstock, a North Sydney girls' school conducted by Edith Hooke, a strict disciplinarian. She developed a strong interest in geology, both at Woodstock, where she was dux in 1912, and during a visit to the volcanic north island of New Zealand in the following year.

In 1913-14 Miss Ralston passed English, French, philosophy and history subjects at the University of Sydney, but did not graduate. During World War I she worked as a photographer, developer and printer for the Young Men's Christian Association's Snapshots from Home League, a volunteer group that produced photographs which families sent to relations serving overseas. Although she was untrained as a teacher, her grounding in geology and her natural ability gained her an appointment in 1918 as part-time geology mistress at Arden College, Neutral Bay. Later that year she joined the full-time teaching staff of Addison College, Strathfield.

In 1920 Miss Ralston paid £20 for the goodwill of Wenona, a small preparatory school for girls in North Sydney and a renamed vestige of Woodstock. She retained the name—which had been inspired by the 'tall and slender maiden' in Longfellow's *Song of Hiawatha* —and also Miss Hooke's school crest (the Australian federation flag of Union Jack and starry cross) and motto, *Ut Prosim* (That I May Serve). By 1922 Wenona had outgrown its rented premises in St Thomas's church hall and Ralston moved her twenty-four students and staff of one to a large, two-storeyed house, purchased by her father, at the summit of Walker Street. Wenona was recognized as a registered secondary school in 1927. By 1930 it had 200 day-girls and boarders from whom a small but growing number of university entrants matriculated each year. The curriculum gave prominence to geology. With an eye to future expansion, Ralston bought two neighbouring properties in the early 1930s and a third in World War II. When Japan entered the war she decided against evacuating the school and cited (Sir) Winston Churchill's slogan, 'Business as usual'.

A short, stout woman, always decorously groomed, with her white hair side-parted and neatly arranged, Ralston was a formidable opponent in argument and a forceful public speaker. She taught her students to be God-fearing, patriotic, hard-working and considerate of others. Ruling her school, staff and students firmly, she claimed to know each girl individually. In the 1950s she was several times president of the State branch of the Headmistresses' Association of Australia. She represented the association at the first annual meeting of the State standing committee in support of 'A Call to the People of Australia'. 'There is nothing really new in it', she said of the Call's affirmation of traditional Christian values. 'Our teachers believe that the Call does not do more than the schools have set out to teach'.

To ensure its continued existence, Ralston sold her school in 1959 to a non-profit company, Wenona School Ltd; by then the school had 650 boarders and day-girls. She remained headmistress for another five years and belonged to the council of governors. At her last speech night, when commenting on (Sir) Harold Wyndham's scheme to emphasize science subjects, she expressed the hope that languages and humanities would continue to be taught. In 1967 she was appointed M.B.E. She died on 16 October that year at her Cremorne home and was cremated with Anglican rites.

N. Souter, *The Wenonians* (Syd, 1984); *SMH*, 28 Nov 1952, 25 Nov 1958, 13 Dec 1963, 1 Feb 1964, 17 Oct 1967.   NGAIRE M. SOUTER

RAMSAY, SIR ALAN HOLLICK (1895-1973), educationist and soldier, was born on 12 March 1895 at Windsor, Melbourne, eldest of five children of Victorian-born parents Charles Ramsay, produce dealer, and his wife Frances Sarah Laura, née Hollick. Alan attended Melbourne Continuation (High) School where he was an above-average student, quiet and unassuming, perhaps even shy. He took little interest in sport, but was enthusiastic about serving in the cadets. Joining the Victorian Education Department, he became a junior teacher (on probation) in 1912 and three years later was appointed to the primary school at Cowleys Creek, near Timboon.

On 1 October 1915 Ramsay enlisted in the Australian Imperial Force. Allotted to the 4th Field Artillery Brigade, he sailed for the Middle East in the following month. He served in Egypt before being sent to the Western Front in March 1916. Promoted corporal in March 1917 and sergeant in October, he was awarded the Meritorious Service Medal in 1918 for his bravery and devotion to duty. While serving with the 2nd Divisional Artillery he was commissioned on 1 January 1919 and promoted lieutenant in April. His A.I.F. appointment terminated on 2 August in Melbourne.

Resuming his teaching career at Lee Street State School, Carlton, Ramsay was transferred to Essendon High School in 1922 and to Coburg High School in 1924. Meanwhile, he studied part time at the University of Melbourne (B.Sc., 1923; Dip.Ed., 1925). At the Congregational Church, Ascot Vale, on 22 December 1924 he married with Presbyterian forms Edna Mary Watson, a chemist. In 1925 he was appointed to University High School. By 1926 he was described as a 'teacher of distinct ability ... [who] gains the immediate interest and co-operation of his pupils'.

Ramsay retained his interest in soldiering. On 31 March 1930 he was given command of the 10th Field Artillery Brigade (Militia). When World War II began he was a temporary colonel heading the 4th Divisional Artillery. He dropped a rank to join the A.I.F. on 13 October 1939 and became commanding officer of the 2nd/2nd Field Regiment. Six months later he took over the medium artillery of I Corps as a brigadier. In October 1940 he was appointed to head the 9th Divisional Artillery.

The division embarked for the Middle East in November, trained in Palestine and moved forward into North Africa. One of the 9th's artillery units became part of the force besieged at Tobruk, Libya. For his enthusiasm and judgement there, and at Mersa Matruh, Egypt, Ramsay was appointed C.B.E. in 1942. In the battle of El Alamein (23 October-5 November) he established his name. Planning artillery support for the major attack on 30 October suited his temperament. It required meticulous attention to detail to co-ordinate the fire of the 360 guns in the fifteen regiments under his control. The result was outstanding, and the British Eighth Army's artillery commander subsequently distributed Ramsay's plan as a model. Further recognition followed, with the award of the Distinguished Service Order (1943) and a mention in dispatches. He was held in such regard that his commander, Sir Leslie Morshead [q.v.15], recommended him to take over the division, but the commander-in-chief, Sir Thomas Blamey [q.v.13], demurred at the proposal because Ramsay's experience had been restricted to the artillery.

Ramsay returned to Australia in February 1943 and commanded II Corps' artillery from June. With Blamey's confidence finally obtained, he was appointed in January 1944 to lead the 5th Division as a temporary major general. In November the division was deployed to New Britain, where Ramsay used deep patrols and gradually established an ascendancy over a much larger Japanese force. He was appointed C.B. (1946) and twice mentioned in dispatches. In April 1945 he was transferred to the 11th Division on Bougainville, but reverted to his previous command in July. His A.I.F. appointment ended on 26 September and he was placed on the Reserve of Officers in the following month.

Back home, Ramsay became principal of Melbourne High School in February 1946. The appointment was a popular one, particularly as he was one of the school's own. In early remarks to parents he stressed the school's academic achievements, but emphasized the need for boys to develop a responsibility to each other and the broader community. He reinstituted the cadet unit and encouraged a wider involvement with other schools. In May 1948 he was appointed State director of education. Deeply attached to his school, he was sad to lose close contact with pupils.

The education system which Ramsay took over had been starved of funds during World War II and faced a massive increase in enrolments. He attacked the problem with characteristic enthusiasm, introducing standardized prefabricated classrooms to meet the immediate need for accommodation; permanent new buildings came much later. Conscious of the need to recruit more professionally trained staff, he introduced a two-year course for those intending to be primary schoolteachers and expected those who were to teach in secondary schools to have university qualifications. A comprehensive programme of in-service residential training was also implemented. Lindsay Thompson, a later premier of Victoria, described him as 'the acme of reliability and sound common sense'.

Ramsay retired in March 1960 and was knighted next year. He gradually became so disappointed at the militancy of teachers in state schools that he insisted his grandson should be educated at Scotch College, outside the system of which he had long been proud. Sir Alan was a trustee of the Shrine of Remembrance, and a member of the Returned Sailors', Soldiers' and Airmen's Imperial (Returned Services) League of Australia and the Naval and Military Club. He served as an elder of the Ewing Memorial Church, East Malvern, and as its Sunday School superintendent. Survived by his wife, and their daughter and son, he died on 19 September 1973 at Armadale and was cremated. His portrait (in military uniform) by Donald Cameron is held by Melbourne High School.

D. McCarthy, *South-West Pacific Area—First Year* (Canb, 1959); D. Dexter, *The New Guinea Offensives* (Canb, 1961); B. Maughan, *Tobruk and El Alamein* (Canb, 1966); Education Dept (Vic), *Vision and Realisation*, L. J. Blake ed (Melb, 1973); A. Inch, *Honour the Work* (Melb, 1977); Melb High School, *Unicorn*, Dec 1944, July 1946; *Education Gazette* (Vic), May 1960; A. H. Ramsay to G. Long, 11 Apr 1951, AWM 76, item B409 (AWM); information from Mrs M. Sandbach, McCrae, Vic, Mr M. Sandbach, Melb, and the Hon L. H. S. Thompson, Glen Iris, Melb.

S. N. GOWER

RAMSAY, ALEXANDER MAURICE (1914-1978), public servant, was born on 27 October 1914 at Parkside, Adelaide, second child of South Australian-born parents Alexander Ramsay, boot-operator, and his wife Bessie Laurance, née Smee. Young Alex was sent to Parkside Public and Unley High schools. Like other contemporaries with the mind but not the means to attend university, he trained (1935-36) at Adelaide Teachers' College. He then taught at Berri Higher Public School (1937-38) and Adelaide High School (1939-42). At St Augustine's Anglican Church, Unley, on 27 December 1939 he married Amy Jane Woithe, whom he had met at college. They were to have four children.

Eventually entering the University of Adelaide (B.Ec., 1941), Ramsay studied economics, history, geology, geography, French and English, and was appointed (1943) assistant-lecturer in economics. In 1942 a group that included Ramsay, G. V. Portus, J. W. Wainwright, Tom Garland and K. S. Isles [qq.v.11,12,14] founded Common Cause. Their manifesto, released in March 1943, aroused much interest with its aims of encouraging collective effort to win World War II and of working 'for a postwar world in which the social evils of . . . poverty, unemployment, bad housing, malnutrition and inequalities of opportunity for education, health and leisure will be banished'. Between 1943 and 1945 the movement attracted almost three thousand members in South Australia. They lobbied governments, carried out community projects and forwarded public education. Common Cause's secretary-treasurer in 1943 and editor of its newsletter from 1945, Ramsay was perhaps the most industrious and outspoken of the founders. He wrote frequently to the press and maintained his involvement until the movement was disbanded in 1949.

In 1943 several of the State's senior public servants recognized Ramsay's talents, dissuaded him from continuing a secondment with the Commonwealth Department of Postwar Reconstruction, and employed him at the South Australian Housing Trust as assistant-secretary and economic planner. He was to remain with that organization for the rest of his life. The trust had been established in 1936 as part of the government's plan to promote the growth of secondary industry in South Australia by keeping wages lower than elsewhere through the provision of low-cost rental housing to workers and their families. Building costs were rigidly contained by pioneering mass-produced cottages. While motivated to some extent by humanitarian concern in a period of acute housing shortages, the trust did not provide accommodation for the poor or the unemployed.

From 1938 a new government, led by (Sir) Thomas Playford, significantly increased the trust's activities and its staff. During World War II the premier learned to use State instrumentalities, such as the trust, in a wide range of development-related initiatives, drawing on the skills and energies of Ramsay and others to create an informal but efficient system of administration. At first Ramsay worked as the trust's supply officer, securing labour and scarce building materials, but he was clearly intended for higher things. Playford considered him 'a brilliant find' because he was intelligent, compassionate and articulate, with the necessary flair for public relations. 'He had opinions and he had principles and he would fight for them'. Moreover, he could build the trust into a 'big show'. Ramsay became acting general manager in 1948 and general manager in January 1949.

Under Ramsay, the Housing Trust reflected Playford's style of administration—informal, accessible and cost-conscious. Although the premier's parsimony and single-mindedness must have frustrated Ramsay at times, he worked creatively within those constraints, retained Playford's support, and became renowned for his skills as a negotiator and manager. He allowed subordinates flexibility on the job, promoted those who showed constancy and commitment rather than mere professional expertise, and concentrated decision-making in his own hands.

Ramsay defined management as 'achieving clearly defined aims as economically as possible by means of other people'. He also encouraged familial loyalties, both within the trust and among home-buyers and tenants. 'Finding people with appropriate qualities, motivating them and making opportunities for them, keeping them conventionally efficient but urging them always to treat each other and all the trust's customers as . . . *real* people . . . was the core of the managerial task as this exceptionally successful manager saw it'. Given the large demands on staff arising from the size of operations and from the acute postwar housing need, these attributes were vital. Most of Ramsay's staff and colleagues remembered him with affection and respect, although some, especially women, criticized his patriarchal style.

Earning wide public recognition and esteem as South Australia's 'Mr. Housing', Ramsay served the successive State governments of Playford, F. H. Walsh [q.v.], D. A. Dunstan and R. S. Hall. With the support of the trust's chairman J. P. Cartledge [q.v.13], he was chiefly responsible for diversifying operations, and for expanding the size and scope of the organization. He came to play a key role in suburban land and housing markets by supplying large numbers of houses for rent and purchase, thereby helping to restrain the cost of public and private housing. The trust moved from building houses near factories and town centres to building factories and town centres near its housing estates, thereby coming into direct competition with private and project builders. Beginning in the 1950s, the trust also took on a new welfare dimension by providing 'cottage flats' for elderly people.

Every aspect of the trust's work and Ramsay's strong personal support were fully engaged during the 1950s and 1960s when the trust built Elizabeth, a completely new town on the northern outskirts of Adelaide. In later years Playford enjoyed recounting the story of Ramsay's unorthodox methods in obtaining land from a reluctant farmer on which General Motors-Holden's [q.v.9] Pty Ltd would build its second South Australian factory. Conscious of the social implications of Elizabeth's rapid urban development and of its predominantly British immigrant population, Ramsay 'jumped hurdles' by supplying trust-built facilities (such as halls and theatres) and selecting tenants to act as community leaders. He was annoyed at the emphasis the press gave to the town's 'youth problems'; to counteract it, he promoted churches and counselling services, and attended many fund-raising functions and celebrations.

In the 1970s, partly through pressure from social-welfare organizations and Dunstan's Labor government, the trust broadened its role by providing a wide range of housing for handicapped people, single mothers, and boarders and lodgers. Keeping future welfare needs in mind, Ramsay retained at least half of the trust's housing stock, and in 1972 succeeded in having the Commonwealth-State housing agreement amended to allow the purchase and rehabilitation of old houses. The trust then bought hundreds of inner-city cottages and terraces for low-cost rental housing.

A slim, brown-haired man with fine features and a gentle smile, Ramsay had great personal charm, reflecting his generous nature and his passionate and practical Christianity. In an article, 'The Public Service as a Vocation', published in *Public Administration* (1969), he asserted that 'man realizes the finest quality of his nature when he forgets himself . . . and concerns himself with his neighbour'. Arguing that the state provided the essential infrastructure for the operations of the market economy, he merged his economic training and Christian principles in public service that was 'both in keeping with the highest ideals of a Christian society and essential for its progress'. He described his work as having two dimensions: honest stewardship of the resources entrusted to him, and care for the public good. It gave him satisfaction that the Housing Trust ran at a profit, built houses as cheaply as any other housing authority, and yet also served the community. If a man could obtain accommodation at one-fifth of his income then he had a fair chance of giving his family a reasonable start in life.

Ramsay felt that his duty lay in South Australia and declined offers of employment interstate, including a request from Prime Minister (Sir) Robert Menzies [q.v.15] to go to Canberra 'to finish off the city'. Instead, (Sir) John Overall, the trust's chief architect (1945-49), was made (1958) first commissioner of the National Capital Development Commission.

In 1958 Ramsay was appointed C.B.E. He was president (1951-52) of the Adelaide branch of the Economic Society of Australia and New Zealand, and vice-chairman (1950-52) of the Australian Institute of International Affairs. In addition he was chairman of the Municipal Tramways Trust, Adelaide (1968-76), and of the short-lived Australian Housing Corporation (1975-76); a member of the Australian Broadcasting Commission (1967-73), the National Gallery of South Australia board (1963-67) and the Libraries Board of South Australia (1962-68); and president of the South Australian branch of the Australian Boy Scouts' Association (1967-73) and of Meals on Wheels Inc. (1970-78). A founding councillor of the Australian Institute of Urban Studies, he prepared reports on national urban and housing issues. He was a churchwarden (1955-71) of St Richard's Church, Lockleys, a member (1956-71) of the Adelaide diocesan synod, a governor (1962-68) of the Collegiate School of St Peter and president (1965-73) of the South Australian council of the Young Men's Christian Association.

An asthma sufferer himself, Ramsay helped to establish South Australia as a leading centre for treating the disease. He was founding head (1959) of Asthmatic Children's Aid and foundation chairman (1963) of its successor, the Asthma Foundation of South Australia. Energetic, even in his leisure, he was a keen yachtsman and rear commodore of the Royal South Australian Yacht Squadron. In a paddock near his Lockleys home he built a three-ton sloop, *Aroona*. While sailing in Gulf St Vincent, he observed the loss of Adelaide's coastal dunes—partly resulting from the trust's broad-scale metropolitan development. He arranged for the surviving North Glenelg dunes to be transferred from Housing Trust ownership to the new West Beach Trust. He followed Australian Rules football, and was an avid reader.

Ramsay died of myocardial infarction on 25 May 1978 at the Adelaide Club and was cremated; his wife, and their son and three daughters survived him. The large sum of money donated in lieu of flowers at his funeral endowed an annual vacation scholarship for university students to undertake asthma research. Robert Hannaford's portrait of Ramsay is held by the South Australian Housing Trust.

S. Marsden, *Business, Charity and Sentiment* (Adel, 1986) *and* Constructing Playford's City: the South Australian Housing Trust and the transformation of Adelaide, 1936-1966 (Ph.D. thesis, Flinders Univ, 1994); *Aust Q*, 50, no 3, 1978; information from Mrs A. Ramsay, Adel.

SUSAN MARSDEN

RAMSAY, MARMADUKE FRANCIS (1860-1947), **ROBERT CHRISTIAN** (1861-1957) and **EDWARD LAUDERDALE** (1865-1941), graziers and sportsmen, were born on 8 December 1860 and 20 December 1861 at Cheltenham, England, and on 27 March 1865 at Five Dock, Sydney, three of ten children of Robert Ramsay [q.v.6], a London-born pastoralist, and his wife Susan, née Lindsay Carnegie, who came from Scotland. Frank and Robert attended Ipswich Grammar School, Queensland, until 1874 when the family moved to England. The three boys were sent to Elstree Preparatory School, Berkshire, and Harrow School, Middlesex; Frank and Robert went up to Trinity College, Cambridge, but neither graduated.

Frank returned to Queensland in 1880. He gained pastoral experience at Wellshot station, near Barcaldine, before taking over management of Eton Vale, near Toowoomba. Robert joined him in 1883. When Lauderdale returned in 1886, they formed the Ramsay Bros partnership to manage the stations they had acquired with (Sir) Arthur Hodgson [q.v.4] in north-west Queensland: Oondooroo and

Elderslie (near Winton), Charlotte Plains (near Hughenden), Burleigh (on the Richmond River) and Disney (near Clermont). About 1887 Ramsay Bros acquired Hodgson's share of the 1027-square-mile (2660 km²) Oondooroo; 'regardless of cost', Robert developed it into the most progressive run in north-west Queensland by introducing private telephone-lines, shearing machines, Humber motorcycles and Serpollet steam-motorcars.

In 1893 the Hodgson-Ramsay partnership in Eton Vale was dissolved. Frank managed the Ramsay share of the property, appropriately named Harrow, and acquired interests in other stations on the Darling Downs. These holdings, including Harrow, were to be gradually resumed for closer settlement after 1897. On a visit to England, Frank married Alice Katherine Angélique Waterfield on 6 June 1895 at Canterbury Cathedral, Kent; they were to have six children. About 1908 he retired to England, settling at Lee Priory, Littlebourne, Kent, near his father's estate, Howletts. Harrow was then managed by Robert Ramsay who, on 23 October 1907 at St James's Cathedral, Townsville, had married 20-year-old Olive Zillah Voss; they were to have two sons and four daughters. When Harrow was sold in 1927, Robert also retired to Howletts. Lauderdale, who never married, remained in Queensland, acquired (1927) a small portion of Harrow station and named it Banchory.

Each brother was an avid sportsman. Frank had played senior cricket and football for Harrow, and cricket for Cambridge. He played —not 'as often as the locals would have liked' —for Toowoomba and the Darling Downs throughout the 1880s and 1890s; he represented Queensland against an Australian team in 1884, against an English XI in 1885, and against New South Wales in 1893, 1894 (as captain) and 1899. An indifferent right-hand batsman, he proved an economical right-arm, medium-pace bowler, but his action was sometimes questioned by critics. His greatest triumphs came in November 1897 when, as captain of a Toowoomba XVIII which played against A. E. Stoddart's touring English XI, he took five wickets for 71, including that of K. S. Ranjitsinhji for a duck, and in November 1899, when playing for Queensland against New South Wales, he captured Victor Trumper [q.v.12] on 77. In later life Frank bred racehorses, and became a keen golfer and fisherman. Noted for his business ability, honesty and personal charm, he was best remembered as a cricketer, for 'no Queensland team was complete without him at least up to 1900 and possibly later'. He died on 31 December 1947 at Lee Priory and was cremated; his wife, their four daughters and one of their two sons survived him. Their elder son John Marmaduke died of wounds in World War I.

Robert also excelled at cricket (as a slow bowler) at Harrow, and at Cambridge where he was awarded a Blue in 1882. That year he took twelve wickets against a touring Australian team and was selected to play for the Gentlemen of England against the Australians. After going down from Cambridge, he represented Somerset. Although he played for Queensland against Australia in 1884, his pastoral pursuits precluded further representative or first-class engagements. A fervent imperialist, he was a founding member (1910) of the Brisbane group of the Round Table. He was a member of the Queensland Recruiting Committee from 1914, but resigned in August 1917 over conscription and became president of the Queensland Reinforcements Referendum Committee. He died on 25 June 1957 at Howletts and was cremated.

Less adept at cricket, Lauderdale played only in Toowoomba club competitions. He was a long-term patron (until 1939) of the Toowoomba Cricket Association. Encouraging the development of tennis, football, hockey, vigoro and basketball, he gave £500 to the Darling Downs Lawn and Hardcourt Tennis Association to build a complex at Toowoomba. He supported the local branch of the Royal Agricultural Society of Queensland and the Toowoomba Choral Society. His main love, however, was horse-breeding and racing. At Banchory, he established a successful racehorse stud, mainly with stock imported from the family estate, Howletts. In the 1930s his horses won races at Toowoomba, and in Brisbane and Sydney. He was a member (1899-1941) of the Queensland Turf Club and a trustee of the Clifford Park (Toowoomba) racecourse.

Lauderdale died on 6 December 1941 at Toowoomba and was buried with Anglican rites in the local cemetery. His estate was sworn for probate at £211 232. He left money to various charities, relations and friends, £200 to every Banchory employee, £100 to each of his trainers, and £50 to each member of staff at the Queensland Club, to which he, like his brothers, had belonged. All debts owing at the time of his death were 'forgiven and released'.

R. Webster and A. Miller, *First-Class Cricket in Australia* (Melb, 1991); *Pastoral Review*, 16 Jan 1942, 16 Apr 1948; *Qld Trustees Q Review*, Mar 1948; *Chronicle* (Toowoomba), 8 Dec 1941; *Courier-Mail*, 13 Jan 1942; *The Times*, 2 Jan 1948, 26, 28 June 1957.

M. FRENCH

RAMSDEN, BARBARA MARY (1903-1971), editor, was born on 27 December 1903 at Annandale, Sydney, eldest of three children and only daughter of Edward Maxwell Ramsden, a Melbourne-born medical student, and his wife Edith Johnson, née Hindley, who came from England. The family moved to Richmond, Melbourne, and later to Adaminaby and Bathurst, both in New South Wales. From 1919 Barbara boarded at Ascham school, Sydney. Her early interest in medicine appeared to wane and in 1924 she enrolled in arts at the University of Sydney. In the following year she moved with her mother and youngest brother to Melbourne and in 1926 entered the University of Melbourne (B.A., 1928). She obtained employment as a clerk in the university's engineering and metallurgy library in May 1928. Transferred to the central library in June 1931, she worked there part time and in the book-room of Melbourne University Press before performing the duties of assistant-reader with the publishers.

In 1941 Ramsden was formally appointed assistant-reader with M.U.P., then under the management of Frank Wilmot [q.v.12]. She had immense respect for him and revealed it in her review, published in the *Australian Quarterly* (June 1943), of Vance Palmer's [q.v.11] *Frank Wilmot (Furnley Maurice)* (1942). Wilmot's death in 1942 had left her effectively in charge of the press but without a corresponding increase in status, a recurring situation that frustrated her throughout her career. In April 1943 she applied unsuccessfully for the position of manager, which was awarded to the historian Gwyn James who had been brought in 'to carry on the work of the Press during Miss Ramsden's absence' on leave.

Ramsden's legacy was seen in the growth of M.U.P., the generation of editors whom she trained, and the meticulous editing that produced such books as Geoffrey Blainey's *The Peaks of Lyell* (1954), Margaret Kiddle's [q.v.15] *Men of Yesterday* (1961), the early volumes of Manning Clark's *A History of Australia* (1962, 1968) and of the *Australian Dictionary of Biography* (1966 and 1967, edited by Douglas Pike [q.v.]), and the *Encyclopaedia of Papua and New Guinea* (1972, edited by Peter Ryan). In 1965 she was appointed M.B.E. Following her retirement in June 1967, she was awarded the university medal for exceptional services.

Described as 'not a bit feminine in the ordinary sense', Miss Ramsden was a chain-smoker, rather short in stature, with 'very blue, very expressive eyes'. She typically wore a severe navy or green serge suit, with a shirt, man's tie and flat 'barges' of shoes. A formidable editor, both in expertise and in manner, she provided 'much of the stability and the authority in scholarship' which M.U.P. enjoyed.

Barbara Ramsden was an intensely private woman who lived for many years at Florida House, 601 St Kilda Road. She had an excellent knowledge of books, loved painting, and was a good horsewoman. A committee-member of the Probus Women's Housing Association and the Batman Business and Professional Women's Club, she was also an active member of the Melbourne Women's Walking Club and treasurer of the Victorian branch of the Fellowship of Australian Writers. She died of cancer on 1 January 1971 in Melbourne and was cremated. That year the F.A.W. established the Barbara Ramsden award for books that reflected 'credit on both author and editor'. In his preface to *Anthropology in Papua New Guinea* (1973) Ian Hogbin wrote: 'If some of my authors write like angels . . . then it is she who deserves much of the credit'.

R. Moye, 'The "Legendary" Barbara Ramsden, Book Editor', in *Melbourne University Mosaic* (Melb, 1998) and for sources.   ROS MOYE

RANCLAUD, DORA; *see* ALLMAN

RANFORD, ROBERT FRANK GORDON (1917-1943), soldier, was born on 29 October 1917 at Semaphore, Adelaide, sixth of seven children of Stewart Galway Ranford, a South Australian-born labourer, and his wife Mary Elizabeth, née Davy, who came from England. As a boy, Gordon was fond of sport, particularly cricket, baseball and swimming. On 2 March 1929 he rescued a woman and her 10-year-old daughter from drowning in the Port Adelaide River at Ethelton; he was awarded the bronze medal of the Royal Humane Society of Australasia. He attended Ethelton Public and Lefevre Peninsula Central schools, then worked as a stationhand on properties in the Clare district.

On 20 May 1940 Ranford enlisted in the Australian Imperial Force. Five ft 8 ins (173 cm) tall and stockily built, he had blue eyes and brown hair, and gave his religious denomination as Presbyterian. His fair complexion earned him the nickname 'Snowy'. Following initial training, he joined the 2nd/48th Battalion and embarked for the Middle East on 17 November. He served at Tobruk, Libya, throughout the siege, from April to October 1941, and was mentioned in dispatches. He was confirmed in the rank of corporal in July.

After the 9th Australian Division withdrew to Palestine, Ranford was admitted to hospital on 19 November. He recovered from his illness in nineteen days and rejoined his battalion. In July 1942 the 2nd/48th was sent to the El Alamein area, Egypt, to block a German advance towards the River Nile. Ranford was promoted acting sergeant on 25 July (confirmed 17 September). The battle of El

Alamein began on 23 October. On the night of 30/31 the 2nd/48th—which had been constantly in action—attacked towards Barrel Hill, south-east of Sidi Abd el Rahman. When his platoon commander was wounded, Ranford took over. He led the assaults on two posts which killed fourteen enemy soldiers, and destroyed two machine-guns and an 88-mm gun. Although he was wounded, he continued to command the platoon (then only seven strong) until he was wounded a second time. For his 'leadership and grim determination' he was awarded the Distinguished Conduct Medal.

Ranford recovered in time to sail for Australia with the 2nd/48th in February 1943. The battalion trained in North Queensland before being deployed to Papua in August to prepare for the Huon Peninsula campaign in New Guinea. In November, during fighting along the Sattelberg Road, west of Finschhafen, Ranford showed bravery and initiative, for which he was again mentioned in dispatches (1945). On 20 November 1943, shortly after Japanese positions at Fougasse Corner had been captured and occupied, he was killed by a sniper. He was buried in Lae war cemetery. Sergeant T. C. Derrick [q.v.13], who won the Victoria Cross four days later, wrote in his diary that Ranford was a dashing, courageous and fearless soldier, 'easily the battalion's best'.

J. G. Glenn, *Tobruk to Tarakan* (Adel, 1960); M. Farquhar, *Derrick, V.C.* (Adel, 1982); G. A. Mackinlay, *True Courage* (Syd, 1992); J. Coates, *Bravery Above Blunder* (Melb, 1999); AWM 52, item 8/3/36 and PR82/190 (AWM); information from Mr L. Ranford, Semaphore, Adel.   ANTHONY STAUNTON

RANKIN, GEORGE JAMES (1887-1957), farmer, soldier and politician, was born on 1 May 1887 at Bamawm, Victoria, tenth child of Irish-born parents James Rankin, farmer, and his wife Sarah, née Gallagher. George was educated at the local state school and later farmed at Nanneella. At the Presbyterian manse, Rochester, on 17 July 1912 he married Annie Isabella Oliver, a 39-year-old dressmaker. He had joined the Militia in 1907 and been commissioned (1909) in the 9th Light Horse Regiment. On 20 August 1914 he was appointed lieutenant, Australian Imperial Force, and posted to the 4th L.H.R.

The unit reached Gallipoli in May 1915. Rankin was wounded in July and promoted captain in December. Appointed major in March 1916, he participated in operations in the Sinai where he showed a brilliant grasp of light-horse tactics. As second-in-command of his unit from August 1917, he was present at the famous charge at Beersheba on 31 October, and subsequently took an important part

in reorganizing the unit and consolidating positions on the town's outskirts. In 1918 he won the Distinguished Service Order for his gallantry in action around Jerusalem. He was also mentioned in dispatches. For his leadership during the capture of Damascus he was awarded a Bar to his D.S.O.

In March 1919 units of the Light Horse were sent to Egypt to help the British put down a rebellion. Rankin sailed for Australia in June and his A.I.F. appointment terminated on 23 September. Resuming his service in the Militia, he gained steady advancement: he commanded the 2nd Cavalry Division as a brigadier (from October 1936) and as a major general (from July 1937).

Rankin developed an interest in politics. In 1928 he helped to form the Bamawm-Rochester branch of the Country Party, over which he presided from the early 1930s. He was elected chief president of the Victorian United Country Party in 1937, but, under party rules, had to resign that year when he won the seat of Bendigo in the House of Representatives. Although he had denounced participation in composite ministries to appease those who wanted the Country Party to remain independent from the United Australia Party, he immediately aligned himself in parliament with Country Party members who sought to form a coalition with the U.A.P. under Prime Minister Joseph Lyons [q.v.10]. His stand angered the State council of the V.U.C.P. which forced him to back down.

Concentrating on issues relating to defence and primary industry, Rankin earned a reputation as an authority on—and unswerving advocate of—the interests of returned servicemen and wheat-farmers. He was placed on the Unattached List in February 1942, but continued to play an active role (until July 1944) as colonel commandant of the North-West Group, Volunteer Defence Corps, Victoria. By 1943 he was again sitting with the federal parliamentary Country Party and had become a tenacious and aggressive critic of the Labor government. He had a number of Labor friends, but the party as a whole viewed him as a thorn in its side.

In 1949 the electoral boundaries of Rankin's seat were redrawn to exclude Rochester and Echuca, towns where he enjoyed overwhelming electoral support. He stood for the Senate in December, and won. In April 1951 he was again returned as a senator, but the number of his speeches and interjections decreased. He served as chairman of committees in 1951-53 before his frequent illness led to absences from parliament. While consolidating his reputation as a bitter anti-communist, he maintained a blunt, fearless and no-nonsense approach which rankled the coalition government headed by (Sir) Robert Menzies [q.v.15], as it had previous Labor ministries. There were some in all three major parties who were relieved when he chose not to contest the 1955 elections, due to poor health.

Survived by his wife, Rankin died of cerebrovascular disease on 28 December 1957 at Rochester and was buried in the local cemetery. His estate was sworn for probate at £50 096. Throughout his adult life he had been loyal to the army and to his district. That loyalty was reflected in the tributes paid to him. Yet many distrusted the big, overweight, genial and abrasive old soldier, who drank heavily and thought nothing of being ejected from parliament after a slanging match with his political opponents. Rankin valued public service, but his rough manners, learned in the country and reinforced by army life, probably disqualified him from higher office.

U. Ellis, *A History of the Australian Country Party* (Melb, 1963); P. Spender, *Politics and a Man* (Syd, 1972); D. Holloway, *Hooves, Wheels and Tracks* (Melb, 1990); N. Smith, *Men of Beersheba* (Melb, 1993); *Rochester Irrigator*, 8 Feb 1957, 8 Jan 1958; *Bendigo Advertiser*, 30-31 Dec 1957; *Countryman* (Melb), 16 Jan 1958; information from Mr G. Rankin, Bendigo, Vic.   MALCOLM SAUNDERS

RANKIN, ROBERT WILLIAM (1907-1942), naval officer, was born on 3 June 1907 at Cobar, New South Wales, second of three children of Australian-born parents Francis John Rankin, sharebroker's clerk, and his wife Florence May, née Harvey. Robert was educated at Merrylands Public School, Sydney, and Parramatta High School. In 1921 he entered the Royal Australian Naval College, Jervis Bay, Federal Capital Territory. Nicknamed 'Oscar', he excelled at Rugby Union football, became cadet captain and graduated in 1924 with prizes for engineering and mathematics. Having served as a midshipman in H.M.A. ships *Brisbane* and *Melbourne*, Rankin undertook training with the Royal Navy in 1926. Next year he attended the junior officers' war-course at the R.N. College, Greenwich, where he was one of six sub lieutenants whose essays were commended by the Admiralty. Following further courses at Portsmouth, he joined the newly commissioned cruiser H.M.A.S. *Canberra* in 1928 and returned in her to Australia where he was promoted lieutenant in August 1929.

Deciding to specialize in hydrography, Rankin joined the survey ship H.M.A.S. *Moresby* on 18 January 1934. Apart from occasional periods on shore, he charted Australian and New Guinea waters until February 1938. His superiors regarded him as a keen, hard-working officer, if somewhat lacking in powers of command. At the Bellevue Hotel, Brisbane, on 4 October 1937 he married with Catholic rites Mary Glennie Broughton, a 25-year-old nurse.

Rankin had been promoted lieutenant commander in August 1937. Sent to Britain on exchange duty, he was posted (March 1938) to the Home Fleet's H.M.S. *Gleaner,* a minesweeper engaged in survey work. After courses at H.M.S. *Dryad,* he was appointed (December 1939) to the repair-ship H.M.S. *Resource* as first lieutenant. Serving in the Mediterranean and South Atlantic under difficult wartime conditions, he proved a 'conspicuous success'.

Back in New South Wales from September 1941, Rankin was employed on a survey of the Broken Bay-Pittwater area. Early in 1942 he was posted to the sloop H.M.A.S. *Yarra*, with the intention that he would succeed (Sir) Hastings Harrington [q.v.14] in command. On 5 February, while under air-attack near Singapore, *Yarra* took on board 1804 people from the burning troop-ship *Empress of Asia*. Harrington commended Rankin's help in organizing the rescue.

Rankin assumed command of *Yarra* on 11 February 1942 and performed escort duties around the Netherlands East Indies. At 6.30 on the morning of 4 March, while escorting a small convoy from Java to Australia, the sloop encountered a Japanese squadron comprising three cruisers and two destroyers. Rankin immediately transmitted a sighting report, ordered the convoy to scatter, and placed *Yarra* between the enemy and the fleeing ships. The sloop made smoke and vainly engaged the enemy with her 4-inch (102 mm) guns, but the convoy was quickly overwhelmed. *Yarra* fought to the last. Some time after 8 a.m. Rankin finally gave the order to abandon ship. A direct hit on the bridge killed him minutes later. Of *Yarra*'s complement of 151 men, only thirteen were rescued. Rankin's wife and daughter survived him. In 2000 a Collins-class submarine was named after him.

F. B. Eldridge, *A History of the Royal Australian Naval College* (Melb, 1949); G. H. Gill, *Royal Australian Navy 1939-1942* (Canb, 1957); R. J. Hardstaff, *Leadline to Laser* (Syd, 1995); *Naval Hist Review*, Sept/Oct 1994, p 17.   RICHARD PELVIN

RANKINE, ANNIE ISABEL (1917-1972), Aboriginal leader, was born on 26 February 1917 at the Aboriginal Station, Point McLeay (Raukkan), South Australia, third of eleven children of Clarence Long, woodcutter, and his wife Polly, née Beck, both South Australian born. One of the Ngarrindjeri people, Annie spent her life at Point McLeay, near the south-eastern shore of Lake Alexandrina. She was educated at the local school, but left in 1928 to care for her siblings after her mother died in childbirth. At the Point McLeay manse on 16 February 1935 she married with Congregational forms Hendle Henry Rankine, a widower and a labourer from the local community; they were to have nine children, four of whom died in early childhood.

Although the Rankines' material circumstances were modest (they lived in a two-roomed house), Annie managed her family's affairs so capably that she was granted a level of independence from bureaucratic control enjoyed by few Aborigines at that time. Her life was one of service—to her family, her community and the Aboriginal people of South Australia. She fostered children in need, cleaned the school and church (of which she was a faithful member), practised traditional medicine, taught crafts and customs to the women and children of Point McLeay and Meningie, and recorded Ngarrindjeri lore. Her generosity and kindness became legendary. After hearing that two little girls had nothing to wear to a school concert, she cut up one of the few frocks she owned to make dresses for them, adding different coloured bows to make each dress special.

Admired for her integrity, fairness and strength of character, Mrs Rankine enjoyed excellent relationships with staff at the reserve and with officers of the Department of Aboriginal Affairs. In her efforts to achieve social benefits for her people, she rejected favouritism and was committed to the rights of all. She believed that Aborigines' interests were best served by developing positive attitudes and rapport with others. In 1968 she was elected founding chairman of the Point McLeay community council and in 1970 was appointed M.B.E. She said that she 'just worked along quietly for her people' and wanted more houses, better conditions and adult education classes to enable them 'to get somewhere' rather than continuing to be 'spoonfed'.

Rankine encouraged her children to adopt her values and commitments. Her daughters Polly, Leah and Harriet worked at the Aboriginal Women's Home, Sussex Street, North Adelaide, in the late 1950s and early 1960s; her son Henry, who succeeded her as chairman of the Point McLeay community council, was awarded the O.A.M. in 1992. Annie Rankine died of pneumonia and myocardial failure on 11 June 1972 at Tailem Bend hospital and was buried in Point McLeay cemetery; two of her five sons and three of her four daughters survived her.

C. Mattingley and K. Hampton (eds), *Survival in Our Own Land* (Adel, 1988); B. Salgado, *Murrundi Voices* (Murray Bridge, SA, 1994); *Advertiser* (Adel), 13 June 1970, 13 June 1972; information from Mrs L. Padman, Murray Bridge, SA; family information.

JUDITH RAFTERY

RAPKE, JULIA RACHEL (1886–1959), feminist and civil rights activist, was born on 11 February 1886 at Christchurch, New Zealand, daughter of Ralph Levoi, an insurance agent from London, and his Melbourne-born wife Miriam, née Levy. Julia attended Wellington Girls' High School before moving with the family to Melbourne. On 28 November 1906 at the Synagogue, St Kilda, she married Abraham Bernard Rapke, a 28-year-old tobacconist from Poland; they were to have two sons and a daughter.

In the mid-1920s Mrs Rapke entered public life, initially in charity work as secretary of the Maternity Patients' Convalescent Home. From 1927 she was active politically as secretary of the Victorian Women Citizens' Movement, the State affiliate of the Australian Federation of Women Voters. She also became a delegate to the National Council of Women of Victoria and convenor (1931) of its standing committee for suffrage and rights of citizenship. In 1929 she was appointed a special magistrate at the Children's Court, St Kilda, and a justice of the peace. As founding president (1938-40) of the Women Justices' Association of Victoria, she brought together influential and public-spirited women to lobby for the welfare of women, adolescents and children.

Although she was committed to non-party political organization for women, Rapke was a conservative in State and national politics. She joined the Brighton Beach branch of the Australian Women's National League, spoke in support of the All for Australia League during the Depression and campaigned periodically for the United Australia Party. In 1937 she considered standing for the Victorian legislature as a party candidate, rather than an Independent feminist, on the grounds that 'parliament legislates for the community as a whole'. She took part in the Constitutional Club's model parliament in the 1930s (one of only three women admitted) and rose to the posts of prime minister and governor-general. Convinced of the value of this organization as a political training ground, she formed the widely publicized women's model parliament in May 1946 and took a leading role in tutoring the participants in public speaking, parliamentary procedure and debate.

Rapke had resigned as secretary of the Victorian Women Citizens' Movement in mid-1931, but continued on the executive as international corresponding secretary and represented the movement on the board of the Australian Federation of Women Voters. As an A.F.W.V. delegate, she served as secretary of the Australian Pan-Pacific Women's Committee, and as secretary and treasurer of the Australian Joint Standing Committee of Women's Federal Organizations (later the Australian Liaison Committee).

The A.P.P.W.C. and the A.L.C. co-ordinated the participation of Australian women in international conferences. In addition, the A.L.C. advised the Commonwealth government on the appointment of appropriate women to international bodies—particularly the League of Nations—and provided ministers with information for reports on the position of women in Australia. Drawing on her experience in these organizations, Rapke broadcast a series of addresses entitled 'Women in Affairs, National and International' on radio-station 3LO in 1936 and delivered a paper, 'Women's Work for World Peace', in 1937. Both the A.P.P.W.C. and the A.L.C. were to be disbanded on her recommendation in 1946, owing to their inactivity during World War II.

Elected president of the V.W.C.M. in 1936, Rapke also became a vice-president of the A.F.W.V. She retained the latter post until 1957. Two speeches she gave to the A.F.W.V. conference in 1936, 'Women and Household Employment—Economic Aspects of Women's Rights and Equalities' and 'Legal Domicile of Married Women', indicated the range of her interests in women's issues. Her extensive contact with the nation's leading women, and a strong sense of the significance of their efforts, stimulated her to interview and to write short sketches on eighteen of them in 1938-40. Held as the Julia Rapke papers at the National Library of Australia, they provide valuable insights into Rapke herself as well as her subjects. Among the women, Ruby Rich (who was Jewish) had a major influence on Rapke and was the recipient of her confidences.

Widowed in 1940, Julia found consolation in an expanded public role. She served as vice-president of the Council for Women in War Work and as a member of the Co-ordinating Committee for Child Welfare in Wartime. Yet, more of her energy was devoted to the Victorian International Refugee Emergency Council and the Australian Open Door Council. She also assumed the federal secretarial responsibilities of the Women's International Zionist Organization, thereby extending her internationalism. Maintaining her abhorrence of war and violence, in 1946 she led a broadly based women's protest movement against the atomic bomb.

While she was deeply committed to assisting Jewish refugees and internees, Rapke remained determinedly integrationist and occasionally came into conflict with Ida Wynn [q.v.12 Samuel Wynn], president of the W.I.Z.O. Federation of Australia. Wynn lamented that Rapke was unable to 'steep herself in W.I.Z.O.', that she was interested in Zionism 'only in the most impersonal way' and that she devoted too much time to other organizations. Rapke, for her part, believed that Jewish women needed to be encouraged to play a larger part in national affairs.

In the months before World War II ended, Rapke had concentrated on strengthening feminist organization in Victoria in order to enlarge women's influence on postwar reconstruction. Between March and June 1945 she convened meetings with representatives of the V.W.C.M., the Women for Canberra Movement and the League of Women Electors. The three bodies merged to form the League of Women Voters of Victoria. It held its inaugural meeting in August and elected Rapke president. Resuming the presidency of the Women Justices' Association in the same month, she reached the pinnacle of her career in the women's movement in the four years that followed.

They were not easy years for Rapke. Both the L.W.V. and A.F.W.V. experienced internal conflict over the content and provenance of Jessie Street's [q.v.] Australian Woman's Charter. In a vulnerable position as a result of the demise of the Australian Liaison Committee, the A.F.W.V. found itself outmanoeuvred by the Charter group during 1947 when it tried to reconstitute the A.L.C. in opposition to the Charter movement's Co-operating Organization. Rapke joined Rich and Bessie Rischbieth [q.v.11] against Street in this Cold War battle for leadership of the women's movement in Australia, but her ability to determine the position of the L.W.V. had been undermined by the presence of Chartists on the league's executive. 'I hate not knowing who I can trust', she wrote to Rich.

Although Rapke continued on the board of the L.W.V. after her term as president ended in 1949, the weight of her public activity began to shift. In 1947 she had organized W.I.Z.O's second national conference. Following a period as Victorian president (1952-54) of this body, she was elevated to the federal presidency in 1954, a position she held until her death. Rapke brought to both offices a wealth of experience in organization, public speaking, leadership and lobbying. W.I.Z.O. 'rose to its greatness' under her. In 1954 Rapke's daughter Betty died. Julia left on a ten-month trip to Europe and Israel: the journey had special poignancy and served to affirm her faith. While in Israel, she was invited to join the world executive of W.I.Z.O. and later served on the executive of the Zionist Federation of Australia and New Zealand. She narrowly failed, however, to gain the franchise for women in her own St Kilda Synagogue.

In 1957 Rapke was appointed O.B.E., particularly for 'raising the status of women' and for improving 'the care and treatment of underprivileged children and delinquent youth'. Survived by her sons, she died on 9 October 1959 at Windsor and was buried in Springvale cemetery. A wing of the Ida Wynn Children's Centre at Mount Carmel, Haifa, Israel, was named after her.

The Rapkes' second son TREVOR GEORGE (1909-1978) was born on 2 September 1909 at Prahran, Melbourne, and raised at St Kilda, home of the city's Anglo-Jewry. Trevor attended Wesley College and entered the University of Melbourne (B.A., 1931; LL.B., 1933). He also went to the St Kilda Hebrew School: Sabbath afternoon services, followed by higher Hebrew classes, formed the basis of his continuing interest and expertise in orthodox learning and culture. A senior member of the Judaean League, he and Maurice Ashkanasy [q.v.13] extended 'its tentacles of dissent into the knitted world of St Kilda and Toorak Road', but he remained committed to traditional Judaism and occasionally gave sermons to his orthodox congregation. He passed on the Jewish faith through the children's services, which he helped to originate in 1924, and through the 3rd St Kilda Scout Group, which he formed to enable Jewish boys to engage in scouting in an appropriate religious context.

While adamantly opposed to a secularism that would submerge Jewish identity, Rapke was a leader in replacing the Victorian Jewish Advisory Board with the lay Board of Deputies, of which he was president (1956-58). He disagreed with many of the beliefs of the liberal congregation, but kept in touch with its members and sometimes acted as a mediator in the interests of communal harmony. In 1957 he was appointed Australia's representative on the Jewish Congress's world executive and elected president of the World Israel Movement. He was also a long-term executive-member of the Zionist Federation of Australia and New Zealand.

Accepting Jacob Danglow's [q.v.8] advice against joining the rabbinate, Rapke had been admitted to the Bar on 1 March 1935. He was appointed paymaster sub lieutenant, Royal Australian Naval Volunteer Reserve, on 19 January 1941 and promoted lieutenant in April. While serving (1942-43) in H.M.A.S. *Australia*, he saw action in the battle of the Coral Sea and acted as secretary to Commodore H. B. Farncomb [q.v.14]. His naval appointment terminated on 22 April 1944. At the Synagogue, St Kilda, on 17 June 1947 he married 19-year-old Betty Ellinson.

On 22 April 1958 Rapke took silk. It was claimed that he was the first Jew to become a judge in Victoria when he was elevated to the bench of the County Court on 3 November. As a judge, he was outspoken and earthy, showing the same concern as his mother for community welfare, civil liberties and just sentencing. The sharp distinction he drew between offences against property and those involving violence brought him into conflict with government ministers. He publicly condemned illegal discipline at Pentridge prison, procedures in trials for rape, and the practice

of keeping juveniles in custody for long periods while awaiting trial. Prepared to make his views known to the press, he antagonized some members of the judiciary by criticizing their remoteness from society.

In 1964 Rapke was appointed judge advocate-general, Australian Naval Forces. The Commonwealth government chose him in 1971 to investigate allegations of 'bastardisation' at the naval training establishment H.M.A.S. *Leeuwin*, Fremantle, Western Australia. Some believed that his close links with the R.A.N. would compromise his impartiality, but his report was characteristically judicious and his recommendations were consistent with the humane principles he employed on the bench.

Rapke was a Freemason, president (1956-57) of the Athenaeum Club and honorary professor of law (1965) at the United States Naval Justice School, Rhode Island. Late in 1977 he was notified that he was to be appointed A.O. in the Australia Day honours list. He died of complications arising from a coronary occlusion on 21 January 1978 at Templestowe and was buried in Springvale cemetery; his wife, and their four sons and two daughters survived him. D. P. Whelan, chief judge of the County Court, eulogized him as 'colourful, strong, fair and fearless'.

Principal Women of the Empire (Lond, 1940); H. L. Rubinstein, *The Jews in Victoria 1835-1985* (Syd, 1986); W. D. Rubinstein, *The Jews in Australia*, 2 (Melb, 1991); *WIZO Review*, Dec 1959, Mar 1960; *Herald* (Melb), 31 Jan 1978; Bessie Rischbieth papers, series 4 and 5, Ruby Rich papers, boxes 1, 9 and 43, *and* Aust Federation of Women Voters papers, boxes 3, 6-7, 9-10 and 15 (NL); League of Women Voters of Vic papers, boxes 872-73 *and* Women Justices' Assn of Vic papers, boxes 1-2 (SLV); information from Mr J. Rapke, Melb.

JUDITH SMART

RATCLIFFE, FRANCIS NOBLE (1904-1970), ecologist and conservationist, was born on 11 January 1904 at Calcutta, India, son of Samuel Kirkham Ratcliffe, journalist, and his wife Katie Maria, née Geeves. Francis was educated at Berkhamsted School, Hertfordshire, England, and at Wadham College, Oxford (B.A., 1925), where he studied under (Sir) Julian Huxley and obtained first-class honours in zoology. After graduating, he spent a year at Princeton University, New Jersey, United States of America, as a J. E. Proctor visiting fellow.

Following a period in London with the Empire Marketing Board, Ratcliffe was brought to Australia in 1929 by the Council for Scientific and Industrial Research to study flying foxes in Queensland and northern New South Wales. He returned to Britain in 1932 to take up a post as assistant in the zoology department at the University of Aberdeen. His affection for the Australian bush drew him back to Australia in 1935 to work for the C.S.I.R. in a free-ranging position which the chief executive officer Sir David Rivett [q.v.11] described as 'biological scout'. Travelling from his base in Melbourne, he researched wind-erosion in north-eastern South Australia and south-western Queensland, and came to the favourable attention of C.S.I.R.'s senior staff. At College Church, Parkville, on 14 January 1936 he married with Presbyterian forms Agnes, daughter of Professor Sir John Marnoch of Aberdeen.

In 1937 Ratcliffe moved to Canberra, where he had been appointed senior research officer in C.S.I.R.'s division of economic entomology. His field-research formed the basis of his classic, *Flying Fox and Drifting Sand* (London, 1938). The book demonstrated his capacity for lively and clear prose, his eye for a sparkling phrase, and his ability to portray people, native animals and the bush. On 21 May 1942 he was commissioned acting captain in the Militia. Transferred to the Australian Imperial Force on 31 August, he was promoted temporary major and appointed assistant-director of entomology at Land Headquarters in May 1943. He travelled extensively in the South-West Pacific Area, directing the fight against malaria, scrub typhus and dengue fever. On 6 December 1945 he was placed on the Reserve of Officers.

Ratcliffe returned to C.S.I.R. and carried out research on termites before accepting a new challenge as officer-in-charge of the wild-life survey section in the recently formed (1949) Commonwealth Scientific and Industrial Research Organization. Remembered as 'a good-looking, charming Englishman', he was for more than a decade the leading figure in attempts to control the number of Australia's rabbits. With Professor Frank Fenner of the Australian National University, he conducted field-studies to test the introduction of the myxoma virus. They described their work in *Myxomatosis* (Cambridge, 1965). During this controversial period of rural politics, critics accused the scientific community of dragging its feet. Ratcliffe's chief adversary was Dame Jean Macnamara [q.v.10] who, he self-deprecatingly said, regarded him as 'a boil on the bum of progress'.

Given his visionary plans for the conservation of Australia's natural heritage, Ratcliffe grew frustrated that so few resources were available for wildlife research and showed that he was uncomfortable with bureaucratic ways. In 1961 he returned to his former division as assistant-chief. While in this post, he made an enduring contribution through his role as founding spirit and honorary secretary (from 1964) of the Australian Conservation Foundation.

Increasingly released from his duties at C.S.I.R.O., he drove the new and independent A.C.F. with dogged determination. He used his network of friends, acquaintances in high places and scientific colleagues to bring together the necessary people and funds. To this end, he needed to win over the 'hot-shots' and to tolerate the 'small-time, emotional conservationists'. From small beginnings the foundation progressed steadily at a time of limited but growing consciousness of conservation issues. Ratcliffe was a perfectionist. He insisted that the foundation's publications should always be of the highest scientific quality and wrote a number of them himself, including the very first, on the conservation of kangaroos.

The nascent conservation movement contained a diverse range of individuals—scientists, grass-roots amateurs, government officials and business leaders—with differing viewpoints. Ratcliffe was not always easy to work with, and was increasingly troubled by ill health. Much of his energy was spent in finding appropriate senior staff and the funds to employ them, which entailed constant negotiations with the Commonwealth government for grants. His dislike of organizational necessities, suspicion of '"front-room" boys' and impatience with those who did not share his vision led to numerous conflicts. His moods ranged from the deepest pessimism to extraordinary optimism. At the same time, his humility and care for his colleagues won him many lasting friends.

In 1957 Ratcliffe was appointed O.B.E. The A.N.U. conferred on him an honorary D.Sc. in 1968. He was president of the Ecological Society of Australia in 1963-64. In January 1969 he retired from the C.S.I.R.O. and in October 1970 relinquished his formal connexions with the A.C.F. He continued to act as technical adviser to the House of Representatives Select Committee on Wildlife Conservation. Survived by his wife and twin daughters, he died of a cerebral haemorrhage on 2 December 1970 in Canberra Hospital and was cremated with Anglican rites.

D. Zwar, *The Dame* (Melb, 1984); B. Broadbent, *Inside the Greening* (Melb, 1999); B. Coman, *Tooth & Nail* (Melb, 1999); Aust Conservation Foundation, *Newsletter*, 3, no 1, Feb 1971; *Search* (Syd), 2, no 3, Mar 1971, p 74; *Hist Records of Aust Science*, 10, no 1, June 1994, p 1; J. Warhurst, 'The Australian Conservation Foundation: The Development of a Modern Environmental Interest Group', *Environmental Politics*, 3, no 1, Spring 1994, p 68; *Quadrant*, Jan-Feb 1998, p 20; *Canb Times* and *SMH*, 3 Dec 1970; Ratcliffe papers (NL).   JOHN WARHURST

RAW, ALAN RAYSON (1902-1964), cereal geneticist, was born on 24 August 1902 at St

Kilda, Melbourne, youngest of three children of John Thomas Raw, a schoolteacher from Scotland, and his Victorian-born wife Esther Maria Maud, née Rayson. After attending state schools—including Richmond Central where his father was headmaster—and Wesley College, Alan entered the University of Melbourne (B.Ag.Sc., 1927; M.Ag.Sc., 1931). For his master's degree he wrote a thesis entitled, 'Endosperm Characters in Wheat: Investigations with Free Gallipoli 1928-31'. His work attracted wide attention and the thesis was published in the *Journal of the Department of Agriculture of Victoria* in 1932.

In 1927 Raw had joined the Victorian Department of Agriculture and begun working with the senior cereal breeder George Gordon at the State Research Farm, Werribee. On 20 January 1932 at St John's Catholic Church, Clifton Hill, Melbourne, he married Nellie Mulrooney, a teacher. Succeeding Gordon in 1946, he continued to develop new cereal varieties for Australian conditions. He produced the Insignia, Olympic, Sherpa, Beacon, Diadem, Stockade and Emblem wheats, Research, Resibee and Anabee barleys, and Algeribee and Orient oats. All these varieties were extensively planted in Victoria. Raw became Australia's leading authority on barley. By 1964 his Research variety comprised 95 per cent of the malting barley grown in southern Victoria, and it had also been important in Tasmania, New Zealand and Kenya.

A geneticist as much as a breeder, Raw took a fundamental approach and frequently employed the genetic modification techniques of his day, which involved irradiation and the use of chemical mutagens such as colchicine. He also sought improvements through the introduction of new germ-plasm. Some of this work led to the production of fertile crosses between wheat and the grass *Agropyron*, and to the introduction of high-yielding wheats which produced flour with good baking qualities. While his major interest lay in cereal crops, staff working under his direction followed his methods in developing new varieties of flax, linseed, potatoes, tobacco, tomatoes and onions.

The results of Raw's work were published in twenty articles in the *Journal of Agriculture, Victoria*. The last of these appeared after his death: it was a report on his presentations at three international conferences held in Europe in 1963, and on his visits that year to plant-breeding and research organizations in India, Greece, Italy, France, the Soviet Union, the Netherlands, Sweden and Britain. Described by his colleagues as thoughtful and kind, Raw was a popular lecturer at the annual field-day at the State Research Farm. He was an archetypal member of a family who made its way in the world through education and paid their debt in professional service. By occupation and by inclination he was close to nature, and liked nothing better than to go fishing. He died of a coronary occlusion on 9 September 1964 at Wagga Wagga, New South Wales, and was buried in Werribee cemetery; his wife, daughter and son survived him.

B. R. Wardle, *The Land that Yielded* (Melb, 1972); *J of Agr* (Vic), Oct 1964, p 469; information from Miss M. and Mr W. Raw, Werribee, Vic.

IAN D. RAE

RAWLING, JAMES NORMINGTON (1898-1966), political activist and writer, was born on 27 July 1898 at Plattsburg, near Newcastle, New South Wales, eighth of nine children of English-born parents James Rawling, coalminer, and his wife Annie Elizabeth, née Normington. Educated at Newcastle High School, Jim enlisted in the Australian Imperial Force on 7 August 1916. He served on the Western Front from October 1917, first with the 36th Battalion and then with the 35th. In a letter from the trenches he told his mother, 'what is known as the glory of war is non-existant [sic]. One sees everywhere one's fellow men lying dead around one and . . . takes no more notice than . . . of a dead dog'. His abomination of war was to be a driving force in his life.

After the Armistice, Rawling gave lectures for the A.I.F. Education Service. He returned to Australia in June 1919 and was discharged from the army on 7 August. In 1920 he entered the University of Sydney (B.A., 1929; M.A., 1946) and in 1921-22 trained as a teacher. At the Saints Church, Rozelle, on 18 February 1922 he married Mary Stewart with Mormon forms. Next year he taught at Crown Street Public School and began tutoring for the Trade Union Educational League. Following three years (1924-27) at Newcastle as an ironworker's assistant, he returned to Sydney where he taught at private schools and colleges.

Rawling lost his religious faith. He joined the Communist Party of Australia in 1925. An active campaigner and publicist for the party and its 'fraternal' organizations, he spoke and wrote about past events and contemporary issues. In 1932-34 he edited *World Survey*, the magazine of the League Against Imperialism, and in 1934-39 *War! What For?* (later *World Peace*), the organ of the Australian Movement Against War and Fascism (later Australian League for Peace and Democracy) of which he was secretary. His pamphlet, *Who Owns Australia?* (1937), enjoyed four editions. The C.P.A. commissioned him to write *The Story of the Australian People* (1938-39), an unfinished series of booklets which sold for one shilling each. Suddenly expelled from the party in December 1939 for expressing unorthodox views, he justified his stance in an article in the *Sydney Morning Herald* on 6 March 1940: 'The Hitler-Stalin pact of last August pulled me up with a jerk . . . the "spear-head of peace" and the spear-head of aggression had coalesced . . . the brutal invasion of Finland was the final determining blow'.

For the next five years Rawling worked as a temporary clerk with the Metropolitan Water, Sewerage and Drainage Board, and studied Australian literary history. He then resumed teaching, mostly in private schools. The university awarded him second-class honours for his thesis on Daniel Deniehy [q.v.4]; his left-wing perspective allegedly found little favour in (Sir) Stephen Roberts's [q.v.] conservative history department. When Rawling was awarded a Commonwealth Literary Fund fellowship in 1947 to write a biography of Charles Harpur [q.v.1], Opposition politicians attacked the Federal government for supporting a former communist. Two years later he appeared as a principal witness before the Victorian royal commission on communism. He told the commission that 'socialism had not been established in Russia', and that international communism as directed by the Kremlin was 'a bigger danger to culture and democracy and freedom than even Hitler and the Nazis'.

J. Normington-Rawling (as he styled himself for a time) finally published *Charles Harpur, an Australian* in 1962. The book expressed his 'commitment to nurturing Australia's cultural traditions' and received generally favourable reviews. In 1962-63, as a visiting fellow at the Research School of Social Sciences, Australian National University, Canberra, he worked on his history of the C.P.A. His manuscript, and his large collection of sources for Australian radical politics between 1869 and 1945, are held by the Noel Butlin Archives Centre, A.N.U.

A loner, a radical pacifist and an ideologue, Rawling had been attracted to communism by intellectual persuasion and by moral outrage at capitalist and imperialist exploitation. His contemporaries saw him as opinionated, stubborn and impractical, and as one who was better at writing propaganda than at public speaking or organization. Following his break with the C.P.A., he was frustrated by his failure to find permanent employment as a schoolteacher or an academic, and believed that he was being punished unfairly for his past associations. In the classroom, he was patient, kindly and tolerant, but determined that his students should understand that art, literature and politics deserved greater prominence in the curriculum, for their own sake and as a means of advancing the wider cause of peace. Survived by his wife and three daughters, he died of a coronary occlusion on 7 March 1966 in Sydney Hospital and was cremated.

S. Macintyre, *The Reds* (Syd, 1999); *Meanjin Q*, 22, no 1, 1963, p 69; *Notes & Furphies*, Oct 1979, p 1, Apr 1980, p 2; *Quadrant*, Dec 1989, p 60, Sept 1998, p 34; J. Pomeroy, 'The Apostasy of James Normington Rawling', *Aust J of Politics and Hist*, 37, no 1, 1991, p 21; Rawling papers MSS 1326 (ML).

JOHN POMEROY

RAYMOND, ARTHUR WILMOT (1892-1954), medical practitioner and air force officer, was born on 19 September 1892 at Palmerston (Darwin), Northern Territory, son of English-born parents Wilmot Hope Raymond, telegraphist, and his wife Edith, née Castle. Arthur was educated at The King's School, Canterbury, England, Sydney Grammar School and the University of Sydney (M.B., 1915; Ch.M., 1925).

Commissioned lieutenant, Royal Army Medical Corps, British Army, on 23 March 1915, Raymond sailed for England that month. In July he was sent to the Western Front where he served as regimental medical officer in several Scottish regiments, the heavy artillery and the Rifle Brigade. He took part in a number of major actions, including the 3rd battle of Ypres and the British retreat of March 1918, and was twice wounded. Promoted temporary captain in March 1916 (substantive September 1918), he was awarded the Military Cross (1917) and Bar (1918) for rescuing wounded men in hazardous circumstances.

In 1919 Raymond resigned his commission. After undertaking postgraduate medical work in London, he returned to Australia in August 1920. At St Stephen's Presbyterian Church, Sydney, on 2 November 1921 he married Jessie Lauraine Kidd, a trained nurse. He qualified in surgery (1925), then practised at Winton, Queensland. Moving to rooms in Wickham Terrace, Brisbane, he accepted positions in the General and Children's hospitals.

With war again threatening, Raymond obtained a commission as surgeon lieutenant, Royal Australian Naval Volunteer Reserve, in March 1939. He grew impatient at the lack of an overseas posting and transferred to the Royal Australian Air Force on 19 February 1940 as a flight lieutenant in the Medical Branch. Appointments to various Australian-based units prompted him to write to England, inquiring about a return to the R.A.M.C., but nothing came of it.

Raymond's superiors in the R.A.A.F. were impressed by his abilities and promoted him squadron leader in October 1941. He continued to long for active service. Eventually, in August 1944, he was given command of No.22 Medical Clearing Station, Aitape, New Guinea. In the landing at Labuan, Borneo, in June 1945, he went ashore under enemy fire with the preliminary reconnaissance party and selected a site for his unit. His clearing station was operational within twenty-four hours. He was promoted wing commander in January 1945. For his consistent devotion to duty, courage and resourcefulness, he was appointed O.B.E. (1946). Late in 1945 he fell ill with heart disease, but recovered sufficiently to serve with the R.A.A.F. component of the British Commonwealth Occupation Force, Japan, in 1946. He was demobilized from the air force on 8 September 1948.

'Doc' Raymond was a friendly and unpretentious man who knew when to disregard regulations. He resumed private practice in Macquarie Street, Sydney, and served part time as principal medical officer, Eastern Area, R.A.A.F., until April 1952. Survived by his wife, two sons and two daughters, he died of a coronary occlusion on 17 January 1954 at Roseville and was cremated with Anglican rites.

AWM 64 and 165 (AWM); WO 338, 339 and 389 (PRO, Lond); information from Mr G. Park, Geelong, Vic, Dr A. W. Raymond, Point Frederick, Miss G. L. Raymond, Gosford, and Miss K. A. Raymond, Winmalee, NSW.   ALAN FRASER

READ, THOMAS ANDREW (1886-1972), metallurgist, was born on 16 February 1886 at Dean, Victoria, son of William Tennyson Read, a farmer from England, and his Scottish-born wife Elizabeth, née Scott. Thomas moved with his parents to Broken Hill, New South Wales, and attended the Church of England and Broken Hill Superior Public schools. Completing his formal education at Broken Hill Technical College, he gained a diploma and associateship in assaying (1906), a diploma in chemistry (1910) and a fellowship in metallurgy (1925) from Sydney Technical College.

In 1901 Read began work in the general store at Broken Hill South Ltd's mine. Because of his interest in and aptitude for chemistry, he was transferred to the assay office in 1905. His enthusiasm and dedication to duty marked him for rapid promotion, from assayer's boy to assayer's assistant and to chief assayer. At St Paul's Anglican Church, Chatswood, Sydney, on 11 April 1912 he married Ivy Viola Grace Dunstan (d.1959); they were to remain childless. When William McBride [q.v.15] enlisted in the Australian Imperial Force in August 1915, Read took over his duties as metallurgist and mill superintendent. In 1922 he was appointed chief metallurgist.

During World War I Read carried out a considerable amount of laboratory and plant experimentation, concentrating on selective lead and zinc flotation methods, the use of compressed air, and ways of improving apparatus and reagents. He put into operation a De Spirlet zinc-concentrate roaster to produce sulphuric acid for the flotation process. His first major success came in 1917 with the introduction of the use of ferric salts in the differential flotation process.

Like McBride, Read was involved in the measurement of suspended dust and in finding methods to prevent its occurrence: his research led to significant improvements in mining conditions. He also experimented (1917-18) with mechanical methods of dust-allaying, and continued this work in the 1920s. Accompanied by the underground superintendent H. H. Carroll, he spent nine months in 1926 visiting mines and mills in South Africa, Europe and North America. In July 1927 Read and his assistants found that the addition of potassium ethyl xanthate and a frothing oil before flotation led to a marked increase in the recovery of lead and silver. This technique was quickly taken up by other mines on the field. Read was largely responsible for the design and construction of the new Broken Hill South concentrating plant, the first in Broken Hill to be built of concrete and steel. Work began in 1928, the gravity section was opened in 1929 and the flotation section commenced operations in 1934. The plant incorporated a sub-aeration flotation machine developed by Read and G. B. Game.

A keen member (from 1918) of the Australasian Institute of Mining and Metallurgy, Read was a stalwart of the Broken Hill branch (chairman 1933-36 and 1942), commenting on standards and encouraging presentations by his colleagues. He was a councillor for New South Wales (1935-52) and a vice-president (1944) of the A.I.M.M. The local branch meetings provided a fruitful field for the promulgation of ideas; discussion of the results of research crossed company boundaries and ensured that the Broken Hill field remained at the forefront of technological development in metallurgy. Between 1921 and 1935 Read published a number of papers in the institute's *Proceedings*: the first—in association with his superintendent W. E. Wainwright [q.v.12]— was on the concentration practices of Broken Hill South. He was for many years a member of Broken Hill Technical College's advisory committee.

Read's loyalty and devotion to the Broken Hill South operations were such that he did not seek wider recognition or more lucrative positions, though he received many offers. In the late 1930s the company agreed to release him as a consultant to North Broken Hill Ltd for the design and erection of a new concentrating plant. His protégés came to hold important assay and metallurgical posts on various Australian mining fields.

After he retired as chief metallurgist in March 1955, Read and his wife moved to

Balwyn, Melbourne. He died on 2 February 1972 at Camberwell and was buried in Springvale cemetery.

O. H. Woodward, *A Review of the Broken Hill Lead-silver-zinc Industry* (Melb, 1962); B. Carroll, *Built on Silver* (Melb, 1986); A'sian Inst of Mining and Metallurgy, *Procs*, 1918, 1920-21, 1925-30, 1933, 1935, 1938, 1941 and 1943; *Barrier Daily Truth*, 16 Mar 1955; W. Hodder, History of the South Mines (ts, 1965, Charles Rasp L, Broken Hill Archives).

D. F. BRANAGAN

REED, CYNTHIA; *see* NOLAN

REED, SIR GEOFFREY SANDFORD (1892-1970), judge and director-general of the Australian Security Intelligence Organization, was born on 14 March 1892 at Port Pirie, South Australia, elder child of William Reed, Wesleyan clergyman, and his wife Elizabeth, née Lathlean, both Australian born. Geoffrey was educated at Prince Alfred College (1901-09) and (on a scholarship) at the University of Adelaide (LL.B., 1913). Articled to his uncle R. H. Lathlean, he was admitted to the Supreme Court of South Australia as a solicitor and barrister on 25 April 1914.

On 18 February 1918 Reed enlisted in the Australian Imperial Force. At the Methodist Church, Malvern, on 22 June that year he married Kathleen Jennie Matthews. He reached England in October and served in France with a supply depot from January 1919. Back in Adelaide, he was discharged from the A.I.F. on 21 May.

Reed continued his legal career as associate to Justice Alexander Buchanan. On 20 February 1920 he became a partner in the law firm McLachlan, Reed & Griffiths. Active in the Law Society of South Australia, he was its secretary in 1924-27, treasurer in 1932-33 and vice-president in 1934. He began lecturing in law at the university in 1928. In 1937 he took silk and chaired a royal commission on transport. An acting-judge of the Supreme Court in 1935-37, he was appointed permanently to the bench on 15 July 1943.

From May 1941 Reed was chairman of the South Australian National Security Advisory Committee. The Federal government appointed him to undertake a number of security-related inquiries: he investigated the lack of co-operation between civilian and military intelligence agencies, heard (1943) charges against Lieutenant Colonel R. F. B. Wake, head of the Queensland office of the Commonwealth Security Service, and examined (1944) breaches of national security regulations in Hobart. In 1945 he carried out an inquiry into the court-martial and detention system in the army, and chaired a royal commission into the Adelaide Electric Supply Co. Two years later he headed a royal commission into allegations of improper payments to the Tasmanian premier (Sir) Robert Cosgrove [q.v.13]. In December 1948 the Commonwealth solicitor-general (Sir) Kenneth Bailey [q.v.13] sought Reed's suggestions about a 'new security service'.

Reed's appointment for a twelve-month term as Commonwealth director-general of security was announced on 2 March 1949. The Australian Security Intelligence Organization came into existence a fortnight later when Reed received a charter from Prime Minister J. B. Chifley [q.v.13] setting out his authority and responsibilities. The principal reasons behind the decision to establish A.S.I.O. lay in a serious but unsolved Soviet espionage case, and increasing allied (especially British) pressure for Australia to address its security shortcomings. Chifley's government was also influenced by widespread industrial unrest fomented by the pro-Soviet Communist Party of Australia. Reed faced a difficult and politically delicate task. He set about his job in a dedicated and methodical manner, his integrity and bipartisan approach winning him the early confidence of his political masters.

The new organization made its presence felt within a few months. By June 1949 the prime minister had authorized the first telephone-interception operations and on 8 July C.P.A. headquarters in Sydney was raided at A.S.I.O.'s direction. Reed was successful in obtaining money and staff. A.S.I.O., modelled on its British counterpart, Military Intelligence 5 (M.I.5), grew rapidly. (Sir) Robert Menzies [q.v.15], who replaced Chifley as prime minister in December 1949, became a strong supporter of the service, and Reed's term as director-general was extended until 30 June 1950.

Reed's last months in office were largely dominated by the government's Communist Party dissolution bill (tabled on 27 April 1950) which occasioned acrimonious debate. He completed his term on 6 July. In a valedictory report to Menzies, dated 27 June, he listed his achievements: the successful establishment and maintenance of the new organization, representative offices in all States and mainland territories, a staff of 141, the introduction of a comprehensive record system based on registries, scrupulous observance of political impartiality, and the consolidation of operational activity. On his departure, he received warm tributes from his American and British counterparts, and from both Menzies and Chifley.

Returning to Adelaide, Reed resumed his role as a judge. In 1953 he was knighted. Two years later he chaired a commission on electoral boundaries. He served as deputy to the governor of South Australia in February and November 1957. In the following year he was judge in the controversial murder trial of the Aborigine, Rupert Max Stuart; in July 1959 he was appointed to the royal commission into Stuart's conviction.

Five ft 5¼ ins (166 cm) tall and compactly built, Reed had been a keen tennis player as a young man. He belonged to the Adelaide, Royal Adelaide Golf and Adelaide Oval Bowling clubs, and the Commonwealth Club, Canberra. Chairman (1940) of the Red Cross Emergency Service Committee, he was founding president (1963) of the Asthma Foundation of South Australia and a life member (from 1942) of the Returned Sailors', Soldiers' and Airmen's Imperial League of Australia. He was also a Freemason and a grand master (1953-56) of the Grand Lodge of South Australia. Throughout his life he retained close links to the Methodist Church. His interest in aviation was also abiding. Sir Geoffrey took leave in December 1961 and stepped down as a puisne judge on 14 March 1962. After travelling abroad, he spent his retirement in Adelaide, caring for his wife who was partially blind. He died on 31 December 1970 in Calvary Hospital, North Adelaide, and was cremated; his wife, and their son and daughter survived him.

D. Ball and D. Horner, *Breaking the Codes* (Syd, 1998); *Argus*, 2 Aug 1945, 3 Mar 1949; *Age* (Melb), 2 June 1950; 'ASIO: a Chronology' *and* R. A. Swan, 'Significant Events in the History of Internal Security Intelligence Organizations in Australia up to the Formation of ASIO on 16 March 1949' *and* 'ASIO—A History 1949-79', (tss, ASIO, Canb); Reed family scrapbook (held by Mrs M. Kerr, Colonel Light Gardens, Adel); information from Mr R. Reed, Dapto, NSW. REX STEVENSON

REES, CORALIE CLARKE (1908-1972), journalist, broadcaster and author, was born on 23 October 1908 in Perth, eldest of six children of Guildford Clarke, a newspaper publisher from South Australia, and his Victorianborn wife Sylvia Frances, née Norton. Coralie attended Perth Modern School where she began her literary career as editor of the magazine *Sphinx*. Finishing equal top in English and history in the Leaving certificate examinations (1925), she attended the University of Western Australia (B.A., 1929). There she was active in the dramatic society and was sub-editor (1927-28) of the undergraduate magazine, *Black Swan*. In 1929 she collaborated with its editor Leslie Rees in writing a play, *Centenaryitis* (a satire on Western Australia's centenary celebrations) in which she played the leading role of Westralia. That year

her one-act play 'Shielded Eyes' appeared in *Black Swan*; it was produced in 1930 with (Sir) Paul Hasluck in the main role.

After graduating, Coralie Clarke edited the *Dawn*, a monthly feminist magazine published in Perth. Her writing convinced Professor (Sir) Walter Murdoch [q.v.10] of her 'outstanding literary ability' and led in 1930 to a travelling scholarship to study dramatic literature at the University of London. On 19 September 1931 at the register office, St Pancras, she married Rees, who was by then working as a journalist. A strikingly attractive woman, with 'masses of curly hair', 'a broad brow and wideset, large greeny-grey eyes', she worked the next five years as a freelance journalist, writing the well-received 'London Woman's Diary' for the *West Australian* and contributing regularly to the Sydney magazine *Woman's Budget* and to the *Australian Women's Weekly*. She published interviews with prominent British women, such as Lady Astor, and Australian writers living in England, among them Henry Handel Richardson and Mary Grant Bruce [qq.v.11,7].

In 1936 Mrs Rees returned to Australia and toured as secretary to the concert pianist Eileen Joyce. She and her husband then settled at Neutral Bay, Sydney. While raising two daughters, she freelanced as a writer and as an occasional broadcaster. She and Leslie produced travel features which were broadcast in Australia, New Zealand, South Africa and Canada. In 1946 she wrote *Silent his Wings*, an elegy in memory of her brother Max who was killed in 1944 while serving with the Royal Australian Air Force in Canada. It is widely regarded as her finest work. Her play for an all-child cast, *Wait Till We Grow Up* (1948), was performed at primary schools in Sydney.

Despite suffering increasingly from ankylosing spondylitis, a crippling spinal condition, Coralie continued to travel with Leslie to remote places, gathering material for their best-selling books: *Spinifex Walkabout* (1953), *Westward from Cocos* (1956), *Coasts of Cape York* (1960) and *People of the Big Sky Country* (1970). She also continued to write children's stories which were published as a collection, *What Happened After? The Nursery Rhyme Sequels* (1972). Survived by her husband and daughters, she died of cardiorespiratory failure on 14 February 1972 in her home at Balmoral and was cremated with Anglican rites.

L. Rees, *Hold Fast to Dreams* (Syd, 1982); *Womanspeak*, Aug-Sept 1987; H. de Berg, Coralie Rees (taped interview, 1968, NL); information from Mr R. Davidson, Fremantle, WA, Ms E. Durack, Claremont, Dr A. Gregg, White Gum Valley, Perth, Mr L. Rees, Balmoral, Ms D. Peterson, East Willoughby, and Ms M. Wintle, Bondi, Syd. LESLEY REECE

REFSHAUGE, JOAN JANET BROWN (1906-1979), medical practitioner and medical administrator, was born on 3 December 1906 at Armadale, Melbourne, eldest of five children of Victorian-born parents Francis Christopher Refshauge, a state school teacher who became an invalid, and his wife Margaret Isabella, née Craig. Joan's parents made every sacrifice to guide their children to higher degrees. Educated at University High School, Presbyterian Ladies' College and the University of Melbourne (B.Sc., 1928; M.Sc., 1929; M.B., B.S., 1939), she taught mathematics at university and in schools, completed a diploma of education in 1930 and turned to medicine in 1935. At the Presbyterian Church, South Melbourne, on 19 May 1937 she married Max Wulfing Bergin, a surveyor; their son Rupert was born in 1942. She worked as a hospital resident until May 1943 when she was commissioned captain in the (Royal) Australian Army Medical Corps. Posted to the 2nd Australian Army Out-Patients Department, she was responsible for the health of servicewomen in and around Melbourne. Her appointment terminated in April 1946.

Max had served in the Australian New Guinea Administrative Unit during World War II and remained in Papua. Joan followed him to Port Moresby in 1947. In order to be employed in the Department of Public Health, she was required to confine herself to maternal and child health. After she divorced her husband in 1948, she continued to practise, and persuaded her widowed mother to join her and Rupert. She was a highly professional doctor and—unlike some of her flamboyant male colleagues—reassuring to her Melanesian patients.

As part of the postwar expansion of the department, Refshauge was deputed to establish the programmes which evolved into the Queen Elizabeth II infant, child and maternal health service. The task required delicate liaison with the missions which had created these services and continued to deliver most of them. She recruited staff, organized the training of indigenous nurses and began school health-services. While assistant-director of the department, she also attended the University of Sydney and obtained a diploma in public health (1954). By 1963, the year in which she resigned, she had established 21 central clinics, 528 village clinics, and 541 centres visited by mobile patrols.

Like others in her family, Refshauge embodied a 'progressive' tradition, working to improve society through professional skill and apolitical public service, despite disruptions caused by marriage, war and motherhood. Although racial segregation was explicit, and tacit distinctions also separated females from males, she quietly ignored the taboo on touching Melanesian men. Some Australians in New Guinea could not believe that women were doctors, and treated her as a nurse. Throughout her service, her salary was less than those of her male counterparts. Characteristically, she did not complain. She devoted time to introducing the Girl Guides and the Young Women's Christian Association to the Territory. In later years she did question the assumptions that underpinned sexual discrimination and steered women into feminine careers.

Refshauge knew that she was a pioneer in public health. She slowly recognized that she was also a role model for Papua New Guinean women. In 1964 she was appointed O.B.E. and awarded the Cilento medal for tropical medicine. That year she joined the Queensland Department of Health. She became deputy-director of maternal and child welfare in 1968 and retired in 1973. Survived by her son, she died on 25 July 1979 at Auchenflower, Brisbane, and was cremated.

C. Bell (ed), *The Diseases and Health Services of Papua New Guinea* (Port Moresby, 1973); L. M. Hellstedt (ed), *Women Physicians of the World* (Washington, 1978); E. Kettle, *That They Might Live* (priv pub, Syd, 1979); D. Denoon, *Public Health in Papua New Guinea* (Cambridge, 1989); *MJA*, 12 Jan 1980; J. Byford, Dealing with Death, Beginning with Birth: women's health and childbirth on Misima Island, Papua New Guinea (Ph.D. thesis, ANU, 1999).   DONALD DENOON

REHFISCH, ALISON BAILY (1900-1975), artist, was born on 23 January 1900 at Woollahra, Sydney, elder daughter of William Baily Green, a native-born hardware agent, and his wife Annie Louisa, née Greenwood, who came from England. The family soon moved to Mosman. Annie, an accomplished painter, woodcarver and musician, believed in women's emancipation and encouraged her daughter's interest in the arts. Alison was devastated by the death (1906) of her younger sister Betty and began to draw pictures of God, angels and heaven.

While a boarder at Redlands school, Cremorne, Alison was taught applied arts and design by Albert Collins, a landscape painter. After leaving Redlands, she studied at Julian Ashton's [q.v.7] Sydney Art School. On 20 August 1919 at St Stephen's Presbyterian Church, Sydney, she married Rodney Eschenburg Rehfisch, a 34-year-old warehouse manager; they were to have one daughter (b.1920). The family settled at Neutral Bay in 1922.

Once her daughter started school, Alison began attending Antonio Dattilo Rubbo's [q.v.11] painting classes at the Royal Art Society of New South Wales where she met GEORGE BERNARD DUNCAN (1904-1974). She shared a studio in the city with him and with

Dora Jarret, a lifelong friend. Known for her vitality and strength of character, and her outgoing nature and flamboyant sense of style, she held her first exhibition (with Jarret) in 1929, at the Blaxland Gallery. She began exhibiting with the Society of Artists in 1931 and held a joint exhibition with Duncan in 1933.

When the Rehfisches separated, Alison moved (1930) into a studio apartment at 12 Bridge Street. There she lived and worked closely with fellow artists such as 'Dorrit' Black, 'Rah' Fizelle, Thea Proctor and Adelaide Perry [qq.v.7,8,11,15]. The rooms were later taken over by Norman Lindsay [q.v.10] who—in 'The Party'—depicted George, Alison and himself at a seemingly risqué gathering of artists, dancers and models at the studio.

In 1933 Alison Rehfisch left for Europe. She studied under Iain Macnab at the Grosvenor School of Modern Art, London, and her highly stylized compositions reflected his teaching. Believing that an artist should not be influenced, but stimulated, by other artists, Rehfisch drew on the work of El Greco, for his colour and elongated shapes, Chagall, for his sense of fantasy, and Braque for his design and simplified reality. She hated 'frills . . . in life and painting, too'. In 1934 she, Duncan and Gerald Lewers [q.v.15] were represented in the 'Six Colonial Artists' exhibition at the Cooling galleries, New Bond Street. She also showed with the Society of Women Artists, the Royal Institute of Oil Painters and the British Empire Society in England, and with the Société Nationale des Beaux Arts in Paris. In 1938 she helped to create a huge felt mural, designed by Arthur Murch for the Australian wool pavilion at the Empire Exhibition, Glasgow; the offer of minimal, but much-needed, wages attracted a team of Australian artists living in London, including (Sir) William Dobell [q.v.14].

Captivated by Europe, Rehfisch embraced the culture and languages of Spain, France and Germany. She spent months at Seville, studying the Spanish masters and at Malaga, on the Mediterranean, where she lived in an old Moorish castle converted into a studio. Her colourful and expansive letters home provided the basis for her mother's weekly radio programme, 'Story of an Artist in Spain', for the Australian Broadcasting Commission. The death of her estranged husband in 1938 prompted her to return to Sydney, where she later took up residence at 214 George Street.

Alison and George Duncan were married on 4 December 1942 at the registrar-general's office, Sydney. Born on 7 January 1904 at Auckland, New Zealand, son of George Mathew Duncan and his wife Mary Anne, née O'Connor, George travelled and studied in Britain and Europe in 1935-39. During World War II he worked as a camouflage artist. He

and Alison continued to exhibit jointly at the Macquarie Galleries. They had an unusually modern, egalitarian relationship. She had an eye for home decoration, but avoided the more mundane chores. George took on the domestic role of provider. In 1947 their studio was destroyed by fire and Alison lost some two hundred paintings. Fellow artists held an exhibition and auction at Desiderius Orban's studio to raise funds to help them. The Duncans moved to the country and began to paint the rolling, rural landscapes of Berrima, Moss Vale, Goulburn and surrounding districts. They returned to Sydney in 1953. He was director (1953-64) of the David Jones' [q.v.2] Art Gallery and president of the Australian Water-Colour Institute for six years, which curtailed his time for painting.

Both Alison and George were active as exhibitors and organizers of the Contemporary Group's affairs. She also belonged to the Contemporary Art Society of Australia and was included in the Australian Women Painters' exhibition, held at the National Art Gallery of New South Wales in 1946. While she painted still lifes, landscapes and some figurative works, she was chiefly recognized for her flower-paintings—a genre low in the hierarchy of art. This, and the modern values in her work, made it less acceptable to the 'establishment'. With her use of generous, but thinly-applied colour, and formalized, finely balanced composition, Rehfisch always maintained her faith in her early principles, of which she stated, 'Simplicity is my aim. The basis of all modern art is design'. Some critics castigated her for pursuing a career and for her use of 'violent colours and dramatic atmospheres', but a number of informed judges praised her exhibited works. In 1950 James Gleeson wrote in the *Sydney Morning Herald*: 'Alison Rehfisch is developing in her flower-pieces an ability to enthral us with a kind of magic nostalgia'.

Despite her disillusionment with emerging trends, Rehfisch continued to exhibit until 1969. She spent her later years at Hillgrove, a house with a beloved garden which she and George had bought at Pymble, where she painted and sought to impart her principles of colour and design to students. George died of cancer on 8 May 1974 at Greenwich. Inconsolable, and suffering from failing eyesight, Alison took poison while 'in a state of severe mental depression' and died on 12 March 1975 at her Pymble home. She was cremated with Anglican rites. Her daughter survived her. A joint memorial retrospective exhibition of Rehfisch's and Duncan's work was held in 1976 at the Macquarie Galleries in Sydney and Canberra.

L. Rees, *The Small Treasures of a Lifetime* (Syd, 1969); Macquarie Galleries, *Duncan and Rehfisch*

(Syd, 1976); J. Burke, *Australian Women Artists 1840-1940* (Melb, 1980); J. Campbell, *Early Sydney Moderns* (Syd, 1988); C. Ambrus, *Australian Women Artists* (Canb, 1992); R. Power, *Alison Rehfisch* (Syd, 2002); *Aust Women's Weekly*, 21 Dec 1946, p 30; *Huntley's Aust Art Investor*, 2, Apr 1989; *SMH*, 21 Apr 1933, 2 Mar 1939, 5 Aug 1946, 5 Feb 1976; H. de Berg, Alison Rehfisch *and* George Duncan (taped interviews, NL).   RACHEL POWER

REICHSTEIN, LANCE ERIC HAROLD (1900-1980), businessman and philanthropist, was born on 31 October 1900 at Morchard, South Australia, youngest of six children of Johann Wilhelm Reichstein, farmer, and his wife Emily, née Wait, both South Australian born. Educated at Morchard Public School, Petersburg (Peterborough) and Adelaide High schools, and the University of Adelaide (B.E. Hons, 1922), Lance worked as a draughtsman for C. A. Smith & Co., engineers, before supervising the drawing-office of the South Australian Gas Co. In 1924-35 he was head of the engineering department at the Gordon Institute of Technology, Geelong, Victoria; his lectures emphasized the practical rather than the theoretical. He helped to form the Gordon Kelvin Club in 1932.

With A. G. Appleby, Reichstein had established Industrial Service Engineers Pty Ltd in 1928 to manufacture tools for use in the automotive industry. In 1929-30 he made the first of many visits to factories abroad, travelling via New Zealand to the United States of America and Canada. He expanded I.S.E. and increased its range of products. A branch was opened in West Melbourne in 1934 and a factory built at Yarraville soon afterwards. Reichstein moved to Melbourne. On 15 October 1938 at St John's Anglican Church, Toorak, he married Esther (Tessa) Frances Smalpage, a 27-year-old musician; they were to be divorced in 1943.

In 1940 Reichstein formed Steelweld Pty Ltd, which produced munitions at West Footscray. Next year he founded Harland Engineering (Australia) Pty Ltd, in association with its parent company in Scotland. His firms employed 750 people by the end of World War II. In November 1946 he, Keith Duncan, F. S. Grimwade, G. F. Maxted, J. B. Arnold and others established Industrial Engineering Ltd as a holding company. Issues of shares in I.E.L. were readily taken up. At the Unitarian Church, East Melbourne, on 21 January 1949 Reichstein married Mavis Lurline Young, a 35-year-old manageress; they were to have a daughter before being divorced.

The I.E.L. group of companies usually manufactured under licence, as Reichstein preferred to supply goods for which there were proven markets rather than to develop original lines. In the postwar period a major affiliation was negotiated between Steelweld and the Caterpillar Tractor Co. of the U.S.A. which resulted in four hundred men being employed for ten years in the production of earth-moving equipment. The loss of the Caterpillar licence was a setback which Reichstein overcame by initiating more joint ventures, diversifying his products to include pressure vessels, doors and industrial gases, and introducing marketing techniques such as annual trade fairs (from 1959). By the late 1950s I.E.L. had factories and outlets throughout Australia. Reichstein was the principal founder and a member (1968-79) of the executive-committee of the Heavy Engineering Manufacturers' Association which lobbied for the protection of Australian manufacturing.

In 1956-71 Reichstein represented Bourke Ward on the Melbourne City Council, becoming identified with the Civic Group and serving on several committees, including one responsible for abattoirs and markets. After being involved in philanthropy in a quiet and inconspicuous way, he chaired (1966-71) an appeal for funds for extensions to the Footscray and District Hospital, directing his charitable impulses towards Melbourne's west, the home of much of his business empire. He established the Lance Reichstein Charitable Foundation in 1970 and in the following year endowed it with 28 000 I.E.L. shares.

Reichstein was a member of the Victoria and Moonee Valley Racing clubs, the Victorian Amateur Turf Club, and the Melbourne Cricket and Victoria Golf clubs. In a civil ceremony on 18 March 1979 at Olinda he married Josephine McGrath, née Garro, a 46-year-old widow. He resigned as chairman of I.E.L. only days before his death. Survived by his wife, and by the daughter of his second marriage, he died on 25 June 1980 at Windsor and was cremated with Anglican rites. The Reichstein foundation was the principal beneficiary of his estate, which was sworn for probate at $5 156 208.

P. Anderson, *Lance Reichstein Remembered* (Melb, 1989); *Herald* (Melb), 8 Mar, 11 Aug 1956, 15 Aug 1967, 28 Nov 1976, 26 June 1980; *Australian*, 19 Aug 1967; *Age* (Melb), 7 Sept 1967, 17 Mar 1970, 26 June 1980, 18 Feb 1989; *Aust Financial Review*, 26 June 1980; *Advertiser* (Adel), 27 June 1980.

MARK RICHMOND

REID, SIR ALEXANDER JAMES (1889-1968), public servant, was born on 12 October 1889 at Glasgow, Scotland, one of five children of David Hay Reid, life-insurance agent, and his wife Jane Boag, née Niven. Alex attended a local Glasgow school and reached Albany, Western Australia, with his widowed mother and brother David in the *Suevic* on 17 April 1909. Employed as a messenger at

the Perth Public Hospital, he joined the De-
partment of Public Works as a clerk in 1911.
Three years later he transferred to the
Friendly Societies section in the Colonial Sec-
retary's Department. At the Congregational
Church, Subiaco, on 17 April 1915 he married
Florence Sarah Jones.

Having duly qualified, Reid was admitted as
an associate (1916) of the Incorporated Institute of Accountants, Victoria. He studied part
time at the University of Western Australia
(B.A., 1924) and retained contact with the university as a tutor (1926-30) for correspondence courses in economics. In 1924 he was
appointed as deputy registrar general. His
authority increased when he became assistant under-treasurer in 1931 and culminated in
his promotion to under-treasurer in 1938, a
position he held until his retirement in 1954.
After the Premier's Department became a sub-
department of Treasury in 1941, he headed
both departments.

Reid was a powerful under-treasurer upon
whose advice Labor and Liberal-Country Party
governments relied during the years of economic recovery, World War II and postwar
development. He played a major role in Commonwealth-State financial relations. Appointed
to provide economic analysis and data on
public finance, he was a member of the committee that prepared the 'Case of the People of
Western Australia' for secession in 1933. That
year, with John Curtin [q.v.13], he drew up
the State's first submission to the new Commonwealth Grants Commission. He was a
careful draftsman of Western Australia's
claims and a persuasive advocate before the
commission. After his retirement he served
on the commission until 1965.

In a small public service Reid's influence
reached far beyond the Treasury. He was
chairman (1935-49) of the Workers' Homes
Board (State Housing Commission from
1946), a member (1938-68) and chairman
(1955-56) of the (Royal) Perth Hospital Board,
and a founding member (1946-68) and chairman (1954-68) of the State Electricity Commission. In addition, he was a board-member
of the Wundowie-based Charcoal Iron & Steel
Industry (1943-67) and of Chamberlain Industries Pty Ltd (1954-56), both government initiatives. Following his retirement, he held a
number of private directorships. Reid's energy,
accessibility, tact, negotiating skills, friendly
manner and wide-ranging personal contacts
made him a most effective committee-man.
His continuing government appointments,
however, occasioned some debate as he grew
older. In 1963 he was invited to be the inaugural chairman of the Metropolitan Water
Board but, when politicians objected because
of his age, declined the post.

As an ex-officio member (from 1944) of the
senate of the University of Western Australia,

Reid was active in university governance; he
oversaw increased State government funding
to the university and was a member (1957)
of the Committee on Australian Universities,
chaired by Sir Keith Murray. As pro-chancellor
(1948-56) and chancellor (1956-68), he was
both a figurehead and a significant force in
university affairs. This involvement flowed
into the field of arts and culture: he became a
director of the Australian Elizabethan Theatre
Trust in 1954, joined the board of Perth's
National Theatre Company in 1956 and
chaired the Festival of Perth committee.

Reid was appointed I.S.O. (1946) and
C.M.G. (1952). In 1958 he was knighted. Survived by his wife, and their son and daughter,
he died on 30 August 1968 at Bethesda Hospital, Claremont, and was cremated. His estate
was sworn for probate at $84 367. The Reid
library at the University of Western Australia
was named after him.

Gazette of Univ WA, 18, no 3, Oct 1968; *West
Australian*, 1 Jan 1952, 20 Sept 1963, 31 Aug 1968,
22 Mar 1969; R. Jamieson, interviews with R. H.
Doig, oral history transcript, 1984-86 (BL).

LENORE LAYMAN

REID, ANDREW THYNE (1901-1964), engineer, businessman and benefactor, was
born on 20 December 1901 at Randwick,
Sydney, eldest of three sons of Scottish-born
parents Andrew Reid, general importer, and
his wife Margaret, née Thyne. Made a partner
in James Hardie & Co. in 1896, Andrew senior
became sole proprietor in 1912 and built the
firm into a large industrial enterprise. In 1920
it was registered as a public company. Among
other building products, the firm manufactured Fibrolite cement sheets.

After attending Sydney Church of England
Grammar School (Shore), Thyne lived at St
Andrew's College, University of Sydney (B.E.,
1924), studied mechanical and electrical engineering, and won a Blue for rowing. He first
worked for a small engineering firm at Sheffield, England. At the Presbyterian Church,
Downing Street, Cambridge, on New Year's
Eve 1926 he married Katharine Mabel, daughter of Professor J. T. Wilson [q.v.12]. Back
home, he joined James Hardie & Co. Ltd in
1927 as an engineer. From 1930 he was one of
its directors.

Thyne and Katharine, who had no children,
lived at Carlingford. Later, he also acquired
a flat in the Astor, Macquarie Street. They
visited Britain in 1932 where he learned to fly.
In the following year he acquired an 'auto-
gyro' (now held by the Powerhouse Museum,
Sydney) in which they flew to remote and virtually inaccessible places. He belonged to the
Institution of Mechanical Engineers, London,

the Royal Sydney Golf and Australian clubs, and the Ski Club of Australia. When his father died in January 1939, Thyne was appointed chairman of James Hardie.

On 19 December that year Reid enlisted in the Australian Imperial Force. Next month he was commissioned lieutenant in the Ordnance Corps. Arriving in the Middle East in December 1940, he was promoted major in March 1941 and took command of the 2nd/1st Field Workshop. He told his officers that 'it is part of my nature never to be satisfied. Anything I have done I have always felt could have been done better. So don't be discouraged if I should ... appear to expect too much from you'. His service included two months at Tobruk, Libya. In September 1942 he returned to Australia as a lieutenant colonel and was attached to the Directorate of Mechanical Maintenance, Army Headquarters, Melbourne.

Transferring to the Reserve of Officers on 5 July 1945, Reid returned to James Hardie as supervising engineer. He and his brother (Sir) John ran the Hardie companies from Sydney and Melbourne respectively. Thyne chaired Hardie Rubber Co. Ltd (from 1948), James Hardie Asbestos Ltd (1953-64) and Hardie Holdings Ltd (1954-64), and was a director of H. C. Sleigh [q.v.11] Ltd (following its takeover of Hardie Rubber Co. Ltd in January 1960). He remained at heart a practical 'hands-on' engineer.

After the war Reid had bought a de Havilland Dragon aeroplane and then a de Havilland Drover. Katharine often navigated for him when they visited the outback; they mostly camped beside the aircraft at night. In the mid-1950s he headed a syndicate to develop the snowfields at Thredbo in the Snowy Mountains. Wearing his prized and 'battered old digger's hat', he repeatedly flew his partners to Cooma to find a suitable site for an alpine village. From 1958 to 1961 he chaired Kosciusko Thredbo Ltd.

Believing 'that only a fool dies a rich man', Reid gave some £1.5 million in the early 1950s to establish a charitable trust in Melbourne. He later set up a similar trust in Sydney. A close friend of Sir Ian Clunies Ross [q.v.13], he was 'passionately' interested in the University of Sydney and a liberal contributor to its faculty of veterinary science. He also donated money to the Commonwealth Scientific and Industrial Research Organization to help finance a radio-telescope at Parkes. Among many other benefactions—large and small—he provided £17 500 to buy premises for the University Boat Club. A councillor (from 1937) of St Andrew's College, Reid had given the college £262 794 in cash or commitments by 1962. Although most of the money was for building, he endowed a special fund that made possible a senior common-room and

supported such activities as Professor J. R. Stewart's [q.v.] excavations in Cyprus. He also helped many individual people 'in trouble, in difficulty, or in need': Rev. Alan Dougan believed that none knew 'the full story of all that he did'.

A man of humility and reticence, Reid was impatient with ceremony and protocol, and shunned publicity. In 1964 he declined to be appointed C.M.G. He lived life to the full, relished fine wine, appreciated good food and cooking, and had a close relationship with the gastronome Sue Du Val. Survived by his wife, he died suddenly of coronary thrombosis on or about 7 December 1964 at the Astor and was cremated. Ray Crooke's portrait (1978) of Reid is held by St Andrew's College. After his death the trusts were renamed the Andrew Thyne Reid Charitable and Thyne Reid Education trusts.

B. Carroll (ed), 'A Very Good Business' (Syd, 1987); R. I. Jack, The Andrew's Book (Syd, 1989); Univ Syd Union, Union Recorder, 1 Apr 1965, p 64; Ski Australia, 6, Apr-May 1965, p 26; Smith's Weekly, 1 Jan 1927; SMH, 10 Dec 1964; Australian, 6 June 2000; Honours, A463, item 1962/6286 (NAA, Canb); A. T. Reid, notebook and papers (AWM); information from Mr J. B. Reid, Univ NSW, Syd, and Mrs F. MacLachlan, Mount Pleasant, SA.

MARTHA RUTLEDGE

REID, ELIZABETH JULIA (1915-1974), Grail worker and journalist, was born on 24 February 1915 at Waverley, Sydney, second of three children of John Francis Reid, journalist, and his wife Annie Catherine, née Phibbs, both born in New South Wales. Sir George Reid [q.v.11] was her great-uncle and she later commented that his generation of Reids included 'an explorer, a parson, a prime minister, and a Poor Clare nun'. Elizabeth was educated at Lourdes Hill convent school, Hawthorne, Brisbane. Influenced by her father's ideas, she wrote letters to local newspapers decrying the injustice of the White Australia policy. She trained (until 1938) as a nurse at Brisbane General Hospital before travelling to Sydney to study with The Grail, an organization for Catholic laywomen who 'wished to play a greater role in the world'.

Accepted as a member of the Grail Nucleus, Reid moved to Melbourne in August 1939. She helped to build up the movement, taught courses in major Australian cities, edited Torchlight—the magazine of the National Catholic Girls' Movement—and instructed leaders of the N.C.G.M.'s Vanguard groups (for girls aged 14 to 18 years). In 1948 she was sent to work in Hong Kong. Her main function was to edit and produce the weekly diocesan newspaper, Sunday Examiner. She also trained a group of student journalists, established a Grail centre to promote the welfare of women and girls, and assisted refugees, particularly Catholics entering Hong Kong from the People's Republic of China. Her experiences strengthened her strong antipathy to communism.

Reid travelled regularly for the *Sunday Examiner*, covering stories in Macao, Taiwan, Korea, Japan, Vietnam, the Philippines, Malaya, Singapore and Indonesia. She visited Australia for Christmas 1955 and reported on Aboriginal missions. Skilled in the use of a camera, she filed photographs and stories with the National Catholic Wire Service in the United States of America, reporting on the exchange of prisoners of war in Korea in 1953, the siege of Dien Bien Phu, Vietnam, in 1954, and the conference of Asian and African countries, held at Bandung, Indonesia, in 1955.

In 1956 Reid moved to New York to take up an assignment with the International Movement for the Fraternal Union of All Races and Peoples, a Catholic aid organization which was consulted by the United Nations. She endeavoured to ensure that a Catholic voice was heard at the U.N. on issues relating to human rights, the family, forced labour, the status of women, and freedom of education. As an accredited correspondent at U.N. headquarters in 1958-66, she continued to be active as a journalist.

From 1960 Reid worked in Africa, teaching journalism and establishing Grail self-help projects for women in Ghana, Tanganyika (Tanzania), Uganda, Botswana and South Africa. At the request of the Catholic bishops of Africa, she provided training for women whose husbands were about to be posted to Western countries as diplomats or were being groomed for civic leadership. By 1966 she was based in New Delhi as executive-secretary of Action for Food Production, an umbrella organization for church- and government-funded assistance projects. She managed a budget that ran to millions of dollars: it was directed towards agricultural projects and training. One of her undertakings was the Grail Mobile Extension Training Unit which instructed villagers in various parts of India. Believing that 'the primary function' of aid was 'development, rather than relief and charity', she described herself as a 'bridge person' who came when she was needed and moved on once local people had been trained to take over.

In her prime Reid was an attractive woman with a broad smile and dark hair plainly styled in a no-nonsense manner. Later in life she became rather plump. Practical and cheerful, she was a committed advocate for many causes. Her autobiography, *I Belong Where I'm Needed* (Westminster, Maryland, U.S.A., 1961), not only gave an account of her life but also invited young Catholic women to join in her enthusiasms.

Although increasingly a citizen of the world, Reid remained in close touch with her family and Grail friends in Australia. Each day she read the Australian news at the High Commission in New Delhi. Writing to her sister Joan in November 1974, she described Prime Minister Gough Whitlam as 'a pain', and the purchase of the painting, 'Blue Poles', for the Australian National Gallery, as wasteful. In December 1974, knowing that she was soon to die of cancer, she visited Goa, the place of enshrinement of St Francis Xavier, to pray for a miracle. When she failed to recover, she asked to be taken to the Tiltenberg, the International Grail Centre, near Haarlem, the Netherlands. She died on 23 December 1974 at The Hague and was buried in the grounds of the Tiltenberg. Archbishop Angelo Fernandez of New Delhi called her 'a great and effective communicator of development, justice and peace'.

S. Kennedy, *Faith and Feminism* (Syd, 1985); *Catholic Weekly* (Syd), 23 Jan 1975; Reid papers and correspondence (The Grail archives, North Syd); information from Mrs J. Dean, Durack, Brisb, Dr A. Healey and Ms M. Merrick, North Syd.

HILARY M. CAREY

REID, ISABELLE BRUCE (1883-1945), veterinary surgeon, was born on 21 December 1883 in Melbourne, youngest of ten children of Robert Joseph Reid [q.v.11], a merchant from Scotland, and his Victorian-born wife Mary Jane, née Clancy. The family owned a large property at Balwyn, bounded on the north by Whitehorse Road and to the south by Mont Albert Road. Growing up in a viticultural, market-gardening and dairying district, Belle developed a passionate interest in animals, particularly horses. She was educated at Genazzano convent school, Kew, where she did well academically, became an accomplished needlewoman and showed potential as a soprano. She wanted to continue to study singing, but her parents considered a career on the stage unsuitable for a young woman of social standing. They did, however, support her decision to enter the Melbourne Veterinary College, Fitzroy, in 1902.

Completing the course in 1906, Reid was one of five final-year students who were examined, and the only one to pass. When she was registered by the Veterinary Board of Victoria on 21 November she was said to be the first formally recognized female veterinary surgeon in the world. She immediately set up practice in a house in Whitehorse Road that had formerly accommodated her family's chauffeur. Driving to her calls by pony and trap, she became a familiar sight around

Balwyn. In 1923 she retired and left the practice in the hands of P. T. Kelynack, husband of her favourite niece Sylvia. The original stables and kennels, and some of her instruments, can be seen at the Balwyn Veterinary Surgery.

In 1911 Reid and her sister Mary ('May') had bought one thousand acres (405 ha) of farmland at Bundoora and named it Blossom Park. Belle moved to the farm in 1925. She engaged Edna Walling [q.v.] to landscape the garden of her home, had stables built to accommodate both her own horses and others on agistment, and supervised the construction of a large dairy. Belle later bought May out. A keen breeder of animals, she imported an Irish cob stallion, Hafron Sensation, which provided the main bloodline of her stud. She also bred stud Jersey cattle: their names all began with Jubilee. As a dog-breeder, she initially kept Pomeranians, but soon turned to Irish wolfhounds. A member of the Royal Agricultural Society of Victoria, she regularly exhibited her cattle, dogs, pigs and harness horses with excellent results. She rode with the Findon Harriers Hunt, took part in show-jumping and played polo, often at Blossom Park.

Late in life Miss Reid still managed the farm, with the help of Sylvia Kelynack. She died of coronary thrombosis on 13 December 1945 at Canterbury and was buried in Box Hill cemetery; her estate was sworn for probate at £101 603. A formidable woman, she only gained limited status in what was then a conservative, male-dominated profession, partly because she retired from practice early. In 1996 her name was included in the National Pioneer Women's Hall of Fame, Alice Springs, Northern Territory.

Sun News-Pictorial, 5 Sept 1924; Roy College of Veterinary Surgeons *and* Veterinary Bd of Vic, records (held by Veterinary Practitioners Bd of Vic); Melb Veterinary College, records (held by Faculty of Veterinary Science, Univ of Melb); information from Dr P. T. and Mrs K. S. Kelynack, Bundoora, Melb, and Mrs J. Taylor, Foster, Vic.

HUGH J. WIRTH

REID, MARY WALKER (1911-1963), grazier and benefactor, was born on 6 November 1911 at Winnipeg, Canada, second of three children of John Geddes, a Scottish-born grain-broker, and his wife Helen Lee, née Tillie, who came from Ireland. Her father served as a captain with the Canadian Expeditionary Force and was killed in action in 1915 at Ypres, Belgium. From early that year Helen and the children lived in London. Like her mother, Mary was educated at Queen's Gate School, South Kensington. She represented England in international fencing matches, including the Championships of Europe, held in Budapest (1933) and Warsaw (1934). At the parish church, Tewin, Hertfordshire, on 31 October 1936 she married George Thyne, youngest brother of Andrew Thyne Reid [q.v.]. George brought his bride to his property, Narrangullen, near Yass, New South Wales, where he and his father had founded (1934) an Aberdeen Angus stud with cattle imported from Scotland.

On 13 May 1940 George was commissioned lieutenant, Australian Imperial Force. He served with the 2nd/17th Battalion in the Middle East and was twice mentioned in dispatches. Captain Reid was killed in action on 14 September 1943 in the advance on Lae, New Guinea. Mary's fourth child was born posthumously. Left a life interest in her husband's estate, she faced the future with fortitude, managing Narrangullen almost single-handed until after the war. She became an accomplished horsewoman and shared her love of the outdoors with her children, taking them riding and camping.

Trading as the Estate of the late G. T. Reid, she developed Narrangullen into one of the foremost studs and regularly visited Scotland to buy stock. Among her many prizes at the Sydney Royal Show, Mary Reid won outright (1953) the Andrew Reid trophy for a sire's progeny with Black Sailor of Broomhall. In 1958 N. Geranium III was senior grand champion female and 'supreme champion Aberdeen Angus exhibit'. That year N. Edensor was grand champion Angus bull at the Melbourne Royal Show. Mrs Reid sat on the panel of Royal Show judges, adjudicated at the Perth and Adelaide shows, and was a member of the State executive of the Angus Society of Australia.

There were few Yass organizations to which Mrs Reid did not give her time, talent and money. She established (1950) and presided over the Yass & District Nursery Kindergarten, helped to re-form (1960) the local Girl Guides' Association, and regularly attended musicales organized by the Yass Music Club. A committee-member of the Yass Pastoral and Agricultural Association, she supported its annual show by competing as a rider and by exhibiting the Narrangullen stud cattle. She was a generous benefactor of the Legacy Club of Canberra and of St Andrew's Presbyterian Church, Forrest. As patron of the local sub-branch of the Returned Servicemen's League of Australia, she gave an annual Christmas party for the war veterans from Linton, Yass.

Between 1956 and 1959 Mrs Reid donated £40 000 to Women's College, University of Sydney, for a new wing which was named after her. An 'active and vital member' of the college council from 1955, she was deeply interested in the welfare and comfort of students. She also contributed funds for research in the university's faculty of veterinary science and towards the establishment of a radio-telescope at Parkes.

'Enthusiastic and energetic', Mary Reid sparkled with fun. She played her piano for hours at night. In Sydney, she maintained a flat in the Astor, Macquarie Street, and belonged to Royal Sydney Golf Club. She died suddenly of heart disease on 9 March 1963 at Narrangullen and was buried with Presbyterian forms in Yass cemetery. Her two sons and two daughters survived her. Keith Henderson's portrait of Mary is held by the family.

C.-L. de Beaumont, *Modern British Fencing* (Lond, 1949); *Pastoral Review*, 15 Mar 1947, p 208, 16 May 1951, p 595, 16 Mar 1953, p 315, 16 Apr 1953, p 439, 16 Mar 1957, p 351, 18 Apr 1958, p 378, 17 Oct 1958, p 1153, 18 Apr 1963, p 359; Women's College, Univ Syd, *Calendar*, 1959, p 11, 1963, p 4; *Yass Tribune*, 11 Mar 1963; information from Mrs F. MacLachlan, Mount Pleasant, SA.

MARTHA RUTLEDGE

REINHOLD, WILLIAM JAMES (1889-1966), army officer and civil engineer, was born on 6 November 1889 at Clayfield, Brisbane, second child of Gustav Theodor Emanuel Reinhold, a draftsman from England, and his Irish-born wife Mary Jane, née Kerlin. Bill was educated at Brisbane Grammar School and—after a short period as a schoolteacher—at the University of Queensland (B.E. Civil, 1916). Selected to join the British Army and serve with the Royal Engineers, he sailed to England and was commissioned on 15 January 1916.

While serving on the Western Front with the 90th Field Company, Reinhold was wounded three times, mentioned in dispatches and awarded the Military Cross. He was promoted temporary lieutenant in February 1917, transferred to the Tank Corps six months later and made acting captain in August 1918. Although he was recommended for a commission in the regular army because of his 'ability, energy and daring', he decided to return to Australia in 1919. On 18 September that year at the Congregational Church, Wharf Street, Brisbane, he married Gladys Isabel Petrie (d.1939); they were to adopt a son (d.1959).

Reinhold worked as an engineer with the Department of Public Lands. He then became supervising engineer for the Main Roads Board, which involved travel by pack-horse to determine where roads would be built through tropical forests in North Queensland. In 1923 he set up as a consultant engineer, operating from his Clayfield home. Next year he was elected a member of the Institution of Engineers, Australia. His personality, diligence and willingness to travel enabled him to collaborate with thirty-seven local authorities in central and southern Queensland. Although he mainly designed and constructed roads and bridges, he also handled industrial and community projects.

Appointed honorary major in the Australian Army Ordnance Corps (Militia) in August 1941, Reinhold was transferred in the following month to the Royal Australian Engineers and appointed commanding engineer, Northern Command. He was called up for full-time duty on 6 October and promoted lieutenant colonel on 12 January 1942. Posted to the 5th Division in March, he joined the Australian Imperial Force on 27 July. In September he was posted to Milne Force (later the 11th Division), Papua, as commanding engineer. For the drive, technical knowledge and leadership he displayed at Milne Bay, he was appointed O.B.E. (1943).

In February 1943 Reinhold was sent to supervise the construction of a 68-mile (109 km) road between Bulldog, Papua, and Wau, New Guinea, a strategically important supply line. About 2000 Australian soldiers and 1500 Papuans laboured in rugged country and frequent heavy rain; most days were torrid, some nights were icy cold; every foot of progress demanded courage, endurance, skill and toil. The road was almost completed by September when General Sir Thomas Blamey [q.v.13] ordered Reinhold to take home leave.

From November 1943 Reinhold served on the staff of the chief engineer, New Guinea Force, Port Moresby. In January 1944 he took command of a works unit in the Wau area and supervised the construction of a road to Labu. He returned to Australia in May and was transferred to the Reserve of Officers on 18 November on medical grounds. After the war his accounts of his road-building projects were published as *The Bulldog-Wau Road* (Brisbane, 1946) and *The Wau-Labu Road* (Port Moresby, 1977).

At St John's Anglican Cathedral, Brisbane, on 2 January 1946 Reinhold married Jean Elaine Barlow, a 42-year-old music teacher. His consulting business continued to thrive. A tallish man, with 'flint-like blue eyes', he belonged to Legacy, and was honorary consultant to Brisbane Grammar and Brisbane Girls' Grammar schools (which his nephews and nieces attended, with his encouragement and financial support). In 1964 he retired. He had been a keen cricketer in his youth; in later life he played golf and went boating on Moreton Bay. His other interests included music, opera, theatre and literature. Survived by his wife, he died on 27 August 1966 at the Repatriation General Hospital, Greenslopes, and was cremated with Anglican rites.

D. McCarthy, *South-West Pacific Area—First Year* (Canb, 1959); R. McNicoll, *The Royal Australian*

Engineers 1919 to 1945 (Canb, 1982); R. L. Whitmore (ed), *Eminent Queensland Engineers* (Brisb, 1984); Reinhold papers (FRYER L).

P. J. GREVILLE

REMBERT, EDWARD HENRY (1902-1966), architect, was born on 12 April 1902 at Hurstville, Sydney, youngest of thirteen children of native-born parents Charles Rembert (d.1902), blacksmith, and his wife Susannah Jane, née Burrell. Harry was raised by his mother and elder sisters, and sent to the local public school. While apprenticed to the architect Thomas J. Darling, he attended Sydney Technical College. On 30 December 1924 he was registered as an architect. After he gained experience working for Henry White [q.v.12], the flamboyant designer of theatres, he joined the Department of Public Works on 3 August 1926. He was finally confirmed in the post of architect in 1942.

Encouraged by Cobden Parkes [q.v.15], the government architect, Rembert designed numerous public buildings—schools, hospitals, court-houses, police stations and technical colleges, mostly during the 1930s and 1940s. In style, his designs of this period were influenced by the Dutch architect Willem Dudok. Of these works, perhaps the most outstanding were the Hoskins block (1937-38) at Sydney Technical College, and major buildings (1934-38) at Newcastle Technical College, including his masterpiece, the H. G. Darling [q.v.8] Engineering Building, in which Dudokian forms were suffused by Rembert's own idiosyncratic spirit.

Rembert designed several private houses for family and friends, but none of them approached the quality of his own remarkable mountain home at Wentworth Falls in the Blue Mountains, where he lived as a bachelor with his elder brother Oscar from 1935. In this most modest dwelling he devised an inventive plan and used the simplest of materials —brick and rough timber-boarded walls— which fitted quietly into a bushland setting. Several decades later the house was seen as inspiring some of the leading practitioners of the 'Sydney School' style of architecture.

On 20 July 1947 Rembert was appointed senior designing architect. Promoted assistant government architect in March 1960, he had responsibility for the entire architectural design output of a very large office. He no longer had the time to design buildings himself, but he played an important role (1957-64) on the Height of Buildings Advisory Committee. More importantly, he acted as guide and mentor to a new generation of young architects, who had joined the government architect's office at a time when it faced the exciting task of designing the universities,

schools, colleges and numerous public buildings needed to serve the needs of an increasing population. The quality of architecture emanating from the office gained it an enviable reputation. Rembert's influence, like his personality, was gentle and discreet, yet pervasive and persuasive.

In his younger days Harry Rembert had been a talented cricketer, playing first grade for St George, (Sir) Donald Bradman's club, and later becoming a champion club golfer. Having suffered from tuberculosis in his twenties, he was never robust in health, and was forced to retire due to bronchial and heart problems in 1965. He died of coronary thrombosis on 12 September 1966 at Katoomba and was cremated with Anglican rites.

G. P. Webber, *E. H. Rembert* (Syd, 1982), and for bib.

PETER WEBBER

REMINGTON, GEOFFREY COCHRANE (1897-1968), lawyer and public benefactor, was born on 27 November 1897 at Summer Hill, Sydney, third child of John Cochrane Remington, a life-insurance manager from Ireland, and his native-born wife Constance Mabel, née Dickinson. Geoffrey was educated at Tudor House, Moss Vale, The Armidale School and Sydney Church of England Grammar School (Shore). He passed the Solicitors' Admission Board examinations and was admitted as a solicitor of the Supreme Court of New South Wales on 16 March 1923. At St Stephen's Presbyterian Church, Sydney, on 7 May 1930 he married Joan Daly; they were to have a son and a daughter.

By 1933 he had founded the firm, Remington & Co., and was well established as a solicitor in the city. A council-member and president (1937-39) of the New South Wales Constitutional Association, he wrote letters, articles and book reviews on a range of topics, including reform of the Legislative Council, and was a founder (1935) and chairman (1947-68) of the New South Wales group of the (Royal) Institute of Public Administration. His newspaper articles advocated the creation of 'an economic general staff' at Federal government level. He was also interested in the Australian Institute of Political Science. In 1935 he sought help from Frank Tate [q.v.12] to gain support for the A.I.P.S. from the Carnegie Corporation of New York. Tate suggested that he should study the report by Ralph Munn and Ernest Pitt [q.v.11] on the libraries of Australia. Remington was 'shocked at what it had to say and fascinated by the way it said it'.

With expert advice and help from John Metcalfe, deputy principal librarian of the Public Library of New South Wales, Remington headed the Free Library Movement. As a result of their energetic campaign, which included visits and speeches to local councils and shires throughout the State, he was appointed (1937) to the Libraries Advisory Committee, which drafted a bill. The Library Act, passed in 1939, provided for State government subsidies to local councils to set up free public library services; it also instituted the Library Board of New South Wales, on which Remington served as deputy-chairman from its establishment in 1944 until 1968. He was a trustee (president 1967) of the Public Library and a member of its Mitchell [q.v.5] Library committee, a member of the Australian Advisory Council on Bibliographical Services and of the Industrial Fund for the Advancement of Scientific Education in Schools, and sometime treasurer of the Library Association of Australia.

During World War II Remington had been based in Melbourne as assistant-director (1941-42), labour resources division, Department of War Organization of Industry, and in Brisbane and Melbourne as assistant-director (1942-43), personnel, of the Allied Works Council. In carrying out his responsibility to obtain manpower for essential works he was not intimidated by threats from employers, trade-union officials, workers, politicians or the military. Having served as liaison officer between the department and the United Nations Relief and Rehabilitation Administration, he was chief administrative officer and acting-director in the South-West Pacific for U.N.R.R.A. in 1945-46.

After helping to reactivate the F.L.M. in 1944 to persuade local councils to implement the Library Act, Remington addressed meetings designed to set up similar movements in Victoria, Queensland and Tasmania. He chaired (from 1945) the executive of the New South Wales Film Council, which acquired and circulated documentary and educational films; and he presided (1948-49) over the Rotary Club of Sydney.

From 1953 Remington worked through Rotary for the establishment of an administrative staff college. The Australian Administrative Staff College was incorporated in 1955, with memorandum and articles prepared by him: Essington Lewis [q.v.10] chaired the company and Remington the college's executive-committee. He canvassed large firms to raise funds, and was delighted when Sir Douglas Copland [q.v.13] was appointed principal of the college. The A.A.S.C. opened at Mount Eliza, Victoria, in 1957. Remington's relationship with Copland degenerated almost from their meeting, and certainly from the point at which he told Copland that academic freedom was not part of the job. Their correspondence revealed the gulf between their views and the anger engendered in both of them.

Except for his wartime absences, Remington managed his busy and successful law practice. In 1955 he referred to his 'law work' as 'often tedious but a necessity'. His business skills led to his appointment to the boards of a number of leading firms, especially in the 1950s and 1960s: he was chairman of Rolls Royce of Australia Pty Ltd and Crane Australia Pty Ltd, and a director of W.R. Carpenter [q.v.7] Holdings Ltd, Standard Telephones & Cables Pty Ltd and the Scottish Australian Co. Ltd.

In reminiscing, Remington described himself as 'a busy man' and—exaggeratedly—as 'a relatively uneducated man'. Widely read, he wrote for journals and newspapers, spoke effectively in public and corresponded widely with influential people, including Beatrice and Sidney Webb whose books he had read and reviewed. He had access to prime ministers and premiers. The people he admired encompassed (Sir) William McKell, Labor premier of New South Wales and governor-general, Paddy Hill, head of the Barrier Industrial Council, (Sir) Robert Menzies [q.v.15] and Lewis. He made extensive use of telephones and cables as he developed and cultivated an impressive network of allies. A friend and confidant to men as diverse as Hartley Grattan and Herbert Vere Evatt [qq.v.14], he was indefatigable in congratulating those who achieved public recognition, and both astute and generous in his praise of those who were not in a position to do so, such as his office staff.

When Remington was appointed C.M.G. in 1960, Sir Norman Nock acknowledged his 'remarkable capacity to get things done'. Notably well dressed and something of a bon viveur, Remington entertained friends and contacts at his clubs—the Union Club, the Royal Sydney Yacht Squadron, the Royal Automobile Club of Australia, and the Commonwealth Club, Canberra. He died of a coronary occlusion on 20 January 1968 at his Woollahra home and was cremated with Anglican rites. His wife and their daughter survived him.

B. and H. Carey, *Educating the Guardians* (Syd, 1985); *Aust Lib J*, 17, no 2, 1968, p 57; *Public Administration* (Syd), 27, Sept 1968, p 195; *SMH*, 12 June 1936, 19 Feb 1943, 2 Feb, 11 June 1960, 23 Jan 1968; *Smith's Weekly* (Syd), 24 Jan 1942, 23 June 1945; *Bulletin*, 23 Dec 1959, p 11; D.J. Jones, William Herbert Ifould and the Development of Library Services in New South Wales, 1912-1942 (Ph.D. thesis, Univ NSW, 1993); Remington papers *and* Doc 1724 (ML); family information.

CARMEL MAGUIRE

RENNIE, BEATRICE LILIAS (1893-1971), headmistress, was born on 21 September 1893 at Belmont, Dubbo, New South Wales, sixth of eight children of native-born parents Charles Edward Rennie, a draftsman with the Department of Lands, and his wife Lilias, née Millar. The family moved to Chatswood, Sydney, and later to Mosman. Beatrice enjoyed outdoor activities, such as boating, fishing, swimming and walking. Educated at Woodstock, North Sydney, she eventually convinced her father to allow her to attend the University of Sydney (B.A., 1916).

In 1918 she became first assistant-mistress at the Glennie [q.v.4] Memorial School, Toowoomba, Queensland; its principal was Miss Grace Lawrance. Miss Rennie taught history, geology and physical culture, and also assisted in the library and with the photography club and school magazine. Her kindly humour and love of scholarship made a deep impression on her students. That she was described as 'tall' was due as much to her imposing presence as to her height.

Misses Lawrance and Rennie travelled to England and the Continent in 1921 and visited many of the best girls' schools. Both women resigned from the Glennie in 1925 with the intention of founding a school in Sydney. They chose a large, old house at 47 Mandolong Road, Mosman, where Queenwood was officially opened on 22 September. Their entrepreneurial courage was remarkable since neither enjoyed perfect health.

The name 'Queenwood' was chosen partly after the school which Miss Lawrance's mother had founded in England and partly because of Miss Rennie's regard for John Ruskin's book, *Sesame and Lilies* (1865), in which he described 'queenliness'—dignity, courtesy and service—as key aims of a girl's education. She observed that 'we are all daughters of the King of Heaven' and described the school motto, *Per aspera ad astra*, as providing fine ideas, high standards and a lasting strength of purpose.

By 1926 Queenwood was a registered secondary school. Three years later Miss Rennie was teaching, running the school and caring for her ailing co-principal. In 1932 a combination of the Depression, Lawrance's death in November, and Rennie's successive illnesses meant that Miss Violet Maude Medway (who had joined the staff in 1929) often assisted in managing the school. The two women became co-principals in 1942. Queenwood prospered despite the Depression and World War II. By 1950 Rennie was president of the State branch of the Headmistresses' Association of Australia. She and Medway bought a holiday cottage near the golf course at Leura where Rennie walked on the links with their cat, Ting, who lived to the age of 21.

Miss Rennie continued teaching English, geology, history, zoology and Scripture, though in later years she no longer took the boarders for an early morning swim at Bal-

moral. The school did well academically. In 1962 Rennie retired as co-principal, but the school remained her home; she worked in the library and helped students, as far as her health permitted. In 1966 the school became a non-profit private company, Queenwood School for Girls Ltd. Miss Rennie suffered from chronic nephritis for many years. She died on 4 September 1971 at Mosman and was cremated with Presbyterian forms.

C. Henderson, *The Glennie, a Work of Faith* (Syd, 1983); V. M. Medway, *Queenwood, the First Sixty Years 1925-1985* (Syd, 1986); *Queenwood Gazette*, 1930, 1936-37, 1939; Queenwood School for Girls archives, Mosman, Syd.   JILL CURNOW

REPIN, IVAN DMITRIEVITCH (1888-1949), coffee-shop proprietor and coffee importer, was born on 5 January 1888 in Novgorod province, Russia, son of Dmitri Ivanovitch Repin, a trader on the River Sheksna, and his wife Maria, née Pavlovna. Ivan studied engineering at the Mining Institute, St Petersburg. In that city on 21 April 1913 he married Alexandra Michaelovna Hrisonopolou, who came from the Crimea; they were to have two sons and two daughters. He was working in the Don basin in the Ukraine when the 1917 revolution broke out; he fled to the Urals, and then to Vladivostok.

Sailing from Shanghai with his wife, two daughters and brother Peter, Repin reached Sydney on 12 October 1925 in the *Tango Maru*. Life was not easy: he worked as a motor driver and later ran his own single bus line. He opened refreshment rooms at 152 King Street in September 1930 and was naturalized on 11 December that year. Repin's Coffee and Tea shops followed in quick succession—by 1934 there were two shops in both King and Pitt streets, and another in Market Street. In 1937 he moved one shop from Pitt Street to George Street and added Repin's Quality Inn at 108 King Street. Douglas Annand [q.v.13] painted a mural in Repin's Elite Lounge Restaurant, 175 Pitt Street (opened 1942).

Many migrants from Europe rejoiced in a real cup of coffee instead of the weak, milky concoction that passed for one in Sydney. During the Depression employers who could no longer afford rented premises began to meet their staff at Repin's in Pitt Street to read the mail they had collected from the General Post Office. Repin's became an important part of the commercial fabric of the city where newcomers began their enterprises and made friends.

Repin visited the United States of America in 1935-36 and 1938-39 to learn about coffee and improve his blends. During World War II visiting American servicemen patronized his shops. In the late 1940s customers 'sat cramped in cubicles with heavy high dark wooden panels separating each table', talking over good coffee or pots of tea, with refreshments such as waffles and raisin toast. The King Street shop 'had a touch of Europe about it largely because it was frequented by European-style, coffee-loving intellectuals', such as George Munster, Eugene Kamenka and George Molnar. Repin bought a coffee-roaster in 1948, began roasting coffee in his shop windows and sold freshly ground beans over the counter.

In time Repin acquired houses at Bellevue Hill (where he lived), Lane Cove, Palm Beach (two) and Paddington. He enjoyed photography and boating. Survived by his wife, daughters and younger son, he died of a cerebral haemorrhage on 20 June 1949 in the Scottish Hospital, Paddington, and was buried in Botany cemetery with Russian Orthodox rites.

Repin's coffee shops had brought to predominantly tea-drinking Sydney a little of the sophistication that characterized the city of St Petersburg in Tsarist Russia. They were the antipodean counterpart of the Russian Tea Room in coffee-drinking New York and the precursors of Australia's Italian espresso-bars. Decades after Repin's death former customers fondly remembered his shops.

B. Brown, *Coffee with Roses* (Syd, 1983); A. Coombs, *Sex and Anarchy* (Melb, 1996); *SMH*, 21 June 1949; naturalization file, A659, item 1943/1/3554 (NAA, Canb); deceased estates, I. Repin, 20/4500 (NSWA); information from, and cuttings held by, Mr G. D. Repin, Clareville Beach, Syd.

IAN J. BERSTEN

REVELL, RAYMOND STEPHEN HENRY (1911-1968), speedcar driver, was born on 9 March 1911 at Newtown, Sydney, son of Australian-born parents Percy Raymond Revell, water-bag maker, and his wife Edith Hilda, née Saxon. Educated at Bexley Public and Kogarah Boys' Intermediate High schools, Ray worked as a motor mechanic. At St Clement's Anglican Church, Marrickville, on 25 March 1937 he married Margaret Gordon Nicol, a laundress; they were to have two children before she divorced him in 1948.

Although Revell had shown promise as a sprinter and Rugby League footballer, he turned to speedcar racing in the mid-1930s. Gaining prominence in the sport during the years of World War II, he played an important part in its revival once peace had been restored. He competed at the Sydney Showground speedway against such stars as (Sir) John (Jack) Brabham, and Frank ('Satan') Brewer who had raced extensively in the United States of America. At a time when many drivers favoured air-cooled, twin-cylinder motorcycle engines to propel their diminutive dirt-track racers, Revell was open to new ideas. In 1946 he experimented with jet propulsion to assist his conventional engine. With a brace of rockets (mounted on either side behind the cockpit) generating extravagant plumes of smoke, his car proved a spectacular drawcard for promoters in Sydney and Brisbane. Revell won the Australian championship in 1947 and the world title in 1948 (without the assistance of rockets).

In 1948 Revell travelled to the United States and raced on the West Coast with some success. He became the first Australian resident to own and import an Offenhauser vehicle. Thus equipped, he won four consecutive national speedway championships in 1950-53, and many New South Wales and Queensland titles. By 1957 he had been awarded a hundred trophies. He once made £160 in a night of racing. Less precise than Brabham, who deferred to his rival's experience and superior vehicle, he was the leading speedcar driver of the period, possessing quick reflexes and the ability to sense danger and avoid collisions. Despite suffering a serious injury in a racing accident in 1945, he acquired a considerable reputation for safe driving, unusual in a 'harum-scarum' sport.

On 24 December 1949 at Wesley Chapel, Sydney, Revell married with Methodist forms Violet Nancy Young, a clerk; she was a widow, and sister of his fellow racing-driver Andy McGavin. Revell dabbled in stock-car racing. He also entered his distinctive, blue-and-white Offenhauser in road-races at Mount Druitt and Bathurst; the car's two-speed gearbox and tiny wheels, while suitable for the speedway, proved serious liabilities in its three appearances at Bathurst. In October 1956 Revell raced a Cooper-MG at that circuit. His fame boosted his motorcar repair business, which was finally based at Woolloomooloo, Sydney.

Red haired and freckled, Revell belonged to a distinguished motor-racing family. His younger brother Aubrey was a leading competitor in Formula Vee in the 1960s; Ray's son Howard was a first-rate speedcar driver; Aub's sons Neil and Phillip excelled in open-wheeler racing. Ray Revell died of cirrhosis of the liver on 18 November 1968 in Sydney Hospital and was cremated with Anglican rites. His wife survived him, as did the son and daughter of his first marriage.

J. Medley, *Bathurst: Cradle of Australian Motor Racing* (Syd, 1997); *Sports Car World*, Oct 1959, p 30; *Aust Speedway News*, no 59, 1974?, p 18; *Racing Car News*, Feb 1980, p 54; *SMH*, 15 Feb 1946, 17 Nov 1948, 16 Apr 1950, 15 Apr 1951; *Sun* (Syd), 3 Oct 1956, 22 Mar 1957, 19 Nov 1968; information from Mr G. Howard, Pymble, Syd, and Mr H. Revell, Brisb.

ANDREW MOORE

REYE, RALPH DOUGLAS KENNETH (1912-1977), pathologist, was born on 5 April 1912 at Townsville, Queensland, youngest of nine children of Carl Albert Hermann Reye, a fruit merchant from Württemberg, and his wife Mabel Mary, née Youngson, who was born in New South Wales. The frequent mispronunciation of Douglas's surname drew his response, 'It rhymes with "eye"'. After attending Townsville Grammar School, he entered St Paul's College, University of Sydney (M.B., B.S., 1937; M.D., 1945), where he 'passed an unruffled and aloof six years'. He rowed in St Paul's challenge VIII, played an occasional game of tennis and owned a new motorcar. Tall, slim and sensitive, he was described as a 'bronzed Apollo of the Barrier Reef', as 'Teutonic' looking, and as 'the aesthete, the epicure, the connoisseur'.

In 1939 Reye joined the pathology department of the Royal Alexandra Hospital for Children; he remained at that institution for the rest of his working life. During World War II he tried to obtain a commission in the Australian Army Medical Corps. Because of a shortage of pathologists in civilian practice, his application proved unsuccessful, but he was appointed honorary captain, Reserve of Officers, in March 1941. When Frank Tidswell, the hospital's director of pathology, died that year, Reye was made acting-director; he was to be confirmed in the post in 1946.

On 3 January 1942 in the chapel of his old college he married with Anglican rites Corrie Saunders (d.1990), a fellow medical practitioner who became director of the Spastic Centre, Mosman, and a notable figure in the treatment and rehabilitation of children with cerebral palsy. Reye wrote a thesis entitled, 'Histiocytic granulomatosis of infants: a comparison of certain ill-defined reticuloendothelial hyperplasias, based on the study of four cases', for his M.D. He also lectured (part time) in pathology at the university.

Reye's publications were comparatively few, but he contributed more than thirty papers to local and international journals, among them the *Archives of Pathology*, the *Journal of Pathology and Bacteriology*, and the *Lancet*. Although he preferred scientific terminology to popular names and eponyms, his own name was given to two medical conditions: the malignant tumours of childhood which he described in 1956 and 1965 were called Reyeoma I and Reyeoma II. With Graeme Morgan and Jim Baral, he published a paper in the *Lancet* (1963) on what was later known as the Reye syndrome (encephalopathy with fatty degeneration of the viscera). In 1966 he, Margaret Menser (later Burgess) and David Dorman described renal artery stenosis in the rubella syndrome —the first time that it had been recognized.

Under Reye's direction, the hospital's pathology department expanded steadily. A micro-biologist, biochemist, virologist, histopathologist, bacteriologist and two haematologists joined the staff, and a cytogenetics laboratory was established. The director's meticulous attention to detail ensured that requests for equipment were usually approved by the hospital administration without question. Initially responsible for all laboratory work, Reye later confined himself to histopathology. In 1965 he was elected a fellow of the Royal Australasian College of Physicians.

Colleagues found Reye shy and retiring, but ready to give advice to those who sought his help. That he kept the door to his office closed created a barrier for many of the hospital's junior staff. A number of registrars and residents lost the benefit of his expertise in paediatrics, 'not knowing how keen he was to share his experiences with them'. To those who knew him well, he was 'a delightful friend with his own brand of whimsical humour'.

Reye enjoyed reading, art, 'classic' motorcars, and his garden of subtropical trees and plants which overlooked the Lane Cove River at Linley Point. Less than twenty-four hours after he retired from the R.A.H.C. he died of a ruptured abdominal aortic aneurysm on 16 July 1977 at Royal North Shore Hospital and was cremated. His wife and their daughter survived him.

Univ Syd Medical Soc, *Senior Year Book* (Syd, 1936); D. G. Hamilton, *Hand in Hand* (Syd, 1979); J. C. Wiseman and R. J. Mulhearn (eds), *Roll of the Royal Australasian College of Physicians*, 2, 1976-90 (Syd, 1994); *Aust Paediatric J*, 14, 1978, p 48; *Lancet*, 14 Jan 1978, p 111; Roy A'sian College of Physicians Archives (Syd); St Paul's College archives, Univ Syd; information from Miss M. O'Halloran, Cronulla, Dr P. Grattan-Smith, Hunters Hill, Dr J. Yu, Mosman, Syd, and the late Dr D. G. Hamilton and Dr A. W. Middleton.   BRENDA HEAGNEY
                        G. N. B. STOREY

RHODES, IAN DESMOND LAURIE (1912-1967), naval officer, was born on 19 August 1912 at Ongaonga, near Waipawa, New Zealand, younger son of Albert Victor Laurie-Rhodes, a sheep-farmer from Victoria, and his New Zealand-born wife Agnes, née McKay. In 1920 the family settled in Victoria. Ian was educated at Geelong Church of England Grammar School where he did well in sport, especially Australian Rules football. He turned to farming before working as a salesman. On 1 April 1939 at Christ Church, South Yarra, he married with Anglican rites June Phillips Allan, a dress designer; they were to have one child before being divorced on 7 November 1947.

Using the surname Rhodes, he attempted to enlist in the army, navy and air force on the outbreak of World War II, but was rejected because of a stomach ulcer. A sympathetic medical examiner cleared him on 17 September 1940 to enter the Royal Australian Naval Volunteer Reserve as an ordinary seaman under the British Admiralty's yachtsmen scheme. Immediately posted to Britain for further training, he joined the destroyer H.M.S. *Kashmir* on 1 April 1941 and in the following month took part in the Royal Navy's attempt to prevent a German seaborne landing on Crete.

On 23 May *Kashmir* came under air-attack while returning to Egypt to refuel. Hit amidships by a bomb, she broke in two and began to sink rapidly. When a German bomber machine-gunned both the rear section of the ship and members of her crew who were struggling in the sea, Rhodes left the port Oerlikon gun (on which he was the gunlayer) as the water rose around it and climbed to the nearby starboard gun. Turning this weapon against the attacking aeroplane, he shot it down in flames. Rhodes was taken to Alexandria in H.M.S. *Kipling*, his only possessions a pair of shorts and a borrowed cap. He won the Conspicuous Gallantry Medal, the highest decoration—next to the Victoria Cross—which could be awarded to naval ratings. No other Australian sailor received this decoration in World War I or II.

Rhodes was commissioned on 22 January 1942 and promoted provisional lieutenant in August. Joining the cruiser H.M.S. *Sheffield* on 10 April, he served in the Atlantic and Arctic oceans, escorting convoys *en route* to Russia. In March 1943 he was transferred to the cruiser H.M.A.S. *Shropshire* which was then being commissioned in England. He remained with that ship until July 1944, winning favourable regard as a 'keen and capable' officer, 'well above average'. Back with the R.N., he served in H.M.S. *Mount Stewart* and on shore in Colombo. By the end of the war he was performing shore duties in Port Moresby.

Demobilized on 26 April 1946, Rhodes became a farmer at Labertouche, Victoria. On 27 November 1947 at the Collins Street Independent Church, Melbourne, he married with Congregational forms Patricia May Worboys, née Huxtable, a divorcee. He joined the United Linen Co. Pty Ltd, importers and wholesalers of Irish manchester, and became a director. Survived by his wife, and by the son of his first marriage, he died of cirrhosis of the liver on 3 January 1967 in Fairfield Hospital and was cremated.

Navy (Syd), Feb 1948, p 32; *J of Aust Naval Inst*, Feb 1988, p 43; *SMH*, 8 Oct 1943.

MIKE FOGARTY

RICE, PERSIA; *see* CAMPBELL

RICHARDS, HARRY (1903-1971), soldier and labourer, was born on 24 December 1903 at Normanville, South Australia, son of Christian William Theodor Richards, farmer, and his wife Edith Maud May, née Treloar. Nothing is known of Harry's education. In 1926 he joined the South Australian police force and was stationed in Adelaide. Five ft 11 ins (180 cm) tall, he had brown eyes, brown hair and a solid build. At the Methodist Church, Edwardstown, on 4 April 1927 he married Elsie Offen, née Smith, a widow; he was to divorce her in 1932. Unemployed and in debt, he lived with his brother during the Depression. On 14 March 1933 at the office of the registrar-general, Adelaide, he married Ada May Mitchell. By then he was a labourer, but was often out of work. He moved to Broken Hill, New South Wales, in 1937 and to Perth in 1938, looking for jobs.

Lowering his age by five years, Richards enlisted in the Australian Imperial Force on 26 March 1940. In the following month he sailed for the Middle East with the 2nd/11th Battalion. After fighting in Greece (April 1941), the 2nd/11th retreated to Crete. The Germans invaded the island on 20 May. Nine days later Richards took part in the withdrawal across the mountains to the beach at Sfakia, all the while half-carrying a hospital patient. Given the option of being evacuated with the patient, he refused, saying that he would 'go back and get someone else who could not walk'.

When orders were issued on 1 June for the remaining allied forces on Crete to surrender, Richards took measures to escape. He found and concealed an abandoned naval barge with about 80 gallons (364 litres) of petrol and decided to take sixty-two men to North Africa, after calling at Gávdhos Island for supplies. They sailed at 9.20 that night. Before dawn next day the vessel—which Richards named the M.V. *Leaving*—ran aground on Gávdhos. Because fuel and food were short, Richards called for volunteers to remain on the island. Ten men did so. The voyage resumed at dusk. When the petrol ran out, Richards rigged a sail of blankets which helped the barge to move at 'a fair speed'. On the 9th the *Leaving* was beached near Sidi Barrani, Egypt. A British Army unit gave the party food and shelter. Richards's care for the men had been 'beyond description' and his exercise of command 'masterly'. In January 1942 he was awarded the Distinguished Conduct Medal.

Richards sailed for Perth in September and was transferred to the South Australian Lines of Communication Area in March 1943. Discharged from the army on medical grounds on 20 November 1944, he did not return to his wife but moved to Whyalla and found a job in the shipyard. His wife petitioned for a divorce, which was granted on 27 March 1946. On

21 July 1947 at the office of the principal registrar, Adelaide, he married Caroline Mann, née Franks, a 54-year-old divorcee from the United States of America. He worked as a barman in her wine-saloon. On 25 September 1951 they were divorced. Richards was employed as a labourer until he reached retiring age. He died of cardio-respiratory disease on 16 May 1971 in Adelaide and was buried in Centennial Park cemetery; the son of his first marriage and the two sons of his second survived him.

G. Long, *Greece, Crete and Syria* (Canb, 1953); AWM 52, item 8/3/11, AWM 88, item AMF 15/R, 3DRL, 7974 (AWM); information from Mrs F. Nache, Kensington Gardens, Adel.   PETER CHARLTON

RICHARDS, JACK CHRISTIAN (1911-1969), engineer, was born on 9 December 1911 at Auchenflower, Brisbane, elder child of Australian-born parents Henry Caselli Richards [q.v.11], university lecturer, and his wife Grace, née Christian. Jack was educated at Brisbane and Melbourne Church of England Grammar schools, and at the University of Queensland (B.E., 1934). A Rhodes scholar, he studied engineering science at Magdalen College, Oxford (B.A., 1936), and ferrous metallurgy at the Technische Hochschule, Berlin (1936-37). The Institution of Civil Engineers, London, awarded him a Telford premium (1936-37) for a paper on structural design. He visited steel-making plants in Britain, Germany and the United States of America before returning to Australia.

On 27 April 1938 Richards joined the Broken Hill Proprietary Co. Ltd as a special (technical) cadet attached to the company's steelworks at Newcastle, New South Wales. At St John's Anglican Cathedral, Brisbane, on 15 April 1939 he married Olivera ('Vebe') Graham Gardner, a schoolteacher. When he nominated for associate-membership (1941) of the Australasian Institute of Mining and Metallurgy, Essington Lewis [q.v.10] testified to his 'probity and personality'; Richards became the A.I.M.M.'s representative for Newcastle and was admitted as a full member of the institute in 1952.

In 1940 Richards had been appointed assistant to (Sir) Ian McLennan, executive-officer and later production superintendent at the steelworks. In addition to his other duties, he gained experience in the field of ferro-alloys. B.H.P. had been unsuccessful in obtaining information on how to manufacture tungsten carbide, a strategic material important to the war effort. Under Richards's direction the Newcastle steelworks launched (December 1940) a research programme to develop tungsten carbide for the tips of steel-cutting tools.

Within a year large numbers of tool tips had been made and used to produce shell cases. In 1943 Richards was promoted production superintendent.

As his company's representative, Richards joined the Australian Scientific and Technical Mission to Germany in 1946; its members examined and collated data of value to Australian industry. Back at Newcastle in mid-year, he was made assistant-manager of the steelworks. On 10 August 1951 he was appointed assistant general manager of B.H.P. at head office, Melbourne. Eight years later he rose to general manager, development and shipbuilding. He upgraded B.H.P.'s shipyard at Whyalla, South Australia, and, when the company decided to explore for oil and natural gas, co-ordinated investigations into the production of offshore drilling platforms. On McLennan's appointment as general manager of B.H.P. in 1967, he made Richards his executive-assistant, but directed him to retain responsibility for oil and natural gas operations in the Gippsland Basin.

Richards was a director (1952-59) of the Lysaght Durham Chemical Co. Pty Ltd, chairman (from March 1967) of Koppers Australia Pty Ltd and a board-member (from January 1968) of the Wiltshire File Co. Pty Ltd. In 1951 he and his wife had joined the University Ski Club. They brought to it enthusiasm and energy. Jack's craftsmanship was seen in the French-polished interiors of the club's lodges at Mount Buller and Mount Hotham. He managed the Hotham lodge in 1962-67. Another of his interests was breeding Aberdeen Angus cattle on his property at Romsey.

A 'sterling character' who always acted with 'absolute fairness', Richards served (1955-69) on the council of Trinity College, University of Melbourne, and was a member (1957) of Sir Keith Murray's committee on Australian universities. He was killed on 19 February 1969 when the motorcar in which he was a passenger overturned at Ruby, near Leongatha. Survived by his wife, and their daughter and three sons, he was cremated.

L. Sheridan, *University Ski Club, 1929-1979* (Melb, 1988); *BHP Review*, Dec 1942, p 2, Mar 1944, p 5, Mar 1946, p 6, June 1947, p 6, June 1951, p 4, Sept 1951, p 8, June 1957, p 22, Autumn 1969, p 25; *Herald* (Melb), 19 Feb 1969; *Age* (Melb), 20 Feb 1969; Trinity College, Univ Melb, *Newsletter*, July 1969; A'sian Inst of Mining and Metallurgy, member records (Clunies Ross House, Parkville, Melb); Richards papers, 1945-50, M085 *and* executive biography files, 6E-1 (BHP Co Ltd Archives, Fishermans Bend, Melb).   HELEN SMITH

RICHARDSON, ARTHUR JOHN (1888-1973), cricketer, was born on 24 July 1888 at Sevenhill, South Australia, son of Irish-born parents Nathaniel Richardson, farmer, and his wife Alice, née Temperly. Arthur played cricket at Sevenhill Public School and then in the Stanley Association. At the age of 17 he made 239, 142 and 150, each not out, in successive months. He batted powerfully—a correspondent recalled no other hit clearing the Clare butter factory—and often opened the bowling. On 18 April 1914 he married with Methodist forms Elsie Maude Trestrail in a private house at St Peters, Adelaide. By this stage he was employed as a water-meter tester in Adelaide.

After interstate cricket resumed in December 1918, Richardson played for South Australia. Despite a forceful 111 against the Marylebone Cricket Club team in 1920 in Adelaide, he was not included in the Australian squad for the 1921 tour of England. In matches against an M.C.C. side in 1922-23 he made 150 in 144 minutes and a hurricane 280, including a century before lunch. His partnerships with V. Y. Richardson [q.v.11] (no relation) were features of Sheffield Shield matches. Tall and bespectacled, with a 'two-eyed', upright stance, 'Roscoe', as he was known, had a full range of strokes; he lofted the ball judiciously and drove 'with the force of a kicking mule'. He bowled accurate, flighted off-breaks, but was slow in the field. A right-handed batsman and bowler, he could also throw and bowl with his left hand. In December 1924 he played in his first Test (against England) and made 98. In the 1926 Test series he scored a century at Leeds, England, and tried 'leg theory' when bowling. His first-class career figures were 5238 runs (average 41.57) and 209 wickets (at 31.97); he played nine Tests, scoring 403 runs (average 31) and taking 12 wickets (at 43.42).

Richardson was based in Adelaide as an insurance inspector and State coach (1923-27) until accepting a playing-and-coaching offer from Western Australia in 1927. In his final first-class appearance at home he represented Western Australia against the M.C.C. in November 1929. Contracts followed in the Lancashire League—he broke its batting record in 1929 and took 10 wickets in an innings in 1932—and in South Africa and the West Indies. In the West Indies (1934-35) he umpired two Tests against England. Returning to Adelaide in 1936, he filled much of his life by coaching, umpiring and watching cricket. Coursing was another of his interests. Cricket had supported him throughout the Depression, but he lost his savings when H. W. Hodgetts's [q.v.14] sharebroking firm collapsed in 1945. Another coaching contract (1946-49) with the South Australian Cricket Association, a testimonial match in 1949—Sir Donald Bradman's last first-class match—and various fund-raising efforts restored him to modest comfort. He was a State selector in

1948-49 and coach of the South Australian women's cricket team in 1955-56.

A man of firm principles and sober habits (he sucked a fruit stone, rather than chewing gum, when playing), Richardson was a worthy example to the young cricketers he coached. He died on 23 December 1973 at Semaphore and was cremated; his wife, daughter and two sons survived him.

L. R. Hill, *Eighty Not Out* (Mount Gambier, SA, 1968); S. Downer, *100 Not Out* (Adel, 1972); J. Pollard, *Australian Cricket* (Syd, 1982); C. Harte, *SACA* (Adel, 1990); *Northern Argus* (Clare), 5 Oct 1906, 5 Apr 1907, 13 Feb 1914, 26 Feb 1926; *Advertiser* (Adel), 11 Oct 1915, 4 Nov 1918, 9, 10 Nov 1920, 4 Mar 1949, 26 Dec 1973; *Register* (Adel), 10 Nov 1920, 16 Mar 1923, 8 Nov, 12, 26 Dec 1924, 1, 4 Jan, 5, 24 Feb 1926; information from Mr B. L. Bowley, Campbelltown, and Mr C. L. B. Starr, Plympton, Adel.   R. M. GIBBS

RICHARDSON, ERNEST BIGGS (1903-1965), banker, was born on 6 July 1903 at Trangie, New South Wales, son of native-born parents Charles Richard Richardson, commission agent, and his wife Lucy Jane, née Robinson. Educated at the local public school, Ernest passed the Institute of Bankers' preliminary examination in September 1918. Next year he attended Abbotsholme College, Killara, Sydney.

Joining the Commonwealth Bank of Australia in 1920 as a junior clerk, Richardson spent two years at the Dubbo branch before moving to the Sydney office. In 1928 he was transferred to the secretary's section in the bank's administration. He accompanied the governor (Sir) Ernest Riddle [q.v.11] and the economic adviser (Sir) Leslie Melville to the 1932 Imperial Economic Conference, held in Ottawa. Richardson spent six months in the bank's London branch before returning to Sydney. At All Saints Church, Woollahra, on 20 November 1934 he married with Anglican rites Emily Constance Spencer, a nurse.

'Rich', as he was affectionately known, was appointed acting-secretary of the bank in 1937. When he became secretary in the following year, he was the youngest man to hold that office. He played a vital part in diffusing 'the gospel of central banking', and in promoting understanding between the board of directors and the departments within the bank—an important function, as the governor was not a member of the board. A succession of governors—Riddle, Sir Harry Sheehan and especially H. T. Armitage [qq.v.11,13]—were to rely on him. Richardson made the secretary's position 'the focal point of decision-making'.

Throughout World War II Richardson was closely involved in major developments in the role of the bank and in maintaining the co-operation of the private banks. From mid-1944 he worked in Canberra and Sydney on legislation, passed in 1945, which abolished the Commonwealth Bank's board and set up a small advisory council of Treasury and bank officials, of which he was one. In 1947 the Chifley [q.v.13] Labor government tried to nationalize banking, but was successfully challenged by the private banks in the High Court of Australia. At the end of the court hearing, the solicitor-general (Sir) Kenneth Bailey [q.v.13] thanked the Commonwealth Bank for its assistance in preparing the defendants' case, and praised Richardson for his 'direction of so much of what was done both on the intellectual and on the material side'. His efficiency, courtesy, composure and good temper had 'won him the admiration, and indeed the affection, of everybody concerned'.

In January 1949 Dr H. C. Coombs became governor of the Commonwealth Bank and Richardson was appointed his deputy. Coombs described it as a natural partnership: Rich's knowledge of the bank, shrewd judgement and capacity for work made him of 'fantastic value' in the two-man team. When a new board was set up by (Sir) Robert Menzies' [q.v.15] government in 1951, Coombs and Richardson became chairman and deputy-chairman respectively. In 1956 they were re-appointed for seven-year terms as governor and deputy-governor. Richardson was appointed C.B.E. (1957).

In 1959 the central and commercial banking functions of the Commonwealth Bank were separated, and the Commonwealth Banking Corporation was established to control the commercial arm. Richardson was made managing director of the Commonwealth Banking Corporation and an *ex officio* member of the board. He left central banking with regret, but brought characteristic energy and enthusiasm to his new tasks. The first five years saw substantial growth under his leadership. Brisk and decisive, he was liked and respected in the bank, and in the wider community.

Richardson served as chairman of trustees of the Anzac Memorial, Hyde Park, Sydney, as a trustee of the Social Science Research Council of Australia, and as treasurer of the New South Wales branch of the National Heart Foundation of Australia. In the bank he was invariably interested in staff activities and welfare. Rather short and solidly built, he had played as a forward in the bank's Rugby League football team and 'attacked like a fox terrier'. Later in life he turned to bowls and golf. He died of cerebrovascular disease on 3 March 1965 at Richmond, Melbourne, and was cremated; his wife and their son survived him. A staff hostel in Canberra was named after him.

C. L. Mobbs (comp), *Commonwealth Bank of Australia in the Second World War* (Syd, 1947); L. F. Giblin, *The Growth of a Central Bank* (Melb, 1951); J. E. Matthews, *The Commonwealth Banking Corporation* (Syd, 1980); H. C. Coombs, *Trial Balance* (Melb, 1981); C. B. Schedvin, *In Reserve* (Syd, 1992); *Bank Notes* (Syd), Apr 1965; *Aust Economic Hist Review*, Sept 1983; information from Mr J. S. Richardson, Gooseberry Hill, Perth.

M. R. HILL

RICHARDSON, MERVYN VICTOR (1893-1972), inventor, was born on 11 November 1893 at Yarramalong, New South Wales, second son of Archibald George Heron Richardson, a schoolteacher from Ireland, and his native-born wife Charlotte Martha, née Griffith. Archibald taught in country schools (1889-99) and in Sydney (from 1912). Mervyn's lack of formal education beyond primary school did not inhibit his flair as an amateur designer and mechanic. After being apprenticed to a jeweller, he worked as a sign-writer. In 1916 he helped his elder brother Archibald to build a low-winged monoplane for which they designed a radial engine with contra-rotating propellers. The brothers were filmed demonstrating the machine at Mascot, Sydney. Later that day Archibald, who had invested everything in the project, crashed the aircraft beyond repair.

In the 1920s Mervyn worked as a motorcar salesman. At the Methodist Church, Concord, on 26 June 1926 he married Vera Marie Bertram, a clerk. Next year he designed the Austin 'Wasp', a sporty, duck-tailed, coupé body for the locally assembled Austin 7 car. Undeterred by previous failures, he set up New South Wales Motors Ltd and opened a showroom in William Street. This venture gave him his first taste of success and financial security, but the business did not survive the Depression. By the early 1930s Mervyn, Vera and their baby son Garry were reduced to living in a single room at North Strathfield. Richardson regularly walked to the city in search of work and eventually became a travelling salesman for the Gold Star Coupon Co. To supplement his income, he studied logarithmic scales so that he could calibrate (by hand) and sell slide-rules.

A new job as an engineering salesman led to improved circumstances. In 1941 the family moved to a house in Bray Street, Concord, that Richardson had designed. When Garry started (1948) a lawn-mowing business during university vacations, his father made two complex reel-type mowers to help him. Driven by the desire to succeed again, Mervyn continued to build lawnmowers in his backyard workshop and registered the name Victa Mowers (a corruption of his middle name) in mid-1950. Over the next two years he built and sold sixty reel-type mowers, powered by imported Villiers two-stroke engines.

In 1948 Richardson had watched a public demonstration of the 'Mowhall' rotary-blade lawnmower, which required two people to push and pull it over long grass and was never a commercial success. In August 1952 he hit upon the idea of putting a Villiers engine on its side to drive a set of rotating blades. Within a few hours he had assembled the prototype of the Victa rotary lawnmower from scrap metal, billy-cart wheels, and a jam tin used as a petrol tank. To his family's amazement the contraption cut fine grass with precision and yet could plough through long grass and weeds.

Within three months thirty mowers had been sold. Burgeoning suburbs created an astonishing demand for the lightweight lawnmower which could turn backyards that had once been cow pastures or bush into civilized swathes of lawn. On Friday 13 February 1953 Richardson gave up his job and became full-time manager of Victa Mowers Pty Ltd. By 1958 the company had moved to a new factory at Milperra and its 3000 employees were building 143 000 mowers a year for export to 28 countries. In the 1960s Victa diversified: in addition to lawnmowers, the firm manufactured the 'red phone' (a private payphone system installed in shops and clubs), the Victa Airtourer (a light aircraft) and, for a short time, Victa project homes.

Richardson enjoyed the fame and trappings of life as a 'self-made' millionaire. He indulged in sports cars and ballroom dancing, yet still took a cut lunch in a paper bag to work each day. His life was the subject of a number of articles in popular magazines. At Pittwater he delighted in showing off the amphibious-aircraft hangar and boatshed of his ultramodern house, Kumale, designed by the architect Peter Muller.

During the early 1960s Garry Richardson played an increasingly important role in the company and succeeded Mervyn as chairman in 1965. The company was sold to the Sunbeam Corporation Ltd in 1970. Survived by his wife and their son, Mervyn Richardson died on 31 December 1972 at St Luke's Hospital, Darlinghurst, and was cremated with Anglican rites. In 1994 the factory moved to Campsie, where the seven millionth Victa lawnmower was built in 1997. The Richardson radial aero-engine and the Victa prototype lawnmower (1952) are held by the Powerhouse Museum, Sydney.

R. G. Cull, *Inventive Australians* (Melb, 1993); R. Renew, *Making it* (Syd, 1993); *Woman's Day*, 30 Mar 1964; *Sun* (Syd), 22 Feb 1957, 8 Feb, 2 Aug 1966; *Sunday Mirror* (Syd), 17 Sept 1961; *Age* (Melb), 8 Dec 1992; information from Mr G. Richardson, Syd.   RICHARD V. WOOD

RICHARDSON, PETER ALFRED (1933-1973), flautist, was born on 29 August 1933 at Crows Nest, Sydney, son of Australian-born parents Frank Alfred Richardson, real-estate agent and later journalist, and his wife Nell Victoria, née Morrison. After his parents' divorce, Peter spent his childhood and adolescence at Thirroul, living with his mother and maternal grandmother. His musical education began at Thirroul Public School with the 'State Schools' Flute Programme'. In his spare time between commuting from Thirroul and attending (1952-54) the New South Wales State Conservatorium of Music, he worked as an orderly at Sydney Hospital where he developed an interest in medicine and drugs. He studied the flute with Victor McMahon, and then with Neville Amadio who influenced him greatly and considered him his finest pupil. In several respects he modelled himself on Amadio: both were debonair, charming, and stylish musicians. Despite his sophistication and the depth of his performing experience, Richardson never intimidated his colleagues.

At St Jude's Anglican Church, Randwick, on 3 September 1954 Richardson married Marilyn Ann Alle, a soprano. He later described it as 'marrying an image'. They were to have three sons before their marriage was dissolved on 15 October 1965. The handsome young couple were prominent contributors to Sydney's musical life, especially during the 1950s and early 1960s. With the pianist-composer Larry Sitsky, they formed the Melba Trio and played for many music clubs. With Richard Meale, they founded the ensemble Musica Nuova which, under Neale's direction, gave the first Australian performance (1959) of Schoenberg's *Pierrot Lunaire*. Nigel Butterley wrote his carol *Joseph and Mary* for the Richardsons in 1959.

Although Richardson disliked playing in orchestras, financial necessity compelled him to undertake that work, which included a number of J. C. Williamson [q.v.6] Ltd's musicals (such as *My Fair Lady* and *The Pajama Game*), casual engagements with the Sydney Symphony Orchestra, and periods as principal flute with the Tasmanian Symphony Orchestra and Clarice Lorenz's National Opera of Australia. He taught at the Canberra School of Music, the University of Sydney, the Conservatorium, Abbotsleigh Church of England School for Girls and Presbyterian Ladies' College, Croydon. Richardson was revered by his students for 'his great skill and patience', and by his professional colleagues for the 'brilliant sheen and exact intonation' of his performances.

His intelligence and musical curiosity soon brought him under the influence of Dene Barnett, who pioneered authentic stylistic practice in early music; thereafter, Richardson was prominent in performances of Bach and

Handel and with the Sydney Baroque Ensemble. He was also a mainstay of new music, especially (but not exclusively) the *avant-garde*. A committee-member (1964-73) of the local chapter of the International Society for Contemporary Music, he was almost a fixture at its regular concerts and at those of Musica Nuova. He premièred Meale's *Flute Sonata*, and gave the first Australian performance of Pierre Boulez's *Sonatine* (with Gordon Watson) and works by Elliott Carter, Goffredo Petrassi, Bruno Maderna and H. W. Henze. Richardson played in the premières of Meale's *Las Alborados* (1963) and Butterley's *Laudes* (at the 1964 Adelaide Festival of Arts).

Following his separation from his wife in 1964, Richardson began to drink heavily and to take drugs, activities which continued after he married Margaret Alison Eyres, a 26-year-old nursing sister, on 22 October 1965 at St Andrew's Scots Church, Rose Bay. Despite his acknowledged success and popularity, he was subject to depression, psychosexual turmoil and feelings of worthlessness. Ambivalent about psychotherapy, he dealt with his depression through drug abuse. He died of 'chloral hydrate poisoning self administered as a sleeping draught' on 11 March 1973 in his home at Paddington and was cremated with Anglican rites. His wife, and their son and daughter, survived him, as did the sons of his first marriage. In 1974 students and colleagues gave a concert in memory of Richardson; it included the première of Raymond Hanson's [q.v.14] *Dedication*.

Music Now, 2, no 2, Dec 1974; *SMH*, 11 Apr 1958, 11 Nov 1964, 13, 14 Mar 1973, 19 Mar 1974; information from Mr N. Amadio, Mr N. Butterley, Mrs M. Newman and Mrs A. van der Vlies, Syd, and Ms M. Richardson, Brisb.   JOHN CARMODY

RICHMOND, ROBERT OLIFFE GAGE (1919-1977), sculptor, was born on 8 November 1919 at Old Beach, Hobart, fifth child of Robert Lawrence Richmond, a farmer from England, and his Tasmanian-born wife Catherine Augusta, née Gage. In 1929 the family moved to New Town. Oliffe attended (1929-36) The Friends' School where he excelled at athletics, cricket, rowing and football, and won a prize for pencil sketching. A female friend recalled that, with his dark hair, olive skin and brown eyes, he was 'much sought after'. After studying (1937-39) art and applied art at Hobart Technical College, and gaining a diploma in 1940, he worked for Amos Vimpany, Hobart's most prominent stonemason, in whose workshop he learned much about materials, tools and methods of carving. He was also influenced by the 'modernistic' ideas of the New Zealand-born sculptor Alison Duff.

Richmond had learned to fly small aircraft while he was a student. On the outbreak of World War II he volunteered for the Royal Australian Air Force, but was rejected because of a slight defect in his vision. Mobilized in the Militia on 19 August 1940, he rose to staff sergeant in the Intelligence Corps, Hobart, before serving (September to November 1944) in New Guinea with the Royal Australian Engineers. The environment excited his sensibilities with its exotic flora and fauna, and different human physiological 'types'. He drew scenes of army life, but his was, fundamentally, a sculptor's perception. Even in his fully resolved chalk or pencil portrait studies of soldiers, he was concerned with the head as a solid form rather than a face as a window to a soul. The native artefacts he collected would continue to influence his work.

Back in Australia, Richmond performed engineering staff duties until he was discharged from the army on 6 March 1946. That year he enrolled at the East Sydney Technical College to study sculpture under Lyndon Dadswell. In 1948 he won a New South Wales government travelling scholarship. He was formally attached to the Royal College of Art, London, but soon set off for the major art centres in Europe. Returning to England, he worked as Henry Moore's assistant until 1951 when he succeeded him as a teacher in sculpture at the Chelsea School of Art. Although he occasionally helped Moore to work on major pieces, he began to build his own career as a sculptor. At the register office, Chelsea, on 22 July 1952 he married Waehlin Fong.

From 1954 Richmond's sculptures were included in major group exhibitions in London and other British cities, and in Paris, Oslo, Zurich, Switzerland, Sydney, Melbourne, Phoenix, Arizona, United States of America. When his first solo showing was held, at the Molton Gallery, London, the critic Edward Lucie-Smith commented: 'it is not very often that an artist springs on us more or less fully fledged'. Other solo exhibitions followed, in Belfast (1964), New York (1964), London (1965), Canberra and Melbourne (1967), and Sydney (1968). The highly textured figurative bronzes of his first exhibition—suggesting intense human energy and inner tension, and described by Dadswell as 'heroic and monumental'—gave way towards the end of the decade to a series of aluminium assemblages made up of machined and extruded industrial components which embodied none of the organic character that had stamped his work to that point. In the new, hard-edged, planar pieces there was no evidence of the artist's hand; instead, this new sculpture paid homage to the machine.

About 1970, at the time of his aluminium constructions, Richmond produced two quite different bodies of work. One comprised intimate little forms carved out of the toughest woods, such as ebony; the other consisted of a series of bronze abstract pieces, cast by means of the lost-wax process from forms manipulated from wax sheets. Despite their small size, these exquisite pieces possessed intimations of much larger scale. A sense of the monumental had long been a characteristic of Richmond's work. It found dramatic expression in his final series, a collection of massive assemblages in wood, first exhibited at the Commonwealth Art Gallery, London, in early 1976. Dadswell was left with a lasting impression of 'a room filled with towering forms' and felt as if he were 'a man amongst the monsters of H. G. Wells' *War of the Worlds*'.

Richmond placed artistic integrity above popular and material success. Laconic and self-effacing, he was rock-solid in maintaining his aesthetic values. He meditated for long periods among the megaliths of Stonehenge and was sustained by the sense of being part of a great and ancient tradition. Survived by his wife, he died of myocardial infarction on 26 February 1977 in his home at Kensington and was cremated. His work is held by major galleries in Britain, the Netherlands and Australia.

G. Sturgeon, *The Development of Australian Sculpture 1788-1975* (Lond, 1978); K. Scarlett, *Australian Sculptors* (Melb, 1979); C. Hogben, *Oliffe Richmond*, exhibition cat (Syd, 1980); C. E. Johannes, *Oliffe Richmond Drawings*, exhibition cat (Hob, 1989); G. Legge, *Oliffe Richmond 1919-77*, exhibition cat (Syd, 1993); *Art and Aust*, 3, no 1, June 1965, 15, no 2, Dec 1977.   LINDSAY BROUGHTON

RICKARD, ARTHUR LANCELOT (1895-1949), businessman and army officer, was born on 18 September 1895 at Waverley, Sydney, son of (Sir) Arthur Rickard [q.v.11], a native-born broker, and his wife Annie Eliza, née Addy, who came from England. Young Arthur attended Barker College, Hornsby, where he shone at Rugby Union football, athletics and tennis. In 1914 he began to study accountancy, probably in his father's real-estate firm, Arthur Rickard & Co. Ltd.

Commissioned in the Militia in March 1915, Rickard was appointed second lieutenant, Australian Imperial Force, on 3 September. He embarked for Egypt that month and accompanied the 3rd Field Artillery Brigade to France in March 1916. For carrying out a hazardous reconnaissance on a Somme battlefield in November, he was awarded the Military Cross. He was also mentioned in dispatches. In July 1917 he was promoted captain and transferred to the 12th Army Brigade. On 28 December he was gassed and admitted to hospital, but returned to duty two months later. Briefly seconded to the 51st (Highland)

Division in April 1918, he rejoined his unit and remained in action until a few days before World War I ended. He was promoted major and appointed commanding officer of the 45th Battery in October, and again mentioned in dispatches. While on leave in England, he had married Charlotte Mary Woodman on 7 September 1918 at the register office, Colchester, Essex; they were to have one son before being divorced.

Rickard returned to Sydney in April 1920 and his A.I.F. appointment terminated in July. Becoming a director and sales manager in his father's firm, he dressed immaculately, liked good cars and—with his intelligence, wit and gentleness—was good company. At St Thomas's Anglican Church, North Sydney, on 23 June 1926 he married 18-year-old Myfvanwy Ison Jolliffe Page.

In March 1939 Rickard was appointed to the 9th Field Brigade, Militia. On 1 May 1940 he transferred to the A.I.F. Given command of the 8th Battery, 2nd/2nd Anti-Tank Regiment, he sailed for the Middle East in October. During the Syrian campaign (June-July 1941) Rickard's battery halted a Vichy French counter-attack at Merdjayoun on 15 June, losing four guns but destroying eight tanks. For his 'quickness and initiative', he was awarded the Distinguished Service Order. He was also mentioned in dispatches.

Returning to Australia in March 1942, Rickard was promoted (May) temporary lieutenant colonel and appointed (June) to command the 103rd Anti-Tank Regiment at Newcastle, New South Wales. The regiment was sent to the Northern Territory in December. In August 1944 Rickard took command of the 106th Tank-Attack Regiment, A.I.F., which was deployed at Scarlet Beach, north of Finschhafen, New Guinea. Next month he was transferred to the 2nd/1st Tank-Attack Regiment at Helidon, Queensland. When that regiment moved to Aitape, New Guinea, in January 1945, its batteries and men were used as field artillery or infantry. On 28 May Rickard was temporarily detached to command the 2nd/6th Cavalry Commando Regiment and Farida Force.

In August Rickard rejoined his anti-tank unit. He relinquished command in November and flew home to Australia. In May 1946 he was appointed officer commanding troops in a ship that was repatriating Japanese prisoners of war. Placed on the Reserve of Officers on 31 July, he was once more mentioned in dispatches, this time for his service in the South-West Pacific Area in April-August 1945.

Rickard formed a small property-development company in Sydney, but he was dogged by ill health. He died of hypertensive cerebro-vascular disease on 9 March 1949 in the Repatriation General Hospital, Concord, and was cremated. His wife, their daughter and two sons survived him; the son of his first marriage was killed in January 1941 while serving with the A.I.F. in Libya.

C. E. W. Bean, *The A.I.F. in France 1918*, vol 5 (Syd, 1937); G. Long, *Greece, Crete and Syria* (Canb, 1953) and *The Final Campaigns* (Canb, 1963); D. M. Horner, *The Gunners* (Syd, 1995); G. McKenzie-Smith, *Australia's Forgotten Army*, 2 (Canb, 1995); information from Mr B. Rickard, Cammeray, Major D. R. Rickard, Darling Point, Ms S. O'Neill, Hornsby, and Ms S. Hughes, Turramurra, Syd.

LAURIE HINDMARSH

RICKETSON, STANIFORTH (1891-1967), stockbroker, was born on 1 August 1891 at Malvern, Melbourne, fifth child of Victorian-born parents Henry Joseph Ricketson, squatter, and his wife Sophia Henrietta, née Sheppard. His maternal great-grandfather J. B. Were [q.v.2] had set an example which would influence Staniforth's career. The boy was given the maiden name of his paternal grandmother Georgina, née Staniforth (d.1882); her widowed husband Henry Ricketson senior married J. B. Were's daughter Edith in 1884, reinforcing the connexion between the two families.

At Prahran North State School, Ricketson received a gold medal as dux (1905) of boys. In 1906 he won Corrigan [q.v.3] entrance and government scholarships to Wesley College. Leaving school in 1907, he worked on pastoral stations in Victoria and New South Wales. In 1908 he found a job as a correspondence clerk with the Australian Mercantile Land & Finance Co. Ltd, Melbourne. Next year he accompanied his brother Lancelot to King Island where they ran the Ricketson Bros general store. Staniforth also edited the local newspaper, *The King Islander*.

In 1910 Ricketson moved to Tasmania where he became a reporter with the *North Western Advocate and Emu Bay Times*. At the invitation of his great-uncle Francis Wellington Were, he returned to Melbourne and joined the staff of J. B. Were & Son on 4 December 1911. Within a year he had charge of the *Australian Stock Exchange Intelligence*, the firm's periodical which summarized news for clients. He expanded the publication and presented additional features under the heading, 'Talks on, 'Change'. On 17 March 1914 he was elected a member of the Stock Exchange of Melbourne and admitted as a partner in J. B. Were & Son.

With the outbreak of World War I, Ricketson and many of his colleagues and relations on the stock exchange immediately volunteered for service. He enlisted in the Australian Imperial Force on 17 August and was posted to the 5th Battalion's 'F' Company which was composed of old boys from Victorian public schools. Sailing for the Middle East in October, he took part in the Gallipoli landing on 25 April 1915. His strength of purpose was readily apparent. When the company's commissioned and non-commissioned officers became casualties that day, he braved heavy fire to rally the men and dig a shelter for a wounded officer. He was commissioned on 27 April and awarded the Distinguished Conduct Medal. For his subsequent services on the peninsula he was mentioned in dispatches.

W. L. Winter Cooke described how, in June, 'a Turkish bullet ploughed a furrow—right across [Ricketson's] scalp—just missing the bone—but he disregarded it, smiled and carried on'. A shell-blast in August left Ricketson partially deaf in the right ear. Evacuated to England in October suffering from diarrhoea, he was sent home in February 1916 to recuperate. At the Presbyterian Church, Prahran, on 6 April that year he married Mary Gwendolyn Brown; they were to have six children before being divorced in 1945. On 4 May 1916 F. W. Were sold the business to his three partners F. J. Fleming, W. F. Geach and Ricketson. Back in England by September, Ricketson was promoted captain in January 1917. He rejoined the 5th Battalion on the Western Front in November and his A.I.F. appointment terminated in Melbourne on 3 September 1919.

In 1923 Ricketson introduced J. B. Were & Son's *Weekly Share Market Letter* to clients. An increasingly strong force in the firm, he urged his partners in 1928 to sponsor the raising of capital for the first of the Capel Court group of companies, Were's Investment Trust Ltd (later Australian Foundation Investment Co. Ltd). The success of this venture encouraged the firm to back National Reliance Investment Co. Ltd, which was registered in December 1929.

In 1930, when Prime Minister J. H. Scullin's [q.v.11] Labor government struggled to cope with the Depression, some ministers and back-benchers advocated financial policies that alarmed Ricketson. As a young man he had met J. A. Lyons [q.v.10] who, by November 1930, was acting Federal treasurer. That month Lyons defied caucus and set about raising a £28 million conversion loan. Ricketson formed and headed a committee to advise Lyons and promote the loan. This cabal, comprising Ricketson, four other businessmen and his friend (Sir) Robert Menzies [q.v.15], became known as 'the Group'.

After the conversion loan had been fully subscribed, Ricketson took a prominent part in moves in Melbourne to form an Australian Citizens' League with the aim of restoring 'political integrity and stability' and creating 'a healthy atmosphere remote from party politics'. As acting honorary secretary of the organizing committee, he advertised 'A Monster Mass Meeting' to be held in the Melbourne Town Hall on 19 February 1931. The meeting was a resounding success, and a council of the league (All for Australia League from March) was elected with Ricketson as honorary treasurer. He and his colleagues in the Group had already begun moves to persuade Lyons to leave the Australian Labor Party. In March Lyons revealed his decision to defect. When the Victorian section of the United Australia Party was formed in May, Ricketson was elected temporary secretary of its central council. Under Lyons's leadership, the U.A.P. won a decisive victory in the Federal elections in December.

In 1935 J. B. Were & Son moved to a new Capel Court building in Collins Street. Additional companies were launched: Capel Court Investment Trust (Australia) Ltd in 1936 and Jason Investment Trust (Australia) Ltd in 1937. Ricketson chaired the newly formed Argus & Australasian Ltd in 1936-39. His 'skill and foresight', especially in building up stocks of newsprint before the price rose, ensured that the business was profitable. He had given evidence in 1936 to the Commonwealth government's royal commission on monetary and banking systems. Among other matters, he explained the operation of the 'outside exchange market'. To demonstrate its benefits, he described how—during the financial crisis in the United States of America —J. B. Were & Son had 'bought for Australian clients some 23 million dollars of Australian [issues of] dollar bonds at about 25 to 40 per cent of their par value, most of these having since recovered to above par'.

In the late 1930s Ricketson directed his firm's successful promotion and underwriting of major companies, including Australian Paper Manufacturers Ltd, Felt & Textiles of Australia Ltd and Imperial Chemical Industries of Australia & New Zealand Ltd. On 26 October 1940 he became sole proprietor of J. B. Were & Son, but in December admitted six new partners. He served on the committee of the Stock Exchange of Melbourne in 1942-46. Having forecast in 1943 that World War II would be followed by a period of 'great industrial expansion', in September 1946 he described 'talk of an early economic depression' as 'moonshine'. On 21 October that year at St Stephen's Presbyterian Church, Caulfield, he married Edna Letitia Holmes, a 35-year-old secretary. His firm marketed a substantial parcel of ordinary shares in Foy & Gibson [qq.v.4,8] Ltd and in 1948 issued a special booklet promoting the expansion plans of Broken Hill Proprietary Co. Ltd and its subsidiary, Australian Iron & Steel Ltd.

For a long period in the 1950s Ricketson advocated the severance of the Commonwealth Bank of Australia's 'central bank function from its trading activities'. The establishment of the Reserve Bank of Australia in 1959 has been attributed in part to his influence and persistence. Late in the decade he was closely involved in setting up the short-term money market. In the 1960s he continued to chair a number of companies, including Capel Court Investment Co. (Australia) Ltd, to whose group had been added Lombard Investments (Australia) Ltd, Brenton Investments (Australia) Ltd, Clonmore Investments (Australia) Ltd and Haliburton Investments (Australia) Ltd.

Ricketson was a staunch Anglican and a teetotaller. He demanded that his firm, partners and staff should not engage in share trading on their own account. Many of his associates and subordinates found him overbearing. His sons Anthony, Michael and John joined the firm only to leave it, as did a number of its senior officers. Sir Keith Murdoch [q.v.10] had told Ricketson in 1948: 'I have a tremendous admiration for your power of organisation, your courage and your integrity, so it has not disturbed me when I have (very occasionally) felt that your remarks or views have been couched in hard words because your work and great undertakings require intensity of thought and effort'.

A member of the Melbourne Club and the Naval and Military Club, Ricketson also belonged to the Australian and Australasian Pioneers' clubs in Sydney. His recreations were tennis, squash, swimming and, in later life, walking. In the 1950s and 1960s he went with associates and friends on excursions to country retreats, at which they studied and discussed ecological and environmental issues, as well as financial and public affairs. Jack Cato [q.v.13] recorded these occasions in photographs and verse. Images of Ricketson reveal a tall, handsome man, generally with an impassive face.

Survived by his wife and their daughter and son, and by the two daughters and three of the four sons of his first marriage, Ricketson died on 6 December 1967 at Kew and was cremated. J. B. Were had died on the same day eighty-two years previously; he, too, was aged 76. When news of Ricketson's death reached the Stock Exchange of Melbourne, members adjourned for two minutes as a mark of respect. His estate, including Toolebewang farm at Launching Place, Upper Yarra Valley, was sworn for probate at $1 994 720, of which $1 153 614 was his interest in J. B. Were & Son. A portrait of Ricketson by Sir John Longstaff [q.v.10] is held by the family; another by (Sir) William Dargie is in the firm's possession.

J. B. Were & Son, *The House of Were, 1839-1954* (Melb, 1954); R. T. Appleyard and C. B. Schedvin (eds), *Australian Financiers* (Melb, 1988); J. B.

Were & Son papers (held by the firm, Melb, *and* at Melb Univ Archives); information from Prof S. Ricketson, Monash Univ, Clayton, Melb.

FRANK STRAHAN

RIDDELL, PERCY DRYDEN (1886-1967), technical education administrator, was born on 31 October 1886 at Marrickville, Sydney, eldest of six children of English-born parents Michael Dryden Riddell, fitter, and his wife Helena, née White. Helena instilled in her five sons and only daughter the determination that none of them was to become a blue-collar worker. After leaving Kogarah Superior Public School, Perce completed a course in speed shorthand, and began to read widely and voraciously. He joined the New South Wales Public Service as a clerk on 23 April 1907, but left in the following year to teach shorthand at commercial colleges in Sydney. In 1911 he entered the Department of Public Instruction's technical education branch as secretary to committees.

Transferred to Broken Hill Technical College as sub-registrar in 1915, Riddell was promoted principal in July 1920. At the Methodist Church, South Bathurst, on 11 January 1916 he married Edith Smith; they were to remain childless. He was foundation president (1917-29) of the Barrier District branch of the Workers' Educational Association. As vice-president of the Barrier Field Naturalists' Club, he arranged scientific expeditions to Central Australia and accompanied some of them as an anthropological observer.

On 18 February 1929 Riddell was appointed principal of Newcastle Technical College. An outstanding administrator, he energetically sought solutions to the problems associated with developing technical education in an industrial centre, and secured the assistance of a number of leaders of commerce and industry. His leisure time was partly filled by community work: he was president of the Rotary Club of Newcastle and of the local branch of the New South Wales Society for Crippled Children.

Riddell was appointed superintendent (director from 1947) of technical education on 23 October 1939. He brought to the position 'experience in various divisions of the service, personal knowledge of the staff of the Technical Education branch', and close contact with industry. He was responsible for implementing the Commonwealth Defence Training Scheme. As State regional director of the Commonwealth Reconstruction Training Scheme, he had to plan courses to suit the needs of the State's industrial structure. A member (from 1941) of the Board of Secondary School Studies, he developed a rapport with Robert Heffron [q.v.14], minister for education (from 1944), and in 1949 was appointed to the council of the New South Wales University of Technology.

Woodwork was one hobby to which Riddell devoted much time. From the workshop of his rented home at Killara he donated each year large numbers of his handmade, moving wooden toys to the Royal Alexandra Hospital for Children. His other hobbies included bowls and anthropology. Following his retirement on 31 October 1949, Riddell and his wife moved to Mount Ku-ring-gai. A tall, slender, but well-built man, he was often seen smoking (or cleaning) his pipe. He was courteous, quietly spoken, considerate and well liked—despite his 'penchant for frankness'. Survived by his wife, he died on 27 November 1967 at Hornsby and was cremated with Presbyterian forms.

SMH, 6 July, 30 Oct, 2 Nov 1949, 19 May 1965, 30 Nov 1967; J. Cobb, History of Technical Education in New South Wales to 1949 (ts, 1988) *and* staff file 13/9344, teachers' records (NSW Dept of Education archives); information from Mrs J. Waters, Bexley, Syd.   MARY McPHERSON

RIDDLE, ARTHUR RAYMOND (1888-1967), biophysicist, and DOROTHY (1894-1979), librarian, were husband and wife. Arthur was born on 24 July 1888 at Yorketown, South Australia, sixth of seven sons of William Riddle, an English-born machinist, and his wife Elizabeth Angel, née Pegler, who was born in South Australia. Educated locally and at Kyre College, Adelaide, he was required to join the family's ironmongery business, but became an accomplished photographer and won medals in several competitions. His work came to the notice of (Sir) Kerr Grant [q.v.9], professor of physics at the University of Adelaide, who secured him employment as a laboratory assistant. Riddle studied science at the university in 1913-14 before enlisting in the Australian Imperial Force. He served (1915-21) as radiographer and physicist with the Australian Army Medical Corps at No.7 Australian General Hospital, Keswick, and rose to the rank of warrant officer.

At the office of the registrar-general, Adelaide, on 24 May 1921 Riddle married Dorothy Lemon; they had no children. Dorothy had been born on 17 December 1894 at Ipswich, England, daughter of Fred Lemon, an officer of the inland revenue, and his wife Eileen, née Jones. Eileen and her three children had emigrated to South Australia during World War I. On the day of their wedding the Riddles sailed for the United States of America. Arthur studied at Cornell University, Ithaca, New York (B.S., 1922; M.S., 1932), while working as an instructor in physics (1921-27). He undertook research in spectrography, ultra-violet fluorescence, X-ray measurement, and the use of photography in solving scientific problems.

Biophysicist (from 1927) at the Hegeman Memorial Research Laboratory, Mount McGregor, Riddle designed special filters for use in assessing biological responses to infra-red and ultra-violet solar radiation. Appreciating the value of applying physics to medicine and biology, he returned to Cornell in 1930 to take advanced courses in physiology and biochemistry. In 1932 he became head of the biophysics department, Payne Whitney Psychiatric Clinic, New York Hospital. The collapse of the hospital's endowment income in the following year led to the retrenchment of its research staff. Riddle decided to return to Australia, but his wife—who was employed as a library assistant at Cornell—refused to leave and they separated. In 1937 Dorothy sought Arthur's consent to a divorce. He declined, and never heard from her again.

In 1934 Riddle went to the Brisbane abattoir, Cannon Hill, to take up a temporary post funded jointly by the Council for Scientific and Industrial Research and the Queensland Meat Industry Board. He investigated the effects of various types of radiation on micro-organisms in beef, and the physical condition of beef during chilling. Appointed to the C.S.I.R.'s permanent staff in 1937, he became officer-in-charge of the food preservation research laboratory at Cannon Hill in 1940. In 1953 he retired. He died on 22 November 1967 in Brisbane and was cremated. Riddle bequeathed between $35 000 and $40 000 to the University of Adelaide for student scholarships. Thousands of his photographic negatives on glass, stored in a shed at Yorketown, had been destroyed by larrikins while he was in America; 258 that survived, and 2000 of his prints, are held by the Mortlock Library of South Australiana.

The diminutive and dynamic Mrs Riddle returned to Adelaide in 1942 and joined the research service at the Public Library of South Australia. Her evidence to the Education Inquiry Committee stressed the need for every school to have its own library and impressed (Sir) Charles Abbott, the State's minister of education. In July 1944 she was appointed organizer of school libraries. Through her articles in Department of Education and South Australian Teachers' Union journals, and her visits to some one thousand schools over the next ten years, she exhorted teachers to apply for grants for library training and preached the value of children having access to school libraries. Insisting that all but one-teacher schools should have at least one room dedicated to library purposes, she advocated voluntary rather than scheduled library visits by pupils. She emphasized that reading was enjoyable and important 'in the mental,

emotional and spiritual life of the child'. As chairman (1945) of the committee which organized the first children's book week in South Australia, she argued that children should be given access to a wide range of material and taught how to find information themselves.

Although the department provided money for buildings, shelving and catalogue cabinets, its funding of book purchases was confined to subsidizing (on a pound for pound basis) what each school could raise locally. Everywhere she went, Riddle convened meetings of parents and citizens. They raised over £2000 in her first year in office, and increasing sums thereafter. Hundreds of schools entrusted her with their book-buying; her enjoyment in wielding that power was resented by booksellers. Little money, however, was collected in drought-stricken and other impoverished areas. In 1950 the American Library Association agreed to send children's books to schools in need. Due to Riddle's efforts, by 1952 the number of government schools with specially designated library areas had risen from 6 to 603. She also promoted the employment of full-time librarians in large schools and teacher-librarians in smaller ones.

After retiring from the Department of Education in 1954, Riddle became director of the Young Women's Christian Association's hostel at Binghamton, New York. In 1957 she was engaged by the Y.W.C.A. of Sydney to catalogue its library. Back in Adelaide, she was teacher-librarian at Nailsworth Girls' Technical High School (1960-61) and Methodist Ladies' College (1962-70). She served on the executives of the Y.W.C.A. of Adelaide (1947-55) and the New Education Fellowship. Convenor (1949-79) of the international committee of the National Council of Women of South Australia, she was a member of the Australian-American and United Nations associations, and a council-member of the Wanslea Emergency Home for Children (1962-68) and of St Ann's College, University of Adelaide (1953-55). In 1969 she was appointed M.B.E. She died on 17 September 1979 in Adelaide and was cremated. The bookroom at Marjorie Black House, Unley, was named after her.

SMH, 20 Jan 1945; *Advertiser* (Adel), 15 Sept 1955, 25 Sept 1968, 1 Jan 1969; J. Brewer, A Critical History of the Development of School Libraries in South Australia (M.Lib. thesis, Monash Univ, 1982), and for bib; Riddle papers (Mort L); information from Mr H. Mincham, Hope Valley, and Miss D. Gum, Ashford, Adel.   P. A. HOWELL

RIDE, SIR LINDSAY TASMAN (1898-1977), physiologist, soldier and university vice-chancellor, was born on 10 October 1898 at

Newstead, Victoria, fifth child of Australian-born parents William Ride, a 'pioneer' Presbyterian missionary, and his wife Eliza Mary, née Best, daughter of a stonemason. After attending three state schools in the country, Lindsay was awarded a scholarship to Scotch College, Melbourne, where he excelled in sport and won a senior government scholarship. Red-headed and 5 ft 10 ins (178 cm) tall, 'Ginger' Ride enlisted in the Australian Imperial Force on 14 February 1917 and joined the 38th Battalion on the Western Front early in 1918. Twice wounded (once severely), he was 'invalided out' of the army on 24 April 1919. In retrospect, he was disgusted by trench warfare, but concluded that sportsmanship and teamwork had been vital to the A.I.F.'s victories.

Enrolling in medicine at the University of Melbourne, Ride took a commission (1921) in the Melbourne University Rifles, represented the university in athletics, rowed and played cricket and football for Ormond [q.v.5] College, and presided (1921-22) over the Students' Representative Council. He was elected Victorian Rhodes scholar for 1922. At New College, Oxford (B.A., 1924; M.A., B.M., B.Ch., 1928; D.M., 1939), 'Blue' Ride was captain of boats and steward of the junior common-room; although his academic results were mediocre, he impressed authorities as 'a good Rhodes Scholar' and a 'first rate fellow'.

At St Columba's Church, Chelsea, London, on 30 June 1925 Ride married with the forms of the Church of Scotland Mary Margaret Louise Fenety, a Canadian. Entering Guy's Hospital, he qualified as a member of the Royal College of Surgeons, England, and as a licentiate of the Royal College of Physicians, London. He showed a flair for medical research. On 21 October 1928 he was appointed professor of physiology at the University of Hong Kong, where he investigated blood groups of the peoples of the Pacific and wrote *Genetics and the Clinician* (Bristol, England, 1938). Committing himself to the colony, 'Doc' Ride was commissioned in the Hong Kong Volunteer Defence Corps and appointed a justice of the peace. He played for the Hong Kong Cricket Club, rowed, and became an elder in the Union Church. An excellent baritone, he helped to found (1934) the Hong Kong Singers.

Foreseeing war, Ride sent his wife and children to Australia in 1938. (The marriage did not survive the long separation). He commanded the Hong Kong Field Ambulance in 1941, but was taken prisoner by the Japanese in December. On 9 January 1942 he escaped to unoccupied China, a feat for which he was appointed O.B.E. (1942). He then formed and commanded (as a colonel in the Indian Army) the British Army Aid Group which helped escapees from Hong Kong, provided medical and other assistance to prisoners of war, and gathered intelligence. Nicknamed 'The Smiling Tiger', Ride was elevated to C.B.E. (1944) for his outstanding leadership. He later served (1948-62) as colonel commandant of the Royal Hong Kong Defence Force.

In April 1949 Ride was appointed vice-chancellor of the university. He set about rebuilding its shattered fabric: during his fifteen-year tenure twenty-two new buildings were erected and student numbers increased threefold. A decisive man, genial but authoritarian, he had a loyal following among older staff but his paternalism was challenged in later years by some more recently appointed. He was knighted in 1962, awarded honorary degrees by the universities of Toronto, Melbourne, London and Hong Kong, and made an honorary member (1962) of the Royal Academy of Music, London.

On 12 November 1954 at the Union Church, Hong Kong, Ride married Violet May Witchell; she had been his secretary before the war. He was a member of the 1967 commission of inquiry into the Kowloon riots, honorary colonel of the Hong Kong Regiment, president and conductor of the Hong Kong Singers, chairman of the Hong Kong Music Society and author of 'a monumental survey' of the old Protestant cemetery at Macao. Sir Lindsay died on 17 October 1977 in Hong Kong and was cremated; his wife survived him, as did the two sons and two daughters of his first marriage.

B. Mellor, *The University of Hong Kong* (Hong Kong, 1980); E. Ride, *BAAG* (Hong Kong, 1981); C. Matthews and O. Cheung (eds), *Dispersal and Renewal* (Hong Kong, 1998); Rhodes Trust, records (Rhodes House, Oxford, and Univ Melb Archives); Ride papers on the British Army Aid Group (AWM); information from Dr W. D. L. Ride (held by ADB).

J. R. POYNTER

RIDGE, CLIVE FARRAN; see FARRAN-RIDGE

RILEY, ALEXANDER (1884-1970), tracker, was born on 26 May 1884 at Nymagee, New South Wales, son of John Riley, labourer, and his wife Mary, née Calligan. Alec was part-Aboriginal and worked as a stationhand. On 11 June 1911 he joined the New South Wales Police Force as a tracker and was based at Dubbo. His tracking skills helped to break a cattle-thieving ring in 1913. He also assisted in the recapture of two escapees from the Dubbo gaol. Although he resigned from the police force on 31 August 1914, he was re-appointed on 1 January 1918.

On Christmas Eve that year, after following her footprints across rough and barren terrain, Riley found a barefooted 6-year-old girl who had been lost for twenty-four hours in the mountains near Stuart Town. He helped to apprehend George Earsman in 1921; Earsman was later sentenced to death for the murder of Alexander Matheson. In the early 1920s Riley was credited with the capture of the 'last of the bushrangers', Roy Governor, a younger brother of the notorious Jimmy Governor [q.v.9]. Roy, an expert bushman, had evaded thirty policemen and 'blacktrackers' for three months until Riley discovered that he tied pieces of sheepskin—wool-side down—to his feet to disguise his tracks.

At the Presbyterian manse, Wellington, on 14 June 1924 Riley married 26-year-old Ethel Taylor. He was a well-known horseman in the Dubbo district, appearing at many country shows and with the travelling rodeo of the Police Boys' Clubs.

In 1939 Riley helped in the arrest of Andrew Moss, who had reputedly killed thirteen people over twenty years. It had taken him more than twelve months of 'painstaking investigation to run this man to earth'. Moss was charged with three murders, convicted and sentenced to death, but his sentence was commuted to life imprisonment. That year Riley was officially commended for 'his excellent tracking work which led to the recovery of property to the value of approximately £80, stolen from a store at Trangie, and also for the arrest of the offenders responsible for the robbery'. In 1940 he was able to demonstrate that the death of a child, whose remains were found in a gorge near Bugaldie, was the result of an accident rather than foul play.

When he was promoted sergeant on 5 August 1941 Riley was the first Aborigine to gain that rank in the New South Wales Police Force. Again officially commended for finding a missing man in April 1942, he was awarded the King's Police and Fire Services Medal for Distinguished Service in January 1943. He lived all his working life at the Talbragar Aboriginal Reserve, by the Macquarie River, near Dubbo, and was permitted to remain there with his wife after his retirement from the police force on 13 July 1950. Survived by his five sons and three daughters, he died on 29 October 1970 at Dubbo and was buried with Anglican rites in the local cemetery. In 1996 Michael Riley made a short documentary film, *Blacktracker*, about his grandfather and his 'legendary skills and deep humanity'. It was screened by the Australian Broadcasting Commission in September 1997.

M. Riley, *Yarns from the Talbragar Reserve* (Dubbo, NSW, 1999); *South West Pacific*, no 22, 1949, p 46; NSW Aborigines Welfare Bd, *Dawn*, 6, nos 6, 7, 8, 1957, 11, no 11, 1962, 16, no 1, 1967; *New Dawn*, Jan 1971; *Canb Times*, 1 Sept 1997; Riley's police service record (NSWA). GEOFFREY GRAY

RILEY, BERNARD BLOMFIELD (1912-1978), barrister and judge, was born on 21 July 1912 at Cairns, Queensland, second child of Australian-born parents Bernard Rocks Riley, manager of the Colonial Sugar Refining Co. Ltd's Hambledon Mill, and his wife Isabella Marion, née Murphy. Bernard was a fifth-generation Australian, through his great-great-grandfather Richard Brooks [q.v.1]. He attended Kersworth Preparatory School, Rose Bay, then boarded at The King's School, Parramatta. A fine middle-distance runner and school captain (1930), he won the Broughton and Forrest [qq.v.1] exhibition. He graduated from Keble College, Oxford (B.A., 1934; M.A., 1951), with second-class honours in jurisprudence, and was called to the Bar at Gray's Inn, London, on 3 July 1935. Back in Sydney, he was associate, successively, to Chief Justice (Sir) Frederick Jordan and (Sir) Colin Davidson [qq.v.9,8]. On 4 May 1936 he was admitted to the New South Wales Bar. He built up a practice (mainly in Equity) from chambers in Phillip Street.

On 21 July 1941 Riley was commissioned in the Militia and posted to the artillery. At St Martin's Anglican Church, Killara, on 15 December that year he married Stephanie Marguerite Cooper Day. He joined the Australian Imperial Force on 17 July 1942. Transferred to the Australian Army Legal Corps as captain, he served in Darwin and New Britain. At Rabaul in December 1945 he prosecuted at the trial of suspected Japanese war criminals. He was placed on the Reserve of Officers in Sydney on 30 May 1946.

Resuming his practice at the Bar, Riley appeared in the Bank nationalization case, and was a junior counsel to (Sir) Victor Windeyer, Q.C., who assisted the (Petrov) royal commission into espionage (1954-55). Riley published *The Law Relating to Bills of Exchange in Australia* (1953), which was used as a textbook for many years, and lectured occasionally at the University of Sydney. Taking silk in New South Wales on 3 August 1960 and in Victoria on 9 October 1962, he presided (1967-69) over the New South Wales Bar Association. In 1968 he was elected to the Legislative Council.

Riley was a director of C.S.R. (1958-73) and the Australian Mutual Provident Society (1963-73), chancellor of the diocese of Bathurst, a member of the Walter and Eliza Hall [qq.v.9] Trust, a governor (1948-62) of King's and honorary secretary (1958-62) of the school council. Widely read, he had a love of spoken and written English: the annual Bernard Riley English language prize at King's was named after him. With his lucid mind, nice turn of phrase and ready wit, he was popular as a guest speaker. He belonged to the Australian Club and the Royal Australian Historical Society.

Appointed a judge of the Federal Court of Bankruptcy from 22 October 1973, Riley was elevated in January 1977 to the bench of the new Federal Court of Australia. His work was largely in the bankruptcy jurisdiction. He also became deputy-president of the Trade Practices Tribunal, where his background in commercial law was valued. As a barrister and as a judge, he treated everyone with tact and good manners. Fearless independence and a high sense of propriety characterized both his professional and private life. Sir Nigel Bowen, his colleague and friend, thought him 'kind, gentle and honourable'.

Riley died of coronary thrombosis on 4 August 1978 in Royal North Shore Hospital and was cremated; his wife, son and daughter survived him.

JRAHS, 46, 1960, p 206; *Aust Law J*, 52, Nov 1978, p 653; *Aust Law Reports*, 19, 1978, p ix; *The King's School Mag*, Dec 1978, p 105; The King's School, Parramatta, Syd, Archives; Trade Practices Tribunal, ts of procs, 8 Aug 1978 (NL); family information.

JONATHAN W. DE B. PERSSE

RILEY, FREDERICK JOHN (1886-1970), political activist and trade unionist, was born on 18 May 1886 at Stirling, South Australia, eldest of six children of Frederick Riley, blacksmith, and his wife Susannah, née Williams. His father was a leading trade unionist, a pioneering Labor Party activist and a municipal councillor. Young Fred left Hindmarsh State School at the age of 12 and worked as a labourer in every mainland State except Western Australia.

In Sydney, Riley associated with Harry Holland [q.v.9] in socialist agitation. At Wollongong in 1914, while defending the principle of free speech, he ignored a policeman's directive to cease addressing a public meeting and 'move on': he refused to pay the fine, and was gaoled for a week. He moved to Adelaide before settling in Melbourne. In 1916 he became secretary of the Victorian council of the Australian Peace Alliance. A 'large, thick-set man' with a prominent chin, he frequently found himself involved in brawls for leading anti-conscription rallies; he was often fined, even when he tried to protect Vida Goldstein [q.v.9] and other women speakers from being attacked by off-duty soldiers.

Riley was a founding member (1918) of the Y Club, a discussion group of socialists and rationalists, which he later served as secretary. In 1919 he took part in the Melbourne waterfront strike. He helped to collect and distribute more than £10 000 in relief, and to negotiate a settlement of the dispute. In a civil ceremony at 362 Little Collins Street, Melbourne, on 27 April 1920 he married Alice Ann Warburton, née Large, a 44-year-old divorcee

and fellow organizer of strike relief. After the unions had appointed him (1919) to collect evidence for the Commonwealth royal commission on the basic wage, his career took a crucial turn in 1922 when he became secretary of the Manufacturing Grocers' Employees' Federation of Australia and of its Victorian branch. He proved an effective defender of the interests of a largely female rank and file. According to one observer, he was 'the most subtle and charming propagandist at Melbourne Trades Hall'.

From the mid-1920s Riley was a powerful force in the Victorian labour movement. President of the Trades Hall Council in 1931-32, he was president of the Victorian branch of the Australian Labor Party in 1941-42. Frank McManus, a Riley protégé, recalled his mentor as 'a wily tactician' who—as chairman of the agenda committee at various conferences—was 'followed like the tail of a comet by delegates who wanted some item on the agenda that Fred did not'. Riley was a member of the Victorian Advisory Committee on Price Fixing (from 1939) and of its successor, the Victorian Prices Decontrol Advisory Committee (until 1954). In January 1942 he was appointed an adviser to (Sir) Douglas Copland [q.v.13], the Commonwealth prices commissioner. A widower from 1940, he married Annie Elliott Warn, a 37-year-old housekeeper, on 17 July 1943 at St Luke's Anglican Church, Fitzroy.

Strongly anti-communist since the 1930s, Riley was one of the delegates of the 'old', right-wing Victorian executive refused admission to the A.L.P.'s federal conference in Hobart in 1955, and one of the few non-Catholics to align himself with the Democratic Labor Party (State president 1960-61). He retired as union secretary in 1961. Between 1913 and 1955 he had made four attempts to enter the New South Wales, Commonwealth and Victorian parliaments, standing once as a socialist, twice as an A.L.P. candidate and once for the D.L.P. Survived by his wife, he died on 2 April 1970 at Reservoir and was cremated. His estate was sworn for probate at $110 713. The political ephemera which Riley had avidly collected is held by the State Library of Victoria.

R. Murray, *The Split* (Melb, 1970); F. McManus, *The Tumult and the Shouting* (Adel, 1977); Riley papers (NL).

FRANK BONGIORNO

RIMMER, WILLIAM BOLTON (1882-1945), astronomer and public servant, was born on 9 November 1882 at Fazakerley, Lancashire, England, son of John Rimmer, farmer, and his wife Sarah Jane, née Bolton. William studied engineering at University College,

Liverpool (B.Sc., 1903; M.Sc., 1906; Victoria University of Manchester), and worked as a surveyor in British Columbia, Canada. Enlisting in the Royal Engineers in 1916, he was commissioned in June 1917 and promoted captain in July 1919. After he was demobilized he decided to become an astronomer and carried out spectroscopic research at the Imperial College of Science, Kensington, London.

In 1921 Rimmer obtained a position as research assistant at the Norman Lockyer Observatory, a small, private astrophysical establishment near Sidmouth, Devon. Selected as assistant to Dr W. G. Duffield [q.v.8], director of the newly established Commonwealth Solar Observatory at Mount Stromlo, Federal Capital Territory, he sailed for Australia and joined the observatory staff in December 1924. In the sacristy of St Gregory's Catholic Church, Queanbeyan, New South Wales, on 14 June 1927 he married 29-year-old Kathleen Anne Hayes.

Until 1939 Rimmer was the only trained astronomer at Mount Stromlo; the other four or five staff-members were solar or geophysicists. In 1926-29 his chief astronomical task was to photograph spectra of the brighter stars, especially in the southern sky, using the Oddie [q.v.5] 9-inch (23 cm) refracting telescope. For this purpose, the telescope had been provided with a glass prism which fitted over its objective to form spectra of stars in the focal plane, where they could be photographed. Over two thousand such spectra were obtained. They were used to estimate absolute magnitudes (luminosities or candlepowers) of the stars, mainly from the appearance of hydrogen lines in their spectra. Rimmer's account of this work—an extensive investigation which did him credit—was only the second paper to be published from the new observatory. For more than twenty years his study remained the only substantial astrophysical programme that had been carried out in Australia.

When Duffield died suddenly in August 1929, it was decided to economize by appointing no new director. Rimmer was made officer-in-charge, a position to which he could hardly have aspired in the ordinary way. With the added responsibilities the post entailed, his research had to be limited to maintaining two programmes concerning the sun. In the first, the sun's brightness was observed around noon every clear day with a pyrheliometer to determine whether its radiation was constant or whether it varied with, for example, the sunspot cycle. In the second programme, a pyranometer made a continuous record of the heating of the earth by the energy supplied by the sun, either directly, or as diffused by the sky and clouds. The results were of interest to agriculturists, meteorologists and others.

Measurements in both projects continued until the outbreak of World War II.

Rimmer had been appointed O.B.E. (1938) for his services to astronomy. A new director was finally selected in 1939 and Rimmer was redesignated first assistant. He was president (1940-41) of the Royal Society of Canberra and a member (from 1930) of the local branch of the Professional Officers' Association, Commonwealth Public Service. He also belonged to Rotary. Survived by his wife, he died of a cerebral haemorrhage on 2 July 1945 at Mount Stromlo and was buried in Canberra cemetery with Baptist forms.

Memoirs of Commonwealth Solar Observatory (Canb, 1935); *Monthly Notices of the Roy Astronomical Soc*, 1920-23; Cwlth Observatory, *Annual Report supplement*, 1950; *Records of Aust Academy of Science*, 4, no 1, 1978; *Canb Times*, 3 July 1945.

S. C. B. GASCOIGNE

RINGROSE, EDWARD COLIN DAVENPORT (1899-1957), educationist, was born on 30 June 1899 at Herberton, Queensland, seventh child of London-born parents Robert Colin Ringrose, barrister, and his wife Lydia Isabella, née Emery. Educated at Townsville and Brisbane Grammar schools, Ted won an open scholarship to the University of Queensland (B.Sc., 1920; B.A., 1926). While teaching at Rockhampton (1920-24) and Ipswich Grammar schools (1925 and 1927) and Brisbane Boys' College (1926), he continued his studies as an external student of the University of Melbourne (Dip.Ed., 1927; B.Ed., 1936). At Ipswich on 27 July 1928 he married with Methodist forms Sylvia Daphne Pratt. From that year he lectured at the Teachers' Training College, Brisbane. He was president of the State Secondary School Teachers' Association (1932-33 and 1935-36) and of the Queensland Teachers' Union (1936-37).

In 1937 Ringrose was appointed lecturer in education and experimental psychology in the department of philosophy, University of Queensland. Although the university refused to release him for military service in 1942, he served as a part-time senior psychologist (1943-45) in the Department of Labour and National Service. He played a central role in the expansion of the university's education programme by developing courses for students who wanted to obtain diplomas and certificates in education, and for those who chose to pursue bachelor's and master's degrees. Promoted associate-professor in 1946, he was appointed dean of the new faculty of education in 1949 and director of external studies in 1950.

In a period of rapid growth in external studies, Ringrose oversaw wide-ranging reforms, including the establishment of a board of external studies, the appointment of academics with appropriate teaching skills, the continued development of the Thatcher [q.v.] Library and vacation schools, the introduction of study circles and centres in regional areas, and the publication of a handbook. Under his direction, courses were made available to armed services personnel, and to residents in the Territory of Papua and New Guinea, the South-West Pacific and South-East Asia. Ringrose was a member (1947-57) of the university senate, an associate-member (1950-57) of the professorial board, chairman of the board of external studies (1949-57) and the library committee (1951-56), and a member of the John Darnell fine-arts committee. Tall, with angular features and a commanding presence, he was intelligent, enthusiastic and thorough, with a capacity for clear thinking and a breadth of outlook and understanding. His organizing ability and leadership qualities enabled him to work well in a team and to harness the talents of others.

Ringrose was chairman of the State branch of the National Association for the Prevention of Tuberculosis in Australia (1956-57) and the education committee of the Crèche and Kindergarten Association of Queensland (1945-57). In addition, he was a member of the Queensland Marriage Guidance Council. A keen gardener and fisherman, he also enjoyed tennis and bushwalking. He died of cancer on 1 May 1957 at Beerwah Private Hospital, Brisbane, and was cremated; his wife and their son survived him. The Ringrose libraries, in Queensland's provincial cities and towns, were named after him.

R. D. Kitchen, *Men of Vision* (Brisb, 1985); M. I. Thomis, *A Place of Light and Learning* (Brisb, 1985); Univ Qld Archives.   JOHN LAVERTY

RIORDAN, WILLIAM JAMES FREDERICK (1908-1973), politician, was born on 8 February 1908 at Chillagoe, Queensland, son of William James Riordan, engine driver, and his wife Annie Helen, née Page, both Queensland born. Educated at state schools at Chillagoe, Mareeba and Gordonvale, and at Brisbane Grammar School, young Bill worked in the Department of Justice, Brisbane, for seven years before becoming secretary to his father, a former trade-union official, who was appointed to the Industrial Court of Queensland in 1933.

Growing up in a family with a trade-union and political background (his father was a member of the Legislative Council in 1917-23 and his uncle Ernest was to enter the Legislative Assembly in 1936), Riordan had become interested in politics at an early age and joined the Australian Labor Party. On the death of

another uncle, David ('Darby') Riordan, in 1936, he interrupted his legal studies at the University of Queensland and won Darby's Federal seat of Kennedy at a by-election on 12 December; at the age of 28 he was the youngest member of the House of Representatives. He was admitted to the Queensland Bar on 22 April 1941, but never practised. On 19 December 1942 at St Mary's Catholic Cathedral, Sydney, he married Kathleen Amelda Garvey (d.1970), an interior decorator; they were to remain childless.

The electorate of Kennedy covered much of Central and North Queensland. Representing his constituents in this vast area, Riordan faced a daunting task—communications were poor, the roads being mostly gravel or worse, and telephone services proved unreliable—but he received valuable support from the powerful Australian Workers' Union. In the late 1930s he was concerned about the vulnerability of northern Australia and, from the Opposition back-benches, urged the government to take measures to bolster defence.

Labor gained office under John Curtin [q.v.13] in October 1941. Riordan was elected chairman of committees and deputy-Speaker in June 1943. He was appointed minister for the navy in the second Chifley [q.v.13] government in November 1946 and held that portfolio until Labor's defeat at the general elections in December 1949. Since postwar defence policy had been broadly settled, his roles as minister were to run his department and implement the re-equipment programme, which included the introduction of a fleet air-arm. Although he knew little about naval matters, he carefully read the papers submitted to him, effectively represented the navy in cabinet, and made himself available to politicians of all parties who sought his assistance.

Riordan adhered firmly to A.L.P. principles and embraced the socialization objective (1921). A member (1941-42) of the joint parliamentary committee on broadcasting, he had endorsed the minority Labor Party report which recommended the nationalization of commercial radio-stations. He backed the government's proposal to regulate the marketing of primary products: in 1946 he spoke approvingly of the sugar industry, in which prices and charges for milling and refining were fixed by the government, and workers' wages were determined by arbitration. Legislation introduced in 1947 to nationalize the private banks also received his support.

An electoral redistribution in 1948 led to Riordan's electorate being halved in size, but it still covered much of Central Queensland. He was able to retain his predominantly rural seat by developing and maintaining strong personal ties with working-class families in the sugar, mining and meat industries, and in the railways. During parliamentary recesses he travelled constantly throughout his electorate, but the strain taxed his health. He retired from parliament in 1966 on medical advice. In the ensuing by-election the Country Party won Kennedy.

A tall, well-built man, Riordan liked people and was unfailingly courteous to them. He had a strong voice, but, due to his impaired hearing, sometimes spoke more loudly in public than he intended. For recreation, he played golf. In 1967 he was appointed C.B.E. He died of pneumonia on 15 January 1973 in Princess Alexandra Hospital, Brisbane, and was buried in Nudgee cemetery.

T. R. Frame et al (eds), *Reflections on the RAN* (Syd, 1991); *PD* (HR), 18 June 1937, p 80, 3 May 1938, p 713, 2 June 1942, p 1882, 10 Apr 1946, p 1321, 6 Nov 1947, p 1792, 11 May 1966, pp 1684, 1687; *Cairns Post*, 31 Oct 1936; *SMH*, 16 Jan 1973; information from Mr J. B. Howse, Griffith, Canb, and Sir James Killen, Chapel Hill, Brisb.   A. N. PRESTON

RITCHARD, CYRIL; see ELLIOTT, LEAH

RITCHIE, DAVE; see SANDS

RITCHIE, ERNEST (1917-1976), organic chemist, was born on 11 February 1917 at Waverley, Sydney, third child of Thomas Wallace Ritchie, a railway guard from Scotland, and his native-born wife Myra Florence Charlotte, née Calf. Ern attended Woollahra Public, Randwick Intermediate and Sydney Boys' High schools. In 1933 he entered the University of Sydney (B.Sc., 1937; M.Sc., 1939; D.Sc., 1954) where he graduated with first-class honours in general and inorganic chemistry, and won a Blue for Rugby Union football. He belonged to a group that included John Cornforth, Arthur Birch, Rita Harradence and (Sir) Ronald Nyholm [q.v.15], all of whom were to make outstanding contributions to chemical research.

On graduation Ritchie joined the staff of the university as a demonstrator and pursued research in synthetic organic chemistry with Francis Lions [q.v.15]. Promoted lecturer (1941) and senior lecturer (1946), he was a stimulating and methodical teacher, 'often speaking without notes'. At the district registrar's office, Waverley, on 7 February 1945 he married Mary Euphemia ('Maisie') Smith.

In 1948 Ritchie embarked on the chemical characterization of Australian plant constituents, including alkaloids, pigments, resins and volatile oils. His first project concerned the pigment class, *anthocyanins*, which were detected in the fruits and flowers of some three hundred Australian and New Guinean species. The broad phytochemical programme was carried on in partnership successively with G. K. Hughes and W. C. Taylor, and involved numerous collecting-expeditions to tropical rain-forests with botanists from the Commonwealth Scientific and Industrial Research Organization. One consignment of collected bark weighed 727 lbs (330 kg).

The attempted elucidation of 'biogenesis'— the elaborate chemical pathways believed to operate in living plants—was a topic widely discussed. This field of research, pioneered by (Sir) Robert Robinson, inaugural professor (1912-15) of organic chemistry at the University of Sydney, became one of Ritchie's interests. Of his many investigations, a decade-long study of alkaloids derived from the Queensland genus, *Galbulimima*, was accorded much praise.

Ritchie's record of fostering high achievement in many of his former research students matched his success as an investigator. He rose to become professor of organic chemistry (1967) and head (1971-72) of the (combined) school of chemistry. On leave, he was twice a research fellow at the University of Oxford: in 1954-55 with Robinson, and in 1970 investigating microbiological chemistry. Unassuming in manner, Ritchie was enthusiastic, cheerful and given to understatement. He was respected as an academic administrator, a role he played reluctantly but effectively. In public and in committee he 'was terse and to the point'. Under his leadership the department of organic chemistry enhanced its reputation for research and received increased grants. As head of school he introduced new committee structures which allowed academic and non-academic members of staff from all levels to participate in policy-making.

His work attracted international recognition. Ritchie was awarded the Edgeworth David [q.v.8] medal (1948) by the Royal Society of New South Wales and the H. G. Smith [q.v.11] memorial medal (1963) by the Royal Australian Chemical Institute. In 1963 he was elected a fellow of the Australian Academy of Science. His publications included 146 research articles and two book-chapters, covering not only natural-product chemistry but also synthetic and mechanistic chemistry. He belonged to the R.S.N.S.W., helped to found (1965) the *Australian Journal of Chemistry* and served as a member of its advisory committee.

A 'congenial companion with a dry sense of humour and simple tastes', Ritchie 'liked his beer', 'rolled his own cigarettes', and enjoyed gardening, fishing, reading, and listening to music. He died suddenly of coronary thrombosis on 9 April 1976 at his Roseville home and was cremated; his wife, and their daughter and two sons survived him.

Univ Syd, *Gazette*, July 1976, p 22; *Records of the Aust Academy of Science*, 3, no 3/4, Nov 1977, p 111; *SMH*, 10 June 1939, 7 May 1946, 10 Mar 1954, 22 Mar 1967; information from Mr T. Robinson, Univ Syd Archives. H. G. HOLLAND

RITCHIE, RUSSEL PETER; *see* SANDS

RITCHIE, SIR THOMAS MALCOLM (1894-1971), electrical engineer and Liberal Party president, was born on 11 June 1894 at Carlton, Melbourne, son of Thomas Ritchie, a tinsmith from Scotland, and his Victorian-born wife Margaret Tascar, née Henry, a tailoress. After attending Lee Street State School, Malcolm won an Arnot [q.v.7] scholarship to the Working Men's College where he obtained a diploma in electrical and mechanical engineering.

At 21 Ritchie formed his own company, the first in Australia to manufacture heavy-duty electrical switchgear. From 1923 he organized mergers with British and American companies, expanding his activities to employ thousands of workers in four States, and helping to pioneer manufacturing in a number of areas, including general and distribution switchgear. At the Presbyterian Church, Armadale, on 22 April 1924 he married Phyllis Elizabeth Brown. In 1934 he was appointed general manager of Noyes Bros Pty Ltd, which was then moving into the supply of radio sets and accessories. Having settled in Sydney, he served as a member (1935-46) of the New South Wales Electricity Advisory Committee and, during World War II, as State business administrator of the Commonwealth Department of Munitions.

A practical man with a precise mind and efficient habits, Ritchie was below average height, beetle-browed and square-jawed, with steel-blue eyes which had an impish glint. As a leading, self-styled 'industrialist', he was often outspoken, using guest appearances around Australia and in Britain to challenge conventional wisdoms. In 1948 he argued that capital would be more effectively utilized by a 56-hour week, with workers employed in weekly shifts of 28 hours each. In 1950 he proposed that Britain should export entire factories to Australia—including the office-boys—to help preserve Australia from 'millions of South-East Asians who are anxious to occupy the country and are all out to win it'.

Ritchie's business peers acknowledged his talents by electing him to official positions with several employer organizations. By 1950 he was chairman and managing director of Noyes Bros and of Crompton Parkinson (Aust.) Pty Ltd, subsidiaries of a British electrical-engineering group. Considered by the better-bred to be 'pushy', he joined exclusive clubs in Sydney and Melbourne, and was knighted in 1951 for his war-work. He involved himself in community life through Rotary, the Boy Scouts' Association and the Fairbridge [q.v.8] Farm Schools.

Opposed to the extremes of both the left and the right of Australian politics, Ritchie made a substantial contribution to the emergence and development of the Liberal Party of Australia. He chaired the party's provisional executive in 1945, raised funds in Sydney and Melbourne to finance the federal secretariat, persuaded a sceptical Queensland People's Party to become the Liberal Party in the northern State, and drafted the plan for the federal organization of the party. And it was Ritchie, unanimously elected the first federal president, who formally inaugurated the Liberal Party on 31 August 1945 in the Sydney Town Hall.

He had a difficult relationship with (Sir) Robert Menzies [q.v.15], the Liberal parliamentary leader. While Menzies believed that businessmen were not 'politics conscious', Ritchie, the self-made man, felt more comfortable among those who worked with their hands. His plans to raise 'millions' for party funds and to popularize 'big business' provoked Menzies to claim that potential supporters would turn away if they detected 'the power of money' in the party. Ritchie resented the implication that he relied on his business associates to gauge public opinion. Having worked closely with the party's branches, and in factories, he claimed to be closer to 'ordinary Australians' than Menzies and some of his parliamentary colleagues.

As federal president, Ritchie pursued two causes. He sought to involve the extra-parliamentary organization in making policy, and to create a truly national party with a 'national spirit'. Menzies helped to defeat the first objective, and the near-autonomous State divisions thwarted the second. Even so, Ritchie managed to translate vague aspirations into a working organization. R. G. (Baron) Casey [q.v.13] succeeded him as president in 1947, but Ritchie was recalled to office when Casey won a seat in the House of Representatives in the coalition's landslide victory of 1949. Ill health forced him to resign the presidency in 1951—just when his frank speaking and determination to involve the organization in policy matters were beginning to irritate the new Menzies government. Ritchie remained, however, a party trustee until 1955.

Sir Malcolm gradually withdrew from his multiple directorships and, in 1962, established a Poll Hereford stud at his property, Trelm, at Bong Bong, near Moss Vale. A keen sportsman, he continued to play golf and laid his own bowling green at Trelm where he entertained Sydney friends. He died on

22 February 1971 at his home and was cremated with Anglican rites. His wife survived him. They had no children.

I. Hancock, *National and Permanent?* (Melb, 2000); *Punch* (Melb), 29 Dec 1921; *SMH*, 24 Feb 1971; Menzies *and* Ritchie papers, *and* Liberal Party of Aust papers (NL).   I. R. HANCOCK

RIVETT, ROHAN DEAKIN (1917-1977), journalist, newspaper editor and author, was born on 16 January 1917 at South Yarra, Melbourne, elder son of Australian-born parents (Sir) Albert Cherbury David Rivett [q.v.11], university lecturer, and his wife Stella, née Deakin. Alfred Deakin and Albert Rivett [qq.v.8,11] were his grandfathers. Rohan pronounced his surname Riv*ett*. At the age of 13, while a student at Wesley College, he visited England with his father and wrote a book-length narrative about the Australian cricketers' 1930 tour. Like other students at Wesley who became writers, he learned a lot from his English master A. A. Phillips. Entering the University of Melbourne (B.A., 1938), he lived at Queen's College, and studied history and political science; he graduated with first-class honours, as did his classmates Manning Clark and A. G. L. Shaw. Clark remembered him as 'an enthusiast'.

He and Clark both embarked on study at Balliol College, Oxford. Just before sailing, Rivett had acted in a Queen's College production of the American dramatist Clifford Odets's anti-capitalist and pro-Soviet play, *Waiting for Lefty*; his brother Ken recalled that he was 'very involved, emotionally as well as theatrically'. The radicalism of the master of Balliol, A. D. (Baron) Lindsay, attracted him. In October 1938, his first month at Oxford, he helped Lindsay campaign as the Independent, anti-Munich candidate at a by-election in which the Conservative majority was nearly halved. Rivett's interest in international affairs, aroused earlier in Melbourne by W. Macmahon Ball's lectures in political science, became intense, and remained so. When World War II began, he and Clark returned to Australia without completing their courses.

Unable to enlist in the Australian Imperial Force because recruiting had almost ceased, Rivett joined the Melbourne morning daily, the *Argus*, as a cadet reporter. On 2 January 1940 at St John's Church of England, Camberwell, he married Gwyneth Maude Terry, a student. He eventually enlisted in the A.I.F. on 7 June, but in August was released on loan to the Federal Department of Information to prepare news bulletins in Sydney for an overseas radio service run by Ball. In 1941 he broadcast news commentaries for this service from Melbourne. After Japan entered the war in

December, he volunteered to work with the Malaya Broadcasting Corporation in Singapore. He was discharged from the A.I.F. that month.

On 9 February 1942 Rivett told the world that Japanese forces had landed on Singapore. Although the British surrendered the island on 15 February, he was not captured until 8 March, in Java, after harrowing journeys by sea and land. His experiences were described vividly in *Behind Bamboo* (Sydney, 1946) by 'Rohan D. Rivett, War Correspondent Prisoner of War on the Burma-Thailand Railway'. The book, 392 pages long, was written in October-November 1945 while its author was recovering from the rigours of captivity; reprinted eight times, it sold more than 100 000 copies. The years of imprisonment left him with an enduring respect for ordinary Australians and an enhanced awareness of Asia.

Rivett had returned to the *Argus,* but in January 1946 was recruited to the Melbourne evening *Herald* by Sir Keith Murdoch [q.v.10], chairman of the Herald & Weekly Times Ltd. He had also returned to a marriage which soon ended in divorce. His ex-wife Gwyneth was to marry the journalist and academic Hume Dow. At South Yarra on 17 October 1947 Rivett married with Methodist forms Nancy (Nan) Ethel Summers, an actress. They were to have a twin daughter and son, Rhyll and David, and another son Keith. David was named for his paternal grandfather, Keith for Murdoch.

At the *Herald* Rivett worked among other able and literate young men chosen personally by Murdoch. Having sent him to China in July 1947 to report on the civil war, Murdoch asked him to work in his London office from 1948. Rivett's dispatches impressed the proprietor, who invited him in 1951 to be editor-in-chief of Adelaide's evening daily, the *News*, almost the only paper in the group which Murdoch personally controlled. Murdoch had become vehemently anti-communist; he was satisfied that Rivett, though radical, had no sympathy with communism.

In late 1951 the Rivetts moved to Adelaide. Rohan was 34, and carried with him a sense of mission which marked him as both a Deakin and a Rivett. Murdoch died in October 1952, leaving the *News* to his 21-year-old son Rupert, then studying at Oxford. He and the Rivett family had been friends in England and became still closer in Adelaide. The young proprietor and the youngish editor shared a radical liberal view of the world and a Melburnian urge to liven up Adelaide. Rivett was allowed a freer hand than any other editor in Australia.

The *News* was an evening tabloid. It offered opinions on domestic and foreign matters (such as the gerrymander which ensured victory for the anti-Labor government of (Sir)

Thomas Playford in election after election, the White Australia policy, and the Anglo-French invasion of Egypt) different from those of the broadsheet morning *Advertiser*, a Herald & Weekly Times publication which seemed to Rivett and Murdoch to be an instrument of an Adelaide Establishment. Kingsley Martin, editor of London's left-wing *New Statesman and Nation*, judged the *News* 'the one genuinely liberal daily in the continent'. In the estimate of David Bowman, one of Rivett's protégés who later edited the *Canberra Times* and the *Sydney Morning Herald*, Rivett and J. D. Pringle were 'the only men of real consequence and capacity for thought' who edited Australian newspapers in the 1950s. 'I thought the sun shone out of him', he said of Rivett.

Listeners to the Australian Broadcasting Commission's radio programme, 'Notes on the News', were familiar with Rivett's earnest and lucid voice. The commentator himself made news when the A.B.C. prevented him from saying on 1 November 1956 that Britain was 'regarded throughout most of the world as an aggressor' against Egypt.

In 1959 the *News* was largely responsible for forcing Playford to set up a royal commission into the conviction for murder of Rupert Max Stuart, an Aborigine. Stuart's counsel J. W. Shand [q.v.] walked out of the commission after complaining that its chairman, Chief Justice Sir Mellis Napier [q.v.15], was impeding his cross-examination of a former policeman. The *News* reported the event in headlines which provoked an astonishing prosecution of the paper and its editor, not only on the unusual offence of criminal libel, but on the practically forgotten one of seditious libel. Beginning on 7 March 1960, the trial lasted for ten days. Cross-examination revealed that Murdoch and Rivett had worked together composing the headlines in question. The jury found the accused not guilty on all but one charge, on which it could not agree. With Rivett on bail, the remaining charge hung in the air for almost three months before being withdrawn on 6 June. Many people believed that Playford dropped the last charge in return for an undertaking from Murdoch that the *News* would go easy on his government.

Two weeks earlier Murdoch had moved from Adelaide to Sydney, where he had bought the *Daily Mirror*. By 1960 the *News*'s circulation and profit were both much higher than they had been before Rivett arrived. In that year, however, Murdoch dismissed him. Murdoch was certainly unhappy with some editorial decisions taken after he had left for Sydney. He said privately that he needed to be on the spot in order to give a steadying hand. 'Headstrong' was his word for Rivett. Even friends and admirers could describe Rivett as over-enthusiastic, or as courageous but unstable; he himself owned up to a 'fairly vol-

canic' nature, and said later that he had not expected the relationship with Murdoch to last forever. His replacement as editor was announced on 12 July 1960. Murdoch offered Rivett more generous terms than contractually required. He would later do the same to others in his long line of dismissed editors, but he appears to have remained singularly uncomfortable about the first.

Rivett never edited another paper and never overcame his sense of loss at having to leave the *News*. Between 1961 and 1963 he worked at Zurich, Switzerland, as director of the International Press Institute. The experience was not altogether happy, partly because he was not suited by temperament to serve many masters, but he drew satisfaction from steering help towards battling editors in Africa and Asia. He and his family returned to Melbourne. From that base, often travelling overseas with his wife, he worked as freelance journalist, broadcaster, public speaker and author, at every opportunity encouraging Australians to be aware of their Asian and Pacific neighbours. For the *Canberra Times* from 1964 he wrote on Victorian politics, international affairs and cricket; later he contributed to the radical weekly, *Nation Review*. He wrote several books, including a life of his father that shone with filial love and admiration, and a life of Herbert Brookes [q.v.7], Deakin's son-in-law. Rivett was 6 ft 1 in. (185 cm) tall, fair-haired, handsome and affable. He died suddenly of a coronary occlusion on 5 October 1977 at his Camberwell home and was cremated. His wife, and their daughter and two sons survived him; his estate was sworn for probate at $100 996.

K. S. Inglis, *The Stuart Case* (Melb, 1961); *Adel Review*, Oct 1995; P. Gifford, Aspects of Australian Newspaper Journalism and the Cold War, 1945-1966 (Ph.D. thesis, Murdoch Univ, 1997); H. de Berg, R. D. Rivett (taped interview, NL); Rohan Rivett papers (NL); family information; personal knowledge.   K. S. INGLIS

ROBERTS, CALEB GRAFTON (1898-1965), civil engineer, public servant and army officer, was born on 31 January 1898 at Balmain, Sydney, only child of Thomas William Roberts [q.v.11], the English-born artist who founded the Heidelberg school, and his wife Elizabeth, née Williamson, who came from Melbourne. The family moved to London in 1903 and set up house at Putney. 'Ca' was educated at St Paul's School, London, and the Royal Military Academy, Woolwich. A keen sportsman and a good scholar, he impressed his father as being a 'model all-rounder'. On 26 August 1916 he was commissioned in the Royal Engineers. He served in Palestine (1917), on the Western Front (1917-18) and in northern Russia (1919). Promoted lieutenant in February 1918, he won the Military Cross (1919) and played Rugby Union football for the British Army.

Back in England, Roberts resigned his commission, entered East London College, University of London (B.Sc.Eng Hons, 1922), and obtained a position as an assistant-engineer with the Ministry of Transport. On 30 September 1922 at the parish church, Kew, he married Norah Joan Watson. They lived near Billericay while he worked as a resident engineer on the reconstruction of the trunk road between London and Southend. With no prospects other than the promise of an interview with William Calder [q.v.7], chairman of the Country Roads Board of Victoria, he left with his family for Melbourne in August 1925. That year he began his employment with the C.R.B. as an assistant highway engineer.

Roberts was promoted to highway engineer in 1928. His responsibilities included the modernizing of road-making techniques and the introduction of cheaper construction methods. In 1937 he prepared the board's 'first 10-year plan for highway development'. An engineer officer (from 1931) with the Citizen Military Forces, he was gazetted acting major on 25 September 1939 and called up for full-time duty. In November he was transferred to the Australian Intelligence Corps. While serving at Army Headquarters, Melbourne, he was raised to temporary colonel and made director of military intelligence in February 1942.

On 1 July 1942 Roberts was appointed controller of the Allied Intelligence Bureau at Douglas MacArthur's [q.v.15] General Headquarters, South-West Pacific Area. The A.I.B. spread propaganda and conducted espionage, sabotage and guerrilla operations in enemy-held territory. By 1944 Roberts had charge of an organization comprising some 2000 men from Australia, Britain, the Netherlands, the United States of America and countries occupied by the Japanese. It was a daunting job. He found it difficult to reconcile the aims and allegiances of the various national groups, and to deal with some highly individualistic and temperamental members of his staff. On 17 October that year he relinquished his appointment and was placed on the Regimental Supernumerary List.

Resuming work at the C.R.B., Roberts was promoted chief engineer on 30 October 1944. He was to hold office in a period when the number of motor vehicles on Australian roads increased enormously. The board sent him to the U.S.A. and Britain from June 1947 to January 1948 to study the latest methods of building and maintaining roads, as well as new measures to improve safety. His report constituted a landmark in the analysis of Australia's needs: it recommended fresh approaches to highway planning, to predicting traffic demand, to constructing and repairing roads, and to developing the skills of personnel involved in these activities.

With prescience, Roberts urged the establishment of a national organization to study roads. After he and (Sir) Louis Loder [q.v.15] submitted a further report to the National Association of Australian State Road Authorities, the Australian Road Research Board was established in 1959. Roberts was also committed to advancing the engineering profession; to that end, he lectured at Swinburne Technical College and the University of Melbourne. Appointed deputy-chairman (1956) of the C.R.B., he became its chairman in July 1962. He retired on 30 June 1963, but was 'co-opted to serve in an advisory capacity' with the A.R.R.B. Survived by his wife and three sons, he died of coronary vascular disease on 23 November 1965 at Kew and was cremated.

Allison Ind, Roberts's deputy at the A.I.B., described him as 'a man of integrity, tremendous energy, and fearless loyalty'. Colleagues at the C.R.B. found him kind-hearted and appreciative, despite his stern manner and military bearing.

G. Long, *The Final Campaigns* (Canb, 1963); Aust Road Research Bd, *'The First 15 Years'* (Melb, 1975); W. K. Anderson, *Roads for the People* (Melb, 1994); Vic Roads Retirees Assn, *Reminiscences of Life in the Country Roads Board* (Melb, 1995); H. McQueen, *Tom Roberts* (Syd, 1996); *Roadlines*, Mar 1966; information from Mr C. P. Roberts, Hawthorn, Melb.

A. (LEN) PUGLISI

ROBERTS, FRANK (c.1899-1968), pastor, was born about 1899 at Blakebrook, near Lismore, New South Wales, eldest of fifteen children of Australian-born parents Lyle Roberts, labourer, and his wife Bella, née Davis. Lyle was a fully initiated Bundjalung who later converted to Christianity. Educated at the segregated school at Cabbage Tree Island station, near Wardell, which was maintained by the Board for Protection of Aborigines, Frank worked as a labourer. On 13 August 1918 at the Presbyterian manse, Ballina, he married Dorothy Hart. He took his family to Lismore, probably in 1925. Armed with character references and a solicitor's letter, he succeeded in enrolling his children in a public school. When the segregation of students resumed in 1928, the Robertses returned to Cabbage Tree Island.

Following a 'violent argument' with the station's manager, Roberts and his family moved in 1937 to the Aboriginal settlement at Tuncester, near Lismore, where there was no board-appointed manager. About 1933 he had committed himself to evangelism under the auspices of the United Aborigines Mission. Frank, his father and brothers held prayer meetings and ran the Tuncester settlement. In an effort to put pressure on families to move to supervised reserves, the Aborigines Protection Board had closed the school and threatened to remove children from their parents. Roberts campaigned against the board's policies.

Tuncester became a refuge for Aborigines who objected to the authority of White managers on stations and reserves. Roberts called the settlement by its Aboriginal name, Cubawee, which meant 'plentiful food'. He thanked God for 'the spiritual food'. With U.A.M. evangelists from Purfleet, he travelled to Sydney in 1938 for the 'Day of Mourning' protest. He later recruited Bundjalung people to the Aborigines' Progressive Association in the hope that 'the Association will smash up the Aborigines Destruction Board'.

In 1940, with his eldest son, Roberts organized—independently of the U.A.M.—a convention at Cubawee 'for the deepening of the spiritual life'. Hundreds participated in what became an annual event and a model for other gatherings. The U.A.M. listed Roberts as a 'native helper' and then as a 'native evangelist' before appointing him a 'native pastor' in 1947. The idea of an autonomous indigenous church gathered support within the mission and in 1950 it was proposed that Roberts work interstate to this end. Nothing came of the plan because of a lack of money. He retired from the U.A.M. in 1956, but remained a 'prayer partner'.

Cubawee was crowded, dilapidated and without sanitation. Neither the Aborigines Welfare Board nor Lismore City Council met its needs. Roberts protested in vain. As official policy gradually came to favour assimilation, the buildings on Cubawee were bulldozed in 1964 to force the remaining residents to move. Land security and Aboriginal independence had been two of Roberts's persistent aims. His achievement—the creation of a relatively autonomous Christian network across Bundjalung communities—underpinned their reassertion of land rights in the 1960s. Suffering from chronic bronchitis and emphysema, Roberts died of a coronary occlusion on 21 June 1968 at Lismore and was buried in the local lawn cemetery with the forms of the Assemblies of God. His wife, and their three sons and two daughters survived him.

M. Reay (ed), *Aborigines Now* (Syd, 1964); H. Goodall, *Invasion to Embassy* (Syd, 1996); Sel Cte on Administration of Aborigines Protection Bd, Procs, *PP* (NSW), 1938-40, vol 7; *Aust Abo Call*, May, July 1938; *United Aborigines' Messenger*, Apr 1939, Sept 1940, June 1947, Feb-Apr, June-July, Sept-Oct 1950, Aug 1953, Dec 1955; Richmond River Hist Soc, *Bulletin*, 47, 1968, p 11.   HEATHER RADI

ROBERTS, FREDERICK HUGH SHERSTON (1901-1972), entomologist and parasitologist, was born on 16 January 1901 at Rockhampton, Queensland, second child of Australian-born parents Richard Ussher Roberts, clerk, and his wife Letitia Julia, née Spicer. 'Bob', as he was nicknamed, was educated at Townsville Grammar School and the University of Queensland (B.Sc., 1923; M.Sc., 1925; Ph.D., 1935). After being employed for six months as a microscopist with the Australian Hookworm Campaign, he joined the Commonwealth Prickly Pear Board as a research entomologist in April 1923 and worked at several field-stations in Queensland. The board's investigation of biological control agents led to the introduction (1925) of the moth, *Cactoblastis cactorum*, and to the destruction (by 1930) of the prickly pear which had infested 65 million acres (26.3 million ha) of the land in Australia. On 6 April 1929 Roberts married Ethel Anne Cornell with Anglican rites in her home at Toowoomba; they were to have a son and daughter.

In 1930 Roberts was appointed veterinary entomologist with the Queensland Department of Agriculture and Stock. From 1933 he was based at the Animal Health Station, Yeerongpilly. Sent abroad in 1938 to study the control of parasitic diseases in livestock, he visited laboratories in North America, Britain, Europe and South Africa. He also studied parasites of domestic animals, discovered a new tapeworm in pigeons and found trichostrongyles in rabbits. Between 1939 and 1941 he lectured part time in veterinary parasitology at the University of Queensland.

Appointed a lieutenant in the Militia on 19 December 1941, Roberts transferred to the Australian Imperial Force on 11 August 1942. He served with various medical units in Australia and New Guinea before being posted in May 1943 to the 2nd Mobile Entomology Unit, with which he studied the behaviour of *Anopheles* mosquitoes. Promoted major in October, he collaborated with his colleague Josephine Mackerras [q.v.15] in experiments to combat malaria. His army service ended on 22 March 1945.

Two months later Roberts rejoined the Department of Agriculture and Stock as acting-director of research in the division of animal industry. In June 1947 he was appointed to the Council for Scientific and Industrial Research's division of animal health and production as principal research officer and officer-in-charge of the newly established veterinary parasitology laboratory at Yeerongpilly. Under his direction, the laboratory gained a worldwide reputation for its studies of the parasitic diseases of cattle. He published a finely illustrated monograph, *Insects Affecting Livestock, with special reference to important species occurring in Australia* (Sydney, 1952), which became a standard textbook in Australia and overseas. He also initiated negotiations and planning for the Commonwealth Scientific and Industrial Research Organization's new laboratories at Long Pocket, Indooroopilly, which were opened on 2 September 1968.

During his career Roberts published 133 papers dealing with ticks, insects and parasitic worms. He was president (1935 and 1946) of the Entomological Society of Queensland and an associate-member of the Queensland division of the Australian Veterinary Association. Following his retirement in January 1966, he became a senior research fellow with the C.S.I.R.O. Over the next three years he wrote an authoritative monograph, *Australian Ticks* (Melbourne, 1970), which described their taxonomy and biology and drew on his research of more than thirty years.

Invariably kind, supportive and encouraging to younger scientists in his division, Roberts was a man of integrity who was gifted with a good sense of humour. He died on 26 July 1972 at Canossa Hospital, Oxley, and was cremated; his wife and son survived him.

Historical Directory of CSIR and CSIRO (Canb, 1978); P. J. Skerman, *The First 100 Years* (Brisb, 1998); *Aust Veterinary J*, 48, 1972, p 641; Entomological Soc of Qld, *News Bulletin*, 88, July-Aug 1972, p 16; series 3, PH/ROB/16, pts 1 and 2, CSIRO Archives, Canb; student records, UQA S157, 171, Univ Qld Archives. BEVERLEY M. ANGUS

ROBERTS, JOHN KEITH (1897-1944), physicist, was born on 16 April 1897 at Kew, Melbourne, elder child of Australian-born parents Henry Charles Roberts, sharebroker, and his wife Winifred Mary, née French. His parents and his sister Winifred were capable musicians. Keith sang and played the violin; music was always an important part of his life. At Camberwell Grammar School he qualified for university entrance in 1913. His father was keen for him to go into commerce and he spent an unhappy year working for a firm in the city before enrolling at the University of Melbourne (B.Sc., 1918; M.Sc., 1920).

Graduating with first-class honours, the Dixson scholarship in natural philosophy and a government research scholarship, Roberts assisted Professor T. H. Laby [q.v.9] in the early stages of the latter's classic redetermination of the mechanical equivalent of heat. Roberts wrote two papers (one jointly with Laby) which were published by the Royal Society of Victoria in 1920. An 1851 Exhibition science research scholarship enabled him to go to England to work at the Cavendish Laboratory, Cambridge (Ph.D., 1923; Sc.D., 1941), under Sir Ernest (Baron) Rutherford.

Roberts became briefly involved in the initial, unsuccessful search for the neutron.

Chiefly, however, his research continued to focus on precision measurement, and he wrote a thesis on conservation of energy in hydrogen discharge. Appointed to Britain's National Physical Laboratory in October 1922, he worked in the heat section, making precise determinations of the thermal properties of metallic crystals. At the register office, Kensington, London, on 5 June 1924 he married Margaret Sylvia Whyte, a divorcee and daughter of the wallpaper manufacturer Harold Sanderson. Later that year Roberts developed a tubercular hip. Seriously ill, he was sent to a sanatorium in Switzerland where he spent much of the next four years lying on his back. In this position he wrote his well-known treatise, *Heat and Thermodynamics* (London, 1928).

In 1928 Roberts returned to England and rejoined the Cavendish Laboratory. An excellent lecturer, and a careful and conscientious teacher, he transferred in 1933 to Cambridge's colloid science laboratory as assistant-director of research. An investigation of energy exchanges between hot surfaces and the gases in contact with them led him into a long and highly successful study of the adsorption of gases by metal surfaces. For this work he was elected a fellow (1942) of the Royal Society.

Following the outbreak of World War II, Roberts became a senior scientific officer with the Royal Navy, working first on the degaussing of ships and then on minesweeping. Late in 1942, at the height of the battle of the Atlantic, he was appointed chief scientist in the Anti-Submarine Experimental Establishment, Fairlie, Scotland, where he oversaw one of the great scientific achievements of the war—the development of improved equipment for detecting submarines. In February 1944 he was elected a fellow of Christ's College, Cambridge. He planned to take up the position when his wartime work finished, but he developed Addison's disease. Survived by his wife and their two daughters, he died of pneumonia and pericarditis on 26 April that year at St Marylebone, London, and was cremated.

Selfless, affectionate and humorous, Roberts was held in high regard by friends and colleagues. In his wartime posts he proved an excellent leader of large and complex projects. 'Had he survived', his obituarist in *The Times* asserted, 'there can be little doubt that the future of the Cavendish Laboratory would have been largely dependent on him'.

Obituary Notices of Fellows of the Roy Soc, 4 (1944), p 789; *The Times*, 28 Apr 1944; family information. R. W. HOME

ROBERTS, MURRAY BERESFORD (1919-1974), impostor and swindler, was born on

10 August 1919 at Brooklyn, Wellington, New Zealand, only child of New Zealand-born parents Andrew Murray Roberts, surveyor, and his wife Annie Isabelle, née Huckstep. On leaving Auckland Grammar School, Murray enrolled in medicine at the University of Otago, but did not complete his degree. One of his contemporaries noted his charming manner and his tendency to make extravagant claims about himself. In 1941 Roberts was fined £50 for acting as a locum tenens for a medical practitioner without being qualified. During World War II he posed as an assistant medical director, with the rank of brigadier, 3rd New Zealand Division, and boasted about having done postgraduate work in brain surgery in Moscow. In 1946 he moved to Australia and taught at several schools.

Falsely claiming university degrees, Roberts was employed in turn by Australian Paper Manufacturers Ltd and Imperial Chemical Industries of Australia and New Zealand Ltd. In Western Australia from 1947, he briefly edited the *Kalgoorlie Miner*. On 21 February 1949 at St Philip's Anglican Church, Cottesloe, he married Dorothy Elizabeth Bright, a typist; he gave his name as 'John Malcolm Cook'. The couple were to have one son before being divorced in 1955.

Always a rogue, Roberts frequently impersonated medical practitioners and schoolteachers even though he was convicted in several States. With his handsome appearance, 'plummy' voice, intelligence and wit, he obtained money and credit in Melbourne by claiming in June 1954 to be 'Professor Sir Leonard Jackson', the 'new prosecutor' at the [Petrov] royal commission into espionage. Next year in New South Wales he posed as a professor of neurosurgery to gain access to Goulburn gaol to interview a prisoner, and arranged to do a muscle graft at Goulburn Base Hospital on the following day, an appointment he did not keep.

In Tasmania on 27 April 1956 Roberts relieved a truck driver, Ernest Stanley Wignall, of £50 as the deposit on a house which Roberts did not own. Departing for the mainland, he reached Sydney where he posed as 'Lord Russell', governor-general designate of Australia, and obtained a luxury hotel suite. Having served another term in gaol, he was extradited to Tasmania. There he told the magistrate that he considered himself to be 'more of a nuisance value than a criminal'. After his release from prison, he claimed to be 'Sir William Penny', 'Sir John Douglas' and 'Dr Bodkin Adams' (in Melbourne) and 'Mr Law, woolbuyer' and 'Justice Adams' of the New Zealand Supreme Court (in Brisbane). Leaving that city without paying his hotel bill, he appeared in November 1958 at Sydney's Central Court of Petty Sessions charged with theft.

Roberts amused Sydney in June 1960 by impersonating Baron Alfred von Krupp: in this role he entertained the mayor of Manly and promised to give the municipality a £250 000 car park. Roberts received another gaol sentence. At Abergeldie Guest House, Bowral, on 29 December that year, as 'John Martin Jackson' he married with Presbyterian forms Beryl Florence Sinclair, a 31-year-old schoolteacher, but in the following March was sentenced to yet another term in gaol for giving false information to the marriage registrar. The marriage ended in divorce.

His fraud turned nastier in November 1962 when Roberts, as 'Lord Porter', a privy councillor and medical attendant of the royal family, persuaded Lionel Coleman, that Coleman suffered from 'deep-rooted cancer of the spine' and to give him £400 towards the cost of an operation. This time Roberts was gaoled for four years, having been extradited from Darwin. Judge C. V. Rooney said: 'One doesn't need a lively imagination to picture the terror you caused in this man's family by falsely telling him he had cancer'.

In 1967 Roberts gained the consent of a widow, Mrs Joyce Derrom Brown (from New Zealand), to a proposal of marriage and persuaded her to give him £4000 to invest. Sydney fraud squad detectives apprehended him at a bank. In his later life Roberts turned to alcohol. He choked on his vomit and died on 5 August 1974 in a hotel room at Papakura, New Zealand; survived by his son, he was cremated. Roberts's autobiography, *A King of Con Men* (Auckland, 1975) was published posthumously.

A. Dettre, *Infamous Australians* (Syd, 1985); *Herald* (Melb), 4 Jan 1954, 6 July 1955, 18 June 1957, 23 Dec 1968; *Age* (Melb), 7 July 1955, 29 June 1960, 29 June 1963, 31 Mar 1967; *Sunday Telegraph* (Syd), 3 July 1960; *Sun* (Syd), 17 Mar 1961; *Truth* (Syd), 25 Mar 1968; *A'sian Post*, 26 Dec 1968; *SMH*, 7 Aug 1974.   MALCOLM BROWN

ROBERTS, SIR STEPHEN HENRY (1901-1971), historian and university vice-chancellor, was born on 16 February 1901 at Maldon, Victoria, son of Australian-born parents Christopher Roberts, miner, and his wife Doris Elsie Whillemina, née Wagener, who were respectively of Cornish and German descent. Stephen attended Castlemaine High School, Melbourne Teachers' College and (on scholarships) the University of Melbourne (B.A., 1921; M.A., 1923; D.Litt., 1930). He found his *métier* in the history department of Professor (Sir) Ernest Scott [q.v.11] and readily absorbed his rigorous empiricism as well as his distinctive European outlook.

A remarkable student with an exceptional memory and ferocious, focused energy, Roberts graduated with first-class honours, Wyselaskie [q.v.6] scholarships in English constitutional history and political economy, and the Dwight [q.v.4] prize in sociology. He was appointed assistant-lecturer and tutor in British history. His master's degree involved original research in Australia's pioneering history, which he duly published as *History of Australian Land Settlement, 1788-1920* (1924). In 1925 he attended the first conference sponsored by the Institute of Pacific Relations, in Honolulu. Roberts's paper, which concentrated on Australia's role in a changing Pacific, soon broadened into a major publication, *Population Problems in the Pacific* (London, 1927). A Harbison-Higinbotham [q.v.4] research scholarship and a free passage enabled him to undertake research at the University of London (D.Sc., 1929). He arrived in England accompanied by his devoted mother and by his younger brother Frederick (who was to become a geographer and to draw the maps in Stephen's early books). Stephen studied at the London School of Economics. The topic of his dissertation, French colonial policy from the 1870s to the 1920s, came from his distinguished teachers Harold Laski and Lillian Knowles, but also related to Scott's interest in French maritime explorers. With his usual industry and application, Roberts wrote his large and original thesis in record time and did much of the archival work in Paris. His capacity to read French and German languages proved invaluable.

At Christ Church, Paddington, London, on 3 August 1927 Roberts married with Anglican rites Thelma Lilian Beatrice Asche, from Toorak, Melbourne; Oscar Asche [q.v.7] was her uncle. After a honeymoon in Germany they came home to Melbourne. Taking up a research fellowship at the university, he worked on the squatting age in Australia. He returned to Paris late in 1928 to investigate the 'Mind of France'. Quite suddenly he received a cable from Scott urging him to apply for the Challis [q.v.3] chair of history at the University of Sydney following the suicide of Professor G. A. Wood [q.v.12]. Appointed in April 1929 (over Wood's son), he had returned to Australia with a particular love of France. His time in England had not Anglicized him and his early anti-English bias mellowed only slowly as he matured.

Whereas Wood had seen history and the arts as civilizing and morally uplifting agents, Roberts was a utilitarian who aimed to train professionals for work. He was truly Scott's pupil: empirical, research oriented, with a concern for international trends and an ability to place Australia in a wider colonial context. The 'Sydney school' around Roberts was proudly a 'hard school', not merely because of its declared standards of data, but in its overt hostility to what it conceived as romantic or literary approaches to the past.

Roberts concentrated his energies on his own research and writing. He was a diligent, but indifferent, undergraduate teacher, strongly interested in his broader role as an educator. In one remarkable burst of scholarly energy, he published six books in eight years —a mixture of original research monographs and texts of synthesis—starting with his doctoral thesis, a two-volume *History of French Colonial Policy (1870-1925)* (London, 1929). Having completed his texts for schools, *Modern British History* (1932), with C. H. Currey [q.v.13], and *History of Modern Europe* (1933), he turned to international studies, *Australia and the Far East* (1935), before reverting to domestic history with *The Squatting Age in Australia, 1835-1847* (Melbourne, 1935). Although his work contained far too many textual errors from hasty writing and proof-reading, each book had an enduring impact in its field by providing standard interpretations or formulating major hypotheses for debate. He was rightly seen as the most prolific historian of his generation in Australia; he was also among the most penetrating and international in outlook.

As second Challis professor, Roberts favoured a broad spectrum of history, from ancient to modern, and from Europe to Asia and the Pacific. He also pioneered American studies in the aftermath of World War II. As a member (1938) of the Board of Secondary School Studies, he influenced the design of the school curriculum and shaped history papers that reflected his world view. His *History of Modern Europe* became a core textbook. He was a trustee of the Public Library of New South Wales and a member of its Mitchell [q.v.5] Library committee.

In the 1930s Roberts was involved with the Australian Institute of International Affairs, the Sydney group of the Round Table, and the Institute of Pacific Relations. Becoming a leading international analyst, he gave public lectures and wrote extensively on political and diplomatic issues, especially for the *Sydney Morning Herald*. From 1932 he presented 'Notes on the News' for the Australian Broadcasting Commission. He spent most of 1936 on study leave, mainly in Britain, but with some three months in Germany. His most famous book, *The House that Hitler Built* (London, 1937), was based on meetings with Nazi leaders, attendance at their awesome rallies and his own teaching knowledge of central European history. He exposed Hitler's Reich, condemned the persecution of the Jews, and warned that Germany was likely to involve the world in war. Aimed at the common reader, the book was translated into a dozen languages and reprinted many times.

Roberts's public commentaries and book brought him fame, influence, and wealth: Thelma happily remarked that their home in Wyuna Road, Point Piper, was the real house that Hitler built!

In the late 1930s Roberts repeatedly spoke presciently of the dangers of appeasement. During World War II, as 'Our War Correspondent', he wrote a column (almost daily) for the *S.M.H.*, in addition to weekly articles under his own name. Gradually, his public roles overshadowed his research and he published no major history after the war.

Dean of arts (1942-47) and chairman of the professorial board (1947), Roberts was appointed acting vice-chancellor late in 1946 and confirmed in office in October 1947; he was also university principal from 1955. He soon proved an able administrator and quickly grasped financial issues. Well informed about what went on in the university, he kept control of the purse, believing that money matters were his concern alone. In the face of a rapid increase in student numbers (particularly returned servicemen and women), inadequate financial resources, cramped facilities and the frayed tempers of overworked academic staff, he showed 'a remarkable capacity for long-sighted improvisation'. He chaired (1952-53) the Australian Vice-Chancellors' Committee when his influence within the higher-education system was at its height.

Roberts invited leaders of commerce, industry and public life to support the university's various foundations. He also welcomed ambassadors and consuls to his university. Although he was an instinctively shy man who rarely left his rooms, except to attend meetings, he was assiduous in accepting invitations to social engagements in the evenings. The result of all his efforts was financial gain and the promotion of the university overseas. He encouraged closer relations with the university colleges and went out of his way to visit them; his wife enthusiastically supported their dramatic societies.

Once the austerity of the postwar years was over, Roberts vigorously pursued the expansion and development of the university. The report (1957) of Sir Keith Murray's Committee on Australian Universities, and consequent funding from the Menzies [q.v.15] government, meant that Roberts had to supervise the structural expansion of the university across City Road into Darlington. In the 1960s he also had to cope with student unrest. He took great pride in celebrating the graduation of Charles Perkins, the first Aborigine to complete a degree at the university, and he worked enthusiastically to support the training of Pacific Islanders and Papua New Guineans in the university's medical faculty.

In an age when many academics were from a middle-class background, with an affinity for Oxford and Cambridge, Roberts had distinctly working-class origins. He relied on a scholarship education and a good marriage to advance him professionally and socially. By 1947 he was a member of the Australian Club. The recipient of numerous honours, he was appointed C.M.G. in 1956, commander of the Danish Order of the Dannebrog (1960), the Lebanese National Order of the Cedar (1961), the Greek Order of the Phoenix (1964) and the Italian Order of Merit (1967), and to the Légion d'honneur (1967). In 1965 he was knighted. The universities of New England (1957) and Sydney (1968) in Australia, Bristol (1948) and Durham (1953) in England, and British Columbia (1956) and McGill (1958) in Canada all bestowed honorary doctorates on him. He chaired the New South Wales State Cancer Council from 1952.

By the time he retired in 1967, Sir Stephen had effectively transformed the old, small, elite University of Sydney into a modern institution of over 16 000 students, with new faculties, new research capacity and new esteem. In his own archives he kept notes for a final *magnum opus* on 'The Mind of France'. It remained one of his few unfinished projects. A 'man who enjoyed life', he was an expert on Australian wines, and an avid stamp collector from boyhood. In his youth Roberts was elegant and handsome; by the time he was vice-chancellor heavy-framed spectacles accentuated his narrow eyes and fleshy features. He took pleasure in foreign travel and attending overseas conferences. He died of hypertensive coronary vascular disease on 19 March 1971 aboard the *Marconi*, near Port Melbourne, while *en route* to Europe with Lady Roberts. Survived by his wife and their three daughters, he was cremated.

Roberts was in many ways an uncommon Australian. For all his contemporary prejudices, he brought a new professionalism to a field of study then dominated by amateurs and antiquarians. Equally, his broader international outlook, which linked Australia to the wider world, was prescient for the new nation. Within the fragile intellectual history of Australia he played a robust but since neglected role. (Sir) William Dargie's portrait of Roberts is held by the University of Sydney: it offers an appropriate view of an august figure in Australian society.

D. R. Wood, *Stephen Henry Roberts, Historian and Vice-Chancellor* (Syd, 1986); D. M. Schreuder, 'A "Second Foundation": S. H. Roberts as Challis Professor 1929-47' in B. Caine et al (eds), *History at Sydney, 1891-1991* (Syd, 1992) and 'An Unconventional Founder', in S. Macintyre and J. Thomas (eds), *The Discovery of Australian History 1890-1939* (Melb, 1995); W. F. Connell et al, *Australia's First*, 2 (Syd, 1995); G. Walsh, *Australia: History & Historians* (Canb, 1997); Univ Syd, *Gazette*, May 1967, p 193; *Aust J of Politics and Hist*, 46, no 1, 2000, p 1; *SMH*, 10 Apr 1929, 8 Sept 1932, 5 Mar 1937, 6 July 1949, 2 Jan 1956, 5 Oct 1963, 1 Jan 1965, 31 Aug 1967, 26 Jan 1968, 20 Mar 1971; Roberts papers (Univ Syd Archives); R. M. Crawford papers (Univ Melb Archives); E. Scott papers (NL).

D. M. SCHREUDER

ROBERTSON, AGNES ROBERTSON (1882-1968), schoolteacher and politician, was born on 31 July 1882 at Stepney, Adelaide, daughter of David Kelly Keay, a stonecutter from Scotland, and his wife Mary Ann, née Thomson. A lone girl among seven brothers, Aggie soon learned 'to fight my way with them all' and became a vocal participant in political discussions around the family table. She was educated at a private school in Adelaide, and at state schools in Brisbane and New South Wales where her father undertook substantial building contracts. The Keays moved to Western Australia about 1895. Agnes qualified as a schoolteacher through the monitorial system. At St Andrew's Presbyterian Church, Perth, on 1 July 1903 she married Robert Robertson, a 29-year-old journalist.

When her husband died of tuberculosis in 1912, Agnes Robertson's life changed dramatically. A widow with three small children, and an uncertain income, she joined the Education Department and taught Class 4B at Thomas Street State School, Subiaco. Inspectors consistently rated her work as excellent. She served on the executive (vice-president 1941) of the Western Australian Teachers' Union and was a member of the Teachers' Appeal Board at a time when equal pay and pension rights were recurrent issues. Although she enrolled at the University of Western Australia, she did not complete a degree, but turned her attention to church and community affairs. She regularly worshipped at the Ross Memorial Presbyterian Church, West Perth, and for many years taught the girls' Bible class. In 1937 she travelled to Edinburgh to attend the General Assembly of the Presbyterian Church and in the mid-1940s became Western Australia's first Presbyterian woman lay preacher.

Robertson's domestic problems had eased when her parents came to live with her and her mother assumed responsibility for managing the household. Each day Agnes walked home for lunch and her habitual half-hour 'cat nap'. She enjoyed needlework and reading, particularly a rattling good yarn. During the 1920s and 1930s her constant mentors were Ethel Joyner and Bessie Rischbieth [q.v.11], who involved her in community activities, and (Dame) Florence Cardell-Oliver [q.v.13], who nurtured her political awareness. With her commanding presence, eloquence and a certain wit, Mrs Robertson proved a consummate committee-woman. In the wider community she lent her name to innumerable social activities—particularly those benefiting women, children, the disabled and the aged—and held high office in the Women's Council of the Liberal and Country League of Western Australia.

Following her retirement from teaching in 1941, Robertson served as part-time secretary of the Presbyterian Children's Homes. In 1947 she accepted the offer of a place on the L.C.L.'s ticket for the Senate. Elected in December 1949, she was the L.C.L.'s first (and the State's second) woman senator, taking her seat on 22 February 1950. In her maiden speech she foreshadowed the areas in which she would show a particular interest, among them the 'tangled skein' of world affairs, peace in an atomic age, and national defence in the face of encroaching communism. As a staunch supporter of (Sir) Robert Menzies' [q.v.15] government, she gave unqualified backing to the Communist Party dissolution bill (1950) and consistently defended the government's budgets, including the so-called 'horror budget' of 1951 which she described as a 'courageous' measure.

While leading a women's delegation in Manila in 1955, Robertson was shocked to learn that she had been dropped from the Liberals' ticket because of her age. In September she switched her allegiance to the Country and Democratic League, which gave her first place on its Senate ballot paper. Pursuing a vigorous forty-day campaign in rural areas, she averaged three speeches a day, in addition to a series of broadcasts on radio. Labor preferences gave her 'a last-minute victory over the candidate the Liberal Party had endorsed in her place'. She was the Country Party's first woman senator. In October 1956 she was the first woman appointed to the Joint Parliamentary Committee on Foreign Affairs. For several years she led Australian delegations to annual conferences of the Pan Pacific and South East Asia Women's Association.

Robertson drew attention to the Cinderella status of Western Australia and advocated substantial support for education, roads, water projects and decentralization in that State. She was pleased in September 1957 to support an amendment to the Gold-mining Industry Assistance Act (1954-56) which would benefit Western Australia, but disheartened in May 1958 that assistance under the Western Australia Grant (Northern Development) bill was a mere £2.5 million. In 1962 she made an impassioned plea for conserving the nation's heritage: she named a number of buildings under threat (including the convict-built barracks in Perth) and urged support for the National Trust of Australia.

The senator addressed other major issues ranging from industrial relations to social welfare. She abhorred strikes, appeared ambivalent about the 40-hour week, advocated the banning of heroin, and continued to promote free milk in schools, both for its nutritional value to children and as a fillip for the dairy industry. Her political philosophy was essentially a manifestation of her religious and social conscience. Defying the risk of being considered old-fashioned, she never hesitated to remind the Senate 'that the Word of the Old Book is still true: "Righteousness exalteth a nation"'.

Throughout her parliamentary years Robertson occupied the same room at the Hotel Kurrajong and rarely missed a sitting in the House. A tall, imposing woman, with dark hair greying by the time she reached the Senate, she wore pearls, pastel-coloured ensembles, a contrasting corsage and sensible laced shoes. She lived by her Christian beliefs. When her god-daughter was orphaned, she took her into her home as a foster child. Robertson died on 29 January 1968 at Mount Waverley, Melbourne, and was cremated; her son and two daughters survived her.

PD (Cwlth), 1950, p 481, 1952, p 513; *Presbyterian* (Perth); 1 Jan 1934; *Aust Women's Weekly*, 16 Mar 1956; *Eastern Recorder*, 27 June 1957; *West Australian*, 31 Jan 1968; Education Dept (WA), 3512/1.46, A. R. Robertson, *and* MN 1070/3306A/45, A. R. Robertson (SROWA); information from Ms B. Grant, Shenton Park, and Mrs M. M. Winter, Cottesloe, Perth.   WENDY BIRMAN

ROBERTSON, EDWARD GRAEME (1903-1975), neurologist and conservationist, was born on 20 October 1903 at Footscray, Melbourne, fifth child of Victorian-born parents John Robertson, draper, and his wife Cecilia Elizabeth, née Hooper. Educated at Scotch College and the University of Melbourne (M.B., B.S., 1927; M.D., 1930), Graeme became a resident medical officer and registrar at (Royal) Melbourne Hospital. In 1930 he travelled to London where he worked and studied at the National Hospital for Diseases of the Nervous System, Queen Square. Returning home in 1934, he began to establish himself as a leading neurologist. On 29 August 1935 at Scots Church, Melbourne, he married with Presbyterian forms Mildred Jane Duce (d.1971), a nurse.

While maintaining his private practice, Robertson accepted appointments as honorary neurologist to four hospitals: the (Royal) Victorian Eye and Ear (1940), the Royal Melbourne (1944), the (Royal) Children's (1944) and the (Royal) Women's (1949). He was also a consultant to the Tasmanian Department of Public Health and the Royal Australian Navy. A foundation fellow (1938) and vice-president (1962) of the Royal Australasian College of Physicians, he played a leading role in forming the Australian Association of Neurologists (1950)—of which he was president (1958)—and the Asian and Oceanian Association of Neurologists (1962). Both the Association of British Neurologists and the American Neurological Association accorded him honorary membership.

Robertson was an authority on the radiological examination of the brain. He published three scientific monographs, *Encephalography* (Melbourne, 1941), *Further Studies in Encephalography* (1946) and *Pneumoencephalography* (Springfield, Illinois, United States of America, 1957), and sixty-six scientific articles. He 'saw in the nervous system a complexity reduced to a perfection of orderliness which fascinated him'.

Interested in 'architecture and furniture and allied things of beauty', and concerned about the destruction of fine nineteenth-century buildings in the name of 'progress', Robertson helped to found the Victorian branch of the National Trust of Australia in 1956. He was a keen photographer who often rose at dawn to take his shots. The play of light on the detail of buildings captivated him and fired his passion for decorative cast iron. Robertson was appalled that councils throughout Victoria were ordering the destruction of cast-iron verandahs in the 1950s and 1960s. His first non-medical book, *Victorian Heritage* (Melbourne, 1960), captured in words and black-and-white photographs the beauty of the State's ironwork. The book sold out. It helped to apply a brake to what he called 'vandalism' committed by those in authority.

Robertson's subsequent books included *Sydney Lace* (1962), *Early Houses of Northern Tasmania* (with Edith Craig, 1964), *Ornamental Cast Iron in Melbourne* (1967), *Early Buildings of Southern Tasmania* (1970), *Adelaide Lace* (1973) and *Carlton* (1974). His daughter Joan co-authored his last books, *Parkville* (1975) and *Cast Iron Decoration: A World Survey* (1977). The Royal Australian Institute of Architects commented: 'by direct and indirect means', Dr Robertson revealed ornamental cast iron 'to thousands of people, raised it to the status of an art form worthy of serious study and influenced the preservation of much of what survives'. In 1969 he became founding chairman of the National Trust's committee for cast iron. Examples that he had gathered over many years formed the nucleus of the trust's collection. It remains in storage, awaiting the fulfilment of his dream that it will be housed in a museum dedicated to cast iron.

In 1950 Robertson had been a founding member of the Society of Collectors, inaugurated by (Sir) Joseph Burke. His special areas of interest were Australiana, and antique English and early colonial furniture. One of his prize possessions was a magnificent desk purchased from Sir Keith Murdoch [q.v.10]. With Clifford Craig and Kevin Fahy, he wrote *Early Colonial Furniture in New South Wales and Van Diemen's Land* (1972). Robertson travelled extensively. While visiting San Francisco, U.S.A., in 1961, he had learned that one of the world's remaining wrought-iron ships, *Rona*, lay berthed at Melbourne. He persuaded the Victorian branch of the National Trust to buy the hulk and chaired (from 1968) the committee which oversaw its restoration under the barque's former name, *Polly Woodside*.

To friends and colleagues, Robertson was a lovable eccentric whose perfectionism verged on the obsessional. In July 1975, although seriously ill with cancer, he attended a meeting of the National Trust's council to argue for the acquisition of an appropriate site for the *Polly Woodside*. Survived by his son and daughter, he died on Christmas Day 1975 at Toorak and was cremated.

MJA, 24 July 1976, p 147; *Procs of Aust Assn of Neurologists*, 13, 1976, p 1; information from Mr J. Cuming, South Yarra, Dr P. Ebeling, Toorak, Dr N. Wettenhall, Toorak, and Mr R. Davidson, Melb.
MARY RYLLIS CLARK

ROBERTSON, SIR HORACE CLEMENT HUGH (1894-1960), army officer, was born on 29 October 1894 at Warrnambool, Victoria, sixth child of Melbourne-born parents John Robertson, schoolteacher, and his wife Annie, née Gray. Family members called him 'Red Robbie' because of the colour of his hair and to differentiate him from his brother John ('Black Robbie'). Educated at Outtrim State School (1905-10) and briefly at Geelong College, he entered the Royal Military College, Duntroon, Federal Capital Territory, in 1912, having barely qualified, academically, for admission.

Due to the outbreak of World War I, Robertson's class graduated early. On 2 November 1914 he was commissioned lieutenant in the Permanent Military Forces and in the Australian Imperial Force. Although he was a minor, on 7 November that year at Collingwood, Melbourne, he married with Presbyterian forms Jessie Bonnar, a 38-year-old nurse; he gave his age as 24 and she gave hers as 31. A second marriage ceremony was performed on 19 October 1916 at the Kasr-el-Nil Chapel, Cairo. They concealed their difference in age from friends and family.

Posted as machine-gun officer to the 10th Light Horse Regiment, Robertson fought in the Dardanelles campaign from May 1915 until the evacuation from Gallipoli. He took a leading role in the fight at Hill 60 in late August when he commanded the depleted remnants of the regiment in a vicious night-attack which resulted in heavy casualties. Reaching Egypt, he was promoted major in May 1916 and given command of a squadron. At the battle of Magdhaba, Palestine, in December, he led the whole regiment in a mounted charge against entrenched Turkish positions and won the Distinguished Service Order (1917). Posted to the headquarters of the Yeomanry Mounted Division, a British formation, in June 1917, he served on the A.I.F. staff in Cairo from September 1918. For helping to supervise the repatriation of light-horse units he was appointed (1920) to the Order of the Nile. He was twice mentioned in dispatches.

Robertson returned to Australia in August 1919 and to a typical series of staff and regimental administrative postings. Attending the Staff College, Camberley, England, in 1923-24, he received an 'A' pass and impressed his superiors as being 'an officer of strong character and high ability'. His capacities as a trainer of troops were often commented upon during his career, and he honed them while he was chief instructor at the Small Arms School, Randwick, Sydney, in 1926-30. From December 1934 he was director of military art at Duntroon, in charge of educating and training the army's future regular officers. In June 1936 he was promoted brevet lieutenant colonel and in March 1939 he became commander of the newly created 7th Military District which encompassed the Northern Territory. He took preliminary steps to place northern Australia on a better defensive footing in the event of war with Japan before volunteering for service with the A.I.F. in April 1940.

That month Robertson was given command of the 19th Brigade. He was the first regular officer to receive a command at this level in World War II. He trained the 19th to his own exacting standards for the rest of the year and led it with style and vigour in the Libyan campaign (January-February 1941). For his contribution to the Australian capture of Tobruk he was to be appointed C.B.E. (1941). Ill health and time in hospital meant that he missed the disaster in Greece, and, on recovering in March, he was posted to command the A.I.F. Reinforcement Depot near Gaza, Palestine. He reformed it from top to bottom. The outbreak of war in the Pacific led to his return in December to Australia, where he became the willing object of some ineffectual plotting to have him made commander-in-chief (the so-called 'revolt of the generals').

Placed in command of the 1st Armoured Division in April 1942, Major-General Robertson oversaw the creation of Australia's first fully-mechanized formation. Originally intended to serve in the Mediterranean, the division never left Australia, but was transferred to Western Australia in February 1943 and disbanded in September. In April 1944 Robertson took over the administration of III Corps. The dwindling threat of a Japanese invasion led to the disbanding of units and formations in Western Australia and to the reallocation of personnel. By the end of the year Robertson's command had been reduced to almost nothing. Another period of illness in mid-1944 further reduced his chances of front-line service, and it was only in April 1945 that he returned to action, in command of the 5th Division in New Britain. He was transferred to the 6th Division in late July and accepted the surrender of the Japanese 18th Army near Wewak, New Guinea, in September. Again, he was twice mentioned in dispatches.

Appointed temporary lieutenant general in December, Robertson supervised the repatriation of Australians serving in New Guinea and came home in February 1946. He briefly headed Southern Command before being appointed in May to relieve Lieutenant General (Sir) John Northcott [q.v.15] in command of the British Commonwealth Occupation Force in Japan. As one of the most senior foreign officers in that country, he had direct access to the supreme commander, General Douglas MacArthur [q.v.15]. His relations with some senior British officers were less cordial. With the re-establishment of civil government in Japan, B.C.O.F. had relatively little to do, and this caused problems for the morale of the force. In April 1950 the Australian government gave notice that it would remove its remaining troops, by then reduced to a single understrength battalion and a Royal Australian Air Force fighter squadron.

Before this could be accomplished the Korean War broke out in June, and the administrative structures of B.C.O.F. had to be hurriedly revived to cope with the influx of troops which various Commonwealth countries had contributed to the United Nations Command. Robertson's administrative ability and his good personal relations with the Americans allowed much to be achieved in a short time. His insistence that the Australian battalion would not be sent to Korea until it had been brought up to strength and given additional training underscored his well-known concern for the welfare of those he commanded. He made frequent trips to Korea to visit Commonwealth troops in his additional capacity as commander-in-chief, British Commonwealth Forces, Korea, an administrative and non-operational role. In 1950 he was appointed K.B.E. He was also to be appointed to the American Legion of Merit and the Korean Order of Military Merit Taiguk in 1952.

In mid-November 1951 Sir Horace finally, and reluctantly, returned to Australia to become director-general of recruiting. He led a campaign to make up the manpower deficiencies which the army had suffered as a result of reductions in the defence vote after 1945. Fresh from Korea and with experience gained in two world wars, he had little time for talk about 'pushbutton warfare', noting that 'it is still the man on the ground that matters'. In January 1953 he was made head of Southern Command, Melbourne. He retired from the army on 30 October 1954.

Jessie died in August 1956 and Robbie seemed to mellow slightly in his final years. While maintaining his links with the army as honorary colonel (from 1954) of the Royal Australian Regiment, he began to write his memoirs, which he described as 'the million pound libel'. He died of a ruptured aortic aneurysm on 28 April 1960 in the Repatriation General Hospital, Heidelberg, and was buried in Springvale cemetery. His estate was sworn for probate at £108 985: he was always canny with money. Robertson was a flamboyant and controversial figure in the army. Few of his contemporaries were neutral in their view of him. He was widely admired and heartily detested, but even those who did not like him conceded his great ability as a trainer of troops and as an administrator. His command in Libya suggests that he possessed considerable ability as a field commander as well.

J. Grey, *Australian Brass* (Melb, 1992), and for bib; Robertson papers (held by author).

JEFFREY GREY

ROBERTSON, JESSIE MARIAN (1909-1976), radio broadcaster and community leader, was born on 1 July 1909 in West Perth, second of three children of Robert Robertson (d.1912), a journalist from Scotland, and his South Australian-born wife Agnes, née Keay [q.v. Robertson], who became a senator. Educated at Thomas Street State and Perth Modern schools, Jess trained as a teacher of home science and set up (1931) Phoebe's School of Domestic Art. From the mid-1930s she was employed by W.A. Broadcasters Ltd as an announcer on Radio 6IX. She became known as 'Phoebe the early cook' to housewives and as 'Aunt Judy' to those who listened to her children's programme. She also conducted 'good housekeeping' parties for Metters Ltd, manufacturers of the 'Early Kooka' gas stove.

In December 1941 Robertson enlisted in the Australian Women's Army Service. Commissioned lieutenant in January 1942, she served at headquarters, Western Australian Lines of Communication Area, until May 1943 when she was transferred to Victoria. On 28 July she was promoted captain. She compiled statistics of prisoners of war and of Australian forces in the field. Her appointment terminated on 21 December 1945. Returning to Radio 6IX, she revived her role as 'Aunt Judy'; her plays, performed by children, were a special feature of the programme. As Jess Robertson, she broadcast a women's session and a music show. She co-hosted (from 1951) the weekly community programme, 'Help your neighbour', and covered the visit of Queen Elizabeth II in 1954.

Miss Robertson was active (often by her mother's side) in numerous women's organizations and civic associations. A foundation member (1946) of the Business and Professional Women's Club of Perth, she led the Australian delegation to the international federation's seventh congress (1956) at Montreal, Canada. She was also a founder of the A.W.A.S. Association of Western Australia (1947), the Soroptimist Club of Perth (1958) and the King Edward Memorial Hospital auxiliary (1958). In addition, she was involved with the Prisoners' Aid, the Silver Chain Nursing and the Presbyterian Women's associations. She served as State president of the National Council of Women (1956-59 and 1966-72) and of the Australian-Asian Association (1960-65), and was international president (1961-64) of the Pan-Pacific and South East Asia Women's Association. Her hobbies included handicrafts, gardening and music.

In 1953 Robertson stood unsuccessfully as a Liberal Country League candidate for the Legislative Assembly seat of Leederville. In 1958 she was defeated for the Senate. She helped to found (1957) the women's auxiliary of the Country and Democratic League and was president (1961-64) of its federal women's council. The first woman to be elected an alderman (1969) of Mundaring Shire Council, she was deputy-president in 1972-74.

Robertson died of hypertensive heart disease on 22 June 1976 at the Alfred Carson [q.v.7] Hospital, Claremont, and was cremated with Presbyterian forms. The *Independent Monitor* claimed that she would be 'remembered as a woman who not only spoke about things of consequence to others but who took action on their behalf'.

Broadcaster, 30 Jan 1946, 29 Nov 1952; *SMH*, 13 Feb, 9 Apr 1958; *Independent Monitor*, 7 July 1976; *West Australian*, 8 July 1976.

MICHAEL STURMA

ROBERTSON, PHILADELPHIA NINA (1866-1951), Red Cross administrator, was born on 27 February 1866 at Wangaratta, Victoria, fourth child of John Dickson Robertson, a Presbyterian clergyman from Scotland, and his English-born wife Amelia, née Spencer. Educated at Presbyterian Ladies' College,

Melbourne, Philadelphia learned typing and shorthand, and took up secretarial work. She also completed first-aid classes, run by the St John Ambulance Association, at Castlemaine. World War I broke out while she was travelling in Britain with her sister and brother-in-law; she immediately offered her services to the British Red Cross Society and the Order of St John, and was employed as a clerk by the latter organization until November 1914 when she left for Melbourne.

In 1915 Robertson took a salaried post with the Australian branch of the British (Australian) Red Cross Society as secretary to the central council and to the president Lady Helen, wife of the governor-general Sir Ronald Munro Ferguson (Viscount Novar of Raith) [qq.v.10]. Working in Government House (the headquarters of Red Cross for the duration), Robertson soon became an invaluable member of staff and a tireless assistant to the indefatigable Lady Helen. With the help of two paid typists and a few volunteers, Robertson dealt with the overseas business of Red Cross, communicated regularly with the State divisions, kept minutes of meetings and edited monthly leaflets. In addition, she was the secretary of the depot committee of the Victorian division of the Red Cross. She was appointed O.B.E. in 1918.

After the war the Australian Red Cross Society was reorganized. In February 1921 Robertson became general secretary of the Victorian division and continued as secretary to the central council. She referred to the new arrangement as the beginning of her 'Jekyll and Hyde Red Cross existence'. The national and State headquarters moved into a refurbished building in La Trobe Street, Melbourne, in 1922.

Granted leave in 1925, Robertson sailed for England where she took the opportunity to interview officers of the British Red Cross Society. She visited London twice more, as an Australian delegate to the British Empire Red Cross Conference in 1930 and to the Sixteenth International Red Cross Conference in 1938. During these trips to Britain she met and stayed with Lady Novar, with whom she continued to correspond. In the 1930s she was a leader in raising funds for a memorial in Melbourne to John Simpson Kirkpatrick [q.v.9], 'the man with the donkey' at Gallipoli in World War I.

In December 1938 Robertson resigned her Red Cross offices; the central council and the Victorian division both granted her life membership. Her retirement, however, was brief. After the outbreak of World War II she returned to the Red Cross as honorary director of its Victorian branches. Co-ordinating their work, she managed an organization which expanded substantially as the war progressed. She retired again in July 1946.

Miss Robertson had contributed articles and verse to newspapers and magazines, and published *An Anzac Budget and Other Verses* (1916) and *Shreds and Patches* (1924). Her autobiography, *Red Cross Yesterdays*, appeared in 1950. She belonged to the Victoria League, the Alexandra Club and the Albert Park Golf Club. A home for seriously disabled ex-servicemen, in Clarendon Street, East Melbourne, was named (1950) after her. She died on 11 January 1951 in St Andrew's Hospital, East Melbourne, and was cremated with Presbyterian forms.

Who's Who in the World of Women (Melb, 1930, 1934); P. Cochrane, *Simpson and the Donkey* (Melb, 1992); Aust Red Cross Soc, *Annual Report*, 1915-51.
MELANIE OPPENHEIMER

ROBERTSON, THOMAS LOGAN (1901-1969), educationist, was born on 12 November 1901 at Balham, London, only son of Andrew Henry Fleming Robertson (d.1911), stockbroker, and his wife Margaret Jane, née Mundell. Contracting pulmonary tuberculosis, Andrew migrated with his family to Western Australia in 1905 and settled at Kalgoorlie. Thomas was educated locally, and at Perth Boys' and Perth Modern schools. In 1919 he joined the Education Department of Western Australia as a monitor and trained (1920-21) at Claremont Teachers' College. He taught at the East Claremont Practising School (1922-26) and at Geraldton, Busselton and Bridgetown, and studied part time at the University of Western Australia (B.A., 1924; M.A., 1936). On 3 May 1927 at St Giles's Presbyterian Church, Mount Lawley, he married Marion Gibson, a schoolteacher.

In 1938 'Blue' Robertson won a Carnegie fellowship and undertook research at the University of London (Ph.D., 1942) on junior county scholarship examinations. He returned home in 1939, completed his thesis while teaching in country schools, and was promoted to inspector at Northam in 1941. Mobilized in the Militia in May 1942 and commissioned in July, he served in the Australian Army Education Service (from March 1944 as a temporary major) until he was placed on the Retired List on 4 January 1945. After investigating (1945) the recruitment of teachers in Australia on behalf of the Department of Postwar Reconstruction, he became assistant-director of the Commonwealth Office of Education in 1946.

On 1 February 1951 Robertson was appointed director of education in Western Australia. He reorganized and modernized the State's education department by using research and long-term planning to win political support for necessary changes. Prominent at interstate conferences, he helped in 1959 to prepare a statement addressing the needs of Australian education and took part in the political manoeuvring that accompanied the States' case for Commonwealth financial assistance to schools. A founding member (1959) of the Australian College of Education, he encouraged the study of educational administration. As a delegate (1961-64) to conferences of the United Nations Educational, Scientific and Cultural Organization, he was aware of the growing significance of the Indian Ocean region for Western Australia, both economically and culturally. He was also a driving-force behind the establishment of the Western Australian Institute of Technology in 1966.

Following his retirement that year, Robertson chaired the interim councils of W.A.I.T. (1967-69) and the Canberra College of Advanced Education (1966-68). He was president (1967) of the Australian Council for Educational Research and director of the national seminar on educational planning, held in Canberra in 1968. In 1969 he was appointed C.M.G.

Robertson's strong physical features and his height (almost six feet, 183 cm) gave him an appearance and demeanour that commanded respect. Survived by his wife, daughter and son, he died of a coronary occlusion on 29 August 1969 in his home at Nedlands, Perth, and was cremated. A bust executed by Theodore Hannan was unveiled on 15 September 1971 at the opening of the T. L. Robertson Library at W.A.I.T.

M. White, *Thomas Logan Robertson, 1901-1969* (Perth, 1999), and for bib.   VICKI WILLIAMSON
LESLEY CARMAN-BROWN

ROBIN, BRYAN PERCIVAL (1887-1969), Anglican bishop, was born on 12 January 1887 at Oxton, Cheshire, England, elder son of Rev. Percival Carteret Robin, clergyman, and his wife Fanny Margaret, née Pollock. Bryan was educated at Rossall School, the University of Liverpool (B.A., 1909; M.A., 1941) and Leeds Clergy School (1909). Sent as assistant-curate to St Margaret's Church, Ilkley, Yorkshire, he was made deacon on 25 September 1910 and ordained priest on 24 September 1911. He sailed to Australia, joined the Bush Brotherhood of St Barnabas in 1914 and ministered to remote communities in North Queensland until 1921. *The Sundowner* (London, 1922), his book about his experiences, was credited with attracting other clergy to the brotherhood. Returning to Ilkley, he married Frances Nathalie Glennie on 12 January 1921 at St Margaret's.

Back in Queensland, Robin served as rector of Hughenden (1921-22), canon and sub-dean of St James's Cathedral, Townsville (1922-25), warden of St John's College, University of Queensland (1926-30), canon of St John's Cathedral, Brisbane (1926-30), and State chairman of the Student Christian Movement. Having returned to England, he was appointed rector of Woodchurch, Cheshire, in 1931; patronage of the incumbency had been held by his family since 1612. He was later rural dean (1936-41) of Wirral North, honorary canon (1940-41) of Chester Cathedral and an air-raid precautions warden during World War II. Consecrated bishop of Adelaide by the archbishop of Canterbury on 25 July 1941 in Westminster Abbey, he was enthroned at St Peter's Cathedral, Adelaide, on 2 December.

Although High Church in his leanings, Robin felt comfortable with the wide range of Anglican 'churchmanship' in the Adelaide diocese. He was enthusiastic and energetic, a spiritual man who 'enjoyed life, his faith, and people'. In manner he was stately—some said imperious—but not pompous. His keen sense of humour disturbed as well as challenged, as did his trademark raising of one eyebrow, well depicted in Ivor Hele's portrait (1956, held at Bishop's Court). Robin encouraged the celebration of the Eucharist as the focus of Sunday worship and preached a gospel that related faith to everyday life.

Early in his episcopate he appointed two commissions (1942-43) which paved the way for important pastoral strategies. The first dealt with the provision of religious education programmes in Church day and Sunday schools, and in state and independent schools. The second commission established a diocesan committee to co-ordinate and develop social welfare services. After 1945, through the Bishop's Home Mission Society, he sought ways to provide priests and resources for rapidly growing communities in new suburbs. To boost the number of his clergy, he invited members of the Society of the Sacred Mission to come from England and establish a theological college: St Michael's House, Crafers, was opened in 1947. As early as 1946 he supported the election of women to synod.

In 1956 Robin retired to England where he officiated as assistant-bishop (1958-67) of Portsmouth. He died on 17 June 1969 in his home at Petersfield, Hampshire, and was cremated; his wife, their two daughters and two of their three sons survived him.

P. Webb, *Brothers in the Sun* (Adel, 1978); D. Hilliard, *Godliness and Good Order* (Adel, 1986); *Adel Church Guardian*, Oct 1956, p 5, Aug 1969, p 8; Robin papers (held by Adel Anglican Diocesan archives); information from Canon C. Chittleborough, Port Willunga, SA, Miss I. Jeffreys, Marryatville, Miss N. Morrison, Toorak Gardens, Adel, Mrs N. Jowett, Yea, Vic, and the late Archbishop T. T. Reed.   ROBIN RADFORD

ROBINSON, ALFRED LAMBTON (1903-1948), government officer and soldier, was born on 7 December 1903 at Townsville, Queensland, son of Charles Frederick Robinson, telegraph-operator, and his wife Ruby Laura, née Lambton, both Queensland born. Alfred was educated at several state schools in North Queensland and at Townsville Grammar School. In 1921 he began work in the Dalby branch of the National Bank of Australasia. After being transferred to St George in 1925, he obtained a post in the public service of the Mandated Territory of New Guinea and left for Rabaul in 1926. There, on 20 December 1927, he married Alice Baxter whom he had met at Dalby. He served as a clerk at Kavieng, Kokopo, Madang, Kieta, Lorengau and Sohano.

By 1941 Robinson was back in Rabaul, in the Department of District Services and Native Affairs. He had joined the local militia unit, the New Guinea Volunteer Rifles, soon after its formation in September 1939. With the threat of a Japanese invasion, his wife and son were evacuated to Dalby. Robinson was called up for full-time service on 20 January 1942. He was stationed near the beach to the south of Rabaul when the Japanese landed three days later. Overwhelmed by their numbers and with his meagre ammunition exhausted, he joined other Australians escaping inland. They had no plans or rations, and chose their own routes through difficult, mountainous country.

On 3 February Robinson and others were at Tol plantation on Wide Bay when they saw Japanese landing barges heading to shore. Many of the Australians were sick and unarmed. A number surrendered immediately, but Robinson was captured while trying to escape. Next morning he and nine others, hands tied behind their backs, were marched into the plantation by a 'shooting party'. He dropped into the scrub on a bend, responded to the advice, 'Lower, Sport', and survived. Unable to free his hands, he was in a desperate condition when some Australians found him on the 6th. He walked to the north coast, joined Keith McCarthy's [q.v.15] men and sailed in the *Lakatoi* to Cairns, Queensland. They arrived on 28 March, with news of the massacre of over 150 prisoners at Tol.

After convalescing, Robinson returned to New Guinea in August 1942. He served first as a sergeant and then as a warrant officer in the Australian New Guinea Administrative Unit. As a member of the advance party that landed on Los Negros Island in February 1944, and during operations on Manus Island (March-May), he proved 'an efficient and daring scout'. He led New Guinean police in attacks on Japanese positions, rescued an American serviceman under fire, and dived into the sea to save a suicidal Japanese soldier.

James McAuley [q.v.15], who served with him on Manus, said that he had 'a record of laconic courage'. Five ft 10 ins (178 cm) tall, lightly built and brown haired, 'Robbie' was commissioned lieutenant on 10 July. His Distinguished Conduct Medal was gazetted in September. He was a devout Anglican who carried a Bible in his top pocket throughout the war.

Having come to think of New Guinea 'as his country', Robinson transferred to the postwar field service after leaving the army on 2 July 1946. He worked as assistant district officer at Gasmata before resigning in April 1948 to take up the lease of Ring Ring copra plantation in south-eastern New Britain. While recruiting labourers at Poi'iong, an area beyond administration control, he was suddenly attacked and killed by villagers on 12 December 1948. He was buried at Kandrian station. His wife and son survived him.

L. Wigmore, *The Japanese Thrust* (Canb, 1957); J. K. McCarthy, *Patrol into Yesterday* (Melb, 1963); I. Downs, *The New Guinea Volunteer Rifles* (Broadbeach Waters, Qld, 1999); *PIM*, Jan, May, June 1949; *Quadrant*, 5, no 3, 1961; *Dalby Herald*, 17 Dec 1948; AWM 76, B423, AWM 54, 607/8/1 and 1010/6/16 (AWM); Dept of District Services and Native Affairs, district annual report, New Britain, 1948/49 (National Archives, PNG); McCarthy papers (Univ PNG L).   H. N. NELSON

ROBINSON, GRACE FAIRLEY; *see* BOELKE

ROBINSON, JAMES ALEXANDER (1888-1971), educationist, was born on 20 January 1888 at Nudgee, Brisbane, second child of Henry Walton Robinson, a Queensland-born farmer, and his wife Esther, née Adams, who came from Ireland. James was sent to New Farm State School, where he became a pupil-teacher in 1901 and an assistant-teacher in 1909. Taking leave in 1913, he entered King's College, University of Queensland (B.A., 1915), as a founding student. He attended evening-classes at university, taught day-classes at the new (Queensland Teachers') Training College, Gardens Point, and tutored in mathematics at King's College. President of the university sports union and of King's College students' club, he captained the university's first XI and won Blues (1913) for cricket and tennis.

On 15 May 1915 Robinson was appointed lieutenant in the Australian Imperial Force. Embarking with the 26th Battalion, he served on Gallipoli (from September) and accompanied the unit to France in March 1916. While serving on the Western Front he was promoted major, awarded the Distinguished

Service Order and thrice mentioned in dispatches. In August 1918 'Old Uniformity' (as he was nicknamed) was given command of the battalion as temporary lieutenant colonel. He was severely wounded in October and evacuated to England. After briefly rejoining his unit in France, he sailed for Australia in March 1919 and his appointment terminated on 27 July. He had supervised the salvage (June 1918) of a German tank named *Mephisto*, which was brought to Brisbane as a war relic and housed in the Queensland Museum.

Back at the training college, Robinson lectured in mathematics, perspective and model drawing, and drill. At St Andrew's Anglican Church, Indooroopilly, on 23 April 1921 he married Alice Clinton, daughter of Sir Arthur Morgan [q.v.10]. He was principal of Rockhampton State High School and Technical College from 1925 before returning to the training college in 1935 as its principal. Guiding the college through the years of World War II and the attendant emergency measures, he oversaw Q.T.T.C.'s expansion and relocation (1942) at Kelvin Grove. A one-year diploma of education was introduced (1937), establishing an important link with the university, entry standards were raised, and teacher-training methods improved. After retiring as principal in 1954, he continued to appraise and advise trainee-teachers until he was 68.

Robinson was a man of conservative values and 'ramrod bearing'. Known as 'Rocks' to his students, he was sometimes eccentric and idiosyncratic in manner, but always energetic, fair and broad-minded. He served on the Queensland Institute for Educational Research, the senate of the University of Queensland (1953-60) and the Board of Adult Education (1957-60). In addition, he taught immigrants by correspondence, and English and mathematics to inmates of Boggo Road gaol until he was in his eighties. In 1966 he was appointed M.B.E.

Survived by his wife, son and four daughters, Robinson died on 14 July 1971 in his home at Chelmer and was cremated with Methodist forms. A likeness (1981), sculpted in sandstone by Rhyl Hinwood, is fixed to the library wall at the Kelvin Grove campus of the Queensland University of Technology.

N. R. Anderson, *Kelvin Grove, Forty Years 1942-1981* (Brisb, 1981); M. Whitmore, *Mephisto* (Brisb, 1989); N. Kyle et al, *A Class of Its Own* (Syd, 1999); Dept of Public Instruction (Qld), *Annual Report*, 1935-54; Robinson file, History Unit (Education Dept, Brisb); Teachers' College records, A/23132 (QA); information from Mrs L. Watson-Browne, Chermside, and Dr M. Dickinson, Brisb.
                                                    NOELINE J. KYLE

ROBINSON, JEAN ELSIE; *see* FERGUSON

ROBSON, EWAN MURRAY (1906-1974), politician, soldier and solicitor, was born on 7 March 1906 at Ashfield, Sydney, second son of William Elliott Veitch Robson [q.v.11], a native-born solicitor, and his wife Mabel Jackson, née Wise, who came from Victoria. Murray proceeded from Newington College to St Paul's College, University of Sydney (B.A., 1927; LL.B., 1930); while there, he rowed for the university. Admitted as a solicitor on 4 June 1930, he practised in the family firm, Robson & Cowlishaw (Robson, Cowlishaw & Macready from 1955). On 31 March 1931 at St Stephen's Presbyterian Church, Sydney, he married Lesley Alison Martin. Both his father and grandfather (William Robson [q.v.11]) had served in the New South Wales parliament. In August 1936 Murray won the by-election for the Legislative Assembly seat of Vaucluse as an Independent United Australia Party candidate. He had an impressive appearance, being good-looking and 6 ft 2 ins (188 cm) tall. Beneath his 'unbending exterior' he had 'a warm and kindly disposition'.

Soon after his election Robson joined the U.A.P., but associated with a group of rebels who were unhappy with the government's economic management and the party's control over pre-selection. He was prominent in the struggle that led to the resignation of the premier (Sir) Bertram Stevens and his replacement by Alexander Mair [qq.v.12,10] in August 1939.

A lieutenant in the Militia from 29 September 1939, Robson was appointed to the Australian Imperial Force on 29 December. He embarked with the 2nd/5th Field Regiment in May 1940, but on reaching Scotland transferred to the 2nd/31st Battalion. In June 1941 Captain Robson received a shrapnel wound to the foot while fighting in Syria. Attached (from October) to the Middle East Tactical School, he rejoined his unit in February 1942 and accompanied it to Australia.

In August 1942 Robson sailed with the 2nd/31st to New Guinea where he suffered bouts of malaria. Promoted temporary major (September), he commanded the battalion as lieutenant colonel from May 1943. He was awarded the Distinguished Service Order for 'courage, coolness, [and] determined and resourceful leadership in the field' throughout the Lae campaign (September-December), and was thrice mentioned in dispatches. In July 1945 he led the unit in the invasion of Balikpapan, Borneo, and in September accepted the surrender of Japanese forces at Bandjarmasin. Relinquishing command, he returned to Sydney and was placed on the Reserve of Officers in November.

Robson found it difficult to adjust to civilian life. During the war he had become estranged from his wife; they lived apart and she di-

vorced him in October 1947. At St Peter's Anglican Church, Watsons Bay, on 8 December 1950 he married Naomi Priscilla Other Gee, a 34-year-old milliner.

While on leave from parliament, Robson had missed the political upheavals of the collapse of the U.A.P. and the foundation of the Liberal Party. Following his return, he persuaded (Sir) Robert Askin, a former sergeant in his battalion, to enter parliament. Robson's political interests were mainly parochial; his most frequent interventions concerned traffic problems and public transport in the Eastern Suburbs. In August 1954, after (Sir) Vernon Treatt had lost three successive elections, Robson was persuaded to accept the leadership of the Liberal Party as a compromise candidate.

Like other senior members of the party, Robson had no experience in government. He had little interest in policy except for Cold War anti-communism. Described by Katharine West as 'swashbuckling', 'fiery and flamboyant', he could be 'unpredictably moody'. His 'extraordinary want of tact and diplomacy' and military style of leadership won him few allies, and he alienated the Liberal Party machine by trying to forge a closer alliance with Colonel (Sir) Michael Bruxner's [q.v.7] Country Party. After months of 'continuous intrigue' Robson was replaced as leader in September 1955. He never had the opportunity to lead his party in a general election.

In July 1957 Robson resigned from parliament and returned to his legal practice. He belonged to the University, Royal Sydney Golf, Rose Bay Bowling and Tattersall's clubs. In 1966 he was appointed C.B.E. Survived by his wife and the two sons of his first marriage, he died of a coronary occlusion on 26 August 1974 at his Rose Bay home and was cremated.

K. West, *Power in the Liberal Party* (Melb, 1965); D. Clune, *The New South Wales State Election, 1941* (Syd, 1995); F. Frost, *The New South Wales State Election, 1956* (Syd, 1999); *PD* (NSW), 27 Aug 1974, p 638; *Aust Q*, Dec 1961; *SMH*, 21 Sept 1955, 27 July 1957, 1 Jan 1966; *Sun-Herald* (Syd), 28 July 1957.

MICHAEL HOGAN

ROBSON, LEONARD CHARLES (1894-1964), headmaster, was born on 17 October 1894 at Waverley, Sydney, third son of James Robson, a clerk from Ceylon (Sri Lanka), and his native-born wife Harriet Clarissa, sister of William Holmes [q.v.9]. After attending Stanmore Superior Public School, in 1907 Len entered Sydney Grammar School where he proved a brilliant mathematician, a prize-winner and a consummate oarsman. At the University of Sydney (B.Sc., 1915), he gained first-class honours in mathematics and formed a lasting friendship with Professor H. S. Carslaw [q.v.7].

On 20 September 1915 Robson enlisted in the Australian Imperial Force. Because of his poor eyesight, he was posted to a medical unit. In March 1916 he was transferred to the 18th Battalion, with which he served on the Western Front. He was commissioned in October, promoted lieutenant in January 1917 and mentioned in dispatches. For his work as adjutant during operations in Flanders in September-October, he was awarded the Military Cross. Robson resigned his A.I.F. appointment on 30 January 1920 in England. Having been elected Rhodes scholar for New South Wales in 1916, he read mathematics at New College, Oxford (B.A., 1920; M.A., 1925); he rowed in the college VIII and gained first-class honours. At St Stephen's parish church, Hampstead, London, on 29 November 1920 he married Marjorie Guelph Grindrod. He returned to Australia and took up an appointment as senior mathematics master at Geelong Church of England Grammar School, Victoria.

In 1922 Robson became the first Australian-born headmaster of Sydney Church of England Grammar School (Shore). He had some difficulty in establishing himself: he had to confront sceptical older masters—many of whose careers went back to the foundation of the school—and improve the school's recent sporting performance. Robson retired many of the longest-serving staff, made his own appointments, and satisfied the Shore Old Boys' Union when the school won all races at the Head of the River regatta in 1928. Shore was to be pre-eminent in schoolboy rowing in New South Wales over the next three decades; Robson himself coached many of the winning crews.

As headmaster, Robson was a conservative reformer who built upon the English public-school tradition. Although he deprecated the effect on school life of centralized, state-controlled examinations, he was aware of competition from the high schools and strove to raise Shore's standing. He taught mathematics to the senior classes and helped his students to achieve many distinguished results in the Leaving certificate. After the Depression, he sought to modernize Shore. Bernhardt Holtermann's [q.v.4] villa and tower, the original boarding-quarters and headmaster's residence, were transformed into a brick collegiate building with modern dormitories. In 1938 Robson visited Europe and the United States of America, and came back convinced that Shore needed to improve its equipment. By 1940 the school had some of the most modern science laboratories of any Australian school. He encouraged drama and music, though he could never fully comprehend their educational purpose. His first school report at Sydney Grammar had noted that he was 'not strong on the imaginative side', and he quoted it against himself.

Robson stressed character formation and the importance of religious and spiritual education. From Albert Weigall [q.v.6], his headmaster at Sydney Grammar, he had developed a distaste for 'ostentatious vulgarity'. Shore boys were taught to show initiative and leadership, but to be self-effacing, and loyal to school, country and monarchy. From his wartime experience Robson drew on the lessons of service and sacrifice which he expected others to follow; in 1940 his insistence that young single masters should volunteer for military service led to James McAuley's [q.v.15] resignation from the staff.

With Julian Bickersteth [q.v.7] of the Collegiate School of St Peter, Adelaide, and (Sir) James Darling, of Geelong Grammar, Robson had been a founder (1931) of the Headmasters' Conference of Australia. Increasingly influential, he sat on the New South Wales committee (1933-36) to inquire into examinations and secondary school courses. It was chaired by (Sir) Robert Wallace [q.v.12], and recommended the establishment of the Board of Secondary School Studies, on which Robson served (1937-49). During World War II he became a leading representative of the 'independent schools' in Australia; in the postwar years he was a legendary figure within the school and among his fellow headmasters. In 1955 Robson was appointed C.B.E. To J. Wilson Hogg, he seemed 'almost Elizabethan' in combining his qualities as a schoolmaster and administrator with his intellectual and athletic achievements.

Tall and thin, Robson exuded nervous vitality. Striding about the school with his gown flowing behind him, he always seemed in a hurry. Even in later life, his hands moved constantly between coat pocket and lapel when addressing the school assembled. Shy, and serious almost to a fault, he held most parents at a distance. Many found his manner brusque. Boys' misdemeanours could bring forth outbursts of rage. His staff certainly knew that 'the chief' was never one with whom to pass the time of day in idle conversation. Beneath his severe exterior he was kind and compassionate to those who had tried and failed, and to those who had suffered grievous personal loss.

A heart attack in 1949 took its toll on Robson's energies and health, but he remained headmaster until 1958. He was a fellow (1958-64) of the Senate of the University of Sydney. In the late 1950s he chaired the advisory committee of the Industrial Fund for the Advancement of Scientific Education in Schools. His advice to the Menzies [q.v.15] government in 1964 provided the basis for the scheme of Commonwealth aid for science laboratories in schools. He was foundation chairman of the Commonwealth Advisory Committee on Standards for Science Facilities in Independent Secondary Schools.

Robson died of cancer on 5 December 1964 in Canberra Community Hospital and was cremated; his wife and their son survived him. Although he had not formally accepted a knighthood, special arrangements allowed his wife to be known as Lady Robson. (Sir) William Dargie's portrait of L. C. Robson, which won the Archibald [q.v.3] prize in 1947, is held at Shore.

G. Sherington, *Shore* (Syd, 1983) *and* 'The Headmasters' in C. Turney (ed), *Pioneers of Australian Education*, 3 (Syd, 1983); I. Palmer (ed), *Melbourne Studies in Education 1984* (Melb, 1984); *Aust Teacher*, June 1965, p 9; *SMH*, 19 Aug 1920, 5 Oct 1922, 1 Jan 1955, 12 Dec 1958, 6 Mar, 7 Dec 1964; Robson papers *and* information from Legends of Shore Project (Syd C of E Grammar School archives).   G. E. SHERINGTON

RODD, JOHN MILLER (1911-1976), solicitor, company director and army officer, was born on 24 November 1911 at Camberwell, Melbourne, elder son of Victorian-born parents Edgar Alfred Rodd, bank manager, and his wife Alexandra, née Miller. John attended Scotch College and won a senior scholarship to the University of Melbourne where he began a law degree before completing (1932) the articled clerks' course. He had been articled to Sir Arthur Robinson [q.v.11] in 1930 and was admitted to practise as a barrister and solicitor on 1 May 1935. His career in commercial law (specializing in the mining industry) and in serving the Law Institute of Victoria was to mirror that of Robinson.

In 1936 Rodd was commissioned lieutenant, Melbourne University Rifles, Militia. On 6 May 1940 he was appointed captain, Australian Imperial Force, and posted to the 2nd/ 14th Battalion. By December he was on the staff of the 7th Division in the Middle East. He undertook a course at the Tactical School and impressed the chief instructor with his 'clear brain', 'inquiring mind', 'strong bent for detail' and 'pleasant manner'. Mentioned in dispatches for his work in February-July 1941, he was promoted major in June 1942 and transferred to British General Headquarters, Middle East, as assistant Australian liaison officer. He was repatriated in February 1943. At Christ Church, South Yarra, on 3 March that year he married with Anglican rites Joan Patricia Berry, a 22-year-old draughtsman. In June-October 1943 he performed staff duties in Port Moresby. Returning to Australia, he was placed on the Reserve of Officers on 30 September 1944.

That year Rodd was made a partner in Arthur Robinson & Co. Recommended by Sir Arthur's nephew Lyell Robinson, he began in 1953 to act for the mining group, Rio Tinto Co. Ltd, London, which then had almost no Australian infrastructure. Initially, Rodd's office in Collins Street, Melbourne, was Rio Tinto's Australian base. He became closely involved in the company's Australian business, especially the complicated financing and floating of Mary Kathleen Uranium Ltd (1955). In the judgement of the firm's historian, he was an 'indefatigable worker with an enormous capacity for detail . . . constantly on the alert for any breaches of law or ethics. His wide experience made him a most valuable member of the team'.

Rodd later played a major role in the formation of Hamersley Iron Pty Ltd. He helped this company to reach a complex agreement (1963) with the Western Australian government for prospecting and leasehold rights, to conclude difficult negotiations with Lang Hancock and Peter Wright for the acquisition of their iron-ore interests, and to formulate sales contracts with the Japanese. In these activities he worked closely with senior officers of the Rio Tinto Mining Co. of Australia Ltd and the Zinc Corporation Ltd, including Struan Anderson [q.v.13], Val Duncan and John Hohnen.

Acting for Rio Tinto involved Rodd in considerable travel, interstate and abroad. He visited Britain at least twice a year. His frequent trips to Mary Kathleen, Queensland, at first took up to three days each way. Roy Wright, vice-chairman of Rio Tinto, noted that he 'was no desk bound lawyer'. Rodd helped to arrange the merger (1962) of the Conzinc and Rio Tinto groups in Australia. With the increase in local staff, and the appointment of (Sir) Maurice Mawby [q.v.15] as chairman of Conzinc Rio Tinto of Australia Ltd, Rodd's involvement with the firm was reduced to that of director and legal adviser. He served on the boards of other public companies, and as honorary Swedish consul (1967) and consul-general (1971) in Melbourne.

A member (1945-67) and president (1952-53) of the council of the Law Institute of Victoria, Rodd sat on a number of its committees and represented the institute on various other bodies. He chaired the Law Institute's committees that advised (Sir) Arthur Rylah [q.v.], the Victorian attorney-general, on the revision of company law which resulted in the Companies Acts of 1958 and 1961. Rodd was appointed C.B.E. in 1968. As the senior partner (from 1975) in Arthur Robinson & Co., he was the head of one of the few firms—all small— that handled most of Australia's work in commercial law. He died of cancer on 16 September 1976 in his holiday home at Anglesea and was buried in Springvale cemetery. His wife, daughter and son survived him.

R. H. Harding, *Wholeheartedly and at Once* (Melb, 1992); *Law Inst J*, 27, 1953, p 264, 42, 1968, p 69, 50, 1976, p 462; R. Campbell, History of Arthur Robinson & Hedderwicks, *and* R. Wright, Reminiscences (both unpublished, held by Arthur Robinson & Hedderwicks, Melb); Rio Tinto Ltd collection (Univ Melb Archives); information from Arthur Robinson & Hedderwicks and Mr M. Rodd, Melb.

ANDREW J. RAY

RODD, LEWIS CHARLES (1905-1979), headmaster, social historian and Christian socialist, was born on 12 March 1905 at Paddington, Sydney, fifth child of English-born parents Lewis Rodd (d.1916), master mariner, and his wife Lillian Amelia, née Waterhouse. 'Roddy' grew into a 'child bookworm'. He left school early, like his hero in *Jude the Obscure*, and read his own way to matriculation.

In 1927 Rodd entered the University of Sydney (B.A., 1931). Trained as a schoolteacher, he taught (1930-32) at Darlinghurst Public School. He excelled at psychology and economics, became fascinated with Anglo-Catholic religious traditions, and formed a friendship with Kylie Tennant. Into her young and eager ears he bubbled an understanding of the pathways to Australian identity, similar to those explored by C. J. Dennis [q.v.8]. Rodd was transferred to Coonabarabran in September 1932. There, at Christ Church, he married Kylie with Anglican rites on 21 November that year. She was to describe their relationship in florid and sometimes contradictory detail in several of her books. Marriage provided him with an anchor of emotional stability and the opportunity to nurture her literary talent.

A founder (1931) of the Educational Workers' League, Rodd sat on the editorial committee of the *Educational Worker*. He achieved, through influencing Kylie's books, a wider audience for the dissemination of his ideas than through his polemical writings. He promoted the importance of teaching—and the role of a questioning and critical approach —through the many political, religious and social organizations to which he belonged, among them the Labor Educational League, the New South Wales Teachers' Federation, the Christian Socialist Movement and the Australian Peace Pledge Union. During World War II he registered as a conscientious objector.

Rodd gained further experience from postings to Canowindra (1934-36), Dulwich Hill (1936-39) and Muswellbrook (1939-41). Even while headmaster of Laurieton Public School (1941-53) and of Hunters Hill (from 1953), he remained adviser, typist and organizer of Tennant's writing. After the war he helped to form the Sirius Publishing Co., which produced cheap Australian editions of popular novels. Described by his wife as 'sardonic'

and 'introverted', and as 'a meticulous planner', he collected early Australiana, the works of Arctic and Antarctic explorers, and the novels of Thomas Hardy. He invariably set off for school wearing 'an immaculate white coat, starched and crisp'.

His breakdown and retirement from teaching in November 1960 altered the balance of their literary partnership. Subject to fits of depression, Rodd attempted suicide by throwing himself under a train: he fractured his skull, and lost an arm and a foot, but survived. His publications included *Australian Imperialism* (Sydney, 1938), *Venturing the Unknown Ways* (Melbourne, 1965) with Donald McLean [q.v.15], and, with Tennant, *The Australian Essay* (Melbourne, 1968). *John Hope of Christ Church* (1972) was his finest book. Hope [q.v.14] had been a close friend since 1945. Rodd saw him as an exponent of a practical theology, well suited to the struggling religious life of the inner-city. *A Gentle Shipwreck* (Melbourne, 1975) contained Rodd's reminiscences of Surry Hills before World War I.

Personal tragedies marked these years of productive writing. Ill health and drugs—legal and illicit—disturbed family affairs, prompting the Rodds to retreat (1977) to Shipley in the Blue Mountains. In 1978 their only son was 'pushed' from an upstairs window of a derelict house in Sydney and died of head injuries. Rodd died on 29 July 1979 at his Shipley home and was buried beside his father in Waverley cemetery; his wife and their daughter survived him.

B. Mitchell, *Teachers, Education, and Politics* (Brisb, 1975); K. Tennant, *The Missing Heir* (Melb, 1986); *Hummer*, no 27, Jan-Apr 1990, p 3; Rodd papers (NL); NSW teachers' records (Education Dept, Syd); Intelligence file, A6126, item 506 (NAA, Canb).

FRANK FARRELL

RODGERS, DONALD KILGOUR (1906-1978), journalist and press secretary, was born on 20 May 1906 at Newcastle, New South Wales, son of Australian-born parents Robert Howden Rodgers, clerk, and his wife Jessie Edith, née Kilgour. Educated locally, Don worked as a journalist on the *Newcastle Morning Herald and Miner's Advocate* and the *Newcastle Sun*. In 1931 he joined the *Labor Daily* in Sydney. While attached to that newspaper's bureau at Parliament House, Canberra, he emerged as an accomplished political reporter. At Scots Church, Sydney, on 21 March 1936 he married with Presbyterian forms Edna Ida Dorothy McNevin, a 22-year-old usherette. In September 1937 he was seconded to assist John Curtin [q.v.13] in campaigning for the forthcoming Federal general election. The transfer was intended to be for one month only, but he 'hit it off' with Curtin and accepted a permanent post as his publicity officer (later press secretary).

Rumours circulated for many years that Rodgers drafted Curtin's article published in the Melbourne *Herald* on 27 December 1941, which contained the famous declaration: 'Australia looks to America, free of any pangs as to our traditional links or kinship with the United Kingdom'. In a letter written in June 1976 and opened after his death, Rodgers confirmed that he had been the 'author' of the statement. He travelled constantly with the prime minister by train, often sharing a sleeping-compartment with him. Curtin had a cast in his left eye, and Rodgers faced the problem of obtaining a publicity shot giving him something like a 'straight-on appearance'. He finally found a 'beauty' in the *Illustrated London News*, 'of all places', and it became Curtin's stock image.

Rodgers also had to counter the inopportune public statements of Curtin's wife Elsie whom he described as a 'champion political brick dropper'. He took long walks with Curtin during his fits of melancholia, lifting the prime minister's mood with disquisitions on reform programmes such as introducing the 'Continental Sunday' to wartime Australia. These 'pipe dreams' were usually shelved as politically unacceptable. Rodgers was privy to most of Curtin's major wartime consultations and attended virtually all of the prime minister's meetings with General Douglas MacArthur [q.v.15]. Curtin discussed his decisions with Rodgers, once explaining why he had given his old rival Eddie Ward [q.v.] the portfolios of transport and external territories: 'the Japs have got the external territories and the army's got the transport'! Rodgers also organized and sustained Curtin's gruelling schedule of twice-daily press conferences.

Following Curtin's death in 1945, Rodgers settled in comfortably as press secretary to J. B. Chifley [q.v.13]. The new prime minister held fewer press conferences and was less receptive generally to the demands of journalists. Rodgers performed his most memorable duty for Chifley in 1947 when he released to the press a statement announcing the government's decision to nationalize the banks. He later recalled: 'I've never seen a man with such a look of pleasure on his face [as on] that Saturday morning . . . he had written it out in his own hand . . . thirty-five words it was, and he said, "Get that out, Don!"' After the Labor government was defeated in 1949, Rodgers believed that he should 'move on', but he could not bring himself to leave the warm, personable Chifley, a man who even exchanged letters with the young Rupert Murdoch about the virtues of socialism. When Chifley died in June 1951, Rodgers worked briefly for H. V. Evatt [q.v.14], whom he disliked.

In September that year Rodgers was appointed to the Australian News and Information Bureau. He moved to Sydney in 1955 as editor of news services for radio-station 2UW. Although he retired in 1971, he continued to work indefatigably, covering local government for the *Manly Daily*, providing political reports for John Laws's radio programme and serving as a press officer for Royal North Shore Hospital. Despite his long association with the Labor Party, he was objective in his political assessments, arguing that the Depression government of J. A. Lyons [q.v.10] had achieved greatness because 'it had got Australia back on its feet'. From the late 1950s Rodgers drew closer to the Liberal Party. A political consultant (1959) to its New South Wales branch, he directed the party's campaign (1965) for the Labor-held seat of Wyong. He admired the political style of Premier (Sir) Robert Askin.

Rodgers followed cricket, and Rugby Union football which he had taken a leading part in bringing to the Federal (Australian) Capital Territory. He was a lifelong member of the Australian Journalists' Association. In 1973 he was appointed M.B.E. A robust, gregarious man, with an acute 'news-sense', Rodgers was a master of political communication at a time when the printed word dominated. He was not the first of Australia's prime ministerial press secretaries, but he was the most influential and effective. Survived by his wife and their three sons, he died on 2 May 1978 in his home at St Ives, Sydney, and was cremated.

Smith's Weekly (Syd), 22 Aug 1942; *SMH*, 29 Sept 1951, 2 June 1973, 3 May 1978; M. Pratt, taped interview with Rodgers, 1971 (NL); Rodgers papers (NL).

C. J. LLOYD*

ROGERS, JAMES STANLEY (1893-1977), physicist, was born on 18 June 1893 at Beaconsfield, Tasmania, eldest of nine children of native-born parents James Rogers, Methodist clergyman, and his wife Agnes, née Caldwell. John David Rogers [q.v.] was his brother. With the father being called to a new parish every five years, the family moved regularly. James received his secondary education in Victoria, at the Bendigo Continuation School (dux 1910). In 1911 he entered the Melbourne Training College and the University of Melbourne (B.A., Dip.Ed., 1919; B.Sc., 1921; M.Sc., 1922; D.Sc., 1945). He completed his B.A. while teaching (1913-15) at country high schools.

On 25 June 1915 Rogers enlisted in the Australian Imperial Force. He sailed for Egypt and joined the 14th Battalion which was transferred to the Western Front in June 1916.

Rising rapidly through the ranks, he was selected for staff duties in January 1917 and promoted captain in April. For his work in June-August at headquarters, 4th Division, during operations around Messines, Belgium, he was awarded the Military Cross. He served as brigade major with the 3rd (British) Tank Brigade before returning to Melbourne where his A.I.F. appointment terminated on 5 October 1919. Resuming his teaching career, he also undertook the additional subjects needed to complete a degree in science. In March 1921 he resigned from the teaching service to do a master's degree in natural philosophy under T. H. Laby [q.v.9] who became a powerful patron. On 12 July 1922 at the Presbyterian Church, Kew, he married Hazel Carr.

Having been awarded an 1851 Exhibition science research scholarship, Rogers sailed with his wife for England. On Laby's recommendation he was admitted as a research student to the Cavendish Laboratory, University of Cambridge. He embarked on a Ph.D., measuring the ranges of alpha particles emitted from various radioactive substances. After only two years, with his research still in an unsatisfactory state, he returned to the University of Melbourne to take up a senior lectureship which Laby had offered him. He continued his study of radioactive emissions, with better results, and in 1925 won the university's David Syme [q.v.6] prize for research. When he submitted his work to Cambridge, however, the examiners deemed it insufficient to rescue his Ph.D., and awarded him an M.Sc. (1928) instead.

Over the next few years Rogers continued his investigations into radioactive emissions. He carried out ground-breaking work on photographic measuring techniques for gamma rays and published a handful of papers for which he was eventually awarded a D.Sc. His real strength was his teaching. In particular, he taught for many years an outstandingly successful course in physics for first-year medical students. The textbook he wrote, *Physics for Medical Students* (1933), enjoyed several editions. Firm but sympathetic in his approach to students, he was able to win respect at the same time as he aroused interest in his subject.

During World War II, while continuing his teaching, Rogers served as secretary and executive-officer of the Optical Munitions Panel (later Scientific Instruments and Optical Panel) which pioneered the production of precision optical equipment in Australia. His unpublished history of the organization is held by the National Archives of Australia. In 1946 he became warden of the university's branch campus at Mildura. Returning to Melbourne in early 1950, he was appointed dean of graduate studies and warden of overseas students. In 1963 he retired. Survived by his wife and their two daughters, he died on 23 July 1977 at Heidelberg and was cremated.

R. W. Home, *Physics in Australia to 1945* (Melb, 1990); *Univ Melb Gazette*, Dec 1977, p 15.

R. W. HOME

ROGERS, JOHN DAVID (1895-1978), army officer and company director, was born on 29 April 1895 at Penguin, Tasmania, second of nine children of native-born parents James Rogers, Methodist clergyman, and his wife Agnes, née Caldwell. James Stanley Rogers [q.v.] was his elder brother. Raised in an austere but loving household at various places in rural Victoria, John won a scholarship to Geelong College (dux 1913) and proceeded to the University of Melbourne (B.Sc., 1922). He undertook compulsory military training with the Geelong College cadets and the Melbourne University Rifles. On 20 August 1914 he interrupted his studies and enlisted in the Australian Imperial Force.

After training in Egypt with the 6th Battalion, Rogers fell ill in a troop-ship off Gallipoli and missed the initial landing at Anzac Cove on 25 April 1915. He rejoined his unit a day or so later and was appointed lance corporal on his twentieth birthday. Following the 2nd Brigade's attack at Cape Helles, he was promoted sergeant and company sergeant major on successive days in May. On 4 August he was commissioned. He became battalion intelligence officer in September and lieutenant in December.

On the Western Front, Rogers won the Military Cross for leading a successful raid on German trenches in June 1916. He was promoted captain in December. From time to time in 1917 he was attached to the 1st Division for staff training before being posted to its headquarters in January 1918 as general staff officer, 3rd grade. During the Menin Road attack (3rd battle of Ypres) in September 1917 he had served as 3rd Brigade intelligence officer. Mentioned in dispatches in May 1918, he joined the Australian Corps headquarters staff that month and worked for Major R. G. (Baron) Casey [q.v.13]. His A.I.F. appointment terminated on 21 February 1919 in Melbourne. He was awarded the Belgian Croix de Guerre that year.

Resuming his university studies, Rogers cut a dashing figure and relished extra-curricular activities. He gained honours in almost every examination and won a Bloomfield scholarship. At the Methodist Church, Balaclava, on 14 September 1922 he married Irene Myrtle Lowe; his father performed the ceremony. Rene had been the first woman to graduate (1918) in agricultural science from the University of Melbourne. In 1923 Rogers joined the Vacuum Oil Co. Pty Ltd. After being employed as head chemist (1924-29) in Sydney, he held increasingly senior management positions in Western Australia, New South Wales and Victoria. He was also active in the Militia in 1920-24, serving as an intelligence officer at the district base headquarters, Melbourne.

With Lieutenant General Sir Thomas Blamey's [q.v.13] encouragement, Rogers was appointed to the A.I.F. on 15 June 1940 and sent to I Corps headquarters in Palestine at the end of September. In November he was promoted lieutenant colonel and became the corps' senior intelligence officer. Next month he was attached to the 6th Division as liaison officer for the attack on Bardia, Libya (3 January 1941). In the Greek campaign (April) he headed the team that co-ordinated the evacuation; he was one of the last Australians to leave for Egypt and was appointed O.B.E. Following the Syrian campaign (June-July), he worked closely with Lieutenant General (Sir) John Lavarack [q.v.15] and Brigadier (Sir) Sydney Rowell [q.v.]. For much of the second half of 1941 he performed liaison duties in the Western Desert.

Recalled to Australia in January 1942, Rogers carried out intelligence work at Headquarters, Home Forces. He was made a liaison officer with General Headquarters, South-West Pacific Area, on 31 March and promoted colonel in May. On 1 July he became director of military intelligence at Land Headquarters, Melbourne, with the temporary rank of brigadier (from September). He remained D.M.I.—the senior intelligence officer in the Australian armed forces—until August 1945, and served with Advanced L.H.Q. in Brisbane and New Guinea, at Hollandia and on Morotai Island.

Rogers' leadership, integrity, thoroughness and diplomacy came to the fore as D.M.I. Trusted by Blamey, the commander-in-chief, he was also respected by Major General Gordon Bennett [q.v.13] and by Staff Corps officers such as Lavarack and Rowell. He successfully promoted co-operation among the many, varied, bureaucratic, and often mutually suspicious Australian, American and British military and civilian intelligence organizations and security services, and the headquarters and forces they supported. In September 1944 he represented Australia at a major intelligence co-ordination conference in Britain. In late 1944 and again in 1945 he acted forcefully to alert the Australian government to Soviet espionage and the ensuing betrayal of allied plans to the Japanese.

During the latter part of World War II Rogers planned for postwar intelligence and counter-intelligence structures, providing for the involvement of regular as well as reserve officers. This approach partly stemmed from his dislike of Staff Corps–Militia jealousies.

In August 1945 he led the Australian mission to South East Asia Command, Ceylon (Sri Lanka), and in September represented his country at the surrender of Japanese forces in Singapore. He was appointed C.B.E. (1947).

In November 1945 Rogers returned to Vacuum Oil as general manager for New South Wales. A director (from 1946), he represented the Australian subsidiary in New York in 1951-52, and became its deputy chairman (1954) and chairman (1958). He also sat on the boards of Moulded Products (Australasia) Ltd (1959-67), Mayne Nickless Ltd (1959-67), David Syme [q.v.6] & Co. Ltd (1960-67) and the Trustees, Executors & Agency Co. Ltd (1959-70). On retiring from Vacuum Oil in August 1959, 'J.D.R.' served as chief executive officer (1959-71) of the building committee of the Victorian Arts Centre, National Gallery of Victoria.

Rogers was honorary colonel of the Australian Intelligence Corps (1956-61), a member of Legacy, and a trustee of the Services Canteens Trust Fund (1957-76) and the Field Marshal Sir Thomas Blamey Memorial Fund. His broader community service was exemplified by a range of honorary appointments on hospital boards, and on committees that handled superannuation and scholarship funds. He also served on the councils of Ormond [q.v.5] College (1950-65) and Geelong College (1943-51 and 1954-60). Survived by his wife, daughter and two sons, he died on 10 April 1978 at Caulfield and was cremated.

C. E. W. Bean, *The Story of Anzac*, 2 (Syd, 1924) and *The A.I.F. in France, 1917* (Syd, 1933); G. Long, *To Benghazi* (Canb, 1952), *Greece, Crete and Syria* (Canb, 1953) and *The Final Campaigns* (Canb, 1963); D. Dexter, *The New Guinea Offensives* (Canb, 1961); D. M. Horner, *High Command* (Syd, 1992); D. Ball and D. Horner, *Breaking the Codes* (Syd, 1998); *Melb Legacy Bulletin*, 18 Apr 1978; *Mobil News*, May 1978; RHSV, *J*, June 1985; family correspondence and information from Mrs J. Thomson, Batemans Bay, NSW.   NEIL JAMES

ROGERS, JOHN NOBLE CORE (1898-1971), surveyor and public servant, was born on 7 October 1898 at Newtown, Sydney, eldest child of Victorian-born parents Henry Havelock Rogers, insurance clerk, and his wife Robina Violet, née Carter. Educated at Sydney Grammar School, Jack was articled as a pupil-surveyor in April 1916 to Frank Wearne at Casino. On 25 June 1918 he enlisted in the Australian Imperial Force; he served at the military camp, Liverpool, until he was discharged from the army on 31 December. Resuming his profession, he joined Dobbie & Foxall [q.v.14] in Sydney in April 1920 and passed the land surveyors' examinations in the following year. At the Presbyterian

Church, Pymble, on 7 October 1925 he married Clara Birchenall Moore.

Rogers practised privately for fourteen years, mainly in Sydney, and was elected a fellow (1933) and councillor of the Institution of Surveyors, New South Wales. In 1935 he joined the Department of the Interior and moved to Canberra. After four years of general surveying in the Federal (Australian) Capital Territory, he became administrative assistant to the head of the property and survey branch which dealt with land acquisition and survey matters connected with the war effort. He was appointed assistant surveyor-general in September 1946 and promoted to surveyor-general and chief property officer on 29 March 1949. In these capacities he supervised the surveying needs of Commonwealth departments and agencies throughout Australia and negotiated the settlement of compensation claims for land and buildings acquired during World War II. He was also director of national mapping and chairman (1949-51) of the National Mapping Council, on which he remained until 1963.

Following reorganization of the Department of the Interior in 1951, Rogers was appointed assistant-secretary in charge of the A.C.T. planning and development branch, while retaining the post of surveyor-general. The government's decision in the late 1950s to transfer a number of departments from Melbourne, together with the growth of Canberra, led to an increased workload, not only in surveying, but also in areas such as parks and gardens, forestry and agriculture, and the sale of leases for business and residential purposes—all of which were functions of his branch.

An executive-member (1953-57) of the National Capital Planning and Development Committee, Rogers served as the department's nominated member (1948-65) on the A.C.T. Advisory Council. For the most part, he was quiet and reserved in manner, but he had an alert and clear mind, and the ability to get to the crux of problems without fuss. While he pulled no punches in expressing his views, he remained 'forever the gentleman'. After retiring in 1963, he was chairman (1965-71) of the Canberra Building Review Committee, deputy-chairman (1969-72) of the Design and Siting Review Committee and a member (1968-71) of the A.C.T. Surveyors' Board.

Rogers was an honorary member (1950) of the Commonwealth Institute of Valuers and a fellow of the (Royal) Australian Planning Institute. In 1960 he became foundation president of the Canberra division of the Institution of Surveyors (Australia). He was appointed I.S.O. in 1964. Survived by his wife and their son, he died on 15 October 1971 in his home at Griffith and was cremated.

Aust Surveyor, June 1934, Sept 1963, June 1972; *Valuer*, Jan 1951; *Australian*, 16 Feb 1965; *Canb Times*, 16 Oct 1971; Rogers correspondence 1951-68 (NL); family papers held by, and information from, Mr J. Rogers, Hunters Hill, Syd; information from Mr E. Wigley, Reid, Canb; personal knowledge.

JACK TAYLOR

ROGERS, JONATHAN (1920-1964), sailor, was born on 16 September 1920 at Vroncy-sylite, near Llangollen, Denbighshire, Wales, fifth of seven children of Jonathan Rogers, labourer, and his wife Sarah Ellen, née Probyn. Leaving Acrefair Central School at the age of 14, he worked at the Ruabon brickyard, boxed and played soccer.

On 22 November 1938 Rogers enlisted in the Royal Navy. Five ft 8 ins (173 cm) tall and heavily built, he had brown hair, blue eyes and a fresh complexion. He spent most of World War II at sea in three coastal vessels: Motor Anti-Submarine Boat No.62 (1940-41), Motor Launch No.204 (1942-43) and Motor Torpedo Boat No.698 (1943-45). Promoted petty officer in 1943, he was awarded the Distinguished Service Medal for his 'coolness and leadership' under enemy fire during an action off Dunkirk, France, on the night of 23/24 May 1944. He was discharged from the R.N. on 23 January 1946.

At the parish church, Pen-y-cae, Denbighshire, on 4 April 1942 Rogers had married Lorraine Williams; they lived in the village and were to have four children. After the war he worked above ground at a local colliery and built pre-fabricated houses. In 1950 he applied to join the Royal Australian Navy. He was accepted on 6 July and posted to the aircraft-carrier H.M.A.S. *Sydney*; his next ship was the frigate *Burdekin*. Service (1952-54) in the destroyer *Tobruk* took him to Korean waters. He was promoted chief petty officer in 1956. His subsequent postings included the ships *Junee* (1956-57), *Anzac* (1957-58), *Warramunga* (1959) and *Barcoo* (1959-61), and the shore establishments *Cerberus* (1958-59), Westernport, Victoria, and *Rushcutter* (1961-62), Sydney. The family finally settled at Ettalong Beach, New South Wales.

In January 1963 'Buck' Rogers joined the destroyer *Voyager* which was commanded by Captain D. H. Stevens [q.v.]. As her coxswain, Rogers was the senior sailor on board and responsible for the 'good order and discipline' of the ship's company. On 10 February 1964 *Voyager* took part in exercises with the aircraft-carrier *Melbourne* off the south coast of New South Wales. That evening Rogers presided over a game of tombola being played by about sixty men in the ship's forward cafeteria. At 8.56 p.m., 20 nautical miles (37 km) southeast of Jervis Bay, *Voyager* collided with *Melbourne* and was cut in two. *Voyager's* severed forward section immediately heeled sharply to starboard and about five minutes later turned upside down. Water began pouring into the cafeteria. Within another five minutes the forward section sank. Rogers was one of the eighty-two men who died. His wife, son and three daughters survived him.

Sailors who escaped from the cafeteria later told how Rogers had taken charge of the situation. He had calmed terrified shipmates, attempted to control the flooding, tried to free a jammed escape hatch with a length of pipe and a spanner, and organized men to move into other compartments with functioning emergency exits. Meanwhile, he knew that he was probably too large to fit through an escape hatch himself. When it was obvious that some of his comrades would not get out in time, he led them in prayer and a hymn, 'encouraging them to meet death' beside him 'with dignity and honour'. His wife remarked: 'It was typical of him—he never thought of himself'. He was posthumously awarded the George Cross.

Report of Royal Commissioner on Loss of H.M.A.S. "Voyager" (Melb, 1964); *Sun News-Pictorial*, 13 Mar 1965; *Canb Times*, 11 Feb 1995; *Navy News*, 24 Mar 1995; information from Naval Hist Branch, Ministry of Defence, Lond; family information.

DARRYL BENNET

ROHAN, CRIENA; *see* CASH, DEIRDRE

RONALD, ROBERT BRUCE (1888-1956), grazier and soldier, was born on 5 May 1888 at Elsternwick, Melbourne, son of Robert Wilson Ronald, a Victorian-born grazier, and his wife Veronica Jane, née McGeorge, who came from England. Bob began his education in England before returning to Victoria, where he was sent to Geelong Church of England Grammar School and Dookie Agricultural College (Dip.Ag., 1907). He gained pastoral experience with the Australian Mercantile, Land & Finance Co. Ltd on Angledool (overseer 1910-12) and Charlton stations in northern New South Wales, then returned to Nap Nap, the family property and merino stud (Flock No.66) west of Hay.

On 26 September 1914 Bob and his younger brother Kenneth enlisted in the Australian Imperial Force. Both left Australia as troopers in the 6th Light Horse Regiment and reached Gallipoli in May 1915; Bob was wounded and evacuated in June; Kenneth was killed there one month later. Bob Ronald served with his regiment in the Sinai and Palestine. He was commissioned in September 1916 and promoted lieutenant in December. In November 1917 he was wounded in the left eye, arm, thigh and ankle; he was awarded (1918) the Military Cross for his 'conspicuous gallantry and devotion to duty'. Unfit for service, he returned to Australia in February 1918 and was discharged from the army on 3 August. He joined his father, brother Ian and sister Mrs S. C. McKehnie in running Nap Nap (42 000 acres, 17 000 ha) as a family company, R. W. Ronald & Co. At St Stephen's Presbyterian Church, Caulfield, Melbourne, on 23 April 1930 he married 24-year-old Gaie Chrisp.

Ronald was a member of the Royal Australian Historical Society and a contributor to its *Journal and Proceedings*. Like his father, he was interested in the history of land settlement in the Riverina. Assisted by his father's investigations in the Mitchell [q.v.5] Library, Sydney, he carried out extensive research in Sydney, Melbourne and the Riverina. He drew on official records, contemporary books, maps and newspapers, and published a number of articles in the *Riverina Recorder* (Balranald) and the *Riverine Grazier* (Hay). A series in the latter in 1929 was reprinted—with changes—in the *Pastoral Review* (February 1930-September 1931); five pieces on the 'Saltbush Plains of Western Riverina' appeared in 1934. These articles formed the basis of his authoritative reference work, *The Riverina: People and Properties* (Melbourne, 1960), which he had begun in 1939 during 'enforced idleness following an accident' and which he dedicated to the pioneers who had 'explored and occupied the land'.

According to a friend, Ronald 'suffered from all that war means', but never complained. He was a member (1925-53) of Waradgery Shire Council and of the Graziers' Association of Southern Riverina, and was active in the development of flood control on the lower Murrumbidgee. (Selfless service meant that he finished up with the worst road in the shire). Well liked by all, he gave generously of his time and money to sporting, cultural and charitable organizations, especially in the Maude district. He belonged to the Australian and the Imperial Service clubs (Sydney) and the Waradgery Club (Hay). Survived by his wife and their two sons, he died of a coronary occlusion on 1 December 1956 at Hay and was buried in the local cemetery.

H. B. Ronald, *Wool Before the Wind* (Mclb, 1987); *Pastoral Review*, Oct 1907, Mar 1915, June 1925, Apr, May, July, Sept, Nov 1934, July 1938, Sept 1948, Dec 1956; Geelong C of E Grammar School, *Corian*, May 1957, p 91; *Riverine Grazier*, 4 Dec 1956, 16 Nov 1977.

G. P. WALSH

RONAN, THOMAS MATTHEW (1907-1976), author, was born on 11 November 1907 in Perth, second child of Victorian-born parents Denis James (Jim) Ronan, station-manager, and his wife Julia, née Richardson (d.1919). Tom's early childhood was spent at Roebuck Plains station, near Broome. His father told the children yarns and anecdotes; his mother, an amateur actress, entertained them with monologues from Shakespeare. He attended Christian Brothers' College, Perth, for five and a half interrupted years and re-called that 'I never fitted in at school, any more than I subsequently did in the Army or in the Government Service'. Fascinated by words, however, he developed a love of reading.

Ronan left school at 14 and went droving with his father in the North-West. Then came four years (1923-26) as a ship's clerk and shell-opener in Broome-based pearling boats. In 1927-34 he helped his father and Mat Wilson to manage the Victoria River depot on Koonbook station where he met many of the 'hard cases' who were to bring life to his books. As one of them said: 'Those of us ... who aren't dodging the police are dodging wives, and we'd nearly all get put in the asylum if we went back to any civilised part of the country'. By 1934 Mat Wilson had com-mitted suicide, Jim Ronan was a pensioner in Darwin hospital and Tom Ronan was 'broke'. He spent six years as a drover and stockman in the Kimberleys and the Northern Territory.

Enlisting in the Australian Imperial Force on 2 July 1940, Ronan was allotted to the 2nd/3rd Anti-Tank Regiment and fought at El Alamein, Egypt. In February 1943 he returned to Australia with his regiment. He was dis-charged from the army on 29 May 1944 to be re-employed in the meat industry, an essential war occupation. Found to have a duodenal ulcer, he spent time in hospital and began writing his first novel, *Strangers on the Ophir* (Sydney, 1945). He went back to the cattle country and became manager of Newry station, near the source of the Keep River, Northern Territory.

At the Star of the Sea Church, Kirribilli, Sydney, on 29 December 1947 Ronan married with Catholic rites Mary Elizabeth ('Moya') Kearins, a 30-year-old writer for radio; they were to have ten children. In 1949 they bought Springvale homestead at Katherine, Northern Territory. While living there, Ronan worked (1950-57) as a technical assistant at the Com-monwealth Scientific and Industrial Research Organization's research station. Elected to the Legislative Assembly for Batchelor in May 1954, he resigned his seat in April 1955. He chaired (1963-65) the Northern Territory Tourist Board and later ran a herd of one hun-dred milking goats.

Ronan had won a Commonwealth Jubilee Literary Competition in 1951 with the manu-script of a novel, *Vision Splendid* (London, 1954). In 1954 and 1963 he was awarded Com-monwealth Literary Fund fellowships. He wrote four of his five novels at Springvale, a biography of his father, *Deep of the Sky* (London, 1962), and two volumes of auto-biography, *Packhorse and Pearling Boat* (Mel-bourne, 1964) and *Once There was a Bagman* (Melbourne, 1966). Moya, who was described as 'beautiful, gracious, steadfast [and] tal-ented', helped to edit her husband's books. They provide the most authentic and prob-ably the liveliest writing about life in the North-West 'big river country', where he 'was at home'. Elizabeth Durack, a friend, de-scribed Ronan as thin, balding, tall and rangy, with penetrating brown eyes, and regarded him as 'a good raconteur'. In 1969 he moved to Adelaide. He died of bronchopneumonia on 15 July 1976 in Royal Adelaide Hospital and was cremated; his wife, six of his seven sons and two of his three daughters survived him.

P. Forrest, *Springvale's Story* (Darwin, 1985); *People* (Syd), 22 Oct 1952; *Walkabout,* 32, no 9, Sept 1966, 34, no 6, June 1968; *West Australian,* 7 Jan 1967, 20 Aug 1968; *Weekend News,* 24 Aug, 25 Sept 1968; *Advertiser* (Adel), 16 July 1976; H. de Berg, Tom Ronan (taped interview, 1974, NL); information from Mr N. Ronan, Box Hill, Melb.

DONALD GRANT

ROPER, ERNEST DAVID (1901-1958), judge, was born on 1 March 1901 at Orange, New South Wales, eighth of twelve children of native-born parents Walter James Roper, a draughtsman in the Department of Lands, and his wife Hannah Marie, née Gray. The family moved to Armidale in 1902 and to Mosman, Sydney, in 1916. Educated at Armi-dale District and North Sydney Boys' High schools, David won the Barker [q.v.1] scholar-ship in mathematics. At the University of Sydney (B.A., 1921; LL.B., 1925), he gradu-ated in arts with first-class honours in math-ematics and philosophy, and was awarded the university medal in each subject.

Admitted to the Bar on 29 August 1925, Roper steadily built up a sound practice in crown lands, valuation, Equity and income tax matters. At St Clement's Anglican Church, Mosman, on 22 December 1930 he married Elizabeth Isabel Daniel; they were to remain childless. He was Challis [q.v.3] lecturer in Equity and company law (1928-36) at the uni-versity and secretary (1935-37) of the Council of the Bar of New South Wales (New South Wales Bar Association from 1936). The Com-monwealth government retained him as coun-sel to assist the royal commission on taxation. Its commissioners, Sir David Ferguson and (Sir) Edwin Nixon [qq.v.8,15], paid tribute in their final report (1934) to his 'invaluable assistance in the consideration and framing of the reports and in dealing with the many constitutional and other legal problems'.

Following the retirement of George Herbert Pike [q.v.11], Roper was appointed to the Land and Valuation Court as deputy-judge from 2 February 1937. He became the sole judge on 25 May. Owing to a decline in the number of cases, he frequently acted as a Supreme Court judge between 1937 and 1940. His appointment as a Supreme Court judge in 1940 was backdated to 25 May 1937. On the bench Roper proved an immediate and conspicuous success: he quickly earned the respect of his fellow judges, the legal profession, and the litigants who appeared before him—often without legal representation. He was equally at home in matters of Equity, statute law and common law, and handled cases with expedition and a minimum of formality. He was, as a colleague said after his death, 'no over-speaking judge' and attracted no attention by public utterances in court.

In the diversity of his judicial functions Roper resolved many contentious issues of public importance: the award of the Archibald prize to (Sir) William Dobell [qq.v.3,14] in 1943 when the judge laid down the essential criteria for a portrait; the Pye brothers' challenge (1945-56) to the validity of the New South Wales government's policy of acquiring land for war-service settlement at its 1942 value; and the 'Red Book' cases (1947-48) involving a dispute over certain ecclesiastical practices followed by Arnold Wylde [q.v.], the bishop of Bathurst. In these and many other cases Roper's decisions were upheld when appealed against in higher courts. Indeed, it was rare that any of his decisions was set aside.

In 1947 Roper succeeded H. S. Nicholas [q.v.11] as chief judge in Equity and as probate judge. He was also called on to sit with the chief justice and other judges as the Full Court to hear appeals and as the Court of Disputed Returns to resolve electoral issues.

Roper devoted valuable time to extrajudicial functions. In 1942 he was a member of the prime minister's Committee of National Morale. A fellow (from 1942) of the senate of the University of Sydney and deputy-chancellor in 1946-52, he presided over the Sydney University Law Society for many years from 1946. In addition, he was a director of the United States Educational Foundation in Australia and of Prince Henry Hospital. Roper was a gregarious man with a wide circle of friends and admirers. He was tall and slight in build, and invariably courteous, modest and discreet in manner. A member of the Union and University clubs, he enjoyed nothing more than a game of snooker with his colleagues.

Survived by his wife, Roper died of cerebrovascular disease on 28 June 1958 in St Luke's Hospital, Darlinghurst, and was cremated. The gates at North Sydney Boys' High School were named (1962) after him, as were prizes at the University of Sydney for students in Equity and corporate law.

H. M. Storey, *History of North Sydney High School 1912-1962* (Syd, 1962); *Aust Law J*, 32, 21 July 1958, p 96, and R. Else-Mitchell, 'Mr Justice Roper and the Land Jurisdiction', 70, Nov 1996, p 902; *NSW State Reports*, 1958, p iii; *Syd Law Review*, 3, Mar 1959; *SMH*, 27 Jan 1937, 18 Feb 1948, 1, 2 July, 29 Aug 1958; *Sun-Herald* (Syd), 29 June 1958; *Bulletin*, 9 July 1958, p 14.   R. ELSE-MITCHELL

ROSALIE, SISTER; *see* NICHOLAS, MABEL

ROSANOVE, JOAN MAVIS (1896-1974), lawyer, was born on 11 May 1896 at Ballarat, Victoria, second of eight children of Melbourne-born parents Mark Aaron Lazarus, barrister and solicitor, and his wife Ruby, née Braham, both non-practising Jews. Educated locally at the Loreto convent school and Clarendon Ladies' College, Joan was articled to her father. In 1917 at the University of Melbourne she completed the subjects in law required to qualify as an articled clerk. She appeared in courts at Ballarat and in Melbourne before she was formally admitted to practice as a barrister and solicitor on 2 June 1919; her registration had been delayed to enable returned servicemen to complete their degrees and add 'gravitas' to the ceremony.

Initially, Joan practised in Melbourne as an 'amalgam', doing the work of both barrister and solicitor. On 2 September 1920 in her parents' Ballarat home she married with Jewish rites Emmanuel ('Mannie') Rosanove, a medical practitioner. He was to specialize as a dermatologist and become a fellow (1978) of the Royal Australasian College of Physicians. The couple moved to Tocumwal, New South Wales. Joan's first daughter was stillborn; the safe arrival of a second daughter did not prevent her from occasionally appearing in court.

In 1923 Mannie bought a home and practice at Westgarth, Melbourne. On 10 September that year Joan signed the Victorian Bar roll, becoming the first woman in the State to do so. She could not obtain rooms in Selborne Chambers, and, in a male-dominated profession, few briefs came her way. In 1925 she reverted to her role as an amalgam. Accepting mainly criminal and matrimonial cases, she established a thriving business: at the peak of her career, she allegedly handled one-eighth of all divorce actions in Victoria. Her advocacy in other jurisdictions added to her reputation for determination, enterprise and acumen. One notable episode was her short but flamboyant appearance on 12 November 1934 in the State's Practice Court when she represented Egon Kisch [q.v.15]. In a series of cases in 1939 she acted for producers and sellers of margarine, winning renown for her inventiveness in finding loopholes in legislation restricting the sale of the product.

The Rosanoves had toured Canada, the United States of America and Britain in 1932-33. After they returned to Melbourne, they lived at Toorak. In 1949 Joan again signed the Bar roll. She achieved her ambition to practise from Selborne Chambers by accepting a position as 'reader' to a male barrister Edward Ellis (although he was her junior in age and experience) and taking over his room when he moved to Western Australia.

From 1954 Mrs Rosanove submitted a number of applications in Victoria to be made a Q.C. That she had to wait until 16 November 1965 to be appointed led many of her peers to conclude that 'she had been shabbily treated'. In 1967 she took silk in New South Wales. Her struggle to achieve equality for female lawyers had influenced the style of advocacy she adopted. Immaculately groomed, a little over five feet (152 cm) tall, pugnacious, effective in defending her clients and penetrating in cross-examining witnesses, she did not hesitate to challenge presiding magistrates and judges.

Mrs Rosanove contributed to legal reform and supported other causes, particularly those affecting the status of women. As early as 1926 she had been a member of a deputation to (Sir) Frederic Eggleston [q.v.8], the Victorian attorney-general, requesting the appointment of female justices. In a concise and hardheaded article in the *Australian Law Journal* (1953-54) she advocated uniform divorce law in Australia and an end to the injustices which wives suffered in court. As president (1951) of the Soroptimists Club of Melbourne and of the Business and Professional Women's Club, she encouraged other women to become involved in 'social action'.

Joan and Mannie made a formidable combination. He did the cooking, and reportedly said of her: 'as a cook she was a brilliant lawyer'. She spent her retirement (from 1969) at Frankston, where she enjoyed fishing and gardening. Survived by her husband and two daughters, she died on 8 April 1974 at Frankston and was cremated.

I. Carter, *Woman in a Wig* (Melb, 1970); R. Campbell, *A History of the Melbourne Law School, 1857 to 1973* (Melb, 1977); S. De Vries, *Strength of Purpose* (Syd, 1998); *Table Talk*, 28 Nov 1929; *People* (Syd), 17 Jan 1951; information from Prof D. Anderson, Yarralumla, Canb, and Mrs P. Lusnick, Euroa, Vic.
                                                    BARBARA FALK

ROSE, ALFRED LIONEL (1898-1980), veterinarian, army officer and public servant, was born on 21 March 1898 at Strathfield, Sydney, fifth child of Herbert John Rose, an Anglican clergyman from England, and his wife Harriett Ethel, née Priddle, who was born in New South Wales. Educated at Sydney Grammar School, Lionel enlisted in the Australian Imperial Force on 15 May 1916 and was allotted to the 117th Howitzer Battery. He served on the Western Front and was wounded in May 1917. Commissioned in November, he was promoted lieutenant in March 1918. In December 1919 he returned to Australia where his A.I.F. appointment terminated on 21 April 1920.

After studying at the University of Sydney (B.V.Sc., 1924), Rose was appointed a veterinary surgeon in the New South Wales Department of Agriculture. At All Saints Church, Woollahra, on 27 March 1925 he married Helen Blaxland with Anglican rites; they were to be divorced in 1950. Promoted district veterinary officer in May 1927, he was based at Orange and (from 1928) at Cootamundra. He made significant advances in the knowledge and control of a number of serious diseases of livestock, in particular black disease of sheep, toxaemic jaundice and enterotoxaemia. His name was widely esteemed by stock-owners in southern New South Wales.

Rose had joined the Militia in March 1924. By 1940 he was commanding the 21st Light Horse Regiment as a temporary lieutenant colonel. On 4 July he was appointed major, 7th Division Cavalry Regiment, A.I.F. Sailing for the Middle East in December, he took part in the Syrian campaign (June-July 1941) before coming home in March 1942. Promoted lieutenant colonel in May 1943, he was posted in January 1944 to I Corps headquarters, New Guinea, as a general staff officer, 1st grade. For his work (from June 1945) at Balikpapan, Borneo, he was appointed O.B.E. (1947). Back in Australia, he was placed on the Reserve of Officers on 28 May 1946.

Joining the Commonwealth Department of Health as chief veterinary officer, Northern Territory, Rose was transferred to the Department of the Interior in June 1947 as director of the animal industry section, with headquarters at Alice Springs. He established a diagnostic and research laboratory, and concentrated on eradicating contagious bovine pleuro-pneumonia (then rampant in the Territory). His successful strategy was adopted by Commonwealth and State governments.

On 20 October 1950 at the court-house, Cootamundra, Rose married Nell Hooper, née White, a divorcee who died in 1951. At the office of the principal registrar, Adelaide, on 4 May 1955 he married 32-year-old Carmel Mary Kerrison. Rose retired in 1958, but maintained many of his activities in the Territory. In July he became a member (chairman 1963-77) of the Reserves Board which oversaw the preservation of parks and wildlife. After serving in the Legislative Council as a nominated member (1954-58), he won the seat of Alice Springs in 1962; he was defeated in 1965 when he stood as a candidate for the North Australia Party which he had formed in August that year. He also worked as a consultant to pastoral interests and the government.

A member (1926) and fellow (1970) of the Australian Veterinary Association, Rose was awarded its Gilruth [q.v.9] prize in 1961. He was elected a foundation life fellow (1971) of the Australian College of Veterinary Scientists. In 1978 he was appointed A.M. Rose died on 2 May 1980 in Alice Springs Hospital; he was accorded a state funeral and was buried with Anglican rites in the local cemetery. His wife and their daughter and two sons survived him, as did the son and two daughters of his first marriage. A virology laboratory at Berrimah was named (1979) after him.

F. Fenner (ed), *History of Microbiology in Australia* (Canb, 1990); *Aust Veterinary J*, 56, no 8, 1980, p 396; *Historia Medicinae Veterinariae*, 8, no 2, 1983, p 53; *Argus*, 29 Aug 1950; *SMH*, 14 Oct 1958; *Canb Times*, 11 May 1980; CP 69 (NAA, Canb); information from Mrs P. K. Lonsdale, Tweed Heads, NSW, and Mrs C. Rose, Alice Springs, NT.

ROBERT I. TAYLOR

ROSEBY, GERTRUDE AMY (1872-1971), headmistress, was born on 20 April 1872 at Dunedin, New Zealand, eldest of ten children of Rev. Thomas Roseby [q.v.6], a Sydney-born Congregational minister, and his wife Sarah, née Hooworth. Thomas ministered at Ballarat, Victoria, from 1885 before returning to Sydney in 1888. He encouraged his children, girls and boys alike, to undertake higher education. Gertrude was privately tutored. She entered the University of Sydney (B.A., 1895) and graduated with second-class honours in logic and mental philosophy.

Miss Roseby taught for eight years at Rockhampton Girls' Grammar School, Queensland, where she was appointed senior assistant mistress. She visited Britain, completed a diploma of pedagogy (1905) at the University of London and taught (1906-07) at Wyggeston School for girls, Leicester. Returning home early in 1908, she became resident headmistress of Ascham, Darling Point, under its principal H. J. Carter [q.v.7]. In April 1911, with her sister Mabel, she bought Redlands, Neutral Bay, a school with 35 day-girls and 8 boarders.

Known as 'Miss G.A.' and affectionately as 'The Bud', Gertrude Roseby was a progressive in her early years, promoting co-education in the kindergarten and introducing a modified Dalton system in the senior school. She took affectionate care of the younger boarders and in 1913 instituted an annual picnic for boarders to (Royal) National Park. Debating (from 1919) and guiding (from 1923) were prominent among extra-curricular activities, and classes were sometimes held in the school's carefully planted gardens. Miss Roseby taught English, Latin, history and Scripture to the upper forms, who remembered inspiring lessons on Shakespeare, and on the Authorized Version of the Bible as literature. Her farewell cards to school-leavers featured hand-written, individually chosen quotations from these and other sources. She encouraged able pupils to go on to university and promoted the artistic and scholastic talents of her girls, among them Ellice Nosworthy [q.v.15], Jean Sulman, Eleanor Dark, Thistle Harris and Elizabeth Liggins. There were few school rules: the 'honour' system prevailed, and Miss Roseby inspired 'Redlanders' to be loyal to herself and the school.

Although her brother Norman had won the Military Medal at Gallipoli, Miss Roseby believed passionately in the cause of peace. In the 1930s she supported the League of Nations and belonged to the Women's International League for Peace and Freedom, and the Congregational (Women's) Peace Fellowship (Congregational Women's Fellowship for the Study of World Affairs). She was president of the Congregational Women's Association in 1942-46 and later a life member.

A woman of dignity and charm, noted for her gentle determination and mellifluous speaking voice, Gertrude Roseby was, for a year, president of the Headmistresses' Association of Australia. In June 1945 she sold the school (which by then had more than three hundred pupils) to the Church of England. She remained headmistress until December. Boarding had ceased in 1941. With her maiden sisters Mabel and Mary, she retired to a garden cottage at Willoughby, but kept in constant contact with the school and its old girls. She was chairman (1946-50) of the Sydney Kindergarten Training College council, a founder and treasurer (1951-63) of Wybalena Hostel for Girls, Burwood, president of the State branch of the Women's Inter-Church Council and an active member of the National Council of Women of New South Wales. In June 1958 she was appointed O.B.E. She quietly assumed that she was the equal of any man in the sight of God. Aged 99, she died on 27 December 1971 at Wahroonga and was cremated with Congregational forms.

Her sister SARAH MABEL (1878-1957), schoolmistress, was born on 26 March 1878 at Dunedin, New Zealand, and educated at the University of Sydney (B.A., 1900). In 1911 she joined her elder sister at Redlands, where she taught mathematics and geology. Called

'Miss May' at school, she was known for her common sense and want of sentimentality. Her humour and wit were remembered by boarders, to whom she often read at breakfast from the latest issue of *Punch*. In the 1920s she played tennis and cricket with the girls and enjoyed charades. With her sister Mary, she visited Britain in 1929, but returned within a year.

Mabel Roseby worked in the central office of the Congregational Church, helping to edit the *New South Wales Congregational Year Book and Calendar*; she was also secretary of the Congregational Women's Association and of the management-committee of a nursery school at Mosman. Her hostility to the 'drink traffic' led her to assist regularly at the Congregational Metropolitan Mission's centre at Alexandria. She died on 11 October 1957 in Sydney.

Gertrude's and Mabel's cousins Clara Roseby (1870-1936) and Mary ('Minnie') Roseby (1873-1966) were graduates of the University of Sydney and co-principals of Kambala school from 1914 to 1926; Clara remained as principal until 1927, then joined her sister Mary in retirement in England.

M. Gillham, R. Dunlop and J. Birkl (eds), *SCEGGS Redlands in Retrospect* (Syd, 1990); *Congregationalist* (Syd), Feb 1972; *SMH*, 29 May 1945, 12 June, 1 Oct 1958, 21 Apr 1967, 29 Dec 1971; Kindergarten Union of NSW, *Annual Report*, 1951; Congregational card index (Uniting Church archives, Parramatta, Syd); O'Reilly papers *and* G. A. Roseby file, Doc 2483 (ML).   RUTH TEALE

ROSENSTENGEL, EDMUND (1887-1962), furniture-maker, was born on 2 February 1887 at Toowoomba, Queensland, ninth of twelve children of Richard Rosenstengel, a Prussian-born cabinet-maker, and his wife Margaret, née Moynihan, who came from Ireland. Apprenticed in 1902 to his father at the Toowoomba firm, Rosenstengel & Kleimeyer, Ed moved to Sydney in 1906 and worked for a time with Edward Verdich, a craftsman at Newtown. He spent a year at Auckland, New Zealand, before travelling in 1908 to Vancouver, Canada, where he took a seasonal job with a timber company and ran a small furniture-repair shop during winter. After visiting Grand Rapids, Michigan, United States of America, a centre of furniture manufacture, he returned via Europe to Queensland and rejoined the family business in 1911. On 28 April 1914 at the Sacred Heart Church, Sandgate, Brisbane, he married with Catholic rites Eveleen Gertrude Smith; they were to have a son (d.1918) and a daughter.

In 1922 Rosenstengel set up a workshop and showroom at New Farm, Brisbane, in a building that had previously been a picture-theatre.

For the next few years he made austere oak furniture in the style of the Arts and Crafts movement, similar to items produced by local competitors. The slogan, 'buy furniture direct from the man who makes it', became a well-known feature of his promotions.

Rosenstengel's work gradually began to reflect his interest in the decorative arts and his admiration for Queensland woods, particularly oak, silver ash and maple. Believing that the 'best results' would come from the informed adaptation of historical styles, he often incorporated elements of different periods or blended aspects from French and English traditions. His best-selling items included black-stained oak dining-tables and sideboards in the Jacobean style, suited to 'Tudor residences' and 'Spanish mission villas' which were built in Brisbane in the late 1920s. Advertisements for his business indicated that he also tried to bring his sense of design and workmanship to the 'man in the street'.

Special commissions executed during the 1930s included a gramophone cabinet for the yacht *Tangalooma*, Louis XVI-style furnishings for the reception room at the Brisbane Hydropathic Baths and furniture for the lord mayor's office. He made a jewellery box of maple and satinwood, ordered by the Queensland government as a gift for the Duchess of York, and a suite of Louis XV-style furniture for the bedroom in Government House, occupied by the Duke of Gloucester during his visit to Brisbane in 1934. The pieces, made entirely of Queensland timber, comprised a bed, dressing-table and chairs of maple, and a standard lamp of silver ash decorated with Australian flora and fauna.

The Queensland Authors' and Artists' Association engaged Rosenstengel to carve a grand frame to accommodate the poem written by Mabel Forrest for the opening (1930) of Brisbane's City Hall. Unveiled in September 1937, it was one of his most important works. The frame was made from silver ash and depicted coastal vegetation. That year he completed a bardic chair, commissioned by the State government for presentation to the winning bard at the (Royal) National Eisteddfod of Wales. The most striking part of this high-backed chair in Gothic style was a panel of satin ash, carved in bas-relief and polychromed with Welsh scenery and traditional Welsh figures, which was surmounted by the Queensland coat of arms and a laurel wreath.

World War II dramatically changed the priorities of craftsman and customer, and reduced manpower and materials. The number of staff at Rosenstengel's workshop declined from about twenty-five to ten and he was required to make standard wartime repeats. In his frustration he wrote: 'I find the aesthetic and creative senses sluggish almost to a state of paralysis'. Despite the restrictions, he was able to produce a jewellery box in French *Régence* style for Colonel Walter Enz of the United States Army, and two armchairs in Queensland maple, presented (1946) by the Queensland division of the Australian Red Cross Society to the retiring governor Sir Leslie Wilson [q.v.12].

Rosenstengel's faithful clientele continued to order new furniture and to bring back old items for refurbishment. He announced his retirement in 1956, but requests from customers for 'last pieces' kept him in business until March 1958. A quiet and private man, he devoted his final years to studying reference books on eighteenth-century decorative arts from his large library. He died on 11 October 1962 at his New Farm home and was buried in Nudgee cemetery; his wife and daughter survived him. In 1972 his collection of furniture, silver and rare porcelain was sold at public auction.

Steering Wheel, 1 July, 1 Aug, 1 Sept, 1 Oct 1932; *Furniture Trades Review*, Apr 1937, p 17; *People* (Syd), 14 Jan 1953, p 36; *Australian Antique Trader*, 15 Oct-15 Nov 1987, p 26; *Antiques & Art in Qld*, no 1, Oct 1994-Feb 1995, p 22; *Courier-Mail*, 30 Nov 1934, 2 Mar 1937, 9 Feb 1956, 6 May 1958, 13 Oct 1962; *Telegraph* (Brisb), 1 Mar 1937, 9 Aug 1954, 27 Mar 1972, 28 June 1979; Rosenstengel papers (OL).   DIANNE BYRNE

ROSENTHAL, ALVORD SYDNEY (1901-1975), naval officer, was born on 16 January 1901 at Lewisham, Sydney, second of three sons of Australian-born parents (Sir) Charles Rosenthal [q.v.11], architect, and his wife Harriet Ellen, née Burston. Alvord was educated at The King's School, Parramatta. In 1915 he entered the Royal Australian Naval College, Jervis Bay, Federal Capital Territory, from which he graduated in 1918.

Promoted midshipman on 1 January 1919, 'Rosie' joined the battleship H.M.S. *Ramillies* in May and was present at Scapa Flow, Orkney Islands, Scotland, when the German fleet was scuttled on 21 June. From February 1920 *Ramillies* operated in the Bosporus Strait and the Black Sea. Rosenthal completed his training in Britain and was promoted lieutenant in October 1923. Back in Australia, he served in the destroyer H.M.A.S. *Anzac*, and as assistant-surveyor in H.M.A.S. *Geranium*.

On 17 December 1925 at Holy Trinity Church, Balaclava, Melbourne, Rosenthal married Audrey Fleming (d.1958) with Anglican rites. Promoted lieutenant commander in October 1930, he was appointed to command the destroyers *Waterhen* in 1933 and *Vendetta* in 1934. Although his superiors had reservations about his ability, he proved an outstand-

ing seaman when he took *Voyager* to sea in a gale on 18 June 1935 to search for a missing ship. On 21 November 1935 Rosenthal joined the cruiser *Canberra*. His performance in that ship earned him promotion to commander in January 1937, but his record in *Waterhen* and *Vendetta* counted against him: on 31 January 1937 he was transferred to the Auxiliary List and appointed district naval officer, South Australia.

Following the outbreak of World War II Rosenthal was placed in command of the armed merchant cruiser *Westralia*, which escorted convoys in Australian and Netherlands East Indies waters. In May 1941 he took over the new destroyer *Nestor*, part of the force which hunted down the German battleship *Bismarck*. *Nestor* then joined Force H in the Mediterranean where she narrowly escaped being torpedoed by a submarine on 21 July. Three days later the convoy she was escorting was attacked by Italian motor torpedo-boats which hit the troop-ship *Sydney Star*. Rosenthal skilfully embarked the troops, convinced the master to keep the ship afloat and escorted her safely to Malta. For his courage and resourcefulness he was awarded the Distinguished Service Order.

On 15 December 1941, south of Cape St Vincent, *Nestor* sighted the German submarine *U-127* on the surface and sank her with depth charges. Rosenthal won a bar to his D.S.O. for his part in the action. *Nestor* sailed for five months with the Far Eastern Fleet before embarking for the Mediterranean to take part in operations to supply Malta. On 15 June 1942 she was damaged near Crete when straddled by two heavy bombs; attempts to tow her to Alexandria failed and she was sunk next day.

From October 1942 until November 1944 Rosenthal served as naval attaché in Washington, where Sir Owen Dixon [q.v.14] considered him 'an unqualified success'. He was promoted acting captain on 29 January 1945 and appointed captain of Garden Island Dockyard, Sydney. After the war ended, he served at Navy Office, Melbourne, as director (1946-56) of naval reserves and director (1956-58) of studies, industrial mobilization course. In 1951 he was appointed O.B.E. and placed on the Emergency List. Granted the honorary rank of commodore in April 1960, he retired from the navy on 16 January 1961.

Five ft 11 ins (180 cm) tall and athletic in build, Rosenthal was cheerful and easy-going when off duty, but at sea he drove his ships hard. On the bridge he developed into a decisive commander, a meticulous navigator and a capable ship-handler. He enjoyed manual work and took a keen interest in the mechanical efficiency of his vessels. A committee-member (from 1959) of the Naval and Military Club, Melbourne, he tried his hand at a business venture without success. At St Andrew's Presbyterian Church, Frankston, on 8 April 1960 Rosenthal married Alison Lucy Urquhart, née Platts, a schoolteacher and a divorcee. He spent his retirement at Frankston, indulging his hobby of model-making. To some, he seemed something of a recluse. Survived by his wife, and by the two sons of his first marriage, he died on 20 July 1975 at Heidelberg and was cremated.

F. B. Eldridge, *A History of the Royal Australian Naval College* (Melb, 1949); J. E. Hewitt, *The Black One* (Melb, 1984); G. H. Gill, *Royal Australian Navy 1939-1942* and *1942-1945* (Syd, 1985); H. Burrell, *Mermaids Do Exist* (Melb, 1986); *Naval Hist Review*, Dec 1975.
                                               J. S. SEARS

ROSENTHAL,   GERTRUD;   *see* BODENWIESER

ROSEVEAR, JOHN SOLOMON (1892-1953), politician, was born on 4 January 1892 at Pyrmont, Sydney, seventh child of native-born parents William John Rosevear, carter, and his wife Maria, née McGuirk. Educated at a local public school, Sol began work in the timber industry. At St Bartholomew's Anglican Church, Pyrmont, on 23 September 1916 he married Clara May White, a machinist. A skilled tradesman and active unionist, he was involved in the timberworkers' strike of 1929; he found himself unemployed in its aftermath and scraped a living from relief work.

Rosevear became an energetic official in the Leichhardt branch of the Australian Labor Party and served as campaign organizer for E. G. Theodore [q.v.12] in the 1929 Federal election. Two years later he contested the seat of Dalley against his former political associate and friend. Standing for the Lang [q.v.9] Labor Party, he defeated Theodore and three other candidates. He sat in the House of Representatives with the 'Langites' led by J. A. Beasley [q.v.13] until they reunited (1936) with the federal Labor Party. In 1936-37 Rosevear was an executive-member of federal caucus. When a further split occurred in 1940, he was elected deputy-leader of the A.L.P. (Non-Communist), again under Beasley, although he had agonized over whether or not to join this Langite splinter group.

In parliament Rosevear distinguished himself as a 'clear thinker, with a good financial brain, quick intelligence and strong personality', but he was 'more interested in the craft and the practice of politics than in any theories or principles'. If somewhat reserved, he was good-humoured and genial. He proved an effective and forceful, rather than a

polished, debater, and was regarded by (Sir) Paul Hasluck as 'one of the ablest' performers in the House. Rosevear was a member of the Bankruptcy Legislation Committee (1932-36) and temporary chairman of committees (1934-43).

When the Beasley group was reconciled with the federal party in 1941 and Labor came to power under John Curtin [q.v.13], many observers believed that Rosevear was unlucky not to secure a post in cabinet. His omission was probably the result of continuing hostility in caucus to his having aligned himself with the Langites in 1940. Although he was a disgruntled and troublesome back-bencher in the early years of the Curtin government, he was appointed controller of leather and footwear in 1942, a position to which he clung tenaciously until 1945, even after he became Speaker on 22 June 1943. He was also chairman (1944-45) of the Post-war Planning Committee of Leather and Footwear Industries.

A controversial Speaker, Rosevear brought to his office 'a new strength and a new power', including many of the tactics perfected in the hurly-burly of New South Wales Labor politics between the wars. Not all of them were well suited to his new role as presiding officer. Symbolically refusing both wig and gown, he was quick to make up his mind and gained a reputation for inflexibility in upholding his rulings. Opposition members and journalists regularly accused him of partisanship. On one occasion in 1946, he left the Speaker's chair to launch a ferocious tirade against his former ally Lang. In the following year, in his capacity as a private member, he made several attacks on judges of the High Court of Australia from the floor of the House. E. H. Cox, a journalist in the Canberra press gallery, claimed that the Speaker was 'frequently quite drunk in the Chair', but had 'an amazing gift for concealing his condition'. Rosevear also allowed illegal gambling in the House, a pastime in which he was an enthusiastic participant.

While enjoying all of the perquisites to which his high office entitled him, and more, Rosevear continued to play an influential role in caucus. He won the favour of federal Labor members after World War II when he spearheaded a movement to increase parliamentary salaries and improved facilities for politicians. By 1947 some believed that he had grown tired of the speakership and was manoeuvring to succeed J. B. Chifley [q.v.13] as party leader, but a number of back-benchers, while impressed by his intelligence and debating skill, regarded 'his taste for grog' as a disqualification. In 1948 he led the Australian delegation to the Empire Parliamentary Association conference, held in London. Following his return, he had to curtail his official activities due to illness. He was twice admitted to hospital in 1949, but remained in parliament and represented Dalley for the remainder of his life.

With the election of (Sir) Robert Menzies' [q.v.15] government in December 1949, Rosevear lost the speakership on 21 February 1950. He died of a coronary occlusion on 21 March 1953 in Lewisham Private Hospital, Sydney, and was cremated; his wife, and their son and daughter survived him. According to Hasluck, when the clergyman at Rosevear's funeral described him as a 'great national leader and statesman', a 'devout Christian' and a 'highly moral character', Fred Daly remarked audibly, 'By God, we're burying the wrong man'. A portrait of Rosevear by Joshua Smith, which won the Archibald [q.v.3] prize (1944), is held by Parliament House, Canberra.

G. Souter, *Acts of Parliament* (Melb, 1988); R. McMullin, *The Light on the Hill* (Melb, 1991); P. Hasluck, *The Chance of Politics* (Melb, 1997); *PD* (Cwlth), 24 Mar 1953, p 1494; *SMH*, 22 Mar 1953; E. H. Cox papers (NL).   FRANK BONGIORNO

ROSS, WILLIAM ANTHONY (1895-1973), Catholic missionary, was born on 23 September 1895 at Whiteport, New York State, United States of America, sixth of ten children of Irish-born parents William Ross, engineer, and his wife Mary Agnes, née O'Laughlin. William's mother died when he was 7. While at the Franciscan Sisters' welfare home at Peekskill, he heard of Fr Damien's work with lepers on Molokai Island, Hawaii, and dreamed of becoming a missionary. After he had completed high school, the Sisters arranged for him to attend college at St Laurent, Montreal, Canada. In 1913 he began an apprenticeship in an electrical-engineering firm. Three years later he entered the seminary run by the missionaries of the Society of the Divine Word (S.V.D.), at Techny, Illinois. Ordained priest on 10 June 1922, he was appointed to the S.V.D. seminary at Duxbury, Massachusetts.

In 1926 Francis Wolf, the German bishop at Alexishafen in the Mandated Territory of New Guinea, wrote to the American province of the S.V.D. requesting an English-speaking priest to be his secretary. Ross volunteered, and arrived in New Guinea on 19 November. Among other responsibilities, he acted as liaison officer between German missionaries and Australian administrators of the former German colony. His cheerful disposition, wry sense of humour and unpretentious manner equipped him for the role.

Although he was only 5 ft 2 ins (157 cm) tall, Ross quickly earned respect for his endurance and his missionary zeal. Armed with a .38-inch (9.6 mm) calibre revolver, he made two exploratory trips into the hinterland of the Alexishafen mission in the early 1930s. When the Australians Mick Leahy [q.v.10], his brother Dan and Jim Taylor opened up the Wahgi Valley to foreigners in 1933, they invited Ross to join them there. Encouraged by Bishop Wolf, who recognized his pioneering aptitude, Ross took part in an expedition in 1934 to Mount Hagen, where he established a station and became the first missionary in the Western Highlands. He was a dedicated priest who walked up to thirty miles (48 km) a day to visit the sick and dying. Like the Hagen men, he grew a bushy beard. Fluent in the local languages, he encouraged the people to retain their traditional culture and mode of dress, and integrated their understanding of good and evil spirits with Christian beliefs.

During World War II Ross and his colleague Fr George Bernarding helped Australian civilians to escape from Japanese troops advancing from the north coast. Despite protests from the Catholic Church, both priests were evacuated to Australia under military orders in February 1943. For the next two years Fr Ross served in the parish of Kogarah, Sydney. In September 1944 he and Bernarding returned to New Guinea. Mount Hagen became a separate vicariate in 1959, under Bishop Bernarding.

Over the years Ross and his fellow missionaries were responsible for the growth of Catholicism in the Western Highlands, which became the third largest Catholic mission in Oceania. Church membership increased from 28 in 1938 to 70 000 by 1968. Ross was appointed O.B.E. in 1971. He died on 20 May 1973 at Rebiamul Catholic mission, Mount Hagen, and was buried in its graveyard.

M. Mennis, *Hagen Saga* (Port Moresby, 1982), and for bib; *Post-Courier*, 14 June 1971, 25, 28 May 1973.   MARY R. MENNIS

ROSSITER, JAMES LEONARD (1887-1962), headmaster, was born on 9 November 1887 at Crystal Brook, South Australia, eldest of four sons of South Australian-born parents Samuel Rossiter, a Wesleyan minister, and his wife Emma Thyrza, née Mitchell. Sent to Prince Alfred College, Adelaide, in 1901, Leonard worked as a pupil-teacher (1905-07) at Flinders Street School before attending (1908-09) the University Training College and studying classics at the University of Adelaide (B.A., 1910; M.A., 1912). From 1910 he taught in turn at Adelaide and Unley District high schools. At the Congregational Church, Glenelg, on 8 April 1912 he married Mary Marguerite Sparkman Jacobs, a schoolteacher.

In April 1913 Rossiter was appointed inspector of schools for the Northern Territory. When the position was abolished in the following year, he joined the New South Wales Department of Public Instruction and was appointed to East Maitland Boys' High School. After gaining a diploma of education (1915) from the University of Sydney, he rose to classics master and then deputy-headmaster (from 1919) at East Maitland, and deputy-headmaster (1922) at Parramatta High School. In 1923 he became principal of Thornburgh College, a joint Methodist and Presbyterian school at Charters Towers, Queensland. Granted study leave in 1927, he visited England, Europe and North America, and was awarded a doctorate of letters by a university in Indiana to which he had submitted a thesis. The identity of the awarding institution remains unknown.

Although highly regarded at Thornburgh, Rossiter moved to Perth in January 1930 to take up the headmastership of Wesley College. He was to earn considerable distinction over the next twenty-two years as the Methodist boys' school experienced a dramatic rise in enrolments and academic standing. Despite the Depression and competition from three longer established non-Catholic schools in the Perth metropolitan area, Wesley trebled its enrolments to three hundred during the 1930s to emerge as the largest independent school in Western Australia. It achieved better results in public examinations than its rivals. Rossiter instilled in his pupils a strong commitment to citizenship and in 1939 founded the Wesley Hundred, a community-service corps of senior boys whose meetings followed a Masonic-like ritual.

Assisted by a commanding physical presence, an authoritative style of public oratory, regular use of his doctoral title, and a shrewd cultivation of politically and socially influential contacts (especially fellow Freemasons), Rossiter became a well known public figure. He was respected, even revered, by successive generations of students, but his treatment of the teaching staff was sometimes gruff and insensitive, and relations with his governing body, the Wesley Church Trust, were soured by his reluctance to relinquish his post at the age of 65. Nor was he popular with fellow headmasters in the Public Schools' Association, the majority of whom refused to approve Wesley's admission, partly because of personal hostility to Rossiter. The veto was lifted only when it was confirmed that he would leave in December 1952.

After his retirement, Rossiter continued to participate in community affairs. A Freemason from 1924, he was grand master (1958-62) of the Grand Lodge of Western Australia of Antient, Free and Accepted Masons. He was a member (1944-56) of the senate of the University of Western Australia and warden of convocation (1954-58). In 1960 he was appointed C.B.E. Survived by his wife, two sons and one of his two daughters, he died on 3 September 1962 in Royal Perth Hospital and was cremated with Anglican rites. His portrait by Margaret Johnson is held by Wesley College.

Rossiter's elder son ROGER JAMES (1913-1976) was born on 24 July 1913 at Glenelg, Adelaide. Educated at Thornburgh and Wesley colleges, and at the University of Western Australia (B.Sc., 1935), he took up his Rhodes scholarship in 1935 at Merton College, Oxford (B.A. Hons, 1938; M.A., B.M., B.Ch., D.Phil., 1941; D.M., 1947). On 16 March 1940 at Rosslyn Chapel, Roslin, Scotland, he married with Episcopalian rites Helen Margaret Randell. After serving in the Royal Army Medical Corps during World War II, he was appointed professor of biochemistry in the faculty of medicine at the University of Western Ontario, London, Canada. Dean of graduate studies, vice-president and provost, he was elected a fellow of the Royal Society of Canada. He died suddenly of arteriosclerosis on 21 February 1976 in Helsinki and was cremated; his wife, daughter and three sons survived him.

His brother Geoffrey George (b.1916) studied at the University of Western Australia (B.A. Hons, 1939), served (1941-46) in the Royal Australian Air Force and won the Distinguished Flying Cross. A Rhodes scholar (1946) at Merton College (B.A. Hons, M.A., 1948), he was executive-officer (1950-65) of the United States Educational Foundation in Australia and warden (1965-81) of Burton Hall, Australian National University, Canberra.

W. G. H. Maxwell, *A School on the Towers* (Brisb, 1988); J. Gregory, *Building a Tradition* (Perth, 1996); P. J. Boyce, *Honest and Unsullied Days* (Perth, 2001); *West Australian Craftsman*, 29, no 2, Sept 1962; G. M. Wild, Dr James Leonard Rossiter (M.Ed. research paper, Univ WA, 1975); B. Carter, The Public Schools Association of Western Australia as an Exclusive Sporting Body (B.A. research paper, WA Inst Technology, 1977); Wesley College, South Perth, Archives; information from Mr G. G. Rossiter, Farrer, Canb.   PETER BOYCE

ROSS-WATT, BLANCHE MURIEL EUGÉNIE (1861-1956), shire president and charity worker, was born on 14 January 1861 at Gisborne, Victoria, seventh of eleven children of Thomas Ferrier Hamilton [q.v.4], a squatter who came from Scotland, and his English-born wife Elizabeth Mary Milner, née Stephen, grand-daughter of John Stephen [q.v.2]. Educated privately at Elderslie, the family property at New Gisborne, Blanche recalled presenting the Duke of Edinburgh [q.v.4] with a posy when the royal train stopped at Gisborne in 1867. She was sent to finishing school at Hanover, Germany, in 1882, the first of her seventeen journeys abroad. Travel enabled her, like others of her background, and generation, to establish a wide and enduring circle of acquaintances overseas.

At St Paul's Anglican Church, Gisborne, on 8 December 1897 Miss Hamilton married her neighbour and second cousin Thomas Riddell Ross-Watt (d.1919), a 47-year-old pastoralist. They lived at his property, Rosslynne. Prominent in nearly every charitable activity in the district, Mrs Ross-Watt helped to organize a Wattle Day drive in Melbourne on 2 September 1912, raising £3000 to build a hall for the children of New Gisborne. On the outbreak of World War I, she established a local branch of the British (Australian) Red Cross Society, of which she remained an active member until her death. She led a campaign to have a cottage hospital built at Gisborne and served for many years on the committee of the Kyneton (District) Hospital.

Following the death of her husband, she established and ran—with her daughter Betty —a small farm, Cathlaw, at New Gisborne; they planned the house and planted a garden which became renowned for its beauty. In 1925 Mrs Ross-Watt was elected to the Gisborne Shire Council. Two years later she was one of the initial group of fourteen women to be appointed justices of the peace in Victoria. When she was elected shire president in 1931, newspaper reports referred to her as the first woman to hold this office in the State; she again served as president in 1939. Appointed O.B.E. in 1949, she retired from the council in 1950.

Although Ross-Watt was a hard-working and supportive member of the Gisborne community, she was by no means uncritical of it. She delighted in debate and controversy, and challenged the patronizing and self-satisfied attitudes of the local male establishment. In an article in the Melbourne *Herald* on 19 March 1927 she had expressed her views on women entering public life: 'The mingled politeness and hostility with which my election and first appearance [on the council] were treated have given place to a liking and tolerance exactly the same as would be accorded to me if I were a man ... I don't want to be treated as a woman, if that involves the hypocrisy that very often accompanies formal deference'.

Widely known for her feminist views, Ross-Watt was a woman of charm and vision who was admired for her energy and leadership. She died on 18 May 1956 at Cathlaw and was buried in Gisborne cemetery. Her daughter survived her.

Aust Municipal J, 31 Mar 1930, p 492; *Aust Woman's World*, 1 Oct, 1 Nov 1931; *Justice of the Peace*, 15 Nov 1946, p 7; *Leader* (Melb), 26 Sept 1931; *Gisborne Gazette*, 25 Mar 1956; family papers (held by author).   N. R. G. ROBERTSON

ROUGHLEY, THEODORE CLEVELAND (1888-1961), zoologist and author, was born on 30 September 1888 at Ryde, Sydney, third son of native-born parents John Roughley, commission agent, and his wife Ann, née Small. Ted attended Sydney Boys' High School, passed the senior public examination and began to study medicine at the University of Sydney (B.Sc., 1933). More interested in zoology than medicine, he joined the staff of the Technological Museum, Sydney, on 21 August 1911 and became 'an outstanding microscopist and photographer'. He played first-grade cricket for Petersham Cricket Club and baseball for the university, studied art under Julian Ashton [q.v.7] and was known for his love of books. At St Philip's Anglican Church, Sydney, on 27 March 1915 he married Olive Lambert.

As the museum's economic zoologist, Roughley focused on the commercial use of 'natural resources', particularly fish and seafood. His *Fishes of Australia and their Technology* (1916), a work of both art and science, contained over 300 pages, 70 colour plates and 60 figures on edible fish. The governor-general Sir Ronald Munro Ferguson [q.v.10] greatly admired 'the beauty of the engraving and plates'.

Roughley published more than fifty scholarly papers, and many other articles in magazines and newspapers. 'The Story of the Oyster' appeared in the *Australian Museum Magazine* in 1925. It was followed by further articles on the Sydney rock oyster that contributed to the growth of the oyster 'industry' in New South Wales. 'The Life History of the Australian Oyster (*Ostrea commercialis*)', published in the *Proceedings* of the Linnean Society of New South Wales in 1933, earned him a B.Sc., and his discovery that oysters change sex during their lives brought him international attention. In 1929 Roughley had mounted a major exhibition on commercial products obtainable from sharks in New South Wales waters. Four years later he published a book, *The Cult of the Goldfish*, which became popular. In the 1930s he was partly responsible for the development of the fish-canning industry. Roughley did not confine his fields of inquiry to one area, as indicated by his work with M. B. Welch on wood borers and his own writing on the pioneer Australian aviator Lawrence Hargrave [q.v.9].

President of the Microscopical (1926-27), the Royal Zoological (1934-36) and the Linnean

(1938-39) societies of New South Wales, and of the Great Barrier Reef Game Fish Angling Club (1937), Roughley belonged to the Aquarium Society, Sydney, and several other sporting and angling associations. He had been elected a fellow (1931) of the R.Z.S.N.S.W. On 13 March 1939 he transferred to the fisheries branch of the Chief Secretary's Department as research officer. He was deputy-controller of fisheries (1943-47) and superintendent of fisheries (from 1947).

Roughley set high standards, and could be critical when they were not met. His observation that the specimens in one particular branch of the museum were 'badly arranged and the labelling dreadfully patchy' was characteristic. He helped to organize the annual cricket match between the staff of the Technological Museum and the Australian Museum, hoping it would foster co-operation and friendship between the organizations. In the first match in 1921 he led his team to an easy victory by scoring 115 not out and taking four wickets.

In cricket whites, Roughley appeared tall, elegant and long of limb. He was known as a witty raconteur whose tales were enhanced by his beautifully modulated voice. Following his retirement in September 1952, he continued to write and pursue various interests in fish and fishing. He was a member (1952-60) of the State committee of the Commonwealth Scientific and Industrial Research Organization. In 1956 he studied the oyster industry in the United States of America and Britain. His article on the *Bounty* descendants on Norfolk Island featured in the *National Geographic Magazine* in 1960. He lived at Vaucluse, collected books and paintings by Australian artists, and belonged to the Vaucluse Bowling and Blackheath Golf clubs. Survived by his wife, and their daughter and son, he died on 14 January 1961 at The Entrance and was cremated with Presbyterian forms.

People (Syd), 28 Mar 1951, p 28; Roy Zoological Soc of NSW, *Procs*, 1960-64, p 39; Linnean Soc NSW, *Procs*, 86, 1961, p 295, and for publications; *Daily Telegraph* (Syd), 2 July 1949; J. L. Willis, 'From palace to Powerhouse: the first one hundred years of the Sydney Museum of Applied Arts and Sciences', ts, 1982 *and* Roughley papers, MRS 311 (Powerhouse Museum Archives, Syd); information from Ms H. Yoxall, Powerhouse Museum, Syd.

MAREE MURRAY
JOHN ROACH

ROUSE, EDGAR JOHN (1894-1974), businessman and philanthropist, was born on 24 October 1894 at Darling Point, Sydney, second child of Melbourne-born parents John Joseph Rouse, merchant, and his wife Anastasia Margaret, née Elsdon. John was a dealer in photographic material who, with Thomas Baker [q.v.7], had founded the firm of Baker & Rouse. In 1908 it became Kodak (Australasia) Pty Ltd. Educated at St Ignatius' College, Riverview, Edgar worked as a radiographer before serving full time (from 1916) in the Militia as a clerk at the Liverpool Concentration Camp. He enlisted in the Australian Imperial Force on 8 May 1917 and reached England in February 1918. Diagnosed as having tuberculosis of the lung, he was repatriated and discharged from the army on 29 July. Later that year he joined Kodak. At St Mark's Anglican Church, Darling Point, Sydney, on 2 April 1924 he married Mary Constance Layton (d.1970).

Unlike his gregarious father, Edgar Rouse was shy and retiring, but he had John's generous and loyal nature, and the same ability to combine business acumen with altruism. He was appointed Melbourne manager of Kodak in 1928 and chairman of the board of the Australasian company in 1938. In the late 1930s, foreseeing that there would be a shortage of radiographical film in the event of war, he visited the United States of America and bought stocks of film base and chemicals. Australia and New Zealand thus had adequate supplies of these products during World War II. Following his retirement in 1959, Rouse continued as honorary chairman of Kodak (Australasia). He had been elected chairman of the Australian board of Eagle Star Insurance Co. Ltd in 1955.

In 1942 Rouse had followed his father as a trustee of the Baker Medical Research Institute. He was chairman of trustees in 1944-71. Prompted by his interest in radiology, he became an early benefactor of the Australian and New Zealand Association of Radiologists (Royal Australasian College of Radiologists). He continued to support it by donating money himself and making grants from the Thomas Baker (Kodak), Alice Baker and Eleanor Shaw Benefactions, of which he was chairman. His generosity led to the establishment of fellowships, professorships and scholarships. Largely due to him, the first chair of radiology in Australia was established in 1964 at the University of Melbourne. It was named after him.

Rouse shared the initial gold medal (1961) awarded by the Faculty of Radiologists, Britain. The Australasian college had elected him an associate (1950) and an honorary fellow (1952). Radiographical societies in Britain, Australia and New Zealand accorded him honorary membership, as did the Australian Medical Association. He served on the board of management of the Alfred Hospital, Melbourne. His long-term support for radiological education and medical research enhanced the status of Australasian radiological sciences, strengthened their international ties and contributed to the reputation of the Baker

Institute. In 1969 Rouse was appointed C.B.E. Survived by his son and daughter, he died on Christmas Eve 1974 in East Melbourne; his body was bequeathed to the University of Melbourne.

J. Cato, *The Story of the Camera in Australia* (Melb, 1955); J. Ryan et al, *Australasian Radiology* (Syd, 1996); A. Tate, *Shadows and Substance* (Syd, 1999); *J of the College of Radiologists of A'sia*, 6, no 1, June 1962, p 7; *A'sian Radiology*, 19, no 2, June 1975, p 114; information from Mr J. L. Rouse, Toorak, Melb.   AUDREY TATE

ROWALLAN, SIR THOMAS GODFREY POLSON CORBETT, 2ND BARON (1895-1977), army officer and governor, was born on 19 December 1895 at Chelsea, London, second of three children of Archibald Cameron Corbett, merchant, politician and benefactor, and his wife Alice Mary, née Polson (d.1902). His father was created Baron Rowallan of Rowallan in 1911. Educated at Eton, 'Billy' joined the Ayrshire Yeomanry at the age of 18 and served at Gallipoli, in Egypt and Palestine, and on the Western Front. On 30 March 1918 near Boyelles, France, he was badly wounded in his left leg when, under 'heavy fire and in full view of the enemy', he dug out wounded soldiers. For his deeds he was awarded the Military Cross. He uncomplainingly endured pain in his leg for the rest of his life.

On 14 August 1918 at the Church of St Andrew, St Andrews, Scotland, Corbett married with Episcopalian forms Gwyn Mervyn Grimond (d.1971). He ran the family estate at Rowallan Castle, Kilmarnock, and developed into an expert dairy-farmer and cattle-breeder. In 1933 he succeeded his father as second baron. He was president of the Royal Highland Agricultural Society of Scotland, chairman of Brown & Polson, grain and flour merchants, and a governor (1951-59) of the National Bank of Scotland.

In 1939 Rowallan raised a battalion of the Royal Scots Fusiliers. By contriving to have himself examined by an elderly army doctor with impaired eyesight, he was passed as medically fit despite his injured leg. In April 1940 he led his men to France as part of the British Expeditionary Force and in June brought them safely back to England. He was involved in training potential officers until he retired from the army in 1944 with the rank of lieutenant colonel. In 1922 he had joined the Boy Scouts' Association. As chief scout (1945-59) of the British Commonwealth and Empire, he devoted himself to reinvigorating and unifying the movement. Appointed K.B.E. (1951) and K.T. (1957), he was awarded the honorary degree of LL.D. by the universities of McGill, Canada (1948), Glasgow, Scotland (1952), and Birmingham, England (1957).

Although the State conference of the Australian Labor Party had resolved (1958) that the next governor of Tasmania should be an Australian, Rowallan was appointed on 28 May 1959. He arrived in Hobart on 21 October and was sworn in that day. Hard working and conscientious, he travelled to most parts of the State and interested himself in virtually every area of endeavour. His speeches, delivered without notes, were thoughtful, pertinent and personal. He developed a genuine affection for the island and a real appreciation of its physical, cultural and economic assets.

Committed to promoting Tasmania and to protecting its interests, Rowallan became a strong defender of States' rights in general and the sovereignty of Tasmania in particular. Following serious floods in 1960, he requested a message of sympathy from the Queen. The casual way in which the secretary of state for Commonwealth relations and the office of the governor-general responded to his request seemed to him to be further evidence of a general erosion of the State's rights. Rowallan began a campaign to reaffirm Tasmania's sovereignty and its right to deal directly with the Monarch. Backed by the opinion of Chief Justice Sir Stanley Burbury, he engaged in extensive correspondence with the governors-general Viscount Dunrossil [q.v.14] and Viscount De L'Isle, the secretary of state for Commonwealth relations, and the Queen's private secretary.

Rowallan found himself caught up in a *cause célèbre* arising from the dismissal (1956) of Sydney Sparkes Orr [q.v.15] as professor of philosophy at the University of Tasmania. He withstood representations from church leaders and, as the university's visitor, dismissed a petition supporting Orr from ten members of convocation.

While in Tasmania, Rowallan maintained his interest in dairy-cattle. Granted registration as a Tasmanian breeder, he built up a stud of Jerseys in the paddocks at Government House. He enjoyed photography, golf and sailing, and bought a Derwent-class yacht, *Nymph,* which he skippered himself and gave to the Sea Scouts. Tall and erect, he had an infectious laugh and was by nature interested in people. Those close to him described him as having 'the eye of a guards sergeant and the heart of a chaplain general'. Like his father, he was teetotal, but was happy to serve liquor at Government House. His popularity was deserved. He received many tributes and honours, including several not usually associated with the office of governor—a railway locomotive was named after him, and he was made an honorary life member (1963) of the Royal Society of Tasmania.

In 1961 Rowallan was diagnosed as suffering from cancer of the palate, for which he received treatment in London. His term of office ended on 25 March 1963 and he returned to Scotland. In 1976 he published his autobiography, *Rowallan*, in Edinburgh. He died on 30 November 1977 at Glasgow and was cremated. His daughter and four of his five sons survived him; his other son, John, a member of the Grenadier Guards, had been killed in action in Europe in 1944.

D.N.B., 1971-1980 (Oxford, 1986); R. Davis, *Open to Talent* (Hob, 1990); *Cwlth Law Reports*, 100, 1957; *Mercury*, 29 May, 22 Oct, 30 Oct 1959, 17 May 1960, 13 Oct 1962, 26 Mar 1963; *The Times*, 1 Dec 1977; NS422/17 and TA315 file AC230 (TA); information from Mr E. E. O'Farrell, Oyster Cove, Tas.

GUY GREEN

ROWE, ALBERT PERCIVAL (1898-1976), radar pioneer and university vice-chancellor, was born on 23 March 1898 at Launceston, Cornwall, England, son of Albert Rowe, sewing-machine agent, and his wife Mary Annie, née Goudge. Young Albert attended the Portsmouth Dockyard School and studied physics at the Royal College of Science, University of London (B.Sc. Hons, 1922). He joined a defence science unit of the Air Ministry, and lectured part time (1927-37) at the Imperial College of Science and Technology. On 18 June 1932 at the parish church, Beckenham, Kent, he married Mary Gordon Mathews, a 26-year-old solicitor; they had no children.

From 1935 Rowe was secretary of the Committee for the Scientific Survey of Air Defence, formed under the chairmanship of (Sir) Henry Tizard to evaluate research in radio direction finding. In 1938-45 he was chief superintendent of the organization which became the Telecommunications Research Establishment and which led much of the development of radar. It employed more than 3000 people, and had to work closely but secretly with the armed services, Treasury, manpower authorities, manufacturers of the new radar devices and their operational users. Rowe was appointed C.B.E. in 1942.

To reconcile inventive research with extensive bureaucratic co-ordination, Rowe developed a management model to which he ascribed much of the success of radar in World War II. He believed that the head of such an enterprise should shape its policies in regular meetings with a small group of leaders—outstanding researchers and divisional heads from within the enterprise and, when necessary, from other institutions. Their sessions should be informal to allow uninhibited mutual criticism. The chief executive would appoint most of the leaders and act alone if they failed to agree. In other respects he was merely *primus inter pares*, the executor of the whole company's best ideas. Inspir-

ation and command would flow down from that leadership to the ranks of second- and third-rate people (his words) whose talents rightly matched their plainer tasks. Even potential leaders among them should obey and learn while they were young and inexperienced. Rowe insisted that, in a large institution, 'be it a university or any other, the transmission lines of enthusiasm must start at the top and be unbroken'.

In 1946 Rowe moved to Australia as chief scientific officer for the British rocket programme; in the following year he was appointed scientific adviser to the Department of Defence. On 1 May 1948 he became, by invitation, the first full-time vice-chancellor of the University of Adelaide. Friends warned him that the university 'had known great days and great men but that in-breeding and impoverishment had reduced its stature'. It was Australia's worst-financed university. It had next to no research students. There was little graduate support, no public-relations and no long-term planning. Its staff had poor pay, poor research funds, no retiring age and inadequate superannuation. A table in the student-union refectory provided their only social meeting-place.

Rowe described his first two years as vice-chancellor as a 'happy honeymoon'. By reproachful comparisons with other States he persuaded Premier (Sir) Thomas Playford to double the university's annual grant. His and others' initiatives achieved a staff retiring age and adequate superannuation, higher salaries, half time for research, better research funding, frequent study leave for approved purposes, and twenty-eight new academic positions. One newcomer celebrated the conditions as 'American pay, British intellectual freedom and Australian study leave'. Rowe also created a staff club, but had an early rebuff when he was not allowed to exclude lecturers and tutors from it. He gave the union an admirable full-time warden, who disappointed him by refusing to 'shop' or punish unruly students.

'A.P.' disliked student misbehaviour, and radical politics which might antagonize governments. The students resisted censorship, and some regretted losing the academics from their refectory. When the Himalayan 'abominable snowman' appeared in the news, the vice-chancellor was dubbed 'the abominable Roweman'. One morning gigantic yellow footprints led from his house across the campus, through a public lavatory, and up the side and steep roof of the Elder [q.v.4] Hall to a life-sized female figure on its weather-vane. Despite all, Rowe and his wife were generally friendly to students and liked their company.

Within three years Rowe had radically improved the university, but not realized his own vision of it. He wanted great scientific research, and believed that it could only come under outstanding leadership: scientists 'of world stature' must be attracted, mostly from Britain, as deans and heads of research centres; they should concentrate resources on a few major projects and thus attract talented researchers. Those outstanding performers should have higher pay. The existing professors should chiefly teach and administer. In his published account, *If the Gown Fits* (Melbourne, 1960), Rowe expressed contempt for research in the humanities and scarcely mentioned the social sciences.

The strategy did not please many of the professors, nor was it adopted. Frustrated, Rowe gave two years notice in 1956. Chairman (1954-55) of the Australian Vice-Chancellors' Committee, he helped to persuade Prime Minister (Sir) Robert Menzies [q.v.15] to commission the inquiry, chaired by Sir Keith Murray, from which Federal funding of Australian universities followed. Rowe was not offered a hoped-for role in that work. On 1 May 1958 he retired. Returning to England, he lived at Malvern, Worcestershire, the last location of his great radar enterprise. He died on 25 May 1976 in Bromyard Hospital, Linton, Herefordshire, and was cremated; his wife survived him. Rex Bramleigh's portrait of Rowe is held by the University of Adelaide.

W. G. K. Duncan and R. A. Leonard, *The University of Adelaide, 1874-1974* (Adel, 1973); M. M. Finnis, *The Lower Level* (Adel, 1975); *The Times*, 31 May 1976; correspondence file, no 364, 1947-76 (Univ Adel).   HUGH STRETTON

ROWE, FRANCIS HARRY (1895-1958), public servant, was born on 20 October 1895 at Bright, Victoria, son of Richard Harry Rowe (d.1906), mine-manager, and his wife Thomasina, née Rodda. Frank grew up in the large household of his relations at Wandiligong. Educated at the local state school, he worked as a teacher with the Victorian Education Department at Bright, Wandiligong, and Collingwood, Melbourne, and held a commission in the senior cadets. On 12 March 1917 he enlisted in the Australian Imperial Force and was allotted to the Army Medical Corps. After making a voyage to England as an orderly in the hospital ship *Kanowna*, he was discharged from the army on 24 September in Melbourne. In 1918 he joined the Commonwealth Repatriation Department as a clerk. At the Presbyterian Church, Numurkah, on 24 September 1920 he married Annie Victoria Callander.

In 1921-32 Rowe was based in Brisbane as deputy-commissioner for repatriation in Queensland. Back in Melbourne, he served (from 1933) as chief war pensions officer for the Commonwealth and assisted W. M. Hughes [q.v.9], the minister for health and repatriation, in formulating new policies. In June 1935 he was appointed deputy-chairman of the Repatriation Commission. He was temporarily transferred in February 1941 to the Department of Labour and National Service as chief administrative officer to co-ordinate the preparation of a new national child-endowment scheme. Appointed secretary of the Department of Social Services on 9 April, he became its first director-general on 11 December. At that time the department administered the Invalid and Old-age Pensions Act (1908-41) and the Maternity Allowance Act (1912-37). While Rowe was in office, major changes occurred in child endowment (1941), widows' pensions (1942), unemployment and sickness benefits (1944) and measures for rehabilitating physically handicapped people (1948).

In 1946 Rowe visited New Zealand as a government adviser to discuss reciprocal social-welfare arrangements. Later that year he spent six months in Canada and the United States of America, investigating social-welfare issues and studying legislation; he also attended the Maritime Session of the International Labour Conference, held at Seattle. He represented Australia at the United Nations Social Commission in Geneva in 1951, and in New York in 1952 and 1955 where the agenda covered welfare developments in member nations. In 1952 and 1955 he attended sessions of the I.L.C. in Geneva.

Rowe was 5 ft 11 ins (180 cm) tall and solidly built. He was endowed with a sense of humour, a deep respect for others, and a humane approach to technical and administrative aspects of social welfare. One colleague remarked, 'I don't know why it is but I feel better when I just know he's in the building'. In 1953 Rowe was appointed C.B.E. He visited London in 1957 to negotiate a reciprocal agreement (1958) on social security between Britain and Australia.

Survived by his wife and two daughters, Rowe died of a coronary occlusion on 24 May 1958 in the Mercy Hospital, East Melbourne, and was cremated. In 1959 a fellowship was named after him: it enabled Australian physicians to undertake postgraduate training in rehabilitation in the United States.

L. F. Fitzhardinge, *The Little Digger 1914-1952*, 2 (Syd, 1979); *Social Services J*, June 1958; *Age* (Melb), 11 Feb 1941, 1 June 1959; information from Mrs G. Moyes, Wahroonga, Syd.   HELEN BOXALL

ROWE, OLIVE DOROTHY (1888-1979), ballroom dancer, was born on 22 April 1888 at Darlinghurst, Sydney, third child of Hogarth

Crawford, a shorthand writer from Scotland, and his Victorian-born wife Rhoda Louisa, née Hummerston. By 1890 the family had moved to Melbourne. Olive's schooling was brief, offering little opportunity for dancing or to indulge her love of music (she played the mandolin). A pattern of family duty was set early in life when she was given responsibility for the care of her invalid mother. She worked in a tobacco factory, rolling cigarettes, and then at the MacRobertson [q.v.11 Robertson] chocolate factory, Fitzroy, where another employee David James Rowe (d.1949) wooed her by 'tossing "Milk Kisses" in her direction'. They were married with Congregational forms on 4 August 1911 at Fitzroy. Three of their children were born in Melbourne. Olive looked after her family while David worked at night as a taxi-driver.

In the early 1920s Mrs Rowe's commitment to her home was challenged by the dance boom of the jazz age and by the public dances held six days a week, afternoons and evenings. Although she later stressed that she 'had never set foot inside a ballroom' until she was in her sixties, according to family accounts she sometimes 'slipped off to the local dance' after the children were asleep, only to be returned home by her 'rather irate' husband in his taxi. At this stage she stopped dancing. In 1927 David secured a better job at W. E. Bramble & Sons Ltd, and the family moved to Newcastle, New South Wales. After the birth of her fourth child in 1929, Olive established a successful pie-making business before being employed by a catering firm.

Aged 62, Olive was 'lonely and depressed' following the death of her husband. She began lessons in modern ballroom dancing at Mr and Mrs J. Lambert's studio, Hamilton. Within two years she had won the bronze, silver and gold medals of the International Dancing Masters' Association (its ballroom branch headquarters were at Blackpool, England). She subsequently added three gold bars to the gold medal, and in 1955, at the age of 67, won the association's gold statuette. Claiming that she was 'not much good at old-time', she embarked on Latin American dancing, adding the cha-cha to her favourite tango.

Despite having battled tuberculosis in her twenties, and health problems in her fifties, Olive Rowe was dancing four times a week in her sixties. Her trim 24-inch (61 cm) waist and slender figure were set off by ballerina-length frocks made by her daughter Dorothy. At the age of 75 she won the I.D.M.A.'s 'highest award for modern ballroom dancing'. She then concentrated on teaching and dancing exhibitions at local clubs and dance halls. A 'woman of great character who was never tired or bored', she 'was known throughout Newcastle for her love of life and her ballroom dancing'. Olive Rowe was still dancing on her ninety-first birthday. On 22 April 1979 she left a dance studio and was struck by a motorcar; she died that day in the Mater Misericordiae Hospital, Waratah, and was cremated. Her two daughters and one of her two sons survived her. While serving in the Royal Australian Air Force her elder son was presumed to have died when his Catalina flying-boat was lost off Formosa (Taiwan) in 1945.

M. Lake and F. Kelly (eds), *Double Time* (Melb, 1985); B. Caine and R. Pringle (eds), *Transitions* (Syd, 1995); *Newcastle Morning Herald*, 8 Sept 1955, 23, 24, 26 Apr 1979.   PATRICIA HALE

ROWELL, SIR SYDNEY FAIRBAIRN (1894-1975), army officer, was born on 15 December 1894 at Lockleys, South Australia, fourth son of James Rowell [q.v.11], an English-born soldier and orchardist, and his Australian-born second wife Zella Jane, née Williams. Syd acted as 'unofficial batman' to his father, who was colonel commanding (1907-11) the South Australian Brigade. Educated at Adelaide High School, he was one of the first cadets to enter the Royal Military College, Duntroon, Federal Capital Territory, in 1911. He and his classmates were commissioned on 14 August 1914 and allotted to units of the Australian Imperial Force. Rowell succeeded in transferring to the 3rd Light Horse Regiment, commanded by his cousin F. M. Rowell.

Misfortune dogged Rowell's career in the A.I.F. After pneumonia prevented him from sailing with his regiment in November, he joined it in Egypt, but broke his leg in February 1915 when his horse fell during training. He did not reach Gallipoli until 12 May. Soon in a hospital in Malta, he managed to return to Gallipoli in August and to command a squadron. In September he was made adjutant. Suffering from typhoid fever, he was evacuated to Egypt in November and thence to Australia. While his Duntroon friends gained experience, promotion and decorations, he taught at an officers' training school at Duntroon until June 1917 before filling a staff post in Adelaide. At the Chalmers Church, North Terrace, on 20 August 1919 he married with Presbyterian forms Blanche May Murison, a nurse.

Rowell sailed for England in 1924 to attend the Staff College, Camberley. His two years there were a rewarding experience, and he was promoted major (January 1926). A five-year posting to Perth on his return was endured in the midst of the Depression and the strains imposed on the army by the suspension of compulsory training in 1929. Furthermore, he did not obtain two appointments for which he believed he was well qualified. He expressed his discontent to (Sir) Julius

Bruche [q.v.7], the visiting chief of the General Staff, and was transferred to Army Headquarters, Melbourne, in 1932.

In the Directorate of Military Operations and Intelligence, Rowell worked with some of the ablest officers of the day—(Sir) John Lavarack [q.v.15], H. D. Wynter and (Sir) Vernon Sturdee [qq.v.]. With Sturdee he formed 'the most profitable partnership' in his career. After a year at the headquarters of a Militia division, he was sent to England in 1935 on exchange as operations staff officer of the 44th Division, Territorial Army. He made a powerful impression on his superior, Major General J. R. Minshull-Ford, who considered him 'undoubtedly a Commander', and on the chief of the Imperial General Staff, Field Marshal Sir Cyril Deverell, who recommended him for the Imperial Defence College. In January 1937 Lieutenant Colonel Rowell joined that college; there one of his friends was W. J. (Viscount) Slim [q.v.].

Returning to Melbourne in 1938, Rowell briefly became director of military operations and intelligence until selected by Lieutenant General E. K. Squires [q.v.12], the newly appointed inspector general, as his staff officer. They visited almost every army station and establishment in Australia, and between them developed an 'elder and younger brother' relationship. That year Rowell was appointed O.B.E. After Squires was made acting C.G.S. in May 1939, Rowell had little inspectorial work until the outbreak of war with Germany. In October 1939 Sir Thomas Blamey [q.v.13] appointed him chief of staff of the 6th Division, A.I.F. When the government decided to form a corps in February 1940, Blamey was given the command. He took Rowell with him as brigadier, general staff.

Blamey and Rowell prepared I Corps for operations in the Middle East, completing the force's structure and forming a sound relationship with the British army. Rowell soon found that Blamey's dual role as corps commander and commander of the A.I.F. presented problems. He wanted to train the corps headquarters for battle, but could not persuade Blamey to establish an A.I.F. administrative headquarters to free them both to concentrate on this task. For his staff work Rowell was appointed C.B.E. (1941).

The tragic campaign in Greece was an exhausting experience for all commanders and staffs, but for Rowell it was something more. The short fighting withdrawal of April 1941, carried out with minimal air support and against overwhelming German forces, convinced him that Blamey was 'quite incompetent as a field commander in modern war'. He recalled sharp differences at critical times and Blamey's poor judgement on certain occasions. Moreover, he had lost his respect for Blamey as a man since their arrival in Palestine. For his part, Blamey wrote: 'Rowell has very great ability; is quick in decision and sound in judgement. There can be no question of his personal courage, but he lacks the reserves of nervous energy over a period of long strain'. The last point may be accounted for by Rowell's having to cope with a commander whom he believed to be failing amid the ceaseless tactical emergencies of the withdrawal in Greece. Back in Palestine, Rowell wrote to Sturdee that he would never again serve in the field under Blamey. He was twice mentioned in dispatches and awarded the Greek Military Cross.

On their return from Greece, Blamey moved immediately to Cairo as deputy to the commander-in-chief, General (Earl) Wavell, leaving Rowell to rebuild the corps headquarters in Palestine. When Rowell learned of the 7th Division's role in the projected invasion of Syria, a country held by the Vichy French, he tried to ensure that the operation should fall under the direction of the Australian corps rather than that of General (Baron) Wilson in Jerusalem. Blamey, however, was not interested. That Blamey later changed his mind, giving Lavarack the command, was surprising. A difficult but brief campaign ended with the surrender of the Vichy forces on 12 July 1941; Rowell had the satisfaction of having again produced 'a smooth-running operational headquarters'. Urgently wanted in Melbourne by the C.G.S., Sturdee, as his deputy, he left by air early in August.

In Australia, Rowell faced the situation in which war with Japan was approaching, but the means of defence were lacking. He was able to bring a degree of order into the General Staff, and to limit access to Sturdee's office so that the C.G.S. could concentrate on major issues. He also played a vigorous part in quelling the so-called 'revolt of the generals' in which some senior officers proposed the retirement of all commanders over the age of 50 and the appointment of (Sir) Horace Robertson [q.v.] as commander-in-chief.

Soon after Blamey reached Melbourne on 26 March 1942, he gave command of the new I Corps to Rowell, saying that he had earned it. Rowell became a temporary lieutenant general responsible for the defence of southern Queensland. The Japanese had already landed in New Guinea, but their major seaborne operation aimed at Port Moresby was turned back in the battle of the Coral Sea (5-8 May). Rowell and others were amazed when a Militia brigade was sent to reinforce Port Moresby on 15 May, leaving the battle-hardened 7th Division near Brisbane. In his memoirs Rowell called the decision a 'cardinal error'. He was dispatched north in July to command New Guinea Force; elements of 7th Division under A. S. Allen [q.v.13] were to follow him.

Rowell took hold of a dangerous situation. The Japanese navy controlled the Solomon Sea and the enemy air force was aggressive. In Papua, Kokoda and its airfield were already lost, and Japanese ground forces were pushing south along the Kokoda Track against partly trained militiamen. Rowell was responsible for the defence of Port Moresby, for holding the Track and for recapturing Kokoda. In addition to the soldiers engaged in these operations, he also commanded the independent companies based on Wau and the force under C. A. Clowes [q.v.13] which protected new airfields at Milne Bay. He could and did visit Clowes by aeroplane, but the brigades on the Track could only be reached on foot after a five-day slog, which he judged was impracticable. Learning that only about 10 per cent of the supplies and ammunition dropped by air was being recovered, he placed the 7th Division on the defensive until stocks for an offensive could be accumulated.

An unwanted burden came through interference by the American supreme commander of the South-West Pacific Area, General Douglas MacArthur [q.v.15], who was based in Brisbane, and who sent tactical instructions (some of them fatuous) to Clowes during the battle for Milne Bay. On 12 September 1942 Blamey arrived on a two-day visit, which passed off smoothly. In a national broadcast he expressed his confidence in the outcome in New Guinea and in Rowell. Yet, nine days later Blamey was back at Rowell's headquarters in an atmosphere of crisis. This second visit arose from MacArthur's advice to Prime Minister John Curtin [q.v.13] that Blamey should be sent to New Guinea to 'energize the situation' and 'to save himself'. Blamey did not argue, but he did send a letter explaining his imminent arrival and hoping that Rowell would 'not think that it implies any lack of confidence in yourself'. To Rowell it did. Blamey was still the man whom he despised and considered incompetent as a field commander. He was not prepared to become his chief of staff when the tide of his battle on the Track was turning. In three 'brawls' Rowell displayed his 'personal animus' towards Blamey. On 28 September Blamey dismissed Rowell, who left that night for Brisbane.

Following interviews with MacArthur and Curtin, Rowell withdrew on leave to his home and garden. Blamey continued to pursue him, demanding that he be reduced to his substantive rank of colonel. Rowell made it clear that he would not accept this, and warned F. M. Forde, the minister for the army, that the affair might become 'a first-class political row'. After Rowell wrote to (Sir) Robert Menzies [q.v.15] about the wretched business, the matter was raised in the Advisory War Council and the War Cabinet. Curtin then told Blamey to find an appointment for Rowell as a major general. He was banished to Cairo as commander of A.I.F. Details and as Australian liaison officer at General Headquarters, Middle East.

In February 1943 Rowell began his exile, discovering that he was not expected, and that he had neither accommodation nor instructions. He found friends at G.H.Q., and in the home of R. G. (Baron) Casey [q.v.13] who was British minister of state. Rowell had a high sounding title, but his post was a sinecure, leaving him free to be useful in his own way. He made himself a conduit for information about operations in the Middle East and the war in the Pacific, and sent weekly reports to Army Headquarters in Australia. He visited allied headquarters in Algiers, and worked briefly in Delhi. Cairo and his travels freed his mind from bitterness, and helped to put the painful past behind him. Thanks largely to Casey, he spent the last two years of the war as director of tactical investigation at the War Office, London. Again among friends, he enjoyed the stimulus of working on top-level committees. As preparations for the invasion of France dominated the military scene early in 1944, Rowell focused his work on battle problems that could be expected in the near future. He served in the War Office until the end of 1945 and was appointed C.B. (1946).

Seeking an appointment in the Australian army, Rowell wrote to Prime Minister J. B. Chifley [q.v.13]. When Chifley later saw him in Canberra, his comment on the affair with Blamey was: 'I hate bloody injustice'. In March 1946 Sturdee became C.G.S. in the post-Blamey army, on condition that Rowell be made vice-chief and his rank restored. The two lieutenant generals set out to build a better army, based on a small regular force with a reorganized Militia as the reserve. Such a fundamental change required developments in the structure upon which the army rested —the production of officers, schools, accommodation and administrative services. It was Rowell who presented the case for the army in 1947 and it was accepted, but recruitment was to be on a voluntary basis without improvements in pay and conditions of service. So continual were the attacks on the army within and outside parliament—and from Blamey— that Rowell was moved to answer them in a public address in April 1949.

While Sturdee was abroad that year, miners went on strike on the New South Wales coalfields. The government ordered the army to cut coal and the railwaymen agreed to transport it. Rowell travelled to Sydney to handle the political problems so that soldiers under Lieutenant General (Sir) Frank Berryman could concentrate on coal-mining. Rowell was aware of the delicacy of the situation. His wise advice to the government against proposals to have the troops paid miners' award rates was accepted, as was that on the provision of beer for them.

In April 1950 Rowell succeeded Sturdee as C.G.S., a significant event in the army's history inasmuch as he was the first Duntroon graduate to hold the post. As the senior of the service chiefs, he was also chairman of the Chiefs of Staff Committee. Becoming C.G.S. during the Cold War, he was faced with the introduction of national service at a time when the new Australian Regular Army was in its infancy, short of everything and yet maintaining a force in the Korean War. The need to see the army at home and abroad, and to attend major conferences, imposed a heavy burden of travel. In 1953 he was appointed K.B.E. On 14 December 1954, the day before his retirement, he took the graduation parade at Duntroon, where he had begun as a cadet 43 years earlier. His wheel had come full circle.

Sir Sydney's first year of retirement in Melbourne was not without difficulty after the pressures of high office, but he turned to his garden, cricket, horse-racing, *The Times* crossword puzzle and reading. Directorships began to be offered—Elder, Smith [qq.v.4,6] & Co. Ltd in 1954 and the Commonwealth Aircraft Corporation in 1956 (chairman 1957-68). In 1958-68 he was chairman of the Australian Boy Scouts' Association and a member of the Rhodes Scholarships Selection Committee for Victoria. He was offered, but declined, the post of Australian consul-general in New York. In 1959 he led the delegation from the Australian Institute of International Affairs to a conference in New Zealand on Commonwealth relations. He was urged by historians and colleagues 'to put on paper some recollections of my army life'. The result was *Full Circle* (Melbourne, 1974). Written with 'modesty and a good deal of charm', the book showed 'dignity and restraint in dealing with his final crisis with Blamey'.

Rowell kept the same lean, trim figure all his life. He continued to be active, but the strain of his wife's illness sapped his strength. He died on 12 April 1975 at his South Yarra home, twelve days before Lady Rowell, and was cremated. Their daughter survived them. (Sir) Ivor Hele's portrait of Rowell is held by the Australian War Memorial, Canberra.

G. Long, *To Benghazi* (Canb, 1952) and *Greece, Crete and Syria* (Canb, 1953); D. McCarthy, *South-West Pacific Area—First Year* (Canb, 1959); J. Hetherington, *Blamey* (Canb, 1973); D. M. Horner (ed), *The Commanders* (Syd, 1984) and *Blamey* (Syd, 1998); Rowell papers (AWM).   A. J. HILL

ROWNTREE, EDWARD FEARNLEY (1894-1966), engineer, was born on 23 January 1894 in Hobart, one of eight children of Francis Rowntree, engineer, and his wife Ann Maria, née Fearnley. Amy Rowntree [q.v.11] was his sister. Ted was educated at the Philip Smith Training College, Hobart, the University of Tasmania (B.Sc., 1914) and the University of Melbourne (B.Mech.E., 1921). He enlisted in the Australian Imperial Force on 21 January 1916 and sailed for England in November. Commissioned as an observer in the Australian Flying Corps on 23 June 1917, he was promoted lieutenant in September and posted to No.3 Squadron in France in January 1918. For carrying out patrols at low altitude in August, he was awarded the Distinguished Flying Cross. He returned to England and completed pilot training after the Armistice. His A.I.F. appointment terminated in Hobart on 4 February 1920.

Twelve days earlier Rowntree had joined the Tasmanian Hydro-Electric Department as an engineering draftsman, on a salary of £250 per annum. He won rapid promotion and by 1924 was principal assistant to the hydraulic engineer. Deployed on surveys of the State's water resources and projects to expand generating capacity, he was involved in the design and construction of Tasmania's second hydro-electric scheme, a subsidiary power-station on the Shannon River. On 25 July 1928 at Christ Church, St Kilda, Melbourne, he married with Anglican rites Mary Catherine Neilson.

In 1933 Rowntree was appointed acting hydraulic engineer, Hydro-Electric Commission, Tasmania. Responsible for design and construction, he began work on what was then Australia's most ambitious hydro-electric undertaking, the Derwent Valley power development project. Next year Commissioner William Maclean restructured the civil engineering branch, effectively demoting Rowntree by appointing him civil engineer, design. Maclean had wide practical experience, but little formal training. He and the university-trained Rowntree soon came into conflict over numerous aspects of the scheme. Maclean continually took the side of his construction engineers against his design chief, often with costly results. Their differences culminated in a disagreement over the design of the second stage of the Derwent development, with Maclean insisting on a conventional concrete arch and Rowntree arguing in favour of a rock-fill dam. The technology which Rowntree advocated was unfamiliar to Australian engineers, and several dams built by that method in the United States had leaked badly. Rowntree was convinced that the new practice of concrete-facing would solve the problem and effect savings of more than £100 000.

Aware that Rowntree was job-hunting while interstate on business for the H.E.C., Maclean called him to his office on 5 June 1940, abolished his £850 per annum position and gave him four weeks notice. Within a few months a board of inquiry examined the

H.E.C.'s administrative structure: it criticized Maclean's overbearing style, his disregard for the opinions and feelings of his senior engineers, and his failure to grasp and act upon the urgent need to expand the State's power-generating capacity. Rowntree, who was praised for his valuable contribution to the inquiry, successfully sued the H.E.C. for wrongful dismissal.

From 1941 Rowntree worked in temporary positions in several Commonwealth government departments. Appointed engineer for major investigations, Department of Public Works and Housing, in January 1947, he was seconded in 1948 to a joint committee of officers from the Commonwealth, New South Wales and Victoria to prepare preliminary proposals for the Snowy Mountains hydro-electric scheme. On 1 December 1949 he joined the Snowy Mountains Hydro-electric Authority as chief investigating and design engineer. According to his senior colleagues, he provided 'remarkably accurate' calculations of river flows and projected power outputs for the scheme.

Apparently disenchanted with the bureaucratic structure of the S.M.H.E.A., Rowntree returned to Tasmania in 1951 and to the H.E.C. as consulting hydraulic engineer. With no administrative responsibilities, and with Maclean replaced, he worked directly to the chief civil engineer on investigation and design problems. Following his formal retirement in December 1958, he continued to be employed by the commission on a part-time basis. Principal executive-officer of the Hobart Rivulet Flood Protection Authority from 1961, he was engaged by the Rivers and Water Supply Commission in 1965 to investigate the State's water resources. In 1964 he was appointed M.B.E.

A quiet, deliberately spoken man with a nicotine-stained moustache and a hacking cough, Rowntree preferred working alone and held firmly to his opinions. He invented the 'Rowntree Control' to reduce turbulence and loss through spillage in overflowing canals, and the 'Draft Tube Plate' to increase the flow of water when storage in dams was low. Survived by his wife, son and three daughters, he died on 30 June 1966 in St John's Hospital, South Hobart, and was cremated.

Report of the Board of Inquiry on the Hydro-Electric Commission, *J & PP* (Tas), 1941; *Examiner* (Launc), 19 July 1941; J. K. Wilkins, A Pride of Engineers, ms, *and* Rowntree file (HEC, Hob); Rowntree biog file (Inst of Architects, Hob); information from Mr H. H. McFie, New Town, Hob.

ROGER LUPTON

ROXON, LILLIAN (1932-1973), journalist and author, was born on 8 February 1932 at Savona, Italy, second of three children of Izydor Ropschitz, medical practitioner, and his wife Rosa, née Breitman. Unable to study medicine in his native Poland because of discrimination against Jews, Izydor had graduated from the University of Padua, Italy, and moved in 1926 to Alassio, on the Italian Riviera, where he built a thriving practice. Following the pact between Hitler and Mussolini, the family fled to Britain in September 1938 and reached Melbourne on 13 August 1940. Settling in Brisbane, Izydor was registered as a medical practitioner on 14 November. Next month he changed his name to Isador Roxon. Lillian boarded at St Hilda's School, Southport, for three years before attending Brisbane State High School.

Hoping to become a journalist, Roxon had sold her first article to *Woman* magazine (later *Woman's Day*) when she was 14. On leaving school in 1949, she failed 'to get even a copy girl's job'. She enrolled at the University of Sydney (B.A., 1955) and found it 'a nice place to hang out and meet boys'. She was drawn into 'the Push', a network of intellectuals and Bohemians whose libertarian philosophy towards sex and politics put it at odds with the restrictive social mores of the 1950s. Some of its most prominent figures, like Roxon, were children of European parents who had emigrated to Australia. Through the Push, she established her reputation as an independent woman, a wit, a seeker-out and promoter of talent, and a person with an almost unrivalled capacity to shock others. Craig McGregor, an Australian journalist, later described her as 'the mistress of the put-down and the send-up, the come-on and the come-uppance, the double-faced about-turn and the blunt, uncompromising insult'.

After working as a publicist for Anthony Hordern & Sons [qq.v.4], a Sydney department store, Roxon broke into journalism in 1957 when hired by Donald Horne, editor of the magazine, *Weekend*. She did not stay long. A visit to New York had convinced her that that city was her milieu, and she left Australia for the United States of America in 1959. At first she freelanced at Hollywood for *Weekend*, then joined the New York bureau of the *Sydney Morning Herald* in 1963. This position enabled her to cover the rebellious social, cultural and political movements that occurred in the 1960s.

At a 1966 press conference, Danny Fields, a publicist and rock band manager, was impressed when Roxon asked Brian Epstein, manager of 'The Beatles': 'are you a millionaire?' The question indicated that she recognized that rock music was no passing fad, but likely to become a multi-billion-dollar industry. Fields introduced her to Max's Kansas City, a New York nightclub at the forefront of the 1960s counter-culture. Its patrons included artists, singers and actors, such as Andy Warhol, Lou Reed, Jane Fonda, John Lennon and Janis Joplin.

Roxon became a central figure at Max's, where she held court among the stars and became a confidante to many influential people in the music business. In 1968 she set out to chronicle the rock scene and counter-culture in what was to be the world's first encyclopaedia of rock music. *Lillian Roxon's Rock Encyclopedia* was published in 1969. Running to 611 pages, it contained 1200 alphabetical entries. It had three printings in hardback edition before appearing as a paperback. The *New York Times* described it as 'the most complete book on rock music and rock culture ever written'. It was the template for many that followed.

The encyclopaedia made Roxon something of a celebrity. Her own portrait for it was taken by one of her famous friends, Linda Eastman, a photographer who later married (Sir) Paul McCartney, the 'Beatle'. The book brought Roxon a regular column on rock music in the *Sunday News* (New York) and another column, 'The Intelligent Woman's Guide to Sex', in *Mademoiselle* magazine. When Germaine Greer published *The Female Eunuch* (London, 1970) she dedicated the book to Roxon, whose independence she admired. The two women (who had started out in the Sydney Push) had a somewhat feisty friendship. Roxon saw Greer's dedication as double-edged; she paid her back in kind in one of her columns.

While working for the *S.M.H.* and writing the encyclopaedia at nights and weekends, Roxon had developed asthma. She was a short woman, noted for her flawless skin and youthful looks, but the asthma attacks, and the weight she developed from the cortisone drugs prescribed for it, imposed severe strains on her. Early in August 1973, dressed in a typically flamboyant gown and feather stole, she attended a singing performance at Max's Kansas City for what proved to be the last time. Alarmed at her failure to return telephone calls, friends summoned the police, broke into her apartment on East 21st Street and found her body. She had died of a massive asthma attack on (or about) 9 August.

A memorial service for Roxon was held at the Universal Funeral Chapel, New York. Her estate was sworn for probate at $44 378. In November 1973 her younger brother Jack set up the Lillian Roxon Memorial Asthma Research Trust in Melbourne to help Australian researchers to study overseas. In 1998 Yvonne Ruskin, in her book, *High on Rebellion* (New York), called Lillian Roxon the 'mother of rock and roll journalism'.

Quadrant, Jan-Feb 1971; *New York Times*, 17 May 1970, 11 Aug 1973; *Nation* (Syd), 15 May 1971; *Rolling Stone*, 13 Sept 1973; *SMH*, 11 Aug, 12 Nov 1973, 7 Mar 1974, 8 Nov 1975; Roxon papers (ML); family information.   ROBERT MILLIKEN

RUBBO, SYDNEY DATTILO (1911-1969), professor of microbiology, was born on 11 September 1911 in Sydney, elder son of Antonio Salvatore Dattilo-Rubbo [q.v.11 Rubbo], an Italian-born artist, and his wife, Mildred Russell, née Jobson, who was born in New South Wales. Educated at Sydney Boys' High School and the University of Sydney (B.Sc., 1934), Syd qualified for membership of the Pharmaceutical Society of New South Wales. He proceeded to the London School of Hygiene and Tropical Medicine, where he gained a diploma in bacteriology (1935). Awarded a scholarship for microbiological research at the University of London (Ph.D., 1937), he studied the biochemistry and taxonomy of fungi in blue-veined cheese. At the register office, Hampstead, on 30 July 1937 he married Ellen Christine Gray, an artist.

Later that year Dattilo-Rubbo was appointed senior lecturer in the department of bacteriology, University of Melbourne. He taught students of medicine, dentistry, science and agricultural science. For science undergraduates, he introduced a pioneering series of lectures—modelled on those he had attended in London—on bacterial metabolism and industrial fermentations. A 'brilliant and provocative lecturer', he inspired a generation of students. In 1939-42 he also studied medicine part time at the university (M.B., B.S., 1943), successfully negotiating his dual role as teacher and student. After completing a years residency at Royal Melbourne Hospital, he returned to the department in 1944 and in the following year was appointed professor of bacteriology (microbiology from 1964).

An 'originally-minded' and 'imaginative' researcher, Rubbo (as he began to style himself) concentrated 'on structure-activity relationships of the acridines and related anti-bacterial drugs'. His investigations (in collaboration with Adrien Albert) led to the production of a new antiseptic, aminacrine, said to be the first Australian drug recognized by the *British Pharmacopoeia*. With J. M. Gillespie, Rubbo isolated para-aminobenzoic acid. He also helped to develop two industrial fermentation processes. The work he undertook with John Cymerman-Craig and others showed the potential value of verazide as a treatment for tuberculosis.

While maintaining his interest in chemotherapy, Rubbo turned his attention to the prevention of tetanus, the reduction of cross-infection in hospitals, and even the sterilization of spacecraft to ensure that terrestrial organisms did not contaminate outer space.

His book, *A Review of Sterilization and Disinfection as applied to Medical, Industrial and Laboratory Practice* (London, 1965), co-authored with Joan Gardner, became a standard text worldwide. For his publications, the University of Melbourne awarded him an M.D. (1955) and the University of London a D.Sc. (1966). He was a founder (1959) and president (1960-61) of the Australian Society for Microbiology.

As professor of bacteriology, Rubbo was also responsible for the Public Health Laboratory (Microbiological Diagnostic Unit). He persuaded the State government to provide funds so that the laboratory's 'diagnostic and epidemiological services for the recognition of notifiable or infectious diseases' could be made freely available to the general community. At the same time, he enhanced the laboratory's role as a reference centre for 'bacteriological and epidemiological aspects of public health'. In addition, he publicly supported efforts to regulate the pasteurization of milk, to control the spread of tuberculosis and to reduce the incidence of food contamination.

Under Rubbo's leadership, the department of microbiology rapidly developed into the largest and best of its kind in Australia. It was a source of deep satisfaction to him that five of his senior staff were appointed to chairs in the late 1960s. His team achieved what it did despite limited funds and a chronic lack of laboratory space. Even after his department moved to a spacious new building in 1965, Rubbo remained a forthright critic of government parsimony in university funding. Although frustrated by repeated failure, he continued to crusade for increased salaries for academics and more money for research.

Outspoken on political and moral issues, Rubbo opposed Australia's involvement in the Vietnam War and campaigned with particular authority against the use of biological and chemical agents in warfare. He was interested in the arts, especially painting, sculpture and the theatre; his pastimes included tennis, woodwork, wine-making and playwriting. As president (1959-64) of the Melbourne branch of the Dante Alighieri Society, he devoted considerable time to fostering cultural relations between Australia and Italy. He was awarded the society's silver medal in 1964 and was appointed to the Order of Merit of the Republic of Italy in 1967.

Rubbo was handsome, tanned and athletic, with a shock of curly, prematurely silver hair. Extroverted, energetic, generous, enthusiastic and exhilarating, he seemed to be 'propelled ... through life at 100 miles an hour'. With abundant plans for the future, he did not dwell either on the disappointments or the successes of the past, and deflected criticism of his 'castles in the air' with 'a disarming grin'. He died of coronary atherosclerosis on 14 April 1969 in the garden of his holiday home at Mount Martha and was cremated; his wife, and their two sons and two daughters survived him. A bronze sculpture (1974) in memory of Rubbo stands in the courtyard near the microbiology and immunology building, University of Melbourne. It was created by Norma Redpath, with whom he had lived at Parkville.

A. J. Woodgyer and J. R. L. 'Joc' Forsyth, *Microbiological Diagnostic Unit 1897-1997* (Melb, 1997); *Univ Melb Gazette*, May 1969, p 10, June 1974, p 9; *Herald* (Melb), 24 July 1945, 9 Jan 1953, 3 Mar 1959, 6 July 1960, 7 July 1962, 15 Feb 1966; *Sun News-Pictorial*, 20 Aug 1949, 13 Aug 1962, 6 Jan 1964; *Age* (Melb), 19 Mar 1953, 17 Aug 1965, 19 Apr 1966, 6 Apr 1967, 4 Apr, 14 Oct 1968; S. D. Rubbo, Application for Chair of Bacteriology, Univ of Melb, 1944 (copy held by author).   CAROLYN RASMUSSEN

RUBENSOHN, SOLOMON ('SIM') (1904-1979), advertising executive, was born on 31 March 1904 at East London, South Africa, son of Samuel Rubensohn, a hotelkeeper from Riga, Russia (Latvia), and his English-born wife Rebecca, née Kluffield. The family migrated to Sydney in 1908. 'Sim' was sent to primary school at Manly and to Sydney Technical High School, Ultimo, where he obtained the Intermediate certificate in 1919.

Starting work as an office clerk with the real-estate firm Raine & Horne Ltd, by 1925 Rubensohn had joined the Goldberg [q.v.14] Advertising Agency; he was promoted manager three years later. About 1929 he founded the Hansen-Rubensohn Co., advertising agents, with Rupert Hansen, but he was not a man suited to partnerships and Hansen left within a year. Rubensohn's strength lay in acquiring clients, even during the Depression. By 1959, when he accepted a handsome takeover offer from the American firm McCann-Erickson Inc., Hansen-Rubensohn Pty Ltd was the third largest agency in Australia. Clients included the Australian Labor Party, New South Wales statutory authorities such as the Metropolitan Water, Sewerage and Drainage Board, and large corporations, among them Australian Consolidated Industries Ltd, Caltex Oil (Australia) Pty Ltd, Marrickville Holdings Ltd, Nestlé Co. (Australia) Ltd, Philips Electrical Industries of Australia Pty Ltd, Samuel Taylor Pty Ltd (Mortein), Trans-Australian Airlines and Victa Mowers Pty Ltd. Typically, it was not the 'pitch' that won the contract; for example, Rubensohn won the Caltex and Nestlé accounts by ensuring that the companies gained access to tins and other scarce resources after the war.

Although Rubensohn was governing director of Hansen Rubensohn-McCann Erickson

Pty Ltd until he retired in 1974, the firm's management was largely controlled by the Americans. As early as 1967 he was said to play little part in the company's day-to-day operations.

Rubensohn's principal interests were political advertising and lobbying. From the late 1920s or early 1930s, in one of the longest associations between an advertising agent and a political party anywhere, he handled the A.L.P.'s account, telling officials what to say, and how and when to say it, and cementing his position by raising money for the party and carrying its debt. He strengthened his position as a lobbyist by converting the donations of clients (or potential clients) into political influence, and by delivering on time and in good measure. He was the 'ultimate master' of his 'Holy Trinity' of political persuasion: 'I know something about you. I need something from you. I have something for you'.

Having been introduced to people in Canberra by Percy ('Pip') Cogger, a brilliant copywriter who had joined him in 1929, Rubensohn became a friend of many Labor leaders, including J. B. Chifley, Arthur Calwell and H. V. Evatt [qq.v.13,14]. A 'great tactician' who knew a good deal about the skeletons in party and union closets, Rubensohn was ruthless, but widely trusted because he was 'utterly discreet'.

Following the 1946 election, R. G. (Baron) Casey [q.v.13] had recruited Rubensohn, who fell out with Chifley over bank nationalization, to organize (for the Liberal Party) the longest and most lavishly funded political campaign ever seen in Australia. In agreeing to switch sides, Rubensohn set three conditions: that he continue to work for Labor in New South Wales, that he have a free hand, and that he start immediately. The campaign was notable, first for separating the longer-term task of destabilizing a government from the short-term challenge of marketing specific policy promises; second, for its use of wireless; and, finally, for being the first to be organized on a national rather than a State basis. Once appointed, Rubensohn not only advised (Sir) Robert Menzies [q.v.15] that advertisements to 'unsell' Chifley and 'sell' Menzies should be 'virile and fearless', but came up with the idea that Menzies should visit electorates where the Liberals were weak. W. S. Howard, whom Rubensohn assigned to accompany the Liberal leader, 'did as much as any ten people to put Menzies back in power'.

Adapting the format of the radio serial, Rubensohn used Cogger to create about two hundred fifteen-minute programmes that went to air, twice weekly, from February 1948 to December 1949, on more than eighty commercial stations. 'Part satire, part serial, part soapbox', the series was built around 'John

Henry Austral', a 'neighbourly but knowledgable' political observer, 'able to see through sham and pretence'. Without acknowledging their provenance, the programmes drove home the threat that communism, Labor's socialism and the welfare state posed to private enterprise, productivity and the 'Australian way'. Incensed by the impersonation of Labor ministers on the programmes, Chifley tightened the provisions of the Broadcasting and Television Act (1942) in relation to the dramatization of current political matters.

Another covert use of radio, developed with Casey and copied from the United States of America, was a 'Country Quiz' which went to air for a similar period on more than fifty stations. From March 1949, until the election in December, large advertisements, carrying Menzies' photograph and signature, as well as points of Liberal policy, appeared in the press every week. In a campaign estimated to have cost several hundred thousand pounds, Rubensohn's commission on outlay was 15 per cent.

In 1951 Rubensohn returned to Labor to promote the 'No' case in the referendum on outlawing the Communist Party of Australia. Sceptical about the existence of a communist threat, he had developed an intense dislike of Menzies, largely because the government he had 'put in' spurned his attempts to extract concessions for his clients. For more than twenty years he was to be responsible for most of Labor's advertising. As early as 1934, possibly inspired by the North Americans, Hansen-Rubensohn had used radio plays to dramatize Labor's appeal. In 1961 Rubensohn and Cogger pioneered the ten-minute television 'documentary' for Labor. The 'Mrs Jones' campaign of 1965 also used the documentary form. Commissioned by Marrickville Holdings's managing director Richard Cribbin, the campaign targeted the dairy industry and the coalition government's margarine quotas. In contrast to the agency's television and radio work, its newspaper advertisements, designed to appeal to the 'rational' side of voters, were often seen as 'dull and prosaic', containing too much detail and too many words. In 1968 Rubensohn introduced five-minute interviews with Labor leaders, with a mix of 60-second and 30-second commercials. In 1969 his agency put 'Westerway', a series of five minute Labor documentaries, to air on television-station ATN-7 in Sydney for six months. The use of this kind of promotion constituted his agency's most distinctive work.

Once Rubensohn had persuaded his American principals that he should accept it, the A.L.P.'s 1972 campaign marked the high point of his Labor years. Organized for the first time by the A.L.P. at a national level, preceded in 1971 by a mini-campaign, and enriched by the agency's earlier work in New South Wales and South Australia, the 'It's Time' campaign was heralded as a watershed in political image-making. The campaign also marked a shift in the A.L.P.'s relationship with the agency. Most of the market research for the campaign was provided, not by Marplan Pty Ltd (McCann-Erickson's subsidiary), but by Spectrum International Marketing Services Pty Ltd, which was engaged by the party following its disappointment with the agency's conduct of the 1970 Senate campaign. Rubensohn accepted the idea because such surveys mattered little to him. The campaign committee was dissatisfied with the agency's newspaper advertisements and commissioned supplementary ones. Accepted by Rubensohn and paid for by Rupert Murdoch, they appeared in newspapers across the country and 'did more damage to the Liberals' cause'—according to the journalist Alan Reid—'than the rest of the A.L.P.'s expensive advertising campaign put together'. E. G. Whitlam attended a huge party given by Rubensohn to celebrate Labor's 1972 victory. After the lacklustre 1974 campaign, however, the party cleared its debt to Hansen-Rubensohn and severed relations with the firm.

If Rubensohn were unusual in working for one side of politics and then the other, he was possibly unique in working for both sides of a campaign at once. In 1971, following criticism from New South Wales Labor leader Pat Hills of the advertising material which the agency had prepared for the forthcoming State election, Rubensohn handed the material to the Liberal premier (Sir) Robert Askin; he also passed on promises from Labor's policy speech twenty-four hours before Hills was to deliver it.

After World War II, as the Rev. (Sir) Alan Walker's 'unorthodox and erratic Jewish-Christian friend', Rubensohn had helped him to communicate with 'ordinary people', encouraged him to set an ambitious budget and to use radio dramas for his 'Mission to the Nation' (1952-57), and contributed to a number of his other ventures.

Charming to clients, Rubensohn was no charmer to his staff. He was described as an 'utter and complete bastard', and remembered by Bryce Courtenay for 'his irascible, high-pitched' voice barking instructions'. Rubensohn made his first calls of the day at 5.00 a.m., left the office in his luxury car at 4.00 p.m., but expected his staff to continue work so that his demands would be met by 7.00 the following morning.

A 'tiny Jewish alcoholic with a gammy leg' (the result of driving while drunk), Rubensohn had married three Gentile wives. In Sydney on 5 December 1927 he married with Methodist forms Audrey Francis Rogers, a typist; they were to have a daughter before being divorced in May 1935. On 12 August that year at the district registrar's office, Paddington, he married Phyllis Amelia Mullis, a publisher, editor and the playwright 'Amery Paul'; they were divorced in September 1946. At St Stephen's Presbyterian Church, Macquarie Street, on 13 November that year he married Catherine Elizabeth Malone, a stenographer who had worked for him as a secretary.

Growing up at Manly, Rubensohn was an outstanding swimmer; he had swum across the Heads with the Olympic freestyle champion Johnny Weissmuller. He was keen on golf until some time after World War II. As a gambler and horse-breeder, and as a member of the Sydney Turf Club and later the Australian Jockey Club, he enjoyed a long association with racing.

In 1963 Rubensohn was appointed C.B.E. (after earlier declining a knighthood). He was an accomplished horticulturalist; a variety of camellia, Ellie Rubensohn, was named after his third wife. Until badly afflicted with arthritis, he tended his large garden at Kelvin Park, Dural. Opened to the public once, in 1969, to aid the Children's Medical Research Foundation, it attracted 12 000 visitors. After selling his property in May 1973, and his extensive collection of Australian paintings, antique furniture, glassware, silver and porcelain in a four-day auction, he was alleged by the Sydney *Sun* to have had inside knowledge of government plans to build an airport nearby at Galston. He sued John Fairfax & Sons [qq.v.4,8] Pty Ltd for libel; a settlement, in his favour, was reached on undisclosed terms.

In 1974 Rubensohn moved to Fiji, but regularly returned to Sydney. He died on 1 March 1979 in Royal North Shore Hospital, and was cremated; his wife and their three daughters survived him, as did the daughter of his first marriage. Ray Crook's portrait of him is held by the family.

L. Oakes and D. Solomon, *The Making of an Australian Prime Minister* (Melb, 1973); S. Mills, *The New Machine Men* (Melb, 1986); D. Wright, *Alan Walker* (Adel, 1997); A. W. Martin, *Robert Menzies*, 2 (Melb, 1999); *Aust Q*, 40, no 2, 1968, p 40, no 3, 1968, p 19, 42, no 2, 1970, p 20; *Aust J of Politics and Hist*, 45, no 3, 1999, p 311; *SMH*, 1 Jan 1963, 20, 25 Aug 1969, 2, 18 May, 27-30 June, 30 Aug, 13 Sept, 29 Nov 1973; *Bulletin*, 24 Feb 1973; A. Lee, Nothing to Offer but Fear? Non-Labor federal electioneering in Australia, 1914-1954 (Ph.D. thesis, ANU, 1997); V. Braund, Themes in Political Advertising: Australian federal election campaigns 1949-1972 (M.A. thesis, Univ Syd, 1978); information from Ms V. Rubensohn, Waverton, Syd.   MURRAY GOOT

RUBEO, ELENA DOMENICA LUISA (1896-1979), community worker, was born on

23 November 1896 in Rome, fourth child and only daughter of Luigi Rubeo, printer and compositor, and his wife Edvige Cecilia, née Marani. Elena arrived in Adelaide with her parents and brother Ricardo on 16 October 1908 in the *Seydlitz*; two of her brothers had migrated earlier. She was educated at the Convent of Mercy school, Angas Street. In 1912 the family moved to Ruthven Mansions, a luxury apartment building in Pulteney Street, where they opened an elegant restaurant, Café Rubeo, which offered authentic Roman cuisine and live music. After her brothers enlisted in the Australian Imperial Force in 1914, she helped to manage the restaurant and became active in the British (Australian) Red Cross Society. She later received a decoration from the Italian Red Cross. In 1920 her parents acquired a large house in Lefevre Terrace, North Adelaide; she was to live there for the rest of her life.

Signorina Rubeo retained affection for Italy and frequently returned to Rome where she had many friends, including members of the Borghese family. Following one trip in 1927, she began to import fine goods, such as linen drapery and silk lingerie, to sell to her friends in Adelaide. She came to the attention of the Customs Office for failing to provide proper documentation for the goods and for importing foreign language publications, as well as the British *Labour Monthly* which was classified as seditious literature.

Intelligent, well-informed on world affairs and fluent in English, Rubeo assisted newly arrived immigrants to cope with Australian laws and regulations, and was occasionally employed by Commonwealth departments as a translator. She taught Italian to Australians and (in 1934) to the children of Italian fishermen living at Glanville. Her school was set up by the consul, who had been directed by the Italian government to promote its cause abroad. Although a loyal Australian citizen (her parents had been naturalized in 1911), Rubeo believed that Benito Mussolini was achieving much for her native country. She stopped teaching in 1935 to care for her ailing parents. During World War II, aware that she was under investigation by the Security Service, Adelaide, she led a retiring life. To help to support herself, she took in boarders, some of whom—like the author Ernestine Hill [q.v.14]—became friends.

From 1945 Rubeo worked with renewed enthusiasm for the welfare of the Italian community. Describing herself as 'a self-appointed mother to them all', she sought work and housing for new arrivals, lent them money interest-free, acted as their confidante and interpreter, found them doctors and lawyers, and visited those who were confined in gaols, hospitals and asylums. Her voluntary work filled a need in a period of large-scale immi-

gration when no appropriate government agency existed.

Rubeo was registered as a business agent in March 1950. She aided Italians by translating documents, preparing wills and applications for repatriation, and arranging passages to and from Australia; for these services she charged a nominal fee. In 1952 she was appointed Italian consular-agent for South Australia (vice-consul from 1955), a position she held without remuneration until 1962. The consulate offices in Gilbert Terrace were transferred to her home so that she could be contacted by day and night. She also ran (from 1960) a travel agency, Arrow Travel Express, in the city.

Five ft 10 ins (178 cm) tall, Rubeo was a good-looking woman with a dignified and gracious manner who commanded the respect and affection both of Italian immigrants and the professionals with whom she came in contact. In 1977 she was awarded the O.A.M. She died on 4 June 1979 in North Adelaide and was cremated with Catholic rites.

Advertiser (Adel), 20 Feb 1952, 11 June 1977, 6 June 1979; D596, item 1929/9662, D1915, item SA14581 (NAA, Adel); information from Mrs M. Boas, Myrtle Bank, Mrs A. Guido, Goodwood, Mr M. Rubeo, Kensington, and Mr B. Stanley, Urrbrae, Adel.   CARMEL FLOREANI

RUBIN, HAROLD DE VAHL (1899-1964), grazier, art-collector and philanthropist, was born on 3 January 1899 at Carlton, Melbourne, younger son of Mark Rubin [q.v.11], a diamond merchant from Kovno, Russia (Lithuania), and his Victorian-born wife Rebecca, née Davis. Harold began his education at Broome, Western Australia, where his father owned a pearling fleet. After the family moved to London, he attended University College School, Hampstead (1908-15), and Eton College (1916). Commissioned in the 5th Battalion, Coldstream Guards, in February 1917, he served with the 38th Battalion, Royal Fusiliers (City of London Regiment), and was promoted lieutenant in January 1918. He returned to civilian life in 1919.

On 8 July 1925 at the Synagogue, Hampstead, Rubin married Marcelle Yvonne Raphael; the marriage was to end in divorce. Left a fortune by his father (who had died in 1919), he set up as a pearl merchant in London in the mid-1920s. During the 1930s he expanded the family's pastoral holdings in Queensland and Western Australia, and began to collect paintings. His next three marriages also ended in divorce: at the register office, Westminster, he married 20-year-old Leila Hyde on 17 October 1940, 25-year-old Elizabeth Wilkie Cameron on 11 July 1945, and 24-year-old Marie Spain on 30 December 1948.

He was again commissioned in the British Army in October 1941. Demobilized in 1945 with the honorary rank of major, he worked as an art dealer at 20 Brook Street, London.

Major Rubin returned to Australia in 1950 to run his extensive grazing interests which included Queensland Pastoral Estates and properties on the De Grey River in Western Australia. He lived at Toorak House, a mansion built by Sir James Dickson [q.v.8] at Hamilton, Brisbane, but regularly visited his 17 000-acre (6900 ha) property Pikedale, near Stanthorpe, and kept a flat at the Astor in Macquarie Street, Sydney. On 18 November 1959 at the general registry office, Brisbane, he married Julia Eleanora Gvozdic, née Hanselman, a 30-year-old divorcee known as Julie Muller.

In 1959 Rubin facilitated the Queensland Art Gallery's acquisition of seven important European paintings from his private collection, comprising works by Picasso, Degas, Renoir, Toulouse-Lautrec and Vlaminck which were valued in all at £126 504. The most significant was Picasso's 'La Belle Hollandaise' (1905), painted in the years between the artist's 'blue' and 'rose' periods. Rubin was prescient in recognizing what he called its 'exquisite tenderness'. The painting is frequently requested for inclusion in major international exhibitions of Picasso's art.

After undergoing a major operation in 1956 at St Vincent's Hospital, Sydney, Rubin became a benefactor of the hospital. In 1958 he financed St Vincent's purchase of Babworth House, Sir Samuel Hordern's [q.v.9] home at Darling Point, and provided the money needed to equip it as an after-care annexe, which was opened in August 1961. Overall, he gave an estimated £500 000 to hospitals and medical research.

Rubin was a man of eccentric habits, but he initiated many of the bizarre stories about himself, making it difficult to distinguish fact from fiction. In the late 1950s he founded the Queensland chapter of the International Goldfish Club (membership was restricted to those who were prepared to swallow a live goldfish) to raise money for the Miss Australia Quest. His city residences were filled with paintings, stacked face to face, as well as with live and stuffed exotic and domestic birds—'parrots, lorikeets, budgies, canaries, finches and sparrows'. He bought entire exhibitions of work by young painters; Robert Hughes, who became an art critic, benefited from his largesse.

In 1962 Rubin was converted to Catholicism. He died of cancer on 7 March 1964 at St Helen's Hospital, South Brisbane, and was buried with Catholic rites in Canberra cemetery. His wife and their son survived him, as did the son of each of his first and third marriages; the son of his fourth marriage predeceased him. Rubin's estate was sworn for probate at $949 342. He bequeathed eighteen paintings to the government of Israel. The bulk of his art collection, which had once numbered four hundred works, including sixty paintings by (Sir) William Dobell [q.v.14], was sold by auction between 1971 and 1973.

Nation (Syd), 18 Apr 1964; *Bulletin*, 19 Nov 1991; J. Hopkins, Centenary History of the Queensland Art Gallery: chronology of events, acquisitions, exhibitions and personalities (ms, 1995) *and* donor file, H. Rubin (Qld Art Gallery Research L).

LYNNE SEEAR

RUDALL, REGINALD JOHN (1885-1955), lawyer and politician, was born on 27 September 1885 at Gawler, South Australia, elder child of Samuel Bruce Rudall, a South Australian-born solicitor, and his wife Margaret, née McNeil, who came from Victoria. Reg attended Queen's School, North Adelaide, the Collegiate School of St Peter, and the University of Adelaide (LL.B., 1906) where he won a Stow [q.v.6] prize. He was articled to his father in 1902 and admitted on 20 April 1907 as a barrister and solicitor. Tallish, lean and athletic, he played football, cricket and tennis, and captained the Gawler hockey team. In 1908 he was awarded a Rhodes scholarship. He read at Christ Church, Oxford (B.Litt., 1911), before working in his father's firm at Gawler. On 20 January 1914 he married Kathleen Clara Sutherland in the chapel of St Peter's College; they were to have two sons, John ('Jake') Glasgow (b.1920) and Peter Sutherland (b.1922).

Prepared by several years membership of a rifle club, and service in the King Edward's Horse at Oxford, Rudall enlisted in the Australian Imperial Force on 11 August 1915 and was commissioned on 16 December. He trained in Egypt and England, and in December 1916 joined the 50th Battalion in France. In January 1917 he was detached to the headquarters of the 13th Brigade; next month he was promoted lieutenant. Sent to London in September 1918, he was appointed assistant-director in the newly formed A.I.F. Education Service. He took charge of the London office, as a captain from January 1919, until he embarked for Adelaide in May.

After his A.I.F. appointment terminated on 29 July, Rudall returned to his practice at Gawler and lectured (1920-25) in constitutional law at the University of Adelaide. In July 1933 he stood as the Liberal and Country League's candidate for Barossa and was elected to the House of Assembly. As a back-bencher he was a fiscal conservative, but he supported the development of free public libraries in South Australia. With the abolition of multi-member electorates, Rudall won the seat of Angas in

March 1938. His 'ability . . . industry, and the charm of his rugged personality' made him an exceptional chairman of committees in the last months of (Sir) Richard Butler's [q.v.7] government.

(Sir) Thomas Playford became premier in November 1938. Rudall was immediately elevated to the cabinet. As commissioner of crown lands (1938-44), minister of lands (1944-46), minister of repatriation (1938-46) and minister of irrigation (1938-46), he was involved in the soldier-settlement scheme in a State that bore the scars of earlier unsuccessful efforts. His credentials as a returned soldier, and his open-minded and judicious approach, alleviated criticism when bureaucratic and financial problems with the Federal government and his own department delayed the selection and purchase of suitable land. He retained warm relations with returned servicemen and became a valuable legal adviser to the Returned Sailors', Soldiers' and Airmen's Imperial League of Australia.

Rudall's life, however, had been shattered by the deaths of his sons (Peter in H.M.A.S. *Sydney* on 20 November 1941, and Jake at Buna, Papua, in December 1942). The premier smoothed his path to the Legislative Council, to which he was elected as a member for Midland in 1944. He helped to steer through a recalcitrant Legislative Council bills to control the dividend rates and share issues of the virtually monopolistic Adelaide Electric Supply Co., to set up a royal commission into, and ultimately to nationalize, the company in the form of the Electricity Trust of South Australia. Invoking protection of the people against exploitation, he endeavoured to guarantee reliable and fairly priced electricity.

For the remainder of his career Rudall served as attorney-general (from April 1946), minister of education (April 1946 to December 1953) and minister of industry and employment (from December 1953). He was tested by the education ministry as the neglected and under-funded state system faced an unprecedented increase in the number of school children. A popular visitor to schools, he travelled as much as he had done when overseeing the far-flung soldier settlements, charming the most disgruntled with his empathy and wit. Although welcomed as an approachable minister by harried teachers' organizations, he was unable to obtain sufficient resources from the government to avert serious overcrowding in dilapidated classrooms or to maintain a supply of properly trained staff. His relations with the teachers deteriorated and in July 1953 he refused to meet an approved deputation. On 15 December he relinquished the portfolio.

Rudall was a heavy smoker. He suffered from emphysema and was increasingly absent from parliament in 1953 and 1954. Survived by his wife, he died of hypertensive ventricular failure on New Year's Day 1955 in Calvary Hospital, North Adelaide; he was accorded a state funeral and was buried in the A.I.F. cemetery, West Terrace. By nature somewhat indolent and unambitious, Rudall might have had a more brilliant career were it not for the deaths of his sons.

B. W. Muirden, *When Power Went Public* (Adel, 1978); S. Cockburn, *Playford* (Adel, 1991); P. B. Wells, *Rudall, the Four Rudalls I Knew* (Adel, 1991); *PD* (SA), 1938, p 13, 1954, p 212, 1955, pp 51, 195, 225; *SA Teachers' J*, May 1946, p 11, June 1946, p 15, July 1953, p 3.   JENNY TILBY STOCK

RUDDER, SUSIE OLIVE; *see* KAYLOCK

RUDDUCK, GRENFELL (1914-1964), architect and town planner, was born on 19 September 1914 at Dromana, Victoria, second of three children of Ernest Rudduck, storekeeper, and his wife Theresa, née Lang, both Victorian born. His parents, staunch Methodists committed to community service, named him after the missionary (Sir) Wilfred Grenfell. Educated at Wesley College and the University of Melbourne (B.Arch., 1939), 'Gren' was awarded a Blue for Australian Rules football, a half-Blue for rowing and a number of prizes from the Royal Victorian Institute of Architects. He was articled in 1937 to Leighton Irwin [q.v.9] and became active in R.V.I.A. affairs. At Queen's College chapel, University of Melbourne, on 2 September 1939 he married Loma Butterworth Amos; her father, a Methodist minister, conducted the service.

In May 1941 Rudduck won the R.V.I.A.'s Haddon travelling scholarship for designing a community health-and-recreation centre which he proposed to construct step by step to enlist public support. Head of architecture at the Working Men's College, Melbourne, from January 1942, he joined (April 1943) the Department of Post-war Reconstruction, Canberra, where he provided theoretical and technical advice on plans for housing. In November 1944 he moved to the regional planning branch. Dr H. C. Coombs, the department's director-general, was impressed by his flair for negotiation.

Backed by Coombs and (Sir) John Crawford, director of research in Coombs's organization, in 1947 Rudduck was granted a research fellowship in social science by the Australian National University to study technical aspects of regional planning. He took leave to attend the 1947-48 session in town planning at University College, London, under Professor William (Baron) Holford, and used his Haddon scholarship to travel to Europe and North America. Back in Australia, he returned to his department (renamed National Development in 1949) and was appointed director of regional development in 1951.

Rudduck helped to organize the inaugural congress of the Australian Planning Institute (held in Canberra in 1951) at which he presented a paper on the growth of Australia's regions. He then toured the country with Holford, believing that he had a stake in the development of the entire continent. His drive and dedication salvaged a faltering project to map Australia's resources. He recruited experienced cartographers from overseas to the team which produced the first *Atlas of Australian Resources* (1952).

After attending the British Commonwealth Economic Conference in London in 1952, Rudduck became attracted by the idea of planning in an international arena. In 1955 he was seconded for three months to a United Nations' technical assistance mission in Malaya. He was then seconded for two years to advise on housing and settlement in Pakistan, where he established a natural rapport with his clients. His appreciation of their country's history, geography and culture informed both his 'urban biographies' of Karachi, Dacca and Lahore and his common-sense approach to building low-cost housing in rural areas. Rudduck's *Towns and Villages of Pakistan* (Karachi, 1961) became a local best-seller. The National Planning Commission of Pakistan invited him back for three months in 1964 to advise on a third '5-year plan'.

At home, Rudduck gave advice on regional planning to the Department of the Army before accepting, with some misgivings, an appointment in March 1958 as associate-commissioner to the new National Capital Development Commission. A Canberra resident since 1943, he moved easily between private and official assignments. From 1951 he served as an adviser to the A.N.U.'s building and grounds committee; in 1955 he worked with Professor Denis Winston [q.v.] on a site plan for the university while reporting to government on the infrastructure needed for airlifting beef in the outback.

Never a bureaucrat—despite his years as a public servant—Rudduck was 'always a compassionate rebel', warm hearted and engaging, interested in people and ideas. He stood by his beliefs. His skills as a mediator gained public acceptance for the commission's transformation of the 'bush capital'. He saw Canberra as a garden city of no more than 100 000 people, and maintained this view despite the pressures of population growth. By 1963 this stance put him in fundamental conflict with the commission's larger plans. Sidelined from its mainstream work, he concentrated on building relations between communities and planners, anticipating popular movements of later decades. He promoted urban research, remained an advocate of regional development in Australia (citing Canberra as an example of what could be done) and pressed planners to regard local communities as clients whom they should heed.

Survived by his wife, daughter and three sons, Rudduck died of myocardial infarction on 19 December 1964 in East Melbourne and was buried in Dromana cemetery. A stone wall and plaque near the West Basin ferry terminal on Lake Burley Griffin, Canberra, commemorate him.

Architecture in Aust, Mar 1965; *Aust Planning Inst J*, Jan 1965, Apr 1967; *Canb Hist J*, no 30, Sept 1992; Rudduck papers (NL).   IAN W. MORISON

RUMBLE, LESLIE AUDOEN (1892-1975), Catholic priest, was born on 24 August 1892 at Enmore, Sydney, third son of English-born parents Harry Humphrey Rumble, civil engineer, and his wife Kate Rosaline, née Knight. Leslie was baptized an Anglican. At the age of 3 he went with his family to Western Australia, where he attended state schools until he was 14. Although there was little religion in the home, his father suddenly became a Catholic in 1908 and insisted that the family did likewise. Leslie was a reluctant convert and after two years reverted to the Church of England. While working as a photographer, he was impressed by a Catholic colleague, rejoined the Catholic Church and felt a call to the priesthood. Judging that Rumble was too English to be happy among secular priests, his parish priest suggested that he try the French Missionaries of the Sacred Heart, in Sydney. The young man entered the juniorate in March 1913.

Soon afterwards Harry announced that he and the family had renounced Rome. For ten years father and son maintained a controversial correspondence, until, just before Leslie's ordination to the priesthood on 26 July 1924, Rumble senior and most of the others returned to the faith. *En route* to Rome to study at the Dominicans' Ponteficio Ateneo 'Angelicum' (D.D., 1927), the new priest gave them Holy Communion.

Returning to Sydney in 1927, Rumble taught theology at the Sacred Heart Monastery, Kensington. As part of the preparations for the International Eucharistic Congress, he began in 1928 a Sunday evening programme on radio-station 2UE, answering queries about Catholicism. Dr Rumble's 'Question Box' was transferred to the Catholic station 2SM and continued until 1968. Interstate Catholic papers carried this material to those outside the range of the radio signal. Four collections of his questions and answers, the first in 1934, sold seven million copies, principally in the United States of America, making him a much-quoted spokesman. He also wrote many pamphlets and magazine articles.

Rumble's knowledge of the varieties of belief (derived from his family's experience) conditioned him to play fair with questioners, whom he always treated as honest inquirers. Using plain language and short sentences, and avoiding rhetoric, he spoke ninety words to the minute in a voice like worn sandpaper, giving an effect of common sense and rationality. When anyone asked what the Church taught about a specific subject, he quoted the Bible—thus quietly claiming it as the book of the Church. He liked to bring in Protestant authorities to support a case and kept the works of many Protestant authors on his shelves.

The shelves were made by Rumble himself, from fruit boxes; just as he repaired his own shoes, he did his own sewing. The simplicity a superior had noted in him as a novice stayed with him to the end. Given a television set, he put it in the monastery's common-room, watching only cricket and boxing occasionally. His recreation was giving retreats. Advancing glaucoma forced him to retire in 1968. In obedience to his religious superior he collated a final book, *Questions People Ask about the Catholic Church* (1972), which read like a temperature chart of the Church after the Second Vatican Council. Dr Rumble, although loyal, was not comfortable in that era. He died on 9 November 1975 in Lewisham Hospital and was buried in the Sacred Heart cemetery, Douglas Park.

N. Bridges, *Wonderful Wireless* (Syd, 1983); J. J. Littleton (ed), *Brotherhood in Mission* (Syd, 1992); Sacred Heart Monastery, *Annals* (Syd), Mar 1953, Nov 1954, Sept 1967; *Parade*, Dec 1971; *Catholic Weekly* (Syd), 19 Feb-2 Apr 1953, 26 Dec 1968, 13 Nov 1975; *Advocate* (Melb), 9 Jan 1969; *Leader* (Brisb), 23 Nov 1975; *SMH*, 20 Dec 1968, 15 Nov, 1, 19 Dec 1975; J. F. McMahon, Life (ms), *and* Rumble papers (Sacred Heart Monastery, Kensington, Syd).

EDMUND CAMPION

RUSSELL, ALEX (1892-1961), grazier, soldier, golfer and golf-course architect, was born on 4 June 1892 at Geelong, Victoria, son of Philip Russell, grazier, and his wife Mary Gray, née Guthrie, both of whom were born at Geelong. The family owned Mawallok, a sheep-station near Beaufort. Alex was sent to Glenalmond College, Perthshire, Scotland, for his early schooling. Returning to Australia, he attended (1908-11) Geelong Church of England Grammar School where he became

a prefect, captain of cricket, and a member of the football and shooting teams; he also gained prizes for mathematics, English and divinity. In 1912 he travelled to England and entered Jesus College, Cambridge, to study engineering.

On 9 October 1914 Russell was commissioned in the Royal Garrison Artillery. While serving on the Western Front, he was wounded twice, awarded the Military Cross and promoted (1918) acting major. At Holy Trinity Church, Chelsea, London, on 14 September 1917 he had married Jess Lucy, daughter of F. W. Fairbairn [q.v.8]. The young couple sailed to Australia and settled at Sandringham, close to the Royal Melbourne Golf Club. Alex won the Australian Open in 1924, the Australian foursomes in 1924 and 1926, and the Victorian and South Australian championships in 1925. Jess won the national ladies' foursomes in 1926 and 1927, and came second in the ladies' amateur championship in 1927, 1930 and 1932.

In 1926 Russell assisted the Scottish architect Alister Mackenzie to design Royal Melbourne's new west course at Black Rock; he and Mick Morcom, the club's greenkeeper, supervised construction and the links were opened in 1931. The new east course, which Russell designed (1930) and helped to build, opened in 1932. He also designed courses at Lake Karrinyup, Perth (1928), Yarra Yarra, Melbourne (1929), and Paraparaumu Beach, near Wellington, New Zealand (1951).

For a short period in the mid-1920s Russell had been private secretary to Prime Minister S. M. (Viscount) Bruce [q.v.7]. In 1932 Alex and Jess moved to Mawallok. He developed the station's merino stud, won prizes for his sheep, and presided (1950-51) over the Australian Sheepbreeders' Association. During World War II he worked for the Australian Red Cross Society as deputy-commissioner (1941-42) in the Middle East and chief commissioner (1943-46) of the field force which operated mainly in the South-West Pacific Area. In the eighteen months between these two appointments he served in the Militia as camp commandant at headquarters, I Corps, joined the Australian Imperial Force on 4 August 1943 and directed amenities organizations at headquarters, New Guinea Force, Port Moresby, and Land Headquarters, Melbourne. In October he was transferred to the Reserve of Officers with the rank of lieutenant colonel. He was mentioned in dispatches.

Russell was appointed a knight of grace of the Order of St John of Jerusalem in 1948. He was president (1936) of the Old Geelong Grammarians, a committee-member (1944-48) of the Melbourne Club, a councillor (1929-55) and life member (1933) of the Royal Melbourne Golf Club, and captain (1946-49) and president (1950-52) of the Barwon Heads Golf

Club. In retirement he lived at South Yarra. Survived by his wife, and their son and two daughters, he died of hypertensive cerebro-vascular disease on 22 November 1961 at Heidelberg and was cremated with Presbyterian forms. His estate was sworn for probate at £223 068. Greg Nuttman's charcoal sketch of Russell is held by the R.M.G.C.

A. D. Ellis, *The History of the Royal Melbourne Golf Club*, 1 (Melb, 1941); J. W. Barnaby, *The History of the Royal Melbourne Golf Club*, 2 (Melb, 1972); J. Pollard, *Australian Golf* (Syd, 1990); J. Johnson, *The Royal Melbourne Golf Club* (Melb, 1991); *Pastoral Review*, 19 Dec 1961, p 1411; information from, and papers held by, Mr P. Russell, Barwon Heads, Vic.   WILLIAM I. WHITTON

RUSSELL, CHARLES WILFRED (1907-1977), grazier and politician, was born on 24 April 1907 at Willambi, Manilla, New South Wales, fourth of five children and only surviving son of Australian-born parents Wilfred Adams Russell, grazier, and his wife Millicent, daughter of Charles Baldwin [q.v.3]. In 1910 the family moved to Dalmally station, near Roma, Queensland. Thirteen years later Wilfred bought the Darling Downs property Jimbour with its large house that had been built by Sir Joshua Bell [q.v.3]. Educated at Cranbrook School, Sydney, Charles jackerooed on his father's sheep-stations in western Queensland before becoming manager of Nardoo station, Cunnamulla, in 1930.

After his father's death in 1932, Russell managed the family's pastoral properties. His practical knowledge made him a confident, if controversial, spokesman for the wool industry. Gaining political experience as a Wambo shire councillor (1933-41), he pushed for the construction of all-weather roads. In 1937 he joined the board of Sturmfels Primary Producers' Co-operative Association Ltd; in 1940 he helped to arrange its merger with Queensland Primary Producers' Co-operative Association Ltd. He was to remain a 'Primaries' board-member until 1975.

A man who enjoyed travelling, Russell had made in 1934 the first of many trips abroad. He learned to fly and returned from the United States of America in 1938 with his first aeroplane, a Beechcraft F17D. On 10 February 1941 he enlisted in the Royal Australian Air Force as an airman pilot. Commissioned flight lieutenant in May, he served as an instructor at training schools in Queensland, Tasmania and New South Wales before being transferred to the R.A.A.F. Reserve on 28 February 1944. At St John's Anglican Cathedral, Brisbane, on 27 July that year he married Hilary Maude, a 22-year-old mothercraft nurse and daughter of Frank Newton [q.v.11].

Russell had been a founder and guarantor of the Queensland Country Party in 1936. He stood unsuccessfully for the Legislative Assembly seats of Warrego (1938) and Dalby (1944). Assisted by his father's reputation—Wilfred had represented Dalby in 1926-32—and a campaign ably organized by (Sir) James Killen, Russell won Dalby in 1947. In parliament he spoke on the concerns which were to occupy him for the rest of his life: transport, land settlement, decentralization and rural industries. Although he found the atmosphere 'friendly', he was frustrated in Opposition and contested the House of Representatives seat of Maranoa at the 1949 election, winning it handsomely.

Idealistic about the Country Party's platform, Russell quickly grew critical of the party's inability to put its election promises into practice. On 7 October 1950 he resigned from the parliamentary party over the government's unwillingness to raise the exchange rate and its decision to impose a wool tax. Ostracized by the Liberal-Country Party coalition government led by (Sir) Robert Menzies and (Sir) Arthur Fadden [qq.v.15,14], he sat on the cross-benches for the rest of his term and saw himself as the lone voice espousing correct policies. In the 1951 election he stood for Maranoa as an Independent, but was defeated. The Country Party expelled him shortly after the election, and his subsequent application to join the Liberal Party was turned down. He campaigned strongly, though unsuccessfully, for the Senate in 1953, for Maranoa in 1954 and 1955, and for the Legislative Assembly seat of Condamine in 1972, publishing his views in newspaper columns, on radio and finally on television.

Russell was a director of the Queensland National Pastoral Co. Ltd (1946-50), the Coca-Cola Export Corporation (1946-72) and Napier Bros Ltd (1953-62). He was also chairman (1951-77) of Barnes [q.v.7] Milling Ltd, the company which built a new flour-mill at Dalby in 1958. A progressive farmer, he developed at Jimbour an irrigation system, a model dairy and piggery, and a feedlot. His wealth and connexions gave him the means to shrug off censure and maintain his firmly held beliefs. He criticized the Country Party trenchantly and was unafraid to challenge government policies. In 1965 he lost an appeal to the High Court of Australia against the validity of the Federal wool tax, but in 1977 he succeeded in having the Queensland government's stock assessment levy declared invalid.

Fiercely anti-socialist and intensely loyal to the British Empire, Russell stood on the extreme right of conservative politics. He united with other men who were disaffected with the major political parties, among them Sir Raphael Cilento, G. H. Griffiths [q.v.9] and the economist Colin Clark. During the 1950s he had helped to form the short-lived Australian Democratic Union and the Australian Democratic Party. In the 1960s he was a leader of the Basic Industries Group and a member of the Federal Inland Development Organization. He kept in contact with various fronts of Eric Butler's Australian League of Rights, but did not join the league because he disagreed with its Social Credit theories. In the 1970s he joined the right-wing Workers Party and the Progress Party.

With his wife, Russell was involved in the social and cultural life of the Dalby district. The restored Jimbour House, classified by the National Trust of Queensland, became a popular venue for fund-raising entertainment. Charles and Hilary expressed their love of their home in *Jimbour: Its History and Development* (1955). Flying remained an important part of his life, and in 1975 he flew a Beechcraft Baron home from the U.S.A., via Europe, the Middle East and Singapore. He belonged to the Queensland and United Service clubs, Brisbane, and Royal Sydney Golf Club. His autobiography, *Country Crisis* (1976), set out his opinions on economics, detailed his political associations, and showed his concern for the decrease in rural population and the erosion of rural prosperity.

Russell collapsed on 20 October 1977 while speaking at a meeting of the Maranoa branch of the Progress Party. He died of a cerebral haemorrhage on the following day in Dalby hospital and was cremated. His wife, and their daughter and four sons survived him.

Courier-Mail and *SMH*, 24 Oct 1977; *Qld Country Life*, 27 Oct 1977; Russell papers (Fryer L, Univ Qld).

ELAINE BROWN

RUSSELL, ERIC ALFRED (1921-1977), economist, was born on 20 December 1921 at Colac, Victoria, second son of William John Russell, stationmaster, and his wife Lillian Rosetta, née Holland, both Victorian born. William's occupation meant that the family moved frequently. Eric was educated at Melbourne High School (1936-38) and the University of Melbourne (B.A. Hons, B.Com., 1943) where he tutored (1943-44) in advanced economics. At Wesley Church, Melbourne, on 8 June 1945 he married with Methodist forms Norma Mary Farrow, a clerk; they were to be divorced in 1948. He proceeded to King's College, Cambridge (B.A., 1947; M.A., 1959), studied under the philosopher Ludwig Wittgenstein, and gained first-class honours in the economics tripos.

Returning to Australia, Russell lectured (1947-50) at New England University College, Armidale, New South Wales. On 18 August 1948 at St Paul's Presbyterian Church, Bris-

bane, he married Judith Roe, a university teacher. He taught at the University of Sydney (from 1951) before being appointed senior lecturer in economics at the University of Adelaide in 1952. He was promoted to reader in 1958 and professor in 1964, and was head of department in 1966-75. A gifted teacher, and a superb but gentle critic, he influenced a generation of undergraduates.

Russell examined the wool boom of the early 1950s, balance of payments, import controls, Australia and the European Economic Community, distribution issues (most noticeably incomes policies), education, international investment and the energy crisis. He published little, yet his was always one of the earliest and wisest voices analysing the major issues of the Australian economy from the 1950s to the 1970s. He was a political economist in the best sense of the term—conscious of the political and institutional settings of any economic problem and interested in economics only in so far as it bore directly or indirectly on policy issues. In a seminal paper (*Economic Record*, April 1957) he and James Meade set out how the Australian economy worked, what the social relationships and relevant institutions were, how the domestic price level was formed and how Australia as a small open economy responded to external pressures.

In 1959 Russell appeared before the Commonwealth Conciliation and Arbitration Commission to present evidence on behalf of wage-earners. His arguments for adjusting money incomes according to effective productivity and prices were to provide the foundation for the wages accord (1983). In his presidential address in 1972 to the economics section at the Adelaide conference of the Australian and New Zealand Association for the Advancement of Science he made evident his deep understanding and intelligence, especially in his views on methodology, the value of economic theory and the use of empirical evidence.

A member (1970-75) of the Australian Advisory Committee on Research and Development in Education, Russell was elected a fellow of the Academy of the Social Sciences in Australia in 1973. In addition to his interest in economics, history, philosophy and politics, he loved the theatre, painting and sport. He was a complex and private man who worked intensely hard. Such intensity took its toll. Survived by his wife and their three sons, he died of myocardial ischaemia on 26 February 1977 in Royal Adelaide Hospital and was cremated.

G. C. Harcourt, *The Social Science Imperialists* (Lond, 1982); *Aust Economic Papers*, 16, 1977, p 159; G. C. Harcourt, 'Eric Russell, 1921-77: A Memoir', *Economic Record*, 53, 1977, p 467.

G. C. HARCOURT

RUSSELL, ROBERT GEOFFREY (1892-1946), manufacturer and distributor, was born on 26 May 1892 at Castlemaine, Victoria, son of Robert Frederick Russell, a school inspector from Ireland, and his second wife Lucy Coles, née Gammon, who was born in Victoria. Geoff grew up at Geelong and at Hawthorn, Melbourne. He completed his schooling at Scotch College, without showing the scholarly aptitude of his father. Instead, from an early age, he developed an intense interest in mechanical engineering. He was both a perfectionist and ambitious, but was not driven by love of money.

After completing an apprenticeship to a fitter and turner at the Glenferrie workshop of A. H. McDonald & Co., Russell worked as a journeyman motor mechanic at Wangaratta. He enlisted in the Australian Imperial Force on 22 March 1915 and served at Gallipoli and on the Western Front, mainly with the 6th Field Ambulance. Promoted sergeant in May 1916, he returned to Australia in June 1919 and was discharged from the army on 9 August. At Holy Trinity Cathedral, Wangaratta, on 14 April 1920 he married with Anglican rites Hazel Margaret Notcutt.

Russell had become a partner in a garage at Wangaratta in 1919. Restless and determined, he sold out after about two years and went into debt to buy a 'tin shed' workshop at Collingwood. There he established a specialist engine-reconditioning business which he registered as the Auto Grinding Co. Pty Ltd. His first equipment, obtained by hire purchase, included a Heald cylinder grinder, a lathe, a vertical drilling machine and a power hacksaw.

In 1924 Russell moved to larger premises in Queensberry Street, Carlton, the centre of Melbourne's motor trade. Two years later he and his friend Bill Ryan formed Replacement Parts Pty Ltd. Its office was located in Elizabeth Street. More genial than the taciturn Russell, Ryan proved an ideal partner. The company distributed automotive spare parts, accessories and general equipment, stocking its own products and those of other firms. Profitable trading enabled the Russell Manufacturing Co. Pty Ltd to be set up (1927) in North Melbourne. By 1930 this piston-making factory had moved to Burnley Street, Richmond. The trade name Repco was registered that year.

Russell embarked on his ventures at a time of small-scale manufacturing in Australia, when proprietors often ate a sandwich lunch with their workers on the footpath; business lunches might consist of a meat pie, an apple slice and a cup of tea in a nearby café. Respected by his employees, Russell was one of the 'hard but fair' employers much valued in the period. He had a talent for welding a team from varied but complementary individuals. Several of his apprentices and trainees became Repco executives.

The number of motor vehicles in Australia grew rapidly: 123 000 were registered in 1921 and 656 000 in 1930. The expansion made Russell and Ryan wealthy. Their businesses catered for the numerous 'niche' requirements of an industry that had a proliferation of motorcar brands, an inconsistent quality of original components and difficulty in meeting the demand for parts. The Depression wrought mixed effects on Repco. More motorists chose to recondition and repair their vehicles rather than buy new ones. The Federal government increased protective tariffs on Australian manufactures. Both these developments enabled the business to survive a severe reduction in liquidity caused by customers who were slow—or failed—to make payments.

The Repco group of companies resumed their growth after the slump. Spare-parts branches were opened at Sale and Hamilton, and, under the umbrella of Replacement Parts (Tasmania) Pty Ltd, at Launceston and Burnie. By the mid-1930s the four companies employed over five hundred people and manufactured 60 per cent of the goods they sold. Russell bought out Ryan in 1936. Next year he floated Repco Ltd as a public company; he was its chairman and managing director. During World War II he worked fervently to supply the armed services' needs for engine parts and repairs. In addition to running Repco, he managed a plant for the Department of Aircraft Production. In spare moments he worked on aircraft cylinder heads at his home. His elder son Tom was killed in action in 1943 while serving with the Royal Australian Air Force.

Russell was one of a band of visionary, innovative and technically gifted entrepreneurs who provided a firm base for Australian manufacturing after World War I. The enterprises which they established helped the economy to adjust to peacetime conditions and later to recover from the Depression. In World War II their productive capacity was critical to the nation's survival. With probing, steel blue eyes and a rigid moral code, Russell became more reserved and aloof as he aged. He fell seriously ill in 1945, resigned from Repco's board, sold his controlling interest for some £200 000 and retired to his mansion, Amberley, at Lower Plenty. Survived by his wife, and their daughter and younger son, he died of a cerebral tumour on 19 April 1946 at Heidelberg and was cremated.

Ms histories of Repco by J. Goode, and by R. Murray and K. White, in R. Murray/K. White papers *and* Repco papers (Univ Melb Archives); information from the late Messrs G. Russell and W. L. Ryan, and the late Sir Charles McGrath.

ROBERT MURRAY

RUTHERFORD, CLARA PADBURY (1878-1975), women's activist, was born on 6 July 1878 in Perth, fourth of eight children of Edward Roberts, farmer, and his wife Charlotte, née Nairn, both Western Australian born. Educated privately and at Pyrmont Girls' School, Albany, Clara trained as a nurse for two years at Perth Public Hospital before returning to the family home, Yathroo station, Dandaragan. There, on 6 April 1910, she married with Anglican rites Douglas Rutherford (d.1961), a surveyor; they were to have three children. After several months in survey camps, the couple moved to Moora. Clara started a club for local women. From 1917 they lived at Belmont, near Perth, where they ran a poultry farm to supplement their income, before settling at Subiaco in 1919.

In 1918 Mrs Rutherford had joined the Western Australian National Council of Women. Prominent in the establishment of the West Australian Housewives' League, she was elected its inaugural president in 1920 and later made a life member of the Western Australian Housewives' Association. She chaired Edith Cowan's [q.v.8] election campaign committees in 1921 and 1924, and presided over the Women's Electoral League. In February 1922 she was appointed a justice of the peace; she became one of the first two women to sit on the Perth police court bench. Between 1930 and 1953 she held various offices in the Western Australian Women Justices' Association.

A founder of the Country Women's Association of Western Australia, Rutherford had been elected a vice-president at the initial conference in 1925. She chaired a C.W.A. committee which endeavoured to provide a seaside home where women and children from the inland could spend holidays: following a successful fund-raising campaign, Sunshine (Lodge) was opened at Cottesloe in August 1929. A regular office-holder in the C.W.A., she was to be given honorary life membership in 1957.

Rutherford had become a member of the executive of the W.A.N.C.W. in 1927. Two years later she represented the council on an international standing committee for suffrage and citizenship rights. Active in affiliated bodies, she was a delegate to the Good Films League and a founding member of the Women's Immigration Auxiliary Council of Western Australia. She served on the W.A.N.C.W. executive for more than forty years and had three terms as president; by 1935 she had been made honorary life vice-president in recognition of her services. In addition, she was a council-member of the State branch of the Girl Guides' Association, a member of the Western Australian Women's Parliament (founded in 1946), a local committee-member of the 'Call to the People of Australia' campaign and president (1953) of the women's auxiliary of the Civilian Maimed and Limbless Association.

A bespectacled, amiable woman, Rutherford was motivated by a genuine desire for public service and a firm belief that married women should have interests beyond the home. 'Go out and broaden your vision', she urged them. She died on 11 June 1975 at Armadale and was cremated; her daughter and two sons survived her.

R. Erickson et al (eds), *Her Name is Woman* (Perth, 1974); National Council of Women of WA, *Centenary Year Report*, 1929; *Daily News* (Perth), 17 Feb 1954; WA Housewives' Assn records (BL).

ANDREA GAYNOR

RYAN, MARY MARGARET (1886-1968), community worker, was born on 15 September 1886 at Timaru, New Zealand, third of eight children of Irish-born parents Jeremiah Kelly, labourer, and his wife Deborah, née O'Connor. Educated to primary level at a one-teacher school, by the age of 13 Mary was managing the household while her mother recovered from the death of newborn twins. She admired her mother's domestic skills, but complained of slavery in 'a house full of children in a much too small home, never enough money and nothing but work, work all day long'. After entering domestic service, she trained (from 1915) at Wellington Hospital and qualified as a registered nurse in December 1919.

Moving to Sydney, Mary Kelly registered as a general nurse with the Australasian Trained Nurses' Association on 14 July 1920. She worked in the small hospital at Portland, a town in which social life was dominated by the largest employer, a cement works. At St Vincent's Catholic Church, Portland, on 15 August 1921 she married Michael Thomas Ryan, a billiard marker. Following the birth of their three children in the 1920s, she worked only intermittently as a relief sister. She was appointed a justice of the peace and became an unofficial social worker.

By means of the library of Portland School of Arts and a subscription to the Left Book Club, Mrs Ryan read the works of the interwar socialists. The indignity and poverty of the Depression sharpened her political commitment. Both she and Michael were active members of the Australian Labor Party. As secretary and later president of the local branch, she attended regional and State A.L.P. conferences, persistently pressing the needs of women and children for education, housing, employment and community facilities. Through the Country Women's Association of New South Wales, she organized a Baby

Health Centre at Portland. From 1941 she served on the Portland District Hospital board.

Mrs Ryan's warm personality, generosity and sense of humour made her a popular and respected figure; J. B. Chifley [q.v.13] was among the regular visitors to her home. As minister for postwar reconstruction, he appointed her to the Commonwealth Housing Commission in 1943. She was propelled into almost two years of intensive travelling, interviewing, correspondence and negotiation. Her own experience in a house with no electricity (save for lighting), no internal water and only a coal-fired stove proved invaluable to the commission in detailing the conditions in which many housewives worked.

As one way of making mothers 'more reconciled to their post', Mrs Ryan advocated the provision of better homes, equipped with electricity and labour-saving devices. She joined the United Associations of Women and the Australian Woman's Charter movement. In 1943, with Jessie Street [q.v.], she tried to increase the voice of women in A.L.P. policy making. Next year she stood unsuccessfully for the Blaxland Shire Council.

In 1944 Mrs Ryan returned to Portland and to her role as a housewife. She later served in a corner store. Although critical of conservative Catholicism and priestly orthodoxy, she remained a practising Catholic; her second son entered the priesthood. In later years she visited Europe and Ireland. Survived by her daughter and two sons, she died on 19 May 1968 at Strathfield, Sydney, and was buried in Northern Suburbs cemetery.

Cwlth Housing Com, *Final Report* (Canb, 1944); Women and Labour Publications Collective, *All Her Labours*, 2 (Syd, 1984); S. Kennedy, *Faith and Feminism* (Syd, 1985); H. Radi (ed), *200 Australian Women* (Syd, 1988); *Aust Women's Weekly*, 15 May 1943; C. Allport, Women and Public Housing in Sydney 1930-1961 (Ph.D. thesis, Macquarie Univ, 1990); Mary Ryan, unpublished autobiography *and* diaries 1943-46 (held by the family).

CAROLYN ALLPORT

RYAN, PATRICK JOSEPH (1904-1969), Catholic priest, was born on 13 March 1904 at Albury, New South Wales, eldest of six children of James Vincent Ryan, a Victorian-born farmer, and his wife Sarah Josephine, née Ryan, who came from Ireland. After attending Albury Public School, Paddy helped on the farm before completing his schooling at the Presentation Convent, Chiltern, Victoria, and St Mary's Towers, Douglas Park, New South Wales. He entered the novitiate of the Missionaries of the Sacred Heart at Kensington, Sydney, in 1923 and was professed in 1924. In Rome from 1927, he studied at the Pontifical Gregorian University (D.Ph., D.D., 1930). On 18 July 1929 he was ordained priest. Returning to Sydney in 1932, he taught philosophy at the Sacred Heart novitiate.

With Oscar Vonwiller and John Anderson [qq.v.12,7], professors of physics and philosophy respectively at the University of Sydney, Ryan took part in the 'Symposium on Science, Philosophy and Christianity' held in 1936. His ability as a controversialist was promptly and widely recognized. In 1937 he helped (Archbishop) Eris O'Brien [q.v.15] to launch Catholic Action in Sydney. The Church used Ryan's skills in a wide range of activities in the 1940s and 1950s—in adult education, pamphlet writing and—with his colleague Dr Leslie Rumble [q.v.]—broadcasting.

From 1940 much of Ryan's effort was spent on anti-communist activity, both public and secret. As director (from 1942) of the Lay Apostolate in the archdiocese of Sydney, he was effectively the founder (about 1945) of the Sydney branch of the Catholic Social Studies Movement, the secret Catholic anti-communist group in the trade unions and Australian Labor Party.

Despite rain, 30 000 people came to the Stadium, Rushcutters Bay, on 23 September 1948 to hear Ryan debate with Edgar Ross, a communist leader. Ross spoke first, in defence of the Soviet Union. Ryan, in a quiet, unimpassioned voice, claimed that communism was based on a degraded philosophy of life, that its programme necessarily involved ruthless and unlimited dictatorship, and that the Communist Party of Australia had no loyalty to God or country, but only to Moscow. 'In saying that the Catholic Church supported Fascism, Mr Ross was [again the quiet, unimpassioned voice] a liar'. Wild applause followed. Ryan addressed many other large audiences, especially during the campaign for the anti-communism referendum of 1951. He also spoke on the positive aspects of Catholic social philosophy, and its incompatibility with *laissez-faire* capitalism.

Ryan remained director of the Sydney office during the years when the 'groupers' in many trade unions brought victory over communist control. Contrary to 'the Movement's' practice in other States, he maintained contact with the security services, and occasionally permitted stacking of union meetings by outsiders who were ineligible to vote. Amid fears in 'the Movement' that Ryan's 'cowboys and Indians' methods (B. A. Santamaria's phrase) would compromise the anti-communist cause, he was replaced as director in 1954. The resulting tension contributed to the Sydney and Melbourne branches parting ways. Ryan was a key speaker at the meetings in 1956 at which the vast majority of New South Wales members decided to remain with the A.L.P.

instead of joining their Victorian and Queensland colleagues in what became the Democratic Labor Party.

In 1954-62 Ryan was director of adult education in the Sydney archdiocese. Suffering from coronary sclerosis, he died of pneumonia on 18 January 1969 at the St John of God Hospital, Richmond, and was buried in the Sacred Heart cemetery, Douglas Park.

J. Franklin, 'Catholic Thought and Catholic Action', *J of the Aust Catholic Hist Soc*, 17, 1996, p 44; *Catholic Weekly* (Syd), 23 Jan 1969; *SMH*, 24 Sept 1948, 20 Jan 1969; Ryan file (M.S.C. Provincial Archives, St Paul's Seminary, Kensington, Syd).

JAMES FRANKLIN

RYAN, RONALD JOSEPH (1925-1967), criminal, was born on 21 February 1925 at Carlton, Melbourne, only son of Australian-born parents John Ronald Ryan, an invalid and former miner, and Eveline Cecilia Thompson, née Young, a domestic servant. Ronald's childhood was dominated by his parents' alcoholism, poverty and poor health, particularly his father's chronic phthisis. He was violently abused by his father and neglected by his mother.

Following the theft of a watch from a neighbour's house at Mitcham in November 1936, young Ryan was made a ward of the state and sent to Rupertswood, Sunbury, the Salesian Order's school for 'wayward and neglected' boys. He did quite well, captaining the football and cricket teams, joining the choir, and impressing other boys as 'a natural leader'. After several failed attempts, he absconded in September 1939 and went to Balranald, New South Wales. He eventually settled there with his mother and three sisters, worked as a labourer and kept out of the hands of the law. Aged about 23, he returned to Melbourne where, by 1950, he was employed as a storeman. On 4 February that year at St Stephen's Anglican Church, Richmond, he married Dorothy Janet George, a secretary; educated at a private school, she had rebelled against her wealthy parents.

In 1953 Ryan was acquitted on a charge of arson. To pay his gambling debts, he uttered a number of forged cheques in 1956 and was placed on a good-behaviour bond. He then took a succession of jobs in the country and the city. By 1959 he was virtually a professional criminal, leading a gang that broke into shops and factories. After being apprehended in April 1960, he and three accomplices escaped from the police, but were recaptured several days later. On 17 June he pleaded guilty in the Melbourne Court of General Sessions to eight charges of breaking and stealing, and one of escaping from legal custody. He was sentenced to eight and a half years imprisonment.

Appearing to want to rehabilitate himself, Ryan was released on parole in August 1963, but soon returned to crime. Following a series of factory-breakings and safe-blowings in Melbourne, he received an eight-year sentence on 13 November 1964. Within ten months his wife divorced him. Ryan and another prisoner Peter John Walker escaped from Pentridge gaol on 19 December 1965; during the break-out, he seized a rifle with which he shot dead a prison officer George Henry Hodson. The media gave extensive coverage to the manhunt. Both fugitives were at large for seventeen days. Reports of their activities caused widespread anxiety, particularly after they robbed a bank at Ormond on 23 December and Walker killed an associate Arthur James Henderson at Albert Park on Christmas Day.

Ryan and Walker were captured in Sydney on 5 January 1966. Brought before the Supreme Court of Victoria, they pleaded not guilty to a charge of murdering Hodson. On 30 March the jury convicted Walker of manslaughter; Ryan was found guilty of murder and sentenced to death. Appeals to the Full Court (June) and the High Court of Australia (October) were rejected. On 12 December 1966 Sir Henry Bolte's Liberal Party government declined to commute Ryan's sentence. The decision sparked large-scale opposition. After an appeal to the Privy Council failed in January 1967, the execution was delayed by a last-minute legal application involving supposedly new evidence. Ryan was hanged at 8 a.m. on 3 February 1967 in Pentridge gaol. Calm and composed on the scaffold, he addressed his last words to the hangman, possibly recalling the injunction of Jesus to Judas before the betrayal: 'God bless you. Whatever you do, do it quickly'. He was buried with Catholic rites in an unmarked grave in the grounds of Pentridge gaol. His three daughters survived him.

Slightly built and 5 ft 8 ins (173 cm) tall, Ryan was a stylish—if 'spivvy'—dresser, who usually wore an expensive, well-cut suit, a silk tie and a fedora. He was always keen to impress as a man of means and consequence. Towards the end of his life he wanted to be known as the 'leading criminal' in the country. He is remembered as the last person to be judicially executed in Australia.

P. Tennison, *Defence Counsel* (Melb, 1975); T. Prior, *A Knockabout Priest* (Melb, 1985); P. Blazey, *Bolte, a Political Biography* (Melb, 1990); B. Dickins, *Remember Ronald Ryan* (Syd, 1994) and *Guts and Pity* (Syd, 1996); M. Richards, *The Hanged Man* (Melb, 2002); *J of Aust Studies*, 33, 1992, p 19; *UTS Review*, 5, no 2, 1999, p 1; family information.

MIKE RICHARDS

RYAN, RUPERT SUMNER (1884-1952), soldier, pastoralist and politician, was born on 6 May 1884 in Melbourne, elder child of Victorian-born parents (Sir) Charles Snodgrass Ryan [q.v.11], surgeon, and his wife Alice Elfrida, née Sumner. His sister Ethel Marian Sumner ('Maie') was to marry R. G. (Baron) Casey [q.v.13]. Rupert attended Geelong Church of England Grammar School in 1895-98, then completed his education in England, at Harrow School, and the Royal Military Academy, Woolwich, where he graduated with the sword of honour.

Commissioned in the Royal Artillery on 21 December 1904, Ryan was serving in England with 'T' Battery, Royal Horse Artillery, when World War I began. In December his unit joined the 7th Division on the Western Front. Ryan was transferred to divisional headquarters in April 1915 and wounded in the battle of Festubert in the following month. He served on the staffs of the XIII Corps (1915-16), Reserve (Fifth) Army (1916), Cavalry Corps (1916-17) and First Army (1917-20), rising from captain (October 1914) to brevet lieutenant colonel (June 1919). Six times mentioned in dispatches, he was awarded the Distinguished Service Order (1918) and three foreign honours.

In 1919 Ryan was appointed chief of staff to the military governor of Cologne in occupied Germany. On 10 January 1920 he was transferred to the headquarters of the Inter-Allied Rhineland High Commission at Coblenz. At the British consulate on 29 May 1924 he married (Lady) Rosemary Constance Ferelith, the 20-year-old daughter of the high commissioner Victor Alexander Hay, Lord Kilmarnock (Earl of Erroll), whom he served as deputy. In 1928 Ryan was appointed C.M.G. Following Kilmarnock's death in February, he acted as high commissioner until the occupation ended. He retired from the army in 1929 and joined Vickers Ltd as an arms salesman; he was probably also an intelligence-gathering agent for the British government. His flair for languages, easy manner and artillery expertise made him a capable representative of Vickers in Moscow (1930), Bangkok (1932-33) and other places, but, discouraged by his lack of success in Siam (Thailand), he resigned in 1934.

After his marriage ended in divorce in 1935, Ryan returned to Victoria where, with Maie, he had inherited a thousand-acre (405 ha) property, Edrington, at Berwick, south-east of Melbourne. While the Caseys remained in Canberra, Rupert and Patrick, his only child, settled at Edrington and built it into one of the largest Romney Marsh studs in the State. He also raised fat lambs, fattened cattle, experimented with pastoral improvement and pioneered the growing of flax in Victoria. With his sister and brother-in-law he learned to fly, and in 1939 built a landing strip on the property.

In World War II Ryan joined the Australian Military Forces and held administrative posts at Army Headquarters, Melbourne, until September 1940, when he stood as the United Australia Party candidate and won the seat of Flinders in the House of Representatives, succeeding J. V. Fairbairn [q.v.8]. He served on the joint committees on social security (1941-46) and foreign affairs (chairman 1952). His parliamentary career was unspectacular, but he won the affection of politicians on both sides for his kindliness and tolerance, and their respect for his knowledge of world affairs. Dame Enid Lyons saw him as 'a doughty champion of women'.

Described by Maie as short, compact and powerful, Ryan rode, fished for trout and continued to fly. With his clipped English accent, Springer spaniels, tweeds and pipe, he was the epitome of the country squire at Edrington, which he shared intermittently with the Caseys. A female journalist and friend admired his 'gay gallantry'. He died suddenly of cardiac failure on the night of 25 August 1952 at his home and was cremated. His son survived him. (Sir) John Longstaff's [q.v.10] portrait (1898) of Ryan is held by the family.

M. Casey, *Tides and Eddies* (Lond, 1966); E. Lyons, *Among the Carrion Crows* (Adel, 1972); D. Langmore, *Glittering Surfaces* (Syd, 1997); *PD* (Cwlth), 26 Aug 1952, p 604, 10 Sept 1952, p 1161; *Corian*, Aug 1952, p 136; *Dandenong J*, 31 July 1946; *The Times, Age* (Melb) and *Sun News-Pictorial*, 27 Aug 1952; Maie Casey papers (NL); information from Mrs J. Macgowan, Darlinghurst, Syd, and Mr R. Davenport-Hines, Lond.   DIANE LANGMORE

RYAN, VICTOR HERBERT (1874–1956), public servant, was born on 10 January 1874 at Paratoo, near Peterborough, South Australia, son of Denis Landers Ryan, an Irish-born boundary rider, and his wife Emma, née Davey. Educated at state schools at Burra and Terowie, Victor worked in a shop at Terowie from the age of 14 before joining the South Australian Railways in 1890 as a junior porter. At the Methodist Church, Terowie, on 17 April 1901 he married Nina Annie Hewett (d.1945). The young couple moved to Adelaide, where he was employed as a ticket clerk at Victoria Square. He became an active member of the St John's Young Men's Literary Society, proved a skilled debater, and was elected to the 'parliament' of the South Australian Literary Societies' Union.

In 1908 Ryan obtained the post of agent at the new Tourist Bureau. Three years later he was appointed director of the combined Intelligence and Tourist Bureau. He provided the agent-general in London with promotional material, such as *South Australia* (1911-13 and 1922), a handbook of information for settlers and tourists and also planned itineraries for dignitaries who visited South Australia. In 1914 he and (Sir) David Gordon [q.v.9] edited the *Handbook of South Australia* for the Adelaide meeting of the British Association for the Advancement of Science.

Under the direction of the State War Council, the bureau was responsible (from 1915) for a wide range of activities, including patriotic appeals, recruitment, and the provision of training and employment for returned servicemen. As secretary of the council in 1916, Ryan dispatched a train loaded with soldiers, a brass band and the premier, Crawford Vaughan [q.v.12], to tour the State, using railway stations as recruiting depots. He oversaw Adelaide's peace celebrations in 1919, which culminated in a military pageant, sporting events, church services and fireworks. In the following year he served on the committee that organized the visit of the Prince of Wales and was appointed O.B.E.

Immigration had been added to Ryan's responsibilities in 1917. He supervised a scheme, launched in 1922 by Sir Henry Barwell [q.v.7], through which youths aged between 15 and 18 were brought from Britain and indentured to South Australian farmers. Responsible for their reception, employment and general welfare, he regularly corresponded with hundreds of 'Barwell Boys' and their parents, and was known as 'Daddy Ryan'. In 1923 he was appointed executive-officer of the Commonwealth-State committee which planned Australia's contribution to the British Empire Exhibition, held (1924-25) at Wembley, London. The Returned Sailors' and Soldiers' Imperial League of Australia protested on the ground that Ryan was not a former serviceman, but he retained the position and toured the country collecting exhibits for the Australian pavilion.

In 1936 Ryan helped to organize South Australia's centenary celebrations and commissioned Frank Hurley [q.v.9] to make a film about the State. A Freemason and a Rotarian, he often officiated at dinners as a master of ceremonies. In 1939 he retired. He died on 24 June 1956 at Unley Park and was buried in Cheltenham cemetery; three of his four daughters and one of his two sons survived him.

Report of the Select Committee of the Legislative Council on the Boy-Migrant Scheme and Nomination Schemes of Immigration, *PP* (SA), 1924; *Aust Lib J*, July 1962, p 145; *Mail* (Adel), 1 Feb 1913; *Advertiser* (Adel), 25 June 1956; Col Sec letters, GRG 24/6/1923/378 (SRSA). KATHRYN GARGETT

RYDER, JOHN (1889-1977), cricketer, was born on 8 August 1889 at Collingwood, Melbourne, fifth child of Henry John Ryder, a Scottish-born carpenter, and his wife Ellen, née Whiteley, who came from England. Educated at Lithgow Street (Abbotsford) State School, Jack started work at the age of 14, apprenticed to a bootmaker in Thomas Davies' firm at Fitzroy; he progressed to storeman and salesman, and later to senior representative of another footwear manufacturer, Whybrow & Co. Pty Ltd of Abbotsford. On 17 June 1916 at the Cairns [q.v.3] Memorial Church, East Melbourne, he married with Presbyterian forms Fanny Douglas Smith, a tailoress. He lost his job during the Depression and was employed intermittently until World War II when—on (Sir) Robert Menzies' [q.v.15] recommendation—he became an inspector of boots. Subsequently, he was a stores clerk with Australian Motor Industries Co., Hawthorn.

In 1906 Ryder had begun playing for Collingwood Cricket Club in the new district competition. About 6 ft 2 ins (188 cm) tall and strongly built, he was a hard-hitting batsman and a handy medium-to-fast bowler. He made his début as a first-class player in 1912. In eighty games for Victoria, he scored 5674 runs at an average of 45.75 and took 150 wickets at 29.69 runs apiece. His most notable display of powerful hitting—295 runs in 245 minutes—occurred on 28 December 1926 in a match against New South Wales, played in Melbourne.

After being selected for the Australian XI in 1920, Ryder played in the five Tests against the visiting Englishmen in 1920-21, but contributed little to his country's victory in the series. Although he toured England in 1921, the selectors overlooked him for the Tests. That year he performed well for Australia in three games against South Africa. After missing—because of injury—the first two Tests in the 1924-25 series against England in Australia, he was chosen for the third, in Adelaide. Coming to the crease in the first innings when his side was 5 for 118, he scored 201 not out. In the second innings he was again top scorer (with 88), ensuring an Australian victory by just eleven runs.

Ryder was a member of the selection panel for the 1926 series in England. He played in the first four Tests, all of which were drawn, but was omitted from the fifth, in which Australia lost the Ashes. Deposed as a selector, he was surprisingly named captain for the 1928 29 home series against England, even though he was not captain of Victoria. The Australians were outclassed in the first two Tests, competitive in the next two, and victorious in the fifth. In that series Ryder played his finest cricket, scoring 492 runs (the highest aggregate by an Australian) and averaging 54.66. As captain, he gained the admiration of his teammates and turned a badly beaten side into one that verged on greatness.

Appointed a selector for the 1930 tour of England, Ryder was omitted from the team by the votes of his colleagues R. L. Jones and C. E. Dolling, probably because of his age. The decision caused an outcry, throughout which Ryder behaved with dignity. It was the end of his Test career: in twenty matches he had made 1394 runs at an average of 51.63, and taken 17 wickets (at 43.7) and 17 catches. He played for Victoria until 1932 and was a State selector in 1931-70. The figures for his first-class career (177 games) were 10 499 runs (average 44.29), 238 wickets (average 29.68) and 132 catches. Apart from two short breaks, he was a member of Collingwood's first XI until 1943. His performances earned him the epithet, 'The King of Collingwood'—a remarkable honour for one who was a cricketer (rather than a footballer) and a Methodist (rather than a Catholic). He remained on the club committee until his death. In 1930 a grandstand at Victoria Park was named after him.

In 1946-70 Ryder served as a Test selector. A number of his decisions were controversial. Sometimes—as with the selection of W. M. (Bill) Lawry for the 1961 tour of England— Ryder was triumphantly vindicated. On other occasions there were suggestions that his enthusiasm for new talent seemed prone to error, especially when the untried youth happened to be a Victorian. He was appointed M.B.E. in 1958. The Victorian Cricket Association instituted the Jack Ryder medal in 1973 to be awarded annually to the best district cricketer. Widely respected, Ryder was abstemious without being puritanical, and 'a father figure to several generations of cricketers'. He led the parade of former Australian Test players at the England-Australia Centenary Match in Melbourne in March 1977. Survived by his wife, daughter and son, he died on 3 April that year at Fitzroy and was cremated.

R. Coleman, *Seasons in the Sun* (Melb, 1993); C. Harte, *A History of Australian Cricket* (Lond, 1993); M. Fiddian, *A Life-Long Innings* (Pakenham, Vic, 1995).   JIM YOUNG

RYDGE, SIR NORMAN BEDE (1900-1980), businessman, was born on 18 October 1900 in Sydney, second son of William Henry Rydge, a native-born blacksmith, and his wife Margaret, née McSweeney, who came from Ireland. Educated at Woollahra Superior Public School and (on a bursary) at Fort Street Boys' High School, Norman joined the Chief Secretary's Department as a clerk in the Master in Lunacy's Office on 16 February 1916 and studied accountancy during his free time. He left the public service within two years. In 1921 he published a book on Federal income tax, the first of several manuals on tax and one on the Sydney Stock Exchange. Having qualified in 1921, he set up in practice as an accountant; by 1924 he was an associate of the Commonwealth Institute of Accountants. At St Vincent's Catholic Church, Ashfield, on 3 July 1926 he married Alys Noad, a 19-year-old musician; they were to have two sons. He was mayor of Canterbury in 1926.

Rydge had taken over the Carlton Hotel, Castlereagh Street, in 1925. Subsequently he acquired a controlling interest in, and chairmanship of, Usher's Metropolitan Hotel Ltd, the Pacific Hotel (Manly Hotels Ltd), and Mockbell's Ltd, coffee-house proprietors and caterers. In 1936 he bought 150 000 shares in the Menzies Hotel, Melbourne, and became managing director. He also acquired a substantial shareholding in Cash Orders (Amalgamated) Ltd (Waltons Ltd from 1959), of which he was chairman (1930-61). In the mid-1930s he was a director of Waldas Shoes Ltd.

His increasing interest in the stock market had led him to launch and edit *Rydge's Business Journal* in 1928 as a source of stock-exchange advice and financial comment. Its monthly editorials were signed 'Norman Rydge' until 1969. In the 1930s Rydge became the leading individual 'player' on the stock market through Carlton Investments Ltd (founded 1928). The company took over Manly Hotels Ltd in 1936. For decades Carlton Investments paid dividends only in the form of bonus share issues. This reinvestment enabled the firm to buy new issues of shares to which it was entitled. More important, in the absence of a capital gains tax, the holder of the bonus shares was able to dispose of them without incurring a tax liability.

In 1936, following a shareholders' revolt led by J. I. Armstrong [q.v.13], Rydge was persuaded by Bernard Curran, his stockbroker and a close friend, to buy a controlling interest in six loss-making cinema operators; he was elected chairman and managing director of the Greater J. D. Williams Amusement Co. Ltd and of Greater Union Theatres Ltd. Within three years Greater Union made a profit, and the box office boomed during World War II. On behalf of Greater Union Theatres Ltd, Rydge established 'a close working relationship' in 1945 with J. Arthur Rank. The development of Greater Union's chain of profitable cinemas led to the creation of subsidiary companies which distributed British, American and Continental films, sold cinema equipment, made and processed television, newsreel and commercial films, and marketed photographic equipment. In 1958 the cinema-operating companies were merged in Amalgamated Holdings Ltd and in 1965 Greater Union Organisation Pty Ltd was set up. Rydge retired as chairman in 1970, but returned in that capacity in 1977.

From 1945 Rydge had begun to dispose of his hotel assets, retaining only the Carlton Hotel (until the early 1970s). Oddly, perhaps, he never extended his publishing beyond *Rydge's* magazine (which his eldest son took over in 1955). With rare exceptions, Rydge avoided diversification. Even with the core cinema business, expansion into other areas of entertainment was notably limited. G.U.O. established only one bowling alley, and that in response to pressure from its partner, the Rank Organisation. Rydge maintained control of Waltons until 1961 when he resigned as chairman because of disagreements with John Walton. He was a commissioner (1961-75) of the Rural Bank of New South Wales and, in the mid-1960s, a director of the Australia Hotel Ltd and City Mutual Life Insurance Society Ltd.

After divorcing his wife in October 1939, Rydge married a 28-year-old nurse, Vincent Lillian Colefax, on 28 December that year at the district registrar's office, Paddington. The marriage ended in tragedy. In October 1949 the coroner found that, in the previous month, she had murdered her 5-year-old son and that she had 'died of poisoning by carbon monoxide, wilfully administered by herself'. On 13 November 1950 at the district registrar's office, Marrickville, Rydge married Phoebe Caroline McEwing, a 39-year-old secretary.

In 1940 Rydge had unsuccessfully contested the House of Representatives seat of Parramatta (for a United Australia Party faction) against Sir Frederick Stewart [q.v.12], the sitting U.A.P. member. Although he joined the Liberal Party, as a businessman he cultivated both sides in politics. For (Sir) Robert Askin's government, Rydge served on an inquiry (1968-69) into establishing an education commission and on another (1971) into the emoluments of senior public servants and politicians. For Neville Wran's government, he chaired (1979) a committee to assess nine applicants for the original Lotto licence.

Appointed C.B.E. in 1955 and knighted in 1966, Sir Norman was president (from 1969) of the trustees of the Museum of Applied Arts and Sciences, and a life governor of the Australian Institute of Management, Royal Prince Alfred Hospital, and the Royal Children's and Alfred hospitals, Melbourne. He belonged to the Australian Golf, American National and Tattersall's clubs; his recreations, when he found time for them, were golf, motorboating, and gardening at his Vaucluse home. In 1961 he moved to Point Piper. He died there on 14 May 1980 and was cremated; his wife and their son survived him, as did the two sons of his first marriage.

T. O'Brien, *The Greater Union Story 1910-1985* (Syd, 1985); *Rydge's*, June 1980; *Kino*, 14, 1985; *SMH*, 29 Feb, 5 May 1936, 21 Nov 1945, 30 Sept 1948, 9 June 1955, 1 Jan 1966, 12 Aug 1967, 6 Feb 1969, 26 Aug 1971, 11 Apr, 15 Aug 1979; *Herald* (Melb), 22 Oct 1948; *Daily Telegraph* (Syd), 8 May 1960; *Financial Review*, 17 July 1979; *Sun-Herald* (Syd), 22 July 1979.   JOHN PERKINS

RYLAH, SIR ARTHUR GORDON (1909-1974), politician and solicitor, was born on 3 October 1909 at Kew, Melbourne, son of Walter Robert Rylah, a Victorian-born solicitor, and his wife Helen Isabel, née Webb, who came from New Zealand. Arthur was educated at Trinity Grammar School and the University of Melbourne (B.A., 1931; LL.B., 1932). Admitted to practice as a barrister and solicitor on 2 May 1934, he joined the family firm of Rylah & Anderson (later Rylah & Rylah). At Holy Trinity Church, Kew, on 10 September 1937 he married with Anglican rites Ann Flora Froude Flashman, a veterinary surgeon.

In 1931 Rylah had been commissioned in the Militia. On 1 May 1940 he was appointed temporary major (substantive in November), Australian Imperial Force. Posted to the 2nd/14th Field Regiment, Royal Australian Artillery, he served in the Northern Territory (July 1941-January 1943), in New Guinea (November 1943-December 1944) and on New Britain (December 1944-December 1945). He was mentioned in dispatches. After his A.I.F. appointment terminated in Melbourne on 30 January 1946, he returned to the law and joined the newly formed Liberal Party. When (Sir) Wilfrid Kent Hughes [q.v.15] transferred to Federal parliament in 1949, Rylah won a hard-fought pre-selection ballot for the seat of Kew in the Legislative Assembly; the strong field included (Sir) Rupert Hamer and (Sir) John Rossiter. He was elected to parliament on 13 May 1950.

Rylah's colleagues quickly recognized his talents. In 1951 he topped the ballot for deputy-leader of the parliamentary Liberal and Country Party. He was denied the position due to a party rule which required the deputy to be a rural member if the leader—at that time Les Norman, a Melbourne businessman—held an urban or suburban seat. The young (Sir) Henry Bolte received the post. Norman lost his seat in 1952. When Trevor Oldham [q.v.15], the new leader of the L.C.P., was killed in a plane crash in 1953, (Sir) Arthur Warner [q.v.] employed all his considerable political skills and influence to ensure that Bolte gained the leadership over Rylah, who became his deputy.

The split in the Australian Labor Party in 1955 destroyed the government of John Cain [q.v.13]. On 7 June Rylah was appointed deputy-premier, chief secretary and government leader in the Legislative Assembly. Next day he was also appointed attorney-general. Over the ensuing years he rose to all these challenges and became the government's most active and successful minister. While a back-bencher, he had served (1950-55) on the Statute Law Revision Committee. As attorney-general (until 9 May 1967), he used this body to initiate wide-ranging reform of the State's laws.

A 'human dynamo', Rylah had a prodigious capacity for work. In 1958 he completed a consolidation of all Victoria's statutes, and was justifiably proud of his companies bill (passed that year) which served as a model for other Australian and foreign jurisdictions. The Chief Secretary's Department administered a wide range of activities. Rylah introduced legal off-course betting (1960), allowed picture theatres to open on Sundays (1964), reformed Victoria's outmoded liquor laws (1965) and liberalized restrictions on Sunday sport (1967). Road safety was of particular concern to him. He prepared legislation to make the wearing of seat-belts compulsory (1970) and to provide for random breath-testing of motorists (1971). The National Motor Vehicle Safety Council of the United States of America presented him with an 'Excalibur' award (1973) for his achievements.

Rylah gave whole-hearted support and loyalty to the premier, Bolte, who confidently left the administrative details of government to his deputy. 'A humane and liberal man', Rylah was a genuine social reformer. Yet, at times, he adopted a reactionary stance. His attitudes to censorship were regarded by many as repressive, and his remark in 1964 that he would not allow his 'teenage daughter' to read Mary McCarthy's novel, *The Group* (London, 1963), became notorious. His commitment to penal reform was compromised in 1967 when he supported the hanging of Ronald Ryan [q.v.]. He was appointed C.M.G. in 1965 and K.B.E. in 1968.

The last years of Rylah's political career were dogged by controversy. In 1967-68 he was criticized in parliament for joining the boards of Easywear (Australia) Pty Ltd and Avis Rent-A-Car System Pty Ltd. Although Bolte vigorously defended him, Rylah resigned from the boards. Separating from his wife in 1968, he moved to his property, Laurieton, at Mount Macedon. On 15 March 1969 Lady Rylah, a prominent member of her profession, was discovered lying in the backyard of her home at Kew. An autopsy found that she had died of subarachnoid haemorrhage. The coroner ordered that her body should be cremated without an inquest, a decision which attracted unfavourable comment in the press. On 9 October that year at the Scots Kirk, Mosman, Sydney, Rylah married Norma Alison ('Ruth') Reiner, née French, a 43-year-old secretary and a divorcee.

In the late 1960s Dr Bertram Wainer began a campaign to reform Victoria's anti-abortion laws, which he claimed promoted misery, graft and corruption. Rylah refused him an audience. Bolte and Rylah were reluctant to antagonize the Catholic-dominated Democratic Labor Party, but came under increasing pressure from the media and the Liberal Party's State council to review the matter. Finally, in January 1970, the government appointed William Kaye, Q.C., to inquire into Wainer's allegations. His report that year led to the prosecution of a number of police officers. The East Kew branch of the Liberal Party showed its dissatisfaction with Rylah's handling of the abortion controversy by challenging (unsuccessfully) his endorsement for the next election.

After announcing on 2 February 1971 that he intended to resign from parliament in the following month, Sir Arthur collapsed at his desk on 5 March and spent the next four months in hospital. He retired to Mount Macedon, pursued his interest in horse-racing, and became a director of several companies. Survived by his wife, and by the daughter and son of his first marriage, he died of a cerebral thrombosis on 20 September 1974 at St Vincent's Private Hospital, Fitzroy. He was accorded a state funeral and was cremated with Anglican rites.

B. Wainer, *It Isn't Nice* (Syd, 1972); B. Muir, *Bolte from Bamganie* (Melb, 1973); *Nation* (Syd), 21 Feb 1970; *Age* (Melb), 17 Mar 1969, 24 Feb 1970, 21 Sept 1974; *Sun News-Pictorial*, 3 Feb 1971, 24 Sept 1974; *Herald* (Melb), 5 Mar 1971, 9 June 1972; *Sunday Observer*, 26 Aug 1973.   B. J. COSTAR

RYLAND, JOHN PETER (1911-1973), pilot and airline administrator, was born on 26 July 1911 at Hawthorn, Melbourne, son of Victorian-born parents Ernest Augustus Ryland, farmer, and his wife Flavie Jeanne, née Borelli. Jack attended Murraydale State School and Xavier College, Melbourne, where he was school captain (1929), and captain of Australian Rules football and boats. After studying at the University of Melbourne (B.Ag.Sc., 1935), he became a research officer in the Victorian Department of Agriculture.

In December 1933 Ryland had enlisted in the citizen component of the Royal Australian Air Force as an air cadet. Gaining his wings, he was commissioned on 1 July 1934. He joined the newly formed Ansett Airways Pty Ltd in 1937 and was soon promoted captain. In July 1938 he was placed on the Air Force Reserve as a flying officer.

Called up for active service as a flight lieutenant on 23 October 1939, Ryland was promoted squadron leader in July 1941. On 10 December he led a detachment of No.13 Squadron to an advanced operational base at Namlea, Buru Island, Netherlands East

Indies. That day the unit's commanding officer was killed in a crash at Laha, Ambon Island, and Ryland was transferred there to replace him. He and his men flew Hudson bombers on raids against the Japanese. For his inspiration, devotion to duty and 'courage and determination in the face of heavy odds', he was awarded the Distinguished Flying Cross (1942).

Ryland was appointed chief instructor at No.1 Operational Training Unit, East Sale, Victoria, in June 1942 and promoted wing commander on 1 October. In January-May 1943 he accompanied (Sir) Daniel McVey [q.v.15] to the United States of America and Britain to determine the types of aircraft that could be manufactured in Australia. On his return in June, he resumed his post at Sale and became the unit's commanding officer in July. Promoted group captain in April 1944, he was posted to No.79 (Bomber) Wing in Darwin in December and led it on operations over Borneo.

On 18 December 1945 Ryland was demobilized from the R.A.A.F. He returned to Ansett Airways as manager of its airline division. In June 1946 he was selected by L. J. Brain [q.v.13] to run a special training school at the R.A.A.F. Station, Point Cook, Victoria, for air and engineering crews of the newly created Trans-Australia Airlines. Succeeding Brain as T.A.A.'s operational manager next month, he rose to assistant general manager later that year and general manager in 1955. At St James's Catholic Church, Gardenvale, on 20 July 1949 he had married June Robinson.

The period in which Ryland was in charge of T.A.A. saw significant developments in civil aviation. He supervised the introduction of pressurized airliners, and turbo-propeller and jet aircraft. Five ft 8 ins (173 cm) tall, rugged in physique and sound in judgement, he proved an excellent administrator. T.A.A.'s outstanding safety record under his management won him acclaim. He was appointed C.B.E. in 1960 and to the Order of Merit of the Republic of Italy in 1969. Survived by his wife, and their son and two daughters, he died of myocardial infarction on 20 October 1973 in his home at Malvern and was buried in Templestowe cemetery.

D. Gillison, *Royal Australian Air Force 1939-1942* (Canb, 1962); I. Sabey, *Challenge in the Skies* (Melb, 1979); *Age* (Melb), 22 June 1946; *Argus*, 17 July 1946; *Herald* (Melb), 25 Mar 1959; *Australian*, 22 Oct 1973; Ryland papers, MS 5020 (NL); A1838/394, item 1535/18/119 (NAA, Canb); information from Mrs J. Ryland, Armadale, and Mr J. L. Watkins, South Melb, Vic; personal knowledge.

RICHARD KINGSLAND

RYMER, GEORGE WALTER (1889-1976), railwayman and trade-union leader, was born on 28 January 1889 at Chesterfield, Derbyshire, England, son of Arthur Rymer, passenger-train examiner, and his wife Emma, née Sadler. After leaving school and serving an apprenticeship to a wagon-builder, George was employed by the Midland Railway Co. He became a carriage inspector at Reading (with the Birmingham Railway Carriage & Wagon Co.) and secretary of the local branch of a wagon-builders' union. Joining the British Army, he served for five years in all, with the Berkshire Royal Horse Artillery and Worcester Royal Field Artillery, Territorial Force. On 28 December 1912 at the Countess of Huntingdon's Free Church, Worcester, he married Jessie Bird, a blouse-maker. The young couple migrated to Queensland in 1914.

Employed at the railway workshops, Townsville, Rymer was dismissed when the men went on strike in April that year. Six months later he was reinstated. He was active in the local branch of the Queensland Railway Union and was northern district secretary by 1917. The Q.R.U. was a militant union imbued with a syndicalist ideology. It advocated direct action rather than the gradual approach of industrial conciliation and arbitration favoured by the Australian Labor Party.

The northern railwaymen staged a three-week strike in August 1917 over a retrospective pay issue. As chairman of the northern combined unions' strike committee, Rymer rose to prominence during this dispute. Following threats of dismissal from the Labor premier T. J. Ryan [q.v.11], the men returned to work. The government's response to the dispute laid the foundation for future confrontation. Two years later the Q.R.U. supported meat-workers at Townsville in their challenge to the arbitration process. On 28 June 1919 a bloody encounter occurred between police and unionists. When Rymer and the northern officials organized a black ban to prevent police reinforcements from reaching Townsville, senior railway staff crewed the train.

In 1920 the Q.R.U. amalgamated with its interstate counterparts to form the Australian Railways Union. Rymer transferred to Brisbane as assistant to Tim Moroney [q.v.10], the union's State secretary. Next year he was raised to the full-time paid post of A.R.U. State president and appointed editor of the union's journal, the *Advocate*. That journal provided him with a vehicle for promoting the A.R.U.'s militant philosophy and for criticizing the A.L.P.'s policies. After visiting Russia in 1923, he reported favourably in the *Advocate* on Russian efforts to build a socialist society.

As the union's delegate to the A.L.P.'s State central executive (1920-23) and to the 1923 Labor-in-Politics convention, Rymer maintained a 'war of words' against E. G. Theodore's [q.v.12] administration, especially after it reduced the basic wage in Queensland by

5 per cent in 1922. Following an A.R.U.-led railway strike, the Gillies [q.v.9] government succumbed to the union's pressure and passed legislation in 1925 restoring the wage to its previous level. The new premier, William McCormack [q.v.10], took a strong stand against the A.R.U. and successfully excluded its delegates—including Rymer—from the 1926 A.L.P. convention because they refused to sign an anti-communist pledge. In 1927 the A.R.U. was further isolated when McCormack reacted to a State-wide railway strike by dismissing all railway employees.

Rymer increased his attacks on the McCormack government, which was defeated at the 1929 election. None the less, dissension within the union over its loss of members, as well as a reorganization due to financial stringencies, drew greater attention to Rymer's role as president. In 1930, at a State council meeting, central district delegates led by Frank Nolan [q.v.15] succeeded in their push for Rymer's removal.

Taking no further part in union affairs, Rymer established a radio retailing business in 1932 in Brisbane—Rymola Radio Co. (later Rymola Radio & Electrical Co. Ltd)—which he ran until 1951. Despite his move to private enterprise, he retained a passion for his early socialist beliefs. He died on 1 July 1976 at his Sunnybank home and was cremated with Anglican rites; his wife, and their daughter and son survived him.

F. Nolan, *You Pass This Way Only Once* (Brisb, 1974); D. J. Murphy et al (eds), *Labor in Power* (Brisb, 1980); D. J. Murphy (ed), *The Big Strikes* (Brisb, 1983); *Advocate* (Brisb), 10 Dec 1923; *Labour Hist*, no 22, May 1972, p 13; Brisb Catholic Hist Soc, *Procs*, 2, 1990, p 52; A. Smith, George Rymer and Labour Politics 1917-1930 (B.A. Hons thesis, James Cook Univ, 1981); information from Prof K. H. Kennedy, Townsville, Qld.   TIM MORONEY

RYMILL, SHYLIE KATHARINE (1882-1959), Girl Guide commissioner, and HENRY WAY (1907-1971), Boy Scout commissioner, were mother and son. Shylie was born on 16 May 1882 at Strathalbyn, South Australia, youngest of four children and only daughter of William Archibald Sinclair Blue (d.1896), an English-born physician and surgeon, and his wife Katharine Gollan, née Gordon, who came from Scotland. In 1898 her mother married (Sir) Samuel Way [q.v.12]. Shylie may have attended schools at Strathalbyn, Semaphore and Hahndorf, country towns in which her father practised, before completing her education at Dryburgh House School, Hackney, Adelaide. A vivacious and beautiful débutante, she became a fun-loving member of society and a successful charity worker. On 18 September 1906 at Christ Church, North

Adelaide, she married with Anglican rites Herbert Lockett ('Cargie') Rymill (d.1951), a golf-course designer.

In 1913 Mrs Rymill won the South Australian women's golf championship. She was associate-captain (1915, 1923 and 1933-34) of the (Royal) Adelaide Golf Club and founding president (1925-30) of the South Australian Ladies' Golf Union. Ladies' captain (1924-28 and 1932) at Kooyonga Golf Club, she won its women's championship in 1925, 1927 and 1928. Her husband had helped to design and build new courses for the A.G.C. at Seaton (1906) and for the Kooyonga Golf Club at Lockleys (1923).

Mrs Rymill was president of the local committee of the Richmond company of the Girl Guides' Association of South Australia in 1927 and commissioner, Western Metropolitan Division, in 1931. As State commissioner from 1938 to 1950, she was involved in organizing the Girl Guides' Thrift Campaign, which raised almost £72 000 for charities during World War II. She was appointed O.B.E. in 1942. Six years later she was awarded the guiding movement's highest honour, the Silver Fish. A generous woman with a sense of humour, she continued to be involved in the Girl Guides' Association after 1950 as a life member of the State council. She died on 3 April 1959 at Thorngate and was buried in North Road cemetery, Nailsworth; her daughter and three sons survived her.

Her eldest son Henry was born on 9 October 1907 in North Adelaide and educated at the Collegiate School of St Peter. Its headmaster K. J. F. Bickersteth [q.v.7] reported that he had 'talents, but not those useful for school lessons'. Joining the Boy Scouts in 1922, Rymill was elected patrol leader of the 2nd St Peter's College troop. He attended the Imperial (1924) and 'Coming of Age' (1929) jamborees in England. In 1924 he began work as a clerk in the dispatch department of Holden's [q.v.9] Motor Body Builders Ltd; by 1935 he was production manager. At St Peter's College chapel on 26 September 1934 he married Alleyne Joan Downer (d.1942) with Anglican rites.

After serving as a Boy Scouts' Association commissioner (from 1930) and Rover commissioner (from 1932), Rymill was appointed South Australian chief commissioner of scouts in 1936. That year he was camp chief at the centenary 'corroboree', held at Belair National Park, Adelaide. While in England on business in 1943, he received the Boy Scouts' highest award, the Silver Wolf. In 1949 he was appointed C.B.E. A governor (1942-71) of St Peter's College and a council member (1950-71) of St Mark's College, University of Adelaide, he was also commodore (1950-54 and 1957-59) of the Royal South Australian Yacht Squadron. He married Barbara Murray

Randell on 22 September 1967 at the Church of the Epiphany, Crafers. In 1968 he was named South Australia's 'father of the year' for his dedication to scouting. He retired from General Motors-Holden's Pty Ltd in the following year.

Rymill collapsed at Leppington, New South Wales, while attending his ninth Australian Scout jamboree as chief commissioner, and died of myocardial infarction on 8 January 1971 at Liverpool District Hospital. Survived by his wife, and by the son and two daughters of his first marriage, he was buried in North Road cemetery, Nailsworth. His estate was sworn for probate at $183 823. A big, genial man, he was remembered for his wit and sense of fun, and for the launching of Rymill 'rockets' at special scouting occasions. The Rymill training centre for scout leaders, at Woodhouse, Stirling, was named (1973) after him.

V. M. Branson, *Kooyonga, 1923-1983* (Adel, 1983); M. Cudmore, *The Royal Adelaide Golf Club, 1892-1992* (Adel, 1992); *SA Scout Leader*, Jan/Feb 1971; *Advertiser* (Adel), 2 Apr 1936, 6 Apr 1959, 19 Aug 1968, 9 Jan 1971; *Sunday Mail* (Adel), 5 May 1974; Girl Guides' Assn of SA, *Annual Report*, 1927-59 (Mort L); St Peter's College Archives (Adel); information from Mr A. Aldous, Gilles Plains, Mr H. Rymill, Stirling, Adel, and Miss K. Rymill, Falmouth, Tas.   JOYCE GIBBERD

S

SAGE, ANNIE MORIAH (1895-1969), army matron-in-chief, was born on 17 August 1895 at Somerville, Victoria, fifth child of Edward Arthur Sage, butcher, and his wife Mary Anne, née Murray, both Victorian born. Educated at Somerville State School, Annie worked as an assistant in a grocer's shop before training at the Melbourne Hospital and studying mid-wifery at the Women's Hospital, Carlton. She was registered as a midwife in September 1924 and granted her nursing certificate in November 1926. After gaining a qualification in infant welfare from the Victorian Baby Health Centres Association, she obtained a diploma of public health from the Royal Sanitary Institute, London. Back home, she was employed (from 1933) in child health, lectur-ing at training colleges and technical schools, and broadcasting to mothers. In 1936 she became matron of the V.B.H.C.A.'s training school.

On 1 January 1940 Sage joined the Aus-tralian Army Nursing Service, Australian Imperial Force. In the following month she was posted as matron to the 2nd/2nd Aus-tralian General Hospital. She sailed for the Middle East in April 1940 and served at Gaza Ridge, Palestine, and at Kantara, Egypt. Made matron-in-chief, A.I.F. (Middle East), in May 1941, she was appointed (1942) a member of the Royal Red Cross for her exceptional administrative ability and 'gallant and distin-guished service'. Sage returned to Australia in May 1942 and was elevated to deputy matron-in-chief at Land Headquarters, Mel-bourne. Appointed matron-in-chief, Australian Military Forces, on 4 February 1943, she was promoted colonel on 23 March. She organ-ized the A.A.N.S. for duty in the South-West Pacific Area and oversaw the training scheme for the Australian Army Medical Women's Service.

Affectionately known as 'Sammie', Sage was 5 ft 5½ ins (166 cm) tall, with blue eyes, fair hair, plain features and a dignified bearing. She was a humane and gentle woman with a salty sense of humour. Following the release of twenty-four of the Australian nurses im-prisoned by the Japanese, she flew to Sumatra in September 1945 to assist with their repatri-ation, thereby realizing an ambition she had held since their capture. For her war service she was awarded the Florence Nightingale medal (1947) by the International Red Cross. She accompanied the A.M.F. contingent to London for the Victory March in June 1946. After her army appointment terminated on 23 January 1947, she became lady superinten-dent (matron) at the Women's Hospital, Mel-bourne. She also continued, part time, as matron-in-chief, Citizen Military Forces. In 1951 she was appointed C.B.E. Ill health forced her to retire in August 1952. Later that year she unsuccessfully sought Liberal Party pre-selection for the Federal seat of Flinders.

Sage was an active member of the Royal Victorian College of Nursing, the Nurses Board of Victoria, the Florence Nightingale Memorial Committee of Australia and the Centaur War Nurses Memorial Fund. Found-ing president (1949-50), treasurer (1950-52) and an honorary fellow (1967) of the College of Nursing, Australia, she helped to establish its War Nurses Memorial Centre in St Kilda Road, Melbourne.

In 1956 Sage became a partner in a grocery shop at Somerville which traded as Sage & Lewis. Maintaining an interest in military nursing, she was honorary colonel of the Royal Australian Army Nursing Corps in 1957-62. She died on or about 4 April 1969 at her Frankston home and was cremated with An-glican rites and full military honours. Part of her estate, sworn for probate at $73 643, was bequeathed to her six nieces and three nephews, to whom she was known as 'Aunty Fam'. In 1969 the College of Nursing estab-lished the Annie M. Sage scholarship.

A. S. Walker, *Medical Services of the R.A.N. and R.A.A.F.* (Canb, 1961); C. Kenny, *Captives* (Brisb, 1986); R. Goodman, *Our War Nurses* (Brisb, 1988); J. Bassett, *Guns and Brooches* (Melb, 1992); R. G. Smith, *In Pursuit of Nursing Excellence* (Melb, 1999); *Aust Women's Weekly*, 13 July 1946; *SMH*, 9 Sept 1952, 5 Feb 1956; A. M. Sage, diary, 1941 (AWM).

JANICE McCARTHY

SAINTHILL, LOUDON (1918-1969), artist and stage designer, was born on 9 January 1918 in Hobart, second of four children of Tasmanian-born parents Willoughby Aveland St Hill, a clerk who became a commission agent, and his wife Honora Matilda, née Horder. By 1920 the family was living in Mel-bourne, first at Toorak and then at East St Kilda. A delicate, nervous child, with a stam-mer that persisted into adulthood (except when talking to children), Loudon contrived to avoid much formal schooling, though he did attend Ripponlea State School for a while. He read widely, painted and drew, and found his way into theatres and concert halls, where he saw Pavlova, heard Melba [q.v.10], and absorbed performances of Ibsen and Chekhov.

In 1932-33 he studied drawing and general design at the Applied Art School, Working Men's College. At his father's insistence he worked as a designer for a sandblasting firm in South Melbourne. By 1935 Sainthill, as he thenceforward spelt his name, was living in a flat at 24 Collins Street and eking out a living by painting murals in a surrealist style reminiscent of Alcimboldo. About this time he met his lifelong partner Harry Karl Tatlock Miller (1913-1989)—a journalist and later an art critic and expert on paintings and antiques—whose connexions and organizing ability were to complement Sainthill's creative talents.

Sainthill's interest in theatre design was fired by the Australian tours (1936-37 and 1938-39) of Colonel de Basil's Ballets Russes de Monte Carlo. An exhibition of his paintings of the dancers and sets led to an invitation to return to London with the company. He and Miller left Sydney in May 1939. During the voyage he painted the dancers and choreographers. In London (Sir) Rex Nan Kivell [q.v.15] organized an exhibition of these studies at the Redfern Gallery, Bond Street, where Sainthill sold fifty of the fifty-two pictures on show. Late that year he and Miller returned to Australia in charge of a major exhibition of theatre and ballet designs, brought together under the auspices of the British Council. It opened in Sydney in February 1940.

In the next few months Sainthill designed the costumes for a performance of Giraudoux's *Amphitryon* at the Comedy Theatre, Melbourne (1941), and the sets for three of Kirsova's [q v 15] ballets, staged in mid-1941. On 4 March 1943 he enlisted in the Australian Army Medical Corps (Militia) and on 20 May joined the Australian Imperial Force. Posted (with Miller) to the hospital ship *Wanganella* in September, he served as a theatre orderly. He transferred to the Australian Army Education Service in November 1945.

After he was discharged from the army on 23 April 1946 in Sydney, Sainthill joined Miller. They lived at Merioola, Edgecliff, with a group of painters who included Alec Murray, Jocelyn Rickards, Justin O'Brien and Donald Friend. In October 1945 Sainthill contributed 'A History of Costume from 4000 B.C. to 1945 A.D.' to the third showing of Theatre Art in Sydney; his thirty-nine water-colours were bought by public subscription and presented to the National Art Gallery of New South Wales in 1946. He held one-man exhibitions at the Macquarie Galleries in April 1947 and July 1948, and—with Miller—produced books on the Australasian tours by the Ballet Rambert (1947-48) and the Old Vic Theatre Company (1948). In 1949 he and Miller sailed for England. Again in London, they rented a house at Belgravia with Rickards and Murray. They

later lived nearby at 8 Chester Street, with Miller's mother and sister Kath, and eventually acquired a country cottage at Ropley, Hampshire.

In 1950 (Sir) Robert Helpmann asked Sainthill to design the décor for the ballet *Ile des Sirènes*, which he and (Dame) Margot Fonteyn took on tour. Sainthill's work attracted the notice of the director Michael Benthall who commissioned him to design *The Tempest* at the Shakespeare Memorial Theatre, Stratford-on-Avon. As preparation he spent three months studying stagecraft with Michael Northen. *The Tempest* opened in May 1951 and was a huge success for Sainthill. His reputation with both critics and the public was firmly established by 1953 with his designs for Shaw's *The Apple Cart* at the Haymarket, London, and Wilde's *A Woman of No Importance* at the Savoy. Among his most brilliant works were the sets and costumes for Helpmann's production of Rimsky-Korsakov's opera *Le Coq d'Or* at the Royal Opera House, Covent Garden (1954), completed at short notice when Chagall withdrew from the commission. For the Old Vic Theatre he designed in 1955 the sets and costumes for *Othello*. In the next fourteen years he designed sets, costumes, or both for a further thirty-two productions, including five more at the Old Vic, pantomimes (*Cinderella*, 1958, *Aladdin*, 1959), films (for example, the interior sets for *Look Back in Anger*, 1959), musicals (among them *Expresso Bongo*, 1958, *Half a Sixpence*, 1963, and *Canterbury Tales*, 1967), and revues. His early designs were described as 'opulent', 'sumptuous' and 'exuberantly splendid', but he declined to be typecast, emphasizing instead that 'no matter how fantastic a figure or scene is, you must make it as believable as possible'. Miller acknowledged Sainthill's special 'quality of enchantment, mixed so often with a haunting sadness that was, in part, characteristic of both the artist and his work'.

Friends spoke of Sainthill's modesty and 'self-contained serenity'. Photographs of him project a sombre and contemplative languor that belied his ability to work prodigious hours against production deadlines. Well built and notably handsome, he dressed suavely, with a penchant for waistcoats of rich silks, brocades and velvets.

Sainthill collaborated with Miller in producing three more books: *Royal Album* (1951), *Undoubted Queen* (1958) and *Churchill* (1959). In the mid-1960s he was a visiting teacher of stage design at the Central School of Arts and Crafts, London. He died of myocardial infarction on 10 June 1969 at Westminster Hospital and was buried at Ropley. An exhibition of his paintings in London in 1973 helped to raise money for a scholarship (named after him) for young Australian designers to study abroad. His work is held in the National Gallery of

Australia, in a number of State and regional collections, and in the Victoria and Albert Museum, London.

H. T. Miller (ed), *Loudon Sainthill, with an Appreciation by Bryan Robertson* (Lond, 1973); C. France, *Merioola* (Syd, 1986); Melb International Festival of the Arts, *Loudon Sainthill* (Melb, 1991); *Home*, May 1940; *Aust National J*, Jan 1946; *People* (Syd), 30 Jan 1952; *Aust Women's Weekly*, 14 Jan 1959; *Theatregoer*, 2, nos 2-3, Dec 1961-Jan 1962; *SMH*, 30 Jan 1940, 6 Oct 1945, 27 Oct 1951, 12 June 1969, 30 Sept 1972; *Sun-Herald* (Syd), 6 Mar 1953; *The Times*, 16 Feb 1959, 11 June 1969; *Sunday Times* (Syd), 11 Dec 1960; *Aust Financial Review*, 29 Sept 1972; information from Mr A. and Mrs S. Murray, Belgravia, Lond, and Dr F. Tait, Tisbury, Wiltshire, Eng.

SALLY O'NEILL

SALISBURY, JOHN RONALD GEORGE (1921-1980), police officer, was born on 29 May 1921 at Caulfield, Melbourne, second of three children and only son of John Thomas Salisbury, a bootmaker from Sydney, and his Victorian-born wife Elizabeth Jane, née Newland. Ron was educated at Tyler Street State School, Preston, and Richmond Technical School. He began to study surveying, but changed to industrial chemistry and worked for a manufacturer of lacquer-finishes used in the shoe and leather industries.

After joining the Militia in March 1939, Salisbury was called up for full-time duty on 31 October 1941. He served with the artillery in Victoria, and with the artillery and engineers in Queensland. In October 1942 he transferred to the Australian Imperial Force. On 28 January 1943 he was discharged from the army to enable him to enlist next day in the Royal Australian Air Force. Having learned to fly in Australia, he undertook advanced and operational training in Canada and Britain respectively. At Pendref Chapel, Caernarvon, Wales, on 19 September 1945 he married with Congregational forms Winifred Williams, a telephone-operator. Promoted warrant officer pilot, he returned to Melbourne and was demobilized from the air force on 18 March 1946.

Fifteen days later Salisbury joined the Victoria Police Force as a recruit constable. His colleague and later chief commissioner S. I. Miller thought that he looked 'more like a benign schoolteacher or bank manager than a policeman'. Salisbury sported a moustache and, at 5 ft 9 ins (175 cm), seemed short for a policeman. Described as 'a thinker', he was dux of his training squad. He completed a range of operational duties, including a term with the scientific section (1946-47), service as a detective (from 1949) and an exchange posting with the South Australian Police Force (1951). In 1962-69 he was officer-in-charge, successively, of the Special Branch, Drug Bureau and Detective Training School. He was promoted inspector in 1969.

Colonel Sir Eric St Johnston arrived from England in 1970 to undertake a review of the administration and organization of the Victoria Police Force. Salisbury was one of the three staff officers who assisted him. Much of St Johnston's 217-page report drew on the ideas of Salisbury, who was subsequently made head of a new inspectorate and future-plans division to implement its recommendations. The restructuring which followed constituted a watershed in modernizing the police service. On 14 December 1977 Salisbury was promoted to deputy-commissioner, administration, a post in which he was able to effect further reform. His eccentricity and wry sense of humour belied an analytical and logical mind, and an incisive ability to manage organizational change.

Commended for outstanding service on numerous occasions, Salisbury was awarded the Queen's Police Medal in 1977. He never achieved his goal of retiring to a cottage in Wales and writing his memoirs: he died of a cardio-respiratory condition on 11 November 1980 in South Melbourne and was cremated with the forms of the Churches of Christ. His wife and their two daughters survived him.

E. St Johnston, *A Report on the Victoria Police Force* (Melb, 1971); R. Haldane, *The People's Force* (Melb, 1986); *Police Life*, Dec 1980; *Sun News-Pictorial*, 16 July 1946; information from Mr S. I. Miller and Ms G. Salisbury, Melb.

ROBERT HALDANE

SALKAUSKAS, HENRIKAS (1925-1979), artist and house-painter, was born on 6 May 1925 at Kaunas (Kovno), Lithuania, only child of Henrikas Salkauskas, army officer, and his wife Ona-Anna, née Sidzikauskas. His father and other patriots were taken away by the Russians in 1940 and never seen by the family again. It was not until 1958 that young Henrikas was informed that his father had died in the Vorkuto concentration camp, Siberia. He and his mother fled ahead of the advancing Russian army in 1944. They settled at Freiburg, West Germany. Henrikas studied at the university and at L'École des Arts et Métiers, specializing in the graphic arts; Ona-Anna graduated in medicine. On 31 May 1949 they reached Melbourne in the *Skaugum*. Henry, as he was known in Australia, worked under contract in a stone-quarry in Canberra for two years. He began to exhibit his linocut prints.

Moving to Sydney in 1951, Salkauskas lived at Kirribilli from 1954. In the mid-1950s he painted stations for the New South Wales Government Railways and Tramways. He worked as a house-painter for the rest of his life. In 1958 he was naturalized. A friend of many artists, he was a committee-member (from 1957) of the Sydney branch of the Contemporary Art Society of Australia and a founder (1961) of the Sydney Printmakers. He eagerly promoted printmaking and helped to organize exhibitions of graphic art, nationally and internationally. In 1960 he met the Lithuanian-born artist, Eva Kubbos. They worked together and showed in group exhibitions and competitions. Of his one-man exhibition at the Macquarie Galleries in June 1961, the *Sydney Morning Herald* critic commented: 'Salkauskas proves himself one of Sydney's best graphic artists'.

Salkauskas represented Australia in major international print exhibitions at São Paulo, Brazil (1960), Tokyo (1960 and 1962), South East Asia (1962) and Ljubljana, Yugoslavia (1963). Yet in 1965 he turned his attention to painting large water-colours in the abstract-impressionist style. He thought that most water-colourists were too cautious. His method was to place a large sheet of Stonehenge paper on the floor; then, using big brushes, sponges and rags, he manipulated the flow of the dense washes of blacks and greys across the paper until his eye was satisfied with the result. In 1963 he joined the Australian Watercolour Institute and proceeded to revitalize the medium.

The reasons why Salkauskas used blacks and greys extensively in his paintings were complex. They involved his anguish at what had happened to his father, the influence of the Lithuanian winter landscape with its sharp contrasts of black silhouettes against snow, and the Lithuanian graphic tradition of printing in black and white. Despite this restricted palette, his tonal paintings were full of vitality and often involved an expressive use of symbols.

In Australia, Salkauskas won over sixty art awards, among them the Perth prize (1963), the grand prize for the Mirror-Waratah Festival (1963), Sydney, and the Maude Vizard-Wholohan prize (Adelaide). The 'big, blond, amiable Lithuanian' never married. He died suddenly of myocardial ischaemia on 31 August 1979 at his Kirribilli home and was cremated. His work is represented in national, State and regional galleries in Australia. The Art Gallery of New South Wales held a retrospective exhibition in 1981 and established the Henry Salkauskas Contemporary Art purchase award.

V. Ratas (ed), *Eleven Lithuanian Artists in Australia* (Syd, 1967); G. Docking, 'Henry Salkauskas' in Art Gallery of NSW, *Henry Salkauskas, 1925-1979*, exhibition cat (Syd, 1981); *SMH*, 7 June 1956, 27 June 1961, 4 Mar 1964, 9 May 1967, 8 Sept 1979; *Daily Mirror* (Syd), 10 Oct 1963; *Herald* (Melb), 7 Mar 1971; *Courier-Mail*, 29 Oct 1971; H. de Berg, H. Salkauskas (taped interview, 1962, NL);

J. Gleeson, H. Salkauskas (taped interview, 1979, National Gallery of Aust); naturalization file, SP1122/1/0, item 57/64313 (NAA, Syd).

GIL DOCKING

SALTER, WILFRED EDWARD GRAHAM (1929-1963), economist, was born on 27 March 1929 at Cottesloe, Perth, eldest of three children of Western Australian-born parents Harold Peter Salter, health inspector, and his wife May, née Dunderdale, a piano teacher. Wilf was educated at Wesley College (1942-46) and at the University of Western Australia (B.A., 1952). He gained first-class honours in economics in 1953 and represented the university in Rugby Union football. At the district registrar's office, Perth, on 5 December 1952 he had married Moira Joan Burke, a welfare officer.

Awarded a Hackett [q.v.9] travelling studentship, Salter entered Clare College, Cambridge (Ph.D., 1956), and won the Stevenson prize in economics in 1954. The originality of his doctoral thesis on labour productivity in relation to technological change so impressed W. B. Reddaway, director of the department of applied economics, that he gave a seminar on Salter's work. A postdoctoral research fellowship at Johns Hopkins University, Baltimore, United States of America, for the academic year 1955-56 enabled Salter to add American data to his analysis.

Salter returned to Australia in September 1956 to take up a research fellowship in the department of economics, Research School of Social Sciences, Australian National University, Canberra. He delivered a paper at the 1958 congress of the Australian and New Zealand Association for the Advancement of Science and published two articles in the *Economic Record* (April and August 1959). The second of these articles, analysing price and expenditure effects, provided an incisive examination of the problems of achieving equilibrium between full employment and balance of payments in a small open economy. As a result of his investigation into capital and labour productivity in Australia's manufacturing industry, he was asked by R. J. L. Hawke, research officer for the Australian Council of Trade Unions, to appear before the Commonwealth Conciliation and Arbitration Commission as a witness in the 1959 basic wage case.

In 1960 Cambridge University Press published Salter's thesis as *Productivity and Technical Change*. M. M. Postan described it as 'one of the most elegant exercises . . . in the theory of investment and innovations to come out of post-war Britain'. Noting that 'behind productivity lie all the dynamic forces of economic life', Salter emphasized that an understanding of these forces was essential in interpreting data relating to productivity. The economics of the process by which new, durable capital equipment replaced older equipment formed a critical part of his analysis. In general, he stressed that understanding of economy-wide productivity trends required study of experience and behaviour at both the firm and industry levels. Another of his major conclusions cast doubt on the popular view of wage determination which held that real wages should rise with labour productivity. Instead, he found that 'industries with above-average increases in productivity have not received above-average increases in earnings'. Productivity gains were distributed to consumers through lower prices of products with high productivity growth.

In January 1960 Salter was appointed to the Commonwealth Public Service as an assistant-secretary in the cabinet division of the Prime Minister's Department. He took an active part in working out economic policies on almost every front; 'his performance deeply impressed the old Canberra hands, even when they disagreed with him'. Obtaining leave in July 1962, he joined Harvard University's development advisory service and was sent to West Pakistan as an economic adviser to the government. He died of heart disease on 10 November 1963 at Lahore; his wife, and their son and daughter survived him.

M. Postan, *Fact and Relevance* (Cambridge, Eng, 1971); *Economic Record*, Dec 1963; *Gazette of Univ WA*, 14, Mar 1964; *SMH*, 12 Nov 1963; Salter papers, held by Mrs C. Roncevich, Coogee, Perth.

JOHN PITCHFORD

SAMBELL, GEOFFREY TREMAYNE (1914-1980), Anglican archbishop, was born on 28 October 1914 at Broadford, Victoria, fourth of seven children of Edgar Shadforth Sambell, butcher, and his wife Barbara Katherine, née McPhee, both Victorian born. The family moved to Glen Iris and Geoff attended Melbourne High School. While working as a commercial traveller (1931-34) for R. H. Mytton & Co. Pty Ltd, a South Melbourne cutlery firm, he developed his organizing abilities, established a network of contacts with business people, and revealed the strong commitment to social justice that was to characterize his later career. The experience of attending Lord Somers' [q.v.12] Camp in 1932 led him to open a club for unemployed youths in South Melbourne.

Called to the Anglican priesthood, Sambell entered Ridley College in 1935, gained his licentiate (1939) from the Australian College of Theology and began studying at the University of Melbourne (B.A., 1947). He was

made deacon in 1940 and ordained priest on 9 February 1941. Following a term (1940-41) as curate at St John's, Malvern, he was appointed chaplain, Citizen Military Forces, on 8 January 1942. In August he transferred to the Australian Imperial Force. He served in New Guinea with the 57th-60th Battalion (1943-44) and the 2nd/11th Battalion (1944-45), performing the duties of canteen officer, arranging competitions and sporting events, and demonstrating a capacity for openness in his relations with servicemen of varying backgrounds. Although he relinquished his A.I.F. appointment on 19 March 1946, he continued to be active in the C.M.F. in 1949-51 and 1958-60.

Sambell's first post on returning to Melbourne in 1946 was a curacy at St Mark's, Camberwell. Archbishop Joseph Booth [q.v.13] responded to his war record and increasing assertiveness by appointing him director of the newly created Melbourne Diocesan Centre on 24 April 1947. Charged with revitalizing four inner-city parishes, and helped by a team of parish clergy, chaplains and lay people, Sambell was assisted by people working in factories, hospitals and law courts. The centre grew under his leadership and took control of many aspects of non-parochial ministry. In 1961 he became director of the newly created Home Mission Board: it incorporated the centre and other diocesan departments that provided services such as counselling and chaplaincy.

Having been appointed to the board of the Brotherhood of St Laurence in 1947, Sambell insisted on sound management. His careful scrutiny of the community's finances stabilized the more erratic approach of its founder G. K. Tucker [q.v.12]. Sambell played a major role in reshaping the brotherhood as director of its social services (from 1949), and as executive-director and deputy-chairman of its board (from 1956). Among measures to make its operations more professional, he began employing trained social workers in 1953, a step which promoted co-operation with government welfare agencies. In 1957, following a study tour of the United States of America, he introduced a salvage division which became a significant source of funds.

Sambell revived the Victorian Council of Social Service as its president (1956-58) and joined the national organization, the Australian Council of Social Service. His increasing prominence was reflected in his appointment as archdeacon of Essendon (1955) and of Melbourne (1961), and his consecration on 24 February 1962 as a coadjutor bishop. In 1964 he attended the meeting of the East Asia Christian Conference, held in Bangkok. Hugh Gough, the Anglican primate in Australia, appointed him local director of Mutual Responsibility and Interdependence in the Body of Christ. Sambell was later made a delegate to the Anglican Consultative Council.

Elected archbishop of Perth, Sambell was enthroned in St George's Cathedral on 24 October 1969, thereby becoming Perth's first Australian-born Anglican prelate. He rapidly restored the morale of his clergy and increased their stipends. Characteristically, he streamlined diocesan administration, developed new parishes, strengthened the position of religious education and broadened chaplaincy services. In 1974 he established the Anglican Health and Welfare Services Board. Projects initiated under his direction included a recycling operation, housing for single-parent families, an Asian Community Centre, and a marriage and family counselling service.

Eager to eradicate the sense of Western Australia's regional isolation, Sambell sent theological students to be trained at colleges in the other States and allowed some to be placed in Asian countries. His initiative for a diocesan programme, Celebration '75, included an Easter Day eucharist to which major prelates from developing nations were invited. Due to the links he forged, Australia was granted full membership in 1976 of the Christian Conference of Asia.

In 1976-80 Sambell chaired the Federal government's National Consultative Council on Social Welfare. His experiences in Western Australia transformed his understanding of Aboriginal communities and their needs. After a magistrate fined the diocesan trustees in 1977 for allowing fringe-dwelling Aborigines to camp in the grounds of a suburban parish church, Sambell publicly criticized Sir Charles Court's government in 1980 over its handling of the Noonkanbah affair. Although gravely ill, he visited England later in the year, assisted by Tao Tong, a Laotian student whose guardian he had become in 1968. He died of cancer on 19 December 1980 in Perth and was cremated. On 31 December he was posthumously appointed C.M.G.

Five ft 10½ ins (179 cm) tall and heavily built, Sambell was at once lonely and gregarious, brusque and welcoming, and often revealed his emotions more tellingly in body language than in words. He was driven both by a vision of the future and by an element of insecurity. Early in his appointment to the Melbourne Diocesan Centre he was nicknamed 'the Boss'. He maintained control by his mastery of financial information, which exceeded that of accountants on his staff. His strategies were sometimes the product of sleepless nights. Convinced that the Church should minister on the basis of need rather than the availability of funds, he pushed for the creation of new positions and roles, and for the appointment of young clergy. Among the junior priests he encouraged were the future bishops Peter Hollingworth, Michael Challen and James Grant.

Sambell's belief in the importance of co-operating with government organizations made him an intelligent pioneer of social-service work. His nationalism—tinged with a sense of alienation from the English expression of Anglicanism—and his growing sympathy with Anglicans from developing nations and the United States were significant in countering provincialism in Western Australia and prophetic in a national context.

J. Handfield, *Friends and Brothers* (Melb, 1980); J. Tonkin (ed), *Religion and Society in Western Australia* (Perth, 1987); Church of England, *Diocese of Perth Year Book*, 1970-81; A. Porter, Biography of Geoffrey Tremayne Sambell, 1914-1980: Archbishop of Perth, 1969-1980 (M.Phil. thesis, Murdoch Univ, 1990); information from Rt Rev. M. Challen, Rt Rev. J. Grant, Rev. D. Robarts, and Mr H. Speagle, Melb.

COLIN HOLDEN

SAMSON, Sir WILLIAM FREDERICK (1892-1974), businessman and mayor, was born on 12 January 1892 at Fremantle, Western Australia, second of four children of Michael Samson, civil servant, and his wife Mary, née Murphy. His grandfather Lionel Samson [q.v.2] had been one of the first Swan River settlers. Educated at Christian Brothers' colleges at Fremantle and in Perth, Freddy studied engineering at the University of Western Australia. In 1915 he abandoned his course, intending to enlist in the Australian Imperial Force, but was declared medically unfit. He then joined the Metropolitan Water Supply, Sewerage and Drainage Department. Between 1918 and 1930 he worked as a surveyor, though his health was impaired from the effects of Spanish influenza, contracted in 1919. In 1931 he set up as an auctioneer and real-estate agent at Fremantle. On 9 January 1935, in the home (built in 1888) he had inherited from his father, he married with Anglican rites Daphne Alice Marks (d.1953), the 27-year-old daughter of his housekeeper. They were childless.

Entering the Fremantle City Council in 1936, Samson was to serve as mayor for twenty-one years: he was elected unopposed in 1951 and remained unchallenged in that office until he retired in 1972. He believed that Fremantle was the best place in the world and Perth its mere adjunct. Each of his council meetings began with the Bible opened at Psalm CXXXIII, verse 1: 'Behold, how good and how pleasant *it is* for brethren to dwell together in unity!' A man of the people and a 'rough diamond', he maintained that a city should be more than a place of commerce and exchange, and made himself accessible to anyone who came to him for advice or help.

He was quixotic in his efforts on behalf of the community and kept a pocket full of coins with which he fed meters on the streets as he passed by, thereby saving motorists from a possible fine.

In the early 1950s Samson oversaw construction of the O'Connor industrial estate, intended to provide work and housing for returned servicemen. From 1958 he campaigned to save the convict-built Fremantle Lunatic Asylum, which was transformed into a museum and arts centre by 1970. As a member of the Cultural Development Council, he ensured that other neglected historic buildings were restored for public use. He served on the committees of at least eleven clubs and associations—sporting, cultural, commercial and charitable. A shrewd businessman, he had helped to form the Home Building Society in 1946; while chairman (1951-74), he saw its assets increase to $70 million. He was also a councillor of the Real Estate Institute of Western Australia (1949-64) and a member of the State Electricity Commission (1954-74).

Short and portly, Samson had an auctioneer's booming voice that carried across a room. He was hospitable but abstemious, preferring tea to wine. In 1962 he was knighted. In 1969 he was appointed the first honorary freeman in the Fremantle municipality. Denied his wish to spend his last moments in the four-poster bed in which he had been born, Sir Frederick died on 6 February 1974 in Fremantle Hospital and was buried in the local cemetery. His home, bequeathed to the trustees of the Western Australian Museum, became the Samson House Museum. A suburb of Perth was named after him.

West Australian, 1 Jan 1962, 7 Feb 1974; L. Troy and L. Wood (oral hist tss, Fremantle L, WA); information from Mrs M. McPherson, Hilton, Perth.

PATRICIA BROWN

SANDES, ANNIE MABEL (1881-1966), technical-college superintendent, was born on 3 December 1881 at Cleveland, Brisbane, youngest of three children of Irish-born parents James Sandes, policeman, and his wife Annie Jane, née Goudy. Francis Percival Sandes [q.v.11] was her elder brother. Sent to Sydney Technical College, Mabel studied art (1895-98), gained honours in advanced cookery (1901) and won numerous prizes. She undertook administrative work at the college, and taught (1903-05) in the department of domestic economy and cooking.

On 10 April 1906 Miss Sandes was appointed superintendent of the (Emily McPherson) College of Domestic Economy, Melbourne. In setting up the institution, she had to overcome problems that stemmed from inadequate funding, conflicting aims, ill-defined lines of responsibility and the selection of unsuitable premises. She oversaw the renovation of the building, purchased equipment, prepared the curriculum and timetables, selected staff and recommended fees. After the college opened on 1 October, she taught day- and evening-classes, set and marked examinations, and recouped costs by selling meals to the public. In addition, she accounted for all funds, supervised an increasing number of students and handled public relations. Although very young, she soon established herself as a forceful and efficient principal.

From 1911 the college helped to train domestic-arts teachers, who did their practical work at a new hostel under Sandes's management. Despite the increase in her duties and responsibilities, she was refused higher pay. She resigned in 1912, but withdrew her resignation when her post was reclassified from £200 per annum to the range of £240-£270. Her work expanded to include exhibitions, travelling demonstrations and specialist classes. The college council and Education Department officials asked each year that her services be fully recognized. Margaret Mountain, president of the council, asserted in 1914 that the college was 'fortunate in having a Superintendent like Miss Sandes ... Her energy is unflagging'.

Announcing plans to marry, Sandes left the college in 1916: the Sydney *Daily Telegraph* noted the departure of a woman with 'truly Napoleonic characteristics'. At Holy Trinity Church, Launceston, Tasmania, on 30 September that year she married with Anglican rites Stanley Clifton Smith (d.1953), a schoolmaster; they were to have three children. He taught in Tasmania, New Zealand and New South Wales before being appointed boarding-house master at Sydney Grammar School in 1926. His wife 'ably and indefatigably assisted him', combining her role as wife and mother with the task of overseeing the domestic staff to ensure that the daily needs of the boarders were met.

From 1938 Mrs Clifton Smith taught domestic science and dressmaking at St Catherine's School, Waverley. Troubled by increasing deafness, she retired in 1944. She spent her time with family and friends, enjoyed a game of bridge and showed a lively interest in current affairs. At the age of 78 she embarked on a world tour with her daughter Shirley, with whom she lived in Port Moresby from 1964. Survived by her son and two daughters, she died on 19 June 1966 at Korobosea and was buried in Hanuabada cemetery.

J. Docherty, *The Emily Mac* (Melb, 1981); *Catherineian*, Nov 1938, p 3, Dec 1945, p 7; *Sydneian*, Nov 1976, p 78; Emily McPherson College of Domestic Economy records (SLV); VPRS 9514/P1, box

27 (PRO, Vic); information from Dr S. Clifton Smith, Potts Point, and Mrs G. Clifton Smith, Haberfield, Syd.   JUDITH BIDDINGTON

SANDFORD, GLADYS (1891-1971), motorist, was born on 4 March 1891 at Summer Hill, Sydney, fourth child of Oswald Coates, an English-born commission agent, and his wife Valerie Albine, née Lassau, who came from South Australia. By 1896 the family had moved to Auckland, New Zealand. At the age of 21 Gladys was employed as a schoolteacher at Napier. On 20 June 1912 at St Barnabas's Anglican Church, Mount Eden, she married William Henning, a widower and a motor salesman. She learned to drive and enjoyed tinkering with engines.

When her husband enlisted in the New Zealand Expeditionary Force in 1914, Gladys offered her services as a motor driver, but was turned down. She paid her own passage, sailed to Egypt with the Volunteer Sisterhood, and worked as a driver at the Ghaza hospital. Reaching England, she was engaged as a driver by the Motor Transport Section of the N.Z.E.F. on 30 May 1917. She rose to be head lady driver, but contracted influenza and was discharged on 19 January 1919. In 1920 she was appointed M.B.E. Her husband, who had won the Military Cross, had died of wounds in 1918.

Tireless and fearless, Gladys was an attractive woman with fair, curly hair and blue eyes. At St Mark's Church, Darling Point, Sydney, on 3 April 1920 she married Frederick Esk Sandford (d.1929), a squadron leader in the Royal Air Force. They lived in England, India and Egypt. In 1924 she returned to Auckland alone. For many years she had wanted to learn to fly. In December 1925, despite strong opposition, she became the first woman in New Zealand to gain a pilot's licence (no.18).

Forced to support herself, Mrs Sandford worked as a motorcar saleswoman and taught her customers to drive. She was dared to emulate F. E. Birtles' [q.v.7] overland trip from Adelaide to Darwin. With a female companion (who could not drive), she left Sydney on 4 March 1927 in a 1926 Essex 6 coach, planning to motor to Perth, Darwin, Adelaide and along the coast to Sydney. 'Their equipment consisted of tinned foods and flour, a frying-pan, a billy and a grid-iron, blankets and a mattress, canvas waterbags, a tomahawk, fencing wire and a wire strainer, a set of bog extractors, a Red Cross outfit, a revolver, and four suitcases of personal luggage. The only spares they carried when they set out were two spark plugs, a coil, and a soldering iron'. Floods and impassable roads necessitated changes to her itinerary. Returning to Sydney on 25 July, she had driven some 10 000 miles (16 000 km) and

undertaken running repairs, including re-assembling the engine. On the one occasion she needed help, she short-circuited the Transcontinental telegraph-line to gain the aid of technicians.

In 1929 Sandford settled in Sydney. During World War II she founded and presided over the Women's Transport Corps. By 1940 it had almost 400 members who had to practise military drill, and pass theoretical and practical examinations in driving and maintenance. The unit was soon brought under the umbrella of the National Emergency Services. By day she censored letters for the Department of the Army.

After the war Sandford ran a poultry farm with a female friend for a few years before obtaining a job with the Department of Repatriation. In 1956 she retired. She moved into the War Veterans' Home, Narrabeen, worked at the home's art-union office, took up painting, and enjoyed sea fishing. A vice-president of the Sydney branch of the New Zealand Returned Soldiers' (later Services) Association, she marched on Anzac Day and acted as an unpaid social worker for the association, visiting sick and distressed soldiers and their families. She died on 24 October 1971 at the Repatriation General Hospital, Concord, and was cremated.

K. J. Cable and J. C. Marchant (eds), *Australian Biographical and Genealogical Record, 1842-1899*, 2 (Syd, 1987); S. Lainé, *Silver Wings* (Wellington, NZ, 1989); *Aust Women's Weekly*, 19 Mar 1940, 18 July 1942, 26 Feb 1969; *Motor in Aust and Flying*, 1 July 1940; *SMH*, 19 Mar 1940; *Sunday Herald*, 6 Sept 1953; *Daily Telegraph* (Syd), 29 June 1967; Sandford papers (ML).   CAROL J. BAXTER

SANDOVER, ALFRED (1866-1958), hardware merchant and benefactor, was born on 24 November 1866 at Plymouth, Devon, England, youngest of five children of William Sandover, a hotelkeeper who became a politician, and his wife Mary Billing, née Bate. His English-born parents had left Adelaide to visit their homeland. Alfred was considered a delicate child. Educated at North Adelaide Grammar School, he gained first-class honours in the senior public examination in 1881.

In 1884 Alfred joined his brother William in Perth where William had established a pharmacy and hardware business. Dismayed by the temperature of 106°F. (41°C.) on the day he arrived at Fremantle, and by the dust and glare of the limestone roads, Alfred vowed that he would not stay a day longer than his five-year contract demanded. Despite his initial reaction, he spent the rest of his life in Perth. William Sandover & Co. expanded rapidly after the opening of the Coolgardie and Kalgoorlie goldfields in the 1890s; the firm was described as 'brimful of all the latest ideas in machinery, mining, agricultural and domestic requisites'. On 11 July 1895 at St George's Church of England, Malvern, Melbourne, Alfred married Rose Allen (d.1943). In the following year he bought an 8-acre (3 ha) property at Claremont, Perth, and built a house which he named Knutsford.

Both brothers were invited to join a group of Fremantle merchants who, concerned about the high freight rates charged by English shipping companies, had formed (1884) the West Australian Shipping Association Ltd. The W.A.S.A. (of which Alfred was sometime chairman) chartered its own ships and came to control much of the Western Australian trade. In 1923 Sandovers Ltd acquired the Perth branch of the Adelaide company, G. P. Harris, Scarfe & Co., and registered it as Harris, Scarfe & Sandovers Ltd. Alfred was appointed chairman; he was to retain the position until he retired in 1957 at the age of 90.

The diminutive Sandover became prominent in the business, philanthropic and sporting life of Perth. A 'dynamic, colourful and kindly businessman', he combined 'shrewd foresight in commercial dealings with unfailing, old-world courtesy'. He was always willing to give a loan to someone down on his luck, but only after asking, 'not a betting loss, is it?' President (1910-11) of the Perth Chamber of Commerce, he served on the committees of the Chamber of Manufactures (1943-46), the Western Australian Employers' Federation and the Perth Children's Hospital, and gave generously to the Home of Peace, Subiaco. He was also a member of the senate of the University of Western Australia (1912-15 and 1919-31) and of the Council for Church of England Schools (1922-50), and provided land from his Knutsford estate for the establishment of Christ Church Grammar School.

In 1921 he had donated the Sandover medal, which has been presented annually to the fairest and best player in the West Australian Football League. Sandover held office in several cricket clubs, collected fine furniture and paintings, and loved to read. In 1951 he was appointed M.B.E. Survived by his daughter and two sons, he died on 4 May 1958 in his Perth home and was cremated; his estate was sworn for probate at £68 978. A building at Christ Church Grammar was named after him. His son (Sir) Eric Sandover succeeded him as chairman of the family firm.

Studies in WA History, 13, 1992, p 49; *West Australian*, 5 May 1958, 2 June 1979; J. S. Pocklington, Sandover Story—Looking Back Over 90 Years (ms, held by Mr R. Sandover, City Beach, Perth); E. M. Goode, Some Record of the Sandover Family (ts, 1989, Claremont Museum, Perth); K. Goode, Reminiscences about her father, A. Sandover (ms, Claremont Museum, Perth); information from Mr R. Sandover.   JENNY MILLS

SANDS, DAVID (1926-1952), boxer, was born on 24 February 1926 at Burnt Bridge, near Kempsey, New South Wales, fifth of eight children of George Ritchie, a rodeo-rider and timber-cutter of mixed Aboriginal and European descent, and his Aboriginal wife Mabel, née Russell, both of whom were born in New South Wales. Dave's brothers Clement, Percival, George, Alfred and Russell also boxed, emulating their father and their maternal great-uncle Bailey Russell, a noted bare-knuckle fighter. Ray Mitchell recorded that, between them, the brothers contested 494 official fights, with 301 wins (209 by knockouts), 27 draws and 163 losses. Colin Tatz claimed that they fought 607 bouts in all. They also toured with boxing troupes.

In 1939 Percy travelled to Newcastle to train with Tom Maguire. He adopted the ring-name of Ritchie Sands, after 'Snowy' Sands, a local railway guard and boxing fan. All six Ritchie brothers fought under the name Sands and wore green satin shorts with a white star. At the age of 15 Dave joined Percy; both lived at Maguire's gym. Maguire also trained Clem, George and Alfie. Clem was to hold the New South Wales welterweight title in 1947-51 and Alfie the middleweight title in 1952-54. Without Maguire's knowledge, Dave fought a four-round preliminary bout in August 1941 at Newcastle Stadium, swinging his way to victory in the first round. Maguire disapproved, but quickly transformed him into a skilled boxer. By the end of 1942 he had knocked out a dozen opponents at Newcastle. On 11 August 1945 he married 18-year-old Bessie Emma Burns at St Paul's Church of England, Stockton.

Sands was soon boxing in twelve-round matches before excited crowds of up to ten thousand people in Brisbane and Sydney. In May 1946 he defeated Jack Kirkham for the Australian middleweight title. Three months later he knocked out Jack Johnson in four rounds to become national light-heavyweight champion. The rematches were even more one-sided: Kirkham was defeated in five rounds and Johnson fell after 2½ minutes of furious punching. By 1948 Sands had beaten all his local opponents and most American 'imports'. His mauling of a French fighter Tony Toniolo in less than two minutes in February 1949 led the English promoter Jack Solomons to take an interest in him.

Despite an enthusiastic reception from the British press, Sands began his campaign for a world title disastrously. In London on 4 April 1949, while suffering from a swollen, recently vaccinated arm, he was outpointed by Tommy Yarosz. Fifteen days later Sands won, dismally, against a spoiler, Lucien Caboche. Maguire then moved him to Newcastle upon Tyne, where friendly locals and a promoter Joe Shepherd restored his confidence. After two solid victories, he returned to London and in July thrashed the much fancied Robert Ville-main in the 'fight of the year'. On 6 September Sands demolished Dick Turpin in 2 minutes 35 seconds for the British Empire middle-weight title.

Shortly after his triumphal return to Aus-tralia in November 1949, Sands survived a serious accident when the steering on his motorcar failed and the vehicle somersaulted into a creek. Over the next eighteen months he contested and won nine fights, one of them a fifteen-rounder in September 1950 in which he took the Australian heavyweight champion-ship from Alf Gallagher. Sands had become a leading contender for the world middleweight title and Maguire vainly sought to arrange a bout with the American champion 'Sugar' Ray Robinson. In the tricky maze of international boxing-promotion, his efforts were marked by a 'paper-chase' of offers and counter-offers. Sands defeated Mel Brown in London in July 1951 in a preliminary to a title-fight between Robinson and another contender Randolph Turpin. Had Maguire's negotiations suc-ceeded, Sands would have been in Turpin's place and probably would have beaten an unfit Robinson, as did Turpin.

In October Sands won two fights in the United States of America. Back home, he hoped for a world title-bout, but he was estranged from Maguire. A new manager Bede Kerr reopened discussions with Robin-son's connexions, but 'the chance never came'. On 11 August 1952 the truck Sands was driving overturned at roadworks near Dungog, New South Wales; he died of his injuries that evening in the local hospital and was buried in Sandgate cemetery, Newcastle. His wife, and their son and two daughters sur-vived him; their third daughter was born in November. Sands had earned about £30 000, but it went on manager's fees, travel costs, tax, family expenses and generosity to his kin. A public appeal raised more than £2500, suf-ficient to pay off his Stockton home and create a trust fund for his family.

Dave Sands was a consummate fighter-boxer. The most gifted of the Sands brothers, he was fast and quick-thinking, full of front-foot aggression and fierce counter-punching. He had the best left hook of his peers, and could punch heavily with both hands while absorbing the blows of the hardest hitters. Overseas commentators and boxers thought that he could beat the best. Robinson wanted 'a lot of money to fight that guy [Sands]'. When Carl 'Bobo' Olson (whom Sands had defeated twice) took the crown on Robinson's retirement, he remarked: 'this title should have belonged to Dave Sands. It would have been his had he lived'. According to Mitchell, Sands fought 104 bouts: 60 won by knockouts, 33 won on points, one drawn, seven lost on points, one lost by a knockout, and two no-contests. According to Tatz, he was defeated only ten times in 110 fights.

The dark-eyed, snubbed-nosed Sands, whose skills kept his handsome features un-scathed, was widely respected for his quiet manliness and dedication. Despite his devas-tating ability in the ring, he was modest and shy. To his family he was fun-loving and a good provider, even helping with domestic tasks such as sewing. He was extremely close to his brothers, with whom he shared a timber-cutting business. Bessie recalled in 1997: 'he was a gentle soul, a gentleman. We only had seven years together'.

Dave's death spurred on his youngest brother RUSSELL PETER (1937-1977). Born on 20 February 1937 at Burnt Bridge, Russell became a featherweight and fought as a southpaw due to his withered left leg. Lacking mobility and a big punch, he developed excel-lent timing and ringcraft, and an uncanny ability to duck and weave. He enjoyed a repu-tation for courage, and showed that it was well earned in his twelve-round battle (1957) with Ray Riojas. In May 1954 he won the New South Wales featherweight title on points; in December that year he—uncharacteristically —knocked out Young Layton in two rounds for the vacant Australian featherweight title. He surrendered it to Bobby Sinn in Novem-ber 1955. After breaking his leg in a motorcar accident, he retired in 1959. Russell Sands had 48 fights; he won 26 (mostly on points), drew three and lost 19. He died of bilateral pneu-monia on Christmas Eve 1977 at Mayfield East, Newcastle, and was buried in Sandgate cemetery with the forms of the Seventh-day Adventist Church.

R. Mitchell, *The Fighting Sands* and *Great Australian Fights* (Melb, 1965); P. Corris, *Lords of the Ring* (Syd, 1980); C. Tatz, *Obstacle Race* (Syd, 1994); *SMH*, 12 Aug 1952, 26 Dec 1977, 11 Jan 1997; *Sporting Globe*, 28 Sept 1955.   RICHARD BROOME

SANDS, JOHN ROBERT (1919-1980), physician, printer and businessman, was born on 22 September 1919 at Manly, Sydney, son of Australian-born parents Grahame Sands, merchant, and his wife Gladys Beatrice, née Carter. Educated at Sydney Church of Eng-land Grammar School (Shore) and the Uni-versity of Sydney (M.B., B.S., 1941), John became a resident medical officer at Royal Prince Alfred Hospital. On 12 November 1941 he was commissioned provisional captain in the Australian Army Medical Corps (Militia); on 13 August 1942 he was seconded to the Australian Imperial Force. He served with the 10th Field Ambulance in New Guinea and on Morotai Island. While on leave, he married Margaret Lesley Brand on 4 December 1944 at St Andrew's Church of England, Lismore, New South Wales.

Transferring to the Reserve of Officers on 29 June 1946, Sands undertook the twelve-month course offered to returning medical officers at R.P.A.H. He worked briefly at the Brisbane Clinic, Wickham Terrace, from July 1947. Back in Sydney in the following year, he established a private practice at Kensington before moving (1956) to Macquarie Street. In 1955 he was appointed honorary assistant physician at R.P.A.H. and began to specialize in nephrology. As a senior physician in charge of a general medical unit from 1963, he oversaw rapid changes in renal medicine with the development of dialysis treatment and organ transplants. Nephrology was transformed from a minor specialty into a major branch of medicine.

A parallel and fundamental shift occurred from honorary consultants to full-time, salaried staff specialists. An honorary of the old school himself, Sands trained as registrars many young physicians who became prominent in academic medicine and led (often against vociferous resistance) the changes in hospital ethos which made these developments possible.

Possessing a restless intellect, a gentle nature and a sharp wit without malice, Sands came from a family of printers and businessmen. He was thin, with dark hair brushed back from his forehead. His voice was soft but had timbre. He behaved to all with kindness and courtesy bordering on courtliness. Having joined the board of John Sands [q.v.6] Pty Ltd, printers, in 1944, he became executive-chairman in 1965. John Sands Holdings Ltd was registered as a public company in 1950. Sands often left his home after a late dinner to spend further hours at the factory. Under his leadership the firm expanded. His business skills led to his appointments as a councillor of the Medical Benefits Fund of Australia in 1955 and as a director of the Bank of New South Wales in 1974.

Sands was prominent in the affairs of the Royal Australasian College of Physicians, of which he was a councillor (1958-78), fellow (1960), treasurer (1960-68) and vice-president (1974-76). In 1978, aware that he was gravely ill, he declined nomination for the presidency. He wrote numerous medical and scientific papers, including reflections on death and grief. His detailed planning ensured that his patients did not lose continuity of care. Suffering from emphysema and cancer, he died of a cerebral haemorrhage on 21 January 1980 at R.P.A.H., Camperdown, and was cremated. His wife, and their daughter and son survived him.

J. C. Wiseman and R. J. Mulhearn (eds), *Roll of the Royal Australasian College of Physicians*, 2, 1976-90 (Syd, 1994); *MJA*, 2, 1980, p 524; *SMH*, 23 Jan 1980; Dr Geoffrey McDonald, Funeral oration, St Stephen's Uniting Church, Syd, Feb 1980 (held by Dr J. Greenaway, Syd); information from Prof D. Tiller, Royal Prince Alfred Hospital, Camperdown, Mrs L. Sands, Bellevue Hill, and Mr R. Sands, Syd.

GRAHAM MACDONALD

SANGER, HERMAN MAX (1909-1980), rabbi, was born on 3 July 1909 in Berlin, only child of Rabbi Jacob Sänger and his wife Hilda, née Heimann. He grew up at Breslau (Wroclaw, Poland). At the age of 16 he won a scholarship to study in Paris at the Bibliothèque Nationale de France and the Sorbonne. He also attended the universities of Geneva and Cambridge, and studied at the Jewish Theological Seminary, Breslau, and the University of Würzburg (Ph.D., 1933). When he was ordained in 1933, seven successive generations of the Sänger family had produced rabbis.

Returning to Berlin, Sänger was formally inducted into his first pulpit on 1 April 1933: he was forced to thread his way to the synagogue on the Oranienburgerstrasse past Nazi thugs bellowing the *Horst Wessel-Lied*. The German Jewish community made the most of his linguistic and diplomatic skills by using him as a courier in its search for aid and for places of refuge. At the funeral of a distinguished scientist who had died in police custody, he concluded the service with words: 'Here lies German culture'. An agent informed him that if he gave another such speech he would be taken to the concentration camp at Sachsenhausen. There were other warnings and Gestapo interrogations until, in 1936, an anonymous call in the middle of the night advised him to leave Germany next day.

Sanger made his way to London where the secretary of the World Union for Progressive Judaism asked him to consider a struggling, non-orthodox congregation in Australia that needed a rabbi. He reached Melbourne on 19 August 1936. The Beth Israel congregation, established at St Kilda in 1930, was on the point of collapse. His impact was immediate and positive. Within two years of his arrival, the congregation was able to build and dedicate its own synagogue in Alma Road.

Given his broad academic and religious training, and his work in Berlin, Sanger was shocked by the bigotry of the Australian orthodox rabbinate. The wider Jewish community quickly recognized him as their most effective rabbinic voice. Among Jewish leaders in Australia before World War II, he was one of the few outspoken Zionists. As founding president (1942) of the Association of Jewish Refugees, he promoted the integration of new arrivals and campaigned against the discrimination implicit in their status as 'enemy aliens'.

Herman Sanger had a profound national impact. A vice-president of the World Union for Progressive Judaism, he inspired the groups which established Sydney's Temple Emanuel and Perth's Temple David. He also founded two suburban congregations in Melbourne. While he never forgot the silence of the Churches in the face of the Nazis, he pioneered dialogue between the Christian and Jewish faiths in Australia. In 1962 he was appointed O.B.E. Six ft 1 in. (185 cm) tall, elegant and imposing, he had a superb command of English, which he spoke with a slight European accent. Every speech he gave was carefully crafted. (Sir) Robert Menzies [q.v.15] declared him to be Australia's greatest orator.

A lover of books, Sanger devoured them, underlined them and questioned them. He took the rabbi's traditional task of teaching very seriously. At the Temple Beth Israel, St Kilda, on 12 June 1962 he married Winifred Eleanor Nathan, née Clements, a widow. In 1974 he retired. Survived by his wife, he died of peritonitis on 24 January 1980 at Prahran and was buried in Springvale cemetery. The hall at Temple Beth Israel was named after him.

Rabbi H. M. Sanger (Melb, 1961); naturalization file, A659, item 1943/1/1056 (NAA, Canb); Sanger papers (Temple Beth Israel, Melb, archives).

J. S. LEVI

SANTO, PETER (c.1861-1966), indentured labourer, was born about 1861 on Espiritu Santo, the largest island in the New Hebrides (Vanuatu), son of Herbert Santo and his wife Orrie. Peter arrived in Queensland as an indentured labourer in 1888. He was one of 2800 people, mostly males, who left Espiritu Santo for Queensland between 1863 and 1904. Although the period from 1863 to the early 1880s was marred by kidnapping and other illegal practices, the Melanesian labour trade was usually well regulated during its later years. Like many of the 22 000 Melanesians who came to Queensland between 1888 and 1904, Santo was employed in the sugar industry. He worked in many areas along the coast, showing mobility typical of the long-staying Islanders, and remained single until relatively late in life. Like most of his compatriots who remained in Australia, he was marginalized to the fringes of White society and forced into a subsistence way of life. His main language was Kanaka Pidgin English and he became a Christian.

Serving his early indenture agreements on sugar-plantations in the vicinity of Bundaberg, Santo worked as a farm labourer and millhand.

He was engaged first by A. H. and E. Young at Fairymead, then, in turn, by Jack Walker at Isis, John Ruddy at Childers and Angus Gibson [q.v.4] at Bingera. By the late 1890s he was employed at Yeppoon, near Rockhampton, and after 1900 at Seaforth plantation, Ayr. In 1906 an amendment to the Pacific Island Labourers Act (1901) allowed any Islander who had arrived before 31 December 1886 to remain in Australia. Santo continued to move north, working at Goondi mill, Innisfail, and (from 1910) at Macknade mill, Ingham, where he also cut cane in the district.

At the Methodist parsonage, East Ingham, on 17 January 1923 Santo married Amy Meredith (née Wathaken), a 29-year-old widow with three daughters. She had been born at Townsville, of mixed Aboriginal and Islander descent. The couple were to have two sons and a daughter. About 1930 the family moved to Ayr and settled at Plantation Creek, joining other New Hebrideans, among them Thomas Lammon [q.v.15]. Santo's son Richard died in 1932 and his daughter Rosie in 1943. A generous and independent man, he became a familiar figure in the area, hawking his bananas from kerosene tins suspended from a pole across his shoulders. He died on 27 March 1966 in Ayr hospital and was buried in the local cemetery with the forms of the Assembly of God; his wife and their son Peter survived him, as did his three stepdaughters. Thought to be about 105 years old, Santo was one of the last Melanesian labourers in Australia.

T. Dutton, *Queensland Canefields English of the Late Nineteenth Century* (Canb, 1980); *Advocate* (Ayr, Qld), 1 Apr 1966.

CLIVE R. MOORE

SARANEALIS, EDWARD WILLIAM (1902-1971), jeweller and dentist, was born on 2 February 1902 on Thursday Island, Queensland, eldest of seven children of Yahatowgoda Baddallegay Saranealis, a jeweller and dentist from Ceylon (Sri Lanka), and his English-born wife Alice, née Stewart. Thursday Island was a pearling centre. Its cosmopolitan population included Japanese, Chinese, Indonesians and Torres Strait Islanders. (Sir) James Burns [q.v.7] had visited Galle in southern Ceylon in 1882 and recruited twenty-five workers for his pearl-shell fishery. By the 1890s a sizeable Singhalese community lived on Thursday Island; most of them, like Y. B. Saranealis, came from Galle and its surrounding villages. The date when Saranealis reached Thursday Island remains uncertain, but in 1897 he advertised the opening of his jewellery, watchmaking and pearl-dealing business in Normanby Street. Reputedly, he enjoyed the patronage of Lord Northcote [q.v.11], the governor-general of Australia.

After the death of his father in 1919, Eddie Saranealis became head of the household and carried on the family business with the assistance of his brother Donsiman Heriverto ('Hubby'). The firm of pearl merchants and manufacturing jewellers continued to trade as Y. B. Saranealis from a two-storey building in Douglas Street. In his spare hours Eddie drew on the books in his father's professional library to study dentistry. After a faculty of dentistry was established at the University of Queensland in 1934, the Queensland government allowed the Dental Board to register graduates in dentistry and, in certain cases, persons who had practical rather than academic qualifications. Saranealis passed a special examination and was authorized to practise as a dentist on 3 November 1936. He set up a dental clinic in Hastings Street.

In 1942 civilians were ordered to evacuate Thursday Island. Saranealis worked for a time as a dentist at Townsville. Returning to the island in 1946, he resumed his dental practice and his jewellery business. He played in the town band and was a member of the local council. A bachelor, he spent a number of his weekends and holidays with his brothers in their launch *Mitzi*. They visited other Torres Strait islands and travelled to the tip of Cape York Peninsula where they hunted ducks. The *Mitzi* was also used for pleasure cruises and for entertaining prominent visitors to Thursday Island.

Saranealis suffered from emphysema. He died of pneumonia on 2 October 1971 at Thursday Island and was buried with Anglican rites in the local cemetery.

J. C. H. Foley, *Timeless Isle* (Thursday Island, Qld, 1982); W. S. Weerasooria, *Links between Sri Lanka and Australia* (Colombo, 1988); A/38244 (QA). REGINA GANTER

SAVAGE, EMILY WINIFRED (1888-1977), home economics teacher, was born on 2 August 1888 at Enfield, Sydney, fourth of five children of English-born parents Harry Nell, engineer, and his wife Emily, née Warcup. Winnie's interest in cookery began early and her mother gave her basic cooking lessons. With four other young women, she won a bursary in 1905 to study cookery under Hannah Rankin at Fort Street Training School. In 1907, while living at Drummoyne, she became assistant-teacher of cookery at Sydney Girls' High School. She went on to teach cookery in public schools at Petersham (1907-08), Erskineville (1908-09), Albury (1910-12), Hornsby (1912-13 and 1919-24), Broken Hill (1914) and Redfern (1915).

In 1925 Miss Nell visited London as an exchange teacher with the London County Council. Back home, she was appointed (June) supervisor of cookery in the Department of Education. She published *A Handbook of Home Management* in 1926; it was used as a text in schools for the next two decades and the tenth edition appeared in 1959. As supervisor, she made a significant contribution during a time when cookery was increasingly taught in schools.

A gracious woman with a pleasant manner and soft grey eyes, Winifred Nell resigned from the department in August 1933. On 11 September that year at the Independent Church, Kew, Melbourne, she married with Congregational forms Henry Savage, a 75-year-old merchant and a widower. After he died in 1934, Mrs Savage moved from Adelaide to Sydney. She lived at Neutral Bay and resumed her career, with the Sydney County Council. From 1936 to 1953 she was employed as lecturer in home economics. By 1945, as supervisor of the home management section, she trained the council's demonstrators.

Mrs Savage became well known to countrywomen from her regular contributions (1945-57) to the monthly, *Countrywoman in New South Wales*. Her articles and recipes ranged from 'Yeast Cooking' and 'Prune and Apricot Upside Down Pudding' to vegetable and meat dishes. For some three and a half years she also broadcast daily in the 'Banish Drudgery' session on radio-station 2GB. Interviewed in 1953 for the *Sunday Herald*, she said that, in her opinion, the most important development in the kitchen in the preceding four decades had been the general use of refrigeration. Having taught thousands of women to cook, she advocated simplifying the process of food preparation.

On a visit to Britain and the United States of America in 1955, Mrs Savage was impressed by packaged foods. She took part (1957-59) in the Australian Broadcasting Commission's 'Cookery Book' segment of the 'Women's Session', and contributed recipes to the *A.B.C. Weekly* and cookery pages to the *Australian Country Magazine* (1956-62). In 1961 she published *A Treasury of Good Recipes*, with a practical, washable cover. She gave her readers the benefit of her knowledge of cookery—accumulated over more than half a century—and urged them to be 'adventurous' in their cooking and to 'impart character and individuality to a meal by doing so'. Winifred Savage died on 16 February 1977 at Mosman and was cremated.

J. I. Peacock, *A History of Home Economics in New South Wales* (Syd, 1982); *Sunday Herald*, 26 July 1953; *Sun-Herald* (Syd), 20 Jan 1955; Education

Dept (NSW), cookery files, 20/12612-33 (NSWA); NSW teachers' records (Education Dept, Syd).

MARY MCPHERSON

SAVIGE, SIR STANLEY GEORGE (1890-1954), army officer and founder of Legacy, was born on 26 June 1890 at Morwell, Victoria, eldest of eight children of Samuel Savige, butcher, and his wife Ann Nora, née Walmsley, both Victorian born. Stan left Korumburra State School at the age of 12 to work as a blacksmith's striker. He subsequently held various casual jobs before being employed in a drapery. Showing an interest in soldiering and community work, he served as a senior cadet (1907-09) and scoutmaster (1910-15).

On 6 March 1915 Savige enlisted in the Australian Imperial Force. Posted to the 24th Battalion, he landed at Gallipoli in September. A series of promotions culminated in his being commissioned at Lone Pine on 9 November. In the following month he commanded one of the battalion's rearguard parties during the evacuation. Sent to France in March 1916, he was intelligence officer (from May) at Brigadier General (Sir) John Gellibrand's [q.v.8] 6th Brigade headquarters. After taking part in operations at Pozières and Mouquet Farm in July-August, he was promoted captain in September. In November he was wounded at Flers. Next month he was admitted to hospital, suffering from influenza. He returned to his battalion and in February 1917 became adjutant. For his 'consistent good work and devotion to duty' in the fighting at Warlencourt, Grevilliers and Bullecourt (February-May), he was awarded the Military Cross. Volunteering for special service, he was sent to Persia in March 1918 as part of Dunsterforce. He won the Distinguished Service Order for protecting refugees while under fire, and later recorded his experiences in *Stalky's Forlorn Hope* (Melbourne, 1920). Thrice mentioned in dispatches, he sailed for Melbourne where his A.I.F. appointment terminated on 24 April 1919. At the Baptist Church, South Yarra, on 28 June that year he married Lilian Stockton.

Savige worked as sole agent for the Returned Soldiers' and Sailors' Woollen & Worsted Co-operative Manufacturing Co. Ltd, Geelong. Prompted by Gellibrand, and by his own concern for the families of his fallen comrades, he founded Legacy in September 1923. He served in a number of key positions as the society grew into a national body, and was to be the leading figure in its development over the ensuing thirty years. Meanwhile, he had joined the Militia in 1920, and was promoted major in 1924 and lieutenant colonel in 1926. He commanded the 37th Battalion (1924-28), the 24th Battalion (1928-35) and, as a colonel,

the 10th Brigade from 1935 until the outbreak of World War II. In 1938 he was promoted temporary brigadier.

Seconded to the A.I.F. on 13 October 1939, Savige was appointed commander of the 17th Brigade, 6th Division, perhaps partly due to his friendship with Lieutenant General Sir Thomas Blamey [q.v.13]. Their association stretched back to their time in the cadets, and he had defended Blamey when the latter was forced to resign from the Victoria Police in 1936. The battle of Bardia, Libya, on 3-5 January 1941, saw the 6th Division's resounding first victory. It was also a chaotic, confused and costly one from the 17th Brigade's perspective. One of Savige's battalions was badly mauled trying to capture a strong Italian position, and his remaining two battalions rapidly became disorganized during the main attack. In the battle's aftermath, Savige was criticized for his role in these setbacks, particularly by George Vasey, (Sir) Horace Robertson [qq.v.] and (Sir) Frank Berryman, all of them senior regular officers in the division. As his ability to cope with the fluid and technically demanding conditions of modern warfare came into question, Savige became increasingly suspicious of his regular army contemporaries and more defensive of his performance. His brigade played supporting roles in the assault on Tobruk on 21-22 January and the subsequent advance to Derna. In 1941 he was appointed C.B.E.

Although the 17th Brigade took only a small part in the disastrous Greek campaign in April, Savige's personal example and bravery helped to steady those around him during the constant withdrawals and air-attacks. He was awarded the Greek Military Cross (1942). Involved in the closing phases of the conflict in Syria, he commanded the brigade in the hard-fought battle of Damour on 5-9 July 1941 when its men drew on 'sheer grit, determination and courage'. Savige regarded it as 'my most successful operation throughout the war'. He was again mentioned in dispatches. In December he embarked for Australia. A number of senior officers thought that, at the age of 51, he should be retired, following three strenuous campaigns in six months.

Japan's entry into the war dramatically altered Savige's fortunes. On 7 January 1942 he was promoted major general and placed in command of the 3rd Division. The training of this unprepared Militia formation suited his strengths as a commander, and he was ably assisted by his brilliant chief of staff, Lieutenant Colonel (Sir) John Wilton. Blamey probably chose Wilton to balance Savige's shortcomings. Their partnership proved successful when the division fought in the region between Wau and Salamaua, New Guinea, in April-August 1943. The harsh terrain and climate slowed the tempo of the campaign, and produced a war in which a general's contribution lay less in tactics than in 'personal inspiration' and in consideration for 'the welfare of the troops'. Believing that his presence was good for morale and important for tactical control, Savige made concerted efforts to visit the front line, something many higher commanders failed to do. His direction of the campaign was characterized by his encouragement of subordinate commanders, by his concern for his men, and by the way his divisional headquarters provided particularly effective artillery support.

Bitter fighting saw the capture of successive Japanese strongholds, among them Bobdubi Ridge, Komiatum and Mount Tambu. By late August, the month in which Savige's headquarters was relieved, his troops were poised to occupy Salamaua. His dealings with his immediate superior, Lieutenant General Sir Edmund Herring, were acrimonious and marred by misunderstanding. Although Herring was also a Militia officer, his vastly different social background and Savige's increasingly prickly manner combined with the normal confusion and frustration of war to produce tensions. While Savige was a difficult and sometimes trying officer, Herring was not without fault. Major General Berryman's report on the conduct of the campaign largely vindicated Savige. For his contribution to the victory at Salamaua, Savige was appointed C.B. (1943).

On 10 February 1944 Savige was promoted temporary lieutenant general and given command of I Corps (II Corps from April). This further promotion provoked comment, many believing that his friendship with Blamey had unduly influenced the decision. After leading New Guinea Force in May-October, he commanded II Corps on Bougainville, where the terrain and political imperative to minimize casualties required patience and understanding, but little military inspiration. In September 1945 he accepted the surrender of the Japanese forces at Torokina.

From October 1945 to May 1946 Savige served as co-ordinator of demobilization and dispersal. He transferred to the Reserve of Officers on 6 June. Resuming his business interests, he was a director (1946-51) of the Olympic Tyre & Rubber Co. Ltd and chairman (1950-51) of Moran & Cato [q.v.7] Ltd. He was also chairman (1946-51) of the Central War Gratuity Board and a commissioner (from 1951) of the State Savings Bank of Victoria. A leader in Melbourne's Anzac Day marches, he was patron of a number of his former units' associations and honorary colonel of the 5th Battalion (Victorian Scottish Regiment). In 1950 he was elevated to K.B.E. Two months after the death of his wife, Sir Stanley died of coronary artery disease on 15 May 1954 in his home at Kew. Survived by his daughter,

he was buried with Anglican rites and full military honours in Boroondara cemetery. His estate was sworn for probate at £66 007.

Savige's forte, at all levels of military command, was his personal leadership and knowledge of men. His ability to inspire and build rapport with his subordinates was helped by the genuine interest he showed in their welfare. His philanthropy was also seen in his community work, particularly with Legacy. As he progressed through the ranks to senior command positions, however, his lack of formal training and comprehension of modern warfare became an issue. Blamey's patronage of Savige was resented by other senior officers; their attempts to remove Savige from command increased his insecurity. John Hetherington [q.v.14] justly concluded: 'Savige did not pretend to be a military genius, but only a commander who knew his way round the battlefield because he had learned his soldiering the hard way'. Alfred Cook's portrait of Savige is held by the Australian War Memorial, Canberra.

K. Burke (ed), *With Horse and Morse in Mesopotamia* (Syd, 1927); W. B. Russell, *There Goes a Man* (Melb, 1959); J. Hetherington, *Blamey, Controversial Soldier* (Canb, 1973); M. Lyons, *Legacy* (Melb, 1978); D. M. Horner, *General Vasey's War* (Melb, 1992); G. M. Keating, The Right Man for the Right Job: An Assessment of Lieutenant General S. G. Savige as a Senior Commander (B.A. Hons thesis, Univ NSW, 1995); Savige papers (AWM).

GAVIN MICHAEL KEATING

SAVILLE, DONALD TEALE (1903-1943), aviator and air force officer, was born on 22 December 1903 at Portland, New South Wales, younger of twin sons and second of five children of English-born parents John Saville, engineer, and his wife Isabella, née Teale. Donald was educated at All Saints' College, Bathurst, Sydney Church of England Grammar School (Shore), the Friends' School, Great Ayton, Yorkshire, England, Bathurst High and Sydney Grammar schools.

Unsettled and restless, Saville worked in several mechanical engineering jobs at Bathurst and in Sydney before finding a post with Commonwealth Portland Cement Co. Ltd in 1925. He joined the Citizen Air Force, Royal Australian Air Force, as a cadet in May 1927 and completed flying training at Point Cook, Victoria. Receiving a short-service commission in the Royal Air Force, he embarked for Britain in December. On his return to Australia in May 1932, he was appointed to a four-year commission as flying officer, C.A.F. Reserve.

Saville was employed testing private aircraft at Mascot, Sydney, until 1935. He had been chosen in 1934 to pilot a twin-engined monoplane, planned to be built for the MacRobertson [q.v.11 Robertson] England-Australia Air Race, but the machine was not finished on time. After working as an assistant flying instructor with the Tasmanian branch of the Australian Aero Club, he became a senior pilot with Australian National Airways Pty Ltd in 1937.

While holidaying in England in 1939, Saville joined the R.A.F. Volunteer Reserve and rose to squadron leader. Because of his age, he was employed ferrying aircraft from factories to air force bases. In 1941 he accepted a reduction in rank to transfer to Bomber Command. Following operational training, Flight Lieutenant Saville was posted to No.12 Squadron, R.A.F., the first of three units equipped with Wellington bombers with which he served. In December that year he joined No.458 Squadron, R.A.A.F.; he became a flight commander shortly before the squadron was deployed to Fayid, Egypt, in February 1942.

In August Saville was promoted acting wing commander and given command of No.104 Squadron, R.A.F., at Kabrit. The unit moved to Malta in November. Within a fortnight Saville had taken part in numerous sorties, including low-level night-attacks against targets in Tunisia and Sicily. In December he was awarded the Distinguished Flying Cross for his inspiring leadership. On completing a full tour of operations in March 1943, with no break he took over No.218 Squadron, which operated Stirling bombers from Downham Market, Norfolk, England. On his fifty-seventh mission, during the night of 24/25 July, his aircraft was hit and caught fire over Hamburg, Germany. He kept the bomber steady until four of his crew parachuted to safety, but he was unable to escape before it crashed. He was buried in Ohlsdorf military cemetery, Hamburg.

Saville was a seasoned pilot with more than 10 000 flying hours. His reputation as a 'fearless commander' who chose to participate in the 'more difficult sorties' was recognized by the award of the Distinguished Service Order, gazetted two days after his death.

J. Herington, *Air War Against Germany and Italy 1939-1943* (Canb, 1954); P. Alexander, *We Find and Destroy* (Syd, 1979); *SMH*, 3 Feb, 31 May 1934; *Weekly Courier* (Launc), 30 May 1935; F. R. Chappell, A Biography of Wing Commander Donald Teale Saville (ms, AWM); Operations record book, 458 Squadron, RAAF, 1939-45 (AWM).　DAVID WILSON

SAWYER, JESSIE FREDERICA PAULINE (1870?-1947), community leader, was born probably in 1870 at Wantabadgery, Gundagai, New South Wales, eldest of at least seven chil-

dren of Andrew John Allen Beveridge, a grazier from Scotland, and his English-born wife Louisa Theresa, née Robinson. On 11 February 1891 at her parents' property, Dollar Vale, near Junee, Jessie married with Anglican rites Matthew Sawyer (d.1941), a grazier. They settled on Eulomo station, Bethungra, where she bore five children.

In 1922 Mrs Sawyer was one of three foundation vice-presidents of the Country Women's Association of New South Wales. That year she also set up the association's Cootamundra branch. She was elected State president in 1928. Throughout the decade of her presidency, she initiated many successful ventures. Following the collapse of the wool market in 1929, the C.W.A.—at her initiative —provided much needed support for the 'Use More Wool Campaign'. She encouraged members to use wool in the handicraft exhibitions mounted by the association, first in country towns and later in Sydney at David Jones [q.v.2] Ltd's Elizabeth Street store. She supported further exhibitions in 1933, 1935, 1936 and 1937.

As president, Sawyer committed C.W.A. members to supporting the promotion of the 'Gift of Lamb' for Christmas 1934, which had been launched in an effort to boost the sale of that meat to Britain. She used these trade promotions to forward the interests of the association, to consolidate links with its counterparts in Britain, and to encourage a sense of solidarity and common purpose among country women. In 1937 she compiled (with Sara Moore-Sims) *The Coronation Cookery Book*; 55 000 copies of the recipe book had been sold worldwide by 1945, the year of its fourth edition. She contributed numerous articles to the C.W.A. section of *Country Life*.

Sawyer considered it her duty to travel extensively to meet members of the association; her trips while president totalled more than 150 000 miles. The C.W.A. flourished: its membership rose from some 7000 to over 18 000, and financial resources and community activities increased. Sawyer was particularly interested in the fourteen maternity hospitals established in country areas and maintained by the C.W.A. Through the C.W.A. she raised funds to aid the New South Wales Bush Nursing Association, and to support maternal health and infant welfare by means of a network of rest and holiday homes, hostels and baby health centres. She was vitally interested in the Australian Aerial Medical Services, for which she raised £1000 by an appeal to members.

Her willingness to work tirelessly for the movement endeared her to its members, as did her loyalty, sympathy, friendship and self-sacrificing service. To cries of 'No, no, we don't want to lose you', Mrs Sawyer retired from the presidency in 1938 and was succeeded by her kinswoman Ada Beveridge [q.v.13]. Sawyer had been appointed O.B.E. in 1934. She remained active in the association and served (1942-47) on the New South Wales divisional council of the Australian Red Cross Society. A member of both the Queen's and Macquarie clubs in Sydney, she enjoyed music and reading, and was usually photographed wearing pearls. Jessie Sawyer died on 28 December 1947 at the Scottish Hospital, Paddington, and was buried in the Church of England cemetery, Cootamundra. Her two daughters and one of her three sons survived her. As a tribute to her commitment, the C.W.A. renamed (1950) its holiday home at Batlow after her.

Country Women's Assn of NSW, *Progress* (Syd, 1938), and *The Silver Years* (Syd, 1947) and *The Golden Years* (Syd, 1972); H. Townsend, *Serving the Country* (Syd, 1988); *SMH*, 19, 20 Apr, 6 Oct 1928, 2 May 1930, 17 Apr 1931, 18 Mar 1932, 25 Sept, 10 Oct 1933, 1 Jan, 4, 5 Apr, 28 Aug, 3 Sept 1934, 11, 27, 29 Apr, 20 Sept 1935, 6 May 1936, 19 Mar 1937, 28 Apr, 22, 24 Oct 1938, 24 Apr 1939, 29 Dec 1947.

JULIE GORRELL

SAYERS, CHARLES EDWARD (1901-1979), journalist and historian, was born on 9 November 1901 at Bendigo, Victoria, second child and eldest surviving son of Charles Sayers (d.1917), miner, and his wife Alice, née Brown, both Victorian born. When Ted was 5 the family moved to Broken Hill, New South Wales. From the local district school he won a scholarship to high school, but at the age of 13 had to find a job to support his mother and two brothers, his father having become a chronic invalid. He worked as a copy-holder at the *Barrier Daily Truth* and after about twelve months was made a cadet reporter. In 1919 he moved to Queensland where he was employed as a reporter by the *Maryborough Chronicle*; deficient in shorthand, he was dismissed in less than a year. He went to Brisbane and worked successively on the *Telegraph* and the *Daily Mail*.

In 1922 Sayers left Brisbane to join the *Age* in Melbourne. On 23 June 1923 at St Saviour's Church, Collingwood, he married with Anglican rites Ivy May Scown, a stenographer. He reported on State and Federal politics for the *Age*. In 1927 he was seconded to the Commonwealth government as official press representative for the visit of the Duke and Duchess of York. That year he became a founding member of the Canberra press gallery as representative of the Sydney *Sun*. While working as a journalist, Sayers wrote four novels: *The Jumping Double* (1923), *Boss of Toolangi* (1924), *Green Streaked Ring* (1930)

and *Desperate Chances* (1930), all published in Sydney.

After a brief attachment to the Melbourne *Herald*, Sayers returned to the *Age* in 1933 and, in the following year, toured as its special reporter with the Duke of Gloucester [q.v.14]. In 1935 he was appointed editor of the *Age*'s rural newspaper, the *Leader*. Although Sayers suspected that he had been sacked from the *Herald* because of his active role (general president 1928) in the Australian Journalists' Association, Sir Keith Murdoch [q.v.10] thought well enough of him to invite him in June 1940 to join the Commonwealth Department of Information; within six months Sayers was appointed editor. On 23 July 1941 he resigned to take a post with the British Foreign Office's Ministry of Economic Warfare. He served in Singapore and India, and briefly at Chungking, China, organizing anti-Japanese propaganda. In March 1944 he was made director-general of the Far Eastern Bureau of the British Ministry of Information, New Delhi. He was appointed editor of the Australian Associated Press service in London in 1947.

Three years later Sayers returned to Melbourne in ill health. He retired to a small farm at Olinda to devote himself to historical research and writing. His centenary supplement of the *Age*, published in 1954, was followed in 1965 by a biography of its co-founder David Syme [q.v.6]. In all, Sayers wrote about twenty books, including histories of the Victorian districts of Donald (1963), Stawell (1966) and Warrnambool (1972 and 1987), and a centenary history of the Royal Women's Hospital, Melbourne (1956). He also edited meticulously for Heinemann reprints of a number of rare books on Victorian history, among them *Letters from Victorian Pioneers* (1969), John Morgan's [q.v.2] *The Life and Adventures of William Buckley* (London, 1969), Rolf Boldrewood's [q.v.3 T. A. Browne] *Old Melbourne Memories* (1969) and James Bonwick's [q.v.3] *Western Victoria* (1970). His major work, a biography of Sir Keith Murdoch, remained unfinished. Survived by his wife and their two sons, he died on 25 February 1979 at Camberwell and was cremated. Their son, Stuart, followed him into journalism on the *Age*.

Journalist, Apr 1979; RHSV, *Newsletter*, May 1979; *SMH*, 30 Dec 1940, 23 July, 28 Aug 1941, 6 Mar 1944, 13 May 1947; *Age* (Melb), 26 Feb 1979; Sayers papers (LaTL); Murdoch and Dumas papers (NL); information from Mr D. Warner, Mount Eliza, Vic.

PETER GIFFORD

SCAMMELL, LUTHER ROBERT (1858-1940), pharmaceutical manufacturer, was born on 20 March 1858 at Port Adelaide, second of twelve children of Luther Scammell, an English-born chemist, and his wife Lavinia Annette, née Bean. After attending J. L. Young's [q.v.6] Adelaide Educational Institution, young Luther joined his father's firm, F. H. Faulding [q.v.4] & Co., and attended chemistry classes run by the public analyst George Francis. In 1877 he travelled to England with his elder brother William to study under Dr John Muter at the South London School of Pharmacy, Kennington. He passed the examinations of the (Royal) Pharmaceutical Society of Great Britain, and was registered as a chemist and druggist on 30 April 1879. Having gained experience at the Public Laboratory, Kennington Cross, he returned to the family business as a manufacturing chemist and became responsible for preparing many compounds that had previously been imported.

In 1885 Scammell was elected a fellow of the Chemical Society, London. Next year he was one of two South Australian representatives at an intercolonial pharmaceutical conference, held in Melbourne. As a result of his father's disastrous pastoral and mining speculations in the 1880s, Faulding & Co. faced bankruptcy. With the Bank of Adelaide demanding the company's sale, young Luther and William acquired the manufacturing and wholesaling operations, and the business name, in 1888. The retail shops were sold to reduce the debt to the bank. On 8 August that year Scammell married 18-year-old Elizabeth Alice Gray with Unitarian forms in her father's house at Reedbeds.

Faulding & Co. expanded under the direction of the two brothers. A branch, established in Perth in 1890, thrived under the management (from 1894) of Walter Wesley Garner. He was admitted to partnership in 1899. New agencies were set up in Sydney and Melbourne. Luther took responsibility for managing the firm's affairs nationally, while William oversaw the Sydney office from 1908. Much of Faulding's success was founded on eucalyptus oil, which formed the basis of an antiseptic marketed as Solyptol. Scammell took credit for coining the name—a contraction of 'soluble eucalyptus oil'—for Faulding's eucalyptus products. Building on the work of Samuel Barbour, a Faulding chemist, he had developed a method in 1892 for determining the eucalyptol content of the oil. His test became the standard in the industry and was included in the *British Pharmacopœia* (1898). Solyptol soap won a gold medal at the Franco-British Exhibition in London in 1908.

Scammell and Faulding were indirectly associated with the introduction of X-ray tubes to Australia. After Barbour had returned from abroad to Adelaide with two Röntgen tubes in May 1896, he helped (Sir) William Bragg [q.v.7] to produce X-ray pictures. Barbour left Faulding & Co. in 1897, taking the new tech-

nology with him. In 1900 the firm opened an office in London; five years later its agents operated in South Africa, India and Canada. A wide range of proprietary products was made and sold, including Pectoral Drops, Kalmint Toothpaste, Quinine and Iron Tonic Diphtheria Powder, Salts of Lemon, and Milk Emulsion. Grocery items—baking, custard and curry powders, vinegar, and cloudy ammonia—were also produced. World War I provided new opportunities, particularly for the manufacture of Epsom salts which represented Faulding's first venture into industrial chemical production.

In June 1921 Faulding & Co. became a private company, with Scammell as chairman and managing director. He continued to run the firm's affairs until 1935. Day-to-day management then passed to his elder son Alfred, but Luther remained chairman of directors until his death. Primarily concerned with fostering the business, he took little part in public life. He was a member and supporter of the Pharmaceutical Society of South Australia, but never held office. Survived by his wife and their two sons, he died on 8 April 1940 in his North Adelaide home and was cremated.

A Century of Medical Progress, 1845-1945 (Adel, 1945); P. Donovan and E. Tweddell, *The Faulding Formula* (Adel, 1995); *News* (Adel), 8 Apr 1940; *Advertiser* (Adel), 9 Apr 1940; F. H. Faulding & Co Ltd records, Adel; A. M. Madden papers (Mort L); information from Mr P. Scammell, Beaumont, Adel.

PETER DONOVAN

SCANTLEBURY, LILIAN AVIS (1894-1964), Red Cross worker, was born on 12 January 1894 at Collingwood, Melbourne, eldest child of Victorian-born parents Arthur Whybrow, boot manufacturer, and his wife Alice Williamina Hook, née Rostron. Lilian attended Ruyton Girls' School, Kew, and entered Trinity College Hostel (later Janet Clarke [q.v.3] Hall), University of Melbourne. She won a half-Blue for tennis.

Stirred by the grief and suffering caused by World War I, Miss Whybrow travelled to London and joined Vera Deakin [q.v. White] at the Australian Red Cross Society's wounded and missing inquiry bureau in 1916. She 'did her bit' by writing letters and handling anxious inquiries from the relations of servicemen. Her written expression—exercised with restraint and compassion—and her competence led to her appointment as head of the letter section, and, in 1919, of the bureau itself.

At St Peter's parish church, Hampstead, on 29 April 1920 she married George Clifford Scantlebury (1890-1976), a medical practitioner and younger brother of Vera Scantlebury Brown [q.v.11]. Cliff had served in the Royal Army Medical Corps during the war. In

1922 the Scantleburys returned to Melbourne. He was to be elected a fellow (1928) of the College of Surgeons of Australasia (Royal Australasian College of Surgeons) and appointed a consulting surgeon (1946) to the ear and throat department, Royal Melbourne Hospital.

Raised by a mother who believed in the equality of the sexes, Cliff supported Lilian's voluntary work. She helped to oversee the growth and development of the Australian Red Cross Society. Following the devastating bush-fires of January 1939, and anticipating another world war, she was 'one of the chief architects' of a scheme to train members of the society to cope with natural disasters or civil-defence emergencies. From 1940 she was deputy-commandant of the Victorian division and a member of its women personnel committee. During World War II the Red Cross established a new inquiry bureau to communicate with the next of kin of servicemen and women listed as wounded, missing or taken prisoner. Scantlebury resumed her letter-writing, and served as co-director (1940) and director (1945) of the Victorian office. Made an honorary life member (1948) of the Victorian division of the A.R.C.S., she was co-opted to the national council in 1950 and elected junior vice-chairman in 1951 (senior vice-chairman 1960). In 1957 she represented Australia at a Red Cross conference in India. She was appointed O.B.E. in 1959.

Scantlebury built strong networks through women's organizations such as the Lyceum Club, and remained interested in higher education. In 1926 she had been elected to the committee of Janet Clarke Hall. She also served (1939-61) on the Trinity College council as a representative of J.C.H. A leader in the movement to establish J.C.H. as an autonomous institution, she joined its inaugural council in 1961. A wing of the hall was named after her.

Imbued with the same humanitarian values as the family into which she married, Scantlebury had a warm nature and sense of humour. She was respected for her judgement, 'clear and unemotional thinking', personal integrity, administrative ability and leadership. Although she was an unassuming and self-effacing woman, she proved an excellent speaker. People turned to her for advice, and found her dignified, charming and gracious. She died of coronary vascular disease on 12 April 1964 in South Melbourne and was cremated. Her husband and their daughter survived her.

H. Y. Daniell, *History of Ruyton 1878-1956* (Melb, 1957?); Aust Red Cross Soc (Vic), *Newsnotes*, no 101, May 1964; *Univ Melb Gazette*, Sept 1964; M. Blackwood, address at memorial service for Mrs G. C. Scantlebury, 3 May 1964 (ts on ADB file, Canb); W. Kapper, interview with Mrs Eileen Lester, 1976, Vera Scantlebury Brown papers (Univ Melb Archives).   PHILIPPA MEIN SMITH

SCARF, EDWARD RICHARD (1908-1980), wrestler and butcher, was born on 3 November 1908 at Quirindi, New South Wales, fourth child of Lebanese-born parents Michael Eli Scarf, grocer, and his wife Amelia, née Zraysarty. His father's surname had originally been Alissis. Eddie was educated at the Marist Brothers' School, North Sydney, where he excelled at sport. Five ft 11 ins (180 cm) tall and 15 st. 8 lb. (99 kg) in weight, with large hands and a chest measurement of 45½ ins (116 cm), he was considered to be ideally equipped for wrestling.

In 1927 Scarf won the New South Wales amateur heavyweight wrestling championship. Although he retained it in 1928, and also won the State middleweight title and an Olympic Games test-tournament, he was not selected for the Olympics that year. In 1930 he took the New South Wales heavyweight championships in both wrestling and boxing. A string of wrestling titles—including the Australian heavyweight championship in 1929 and 1932—earned him a place in the national team for the 1932 Olympics, held at Los Angeles, United States of America. He won a bronze medal in the light-heavyweight freestyle event, Australia's first Olympic medal in wrestling: in an impressive and cheerful display, he was defeated in his final bout by the American Peter Mehringer.

Returning to Sydney, Scarf built up the family's butchery business at Narrabeen and consolidated his wrestling career. He won his third Australian heavyweight championship in 1935 and the New South Wales and national light-heavyweight titles in 1937 and 1938. Continuing to excel at boxing, he gained the State heavyweight championship in 1934 and 1938. His performances at the 1936 Olympic Games in Berlin aroused considerable excitement. In a tough and contentious wrestling tournament —during which several countries protested against decisions by the judges—a number of questionable decisions went against him and he finished sixth in the light-heavyweight division. He won the gold medal in that division at the 1938 British Empire Games in Sydney.

Turning professional, Scarf won a competition promoted by Stadiums Ltd to decide the Australian heavyweight wrestling championship in 1938. He drew large, animated crowds, especially on 11 November 1940 when he defeated 'Chief Little Wolf' (Ventura Tenario) on points and took home £100 from a side-wager on the match. A supporter had cried out, 'Cut him up, Butch!', as Scarf executed a new hold which looked as if he was 'trussing a side of beef in his butcher's shop'. The crowd 'cheered wildly' when he applied Little Wolf's signature hold, the 'Indian Death Lock', to the Chief himself. On 29 April 1941 Scarf enlisted in the Royal Australian Air Force and was employed as a storekeeper. He served (1943-45) with the Parachute Training Unit and was discharged from the R.A.A.F. on 7 February 1945.

At the Church of Our Lady of Dolours, Chatswood, on 30 July 1942 Scarf had married with Catholic rites Edna May Gale, a munitions worker. After the war, he briefly resumed wrestling before concentrating on his business and opening shops at North Narrabeen, Dee Why and Palm Beach. Involved in community and charity work, he was a founding member of the Warringah Rotary Club, and president and first patron of the House With No Steps. He belonged to the Dee Why Surf Life-Saving Club and played golf like a 'ploughman'. In semi-retirement, he moved to Muswellbrook in 1969 and ran a feedlot. He died on 7 January 1980 at Camperdown and was buried in Mona Vale cemetery; his wife, and their daughter and two sons survived him. Noted sportsmen, among them Tommy Burns, Frank 'Bumper' Farrell and Jim Armstrong, attended his funeral.

D. Cameron, *The Science of Wrestling* (Syd, nd); L. Ayoub, *100 Years of Australian Professional Wrestling* (Syd, 1998); *Manly Daily*, 12 Feb 2000; information from and papers held by Mr M. Scarf, Saratoga, NSW, and Mr R. Scarf, North Narrabeen, Syd.   TOM SEAR

SCARFE, WARREN JAMES (1936-1964), cyclist, was born on 11 December 1936 at Newcastle, New South Wales, son of Australian-born parents Arthur Parsonage Scarfe, engineer, and his wife Eva Frances Macmillan, née Bryden. Educated at Hurstville South Public and Sydney Technical High schools, Warren began work as a cadet draftsman in the Postmaster-General's Department. He studied at night at Sydney Technical College, gaining a diploma in electrical engineering (1955) and the P.M.G. draftsman's certificate (1957). At St Mark's Church of England, Hurstville, on 1 October 1956 he married 18-year-old Margaret Jessie Goldsworthy, with whom he built a house in Tonitto Avenue, Peakhurst. The home remained their permanent residence and there they raised three children. Scarfe was a devoted breadwinner who did not squander his earnings: he made advance payments on the mortgage and built his own furniture. A much-loved husband and father, he balanced, with equanimity, his work, study, family commitments and passion for cycling.

Scarfe had joined the powerful St George Amateur Cycle Club as a junior and shown great promise. Blond haired and 6 ft (183 cm) tall, he was a lightly built rider and seemed naturally athletic, but he worked hard at maintaining fitness and honing his technique. He was adept at both road and track riding, and held four national records: a distance of 26 miles 655 yards (42.44 km) over one hour (1958), the 1000m time trial in 1 minute 9.7 seconds (1958), the 4000m individual pursuit in 5 minutes 2.3 seconds (1959) and the 4000m four-man team pursuit in 4 minutes 42.2 seconds (1960). He won two Australian titles, the 1000m time trial (1956) and the 4000m individual pursuit (1958). Scarfe represented Australia at the Olympic Games in Melbourne (1956), where he finished a creditable fourth in the 1000m individual pursuit. At the 1958 British Empire and Commonwealth Games at Cardiff, Wales, he won the silver medal in the 1000m time trial. After suffering equipment failure, he was unplaced in the 4000m team pursuit at the Olympic Games in Rome (1960).

In his frugal manner, Scarfe had tried to cover legitimate expenses associated with representative competition and remained an amateur. In 1959 he was dropped from the New South Wales team to compete at the Australian Cycling Championships in Perth for failing to pay the required £5 towards his expenses (£100) by the due date. During the half-time break of a St George Rugby League match he provided a riding exhibition while bags were carried around the ground to collect money from spectators to support his Olympic campaign.

In 1961, riding through Newtown, Scarfe swerved to avoid a pedestrian, crashed heavily, and fractured his skull. For the next three years he devoted most of his time to coaching junior cyclists at the St George club, and to supporting his younger brother Ian, winner of the 1963 State amateur road cycling championship. Warren was lured back to racing, but fell while training at Wiley Park on 4 November 1964 and died of head injuries before reaching hospital. Survived by his wife, and their daughter and two sons, he was cremated.

The New South Wales Cycling Federation quickly set up a 'Warren Scarfe Appeal', which received enough money for Margaret to clear the mortgage on the house. Characteristically, Warren had already paid other bills in advance and stowed away Christmas presents for his children. His son David competed at the Olympic Games in Moscow (1980) and the Commonwealth Games in Brisbane (1982). The St George club stages the Warren Scarfe memorial race annually.

W. T. J. Uren (comp), *Australian Olympic Team at Melbourne* (Melb, 1957); F. Tierney (comp), *Australian Olympic Games Team, Rome, 1960* (Melb, 1960); *Aust Cyclist*, Dec 1956, Jan, Feb 1957, May, June 1958, Mar 1959, Dec 1964, Jan 1965; *SMH*,

23 Aug 1956, 13 Jan, 12 May 1957, 14 Feb, 24 July 1958, 18 Feb 1960, 5 Nov 1964; *Sun* (Syd), 10 Mar 1959; *Daily Telegraph* (Syd), 5 Nov 1964; information from Mr I. Scarfe, Lugarno, and Mr P. Bates, Gymea Bay, NSW.   DARYL ADAIR

SCERRI, GEORGE (1910-1980), Catholic priest, was born on 16 May 1910 at Qormi, Malta, and registered as Francesco, second of six surviving sons of Carmelo Scerri, shopkeeper, and his wife Vincenza, née Zerafa. Educated at St Aloysius' College, Birkirkara, and St Mark's Theological School, Rabat, he joined the Missionary Society of St Paul in January 1929 and took the religious name of George. He was ordained priest on 2 April 1938 and assigned to St Joseph's Technical Institute, Hamrun, a home for orphans and underprivileged children. While there, he ran a printing-press which published a daily Catholic newspaper.

In 1958-61 Fr Scerri served as chaplain in a number of ships which took thousands of Maltese migrants to Australia and Canada. Based in Canada in 1960-62, from time to time he also attended to the spiritual needs of immigrants at London, Ontario, and Detroit, Michigan, United States of America. In 1963, through an arrangement between the M.S.S.P. and Cardinal (Sir) Norman Gilroy [q.v.14], archbishop of Sydney, Scerri arrived in Australia. He was sent to minister in East Sydney, a district known for its concentrations of newly arrived immigrants, crowded boarding-houses, gambling dens and brothels. Next year he opened a small chapel in a property purchased at Stanley Street and named De Piro House after the society's founder, Monsignor Joseph De Piro.

Appointed provincial of the M.S.S.P. in Australia in 1971, Scerri moved from Sydney to Melbourne. The society had been established there in 1948 and the city was home to Australia's largest number of Maltese (about 23 000 born in Malta). He had a major impact, not only as a priest who developed trust and respect, but as an individual who was determined to unify the Maltese community. The handsome and modern *Centru Malti* (Maltese Centre), built on M.S.S.P. premises in Royal Parade, Parkville, testified to his dedication towards this goal.

On 13 July 1980 Scerri was savagely assaulted in the society's residence, St Mary's Mission House, Sydney Road, Brunswick, by a person or persons unknown. He died from his injuries on 4 August that year in Royal Melbourne Hospital and was buried in Melbourne general cemetery. The death of 'Dun Gorg' (Father George), as he was affectionately known, horrified and stunned the Maltese community and the public at large.

His death was also reported in Malta, where a requiem Mass was held.

Remembered as having a kind smile for everyone, Scerri was, at the time of his death, one of the most experienced of the M.S.S.P.'s seventeen priests in Melbourne, Sydney and Perth. Like other members of the society, he led a frugal life. He had the ability 'to listen and to offer advice'. Fr Stanley Tomlin, the M.S.S.P.'s superior general in Malta, praised him as a man who 'never drove a car, and yet could be seen in any church, hospital and home at any time'. An obituary in the *Times* (Malta) described his life as 'saintly and exemplary'.

B. York, *Maltese in Australia* (Melb, 1998); *Link*, 6 Apr 1981; *Footprints*, Nov 1990; *Times* (Malta), 5 Aug 1980; *Catholic Weekly* (Syd), 21 Sept 1980.
BARRY YORK

SCHAAF, FRANK RONALD (1915-1978), air force officer, was born on 22 July 1915 at Tenterfield, New South Wales, elder child of Frank Otto Schaaf, tram guard, and his wife Ivy Beatrice, née Hill, both born in New South Wales. Young Frank attended Clovelly Public and Sydney Technical High schools, and studied accountancy at the Metropolitan Business College. He passed the Federal Institute of Accountants' examinations and worked as a clerk with a number of Phillip Street barristers, with export firms and with a transport company. Having served in the cadets, he transferred to the Militia, became a gunner with the 18th Field Brigade, reached the rank of warrant officer, class 2, and was discharged from the army in 1936. At the district registrar's office, Chatswood, on 10 May 1937 he married May Rachel Donnelly; they were childless and divorced in March 1945.

On 21 March 1938 Schaaf had joined the Royal Australian Air Force as an aircraftman 1, clerk. He was posted to No.3 Squadron at Richmond, where he was promoted corporal in January 1940 and sergeant in July. Two months later he applied for aircrew training. Sent for flying instruction to Mascot in December and to Wagga Wagga in February 1941, he was commissioned on 3 June. He arrived in Britain in August and, after operational training, was posted in November to No.452 Squadron, R.A.A.F., based at Redhill, Surrey. The pilots in this Spitfire unit included Keith ('Bluey') Truscott [q.v.] and C. N. ('Bardie') Wawn.

In February 1942 Flying Officer Schaaf was sent to Egypt. There, on 6 June, he joined No.450 Squadron, an R.A.A.F. fighter-bomber unit which flew Kittyhawks. Within three weeks he claimed his first aerial victory, for damaging a Messerschmitt 109. On 22 January 1943 he shot down one Me-109, shared in shooting down another and damaged a third. During the advance to Tripoli, Libya, he held temporary command (January-February) of the squadron and led it 'with great distinction'. By the end of his period in the Western Desert he had destroyed three enemy aircraft in aerial combat and won the Distinguished Flying Cross.

Reaching Melbourne on 21 March 1943, Schaaf was employed as an instructor at No.2 Operational Training Unit, Mildura. He was promoted flight lieutenant in June. After training as a fighter controller at New Lambton, New South Wales, he served with No.104 Fighter Sector Headquarters at Port Moresby from October and with No.111 Mobile Fighter Control Unit at Aitape, New Guinea, from April 1944. He returned to Australia in August. In May 1945 he was posted to No.82 Squadron at Noemfoor, Netherlands East Indies; he commanded the unit at Labuan, Borneo, from July and was made acting squadron leader in October. He led a strike against Kuching on 8 August, which entailed a long return trip of 950 miles (1530 km) for the Kittyhawks. Three enemy aircraft were destroyed on the ground. For 'exceptional operational ability, leadership and courage' Schaaf was awarded a Bar to his D.F.C.

At the end of World War II No.82 Squadron was re-equipped with Mustang fighters in anticipation of its deployment to Japan as part of the British Commonwealth Occupation Force. On 18 October 1945 at Glenferrie, Melbourne, Schaaf married with Presbyterian forms Margaret Florence McKenzie, a hairdresser. In March 1946 he took his squadron to Bofu, Japan. He acted from time to time as temporary commander of No.81 (Fighter) Wing before returning to Australia in February 1947 to commence a series of instructional, test-flying and staff appointments, including postings to the Central Flying School, Point Cook, Victoria, No.78 Wing headquarters, Williamtown, New South Wales, and the Aircraft Research Unit, Laverton, Victoria. Promoted wing commander in July 1954, he served on the staff of the Australian air attaché, Washington, and on exchange with the United States Air Force in 1956-59. He was later employed at the Department of Air, Canberra, in the directorate of organization and the electronic data processing centre. On his retirement on 10 November 1964, he was made honorary group captain.

After working for R. A. Irish & Michelmore, a firm of chartered accountants in Sydney, Schaaf moved to Canberra in 1970 and joined the Commonwealth Public Service. He died of myocardial infarction on 18 April 1978 in Canberra Hospital and was cremated with Anglican rites; his wife, and their daughter and son survived him.

G. Odgers, *Air War Against Japan 1943-45* (Canb, 1957); Operations record book, 82, 450, 452 Squadrons, RAAF, 1939-45 (NAA); information from Mrs K. M. Cockle, Drummoyne, Syd.

DAVID WILSON

SCHERF, CHARLES CURNOW (1917-1949), grazier and air force officer, was born on 17 May 1917 at Emmaville, New South Wales, sixth child of Charles Henry Scherf, a New South Wales-born grazier of German descent, and his wife Susan Jane, née Curnow, who came from England. Young Charles attended the one-teacher school at Emmaville and gained the Intermediate certificate. Five ft 9 ins (175 cm) tall, he became a well-known local sportsman. From 1934 he served in the 12th Light Horse Regiment (Militia), in which he reached the rank of corporal. At Holy Trinity Church, Glen Innes, on 23 August 1939 he married with Anglican rites Florence Hope O'Hara.

When World War II broke out, Scherf was working on his father's property. On 12 September 1941 he enlisted in the Royal Australian Air Force. Following training at Temora and at Mallala, South Australia, he obtained an 'above average' rating, received his pilot's brevet on 2 July 1942 and was commissioned on 17 September. Next month he was sent to Britain where he undertook advanced flying and operational training. He joined No.418 Squadron (a Royal Canadian Air Force attack unit equipped with Mosquito light bombers) on 13 July 1943.

In August Scherf began 'Intruder' operations against enemy airfields in France. He flew an escorting Mosquito on 15 September when eight Lancaster bombers of No.617 Squadron attacked the Dortmund-Ems Canal, Germany, at low level and suffered heavy losses. On 29 December he was promoted acting flight lieutenant. By the end of February 1944 he had destroyed seven German aircraft on the ground or in the air, and shared the credit for shooting down an eighth. He was made acting squadron leader on 13 March and posted to headquarters, Air Defence Great Britain, as a controller of 'Intruder' operations. When he was off duty he revisited No.418 Squadron and flew combat sorties. During three such so called 'holiday excursions'—on 5 April, and 2 and 16 May—he added a further sixteen German aircraft to his tally. On 4 April he won the Distinguished Flying Cross for his performance on night missions. He was awarded a Bar to his D.F.C. in May for displaying 'the greatest qualities of gallantry and skill'. His Distinguished Service Order, gazetted in June, recognized his 'enterprise and fearlessness'. In a total of 38 operational sorties, he was credited with 14½ kills in the air, nine aircraft destroyed on the ground, and a further seven damaged.

Scherf returned to Australia in September 1944. Next month he was posted as chief flying instructor to No.5 Operational Training Unit, Williamtown, New South Wales. On 11 April 1945 he transferred to the R.A.A.F. Reserve and went home to Emmaville. He found it difficult to adjust to peacetime life and showed signs of stress. At night he spoke about the war in Europe and the death-toll of people he knew. He also said that 'the Germans he had killed seemed to march across his bed in the darkness'. Subdued and restless, he drank heavily and began to drive his motorcar at high speed. On 13 July 1949 his car hit a tree and overturned on the Inverell road, two miles from Emmaville; he died later that day from his injuries and was buried in the local cemetery. His wife, and their son and three daughters survived him.

J. Herington, *Air Power over Europe 1944-1945* (Canb, 1963); L. McAulay, *Six Aces* (Melb, 1991); *Aircraft*, 22, Aug 1944; *SMH*, 29 Feb, 7 Apr, 4, 18 May, 18 Oct 1944.   JOHN MCCARTHY

SCHLUNKE, ERIC OTTO (1906-1960), farmer and author, was born on 5 May 1906 at Duck Creek (Trungley Hall), a German community near Temora, New South Wales, fourth child of Albert Hermann Schlunke (d.1927), farmer, and his wife Hilda Amelia, née Stockman, both South Australian born and of German descent. Eric was educated at the local Lutheran school and (in 1922-23) at Hurlstone Agricultural High School, Summer Hill, Sydney. He then joined his father and brothers on Hope Vale, a 2300-acre (930 ha) wheat and sheep property at Reefton.

The 1920s were boom years, but Eric and his brother Herbert had a hard struggle during the Depression. Eric began to write humorous stories for the *Bulletin*. He was so excited by his first cheque in 1933 that he crashed the car on the way home from town. More stories followed, first for the *Bulletin* and later *Meanjin,* and from 1944 he was regularly represented in the anthologies *Coast to Coast*. At the Lutheran Trinity Church, Albury, on 15 April 1939 he had married Olga Ottilie Huf with the forms of the Evangelical Lutheran Church.

All this time Schlunke (pronounced 'Slunky') was a hard-working and enterprising farmer. Carrying out extensive pasture improvement and soil conservation at Hope Vale, he pioneered the use of contour ploughing (with a chisel plough), flumes (grassed waterways) and holding dams—to maximize rainfall effectiveness and check erosion. He wrote about his work and spoke on the Australian

Broadcasting Commission's radio series the 'Land and its People'.

Schlunke's life, like his range as a writer, was virtually confined to the wheat and sheep country of the Riverina, its towns and its people. He described the taciturn farmers and farm labourers (especially those of the sober-minded German community), the pastors, schoolteachers, bank managers, stock-and-station agents and the womenfolk with a gentle, dry and mildly satirical humour. A number of his stories were about Italian prisoners of war who worked as farm hands during World War II. He published two collections of stories, *The Man in the Silo* (Sydney, 1955) and *The Village Hampden* (Sydney, 1958). Some of his stories were translated and published in Germany, Denmark, Czechoslovakia and the Soviet Union.

Schlunke also wrote five novels, though none appeared in book form. Two of them, 'Rosenthal' and 'Foray on Freeling', were serialized in the *Sydney Morning Herald* in 1939, and 'Feather Your Nest' in the *Bulletin* in 1954. His best work, 'Rosenthal', told the story of three generations of German-Australian farmers: Adolph Weismann who established Rosenthal, his son Karl, and grandson Otto (Schlunke himself) on whom the story centred. An impressive chronicle of the effects of fundamental Lutheranism on its adherents, and a compelling study of a rural childhood, it 'glows', according to one critic, 'as does all Schlunke's writing, with affection for the landscape and the rural life'. As a regional writer, Schlunke has been favourably compared with F. D. Davison [q.v.13] and Peter Cowan. Schlunke's unpublished diaries are very georgic; they provide a valuable record of his literary progress and of the practicalities of farming in mid-twentieth century New South Wales.

Recognition largely eluded Schlunke during his lifetime. The tyranny of the farmer's routine meant that he rarely left Hope Vale. Ill health dogged him for much of his life, and he suffered from depression. On 18 November 1960 he shot himself in the head at his Reefton property while 'his mind was unbalanced'. He was buried with Anglican rites in Temora cemetery. His wife (who contributed poems to the *Bulletin*), and their daughter and two sons survived him. A selection from Schlunke's first two collections, with seven additional tales, was published posthumously as *Stories of the Riverina* (Sydney, 1965).

C. Semmler, *For the Uncanny Man* (Melb, 1963); J. B. Koch, *The German Pioneers in the Temora District, 1880-1914* (Temora, 1968); *Meanjin Q*, Dec 1961, p 407; *SMH*, 19 Apr, 16 Aug 1939, 29 Mar 1958, 19 Mar 1966; *Bulletin*, 15 Aug 1951, 8 Dec 1954, 10 Aug 1956, 11 Jan 1961; *Sun-Herald* (Syd),

15 May 1955; *Temora Independent*, 18 Jan 1971; *Australian*, 2-3 Apr 1988; Schlunke papers (ML).

G. P. WALSH

SCHMELLA, JOHN MATTAO (1908-1960), Labor Party secretary, was born on 24 February 1908 at Charters Towers, Queensland, youngest of three children of John Mattao Sciarmella, an Italian-born miner, and his wife Mary, née Brahan, who came from Ireland. Educated at the Christian Brothers' Mount Carmel College, Jack entered the Department of Public Instruction in 1924. He taught in turn at Cloncurry, Hughenden and Townsville North state schools. On 20 August 1929 at St Mary's Catholic Church, Townsville, he married Gladys Mary Parsons, a nurse. After working as a jackeroo, prospector and miner, he became a shift-foreman with Mount Isa Mines Ltd, joined the Australian Workers' Union and the Australian Labor Party, and began to style himself John Matthew Schmella.

In 1945 C. G. Fallon [q.v.14] recruited him as a research officer for the A.W.U. Within five years Schmella was the union's industrial officer. Elected State secretary of the A.L.P. in June 1952, he was a delegate to the party's federal executive from November that year. The *Courier-Mail* reported that he was regarded in Labor circles as 'popular, practical and brilliant'. Campaign director for the State election in 1953, he brought to the task a capacity for hard work, considerable industrial experience and the support of the A.W.U. Labor achieved a majority of 25 in the 75-seat Legislative Assembly, assisted by the zonal system of redistribution introduced in 1949. Schmella soon developed a relationship of trust and respect with other unions and the party branches. At the Labor-in-Politics convention held at Rockhampton in 1953, he reported that the party had gained a thousand new members, formed fifty new branches, affiliated five additional unions, launched a youth movement and improved the performance of its radio-station, 4KQ. By a vote of 105 to 7, the convention approved the report of the industrial groups (which had been formed to fight communism in the trade unions) and carried without debate a resolution supporting the extension of three weeks annual leave to workers under State awards.

Schmella was elected secretary of the party's federal executive in July 1954. Three months later Dr H. V. Evatt [q.v.14], leader of the parliamentary Labor Party, made a dramatic attack on the industrial groups, precipitating the most profound crisis in the A.L.P. since the split over conscription in 1916. The federal executive intervened to establish a new central executive in Victoria and facilitated a compromise between the left and right factions in New South Wales. At a special conference in Hobart in March 1955, Schmella played a central role in negotiations and decisions which were to weaken the power of the groups. He did so despite the decision of five Queensland delegates, including the premier V. C. Gair [q.v.14] and treasurer E. J. Walsh [q.v.], not to take part in the proceedings. Eight members of the Federal parliament subsequently resigned from the A.L.P. and formed the Anti-Communist (later Democratic) Labor Party.

In September 1955 the A.L.P.'s Queensland Central Executive raised the issue of three weeks leave with the State government. Cabinet supported the proposal in principle, but felt that economic conditions did not allow its immediate introduction. The trade unions then united against the government. Organized by Schmella, Joe Bukowski [q.v.13] and (Sir) John Egerton, the Labor-in-Politics convention held at Mackay in February-March 1956 overwhelmingly endorsed the proposal for three weeks leave. Despite undercurrents in the party, Labor was returned to office in Queensland two months later, with a large majority, after an election campaign run by Schmella. On 28 February 1957 the Q.C.E. issued an ultimatum to the parliamentary party, demanding the introduction of three weeks leave. The government refused to be bullied and on 18 April the Q.C.E. passed a vote of no confidence in Gair. In the early hours of 25 April Schmella successfully moved a resolution to expel Gair from the A.L.P. Gair formed the Queensland Labor Party. Following a bitterly fought campaign, the Liberal-Country Party coalition won office at the election on 3 August.

Over the next three years the federal executive and federal conference began operating more efficiently. Schmella worked towards the formation of a national secretariat, which was approved in principle in August 1958. In Queensland, he and George Whiteside, the president of the Q.C.E., encouraged branch members to become more involved in the union-dominated party. Five years of trauma and the effects of heavy drinking took their toll on Schmella's health, forcing him to enter hospital in December 1959. He died of hypertensive renal disease on 18 July 1960 at his St Lucia home and was buried in Toowong cemetery; his wife and their two daughters survived him.

C. Lack (comp), *Three Decades of Queensland Political History, 1929-1960* (Brisb, 1962); R. Murray, *The Split* (Melb, 1970); D. J. Murphy et al (eds), *Labor in Power* (Brisb, 1980); *Courier-Mail*, 1 Aug 1952, 19 July 1960; ALP federal executive records (NL); ALP (Qld) central executive records (OL); information from Miss K. Gallogly, Ascot, Brisb.

MANFRED CROSS

SCHNAARS, STEPHEN FREDERICK (1907-1980), industrial commissioner, was born on 16 December 1907 at Broken Hill, New South Wales, second of four children of South Australian-born parents James Schnaars, silverminer, and his wife Martha Harriet, née Rickard. The family moved to Western Australia where Fred was educated at Albany State and Albany District High schools. During the 1930s he was secretary of several small trade unions, including the Western Australian branch of the Merchant Service Guild of Australasia and the Coach, Car and Rolling Stock Builders' Union. From 1938 he appeared before the Western Australian Court of Arbitration as an industrial advocate for various unions. In 1947 he became the employees' representative in that court. On 23 April 1949 he was appointed a conciliation commissioner. After (Sir) David Brand's [q.v.13] government replaced the Arbitration Court with the Western Australian Industrial Commission, Schnaars was made chief industrial commissioner on 24 January 1964. He was to serve for only four years before resigning in January 1968 on the grounds of ill health.

As an advocate Schnaars had been competent; as an industrial commissioner he gained a reputation for firmness and fairness. He maintained links with union officials, among them Paddy Troy [q.v.], secretary of the West Australian branch of the militant Federated Ship Painters' and Dockers' Union of Australia, from whom he sometimes sought advice on cases. Schnaars was proud of his willingness to 'go anywhere to inspect a claim'. While he was conciliation commissioner, he responded to Troy's challenge to don a diving-suit and inspect the bottom of Fremantle harbour before making a judgement on an award claim by divers. According to one version of events, he panicked under water and was pulled up 'almost expired from fear and exhaustion'. In 1960 he reinstated eight trade unionists whom the Fremantle Harbour Trust had suspended for refusing to work on a ship that had been refitted at sea. He could also be tough. In a similar case in 1963 he ordered the striking union to return to work. When bus drivers and conductors had applied for a new award in 1961, he departed from court precedent to grant male workers an increased margin, but refused to grant conductresses the male wage, despite acknowledging that they did the same work as conductors.

Schnaars' appointment as chief industrial commissioner was seen by some as an attempt by the ruling Liberal-Country Party to placate a union movement hostile to the government's sweeping changes to the industrial system. As the State's most experienced arbitrator, however, his selection was a pragmatic one. On his retirement, Schnaars was praised by Brand

for his 'sense of impartiality and responsibility'. In 1968 he was appointed C.B.E.

Pictured in his mid-forties, Schnaars had a good-natured face, with a wide mouth and large ears. In later life he wore spectacles. He enjoyed bowls and swimming. At the Presbyterian Church, East Fremantle, on 8 October 1938 he had married Isabella Munro Lindsay, a 32-year-old clerk. After her death in 1970, he moved to Heathmont, Melbourne. On 21 February 1972 at the office of the government statist he married Patricia June Hood, née Peck, a widow who had previously changed her surname to Schnaars by deed poll. Survived by his wife, he died on 3 June 1980 at Croydon and was cremated.

S. Macintyre, *Militant* (Syd, 1984); *WA Industrial Gazette*, 29, 1949, 43, 1963/64, pt 4; *West Australian*, 8 Dec 1967, 1 Jan 1968, 6 June 1980; information from Mr W. S. Latter, Fremantle, WA.

BOBBIE OLIVER

SCHNEIDER, FRANZ XAVIER (1895-1952), public servant, was born on 4 December 1895 at Hawthorn, Melbourne, second child of Vincent Schneider (d.1920), a butcher from Württemberg (Germany), and his Victorian-born wife Annie, née O'Callaghan (d.1896). In 1903 Vincent married Annie's sister Minnie; they were to have two sons. Franz was educated at a private school run by Miss Kate O'Connor and at Xavier College, Kew. A small youth—even as an adult he was less than 5 ft (152 cm) tall—he coxed the college VIII, and played cricket and Australian Rules football.

In September 1914 Schneider obtained temporary employment in the deputy crown solicitor's office, Commonwealth Public Service, Melbourne. On 7 January 1915 he was appointed a clerk in the office of the public service commissioner (Public Service Board from 1922). He tried to enlist in the Australian Imperial Force on 9 March 1916, but was rejected on the grounds of his height. Despite being a naturalized British subject, Vincent Schneider was compelled by anti-German prejudice to move alone to Mount Gambier, South Australia, shortly after the outbreak of World War I; he was to return in 1920, broken in health and spirit. Meanwhile, Franz and his elder sister Theresa supported their stepmother and half-brothers, enabling the boys to attend Xavier College. At St Mary's Catholic Church, Hawthorn, on 5 February 1925 Franz married Eileen Martha Cummins, née Payne, a widow.

The Public Service Board was transferred to Canberra in 1928. In his spare time Schneider enjoyed sport. He played for the Ainslie Football and Northbourne Cricket clubs, and was honorary secretary (1932-40) of the (Royal) Canberra Golf Club. Through golf, he met the prime minister J. A. Lyons [q.v.10]; their children often played together at The Lodge. In November 1938 Schneider was appointed Lyons' private secretary. He remained in that post until Lyons died in April 1939, but declined (Sir) Robert Menzies' [q.v.15] invitation to stay on as his private secretary and returned to the Public Service Board.

In 1947 Schneider became secretary of the board. He proved to be a strong and influential figure: 'more than simply the voice of the board—he *was* the board in many respects'. The public service unions regarded him as sincere, fair and impartial in his dealings with them. He laid the foundations for a joint council, comprising representatives of the board, major departments and the unions, to assist staff relations. In 1951 the Menzies government reduced the Commonwealth public service payroll by a flat 10 per cent. Schneider had to oversee the ensuing retrenchments. One of his officers found his manner correct and strict, but bordering on the irascible. From 1947 Schneider suffered from a duodenal ulcer. Towards the end of his life he occasionally drank to excess.

Survived by his wife and their three daughters, and by his step-daughter, Schneider died of a subarachnoid haemorrhage on 16 May 1952 at Canberra Community Hospital and was buried in Canberra cemetery. The fact that he was the third in succession of the board's secretaries to die in office indicated the strains imposed on senior public servants.

G. E. Caiden, *Career Service* (Melb, 1965); W. Dunk, *They Also Serve* (Canb, 1974); *Canb Times*, 6 Aug, 27 Sept 1929, 17 May 1952; *SMH*, 9 Nov 1938, 8 Apr 1939; A7581, item Schneider, F. X. (NAA, Canb); information from Mrs J. P. McCrone, Pearce, and Mr R. Hyslop, Yarralumla, Canb. PETER ELDER

SCHOENHEIMER, HENRY PHILIP (1918-1976), educationist, was born on 12 October 1918 in South Brisbane, son of Australian-born Jewish parents Ferdinand Arthur Schoenheimer, motor mechanic, and his wife Abigail Elizabeth, née Moss. Henry's childhood was at times unhappy, and he left home and Brisbane Grammar School in 1934. He began teaching in North Queensland, at Bloomsbury State School, then transferred to Beatrice River, near Innisfail, in 1936, to Taringa, Brisbane, in 1941, and to Charleville in 1946. While teaching, he studied at the University of Queensland (B.A., 1952) as an external student. As he gained experience, he came to value highly the student-teacher relationship within the learning process and to see education as a dynamic and interactive experience.

Moving to Melbourne in 1951, Schoenheimer taught in turn at Mount Scopus Memorial College and Malvern Grammar School, and studied at the University of Melbourne (Dip.Ed., 1955; B.Ed., 1956; M.Ed., 1961). On 12 October 1954 at the office of the government statist, Queen Street, he married Elizabeth Linda Andernach, a typist and stenographer. He lectured at Swinburne Technical College, and at Monash (1964-71) and La Trobe (1971-73) universities. An enthusiastic proponent of educational reform, he embraced the child-centred theories of thinkers such as Erich Fromm and A. S. Neill, and practices of such Australian schools as Margaret Lyttle's [q.v.15] Preshil. He used Karl Popper's criticism of Plato to support arguments in his lectures. Many students were drawn to his radical ideas. He strongly believed that university lecturers in education should have a background in teaching to enable them to relate theory to practice.

Schoenheimer published school texts, articles and children's books. In 1965-75 he was education correspondent for the *Australian*. He became a full-time writer and consultant in 1973 and joined the staff of the Australian Council for Educational Research in 1975. Two of his most influential books, *Good Schools* (Melbourne, 1970) and *Good Australian Schools and their Communities* (1973), discussed schools at home and abroad where teaching was student-based rather than curriculum dominated. As a leader in the alternative education movement of the 1960s and 1970s, he supported the development of innovative schools, among them the Education Reform Association's school at Donvale. He emphasized that schools should provide links between communities and students.

A secular humanist and an independent thinker, Schoenheimer held high hopes for humanity, but had difficulty in reconciling his ideals with his experiences. He thought that educators had a particular responsibility to find new ways of addressing issues such as over-population, the degradation of the natural environment and the exhaustion of non-renewable resources. In his last public address —given to the Australian School Library Association conference in 1976—he expressed his anxiety about the survival of civilization in the face of the Western world's increasing expectation of affluence and its apparent lack of concern for peace and social justice.

Schoenheimer was a striking figure. That he wore his clothes slightly awry indicated his indifference to social convention. Phillip Adams described him as 'one of those rare people who was greedy to give'. To Stephen Murray Smith, he was 'the sanest, most humane and thoughtful of all critics of the Australian education system'. Schoenheimer committed suicide by inhaling carbon monoxide gas on 24 September 1976 at Kangaroo Ground. Survived by his wife, and their two daughters and two sons, he was cremated.

Herald (Melb), 1 Oct 1976; *Age* (Melb), 6 Oct 1976; information from Mr E. and Mrs J. Schoenheimer, Main Beach, Qld, Prof J. Cleverley, Syd, Ms R. Schoenheimer, Balwyn, Mr D. and Miss M. Lyttle, Kew, and Mr G. Tickell, St Kilda, Melb.

MARGARET H. WHITE

SCHONELL, SIR FRED JOYCE (1900-1969), vice-chancellor and educationist, and FLORENCE ELEANOR (1902-1962), educationist, were husband and wife. Fred was born on 3 August 1900 in Perth, son of Edward William Schonell, a schoolmaster from Victoria, and his English-born wife Agnes Mary, née Mawer. He attended (on a scholarship) Perth Modern School, qualified as a teacher at the Training College, Claremont, in 1920, and taught in turn at Perth Boys' and Highgate State schools. Eleanor was born on 31 October 1902 at Durban, South Africa, daughter of Francis William de Bracey Waterman, a furniture-dealer from England, and his wife Maud Rebecca, née Turner. After arriving in Perth, she completed teacher-training at Claremont in 1922, and taught (1923-26) at primary schools at Subiaco and Jolimont. She and Fred were part-time students at the University of Western Australia and graduated (B.A., 1925) together. They were married on 21 December 1926 at St Alban's Anglican Church, Perth, and were to have two children.

When Fred was awarded a Hackett [q.v.9] studentship, the couple sailed for England in 1928. He studied at King's College and the London Day Training College, University of London (Dip.Ed., 1929; Ph.D., 1932; D.Lit., 1944). His Ph.D. thesis was on the diagnosis and remediation of difficulties in spelling. A lecturer (from 1933) at Goldsmiths' College, he carried out an extensive programme of research in schools. In 1942 he was appointed professor of education at the University College of Swansea, University of Wales. He rejuvenated a department suffering from the disruption caused by World War II. While his educational interests broadened from remedial education to include 'adolescence' and 'community involvement', he continued to be mainly concerned with the learning problems of primary-school children. *Backwardness in the Basic Subjects* (Edinburgh, 1942) and *The Psychology and Teaching of Reading* (Edinburgh, 1945) were his most important publications. His two series of reading books for children, the *Happy Venture* (Edinburgh, 1939-50) and *Wide Range* (Edinburgh, 1948-53), were used for several decades in schools throughout the English-speaking world, apart from the United States of America. A number of his books—some of which were co-authored with Eleanor—ran to several editions and reputedly sold 'millions' of copies.

In 1947 Schonell became professor of education at the University of Birmingham. Taking major responsibility for expanding the research activities of its institute of education, he developed a project that covered a wide range of topics: methods of teaching English to boys, the reading interests and library borrowings of children, the suitability of textbooks and leisure-reading books, selection of entrants for the teaching profession, and methods of teaching English and history. He was founding director of a remedial education centre: it tested and helped local students, and provided a base for research and in-service activities. To train teachers in aspects of remedial education, he instituted a diploma in educational psychology in 1948. That year he also established a journal, *Educational Review*.

Schonell received many invitations to lecture abroad. He declined the offer of a chair at the University of London to return to Australia where he became foundation professor of education at the University of Queensland in 1950. By 1952 a remedial education centre had opened with a former student from Birmingham, J. A. Richardson, as deputy-director. Schonell inaugurated a journal, *The Slow Learning Child* (first published in 1954), and introduced certificate courses to train remedial teachers and teachers of children with intellectual disabilities.

As head of the department of education, Schonell again displayed a broad range of interests. Projects included the oral language of Australian labourers, education of young Aborigines, maladjustment and school failure of intelligent children, social and educational problems of migrants' children, and the effect of the Queensland state scholarship examination on curriculum and teaching methods. The talented researchers whom he recruited included Betty Watts and R. J. Andrews. Schonell published *Essentials in Teaching and Testing Spelling* (Edinburgh, 1953) and, with Eleanor, *Diagnosis and Remedial Teaching in Arithmetic* (Edinburgh, 1957). He influenced teacher-training in Queensland by introducing a postgraduate diploma in education and a bachelor of education degree available to teachers by correspondence.

Eleanor Schonell had enrolled at University College, London (B.A. Hons, 1938; M.A., 1940), and written her master's thesis on the diagnosis of difficulties in written English. She collaborated with her husband in producing standardized ways to test children's academic attainment; these tests were published in *Diagnostic and Attainment Testing* (Edinburgh, 1950). At the University of Birmingham (Ph.D., 1950), she began to study children with cerebral palsy. With the support of J. M. Smellie, professor of paediatrics and child health, she developed procedures for assessing the intellectual and educational characteristics of such children. She also conducted surveys on cerebral palsy. While holding a research fellowship at the university, she worked (part time) as an educational psychologist at the Carlson House School for Spastics, which she had helped to establish in 1948 with funding from Paul Cadbury.

On her return to Australia, Dr Schonell took an active interest in the Queensland Spastic Children's Welfare League; she served on its medical and educational house committee (1951-61) and as honorary psychologist (1958). Her book, *Educating Spastic Children* (Edinburgh, 1956), found a receptive audience in the U.S.A. as well as in Commonwealth countries. She initiated educational and psychological testing of children with cerebral palsy, and wrote a chapter on the subject in *Recent Advances in Cerebral Palsy* (London, 1958), edited by R. S. Illingworth. Committed to providing special education for these children, she saw it as a means of taking them from institutions into the community. Her approach to life was generous and humane. She died of cerebral glioma on 22 May 1962 in Brisbane and was cremated.

After serving as president of the professorial board, Fred Schonell was appointed the first full-time salaried vice-chancellor of the University of Queensland in 1960. One of his biggest challenges was to address the budgetary problems facing a university at which enrolments more than doubled between 1957 and 1963. He recognized the importance of an alumnae association, oversaw the process of moving the remaining departments from George Street to the St Lucia site and recommended the purchase of nearby houses to permit expansion of the campus. Appreciating that too many able secondary school students in Queensland were not proceeding to university, he advocated an increase in the proportion of females in the student body and proposed that a film be made about university education for screening in high schools around the State. He was a member (1961-65) of Sir Leslie Martin's committee on the future of tertiary education in Australia.

In Schonell's nine years as vice-chancellor the number of students at the university grew from 7000 to 15 000. His initiative led to the creation of a student counselling service. He wrote *How to Study at the University* (Brisbane, 1961), urged residential colleges to cease 'initiation' practices, and promoted new courses in Asian Studies, social work and speech therapy. By carrying out a six-year study of the experiences of students, *Promise and Performance* (Brisbane, c.1962), he drew attention at home and abroad to ways of improving tertiary education. He supported better teaching methods and training courses for university lecturers. Responding cautiously to the rise of student radicalism, he offered students the opportunity to participate in a liaison committee, while warning them against violence and treason.

Outside the university, Schonell worked in community groups (especially the Queensland Sub-Normal Children's Welfare Association) which struggled to secure educational and related services for intellectually impaired children and their families. A founding member (1954) of the Australian Elizabethan Theatre Trust, he was a director of the Winston Churchill Memorial Trust and chairman (1966) of its Queensland and national selection committees. He was awarded an honorary D.Litt. (1963) by the University of Western Australia and an honorary LL.D. (1965) by the University of Sydney. In 1962 he was knighted. That year he received the Bancroft [q.v.3] medal from the Australian Medical Association and the Alexander Mackie [q.v.10] medal from the Australian and New Zealand Association for the Advancement of Science. An inaugural fellow (1960) of the Australian College of Education, he was an honorary fellow of both the Australian and British Psychological societies.

In spite of illness, Sir Fred carried on as vice-chancellor, with increasing assistance from his deputy Professor Hartley Teakle [q.v.]. Survived by his son and daughter, he died of Hodgkin's disease on 22 February 1969 at his Indooroopilly home and was cremated. Like his wife, he was remembered for his warm nature and his interest in people. The Fred and Eleanor Schonell Educational Research Centre at the university was named (1967) after them.

M. I. Thomis, *A Place of Light and Learning* (Brisb, 1985); *Univ Qld Gazette*, no 50, 1962, p 4, no 69, 1969, p 1; *Exceptional Child*, 29, 1982, p 155, 30, 1983, p 3.

JOHN ELKINS

SCHRAMM, LEO PAUL (1892-1953), pianist and composer, was born on 22 September 1892 in Vienna, son of Marie Hofmann. His father was probably Gustav Schramm whom his mother subsequently married. After studying piano with Rudolf Kaiser, Paul made his concert début at the age of 8: his performance included some of his own compositions. At 10 he became a pupil of Theodor Leschetizky and at 15 moved to Berlin. His career as a soloist and accompanist was interrupted by World War I, during which he spent two years entertaining Austrian soldiers. In 1916 he married Marie Hahn, a cellist. Before their divorce in 1927, they and the violinist

Stefan Frenkel formed a musical trio. Schramm travelled widely, giving more than seventy concerts each season in the 1920s.

Late that decade Schramm taught intermittently at German conservatoria and at Rotterdam, the Netherlands, where he met the Dutch pianist Bernardina (Diny) Adriana Soetermeer. They were married in a civil ceremony in Berlin on 31 October 1928. Performing light music in addition to a classical repertoire, the couple toured and broadcast as a piano duo. From 1933 they lived in Batavia (Jakarta) where Paul formed and conducted an orchestra, and composed for films. In 1937-38 he twice toured Australia (on the second occasion in company with Diny) for the Australian Broadcasting Commission, completed a Javanese suite for piano and arranged for the publication of two sets of teaching pieces, *Seven Contrasts* and *Old Holland* (Melbourne, c.1938).

The Schramms set up a teaching studio in Wellington, New Zealand, in 1938 and Paul continued to perform. In World War II he was banned from broadcasting and restrictions were placed on his movements, reducing him to doing menial work. He travelled alone to Sydney in March 1946 to revive his international career. Promoted as 'The Pianist of 1946', he gave a series of recitals which received generally favourable reviews. Later, he broadcast on radio. People filled halls in the State capitals to hear his innovative, informal lunch-hour concerts. His more serious programmes consisted mainly of classics by Bach, Beethoven and Chopin, with works (including his own) by modern composers after the interval.

The privations of wartime affected Schramm's technique as well as his morale. Critics soon complained of lightweight programming and of 'superficial rhetoric' in his playing. His performance of Beethoven's 'Emperor' concerto with the Sydney Symphony Orchestra in November 1946 was compared with a race for the Melbourne Cup—Schramm was the winner and Beethoven came last.

In August 1947 Schramm was naturalized. Working to create 'a new musical public', he continued his lunch-hour recitals. Next year he toured Western Australia for the Adult Education Board, taking his Bechstein upright piano. He resumed his evening concerts in March 1949 in Sydney, where one reviewer accused him of having 'debased the musical values of his playing to the point of bankruptcy'. His radio series, 'Presenting Paul Schramm', began in September on station 2GB; he played popular classics by request, performed some of his own jazz-influenced compositions and exchanged banter with the show's compere.

Appalled at the deterioration in his playing, Schramm put music behind him. By 1951 he was investing in property in Sydney to try to make ends meet. A milk-bar venture at Manly in 1952 failed disastrously and in January 1953 he headed north by motorcar. In Brisbane he contemplated a career as a bookmaker 'at the dogs' before obtaining a hawker's licence. He sold clothing from a caravan in south-eastern Queensland and sent money to Diny in New Zealand. Survived by his wife and their son, he died of myocardial infarction on 30 November 1953 at Woolloongabba, Brisbane, and was cremated with Anglican rites.

Schramm was a convivial man, 5 ft 8¾ ins (175 cm) tall and of medium build, with twinkling grey eyes and horn-rimmed spectacles. A chain-smoker, he liked to 'show off' by playing a piano without removing his cigarette from his fingers. Bridge was his favourite pastime. Recordings of his broadcasts demonstrate his powerful technique, his rushed performances and his dry wit. His compositions, mostly unpublished, include operatic, orchestral and chamber works, and a number of short piano-pieces that show the influence of Sergei Prokofiev and Billy Mayerl. A gifted artist, though not of the first rank, he worked hard to 'bring music to the people' of Australasia.

J. M. Thomson, *Biog Dictionary of NZ Composers* (Wellington, 1990); R. Somerville (comp), *Slightly Jazzed* (Wellington, 1992); *Dictionary of NZ Biog*, 4 (Auckland, NZ, 1998); *Fontes Artis Musicae*, 39, nos 3-4, July-Dec 1992, p 226; *SMH*, 22 May 1937, 2, 18 July 1938, 16, 18, 22, 29 Mar, 1 Apr, 20 Aug, 26, 27 Sept, 6, 28 Nov 1946, 4 Mar 1947, 3, 5, 10 Mar 1949; *Sun* (Syd), 2 Dec 1953; Schramm papers (Alexander Turnbull L, Wellington); SP1011/2, box 91, SP1558/2, box 20, SP368/1, box 13 (ABC Archives, Syd); AAAC 489/13870, Paul Schramm, IA1, 115/966, Paul, Diny and Hans Schramm (Archives NZ, Wellington).   ROSS SOMERVILLE

SCHREIBER, OSCAR FERDINAND GORDON (1887-1963), cabinet-maker and trade unionist, was born on 7 October 1887 at Forbes, New South Wales, sixth child of John Schreiber, a grocer from Saxony, Germany, and his Scottish-born wife Annie, née Fraser. Oscar completed an apprenticeship to a cabinet-maker and worked in Sydney for Beard Watson [q.v.12] Ltd. In 1913 he became secretary of the Furnishing Trade Society of New South Wales. On 7 March 1916 in a civil ceremony in North Sydney he married Lilian Goodere, a teacher of dressmaking; they were to remain childless.

As a member of the Australian Labor Party, a delegate to the Labor Council of New South Wales and president of the Trade Union Secretaries' Association, 'Ossie' Schreiber wielded considerable influence in the labour movement. He was relatively self-effacing, however, and seems never to have aspired to high public office. In the early 1920s he held left-wing views and allegiances. About 1925, while remaining a 'sincere socialist', he emerged as a leader of moderate union opinion. By 1927 he had helped to restructure the A.L.P. in New South Wales, reducing the power of the Australian Workers' Union and consolidating Jack Lang's [q.v.9] leadership.

At the special State conference of the A.L.P. in November 1926 Schreiber moved the extraordinary motion confirming Lang's leadership and authorizing him 'to do all things and exercise such powers as he deems necessary in the interests of the [labour] movement'. The motion was carried by 274 votes to 4. From that time Schreiber and his new ally J. S. Garden [q.v.8] belonged to Lang's 'inner group' of advisers. After 1930 Schreiber's influence was critical in ensuring that moderate unions backed the Labor Council's leaders against their left- and right-wing opponents. He and Garden provided Lang with a strong union base. Lang responded with grants of government money for unemployed members of Schreiber's union. In 1936—reacting against the disastrous leadership of the State parliamentary Labor Party—the Labor Council, Garden and most other union leaders withdrew their support from Lang. Schreiber did likewise and was expelled from the A.L.P.

Schreiber was readmitted to the party that year. His subsequent struggle against Lang involved extensive co-operation with communists. Nevertheless, he opposed communist influence in the A.L.P. and in 1940 endorsed action by the federal executive to discourage joint public platforms in political campaigns and to replace communist sympathizers on the State executive. In 1947 he joined right-wing union leaders in publicly opposing communist attempts to ban the construction of the rocket range at Woomera, South Australia. Two years later he urged Prime Minister J. B. Chifley [q.v.13] to attack the Communist Party of Australia more forthrightly, in part to shore up electoral support for the A.L.P.

The Federal government had appointed Schreiber a member of the Commonwealth Disposals Commission (1944-49) and of a committee to advise on the development of a plywood industry in the Territory of Papua-New Guinea. He was a driving force behind the agreement, reached in 1946, between his union and the Associated Furniture Manufacturers of New South Wales on a voluntary code of standards for the trade. Implemented by the Standards Association of Australia, the code was overseen by a joint panel of employer and union representatives. Schreiber was also credited with being largely responsible for several legislative measures to protect consumers. These activities earned him the respect of a number of employers and senior government officials.

In the 1930s Schreiber had been a staunch advocate of shorter working hours to aid economic recovery and generate employment. He argued that increased productivity would neutralize the cost. Following World War II, he emerged as an outspoken critic of the growing movement for equal pay for women. He contended that most women's work was not 'competitive' with that of men and that paying women the male basic wage was unjustified as they were usually not family breadwinners.

Although he retired as secretary of his union in 1948 because of ill health, Schreiber continued as part-time country organizer and maintained his political connexions. He developed a warm friendship with Chifley, with whom he corresponded in the late 1940s. In the early 1950s he was a confidant of New South Wales A.L.P. leaders, notably Joe Cahill [q.v.13] and Reg Downing. Survived by his wife, he died on 2 July 1963 at his Roseville home; his body was bequeathed to the medical school at the University of Sydney and later cremated.

H. Radi and P. Spearritt (eds), *Jack Lang* (Syd, 1977); B. Nairn, *The 'Big Fella'* (Melb, 1986); R. Markey, *In Case of Oppression* (Syd, 1994); *SMH*, 4 Oct 1934, 15 Feb, 11 Sept 1935, 12 June 1940, 5, 17 Oct, 8, 9, 12, 15, 19, 30 Nov 1946, 14 May 1947, 10 July 1963; correspondence, leaflets, pamphlets and newspaper cuttings, MSS 4318 (ML).

RAY MARKEY

SCHRODER, CHARLES GEORGE (1893-1962), water-board official, was born on 26 March 1893 at Fernmount, New South Wales, son of Carl Hammer Schroder, a Danish-born engineer, and his Scottish wife Barbara McKay, née Donald. Carl was a dredge-master who worked in the Northern Rivers region. In 1903 the family moved from Bellingen to Newcastle where Charles attended Wickham Superior Public School. After being briefly employed by Carrington Municipal Council, he joined the Hunter District Water Supply and Sewerage Board as a junior clerk in 1909.

On 9 June 1915 Schroder enlisted in the Australian Imperial Force. Landing at Gallipoli, he served with the 3rd Battalion (September-October) and at Anzac Corps headquarters. In 1916-18 he performed staff duties at the headquarters of II Anzac (later XXII) Corps on the Western Front. He was awarded the Meritorious Service Medal (January 1917), promoted warrant officer, class one (December), and mentioned in dispatches (1918). For his work with the French Fifth Army in the 2nd battle of the Marne (July-August 1918), he won the Croix de Guerre (1919). Returning to Newcastle, he was discharged from the A.I.F. on 6 June 1919. At the Methodist Church,

Mayfield, on 20 November 1920 he married Ella Elizabeth Gilbert.

Qualifying for membership of both the Federal Institute of Accountants and the Australasian Institute of Secretaries, Schroder became the water board's principal book-keeper (1924), accountant (1934) and secretary (1936), and was responsible for mechanizing its accounting procedures. His 'confidence and determination' convinced the board in 1938 to proceed with a three-year programme costing £2.33 million: the plan envisaged the extension of water mains and sewerage services to outlying areas, and the building of large trunk mains to meet future demand. On 7 December 1938 Schroder took office as president of the reconstituted Hunter District Water Board. His appointment, initially for seven years, was to be renewed in 1945 and again in 1952.

Schroder vigorously supported the construction of the Tomago Sandbeds Water Supply Works, which was completed in 1944. During World War II he served on the State War Effort Co-ordination Committee and as chief executive officer of the Northern District Co-ordination Control. He later belonged to the Newcastle Regional Development Committee. Following three years of poor health, he retired in March 1953, lauded for his 'ability, drive and capacity for work'. A newspaper columnist said that, by industry and private study, he had 'fitted himself for one upward step after another until he reached the top'.

Living at Toronto, on Lake Macquarie, Schroder enjoyed fishing and sailing. Photographs reveal a bespectacled man with close-cropped hair and a face filled with character. Survived by his wife and their three sons, he died of cancer on 22 November 1962 at Toronto and was cremated with Presbyterian forms. His successor Frank Finnan [q.v.14] said that he left 'a monument of service behind him'. A reserve at Waratah and a pumping station at the Grahamstown reservoir were named after Schroder.

Hunter District Water Board (NSW), *Tomago Sandbeds Water Supply Scheme* (Newcastle, 1948); Report of the Hunter District Water Board for the Year Ended 30 June 1953, *PP* (NSW), 1954; *Newcastle Morning Herald*, 8 Feb 1950, 27 Nov 1962; *SMH*, 13 Mar 1953.   MARGARET STEINBERGER

SCHULZ, JOHANN FRIEDRICH WILHELM (1883-1964), schoolteacher and printer, was born on 19 March 1883 at Point Pass, South Australia, youngest of four children of Prussian-born parents Gottfried Schulz, labourer, and his wife Maria, née Späde. Educated at the Lutheran School and Immanuel College, Point Pass, Johann was appointed a teacher at the former school in 1901. He moved to Queensland in 1904 and taught at the Bethania Parish School. At the Evangelical Lutheran Chapel, Lights Pass, South Australia, on 26 April 1906 he married Ernstine Caroline Kruschel (d.1956). While continuing to teach at Bethania, he became a freelance reporter for the Brisbane *Courier-Mail* in 1907. Back in South Australia, he taught at the Tanunda Lutheran Day School from 1912 until the wartime closure of all Lutheran schools in the State on 30 June 1917.

After working for several local businesses, Schulz spent eighteen months in 1921-22 as storekeeper at the Lutheran Mission, Finschhafen, Mandated Territory of New Guinea. In 1926 he was employed at Auricht's [q.v.3] Printing Office, Tanunda, as manager and journalist. He knew his fellow townsman Dr Johannes Becker [q.v.13] and filmed German visitors, including Hans Bertram in 1932 and Count Felix von Luckner in 1938. Fluent in German, he frequently spoke at functions in the Barossa Valley and served as a committee-member (1937-44) of the South Australian German Historical Society.

In 1940 Schulz joined the Australian Labor Party. He gained pre-selection for the House of Assembly seat of Angas at the ensuing election. On 13 December he was arrested at Tanunda under the provisions of the National Security Act (1939). The Commonwealth Security Service claimed that he had attended meetings of the Nazi Party in Adelaide, kept Nazi propaganda at his home and visited Germany. His house was searched, various items were confiscated and he was taken to the Wayville detention camp, Adelaide. Although he was unable to campaign for the election on 29 March 1941, he polled 723 of the 3733 votes. Two appeals against his internment were rejected. In May 1941 he was sent to Tatura, Victoria. In April 1942 he was transferred to Loveday, South Australia. He wrote numerous letters to State and Federal politicians in which he asserted his loyalty.

Released on probation in January 1944, Schulz was directed to work and live in Adelaide, but he was permitted weekend visits to Tanunda, except during the State election that year. He was allowed to return home in May because of his age and ill health. On his release, some of his confiscated possessions were returned: two incriminating German badges which did not belong to him were among them. Despite a two-year correspondence with various government departments, he never learned why he was interned or how the badges came to be with his belongings.

Schulz managed Auricht's at Tanunda before retiring to Adelaide. He died on 3 October 1964 at Royal Adelaide Hospital and was buried in Langmeil Lutheran cemetery, Tanunda. His son and two daughters survived him. Inquiries after his death revealed that it had been alleged that he belonged to an organization inimical to the interests of the British Empire and had made disloyal utterances and pro-Nazi statements. The accusations were not proven.

E. M. Schulz, Guilty Till Proven Innocent (B.Ed. thesis, Salisbury CAE, 1987); A367, item C66704 (NAA, Canb); D1915, items SA18743 and SA20419, D1919, item SS827 (NAA, Adel); family papers (held by Ms E. M. Schulz, Port Augusta, SA).

IAN HARMSTORF
LIZ SCHULZ

SCOLLEN, MARY MAY (1887-1967), Sister of Mercy, nurse and hospital administrator, was born on 11 May 1887 at Redfern, Sydney, second child of Irish-born parents Patrick Scollen, a labourer who became a contractor, and his wife Susan, née Smith. Educated at Newtown Superior Public School, Mary entered the novitiate of the Sisters of Mercy, North Sydney, in 1905 and took the religious name of Mary Justinian. She was professed on 26 December 1907 while training as a nurse at the Mater Misericordiae Hospital, which at that time cared for women and children at premises in Willoughby Road, Crows Nest. On 5 May 1911 she was registered by the Australasian Trained Nurses' Association.

In 1919, aged only 32, Sister Justinian was appointed matron of the Mater. The hospital had been moved to Lane Cove Road (Pacific Highway) and extended to comprise private as well as public sections. The influenza pandemic reached Sydney that year. A ward at the hospital was set aside for the victims, and both Sisters and nurses volunteered to attend the sick poor. Of 262 patients admitted to the hospital with influenza, 228 recovered. During Sister Justinian's term of office the Mater was enlarged as the Sisters gradually acquired surrounding properties, despite the sectarianism that made some Protestant householders unwilling to sell to Catholic institutions. The Mater, however, provided for the sick and needy of all denominations; only about 27 per cent of its patients were Catholics.

Small and slightly built, Sister Justinian proved capable and competent, both as a nurse and an administrator. She was a dignified, wise and compassionate woman, with a direct but kindly manner, and it was said of her: 'The Matron is just by name and just by nature'. Yet, she never felt comfortable in the presence of dignitaries. Christian attitudes and values inspired her and informed her nursing practice. Her special concern was the training of nurses. She reminded them: 'To us who know Christ we have the obligation of seeing Him in our neighbour . . . To be kind, generous, just, thoughtful and fair in the name of Christ spells our Catholic hospital service for us'. She opposed what she considered to be a worldwide trend to remove the personal touch from nursing, being alarmed at over-specialization in the profession.

A founding fellow (1955) of the New South Wales College of Nursing, Sister Justinian was appointed M.B.E. in 1958. She relinquished the role of matron to become superior of her community and administrator of the hospital in 1963. Mother Justinian retired in 1967. When her health began to fail, she obtained treatment in the Mater's out-patients department, waiting her turn to see the doctor, though he had served under her. She died on 22 October 1967 at that hospital and was buried in Northern Suburbs cemetery. One of her former medical colleagues described her as 'a great nun, a great nurse and a great woman'.

H. M. Carey, In the Best of Hands (Syd, 1991); Sisters of Mercy archives and Mater Misericordiae Hospital archives, North Syd; information from Dr P. Rogers, Killara, and Sr M. P. Ryman, Hornsby, Syd.
SOPHIE MCGRATH

SCORFIELD, EDWARD SCAFE (1882-1965), cartoonist, soldier and sportsman, was born on 21 April 1882 at Preston, Northumberland, England, son of Joseph Scorfield, insurance agent, and his wife Rebecca Jane, née Taylor. Educated at the Royal Grammar School, Newcastle upon Tyne, Ted became a marine architect. An active member of the Tynemouth Amateur Rowing Club from 1906, he was to be made a life member in 1925. He captained (1910-12) the celebrated Percy Park Rugby Football Club, represented (1910-13) Northumberland County and played lock-forward for England against France in 1910. In the following year the Royal Humane Society commended him, on parchment, for his part in the rescue at Tynemouth of a drowning man who was being carried seaward.

In August 1914 Scorfield enlisted in the British Army. He served with the 66th Field Company, Royal Engineers, at Gallipoli (in the landing at Suvla Bay), Salonika (Thessaloniki), Greece, and Palestine. Promoted sergeant, he was twice mentioned in dispatches and was appointed to the Russian Order of St George.

After World War I, while employed in a Tyneside shipyard, he began to draw cartoons for the Newcastle Weekly Chronicle. On the advice of his agent Percy Bradshaw, he came to Sydney in 1925 and joined the Bulletin as a cartoonist and illustrator, replacing Norman Lindsay [q.v.10]. At St James's Church of England, Sydney, on 4 October 1928 he married Helen Cecilia Olga Louise Pillinger, a 24-year-old Englishwoman; they were childless.

Scorfield's supple line, eye for detail and kindly humour made him a popular jokesmith. He used, with an infectious flourish, the stock devices of his time—philandering husbands, relaxed gaolbirds, punch-drunk boxers, blackened-eyed wives, devious fortune-tellers, stingy Scots, dopey Pommies, canny Jewish bookmakers, pitiless wowsers, prolific Catholics, 'mine-tinkit' Aborigines, flirtatious flappers and naughty ragamuffins. His comic sketches of animals, especially his cheeky dogs, were famous. He drew with a pen and dry brush, and his settings ranged from city slums to outback farms.

His political cartoons cheerfully followed the *Bulletin* line of the period, a combination of Australian nationalism and British conservatism. In the desperate days of World War II Scorfield lionized the Digger, exalted the Allies against the Japanese, and lampooned black-marketeers, strikers and 'white-feather conchies'. But he was almost never malicious: even his sinister Hitler, Stalin and Hirohito had a human, almost redeeming, fishiness about them. His acclaimed caricature of Dr H. V. Evatt [q.v.14]—short, beefy, bespectacled, with a big head and jutting chin personifying relentless folly—was both devastating and affectionate. He published two collections of cartoons, *A Mixed Grill* (1943) and *A Mixed Grill, No. 2* (1952).

A self-effacing man and a generous friend, Scorfield regularly bought the work of hard-up artists for the *Bulletin* simply to give them an income. He was tall, muscular and slow to anger, but a formidable 'knuckleman' when aroused. Always a Geordie, he retained the regional accents of his youth and decorated his office with a picture of the Blaydon races. He resigned in 1961, soon after Sir Frank Packer [q.v.15] bought the ailing *Bulletin* and began to transform the magazine. Scorfield died on 11 December 1965 in hospital at Mosman and was cremated; his wife survived him.

V. Lindesay, *The Inked-in Image* (Melb, 1970); J. Kerr, *Artists and Cartoonists in Black and White* (Syd, 1999); *Bulletin*, 25 Dec 1965; Roy Humane Soc, Lond, cte minutes, 10 Oct 1911; information from Mr J. Frith, Hawthorn, Melb, Mr N. Hetherington, Mosman, Syd, and Mr W. Prior, Dunsborough, WA.   PETER COLEMAN

SCOTT, THOMAS HENRY (1907-1979), army officer, was born on 16 September 1907 at Broken Hill, New South Wales, eldest of four children of South Australian-born parents William Henry Scott, carpenter, and his wife Janet, née Crawford. Nothing is known of Tom's education or early employment. On 1 July 1925 he enlisted in the 27th Battalion,

an Adelaide-based Militia unit; he was then 5 ft 8 ins (173 cm) tall, with a fair complexion and brown hair. Within three years he had risen from private to warrant officer, class two. Commissioned as a provisional lieutenant in July 1932, he was promoted captain on Armistice Day 1937. He lived at Glenelg and worked as a purchasing clerk. At the Unitarian Christian Church, Adelaide, on 1 June 1935 he had married Gladys Winifred Hinde, a tailoress; they were childless.

On the outbreak of World War II, Scott was mobilized for full-time duty. He transferred to the Australian Imperial Force on 1 September 1940 and was posted to the 2nd/48th Battalion. In November the battalion embarked for the Middle East, where Scott became adjutant in March 1941. A bespectacled, bookish-looking officer, he was noted for his quiet but firm efficiency. The 2nd/48th took part in the defence of Tobruk, Libya, in April-October 1941; Scott was mentioned in dispatches for his services between February and July. In September he was promoted major and given command of a rifle company. From July 1942 his battalion saw action in Egypt, at Tel El Eisa and El Alamein.

In September 1942 Scott was seconded to command the 26th Training Battalion in Palestine. Promoted lieutenant colonel in November, he led the 2nd/32nd Battalion, which sailed for Australia in January 1943. After regrouping and training in North Queensland, the 2nd/32nd fought at Lae and Finschhafen, New Guinea, from September. Slightly wounded by shell-fire on the 14th of that month, Scott remained on duty. His levelheadedness and organizing ability won the wholehearted confidence of his men, and his determined leadership and efficiency impressed his superiors. He was awarded the Distinguished Service Order (1945).

Returning to North Queensland in February 1944, the 2nd/32nd resumed training. The battalion embarked for Morotai Island, Netherlands East Indies, in April 1945 and saw active service in British North Borneo in June-August. On 29 September Scott was detached to the 24th Brigade's headquarters, of which he was given command on 4 December. Suffering from a chest complaint, he was evacuated to Sydney in December. He remained in hospital until April 1946 and was placed on the Reserve of Officers on 1 May.

Scott became manager of the Garden City Flour Mill at Ballarat, Victoria. On 1 April 1948 he took over the newly formed 8th/7th Battalion (Militia). In June 1950 he was made temporary brigadier and appointed to command the 6th Brigade, which he led until his retirement from the Citizen Military Forces on 1 July 1953. Predeceased by his wife, he died on 14 May 1979 in Holdfast Hospital, Glenelg, Adelaide, and was cremated.

J. G. Glenn, *Tobruk to Tarakan* (Adel, 1960); D. Dexter, *The New Guinea Offensives* (Canb, 1961); G. Long, *The Final Campaigns* (Canb, 1963); B. Maughan, *Tobruk and El Alamein* (Canb, 1966); S. Trigellis-Smith, *Britain to Borneo* (Syd, 1993); War diaries, 2/32nd and 2/48th Battalions, AIF (AWM).

GARY McKAY

SCOTT GRIFFITHS, JENNIE (1875-1951), journalist and political activist, was born on 30 October 1875 near Woodville, Texas, United States of America, daughter of Stephen Randolph Wilson, cotton-farmer, and his wife Laura, née Nettles, who had been born in France. Apparently a precocious child, Jennie recalled—in a memoir written at the end of her life—busking in the 1880s at town fairs as 'The Baby Elocutionist of Texas', studying Charles Darwin, T. H. Huxley, Henry George [qq.v.1,4], Thomas Paine and Edward Bellamy with a tutor at home, and bungling an elopement with the tutor at the age of 15. She also claimed that she entered the school of law at the University of Texas at Austin in 1890; she probably acquired her knowledge of law while attending classes with her elder half-brother Tom Cowart. When not mixing in student circles, she wrote a column for children in a local newspaper and visited prisons with her father. She then trained as a stenographer and worked as a court reporter.

On a world tour with her brother, Jennie Scott Wilson arrived in Fiji and met Arthur George Griffiths, whom she married on 9 November 1897 at Levuka; they were to have ten children. The Griffiths family owned the *Fiji Times*. When Arthur became the proprietor in 1909, Jennie worked as editor, always with a small child at her feet. After the *Fiji Times* was sold in 1912, she moved to Sydney where her youngest child was born in March 1913.

Scott Griffiths was soon prominent in feminist, pacifist, labour and socialist organizations. Under her editorship (from 1913) the *Australian Woman's Weekly* became a forum for discussions of sex hygiene, infant welfare centres, education for motherhood and equality of the sexes. In 1916 she was sacked for opposing conscription. She served with Kate Dwyer [q.v.8] on the Women's Anti-Conscription Committee that year and with Vida Goldstein [q.v.9] in the Women's Peace Army, and also belonged to the Social Democratic League and the Feminist Club. A regular writer for the *Australian Worker*, she sometimes replaced (Dame) Mary Gilmore [q.v.9] as editor of its women's page.

By 1917 Scott Griffiths was calling herself a revolutionary. She supported the general strike in New South Wales, wrote for the socialist press, and told the members of the Children's Peace Army that women should 'take over control of State affairs and put men in the kitchen to cook'. She also criticized racism, reversing her earlier warnings that the British were under threat from 'invading hordes of Eastern peoples'. Late in 1917 she joined the migration of revolutionaries to Queensland, where opportunities for socialism seemed to rest with the one remaining Labor government. Noted for her small stature (4 ft 8 ins, 142 cm), American accent and passionate conviction, she spoke at meetings to mark the Bolshevik revolution, May Day and the imprisonment of the 'Twelve' Industrial Workers of the World. She also combined membership of the Labor Party with attempts to revive the Queensland Socialist League.

With the help of the Children's Peace Army, Scott Griffiths made the red pennants that sparked three days of riots in Brisbane in March 1919 when returned soldiers attacked militant unionists, radicals and Russian immigrants who insisted on displaying the red flag in defiance of the War Precautions Act (1914). M. H. Ellis [q.v.14] saw her at an outdoor meeting during these events and described her as 'a bit hysterical': 'she pulled down a big man and put a red ribbon round his neck'. She subsequently led the successful campaign to free the 'Red Flag' prisoners.

In June 1920 Scott Griffiths left for the U.S.A., disappointed at the ebbing of the revolutionary tide, but still committed to her principles. By 1923 she was living with her husband at San Francisco. They took American citizenship in 1928. Active in the I.W.W., she contributed to the history of California produced by the Federal Writers' Project (1947), sent poems to the *Industrial Worker* (Chicago) and served as secretary of the Californian branch of the National Women's Party. She died on 29 June 1951 at San Francisco and was buried in Woodland Memorial Park; her husband, six sons and three of their four daughters survived her. More committed to action than doctrine, she had joined any organization that seemed to promise change. Although she was a rationalist, her funeral oration was delivered by a lifelong Quaker friend who said, 'No church was big enough to hold this little woman'.

R. Evans, *The Red Flag Riots* (Brisb, 1988); J. Damousi, *Women Come Rally* (Melb, 1994); *Aust Woman's Weekly*, 19 June, 18 Sept, 6 Nov 1915, 1, 15 Apr, 15 July, 11 Dec 1916; *Aust Worker*, 26 Oct, 30 Nov 1916; *Socialist* (Syd), 9 Feb 1917, 29 Nov 1918; *Daily Standard*, 1 Mar, 22 Apr, 29 Aug, 17, 23 Sept 1918, 9 May, 26, 30 June 1919; *Industrial Worker* (Chicago), 5 July 1951; B. Sutton, She Fought Where She Stood (ms, nd, Fryer L, Univ Qld); Scott Griffiths papers (NL); Censor's secret intelligence reports, MP95/1, items 169/43/48, 169/56/63 and 169/74/90 (NAA, Melb).   T. H. IRVING

SCOTT WAINE, CECIL (1888-1964), accountant and businessman, was born on 30 January 1888 in Sydney, fourth child of John Charles Waine, a builder from England, and his native-born wife Medora Margaret Lucy, née Chatfield. Cecil later styled his surname as Scott Waine. Educated at Sydney Grammar School, he joined the Union Steam Ship Co. of New Zealand in 1905 as an accountant. In the following year he was articled to Troup, Harwood & Co., public accountants. He was fond of sport and helped to form the Coogee Surf and Life-Saving Club.

On completing his articles in 1911, Scott Waine was admitted as an associate (fellow 1918) of the Australasian Corporation of Public Accountants. In 1913 he established his own business; C. R. Mitchell joined him in partnership two years later. At St James's Anglican Church, King Street, on 25 October 1916 Scott Waine married Florence Elizabeth Christmas. They had two daughters before Florence died in 1920. The association with the Christmas family was to have a significant effect on his career. On 10 January 1923 he married Margaret Giles Dixon at St Philip's Church, Sydney. He remained senior partner of C. Scott Waine & Mitchell until his death.

About 1919 Scott Waine had formed a partnership with his brother-in-law Harold Christmas [q.v.7] and S. E. Chatterton to establish a retail business in ladies' wear. It flourished and Christmas presided over its transition to Woolworths Ltd, which began with a modest shop in the basement of the Imperial Arcade in 1924. Scott Waine was one of five directors of Woolworths, and its chairman from 1932. He was to become chairman or a director of Woolworths' subsidiary firms and several other public companies.

In the 1930s Woolworths developed into a chain of variety stores. J. A. Browne [q.v.13], president of the Industrial Commission of New South Wales, investigated chain stores in 1937. Scott Waine publicly defended Woolworths' stores as superior in location, appearance and display, and as offering goods at competitively low prices. His belief in market forces coincided with his bitter criticism in 1942 of the Commonwealth government's proposal to restrict company profits to 4 per cent.

By 1950 Woolworths had 114 variety stores, in most Australian States and New Zealand. Competition with G. J. Coles [q.v.13] & Co. Ltd came about as each extended its operations interstate, and Coles led by diversifying into groceries. Scott Waine presided over Woolworths' acquisition of B.C.C. Stores Holding Co. Ltd (the successful Brisbane cash-and-carry business) in 1958, its expansion into further grocery chains in New South Wales and Western Australia in 1960, and its diversification into clothing and Manchester

with the purchase of Rockmans Ltd in 1961. The postwar growth of Woolworths had been assisted by Scott Waine's financial acumen and by (Sir) Theo Kelly's drive as managing director.

A member of the Australian and Royal Sydney Golf clubs, Scott Waine lived at Warrawee. He owned and collected Georgian silver, antique Dutch and English furniture and Venetian glass. After thirty-one years as Woolworths' chairman, he retired in 1963. He died on 6 September 1964 at Warrawee and was buried in Randwick cemetery; his wife, and their son and daughter, survived him, as did the two daughters of his first marriage.

Retail Merchandiser, 14, no 2, 1966, p 4; *SMH*, 20 Feb 1937, 22, 29 Apr, 25 July 1942, 24 Sept 1960, 9 Sept 1964.   PETER SPEARRITT
                                                            JOHN YOUNG

SCRYMGEOUR, JAMES TINDAL STEUART (1885-1965), cattle-breeder, was born on 14 August 1885 at Meadowbank, near Oamaru, New Zealand, second of four children of Scottish-born parents William Tindal Scrimgeour, sheep-farmer, and his wife Mary, née McGregor. His father owned properties in the Otago and Hawkes Bay regions. Jim was educated at Otago Boys' High School, Dunedin, and Canterbury Agricultural College, Lincoln. An enthusiastic sportsman and horse-rider, he obtained a job with Dalgety [q.v.4] & Co. Ltd. He later wrote about his early life in *Memories of Maoriland* (Ilfracombe, England, 1960).

The family moved to Queensland in 1908 and Jim worked on his father's stations at Goondiwindi. On 21 October 1916 he enlisted in the Australian Imperial Force. He embarked for Egypt in September 1917 and joined the 2nd Light Horse Regiment in January 1918. During fighting in July at 'The Bluff', near Musallabeh, Palestine, he was shot in the face and blinded. Invalided home, he was discharged from the army on 24 October. At the Ann Street Presbyterian Church, Brisbane, on 25 November that year he married Helen Marjorie Brown (d.1962), an expert horsewoman whom he affectionately dubbed the 'commanding officer'.

The couple travelled to London where, in October 1919, Scrymgeour entered St Dunstan's Hostel for blinded servicemen. Over the next year he distinguished himself in the curriculum (Braille, touch-typing, poultry-raising and carpentry) and in sport, especially sculling. Back in Queensland, he settled at Netherby, a property at Warwick bought by his family in 1922, and established a Shorthorn cattle stud, using Scottish lines imported in 1915 by his father. In 1930 his bull, Netherby Royal Challenge, won the first of six championships at the Royal National Show, Brisbane; by 1934 the *Pastoral Review* was describing Scrymgeour's heifers as 'easily the best' in Australia. He adopted the system of guide-wires used at St Dunstan's athletics events to find his way around the buildings and stables on his farm. The hostel had emphasized the training of memory, hearing and touch. When Scrymgeour judged at provincial shows, there was debate as to whether he could sense hair colour, but none about how he could 'see' cattle through his hands. A 'walking stud book', he also bred Clydesdale and trotting horses.

In 1937 Scrymgeour began to replace most of Netherby's stock with Poll Shorthorns. Between 1939 and 1955 he won thirteen senior championships at the Royal Easter Show, Sydney. Netherby and Arthur Langmore's Prospect stud at Jondaryan dominated competition in Brisbane. Scrymgeour served (1938-56) on the council of the Poll Shorthorn Society of Australasia. In October 1955 he suffered severe scalds in an accident at his home. The Netherby stud was dispersed, with record prices, on 13 March 1957, after which he moved to the town of Warwick.

Although Scrymgeour wrote sardonically about officers in his *Echoes of the Australian Light Horse in Egypt and Palestine* (Cairo, 1918), he was deeply patriotic. He was president and later patron of the Warwick sub-branch of the Returned Sailors' and Soldiers' Imperial League of Australia. Soft spoken and genial, with a pipe and battered felt hat, he wrote another three volumes of autobiography, among them *Men, Mokes, Hooves, Horns and Hides* (Ilfracombe, 1959). In 1954 he was appointed O.B.E. Survived by his two daughters, he died on 27 March 1965 at Warwick and was buried in the local cemetery.

Lord Fraser of Lonsdale, *My Story of St Dunstan's* (Lond, 1961); H. S. Gullett, *The Australian Imperial Force in Sinai and Palestine, 1914-1918* (Brisb, 1984); *Pastoral Review*, July 1923, Jan 1930, Apr 1934, Apr 1957, Apr 1965; *Reveille* (Syd), 1 Apr 1940; *People* (Syd), 22 Sept 1954; *Qld Country Life*, 25 Oct 1956, 14 Mar 1957, 1 Apr 1965.   S. J. ROUTH

SCULLY, WILLIAM JAMES (1883-1966), farmer and politician, was born on 1 February 1883 in Sydney, fourth of fourteen children of native-born parents Thomas James Scully, a labourer who turned to farming, and his wife Sarah Lucy Rutherford. William was educated at a small school on Bective station, near Tamworth, until the age of 14. Between harvests, he and his brothers worked as contract labourers—building roads, sinking dams, erecting fences and ring-barking trees to clear the land. An enterprising young man, he tried share-farming at Nemingha. By the age of 21

he was a contractor; eight years later he was a justice of the peace. He served as secretary of the Tamworth Progress Association and became a founding member of the Primary Producers' Union of New South Wales.

Joining the Tamworth Political Labor League about 1903, Scully was soon elected president and sent as a delegate to annual State conferences. After thrice unsuccessfully standing for the Legislative Assembly, he won the seat of Namoi in September 1923 on the resignation of the incumbent, his brother Patrick. When dissension over economic policy split Labor ranks in New South Wales, he remained loyal to Prime Minister J. H. Scullin [q.v.11] and the Australian Labor Party, even though he sympathized with the views of Premier J. T. Lang [q.v.9]. In the 1932 election Scully was defeated. At St Nicholas's Catholic Church, Tamworth, on 15 June 1925 he had married 27-year-old Grace Myrtle Kilbride.

Before entering parliament, Scully had been a judge with the New South Wales National Coursing Association. He also raced horses throughout the State's north-west, as well as at Newcastle and in Sydney. His trotters won feature events at Harold Park. From 1932 he concentrated his efforts on breeding horses and selling them in and around the Tamworth district. On 8 May 1937 he won a by-election for the seat of Gwydir in the House of Representatives.

John Curtin [q.v.13] appointed him minister for commerce on 7 October 1941. Scully held the expanded portfolio of commerce and agriculture (from 22 December 1942) under Curtin, F. M. Forde and J. B. Chifley [q.v.13]. In this capacity he chaired the Australian Food Council which supplied Australia's armed services and allied forces throughout the South-West Pacific Area, and made large contributions to Britain. In 1942 the 'Scully Plan' was introduced to stabilize the wheat industry by guaranteeing farmers a minimum price of four shillings per bushel. After World War II ended, he arranged for surplus farm machinery to be distributed to producers' co-operatives at reduced prices; this practical assistance helped to lower capital costs on small holdings.

On 1 November 1946 Scully was appointed vice-president of the Executive Council. He held the post until 19 December 1949. Defeated at the general election that year, he retired to Tamworth, where he grew lucerne. He served on the Tamworth City Council (1950-56), on the council of the New England University College (1942-53), as president (1955-57) of the Tamworth and District Workmen's Club, and as vice-president and patron of the Tamworth Cricket Association. Continuing his interests in coursing and breeding horses, he was made a life member of the Tamworth Jockey Club.

A 'simple and a humble' man, a non-smoker and a teetotaller, Scully was renowned for his integrity, sincerity and directness. He died on 19 March 1966 in Tamworth Base Hospital. Accorded a state funeral, he was buried in the local cemetery; his wife and two of their three sons survived him. A park in West Tamworth was named after him.

P. Hasluck, *The Government and the People 1939-1941* (Canb, 1952); J. T. Lang, *I Remember* (Syd, 1956); S. J. Butlin and C. B. Schedvin, *War Economy 1942-1945* (Canb, 1977); *SMH* and *Northern Daily Leader*, 21 Mar 1966; information from Mr J. Scully, Garran, ACT.   JANICE BOYLE

SEABROOK, NORMAN HUGH (1906-1978), architect, was born on 12 January 1906 at Northcote, Melbourne, third of four children of Charles William Seabrook, a clerk from Tasmania, and his Melbourne-born wife Catherine Jane, née Brown. Norman attended Brighton State School, Wesley College, and Hassett's Commercial College, Prahran. While at Hassett's, he worked for the architect A. R. Barnes, with whom he served his articles in 1924-26.

In 1927 Seabrook enrolled at the University of Melbourne Architectural Atelier, then under the directorship of Leighton Irwin [q.v.9]. He gained his diploma in architectural design in 1931. On 26 January that year at her parents' Brighton home he married Linda May Millis with the forms of the Churches of Christ. Soon after, he and his wife sailed for England, where he worked in London and Birmingham. While in Europe, they cycled two thousand miles (3200 km) through the Netherlands, Germany and Belgium to study architecture.

Back in Melbourne, Seabrook was admitted as an associate of the Royal Victorian Institute of Architects in 1933. He set up practice in Little Collins Street and returned to the atelier as senior demonstrator in design. A brilliant renderer, he won a competition to design a girls' secondary school at Albert Park. Sponsored by Sir Macpherson Robertson [q.v.11] and completed in 1934 to mark Victoria's centenary, MacRobertson Girls' High School was an early Australian application of *de Stijl* architectural principles and the first Australian example of the modern functionalist style of architecture developed by the Dutch architect Willem Dudok. The building was characterized by dramatic cubistic juxtapositions of horizontal and vertical forms, all in cream brick, with contrasting bands of blue-glazed brick and vermilion-painted steel windows.

This striking style, later claimed by Robin Boyd [q.v.13] to have heralded the '1934 Revolution' of modern architecture in Vic-

toria, became a Seabrook signature. Notable examples of the idiom included his own home at Hawthorn (1934-35); fire stations and associated flats at Brunswick (1937), Brighton (1939) and Windsor (1939-40); commercial premises such as those of Gair Manufacturing Co. Pty Ltd, Melbourne (1935-36), the Bank of New South Wales, Moreland (1936), the Royal Exchange Assurance, Pitt Street, Sydney (1936-37), and a store for Miller & Co. at Hamilton (1937); and the largest rural example of the Dudok idiom, Warracknabeal Town Hall (1939). A technically unusual design was that of Barnett's Building, 164 Bourke Street, Melbourne (1937-38), an early example of a curtain-walled, high-rise building with a roof-top squash court and gymnasium.

In 1936 Seabrook had formed a partnership with Alan Fildes at 84 William Street. Tall and bespectacled, Seabrook was the chief designer: he attracted clients while Fildes took care of production and office management. The practice prospered in the late 1930s with major projects for (Sir) Reginald Ansett, including terminal and hangar buildings (1937) at Essendon Aerodrome. Seabrook also designed another innovative house for himself at Croydon (1941). After World War II Fildes's involvement decreased. Newer associates, among them Eric Atlee Hunt, became prominent in the firm, which moved to Little Collins Street in 1954. In the following year Seabrook, Fildes & Hunt was formed. After Fildes died in 1956, the firm became Seabrook, Hunt & Dale (1958). It moved to Albert Park and then to South Melbourne. The practice undertook further work for Ansett Transport Industries Ltd and St Kevin's College, Toorak, but never regained the momentum for innovation seen in the 1930s. It closed in 1975, following Seabrook's retirement in the previous year.

Seabrook had been divorced on 18 March 1943. Later that day, at the office of the government statist, Melbourne, he married Mavis Black, née Devling, a photographic retoucher and a divorcee. Survived by his wife, and by the daughter of each of his marriages, he died on 9 September 1978 in South Melbourne. He had bequeathed his body to the University of Melbourne.

R. Boyd, *Victorian Modern* (Melb, 1947); D. L. Johnson, *Australian Architecture 1901-51* (Syd, 1980); *Aust Home Beautiful*, July 1935, p 6; *Art in Aust*, 61, Nov 1935, p 91; *Herald* (Melb), 9, 13, 14 Dec 1933; P. Dredge, Biography—Seabrook and Fildes (research report, 1981, Architecture L, Univ Melb); Seabrook and Fildes files (National Trust of Aust, Vic branch, Melb).   PHILIP GOAD

SEABROOK, THOMAS CLAUDIUS (1886-1967), wine merchant and wine judge, was born on 8 June 1886 at Hawthorn, Melbourne, eighth child of Tasmanian-born parents William John Seabrook, clerk, and his wife Mary Sophia, née Mason. After attending state school at Prahran, Tom joined his father as a vignerons' agent and winebroker. Taught tasting by his father, he picked grapes and worked on vintages in the Rutherglen district. He studied analytical chemistry and fermentation at the Working Men's College, Melbourne, and at the Carlton brewery. Modelling his life on that of his elder brother Will, he took up gymnastics, enlisted in the Victorian Scottish Regiment, Militia, in 1902 (commissioned 1912), and became a teetotaller and non-smoker. Will was drowned at Point Lonsdale on 3 January 1914 when he and Tom attempted to save two people swept out to sea; Tom was awarded the bronze medal of the Royal Humane Society of Australasia.

On his father's death in 1914, Tom took over the family business in Queen Street, Melbourne. At the Presbyterian Church, Newtown, Geelong, on 8 June 1915 he married Dorothy (Dora) Sidel Baird (d.1942), a saleswoman. Appointed lieutenant, Australian Imperial Force, on 1 June 1916, he joined the 24th Battalion on the Western Front in January 1917. On 7 December he was promoted captain. In August-December 1918 he served on the staff of the British 87th Infantry Brigade. Having studied French and German for the wine business, he acted as an interpreter for the British. Although he was twice wounded, he regained his health and discovered the delights of drinking wine (as distinct from merely tasting it) on leave in Paris with his friend Frank Menzies [q.v.15] in 1918. His A.I.F. appointment terminated in Melbourne on 11 May 1919.

As a broker, Seabrook assessed fortified and table wines sent to him, and relied on his extensive contacts with vignerons, hoteliers and restaurateurs. Typically, his trade was in hogsheads, but wicker-covered, ceramic demijohns and special bottles of wine were sold direct to the public. After 1940 W. J. Seabrook & Son (Pty Ltd) evolved more along the lines of a classic English wine merchant. The firm imported and exported wines, and produced its own blends. On 28 April 1945 at Knox Church, Ivanhoe, Seabrook married Amy Maclaren, née Edgar, a widow.

Five ft 11 ins (180 cm) tall and lean, Seabrook was meticulous about wine and rarely drank a glass without appraising it. He became one of an influential group of connoisseurs who helped to keep the trade alive when it was threatened by temperance restrictions, failing vineyards and a beer-drinking society's lack of understanding. A friend and associate of Samuel Wynn, François de Castella [qq.v.12,13] and Eric Purbrick, he was honorary secretary (1910-35) and president (1964-67) of the Viticultural Society of Victoria. In 1963 he was appointed O.B.E. Like his father before him and his son Douglas (d.1984) after him, he was chairman of wine judges at the Royal Agricultural Society of Victoria's annual shows in Melbourne and was regularly invited to judge in other capital cities. He died on 6 February 1967 at Bundoora and was cremated. His wife survived him, as did the three daughters and two sons of his first marriage. Douglas, who suffered from the effects of poliomyelitis, sold the family business in 1976.

H. Cox, *The Wines of Australia* (Lond, 1967); *Wine and Spirit News and Aust Vigneron*, 25 May 1914, p 199; *Age* (Melb), 7 Feb 1967, 3 July 1984; information from Mrs D. Paton, Armadale, Melb, and Mr I. Seabrook, Tanunda, SA.

DAVID DUNSTAN

SEAR, HERBERT ROY (1886-1962), radiologist, was born on 16 February 1886 at Medindie, Adelaide, second son of Walter George Sear, draper, and his wife Harriett, née Jones. The family moved to Sydney in 1897. Educated at Sydney Grammar School and at the University of Sydney (M.B. Hons, 1910) where he won a Blue for boxing, Roy worked as a junior resident medical officer at Royal Prince Alfred Hospital, Camperdown. In 1912 he was appointed resident radiologist at the hospital, in a period before formal radiological qualifications had been established. He later became senior radiologist and head of the department at R.P.A.H., and honorary radiologist at other Sydney hospitals. As a captain in the (Australian) Army Medical Corps, Militia, he played a major part in setting up the radiology department of the 4th Australian General Hospital, Randwick, during World War I.

On 20 May 1918 Sear was appointed temporary major, Australian Imperial Force. He served in England with the 3rd Australian Auxiliary Hospital, Dartford, before returning to Sydney where his A.I.F. appointment terminated on 15 July 1919. At St Paul's Anglican Cathedral, Rockhampton, Queensland, on 3 September that year he married Dorothy Muriel, a medical practitioner and daughter of F. H. V. Voss [q.v.12]. From 1912 Sear had assisted the radiologist Herschel Harris [q.v.9]; made a partner, he took over the practice when Harris died in 1920. He carried out both diagnostic radiology and radiotherapy, and, in association with a number of surgeons, treated thyrotoxicosis.

In 1935 Sear was elected president of the radiology section of the British Medical Association's congress, held in Hobart. That year he helped to establish the Australian and New Zealand Association of Radiology. When the association became the College of

Radiologists (Australia and New Zealand) in 1949, he was made a foundation fellow; he was to be president (1951-52) and a life member (from 1957) of the renamed College of Radiologists of Australasia. He was also a foundation fellow of the Royal Australasian College of Physicians (1938) and of the Faculty of Radiologists, Britain (1939), and an honorary member (1939) of the Australian Orthopaedic Association. The University of Sydney had awarded him a diploma in radiology in 1938.

Despite chronic heart disease—the legacy of rheumatic fever in childhood—Sear earned worldwide recognition as a radiologist, particularly for his work on bone diseases and congenital abnormalities of the skeleton. In London in 1952 he delivered the Skinner lecture to the Faculty of Radiologists of Great Britain: he spoke on congenital bone dystrophies and their correlation. As a young man he had attended evening-classes at Julian Ashton's [q.v.7] Sydney Art School under Ashton and Elioth Gruner [q.v.9]: diagrams thus became an important feature of his lectures, adding to his reputation as a gifted teacher.

A 'thorough gentleman', invariably courteous and punctual, Sear brought to radiology high ideals, a sense of duty and a 'staunch code of conduct'. He enjoyed golf, gardening and philately. Survived by his wife and their two daughters, he died on 24 November 1962 at Rose Bay and was cremated.

G. L. McDonald (ed), *Roll of the Royal Australasian College of Physicians*, 1 (Syd, 1988); J. Ryan et al, *Australasian Radiology* (Syd, 1996); A. Tate, *Shadows and Substance* (Syd, 1999); *MJA*, 27 Apr 1963, p 635; *J of the College of Radiologists of A'sia*, 7, 1963, p 7.   AUDREY TATE

SECHIARI, LUCY; *see* DE NEEVE

SECOMBE, VICTOR CLARENCE (1897-1962), army officer, was born on 9 January 1897 at Glen Wills, near Omeo, Victoria, third son of William Secombe, miner, and his wife Katie, née Schlitz, both Victorian born. As a young man Victor was a good Australian Rules footballer, a successful middle-distance runner and an outstanding horseman. He attended Swifts Creek State School, boarded at St Patrick's College, Ballarat, and entered (1915) the Royal Military College, Duntroon, Federal Capital Territory, from which he graduated in December 1917. Appointed lieutenant in the Australian Imperial Force on 1 January 1918, he embarked for England in the following month. He joined the 15th Field Company, Engineers, in France in September and became adjutant of the 5th Divisional Engineers in January 1919. After undertaking a course at the School of Military Engineering, Chatham, England, he returned to Australia in December.

A series of staff and command postings with the Royal Australian Engineers in coastal defence and field units took Secombe to Western Australia (1920 and 1926-28), Tasmania (1920-21), Victoria (1921-25) and New South Wales (1928-32). He studied civil engineering at the University of Melbourne in 1922-23 and was promoted captain in 1926. At St Mary's Catholic Cathedral, Perth, on 22 May 1929 he married Dorothea Mary Teresa Hayes.

In 1932 Secombe was a member of a party sent to Darwin to construct coastal defences. He became assistant-director of works at 2nd District Base, Sydney, in 1934. Two years later he was promoted major and posted to Duntroon. As staff officer, engineer services, he supervised the reconstruction of the college. In December 1936 he became engineer instructor. G. D. Solomon recalled 'Sec' as having 'a gravelly voice, a welcome sense of humour and a temper which was always quick'. With a lifelong interest in breeding and racing thoroughbreds, he took an active role in local riding events. Promoted temporary lieutenant colonel in November 1939, he was transferred to Army Headquarters, Melbourne, next month.

On 4 April 1940 Secombe was seconded to the A.I.F. and given command of the 7th Divisional Engineers. In October he sailed for the Middle East. From January 1941 the engineers of the 7th served in North Africa where, in addition to his field engineering duties, Secombe took charge of works at Tobruk and Benghazi, Libya, and Mersa Matruh, Egypt. Promoted colonel and appointed the division's assistant-adjutant and quartermaster general in May, he participated in the Syrian campaign (June-July). He was appointed C.B.E. and mentioned in dispatches for his work in the Middle East. In November he was made temporary brigadier and appointed deputy-director, supply and transport, at I Corps headquarters, with which he moved to Java in January 1942 and to Australia in March.

After six months as senior administrative staff officer at Headquarters, Second Army, Secombe was sent to Port Moresby in October 1942 as deputy-head of the Combined Operational Service Command, which coordinated all construction and lines of communications activities for allied forces in Papua and New Guinea. From March 1943 he filled administrative posts, first at I Corps and New Guinea Force, and then at Land Headquarters, Brisbane. Attached to Northern Territory Force in April 1944 for logistics planning, he returned to Brisbane in September as acting deputy quartermaster general. In October he was posted to Advanced Land Headquarters, which were located first at Hollandia, Netherlands East Indies, and later at Morotai whence he organized administrative support for operations in Borneo and Brunei. By July 1945 he was back at Land Headquarters as D.Q.M.G. He was twice mentioned in dispatches (1943 and 1947), and was awarded the American Medal of Freedom with Silver Palm (1948).

In March 1946 Secombe became engineer-in-chief at Army Headquarters. He supervised the transition of the R.A.E. from war to peace. Promoted temporary major general in January 1949 (substantive September 1950), he was appointed master-general of the ordnance and fourth military member of the Military Board. In November 1950 he moved to Brisbane as general officer commanding, Northern Command. Twelve months later he was transferred to Sydney as G.O.C., Eastern Command, and made temporary lieutenant general. He returned to Northern Command in May 1952. Of middle height, Secombe was immaculate in appearance and in bearing. He had the ability to be friendly with subordinates, without losing their respect, and gained the trust of all.

Secombe retired from the army on 4 April 1954 as an honorary lieutenant general. In 1955 he was appointed C.B. and colonel commandant of the R.A.E. After breeding Herefords on a 10 000 acre (4050 ha) property near Gatton, Queensland, he bought a small orchard at Kenmore. He died of cancer on 3 February 1962 in the Mater Miscricordiae Hospital, South Brisbane, and was buried in Toowong cemetery. His wife, and their daughter and elder son survived him; their younger son, also a graduate of Duntroon, predeceased him.

J. E. Lee, *Duntroon* (Canb, 1952); A. S. Walker, *Middle East and Far East* (Canb, 1953); D. McCarthy, *South-West Pacific Area—First Year* (Canb, 1959); G. D. Solomon, *A Poor Sort of Memory* (Canb, 1978); R. McNicoll, *The Royal Australian Engineers 1919 to 1945* (Canb, 1982); *SMH*, 5 Feb 1962; information from Mrs M. James, Toowoomba, Qld.
                                                    P. J. GREVILLE

SEDDON, HERBERT ROBERT (1887-1964), veterinarian, was born on 26 May 1887 at Tauranga, New Zealand, eldest of three children of Robert Seddon, a New Zealand-born bank accountant, and his wife Sarah Louisa, née Swarbrick, who came from England. Educated at Auckland Grammar School, Bert joined the Department of Agriculture in 1904 as a cadet. In 1907 he became laboratory-assistant to J. A. Gilruth [q.v.9]. From 1909 he worked in the same capacity in Victoria

and studied at the University of Melbourne (B.V.Sc., 1913; D.V.Sc., 1921), where he lectured (1916-17) on veterinary pathology, bacteriology, materia medica and pharmacy.

At the Presbyterian Church, South Yarra, on 28 November 1914 Seddon had married Ethel Marian Munn, a milliner; they were to have a son and daughter before he divorced her. Appointed captain, Australian Army Veterinary Corps, Australian Imperial Force, on 15 January 1918, he served in the Middle East and commanded (from July) the 10th Mobile Veterinary Section which cared for camels. In 1919 he attended the Royal (Dick) Veterinary College, London. He was demobilized from the army on 3 February 1920 in Melbourne and returned to the university as lecturer in veterinary pathology and bacteriology.

Appointed veterinary pathologist in the New South Wales Department of Agriculture in 1923, Seddon headed operations at Glenfield Veterinary Research Station. Next year he became director of veterinary research. From 1928 to 1936 he was an honorary lecturer at the University of Sydney. By 1936 he had published over 130 papers dealing with diseases of livestock. These included articles on tuberculosis, blackleg, contagious abortion (brucellosis), botulism, sheep blowfly and a wide range of disease conditions, including nutrition and poison plants. He married Verlie Victoria Watts on 12 January 1935 at St Michael's Anglican Church, Sydney.

Seddon was appointed to the new chair of veterinary science at the University of Queensland in 1936. Limited funds and the lack of suitable buildings inhibited his plans for the course, but he carried out his duties single-handed, and with characteristic enthusiasm and energy. The initial classes were held in a converted stable. His lectures reflected his experience and humour. In 1940 five of his first class graduated. A lack of students and staff during World War II forced the school to close in 1943.

From 1937 Professor Seddon was also veterinary adviser to the Department of Agriculture and Stock, government director of veterinary services and a member of the Veterinary Surgeons' Board of Queensland. He served on the National Health and Medical Research Council's nutrition committee and as officer-in-charge (from 1943) of the food section, Rationing Commission, Melbourne. In 1946 he joined the division of veterinary hygiene, Commonwealth Department of Health, Canberra. Eight years later he became technical director of the McGarvie Smith [q.v.11] Institute at Ingleburn, New South Wales, and built up an active veterinary practice at Campbelltown.

A foundation member (1921), honorary secretary (1924-28), president (1929-31) and fellow (1950) of the Australian Veterinary

Association, Seddon was awarded its Gilruth prize in 1950. He sat on the Australian National Research Council, belonged to Rotary and enjoyed playing golf. Survived by his wife and by the son of each of his marriages, he died on 25 October 1964 at his Campbelltown home and was cremated with Anglican rites. Lola McCausland's portrait of Seddon is held by the University of Queensland.

Aust Veterinary J, 35, May 1962, p 300, 41, Jan 1965, p 23; *Aust J of Science*, 27, no 9, Mar 1965, p 252; *SMH*, 4, 16 Jan 1923, 12 Feb 1936; *Courier-Mail*, 7 May 1943; information from Rev J. Seddon, Mosman, Syd, Dr R. M. Watts, Ingleburn, NSW, and the late Mrs V. Seddon; personal knowledge.

ROBERT I. TAYLOR

SEIDEL, WALDEMAR CARL (1893-1980), pianist and music teacher, was born on 11 March 1893 at St Kilda, Melbourne, eldest of three children of Alfred Carl Seidel, a German-born pianist and choral conductor, and his Victorian-born wife Susan Ann, née Miller. A graduate of the Royal Conservatorium of Music, Leipzig, Alfred had migrated to Australia at the age of 19. Wally was educated at Xavier College, Kew. He received his early piano lessons from his father and became the protégé of J. Alfred Johnstone, a well-known teacher and author of piano-tutors. Seidel received additional training from Benno Scherek—with whom he also studied the art of accompaniment—and from Edward Goll [q.v.9].

On his departure for England in 1924, Johnstone turned over his entire teaching practice to Seidel, who hired a room in the music warehouse of W. H. Glen & Co. Pty Ltd, Collins Street, and combined teaching with work as a professional accompanist. He toured with such performers as Amy Castles [q.v.7] and Stella Power [q.v.]. At the Presbyterian Church, St Kilda, on 10 January 1925 he married Irene Olive Zoe Barlow, a 19-year-old milliner. That year he was appointed to the staff of the Albert Street Conservatorium, East Melbourne. His touring career over, teaching became his 'chief aim and ambition in life'. He supplemented his income by selling pianos and gramophones. The notable success of his students prompted Professor (Sir) Bernard Heinze to appoint him to the staff of the University Conservatorium in 1931.

In a golden age of piano-teaching in Melbourne, Seidel stood apart from his colleagues for resolutely imposing no particular school of pianism upon his pupils. Instead he strove to develop the technical and interpretative individuality of each student, regardless of ability. He published his views in 1931 in the *Australian Musical News*. Those who studied under him and went on to establish prominent careers included Don Banks, Phyllis Batchelor, May Clifford, Douglas Gamley, Peggy Glanville-Hicks, Bernice Lehmann, Noel Mewton-Wood [q.v.15] and Margaret Schofield. Seidel also became adept at teaching blind pianists, a skill he passed on to others.

For Seidel, music was at root a spiritual activity, but one associated with no particular doctrine. Although he had been baptized a Lutheran, organized religion of any kind did not sit well with a pedagogical philosophy based on the primacy of independent thinking. His few interests, outside music and family life, included the Savage Club (member 1932-66) and Freemasonry. Following a serious motorcar accident in 1937, he took up golf and it quickly became an abiding passion. At work and at home he cut a cultured, if unobtrusive, figure of almost unshakeably affable temperament. Essentially a very private man, he had few close friends but was well liked by his colleagues. He retired from the conservatorium in 1974 and taught privately for the rest of his life. Survived by his wife and their two sons, he died on 17 September 1980 at Malvern and was cremated.

P. J. Tregear, *The Conservatorium of Music University of Melbourne* (Melb, 1997); *Aust Musical News*, Apr 1924, p 19, Mar 1931, p 17; *Music and the Teacher*, Dec 1980; information from Miss M. Clifford, East Ivanhoe, Mr C. Seidel, Glen Iris, Melb, and Mrs V. Crawford, Neutral Bay, Syd.

PETER JOHN TREGEAR

SEIFFERT, JOHN WESLEY (1905-1965), prison warder and politician, was born on 9 September 1905 at Goulburn, New South Wales, third son of locally born parents Frederick Emil Seiffert, gardener, and his wife Sarah Jane, née Walker. Jack attended Goulburn Superior Public School and began work as a storekeeper. At St Andrew's Presbyterian Church, Goulburn, on 8 September 1928 he married Ada Fedoris Brown, a typiste. Intensely sport-minded and gifted with considerable prowess, he excelled at hockey and Rugby League, but injuries cut short his career as a representative footballer. He was the one-mile (1.6 km) Australian amateur track cycling champion in 1926 and treasurer (1935-38) of the New South Wales Country Rugby League.

Seiffert worked as a warder (1931-41) at Goulburn gaol, and served as an alderman (1934-37) on Goulburn Municipal Council. In May 1941 he won the Legislative Assembly seat of Monaro as a Labor candidate. His electorate, based on Queanbeyan, had been a Country Party stronghold, but he increased his majority in each election and held the seat until his death.

Although more at home in his electorate than the inner circles of State Labor politics, Seiffert was a vigorous debater with an impressive command of language acquired by persistent effort. Tall and well built, he never hesitated to speak his mind, even to the extent of criticizing his colleagues: he was loyal to the party and its principles rather than to its personalities. Often in conflict with the State executive, he lost endorsement in 1950, held his seat as an Independent and was soon afterwards readmitted to party ranks. His temperament and outspokenness caused him to be known as the 'Gladiator' and the 'Man from Snowy River'. Perhaps his best known prank in parliament was to exchange the false teeth of two sleeping members.

Resenting privilege in any sphere, Seiffert called the Chalet at Charlotte Pass a 'breeding ground for snobocracy'. By public criticism he obtained a reduced bus fare to the area, thus opening the snowfields to those of lesser means. He was a trustee of Kosciusko State Park from 1948. In July 1956 he demanded an inquiry into the strength and position of the ski-lodges, following the death of a girl in an avalanche. A founder (1961) and director of the Queanbeyan Leagues Club, he was one of the first to call for the legalization of poker machines and the introduction of late-night trading on Fridays. After visiting Europe in 1961, he suggested the construction of a monorail in Sydney. Mindful of his experience as a warder, he insisted on an independent inquiry into an alleged bashing by police at Cooma in 1963. The Labor premier Robert Heffron [q.v.14], stung by this attack on his government, offered to present Seiffert to any political party willing to accept him. No offers were forthcoming.

Seiffert was devoted to the underprivileged and gifted with an intense love for children; he befriended everyone he met, including his political opponents. He died of cancer on 10 January 1965 at his Queanbeyan home and was buried in Riverside cemetery; his wife, their son and two of their three daughters survived him. Many people credited him with the remarkable development of the Monaro electorate during his twenty-three years as its member. The Queanbeyan Rugby League ground, Seiffert Oval, was named after him.

PD (NSW), 11 Sept 1963, p 4885, 26 May 1965, p 19; SMH, 14 Mar, 15, 18, 26 June 1950, 5 Jan, 26 July 1956, 11 Sept 1959, 7 July 1961, 5, 7, 12 Sept 1963, 11, 14 Jan, 14 Oct 1965; Sun (Syd), 2 Sept 1960, 11, 12 Sept 1963, 11 Jan 1965; Canb Times, 11, 14 Jan 1965.
JOHN N. MOLONY

SELBY, ARTHUR ROLAND (1893-1966), army officer, was born on 16 March 1893 at Armidale, New South Wales, third child of native-born parents John Selby, builder, and his wife Elizabeth, née Vaughan. In the mid-1890s the family moved to Leederville, Perth. Arthur attended Scotch College, Claremont, and in June 1911 was among the first intake at the Royal Military College, Duntroon, Federal Capital Territory. When World War I broke out, the senior cadets at R.M.C. graduated early to be available for active service. Lieutenant Selby joined the Australian Imperial Force on 14 August 1914 and sailed for the Middle East with the 11th Battalion in November. At the Garrison Church, Kasr-el-Nil, Cairo, on 24 February 1915 he married with Anglican rites Susanna Gertrude Bryant whom he had met in Perth; they were to have a daughter.

After landing at Gallipoli on 25 April 1915, Selby was severely wounded in the right elbow on 7 May near Lone Pine. Evacuated to Egypt and thence to England, he was repatriated in November. In 1916 he was appointed adjutant of the wartime officers' training school, near Duntroon. For the rest of the war he held staff posts in Western Australia and Tasmania.

Promoted captain and brevet major in early 1920, Selby was sent in 1923 to the Staff College, Quetta, India, where he became a popular officer. He returned to Australia in 1925 and in the following year was invited back to Quetta as an instructor; he took up the four-year post in September 1926, with the temporary rank of lieutenant colonel. Because opportunities for advancement in the Australian Military Forces were limited, he resigned in September 1930 to join a British regiment, the Royal Ulster Rifles. He served in England in 1932-36, attended the 1937 course at the Imperial Defence College, London, and returned to India.

When World War II began, Selby was a temporary brigadier on the British staff in Egypt. In 1940-41 he commanded an infantry brigade around Mersa Matruh and Sidi Barrani. Granted the acting rank of major general in March 1941, he served as an area commander and then as deputy quartermaster general at General Headquarters, Middle East. Following a period in Eritrea, he moved to Persia and Iraq Command where he was acting commander-in-chief (as temporary lieutenant general) in 1943-44. Mentioned six times in dispatches in 1941-43, he was appointed C.B.E. (1941), C.B. (1943), and to the Russian Order of Kutuzov (1944). His final appointment was that of major general, administration, at Headquarters, Western Command, England.

In February 1946 Selby retired and moved to South Africa. He took up a citrus farm at Muden, Natal, but his dreams of a quiet life were disrupted by the election (1948) of a Nationalist government intent on making South Africa a republic. Selby became a prominent member of a militant opposition group, the Torch Commando. In 1953 he helped to found the Union Federal Party which failed to win any seats at provincial council elections.

Never one to change direction, Selby clung to the imperial ideal. He resigned from the U.F.P. in 1955 to devote his efforts to the Anti-Republican League, but failed to stem the nationalist tide which took South Africa out of the British Commonwealth in 1961. Weakened physically and financially by his dedication to a lost cause, Selby retired to New Hanover, Natal. He died on 30 August 1966 at Greytown and was buried in a Pietermaritzburg cemetery.

C. E. W. Bean, *The Story of Anzac* (Syd, 1921, 1924); W. C. Belford, *Legs-eleven* (Perth, 1940); J. E. Lee, *Duntroon* (Canb, 1952); I. S. O. Playfair, *The Mediterranean and the Middle East*, 1 (Lond, 1954); B. Pitt, *The Crucible of War* (Lond, 1980); *The Times*, 11 May 1953, 24 May 1955; *West Australian*, 12 Sept 1966; A10302, item 1956/1248 *and* A1838, items 201/2/2/9 and 201/2/7/1 (NAA, Canb).

PETER LONDEY

SELBY, ISAAC (1859-1956), lecturer and historian, was born on 3 November 1859 at Greenwich, Kent, England, son of Isaac Selby, joiner, and his wife Isabella, née Gilhome. In 1868 the family migrated to New Zealand. Young Isaac attended school at Dunedin, studied at night, and began to accumulate a vast store of information about history, religion, philosophy, science, literature and the arts. He moved to Melbourne in 1882, then returned to Dunedin. At the office of the registrar of marriages, Auckland, on 28 October 1885 he married Jessie Beatrice Chapman; they were to have a daughter and two sons.

Back in Melbourne, Selby made a living from public lecturing and debating. He praised the virtues of Unitarianism and teetotalism, and attacked Catholicism in general and the Jesuits in particular. In the late 1890s he and his family travelled to San Francisco, United States of America, where a businessman Donald McRae introduced them to the Universal Spiritual Association. Isaac repudiated the society as Catholic, but Jessie came under its influence and refused to leave San Francisco. He sailed to Australia alone in 1901. After standing unsuccessfully against H. B. Higgins [q.v.9] for the House of Representatives seat of Northern Melbourne at the Federal election in March, he attributed his defeat to 'the sinister hand of Rome'.

In 1904 Selby returned to San Francisco. When his wife petitioned for divorce, he countered by suing McRae for alienating her affections. Judge James Hebbard found against Selby, granted the divorce and gave Jessie custody of the children. On 28 November Selby entered Hebbard's court and fired a revolver at him: the bullet lodged in the back of the judge's chair. He was sentenced to seven years imprisonment, transferred to a hospital for the insane, and released in 1910 on the condition that he immediately leave for Australia.

Selby resumed lecturing and debating, in Melbourne and at country centres. His performances, often supported by musicians, singers and photographic slides, continued until the 1950s. As part of a protest against the planned resumption of the old Melbourne cemetery, he formed the Old Cemetery and Soldiers' Memorial Union in March 1918 to 'Save the Old Cemetery and build in the centre of it a monument to the Heroic men who have fallen at the front'. In 1920 he joined the (Royal) Historical Society of Victoria. About that time he inaugurated the Old Pioneers' Memorial Fund to promote the study of history and to lobby for the erection of a statue of John Batman [q.v.1] in the Flagstaff Gardens. In 1924 the fund published Selby's book *The Old Pioneers' Memorial History of Melbourne*, in which he commended the growth of charitable organizations, praised developments in literature, the arts, science and industry, and endorsed free education, the eight-hour day and the White Australia policy. In the following year he published a panto-mime, *Hinemoa*, in the same volume as his history, *Memories of Maoriland*. His other works included *The Old Pioneers Memorial Almanac* (1935).

Selby never remarried. A disappointed lover named Gertie had written to him in 1924: 'You seem to overrule my thoughts when we are together'. He was sometime minister of the Church of Christ, Carlton. During World War II he lectured on the history of warfare and presided (1941-42) over the Russian branch of the Victorian division of the Australian Red Cross Society. He died on 26 March 1956 at Parkville and was buried in Fawkner cemetery.

San Francisco Chronicle, 29 Nov 1904; *Argus*, 4 Mar 1954; *Age* (Melb), 27 Mar 1956; Selby papers (Univ Melb Archives *and* RHSV).

FRANK STRAHAN

SELLECK, SIR FRANCIS PALMER (1895-1976), accountant, businessman and lord mayor, was born on 20 August 1895 at Nathalia, Victoria, son of Christopher Selleck, a miller from England, and his Victorian-born wife Emily, née Latimer. His father and uncle ran Numurkah Roller Flour Mills. Educated at Numurkah State and Shepparton Agricultural High schools, Frank wanted to be a lawyer, but his family could not afford the fees. He moved to Melbourne, joined the army's senior cadets and in October 1912 found a job as a clerk in the Victorian Audit Office.

On 9 March 1915 Selleck enlisted in the Australian Imperial Force. Posted to the 24th Battalion, he served (from September) at Gallipoli as quartermaster sergeant. In May 1916 he was sent to the Western Front where he was commissioned (September), appointed adjutant (September 1917), promoted captain (January 1918), mentioned in dispatches (May) and wounded in action (July). For his work between March and September 1918—making reconnaissances under enemy fire and organizing the battalion's movements—he was awarded the Military Cross. His A.I.F. appointment ended on 23 April 1920. In 1923 he helped to form the Legacy Club of Melbourne, of which he was inaugural treasurer. He has been credited with suggesting the name, 'Legacy'. At All Saints Church, St Kilda, on 22 December 1923 he married with Anglican rites Mollie Constance Maud Miller.

Selleck studied part time and qualified as a fellow of the Federal Institute of Accountants (Australian Society of Accountants). On 11 July 1924 he resigned from the Audit Office. He worked (as accountant and secretary) for a company that made ladies' hats before establishing his own accountancy firm in 1934. Three years later he embarked on a joint venture with cinema interests in Sydney, acquiring a picture theatre in Melbourne, and several in the suburbs and in country towns. He was president of the Victorian Independent Exhibitors' Association in 1942-43. Shortly after the outbreak of World War II, the Federal government had formed a Board of Business Administration to oversee expenditure on defence. Selleck joined the staff as chief inspector of administration and became a board-member in 1944.

In 1949 he was elected to the Melbourne City Council. He improved its management practices and chaired a committee which recommended ways to achieve economies and raise additional revenue. On 30 August 1954 he was elected lord mayor. He held office for three, consecutive, one-year terms. The third term was unexpected: councillors had intended that Sir Frank Beaurepaire [q.v.7] would be lord mayor during the Olympic Games, but he died in May 1956. Selleck presided over the redevelopment of the city centre, including the neglected sites of the Eastern and Western markets. Recognizing the potential of postwar Melbourne, he advocated increased loans as a means of providing municipal infrastructure. He took advantage of the Olympic Games and the attendant publicity to promote his city.

Selleck gained a reputation for directness and efficiency, characteristics which were sometimes interpreted as irascibility by council staff. He was a self-made man, and his success had been earned. In 1956 he failed to win Liberal and Country Party pre-selection for a seat in the Legislative Council. He was knighted that year and appointed K.B.E. in 1957. Despite these distinctions and his military background, he asked uniformed council attendants to stop saluting him. In 1954-56 he was treasurer of the Victorian branch of the Returned Sailors', Soldiers' and Airmen's Imperial League of Australia.

Retiring from the council in 1958, Sir Frank became a director of a number of companies; several of them were involved in retailing, including Foy & Gibson [qq.v.4,8] and Cox Bros (Australia) Ltd. The crash of the latter in the mid-1960s tested him severely. In 1959-67 he was a member of the board of the Commonwealth Banking Corporation. Although a heart attack in 1965 reduced his mobility, he recovered substantially through sheer willpower. He died on 2 October 1976 at Armadale and was cremated; his wife, and their daughter and son survived him.

C. Blatchford, *Legacy* (Melb, 1932); *The Annual Report of the Melbourne City Council*, 1955-56; *SMH*, 14 Dec 1944, 10 June 1955, 26 June 1959, 20 July 1967; *Herald* (Melb), 30 Aug 1954; *Age* (Melb), 31 Aug 1954; information from Messrs C. O. Harry, Balwyn, J. L. Mills, Parkdale, and G. Tolson, Prahran, Melb.   JOHN YOUNG

SELLHEIM, GERT HUGO EMMANUEL (1901-1970), architect and graphic designer, was born on 31 December 1901 at Viljandi (Vil'yandi), Estonia, then part of the Russian Empire, son of Bruno Sellheim, medical practitioner, and his wife Helene, née Moritz, both of whom were of German descent. Gert fought in the White Army in the Russian Civil War in 1918-20. After studying architecture in Berlin, Munich, Vienna, Graz and Paris, he arrived at Fremantle, Western Australia, in December 1926. Because his architectural qualifications were not immediately recognized, he worked as a farm labourer near Pingelly. Registered as an architect on 21 May 1929 in Perth, he joined R. H. Alsop [q.v.7] and F. J. Glennon as a site architect for the University of Western Australia.

In 1931 Sellheim moved to Melbourne. He practised as an industrial and commercial designer, and began producing posters, principally for the Australian National Travel Association. His most famous posters—'Australia Surf Club' (which showed stylised figures hauling a surf-rescue line) and 'Corroboree Australia' (which featured black stick-figures with Aboriginal markings)—were hard-edged, coloured lithographs that revealed his European training and the influence of cubism. They marked a striking contrast to Percy Trompf's and James Northfield's [qq.v.12,15] work in the more conventional illustrative tradition. Trompf and Northfield embellished the Australian landscape; Sellheim represented it, sometimes using photomontage in his compositions. The three of them came together at the Art Training Institute, Melbourne, which marketed their talents. Sellheim's 'dynamic treatment of colour' enabled him to uphold 'the best trends in modern design'.

At the German Evangelical Lutheran Church, East Melbourne, on 15 January 1938 Sellheim married Sally Irene Evans, a fashion model. He won the 1939 Sir John Sulman [q.v.12] prize for his decoration of the interior of the Victorian Government Tourist Bureau's building in Collins Street. Sellheim designed a sundial and painted murals for the Newburn Flats, Queens Road, South Melbourne, in 1941. From the mid-1930s he had worked with the publisher Oswald Zeigler on a variety of commemorative books, including *Australia 1788-1938* (Sydney, 1938), a lavish mix of text, image and photomontage, with line drawings by Sellheim featuring Aboriginal images. Its successor, *This is Australia* (1946), was revised and reprinted a number of times.

Sellheim pioneered the use of Australian Aboriginal imagery, not as a straight copy, but as a motif in his posters, interior decoration and book design. As an A.T.I. prospectus put it: 'Sellheim has proved that out of this country's strange and wonderful past can be drawn endless inspiration'. Interned as a Nazi sympathizer in May 1942, he claimed to abhor Hitler's views. Following his release four months later, he lived in Adelaide, applied for Australian citizenship in 1944 and moved to Sydney in 1945. His flying-kangaroo logo for Qantas Empire Airways Ltd first appeared on the airline's new Lockheed Constellations in January 1947. Sellheim's winning entry in a stamp-design competition became in 1948 the two-shilling stamp celebrating Aboriginal art. In 1963 Qantas sent him overseas to produce posters and brochures on some of its major ports of call, including Singapore, London and Rome.

Survived by his wife, and their son and daughter, Sellheim died of myocardial infarction on 3 January 1970 in his Lane Cove home and was cremated with Anglican rites. Posters and books designed by Sellheim are held by major public galleries and libraries in Australia. One of the country's most influential graphic designers in the twentieth century, he produced work that continues to influence the way artists imagine and depict the continent and its people.

P. Spearritt (ed), *Trading Places* (Melb, 1991); R. Butler, *Poster Art in Australia* (Canb, 1993); *Art in Aust*, Nov 1940; *Walkabout*, Nov 1957; A11797, item WP6419 (NAA, Canb); D1915, item SA10941 (NAA, Adel); information from Mr N. Sellheim, Turramurra, Syd.   PETER SPEARRITT

SELLWOOD, NEVILLE FRANCIS (1922-1962), jockey, was born on 2 December 1922 at Hamilton, Brisbane, fifth child of Queensland-born parents Charles Sellwood, labourer, and his wife Amy Elizabeth Sherman, née Goan. Apprehensive about the financial and physical risks involved in a career in horse-racing, Neville's mother wanted him to become a solicitor, but he deliberately performed poorly at school in an attempt to thwart her ambitions for his future. Perhaps at his mother's insistence, he began work in a pharmacy: he was soon dismissed, after pouring cascara into bottles intended for cough medicine. In 1938 he was apprenticed to Jim Shean, a horse-trainer in Brisbane. His first ride was at Bundamba racecourse, Ipswich; his first win was on Ourimbah, at Doomben, Brisbane, on 11 March 1939.

Called up for full-time duty in the Militia on 19 January 1942, Sellwood served with postal units in Brisbane and at Townsville where a sympathetic commanding officer allowed him to ride trackwork and take mounts at local race-meetings. He topped the jockeys' premiership at Townsville in three successive years, winning 140 races from 290 mounts. Rather than calling different odds for each horse he rode, the bookmakers laid 'even-money Sellwood' for them all. At St James's Anglican Cathedral, Townsville, on 21 October 1944 he married Alwyn Grace Dinnar, a waitress; they were to have two daughters and a son.

By the time he was discharged from the army on 2 May 1946, Sellwood enjoyed a growing reputation as a talented jockey. That year he joined the stables of Maurice McCarten [q.v.15], a Sydney trainer. The pair formed an extraordinary partnership. Within two years Sellwood had won the Sydney jockeys' premiership, a feat he would repeat five times. His first major wins were on Delta in 1949, in the Victoria Racing Club Derby and the W. S. Cox Plate. Riding the same horse, he won the Melbourne Cup in 1951 and was rewarded by the owner (Sir) Adolph Basser [q.v.13] with a Rolls Royce motorcar. He won three more V.R.C. Derbys (1953, 1959 and 1960), three Caulfield Cups (1950, 1951 and 1957), two Australian Jockey Club Derbys (1952 and 1953), two A.J.C. Epsom Handicaps (1956 and 1959), two A.J.C. Metropolitans (1951 and 1958), and the Queensland Turf Club Derby (1959). His second Melbourne Cup win in 1955, on Toparoa (trained by T. J. Smith), was controversial. The lightly weighted Toparoa just held off the fast finishing topweight, Rising Fast. Sellwood was subsequently suspended for causing interference to Rising Fast, but, to the surprise of many, Toparoa was not disqualified and its connexions kept the cup.

Sellwood rode the champion horses, Tulloch and Todman, to twelve and ten victories respectively, including Todman's win in the inaugural Golden Slipper Stakes in 1957. Described by one English racing journalist as the 'complete jockey', he had an uncanny ability to read and judge pace and tactics in distance races. He was also shrewd in other ways. His ledgers, recording the form of every horse he had ridden, assisted him in choosing mounts. His manner was confident and easy, and he charmed owners and trainers alike. Enjoying the publicity and wealth that came with success, he wore expensive suits and earned the nickname 'Nifty', but he was no spendthrift, investing much of his earnings in shares, and in a sheep-property at Cudal, New South Wales.

In 1950 Sellwood had travelled overseas, and won races in the United States of America and Britain. He returned to England in 1962 and achieved what was perhaps his greatest success, victory on Larkspur in the Derby. That year he also rode in France for the Aga Khan's stable and led the French jockeys' premiership with 102 winners. On 7 November 1962 he rode the misnamed Lucky Seven on a wet track at Maison Lafitte racecourse, near Paris. The horse slipped, fell and rolled on him, causing severe internal injuries. Sellwood was carried unconscious from the track and died on the way to hospital. Accompanied by his wife and their three children, his body was returned to Australia and buried with Catholic rites in Cudal cemetery. Yves St Martin, who also rode 102 winners to share the premiership, presented the prize, a golden whip, to Sellwood's widow.

N. Penton, *A Racing Heart* (Syd, 1987); J. Pollard, *Australian Horse Racing* (Syd, 1988); M. Painter and R. Waterhouse, *The Principal Club* (Syd, 1992); *People* (Syd), 26 Aug 1953; *SMH*, 7 Nov 1955, 8, 9 Nov 1962; *Daily Telegraph* (Syd), 7 Oct 1958, 9 Nov 1962.   RICHARD WATERHOUSE

SEMMENS, EDWIN JAMES (1886-1980), forester, local historian and community leader, was born on 20 January 1886 at Toongabbie, Victoria, eldest of nine children of Josiah Semmens, storeman and later inspector of forests, and his wife Agnes, née Veitch, both Victorian born. Educated at the Maryborough School of Mines, Ted became a state primary school teacher in 1902. After attending the Melbourne Training College in 1909-10, he taught in metropolitan and country high schools. He studied part time at the University of Melbourne (B.Sc., 1925), won a (Godfrey) Howitt [q.v.4] natural history scholarship in zoology, and played tennis and golf. On 8 May 1915 at Armadale he married, with the forms of the Australian Church, Florence Bilton, a teacher; they were childless.

In 1927 Semmens—who was known affectionately as 'Teddo', 'E. J.' and 'Jacko'—was appointed principal of the School of Forestry, Creswick. Introducing a broad curriculum for the three-year, residential course, he set high standards and made himself available outside normal working hours to guide the study habits and interests of his exclusively male students. During his tenure the school produced some of Australia's best-known botanists, including James Willis and Richard Bond, as well as numerous foresters working in the public and private spheres. Semmens concentrated his research on the composition of Eucalyptus oils. An active field-botanist, he accumulated a valuable collection of plants which he presented to the school. In 1935 he was elected a fellow of the Linnean Society of London.

At a time when relatively few Australians were interested in preserving their country's historical records, Semmens collected letters, diaries, reports, account-books, photographs, paintings, maps, publications and objects relating to the history of the region around Creswick, Allendale, Smeaton, Bloomfield, Clunes, Daylesford, Ballarat and Eaglehawk. He gathered documents and artefacts associated with local government, religion, education, sport, community organizations, individuals, and industries—including agriculture, grazing, gold-mining, forestry, retailing and manufacturing.

Although he published little, Semmens 'saw relationships between the different types of documents long before others were aware of them'. He gave part of his collection to the Creswick Historical Society and donated the bulk of it to the archives at the University of Melbourne. Occupying some 200 ft (60 m) of shelving, this gift to the university has been described as 'one of the most important collections of local history source material assembled in Australia'. In 1977 the university conferred on Semmens a doctorate of forest science *honoris causa* for his contributions to forestry and history.

Semmens was a councillor (1951-75) and president (1956) of the shire of Creswick. He 'loved nothing better than a good debate' and 'was happy to keep talking' until it was time for a scotch. Prominent in a number of community organizations, he presided (1948-51) over the Creswick District Hospital. In 1968 he was appointed M.B.E. He and Florence created a beautiful garden at their home on the town's Eastern Hill. Predeceased by his wife, he died on 31 December 1980 at Creswick and was cremated with Anglican rites.

Age (Melb), 7 Dec 1977; *Creswick Advertiser*, 29 Jan 1981; cuttings from *Creswick Advertiser* and *Courier* (Ballarat) (held by Creswick Hist Soc); information from Mr J. Sewell, Creswick, Vic; family information; personal knowledge.

FRANCIS ROBERT MOULDS*

SEPPELT, OSCAR BENNO (1873-1963), winemaker and viticulturist, was born on 13 July 1873 at Seppeltsfield, South Australia, second (and eldest surviving) of sixteen children of Oscar Benno Pedro Seppelt [q.v.6], a spirits merchant from Lower Silesia, and his wife Sophie Helene Henriette, née Schroeder, who was born in South Australia. Educated at Prince Alfred College, Adelaide, young Oscar spent several years studying viticulture in Vienna. In 1895 he returned to South Australia where he joined his father and brothers at their winery at Seppeltsfield, in the Barossa Valley. On 25 June that year at the Flinders Street Lutheran Church, Adelaide, he married Hedwig Cecilia Leichter Müller (d.1955) from Vienna. They were to remain childless.

In 1902 the family business was registered as B. Seppelt & Sons Ltd. Oscar junior took charge of operations at Seppeltsfield and his brothers managed branches in other States. The enterprise expanded rapidly. In 1914, in the first of a series of property acquisitions, Seppelt bought Clydeside Cellars, at Rutherglen, Victoria. When his father retired in 1916, Oscar became managing director. That year, in a bold move, he arranged the purchase of Chateau Tanunda, which brought the firm substantial stocks of spirits and enhanced its production capability. In 1918 the company bought the Great Western vineyards, near Ararat, Victoria. A Sydney office was opened in 1922, more land was acquired at Barooga, New South Wales, and winemaking began at Rutherglen in 1929 after the Clydeside Cellars were renovated and new vines were planted. While directing these developments, Seppelt retained his interest in the practical and scientific aspects of production: he designed and patented a wine-pasteurizer which began to be manufactured for sale in 1927.

Involved in trade organizations from an early stage, Seppelt had represented the South Australian Vinegrowers' Association at the first meeting of the Federal Viticultural Council of Australia in 1918; three years later, at the second meeting, he presented a review of the 1921 vintage and the wine trade generally. He was president of the council in 1938-39. As chairman (1931-39) of the Wholesale Winemakers' and Brandy Distillers' Association (Winemakers' Association of South Australia

from 1935), he supported the introduction of a diploma course in oenology at Roseworthy Agricultural College in 1936. Industry also benefited from his terms as president of the South Australian Chamber of Manufactures (1930-32) and of the Associated Chambers of Manufactures of Australia (1933). For twenty-three years, as a well-respected leader of the wine and spirits business, he showed energy, determination, common sense, generosity and impartiality.

Seppelt regularly contributed articles to the *Wine and Spirit News and Australian Vigneron*. He wrote about viticulture and its prospects in South Australia, the wine industry at home and abroad, and the effect of government policies on Australian production and sales. In 1939 he retired and moved from Seppeltsfield to the Adelaide suburb of Tusmore. His brother Leo succeeded him as chairman of the company. Oscar served (1931-58) as consul for Greece in South Australia and was appointed to the Royal Order of George I in 1958. Survived by his adopted daughter, he died on 26 July 1963 in a private hospital at Toorak Gardens and was cremated. His estate was sworn for probate at £122 652.

The House of Seppelt, 1851-1951 (Adel, 1951); A. Aeuckens et al, *Vineyard of the Empire* (Adel, 1988); *Aust Wine, Brewing and Spirit Review*, 81, 1963, p 46; B. Seppelt & Sons Ltd records (SLSA).

M. J. EMERY

SETON, CARDEN WYNDHAM (1901-1970), coastwatcher, was born on 14 June 1901 at Wellingrove station, near Glen Innes, New South Wales, tenth child of Leonard Miles Cariston Seton, an English-born grazier, and his Australian-born wife Eleanor, née Wyndham. Educated at New England Grammar School, Armidale, Carden worked as a woolpresser. In 1927 he travelled to Shortland Island, British Solomon Islands Protectorate, to manage Lofung plantation at Faisi for Burns, Philp [qq.v.7,11] & Co. Ltd. On 21 May 1929 he married Kate Walker Cameron with Presbyterian forms at Matheson, New South Wales.

Moving from Faisi to Sydney when the Japanese invaded the Solomons, Seton enlisted in the Australian Imperial Force on 9 March 1942. In September he embarked with the 30th Employment Company for Port Moresby. Within twelve days of his arrival he was sent to Brisbane. His intimate knowledge of the Solomon Islands led him to be seconded on 5 October (as acting sergeant) to the Allied Intelligence Bureau which co-ordinated intelligence-gathering and subversive activities behind enemy lines in the South-West Pacific Area.

On 20 October Seton was landed by an American submarine on enemy-occupied Choiseul Island to join the network of coast-watchers in the islands to the north-east of Australia. He and Lieutenant (Sir) Alexander Waddell, Royal Australian Naval Volunteer Reserve, established a radio station overlooking Bougainville Strait. Their reports on Japanese naval and air traffic assisted American forces during the battle for Guadalcanal. They also contributed to the rescue of many allied pilots, twenty-three of them on Choiseul.

Seton was attached to 'M' Special Unit in May 1943. Bearded, 6 ft 2 ins (188 cm) tall and weighing about 14 stone (89 kg), he was formidable in appearance. The local scouts, whom he organized, trained and led, inflicted heavy casualties on the enemy and destroyed much of their equipment. Seton's 'fearless and aggressive spirit', and his success in combat, helped to keep local inhabitants loyal to the Allies. He won the Distinguished Conduct Medal. On 14 October he was commissioned acting lieutenant. From January 1944 he pinpointed targets for a number of successful dive-bombing raids, as a result of which Choiseul Bay ceased to be an important enemy base.

In March 1944 Seton returned to Brisbane. Four months later he was posted to New Britain where he conducted guerrilla operations against enemy outposts until March 1945. Judged 'eminently suited to lead a band of killers', he was sent in May to relieve Lieutenant Paul Mason [q.v.15] as guerrilla leader in the Kieta area of Bougainville. In June he was promoted captain. During his time on Bougainville he was responsible for killing 708 Japanese.

Placed on the Reserve of Officers on 9 December 1945, Seton returned to Choiseul in the following year to run Lutie plantation at the mouth of the Vurulata River. He was a member (1947-49) of the B.S.I.P. Advisory Council. Back in Queensland from 1955, he farmed at Upper Mount Gravatt, worked for a shearing co-operative, Grazcos Ltd, at Longreach for two years and moved to Brisbane in the mid-1960s. He died of coronary thrombosis on 24 October 1970 at Slacks Creek and was cremated with Anglican rites. His wife and their two sons survived him.

G. Long, *The Final Campaigns* (Canb, 1963); E. Feldt, *The Coast Watchers* (Syd, 1967); W. Lord, *Lonely Vigil* (NY, 1977); G. H. Gill, *Royal Australian Navy 1942-1945* (Canb, 1985); information from Mr G. D. Seton, Tea Tree Gully, Adel.

SHIRLEY LITHGOW

SEYLER, ALBERT JAKOB (1913-1977), telecommunications scientist, was born on 24 July 1913 at Dudweiler, Saarland, Germany, only child of Jakob Johannes Seyler, railway official, and his wife Elizabeth Katarina, née Schmidt. Albert learned French at an early age, and was fond of music and outdoor pursuits. At Ludwigs Gymnasium, Saarbrücken, he studied Latin, Greek, mathematics and science. Graduating in 1932, he won a scholarship to the Technische Hochschule, Munich, where he obtained a diploma in electrical engineering in 1938.

Employed by the Flugfunk-Forshungsinstitut (Aeronautical Wireless Communication Research Institute) at Oberpfaffenhofen, near Munich, Seyler initially undertook research into air navigational aids, especially wireless. During World War II, with the rank of captain (March 1941) in the *Luftwaffe*, he worked as a radar engineer in France, Norway and Italy. He developed a radar-controlled method for guiding night-fighters from the ground, and designed radar-jamming equipment and transmission stations. In Munich on 27 October 1941 he married Franciska Georgiana Klapperich, a secretary at the Forshungsinstitut.

At the end of the war Seyler was interned briefly by the British Army, but soon found a job as a radio engineer at the American airbase at Oberpfaffenhofen. In December 1947 he was contracted under the Australian government's programme of employing 'enemy aliens' with scientific and technical backgrounds. At the time of his recruitment he was described as 'tall', 'angular', 'well built' and 'somewhat serious'. A security check confirmed his involvement as a student in several National Socialist organizations. Seyler rejected militarism and made a commitment to science for socially constructive purposes. He chose Australia in preference to other nations offering him settlement because he believed that he was less likely to be employed on defence projects there. He later refused to allow his son to belong to the cadet corps at school.

In 1948 Seyler arrived in Melbourne where he joined the research laboratories of the Postmaster-General's Department. Acquiring excellent English, he worked as a member of the team engaged in planning for the introduction of television in 1956. He was quick to recognize the inappropriateness of the P.M.G.'s techniques for testing television generation and transmission facilities, and steered his section toward finding the best frequency to use. In the early 1950s he contributed to the development of an innovative concept for waveform testing, and later produced the first solid state operational 'pulse and bar' waveform test-signal generator. He also conducted research into video transmission circuits and relay links. In 1956 he was responsible for ensuring that Sydney received television pictures of the Olympic

213

Games in Melbourne by arranging for a commercial airliner, equipped with a radio transponder, to circle over the Australian Alps. His work helped to establish the P.M.G. laboratories as a major contributor to television-signal research.

Seyler was naturalized in 1955. He studied at the University of Melbourne (M.Elec.Eng., 1956; D.App.Sc., 1966), and added to the stature of the P.M.G. laboratories by his publications and his participation in conferences. The Institution of Radio and Electronics Engineers Australia twice awarded him the annual Norman W. V. Hayes memorial medal (1960 and 1964) for the most meritorious paper published in its *Proceedings*. In 1964 he became assistant director general of the research laboratories, a post which he held until his death. Some colleagues found him 'arrogant' and 'impatient'; others considered him to be an 'inspirational' and 'remarkable scientist' who delighted in solving complex problems. As early as 1954 he had examined over-the-horizon high frequency radio and broad-band communication by means of a geostationary satellite.

In the 1960s Seyler began to receive widespread recognition for his achievements. A fellow (1967) and president (1972) of the I.R.E.E.A., he was a member (from 1964) of the faculty of engineering at Monash University and an honorary consultant in communication engineering (from 1966) at the University of Adelaide. He was also a foundation fellow (1975) of the Australian Academy of Technological Sciences, and an adviser to Bell Telephone Laboratories, United States of America (1968-69), and Bell-Northern Research, Canada (1973-74), on human communication systems and teleconferencing.

Although he was convinced of the potential of modern technology to overcome communication problems, Seyler was concerned at the dangers arising from the misuse of this knowledge. He appreciated the importance of inter-disciplinary approaches to understanding the impact of technology on human beings and was a committed conservationist. A skilled carpenter and gardener, he had built his own home at Burwood, before moving to Emerald. He died of coronary vascular disease on 26 April 1977 at Emerald and was buried in Springvale cemetery; his wife and their son survived him. Tom Grochowiak's portrait (1944) of Seyler is held privately.

A. Moyal, *Clear Across Australia* (Melb, 1984); Inst of Radio and Electronics Engineers Aust, *Procs*, 1964-65; Aust Academy of Technological Sciences, *Annual Report*, 1976-77; Telecom Research Laboratories, *Annual Report*, 1977; U. von Homeyer, The Recruitment, Deployment and Experiences of German Scientists in the Post World War Two Period: an historical evaluation (M.A. thesis, Flinders Univ, 1995); A6119, item 1047 (NAA, Canb); MT105/8, item 1/6/3707 (NAA, Melb); papers held by, and information from Mr P. Seyler, Brighton, Melb.   GRAEME OSBORNE

SHACKLETON, GREGORY JOHN (1946-1975), journalist, was born on 24 August 1946 in Brisbane, son of Queensland-born parents William Joseph Hogg, bank clerk, and his wife Olwyn Rebecca, née Schoenheimer. After leaving school, Greg worked as a copy-boy with radio-station 3AW, Melbourne. He changed his surname three times by deed poll: from Hogg to Smith, then to Sugar and finally to Shackleton. In 1964 he enrolled as a part-time student at the University of Melbourne (B.A., 1976).

At St Peter's Church of England, Glenelg, Adelaide, on 7 May 1966 Shackleton married Shirley Doreen Venn, a 34-year-old publicity manager. After a stint as a public-relations officer with the Australian Tourist Commission, San Francisco, United States of America, he returned to Melbourne in 1968 to work as a general reporter and news presenter with television-station HSV-7. By his wife's account, he reached A-grade level at the age of 22.

Although Shackleton was apparently a capable journalist, he achieved national prominence only after his death. On 10 October 1975 he was sent to Portuguese Timor to report on the civil war between the Revolutionary Front of Independent East Timor (Fretilin) and factions covertly supported by Indonesia. At the town of Balibo, Shackleton, his cameraman Gary Cunningham (aged 27) and sound recordist Tony Stewart (21) joined another journalist Malcolm Rennie (29) and his cameraman Brian Peters (30), both from TCN-9, Sydney. All of them died on 16 October that year during or immediately following an assault by Indonesian soldiers and their East Timorese allies against a Fretilin force at Balibo. Their remains were later buried in Jakarta. Shackleton's wife and son survived him.

The five young newsmen had found little time to familiarize themselves with local conditions and only Cunningham had previously worked in a war zone. Yet their initial reports indicated sufficient competence to gainsay one newspaper colleague who dismissed them as having 'come straight from chasing fire engines' in Australia. Shackleton may have been carrying documents on behalf of Fretilin; if so, this action may have contributed to his death. The question as to whether he and his four companions were killed in the battle or subsequently murdered remained unresolved for more than twenty-five years.

Shackleton's mother complained to Australian authorities and his widow campaigned unrelentingly for the truth to be revealed. The Australian Journalists' Association and prominent members of the profession, such as John Pilger and Rohan Rivett [q.v.], criticized successive Australian governments for their failure to exert real pressure on the Indonesians to hold a full inquiry into the killings. In 2000 the Department of Foreign Affairs and Trade published Commonwealth government documents relating to the Indonesian invasion and subsequent annexation of East Timor, but excluded intelligence material. It has been alleged that Australian authorities received intelligence reports, before and after the attack on Balibo, indicating that Indonesian officers planned and supervised the murder of the five newsmen. Their common headstone bears an inscription: 'No words can explain this pointless death in Balibo'.

D. Ball and H. McDonald, *Death in Balibo, Lies in Canberra* (Syd, 2000); W. Way (ed), *Australia and the Indonesian Incorporation of Portuguese Timor, 1974-1976* (Melb, 2000); *SMH*, 13, 18 Oct, 13 Nov 1975, 14 Oct 1995; *Age* (Melb), 18, 21 Oct, 6 Dec 1975, 25 Nov 1981, 21 Oct 1998; *National Times*, 25 Aug 1979.   PETER GIFFORD

SHAND, DONALD MUNRO (1904-1976), grazier and airline founder, was born on 20 September 1904 at Drummoyne, Sydney, fourth child of James Barclay Shand, a native-born accountant, and his wife Ann, née Donald, who came from Scotland. James was later a member (1926-44) of the Legislative Assembly. Don was sent to Epping Public, Cleveland Street Intermediate High and Burwood Commercial schools. While employed by a Sydney wool firm, he attended classes at Sydney Technical College. He worked on various grazing properties in the Armidale district before becoming a wool and skin buyer. At St Stephen's Presbyterian Church, Sydney, on 24 May 1927 he married the twice widowed, 48-year-old Evelyn Wigan, née Hawkins, formerly Hyde. They settled at Woodville, a 4000-acre (1600 ha) property at Puddledock, near Armidale.

Prompted by an article on improved pastures in *Farm Topics* (1928), Shand began the arduous task of converting heavily timbered country into agricultural tillage and supplemented his income by selling wood to residents of Armidale. Through the Depression, he worked long and hard hours. In 1935 he started to produce fat lambs. By 1939 he had acquired a considerable reputation for cultivating large-scale crops of soy beans and peas, as well as chrysanthemums for pyrethrum and opium poppies for morphine.

Shand contested the House of Representatives seat of New England for the Country Party in 1940 and 1949; on each occasion his preferences helped the co-endorsed candidate, respectively Joseph Abbott and David Drummond [qq.v.13,8], to victory. During World War II Shand had set up Women's Agricultural Security Production Services groups, using female students from Teachers' College, Armidale, and local women to harvest crops and as casual labour. With the co-operation of other landholders, he organized mass production of primary products as part of the war effort.

Believing that Australia could not reach its potential without regional development, Shand became founding chairman of East-West Airlines Ltd in 1947. His cousin J. W. Shand [q.v.] was a director. The company had planned to fly between Grafton and Moree, but switched to Tamworth-Sydney and other routes. Low population densities and too few paying customers proved obstacles. Backed by local graziers including A. S. Nivison [q.v.15] and P. A. Wright [q.v.], East-West expanded into aerial agriculture—spreading superphosphate, seeding, and crop dusting. Shand oversaw the successive purchase of Avro Anson, Lockheed Hudson, Douglas DC-3 and Fokker Friendship aircraft. He developed a close link with Trans-Australian Airlines and in 1960 Lester Brain [q.v.13] became a director of East-West. Next year, with the support of the New South Wales cabinet, Shand withstood pressure from Senator (Sir) Shane Paltridge [q.v.15] and the Commonwealth government to accept a takeover offer from Ansett Transport Industries Ltd. In the early 1970s East-West extended its routes to Maroochydore, Queensland, and Alice Springs, Northern Territory, and emerged as an innovator in providing cheap, direct charter flights, with bulk-booking of hotel and resort accommodation.

During World War II the Federal government had appointed Shand to an advisory body to investigate new crops. On a visit to the United States of America in 1943, he realized that Australia was ignoring a prospective commercial industry. He smuggled home grains of hybrid sorghum maize and established a trial plot on Woodville. Helped by correspondence with Eugene Funk, and other plant-breeders at the Iowa State College of Agriculture and Mechanic Arts, Ames, U.S.A., and at the Max-Planck-Institut für Züchtungsforschung, Scharnhorst, West Germany, he built a base from which the Shand Selected Seed Co. (from 1969 Dekalb Shand Seed Co. Pty Ltd) sold hybrid maize seed. By the early 1970s, as beef prices plummeted and the sheep and wool industry endured crisis, his Woodville field-days attracted thousands of visitors from all parts of eastern Australia. In 1976 he was appointed C.M.G.

Shand was a man of ideas, always looking for new ventures. Some projects, such as promoting the outback as a tourist destination and the water-bombing of bushfires, came to fulfilment; others, such as growing orchids and daffodils for the North American market and stocking dams with South African 'Tirasia' fish, proved unviable. Shand relaxed from the rigours of a taxing life by building over one hundred dams with a bulldozer he kept at Puddledock. Evelyn died in 1951. On 24 May 1952 at St Paul's Church, Armidale, Shand married another 48-year-old widow Beryl Constance Downe, née Coventry. He was 'a burly six-footer [183 cm], with ruddy cheeks and matching laughter'. An entertaining, colourful raconteur, he held court in Tattersall's Hotel with grazing families who came to town for the Thursday sales and shopping forays. He died on 7 November 1976 at Woodville and was cremated. His wife survived him; both his marriages were childless.

A. J. Smith, *East-West Eagles* (Brisb, 1989); *Farm Topics*, 15 May, 1 Aug 1928; *Armidale Express*, 26, 28, 30 Aug, 6 Sept 1940, 11, 16 Nov, 7, 12 Dec 1949, 8, 10, 12 Nov 1976; *SMH*, 24 Nov 1943, 23 Jan 1945, 4 June 1951, 25 Oct 1961; *Sun-Herald* (Syd), 29 Oct 1961, 4 Dec 1969; *Bulletin*, 4 Mar 1972; *Northern Daily Leader*, 9, 11 Nov 1976; Shand papers (ML); information from Mr D. and Mrs J. Cooper, Puddledock, and Mr A. Wood, Woodville, Armidale, NSW.

JOHN ATCHISON

SHAND, JOHN WENTWORTH (1897-1959), barrister, was born on 4 September 1897 at Lewisham, Sydney, second child of native-born parents Alexander Barclay Shand, barrister, and his wife Florence Amelia, née Brierley. Jack was educated at Sydney Grammar School and St Paul's College, University of Sydney (B.A., 1918; LL.B., 1921). In 1918, after training at the State Aviation School, Richmond, he sailed for Egypt where he was commissioned in the Royal Air Force on 25 October as a kite-balloon officer. He returned to the University of Sydney and was admitted to the Bar on 3 November 1921.

At St James's Church of England, King Street, on 9 February 1926 Shand married Enid Mary Holt; they were to have four children before being divorced in November 1939. He never lost his frolicsome ways and zest for life; he had a passion for fast cars and belonged to the Killara Lawn Tennis Club, where he met Judith D'Arcy Westgarth. She was aged 28 when they were married with Presbyterian forms on 20 December 1939 in her father's house at Pymble.

Shand became adept at compensation cases and an expert on laws of libel and contempt. He won against (Sir) Garfield Barwick in several important commercial suits and proved formidable in criminal cases. His reputation as a courtroom tactician rested not only on his many victories, but also on his willingness to accept difficult and often seemingly impossible briefs. Tenacity and a preparedness to take risks counted in his professional success. He was appointed K.C. in January 1943.

In 1946 Shand defended Major Charles Hughes Cousens [q.v.13], a popular radio announcer who had been compelled, while a prisoner of war, to make propaganda broadcasts for the Japanese and was subsequently charged with treason. Shand cast enough doubt at the committal hearing for the charge later to be dropped. Between 1947 and 1949 he reputedly earned £12 000 from assisting government investigations, including the Air Court of Inquiry (1948) into the crash of Australian National Airways Pty Ltd's airliner *Lutana* and the royal commission (1949) into certain transactions in relation to timber rights in the Territory of Papua-New Guinea.

At the 1951 royal commission into the case of the shearer Frederick Lincoln McDermott who had been sentenced to life imprisonment in 1947 for the murder (1936) of a Grenfell storekeeper, Shand reduced a detective-inspector to tears in cross-examination and persuaded the commission that the trial had miscarried. McDermott was freed in 1952. In other notable successes, Shand secured the acquittal in 1951 of Thomas Langhorne Fleming, a wealthy grazier accused on strong circumstantial evidence of murdering his wife by lacing her beer with cyanide, and in 1954 of Shirley Beiger, a model who shot her lover at point-blank range outside Chequers Restaurant, Sydney.

Even Shand's warmest admirers saw his courtroom demeanour as unprepossessing—his style was often contrasted with that of his tall and handsome father. Jack Shand was short and stout, red-faced and freckled. He sometimes seemed to mumble, and in later life became hard of hearing. Barwick observed that 'Shand had a thin-piped voice but great vigour as an advocate and the capacity of insinuation in tone which could annoy and bring a witness into antagonism'. Others heard him as shrill and piercing, with a slight lisp. Nevertheless, he was brisk to the point of rudeness when necessary and widely acknowledged as the most successful criminal barrister in Sydney.

By the time of his last big case Shand had only a few months to live. He appeared before the South Australian royal commission in regard to Rupert Max Stuart, an Aborigine convicted in April 1958 of the brutal murder of a 9-year-old girl. The commission was chaired by the chief justice Sir Mellis Napier [q.v.15] who had earlier heard the unsuccessful appeal against Stuart's conviction. The case became a test of South Australia's criminal trial procedures and the retention of capital punishment. Shand clashed frequently with Napier. Eventually, after being stopped during cross-examination of a witness, he withdrew, in effect accusing Napier of making it impossible for a proper inquiry to be held under his chairmanship. Although Napier protested at this 'sabotage', Shand's tactics heightened public controversy and made it unfeasible for Stuart's execution to be carried out.

From 1947 Shand was a director of East-West Airlines Ltd, run by his cousin Donald Shand [q.v.]. In 1949 he became chairman of Air-Griculture Control Ltd. He died of cancer on 19 October 1959 at his St Ives home and was cremated with Anglican rites. His wife and their son and daughter survived him, as did the daughter and three sons of his first marriage.

K. S. Inglis, *The Stuart Case* (Melb, 1961); I. Chapman, *Tokyo Calling* (Syd, 1990); *SMH*, 17 Jan 1939, 1 Jan 1943, 4 Nov 1948, 21 May, 22 Nov 1949, 7 Sept 1951, 20, 22 Oct 1959, 6 Feb 1960; *Nation* (Syd), 29 Aug 1959; *Mirror* (Syd), 19, 21, 25 Oct 1959, 29 Oct 1973; *Daily Telegraph* (Syd), 20, 29 Oct 1959; *Sun* (Syd), 5 Feb 1960; family information.
JOHN SLEE

SHARKEY, LAWRENCE LOUIS (1898-1967), communist leader, was born on 19 August 1898 at Warry Creek, near Cargo, New South Wales, son of native-born parents Michael Sharkey, farmer, and his wife Mary, née Teefy. Little is known of Sharkey's early life apart from communist apocrypha. His parents were both of Irish descent and raised him as a Catholic. Leaving school at the age of 14, he commenced an apprenticeship to a coachmaker at Orange and subsequently worked in the trade. He later claimed that itinerant bushworkers drew him into the conscription struggle during World War I and into support for the Industrial Workers of the World.

At the end of the war Sharkey moved to Sydney and obtained a job as a lift-attendant. In 1922 he joined the Communist Party of Australia. It had only a few hundred members, mostly in Sydney, where its chief strength lay in left-wing unions. Sharkey became a member of one of them, the Federated Miscellaneous Workers' Union of Australia, and was elected to its executive. He lost the post in 1925 after organizing the Trades Hall cleaners —who were sacked and then reinstated—but was to be made a union delegate to the Labor Council of New South Wales in 1928.

'Lance' Sharkey was elected to the executive of the Communist Party in 1926. He was dumped in 1927 when he resisted the turn from a 'united front' with the Australian Labor Party. Scruffy, inarticulate and unconfident, he attached himself to stronger personalities. He boarded with Esmonde Higgins [q.v.14]

and Joy Barrington, and mixed with their circle of lively, hospitable and incurably optimistic activists. Jack Kavanagh [q.v.14], the leader of the circle, attributed Sharkey's reluctance to appear on the picket line as evidence of his 'indecision and vacillation'.

In 1928, however, Sharkey re-emerged as a strong advocate of the Communist International's new line of forthright opposition to all kinds of reformism. He rose to prominence behind Bert Moxon and J. B. Miles [q.v.15], the chief critics of the Australian leadership. After they won control of the party in December 1929, he became editor of its newspaper, *Workers' Weekly*. In 1930 he visited Moscow as a delegate to the congress of the Red International of Labour Unions. Moxon's downfall in 1931 confirmed Sharkey as second only to Miles in the Australian party's hierarchy.

Thereafter Sharkey remained an unshakeably orthodox communist in the Stalinist mould, unswerving in his support for the Soviet Union and willing to follow the Kremlin in every change of direction it imposed on the Communist International. In the early 1930s he was a fierce exponent of sectarian opposition to Labor reformism, notwithstanding being tossed into a creek by factory workers when he stood against Jack Lang [q.v.9] for the Legislative Assembly seat of Auburn in 1932. Chief Australian representative at the congress of the Communist International in 1935, he brought back news that national parties were to return to the strategy of a united front.

At the congress Sharkey had been elected a member of the executive-committee of the International, much to the surprise of Australian members who expected Miles (as party secretary) to receive that honour. According to other Australians present, Sharkey argued that Miles was a married man with family responsibilities, while he was single and better able to represent the party. By this time Sharkey had given up his job to become a full-time party worker on a subsistence wage. A hard, driving disciplinarian, he insisted on absolute obedience, claiming that: 'We have no personal ties in the Communist Party'. Yet on 10 December 1936 at the district registrar's office, Petersham, he married Catherine Craig Maxwell, a stenographer; they had no children.

Following the signing of the non-aggression pact between Germany and the Soviet Union in August 1939, the C.P.A. dropped its call for united action against fascist aggression. Next month the party swung behind the Soviet policy of opposing World War II as an imperialist conflict. When the Australian government declared the C.P.A. illegal in June 1940, Sharkey went underground with other leading members. He resumed open activity after the Germans invaded the Soviet Union in

June 1941. That year the ban on the party was relaxed; in 1942 it was removed. The Australian Communist Party (as it styled itself from 1944 to 1951) backed the national war effort and grew in numbers.

With the onset of the Cold War, the party withdrew its conditional support for the Labor government's programme of postwar reconstruction. By 1948 the A.C.P. was forthright in criticizing reformist tendencies in its British and American counterparts. That year Sharkey allegedly gave instructions to the Malayan Communist Party to conduct insurgency and displaced Miles as general secretary of the Australian party. Deteriorating relations with the A.L.P. broke down completely when the communist-led Miners' Federation went on strike in June 1949 and the Chifley [q.v.13] government gaoled the union's leaders.

In March 1949 Sharkey had told a Sydney journalist that if 'Soviet Forces in pursuit of aggressors entered Australia, Australian workers would welcome them'. He was tried in the Central Criminal Court and found guilty of uttering seditious words. The High Court of Australia upheld his conviction and in October he was sentenced to three years imprisonment. The term was later reduced and he served thirteen months. On his release he embarked on a national tour. He then spent six months at a sanatorium in the Soviet Union for treatment of a heart condition.

Despite these absences, Sharkey outmanoeuvred his critics within the C.P.A. to consolidate his leadership and ensure that the party minimized the impact of Khrushchev's repudiation of Stalin in 1956. Sharkey sympathized with the Chinese party's criticisms of Khrushchev's revisionism, but, succumbing to majority opinion in the Australian party and to intense pressure while in Moscow in 1961, he rejected the Chinese position in the subsequent Sino-Soviet split. As the party liberalized its policies and practices, Sharkey's limitations were cruelly exposed by a halting performance on national television. He ceded the post of secretary to Laurie Aarons in 1965.

Sharkey was lauded in his heyday as a heroic communist leader, but his reputation sank with the fortunes of his party. His own dogmatism and deviousness added to his consistent support for the worst abuses of Stalinist dictatorship. He had directed the activity of the C.P.A. under repressive circumstances that included constant surveillance by the Australian Security Intelligence Organization, and the strain took its toll—his drunken binges on visits to the Soviet Union were notorious. The close watch on his activities had worked to his advantage in 1954 when the Soviet intelligence officer Vladimir Petrov defected; Petrov alleged that Sharkey had received $US25 000 from the Soviet Union on a night when A.S.I.O. agents had him under continuous observation.

Five ft 6 ins (168 cm) tall, with dark brown hair, Sharkey was described as 'a rugged, forceful speaker' who had 'a gift for expounding the Marxist classics in terms understandable to any worker'. He was a prolific journalist, pamphleteer and expositor of Marxism-Leninism. His more substantial writings, *Dialectical Materialism* (Sydney, 1942), *The Trade Unions* (1942) and *An Outline History of the Australian Communist Party* (1944), were faithful renditions of orthodoxy.

Sharkey died suddenly of coronary atherosclerosis on 13 May 1967 in Sydney and was cremated. His wife survived him. Lacking the warmth and companionableness of communist union leaders such as Jim Healy [q.v.14], he was nevertheless respected for his courage and dedication. A largely self-educated boy from the bush, with strong national roots and popular tastes, he owned a shack on the New South Wales coast, and was fond of surfing and fishing; chess was a Bolshevik accretion, a marker of the unusual path he took from Warry Creek to the Kremlin.

W. A. Wood, *The Life Story of L. L. Sharkey* (Syd, 1950); A. Davidson, *The Communist Party of Australia* (Stanford, California, US, 1969); S. Macintyre, *The Reds* (Syd, 1998); C. Sheil, The Invisible Giant: A History of the Federated Miscellaneous Workers' Union of Australia, 1915-1985 (Ph.D. thesis, Univ Wollongong, 1988); J. N. Rawling papers (ANUABL); L. L. Sharkey files in series A6119 (NAA, Canb).

STUART MACINTYRE

SHAW, CHARLES HERBERT (1900-1955), journalist and author, was born on 10 August 1900 in South Melbourne, third child of Frederick Francis Shaw, a Tasmanian-born horse-trainer, and his wife Mary, née Murphy (d.1915), who came from South Australia. From about 1904 the family eked out a precarious living on a small wheat-farm near Beulah in the Mallee district. When they moved to St Arnaud, Charlie briefly attended the high school, but after his father died in 1914 he had to fend for himself. He struggled to make a living by 'driving horse lorries, pruning, ploughing, harvesting, clearing and fencing, dairying . . . and lumping goods in a railway yard'. During the Depression he humped his swag for more than 2000 miles (3200 km) around south-eastern Australia. Wherever he got the chance, he played Australian Rules football.

While working on a sheep-station in New South Wales, Shaw helped to found an Australian Rules team at Forbes in 1931. One of its members, the co-proprietor of the *Forbes Advocate*, encouraged him to write, then gave him a job. On 18 January 1932 at the Presbyterian Church, Auburn, Sydney, Shaw married Phoebe Matilda ('Maxie') McLachlan, a schoolteacher. Back at Forbes, he gained experience in most kinds of newspaper work, and sent stories to *Smith's Weekly* and the *Bulletin*. In 1936 he bought a Singer Bantam motorcar.

Shaw moved to Sydney in 1939 to work on the *Farmer and Settler*, but soon joined the staff of the *Bulletin*. As its rural editor, he wrote on various subjects under different pen-names—on wheat as 'Ben Cubbin', on cattle as 'Cowpuncher' and on motorcars as 'B.S.' (after his own vehicle). He also wrote sketches and verse based on his outback experiences. During World War II he published two collections of short stories, *Outback Occupations* (1943)—illustrated by Ted Scorfield [q.v.]— and *A Sheaf of Shorts* (1944), a volume of verse, *The Warrumbungle Mare* (1943), a detective story, *Who Could Hate Purcey?* (1944), and two adventure stories for his sons, *The Green Token* (1943) and *The Treasure of the Hills* (1944).

The *Bulletin* staff had low rates of pay, but less pressure of work than those in daily journalism. After publishers rejected several of his manuscripts, Shaw decided that the outback was 'too parochial to hold much interest for people outside Australia'. His next book, *Heaven Knows, Mister Allison* (London, 1952), was a novel about an American marine and a nun, stranded on a Pacific island during World War II, who formed an improbable alliance against the Japanese. It became an international best seller and he reportedly sold the film rights to Eastern Film Enterprises Inc. for $US25 000. Meanwhile, as 'Bant Singer', he published an action-packed detective story, typed for him by Nancy Keesing: *You're Wrong, Delaney* (London, 1953) was set in an Australian country town and centred on Dennis Delaney, Shaw's strong-arm investigator, 'a two-fisted, fast-living Australian'. Written in 'terse, laconic prose', the book was an immediate success and his publisher, Collins, hailed him as a successor to the late Peter Cheyney. It was followed by *Don't Slip, Delaney* and *Have Patience, Delaney!* (both published in London in 1954).

An unobtrusive, 'studious-looking, gentle little man', with 'greying hair and spectacles', Shaw liked to bet, to go fishing occasionally and to play golf. He was a committee-member of Eastlake Golf Club. All he wanted from his royalties was 'to buy his own home', and 'perhaps a new car' to replace the Singer. The pace proved too great. He died of cerebral haemorrhage on 1 August 1955 in Sydney Hospital and was cremated. His wife and their two sons survived him. One more 'whodunit' appeared posthumously, *Your Move, Delaney* (London, 1956). *Heaven Knows, Mr Allison*

was released by Twentieth Century Fox Film Corporation in 1957, starring Deborah Kerr and Robert Mitchum.

N. Keesing, *Riding the Elephant* (Syd, 1988); *People* (Syd), 25 Aug 1954, p 9; *SMH*, 13, 27 Sept, 31 Oct 1953, 8 Jan, 2 Aug 1955, 21, 22 July 1957.

MARTHA RUTLEDGE

SHAW, JOHN HENRY (1927-1977), town planner, was born on 3 April 1927 at Manly, Sydney, elder son of New South Wales-born parents John Alexander Lachlan Shaw, civil engineer, and his wife Nellie Violet, née Hicks. Young John attended Sydney Grammar School and studied civil engineering at the University of Sydney (B.E., 1950). In 1951-52 he designed reinforced concrete and steel structures for the Commonwealth Department of Works. Stimulated by the lectures of Professor Denis Winston [q.v.] at the university, Shaw gained a diploma in town and country planning (1952). He travelled to England and graduated master of civic design (1954) at the University of Liverpool. From July 1954 to October 1957 he was a planning officer with the Cambridgeshire and Isle of Ely County Council.

Back in Sydney, on 16 December 1957 Shaw took up an appointment as lecturer in town planning at the New South Wales University of Technology (University of New South Wales from 1959). He was to be promoted to associate professor in 1963. At St James's Church of England, King Street, on 17 January 1959 he married Jill Douglas McAdam, a librarian. In 1965 the university introduced postgraduate training in housing and neighbourhood design. Next year an undergraduate degree course was initiated to serve the growing need in State and local government for urban planners with interdisciplinary skills. After obtaining a Ph.D. from the U.N.S.W. in 1970 (his thesis was on residential land subdivision), Shaw became inaugural professor in the School of Town Planning, which was established in 1971.

Active in university life, Shaw was involved in the staff association and his beloved Kite Club. With F. E. A. Towndrow, he had founded the university's Civic Design Society in 1962. He delivered numerous addresses to councils, professional institutes, societies and community clubs. A fellow of the (Royal) Australian Planning Institute, he made diverse contributions as a vice-president (1958-63) of its Sydney division, as associate-editor (1962-68) of the *Australian Planning Institute Journal*, and as a member (1965-71) of the institute's board of education. Shaw wrote articles on the theory and practice of town planning. He helped Alfred Brown [q.v.13] and H. M. Sherrard to revise their *Town and Country Planning* (Melbourne, 1951) as *An Introduction to Town and Country Planning* (Sydney, 1969).

Shaw made practical contributions as a senior adviser to governments. From 1964 to 1972 he was a member of the State Planning Authority which produced an outline plan for metropolitan Sydney in 1968. His expertise was recognized by his position as deputy-chairman of the Housing Commission of New South Wales in 1970-77, turbulent years in the development of both greenfields and high-rise estates. He also served two terms (1970-76) on the National Capital Planning Committee.

An unassuming man of slim build, Shaw was widely respected by his colleagues and students. He died of cancer on 16 September 1977 in Sydney and was cremated; his wife and two of their three sons survived him. The John Shaw memorial prize is awarded annually by the U.N.S.W. for the best undergraduate thesis in town planning.

E. Daniels, *A History of the Faculty of Architecture* (Syd, 1988); *Roy Aust Planning Inst J*, Feb 1978, p 20; Univ NSW Archives; information from Mrs J. Shaw, Kensington, Syd. ROBERT FREESTONE
ROBERT ZEHNER

SHAW, SIR PATRICK (1913-1975), diplomat, was born on 18 September 1913 at Kew, Melbourne, fourth child of Patrick Shaw, a Melbourne-born physician, and his wife Janet Steedman, née Denholm, who came from Scotland. Young Patrick was educated at Ballarat and Scotch colleges, and at the University of Melbourne (B.A. Hons, 1935; diploma of public administration, 1939). He joined the Commonwealth Public Service in May 1936 and in 1937 transferred from the Postmaster-General's Department to the Prime Minister's Department. On 9 April 1938 at Scotch College chapel he married Catherine Helen Jeffree with Presbyterian forms. After working as private secretary to Alexander McLachlan and George McLeay [qq.v.10,15], successively leaders of the government in the Senate, he was accepted into Australia's fledgling foreign service, the Department of External Affairs, in 1939.

In November 1940 Shaw was posted to Tokyo as third secretary of the newly opened Australian legation. At a time of mounting tension between Japan and Australia, he reported developments, walked to keep fit and attempted to learn Japanese. When Japan entered World War II in December 1941, the legation's staff was interned until exchanged for Japanese diplomats in August 1942. Shaw served as official secretary at the Australian High Commission in New Zealand in 1943-45.

While he was in Wellington the Australian-New Zealand Agreement was negotiated and signed. In 1945 he was sent as first secretary to the Australian legation in China, located first at Chungking and then at Nanking.

Hurriedly sent back to Tokyo in 1947, Shaw replaced W. Macmahon Ball as head of the Australian mission and became British Commonwealth representative on the Allied Council for Japan. He strove energetically, albeit unsuccessfully, to prevent General Douglas MacArthur [q.v.15] from ignoring Australia's views in making policy for the reconstruction of occupied Japan. In 1948 he acted as adviser to Dr H. V. Evatt [q.v.14] at the meeting of British Commonwealth prime ministers in London. Next year he was appointed Australian delegate to, and chairman of, the United Nations Commission on Korea. The commission had little chance of uniting the divided nation.

After two years in Canberra, Shaw was posted to Geneva in 1951 as consul-general in Switzerland and permanent delegate to the European headquarters of the United Nations. He returned in 1953 and worked as assistant-secretary in the Department of External Affairs, helping to promote the Australia-Japan Agreement on Commerce, which was finally concluded in 1957. From 1956 to 1959 he served as Australian ambassador to the Federal Republic of Germany and head of the Australian Military Mission in Berlin. During his term (1960-62) as Australian ambassador to Indonesia he became committed to the policy—still unpopular with most of (Sir) Robert Menzies' [q.v.15] cabinet—of acceding to Indonesia's wish to incorporate Netherlands New Guinea (Irian Jaya). He also rejected widespread fear in Australia that communists were gaining the upper hand in Indonesia, and recommended the retention of friendly links between the two countries through such schemes as the training of Indonesian students in Australia.

Shaw returned home as first assistant secretary. He was deputy-secretary to Sir Arthur Tange in 1964-65, a time when the Australian government backed Britain against Indonesia's confrontation of Malaysia and supported the United States of America's military intervention on behalf of the Republic of Vietnam (South Vietnam). In 1965 he was appointed permanent representative to the United Nations in New York. His term (1970-73) as high commissioner to India and ambassador to Nepal preceded his posting in 1974 as ambassador to the United States. Relations between the two countries had soured because E. G. Whitlam's Labor government had criticized U.S. policy in Indo-China. Shaw helped to soften American antagonism towards Australia, but still presented his government's policies firmly, particularly its opposition to the expansion of the U.S. naval base at Diego Garcia in the Indian Ocean.

In 1960 Shaw had been appointed C.B.E. He was knighted in 1972. Sir Patrick loved music, played golf and acquired a passion for tennis. A dapper dresser who retained into middle age a boyish look, he was punctilious about diplomatic etiquette, but his formality was leavened by an earthy sense of humour. Shaw was widely respected for the way he represented Australia and for his solicitude for younger colleagues. He died of heart disease on 27 December 1975 at Georgetown University Hospital, Washington, and was cremated. His wife and two of their three daughters survived him.

R. N. Rosecrance, *Australian Diplomacy and Japan, 1945-1951* (Melb, 1962); H. S. Albinski, *Australian External Policy under Labor* (Brisb, 1977); W. J. Hudson (ed), *Australia in World Affairs, 1971-75* (Syd, 1980); G. Pemberton, *All the Way* (Syd, 1987); P. Edwards with G. Pemberton, *Crises and Commitments* (Syd, 1992); *Aust Foreign Affairs Record*, 46, no 12, Dec 1975; *SMH*, 14 Nov 1968, 21 Mar 1970, 29 Dec 1975; *Australian*, 29 Dec 1975; R. Harry, Historian Diplomat (ms, copy held in ADB file); Ralph Harry papers (NL).   DAVID LEE

SHEA, FREDERICK JAMES (1891-1970), railway engineer and public servant, was born on 6 July 1891 at Moonee Ponds, Melbourne, third of nine children of Victorian-born parents Frederick Shea, compositor, and his wife Ellen, née Crofts. Young Fred won a scholarship to the Melbourne Continuation School where he developed his technical abilities and a talent for mathematics and physics. In 1907 he was apprenticed to a fitter and turner in the Victorian Railways' workshops, Newport. After obtaining a diploma in mechanical engineering (1914) at the Working Men's College, he moved to head office as an engineering-assistant and worked under (Sir) Harold Clapp [q.v.8] and A. E. Smith. During his sixteen years with the Victorian Railways he contributed to three innovations that changed the face of railway engineering: electrification, modern workshop methods and the railway engineering-defence connexion. On 21 October 1916 at St Mary's Catholic Church, Hawthorn, he married Eileen Marjorie Smythe (d.1951).

In 1923 Clapp recommended Shea to the chief commissioner of South Australian Railways, W. A. Webb [q.v.12], who was planning to modernize the State's rail system. As chief mechanical engineer (1923-39), Shea oversaw the transformation of the S.A.R. Initially, he overhauled the Islington workshops and tool-room. He then designed three types of loco-motives—the 4-8-2 Mountain 500 class, the 4-6-2 Pacific 600 class and the 2-8-2 Mikado 700 class—and assorted carriages, supervised their construction (overseas and later at Islington) and adapted them to local conditions. These designs earned him a reputation as a 'big power man'. For nearly thirty years (from 1924) he was an honorary lieutenant colonel in the Engineer and Railway Staff Corps, Citizen Military Forces. He also served (1932) on a committee of inquiry into the Adelaide Electric Supply Co. Ltd.

World War II extended Shea's career. His mentor, Clapp, general manager (from 1939) of Commonwealth aircraft production, asked him to help with the Bristol Beaufort bomber project. Following the formation of the Aircraft Production Commission under Essington Lewis [q.v.10], Shea managed (1940-41)—from his base at Fishermens Bend, Melbourne—the vast network of government and commercial workshops that comprised the Beaufort division. He was responsible for converting much of Australian industry to a war footing. From January 1942 he was director of aircraft maintenance, Department of Aircraft Production. Augmenting his professional roles with a number of honorary consultancies in government and semi-government service, he published (in 1934) 'The Modern Dynamometer Car' in the *Journal of the Institution of Engineers, Australia*, and (in 1946) 'The Case for the Iron Horse' in the *Journal of the Institute of Transport*.

Towards the end of the war Clapp, by then director-general of land transport, again called on Shea. He needed a chief mechanical engineer to implement the Commonwealth government's proposal to standardize Australia's railway gauges. Shea joined the venture as director of mechanical engineering in the railway standardization division. Once back in railway work, however, he attracted the attention of the Clyde Engineering Co. Pty Ltd which, in association with General Motors Corporation, was manufacturing locomotives at Granville, Sydney. He worked for that company as director of engineering from 1946 until his retirement in 1958, after which he continued as a consultant to the firm. A Clyde-Maybach diesel hydraulic locomotive was named the *F. J. Shea* in his honour.

Shea's life was driven by his energy. A slim youth of middle height who filled out in later life, he was known as a fast mover, talker and thinker. He loved Gilbert and Sullivan, and relaxed by listening to records of their operettas and by copious reading, especially about the engineering feats of ancient civilizations. His daughter Betty remembered him as a generous and kind man 'with an unquenchable sense of humour' and as one who was so 'totally absorbed in his work' that he 'did not have much time for sport or hobbies'. On the job he was a rigorous perfectionist and a stickler for detail. As a manager these attributes sometimes made him a hard taskmaster and a grim, rather awesome colleague.

In retirement Shea lived at Clareville Beach. He died on 6 September 1970 at Mona Vale and was buried in Northern Suburbs cemetery. His son and two daughters survived him.

D. P. Mellor, *The Role of Science and Industry* (Canb, 1958); D. Burke, *Kings of the Iron Horse* (Syd, 1985); D. A. Cumming and G. C. Moxham, *They Built South Australia* (Adel, 1986); *Annual Report of the SA Railway Commissioners*, 1923-39; *Railway Transportation*, no 2, 1959; *SMH*, 8 Sept 1970; Aircraft Production Com files, in particular series MP407/6 (NAA).   CAROL FORT

SHEAHAN, WILLIAM FRANCIS (1895-1975), barrister and politician, was born on 3 September 1895 at Tumut, New South Wales, younger twin and eleventh child of native-born parents Jeremiah Sheahan (d.1896), butcher, and his wife Mary Ann, née Downing. Mary later kept a hotel at Jugiong. Educated at Tumut convent school and Jugiong Public School, and at St Patrick's College, Goulburn, Billy began work on 14 August 1913 in Sydney as a junior clerk in the Treasury. In the following year he transferred to the petty sessions branch of the Department of the Attorney-General and of Justice.

On 20 March 1916 Sheahan enlisted in the Australian Imperial Force. He served (1916-18) on the Western Front with the 17th Battalion and at 5th Brigade headquarters before returning to Sydney where he was discharged from the army on 24 November 1919. His comrades long remembered his courage under fire. Resuming his post in the public service, he studied part time at the University of Sydney (LL.B., 1930), and was admitted to the Bar on 8 May 1930. He soon established a large practice, particularly in criminal law, and appeared before several royal commissions. At the Church of Our Lady of the Sacred Heart, Randwick, on 10 September 1932 he married Ellen Imelda Byrne, a 20-year-old stenographer.

From the age of 16 Sheahan had been a member of the Australian Labor Party. He became an influential figure in the party during the period of J. T. Lang's [q.v.9] dominance in New South Wales. In 1939 he was a State delegate to and vice-president of the federal executive, and a representative at the federal conference. Breaking with Lang, he was one of the federal officers who conducted the unity conference in August which brought about Lang's downfall. Sheahan had unsuccessfully contested the Legislative Assembly seat of Petersham in 1935 and 1938. In 1941, with Petersham abolished due to a redistri-

bution, he decided to contest Yass where he claimed to have more than two thousand relations. He won the seat (renamed Burrinjuck in 1950) and held it for the rest of his career.

With 'his quick wit, his unusual capacity to grasp the details of a situation and his tenacity', Sheahan quickly made his mark in parliament. He became a prominent opponent of Premier (Sir) William McKell: his antagonism was sharpened by his failure to gain ministerial office. When there was speculation in 1947 that McKell would be appointed governor-general, Sheahan caused a furore by publicly stating that the post should go to an ex-serviceman.

A strong supporter of McKell's successor James McGirr [q.v.15], Sheahan was appointed secretary for lands on 19 May 1947; in this capacity he made an important contribution to the success of soldier settlement. On 30 June 1950 he became minister for transport, a difficult portfolio which he tackled with energy and vision; his term in office, however, was not an unqualified success, due in part to the growing problem of public-transport deficits. Given the attorney-generalship by J. J. Cahill [q.v.13] on 23 February 1953 and appointed Q.C. that year, he carried through a programme of law reform, including the abolition (1955) of the death penalty for all offences except treason and piracy. From 15 March 1956 to 13 May 1965 he served as minister for health. Once again, he implemented major changes, such as the Mental Health Act (1958) and the Clean Air Act (1961).

Despite his achievements, Sheahan had a turbulent ministerial career because of his combative personality, scathing tongue and flair for publicity. He feuded openly with premiers, colleagues, bureaucrats, interest groups and the press. Recalling that he had been described as 'testy, irritable and controversial', he added, 'thank God no one has said I was peculiar [and] I have never been accused of dishonesty'. Frustrated ambition played a part in his decision in October 1959 to stand against J. B. Renshaw, the right wing's candidate for deputy-premier. He failed by one vote. Thereafter he allied himself with a rebel group in caucus and challenged cabinet decisions on a number of occasions. In April 1964 he contested the deputy-premiership against P. D. Hills, but lost by a wider margin. Sheahan retired from parliament in October 1973. His son Terence succeeded him as member for Burrinjuck.

'Short, ruddy-faced' and 'exuberant', with 'a warm and friendly smile', Sheahan was known as 'the Burrinjuck bunyip'. He was a keen follower of sport, and a member (from 1950) and chairman (1962-65) of the Sydney Cricket (and Sports) Ground Trust. Survived by his wife, and their son and three daughters, he died on 27 December 1975 at Darlinghurst; he was accorded a state funeral and was buried with Catholic rites in Jugiong cemetery.

PD (NSW), 24 Feb 1976, p 3583; *People* (Syd), 9 Apr 1952, p 16; *ALP Journal*, Dec 1961, p 7; *Smith's Weekly* (Syd), 8 Mar 1941; *Sunday Herald*, 9 July 1950; *Daily Mirror* (Syd), 25 Mar 1954; *SMH*, 20 Apr 1961, 27 Jan 1972, 29 Dec 1975; Sheahan papers (ML); information from Justice T. W. Sheahan, Land and Environment Court, Syd.   DAVID CLUNE

SHEDDEN, SIR FREDERICK GEOFFREY (1893-1971), public servant, was born on 8 August 1893 at Kyneton, Victoria, youngest of five children of George Shedden, a Victorian-born wheelwright, and his wife Sarah Elizabeth, née Gray, who came from England. Fred was educated at Kyneton State and Kyneton Grammar schools. Placed fourth out of 300 candidates in the Commonwealth public service examination, he began work in the Department of Defence at Victoria Barracks, Melbourne, in March 1910. Apart from service overseas, he was to work at the barracks until 1971. In his spare time he studied accountancy and learned shorthand, but the heavy workload caused by the outbreak of World War I forced him to abandon his law studies at the University of Melbourne.

Promoted in the finance branch, Shedden arranged a temporary exchange with a member of the pay staff at Australian Imperial Force Headquarters, London. On 19 March 1917 he was appointed lieutenant in the Australian Army Pay Corps. He reached London in May, visited pay offices in France, and served as acting paymaster of the 4th Australian Division in August. Returning home, he was discharged from the A.I.F. on 24 December. In later years he was proud of this limited military experience.

Shedden continued to rise in the finance branch while studying part time at the University of Melbourne (B.Com., 1932). On 14 December 1927, at her parents' St Kilda home, he married with Congregational forms Anne Cardno Edward, a book-keeper. Later that day he sailed for England to undertake the course at the Imperial Defence College, London. The first Australian civilian to attend the college, he was deeply influenced by its commandant, Vice-Admiral Sir Herbert Richmond, who reported that he worked 'indefatigably', and with 'acuteness and zeal'.

After the year-long course, Shedden spent a further nine months in London, studying financial administration and preparing a paper on the principles of Imperial defence with special reference to Australia. Back in Melbourne in October 1929, he was appointed secretary of the Defence Committee, which included the chiefs of staff of the three services. He witnessed the efforts of the new Labor government to cut costs during the Depression and took part in debates between senior naval and army officers over the most appropriate strategy for defending Australia. Shedden was an advocate of Imperial defence: he argued that the Australian navy should be built up so that it could co-operate with the Royal Navy in times of threat.

Following the defeat of the Labor government in December 1931, the new minister for external affairs (Sir) John Latham [q.v.10] was nominated to attend the League of Nations' disarmament conference in Geneva in 1932. Shedden accompanied him as his assistant, but Latham was absent for much of the conference and Shedden acted in his stead. He was also appointed Australian representative to the British Cabinet Office, and to the Committee of Imperial Defence at which he established a friendship with Sir Maurice (Baron) Hankey. In 1933 he was secretary to the Australian delegation at the World Monetary and Economic Conference, held in London. For his work in London and Geneva, he was appointed O.B.E. (1933).

In December 1933 Shedden resumed work with the Defence Committee in Melbourne. Next year he accompanied Hankey during the latter's visit to Australia. Shedden tried to model himself on Hankey, and was later nicknamed 'the pocket Hankey'. In November 1936 Shedden was appointed first assistant secretary. He set about preparing the department's briefing papers for the 1937 Imperial Conference in London. The Australian delegation included the prime minister Joseph Lyons, the minister for defence Sir Archdale Parkhill and the treasurer R. G. (Baron) Casey [qq.v.10,11,13]. Shedden was the delegation's defence adviser. While in London, he discussed Australia's war preparations with Hankey.

On 17 November 1937 Shedden succeeded Malcolm Shepherd [q.v.11] as secretary of the Department of Defence. Since 1929 he had worked to expand the secretary's influence and authority. He had proven to be a skilful bureaucrat, unafraid to challenge the military chiefs and usually working behind the scenes. Preparations for war dominated his first twenty months as secretary, and he accelerated work on the Commonwealth War Book, which set out procedures to be followed when hostilities began. He assisted in the appointment of inspector-generals for the army, and for defence works and supplies, and helped to arrange the visit of a senior British air force officer to report on the Royal Australian Air Force. On becoming secretary of the Council of Defence—which included senior ministers, military chiefs, defence officials and representatives of industry—he encouraged it to meet more frequently.

As defence secretary, Shedden was an aloof and distant figure who 'eschewed publicity'. His whole life revolved around his work, and he spent most of his time at the office. The Sheddens had no children and lived modestly. Fred was 5 ft 7 ins (170 cm) tall, always well dressed in suit and tie, and conscious of his status. Some military chiefs, among them Major General (Sir) John Lavarack and Air Vice-Marshal (Sir) Richard Williams [qq.v.15, 12], resented his power. Admiral Sir Ragnar Colvin [q.v.8] noted that Shedden 'always had the ear of the Prime Minister and could generally get the Chiefs of Staff's view and wishes overridden. Still . . . he was an able and knowledgeable man and though one couldn't trust him personally his views were generally sound'.

The outbreak of World War II made Shedden his country's most important public servant. As the head of the Department of Defence, he played a crucial role in bringing Australia to a war footing over the ensuing months, but the prime source of his power and influence was his position as secretary of the War Cabinet, a post he held throughout the war. It was his task to ensure that War Cabinet decisions were promulgated and executed by various government departments. The prime minister, (Sir) Robert Menzies [q.v.15], took over the defence portfolio, by then called Defence Co-ordination, and new ministries were formed to administer the three services. As secretary of the Department of Defence Co-ordination, Shedden exercised a measure of control over other defence-related departments. He was at the heart of the strategic decision-making process, co-ordinating advice from the service chiefs, preparing War Cabinet agenda papers, contributing to War Cabinet discussions and preparing minutes for action. After the federal election in September 1940, he also became secretary of the Advisory War Council, which involved the Opposition in key decisions affecting the nation's security. In 1941 he was appointed C.M.G.

Menzies left on a trip to the Middle East and Britain in January 1941, during which he hoped to persuade the British government to reinforce Malaya and Singapore. Shedden was his principal adviser throughout this journey. They visited Australian troops in the Middle East, and discussed war developments with Lieutenant General Sir Thomas Blamey [q.v.13] and senior British officers. In London, Menzies approved the decision to send forces to Greece. Shedden gained first-hand experience of how the British government was conducting the war. He was critical of British generalship in the Middle East. After they returned, Menzies created five additional ministries. In July Shedden was made secretary of the new Department of Home Security,

while retaining his other responsibilities. Menzies agreed to allow a minute-secretary to attend the War Cabinet meetings, thus relieving Shedden of that burden. Throughout the next four years Shedden played a significant role in War Cabinet discussions.

When the Labor party came to office in October 1941, Shedden soon established himself as principal adviser to the prime minister and minister for defence, John Curtin [q.v.13]. His influence was demonstrated after Japan entered the war. Following a War Cabinet meeting on 8 December, he advised Curtin that the information presented by the chiefs of staff was 'scrappy and meagre ... the Government must press it right home that this is a new war'.

When General Douglas MacArthur [q.v.15] became commander-in-chief of the South-West Pacific Area in April 1942, Shedden assumed an even more important role. Curtin established the Prime Minister's War Conference, which consisted of himself, MacArthur and any other minister he thought should be invited. Shedden attended every meeting of the conference. Curtin notified MacArthur, 'if I should not be readily available, Mr Shedden has my full confidence in regard to all questions of War Policy'. In July MacArthur moved his headquarters to Brisbane. The conference met less frequently, but Shedden travelled to Brisbane on several occasions for discussions with MacArthur. Curtin told Shedden in December that, without his assistance, 'he could not have carried on'; he later said that Shedden was his 'right and left hand and head too'. Shedden was elevated to K.C.M.G. in 1943. He was the only civilian to be knighted by the Labor government during the war.

In the second half of 1943 Shedden helped the War Cabinet to establish principles for reshaping the war effort. He then accompanied Curtin to Washington and London in April-May 1944 to seek allied approval for these measures. On his return, he tried to ensure that the government redeployed manpower from the services to essential industries, but his attempts were hindered by Curtin's illness. Shedden provided valuable assistance to the acting prime minister, Ben Chifley [q.v.13], and continued to do so after Curtin died and Chifley became prime minister.

Shedden believed that Australia's future defence policy should be based on three pillars: collective security through the United Nations, British Commonwealth co-operation, and local defence. The government approved these principles, and, after the war, he restructured the Department of Defence to improve co-operation with Britain. Chifley and John Dedman [q.v.13], the minister for defence, largely gave him a free hand. He accompanied Chifley to the Commonwealth Prime Ministers' Conference in London in

April 1946. Continuing to gain added power and authority, he was appointed chairman of the Defence Committee in February 1948—the first non-serviceman to hold the position. Admiral Sir Louis Hamilton, the chief of Naval Staff, claimed that he engineered this appointment to lock 'that little bastard Shedden' into the committee's decisions so that he would not undermine them. In fact, Shedden had already arranged his appointment long before Hamilton proposed it.

In 1948-49 Shedden spent time dealing with a leak of documents to the Soviet Union and the consequent reduction in the flow of classified information from the United States of America. He helped to form the Australian Security Intelligence Organization in March 1949, and later that year travelled to the U.S.A. and Britain in an effort to restore access to intelligence material. Initially, he was unsuccessful. American information only began to be released in December, after Menzies was elected prime minister.

Frustrated by the Chifley government's reluctance to enter into full-scale defence planning with Britain (particularly over the issue of committing forces to the Middle East), Shedden welcomed the new Liberal-Country Party ministry. For several years he was in his element. In June 1950 the Korean War began. The government increased defence preparations and in January 1951 Shedden accompanied Menzies to another prime ministers' conference in London. Back home, Menzies claimed that the nation had only three years to prepare for war. In December cabinet finally agreed to commit forces to the Middle East in time of conflict.

The threat of world war diminished, however, and the government began to focus more on strategic planning in South-East Asia. The signing of the Australia-New Zealand-United States pact offered the prospect of increased co-operation with the U.S.A. Shedden was closely involved in these aspects of defence planning, but his personal influence was waning. He and his department remained in Melbourne, while Menzies sought advice from the senior ministers and departmental secretaries located in Canberra. During a trip abroad with Menzies in January-March 1955, Shedden was disappointed to find that (Sir) Arthur Tange, secretary of the Department of External Affairs, received more attention than he did. Shedden had to fight off several attempts to remove him as chairman of the Defence Committee. Menzies thought that the problem with defence was 'the dead hand of Fred Shedden'. He tried unsuccessfully to persuade him to become ambassador to Japan or high commissioner to Canada. In July 1956 the government announced that Shedden would step down as secretary to write a history of Australian defence policy. After serving as defence secretary for almost nineteen years, he handed over to (Sir) Edwin Hicks in October.

Shedden failed in his task of writing the history, but not through lack of effort. He carried out research in the United States and Britain in 1958. Although he received full pay only until he reached retirement age in August, he continued collecting documents, conducting research and writing. When he submitted the first volume (covering the years 1901-39) to the publisher in October 1967, he was told that it was unpublishable: it was more a stringing together of documents than a history. He kept working until May 1971 (two months before his death), by which time he had brought the narrative (over 2400 typed pages) to the end of World War II. The manuscript is held by the National Archives of Australia, with more than 2400 boxes of his official papers.

Dedicated to his work, Sir Frederick appeared to take little recreation. He enjoyed gardening, and occasionally found time to play golf, or to watch cricket, football or tennis. At the Presbyterian Church, Deepdene, which he attended regularly, he was regarded as a 'gracious man' and 'a disciple of Jesus Christ'. Survived by his wife, he died on 8 July 1971 in St Andrew's Hospital, East Melbourne, and was cremated.

Shedden had long dominated defence decision-making, giving it purpose and consistency. He shaped a defence organization that persisted largely unaltered until the 1970s. To Sir Paul Hasluck, he was 'one of the few outstanding men in the civil side of the Australian war effort. Discretion, orderly arrangement and careful groundwork were so large a part of his training and his method that his achievement was often hidden'. Sir Frederick Chilton, who worked under Shedden for more than a decade, wrote that he:

> had a real presence and powerful personality. He was ruthless with those who crossed him, and devastating with those in his Department who could not rise to his exceptional standards of performance ... Shedden's 'forte' was top level policy and its broad application. He was not a good administrator in the sense of leadership of a team ... He ruled by fear—and this stultified initiative. But as a head of a small policy Dept of Defence, he was superb.

Chilton thought that Sir Robert Garran [q.v.8] and Sir Frederick Shedden were Australia's most outstanding public servants, 'the first as the architect and interpreter of the constitution, the other for his unique role and contribution during Australia's darkest hour'. Shedden devoted his life to the defence of Australia. No other person has played, or is likely again to play, such an important role in the making of Australian defence policy for so long a period.

P. Hasluck, *The Government and the People 1939-1941* (Canb, 1952) and *The Government and the People 1942-1945* (Canb, 1970); D. M. Horner, *High Command* (Canb, 1982) and *Inside the War Cabinet* (Syd, 1996) and *Defence Supremo* (Syd, 2000); *VHM*, 42, no 3, Aug 1971, p 632; *Defence Force J*, no 50, Jan/Feb 1985, p 21, no 83, July/Aug 1990, p 38; Shedden papers (NAA, Canb, and Univ Melb Archives).   DAVID HORNER

SHEEAN, EDWARD (1923-1942), sailor, was born on 28 December 1923 at Lower Barrington, Tasmania, fourteenth child of James Sheean, labourer, and his wife Mary Jane, née Broomhall, both Tasmanian born. Soon afterwards the family moved to Latrobe. Teddy was educated at the local Catholic school. Five ft 8½ ins (174 cm) tall and well built, he took casual work on farms between Latrobe and Merseylea. In Hobart on 21 April 1941 he enlisted in the Royal Australian Naval Reserve as an ordinary seaman, following in the steps of five of his brothers who had joined the armed forces (four of them were in the army and one in the navy). On completing his initial training, he was sent to Flinders Naval Depot, Westernport, Victoria, in February 1942 for further instruction.

In May Sheean was posted to Sydney where he was billeted at Garden Island in the requisitioned ferry *Kuttabul*, prior to joining his first ship as an Oerlikon anti-aircraft gun-loader. Granted home leave, he was not on board *Kuttabul* when Japanese midget submarines raided the harbour and sank her on 31 May. Eleven days later he returned to Sydney to help commission the new corvette H.M.A.S. *Armidale*, which carried out escort duties along the eastern Australian coast and in New Guinea waters. Ordered to sail for Darwin in October, *Armidale* arrived there early next month.

On 29 November *Armidale* sailed for Japanese-occupied Timor—in company with the corvette H.M.A.S. *Castlemaine*—to withdraw the exhausted Australian 2nd/2nd Independent Company, evacuate about 150 Portuguese civilians and 190 Dutch troops, and land soldiers to reinforce Dutch guerrillas on the island. Arriving off Betano before dawn on 1 December, the ships rendezvoused with the naval tender H.M.A.S. *Kuru*, which had already taken the civilians on board. When these people were transferred to *Castlemaine*, she sailed for Darwin, leaving the other two vessels to carry out the rest of the operation. From 12.28 p.m. *Armidale* and *Kuru* came under repeated attack from Japanese aircraft. Despite requests, no air cover was received.

Shortly before 2 p.m. on 1 December 1942 *Armidale*, by then separated from *Kuru*, was attacked by no less than thirteen aircraft. The corvette manoeuvred frantically. At 3.15 a torpedo struck her port side and another hit the engineering spaces; finally a bomb struck aft. As the vessel listed heavily to port, the order was given to abandon ship. The survivors leapt into the sea and were machine-gunned by the Japanese. Once he had helped to free a life raft, Sheean scrambled back to his gun on the sinking ship. Although wounded in the chest and back, the 18-year-old sailor shot down one bomber and kept other aircraft away from his comrades in the water. He was seen still firing his gun as *Armidale* slipped below the waves. Only forty-nine of the 149 souls who had been on board survived the sinking and the ensuing days in life-rafts.

Sheean was mentioned in dispatches for his bravery. A Collins-class submarine, launched in 1999, was named after him—the only ship in the R.A.N. to bear the name of an ordinary seaman.

G. H. Gill, *Royal Australian Navy 1942-1945* (Canb, 1968); F. B. Walker, *HMAS Armidale* (Budgewoi, NSW, 1990); *Sun-Herald* (Syd), 21 Oct 1990, 18 Apr 1999; AWM 76, B444 (AWM); information from Mr V. Jeffries, Jarrahdale, Perth, Mr R. Milton, Hazelwood Park, Adel, and Mr R. Pullen, Glenorchy, Hob.   N. WATSON

SHEEHAN, JAMES MICHAEL (1885-1967), trade unionist and politician, was born on 24 July 1885 at Clinkers Hill, Castlemaine, Victoria, eldest of six children of Michael Sheehan, a blacksmith from Ireland, and his second wife Ellen, née Ferminger, who was born in Victoria. Jimmy attended St Mary's Catholic School, Castlemaine, until the age of 13 when he obtained a job with the Victorian Railways. As a young man he helped to establish the local branch of the Rural Workers' Union of Australia.

In 1910 Sheehan left Castlemaine. After being briefly employed by the State Rivers and Water Supply Commission at Nyah, he went to Melbourne and resumed work with the railways. He was elected to the council of the Victorian Railways Union in 1915. Joining the Victorian Socialist Party, he moved in the same political and ideological circles as Frank Hyett, Robert Ross, John Curtin and John Cain [qq.v.9,11,13]. He and Cain became close friends. Sheehan shared Hyett's and Curtin's passion for sport, and was later president of the Richmond District Cricket Club and vice-president (1940-67) of the Richmond Football Club. A regular speaker for the V.S.P., he was involved—'up to his ears'—in the anti-conscription campaigns of 1916-17.

Following Hyett's death in 1919, Sheehan was appointed a V.R.U. organizer. A vigorous advocate of industrial unionism, he played an important part in founding the Australian

Railways Union in 1920. He retained his role in the State branch of the A.R.U. and was said to be 'the most travelled union organiser in Victoria'. In 1931 he stood unsuccessfully for the Senate as an Australian Labor Party candidate. On 12 July 1938 he achieved his long-cherished ambition when the Victorian parliament chose him to fill a casual vacancy in the Senate. Defeated at the 1940 elections, he was returned to the Upper House in 1943 and was to serve continuously until his retirement on 30 June 1962. He led the Australian delegation to the first session of the International Labour Organization's inland transport committee, held in London in 1945, and revisited that city in 1961 to attend the Commonwealth Parliamentary Association's conference.

President (1940-41) of the A.L.P.'s Victorian branch and a member from time to time of the party's central executive, Sheehan maintained close links with the A.R.U. and the broader industrial labour movement. In 1943-44 he presided over the Trades Hall Council in Melbourne. When the Labor Party split in 1955, he took a moderate, non-sectarian line. He had been elected to the Castlemaine Town Council in 1951, joining his youngest sister Nellie (1895-1959) who in 1942 had become the first woman to sit on the Castlemaine Borough Council. Nellie went on to be the municipality's first female mayor (1954-55). Neither she nor her brother married. When Sheehan served as mayor in 1957-58, she acted as mayoress.

Sheehan died on 10 April 1967 in his home at Clinkers Hill and was buried with Catholic rites in Castlemaine cemetery. A skilful orator who expressed his views forcefully, but without rancour, he was known in the labour movement as 'genial Jimmy'. He was widely liked, not least for his 'kindly nature' and ready smile. 'Mateship' was his creed; 'faith in human reason, and effort for mankind's progress [were] his guides'.

PD (Senate), 11 Apr 1967, p 693; *Railways Union Gazette*, 20 June 1919, 20 Jan 1920, 10 Aug, 10 Oct 1938; *Herald* (Melb), 13 July 1938; *Labor Call*, 20 June 1940, 10 June 1943, 29 Mar 1951; *Castlemaine Mail*, 28 Aug 1942, 2 Sept 1954, 21 July 1959, 31 Aug 1965, 19 Apr 1966, 11, 13 Apr 1967; Sam Merrifield papers (SLV); information from Castlemaine Hist Soc. PAUL STRANGIO

SHELDON, ELIZA JEANETTIE (1885-1974), art-dealer, and EDWIN ARTHUR VINCENT (1895-1945), artist, were born on 24 May 1885 at Williamstown, Victoria, and 3 July 1895 in South Brisbane, eldest and youngest of five children of English-born parents Edwin Arthur Sheldon, jeweller, and his second wife Phoebe Emily, née Fisher. By 1890 the family had settled in Brisbane, where Edwin ran a jewellery business at Fortitude Valley. He claimed that his ancestry could be traced to King Edward II and to a seventeenth-century lord mayor of London. In 1893 he inherited £625 from his mother.

Jeanettie studied art at Brisbane Technical College. Between 1909 and 1919 she exhibited oils, sketches and painting on porcelain at shows held by the (Royal) National Agricultural and Industrial Association of Queensland. She established herself as a prominent identity in the small, divided and struggling art community in Brisbane, and opened the Sheldon Gallery in 1921. Elected to the (Royal) Queensland Art Society, she served as vice-president (1922), secretary (1923-31 and 1937-43) and a council-member (1932-36), proving reliable and trustworthy. From 1923 to 1960 she exhibited pottery, oils and watercolours at its shows. Through the R.Q.A.S. she met the people who formed the clientele for her galleries.

After the Sheldon Gallery closed in 1923, Jeanettie held exhibitions in rented rooms before setting up the Gainsborough Gallery in 1928. She showed paintings by local and interstate artists, including Vida Lahey, (Sir) Lionel Lindsay, Gwendolyn Grant [qq.v.9,10, 14] and Lloyd Rees. In 1921 she had staged Jessie Woodroffe's solo exhibition of pottery; from 1928 she displayed pottery every year, at Christmas. She promoted modern art in Brisbane to some degree, though her own work never paid homage 'at the altars of any of the false gods'. Jeanettie closed the Gainsborough Gallery in 1939, moved to Melbourne in 1944 and returned to Brisbane four years later. By 1952 she was living at Broadbeach. She died on 30 July 1974 in Southport Hospital and was buried with Catholic rites in Toowong cemetery.

Vincent was educated by the Christian Brothers at St James's School, Brisbane. He studied commercial art in the United States of America (1920) and England (1924), and worked as a freelance cartoonist in Brisbane in 1924-26. With his close friends Vincent and George Brown, he took up etching. He visited London in 1929 to learn drypoint under W. P. Robins at the Central School of Arts and Crafts, Holborn. The British Museum acquired three of his etchings, and the Victoria and Albert Museum two monotypes.

Back in Brisbane, Sheldon taught printmaking at his home at Clayfield. In 1931 he was elected a member of the Australian Painter-Etchers' Society. His drypoints of country scenes, and of Brisbane and its landmarks, were described in 1934 as being executed with 'rare skill' and 'joyous animation'. On 9 July 1934 at All Saints Church, Wickham Terrace, he married with Anglican rites Cynthia Ruth Sturtridge; they were childless.

Jeanettie unflaggingly praised his work and arranged five solo exhibitions at the Gainsborough Gallery. He firmly believed in the fundamental importance of sound draughtsmanship and aesthetic beauty. His reaction to modern art was to say, 'bah!'

During World War II Sheldon worked in a munitions factory until illness forced him to resign. Survived by his wife, he died of a coronary occlusion on 19 July 1945 at Boolarong, near Caboolture, and was buried with Catholic rites in Toowong cemetery. A memorial exhibition of his work was held in Brisbane in 1948. The University of Queensland holds a collection of Sheldon's prints, donated by Archbishop (Sir) James Duhig [q.v.8]; in 1981 Sheldon's widow gave more than two hundred of his works to the Queensland Art Gallery.

Australiana, Aug 1997, p 63; Sheldon papers (OL); Sheldon file (Qld Art Gallery).

KEITH BRADBURY

SHELLSHEAR, JOSEPH LEXDEN (1885-1958), army officer and professor of anatomy, was born on 31 July 1885 at Stanmore, Sydney, third of eleven children of London-born parents Walter Shellshear [q.v.6], civil engineer, and his wife Clara Mabel, née Eddis. Joe boarded at King's College, Goulburn. From 1902 he was Renwick [q.v.6] scholar in medicine at the University of Sydney (M.B., Ch.M., 1907; M.D., 1929). Following a year as a resident medical officer at Sydney Hospital, he set up a practice at Albury in 1908. At the Catholic Apostolic Church, Melbourne, on 23 July that year he married Hildred Muriel Christina Robertson; their only child, a son, died in infancy.

Having served as an artillery officer in the Militia, Shellshear was appointed major, Australian Imperial Force, on 20 October 1915 and posted to the 5th Field Artillery Brigade. By July he was commanding a battery on the Western Front. In April 1917 he was promoted lieutenant colonel and given command of the 4th F.A.B. For ably leading his men and providing accurate fire, particularly at Bullecourt, France, in May, and at Ypres, Belgium, in August-September, he was awarded the Distinguished Service Order. He was twice mentioned in dispatches. On 3 April 1918 he reverted to major at his own request and transferred to the Australian Army Medical Corps. His A.I.F. appointment terminated in England on 3 January 1920.

To refresh his medical training, Shellshear undertook research at University College, London, as a Rockefeller fellow and subsequently as a senior demonstrator in anatomy. He and another Sydney graduate

Raymond Dart worked together in Professor (Sir) Grafton Elliot Smith's [q.v.11] department and became deeply interested in the embryology of the nervous system and in anthropology. In 1921 they jointly lectured in the United States of America as Rockefeller fellows. Shellshear accepted the chair of anatomy at the University of Hong Kong in 1922, turned to the study of the brain 'of modern humans' and also carried out field-work in prehistory. He represented the university at the golden jubilee of the University of Adelaide in 1926 and was awarded the *ad eundem* degree of M.S. (Adel.). In 1929 he gained his doctorate *in absentia* from the University of Sydney. He remained in Hong Kong until 1936. Twice dean of the faculty of medicine, he presided (1929-30) over the local branch of the British Medical Society. He published prolifically on the comparative morphology and blood supply of the cerebrum (forebrain).

Back in Sydney in 1936, without a formal position, Shellshear served in an honorary capacity as prehistorian at the Australian Museum and in the department of anatomy at the University of Sydney. In May 1937 he was appointed research professor in the department. Meanwhile, he resumed private medical practice, working in radiology with his brother Kenneth in Macquarie Street until 1958.

In more than twenty major scientific articles in learned journals, Shellshear continued his interest in the anatomy and blood supply of the brain, especially the cerebrum. His research on comparative brain structure was detailed, comprehensive and disciplined. He documented and published his findings on the the differences in brain structure of distinct groups of humans—Chinese, Africans and Australian Aborigines. It was his hope that knowledge would ease rather than exacerbate racial or ethnic tensions. In the 1930s he wrote: 'If anthropologists studying the history of man, ethnologists studying the customs of the races, and anatomists examining the structure of the body, can tell one race why another race does certain things, thinks certain thoughts, science will have helped the world a long way to peace, particularly in the Pacific, where so many peoples are watching each other'.

During World War II Shellshear provided classes for young surgeons-lieutenant to help them to gain their formal surgical qualifications. The teaching dossiers he prepared for their use were published as *Surveys of Anatomical Fields* (1949), co-edited by N. W. G. Macintosh [q.v.15]. Shellshear also taught extensively in the department of anatomy during the resource-starved war years. His distinguished scholarly work included his painstaking cataloguing of the department's major anthropological collection. He retired from the university in 1948.

A quiet and unassuming man, with an infectious keenness for his work, Shellshear was recalled with affection by his colleagues and by surgeons of the Australian armed forces. He enjoyed playing golf, and belonged to the Imperial Service and University clubs. Survived by his wife, he died on 22 March 1958 at Royal North Shore Hospital, St Leonards, and was buried in Northern Suburbs cemetery. The J. L. Shellshear Museum of Comparative Anatomy and Physical Anthropology, University of Sydney, was named after him.

G. E. Hall and A. Cousins (eds), *Book of Remembrance of the University of Sydney in the Great War, 1914-1918* (Syd, 1939); *British Medical J*, 16 Aug 1958, p 453, 23 Aug 1958, p 517, 6 Sept 1958, p 643; *SMH*, 4 Aug 1922, 23 July 1926, 18 Aug 1928, 10 May 1938, 24 Mar 1958; Shellshear papers (Shellshear Museum, Dept Anatomy, Univ Syd).

JONATHAN STONE

SHELTON, MOIRA LENORE; *see* DYNON

SHEPHARD, JOHN (1852-1940), manufacturing engineer and microscopist, was born on 2 December 1852 at Masbrough, Yorkshire, England, son of William Shephard, grocer, and his wife Ann, née Rickett. John was sent to school at nearby Rotherham and apprenticed at the age of 10 to local engineers Guest & Chrimes. The firm made plumbing equipment, scientific instruments (such as photometers), and glass prisms (for use in chandeliers). With a co-worker Ralph Davies, Shephard studied metallurgy, mechanical engineering, electricity and magnetism at Firth College, Sheffield.

In 1883 Shephard emigrated to Australia. Next year he and Davies set up an engineering business in South Melbourne. At the office of the registrar of marriages, Carlton, on 31 January 1885 Shephard married Alice Emma Roberts, a domestic servant. Davies Shephard & Co. (later Davies Shephard Pty Ltd) manufactured and repaired water meters, made brass fittings, cut gears, and designed and built scientific instruments. The rapid expansion of the urban water-reticulation system and the formation of the Melbourne and Metropolitan Board of Works in 1890 led to an increased demand for the firm's plumbing products. Davies opened a branch in Sydney. In 1904 the partnership was dissolved: Davies took over the Sydney offshoot and Shephard retained the Melbourne operation. About 1930 Shephard handed day-to-day control of the business to his son Caleb, but continued as the firm's managing director. The company

began to manufacture Kent rotary-piston water meters in 1933, a product which gained nationwide sales.

In 1889 Shephard had joined the Field Naturalists' Club of Victoria (president 1899-1901). Specializing in the descriptive study of freshwater *Rotifera*—a phylum popular with microscopists—he published his findings in the proceedings of the Royal Society of Victoria (member 1894, president 1912). Although he was an amateur and regarded microscopy as a form of relaxation, he became 'one of the mainstays' of the Microscopical Society of Victoria and joined the Quekett Microscopical Club, London.

Like his friend H. J. Grayson [q.v.9], Shephard was interested in the problems of resolving microscopic images. Optical microscopes were calibrated using a slide with parallel lines drawn at known distances apart; some lines had to be less than 0.00004 inch (1 micron) apart. By 1891 the firm of Davies Shephard had manufactured a microtome. The experience gained in making this instrument, and in using it to cut specimens one micron in thickness, gave Shephard the confidence to convert its basic structure into a micro-ruling engine with which he could scratch lines on slides for microscopes. His engine was in service by 1894, making glass rulings at an astonishing 100 000 lines to the inch, that is, about 0.25 micron apart. This high-precision instrument was as good as, if not better than, any of its kind in the world.

Shephard ruled a graticule for the transit telescope at Melbourne Observatory and a micrometer for the University of Adelaide. His laboratory notebook reveals that he also made a diffraction grating, but it has not been found. Survived by his wife, and their son and daughter, he died on 15 May 1940 at Brighton and was cremated; his estate was sworn for probate at £51 923.

H. C. Bolton, 'The Development of Ruling Engines in Melbourne, 1890-1940: A Link between Amateur and Professional Science', *Hist Records of Aust Science*, 6, no 4, July 1987, p 493, and for sources.

H. C. BOLTON*

SHEPHERD, ALFRED ERNEST (1901-1958), community leader and politician, was born on 6 January 1901 at Bendigo, Victoria, eldest of eight children of Victorian-born parents Alfred Shepherd, miner, and his wife Rebecca Josephine, née Neilson, both active Presbyterians. Leaving Violet Street State School at the age of 14 to help support his family, Ernie worked for Robert Harper [q.v.9] & Co., and studied maths and carpentry at night at the Bendigo School of Mines.

He joined the Labor Party, became secretary of the Newsboys' Union (to secure a pay rise for fellow paper-boys) and supplemented his income by driving for political candidates, including Tom Tunnecliffe [q.v.12]. In 1916 he went to Melbourne, lived with an aunt at Footscray and attended anti-conscription meetings. At 17 he began an apprenticeship as a pattern-maker in the Victorian Railways' workshops at Newport.

An enthusiastic sportsman, Shepherd swam and dived competitively, and played football with the Footscray and North Melbourne second XVIIIs. He was honorary secretary of the Footscray Swimming Club (1918-30), Footscray Football Club (1930) and Footscray District Football League (1933-45). In addition, he was a Victorian Football League umpire (for matches in the second division), and a judge and registrar of the Victorian Amateur Swimming Association. The F.F.C., F.D.F.L. and Victorian Football Union were to award him life memberships. At Ballarat East on 9 April 1927 he married with Presbyterian forms Beatrice Vera Hancock, a dressmaker. By 1929 they had their own home at Footscray. The nearby St Andrew's Presbyterian Church became the family's place of worship.

This leading-hand pattern-maker, staunch member of the Amalgamated Engineering Union, indefatigable secretary, and family man, emerged as 'Labor's trump card' at the 1943 Footscray municipal election: 'The most prosperous city was that with the greatest number of contented individuals', Shepherd declared, 'and Labor stood for making the home life all that it should be'. He served five terms (mayor 1948-49) before retiring from the council in 1955 with an unrivalled reputation for assiduous attention to residents' concerns. A strong supporter of home-ownership as a stabilizing social and political influence, he was made a director (from 1945) of four district co-operative housing societies. He befriended and praised businessmen who lived in and contributed to the community from which they made their money; he supported postwar immigration, but drew attention to overcrowded schools and the housing shortage; and he worked hard to establish youth clubs and elderly citizens' centres.

A non-smoker and teetotaller whose recreations were gardening and reading, Shepherd never owned a car, preferring to cycle, walk or use public transport. His plain style of living, approachability and network of friends stood him in good stead, and helped him to win the seat of Sunshine in the Legislative Assembly in 1945. Redistributions saw him move to the seats of Ascot Vale (1955) and Footscray (1958). He proved a tireless local member, renowned for innumerable silent acts of generosity. John Cain [q.v.13], the leader of the Australian Labor Party, groomed him as his successor and allocated him the education portfolio when Labor won government in December 1952. A hard-working minister, he revitalized his department's building programme, travelling widely to open new classrooms and schools, and to assess local needs. He retained the portfolio when Cain reorganized the government in March 1955, following the split in the A.L.P. 'No country could be over-run by Communism', Shepherd said while campaigning for the general election in May, 'if the people could be given a high standard of education, decent living conditions, an impartial press and the opportunity of home ownership'. His wife broadcast with him on radio-station 3KZ, extolling the government's progressive education policy.

The election result consigned Labor to Opposition. L. W. Galvin [q.v.14] lost his seat and Shepherd succeeded him as deputy-leader. Although he deplored sectarianism, lamented the split and was devastated by the fracturing of lifelong friendships, his relations with local right-wingers remained cordial. On Cain's death in August 1957, Shepherd was unanimously elected leader. Opening Labor's 1958 election campaign at Footscray, he announced a 'family first' platform, promising improved employment, housing and schools. He repudiated attempts to link his party with communism and ascribed the A.L.P.'s defeat to the 'unity ticket' of the Democratic Labor Party and the Liberal and Country Party. While opening a youth centre in his electorate, he died suddenly of myocardial infarction on 12 September 1958 at West Footscray. He was accorded a state funeral and was cremated. His wife and their two daughters survived him.

Stockily built, quietly spoken, bespectacled and well groomed, 'Shep' was a disarmingly fair-minded Labor man propelled to party leadership in turbulent times. He earned considerable respect as a committeeman, a councillor, and a parliamentarian dedicated to the interests and welfare of the common man and the family. A staunch Empire loyalist who upheld the monarchy, Australia Day and the Anzac spirit, he was seen as an asset to a party accused of leftist extremism. He was a home-loving man whose parliamentary and ministerial duties undermined his uncertain health. An education trust, a bridge over the Maribyrnong River, a memorial garden at Maidstone and a reserve at Footscray Park were named after him.

K. White, *John Cain & Victorian Labor 1917-1957* (Syd, 1982); J. Lack, *A History of Footscray* (Melb, 1991); *PD* (Vic), 10 Sept 1958, p 407; City of Footscray, *Mayoral Report*, 1948-49; *Footscray Advertiser*, 21 Aug, 11 Sept 1943, 6, 20 May, 15 July 1955, 8 Aug 1957, 18 Sept 1958, 21 May 1959; *Age*

(Melb), 21 Aug 1957, 3 May, 13, 15, 17 Sept 1958; information from Mrs D. Lole, West Heidelberg, and Mrs N. Woods, Sunshine, Melb.

JOHN LACK

SHEPHERD, CATHERINE (1901-1976), playwright, was born on 28 October 1901 at Enkeldoorn, Southern Rhodesia (Zimbabwe), only child of English-born parents Edgar David Shepherd, Anglican clergyman, and his wife Margaret. The death of her father, when Catherine was an infant, left her mother in straitened circumstances. Margaret took her daughter to England and lived with relations in Yorkshire. Catherine was educated at Howell's School, Denbigh, Wales, and (on a scholarship) at University College, London (B.A., 1923; Dip.Ed., 1924). She travelled extensively during the 1920s before migrating to Australia with her mother and settling in Hobart in 1931. By 1936 she had begun writing scripts for the Australian Broadcasting Commission; she also taught at the Collegiate School for girls in the late 1930s.

Olive Wilton [q.v.12], the Hobart Repertory Theatre Society's dynamic producer, met Shepherd in 1937 and was immediately impressed with her script for a three-act play, set in Van Diemen's Land. Wilton produced Shepherd's *Daybreak* to critical acclaim in Hobart in the following year. The play won a competition run by the Australian National Theatre Movement. It was performed on stage around Australia, broadcast in 1938 on the A.B.C., published twice (Melbourne 1942 and 1946) and presented in Hobart in 1954 as part of Tasmania's sesquicentenary celebrations. In 1943 Shepherd had directed the H.R.T.S.'s production of her play *Delphiniums*, which was published in *Six Australian One-Act Plays* (Sydney, 1944). Gracious, unassuming and gentle, she continued to be actively involved in repertory theatre, usually in backstage capacities, which probably suited her shy disposition. Her other well-known stage play, *Jane, My Love*, was commissioned for the jubilee of Federation celebrations (1951) in Hobart: based on the lives of Sir John and Lady Franklin [qq.v.1], it attracted only qualified enthusiasm from local audiences. She adapted it for radio, renaming it *The Franklins of Hobart Town*.

Radio plays and serials, Shepherd's main body of work, brought her a national audience. With a gift for creating dialogue, she adapted novels such as Charles Dickens's [q.v.4] *David Copperfield* and wrote dramas based on the lives of literary and historical figures. Leslie Rees considered that she made a 'sustained and important though never spectacular contribution to stage and radio drama', and that she wrote with 'probing thoughtfulness'

about the human condition, the search for self-realization and 'the need for freedom in a wide social sense'. Shepherd preferred writing for radio rather than the stage because it provided greater scope for freedom of action and movement, and reached a wider audience. She published one novel for children, *Tasmanian Adventure* (London, 1964).

An executive-member (1947) of the Hobart branch of the Fellowship of Australian Writers, Miss Shepherd was made a life member in 1975. She died on 18 February 1976 at St Ann's Rest Home, Hobart, and was cremated with Anglican rites. Her estate, sworn for probate at $58 353, was bequeathed to St Ann's. Edith Holmes's portrait (1956) of Shepherd is held by the Art Society of Tasmania: it captures her meditative reserve, and also suggests courage and humour.

L. Rees, *The Making of Australian Drama* (Syd, 1973); M. Giordano and D. Norman, *Tasmanian Literary Landmarks* (Hob, 1984); *Mercury* (Hob), 24 Sept 1951, 21 Feb 1976; *Saturday Evening Mercury*, 7 Aug 1954; Hobart Repertory Society records (TA).

GILLIAN WINTER

SHEPHERD, GEORGE FREDERICK (1886-1971), engineer, inventor and benefactor, was born on 13 December 1886 at Richmond, Surrey, England, son of Timothy Shepherd, shop-manager, and his wife Elizabeth Alice, née Dale. George trained as a general engineer at Birmingham before travelling to Sydney in 1924 with the intention of selling convertible motorcars. In the following year he moved to Melbourne where he worked for the Shell Co. of Australia Ltd. He married Mary Louisa Campbell about 1928 in Ceylon (Sri Lanka); they were to remain childless. In 1930 he patented a device to improve the operation of petrol pumps. Losing his job in the Depression, he joined three other former officers of Shell in establishing Pacific Oil Co. Pty Ltd in 1931. The firm distributed petrol in Victoria under the brand name Pax. Although it was taken over by Alba Petroleum Co. of Australia Pty Ltd in 1935, Pacific Oil continued to trade under its own name until 1942.

Finding that his enjoyment of the game of bridge was reduced by the rickety chairs and tables usually provided for players, Shepherd built a more sturdy, adjustable card-table and designed comfortable armchairs, mounted on castors, for parties at his home. In the 1930s he set out to make a better type of swivelling wheel. When his wife broke her leg, he fitted four of his experimental castors to a chair, enabling her to move easily around the house, over carpets, linoleum, mats and concrete.

Shepherd realized that his invention had commercial possibilities. He concentrated on problems of lubrication, dust-proofing and appearance. After years of experiment, hampered by World War II, he produced a standard, two-and-a-half-inch (6.4 cm) castor. It consisted of an inclined, domed wheel—within which there was a bearing with an oil trap—and a domed cover that fitted inside the rim of the wheel to enclose the working parts. Shepherd arranged for the castors to be mass-produced under licence by a friend, Mark Cowen, who began selling them in Australia in 1946.

Although the castors were not an instant success, they gradually became popular. In 1950 an English firm was licensed to manufacture them for the British market. Similar arrangements followed with companies in France, the United States of America, Canada, Mexico, New Zealand, Israel and Italy. Shepherd travelled to England in 1954 to celebrate production of the millionth castor at Birmingham. He continued to improve his design. Later models incorporated rubber treads and brakes; a slightly smaller version was manufactured for lightweight furniture. Fitted to furniture and machinery in offices, homes, hotels, hospitals and factories, tens of millions of Shepherd's castors were eventually sold worldwide, making their inventor a wealthy man.

Towards the end of his life Shepherd decided that he would like to set up in Melbourne something similar to the Mayo Clinic at Rochester, Minnesota, U.S.A. He donated $250 000 to establish the Shepherd Foundation, a 'multiphasic' health-screening centre. Opened in South Melbourne in 1971, the non-profit centre aimed to help in the prediction and early diagnosis of disease by testing about seventy-five people a day. The foundation continues to operate.

Elizabeth Shepherd described her husband as exacting, determined, single-minded and methodical. He was a very private person who loved classical music. Survived by his wife, he died on 20 June 1971 in his home at Brighton and was cremated. His estate was sworn for probate at $187 008.

L. W. Port, *Australian Inventors* (Syd, 1978); E. Gold and R. Greener (comp), *Inventive Vics Exhibition*, cat (Melb, 1985); *Woman's Day*, 10 Sept 1973; information from the Shepherd Foundation, South Melb.   BRIAN WIMBORNE

SHER, WILLIAM PETER (1902-1977), engineer and businessman, was born on 6 November 1902 in Vienna and named Wilhelm Peter, second son of Skender Schlesinger, accountant, and his wife Emilie, née Kohn. Wilhelm studied electrical engineering at the Technische Hochschule (later Technical University of Vienna) and graduated in 1922.

After working as a lighting engineer, he took a job with the French railways at Marseilles. In 1926 he joined the Mecox engineering company, which manufactured power tools. Lacking a permit to work in Paris, he moved to Switzerland and then to Berlin where he assembled electric-power and automotive tools. He changed his surname to Sher and used it on his products. On 3 September 1928 he married Elsa Rabinovicz in Vienna. Fearing persecution by the Nazis, they migrated to Australia in 1939. William was to be naturalized in 1944.

After arriving in Melbourne, Sher was employed by Richardson Gears Pty Ltd at Footscray. His engineering experience, enthusiasm and drive were matched by his alertness to business opportunities. World War II restricted supplies from abroad and created an urgent need for power tools in Australia. In 1940 Sher formed a partnership with Alexander Faill and set up a small workshop in Little William Street, Melbourne. The firm soon produced a three-eighth-inch (9.5 mm) portable electric drill which Sher claimed was the first hand-held power tool to be manufactured in Australia. Problems arising from the unavailability of basic components, such as switches and commutators, were swiftly overcome. Sher and Faill incorporated their venture as the Red Point Tool Co. Pty Ltd and moved to Prahran, where they produced power tools and alarm sirens for the war effort. Eliza Tinsley Pty Ltd was their main supporter and distributor.

In the years of postwar suburban expansion Sher realized that large manufacturers were not meeting the needs of a growing number of home handymen. Returning from a visit to Japan in 1951, he designed the small and light quarter-inch (6.4 mm) Drillmaster. The partners bought a new factory at Collingwood in 1952 and changed the firm's name to Sher Power Tools Pty Ltd in 1957. A two-speed drill, the Shermatic—intended for industry, farm and home use—was marketed in 1958. The rapid development of the Sher range reflected the increasing demand for 'do-it-yourself' tools. With a net profit of £101 464 in 1962, the company had become the largest manufacturer of portable power tools produced wholly in Australia.

On 13 March 1963 Sher Tools Australia Ltd was incorporated as a public company to acquire the whole of the issued capital of Sher Power Tools Pty Ltd. A subsidiary, Malvern Non-Ferrous Foundries Pty Ltd, bought Malvern Brass Foundry in September 1964 and began to manufacture castings for its parent company's products. Sher believed that tools imported from the United States of America were designed with 'inbuilt obsolescence'. He was determined that his products would continue to provide years of service for the home handyman. In 1967 the American Skil Corporation took over Sher Tools Australia, buying every share except those owned by Sher and Faill. Sher remained a director and chairman until 1972 when he and his son Ronald quit the firm and formed Ronald Sher Pty Ltd. They manufactured electric bench-tools (which Skil-Sher Pty Ltd did not make) to avoid competing with their former company. In 1977 Sher was appointed A.M. He belonged to the Institute of Machine Tool Makers, to the Graduate Union of the University of Melbourne and to Rotary. Survived by his wife and their son, he died on 26 June 1977 at Prahran and was cremated with Presbyterian forms.

Aust Hardware J, 15 Sept 1968, p 66; *Herald* (Melb), 13 Mar 1963, 5 Dec 1972; *Age* (Melb), 11 Apr 1968; Sher Tools Aust Ltd records (Univ Melb Archives); information from Mr R. J. Sher, Brighton, Melb.   FAY WOODHOUSE

SHERLOCK, WILFRED HOLDEN (1908-1943), grazier and soldier, was born on 20 May 1908 at Malvern, Melbourne, elder son of Harold Herbert Sherlock, a public accountant from England, and his Fiji-born wife Olive Ruth, née St Pinnock. Wilfred, who was nicknamed 'Bill', was educated at Lauriston State School, near Kyneton, and at Melbourne and Geelong Church of England Grammar schools. A keen debater and member of the cadet unit, he ran the mile (1.6 km) in 4 minutes 42.5 seconds and rowed in the senior VIII.

In 1928 Sherlock entered the University of Melbourne to study commerce. He stroked the university VIII to victory in the intervarsity championship in 1929. On 26 July that year he was appointed lieutenant in the Melbourne University Rifles. Deciding against a career in accounting, he withdrew from his course, resigned his commission on 22 January 1930 and turned to the land. He joined Goldsbrough, Mort [qq.v.4,5] & Co. Ltd and worked as a jackeroo in western New South Wales. After several years as an overseer and manager, he bought his own property, Bundilla, near Coleraine, Victoria, in 1937.

Enlisting in the Australian Imperial Force on 6 November 1939, Sherlock was allotted to the 2nd/6th Battalion and promoted sergeant. On 17 November he was commissioned lieutenant. In April 1940 he sailed for the Middle East, where he saw action in Libya—at Bardia and Tobruk—in January 1941. During the Greek campaign (April) he showed initiative, bravery and leadership while under heavy fire. Made temporary captain in May (substantive 18 September), he was appointed to command 'A' Company of the 2nd/6th. He returned to Melbourne on 4 August 1942.

Nine days later, at Christ Church, South Yarra, he married with Anglican rites Elaine Knox-Knight.

Sherlock's battalion was based at Milne Bay, Papua, from October 1942 until January 1943 when it was sent to Wau, New Guinea, to secure the airfield against a possible Japanese thrust from Lae and Salamaua. The troops were flown in and made ready for immediate action. At Wandumi, on the morning of 28 January, Sherlock's under-strength company, bolstered by twenty men of the 2nd/5th Independent Company, was attacked by the main body of a Japanese force which was approaching Wau from the east along a disused track not known to the Australian defenders.

Despite being reinforced during the afternoon, Sherlock's party remained heavily outnumbered, but held its ground until early next morning. When one of his platoons had been overrun at 3 p.m., he had led a counter-attack with fixed bayonets. Forced to withdraw shortly after 3 a.m. on 29 January, he took his troops across a single-log bridge over the swollen Bulolo River. Pursuing Japanese machine-gunners fired on them. Sherlock turned to face the enemy and was heard shouting defiantly above bursts of gunfire until he was killed.

The grim determination, resolution and courage of Sherlock and his men enabled the Australian command to build up sufficient forces at Wau to defeat the Japanese assault over the next two days. Sherlock's leadership accounted in large part for this achievement. Survived by his wife, he was buried in Lae war cemetery. He was posthumously mentioned in dispatches.

D. McCarthy, *South-West Pacific Area—First Year* (Canb, 1959); D. Hay, *Nothing Over Us* (Canb, 1984); S. Trigellis-Smith, *All the King's Enemies* (Melb, 1988); *Aust Army J*, no 49, June 1953, p 6; *Parade*, Jan 1956, p 12; J. Littlewood, Sherlock (ms, held by author, Caringbah, Syd).   P. R. CAREY

SHERRARD, KATHLEEN MARGARET MARIA (1898-1975), geologist, was born on 15 February 1898 at North Carlton, Melbourne, only child of John McInerny, an Irish-born, American-qualified medical practitioner, and his Victorian-born wife Margaratta Wright, née Brayshay. After passing the senior public examination in December 1914, Kathleen entered the University of Melbourne (B.Sc., 1918; M.Sc., 1921), graduated with honours, and won Kernot [q.v.5] and Caroline Kay research scholarships. She spent 1919 doing research, joined the staff of the university as a demonstrator and rose to be assistant-lecturer in geology. Honorary secretary of the Victorian Women Graduates' Association (1920-28) and of the Australian

Federation of University Women (1928-38), she maintained a continuing interest in and membership of the International Federation of University Women.

In 1927 Kathleen spent six months in England at the mineralogical laboratory, University of Cambridge, working on crystallography under Professor Arthur Hutchinson. She then travelled in Europe with her mother. Back in Melbourne, on 20 December 1928 at the Sacred Heart Church, Kew, she married with Catholic rites Howard Macoun Sherrard, a civil engineer; they lived in Sydney and were to have two sons.

Professor Leo Cotton [q.v.8] enabled Mrs Sherrard to use the facilities of the department of geology at the University of Sydney. A member of the Royal societies of New South Wales and Victoria, the Linnean Society of New South Wales and the Geological Society of Australia, she published scholarly articles mostly on graptolites (extinct marine fossils), attended conferences at home and abroad, and persevered with field-work, sometimes taking her children on the expeditions. In 1950 she worked in the Sedgwick Museum with Dr Gertrude Elles at Cambridge, England; in 1963 she visited Moscow; and in 1967 she studied fossil collections in Peking (Beijing).

Sherrard had helped to establish the Australian Association of Scientific Workers in 1939. She convened a sub-committee which studied the effects of nutrition on child growth. In addition, she worked on the problems of food storage and distribution in the event of any large-scale evacuation from the cities during World War II. She joined her friend Jessie Street [q.v.] on the Status of Women Council in 1949 and also belonged to the United Associations of Women and the Women's International League for Peace and Freedom. Sherrard became involved with the Children's Library and Crafts Movement, contributed to publications as diverse as *Australian Quarterly* and *Australian Women's Digest*, wrote an (unfinished) autobiographical novel, and filled long letters with sharp observation, thoughtful musings and practical instructions.

Well read, Sherrard spoke French and German, relished theatre, music and art, and made lively and provocative conversation. Her friendship, thoughtfulness, gifts and hospitality were widely appreciated. Survived by her husband and their sons, she died on 21 August 1975 at her Centennial Park home and was cremated. Her colleagues named *Monograptus sherrardae* in honour of her pioneering work in the study of graptolites.

Records of the Geological Survey of NSW, 16, 1975, p 231; Roy Soc NSW, *J*, 109, 1976, p 168; Roy Soc Vic, *Procs*, 89, 1977, p 208; Sherrard papers (ML).

RACHEL GRAHAME

SHERRIFF, RONALD (1931-1968), bushman and axeman, was born on 11 January 1931 at Launceston, Tasmania, eldest of fifteen children of Roy Joseph Sherriff, timber-cutter, and Phoebe Dorothy Barrett. Ron attended Lefroy State School until the age of 13 when he went to work for his father, cutting and splitting up to ten tons of 6-ft (1.8 m) firewood a week. Boyhood amusements, such as long-distance running, skipping and hitting a punching-bag, developed his endurance and stamina. He later worked as a blacksmith-striker on the construction site of the Australian Aluminium Production Commission's smelter at Bell Bay. In 1951 he was employed by the Hydro-Electric Commission as a bulldozer driver; he also used axes and cross-cut saws to clear trees for transmission lines. At the Methodist Church, Claude Road, on 13 November 1954 he married Myrtle Alma ('Toby') McCoy. From 1955 he cut timber for mine-shafts at Rossarden; by 1958 he was a contract tree-feller with Australian Newsprint Mills Ltd, Maydena.

In 1947 Sherriff won his first 'chop' at Pipers River, but he did not take up woodchopping seriously until 1953. Through work and intensive training, he built his 5 ft 10 ins (178 cm) frame into a compact 13-14 stone (83-89 kg). He went into the bush, accompanied by a fellow axeman, and learned the best angles to cut; he even analysed the reasons for his defeats. His competitive temperament, profound self-belief and fierce desire to succeed—driven, perhaps, by his father's jibe that he would never be an axeman—made him one of the best all-rounders in Australia.

During his career Sherriff reputedly held 55 State, 10 Australian and 4 world titles, in standing, underhand, sawing and tree-felling events. He won 'Oscars' for the most points at royal shows in Melbourne (1962), Sydney (1966 and 1967) and Hobart (1967), took the all-round Tasmanian title (1964-66), and was named champion of champions (1967) at the Royal National Show, Brisbane. In 1967 he captained the Tasmanian and Australian teams at the Royal Easter Show, Sydney. He was a member of the Australian teams that toured New Zealand in 1961, and Britain and South Africa in 1966. Two of his world records —the 24-ins (61 cm) standing block (Somerset, Tasmania, 1962) and the 18-ins (46 cm) standing block (Lietinna, 1966)—still stood in 1999.

Sherriff competed in a period of intense rivalry between axemen such as Doug and Ray Youd and Jack O'Toole. He was widely respected for his encouragement of fellow-axemen and for his community spirit. With Doug Youd, he founded the Maydena Youth Club, and was its chief instructor. On 13 January 1968 at Deloraine he won the (unofficial) world 15-ins (38 cm) standing-block championship. Four days later, while clearing trees for the Hydro-Electric Commission dam in the Forth Valley, he was killed in a logging accident; his wife, and their son and two daughters survived him. Politicians, sporting officials and axemen attended the funeral at the Latrobe Methodist Church which preceded his cremation. In 1994 Sherriff's name was listed in the Tasmanian Sporting Hall of Fame, Launceston.

P. Adam-Smith, *Tiger Country* (Adel, 1968); J. Preston, *Racing Axemen* (Melb, 1980); R. Beckett, *Axemen, Stand by your Logs!* (Syd, 1983); *Examiner* (Launc), 18, 22 Jan 1968; *Mercury* (Hob), 18 Jan 1968; *Sunday Examiner-Express*, 20 Jan 1968; information from Mrs S. Dobbie, Gowrie Park, Mr A. Sherriff, George Town, Mr D. Youd, Hadspen, Mrs T. Lauder, Launceston, and Mr G. Sherriff, Perth, Tas.   TIM JETSON

SHERWOOD, LIONEL CECIL; *see* CECIL

SHILLITO, PHYLLIS SYKES (1895-1980), designer, was born on 28 April 1895 at Halifax, Yorkshire, England, daughter of George Sykes Shillito, a 'thick wire drawer', and his wife Elizabeth, née Sealey. Phyllis left Rishworth School in 1907 and enrolled in art and design at Halifax Technical College five years later. On completing full-time studies, she remained at the college as a student and part-time teacher (1915-18). In 1917 she gained first-class honours in the examination of the City and Guilds of London Institute. Noel Lecurer, a colleague, wrote that her 'intense love for the subjects she has studied has enabled her to gain a good store of ideas in Design; a fund of material in historic ornament; and a thorough grasp of all the underlying principles of Art, both pure and applied . . . As a teacher she possesses the qualities of patience and tact'. She taught at Winchester School of Art in 1919-22, and lectured (from 1922) in design and craft at the Liverpool City School of Art where she was the only woman on a staff of fifteen.

On 3 March 1923 Shillito sailed with her parents in the *Osterley* for Brisbane, to visit her brother John. She stayed there for two years and taught part time at Brisbane Technical College. On 4 August 1925 she began teaching at the Darlinghurst branch of Sydney Technical College (East Sydney Technical College from 1935), having gained permission from the Public Service Board to continue painting and to hold solo exhibitions. In April 1930 Shillito showed 'a small but very creditable collection of water colours', with a few etchings and drawings, at the Beaux Arts gallery, Mel-

bourne. Her paintings included studies of 'Old English and French provincial towns', as well as Australian scenes—'Cliffs, Bondi' and 'The Dry Creek'. In May 1933 she showed her work at the Sedon Galleries, Melbourne. She drew the illustrations for Coral Fish, Diamond Snake, The Brolga, Penguin, Shark, Sea Horse and many other Australian fauna for Nelle Grant Cooper's books of rhyme for children, *More Australians* (1935) and (with Dorothy Wall [q.v.12]) *Australians All* (1939). Shillito also produced numerous bookplates, among them one for Captain Francis de Groot in which she depicted the opening of the Sydney Harbour Bridge.

Following a request from the superintendent of technical education, Shillito established the diploma of design and crafts at Darlinghurst. Four students qualified in 1936. At first the course included graphic and mural design, relief carving, textile design and use of colour; in the 1940s and 1950s it evolved to incorporate interior, industrial and fashion design. Textile design and colour courses strengthened during this period, while others from the 1930s were abandoned or moved to different schools.

Promoted to head teacher (art) in 1940, Shillito was appointed lecturer in art (1947), senior lecturer (1954) and acting-head of the school of women's handicrafts (1958). The Commonwealth Reconstruction Training Scheme gave impetus to her teaching. Design courses were popular with war widows and many returned servicemen and women. Frequent reports in the press told of the success of these mature-age students and the careers that they were establishing. Several of her former students were employed to teach the expanded number of classes.

Shillito centred her life on promoting an awareness of good design. In addition to working through her students, she wrote for magazines and newspapers; she also published *Sixty Beach and Holiday Homes* (1954) and a chapter, 'Colour Tuning', in Clive Carney's *International Interiors and Design* (1959). From time to time she appeared on the Australian Broadcasting Commission's television programme, 'Woman's World'. She compered a fashion parade in January 1960 and demonstrated how to design and cut dress patterns in August 1961.

In 1960 Miss Shillito retired from the Technical College. She opened the Shillito Design School at 36 Grosvenor Street, Sydney, in 1962. In an interview she said that its curriculum borrowed progressive ideas from fashion schools at Ulm and Munich, Germany, and in Stockholm and Paris. When outlining her school's objectives, she affirmed that students would learn 'basic design and basic colour drawing . . . A student who has mastered the basic principles . . . can design anything from a dress to a kitchen stove'. Of those who satisfactorily completed three years of study, a number went on to make a significant contribution to Australian life. Phyllis Shillito died on 13 March 1980 at Bondi and was cremated.

C. J. Kent, Phyllis Shillito, 1895-1980: a review (M.Design thesis, Univ Technology, Syd, 1995), and for bib.   CHRISTOPHER J. KENT

SHIPP, GEORGE PELHAM (1900-1980), classical scholar and philologist, was born on 21 February 1900 at Goulburn, New South Wales, eldest of five children of native-born parents George William Shipp, schoolteacher, and his wife Frances Emily, née Pallett. From Sydney Boys' High School, George proceeded to the University of Sydney (B.A., 1921; D.Litt., 1959) where he gained first-class honours in Greek and Latin, and won a Cooper [q.v.3] travelling scholarship. He entered Emmanuel College, Cambridge (B.A., 1924; M.A., 1948), attaining a first in the classical tripos with special merit in language. Two small grants enabled him to study philology in Europe, mainly in Copenhagen. On 17 August 1924 at Horsens, Denmark, he married Anna Margrethe ('Bib') Brill (d.1980).

Returning to Sydney in 1925, Shipp was appointed lecturer in Latin at the university and began a career of forty years on the staff. His early publications reflected his interest in the vocabulary of Latin. Most notable was his edition, with commentary, of *The Andria of Terence* (Melbourne, 1938, second edition 1960) which contained valuable observations on the language of comedy. His lectures, delivered with few notes, were, like his books, clear and concise in style and illustrated from an abundant store of examples; he also liked to invite contributions from the class. Over the years many students were drawn to language research by their contact with his learning.

In 1945 Shipp was appointed reader in comparative philology, a specially created post that gave him more time for research and for advanced teaching in Greek and Latin, as well as occasional tuition in Sanskrit or Old Norse. The main focus of his research turned to the Greek language. In his *Studies in the Language of Homer* (Cambridge, 1953) he examined the *Iliad*. His finding that linguistically late features occurred predominantly in similes and other non-narrative passages had major significance for the question of the poem's development. In 1953 he and Dr Arthur Capell introduced the university's first course in linguistics. By invitation of the university senate, Shipp was appointed to the chair of Greek on 9 August 1954.

In *Essays in Mycenaean and Homeric Greek* (Melbourne, 1961) Shipp entered the linguistic debate generated by the decipherment of the Linear B tablets, convincingly rejecting attempts to find specifically Mycenaean elements in Homer's language. His years of retirement (from 1965) were productive. Besides many articles, he had time to complete two books. A much enlarged second edition of his *Studies* (Cambridge, 1972) examined the language of Homer more extensively by treating the *Odyssey* as well as the *Iliad*. His *Modern Greek Evidence for the Ancient Greek Vocabulary* (Sydney, 1979) brought together from modern demotic Greek and its dialects a unique collection of material throwing light on ancient Greek words and their usage.

The interests of research and scholarship in the humanities were especially close to Shipp's heart. He was an original member (1956) of the Australian Humanities Research Council, a foundation fellow (1969) of the Australian Academy of the Humanities and a foundation director (1962) of Sydney University Press. A modest man, he did not seek the public eye, but he enjoyed convivial company; with Bib he gave generous hospitality to colleagues and students at their Longueville home. His favourite recreations were tennis and bushwalking, both of which he pursued with vigour until late in life. He died on 29 August 1980 at Hunters Hill and was cremated; his son survived him.

W. F. Connell et al, *Australia's First*, 2 (Syd, 1995); *SMH*, 13 Apr 1918, 10 May 1922, 3 July 1924; Univ Syd Archives; information from Mrs A. Shipp, Lane Cove, Syd; personal knowledge.
                                          W. RITCHIE

SHIRLEY, ARTHUR (1886-1967), actor and film producer, was born on 31 August 1886 in Hobart and registered as Henry Raymond, eighth of thirteen children of Henry Shirley, civil servant, and his wife Sarah Ann, née Morton. He was baptized Arthur, educated at a Catholic school, and employed with George Adams's [q.v.3] Tattersall's lottery and then as a junior solicitor's clerk. Stage-struck, he went to Melbourne, haunted managements and in 1905 secured a three-line part in *Sweet Nell of Old Drury* with Nellie Stewart [q.v.12]. He toured with William Anderson's [q.v.7] company, appeared in 'Bland' Holt's [q.v.4] melodramas in 1907 and played with Lilian Meyers at the Theatre Royal, Hobart, where he was variously billed as 'H.', 'R.', or 'A.' Shirley. After touring the backblocks (1909-10), he worked in 1911-13 with the companies of George Marlow, Beaumont Smith [q.v.] and George Willoughby. At St Mary's Catholic Cathedral, Sydney, on 22 December 1913 he married Ellen Newcomb Hall, a singer from New Zealand; they had a son before separat ing in 1920 and eventually being divorced in 1940.

Unable to pay a debt of almost £23, Shirley had been declared bankrupt in December 1913. Next year he was involved in litigation with Willoughby. He won romantic leads in two silent feature films, as Dr Henry Everard in *The Silence of Dean Maitland* (directed by Raymond Longford [q.v.10]) and in the title role in Cosens Spencer's [q.v.12] *The Shepherd of the Southern Cross*. Both films opened on 13 June 1914. The former was a success, the latter a failure. Leaving in June with his wife for the United States of America, Shirley was contracted to Hollywood's Kalem and Universal companies. He was 'over six feet [183 cm] tall, blue-eyed and handsome', with 'matinée-idol looks'. His films included a melodramatic, two-reel western, *One Man's Evil* (1915), *Bawb O' Blue Ridge* (1916), *The Fall of a Nation* (1916)—in which he played a soldier—and *Branding Broadway* (1918) with William S. Hart.

Shirley settled in Sydney in April 1920 with grandiose plans for his own company, including an American production team and 'full equipment such as lights, cameras, printing machine and laboratory outfit'. He styled himself 'the Big Australian' and set up a film studio in a property at Rose Bay. Under the slogan 'Moving Pictures Made in Australia for the World', he began to produce an ill-fated feature, 'The Throwback', which was beset by financial problems. Following court action against his cinematographer Ernest Higgins [q.v.9], Shirley was unable to pay costs and was declared bankrupt in 1925. He attributed his insolvency to Higgins's 'hatred, spleen and malice'. The film was never completed.

Returning to the stage as Steve Gunn in *The Sentimental Bloke* (January 1923), Shirley gained financial backing from Pyramid Pictures Pty Ltd, a Melbourne syndicate, for another foray into film-making. His best-remembered and best-regarded cinematic effort was a remake of a popular stage melodrama, based on the detective novel by Fergus Hume [q.v.4], *The Mystery of a Hansom Cab* (Melbourne, 1886). Playing the chief suspect Brian Fitzgerald, Shirley also directed, produced and wrote the screenplay. The commercial success of the film, released in 1925, enabled him to write, produce and direct another feature, *The Sealed Room* (1926), in which he again took the lead.

In 1927-30 Shirley was based in London. Failing to gain releases for his films in Britain, he tried in 1928 to establish a new production company in Rhodesia (Zimbabwe). From 1930 he spent four years at Hollywood. Conveniently believing that his wife was dead (although he had been sued for maintenance in London in 1929), he married Frances Clayton at Hollywood in 1934; her previous mar-

riage had been annulled. He returned alone to Sydney that year. His plans to make more films came to nothing. In 1940 he adopted a son, who supported him. Three years later, standing as an Independent, Shirley unsuccessfully contested East Sydney, Eddie Ward's [q.v.] seat in the House of Representatives.

By 1965 Shirley's main interest lay in archaeology and ancient Egypt. Survived by his adopted son, he died on 24 November 1967 at his Rose Bay home and was buried in Waverley cemetery.

H. Porter, *Stars of Australian Stage and Screen* (Adel, 1965); G. Shirley and B. Adams, *Australian Cinema* (Syd, 1983); *Theatre* (Syd, Melb), 2 Aug 1909, 1 Sept, 1 Oct, 1 Nov 1911, 1 Jan, 1 Feb 1913, 1 Mar 1915, 1 Feb, 1 Nov 1916, 1 Oct 1918, 1 Apr, 1 Sept 1919, 1 June 1920, 1 Dec 1921, 2 Aug 1926; *Motion Picture News* (NY), 22 May, 7, 14 Aug 1915; *Picture Show*, 1 May, 1 July 1920, 1 Jan, 1 June, 1 Mar, 1 Dec 1921, 1 Feb 1922; *Everyone's*, 4 Feb 1925, 26 Jan, 2 Feb 1927; *Film Weekly*, 14 Oct 1926; *SMH*, 25 Feb, 2 July 1925, 27 July 1928, 14 Nov 1929, 5 Nov 1935, 19 Feb 1936, 4, 6 Sept 1937, 14 May 1941; bankruptcy files, nos 19775 (1913) and 24837 (1925) (NSWA); film and stills collections (ScreenSound, Canb).

MARILYN DOOLEY

SHOEBRIDGE, ALFRED ARTHUR (1894-1970), public servant, was born on 14 January 1894 at Marulan, New South Wales, son of Australian-born parents Alfred Allen Shoebridge, railway porter, and his wife Rose, née Moore. Educated at Nelligen Public School, young Alfred was appointed a junior clerk in the New South Wales Department of Public Works on 15 May 1911. He began to study economics and commerce part time at the University of Sydney in 1914 before enlisting in the Australian Imperial Force on 24 August. Posted to the 1st Field Artillery Brigade, he served at Gallipoli from April 1915 until he was admitted to hospital in October suffering from dysentery. In 1916-20 he worked in the A.I.F. Kit Store, London, and rose to warrant officer, class one. He was discharged from the army on 5 June 1920 in Sydney.

Returning to the Department of Public Works, Shoebridge advanced rapidly to inspecting accountant and assistant chief accountant. At the Methodist Church, Lindfield, on 24 October 1925 he married Annie Hicks (d.1957). He transferred to the office of the commissioner for road transport (and tramways) as accountant in 1930. Two years later he was promoted to head the road transport branch. In September 1944 he was appointed assistant-commissioner. During World War II he was a member of the Commonwealth's War Road Transport Committee and chairman of the State's Automotive Industry War Advisory Committee. On 22 May 1950 he became commissioner for road transport and tramways (commissioner for government transport from May 1952).

The two decades following the war were marked by commuters' increasing reliance on private motor vehicles at the expense of mass transit systems. Shoebridge faced public outcries over increasing costs of tram and bus travel, worsening traffic congestion in the city and delays to services. His strategy was to accept the shifting balance between public and private transport and to arrest the decline of the former by rationalizing services and implementing efficiencies. As a means to this end, he gave the 'highest priority' to replacing Sydney's trams with buses.

Shoebridge decided on the gradual introduction of one-man, single-deck buses from 1952. In the ensuing industrial unrest, which saw the dismissal of six hundred striking bus drivers in November 1955, he succeeded in imposing his measures, but only with the support of a committee of inquiry hastily convened by the Cahill [q.v.13] Labor government. While the cost of public transport fell slightly, deep-seated revenue problems remained. On 13 January 1959 Shoebridge retired as commissioner and as chairman of the Sydney Harbour Transport Board, a post he had held since 1952.

On 9 September 1959 at the office of the government statist, Melbourne, Shoebridge married Gladys Reece Jones, née Lomax, a widow. President of the Roseville Golf Club and of the New South Wales branch of the Professional Golfers' Association of Australia, he also presided over the Roseville Returned Servicemen's Memorial Club. He died on 13 December 1970 at Killara and was cremated with Methodist forms; his wife survived him, as did the son and daughter of his first marriage.

Report of the Commissioner for Road Transport and Tramways, *PP* (NSW), 1944, 1945, 1947, 1950; Report of the Commissioner for Government Transport, *PP* (NSW), 1952-57, 1959; *SMH*, 25, 26 Oct 1956, 14 Jan 1959, 15 Dec 1970.

MICHAEL DI FRANCESCO

SHORT, GORDON HERBERT (1912-1959), press photographer, was born on 23 April 1912 at Petersham, Sydney, youngest of four children of Herbert George Short, a civil servant from England, and his native-born wife Lilian, née Greer. Gordon attended Stanmore Public School and in 1928 became a messenger in the pictorial department of the *Sydney Morning Herald*. Known as 'Shorty', he formally began a cadetship in 1930 and moved quickly from the duties of the darkroom into general photography. He covered the 1934 royal tour of the Duke of Gloucester [q.v.14], from Melbourne to Sydney. His photograph of the duke open-

ing the Anzac Memorial in Hyde Park was the largest photograph that the *Herald* had ever published, wrapped around the entire paper. As the 1930s advanced so did his skill.

Although he was an Anglican, on 20 November 1937 at St Mary's Cathedral, Sydney, Short married Eileen Margaret Phillips, a stenographer; their six children were raised in their mother's faith. In April 1943 he was released by John Fairfax & Sons [qq.v.4,8] Ltd to act as an official war photographer with the Department of Information, for which he covered fighting in the Pacific and New Guinea. The *S.M.H.* persistently tried to get him back, and succeeded in June 1945—in time for him to photograph victory celebrations on the streets of Sydney.

As a senior photographer Short enjoyed some choice in the types of stories he covered and tended to do the day shifts. His skilful use of the large format Graflex Speed Graphic (with its supply of spare plates) worked well for his carefully constructed shots. He was an expert at the 'roving story', capturing its action and warmth. Well dressed, with a trim moustache, he moved easily in the society haunts of Prince's and Romano's [q.v.11] restaurants. Connie Robertson [q.v.11], editor of the *S.M.H.*'s women's supplement, had confidence in his ability, respected his belief in the dignity of the press, and understood his refusal to use tradesmen's entrances. He was a dynamic character, who could easily dominate a room.

Although fiercely competitive with his rivals on the *Daily Telegraph*, Short regularly met them for a drink at the Journalists' Club or nearest pub. He was passionate about photography, the Royal Australian Navy, and the snow: he covered fleet exercises and carried out public-relations assignments for the navy, and, on holidays at the snowfields, photographed his sons under the name 'Long', an example of his sense of humour. Short accompanied Queen Elizabeth II's gruelling tour (1954) from Fiji to New Zealand and around Australia. His photographic images of the young Queen and Prince Philip gained an enthusiastic response. He covered other significant events, including the 1953 British atomic-bomb tests at Woomera, South Australia, and the 1956 Olympic Games in Melbourne.

At the end of 1957 Short suffered an undiagnosed illness. After a long convalescence, he returned to work, but died of ascending polyneuritis on 28 October 1959 at Royal North Shore Hospital and was cremated. His wife, and their daughter and five sons survived him.

G. Souter, *Company of Heralds* (Melb, 1981); V. Lawson, *Connie Sweetheart* (Melb, 1990); W. Irving, *The Pictures Tell the Story* (Syd, 1995); K. Evans,

'The Shadow of the Photographer—Images on Paper', in A. Curthoys and J. Schultz (eds), *Journalism* (Brisb, 1999); *Journalist*, Dec 1959, p 3; John Fairfax Holdings Ltd archives, Syd; information from Mr A. Short, North Steyne, Mr E. McQuillan, Abbotsford, Mr W. Irving, Avalon, Syd, and Mr D. Baglin, Mudgee, NSW.   KATE EVANS

SHUMACK, CLARA JANE (1899-1974), army matron, was born on 17 June 1899 at Dark Corner, New South Wales, eighth of eleven children of native-born parents John William Shumack, farmer, and his wife Catherine, née Lewis. Educated at a Bathurst school, Clara trained at the St George and the Coast (Prince Henry) hospitals, Sydney, and was registered as a nurse on 4 November 1926. She worked, in turn, at the St George, as assistant-matron at Canterbury hospital and in a private doctor's surgery. Late in 1935 she left Australia to spend a working holiday in Europe.

In 1937 Shumack returned to the St George where she gained a reputation as a first-rate theatre sister. Five ft 9 ins (175 cm) tall and broad shouldered, she had a 'purposeful stride and upright bearing'. On 20 July 1940 she was appointed matron, Australian Army Nursing Service, and posted to the hospital ship *Manunda*. After a 'shakedown' voyage to Darwin in August, the vessel made four trips to the Middle East between October 1940 and September 1941. The *Manunda* sailed for Darwin in January 1942. During the first Japanese air-raid on the town on 19 February, she suffered several hits; twelve people on board were killed and eighteen seriously wounded. Throughout the attack Shumack calmly and efficiently supervised the nursing of the wounded and dying.

Following a period ashore while the *Manunda* underwent repairs, Shumack reboarded the ship in August for what was to be the first of twenty-seven voyages to Papua and New Guinea. On the second of these trips the hospital ship anchored in Milne Bay, Papua, on 6 September. Enemy warships entered the harbour that night and fired over the *Manunda* while patients were being ferried from the shore in her lifeboats. Although 'no splinters' came 'near enough to hurt', Shumack expressed her fury 'at the Japs for interrupting our work'.

Appointed major in March 1943, Shumack was transferred to the 128th Australian General Hospital, Port Moresby, as matron in April 1944. She was evacuated to Sydney suffering from a skin disorder in July, but rejoined the hospital—which had relocated to Redbank, Queensland—in January 1945. Promoted temporary lieutenant colonel in April (substantive in September), she was awarded the Royal Red Cross in June: the citation emphasized her 'exceptional devotion to duty', especially when the *Manunda* was bombed in Darwin. On 5 September 1945 she was sent as matron to the 113th A.G.H., Concord, Sydney, a post she held until December 1946. She was transferred to the Reserve of Officers on 17 January 1947.

Shumack served as matron, first of the Lithgow District Hospital and then of the Lucy Gullett [q.v.9] Convalescent Home, Bexley. A foundation fellow (1950) of the College of Nursing, Australia, she was a member of the Royal Empire and the Musica Viva societies. To her staff in the *Manunda* she was loyal but 'very regimental'; while she was 'strict', she 'often unbent afterwards'. She died on 23 December 1974 at Strathfield and was buried with Catholic rites in Northern Suburbs cemetery.

R. Goodman, *Our War Nurses* (Brisb, 1988) and *Hospital Ships* (Brisb, 1992); E. White, *A Shumack Family c.1668-1992 & Connected Families* (Syd, 1993); *SMH*, 14 June 1945; information from Ms K. Rowen, Narrabeen, Syd; personal knowledge.
                    PERDITTA M. MCCARTHY

SHUTE, NEVIL; *see* NORWAY

SIDDONS, ROYSTON (1899-1976), manufacturer, was born on 15 December 1899 at Williamstown, Melbourne, eldest child of Joseph Siddons, a miner from England, and his Victorian-born wife Florence Rees, née Gibbs. Royston attended state schools in Western Australia and Victoria, but left at the age of 14 to help his father's troubled carrying business in Melbourne. Two years later the family moved to Wonthaggi where he worked for the State Coal Mine, eventually as a shift engineer. In the evenings he continued at the local technical school the electrical engineering studies he had begun at Swinburne Technical College.

At the Presbyterian Church, Wonthaggi, on 25 July 1923 Siddons married Agnes Emily Smith, a schoolteacher. That year he set up as an electrical contractor with his own shop, but sold out in 1927 and returned to Melbourne. He and his family lived with his parents while he worked in wireless manufacture. In 1931 he leased a metal-casting factory at Collingwood and, with a staff of four and an annual wages bill of £1014, began producing hardware for cabinet-makers. Bolstered by his Methodist principles, a supportive extended family and a talent for cost-saving innovation, he survived the worst years of the Depression and began to prosper. He moved to larger premises at Clifton Hill in 1934. Having perfected the die-casting of padlocks from zinc alloy, he manufactured them under the brand name, Sidco. In 1939 he formed R. Siddons Pty Ltd.

A fire at the factory in 1941 and wartime controls forced a new departure. Siddons obtained Commonwealth approval to rebuild, on condition that a drop forge was installed to manufacture hand tools for the armed services. Friends provided the bulk of the capital to establish and equip Siddons Drop Forgings Pty Ltd (1942). As well as hand tools, the company contributed gun parts and bomb caps to the war effort. By 1945 Siddons was supplying the domestic market, in which postwar shortages of imported tools offered the opportunity for expansion. Sidchrome spanners, pliers, chisels, wrenches, hammers and screwdrivers soon became the firm's main profit earners.

In 1948 a new site was purchased at West Heidelberg. Next year the business became a public company, with Siddons as managing director in charge of 145 employees, including 35 tool-makers. He transferred parcels of shares to senior managers, and continued to enjoy congenial relations with shopfloor workers. His only son, John, trained on the job, starting as a forgehand in 1945 and passing through the major departments. The father's methods of promoting a harmonious workplace were to be developed by the son as a creed of industrial democracy.

Innovations at Siddons included low-voltage resistance heating (a technique in forging invented by Merrill Hanna, the company's laboratory head), a continuous 'austempering' furnace, automatic electroplating, and advanced forging presses from the United States of America. In 1949, while touring factories in the U.S.A., John Siddons encountered the revolutionary Ramset fastening system. He bought a machine and was offered the Australian franchise. Ramset Fasteners (Australia) Pty Ltd was incorporated as a division of Siddons Drop Forging in 1952, with John as general manager of Ramset, and Royston as chairman of Siddons. Import restrictions forced the company to manufacture Ramset guns and pins in Australia much earlier than intended, a technologically demanding transition that was achieved rapidly and smoothly under John's superintendence. Although Siddons tools were being exported to the Pacific Islands, South East Asia and the Middle East, by 1954-55 Ramset profits exceeded those of the hand tools division. Ramset subsidiaries were established in New Zealand and South Africa.

John Siddons oversaw the installation at West Heidelberg of a new forge and a steel-rolling mill (the second such mill in Australia). When he became a director of Siddons in 1953, the emerging tensions between father and son over management and market-ing were transferred to board level. In 1955 Royston moved John from the highly successful Ramset subsidiary and made him general manager of the parent company, while retaining for himself overall control as chairman and managing director.

The resulting clash of generations, hurtful for the participants and potentially debilitating to the business, was recalled by John Siddons in his autobiography, *A Spanner in the Works* (Melbourne, 1990), as 'a period of great personal anguish'. The founding father —admired by the son for his physical and mental stamina, pioneering innovations and astute business judgement—seemed to have hardened into a dogmatic and dictatorial taskmaster, one who insisted on personal, centralized control and was given to maverick decisions. Following disagreements with five successive general managers of Sidchrome, Royston handed their post to his son and left on an overseas trip. During his absence advertisers coined the famous jingle, 'Y' canna hand a man a grander spanner'. Promotion by the television entertainer Graham Kennedy pushed sales to new heights. The Sidchrome trade mark became a household name throughout Australia.

Returning reinvigorated from his travels, Royston outflanked John with a corporate restructure that installed himself as chairman of a holding company, Siddons Industries Ltd, and its subsidiaries, Siddons Drop Forgings and Siddons Rolled Steel, and as managing director of his son's Ramset initiative. In 1957-58 Royston bought a group of William Buckland's [q.v.13] companies which distributed automotive components. The expansion halved the Siddons family's equity in S.I.L. to 15 per cent, threatened long-established investors and left the company vulnerable to takeover. John spent 1959-60 setting up the Ramset business in Britain and returned in time to prevent the sale of S.I.L. to Repco Ltd during the 1960-61 'credit squeeze'. The board deposed Royston as managing director on 10 January 1963 and gradually eased him out of management. He passed the chairmanship to his son in 1968 and left the board in 1972.

Although Siddons had moved from Ivanhoe to Mornington, he still drove regularly to the West Heidelberg plant. From the 1960s he pursued other business interests, with limited success, in gold- and opal-mining, and in citrus- and olive-farming. He was a director of various companies connected with his business, and of others including Freighters Ltd, Ring-Grip Ltd and the Leviathan Ltd. For recreation he sailed and played bowls. He was a council-member of Wesley College.

Siddons died on 24 November 1976 at his Canterbury home and was cremated; his wife, and their son and two daughters survived him. A service was held at the Ivanhoe Methodist Church—where Siddons had been a lay preacher, trustee and Sunday-School superintendent. 'And what has this man contributed?' asked the preacher. 'He gave his country a tool with which to build . . . he gave his country the common spanner'. That year Siddons Industries Ltd, with subsidiaries in six countries, 1500 employees and a wages bill of $12 million, made a pre-tax profit of $3 million and paid $600 000 in dividends. Siddons' estate was sworn for probate at $696 899. One of his bequests helps students training for the ministry of the Uniting Church in Australia. Bram Leigh's portrait (1975) of Siddons is held by the family.

B. Carroll, *Australian Made* (Melb, 1987); *Metals Aust*, 10, no 2, Feb 1978, p 36; *Herald* (Melb), 25 Oct 1969, 25 Nov 1976; *Australian*, 14 Nov 1970; *Age* (Melb), 25 Nov 1976; *Sun News-Pictorial*, 26 Nov 1976; *Heidelberger*, 1 Dec 1976; *Sunday Age* (Melb), 5 Jan 1992; A. P. J. Dixon, Siddons Industries Limited: A History (ms, held by Mr J. R. Siddons, Shoreham, Vic); information from Mr J. R. Siddons.
JOHN LACK

SIMMONDS, KEVIN JOHN (1935-1966), gaol escapee, was born on 22 August 1935 in Sydney, son of Australian-born parents John Simmonds, labourer, and his 16-year-old wife Sheila Mary, née Finn. After years of travelling the State looking for work, Jack settled with the family at Griffith in 1941. He used his horse and cart to carry produce from the surrounding farms to the railway station. Kevin attended Griffith Public School, where he was nicknamed 'Simmo'.

At the age of 14 Simmonds was sent to Boys' Town, Engadine, for stealing. While there, he learned many dishonest tricks. At 18 he was sentenced to two years at Mount Penang Training School, Gosford, for stealing, and breaking and entering. Boyish looking, with a courteous manner and a passion for fitness and fast cars, he quit home soon after his twenty-first birthday and left a trail of safe-crackings, robberies and car thefts through two States. In May 1957 he was sentenced in Sydney to three years imprisonment. He was released in February 1959, but was in court again in the following August, answering three charges of armed robbery, seventeen of breaking and entering, and thirty-five of car stealing. He was sentenced to fifteen years in Long Bay gaol.

On 9 October 1959 Simmonds escaped with a fellow inmate, Leslie Alan Newcombe, from the inner section of the gaol, a feat few had performed. Next day they killed a warder at Emu Plains prison farm and took his gun. After two weeks hiding in Sydney, Newcombe was recaptured. The chase for Simmo became frenzied, involving nearly 500 policemen, armed with guns, bulletproof vests and fast cars. They also had an aeroplane and a helicopter on call.

Two men found Simmonds in Kuring-gai Chase on 5 November. He was digging a hole in which to hide a caravan that he planned to steal and use as a home. Apologizing for tying them up, he drove off in their utility truck. Twelve hours later he crashed through a road block near Wyong. Barefoot, and wearing only shorts and singlet, he was pursued through rugged, leech- and snake-infested country by shifts of police. Tracker dogs were flown in, but continual rain washed away the scent.

Simmonds's ability to keep at bay hundreds of police earned him some public sympathy. The police were lampooned for failing to apprehend him. He spent more than five weeks on the run. Detective Sergeant Ray Kelly [q.v.14], with seven carloads of police and tracker dogs, finally captured him at Mulbring early on 15 November. Townsfolk applauded him at Kurri Kurri police station and crowds greeted him at the Central Criminal Court, Sydney, where he was charged with murder.

In March 1960 a jury found Simmonds and Newcombe guilty of manslaughter. Justice J. H. McClemens [q.v.15] plainly disagreed with the verdict, and sentenced them to penal servitude for life. Two months later Simmonds's appeal against the severity of his sentence was rejected by the Full Court. The six years Simmo spent in the section for 'intractables' at Grafton gaol reduced him to a shuffling, vacant-eyed mumbler who burned his arms with cigarettes. He was found hanged in his cell on the morning of 4 November 1966 and was buried with Catholic rites in South Grafton cemetery.

L. Newcombe, *Inside Out* (Syd, 1979); J. Simmonds with A. Gollan, *For Simmo* (Syd, 1980); *SMH*, 18 May 1957, 10 Oct-17 Nov 1959, 16, 19 Mar, 18 May 1960, 5 Nov 1966.
ANNE GOLLAN

SIMMONDS, ROSE (1877-1960), photographer, was born on 26 July 1877 at Islington, London, second daughter of Millice Culpin, medical practitioner, and his wife Hannah Louisa, née Muncey. The family migrated to Brisbane about 1891 and Dr Culpin established a practice at Taringa. Rose studied art with Godfrey Rivers [q.v.11] at the Brisbane Technical College. On 30 March 1900 in her father's house she married with Baptist forms John Howard Simmonds (d.1939), a 37-year-old stonemason. John kept a photographic record of his commissioned headstones, and maintained a darkroom at home for developing and printing negatives. Rose was soon processing her own photographs, mainly snapshots of her sons.

From about 1927 Mrs Simmonds submitted photographs to the monthly competitions run by the Queensland Camera Club and the *Australasian Photo-Review*. Although her early entries in Q.C.C. competitions were ranked either first or second in the B-grade section, she quickly won awards in the A-grade division. She was elected to the club's committee in 1928. In May that year her 'Pear Blossom' was placed fourth in a special still-life contest run by the *A.P.R.* and in the August issue her 'Playground of the Shadows' came first. For twelve years her work regularly won prizes or received special mention in *A.P.R.* competitions, which attracted entries from such noted photographers as Harold Cazneaux [q.v.7] and Max Dupain. The editor commented on her photograph 'Still Life' in 1929: 'this certainly would have had a prize but for the fact that Mrs Simmonds won the competition with another fine print'.

Her photographic interests were those of the pictorialist and her evolving style was guided by the artist's vision. Simmonds regularly attended monthly excursions to locations in south-east Queensland which were conducted by the Q.C.C. to provide members with inspiration and recreation. Through its competitions the club passed judgement on the work produced on these outings. Artists were invited to monthly meetings of the Q.C.C. to speak about accentuation, atmosphere, balance, gradation, genre, subordination, point of interest and suggestiveness. Simmonds's work was grounded in her knowledge of Queensland painting. 'Playground of the Shadows' owed much to the Impressionist style championed by William Grant in the 1920s; her well-known photographs, 'Morning Light on the Sand Dunes' (1930) and 'Last Rays on the Sand Dunes' (c.1940), had an affinity with the paintings of Kenneth Macqueen [q.v.15].

Simmonds's reputation won her selection in national photographic exhibitions, including one run by the Photographic Society of New South Wales in 1932, and another organized by that society, the Professional Photographers' Association of New South Wales and the Sydney Camera Circle in 1938. An associate (1937) of the Royal Photographic Society of Great Britain, she was also represented in an exhibition of pictorial photography held in Adelaide in 1940.

Survived by her two sons, Simmonds died on 3 July 1960 at Auchenflower and was cremated with Presbyterian forms. A collection of her photographs is held by the Queensland Art Gallery.

B. Hall and J. Mather, *Australian Women Photographers 1840-1960* (Melb, 1986); B. Larner, *A Complementary Caste* (Surfers Paradise, Qld, 1988); *A'sian Photo-Review*, Sept 1927, May, Aug 1928, May, Aug 1929, May, June, Sept 1930; Simmonds file (Qld Art Gallery L).   KEITH BRADBURY

SIMMONS, ROY THOMAS (1906-1975), medical scientist, was born on 29 April 1906 at Heidelberg, Melbourne, second son of Victorian-born parents Thomas Edwin Simmons, saddler, and his wife Isabella May, née McGuiness. Roy was educated at Heidelberg State School and (on a scholarship) at the Working Men's College (diploma of organic and inorganic chemistry, 1926), Melbourne. In 1924 he was appointed a laboratory assistant at the Commonwealth Serum Laboratories, Parkville. He completed training in bacteriology and biochemistry before taking a series of secondments (1927-35) to Commonwealth health laboratories in every State. At Holy Trinity Church, Kew, on 23 September 1932 he married Iris Ethelwyn Dunstan with Anglican rites.

In 1936 Simmons returned to the new research department in the C.S.L., under E. V. Keogh [q.v.15]. After initially working in bacteriology, he undertook blood-group research from 1940, and accepted the added responsibility (until 1956) for the production and quality control of C.S.L. products. His first research paper (1938) concerned the diphtheria bacillus; others followed on the haemolytic streptococci; but from the early 1940s his publications related almost entirely to blood groups. His rank was consultant from 1947 and senior consultant (principal scientific officer) from 1961.

Simmons was best known for his work on the Rh blood group and on the devastating results of incompatibility between a baby's blood that is Rh-positive and a mother's that is Rh-negative. He was one of a team of researchers, drawn mainly from transfusion services and hospitals, who developed an exchange-transfusion technique which, by replacing an affected newborn baby's blood, saved many lives. A later group, again including Simmons, produced anti-Rh (D) gamma globulin which prevents haemolytic disease of the newborn.

His work in applying serological techniques to anthropological research, which helped to chart the distribution of blood-group genes among the peoples of Asia and the Pacific, won Simmons international recognition. For more than twenty years he collaborated with noted anthropologists and attracted research grants from the United States of America. Between 1943 and 1971 he provided a free blood-group reference service for Australia. From 1965 the World Health Organization used his laboratory as its blood-group reference centre for the South Pacific region. In 1957-70 he worked with an American team, studying the fatal neurological disorder kuru ('laughing sickness') in New Guinea: they excluded any blood-group association. As principal or co-author, he published more than 160 scientific papers, mostly in the *Medical Journal of Australia*. His most prized, and unquestionably deserved, academic distinction was an honorary D.Sc. awarded by the University of Melbourne in 1965. He retired in 1971.

Handsome, alert and neatly dressed, Simmons saw himself as a person 'with average ability, application, and a will to succeed'. He delivered scientific papers at numerous conferences and relaxed by gardening at his Heidelberg home. About 1965 he developed diverticulitis. Survived by his wife and their three daughters, he died of septicaemia on 28 February 1975 in East Melbourne and was cremated. His daughters endowed the Roy and Iris Simmons award for students in applied chemistry at the Royal Melbourne Institute of Technology.

A. H. Brogan, *Committed to Saving Lives* (Melb, 1990); *Health*, 4 Dec 1965; *MJA*, 22 Nov 1975; *Aust Inst of Aboriginal Studies Newsletter*, 1975; *American J of Physical Anthropology*, 45, no 1, July 1976; *Pathology*, 8, 1976; Simmons papers (held by Ms A. Simmons, Hawthorn, Melb); information from Mr A. H. Brogan, Glenroy, Melb, and Mr D. S. Ford, Port Macquarie, NSW.   BRYAN EGAN

SIMONDS, JUSTIN DANIEL (1890-1967), Catholic archbishop, was born on 22 May 1890 at Stonehenge, near Glen Innes, New South Wales, youngest of six children of Irish-born parents Peter Simonds and his wife Kate, née Troy, both schoolteachers. Justin received his early education at home and at public schools where his father was in charge, at nearby Deepwater and at Blacktown, Sydney. He then attended Sydney Boys' High School. About 5 ft 5 ins (165 cm) tall and muscular in build, he proved a good Rugby Union footballer. He began studying for the priesthood at St Patrick's College, Manly, in 1907 and was ordained on 30 November 1912 in St Mary's Cathedral, Sydney.

The young priest spent his first year of ministry as curate in the parish of Bega. In 1914 he was appointed to his former seminary as professor of introductory sacred scripture and Greek. He became professor of philosophy and hermeneutics at St Columba's College, Springwood, in 1916. Transferred back to Manly in 1921 as dean and professor of sacred scripture, Simonds returned to Springwood in 1923 as vice-rector and professor of philosophy. From 1928 he studied at the Catholic University of Louvain (Ph.D.,

1930), Belgium, where his thesis on the influence of Philo on Christian apologists was awarded first-class honours. Home again, he resumed his positions at Springwood and was promoted to rector in 1934. He also carried out pastoral duties in the local parish. During his seminary years he contributed articles on theological and philosophical issues to the *Australasian Catholic Record* and the *Manly* magazine.

In February 1937 Simonds's appointment as archbishop of Hobart was announced. The first Australian-born Catholic priest to reach the rank of archbishop, he was consecrated on 6 May by Archbishop (Cardinal) Giovanni Panico, the apostolic delegate. Although Simonds's duties in Tasmania were 'not particularly burdensome', he 'maintained an active schedule of pastoral activity'. He had a deep knowledge of the philosophical and theological principles underlying the lay apostolate and of the papal teachings on social issues. At Louvain he had become an admirer and supporter of the Young Christian Workers' (Jocist) movement. He fostered the observance in Australia of Social Justice Sunday and wrote (1940) the first of the bishops' annual statements on social justice. In September 1942 Panico informed him that he had been appointed coadjutor archbishop of Melbourne, with the right of succeeding Archbishop Daniel Mannix [q.v.10]. Neither Mannix nor Simonds had been consulted about the move.

Although his talents were not fully used during the twenty-one years in which he waited, as parish priest of West Melbourne, to replace Mannix, Simonds accepted his unenviable situation with grace and patience. The period did not lack highlights or productivity. On behalf of the Church in Australia, he toured war-ravaged Europe in 1946 to bring relief to the suffering, to assess the future of Catholic migration and to discuss the sending of orphaned children to Australia. Three years later he attended the second part of the third session of the United Nations General Assembly, held at Lake Success, New York, as a special adviser to the Australian delegation headed by Dr H. V. Evatt [q.v.14]. Simonds's subsequent travels included official visits and the leadership of pilgrimages to Rome and other centres in 1950, 1953 and 1960. He also attended all four sessions of the Second Vatican Council in 1962-65. On learning in Rome that Mannix had died on 6 November 1963 (at the age of 99) and that he was archbishop of Melbourne, he immediately returned home to preside over and to preach a memorable panegyric at Mannix's funeral service.

While he attempted throughout his life to reconcile the secular and religious worlds, Simonds also defended the separation of church and state. He abhorred the involvement of the Church in party politics and vigorously opposed any attempt to use the youth movements of Catholic Action to combat communism in the political and industrial spheres. In contrast with Mannix and the other Victorian bishops, he was critical of the Catholic Social Studies Movement, headed by B. A. Santamaria, especially after the Australian Labor Party split in 1955. His most courageous and controversial act as archbishop of Melbourne, carried out within days of taking office, was to terminate Santamaria's weekly contribution to a Catholic television programme, 'Sunday Magazine'.

Simonds's brief term at the head of a major see was to be unduly onerous because of failing health and weakening sight. Nevertheless, he was able to restructure the management of the burgeoning Catholic education system, to establish twelve new parishes to cater for the needs of a growing population, and to begin implementing the reforms of Vatican II, notably in the areas of liturgy and ecumenism. Invoking the principles of the Universal Declaration of Human Rights (1948), he strongly advocated state aid for religious schools. After officiating, with difficulty, at several functions in the first half of 1966, he suffered a series of strokes and spent most of the last twelve months of his life as a patient in the Mercy Hospital, East Melbourne. His resignation as archbishop was announced on 13 May 1967. He died on 3 November that year at the Mercy and was buried in the crypt of St Patrick's Cathedral.

Regarded as one of the most scholarly of the Australian bishops, Simonds was revered by generations of clerics whom he had taught at Springwood and Manly, and by the Catholic priests, religious and laity of Tasmania and Melbourne. All of them valued his intelligence, kindness and pastoral concern. Neither Roman nor Irish, he was proudly Australian, and blessed with urbanity and wit. Paul Fitzgerald's portrait of Simonds, held by the cathedral, captures something of the archbishop's dignity and composure.

D. F. Bourke, *A History of the Catholic Church in Victoria* (Melb, 1988); F. A. Mecham, *The Church and Migrants 1946-1987* (Syd, 1991); M. Vodola, *Simonds* (Melb, 1997); K. J. Walsh, *Yesterday's Seminary* (Syd, 1998); A. O'Brien, *Blazing a Trail* (Melb, 1999); Simonds papers (Melb Diocesan Hist Com).   MICHAEL COSTIGAN

SIMPSON, COLIN HALL (1894-1964), pharmacist and army officer, was born on 13 April 1894 at St Kilda, Melbourne, son of Colin Simpson, a plumber from Scotland, and his Victorian-born wife Elizabeth Fulton, née Jordan. Young Colin was educated at Caulfield Grammar School and apprenticed to a pharmacist. After serving in the cadets (1909-14) and the Militia, he was appointed second lieutenant, 3rd Pioneer Battalion, Australian Imperial Force, on 1 May 1916. Next month he embarked for England. In November he transferred to the 3rd Divisional Signal Company, Australian Engineers, which was sent to the Western Front. He was mentioned in dispatches in January 1917 and won the Military Cross for maintaining communications during the battle of Messines, Belgium, in June. In October 1917 he was gassed at Passchendaele, and evacuated to England. He returned to Melbourne in February 1918. His A.I.F. appointment terminated on 9 August.

Registered as a pharmacist in July 1918, Simpson set up as a retail chemist at Brunswick. At the Congregational Church, Ascot Vale, on 12 August 1919 he married Jean Elizabeth Watson. In 1937, in collaboration with D. E. Robertson and A. E. Moore, he formed Allied Master Chemists of Australia Ltd which sold products to fellow pharmacists to enable them to compete against other retailers.

Meanwhile, Simpson remained active in the Militia. In October 1918 he was posted to the 2nd/14th Battalion. Promoted captain in 1920, he was transferred to the Australian Engineers (signal duties) in 1921. As a lieutenant colonel (from 1923), he commanded the 3rd Divisional Signals (1923-29 and 1935-39) and the 39th Battalion (1929-33). In May 1939 Colonel Simpson was appointed commander of the 6th Brigade. He had become a confidant of Major-General Sir Thomas Blamey [q.v.13] in the 1920s. They were both involved in the 'White Army', a secret organization formed principally by ex-servicemen to maintain law and order in the event of civil unrest.

On 14 October 1939 Blamey appointed Simpson to command the 6th Divisional Signals, A.I.F., in the rank of lieutenant colonel. With the expansion of the force, Simpson was promoted colonel and made chief signals officer, I Corps, in April 1940. He sailed for the Middle East in September 1940. Based in Palestine, he ensured that every signals unit in the corps was trained to the highest standards, militarily and technically. During the Greek campaign (April 1941) he did his best with scant resources. His own radio receiver, housed in a packing case for kerosene cans, provided news from the British Broadcasting Corporation on 15 April that Yugoslavia had sought an armistice with Germany, thereby exposing the Anzac Corps' left flank. Thus warned by Simpson, Blamey took measures to meet the new danger before official notification was received two days later. Simpson was appointed C.B.E. (1941) for his work in Greece.

Back in Palestine, I Corps headquarters took command of the invasion of Lebanon and Syria, launched on 8 June. The operation involved Australian, Indian and Free French forces moving over three main routes, on a wide front, in difficult terrain. As C.S.O., Simpson solved the numerous communications problems that arose. For his services between February and July 1941 he was mentioned in dispatches. In September he was injured in an accident and incapacitated for four months. On the 11th of that month, while in hospital, he was promoted temporary brigadier—the first officer in the Australian Corps of Signals to achieve that rank. He was evacuated to Australia in November. Even during his convalescence he made arrangements to improve the training of signals reinforcements.

In January 1942 Simpson joined a team of senior officers, from I Corps headquarters, in Java, Netherlands East Indies. They consulted General Sir Archibald (Earl) Wavell, the newly appointed supreme commander of the Australian-British-Dutch-American Command, about the deteriorating situation that followed Japan's entry into the war. Faced with the continued success of the Japanese offensive, I Corps headquarters was withdrawn to Australia. Simpson reached Adelaide on 14 March.

Appointed commander-in-chief, Blamey chose Simpson as the army's signals officer-in-chief and promoted him major general on 6 April 1942. Acting with drive and determination, Simpson expanded the signals component of the army to over 25 000 personnel (including large numbers of women) to meet the demands of the war. He formed the signals intelligence organization, which yielded valuable information about enemy intentions; he made further provision for communicating with aircraft supporting ground forces; and he integrated women into an extensive fixed-communication-system.

The close relationship between Blamey and Simpson was based on mutual respect. It has been said that Simpson was Blamey's 'eyes and ears'—a quasi inspector-general. Simpson was kept constantly aware of Blamey's thinking. In his frequent visits to formations and units, Simpson inquired into matters of fundamental interest to the commander-in-chief, and reported in detail by semi-official letter, telephone, or face to face.

In the course of his wartime duties, Simpson travelled widely, visiting outlying camps, and making trips to Britain and the United States of America. The pace took its toll and he spent at least three terms in hospital. After the war ended in August 1945, the tasks of demobilization, the repatriation of troops and prisoners of war, the return of equipment from overseas, and the organization of an occu-

pation force in Japan all demanded a continuing, flexible and effective communication service. Simpson fixed his attention on these problems until he was placed on the Reserve of Officers on 8 November 1946. Blamey had recommended in October 1945 that Simpson be appointed C.B. Like a number of his recommendations, this one was not approved by the government.

In the postwar years Simpson was involved (1947-52) in another secret army, 'The Association', which came into being to counter a possible communist coup. Blamey was its titular leader, Simpson its main organizer. He resumed his role as a pharmacist and a director of A.M.C.A.L. In addition to supporting the Carry On clubs in Victoria, he was president of the Australian Legion of Ex-Servicemen and Women, and colonel commandant (1958-63) of the Royal Australian Corps of Signals. He barracked for the Essendon football team.

Simpson died of cancer on 23 August 1964 in the Repatriation General Hospital, Heidelberg, and was buried in St Kilda cemetery. His wife and their daughter survived him; their son had died in infancy. Geoffrey Mainwaring's portrait of Simpson is held by the Defence Communications Training Centre, Watsonia.

Members of the Australian Corps of Signals, *Signals* (Canb, 1944); J. Hetherington, *Blamey* (Canb, 1973); D. Horner, *Crisis of Command* (Canb, 1978) and *High Command* (Syd, 1982) and *Blamey* (Syd, 1998); T. Barker, *Signals* (Melb, 1987); G. Haines, *A History of Pharmacy in Victoria* (Melb, 1994); C. Coulthard-Clark, *Soldiers in Politics* (Syd, 1996); A367, item C94121 (NAA, Canb); information from Maj Gen R. P. Woollard, Kingston, Canb, Mr A. W. Sandbach, Canterbury, Melb, Mr I. K. Wallis, Wurruk, and Prof R. L. Wallis, Warrnambool, Vic.

J. WHITELAW

SIMPSON, DOROTHY MARY KELL; *see* FINNIS

SIMPSON, EDWARD TELFORD (1889-1965), solicitor and company director, was born on 13 March 1889 at Double Bay, Sydney, second of four children and only son of native-born parents Edward Percy Simpson [q.v.11], solicitor, and his wife Anne Maria Alexandra Guerry, daughter of the Marquis de Lauret. Helen Simpson [q.v.11] was his sister. Telford grew up at St Mervyns, his parents' home at Double Bay, and attended W. A. Inman's preparatory school at Rose Bay.

In 1900 he was sent to Barker College, Hornsby. On his doctor's orders his luggage included a case of port, as he was considered a sickly child. Simpson's activities soon dispelled fears of serious illness: he became a prefect, and an accomplished footballer, cricketer and rower. He entered St Paul's College, University of Sydney (B.A., 1911; LL.B., 1914), and was admitted as a solicitor on 6 May 1915. Determined to serve in World War I, he sailed to London, trained as a pilot in the Royal Flying Corps and obtained his commission on 17 March 1917. He logged nearly seven hundred flying hours while posted (September 1917-July 1918) to No.52 Squadron on the Western Front. In March 1918 he was promoted temporary captain and in September was awarded the French Croix de Guerre (avec palme). He was demobilized from the air force on 21 August 1919.

Back home, Simpson—who had been admitted to partnership at Minter, Simpson & Co. in 1916, while on active service—practised with the firm from 1919 until his retirement in 1960. He was a founder (1920) and committee-member of the State section of the Australian Aero Club and an organizer of the first Aerial Derby flown at Mascot aerodrome in November 1920. At St Mark's Church of England, Darling Point, on 21 November 1921 he married Edith Ursula Hammond Catterall. Shortly afterwards they built their home on the Cranbrook estate, Bellevue Hill.

Like his father, but without the same influence, Simpson took an interest in public affairs, mixed in conservative political circles, chaired (1936-41) the National Consultative Council and supported various anti-communist causes. A friend of (Sir) Robert Menzies [q.v.15], he corresponded with business and political leaders to further the cause of the United Australia Party.

In 1934 Simpson bought Newbury, a property at Sutton Forest, where he established a Southdown flock and enjoyed family holidays. As founder and first president (1952-62) of the New South Wales Southdown Stud Breeders' Association, he was a familiar competitor in the show-ring, wearing his beret and leggings. On one occasion he was so incensed at losing a championship (because his ram's muzzle lacked the required mouse colour) that he sent a pinned-out mouse-skin to the judge.

Simpson was sometime chairman of directors of Northern Collieries Ltd, Richardson & Wrench Ltd, Australian Paper Manufacturers Ltd and Mort's [q.v.5] Dock & Engineering Co. Ltd. Playing a prominent role on these boards, he expressed views in letters to the *Sydney Morning Herald*, particularly criticizing excessive wartime regulations and control of real estate. He chaired the difficult shareholders' meeting that followed the closure of the historic dock in November 1958, after years of strikes by the Building Workers' Industrial Union of Australia and heavy financial losses.

A short man with a friendly disposition, though liable to peppery outbursts, Simpson was a witty raconteur who enjoyed writing doggerel. His reverence for old families prompted him to trace his ancestry in France and England, and his love of Australian history led him to collect paintings by Conrad Martens [q.v.2]. He belonged to the Union, Australian Jockey, Royal Sydney Golf and Melbourne clubs. Simpson died on 11 May 1965 in his home at Potts Point and was cremated. His wife and their two sons, both solicitors with Minter, Simpson & Co., survived him. John St Helier Lander's portrait (1919) of Simpson in the uniform of the Royal Flying Corps is held by the family.

G. N. Griffiths, *Point Piper, Past and Present* (Syd, 1947) and *Some Southern Homes of New South Wales* (Syd, 1952); Minter, Simpson & Co., *One Hundred and Fifty Years of Law, 1827-1977* (Canb, 1977); A. Moore, *The Secret Army and the Premier* (Syd, 1989); *College Barker*, 1911, 1913-14, 1916 and 1922; *SMH*, 29 Aug 1951, 19 Dec 1956, 16, 19 Nov 1957, 6 Nov, 17 Dec 1958; Minter, Simpson & Co., Letterbooks (ML); family papers (held by Mr E. P. T. Simpson, Bellevue Hill, Syd); information from Mr K. McIntosh, Laggan, NSW.   CAROLINE SIMPSON

SIMPSON, GEORGE (1899-1960), obstetrician and gynaecologist, was born on 14 May 1899 at Clifton, near Hamilton, Victoria, third of six children of Archibald Joseph Simpson, grazier, and his wife Mary, née Robertson, both Victorian born. George's grandfather had been a moderator of the Presbyterian Church of Victoria, and the boy came under the spiritual influence of two other Presbyterian ministers, Andrew Barber and John Flynn [qq.v.7,8]. While boarding at Scotch College, Melbourne, he began a lifelong association with the family of the headmaster, W. S. Littlejohn [q.v.10].

After graduating from the University of Melbourne (M.B., B.S., 1922) in tenth place in a medical class which included (Dame) Jean Macnamara, (Sir) Roy Cameron [qq.v.10,13], (Professor) Rupert Willis [q.v.], (Sir) Macfarlane Burnet and (Dame) Kate Campbell, Simpson held residencies at the Melbourne and Children's hospitals. He travelled to Britain and qualified as a member (1926) of the Royal College of Physicians, London. A residency at Queen Charlotte's Maternity Hospital and further study at the Rotunda Hospital, Dublin, drew him to specialize in obstetrics and gynaecology.

In 1927 Simpson returned to Melbourne. He obtained a diploma of gynaecology and obstetrics (1933) from the university, and became a member (1935) and fellow (1951) of the British (Royal) College of Obstetricians and Gynaecologists. At Holy Trinity Church, Kew, on 18 May 1931 he married with Anglican rites Nesta Cecil Annie Miller. Next year he joined the honorary staff of the (Royal) Women's Hospital. Appointed flight lieutenant, Royal Australian Air Force Reserve, on 25 November 1940, he served full time in 1942-44 with medical units at Daly Waters, Northern Territory, and Heidelberg, Melbourne, and rose to squadron leader.

Simpson's boyhood spiritual mentor, Flynn, had asked him in 1927 to be medical adviser to the Australian Inland Mission. That year Simpson and Barber undertook a three-month survey by motorcar of the medical needs of the outback. Their report convinced the A.I.M.'s councillors to authorize in 1928 experimental flights for what became the Aerial Medical Service (Royal Flying Doctor Service of Australia). Simpson remained close to its administration for the rest of his life and presided over the federal council in 1947.

The A.M.S. was the first of a series of commitments which Simpson made to outreach-medicine for those denied professional care, either by distance or poverty. In 1930 he was appointed honorary obstetrician to the antenatal department of the Melbourne District Nursing Society (Service), the only provider of home midwifery to the poor. Over the next thirty-two years, until it was disbanded in 1952 due to the wholesale move to hospital births, the midwifery service delivered 7617 babies, with the loss of only five mothers. With Dr (Dame) Mary Herring and Dr Victor Wallace [q.v.], Simpson succeeded in 1934 in persuading the M.D.N.S. to open the Women's Welfare Clinic, Melbourne's first birth-control centre. He was a serving brother (from 1936) of the Order of St John of Jerusalem and secretary (from 1945) of the Victorian Bush Nursing Association.

Driven by a deep compassion for women, Simpson was a gifted clinician who championed home midwifery and argued for judicious intervention at a time when many doctors trusted almost everything to nature. He was an elder of the Presbyterian Church and lived his faith daily. In 1957 he was appointed O.B.E. Nesta supported his outreach-work, and served as president of the M.D.N.S. in 1952-64. Simpson died of haematemesis on 24 November 1960 in East Melbourne and was cremated; his wife and their two daughters survived him.

N. Rosenthal, *People—Not Cases* (Melb, 1974); *Walkabout*, Jan 1963, p 35; Simpson papers, Archives of Roy Aust and NZ College of Obstetricians and Gynaecologists, East Melb.   JANET MCCALMAN

SIMPSON, HUGH LESLIE (1894-1968), farmer and soldier-settlement administrator, was born on 3 October 1894 at Birchip, Victoria, son of Albert Edward Simpson (d.1905), bookseller, and his wife Ellen, née Campbell, both Victorian born. Educated at Birchip State, Ballarat Agricultural High and Stawell High schools, Les worked on the family farm. On 30 June 1915 he enlisted in the Australian Imperial Force. He served on the Western Front with the 5th Battalion from March 1916 and was severely wounded in August 1918. Lieutenant Simpson's A.I.F. appointment terminated in Victoria on 21 August 1919.

He resumed farming, at Birchip and Berriwillock. On 1 March 1924 at All Saints Church, St Kilda, he married Barbara Catherine Jane Catto, a nurse. As chief president of the Victorian Wheatgrowers' Association (1934-35) and the Australian Wheatgrowers' Federation (1935-36), he campaigned for farmers to control the marketing of their product. Simpson joined the Returned Sailors' and Soldiers' Imperial League of Australia, served as a Wycheproof shire councillor (1932-46), led the United Country Party as chief president (1938-40 and 1944) and stood unsuccessfully for the Legislative Assembly seat of Walhalla in 1943.

In 1935-46 Simpson was a member (chairman 1941-46) of the Victorian Farmers' Debts Adjustment Board. During World War II he was an adviser (1942-44) to the Federal prices commissioner (Sir) Douglas Copland [q.v.13] and (in 1944-46) was one of the Federal treasurer J. B. Chifley's [q.v.13] delegates for the control of land sales. On 13 February 1946 John Cain's [q.v.13] State Labor government appointed him chairman of the new Soldier Settlement Commission.

A wily political operator, Simpson persuaded the government to allow the S.S.C. to engage and dismiss its staff independently of the Public Service Board. The commission chose good quality land and capable farmers. Property valuations were written down and generous loan-repayment terms were established—1 per cent of capital and 2 per cent interest over 55 years. Simpson insisted that these measures were vital to allow soldier settlers to pay their debts and to enable them to survive the inevitable tough periods. At the same time, the S.S.C. controlled farmers' borrowings to prevent them from over-extending themselves. One Robinvale settler, expressing a general view, said that the commission 'stopped us going bust'.

Simpson was determined that the social and economic disaster of soldier settlement in Victoria after World War I should never be repeated, for the sake of taxpayers as well as ex-servicemen. Largely due to his shrewd planning and the S.S.C.'s tight administration, the Victorian scheme that followed World War II succeeded. Some six thousand ex-servicemen were placed on farms; 96 per cent of them eventually owned their properties.

A staunch member of the Presbyterian Church, Simpson believed in hard work and thrift, and in the individual's responsibility to the community. In 1963, the year of his retirement, he was appointed C.B.E. A widower, he died on 7 June 1968 in his home at Hampton, Melbourne, and was cremated. His two daughters and three sons survived him. A township near Cobden was named after him.

R. Smallwood, *Hard to go Bung* (Melb, 1992), and for sources; information from Mrs J. Garrow, Brighton East, Melb, and Mr H. Brown, Robinvale, Vic.   ROSALIND SMALLWOOD

SIMPSON, NOEL WILLIAM (1907-1971), bank inspector and army officer, was born on 22 February 1907 at Balmain, Sydney, younger of twin sons of Harry Simpson, a Sydney-born orchardist, and his wife Annie Cecilia, née Thomas, who came from New Zealand. Noel attended North Sydney Boys' High School and began work with the National Bank of Australasia Ltd on 27 December 1922. A member (from 1925) of the Militia, he was commissioned lieutenant in March 1926 and promoted captain in August 1930. By November 1939 he was a temporary major in the 45th Battalion.

On 1 May 1940 Simpson transferred to the 2nd/13th Battalion, Australian Imperial Force, as second-in-command. Within five days, however, he was attached to the headquarters of the 20th Brigade. Embarking for the Middle East in October, he joined the staff of the 7th Division in January 1941 and became deputy assistant adjutant-general two months later. In June-July he took part in the Syrian campaign. At Latakia, in March 1942, he was promoted lieutenant colonel and given command of the 2nd/17th Battalion. He acquired the nickname 'Red Fox' from the emblem painted on his Bren-gun carrier. Under his direction the battalion carried out intensive training until July when it moved to Egypt. During the battle of El Alamein, which began on the night of 23 October, the 2nd/17th secured its objectives and, despite considerable casualties, withstood strong counter-attacks by enemy tanks and infantry. For his outstanding leadership Simpson was awarded the Distinguished Service Order.

Arriving back in Australia in February 1943, the men of the 2nd/17th were trained in amphibious warfare in Queensland and at Milne Bay, Papua. In September they landed in New Guinea, first at Lae and then at Finschhafen, both held by the Japanese. During the advance along the Huon Peninsula, Simpson continued to lead the battalion, despite a wound to his scalp, sustained at Finschhafen. His skill in command was again evident in

October when the unit inflicted heavy casualties on the enemy in the Kumawa area and, for seventeen days, successfully defended Jivevenang ridge, a position vital to future operations against Sattelberg. He won a Bar to his D.S.O.

From November 1943 Simpson administered command, in turn, of the 24th and of the 20th brigades before rejoining the 2nd/17th in January 1944. Next month he was posted to the 2nd/43rd Battalion, which he zealously retrained in Queensland. Made temporary brigadier and given command of the 29th Brigade in March 1945, he took it to Bougainville that month. The 29th was scheduled to relieve the 15th Brigade in July and to secure the line of the Mivo River, but torrential rain delayed the operation until August, the month in which World War II ended. In reviewing the operations on Bougainville, Simpson criticized officers who had questioned the need for the campaign. Transferred to the 23rd Brigade in November, he was placed on the Reserve of Officers on 15 May 1946 and mentioned in dispatches in 1947.

Simpson returned to the National Bank. Active in the Citizen Military Forces, he commanded the 6th Brigade (1953-58) and the 3rd Division (1959-60), the latter as temporary major general. He was appointed C.B.E. in 1956 and C.B. in 1963. From 1960 to 1962 he represented the C.M.F. on the Military Board. He retired from the army on 23 February 1964. After almost ten years as an assistant-inspector, he retired from the National Bank in 1966.

Five ft 9 ins (175 cm) tall, with a fair complexion, blue eyes and fair hair, Simpson was physically fit and energetic, though not robust in appearance. He was an intelligent and articulate officer whose directions were precise and unambiguous. Well versed in the doctrines of desert and jungle warfare, he adopted training programmes that brought success in operations. Although he was a strong disciplinarian who showed no tolerance of inefficient officers, he was compassionate and knew when to relieve those under sustained battle-stress. He was highly regarded by his seniors, as well as by his own officers and men. When he was about to take over command of the 2nd/43rd Battalion, his soldiers said: 'You can borrow him for training . . . but let's have him back when we go into action'.

Simpson died of myocardial infarction on 18 November 1971 at the Repatriation General Hospital, Heidelberg, Melbourne, and was cremated with Anglican rites. His twin, Major Grosvenor Harry Simpson, was killed at Anzio, Italy, on 31 May 1944 while serving with the British Army.

G. H. Fearnside (ed), *Bayonets Abroad* (Syd, 1953); D. Dexter, *The New Guinea Offensives* (Canb,

1961); G. Long, *The Final Campaigns* (Canb, 1963); B. Maughan, *Tobruk and El Alamein* (Canb, 1966); G. Combe et al, *The Second 43rd Australian Infantry Battalion 1940-1946* (Adel, 1972); *'What We Have—We Hold!'* (Syd, 1998); J. Coates, *Bravery Above Blunder* (Melb, 1999); *SMH*, 19 Nov 1971; information from Maj Gen J. R. Broadbent, Lindfield, and Lt Cols R. S. Rudkin, Maianbar, Syd, and A. C. Newton, Dickson, Canb.   R. SUTTON

SIMPSON, RAYENE STEWART (1926-1978), soldier, was born on 16 February 1926 at Redfern, Sydney, third child of New South Wales-born parents Robert William Simpson, labourer, and his wife Olga Maude, née Montgomery. Olga deserted her husband and children about 1931. Ray was separated from his siblings and placed in the Church of England Home for Boys, Carlingford. Educated at a local school and at Dumaresq Island Public School, Taree, he worked as a labourer.

On 15 March 1944 Simpson enlisted in the Australian Imperial Force. He served on Morotai, and at Tarakan, Borneo, and Rabaul, New Guinea, and was demobilized on 20 January 1947 in Sydney. After taking various jobs, he joined the Australian Regular Army in January 1951. Five months later he was sent to Korea as a reinforcement for the 3rd Battalion, Royal Australian Regiment. On 16 January 1953 at Kure, Japan, he married Shoko Sakai, a divorcee. Next month he was promoted temporary sergeant. Returning to Australia in April 1954, he served with the 2nd Battalion, R.A.R., in Malaya (1955-57), then with the 1st Special Air Service Company, near Perth. In July 1962, promoted warrant officer, class two, he flew to Saigon for duty with the Australian Army Training Team Vietnam.

Home again from July 1963, Simpson left for a second tour with the A.A.T.T.V. twelve months later. Based at Tako, he accompanied South Vietnamese patrols in the country's north-west. On 16 September 1964 his patrol was ambushed by soldiers of the People's Liberation Armed Forces (Viet Cong). Although severely wounded in the right leg, he rallied his men and led them in repelling repeated assaults until help arrived. For this action he was awarded the Distinguished Conduct Medal. After recovering in a military hospital in Tokyo, he came back to Australia in June 1965. He was posted to the 1st Commando Regiment, Sydney, in January 1966, but was discharged from the army (at his own request) in May. Deciding to rejoin the A.R.A., he made his way to Saigon where, in May 1967, he enlisted and was reappointed to the A.A.T.T.V.

On 6 May 1969 Simpson commanded a Montagnard company during an operation near the Laos-Cambodia border. When the leading platoon came under heavy fire, he led the remainder of the company to its assistance. He dashed forward, reached a fellow-Australian adviser who had been wounded, and carried him to safety. Having tried unsuccessfully to subdue the enemy position with grenades, he covered the withdrawal of his company while still carrying his wounded colleague. In further fighting on 11 May he organized the rescue of wounded men trapped by enemy fire, placing himself between them and the enemy until the withdrawal was completed. For his bravery in both actions he was awarded the Victoria Cross.

Simpson's character was complex. At times he was diffident in company, at others direct and blunt. He was tough, fit and dependable, but also rude, mischievous and exasperating. A proud, moral and compassionate man who was devoted to his wife, he was completely free of pretension and had simple material needs. He was well read in tactics and military history, as indicated by his infantry skills. His colourful language was legendary.

'Simmo' was discharged from the army on 4 May 1970. He obtained an administrative post in the Australian Embassy, Tokyo. Survived by his wife, he died of cancer on 18 October 1978 at the University of Tokyo medical clinic and was cremated. The Australian War Memorial, Canberra, holds his medals and his portrait by Joshua Smith.

I. McNeill, *The Team* (Canb, 1984); L. Wigmore (ed), *They Dared Mightily*, 2nd edn, revised and condensed by J. Williams and A. Staunton (Canb, 1986); D. M. Horner, *SAS* (Syd, 1989); J. L. Menadue, funeral eulogy (1978), copy held by author; information from Mrs J. Fletcher, Green Point, NSW.
          BRIAN KELLY

SIMPSON, WILLIAM BALLANTYNE (1894-1966), army officer, director-general of security and judge, was born on 12 June 1894 at Balmain, Sydney, eldest child of William Morrison Simpson, a Queensland-born solicitor, and his wife Margaret McBride, née McNeill, who came from Scotland. Young Bill was educated at Fort Street Model (Boys' High) School and the University of Sydney (LL.B., 1920). Having been commissioned in the Militia in 1914, he interrupted his studies to enlist in the Australian Imperial Force on 11 December 1916. He served as a driver in the 11th Field Company, Engineers, on the Western Front from January 1918 and returned to Australia in April 1919. On 18 May he was discharged from the A.I.F.

· Admitted to the New South Wales Bar on 6 May 1920, Simpson specialized in cases concerning motor-vehicle accidents, sometimes using model cars to demonstrate his arguments in court. He joined the National Party and in 1922-25 unsuccessfully contested three State and Federal elections. At Scots Church, Sydney, on 8 July 1925 he married with Presbyterian forms Dorothy Margaret Peel Blackley.

A legal officer in the Militia from 1922, Simpson rose to lieutenant colonel in 1928. He was seconded to the A.I.F. as a temporary brigadier on 17 February 1941 and made deputy judge advocate-general of the A.I.F. in the Middle East. Back in Australia in June 1942, he became D.J.A.G. at Land Headquarters, Melbourne. On 23 September he succeeded W. J. MacKay [q.v.10] as director-general of security. As head of the Commonwealth Security Service, based in Canberra, he was answerable to the attorney-general H. V. Evatt [q.v.14] of whom he was 'a school and university associate'. He was responsible for investigating subversive and pacifist individuals and organizations, detecting and averting espionage, preventing sabotage and harmful rumours, vetting defence personnel and workers in defence-related industries, controlling the issue of passports and visas, and ensuring the security of airports, wharves, and factories engaged in war production. In addition, he identified enemy aliens for internment and exercised control over their release.

The recently formed C.S.S. was subject to intense interdepartmental jealousy and critics in the army complained that Simpson 'pulled rank' as an army officer when it suited him and at other times emphasized that he ran a civilian organization. He overcame the personnel problems that had troubled his predecessor, but his task was made more difficult by MacKay's removal of policemen and files from the service when he had left office. At the end of 1942 Simpson established an organizations section, led by J. C. G. Kevin [q.v.15], to make informed predictions about the activities of various groups in Australia. By mid-1943 Kevin had eight hundred organizations on his files, but a few months later reported to Simpson 'the unpalatable fact' that the C.S.S. had been 'unable to locate one known enemy agent or one major instance of sabotage'. Faced with other critical reports within the service, Simpson centralized the work of counter-espionage, established a group of special investigators and drastically reduced the secretarial staff.

Simpson was also responsible for radio security measures in Australia. He took direct control of the 1st Discrimination Unit, formed in February 1944, which examined all intercepted radio traffic within the country. No Japanese agents were discovered broadcasting from Australia. On 16 November Simpson transferred to the Reserve of Officers, but remained director-general as a civilian.

Late in 1944 the army and the security service learned that top-level information was being leaked to the Japanese. In January 1945 Simpson was briefed in general terms on 'Ultra' intelligence (received by the interception and deciphering of Japanese radio traffic) which revealed that the sources of the leaks were a Chinese liaison officer and the Soviet legation. To maintain the secrecy of Ultra, however, he was instructed to take no action. Instead, he produced a report in June on the Communist Party of Australia, in which he warned of the dangers it posed to democracy.

On 23 October 1945 Simpson resigned as director-general of security. Next day he was appointed sole judge of the Supreme Court of the Australian Capital Territory. He was conscientious and respected; lawyers enjoyed appearing before him. From 1946 he was also judge advocate-general of the army and air force, in which capacity he advised on the findings of war crimes tribunals and made recommendations concerning sentences. He chaired (1947-48) a committee inquiring into the cost of producing wheat in Australia, presided (1948) over a court of inquiry into the crash of the DC-3 airliner *Lutana* and served as judge of the Supreme Court of Norfolk Island.

Of middle height, thickset and jowly, Simpson suffered from Parkinson's disease during his later years. He retired due to ill health on 30 April 1960 and moved to Sydney. His recreations included gardening and reading. Survived by his wife and their two sons, he died on 24 November 1966 at Marrickville and was cremated.

F. Cain, *The Origins of Political Surveillance in Australia* (Syd, 1983); M. Bevege, *Behind Barbed Wire* (Brisb, 1993); D. Ball and D. Horner, *Breaking the Codes* (Syd, 1998); J. Thomson, *Winning with Intelligence* (Syd, 2000); *Defence Force J*, no 16, May-June 1979, p 23; *SMH*, 29 Nov 1922, 19 Sept 1942, 25 Nov 1945, 11, 29 Mar, 27 Aug 1946, 15 Sept, 20, 25 Nov 1948, 25 Nov 1966; *Canb Times*, 25 Nov 1966; C. Pappas, Law and Politics: Australia's War Crimes Trials in the Pacific, 1943-1961 (Ph.D. thesis, Univ NSW, 1998); Royal Commission on Intelligence and Security, 7th Report, vol 1, 1977, series A8908 (NAA, Canb); information from the Hon R. Else-Mitchell, Duffy, Mr R. G. Bailey, Yarralumla, Canb, and the Hon J. F. Gallop, Queanbeyan, NSW.

JOLYON HORNER

SINCLAIR, FRANK ROY (1892-1965), public servant, was born on 6 December 1892 at Nurrabiel, near Horsham, Victoria, eleventh child of Alexander Sinclair, a clerk from Scotland, and his English-born wife Mary Ann, née Featherby. Educated at the local state school and the Continuation School, Melbourne, Frank joined the Department of Defence as a junior clerk in 1910. He worked initially in the correspondence section and later the finance branch. At the Methodist Church, North Melbourne, on 15 September 1917 he married

Louisa May Pearce (d.1946); they were to have six children.

Sinclair rose to accountant (army) in 1929 and became secretary of the Defence Committee in 1937. Promoted assistant-secretary in March 1938, he served on the secretariat of the War Cabinet and the Advisory War Council in 1940, and acted as head of the department in January-May 1941 while (Sir) Frederick Shedden [q.v.] was abroad. On 21 August 1941 Sinclair was appointed secretary of the Department of the Army. As head of a service department in wartime, he carried heavy responsibilities and proved an effective and shrewd adviser to his ministers F. M. Forde and J. M. Fraser [q.v.14]. In periodic disputes with the military staff he strictly insisted on civilian oversight of departmental administration: 'command' lay unarguably in the hands of the commander-in-chief General Sir Thomas Blamey [q.v.13], but 'control'— with its political, financial and administrative implications—continued to be the responsibility of the minister and his departmental secretary.

For its part, the army warned Sinclair of the gravity of civil interference in operational matters. His advocacy in December 1941 of guerrilla warfare in the event of a Japanese invasion had been criticized as defeatist by the chief of the General Staff (Sir) Vernon Sturdee [q.v.]. The report Sinclair wrote (after a visit to New Guinea in October 1942) which detailed alleged army wastefulness was sternly rebutted by Blamey, who asked that his response be circulated to members of the War Cabinet. None the less, Sinclair proved a highly capable defence administrator who handled the difficulties of wartime army staff with care and effectiveness.

After World War II ended, Sinclair set out to devise an effective modern administration for the army. He still challenged aspects of military policy, but (Sir) Sydney Rowell [q.v.], vice-chief and later chief of the General Staff, readily acknowledged his support and help. Sinclair also retained the confidence and respect of his postwar ministers Cyril Chambers and (Sir) Josiah Francis [qq.v.13,14].

On 19 May 1950 at St Cuthbert's Presbyterian Church, Brighton, Melbourne, Sinclair married Joan Marie Robinson, a 33-year-old teacher. In 1952 he was appointed C.B.E. Robust in build, and gifted with a warm and friendly nature, he was a keen cricketer and an active participant in public-service social functions. Towards the end of his life he took up bowls. On 29 January 1955 ill health forced him to resign as secretary; he remained on the unattached list until his formal retirement in April 1956.

Sinclair died on 21 March 1965 at Avoca Beach, New South Wales, and was cremated. His wife, and the three daughters and one of the three sons of his first marriage survived him.

J. A. Hetherington, *Blamey* (Melb, 1954); D. M. Horner, *Blamey* (Syd, 1998); *SMH*, 18 Mar 1938, 6 Aug 1941, 12 June 1946, 14 Jan 1955; *Age* (Melb), 23 Mar 1965; A5954, item 70/5 (NAA, Canb); information from Mr and Mrs A. Salisbury, Campbell, Miss F. Whelan, Weston, Canb, and Mrs S. O'Connor, Mansfield, Vic.   ROBERT HYSLOP

SINGH, DAYAL (1901-1962), engineering contractor, was born on 1 July 1901 at Wyrallah, New South Wales, only child of Indian-born parents Diyal Singh, farmer, and his wife Patapa, née Singh (d.1924). Among the first Indian families to settle in the Richmond River district, the Singhs moved to Lismore about 1904. Diyal gradually gave up market gardening for building. He was an experienced carpenter, having worked for Lewis Jones & Co. on the Assam-Bengal Railway. Despite efforts to deny Indian-born British subjects the vote, his name was entered on the Commonwealth electoral roll in 1906 and his wife's in 1909. Young Dayal attended Lismore Public School, then joined his father as a carpenter—building glasshouses, cow bails, cottages and schoolhouses. A motorbike enthusiast, he won the North Coast Motor Cycle Club's 100-mile (161 km) reliability trial at the age of 21. On 21 June 1924, against her father's wishes, he married Ethel Agnes Vidler at St Andrew's Church of England, Lismore.

Diyal Singh moved to Tenterfield in 1931, leaving his son to run Diyal Singh & Son. Dayal expanded the joinery and developed other interests. Exempted from military service because he was a diabetic, he undertook building contracts at the Royal Australian Air Force base at Evans Head during World War II. He had an inventive nature, kept a notebook and pen by his bed to jot down ideas, and designed a hole-digger for transmission poles.

On 1 July 1951 he established Dayal Singh Transmissions Pty Ltd (transmission lines), Dayal Singh Constructions Pty Ltd (civil engineering) and Dayal Singh Pty Ltd (joinery works). He set up Dayal Singh Tyre Service Pty Ltd (tyre-retreading) in 1954 and later acquired a ready-mixed concrete plant. Major public-works contracts completed under his direction included an earth dam at Rocky Creek for Lismore's water supply, the Dungowan Dam for Tamworth, wharves in the Territory of Papua and New Guinea, and sixty miles (97 km) of road in the Northern Territory. In 1962 Dayal Singh Constructions was engaged in building a lift-span bridge where the Pacific Highway crosses the Richmond River at Wardell, at a cost of more than £360 000.

After attending an open-air meeting conducted by John Ridley, a Baptist evangelist, in October 1929 at Lismore, Singh had become a Christian. For three decades the Baptist Church benefited from his initiative and industry; at different times he served as deacon, treasurer and cemetery trustee. In 1955 he and his wife attended the Baptist World Congress in London, following which they visited the Punjab, India, in an unsuccessful search for family connexions. Five years later the large family house of his youth at 136 Orion Street, Lismore, became a rest home for the aged. He was a member of the Northern Rivers Aero Club, the Rotary Club of Lismore, and the North Coast National Agricultural and Industrial Society.

Singh died of a cerebral haemorrhage on 3 October 1962 at Lismore hospital and was buried with Baptist forms in the local cemetery; his wife, and their son and three daughters survived him. An obituarist described him as 'one of Lismore's great citizens'. A memorial window in the Baptist chapel at Evans Head bears witness to his faith.

Goodyear News, Feb-Mar 1963; Richmond River Hist Soc, *Bulletin*, Dec 1993; *Northern Star* (Lismore), 12, 19 Oct 1929, 5, 6 Oct 1962; *Northern Daily Leader*, 5 Oct 1962; Singh papers (Richmond River Hist Soc, Lismore); information from Dr R. Bingle, Mill Hill, Lond, Mr R. Gower, Lismore, Mrs L. S. Kyle, Tregeagle, NSW, and the late Mr F. Wiltshire.

ANNETTE POTTS

SISSONS, ALFRED THOMAS STANLEY (1888-1975), chemist and college dean, was born on 22 April 1888 at Malvern, Melbourne, second son of Victorian-born parents Alfred Francis Sissons, a draper who became a builder and real-estate agent, and his wife Annie, née Stanley. Young Stanley grew up at Brunswick. Educated at Moreland State School, at Thomas Palmer's [q.v.11] University High School, and at the Continuation School, he began teaching in 1907. He attended (1908-09) the Melbourne Training College (where he was Gladman [q.v.4] prize-winner), joined (1910) the staff of the new University Practising (University High) School and studied at the University of Melbourne (B.Sc., Dip.Ed., 1915). At Scots Church, Melbourne, on 15 September 1916 he married with Presbyterian forms Jessie Taylor Tope, a public servant.

That year Sissons was granted leave to take a post as a research chemist with the British government's cordite-production complex at Gretna, Scotland. In 1920, after returning to Melbourne, he was appointed director of studies (retitled dean in 1937) at the College of Pharmacy, Swanston Street. The college was owned and operated by the Pharmaceuti-

cal Society of Australasia, as Victorian pharmacists then proudly styled their professional body. Sissons was one of the few full-time staff and soon won the respect of his employers.

Working closely with Byron Stanton [q.v.], the college's lecturer in materia medica, Sissons made innovative changes to the curriculum. In 1928 he added biology and practical botany. Eight years later he redesigned the course around a four-year apprenticeship. The change reflected developments in pharmaceutical chemistry (especially the advent of 'sulpha-drugs'), provided for 'postgraduate' studies leading to a fellowship of the pharmaceutical society, and included lessons in the history of pharmacy. Sissons' curriculum was recognized as a model for education in pharmacy. From 1960 the college provided a three-year, full-time course.

In 1939 Sissons had been elected a fellow of the (Royal) Australian Chemical Institute. Through his efforts as science editor of the *Australasian Journal of Pharmacy*, and his help with various editions of *The Australian and New Zealand* (later *Australian*) *Pharmaceutical Formulary*, he did much to raise the scientific standing of the profession. He was a member of Stanton's group which compiled an emergency formulary and a war pharmacopoeia for the Medical Equipment Control Committee during World War II. The team worked in the evenings—often until after midnight—and Sissons trudged home in the brownouts to sleep before the next day's classes.

Sissons helped to transform pharmacy from a hand-me-down craft to a practice which used, and responded to, the latest scientific developments. One of the founders of the pharmaceutical science section of the Australasian (Australian and New Zealand) Association for the Advancement of Science, he presided over that section at A.N.Z.A.A.S.'s 1946 congress in Adelaide. He suggested that, as Britain's strong organic-chemical industry was founded on coal tar and America's on petroleum, Australia might base a similar industry on the alcohols. The potential of radioactive chemistry excited him, as did discoveries in organic chemistry (especially the adaptations of the phenanthrene ring) which were beginning to influence medicine.

Perhaps Sissons' most enduring legacy was as a teacher. 'A. T. S.' (or 'Sisso') and Jessie were beloved by many students. The couple attended the weddings and reunions of former pupils, kept scrapbooks recording their careers, and sent parcels to those on active service in wartime. Following his retirement in 1962, she spoke of their forty-two years at the college happily immersed in 'the stream of youth that we have been able to enjoy'. By then he had taught more than two-thirds of Victoria's practising pharmacists, seen several expansions of the college, and supervised its move to Royal Parade, Parkville, in 1960.

Sissons contributed articles on the history of pharmacy to the *Australasian Journal of Pharmacy*. His love of literature, especially the Romantics, influenced his historical writing, but not his scientific prose. A preference for Romanticism was also evident in his appreciation of music. Survived by his wife and their two sons, he died on 30 June 1975 at Griffith, Canberra, and was cremated. A mural by Leonard Annois [q.v.13] in the main hall of the College of Pharmacy, Monash University, commemorates his work. The college holds Laurence Pendlebury's portrait of Sissons.

G. Haines, *A History of Pharmacy in Victoria* (Melb, 1994); *Aust J of Pharmacy*, Aug 1975, p 461; *Procs of the Roy Aust Chemical Inst*, 42, no 9, Sept 1975, p 271; *Age* (Melb), 2 July 1975.

GREGORY HAINES

SKELTON, WALTER PEDEN JOYCE (1883-1979), railway officer and politician, was born on 28 March 1883 at Boggabri, New South Wales, ninth child of native-born parents John Skelton, railway fettler, and his wife Margaret, née Seckold. Walter attended Boggabri Public School and received a stern religious upbringing from his parents. In 1898 he followed his father into the New South Wales Government Railways and Tramways. At the Presbyterian manse, Hamilton, on 26 October 1904 he married Annie Porter Gray (d.1912); they were to have a son and four daughters.

Promoted to stationmaster in 1908, Skelton frequently moved with his family—to Matong (1911), Jerilderie (1912), Boggabri (1913), Carrathool (1916) and Cockle Creek (1919). He played Australian Rules football, joined the Jerilderie rifle club and became a member of the Loyal Orange Institution of New South Wales. On 8 March 1916 at the Methodist Church, Boggabri, he married Alexie Muriel Stewart.

In 1921 Skelton and fellow members of the New South Wales Protestant Federation were disturbed by the case of Sister Liguori [q.v.11 Partridge], 'the escaped nun'. They interpreted enforcement of the 1908 *ne temere* papal decree as 'declaring mixed marriages adulterous and the children illegitimate'. Skelton founded and presided over the Protestant Independent Labour Party. At the 1922 Legislative Assembly elections he topped the poll for the five-member Newcastle electorate (ahead of the chief Australian Labor Party candidate, J. M. Baddeley [q.v.7]). In parliament he vigorously supported free education and prohibition by referendum (without compensation for 'King Booze'). He frankly upheld the interests of all railwaymen and asked endless questions on their behalf. In 1924 he criticized the Catholic Church in debates over the marriage amendment [*ne temere*] bill, introduced by T. J. Ley [q.v.10]. Skelton was re-elected in 1925, but stood unsuccessfully—with the resumption of single-member seats—for Wallsend (1927) and Hamilton (1928), and for the Federal seat of Newcastle (1928 and 1931).

A justice of the peace (from 1925), Skelton was a member (1922-31) of the New South Wales Government Railways Superannuation Board. In Sydney in 1927 he helped to establish the Railway and Tramway Employees and Associates' Agency, which in 1930 combined with two trade unions to form the Railway Service Association (National Union of Railwaymen of New South Wales from 1933), of which he was general president (1930) and assistant-secretary (1931-46). In 1928 he had founded the *Agency*. He continued to edit and write the paper (renamed the *Railway Advocate*) for the N.U.R. until 1957. As a Railways and Tramways Appeals Board advocate, he appeared for hundreds of appellants and represented the union in arbitration courts in New South Wales, Victoria, South Australia and Tasmania. From 1946 to 1957 he was both general and State secretary of the N.U.R.

Skelton was an authorized Methodist lay preacher. He had attended the general conference of the Methodist Church of Australasia in 1923 and 1926. In addition to serving as grand master of the L.O.I. of New South Wales (1930-31) and of Australasia (1931-32), he was a Freemason, an Oddfellow, and treasurer (1969-76) of the New South Wales Prohibition Alliance. He launched and managed (1946-74) the Eventide Homes Appeal which built accommodation for aged pensioners. In 1962 he was appointed M.B.E. Ten years later he was named 'Senior Citizen of the Year'. He died on 21 May 1979 at Greenwich and was cremated; his wife and their three sons and three daughters survived him, as did two daughters of his first marriage.

PD (NSW), 12 July 1922, p 269, 21 Aug 1923, p 318; *Railway Advocate* (Syd), 20 June 1946, 20 Aug, 20 Nov, 20 Dec 1957, 20 Feb 1958, May-June 1979; *Newcastle Morning Herald*, 6, 27 Mar 1922, 24 May 1925; *SMH*, 22 Apr, 29 Sept 1922, 16 Dec 1931, 1 Jan 1962, 27 Oct 1972; W. P. J. Skelton, Autobiography (ms, 1970, NL); National Union of Railwaymen of Aust records (ANUABL); personal knowledge.

L. E. FREDMAN

SKEMP, JOHN ROWLAND (1900-1966), naturalist and social historian, was born on 2 July 1900 at Launceston, Tasmania, son of Benjamin Rowland Skemp, a farmer from England, and his native-born wife Florence, née Kearney, a descendant of Van Diemen's Land pioneers William Kearney and Esh Lovell [qq.v.2]. His father and uncle owned a small farm at Myrtle Bank, near Launceston. At Myrtle Bank State School, Jack was taught by his mother who encouraged his interest in natural history. He went on to Launceston State High School and the University of Tasmania (B.Sc., 1924). Interrupting his studies in 1921, he worked for the Education Department as a temporary teacher in charge of primary schools at Fonthill and Myalla, and as an assistant at Huonville and Burnie High schools. He resigned at the end of 1922 to complete the surveying requirements needed for his degree. After a brief trip to Britain and Europe in 1924, he returned to the family farm. He remained a bachelor.

In 1939 Skemp rejoined the department as education officer at the Queen Victoria Museum and Art Gallery, Launceston. He gave talks on natural history to visiting school parties and toured country schools in northern Tasmania with an exhibition of specimens—live, stuffed and bottled—with which he 'fascinated and bewitched children'. In late 1946 his post was abolished, and he took leave to care for his ailing father and uncle. In 1949 he resigned from the department. His first book, *Memories of Myrtle Bank* (Melbourne, 1952), a record of his father's and uncle's farming experiences, was a sensitive and amusing depiction of people and life in a rural community. In addition, he edited a selection of his father's verse, *Poems of a Pioneer* (Launceston, 1954). While employed as a science teacher at Launceston Technical High School (1955) and Scottsdale District School (1955-59), he produced *Letters to Anne* (Melbourne, 1956), a book based on the correspondence received by his grandmother in 1846-72, and *Tasmania Yesterday and Today* (Melbourne, 1958).

In his retirement Skemp lived at Myrtle Bank and continued to write about nature and local history. With T. E. Burns, he edited *Van Diemen's Land Correspondents* (Launceston, 1961), which contained letters from R. C. Gunn, Sir John Franklin, Jorgen Jorgenson [qq.v.1,2], R. W. Lawrence and others to Sir William Hooker, director of the Royal Botanic Gardens, Kew, London. Much of Skemp's other work complemented the Tasmanian school syllabus: 'A History of the North-West Coast', serialized in *Tasmanian Education* (1962-66), and *A History of Deloraine* (Launceston, 1964). He wrote three articles for the *Australian Dictionary of Biography*.

Although something of a hermit, Skemp was an empathetic and pleasant man who enjoyed cricket. A member (1932-36 and 1954-66) of the Royal Society of Tasmania, he was also a founding member of the Launceston Field Naturalists Club. He died of cancer on 12 May 1966 at Launceston. His body was bequeathed for scientific research and later cremated; his Myrtle Bank property was left to the Field Naturalists Club; his last book, *My Birds* (Launceston, 1970) was published posthumously.

L. Robson, *A History of Tasmania*, 2 (Melb, 1991); *PTHRA*, 3, no 1, 1954, p 12; *Examiner* (Launc), 14 May 1966; *Mercury* (Hob), 16 May 1966; information from Mrs M. Cameron, Mrs E. Walker, Mr H. S. and Mrs B. Payne, Launceston, and Mrs N. Eade, Devonport, Tas.   GWENDA M. WEBB
                                             PETER G. WEBB

SKENE, LILLIAS MARGARET (1867-1957), women's activist and welfare worker, was born on 28 March 1867 at Smythesdale, Victoria, third child of John Prendergast Hamilton, a Scottish-born police magistrate, and his wife Agnes Margaret, née Buchanan, who came from England. After her father had been posted to Hamilton, Lillias was educated locally at Alexandra College. On 7 November 1888 at St Mary's Anglican Church, Caulfield, she married David Alexander Skene, the 33-year-old sheepmaster of Pierrepoint station, near Hamilton; they were to have two daughters and two sons. Thomas Skene [q.v.11] was his brother.

Unable to make the second payment on the property he was buying when the banks collapsed in the early 1890s, David was forced to work as a station-manager in New South Wales. Lillias and their children stayed at Hamilton. They rejoined him at Curraweena station, near Bourke, in 1896 before moving to Glenariff and then in 1900 to Manly, Sydney. There they invested in a small dairy and leased 25 acres (10 ha). In the face of drought and the high cost of fodder, they sold out in 1906 and moved to Melbourne, where David set up as a woolbroker and stock-and-station agent. In 1910, with money inherited from her mother, Lillias acquired a house for the family at South Yarra.

Like that of many progressive reformers in the early twentieth century, Mrs Skene's work among the poor—initially through the Charity Organisation Society, which she joined in 1910—focused on the child as the vehicle for social and racial improvement. She represented the Guild of Play on the National Council of Women of Victoria until the 1920s. Her first paper to a general meeting of council in 1908, 'A City Milk Supply', contributed to the foundation of the Lady Talbot Milk Institute, which supplied fresh milk to babies and aimed to educate their mothers on appropriate feeding methods. In a period of heightened concern about community health during World War I, she presented another paper to council, in June 1915, on advances in child welfare work in New South Wales, a State that had already established baby clinics. In 1917 Skene represented the N.C.W. at a conference called to discuss the establishment of such clinics in Victoria. She also played a leading part in N.C.W. agitation about the 'frightful menace of the Social Evil' and the spread of venereal diseases among soldiers. With other prominent members, she worked to exclude delegates and organizations with pacifist or socialist sympathies from the N.C.W.

As assistant-secretary of the Victorian N.C.W., Skene had accompanied its secretary, Dr Edith Barrett [q.v.7], to the inaugural meeting of the council of the British (Australian) Red Cross on 25 August 1914. In 1915 she was appointed honorary manager and storekeeper for the Home Hospital, based at Government House, Melbourne. She remained dedicated to Red Cross work after the war and was to serve on council, as outreach officer in 1939, and to chair the home hospital committee from 1943.

Skene's wartime experience also led to her appointment in 1919 as honorary secretary of the Women's Hospital Committee's board of management, a position she held for thirty years. She represented the hospital on the N.C.W., the council of the Victorian Baby Health Centres Association, the Metropolitan Hospitals Association, the Victorian Hospitals' Association and the Hospital Benefits Association of Victoria. She was the only woman to serve on the special committee of hospital representatives, which was convened in 1933 to advise the government on hospital finance. A ward in the Gertrude Kumm [q.v.15] wing of the Women's Hospital was named after her.

For her patriotic work during the war, Skene had been appointed M.B.E. in 1919. She was one of Victoria's first seven women justices of the peace (1927), as well as a member of the Victorian Nursing Board (1927) and the State Relief Committee (1929). According to the *Australasian*, she was 'entitled to first place in a gallery of those women who are the leaders of their sex in the public life of the Commonwealth'.

Having succeeded Barrett as honorary secretary of the N.C.W. in 1916, Skene became vice-president in 1921 and president in 1924. When the State councils, on Victoria's initiative, established a preliminary federal council in 1924, Skene was elected its foundation president. After relinquishing office in 1927, she received the Victorian council's gold badge for long and distinguished service. In 1933-34 she was organizing secretary of the executive of the Victorian Women's Centenary Council. She was grateful for the salary of £5 per week, as the family business which she had taken over on her husband's death in 1921 declined during the Depression and she

had incurred heavy medical expenses on behalf of two of her children.

Other organizations in which Mrs Skene played an active role included the Women Justices' Association, of which she was secretary in 1940. She resigned from most of her public positions in 1949 and retired to Brighton. Survived by a son, she died on 25 March 1957 at Armadale and was buried with Presbyterian forms in Brighton cemetery.

H. Gillan, *A Brief History of the National Council of Women of Victoria 1902-1945* (Melb, 1945); A. Norris, *Champions of the Impossible* (Melb, 1978); D. M. Halmarick (comp), *Thos Robertson and Sons* (Melb, 2000); *Woman*, June 1917, Oct 1918, May 1921; *Australasian*, 1 Oct 1927; *Sun News-Pictorial*, 16, 18 Dec 1948, 26 Mar 1957; *Age* (Melb), 26 Mar 1957; K. F. Gray, The Acceptable Face of Feminism: The National Council of Women of Victoria, 1902-18 (M.A. thesis, Univ Melb, 1988); National Council of Women of Vic, Minute Books, 1915-16 (NL); Women Justices Assn of Vic, Correspondence and Minute Books, 1940-46 (LaTL); information from Mrs J. Durham, Elsternwick, Melb.   JUDITH SMART

SKINNER, ROSE (1900-1979), art-dealer, was born on 30 December 1900 in Perth, sixth child and only daughter of Samuel Dvoretsky, a woodcutter from Russia who became a farmer, and his wife Mary, née Coyle. Rose was raised at Rockingham and educated at Methodist Ladies' College, Perth. At the district registrar's office, Perth, on 17 September 1924 she married Herbert Drysdale Varley, a businessman; they were divorced in 1930. On 5 September 1934 at Kegalla, Ceylon (Sri Lanka), she married John Wastell Harrison. Back in Perth by 1939, she worked as a censor during World War II and divorced her husband in November 1945.

On 11 June 1946, in his home at 40 Mount Street, Perth, Rose married with Methodist forms Josiah James Skinner, a divorcee. They had both belonged to the Workers' Art Guild, an association of left-wing intellectuals. 'Joe' Skinner, a builder and real-estate agent, collected art, antique silver and books. When he decided to develop his Mount Street property, Rose persuaded him to build a gallery. An attractive, exposed brick and glass edifice, it reflected his interest in contemporary architecture and design. The Skinner Galleries, opened on 14 October 1958, held 214 exhibitions over the next eighteen years. Furnished with a grand piano, they were frequently used for concerts and literary events. In the early years they also housed a bookshop. The Skinners lived in one of the flats in the same building.

From the beginning the galleries were financially successful. Rose Skinner insisted on selling on commission. In 1959 the artists

Robert Juniper, Brian McKay, Guy Grey-Smith, Tom Gibbons and Maurice Stubbs, all members of the Perth Group, held an exhibition at the galleries. The group broke up within three years, mainly because Grey-Smith objected to Skinner's management. Following a showing in 1962 of (Sir) Sidney Nolan's paintings (which netted £10 000 in sales), Skinner was able to employ an assistant. Nolan and other leading artists—Arthur Boyd, Albert Tucker, Fred Williams and Hal Missingham—were frequent exhibitors.

Quick to spot talent and ready to listen to advice, Skinner fostered the careers of Western Australian artists, among them Juniper, McKay, Howard Taylor and George Haynes. She helped Juniper in particular, but restricted the exhibition of his work in other Australian galleries, and emphasized its more superficial and commercially attractive aspects. By supporting the Perth Society of Artists, to which most of Western Australia's professional artists belonged, she did much to encourage the visual arts in Perth. She was energetic, informed and persuasive, and had wide national and international connexions. In 1965-67, in association with the Festival of Perth, she co-ordinated arrangements for the T. E. Wardle Invitation Art Prize at her galleries.

In 1972 Skinner was appointed M.B.E. The Skinner Galleries were closed in 1976, after her health deteriorated. Survived by her husband, she died on 17 September 1979 at Subiaco and was cremated with Anglican rites. She bequeathed her collection of paintings to the University of Western Australia.

P. O'Brien, *Robert Juniper* (NY, 1992); J. Mills, *I Buried My Dolls in the Garden* (Perth, 1999); Univ WA, *Univ News*, 9, no 6, Aug 1978, p 1; *Art and Aust*, 17, no 2, Dec 1979, p 136; *West Australian*, 27 Sept 1979; Skinner Galleries records (BL); family information.   PHILIPPA O'BRIEN

SKIPPER, HERBERT STANLEY (1880-1962), solicitor and promoter of libraries, was born on 8 February 1880 in Adelaide, eldest of four children of Spencer John Skipper, a South Australian-born journalist, and his wife Emma Frances, née Cox, who came from England. John Skipper [q.v.6] was his grandfather. Stanley was educated at Pulteney Street School, the Collegiate School of St Peter, and the University of Adelaide (LL.B., 1901) where he won three Stow [q.v.6] prizes and the Stow medal. Admitted as a barrister and solicitor on 25 November 1901, he practised in Port Adelaide. On 28 September 1910 at St Clement's Church of England, Mosman, Sydney, he married Elizabeth Kathleen Beach Beach.

Appointed a lieutenant in the Militia on 1 January 1916, Skipper acted as a military prosecutor before joining the Australian Imperial Force as a private on 10 September 1917. He regained his commission on 14 August 1918 and performed staff duties in Britain and France after the Armistice. His A.I.F. appointment terminated in Adelaide on 30 December 1919. He served in the Militia as a legal officer from 1923 to 1940 and retired with the rank of lieutenant colonel.

Clubbable and public spirited, Skipper was a lifelong supporter and president (1922-25) of the Port Adelaide Football Club. He was also president of the local Commonwealth Club (1923-26) and of the Naval and Military Club (1944-46), and an active member of the Returned Sailors' and Soldiers' Imperial League of Australia. In 1948 he was elected to the Adelaide Club. Passionately interested in libraries, he was president (1911-12) of the Port Adelaide Institute. After moving to the city, he joined the North Adelaide Institute. In 1910 he had helped to form the Institutes Association of South Australia; he served on its council (1910-62) and as its president (1943-45). He sat on the board of the Public Library, Museum and Art Gallery of South Australia (1934-39) and on the Libraries Board of South Australia (1940-62).

In their 1935 report Ralph Munn and Ernest Pitt [q.v.11] had described Australia's institute libraries as 'cemeteries of old and forgotten books'. They declared that a library service available only to subscribers was 'fundamentally wrong' and estimated that free libraries would reach at least 40 per cent of the population compared with the 5 per cent who used the institutes. (Sir) Archibald Grenfell Price's [q.v.] ensuing report (1937) broadly endorsed the Munn-Pitt recommendations for South Australia, but successive governments and a rearguard action by the Institutes Association preserved the *status quo*. From that quarter only Skipper saw the need for reform.

Although the Free Library Movement achieved its aims in New South Wales, Tasmania and Victoria in the 1940s, it failed in South Australia. From 1953 a frustrated Skipper mounted almost a one-man crusade. It culminated in 1955 when he persuaded Premier (Sir) Thomas Playford to take the State's libraries out of 'the hillbilly category' by supporting the Libraries (Subsidies) bill which allowed grants for buildings as well as books. South Australia's first free local library, opened at Elizabeth on 11 December 1957, was Skipper's monument.

Skipper was appointed C.B.E. in 1960. Survived by his wife and two of their three sons, he died on 27 January 1962 in North Adelaide and was cremated. His other son, Captain Justin Skipper, A.I.F., had been killed in action in Papua in 1942.

R. Munn and E. R. Pitt, *Australian Libraries* (Melb, 1935); A. G. Price, *Libraries in South Australia* (Adel, 1937); C. Bridge, *A Trunk Full of Books* (Adel, 1986); M. R. Talbot, *A Chance to Read* (Adel, 1992); *SA Institutes J*, 30 Nov 1943, 31 Jan 1961, 30 Apr 1962; *Advertiser* (Adel), 29 Jan 1962.

CARL BRIDGE

SLATER, WILLIAM (1890?-1960), solicitor and politician, was born probably on 20 May 1890 at Wangaratta, Victoria, son of William Slater, a travelling salesman who was born in Ireland, and Marie Agatha O'Reilly (or Reilly). About 1894 William abandoned Marie, leaving her to raise three children in extreme poverty at Prahran, Melbourne. Young Bill learned to read and write, but was forced to leave school and work barefoot as a newsboy at South Yarra. Fined for bathing naked in the Yarra River, he decided to enter the law and educated himself at night in the Prahran Free Library where he met Maurice Blackburn [q.v.7]. Both became lifelong socialists and temperance advocates.

Charity workers with the Try Boys' Society found Slater a regular job as an office-boy. In 1910 a sympathetic Mildura solicitor Percy Park employed him as a clerk and resisted occasional attempts by clients to have him dismissed because of his socialist convictions. By this time Slater was muscular and 5 ft 9½ ins (177 cm) tall. He joined the local football team and participated in four-mile (6.4 km) swimming races along the Murray River. Saving his salary, he bought a partnership in two small fruit-growing blocks near the town; the venture rarely showed a profit.

Slater regarded World War I as an inevitable outcome of capitalist imperialism and refused to join friends in volunteering for active service. After the death toll at Gallipoli mounted, however, he enlisted in the Australian Imperial Force on 11 December 1915 and was posted to the 10th Field Ambulance. By November 1916 he was serving in France. In intervals between carrying the dead and wounded back from the front line, he kept a diary in which he recorded 'the hellishness of war'. He inhaled mustard gas at Tissages, and on 28 July 1917 at Messines, Belgium, suffered a wound in the leg.

Sent to hospital in England, Slater agreed by cable to stand as a Labor candidate in the forthcoming Victorian general elections. The polls were held on 15 November 1917. Eleven days later he was stunned to learn that he had won the seat of Dundas in the Legislative Assembly. In February 1918 he sailed for Australia, medically unfit. Landing first in Perth, he was arrested by military police for speaking at a public meeting in support of John Curtin [q.v.13], but was released when he promised to return promptly to Melbourne. He was discharged from the A.I.F. on 17 May.

Blackburn appointed Slater an articled clerk in his legal firm's branch office at Hamilton. The young man rode his bicycle around the district to visit clients and the electors who had voted for him sight unseen. When he was admitted to practice as a barrister and solicitor on 1 March 1922, Blackburn made him junior partner and named the firm Blackburn & Slater. In 1923 the Victorian branch of the militant Australian Railways Union offered Slater its legal work, enabling him to open his own business in Unity Hall, the A.R.U.'s building in Bourke Street, Melbourne. At the Presbyterian Church, Mildura, on 19 December that year he married Mary Gordon, a 26-year-old senior demonstrator in botany at the University of Melbourne.

In 1924 Slater became attorney-general and solicitor-general in the short-lived (July-November) Prendergast [q.v.11] Labor government. He held the same portfolios, and that of agriculture, in the Hogan [q.v.9] ministries of 1927-28 and 1929-32. Slater pushed through Victoria's first Adoption of Children Act (1928) and attempted (1931) to establish a solicitors' guarantee fund (eventually introduced in 1948). Even his political opponent (Sir) Robert Menzies [q.v.15] described him as having 'a reputation for personal integrity that could scarcely be higher'. In May 1940 Slater was named Speaker of the Legislative Assembly to widespread acclaim. Curtin's Federal Labor government announced his appointment as the first Australian minister to the Soviet Union in October 1942. Resigning the Speakership but not from parliament, he flew to Russia and took office on 13 January 1943. He reported on the magnificent struggle of the Russian people against the German invaders, but falling seriously ill, relinquished his post on 15 April and returned home in June.

After Labor regained power in Victoria, Slater's close friend John Cain [q.v.13] appointed him chief secretary, attorney-general and solicitor-general on 21 November 1945. Slater's main achievement was the strengthening in 1946 of the State's outdated Workers' Compensation Act to cover industrial diseases (such as asbestosis) for the first time. He also set up an independent tribunal to determine wages and conditions for police officers. In addition, he introduced government controls over gambling which severely reduced the financial and political power of John Wren [q.v.12]. A massive campaign in the Dundas electorate allegedly financed by Wren contributed to Slater's defeat in the election in November 1947. The Labor Party found him a safer seat—Doutta Galla, in the Legislative Council—which he retained from 1949 until his death. In 1952-55 he was again attorney-general, with the extra portfolios of immigration and prices.

Slater had taken his brother-in-law Hugh Gordon into partnership in 1935; he retained the name Slater & Gordon after Hugh was killed in action in World War II. The firm specialized in cases involving trade unions and workers' compensation. Some of the junior partners and employees were overtly or secretly members of the Communist Party of Australia; a number of them figured prominently in the Petrov affair. Slater held that his colleagues' political views were their own business. For all that, the firm's radical reputation attracted many briefs from communist-led unions. In the mid-1950s Slater was forced to refute whispering campaigns which 'branded him as associating with Catholics, Freemasons and Reds all at the same time'. His own political philosophy remained that of gradual reformism towards the hoped-for utopia of socialism.

Suffering from cancer, Slater died of a coronary occlusion on 19 June 1960 in South Melbourne and was cremated with Unitarian forms; his wife, and their daughter and two sons survived him. Members of the Police Association (Victoria)—for which he had acted as honorary solicitor—blocked every intersection on the route from the St Kilda funeral parlour to the crematorium at Springvale to ensure an easy transit for the cortège.

M. Cannon, *That Disreputable Firm* (Melb, 1998), and for bib; Slater papers (NL); Slater memorabilia (held by Mrs H. Widdowson, Strathmore, Melb).   MICHAEL CANNON

SLEEP, ALFRED REGINALD (1893-1959), home missionary and private detective, was born on 23 September 1893 at Plymouth, England, one of seven children of Alfred Josiah Sleep, a driller at the naval dockyard, and his wife Thirzena, née Snell. Alfred grew up in a zealous Congregational family and at 16 gave his first sermon as a lay preacher. Under the auspices of the Colonial Missionary Society of London, he reached Western Australia with his brother Harold in July 1913 and was sent as a home missionary to the Nungarin district, on the north-eastern edge of the wheatbelt. Provided with a horse (which at first he could not ride) and some hymn books, he enthusiastically spread the Congregational message and won commendation as 'a preacher of promise'. Late in 1914 he travelled to Adelaide, intending to enter Parkin [q.v.5] Theological College, but decided instead to accept a posting to the Tumby Bay Congregational Church.

On 25 March 1916 Sleep enlisted in the Australian Imperial Force. Joining the 10th Battalion on the Western Front in October, he was evacuated to England next month with chronic gastritis. He could neither eat hard rations nor march well, and medical authorities concluded that he was 'useless for general service'. Transferred to A.I.F. Administrative Headquarters, London, in January 1917, he performed welfare work at the War Chest Club where his 'amiable and tactful disposition' made him a great success with the soldiers. He was promoted acting sergeant before ill health led to his return to Australia in the following year. On 4 October 1918 he was discharged from the A.I.F. in Adelaide. At St George's Church of England, Goodwood, on 15 November that year he married Gwendoline Hannah Sauerbier; he was to divorce her on 3 December 1930.

After working as a secretary for the Young Men's Christian Association, Sleep went back to Western Australia, became a Methodist home missionary, and served at Gnowangerup (1924-25) and Merredin (1926-27). When church officials fell behind in paying his stipend, he abandoned his calling and moved to Perth. By 1929 he was a private detective. On 6 December 1930 at the Charles Street Methodist Church, West Perth, he married Edith Alice Stump, a former parishioner who had been moved to tears by his sermons.

Sleep prospered as he gathered material for divorce hearings. His evidence was invariably accepted by the courts. In his new profession he became more worldly. He grew portly and began to dress well; he also discovered beer and whisky, developed a taste for good food, and sharpened his talent for one-liners. A former parishioner met him in Perth and remembered the fragile figure whom he had known ten years earlier. 'You seem to be flourishing, Alfred. How is that?' Sleep replied: 'In a word—adultery'.

Alfred R. Sleep—with his trusty torch— was built into a Perth identity. The *Mirror*, which specialized in reporting divorce cases beneath punned headings, promoted stories about his amiable and tactful raids on hotel rooms and motorcars, his investigations in parks and at beaches, and his subsequent efforts at marriage counselling. The stories became more frequent with the arrival of American servicemen who caused considerable domestic disruption during World War II. Suffering from cirrhosis of the liver, Sleep retired in 1958 to tend his three hundred roses. He died of coronary disease on 26 October 1959 at Claremont and was buried in Karrakatta cemetery. His wife and their daughter survived him, as did the daughter of his first marriage.

R. Davidson, *High Jinks at the Hot Pool* (Fremantle, WA, 1994); *Western Congregationalist*, Aug, Sept 1913; *People* (Syd), 27 Sept 1950; *Mirror* (Perth), 8 May, 14 July, 29 Sept 1945; Methodist

Church of Aust, Minutes of WA Conference, 1924-27 (Uniting Church Archives, Perth); family and personal information.   RON DAVIDSON

SLEIGH, SIR HAMILTON MORTON HOWARD (1896-1979), company director, was born on 20 March 1896 at South Yarra, Melbourne, only child of English-born parents Harold Crofton Sleigh [q.v.11], shipping agent, and his wife Marion Elizabeth, née Chapple. Hamilton's education and early experience of work were designed to prepare him for assuming his father's interests in shipping, timber and petroleum. After attending St Oswald's Preparatory School at Clifton, near Bristol, England, and the Grange Preparatory School, South Yarra, he travelled with his parents on the Trans-Siberian Railway to England again in 1909 and entered Sherborne School, Dorset, in 1911.

In 1913 Sleigh worked for the Westinghouse Bremsen Gesellschaft at Hanover, Germany, lived with a German family and learned the language; a similar sojourn with a French family was prevented by World War I. Following a year in London with Arbuthnot, Latham & Co., merchant bankers, he went to sea in 1915 as a 'very junior purser', came to Australia in the *Parattah* and joined his father's firm. On 14 December 1917 he enlisted in the Australian Imperial Force. In 1918-19 he served in England as an air mechanic in the Australian Flying Corps. He returned home via the United States of America Discharged from the A.I.F. on 26 September 1919, he resumed work with H. C. Sleigh Pty Ltd. In 1924 he was made a partner. Two of his earliest tasks were to supervise the export of cattle from Darwin to the Philippines and of railway sleepers from Bunbury, Western Australia, to Ceylon (Sri Lanka). At the Presbyterian Church, Toorak, Melbourne, on 17 December 1926 he married Doris Marguerita Halbert (d.1968).

Chairman and chief executive after his father's death in 1933, Hamilton expanded the firm's operations. A wholly owned subsidiary firm, H.C.S. Coasters Pty Ltd, was formed and three ships were bought for the trans-Tasman timber trade. New seaboard facilities were constructed to handle petroleum imports and arrangements were made (1939) to distribute Golden Fleece products in Tasmania. During World War II the firm developed and sold gas producers for motor vehicles. H. C. Sleigh became a public company in 1947, with a paid up capital of £800 000. The Singapore Navigation Co. Ltd, another subsidiary, took delivery in 1952 of an ocean-going tanker, the *Harold Sleigh*. More bulk-carriers were acquired. In the 1950s the parent company introduced modern, 'one brand only', drive-in service stations, began selling better quality petrol, built additional ocean terminals, moved to new offices in Melbourne, and took over Purr Pull Oil Pty Ltd in New South Wales and Queensland.

Sleigh's other business interests included directorships of Amalgamated Petroleum N.L., Associated Australian Oilfields N.L., Australian Lubricating Oil Refinery Ltd, Botany Bay Tanker Co. (Australia) Pty Ltd, Flinders Shipping Co. Pty Ltd, Australian & Eastern Insurance Co. Ltd, Bath Holdings Ltd, Derby Holdings Ltd and Petersville Australia Ltd. He was president (1961-69) of the Australian Hospital Association and vice-president of the Royal Melbourne Hospital. For his services in Melbourne as honorary consul for Finland, he was appointed to the Order of the White Rose and the Order of the Lion of Finland. The doyen of the Australian petroleum industry, he was knighted in 1970 and retired in favour of his son Peter in June 1975.

On 28 March 1973 at St John's Church of England, Toorak, Sleigh had married Brenda Dodds (d.1976), née Wood, a widow. Tall and slim, he was a kindly, soft-spoken, urbane and conservative man, though he could be blunt and hard hitting, especially against the Whitlam government and its royal commission into the petroleum industry. In an interview on the eve of his retirement he criticized modern social trends, youth and education, but wisely admitted that he did not know the answers. Sir Hamilton was a member of the Australian clubs in Melbourne and Sydney. Farming on his property, Bayunga, near Nagambie, was his main recreation. He died on 24 November 1979 at Parkville and was cremated with Anglican rites. The two sons of his first marriage survived him.

H. C. Sleigh Ltd, *The First Sixty Years* (Melb, 1956?); *People* (Syd), 29 Dec 1954, p 42; *Petroleum Gazette*, 18, no 3, 1974, p 85; *SMH*, 30 Dec 1946, 15 Mar, 17, 20 Aug 1951, 30 Aug, 26 Oct 1959, 26 May 1960, 20 May 1963, 7 Mar 1964, 13 June 1970, 4 June, 9 Nov 1974; *Age* (Melb), 31 Aug 1967, 26 Nov 1979; information from Mr P. H. Sleigh, Mt Eliza, Vic.
                                        G. P. WALSH

SLESSOR, KENNETH ADOLF (1901-1971), poet and journalist, was born on 27 March 1901 at Orange, New South Wales, second son and eldest of three surviving children of Robert Schloesser, mining engineer, and his native-born wife Margaret Ella, née McInnes, whose parents came from the Hebrides. Robert was born in London, where his father Adolphe had moved from Germany. The Schloessers were German-Jewish in origin, but without particular interest in Judaism; they were free-thinking, and included professional musicians in their ranks. Robert had studied at Liège, Belgium, and made his children speak French at meals. He changed the family surname to 'Slessor' on 14 November 1914, just after the outbreak of World War I. Ken's father encouraged him to love music, food and books, and instilled in him a European sophistication.

The family moved to Sydney in 1903. Ken, a voracious reader, began writing poetry as a child and edited a school magazine while at Sydney Church of England Grammar School (Shore). In 1917 his first publication, a dramatic monologue (spoken by a digger dying in Europe and remembering Sydney Harbour and Manly Beach) appeared in the *Bulletin*. Next year, when he won the Victoria League's prize for a patriotic poem, 'Jerusalem Set Free', his poetry received attention in Australian newspapers.

Gaining first-class honours in English in the Leaving certificate in 1918, Slessor joined the *Sun* newspaper as a cadet journalist, and studied shorthand and typing at the Metropolitan Business College. His early journalistic writing was full of brilliant description and poetic flourishes. In 1919 he had six poems published in the *Bulletin* and one in *Smith's Weekly*; they indicated his interest in satire. Three of his poems in the *Triad*—rewritings of translations from the Chinese by Arthur Waley—demonstrated his interest in poetic imagery, which would become the central pillar of his aesthetics.

In 1920 Robert's work took him to China, where his wife and younger children joined him in 1922. Ken remained in Sydney. As a young man, he was 5 ft 10 ins (178 cm) tall, with blue eyes, reddish hair, a ruddy complexion and a moustache. On 18 August 1922 at the Methodist parsonage, Ashfield, he married 28-year-old Noëla Beatrice Myee Ewart Glasson, who used her stepfather's surname, Senior. Theirs was to be a sometimes tempestuous relationship, but Slessor was devoted to her, even after her death. They were childless. Noëla, a slim brunette with grey eyes, was a Catholic—a source of anguish to Ken's Presbyterian mother.

That year Slessor met Norman Lindsay, Hugh McCrae [qq.v.10] and Jack Lindsay. He was to remain friendly with the controversial Norman, and loyal to some of his aesthetic and philosophical ideas. Many of Slessor's early poems were strongly influenced by Lindsay, but he had none of Lindsay's giant egocentricity, and was as devoted to experiment as Lindsay was opposed to it. Lindsay was anti-Semitic and aggressively anti-Christian, while holding to a vaguely Platonic view of an afterlife. Slessor remained agnostic to the end of his days.

He dismissed the poems of 'Banjo' Paterson, Henry Lawson [qq.v.11,9] and all the bush balladists. To Slessor, poetry had only

begun 'any consistent growth in Australia' 'with the publication of McCrae's *Satyrs and Sunlight*' (1909). In 1923-24 he helped Jack Lindsay and Frank C. Johnson, a bookseller, to edit *Vision: a Literary Quarterly*, which ran for only four issues. It was strongly influenced by Norman Lindsay; it tried to jolt Australian writing out of the bush and into the city, and it promoted Nietzschean ideas, discussion of sexuality, debate about aesthetics, and writing about the inner life. Allied to the magazine, and creating the same sort of stir, was an anthology edited by the trio, *Poetry in Australia, 1923*.

While McCrae and Jack Lindsay were living out Norman's ideas of artistic purity and a consequent bohemianism, Slessor was getting on with his life as a journalist. In 1922 he declined the editorship of the magazine *Art in Australia*. He spent some time in Melbourne in 1924-25, writing satirical and light verse for the *Herald* and sub-editing *Punch* (where he met the illustrator, Joe Lynch [q.v.15, F. E. Lynch]). Late in 1925 *Punch* closed, and in 1926 Slessor returned to Sydney and the *Sun*. His first book of poetry, *Thief of the Moon*, had been published in 1924, printed on a handpress by J. T. Kirtley in his Kirribilli bathroom. Its sales, though meagre, were aided by the inclusion of three Norman Lindsay woodcuts. Slessor culled what he thought the best of these poems and added many others, publishing *Earth-Visitors* (1926): it, too, was illustrated by Lindsay, and was produced by Jack Lindsay's Fanfrolico Press in London. The book included poems on Heine, Dürer and music.

Slessor joined the idiosyncratic *Smith's Weekly* in 1927 and remained there until 1940, serving as an editor from 1935. He enjoyed its unconventionality, interest in film and humour, and, probably, its 'knock-'em-down' vulgarity; he later described the period as 'the happiest chapter of my existence'. During these years he wrote most of his major poetry, the bulk of his light verse (which was published in *Smith's*, with illustrations principally by Virgil Reilly), numerous articles and film reviews.

Slessor's 'Five Visions of Captain Cook' was included in a booklet, *Trio* (1931), with poems by Harley Matthews and Colin Simpson. In 1932 he published his third major collection, *Cuckooz Contrey*, a collection of illustrated light verse. *Darlinghurst Nights* (1933) and a collection of children's verse, *Funny Farmyard* (1933), followed. In 1939 the small paperback *Five Bells: XX Poems* appeared. Norman Lindsay again provided drawings for *Cuckooz Contrey* and *Five Bells*, but Slessor's work increasingly seemed to belong to another world from that of Lindsay. The elegy 'Five Bells', a meditation prompted by the death from drowning of Joe Lynch in Sydney Harbour in 1927, is generally agreed to be his finest poem. It placed him among Australia's foremost poets:

I looked out of my window in the dark
At waves with diamond quills and combs of
    light
That arched their mackerel-backs and
    smacked the sand . . .
And tried to hear your voice, but all I heard
Was a boat's whistle, and the scraping squeal
Of seabirds' voices far away, and bells,
Five bells. Five bells coldly ringing out.

Appointed official war correspondent by the Commonwealth government in February 1940, Slessor sailed for Britain in May. He served, frequently with Ron Monson [q.v.15], in North Africa, Greece, Crete and Syria until 1943, and was in Papua and New Guinea for some months in 1943-44. Regarding the position as a great honour, he was loyal to the traditions and mythology of the Anzacs. He saw a good deal of action. His admiration for the ordinary soldier combined with his sharp eye and linguistic skill to make him a distinctive correspondent, but his dislike of military authority, and his frustrations with wartime censorship and military bureaucracy, led to disputes.

In November 1943 Brigadier (Sir) Victor Windeyer complained that an account attributed to Slessor and published in *Fact* 'of the operations leading up to the capture of Finschhafen . . . is most inaccurate'. Slessor defended himself and asked for an official apology. When he learned that the army had sought his disaccreditation as a war correspondent, he resigned on 21 February 1944 in protest against 'the whole of the present attitude and working of the Army Public Relations Branch'. His resignation was controversial and the matter was raised in the House of Representatives.

Slessor became an editor at his old newspaper, the *Sun*, in April. During the war he had written only two poems, 'An Inscription for Dog River' (a critique of Sir Thomas Blamey [q.v.13]) and the powerfully elegiac 'Beach Burial'. Noëla had joined him in England and Egypt, but after Slessor was sent to New Guinea it was some time before they were reunited, in Sydney. He was devastated when she died of cancer in October 1945.

That year Slessor edited the anthology *Australian Poetry 1945*. In 1946-47 he lived with Kathleen McShine, the subject of the last new poem published in his lifetime, 'Polarities'. A selection of his poetry, *One Hundred Poems, 1919-1939*, had been published in 1944. The book was popular enough to be reprinted in 1947. After the addition of his three last poems, in 1957, it was reissued many times under the titles *Poems* and *Selected Poems*. It was the book by which Slessor was

known for many years and it provided the basis for his steadily growing reputation. The first of his series of general interest books, *Portrait of Sydney* (1950), was commissioned by Sam Ure Smith. Other such books in the years that ensued included *Life at the Cross* (Adelaide, 1965), *Canberra* (Adelaide, 1966) and *The Grapes are Growing* (Sydney, 1960s).

At the district registrar's office, Chatswood, on 15 December 1951 Slessor married Catherine Pauline Wallace, née Bowe, a 31-year-old stenographer and a divorcee. Their son Paul was born in 1952. The marriage was unhappy, broke down in the late-1950s and ended in divorce in 1961. In the late 1960s Pauline Slessor, who was suffering from cirrhosis, returned to live in the same house as Ken, the old Slessor family home at Chatswood—but as a housekeeper. Paul, of whom Slessor had custody, attended Shore (1964-69) and resided with his father.

Although he did not write any new poetry, Slessor kept up many literary activities. He was editor (1956-61) of the literary magazine *Southerly* and, with John Thompson [q.v.] and R. G. Howarth [q.v.14], edited an anthology, *The Penguin Book of Australian Verse* (Melbourne, 1958), revised as *The Penguin Book of Modern Australian Verse* (Melbourne, 1961). Slessor served (1953-71) on the advisory board of the Commonwealth Literary Fund and in 1954 gave a provocative series of six lectures on Australian poetry for the C.L.F. In 1959 he was appointed O.B.E. Ironically, he agreed to serve on the National Literature Board of Review (a Commonwealth government censorship board) in 1967 because he had always opposed censorship.

A successful senior journalist and editor, Slessor had left the *Sun* in 1957 for the *Daily Telegraph*, where he stayed until 1971. He was president (1956-65) of the Journalists' Club, Sydney. With A. J. H. Macdonald [q.v.15], Edgar Holt, Cyril Pearl and others, he formed the Condiments Club. Nancy Keesing appreciated 'his wide culture, his enjoyment of people and situations, his wit that was both lusty and subtle'. She described him as 'a neat, fastidious man who chose pens and paper for his work with care and discrimination, who valued (and cooked) beautiful food and drank and offered fine wine. He was a connoisseur who loved and collected books, pictures, music, objects and created a beautiful and truly civilized background for his life'. After years of cajoling by Douglas Stewart, he published *Bread and Wine* (Sydney, 1970), a selection of his articles, literary essays, comments on his own poetry, and his war dispatches.

Kenneth Slessor died suddenly of myocardial infarction on 30 June 1971 at the Mater Misericordiae Hospital, North Sydney. In accordance with his will, he was cremated after a secular service and his ashes were placed next to those of Noëla in Rookwood cemetery. His son survived him and inherited his estate, sworn for probate at $99 216.

Slessor's stature as a poet has steadily increased since his death. Posthumous publications included a collection of his light verse, *Backless Betty from Bondi* (Sydney, 1983). His war diaries and dispatches were edited by Clement Semmler in separate volumes, *The War Diaries of Kenneth Slessor* (Brisbane, 1985) and *The War Despatches of Kenneth Slessor* (Brisbane, 1987). A selection of his writing across all genres, *Kenneth Slessor* (Brisbane), appeared in 1991 and an annotated *Collected Poems* (Sydney) in 1994. There have also been a number of critical studies of his poetry and at least two biographies.

A. K. Thomson (ed), *Critical Essays on Kenneth Slessor* (Brisb, 1968); D. Stewart, *A Man of Sydney* (Melb, 1977); A. Taylor, *Reading Australian Poetry* (Brisb, 1987); G. Dutton, *Kenneth Slessor* (Melb, 1991); A. Caesar, *Kenneth Slessor* (Melb, 1995); P. Mead (ed), *Kenneth Slessor* (Brisb, 1997); *Southerly*, 31, no 4, 1971; D. Haskell, 'Sheer Voice and Fidget Wheels', *Aust Literary Studies*, 13, no 3, 1988, p 253; *SMH*, 25 Jan 1919, 2 Apr 1940, 25 Feb, 3 Mar 1944, 5 Nov 1953, 1 Jan 1959, 30 Dec 1967, 17 Sept 1971; Slessor papers (NL); SP109/3, item 392/17, and resignation of Mr Kenneth Slessor, A5954, item 609/3 (NAA, Canb).

DENNIS HASKELL

SLIM, SIR WILLIAM JOSEPH, 1ST VISCOUNT (1891-1970), army officer, governor-general and author, was born on 6 August 1891 at Bristol, England, younger son of John Benjamin Thomas Slim, commercial traveller, and his wife Charlotte Amelia, née Tucker. Educated at St Philip's Catholic school, Edgbaston, and King Edward's School, Birmingham, Bill showed literary ability, little aptitude for sport, and an interest in the army, but lacked the means to proceed to a military academy. He taught in an elementary school, worked as a clerk with a firm of engineers, and joined the University of Birmingham Officers' Training Corps. On 22 August 1914 he was gazetted second lieutenant, Royal Warwickshire Regiment.

Seriously wounded at Gallipoli in August 1915, Slim was invalided to England. He was granted a regular commission in the West India Regiment, but in October 1916 rejoined his old battalion in Mesopotamia. In the following year he was wounded again, awarded the Military Cross, and evacuated to India. After recovering, he served with increasing boredom at Army Headquarters, Delhi. He transferred to the Indian Army in 1919. Next year he was posted to the 1st Battalion, 6th Gurkha Rifles, of which he became adjutant in 1921. At St Andrew's Church, Bombay, on

1 January 1926 he married Aileen Robertson (1901-1993) with the forms of the Church of Scotland; although the service was followed by a ceremony in the Catholic church at Quetta, he regarded himself as a lapsed Catholic.

Slim's brilliant success in 1926-28 at the Staff College, Quetta, was followed by a term at Army Headquarters and by his attachment (1934-36) to the Staff College, Camberley, England, as Indian Army instructor. From the 1937 course at the Imperial Defence College, London, he returned to India. He was promoted lieutenant colonel (1938), given command of the 2nd Battalion, 7th Gurkha Rifles, and appointed (1939) commandant of the Senior Officers' School, Belgaum, as temporary brigadier. Meanwhile, he also developed as a writer. To supplement his income, he contributed stories and articles under the pen-name 'Anthony Mills' to English newspapers, particularly the *Daily Mail,* and to periodicals such as *Blackwood's Magazine.*

On 23 September 1939 Slim assumed command of the 10th Indian Brigade. In November 1940 he led a force which captured Gallabat (on the border between Ethiopia and the Sudan) from the Italians. In failing to capitalize on this success and take nearby Metemma as well, he blamed no one but himself: 'When two courses of action were open to me I had not chosen, as a good commander should, the bolder. I had taken counsel of my fears'. Wounded soon after in an air-attack, he sent a stoical telegram to his mother: 'Bullet Bottom Better Bill'. He was promoted acting major general and appointed to command the 10th Indian Division in May 1941. A successful campaign (June-July) against Vichy French forces in Syria preceded an easier one (August) in Persia, described by him as *opéra bouffe.*

Recalled to India in March 1942, Slim was promoted acting lieutenant general and given command of I Burma Corps (Burcorps), then in retreat from Rangoon before the advancing Japanese. Against great difficulties, he brought the exhausted but defiant survivors to Imphal, India. His pre-eminent contribution, as in subsequent campaigns, was in maintaining morale. He spoke to as many soldiers as possible, man to man, and enabled them to hope 'when hope seemed absurd'. Their 'will to live sustained a will to fight'. On Burcorps' disbandment in May, Slim was appointed to command XV Corps. During the Arakan campaign of 1942-43, he clashed with his army commander, Lieutenant General Noel Irwin, who attempted to have him relieved. The outcome was tersely expressed in Irwin's message to Slim: 'You're not sacked. I am'.

In October 1943 Slim was appointed to command the Fourteenth Army. He smashed the fraying legend of Japanese invincibility at Imphal and Kohima (May-July 1944), and at Mandalay and Meiktila (February-March 1945), Burma. The reoccupation of Rangoon in May 1945 completed a series of victories that brought him fame. Lord Louis (Earl) Mountbatten considered him 'the finest general World War II produced'. The transformation of a defeated force into a proud army was Slim's greatest achievement, and he had come to be known by his soldiers as 'Uncle Bill'. After Rangoon was taken, Sir Oliver Leese, commander-in-chief, Allied Land Forces, South East Asia, decided that he would replace Slim. The decision was greeted with dismay and incredulity by officers and men of the Fourteenth Army, and was quashed in London. Promoted general on 1 July 1945, Slim took over from Leese just as the war ended on 15 August. He had been appointed C.B.E. in 1942 and awarded the Distinguished Service Order in 1943; he was appointed C.B. and K.C.B. in 1944, and G.B.E. in 1946.

Early in 1946 Slim was sent to London to resuscitate the Imperial Defence College as its commandant. He retired on 1 April 1948. An ensuing term as deputy-chairman of the Railway Executive ended seven months later with his recall to the army as chief of the Imperial General Staff. He was promoted field marshal on 4 January 1949. During the next four years he visited British commands abroad and a number of other countries. In Australia he impressed many people, including Prime Minister (Sir) Robert Menzies [q.v.15]. He was appointed G.C.B. (1950) and G.C.M.G. (1952).

On 8 May 1953 Slim was sworn in as governor-general of Australia. Menzies had sought a man of stature, one who had no involvement in Australian politics, and one who would represent the monarch effectively. Slim was to see no change of prime minister over his term of nearly seven years. Despite occasional friction, a relationship of trust developed between him and Menzies, based on a healthy respect for each other's intellect and integrity.

Partly because of the royal visit of 1954—the first by a reigning monarch to Australia—but also owing to his own combination of authority and humanity, Slim's governor-generalship was judged to be notably successful, even by those who believed that the office should be held by an Australian. His humanity came to be as apparent to the Australian people as it had been to his soldiers in Burma. Early in his term, however, he occasioned some surprise by the unflattering remarks he made 'about anything or anybody in Australia he regarded as below par'. As a field marshal he was well qualified both to inspire and to rebuke the Returned Sailors', Soldiers' and Airmen's Imperial League of Australia.

The Slims travelled widely throughout Australia. Sir William's speeches impressed by their cogency, dry humour and directness, as did his off-the-cuff remarks to journalists (when implored by one photographer to smile, he replied, 'Dammit, I *am*!'). His craggy appearance, upright bearing, and jutting chin barely disguised his kindness and approachability. What they did disguise was the pain he continually felt as a result of his wounds. He and his wife both possessed fortitude. She suffered a succession of illnesses, beginning with a serious haemorrhage on their arrival in Canberra. Her determination and perfectionism matched his, and were seen in the improvements she made to Government House, Canberra, and Admiralty House, Sydney. A warmth of heart and manner characterized her presence, whether as hostess or guest, at the many functions attending the vice-regal office.

Slim's three books were all published during his time in Australia. The first, *Defeat into Victory* (London, 1956), about the Burma campaign, sold more than 100 000 copies and was hailed as one of the best, and best-written, on World War II; he dedicated the book to Aileen, 'a soldier's wife who followed the drum and from mud-walled hut or Government House made a home'. He included a number of his speeches in Australia in *Courage and Other Broadcasts* (1957). Accounts of his earlier and smaller battles, some previously published in *Blackwood's Magazine*, appeared in his reminiscences, *Unofficial History* (1959). The Slims were also interested in the arts and education; the former teacher enjoyed visiting schools and talking to pupils and principals alike.

Appointed G.C.V.O. (1954) and K.G. (1959), Slim left office on 2 February 1960 and returned to England. On Menzies' initiative, Sir William and Lady Slim received Australian pensions and passports. In 1960 Slim was raised to the peerage, taking the title Viscount Slim of Yarralumla and Bishopston. He was appointed deputy-constable and lieutenant-governor of Windsor Castle in 1963 and was promoted constable and governor in 1964. His other posts included chairmanship of the council of the Fairbridge [q.v.8] Society, and directorships of the National Bank of Australasia Ltd and Imperial Chemical Industries Ltd. He held nine honorary doctorates, including four from Australian universities. He retained his affection for the Gurkhas and friendships with former colleagues.

Failing in health, Slim retired from his posts at Windsor shortly before he died on 14 December 1970 at St Marylebone, London. He was accorded a full military funeral at St George's Chapel, Windsor, and was cremated. His wife, and their son and daughter survived him. (Sir) Ivor Hele's portrait of Slim is held by the family, Leonard Boden's by the National Army Museum, London. Slim is further commemorated by a plaque in the crypt of St Paul's Cathedral and by a statue at Whitehall unveiled by Queen Elizabeth II in 1990.

R. Lewin, *Slim* (Lond, 1976), and for bib; C. D. Coulthard-Clark (ed), *Gables, Ghosts and Governors-General* (Syd, 1988), J. Keegan (ed), *Churchill's Generals* (Lond, 1991); B. Foott, *Ethel and the Governors' General* (Syd, 1992); J. Colvin, *Not Ordinary Men* (Lond, 1994); A. W. Martin, *Robert Menzies*, 2 (Melb, 1999); *Canb Times* and *The Times*, 15 Dec 1970; *SMH*, 19 Mar 1977; personal knowledge.   MICHAEL D. DE B. COLLINS PERSSE

SLY, KATHLEEN ISABEL ALICE; *see* PARKER

SMALL, SIR ANDREW BRUCE (1895-1980), bicycle manufacturer, land developer and politician, was born on 11 December 1895 at Ryde, Sydney, second of six children of William Andrew Small, a native-born gardener, and his wife Annie Elizabeth, née Martin, who came from Victoria. William and Annie were ardent Salvationists, and by the age of 6 Bruce was playing the tenor horn in Salvation Army bands. He was to hold the post of solo euphonium player in the Territorial Staff Band of Victoria for twenty-two years. The family was always on the move. In later life Bruce recalled that he attended fourteen schools before he finished his formal education at the age of 13. He found work in Melbourne as a printer's devil, earning six shillings a week. He then operated a milk run before becoming a commercial traveller. On 3 September 1919 at the City Temple, Melbourne, he married with Salvation Army forms Eileen Hayman, a nurse. They had one son before being divorced.

By 1920 Small had saved enough to buy a bicycle shop at Malvern for £200. At first he manufactured twelve bicycles a week. With the slogan, 'You'd be better on a Malvern Star', the business blossomed and he formed a company, Bruce Small Pty Ltd, in 1926. Five years earlier he had hired a young telegraph messenger, (Sir) Hubert ('Oppy') Opperman, whose national and international feats as a racing cyclist brought fame to Malvern Star. Small, Oppy and a promotional team toured the world six times and successfully marketed bicycles abroad. In 1936 Allied Bruce Small Ltd was registered as a public company. At the 1st Congregational Church, San Francisco, United States of America, on 11 August 1939 Small married Lillian Ada Mitchell, a clerk from Sydney.

During World War II Small's factories produced bicycles, both for the armed forces and for civilians. Demand surged due to petrol rationing. Malvern Star also made radio-location sets, tubular tent frames and radio-masts for defence purposes. The business eventually comprised six factories, a wholesale warehouse and a chain of forty-five retail shops, supplemented by about one thousand dealerships. A successful manufacturer and exporter, he was a fervent proponent of Australian industrial self-sufficiency.

Described as a 'non-swearing, non-drinking, God-fearing Christian', Small showed a lifelong concern for the less fortunate. He was a director of the Association for the Blind of Victoria for twenty-five years. As its president (1955-64), he was closely involved with the construction of homes for the elderly at Brighton, Bendigo and Ballarat. For many years he was a board-member of the Young Men's Christian Association of Melbourne.

By 1958 Small was a millionaire. He sold his holding in Allied Bruce Small and moved to the Gold Coast, Queensland. He soon acquired 100 acres (40 ha) of low-lying dairy land and mangrove swamps at Bundall, across the Nerang River from Surfers Paradise. Over the next eight years his companies bought more land, reclaiming and developing 500 acres (200 ha) as Paradise City. At the Isle of Capri, part of the project, he built the palm-flanked Wanamara, which remained his home until his death. Flamboyant and extroverted, he soon fell foul of the Southport-dominated Gold Coast City Council by calling for an overall town plan and for co-operation between developers, local government and the Crown.

Using the slogan 'Think Big, Vote Small', Small stood successfully for mayor of the City of the Gold Coast on 29 April 1967. His efforts during the disastrous cyclone in June that year, when he marshalled 5000 civilian volunteers and 187 soldiers to fill and place thousands of sandbags along the eroded beachfront, won him added support. He became known as 'Boulder Bruce' for his efforts to have permanent rock walls constructed along vulnerable Gold Coast beaches. Determined that the Gold Coast's image as a holiday resort would not suffer as a result of the erosion crisis, he toured Australia in 1968 with a bevy of 'meter maids', clad in gold lamé bikinis. He was also often accompanied by his beloved poodle Mimi. By 1969 his promotional tours had spread farther afield to include New Zealand, the Philippines, Hong Kong, Japan and Singapore. At home, he participated in dance marathons and rode a penny-farthing bicycle through Surfers Paradise at the head of a circus parade. He laid the foundation for the development of the Gold Coast as an international tourist destination and did much to Americanize the way of life of Surfers Paradise. In 1974 he was knighted.

Immensely popular, Mayor Small had been re-elected unopposed in 1970. In May 1972, at the age of 76, he won the Legislative Assembly seat of Surfers Paradise for the Country Party. He stood down as mayor in 1973, but remained an alderman. In 1975 he retained his seat in parliament, but narrowly lost it to the Liberal Party candidate, Bruce Bishop, in November 1977. He had again stood for mayor in March 1976, easily defeating his arch political foe, Robert Neumann. While mayor, Sir Bruce bought an official car, a Mercedes 450SL coupé. He claimed that it was for his sole use; when he went interstate or overseas, he refused to make it available to the acting-mayor. His relations with councillors progressively deteriorated over the next two years. Many complained that he acted more as a managing director of his own business than as head of an elected team. Small eventually approached (Sir) Johannes Bjelke-Petersen's government and laid sixteen charges against his fellow councillors. The government dismissed the council and appointed an administrator in March 1978.

Later that year Small fell gravely ill with cancer. Increasingly frail, and reliant upon his son and company secretary Bruce ('Kelly') Small to handle his affairs, he made his final public appearance at a dinner held in his honour on 13 March 1980. His last request to the council, to receive the freedom of the city, was stubbornly refused. Three days before his death, however, he was granted the freedom of the town of Hervey Bay, some 250 miles (400 km) to the north of Surfers Paradise. Survived by his wife and by the son of his first marriage, he died on 1 May 1980 at Benowa and was cremated with Salvation Army forms. Some years passed before his role in the development of the Gold Coast was officially recognized: Mark Andrews' statue of Small was erected in Elkhorn Avenue, Surfers Paradise, in 1986.

V. Freeth, *The Silver Anniversary* (Melb, 1945); A. McRobbie, *The Surfer's Paradise Story* (Surfers Paradise, Qld, 1982); *Courier-Mail*, 18 May 1960, 2 May 1980; *Age* (Melb), *Australian*, *Gold Coast Bulletin*, and *Telegraph* (Brisb), 2 May 1980; *Sunday Sun* (Brisb), 11 Sept 1988.

ROBERT I. LONGHURST

SMART, SIR ERIC FLEMING (1911-1973), wheat-farmer and grazier, was born on 12 October 1911 at Narridy, South Australia, third child of Australian-born parents Percival Horace Smart, farmer, and his wife Lilian Louise, née Rogers. Educated at Washpool Public School and (as a boarder) at Prince Alfred College, Adelaide, Eric worked on the family farm at Jamestown. By the age of 18 he was share-farming and running a thriving business delivering salt. Responding to a land-owner's advertisement in a newspaper calling

for a share-farmer with plant, he travelled to Watheroo, Western Australia, in 1935. He had only £200, and spent all but £25 in making a deposit on a tractor and buying a utility truck. The landowner paid for a seeder and fuel, a friend lent a plough, and a lad helped in return for payment after harvest.

With fair crops but low prices in 1935 and 1936, Smart barely covered his costs. In 1937 an opportunity arose for larger-scale share-farming on Tootra station at Bindi Bindi. A 3500-acre (1400 ha) crop and better prices yielded a profit of £10 000 which became the springboard for further expansion on leased and purchased land. On 15 September 1938 at the Pirie Street Methodist Church, Adelaide, Smart married Jean Constance Davis. He bought Mount Rupert, a 10 000-acre (4000 ha) station at Wongan Hills, Western Australia, in 1940. Six years later his bank invited him to buy 25 000 acres (10 000 ha) near Mingenew, comprising Fairview station, on heavy soil to the east of the town, and an adjoining, virgin, sand-plain block known as The Dip. He renamed the station Erregulla Springs, moved there in 1949 and built a new homestead in 1950. Further purchases of unimproved light land brought the area to 80 000 acres (32 000 ha), in addition to which he leased another 7000 acres (2800 ha) of heavy land.

The Western Australian blue lupin had been long naturalized and sown on the red soils around Geraldton and Gingin for feeding sheep. Smart showed that, by using super-phosphate, lupins would also thrive on sand-plains and build up fertility for cereal cropping. The Department of Agriculture showed little interest in lupins and at first did not share his vision or welcome his field-days. For his part, Smart supported scientific research and hosted departmental trials at Erregulla Springs which showed how, after initial fertility build-up, introduced clovers gave a more diversified and productive agriculture. The practices pioneered included aerial spraying of insects and fertilizing of cereals with nitrogen.

In 1950 the grain production from Smart's properties set an Australian individual record of 102 000 three-bushel bags (8200 tons). This figure regularly increased and passed 500 000 bushels (13 400 tons) in 1967. That year Smart also produced nearly 3000 bales of wool from 105 000 sheep. By 1955 Erregulla Springs had twenty-four houses and a resident population of 120; it boasted a swimming-pool, a tennis-court, a cricket field and a community bus.

Smart detailed his methods and philosophy in a booklet, *West Australian Wasteland Transformed* (Geraldton, 1960). Two points stood out. First, the importance of appreciating the value of labour—to look after one's employees, to pay them well, and to give credit where due. Second, the need to make the best use of machinery. Underlying his success was a firm Protestant ethic, born of his Methodist background, of hard work, integrity, and community involvement. He served on the Wongan-Ballidu (1947-49) and the Mingenew (1950-56 and 1958-60) road boards, and on the Mingenew Shire Council (1961-67). In 1955 he was appointed O.B.E. He was knighted in 1966.

Of middle height and solid build, with brown receding hair and a florid complexion, Sir Eric had piercing blue eyes. He possessed restless energy, a quick mind and the capacity for lightning calculation. Although generous, he could be impatient. Devoted to his family, he loved tennis, golf, the company of friends, travel, his pipe, a fine cigar and a good whisky. Ill health forced him into semi-retirement in Perth in 1966. Survived by his wife, and their son and two daughters, he died of a coronary occlusion on 10 June 1973 at his Dalkeith home and was cremated with Anglican rites. He bequeathed $200 000 to the University of Western Australia for continued research on the West Midlands light lands, with particular attention to the role of lupins.

L. Hunt (ed), *Westralian Portraits* (Perth, 1979); *West Australian*, 31 Dec 1960, 25 Jan 1966, 11 June 1973, 23 Oct 1973; *Countryman* (Perth), 10 Jan 1963; information from Mrs H. Cooksey, Applecross, Perth.   JOHN GLADSTONES

SMERD, STEFAN FRIEDRICH (1916-1978), physicist, was born on 28 July 1916 in Vienna, second son of Rudolf Smerd, mathematician, and his wife Marie, née Pollack. Stefan showed an early love of science and went on to study physics at the Technische Hochschule in 1935-37. Due to the deteriorating political situation in Europe, he and his elder brother Hans migrated to Britain in 1938. There he won a scholarship to the University of Liverpool (B.Sc., 1942; D.Sc., 1965). Although he was interned in Canada for almost a year owing to his nationality, he successfully completed his degree with first-class honours in physics.

For the remainder of World War II Smerd worked at the University of Birmingham and at the Admiralty Signals Establishment at Witley, Surrey, on secret projects connected with the development of radar. His experience enabled him to obtain a position in the division of radiophysics with the Council for Scientific and Industrial Research (Commonwealth Scientific and Industrial Research Organization from 1949). He arrived in Sydney on 29 May 1946, nine days after his widowed father reached Melbourne from Egypt. At St Jude's Church of England, Randwick, on 6 December 1947 Steve married Elizabeth Mary Fraser, a C.S.I.R. laboratory-assistant.

By 1948 Smerd was working with Joe Pawsey [q.v.15] on theoretical aspects of the new field of radio astronomy. Acquiring a strong interest in radio emission from the sun, he rapidly gained an international reputation for his work on thermal processes in the 'quiet' sun, and for that on the extremely energetic non-thermal phenomena associated with solar disturbances. Although his work was largely theoretical, he was particularly fascinated by the observational side of solar radio astronomy. He applied his theories to many practical problems and developed a deep insight into the sun's physical processes.

As one of the world's leading solar physicists, Smerd received numerous invitations to attend conferences and join scientific committees. He established a world data centre for solar radio emission during the International Geophysical Year (1957-58), became an active member of the International Astronomical Union, travelled extensively, and formed close professional and personal contacts with scientists throughout the world.

In 1971 Smerd succeeded his long-term colleague J. P. Wild as head of the solar radio astronomy group and director of the C.S.I.R.O. solar observatory at Culgoora, near Narrabri, New South Wales. Although the administrative responsibilities increased his workload, he accepted this new challenge with enthusiasm and used his knowledge as a catalyst to stimulate and motivate those around him.

Beyond his scientific pursuits, Smerd maintained his interest in politics, sport and community activities. Stemming from a humane and slightly old-fashioned form of socialism, his social philosophy championed the cause of the underprivileged. His keen sense of humour, rich, deep voice and charming nature endeared him to his friends and colleagues. He died on 20 December 1978 while undergoing heart surgery at Royal Prince Alfred Hospital, Camperdown, and was cremated; his wife, and their daughter and three sons survived him.

K. Bittman (ed), *Strauss to Matilda* (Syd, 1988); *SMH*, 30 May 1946; Smerd personal file (CSIRO, Syd); naturalization file, A435, item 1947/4/3526 (NAA, Canb); C3830, item F1/4/SME, SP11/2, item Austrian-Smerd, S. F. (NAA, Syd).
                                        PETER ROBERTSON

SMITH, ADDIE VIOLA (1893-1975), solicitor and trade commissioner, was born on 14 November 1893 at Stockton, California, United States of America, daughter of Rufus Roy Smith, publisher, and his wife Addie Gabriela, née Brown. Viola qualified in business administration at Heald's Business College, San Francisco, in 1908. Employed (from 1910) by a large merchandising firm in California, she moved to the United States Department of Labor, Washington, D.C., in 1917 and studied part time at the Washington College of Law, American University (LL.B., 1920). In October 1920 she was the first woman to join the U.S. Foreign Service, being appointed as clerk to the trade commissioner in Peking (Beijing). Promoted to assistant trade commissioner at Shanghai in 1922 and to trade commissioner in 1928, she was also registrar of the China Trade Act (1922). In 1934 Smith was admitted to practise in the U.S. Court for China. She was American consul and secretary at Shanghai from 1939.

In 1926 Smith had met Eleanor Hinder [q.v.9], who had come to China as industrial secretary of the Young Women's Christian Association. They worked together to re-form the Joint Committee of Shanghai Women's Organizations, and ran its campaign against the use of child labour in foreign-owned silk mills and match factories at Shanghai. Continuing to live and work in that city until 1941, they became devoted to each other, shared a house, and created a garden.

Back in Washington, Miss Smith worked (1942-43) as a China economic specialist for the American government. From 1944 to 1945 she represented the China-America Council of Commerce and Industry in Washington. She returned to China in 1946 to establish its headquarters at Shanghai. Eleanor, who had been repatriated in 1942, joined her there. Based in Bangkok in 1949-51, Smith inaugurated and directed the trade promotion division of the secretariat for the United Nations Economic Commission for Asia and the Far East. At the U.N. in New York, she represented the International Federation of Women Lawyers in 1952-64 and was a member of the I.F.W.L.'s executive-committee.

Following Hinder's failure to gain permanent entry to the United States, she and Smith acquired the top floor of her niece's house at Neutral Bay, Sydney, in the mid-1950s. They lived mainly in New York until 1959, continued to travel frequently (often on U.N. business) and attended conferences. Eleanor's relations, especially her sister Marie Farquharson [q.v.14], welcomed Viola as a member of the family. After Eleanor died in April 1963, Viola acted as executrix of her estate. A member of the Royal Australian Historical Society, she continued to research the Hinder genealogy. She also arranged and annotated her friend's papers, and deposited them in the Mitchell [q.v.5] Library.

A long-time member of the League of Women Voters, Sydney, Smith was vice-president (1968-70) of the Australian Local Government Women's Association. In 1975 she published *Women in Australian Parliaments and Local Governments, Past and Present*. She died on 13 December that year at Mosman and was cremated. Her friends placed two stone seats in the E. G. Waterhouse [q.v.12] National Camellia Gardens, Carlingford, as a memorial.

New York Times, 5 Nov 1920, 23 Feb 1930, 18 Oct 1937, 23 Feb 1946; *SMH*, 20, 22 Mar 1929, 26 Nov 1940, 5 Apr 1977; *Sun-Herald* (Syd), 19 Aug 1962; Hinder papers (ML); immigration files, SP606/2, item 56/34960, SP908/1, item American/Smith A. V., SP1122/1, item N1958/60847 (NAA, Syd); Twelfth Census . . . 1900, San Joaquin, California, US, vol 108, ED 112, p 3 (National Archives, Washington DC).   HEATHER BARKER

SMITH, ARTHUR SYDNEY VICTOR (1893-1971), public servant and businessman, was born on 22 January 1893 at Coburg, Melbourne, son of Victorian-born parents Oscar Victor Smith, printer, and his wife Mary, née Collins. Arthur began work at the age of 14 as a telegraph messenger in the Postmaster-General's Department and transferred to the Department of Defence in 1910. At St John's Church of England, Sorrento, on 11 June 1918 he married Gladys Lavina Muriel Ford, a typiste. On being appointed secretary of the Contract Board in 1925, he began a long association with (Sir) John Jensen and A. E. Leighton [qq.v.14,10].

In 1933 Smith became secretary of the Principal Supply Officers' Committee. He was to play a key role in planning Australia's industrial mobilization in the event of war. Promoted departmental assistant-secretary in 1938, he moved to the new Department of Supply and Development in the following year. When World War II broke out, he was chairman of the Contract Board, and a member of the Factories Board and the Defence Supply Planning Committee. From 1940 he was also a member of the Aircraft Production Commission. Smith travelled to New Delhi in October 1940 as a member of the Australian delegation to the Eastern Group Conference, and revisited India in 1941 to assist Sir Bertram Stevens [q.v.12] in forming the Australian section of the Eastern Group Supply Council which co-ordinated logistic support for the war effort. An unpretentious man, Smith responded to a request from Indian officials for biographical details: 'I was born in Carlton, educated in Fitzroy, and by choice . . . should still be living in Footscray'.

On 1 July 1941 Smith was appointed secretary of the Department of Supply and Development (Supply and Shipping from 1942). With an annual expenditure of over £200 million, the department was responsible for the control of shipping and navigation, the supply of stores and materials (other than munitions) to meet defence and civilian requirements, the production and export of minerals, and the management of liquid fuels, coal and goods in short supply. It also monitored the nation's industrial capacity.

In March 1942 Smith accompanied Dr H. V. Evatt [q.v.14] to Washington in an effort to secure greater collaboration between the United States of America, Britain and Australia in fighting the war in the Pacific. The mission led to the establishment of the Pacific War Council. While Evatt proceeded to London, Smith remained in Washington as Australia's representative at council meetings, and communicated directly with Prime Minister John Curtin [q.v.13] on the acquisition of equipment and supplies for Australia's armed forces. Allan Dalziel [q.v.13] considered that Smith's and W. S. Robinson's [q.v.11] efforts to negotiate with American supply and service chiefs, to obtain shipping space, and to speed up production of essential equipment were 'invaluable factors in Australia's race against time as the Japanese drew nearer'.

Back home in June 1942, Smith served as chairman of the Allied Supply Council, as secretary of the Standing Committee on Liquid Fuels, and as a member of the Allied Consultative Shipping Council and the Oil Advisory Committee. Appointed chairman of the Commonwealth Disposals Commission in 1944, he oversaw the sale of surplus matériel. He resigned from the public service in April 1945 on the grounds of ill health.

Moving to Sydney, Smith became a director of a number of companies, among them Electricity Meter & Allied Industries Ltd, Associated Rural Industries Ltd and Petroleum & Chemical Corporation (Australia) Ltd. Prime Minister (Sir) Robert Menzies [q.v.15] appointed him to the National Security Resources Board in 1950 and, next year, informally commissioned him to investigate security resource management in the United States. In 1951 Smith was appointed C.B.E. Two years later he was engaged as business adviser to the minister for supply on matters relating to long-range weapons projects.

Smith was stocky in build and had a distinctive walk—'a sort of deep sea roll of the shoulders with a habit of carrying his head forward in a semi-aggressive manner'. He was 'a clear thinker, and a quick thinker, with no trace of swank in his make-up' and a smile which came 'suddenly and cordially'. A trusted and competent official, he typified the group of able public servants who had administered Australia's war effort in 1939-45. Survived by his wife and their son, he died on 9 February 1971 at St Vincent's Hospital, Darlinghurst, and was cremated. His estate was sworn for probate at $250 557.

S. J. Butlin, *War Economy 1939-1942* (Canb, 1955); D. P. Mellor, *The Role of Science and Industry* (Canb, 1958); A. Dalziel, *Evatt the Enigma* (Melb, 1967); T. Lawrence, *The Department of Supply, Its Origins and Functions* (Canb, 1971); S. J. Butlin and C. B. Schedvin, *War Economy 1942-1945* (Canb, 1977); A. T. Ross, *Armed & Ready* (Syd, 1995); *Smith's Weekly* (Syd), 29 May 1943.

JUDY POULOS

SMITH, CECILIA (1911-1980), matriarch and Aboriginal activist, was born on 24 March 1911 at Beaudesert, Queensland, second of five children of Aboriginal parents William Hatton, labourer, and his second wife Dolly, née Tate. William, known as 'Pompey', was employed as a stockman and noted for his veterinary skills. Dolly came from Tambo. She had been removed from her family as a child and had worked in Brisbane before her marriage. Educated at Beaudesert and confirmed in the Church of England, Celia found employment as a domestic servant. On 8 August 1932 at Christ Church, Boonah, she married with Anglican rites Ernest Smith, a farm hand. The young couple lived at Dalby and then at Toowoomba. They had separated by 1943 when Celia moved with their four children to Fortitude Valley, Brisbane.

Compassionate and generous, Mrs Smith kept open house where anyone could obtain a hot meal, play a game of cards and receive a few shillings or some second-hand clothing. People needing accommodation stayed for a few days and occasionally longer. Smith visited prisoners in gaol, sometimes sought their release, and welcomed them back into the community. After her only daughter Betty died in the 1950s, she took custody of two of her three children and also cared for several other grandchildren over extended periods. From about 1960 she lived at Carina where she continued to provide hospitality: she grew vegetables and fruit, and cooked meals outdoors on a wood stove for large groups of people.

Joining the Queensland Council for the Advancement of Aborigines and Torres Strait Islanders soon after its formation in 1958, Smith served as honorary secretary (1972-75) and sat on the social committee, helping to run dances to raise money for various causes. She wrote a column (from 1970) in the council's monthly newsletter in which she discussed issues of land rights, wages, conditions on reserves and housing for Aborigines. A member of the Federal Council for the Advancement of Aborigines and Torres Strait Islanders, she attended conferences in Canberra in the 1960s and at Alice Springs, Northern Territory, in 1972. As an executive-member of F.C.A.A.T.S.I.'s women's council, she was a delegate at the fourth national conference of Aboriginal and Islander women, held in Melbourne in 1974.

Smith had campaigned vigorously for a 'Yes' vote in the successful 1967 referendum to empower the Commonwealth government to legislate on Aboriginal affairs. She was often 'on duty' at the 'tent embassy' set up in 1974 at King George Square, Brisbane, to publicize the need for more Aboriginal housing in the city and to protest against the State's repressive Aborigines and Torres Strait Islanders' Affairs Act (1965). In the 1970s she belonged to the Queensland branch of the Union of Australian Women, and kept the organization informed of matters affecting Aborigines. Following abdominal surgery, she died of renal failure on 23 December 1980 in Princess Alexandra Hospital, Brisbane, and was cremated. Her three sons survived her.

J. Bell, *Talking about Celia* (Brisb, 1997); *U.A.W. News*, Feb, June 1974; Qld Council for the Advancement of Aborigines and Torres Strait Islanders, *Newsletter*, June 1971, May 1972, Nov/Dec 1975; *Sunday Mail*, 28 Dec 1980.   YSOLA BEST

SMITH, CHRISTINE IDRIS (1946-1979), skier and interior decorator, was born on 13 December 1946 at Cooma, New South Wales, only child of Gordon Edward Irvine Smith, clerk, and his wife Eunice, née Sturgeon, both of whom were born in New South Wales. Educated at St Patrick's Brigidine convent school, Cooma, and Sydney Church of England Grammar School for Girls, Moss Vale, Christine lived on her maternal family's property at Berridale, close to the snowfields, and learned to ski at an early age.

In January 1962 Smith competed for Australia in the Commonwealth Winter Games at St Moritz, Switzerland. A member of the Australian team at the 1964 Winter Olympic Games, held at Innsbruck, Austria, she was placed 28th in the slalom and 27th in the downhill: her performances were affected by the death of a fellow competitor Ross Milne in the downhill practice. She had wins at home in the 1964 Australian National Alpine Ski Championships (slalom, downhill and giant slalom) and the Thredbo Cup (1963 and 1964). While recuperating from a skiing accident in Europe in 1965, she taught 'The Beatles' to ski for their film, *Help*, and performed in a short skiing sequence. She was unplaced in the 1966 World Ski Championships at Portillo, Chile.

Pre-selected for the 1968 Olympics at Grenoble, France, Smith did not compete when the team was reduced from four to one for the downhill events. She retired from international competition, taught skiing briefly at the dry ski-slope at Brookvale, Sydney, and then instructed children at Thredbo.

In 1974 she established Christine Smith Interiors Pty Ltd. She specialized in bathroom accessories, which she sold from her shop at St Peters, Sydney. Two years later she moved to Bay Street, Double Bay. Described by those in the fashion business as inventive, she added stuffed birds to the décor of one bathroom and used silvery wallpaper and luxuriant plants in another. She gained some notoriety at an interior designer's exhibition with her design for a black bathroom, complete with a nude dummy draped over the bath.

A long-haired blonde with an 'all-Australian girl next door' image, Smith was a stylish and aggressive skier who benefited from overseas competition, but was held back by injury and lack of support. She appeared in fashion magazines and television advertisements promoting ski fashions and products. In 1977 she married an advertising executive Wayne Arthur Garland at Farmington, United States of America; they were to remain childless. She moved her shop to Bondi Junction in 1979, hoping to benefit from the opening of the Eastern Suburbs railway. The opening was delayed.

Depressed by the downturn of her business, Smith committed suicide by swallowing chloralhydrate and paracetamol with salicylic acid on 8 May 1979 in a motel at Crows Nest. She was buried in Berridale cemetery, close to the skifields. In an article published posthumously in the fashion magazine, *Sheila*, she likened skiing to a trip in which 'you reach this curious state between being totally alert and aware of your own body, and being drunk in a dream. Sometimes I feel that if I made a mistake and went over a crevice, I'd be quite happy, just to die like that'.

D. Wynne (ed), *Bathrooms: The Best of Australian Home Journal's Decorating Ideas* (Syd, 1978); *Ski Aust*, Oct, Nov 1961, Aug 1964, Dec 1967, Oct 1968; *Vogue Living*, 15 June-14 Aug 1976, p 64; *Sheila*, Winter, no 2, 1979, p 22; *SMH*, 4 Feb 1962, 8 Dec 1963, 24 Aug 1964, 17 July 1966, 7 Aug 1971, 26 Oct 1978, 20 May 1979; *Sun* (Syd), 15, 16 May 1979; information from Mr P. Kobold, Mawson, Canb.

KERRY REGAN

SMITH, DONALD IAN ROBERTSON (1892-1947), radiologist, was born on 1 March 1892 in North Sydney, son of Scottish-born parents Donald Smith, a civil service clerk who became a dentist, and his wife Jessie, née Fell. Young Donald was educated at Sydney Church of England Grammar School (Shore) and at the University of Sydney (M.B., Ch.M., 1914) where his mentor was (Sir) Thomas Anderson Stuart [q.v.12]. After working as registrar at Sydney Hospital, he was appointed captain, Australian Army Medical Corps, Australian Imperial Force, on 1 March 1916. He served on the Western Front with the 2nd Australian General Hospital and 4th Field

Ambulance, and as regimental medical officer of the 4th Machine Gun Battalion. At the parish church, Harefield, London, on 25 July 1918 he married Frances Margery Chennell, Australian Army Nursing Service, whom he had met at Sydney Hospital. While in England, he trained in the use of X-rays before returning to Sydney. His A.I.F. appointment terminated on 14 November 1919.

Shortly afterwards, Smith moved to Perth and set up a private radiology practice in St Georges Terrace. He was the first medically qualified radiologist in Western Australia. In 1920 he was appointed to the Perth Public Hospital; W. J. Hancock [q.v.9] was its honorary consulting radiologist. Smith guided the development of radiology and extended facilities at the public hospital, and also at St John of God Hospital, Subiaco. In 1933 he relocated his practice to Chennell House, St Georges Terrace. Described as innovative, meticulous and full of boundless energy, he was said to have pioneered the application of valve rectification techniques. Smith's colleagues were impressed by his 'intellectual grand tours' and by rigorous debates over radiology reports at the hospital. He was president (1932-33) and treasurer (1934-43) of the Western Australian branch of the British Medical Association.

Beyond the medical profession, Smith contributed to amateur theatre, and was a competent and enthusiastic pianist, organist and concert performer. A council-member of the West Australian Society of Concert Artists, he played in a number of musicals, including *The Arcadians* (1922). He suffered from Buerger's disease and had one of his legs amputated in 1932, which curtailed his musical-comedy appearances and added a frustrating element of pain to his life. Despite this, he continued to work and to hold posts in theatre companies: he produced *The Girl in the Taxi* (1940) and *Our Miss Gibbs* (1941).

Smith was renowned for his wit. A friend from A.I.F. days related how he had rounded the corner of a recently captured and badly damaged château in France to find Smith playing a tune on a piano as it sank in the mud. Another recalled B.M.A. meetings held at Smith's home, when members moved quickly through the agenda in order to finish the night singing Gilbert and Sullivan songs around the Bechstein piano. Survived by his wife, and their daughter and two sons, Smith died of complications arising from malignant hypertension on 3 January 1947 in Perth and was cremated with Presbyterian forms.

G. C. Bolton and P. M. Joske, *History of Royal Perth Hospital* (Perth, 1982); G. E. Bennett, *A History of Medical X-rays in Western Australia 1896-1970* (Perth, 1983); *MJA*, 3 May 1947, p 574; *Roy Perth Hospital J*, Dec 1958, p 489.

MARY ANNE JEBB

SMITH, FRANK BEAUMONT (1885-1950), producer, director and exhibitor of films, was born on 15 August 1885 at Hallett, South Australia, son of Adelaide-born parents Francis Stringer Smith, postmaster, and his wife Mary Julia, née Blott. Educated (1893-1900) at East Adelaide Public School, 'Beau' became a journalist, working briefly on the staff of the *Critic* and helping to found the *Gadfly*. By 1908 he was press representative for the theatrical entrepreneur William Anderson [q.v.7]. In 1911 he brought from Europe a troupe of midgets, billed as 'Tiny Town'. At Ascot Vale, Melbourne, on 11 March that year he married Elsie Fleming with Presbyterian forms; they were to remain childless. He produced a number of plays after 1913, some of them Australian and others English.

In 1917 Smith turned to film production with *Our Friends the Hayseeds*, inspired by the stories of 'Steele Rudd' [q.v.8 A. H. Davis]. He had previously collaborated in dramatizing them as a play, *On Our Selection*. As a filmmaker, he was producer, director, writer, editor and publicist from the outset. Elsie helped with the scripts and his brother Gordon managed company finances. Of Beau's seventeen silent films (1917-25) and two sound productions (1933-34), the seven about the bucolic Hayseeds were his surest box-office 'hits'. He became Australian silent cinema's most commercially successful producer, due to his rapid, low-cost and regular output of formula films, and to the enthusiasm with which distributors and exhibitors greeted his work. Unlike his creatively superior but financially less secure contemporary, Raymond Longford [q.v.10], he numbered film distribution managers among his closest friends.

Seeking an overseas market in the early 1920s, Smith toyed with the idea of making expensive 'super films', but soon returned to the style of production that earned him the nickname 'One-take Beau'. His output included a horse-racing drama, *Desert Gold* (1919), an anti-German pot-boiler, *Satan in Sydney* (1918), and an inter-racial romance, *The Betrayer* (1921). The latter and *The Adventures of Algy* (1925) were filmed in New Zealand as well as Australia. Nationalism featured in many of the films, notably those adapted from works by A. B. Paterson [q.v.11] (*The Man from Snowy River*, 1920) and Henry Lawson [q.v.10] (*While the Billy Boils*, 1921, and *Joe*, 1924). Of Smith's three films that survive complete, *The Adventures of Algy* can still send an audience into gales of laughter. The sentimental stodge in *The Hayseeds* (1933) is redeemed by flashes of bizarre comedy and genuine affection for rural Australians.

Shrinking profits forced Smith to suspend his film-making in 1925 and to begin exhibiting. That year he was appointed resident managing director of Williamson [q.v.6] Films

(New Zealand) Ltd (later J. C. Williamson Picture Corporation Ltd), Wellington. Although he retired to Sydney in 1938, he continued as a consultant to the company. His genial outlook 'endeared him to all with whom he came in contact'. Dark haired and of medium build, he was gregarious, sentimental, a good storyteller and nobody's fool. On the walls of his home at Killara he kept a representative selection of Australian art. He died of heart disease on 2 January 1950 in Royal North Shore Hospital and was cremated with Anglican rites. His wife survived him.

A. Pike and R. Cooper, *Australian Film 1900-1977* (Melb, 1980); J. Tulloch, *Legends on the Screen* (Syd, 1981); G. Shirley and B. Adams, *Australian Cinema: The First Eighty Years* (Syd, 1983); *Everyones*, 18, 25 Nov 1925; *Dominion* (Wellington, NZ), 6 May 1938; *Showman*, Jan 1950; information from Mrs M. Smith and Ms E. Smith, Lindfield, Syd, and Mr C. Sowry, Ngaio, Wellington, NZ.

GRAHAM SHIRLEY

SMITH, HUGH McCLURE-; see McCLURE SMITH

SMITH, IVOR WARNE; see WARNE-SMITH

SMITH, JACK CARINGTON; see CARINGTON SMITH

SMITH, NORMAN WALTER (1915-1973), Australian Rules football coach, was born on 21 November 1915 at Clifton Hill, Melbourne, second son of Melbourne-born parents Victor Smith, ironworker, and his wife Ethel May, née Brown. Educated at Westgarth Central School, Norm completed an engineering apprenticeship and obtained a job at the Brunswick rope-works of James Miller & Co. Pty Ltd. In 1943 he took over his father's engineering business, moving it from Northcote to North Coburg in 1954. As a young man he had excelled at cricket (which he played at district level) and Australian Rules football. He first played club football for Dennis in the sub-district competition and collected 'a few welts across the ears'. Joining the Melbourne Football Club in the Victorian Football League, he was selected for the first XVIII in 1935. At Wesley Church, Melbourne, on 19 October 1940 he married with Methodist forms Marjorie Victoria Ellis, a typiste.

Frequently chosen as full-forward, Smith played 210 first-grade games and kicked 546 goals for Melbourne. In 1941 he topped the V.F.L. goal-kicking list with 88. He helped Melbourne to four premierships (1939-41 and 1948) and captained the club for three seasons (1945-47). In 1949 he transferred to Fitzroy as captain-coach, but played only seventeen games before retiring as a player in 1950. Two years later he returned to Melbourne as coach. Benefiting from the recruitment of some of the best players in the club's history, he and Melbourne dominated the V.F.L. for a decade, during which the club won six premierships—1955-57, 1959-60 and 1964.

A strong disciplinarian, Smith was known as the 'Demon Dictator' and the 'Martinet of Melbourne'. His canniness and 'stiff auburn hair' earned him a further nickname, the 'Red Fox'. He believed that the club came first and the player second, but had close-knit teams in Melbourne's years of greatness. The development of a quicker, play-on style of football was largely attributable to him. Melbourne sides under Smith were fast, fit and accustomed to success. The crowds watching Australian Rules football grew, with Melbourne-Collingwood games attracting record attendances (115 802 in 1956).

From 1964 tension increased between Smith and a number of influential figures at the club. One factor was the decision by a champion Melbourne player, Ron Barassi, to move to Carlton in 1965 as captain-coach. The Smiths had raised Barassi as a 'son from the time he was 15'. Smith supported his aspirations and even offered to make way for him as coach of Melbourne. When Barassi struck out on his own, some Melbourne officials unfairly accused Smith of ridding himself of a potential rival. In July he was sacked. Although he was reinstated within a week, he never again enjoyed his old relationship with the club. Melbourne's years of glory had passed.

Heart disease compelled Smith to resign from Melbourne in 1967. He recovered sufficiently to coach South Melbourne in 1969-72, taking the Swans to an appearance (1970) in the finals, their first since 1945. Smith was planning to assist Barassi in coaching North Melbourne when his health again deteriorated. He died of a cerebral tumour on 29 July 1973 in his home at Pascoe Vale and was cremated with Presbyterian forms; his wife and their son survived him. Smith's estate was sworn for probate at $22 683.

When coaching, Smith dressed in a suit and tie (and sometimes a cardigan) on fine Saturday afternoons; he donned an old, crumpled raincoat in wet weather. With his beaky nose, furrowed brow and slicked-back hair, he could be both fiery and calculating. To him, teamwork was all. He firmly maintained that 'weak men can't win premierships'. Although he was renowned as a football orator and a stern taskmaster, he was a quiet and retiring man away from the field. Paradoxically, for one who played and coached largely for the love of the game, he did much to professionalize the sport. In 1979 the V.F.L. instituted the Norm Smith medal, awarded annually to the best player in the grand final. Smith's elder brother Len played for Melbourne (1934-35) and Fitzroy (1937-43 and 1945), and coached Fitzroy (1958-62) and Richmond (1964-65). Norm's son Peter played for Melbourne (1966-67) and Carlton (1968-70).

E. C. H. Taylor, *100 Years of Football* (Melb, 1958); J. Dyer and B. Hansen, *The Wild Men of Football* (Melb, 1968); R. Holmesby and J. Main, *The Encyclopedia of AFL Footballers* (Melb, 1998); L. Carroll, *The Grand Old Flag* (Melb, 1999); *Sun News-Pictorial*, 30 July 1973; *Nation Review*, 10-16 Aug 1973; information from Mr P. Smith, Pascoe Vale, Melb.   RICHARD TREMBATH

SMITH, SIR ROSS GREY; *see* GREY-SMITH

SMITH, ROY SHARRINGTON (1892-1971), architect, was born on 24 November 1892 at Launceston, Tasmania, third of six children of Sydney Herbert Smith, commercial traveller, and his wife Grace, née Spong. Roy was educated at The Friends' School, Hobart. Indentured in 1909 to Robert Ricards of Ricards & Heyward, architects, he attended (from 1915) evening-classes under Lucien Dechaineux [q.v.8] at the Hobart Technical School. In 1917 he was admitted to the Tasmanian Institute of Architects. At Holy Trinity Church, Hobart, on 23 August 1922 he married with Anglican rites Isobel Vera Stuart (d.1969), a nursing sister.

After working for a number of local architects, Smith served as an assistant-architect (1925-30) with the Federal Capital Commission, Canberra. In 1930-32 he practised successively in Sydney, London and Dublin. Returning to Launceston, he formed a partnership with Hubert East; Gordon Willing, Jack Newman and Denys Green later joined the firm. With his partners, Smith ran a general practice and designed numerous schools, churches, houses and commercial buildings in northern Tasmania, including Holyman [qq.v.4,9] House, Launceston. His houses were often in a refined vernacular style with Georgian references; his commercial buildings exhibited a restrained Art Deco.

Smith sat for many years on the council of the T.I.A. and was president of the Tasmanian chapter of the Royal Australian Institute of Architects in 1938-40. A founder (1929) of the R.A.I.A., he was a councillor for fourteen years, vice-president (1938-39, 1942-44) and president (1944-46). In 1947 he was elected a fellow of the Royal Institute of British Architects; in 1966 he was made a life fellow of the R.A.I.A.

An active parishioner of St Aidan's Anglican Church, Launceston, Smith became involved in community organizations. For more than twenty years he served on the committees of the (Glenara) Northern Tasmanian Home for Boys (president 1961-68) and the Society for the Care of Crippled Children (vice-president 1966-71): he was responsible for the design of additions and alterations to their buildings. A council-member and chairman (1954-56) of the northern branch of the Royal Society of Tasmania, he also belonged to the Rotary Club of Launceston.

In 1960 Smith helped to found the Tasmanian branch of the National Trust of Australia. For the rest of his life he was its senior architect. His firm carried out restorations on some of Australia's finest colonial houses, among them Franklin [q.v.1] House and Staffordshire House, at Launceston, Clarendon, at Evandale, Malahide, at Fingal, Mount Morriston, at Ross, and Fairfield, at Epping Forest. He revealed his love of the State's architectural heritage in his books, *John Lee Archer, Tasmanian Architect and Engineer* (1962), and *Early Tasmanian Bridges* (1969). Smith was a man of fastidious taste and a skilled photographer; he had gained much from his earlier association with Frank Heyward and East, both of whom appreciated a historical approach to architecture. Survived by his son, he died on 13 September 1971 at his Launceston home and was cremated; his estate was sworn for probate at $54 478. In 1973 the National Trust established a biennial lecture in honour of Smith, Isabella Mead and Karl von Stieglitz.

J. M. Freeland, *The Making of a Profession* (Syd, 1971); *National Trust of Aust (Tas) Newsletter*, 32, Dec 1971, p 1; *Examiner* (Launc), 14 Sept 1971; Smith papers (Launc L); information from Mr J. Newman, Launc, Tas.   BARBARA VALENTINE

SMITH, STANLEY GREIG (1884-1970), charity organizer, was born on 12 August 1884 at Glasgow, Scotland, eldest of three children of James Lockhart Smith, a drapery warehouseman who turned to journalism, and his wife Jessie Annabella, née Gemmell. Educated at Stranraer, Greig wrote for the local newspaper edited by his father. At the age of 16 he joined the civil service in London. On 4 November 1908 at the parish church, Enfield, he married Frances Clara Harris, with whom he migrated to Australia.

In May 1909 Smith became secretary of the Charity Organisation Society, Melbourne. Drawing on his civil-service experience, he enhanced the society's position as the key co-ordinating body for private charities and promoted co-operation with statutory welfare services. He read widely and wrote prolifically. In 1912 he organized the Child Welfare Exhibition in Melbourne and helped to establish the Children's Welfare Association of Victoria. During World War I he held a temporary commission as a lieutenant in the Militia, raised funds for patriotic charities, and investigated the needs of the homeless and the unemployed. He was a foundation council-member (1923) of the Lord Mayor's Metropolitan Hospitals Fund and secretary (1923-58) of the Victorian Society for the Prevention of Cruelty to Children.

Smith played a major role in professionalizing Melbourne's charities. Describing the motives of his co-workers as good but their methods as chaotic, he had established (1913) at C.O.S. headquarters a central register of cases. From 1926 he convened regular case conferences. He lectured to trainee nurses and deaconesses, and, at the University of Melbourne, led a study circle on social-welfare problems. After supervising (from 1929) part of the practical training provided by the Victorian Institute of Hospital Almoners, he helped to found (1931) the Committee for Training on Social Work (Victorian Council for Social Training). He served on the council's board of social studies which introduced a general course in social work in 1933, a course that was transferred to the university in 1941. Founding president (1935) of the Victorian Association of Social Workers, he was admitted as a member (1946) and life member (1965) of the new professional accreditation body, the Australian Association of Social Workers, despite his lack of formal qualifications.

In London in 1936 Smith had attended the Third International Conference on Social Work, addressed a special meeting of the local C.O.S. and visited the National Society for the Prevention of Cruelty to Children. An enthusiastic participant in Australia's postwar reconstruction, he oversaw the transformation (1946) of the Council for Social Training into the Victorian Council of Social Service, advised the Federal government on immigration and citizenship issues, and chaired (1953) a committee which made recommendations to the Victorian government on the Children's Welfare Act (1954). He also reshaped (1946) the C.O.S. as the Citizens Welfare Service of Victoria. While welcoming the expansion of state social security, he foresaw that the public sector would be unable to meet rising expectations.

Smith retired from the C.W.S. in 1957 and from the V.S.P.C.C. one year later. In 1962 he was appointed M.B.E. A widower, he died on 10 August 1970 at Camberwell and was cremated with Presbyterian forms; his daughter and one of his two sons survived him.

P. Anderson, *The Greig Smith Social Work History Collection* (Melb, 1987); Citizens Welfare Service of Vic, *Annual Report*, 1957-58; *Herald* (Melb), 23 Jan 1915, 28 Sept 1957; S. G. Smith memorial file, L. J. Tierney papers (Dept Social Work, Univ Melb).

SHURLEE SWAIN

SMITH, SYDNEY TALBOT (1861-1948), solicitor, freelance journalist and civic worker, was born on 21 April 1861 at Burnside, Adelaide, son of English-born parents (Sir) Edwin Thomas Smith [q.v.6], merchant, and his first wife Florence, née Stock. When Florence died nine months later, Edwin took Sydney and his 2-year-old sister to England, to be reared by relations in Staffordshire, and immediately returned to business in Adelaide. Educated at Tettenhall College, Wolverhampton, and Trinity College, Cambridge (B.A., LL.B., 1884; M.A., 1889), Sydney exhibited the boundless energy, wide interests, phenomenal reading speed and retentive memory that characterized the rest of his life.

While studying law, Smith attended more than 250 theatrical productions and many art exhibitions in London, Manchester and Birmingham, developed a passion for literature, cricket and soccer, did much debating, choral singing, swimming, running, hiking, cycling, sculling and coxswaining, represented his university at lacrosse and chess, became proficient at the piano, organ, languages, billiards and cards, spent summer holidays travelling in Europe and the United States of America, and wrote reviews and sports reports for two British weeklies. He also forsook his parents' Congregationalism and became a devout Anglican.

Called to the Bar at the Middle Temple in June 1885, Talbot Smith (as he was to style himself) arrived in Adelaide on 23 December that year. He spent Christmas Day serving food and washing dishes at the annual banquet his father gave for the city's poor. It marked the beginning of a lifetime of community service. Admitted to the South Australian Bar on 24 July 1886, he entered a limited-term partnership with his uncle, as (W. F.) Stock & Talbot Smith, Glenelg. On 2 June 1887 at St Matthew's Anglican Church, Kensington, he married Florence Oliver Chettle, who had been his sweetheart for many years. The couple lived in a modest house at Kensington Park, enjoyed a busy social life, and had four sons. Dubbed 'this mighty little man', Smith soon emerged as the prime exemplar of the public-spiritedness of the Adelaide gentry. For decades he served many community organizations. He presided over district cricket, football and athletics clubs, and refereed intercollegiate sports. In 1886 he had joined the education committee for the Adelaide Jubilee

International Exhibition, and the committees of the Kensington and Norwood Institute, and St Luke's Boys' Rescue (the 'Larrikin Tamers'); he also organized cycling and lacrosse competitions, appeared in amateur theatricals, and conducted Sunday services for Anglican clergymen who were absent or ill.

From 1891 Smith practised alone, chiefly as a solicitor. During World War I he was to draw up, without fee, four thousand wills for people who enlisted. More interested in world affairs and the arts than the law, he wrote thousands of leading articles and book reviews for the *South Australian Register* (*Register* from 1901) in 1886-1920 and the *Advertiser* in 1891-1941. He contributed light verse and 'Notes on Books' to magazines such as J. C. Wharton's *Truth*, and, in 1941-43, weekly reminiscences of the pre-Federation era to the Adelaide *News*. For more than fifty years he wrote all the reports on South Australian sporting and theatrical events for the Sydney *Bulletin*.

As president of the South Australian Literary Societies' Union (1904-05) and the Amateur Athletics Association (1905-07), and as vice-president (1937-45) of the South Australian School of Arts and Crafts, Smith was always ready to muck in with the chores. He sat (1903-25) on the council of the University of Adelaide, and chaired its finance committee. From 1908 he wrote programme notes on 'The Play' and 'The Author' for every production of the Adelaide Repertory Theatre. Chairman (1919-24), vice-president (1929-30) and president (1931-48) of that society, he kept it afloat through the Depression.

From 1910 until his death, Smith was government representative on the council of the Institutes Association of South Australia and chairman of its literature committee. Throughout that period every one of the 420 000 new books purchased with public money for South Australia's three hundred institute libraries had to meet with his approval. He wrote a vast amount for the association's *Journal* and, as its president (1939-43), inspected institute premises throughout South Australia, using his own motorcar at a time when many country roads were little better than tracks. A gifted and witty public speaker, he accepted innumerable invitations to lecture in most parts of the State.

Smith's father had declined a baronetcy, saying that he 'did not approve of the hereditary principle'. He provided for his grandchildren in his will, but, on his death in 1919, bequeathed to his son a mere £2000 from an estate that was sworn for probate at £238 000. Talbot evinced no bitterness, acknowledging that he had been given a good start in life. He served (from 1921) on the board of governors of the Public Library, Museum and Art Gallery of South Australia, and was president in

1926-29 and 1937-39. He chaired the Libraries Board of South Australia (1940-48), and the central committee of the Commonwealth Literary Fund (1931-39) and its advisory board (1939-44). At the Adelaide Club, he waged a long (twenty-four years) and ultimately successful campaign to have some Australian wines stocked and offered as an alternative to the imported products served at club functions. A member (1913-15) of the ground and finance committee of the South Australian Cricket Association, he endowed the Talbot Smith Fielding Trophy in 1930, still awarded for the best performance in the State's A-grade district competition. In 1940-48 he was widely known and admired as 'The Man Who Remembers' for his participation in the top-ranking commercial radio show 'Information Please'. In 1941 he was appointed O.B.E.

Despite his varied skills, Smith was an appalling driver; his carelessness had caused the accident in 1935 which resulted in the death of his wife. Two delights of his latter years were serving on the South Australian advisory committee of the Australian Broadcasting Commission and having his hero (Sir) Donald Bradman as a next-door neighbour and billiards partner. Survived by three sons, he died on 3 October 1948 in his Kensington Park home and was cremated. His other son Lieutenant Eric Wilkes Talbot Smith had died on 30 April 1915 from wounds received at Gallipoli.

M. J. Doherty, *The Talbot-Smith Fielding Trophy* (Adel, 1984); M. R. Talbot, *A Chance to Read* (Adel, 1992); *SA Institutes J*, 30 Nov 1948; *The Times* and *Advertiser* (Adel), 4 Oct 1948; Smith papers (held by Messrs J. Talbot-Smith, Yankalilla, and I. Talbot-Smith, Goolwa, SA); information from the late Sir Donald Bradman. P. A. HOWELL

SMITH, SIR TOM ELDER BARR (1904-1968), pastoralist and company director, was born on 28 April 1904 at Glen Osmond, Adelaide, fifth of six children of Tom Elder Barr Smith [q.v.11], a South Australian-born pastoralist, and his wife Mary Isobel, née Mitchell, who came from Scotland. His grandfather was Robert Barr Smith [q.v.6]; his great-uncle was Sir Thomas Elder [q.v.4]. The dynasty into which young Tom was born shaped both his education and subsequent career. He was sent to Queen's School, Adelaide, then to Geelong Church of England Grammar School, Victoria, and in 1924 to Trinity Hall, Cambridge. He did not graduate. Having undertaken a business course in the United States of America, he returned to South Australia and became involved in the family's pastoral and financial concerns.

Commissioned lieutenant, Australian Field Artillery, Militia, in 1930, Barr Smith (as he styled his surname) was made honorary captain while serving (1931-33) as aide-de-camp to Sir Alexander Hore-Ruthven [q.v.9 Gowrie], governor of South Australia. On 3 March 1936 at St John's Church of England, Toorak, Melbourne, he married Nancy Leland Green (d.1960). They lived in the family mansion, Birksgate, at Glen Osmond and were to have four children. Following his father's death in 1941, he became chairman of several family firms, among them the Mutooroo, Beltana and Milo pastoral companies, Lake Victoria Proprietors, Auchendarroch Pty Ltd and Mundabullangana Ltd.

Barr Smith was a board-member (from 1941) of Elder, Smith & Co. Ltd. After it merged (1962) with Goldsbrough Mort [qq.v.4,5] & Co. Ltd, he continued as a director until 1968. At various stages he chaired Cellulose Australia Ltd, Elder's Trustee & Executor Co. Ltd and the Stockowners' Co-operative Shearing Co. Ltd, and sat on the Adelaide board of the Commercial Union Assurance Co. of Australasia Ltd. He was also deputy-chairman (1960-68) of the Adelaide Steamship Co. Ltd and a director (1960-68) of Lensworth Finance Ltd.

A member (1944-49) of the Adelaide City Council, Barr Smith served (1945-56) on the committee of the South Australian division of the Australian Red Cross Society, presided over Toc H and chaired the livestock section of the Food for Britain appeal. He was a member (from 1922) and benefactor of the Adelaide Club, and sometime president of the Queen's School Old Boys' Association. Keen on sport, he sat (1942-54) on the committee of the South Australian Jockey Club, belonged to the Royal South Australian Yacht Squadron, and enjoyed playing golf. A friendly and generous man, he was noted for his philanthropy, much of which went undisclosed. He endowed the University of Adelaide with a scholarship (1953), in memory of his father, to study agriculture at the University of Cambridge, and with a cancer-research scholarship (1962), named after his wife. In 1959 he was knighted.

From 1948 Barr Smith had been consul for Sweden in South Australia. In 1960 he was appointed to the Royal Order of Vasa. Suffering from pulmonary tuberculosis, he died of emphysema on 5 March 1968 at Victor Harbor and was cremated. Sir Tom's son and three daughters survived him. His estate was sworn for probate at $1 410 560.

M. I. Legoe, *A Family Affair* (Adel, 1982); *Pastoral Review*, 18 Apr 1968; *Bulletin*, 6 Mar 1979.

MARTIN SHANAHAN

SMITHERS, SIR ARTHUR TENNYSON (1894-1972), public servant, was born on 30 June 1894 at Echuca, Victoria, fourth of five sons of Frederick Smithers, a piano-tuner from England, and his Victorian-born wife Rachel, née Spearritt, late Cocks. Arthur was educated at Echuca State School and, after the family moved to Melbourne, at Prahran College. His first job was with a South Yarra estate-agent, A. E. Oakley, who collected the rent for the Smithers' family home in Domain Road. On 25 May 1911 he joined the Victorian Public Service as a clerk in the Treasury. His younger brother (Sir) Reginald said that he 'had plenty of brains'. 'Tenny' improved his prospects by studying at night and qualifying as an associate of the Commonwealth Institute of Accountants.

At St Mary's Church of England, Caulfield, on 21 April 1920 Smithers married Constance Helen Wise, an artist. His diligence, patience, competence and commitment to his work were rewarded with regular promotions. In 1927 he attended the meeting of the Australian Loan Council, the body which determined borrowings by the Commonwealth and the States. He took part in each of the council's annual meetings until 1959. Appointed State director of finance on 1 September 1937, he became adviser to six different premiers (all of whom held the additional portfolio of the Treasury) in eleven successive governments. In a period when it was common for departmental heads to retain office for long terms, he remained director of finance for twenty-two years.

At that time State government ministers had no private advisers to reflect the views of interest groups or the general community. They depended on their public servants. Treasury was the key department, regarded as the repository of wisdom and authority. As its head, Smithers was seen as being very much 'in control'. He signed the cheques. Ministers asked him whether he could provide the funds they needed. The Treasury's relatively simple set of accounting-books was kept in a room at 2 Treasury Place, Melbourne, in which clerks sat on stools at a long, sloping desk, and prepared invoices, cheques and receipts. The room led to the office of the director of finance. Accounts and statements from every department were delivered by hand to that office. Throughout his career Smithers kept above the sectarianism that was rife in the public service. In 1949 he was appointed C.B.E. He was knighted in 1959, the year of his retirement.

A trustee (from 1937) of the Shrine of Remembrance, Smithers had joined the Royal Melbourne Hospital's management-committee in 1941. He was appointed a trustee of the National Gallery of Victoria in 1945 and a director of the Australian Elizabethan Theatre Trust in 1954. After retiring from the public service, he was chairman (1961, 1965 and

1970) of the State Savings Bank of Victoria and a director of several companies, including Portfolio & Development Ltd and Southern Cross Properties Ltd.

Smithers loved to sing. As a boy and young man he had performed at Ballarat in the South Street competitions and was said to have considered a career in the theatre. He was lead tenor in the choir of St Mary's, Caulfield, for most of his adult life. Accompanied by his wife at the piano, he frequently sang at weddings and birthday parties. They visited and received friends on Saturday nights for cards and supper. The family spent summer holidays at Point Lonsdale, where Arthur swam, and played beach-cricket and golf. He was fond of Shakespeare and supported the Melbourne Football Club.

Survived by his wife and their two daughters, Sir Arthur died on 28 June 1972 at Parkville and was cremated. A journalist noted that his birth and cremation had both occurred on 30 June—the end of the financial year.

Age (Melb), 29 June 1972; *Herald* (Melb), 29 June, 1 July 1972; unpublished autobiog of Sir Reginald Smithers (ts held by Mr R. Bailey, St Andrews, Vic).   JOHN CAIN

SMORGON, NORMAN (1884-1956), businessman, was born on 17 December 1884 at Heidelberg, Ukraine, Russia, and named Naum, son of Gershon Smorgon, butcher, and his wife Leah, née Batagol. Naum received a traditional Jewish education—predominantly involving religious studies that focused on the Bible, the Talmud and the Hebrew language—and learned to read and write Russian. The region around the village of Heidelberg was inhabited by German farmers, in whose language he also became fluent.

As a young man, Smorgon followed his father's trade and helped in the family's small business. On one of his rounds with the butcher's cart, he met Tzippa Mejov, from the neighbouring village of Blumental. Breaking tradition, they made their own courting arrangements without a matchmaker. They were married at Blumental in 1908 and were to have four children. Naum and Tzippa lived at Heidelberg and opened a small mixed-goods store in a shed adjacent to their cottage. Russian laws which restricted the movement and occupations of Jews were abolished in March 1917. In the following year the Smorgons settled at Bol'shoy Tokmak, where Naum established a tannery with his youngest brother, Isak. The two then went into the flour-milling business with their brothers Abram and Moses.

To escape anti-Jewish violence during the Russian Civil War, the extended Smorgon family moved to Mariupol (Zhdanov) on the Sea of Azov. Naum and his brothers again took up flour-milling. Tzippa suffered from paralysis. Because her husband was unable to care for her, she returned to her own family. He divorced her in 1925. Within a year he married Vera Naumovna Feldman at Mariupol; they were to remain childless. After political and economic turmoil caused the mill to close, the brothers eventually re-established themselves in tanning. The rise of Josef Stalin worried Naum deeply. In 1927 he persuaded the family to migrate to Australia, where his sister Bertha had settled.

Having worked as a hawker in Victoria, Smorgon established a kosher butcher's shop in 1927 at Carlton, Melbourne, in association with Moses, Abram and some cousins. The business expanded rapidly and Norman's younger son Victor developed a wholesaling arm. When the original partnership broke up, Norman, and his sons Eric and Victor turned to meat canning and exporting. In 1944 they built large meatworks at Brooklyn. About that time the family reunited and the enterprise continued to grow. Norman Smorgon & Sons Pty Ltd began to export rabbit meat and canned fruit, competing with larger concerns such as the Shepparton Preserving Co. Ltd.

Smorgon was a heavy-set and powerful man, the acknowledged leader of the family. He pushed those around him to try new ventures and improve their lives. In the early 1950s he began to spend much of his time in London, overseeing the family company's export operations. He divorced Vera in 1954. That year, at Honolulu, Hawaii, he married Michelle Langer, a Polish-born divorcee. His first wife Tzippa had recovered from paralysis and migrated to Australia; she lived with their daughter Annia Castan and her family. While holidaying in Israel, Smorgon suffered a stroke and died on 11 March 1956 at Tel Aviv and was buried there. His wife survived him, as did the two sons and two daughters of his first marriage.

Over the next forty years the family enterprise diversified into the manufacture of paper, cardboard, steel, glass, plastic and electronic equipment. Prominent in philanthropic causes, Smorgon Consolidated Industries was one of the largest private industrial corporations in Australia by 1995 when the family decided to sell its operational arms.

R. Myer, *Living the Dream* (Syd, 2000); *Age* (Melb), 18 Feb 1995; naturalization file, series A435/1, item 1945/4/6996 (NAA, Canb).

                                           ROD MYER

SNEDDON, ANDREW WILLIAM (1880-1945), insurance manager, was born on 2 January 1880 at Wallsend, New South Wales, second of ten children of Alexander Sneddon, a blacksmith from Scotland, and his native-born wife Christina, née Johnson. Educated at Sydney Boys' High School, Andrew joined the Australian Mutual Provident Society on 4 January 1897 as a clerk. In 1908 he was transferred to the A.M.P.'s London office. Three years later he qualified as a fellow of the Institute of Actuaries. At St John's Presbyterian Church, Forest Hill, London, on 20 September 1913 he married Amelia Mary Esdale Dunn. Returning to Sydney in 1914, he worked in the A.M.P.'s actuarial department. He completed (1916) the examinations of the Institute of Incorporated Accountants of New South Wales.

In December 1926 Sneddon was appointed manager of the industrial insurance department. He rose rapidly to become general manager of the A.M.P. Society in 1934. Made the actuary in 1938, he held the dual positions until his death. By the 1930s the A.M.P. had lost much of the vigour that had made it one of the largest life-insurance organizations in the world. Management was lacklustre. The society had grown staid, content to follow its competitors' innovations.

Taking control just as the Australian economy was starting to recover from the Depression, Sneddon promoted an active sales strategy. Under his leadership, selling was coordinated centrally, with new incentives for staff. He recognized the strategic importance of industrial life insurance: this took the form of small policies, with premiums collected weekly, door-to-door, and was designed for those who could not afford ordinary life insurance.

Sneddon liked to describe himself as a 'bush' actuary. He was unpretentious and pragmatic, with a shrewd understanding of business. Stoutly built, with a bald head and a bristling moustache, he had rowed and played lacrosse as a young man. He later served as president of the Sydney Rowing and Long Reef Golf clubs, and belonged to the Australian Golf and the Australian clubs. Sometime president of the Incorporated Australian Insurance Institute, the Life Officers' Association of Australia and the Actuarial Association of Australia and New Zealand, he also chaired (1941-45) the council of Women's College, University of Sydney.

From his experience in London, Sneddon knew that British life-insurance offices had wider powers of investment than their Australian equivalents. He persuaded the board of the need to change, but, due to the A.M.P.'s constitution, implementation required legislation. The Australian Mutual Provident Society's (Amendment) Act of 1941 empowered the society to purchase shares. This important step had no immediate effect because, during World War II, all new investments were channelled towards government war loans.

The war also meant that life-insurance companies had to carry out additional work with far less staff. Sneddon not only held the A.M.P. together, but positioned it to become a dominant presence in the Australian share-market. The work, however, impaired his health. He died of a coronary occlusion on 10 November 1945 at his Mosman home and was cremated. His wife and their daughter survived him.

Notable Citizens of Sydney (Syd, 1940); G. Blainey, *A History of the AMP 1848-1998* (Syd, 1999); *Mutual Provident Messenger*, July 1903, July 1904, July 1910, June 1911, Feb 1914, Mar 1916, Jan 1927, July 1931, Oct 1933, Sept, Dec 1934, May 1938; *A'sian Insurance and Banking Record*, 69, no 11, 1945, p 549; *Inst of Actuaries Year Book* (Britain), 1946-47, p 236.   CLARE BELLIS

SNELLING, HAROLD ALFRED RUSH (1904-1979), solicitor-general, was born on 12 September 1904 at Petersham, Sydney, son of Alfred John Snelling, a compositor from England, and his wife May Martha, née Rush, who was born in New South Wales. Educated at Fort Street Boys' High School and the University of Sydney (LL.B., 1926), Harold graduated with first-class honours. He was admitted to practice as a solicitor on 26 August 1927 and entered into partnership with Alexander Stanley Gourlay as Gourlay & Snelling.

At St Thomas's Church of England, North Sydney, on 19 November 1932 Snelling married Ruth Neilley. More ambitious than Gourlay, he transferred to the Bar on 19 December 1933 and took chambers successively at 170, 167 and 148 Phillip Street. He was an imperturbable advocate, with a relaxed, engaging manner, who built up a successful practice.

Mobilized in the Militia on 22 August 1940, Snelling suspended his practice in 1942 and transferred to the Australian Imperial Force on 25 February 1944. He served in Australia and Papua in the Ordnance Corps, of which, as lieutenant colonel, he became deputy director. Following his demobilization on 1 May 1945, he soon expanded his diverse practice. He took silk on 4 May 1952. On the retirement of C. E. Weigall [q.v.12] as solicitor-general, Snelling was appointed to the vacancy in August 1953. He brought to the office not only great ability, but also his individual style, being invariably attired in morning dress and, out of doors, a homburg hat. Almost half of Snelling's tenure coincided with that of his contemporary Robert Reginald Downing as State attorney-general. Downing, an able lawyer, himself conducted in court many State constitutional and public law cases. Snelling's particular forte was in crown fiscal matters, in which he appeared frequently in the Supreme

Court, the High Court of Australia and the Privy Council (he habitually took mid-year cruises to England).

When Chief Justice Sir Kenneth Street [q.v.] retired in 1960, it was an open secret in the legal profession that Snelling was favourably considered—and supported by ancient Crown Law Office convention—as his successor. Political considerations, however, attended the installation of the ailing Herbert Vere Evatt [q.v.14] in the high judicial office for which Snelling was so well fitted.

Snelling lived at Vaucluse and found recreation in gardening at his Leura retreat, and in swimming. He was president of the Australian branch of the International Law Association, a leader in the Australian Academy of Forensic Sciences, president of the Nielsen [q.v.11]-Vaucluse Park Trust and a vice-president of the Millions (Sydney from 1963) Club.

On attaining statutory retiring age in 1974, Snelling relinquished the solicitor-generalship, having advised governments of contrary political persuasions with unvarying distinction and professionalism. In 1975 he was appointed C.B.E. He did not long enjoy retirement, being afflicted with Parkinson's disease. Survived by his wife and their three daughters, he died on 26 April 1979 in the Scottish Hospital, Paddington, and was cremated. Sir Kenneth McCaw, a former attorney-general, judged him to have been 'a gentle and good man of deep humility, patience and compassion'. Snelling's daughter Mrs Priscilla Flemming became the first woman to practise privately as a Q.C. in New South Wales.

Aust Law J, 53, Aug 1979; *Bar News* (NSW), 22, 1988; *SMH*, 5 May 1952, 19 Mar 1953, 3 Oct 1967, 30 Apr 1979; information from Mrs P. Flemming, Wollombi, NSW.   J. M. BENNETT

SNIDER, LEON SAMUEL (1896-1965), theatre proprietor, entrepreneur and politician, was born on 6 February 1896 in Melbourne and named Samuel, sixth child of Polish-born immigrants Samuel Phillip Snider, fruiterer, and his wife Rose Dinah, née Palitz. Educated at St Mary's school, West Melbourne (where he established a lifelong friendship with Arthur Calwell [q.v.13]) and at Scotch College, Sam joined his elder brother Mendel in the family's diverse businesses, which included a cider brewery. During World War I he served as a lieutenant in the Militia, based in Melbourne. Following the Armistice, he travelled through Berlin to White Russia, carrying suitcases of cash to assist relations to escape from the Bolsheviks to the United States of America.

On his return to Melbourne, Snider joined Hoyts Theatres Ltd. By the late 1920s he was managing Hoyts in Sydney. Rivals vied to create the most lavish 'picture palace': Snider oversaw the construction of the Regent (1928) and Plaza (1930) theatres in George Street; S. F. Doyle [q.v.8] built the State Theatre (1929) in Market Street. Styling himself Leon Samuel, Snider married 22-year-old Ruth Etta Noreen Cohen on 15 May 1930 at the Great Synagogue, Sydney. They lived first at Bellevue Hill and then at Point Piper, and spent holidays at Jervis Bay where Snider leased (1936-43) a cottage from the Commonwealth government on the site of the former Royal Australian Naval College. In 1937 he helped to found the Temple Emanuel, Woollahra. Increasing anti-semitism in Europe prompted him and others to lobby the Commonwealth government to permit the immigration of central Europeans, many with professional qualifications.

In 1935 Snider resigned from Hoyts. With George Dean, he established Snider & Dean Theatres Pty Ltd, theatrical entrepreneurs and independent film distributors. They bought picture theatres from Sir Benjamin Fuller [q.v.8] in Brisbane, Newcastle, Sydney, Melbourne, Adelaide and Perth. Snider & Dean imported the successful American revue the *Marcus Show* in its entirety in 1937. Two members of its chorus were to have prominent careers—Daniel Kaminski (Danny Kaye) and a hill-billy singer called Bob Dyer. Snider negotiated contracts to assist Jewish musicians, among them the Weintraub Syncopators who settled in Sydney in 1939 and later played at Prince's Restaurant.

Snider's plans to bring cinema to the country encompassed special Friday-night shows at the School of Arts, Carcoar. He owned two theatres at Bathurst, and used bicycle couriers to show—reel by reel—one movie between them. In 1940 he bought Stokefield, a property at Carcoar, and used it as a base from which to supervise the chain of thirty-five 'hardtop' cinemas he had developed throughout western New South Wales. That year he chaired the Film Exhibitors' Council of Australia.

An alderman (1942-48) on Woollahra Municipal Council, Snider was mayor in 1944. He had been elected (1942) as an Independent to the Legislative Council for twelve years, but later joined the Liberal Party. Generous to his political opponents, he also tried to help immigrants and successfully campaigned for refugees to be reclassified as 'friendly aliens'. He served on the select committee on the local government (areas) bill that investigated boundaries within the County of Cumberland. Re-elected for a further twelve years in 1954, he crossed the floor and joined the Country Party in 1959 when some Liberals supported the Australian Labor Party's proposal to abolish the council.

The interests of Snider & Dean expanded to include importing (beer, wine and spirits)

and hotels (in Sydney and the country). After World War II, Snider was agent for Adler Business Machines Inc., a director of Hale's Secretarial Colleges Pty Ltd, Andersons Seeds Ltd and Stenex Business Equipment Co., and chairman of Williamson Gerard (Australasia) Ltd, wine and spirit merchants. By 1956, when it appeared that television would affect attendance at cinemas, he converted to new wide-screen systems and showed such blockbusters as *The Robe* (1953).

A keen racegoer and racehorse-owner, Sam Snider belonged to Tattersall's Club, and to the Monash Country Club for golfers, near Narrabeen. His wife was a foundation member of the American National Club, Sydney. He died of cerebral thrombosis on 9 August 1965 at Rose Bay and was buried in Rookwood cemetery; his wife, and their daughter and two sons survived him.

S. D. Rutland, *Edge of the Diaspora* (Syd, 1988); *PD* (NSW), 24 Aug 1965, p 9; *SMH*, 9 Sept 1935, 20 June 1936, 17 June 1937, 7 Apr 1939, 19 July 1940, 30 Sept 1959, 10 Aug 1965; *Syd Jewish News*, 13 Aug 1965; Dept of Air, A705, item 171/93/556 (NAA, Canb); information from Mrs D. Orr, Carcoar, NSW, Messrs D. and P. Snider, Ultimo, Syd.

ROSSLYN FINN

SNOW, CHARLES SMETHURST (1882-1953), Boy Scout commissioner, was born on 20 September 1882 in Brisbane, eldest of four children of English-born parents Charles William Snow, jeweller, and his wife Lucy Emily, née Garn. Educated at Brisbane Normal and Brisbane Grammar schools, young Charles was apprenticed to his father, and worked as a watchmaker and jeweller in the family business. While serving as organist and choirmaster at St Mary's Church of England, Kangaroo Point, he formed a scout patrol from the lads of the choir and boys' club in 1908. In the following year he helped to establish a controlling body, the Queensland Section of the Australian League of Boy Scouts, and was elected chief scoutmaster. During a visit to Queensland in 1912, Sir Robert (Lord) Baden-Powell presented him with the medal of merit. In 1917 Snow was awarded scouting's highest honour, the Silver Wolf. Scouts competed in campfire and campcraft activities for two trophies named after him, the Snow Cup (1913) and Snow Casket (1918).

Enlisting in the Australian Imperial Force on 17 July 1917, Snow reached England in February 1918. He served as a mechanic with the Australian Flying Corps and was posted to No.1 School of Navigation and Bomb-dropping before being discharged from the army on 13 July 1919 in Brisbane. Resuming his scouting interests, he was made commissioner in September. He was also to hold the offices of commissioner of sea scouts (1921-23), commissioner for adult leader-training (from 1923) and chief commissioner (from 1925). Wearing his scout uniform, he married 22-year-old Una Catherine Gibson on 19 January 1924 at St Andrew's Church of England, Ormiston.

In 1925, at Canungra, he organized the Queensland scouts' first 'corroboree'. Having run classes for scout leaders from 1913, Snow encouraged the Boy Scouts' Association to acquire (1928) Eprapah, a 99-acre (40 ha) bushland property by a creek at Victoria Point, as a training ground for the State's scouts and their leaders. He had a long and practical association with Eprapah, where he showed that he could 'turn his hand to anything'. Although he had limited formal education, he was a 'natural teacher'. In 1930 he was master-in-charge of the Church of England Grammar School's preparatory school, East Brisbane.

Tradition was broken in 1931 when Snow's position of chief commissioner became salaried and full time. He had the vitality, magnetism and autocratic manner to command attention, and was an 'exceptional communicator', able to 'work his audience' as well as involve them. To scouts and scoutmasters, he seemed a local Baden-Powell. In 1933 he led the Australian contingent to the world jamboree at Gödöllö, Hungary. In 1943, after the State governor and chief scout, Sir Leslie Wilson [q.v.12], took exception to having a paid chief commissioner, Snow relinquished the position. He continued as commissioner for training until ill health forced him to retire in 1952.

Survived by his wife, and their son and daughter, Snow died of tonsillar neoplasm on 7 June 1953 at his Hendra home and was cremated. Eprapah was renamed the Charles S. Snow Scout Environmental Activities Centre in 1978; a training centre at Samford for scout leaders was also named (1979) after him.

L. E. Slaughter, *Baden Powell* (Brisb, 1957); R. Fones, *In the Light of all the Years* (Brisb, 1992) and (ed), *Vic Waddell as the Old Timer* (Brisb, 1996); Boy Scouts' Assn (Qld), Minutes, 1909-43 (Brisb); T. Roberts, Peter Snow and Anne Stone (taped interviews, 1995, Qld Scout Centre, Auchenflower, Brisb); family papers held by Mrs A. Stone, Fig Tree Pocket, Brisb.

RALPH FONES

SODERSTEN, EMIL LAWRENCE (1899-1961), architect, was born on 30 August 1899 at Balmain, Sydney, second of seven children of Emil Gustavus Sodersteen, a master mariner from Sweden, and his Sydney-born wife Julia, née Dolleen. From 1915 young Emil studied part time at Sydney Technical College while employed by the architects Ross &

Rowe. In 1921 he attended lectures by Leslie Wilkinson [q.v.12] at the University of Sydney. Form, proportion and the historic styles formed the basis of his training.

With C. B. Dellit [q.v.13], Sodersteen joined F. R. Hall [q.v.9] & Prentice, Brisbane architects, and helped to design the City Hall. In 1923 he returned to Sydney. He was registered as an architect on 26 June that year and worked for John P. Tate [q.v.] & Young on classically designed office-buildings. In 1925 he set up in private practice and executed presentation drawings for other architects. He was a council-member (1927-28) of the Institute of Architects of New South Wales and a fellow (1931) of the Royal Australian Institute of Architects. An outstanding sportsman, he particularly enjoyed skiing and playing polo.

In 1925 Sodersteen had closed his office to prepare a set of drawings for the international competition to design a national war memorial and museum in Canberra. None of the sixty-nine entries satisfied all the requirements of the adjudicators. Only one, by John Crust, remained within budget. C. E. W. Bean [q.v.7] praised Sodersteen's design. It met most of the requirements and his architecture was judged to be 'exceptionally restrained and expressive of the purposes of the building'. Breaking with stylistic tradition, his domed hall of memory rose from a fortress-like base.

An architectural marriage between Crust's economy and Sodersteen's flair was arranged: they were commissioned to produce an amended joint-plan. While Crust managed the project, Sodersteen took control of design. Even more monumentally austere than his original concept, the new version was accepted in 1928, but the Depression delayed work on the building until 1934. Conflict arose between the two architects. Sodersteen withdrew in 1938, leaving Crust to complete the building. The Australian War Memorial was officially opened in 1941, but its Hall of Memory was not completed until 1959. Sited at the top of Anzac Parade on Walter Burley Griffin's [q.v.9] Parliament House axis, Sodersteen's building was the first national architectural monument in Australia.

In Sydney, Sodersteen executed residential buildings, such as the impressive, nine-storey Birtley Towers (1934) at Elizabeth Bay. By imaginative planning and massing, the Art Deco design featured lavish brickwork and earned him 'the contemporary appellation of a modern Horbury Hunt' [q.v.4]. Working with the architects Robertson & Marks [q.v.10] on an extension (1935) to the Australia Hotel, Sodersteen used black glass embellished with silver to create an interior where everything sparkled and shone. Innovative mechanical ventilation of bathrooms allowed living-rooms and bedrooms to have maximum window areas.

Sodersteen's 'skyscraper style' tower for the City Mutual Life Assurance Society Ltd's offices (1936) was one of the first buildings in Sydney to incorporate fully ducted air-conditioning and automatically controlled lifts. During its construction, he had the assistance of his brothers Erik Magnus, an architect, and Karl Arva, a structural engineer. Leaving Erik in charge, Emil left by aeroplane for England in 1935. During his travels he came under the spell of the Functionalist style of the Dutch architects Willem Dudok and H. P. Berlage. On returning to Sydney, he abandoned Art Deco and designed Nesca House (1939), Newcastle, in an uncompromising version of the Functionalist.

Five ft 3 ins (160 cm) tall and about 12 stone (76 kg) in weight, Sodersteen enlisted in the Royal Australian Air Force on 12 June 1942 and was commissioned in August. He served in Papua and New Guinea with No.13 Survey and Design Unit, and performed works inspection duties in Queensland. On 30 August 1945 he was demobilized from the air force with the rank of flight lieutenant. He and his brothers Erik and Karl had changed their surname by deed poll to Sodersten on 19 November 1943. At the Sacred Heart Church, Pymble, on 7 July 1951 Emil married with Catholic rites Elsie Vera Wynn, a 37-year-old secretary. He designed few buildings after the war. The government of Pakistan approved, in 1951, his plans for a chancellery and residence for the high commissioner in Canberra (which was never built) and invited him in 1953 to assist in planning new cities in Pakistan.

Always groundbreakers, Sodersten and Dellit had been the leading Australian architects working in the Art Deco style. They formed a link between Victorian conventions and Modern architecture. A clever and quick draftsman, Sodersten had an acute eye for detail and was a skilled painter. His presentation perspectives rivalled those of professional artists. Survived by his wife, he died of a coronary occlusion on 14 December 1961 at his Manly home and was cremated without religious rites. His estate was sworn for probate at £51 522.

H. Tanner (ed), *Architects of Australia* (Melb, 1981); M. McKernan, *Here is Their Spirit* (Brisb, 1991); *Architecture*, 16, Apr 1927, p 57, 23, Apr 1934, p 79; *Art in Aust*, 15 Nov 1934, p 91; *Building* (Syd), 57, Jan 1936, p 24, 59, Oct 1936, p 28; K. Sodersten, Emil Sodersten FRAIA (B.Arch. thesis, Univ Syd, 1967); P. Biazos (Becerra), The Life and Works of Emil Lawrence Sodersten (B.Arch. thesis, Univ NSW, 1987). PETER REYNOLDS
POPPY BIAZOS BECERRA

SOLE, MARY; *see* LINDSAY

SOLLY, ROBERT HENRY (1883-1968), architect, businessman and lord mayor, was born on 14 December 1883 in Adelaide, eldest of seven children of Robert Henry Solly [q.v.12], an English-born bootmaker who became a Labor politician, and his wife Mary, née Graham. The family moved to Melbourne in 1885. Young Robert was educated at St Ignatius' School, Richmond, and (on a scholarship) at St Patrick's College, East Melbourne, where he proved a brilliant scholar and a champion athlete.

In 1901 Solly began work as a junior draughtsman in the office of I. G. Beaver, architect. He served as Beaver's principal draughtsman for four and a half years before joining Wunderlich [q.v.12] Ltd in 1908 and taking charge of its architectural department. At St Ignatius' Catholic Church, Richmond, on 15 November 1909 he married Victoria O'Brien, a machinist. Solly exemplified Wunderlich's policy of retaining staff who grew with the concern and assimilated its methods, aims and ideals: he became sales manager in 1923, Victorian manager in 1933 and a director in 1948, and he remained on the board until 1963. He was respected in the building industry for the way in which he integrated his knowledge of architectural principles with his grasp of technology. In 1958 he was elected an honorary member of the Master Builders' Association of Victoria.

Eschewing the partisan politics of his father, Solly had been elected to the Melbourne City Council in 1934 as an Independent candidate for Victoria Ward. By 1968 he was the council's longest-serving member. He chaired the finance committee in 1943-53, keeping a 'housewife's eye on the civic purse'. In addition, he represented the council as a commissioner of the Melbourne and Metropolitan Board of Works and a trustee (chairman 1965-67) of the Exhibition Building. Although he remained unaligned with any political party, he was a foundation member of the (non-Labor) Civic Group in 1940. He became something 'of a father figure', 'always ahead of his papers for a meeting' and 'evenly balanced in his judgements'.

On 31 August 1953 Solly was elected lord mayor, for the customary one-year term. He had accepted nomination on the understanding that he would not solicit votes. Of middle height and solid build, he exuded dignity with his erect carriage, silver hair, grave demeanour and measured tread. He was a fluent speaker whose mastery of language was unequalled by his fellow councillors. His reputation for poise and polish made him an appropriate choice to host the visit of Queen Elizabeth II in 1954. Under the chairmanship of Maurice Nathan, he established the Olympic Civic Committee to prepare the city for the 1956 games.

Solly was a warm and generous man, deeply devoted to his family and always anxious to help the young. A smoker and moderate drinker, he had been a leader of his parish's 4-T Club ('teetotal till twenty-two') in his youth. He was a member of the Melbourne Cricket Club, the Fitzroy and Carlton football clubs, the Royal Automobile Club of Victoria and the Melbourne Swimming Club. Survived by his wife and their two daughters, he died on 2 November 1968 in East Melbourne and was buried in Fawkner cemetery.

E. Wunderlich, *Forty Years of Wunderlich Industry, 1887-1927* (Syd, 1927); J. C. Elden, *The Exhibition Trustees, Royal Exhibition Building, Melbourne* (Melb, 1984); *Patrician*, 3, no 3, Dec 1934, 4, no 5, Dec 1941; *Sun News-Pictorial*, 31 Aug 1953; *Advocate* (Melb), 3 Sept 1953, 14 Nov 1968; *Age* (Melb), 4 Nov 1968; Stock Exchange papers, Wunderlich Ltd (Univ Melb Archives); Architects Registration Bd, series 8838, unit 14 (PRO, Vic); information from Mr R. H. Solly, Balwyn, and Mr J. C. Elden, Hawthorn, Melb; personal knowledge.

F. J. KENDALL

SOUTHEE, ETHELBERT AMBROOK (1890-1968), college principal, was born on 6 August 1890 at Cootamundra, New South Wales, eleventh (and fourth surviving) child of Frederick Southee, a baker from England, and his native-born wife Catherine Charlotte, née McCutcheon. Educated at Cootamundra Superior Public School, Sydney Boys' High School and the University of Sydney (B.Sc., 1912; B.Sc.Agr., 1919), Bert won a Rhodes scholarship in 1913 and proceeded to St John's College, Oxford (B.A., M.A., 1919). On 30 November 1914 he was commissioned in the (Royal) Army Service Corps. He served on the Western Front and in Italy, and rose to acting major; he was twice mentioned in dispatches, and appointed O.B.E. in 1919.

Senior athletic champion (1907) of his high school, Southee had won the Australian long-jump championship (1911), gained Blues for Rugby Union football and athletics at the universities of Sydney and Oxford, and become 100-metres champion of the allied forces in Italy (1919). At the University of Sydney he had been president of the Men's Christian Union, vice-president of the Athletic Club, a councillor of the Science Society, and a founder and first secretary-treasurer of the Agricultural Society; at St John's he was president of the Athletics' Club and a member of the advisory council. Lieutenant Colonel Neville Leese, his superior officer in World War I, said of him: 'He is one of the best organisers I have met in the Army or out of it'.

On 12 June 1918 Southee had married Charlotte Elizabeth Lappin (d.1944) at St Stephen's Presbyterian Church, Sydney. In

1919 he was elected a fellow of the Linnean Society of London. That year he moved to Cornell University, Ithaca, New York State, but cut short his studies in plant-breeding to accept the principalship of Hawkesbury Agricultural College, Richmond, New South Wales. He took office in February 1921 at the age of 30.

Devoting his life to the college and its all-male students, Southee improved courses, introduced subjects such as agricultural geography and economics, and oversaw the construction of new buildings, notably a block of science laboratories. His encouragement of sport ensured that the college colours of maroon and gold ('blood and mustard') commanded respect, but his conservative, even autocratic, management raised hackles, especially when he resorted to cat-and-mouse tactics to apprehend students engaged in 'nocturnal escapades'. Many people idolized him; some tolerated him; others regarded him as arrogant and overbearing, as anti-intellectual and as a male chauvinist. About 2500 students graduated during his term as principal. He was especially supportive of the Old Boys' Union, of which he was president (1921-26) and later an honorary life member. He was also a founding member (1935) of the Australian Institute of Agricultural Science.

Southee retired in 1954 and moved to Eastwood, Sydney. He died on 27 December 1968 at Newport and was buried in Mona Vale cemetery with Anglican rites; his son and one of his two daughters survived him. A trust to fund scholarships for H.A.C.'s students was named after him, as was the Southee Horticultural Pavilion at the Sydney Showground, Homebush, in recognition of his long service as a councillor (1923-39) and a vice-president (1939-68) of the Royal Agricultural Society of New South Wales.

R. N. Dart, *Hawkesbury Agricultural College* (Syd, 1941); J. L. Boland, *Hawkesbury Harvest* (Syd, 1970); B. M. Braithwaite, *Challenge & Change* (Syd, 1991); *Agr Gazette of NSW*, Jan 1969, p 42; *SMH*, 20 Nov 1920, 18 Feb 1921.

SPAFFORD, FREDERICK MICHAEL (1918-1943), air force officer, was born on 16 June 1918 in North Adelaide, only child of James Michael Burke (d.1923), tannery foreman, and his wife Vida Muriel, née Spafford (d.1926), both South Australian born. Little evidence survives of Fred's childhood and education. On 19 September 1929 he was adopted by his maternal grandfather Frederick Blaker Spafford, a 70-year-old ironworker, and given his surname. In time, he worked as a fitter.

On 14 September 1940 Spafford enlisted in the Royal Australian Air Force. His grand-father had died on 25 March that year and Fred named his uncle Walter James Spafford (1884-1962), South Australia's director of agriculture, as his next of kin. After training in wireless at Ballarat, Victoria, and in air gunnery at Evans Head, New South Wales, he arrived in England, under the Empire Air Training Scheme, in August 1941 as a sergeant air gunner.

Sent to No.5 Bomber Group, Royal Air Force, in the East Midlands, Spafford spent short periods with a number of units. In May 1942 he was posted to No.50 Squadron, R.A.F., with which he flew in Manchesters and later Lancasters as a specialist bomb-aimer. The four-engined Lancaster bomber became the principal weapon in Britain's air offensive against Germany by night. Following fifteen sorties, Spafford was awarded the Distinguished Flying Medal in October for his skill and 'praiseworthy example'. He was commissioned in January 1943. Having survived his tour of thirty operations, he could have expected a respite from combat, but in March he was invited to join an elite R.A.F. squadron, No.617, being formed for a special mission against dams in the Ruhr and Weser valleys. (Sir) Barnes Wallis had designed a new type of mine or 'bouncing bomb' able to skip over defensive torpedo-nets and explode at depth against the wall of a dam.

On the night of 16 May Spafford flew with Wing Commander Guy Gibson, who led a formation of nineteen Lancasters in attacks on the Mohne, Eder and Sorpe dams. Bombs had to be released at the dangerously low height of 60 ft (18 m) at a set speed, line and distance from the wall of each targeted dam. Gibson regarded Spafford (whose nickname was 'Spam') as 'the best bomb-aimer there is'. The Mohne and Eder dams were successfully breached, flooding a large stretch of country. The daring and spectacular 'Dam Buster' raid was acclaimed as a triumph, boosting allied morale. Interviewed by the press and on the radio, Spafford described the secrecy and hazards of No.617's training for low-level flying, the elaborate briefings, and the attack which was carried out in bright moonlight against enemy fire. Gibson was awarded the Victoria Cross and, among the other decorations presented at Buckingham Palace, Spafford received the Distinguished Flying Cross. Five ft 8½ ins (174 cm) tall, stockily built and square shouldered, with a fair complexion, hazel eyes and brown hair, he had an open face and wore his cap at a rakish angle. Crew mates spoke of his nonchalance in the face of danger.

Despite high losses in the dams raid—nine of the Lancasters which had set out did not return—No.617 Squadron was kept in commission for similar tasks. On the night of 15/16 September 1943 the British attacked the

Dortmund-Ems Canal, using substantially the same tactics. In patchy fog and poor visibility, and against alert defences, five of the eight attacking aircraft were shot down. Hit by flak, Spafford's plane caught fire, crashed, and blew apart on the ground. There were no survivors. Spafford was posthumously promoted flying officer.

G. Gibson, *Enemy Coast Ahead* (Lond, 1946); P. Brickhill, *The Dam Busters* (Lond, 1951); C. Webster and N. Frankland, *The Strategic Air Offensive Against Germany, 1939-1945*, 2 (Lond, 1961); E. Fry, *An Airman Far Away* (Syd, 1993); *Advertiser* (Adel), 1 Apr, 22, 28 May, 9 Sept, 1 Oct 1943.   ERIC FRY

SPARGO, WILLIAM BENJAMIN (1888-1959), skier and prospector, was born on 16 July 1888 at Bairnsdale, Victoria, eldest child of William John Spargo, a Victorian-born brewer, and his wife Mary Isabella, née Greenaway, who came from England. Bill was raised and educated at Bairnsdale before the family moved to Brunswick, Melbourne; his roots and heart remained in the Gippsland mountains and the Australian Alps. In his twenties he worked on the roads between Omeo and Mount Beauty. Norwegian miners in the area taught him to ski and he probably did some prospecting.

By the 1920s Spargo was employed with the Victorian Country Roads Board. In 1923 the board took responsibility for the Alpine Road between Harrietville and Omeo, and appointed him supervisor. Based at Hotham Heights, he lived in a stone cottage which served as his depot. At his request, the building was enlarged to accommodate up to twenty visiting skiers. From 1925 the C.R.B. allowed him (when he was not engaged on road patrols) to use the premises as a guest-house, Hotham Cottage (Hotham Heights Chalet). He ran it in partnership with a ski instructor for a short period, then brought in his brother Cecil to assist him. Within a few years the chalet became a favourite stop-over for skiers, and Bill was a well-known and popular identity.

Spargo was variously described as 'strange, weird and erratic, but very lovable', and as 'a lean and wiry man of the mountains with a dry sense of humour, outgoing and ... cheerful'. He had joined the Ski Club of Victoria in 1925. Two years later he donated the Spargo Cup for a ski race which was to be held annually until 1948. A skiers' hut in the Mount Hotham district was named after him.

The C.R.B. decided in 1933 to discontinue the operation of the joint road depot and guest-house, and handed the chalet to the Victorian Railways. Spargo was deeply disappointed, but stayed on as the chalet's handyman and did a bit of prospecting for gold. He claimed to have mining in his blood, for his grandfather had been a miner from Cornwall. After he survived the 1939 bushfire (Hotham Heights Chalet did not), he turned to prospecting virtually full time. His perseverance was rewarded in 1941 when he discovered a reef at Mount Loch and named it Red Robin. At St James's Old Cathedral, West Melbourne, on 27 February 1946 he married with Anglican rites Evelyn Maud Piper, née Davies, a 45-year-old widow.

Turning down offers of purchase, Spargo worked the mine profitably himself. In 1951 he sold out and retired to Magnetic Island, Queensland. It was a strange choice for a man who loved the mountains and had taken pride in living in what had been Australia's highest residence. He died on 7 January 1959 at Mount Olivet Hospital, Kangaroo Point, Brisbane, and was cremated.

H. Stephenson (comp), *Skiing the High Plains* (Melb, 1982); J. M. Lloyd, *Skiing into History, 1924-1984* (Melb, 1986); M. Hull, *Mountain Memories* (Melb, 1990); Ski Club of Vic, *Year Book*, 1926-27, p 80, 1927-28, p 20, 1930, p 69.

DONALD S. GARDEN

SPARKES, SIR WALTER BERESFORD JAMES GORDON (1889-1974), cattle-breeder and politician, was born on 26 April 1889 at Murrumbidgerie, near Dubbo, New South Wales, youngest of ten children of native-born parents James Sparkes, station-manager, and his wife Mary Jane, née Yates. Educated at St Joseph's College, Sydney, young James worked on stations in the north-west of the State before buying a property near Jandowae, Queensland, in 1910. Within two years he had established the Lyndley Hereford stud. On 28 February 1912 at Scots Church, Melbourne, he married Jessie Elizabeth Lang. After she died, leaving him with a daughter and a son, he married Alice Goongarry Scott on 15 December 1920 at St Andrew's Presbyterian Church, Brisbane.

Conscious of the importance of registering pedigree stock, Sparkes had been a founding member of the Australian Hereford Society in 1918. He was to be a councillor of the A.H.S. for forty-six years, and its vice-president (1923-24 and 1970-73) and patron (1974). Following the example of other Queensland breeders, among them William Beak [q.v.13], he began to import poll Herefords from the United States of America in 1932. An inaugural member (1933) of the Australian Poll Hereford Society, he served on its council and became its patron.

Sparkes sat on the council (1949-74) of the Royal National Agricultural and Industrial Association of Queensland; he was a trustee (from 1957) and chairman (1953-73) of its beef-cattle committee. For many years he exhibited and judged cattle at shows in Brisbane, Sydney and Melbourne. Taking a practical approach to cattle-breeding, he held that 'length is weight . . . the butcher wants meat and the grazier wants money'. He was also a board-member (1952-69) of the Queensland Primary Producers' Co-operative Association Ltd.

In 1916 Sparkes had been elected to the Wambo Shire Council. As well as being its chairman (1922-50), he was president (1930-32) of the Local Government Association of Queensland. Representing the Country and Progressive National Party, he won the Legislative Assembly seat of Dalby in 1932, but did not seek re-election in 1935 or 1938. He won Aubigny for the Country Party in 1941 and held that seat for nineteen years, during which he was Opposition whip (1950-57). In the 1960 election he was defeated by the Queensland Labor Party candidate.

By the 1960s Lyndley was one of the oldest and largest Hereford studs in Australia. Sparkes was knighted in 1970. Tennis was his major recreation. He died on 15 June 1974 at St Vincent's Hospital, Toowoomba, and was cremated with Anglican rites; his wife and their three sons survived him, as did the daughter of his first marriage. Premier (Sir) Johannes Bjelke-Petersen told members of parliament that Sparkes 'spoke almost daily in this Chamber on behalf of the working man and the man on the land. He always fought their case, and fought it hard'. Sir Gordon Chalk, leader of the Queensland Liberal Party, said that Sir James never lost 'the spirit of the bush'. Sparkes's son, (Sir) Robert, presided (1970-90) over the Queensland branch of the Country (National) Party.

PD (Qld), 1975, p 15; *Chronicle* (Toowoomba), 17 June 1974; Aust Hereford Society Ltd archives, Brisb.   KIERAN MCCONVILLE
SIMON PATON

SPECKMAN, CARL RUDOLPH (1893-1958), army officer, was born on 30 July 1893 at Paddington, Sydney, only child of Rudolph Speckman, a musician from Germany, and his Queensland-born wife Annie Henrietta Frances Dorothea, née Michaelson. Educated at Paddington Superior Public School, Fort Street Model School and Sydney Technical College, Carl became a fitter and turner. On 6 June 1912 he enlisted in the Royal Australian Engineers. He transferred to the 1st Field Company, R.A.E., Australian Imperial Force, on 2 September 1914. One week later at St George's Church of England, Hurstville, he married Ethel Annie Godfrey, a photo-

grapher's assistant, aged 30. In the following month he embarked for Egypt as quartermaster sergeant.

From June to September 1915 Speckman served at Gallipoli before being admitted to hospital and taken to Egypt. In March 1916 he joined the 1st Pioneer Battalion. That month he was commissioned and sent to France. At Pozières on 25-26 July he displayed 'great coolness and courage' in directing the clearing and deepening of a captured enemy trench while under fire; he was awarded the Military Cross and promoted captain. A further advancement, to major, followed in August 1917, as did a mention in dispatches in May 1918. Based in London in 1919-20 as a staff officer with the Australian Department of Repatriation and Demobilization, he helped to acquire equipment for the postwar army.

After his A.I.F. appointment terminated in Australia on 16 April 1921, Speckman served as adjutant and quartermaster to Militia engineer units in New South Wales (1922-31) and Queensland (1931-36). In 1936 he was posted to Army Headquarters, Melbourne. He worked in the quartermaster-general's branch and (from 1938) as deputy assistant director of mechanization. Having been secretary of the inventions board, 1st Military District (Queensland), in 1932-36, he performed the same role at Army Headquarters in 1936-40. In 1939 he was appointed M.B.E.

On 1 May 1940 Speckman joined the Australian Army Ordnance Corps, A.I.F., in command of the 2nd/1st Ordnance Stores Company. He was elevated to lieutenant colonel in July and transferred to 7th Division headquarters in August as deputy assistant director of ordnance services. In October he sailed for the Middle East. Recalled to Australia in January 1942—shortly before his eldest son Charles was taken prisoner at Singapore—he was promoted colonel in April and subsequently held senior ordnance posts with I Corps and New Guinea Force, in the Queensland Lines of Communication Area, and at Land Headquarters and Advanced Land Headquarters. He was twice mentioned in dispatches in World War II.

In August 1945 Speckman was appointed assistant-director of army disposals. He became director in February 1946, with the temporary rank of brigadier from June. The disposal of surplus stores was a crucial task, realizing over £54 million from September 1944 to July 1949. Speckman had few interests outside the army. An intelligent, forthright and capable officer, with the ability to get things done, he was frank, unpretentious, and considerate towards his staff. Retiring from the army in December 1949, he subsequently managed the sewage-disposal farm at Werribee, Victoria. He died suddenly of a coronary occlusion on 13 May 1958 at Sorrento and was cremated; his wife, and their three sons and two daughters survived him.

C. E. W. Bean, *The A.I.F. in France, 1916* (Syd, 1929); R. McNicoll, *The Royal Australian Engineers 1902-1919* (Canb, 1979); J. D. Tilbrook, *To the Warrior his Arms* (Canb, 1989); *SMH*, 8 June 1939, 27 Jan 1942; AWM 76, items A20 and B458, AWM 119, item 147A pt 1, AWM 183, item 43, AWM 256, item 17/1/85 (AWM); information from Mr C. Speckman, Bongaree, Qld, and Brig E. L. Palmer, Leeming, Perth. W. H. EDWARDS

SPENCE, LOUIS THOMAS (1917-1950), air force officer, was born on 4 April 1917 at Bundaberg, Queensland, fifth child of Robert John Spence, a farmer from Ireland, and his German-born wife Louise Margaretta Marie, née Koob. Lou was educated at Longreach State School (1924-31) and Thornburgh College, Charters Towers (1932-34). A tall, athletic youth, he was nicknamed 'Silver' because of his very fair hair. He topped his class, won colours for tennis, and played cricket with the first XI and Rugby League football with the first XIII. After joining the Bank of New South Wales as a clerk at its Queensland head office in Brisbane in February 1934, he passed three subjects at the Bankers' Institute of Australasia examinations in 1937-38. He also became a surf lifesaver.

Enlisting in the Royal Australian Air Force on 6 March 1940, Spence trained as an air cadet at Archerfield, Brisbane, and at Point Cook, Victoria. He was commissioned in August. Two months later he received his wings and was posted to No.25 Squadron, at Pearce, Western Australia. On 24 May 1941 at St George's Cathedral, Perth, he married with Anglican rites Vernon Rima Howarth Swain, a nurse. In August he was sent to the Middle East. Having completed operational training in Khartoum, Sudan, he joined No.3 Squadron, R.A.A.F., with which he flew Kittyhawk fighters. One daring exploit, on 26 January 1942, involved landing his aircraft to rescue a colleague who had crash-landed in the Western Desert; the two of them crammed into his one-man cockpit and returned safely to base. A brave and vigorous pilot, Spence won the Distinguished Flying Cross for leading numerous raids and destroying two enemy aircraft.

Flight Lieutenant Spence returned to Australia in September 1942. He spent almost fifteen months as an instructor at No.2 Operational Training Unit, Mildura, Victoria. In January 1944 he was given command of No.452 Squadron, a Spitfire unit based in Darwin. He was promoted acting squadron leader in the following month. During March his unit was ordered to fly urgently to Perth: for his inspiring airmanship on this long flight

through cyclonic weather, he was mentioned in dispatches. In February 1945 he was posted to No.8 O.T.U., Parkes, New South Wales, as chief instructor. He was demobilized from the R.A.A.F. on 19 November.

Refusing to return to his job with the bank, Spence worked in Canberra as aviation correspondent for the Commonwealth Department of Information. On 17 October 1946 he accepted a commission in the air force. He was appointed senior administrative officer at Fairbairn air base, Canberra. In September 1947 he was attached to the United Nations military mission in Java to help to supervise the cease-fire in Indonesia. Returning home in November, he was chosen by Air Commodore (Sir) Valston Hancock to command the Cadet Squadron at the newly formed R.A.A.F. College, Point Cook.

On 20 February 1950 Spence was promoted wing commander and placed in command of No.77 Squadron, at Iwakuni, Japan. The unit formed part of the British Commonwealth Occupation Force. On 25 June the Democratic People's Republic of (North) Korea invaded the Republic of (South) Korea. Spence immediately readied the squadron for action. Following the Menzies [q.v.15] government's agreement for the 77th to be committed in support of U.N. forces in Korea, he personally led his pilots on many more operations than a commanding officer would normally have been expected to do.

Spence's workload rose as other allied forces were relocated at Iwakuni. He also had to receive an increasing number of important visitors. Under his leadership the morale of No.77 Squadron remained high. On 9 September 1950 he led four Mustangs in an attack on storage facilities at An'gang-ni, South Korea, which had recently been captured by the communists. While he was operating at low level because of poor visibility, his aircraft failed to pull out of a steep dive and he was killed when it crashed into the centre of the town. His wife, and their son and daughter survived him. He had been appointed to the American Legion of Merit (1950), and was posthumously awarded the American Air Medal and a Bar to his D.F.C. Lieutenant General George Stratemeyer, commander of (American) Far East Air Forces, praised him as 'one of the noblest and finest officers of any service' he had ever known.

G. Odgers, *Across the Parallel* (Melb, 1952); J. Watson and L. Jones, *3 Squadron at War* (Syd, 1959); R. J. O'Neill, *Australia in the Korean War 1950-53* (Canb, 1985); *Blackthorn Mag*, 1933, p 3, 1934, p 9, 1950, p 14, 1952, p 35; information from Mrs V. Hillman, Kew, Melb, Miss J. Landsberg, Charters Towers, Wing Commander A. W. Barr, Palm Meadows, Qld, Air Vice Marshal W. H. Simmonds, Isaacs, and Air Vice Marshal J. H. Flemming, Campbell, Canb. P. J. SCULLY

SPENCER, FRANK BREESE (1886-1965), company director, was born on 14 September 1886 at Goodna, Queensland, eighth child of English-born parents Thomas Spencer, leather-dresser, and his wife Annie Maria, née Breese. Educated at public schools, Frank worked as a clerk. On 7 December 1904 at Holy Trinity Church, Fortitude Valley, Brisbane, he married Emily Mary Bogue with Anglican rites.

Spencer joined Nestlé & Anglo-Swiss Condensed Milk Co. as branch manager in 1913. He proved an efficient executive and managed (1914-26) the company's New Zealand operation. In 1921 the Nestlé & Anglo-Swiss Condensed Milk Co. (Australasia) Ltd was formed to acquire the Australasian business of the Swiss-based parent company. Moving to Sydney, Spencer became joint manager of Nestlé for Australasia in 1926 and sole general manager in 1929; he was managing director in 1933-52 (and deputy-chairman from 1934). From 1942 he was chairman of directors of Nestlé in Australasia. After he was appointed a director of the parent holding company in Switzerland in 1946, he made annual visits to Europe. When he retired from the Nestlé Co. (Australia) Ltd in 1962 he was made honorary chairman.

A dynamic personality in the Australian confectionery trade, Spencer had come into the Manufacturing Confectioners' Association 'as smoothly and silently as a Rolls Royce' and 'burst into a veritable blaze of fireworks'. He built on the success that Nestlé had achieved under A. C. Hargrove, who had overseen the construction of a large plant at Abbotsford, Sydney, in 1917. Spencer had responsibility for guiding the business through the difficult times of the Depression and World War II. A convivial man, with a 'beatific smile', he strongly believed in the advantages of vigorous competition in his industry and admitted to being 'perhaps a little outspoken at times'.

Spencer was receptive to new ideas and quick to translate them into action. In 1934 Nestlé introduced an all-Australian innovation, Milo, a drink invented by Tom Mayne of Sydney. Made from a mixture of malt, cocoa and milk, it became a successful product, not only in Australia—which by 1999 was its third largest market behind Malaysia and the Philippines—but in some thirty other countries. Another product that Spencer had seen into production was the Winning Post assortment of chocolates (five ounces for a shilling) in 1933. That year Nestlé began advertising in cinemas.

'Greatly interested in matters of educational value', Spencer was elected a trustee of the Australian Museum in 1939; he became a crown trustee in 1958 and was president in 1960-61. He was a director (1939-48), deputy-chairman (from 1941) and chairman (1947-48) of the Australian Gas Light Co. through times of supply and labour difficulties. A member of the Union and New South Wales clubs (sometime president of the latter), and of the Auckland Club, New Zealand, he also belonged to the Australian Golf and Australian Jockey clubs, Sydney.

Spencer lived at Kirribilli until 1956 and then at Darling Point. Survived by his two daughters, he died at his home on 15 January 1965 and was buried in Northern Suburbs cemetery; his wife and son predeceased him. Nestlé continued to expand and to buy out its competitors.

Aust Museum, *Report of Trustees, 1964* (Syd, 1964); J. Heer, *Nestlé* (Vevey, Switzerland, 1991); *A'sian Confectioner and Soda Fountain J*, 24 Feb 1928, 22 Mar, 22 June, 22 July 1933, May, July 1962, Feb 1965; *Aust Museum Mag*, 1 Sept 1939, p 72; *SMH*, 1 July 1921, 16 Jan 1965. CHRIS CUNNEEN

SPENCER, GWENDOLINE GLADYS (1888-1974), journalist and managing editor, was born on 1 April 1888 in Hobart, second child of Alexander Morton [q.v.10], a museum director from the United States of America, and his Sydney-born wife Caroline Eliza, sister of Stephen Mills [q.v.10]. Gwen was educated at the Collegiate School, Hobart. On 1 February 1909 at St David's Cathedral she married with Anglican rites Henry John Spencer, a 40-year-old electrical engineer. Their twin sons died at birth. By 1922 she was contributing articles and sketches to the new publication *Woman's World*, edited by Frances Taylor [q.v.12]. Her first piece reported an interview with Ada Cambridge [q.v.3].

The Spencers moved to Sydney about 1924. For thirty years from December 1924 Gwen contributed occasional articles to the *Sydney Morning Herald*, signing them as Gwen Morton Spencer from 1933. In the early years she wrote from her personal experiences on such topics as 'A country holiday. Dipping for sheep', life in boarding-houses, and her delight in Sydney and its suburbs. Her younger sister married J. D. M. Moore [q.v.10] in 1924; through this connexion Gwen met Sydney Ure Smith [q.v.11]. In September 1927 she was appointed sub-editor of his stylish and influential magazine, the *Home*.

Mrs Spencer sailed for Britain in the *Oronsay* in May 1932 intending to stay for a year, but in 1933 accepted the position of fashion editor in London of the long-running *Queen*. Subtitled the *Lady's Newspaper & Court Chronicle*, the magazine was an illustrated weekly, with sections on gardening, hunting, fashion and the world of art. It also published poetry and fiction. Spencer reported fashion shows in London and Paris, and found life in both cities stimulating. She flew to Paris twice a year for the dress shows and thought that flying was 'fun'. The flight took three hours, during which a five-course meal was served to the forty-two passengers. There were four fashion shows a day, the last one ending at midnight. In 1934 she experienced excitement and danger when 60 000 Parisians rioted and the army took over from the police.

A studio portrait of Spencer, taken in London in 1934, showed a beautiful, elegantly dressed woman with immaculately waved hair, her face framed by a large fur. In 1935 she was a foundation member of the Fashion Group, Great Britain. She resigned from the *Queen* because of ill health and moved in 1936 to Sussex where she continued to write articles for English and Australian papers. In December that year she became a foundation committee-member when an Australian group of the Over-Seas League was formed in London.

Returning to Sydney in 1937 for a holiday, Mrs Spencer accepted the posts of social editor and feature writer for *Woman*, under the editorship of Vera Hamilton. In 1939 she resumed her working relationship with Ure Smith who had that year formed a company, Ure Smith Pty Ltd. Together they edited (1939-47) the *Australia National Journal*. For most of its life it appeared monthly. In spite of Ure Smith's plans to appeal to a wider audience than the readers of the *Home*, the *A.N.J.* was in financial difficulties by 1940. Ure Smith wrote to a director that 'Mrs Spencer would have to take £4 or at the most £5 per week'. She and Ure Smith produced five annual issues of the *Australia Week-End Book* (1942-46), consisting largely of material that had appeared in *Australia*.

In addition to her editorial duties, Spencer contributed occasional general and fashion articles to *Australia*. For both publications she selected contemporary poems for 'Anthology in Miniature'. By 1944 Ure Smith was director of the Empire-United States of America Art Trust, of which Sir Keith Murdoch [q.v.10] was president. Spencer, as its paid secretary, had written an article for the *Society of Artists Book* (1942), setting out its aims and proposed activities. As Ure Smith's health failed, Gwen's responsibilities increased. She wrote the introduction to *Margaret Preston's Monotypes* and the commentary for *Alec Murray's Album*. By 1949 she was managing editor (with Ure Smith's son Sam) of Ure Smith Pty Ltd.

Spencer retired from that position in 1951, but retained a director's interest. In February she visited England for a years holiday. Letters to the firm reported on a busy social life, interspersed with visits to publishers and sales managers, and attempts to meet (Sir) Robert Helpmann to discuss a book on his career.

She spent eight weeks in Italy 'ghosting' a book for the art patron Captain Neil McEacharn: the result was *The Villa Taranto: a Scotsman's Garden in Italy.*

After her husband's death in 1941, Spencer had moved to a Potts Point penthouse where she proof-read for Ure Smith and, in later years, ghosted other books. She enjoyed meeting artists and writers, collected books of poetry and was 'president of a poets' corner'. A member of the Fellowship of Australian Writers of New South Wales and of the Sydney P.E.N. Club, she also belonged (from 1940) to the Society of Women Writers. As late as 1970, while a vice-president and honorary life member of the society, she spoke on 'ghosting'. Mrs Spencer died on 15 August 1974 at Mosman and was cremated.

I. North et al, *The Art of Margaret Preston* (Adel, 1980); N. Underhill, *Making Australian Art 1916-49* (Melb, 1991); *SMH*, 6 Dec 1924, 28 Jan 1928, 13 July 1929, 11 Jan, 15 Mar 1934, 7 Jan, 9 Apr 1937; Ure Smith Pty Ltd papers *and* Society of Women Writers records (ML); information from Mrs M. Alford, Durong South, Qld, and Mrs J. Yeomans, Balgowlah Heights, Syd.   MARGARET BETTISON

SPICER, SIR JOHN ARMSTRONG (1899-1978), barrister, politician and judge, was born on 5 March 1899 at Prahran, Melbourne, son of Henry Spicer, a photographer from England, and his Victorian-born wife Helen Jane, née Armstrong. The family travelled to England in 1905 and returned in 1911. John was educated at Chelston School, Torquay, England, and at Hawksburn State School, Melbourne. A course at a business college was to follow, but in 1913—through the agency of Leonard Townsend, vicar of Christ Church, South Yarra—he secured a job as office-boy with the legal firm of (Sir) Arthur Robinson [q.v.11] & Co. He took an articled clerk's course at the University of Melbourne in 1916-18. Admitted as a barrister and solicitor on 1 March 1921, he signed the Bar roll on 5 May 1922. At Christ Church, South Yarra, on 27 June 1924 he married Lavinia May Webster with Anglican rites.

While Spicer was establishing a solid practice at the Bar, his friendship with (Sir) Robert Menzies [q.v.15] stimulated his political activity. According to Spicer, they 'grew up in politics together'. A member (president 1939) of the 'Constitutional Club', Spicer was a founder in 1930 of the Young Nationalist Organisation (Victorian president 1933 and 1937) and a regular and effective platform speaker during election campaigns. In 1940, as a United Australia Party candidate, he was elected to the Senate. There his quick, logical mind and well-developed debating skills brought him to notice. He chaired the Senate

Standing Committee on Regulations and Or- dinances in 1940-43.

Spicer appeared to be the epitome of Vic- torian right-wing conservatism. He empha- sized patriotism, joined the Round Table in 1943, and characterized the Australian Labor Party as aiming to impose a 'dictatorship of the Trades Hall' which would create a 'monster State'. As a senator much concerned with 'sound and honest finance', he spoke fre- quently on tax matters.

At the general election in August 1943 Spicer was defeated. His term concluded in June 1944. He returned to the Bar, and took silk in 1948. Bitterly opposed to bank nation- alization, he acted as a junior counsel for the English banks in the ensuing court action. In December 1949 he was re-elected to the Senate and appointed attorney-general in Menzies' coalition government. One of his first tasks was to draft a bill banning the Com- munist Party of Australia. The legislation was subsequently declared unconstitutional by the High Court of Australia. In 1952 Spicer drafted an official secrets bill which provided the option of the death penalty for spying, and permitted wide powers of search and arrest without warrant. Cabinet rejected it. Spicer was also involved in planning for the intern- ment of thousands of communist 'associates' in the event of war with the Soviet bloc. In this instance, however, he was more mindful of civil liberties. Anxious that the 'blanket approach' favoured by the Australian Security Intelligence Organization might lead to wrongful incarceration, he insisted that a sep- arate file be kept for each potential internee, a decision which consumed 'huge amounts of ASIO time'.

In 1956 Spicer was offered the post of chief judge of the newly founded Commonwealth Industrial Court. He accepted after some hesi- tation, later writing to Menzies (who had been overseas at the time) that 'quite frankly I would have welcomed your advice and guidance in reaching a decision'. In 1963 he was knighted. He also presided over inquiries into naval and air disasters, most notably the royal com- mission in 1964 into the sinking of H.M.A.S. *Voyager*. Spicer found that officers in both the *Voyager* and the *Melbourne* had been at fault. A second royal commission in 1967-68 heard fresh evidence and absolved the *Melbourne*'s officers of any blame.

Tall, bespectacled and quiet in manner, Sir John named reading and walking as his prin- cipal recreations. In 1976 he retired from the Industrial Court. He died on 3 January 1978 at Armadale, Melbourne; he was accorded a state funeral and was cremated. His wife and their son survived him. Sir Paul Hasluck (a severe judge of character) wrote that Spicer had 'a quiet authority on any constitutional question or legal argument' and that Menzies

valued anything he said 'whether on the law or on politics'. Hasluck was impressed by Spicer's readiness to listen to reasoned argu- ment. Spicer 'never minded being in a minor- ity'. He was a man of professional probity who thought that 'sound practice and good law were more important than political advan- tage'. Despite these qualities, his record as attorney-general was not outstanding. When he attempted to deal with communism and related security questions, his political views sat uneasily with his professional instincts.

D. Whitington, *The Rulers* (Melb, 1964); D. McKnight, *Australia's Spies and their Secrets* (Syd, 1994); P. Hasluck, *The Chance of Politics* (Melb, 1997); *Age*, 3 Nov 1942, 4 Jan 1978; *Herald* (Melb), 24 Feb 1948, 27 Sept 1969, 28 Oct 1976, 4 Jan 1983; *SMH*, 4 Jan 1978; Sir Robert Menzies papers, MS 4936/1/234 (NL).   GEOFF BROWNE

SPIVAKOVSKY, JASCHA (1896-1970), pianist, was born on 18 August 1896 at Smela, near Kiev, Russia (Ukraine), fifth of nine chil- dren of David Spivakovsky, synagogue cantor, and his wife Rahel. Descended from gener- ations of musicians, Jascha showed musical ability very early and began learning the piano when he was 3. The family survived the pogrom at Odessa in 1905 and later moved to Germany. Jascha studied in Berlin with Pro- fessor Moritz Mayer-Mahr at the Klindworth- Scharwenka Conservatorium. In 1910 he outclassed an adult field to win the coveted Bluethner prize. His career as a concert per- former blossomed until he and members of his family were interned as enemy aliens in World War I.

After the war Spivakovsky presented a series of concerts in Berlin, tracing the histori- cal development of the concerto from Bach to Brahms. The success of the performances established him as one of Europe's foremost pianists. In the 1920s he appeared as a soloist with leading orchestras in Europe, Scandi- navia and Britain. He and his brother Nathan ('Tossy'), a violin prodigy, formed the Spiva- kovsky Duo and gave recitals of the violin and piano repertoire in a number of European countries. Jascha made two triumphant Aus- tralasian tours in 1921 and 1929, performing demanding programmes. In 1926 he married Leonore Krantz in Czechoslovakia. They had met in Adelaide, and were to have a daughter and two sons.

In 1930 Jascha, Tossy and the cellist Edmund Kurtz established the Spivakovsky- Kurtz Trio which came to be highly regarded for its outstanding ensemble-playing and the flawless musicianship of its members. The trio left Germany to tour Australia in 1933, shortly before Adolf Hitler was appointed chancellor. Settling in Melbourne, Jascha joined the staff of the University Conservatorium where he introduced new methods of teaching, including master-classes. He also performed regularly on radio for the Australian Broadcasting Commission. In 1938 he was naturalized. Before World War II began, he helped most of his family and a dozen other people to migrate from Germany to Australia. During the war he served as an air-raid warden, and gave charity concerts for the Australian Red Cross Society and allied troops.

A successful Australian tour in 1947 preceded Spivakovsky's return to the international stage. He played in New Zealand, the United States of America, Canada, Iceland, Scandinavia, Britain, Europe, Israel and Africa. He was 5 ft 8 ins (173 cm) tall, with a powerful build and somewhat ferocious appearance. His hands were unusually large, with chunky fingers, which necessitated his use of unconventional fingering patterns when playing the piano, and which discomforted those who felt his 'vice-like' grip in a friendly handshake. Contrary to his appearance, he was kind, gentle and good-humoured. He was fluent in five languages: English was not one of them, although later in life his grasp of it improved noticeably. Illness curtailed his international career in 1960, but he continued to perform in Australia. At the time of his death he was planning to record Beethoven's violin and piano sonatas with Tossy. Jascha died on 23 March 1970 at Toorak, Melbourne, and was cremated; his wife and their sons survived him.

In performance, Spivakovsky's extraordinary legato technique, extensive tonal command and remarkable intellectual and physical powers were all employed to convey the emotion and passion of the music. His expressive interpretations of works from the Baroque period to the twentieth century won acclaim from audiences and critics. With even the most complex and difficult pieces, he brought out the lyrical and emotional aspects in a way that made sense of the whole. He excelled in communicating with his audience, and made a significant impact on the musical life of Australia, and Melbourne in particular.

Tossy Spivakovsky (1907-1998) studied violin in Berlin with Willy Hess at the Hochschule für Musik. From 1920 he toured as a soloist and as a member of the Spivakovsky Duo. He became concert-master of the Berlin Philharmonic Orchestra in 1926, but resigned in the following year. When the Spivakovsky-Kurtz Trio decided to remain in Melbourne in 1933, Tossy was appointed to the teaching staff of the University Conservatorium, as was Kurtz. He migrated to the U.S.A. in 1941. After World War II he appeared as a soloist (playing his 1721 Stradivarius) with major American orchestras. He held teaching positions at Fairfield University, Connecticut, and the Juilliard School, New York. Handsome and intense, elegant and graceful in his movements, he had an idiosyncratic bowing technique and a striking stage presence. His repertoire included numerous twentieth-century works in addition to the classics. Critics considered his interpretations of the concertos of Tchaikovsky and Sibelius to be his finest.

His brother Isaac ('Issy') Spivakovsky (1902-1977) studied violin under Willy Hess, and cello with Hugo Becker and Gregor Piatigorsky. Issy possessed the traditional family genius for music, but suffered from poliomyelitis as a child and did not pursue a career as a performer. He held a violin teaching position at the Royal Conservatorium of Music, Leipzig, before migrating to Australia in 1934. From 1937 to 1965 he taught violin, viola and cello at Scotch College, Melbourne, contributing much to the development of music at the school. Charming and sensitive by nature, he was warmly regarded by his students despite the rigorous demands he placed on them.

Another brother Adolf Spivakovsky (1891-1958) was a bass-baritone. His stage career was cut short by a stress-related ulcer while he was still in his twenties and he devoted the remainder of his life to teaching. He migrated to Melbourne in 1934 and taught at the University Conservatorium where his students included the sopranos Glenda Raymond, Kathleen Goodall and Sylvia Fisher.

G. Yost, *The Spivakovsky Way of Bowing for Violinists and Violists* (Pittsburgh, US, 1949); G. Kehler (comp), *The Piano in Concert* (Metuchen, US, 1982); C. Stevens, 'Spivakovsky, Jascha', in W. Bebbington (ed), *The Oxford Companion to Australian Music* (Melb, 1997); *Aust Musical News*, 1 Nov 1936, p 9, Oct 1958, p 16; *Scotch Collegian*, June 1966, p 4; *Music and the Teacher*, June 1985, p 3, Dec 1985, p 3; *J of Aust Jewish Hist Soc*, 11, pt 1, 1990, p 128; *Strad*, 109, no 1303, Nov 1998, p 1212; naturalization files, A435, item 1947/4/3896, A659, item 1939/1/11911 *and* A446, item 1960/53/136.

CATHERINE J. STEVENS

SPOONER, SIR WILLIAM HENRY (1897-1966), accountant and politician, was born on 23 December 1897 at Surry Hills, Sydney, fifth child of native-born parents William Henry Spooner, composer, and his wife Maud Ann, née Dubois. Eric Spooner [q.v.12] was his elder brother. Educated at Christ Church School, Sydney, Bill overstated his age to enlist in the Australian Imperial Force on 8 June 1915. He served with the 5th Field Ambulance at Gallipoli and, on the Western Front in 1916-17. For attending to a wounded man while under heavy shell-fire at Bellewaarde Ridge, Belgium, on 20 September 1917, he was awarded the Military Medal.

Next month he was wounded at Polygon Wood. He transferred to the Australian Flying Corps in 1918 and was promoted second lieutenant in April 1919. His A.I.F. appointment terminated in Sydney on 14 August 1919.

In 1922 Bill and Eric helped to found the firm which was to become Hungerford, Spooner & Co., one of the most successful accountancy businesses in Sydney. Bill studied part time at the University of Sydney (Dip.Econ., 1923). At St James's Church of England, King Street, on 30 April 1924 he married Catherine Frier Vera Bogle. After joining the Legacy Club of Sydney in 1935, he chaired (1941-42) its finance committee and had one term as president (1942-43).

Like his brother, Bill Spooner was attracted to the United Australia Party. He took a leading part in gathering together the various competing groups and factions left in the wake of the U.A.P.'s collapse and was prominent in the formation of the Liberal Party of Australia in 1944-45. He became the party's first New South Wales president, federal treasurer and chairman of the federal finance committee in 1945. In his view, the success of the new party depended on avoiding internal factionalism and on accepting donations only when given without conditions, thus ensuring 'complete freedom' from outside influence or control. When he relinquished his offices in 1949, the federal president (Sir) Malcolm Ritchie [q.v.] acknowledged that 'the principles and standards which he set have been a sure guide in developing the financial policy of the Party and have, in no mean degree, contributed largely to the stability which exists today'.

Heading the New South Wales Liberal ticket, Spooner was elected to the Senate on 10 December 1949. Nine days later he was appointed minister for social services in the Menzies [q.v.15] government. Thus, when he took his seat in the Senate on 22 February 1950, he already held a portfolio. In January 1951 he was given responsibility for war service homes. On 11 May he became minister for national development. He retained this portfolio for the next thirteen years, overseeing the reorganization of the coal industry, the development of uranium and iron ore deposits, the search for oil, and the work of the Snowy Mountains Hydro-electric Authority, the Australian Atomic Energy Commission, the River Murray Commission, the Joint Coal Board and various development projects, especially in northern Australia. In addition, he was a member (1951-64) of the Council of Defence, vice-president (1958-64) of the Executive Council and acting prime minister, briefly in 1962. He had become deputy-leader of the government in the Senate in 1956 and leader on 17 February 1959.

In 1963 Spooner was appointed K.C.M.G. He resigned from the ministry in June 1964

and from the Senate in July 1965, and was appointed a privy counsellor in 1966. Resuming his business interests, he was chairman of the Mutual Acceptance Co. Ltd and Duly & Hansford Ltd, and a director of Mercantile & General Reinsurance Co. of Australia Ltd. He was a snowy-haired, bespectacled, firm-jawed and friendly man, who enjoyed playing golf. Survived by his wife, and their son and two daughters, Sir William died of cancer on 14 July 1966 at Manly District Hospital, Sydney; he was accorded a state funeral and was cremated. His estate was sworn for probate at $203 419.

E. Hilmer Smith, *History of the Legacy Club of Sydney*, 2 (Syd, 1950); K. West, *Power in the Liberal Party* (Melb, 1965); G. Starr, *The Liberal Party of Australia* (Melb, 1980); S. McHugh, *The Snowy* (Melb, 1989); G. Barwick, *A Radical Tory* (Syd, 1995); *PD* (Cwlth), 16 Aug 1966, p 6; *Australian* and *SMH*, 16 July 1966; *Bulletin*, 23 July 1966.

GRAEME STARR

SPOWERS, ALLAN (1892-1968), army officer and company director, was born on 9 July 1892 at South Yarra, Melbourne, only son and third of six children of William George Lucas Spowers, a journalist from New Zealand, and his London-born wife Annie Christina, née Westgarth. Ethel Spowers [q.v.] was his elder sister. Allan attended Miss Turner's school and boarded (from 1905) at Geelong Church of England Grammar School. Nicknamed 'Jiggie', he became a prefect and captain of boats. He entered the University of Melbourne (B.A., 1920) in 1912, but interrupted his studies to travel to England where he enlisted in the British Army and was commissioned in the East Lancashire Regiment on 4 May 1915.

Attached to the regiment's 6th Battalion, Spowers fought at Suvla Bay, Gallipoli, in August and in Mesopotamia in the following year. He won the Military Cross (1916) for leading his men in a night-attack during which he was twice wounded. In addition, he was awarded the Distinguished Service Order (1916) and was mentioned in dispatches. He was promoted lieutenant in April 1917 and demobilized from the army in July 1919. Returning to Melbourne, he worked as a journalist on the *Argus* and *Australasian*. At the 1930 Imperial Press Conference in London he represented these newspapers; within a few years he was a director of the company that ran them. On 29 April 1922 at St Marks Church of England, Darling Point, Sydney, he had married Rosamond Sandys Lumsdaine, a niece of A. B. ('Banjo') Paterson [q.v.11].

In 1928-33 Spowers served in the Militia. He was mobilized as a captain in the 46th Battalion in September 1939 and promoted major in November. Transferring to the Australian Imperial Force in May 1940, he was promoted lieutenant colonel and appointed commander of the 2nd/24th Battalion in July. Six ft 1 in (185 cm) tall and sparely built, with penetrating grey-blue eyes and a commanding voice, he maintained high standards of conduct, insisted on mental and physical toughness, and disdained pretentiousness.

The 2nd/24th arrived in the Middle East in December 1940, withdrew to Tobruk, Libya, in April 1941 and was besieged there until October. In January 1942 the battalion was sent to Syria for intensive training. Spowers was twice mentioned in dispatches for his services. Ordered back to the Western Desert in June in response to the German advance into Egypt, he and his men played a leading role in the battle of Tel el Eisa. Lieutenant General Sir Leslie Morshead [q.v.15] described Spowers's leadership as 'outstandingly meritorious' and he was to be awarded a Bar (1945) to his D.S.O. On 12 July 1942 he became a prisoner of war when his jeep was inadvertently driven into enemy territory.

Freed in Germany in March 1945 and repatriated in August, Spowers was appointed temporary colonel and director of amenities, Army Headquarters, Melbourne. He transferred to the Reserve of Officers on 17 July 1946. Although he resigned from the board of the Argus and Australasian Ltd in 1949, he held a number of other directorships and chaired (1951-59) the Victorian division of the Australian Red Cross Society. In 1956 he was appointed C.M.G. and to the Swedish Royal Order of Vasa. He died on 4 May 1968 at Golden Ball, his property at Everton, and was buried in Wangaratta cemetery; his wife, and their daughter and two sons survived him.

R. P. Serle (ed), *The Second Twenty-Fourth Australian Infantry Battalion of the 9th Australian Division* (Brisb, 1963); B. Maughan, *Tobruk and El Alamein* (Canb, 1966); J. J. Corfield and M. Collins Persse (comps), *Geelong Grammarians*, 1 (Geelong, Vic, 1996); *SMH*, 10 Nov 1930, 21 Oct 1949; L. J. Morshead papers (AWM); information from Mrs R. Fraser, Frankston, Mclb, Mr A. Spowers, Scullin, Canb, and Major W. Spowers, Windlesham, Surrey, Eng.   HARRY TAPLIN

SPOWERS, ETHEL LOUISE (1890-1947), painter and printmaker, was born on 11 July 1890 at South Yarra, Melbourne, second of six children of William George Lucas Spowers, a newspaper proprietor from New Zealand, and his London-born wife Annie Christina, née Westgarth. Allan Spowers [q.v.] was her only brother. She was educated at the Church of England Girls' Grammar School, Melbourne, and was a prefect in 1908. Wealthy and cultured, her family owned a mansion in St Georges Road, Toorak. Ethel continued to live there as an adult and maintained a studio above the stables.

After briefly attending art school in Paris, Miss Spowers undertook (1911-17) the full course in drawing and painting at Melbourne's National Gallery schools. Her first solo exhibition, held in 1920 at the Decoration Galleries in the city, showed fairy-tale drawings influenced by the work of Ida Outhwaite [q.v.11]. In 1921-24 Spowers worked and studied abroad, at the Regent Street Polytechnic, London, and the Académie Ranson, Paris. She exhibited (1921) with fellow Australian artist Mary Reynolds at the Macrae Gallery, London. Two further solo shows (1925 and 1927) at the New Gallery, Melbourne, confirmed her reputation as an illustrator of fairy tales, though by then she was also producing woodcuts and linocuts inspired by Japanese art and covering a broader range of subjects.

A dramatic change in Spowers' style occurred in 1929 when she studied under Claude Flight (the leading exponent of the modernist linocut) at the Grosvenor School of Modern Art, London. Her close friend Eveline Syme [q.v.] joined her there. Following further classes in 1931, during which Spowers absorbed modernist ideas of rhythmic design and composition from the principal Iain Macnab, she published an account of the Grosvenor School in the *Recorder* (Melbourne, 1932). In the 1930s her linocuts attracted critical attention for their bold, simplified forms, rhythmic sense of movement, distinctive use of colour and humorous observation of everyday life, particularly the world of children. They were regularly shown at the Redfern Gallery, London. The British Museum and the Victoria and Albert Museum purchased a number of her linocuts.

Stimulated by Flight's proselytizing zeal for the medium, Spowers organized in 1930 an exhibition of linocuts by Australian artists, among them Syme and Dorrit Black [q.v.7], at Everyman's Library and Bookshop, Melbourne. A founding member (1932-38) of George Bell's [q.v.7] Contemporary Group, Spowers defended the modernist movement against its detractors. In an article in the *Australasian* on 26 April 1930 she called on 'all lovers of art to be tolerant to new ideas, and not to condemn without understanding'.

Frances Derham remembered Spowers as being 'tall, slender and graceful', with 'a small head, dark hair and grey eyes'. A rare photograph of Spowers, published in the *Bulletin* (3 September 1925), revealed her fashionable appearance and reflective character. In the late 1930s she stopped practising as an artist due to ill health, but continued her voluntary work at the Children's Hospital. She died of cancer on 5 May 1947 in East Melbourne and was buried with Anglican rites in Fawkner cemetery. Although she had destroyed many of her paintings in a bonfire, a memorial exhibition of her water-colours, line-drawings, wood-engravings and colour linocuts was held at George's Gallery, Melbourne, in 1948. Her prints are held by the National Gallery of Australia, Canberra, State galleries in Melbourne and Sydney, and the Ballarat Fine Art Gallery, Victoria.

C. Deutsher and R. Butler (comp), *A Survey of Australian Relief Prints 1900/1950*, exhibition cat (Melb, 1978); J. Burke, *Australian Women Artists 1840-1940* (Melb, 1980); S. Coppel, *Linocuts of the Machine Age* (Aldershot, Eng, 1995); *Argus*, 22 June 1920, 2 Nov 1921, 24 Sept, 9 Dec 1930, 7 Sept 1948; *Bulletin*, 3 Sept 1925; *SMH*, 6 Dec 1932, 10 July 1936; *Sun News-Pictorial*, 28 Nov 1933; *Age* (Melb), 6 May 1947, 8 Sept 1948; information from Dr T. Quirk, Melb, and Mrs B. Keats, Longwood, Vic.

STEPHEN COPPEL

SQUIRE, JOCELYN; *see* HENDERSON

SQUIRE, NORMAN POWELL (1909-1974), billiard and snooker player, was born on 22 November 1909 at Christchurch, New Zealand, son of Harold Percival Squire, bricklayer, and his wife Harriet Rose, née Downing, both New Zealand born. Norman attended a public school and spent a year at technical college. From an early age he developed a reputation as a superb cueist. Noticing his ability, a fellow New Zealand professional Edward James ('Murt') O'Donoghue encouraged him to try his hand on the Australian club circuit.

About 1935 Squire settled in Sydney. He made an immediate impression as a 'hustler' who habitually conceded mammoth starts for high stakes. Soon virtually unbeatable in snooker, he became a familiar figure, always ready to take on any challenger, at City Tattersalls and other clubs. A tall, heavy man with brushed-back hair, he had a good reach and a deft touch. He used a long-butted cue, specially made in New Zealand. On 22 August 1939 at St Barnabas's Church of England, Broadway, Sydney, he married Annie Ross (d.1965). He was employed as a fitter and turner when he enlisted in the Royal Australian Air Force on 15 March 1943. Qualifying as a flight mechanic, he served with units in New South Wales and Victoria before being discharged from the air force on 28 August 1945 in Sydney.

World War II restricted Squire's opportunities to perform at the highest level. Horace Lindrum had allegedly been reluctant to accept his challenge for the Australian snooker title in 1944. The sport recovered only slowly in the next decade. It was not until the 1960s, when Squire was over 50, that he recorded his best performances in international competition. On a tour of South Africa in 1963, he achieved a maximum break of 147. Back in Sydney in the following year, he defeated a 'class' field in a snooker competition which included Eddie Charlton and Lindrum, winning all ten frames and losing none. In July 1969 he won the Australian professional billiard championship, beating Warren Simpson and Charlton in a round-robin tournament; next month he defeated the celebrated New Zealand player Clark McConachy for the Australasian billiard title.

At the registrar-general's office, Sydney, on 11 March 1969 Squire married Paula Margaret Taylor, late Lyons, née Coutts, a 38-year-old variety entertainer and a divorcee. He loved gambling, and regularly patronized horse-racing, the dogs and the 'trots'. Always prepared to back himself, he would bet at almost any stage of a match, and once played a single frame on which he and his backers collectively wagered $10 000. 'Norman was terribly hard to live with', Paula remarked, because 'he'd earn $500 playing snooker at Lithgow on Friday night and lose the lot on the first race at Rosehill the next day'. We were 'always short of money', she added.

While in the middle of a frame worth $6000 at City Tattersalls Club, Squire collapsed and died of acute myocardial infarction on 23 December 1974. Survived by his wife, their daughter and his stepson, and by the two daughters of his first marriage, he was cremated. During his career he had made over two thousand century-breaks at snooker, sometimes as many as twenty in a week, most of the time playing for money.

C. Everton, *The Story of Billiards and Snooker* (Lond, 1979); *SMH*, 14 Mar, 25 July 1969, 24 Dec 1977; information from Mr L. Wheeler, Chifley, Syd.

R. I. CASHMAN

STANLEY, MURIEL CONOMIE (1918-1979), home missionary and nurse, was born on 6 April 1918 at Yarrabah, Queensland, daughter of Aboriginal parents Luke Stanley and his wife Jessie Ross, née Kepple. The Yarrabah Anglican mission, near Cairns, had been founded in 1892 by Rev. John Gribble [q.v.4]. Educated at the mission school, Muriel was an assistant-teacher by 1937. She travelled to Newcastle, New South Wales, in 1938 to attend the training college of the Church Army in Australia. After finishing the course, she worked in Church Army children's homes in the Hunter Valley and at Armidale, and became in turn deputy-matron and matron of an orphanage in Hobart.

Miss Stanley decided that she could do more for her people as a nurse. Because of prejudice against her colour, she found difficulty in realizing her ambition until she was eventually accepted by the South Sydney Women's Hospital. She completed an eighteen-month course, passed the final examination in November 1944, and was registered as an obstetric nurse in March 1945. Reputedly, she was the first Aborigine to qualify in midwifery. Matron R. M. Keable was impressed by Stanley's 'character and determination', and declared that it had been a privilege to train her.

Back at Yarrabah, Sister Stanley was appointed matron of the hospital. In addition to her duties there, she visited chronic invalids in their homes and led the St Mary's Girls' Guild. She was granted a certificate of exemption from the provisions of the Queensland Aboriginals Preservation and Protection Act (1939), which stipulated that the wages of Aborigines should be paid into trust accounts; these accounts were managed by the police, acting as agents for the chief protector's office. In 1959 she sailed for England, under the auspices of the Church Army, to undertake a two-year course in moral welfare. While in London, she was a guest at a garden party at Lambeth Palace when Geoffrey Fisher, the archbishop of Canterbury, entertained more than two hundred missionaries from abroad.

Again in Queensland, Stanley became a social-welfare officer and worked among Aboriginal families at Cairns. Supported by the Anglican Church, she was its only full-time welfare worker with the Aboriginal people in Queensland. From 1967 she was based at the Woorabinda mission, south-west of Rockhampton, as a liaison officer with the Queensland Department of Aboriginal and Islander Affairs. The department transferred her to Brisbane in 1970, but she returned to North Queensland. On 19 December that year at St Alban's Church of England, Yarrabah, she married Norman Gresham Underwood, a canecutter and a widower. Mrs Underwood, who suffered from hypertension, died of a coronary occlusion on 18 May 1979 at Gordonvale and was buried in the local cemetery. Her husband survived her.

A. W. Batley, *The Boomerang Returns* (Newcastle, NSW, 1955); M. Coleman, *Green Meat & Oily Butter* (Redcliffe, Qld, 1999); *Aust Aboriginal Studies*, no 2, 1985; D. Huggonson, 'Aboriginal Trust Accounts in Queensland: How "Protection" became "Oppression"', *Aust Q*, Summer, 1990; *Sunday Sun* (Syd), 10 Dec 1944.   DAVID HUGGONSON

STANTON, BYRON LIONEL (1891-1963), physician and pharmacist, was born on 7 July 1891 at Palmerston North, New Zealand, son of William Shepherd Smith Stanton, a general dealer from England, and his New Zealand-born wife Annie Ada, née Brown. After the family moved to Melbourne, Byron was sent to Scotch College. He proceeded to the College of Pharmacy, where he was influenced by F. H. Cole, Daniel McAlpine [qq.v.8,10] and William Osler, and topped his final year (1913). In 1915 he entered the University of Melbourne (M.B., B.S., 1921), but he interrupted his course and enlisted in the Australian Imperial Force in November 1916.

As a staff sergeant, Australian Army Medical Corps, Stanton dispensed medicine aboard troop-ships and in England before being discharged in Melbourne on 19 September 1917. Two years later he was appointed lecturer in pharmacy and materia medica at the university, and found himself teaching his own classmates. He was also the Pharmacy Board of Victoria's representative on the faculty of medicine. In 1927 he was made head of the department of materia medica at the College of Pharmacy. There he became a confidant of the dean A. T. S. Sissons [q.v.]. He was to retain his posts at the university and the college until 1963.

Following his graduation, Stanton had worked as a resident medical officer (1921-22) at the Melbourne Hospital, and as a resident medical officer (1922-24) and assistant-pathologist (1925) at the Children's Hospital. On 25 March 1926 at Auburn he married Alice Mary Mills with Presbyterian forms. He travelled to England and qualified as a member (1926) of the Royal College of Physicians, London, then built up a practice as a consultant in Melbourne. In 1943 he was elected a fellow of the Royal Australasian College of Physicians.

While in England, Stanton had met W. H. Martindale who authorized him to handle all queries in the Australasian region relating to the *Extra Pharmacopoeia*. He later served as the British Medical Association's representative on the Australian committee which helped in the revision of the *British Pharmacopoeia*. In 1930 he was elected a fellow of the Pharmaceutical Society of Victoria. During World War II he headed a group which produced the *Emergency Formulary of Australia* (Sydney, 1941) and the *Australian War Pharmacopoeia* (Melbourne, 1942). Much of this work was carried out at his Camberwell home, as was his work for the Medical Equipment Control Committee. He contributed to *The Australian and New Zealand* (later *Australian*) *Pharmaceutical Formulary* and was largely responsible for its 1947 edition. With his vast knowledge of the nature, action and use of drugs, he served on numerous bodies, among them the Pharmaceutical Benefits Advisory Committee.

An eloquent speaker who showed 'flashes of pungent humour', Stanton was interested in painting, bookbinding, origami, botany, literature and music; he enjoyed playing the piano at gatherings of his friends, many of whom were former students. His greatest love, however, was his 'digest of digests', materia medica; he had difficulty in accepting that, from 1963, it was no longer to be taught as a separate subject. For all his brilliance, energy and organization, he failed to realize that materia medica had become turgid, ravelled and too reliant on memory. He died on 20 April 1963 at Kew and was cremated; his wife and their daughter survived him. The College of Pharmacy, Monash University, holds Laurence Pendlebury's portrait of Stanton.

G. L. McDonald (ed), *Roll of the Royal Australasian College of Physicians*, 1 (Syd, 1988); G. Haines, *A History of Pharmacy in Victoria* (Melb, 1994); *MJA*, 4 Jan 1964, p 22.   GREGORY HAINES

STAPLETON, JAMES LAWRENCE (1904-1979), librarian, was born on 16 March 1904 at Mount Gambier, South Australia, elder son of Percival de Soligny Stapleton, telegraph-operator, and his wife Louisa, née Lyford, both South Australian-born. Educated at Norwood District High School, James passed the junior public examination in 1920 and joined the staff of the Public Library of South Australia in the following year. His training as a librarian was practical rather than academic; he worked as a cadet until 1927 and then as a junior library assistant. On 7 May 1935 at Holy Trinity Church, Adelaide, he married with Anglican rites Euthene Breton Grosser, a stenographer.

From 1938 Stapleton managed the library's country lending service, gaining experience which contributed to his appointment as State librarian in Queensland in 1947. In their 1935 report, *Australian Libraries*, Ralph Munn and Ernest Pitt [q.v.11] had excoriated the Public Library of Queensland. Free library services were almost non-existent, subscription libraries were run by local schools of arts, and the Queensland Bush Book Club was only able to reach a limited number of people in isolated areas. In 1945 the Library Board of Queensland commissioned John Metcalfe, principal librarian of the Public Library of New South Wales, to report on the public library service 'in and from Brisbane'. He recommended that year that the Public Library of Queensland be renamed the State Library of Queensland, that the Oxley [q.v.2] Library be incorporated within it as a separate historical collection, and that the State Library should include a country reference and circulation department.

Shortly after Stapleton took up duty in Queensland in May 1947, the Library Board approved the establishment of the Country Lending Service to provide reference books for individuals in remote communities. In an effort to promote libraries Stapleton travelled around the State. He arranged for a 'model children's library'—designed to demonstrate the benefits of free municipal libraries—to tour Queensland in 1951 on the Jubilee (of Federation) Art Train. The development of free library services, however, was hampered by insufficient government funding. In addition, the Library Board's decision not to impose minimum standards of service meant that there was no differential scale of subsidy for free and subscription libraries. Despite a continuing struggle due to the Public Library's being housed in an unsuitable building, the structure for the State Library was put in place during Stapleton's term of office. Training classes in librarianship were introduced and the archives section commenced operations in 1959.

While still a relatively young man, Stapleton had suffered the first of a number of heart attacks, but he continued working until 1970. By then, the Public Library had a staff of 120 and all but six of the eighty-three local authorities responsible for libraries offered free lending services. Stapleton was essentially a very private man, although genial and kindly. In later years he was a keen fancier and grower of orchids. After his retirement he served (1970-72) on the Oxley Memorial Library Advisory Committee. Survived by his wife and their son, he died on 15 March 1979 in Brisbane and was cremated.

J. Metcalfe, *Public Library Service in and from Brisbane, 1945* (Brisb, 1974); *Annual Report of the Lib Bd of Qld*, 1945/46, p 1, 1950/51, p 3; *Aust Lib J*, June 1967, p 98; *Quill*, 11, no 2, July 1970, p 6; Library Board of Qld, Minutes of Meetings, 21 Mar 1947, 7 Dec 1950, 5 Apr 1951 (QA).

SHIRLEY McCORKINDALE

STARR, SIR KENNETH WILLIAM (1908-1976), surgeon, was born on 9 January 1908 at Wellington, New South Wales, eldest of four children of native-born parents William Stanley Starr, machine agent, and his wife Mildred, née Jennings. His father was an itinerant mechanic who travelled through the western region of the State, repairing heavy agricultural machinery on sheep- and cattle-stations. An unreliable man, he drank too much and went missing, leaving his family without support. Mildred worked as a housekeeper for relations near Cowra. At the age of 9 Ken was allowed to move to a boarding-house at Marrickville, Sydney, where he attended the local public school.

In 1920 Mrs Starr bought a house at Stanmore, Sydney, which she ran as a boardinghouse. Ken excelled at Fort Street Boys' High School; his curriculum included much Latin and Greek, and he retained a love of the classics. At the University of Sydney (M.B., B.S., 1930), he won numerous prizes and graduated with first-class honours and the university medal. When he was at school and university he worked at nights, at weekends, and in holidays to help to support the family.

Starr served as a resident medical officer (from 1930) at Royal Prince Alfred Hospital before becoming surgeon superintendent (1933) at (Royal) Newcastle Hospital. In 1936 he travelled to London and gained a fellowship of the Royal College of Surgeons, England, taking the primary and final examinations in successive months and winning the Hallett prize. After further study in Europe and the United States of America, he returned to Newcastle in 1937 as assistant-surgeon.

From 1926 Starr had been active in the Militia. Called up on 23 October 1939 for full-time service as major, Australian Army Medical Corps, he was posted to headquarters, Southern Command, Melbourne. In 1940 he became a fellow of the Royal Australasian College of Surgeons and graduated M.S. from the University of Melbourne. On 10 May that year at All Saints Church, St Kilda, he married with Anglican rites Alison, daughter of Sir Neville Howse [q.v.9]. That day he transferred to the Australian Imperial Force. Sailing for the Middle East in October, he was appointed assistant-director of medical services and promoted temporary lieutenant colonel in January 1941 (substantive August). He served in Eritrea with the 2nd/5th Australian General Hospital, then studied plastic and faciomaxillary surgery in Britain (February-July 1942) and North America. In 1942 he was appointed O.B.E.

In November 1942 Starr was posted as officer commanding, surgery division, 113th A.G.H., Sydney. He set up a facial maxillary and plastic surgery unit at that military hospital. In 1944 he was awarded the Jacksonian prize by the Royal College of Surgeons for his essay, 'Delayed Union of Fractures'. Following a strong disagreement with his superiors about the clinical management of cases, he was sent back to the 2nd/5th A.G.H. in November 1944 and embarked for Morotai in March 1945. During the Borneo campaign he treated many wounds with the newly available drug penicillin. He transferred to the Reserve of Officers on 20 February 1946.

Starr leap-frogged over other staff members to become a senior honorary surgeon at Sydney Hospital in 1946. While none denied his erudition and technical skill, the appointment caused considerable resentment. He was also visiting surgeon at the Repatriation General Hospital, Concord. In addition, he ran a successful general surgical practice. He was a quick operator and did not suffer fools gladly, but was very gentle with children. In 1955, at the invitation of the New South Wales government, he created a special unit for cancer research and treatment at the Prince of Wales Hospital, Randwick, and became its honorary director. Three years later he was made a consultant at Sydney Hospital.

A member from 1962 and chairman (1967-72) of the New South Wales Medical Board, Starr was president (1964-66) of the R.A.C.S. As chairman of the Medical Advisory Committee, he wrote its majority report (1958) recommending the establishment of a new medical school, to be located at the New South Wales University of Technology (University of New South Wales). Many leading medical practitioners regarded the report as an affront to the University of Sydney. In the 1960s Starr chaired other government committees.

The Starrs lived at Turramurra on a large block of land (with horses) until moving to Coogee in 1958 to be near the special unit. Ken belonged to the Australian Club and the Elanora Country Club, and was a fine golfer. He published several books and a number of articles in medical journals, and was a consulting editor to two overseas surgical journals. In 1956 he was appointed C.M.G. He was knighted in 1971.

Suffering from cerebral thrombosis and hypertensive vascular disease, Starr gave up surgery in 1966 and restricted himself to administration and research in the special unit. Over the next few years his health deteriorated, despite the devoted care of his wife. Sir Kenneth died of bronchopneumonia on 16 June 1976 at the Lochinvar Nursing Home, Coogee. His wife, and their three daughters and two sons—one of whom followed him into medicine—survived him. A posthumous portrait of Starr by Robert Hannaford is held by the R.A.C.S., Melbourne.

A. S. Walker, *Clinical Problems of War* (Canb, 1952); *Lives of the Fellows of the Royal College of Surgeons of England 1974-1982* (Lond, 1988); D. Starr, *Kenneth W. Starr* (Georgetown, Texas, US, 1998); *MJA*, 1, 1977, p 560; Starr papers (NL); Univ NSW Archives; information from Dr D. Starr, Georgetown, Texas, US, Dr R. P. Melville, Double Bay, Prof R. Blacket, Wollstonecraft, Prof P. Korner, Woolwich, and Sir Rupert Myers, Castle Cove, Syd.

ROBERT A. B. HOLLAND

STEDMAN, IVAN CUTHBERT (1895-1979), swimmer, was born on 13 April 1895 at Oakleigh, Melbourne, second son of Victorian-born parents James Cuthbert Stedman, merchant, and his wife Lesbia, née Allee. Ivan was educated at Brighton Grammar School and briefly (1905-07) at Sydney Church of England Grammar School (Shore). At the age of 12 he contested his first race, a 50-yard event for boys, at Melbourne's Middle Park Baths, but 'got kicked in the face and pulled out'. In 1910-11 he won Victorian junior championships over 100, 200 and 300 yards.

Swimming styles began to change in the first decade of the twentieth century. Variations of side-stroke were followed by the English trudgen—which involved a frog-like kick and alternate sweeps out of the water with either arm—and finally the crawl, pioneered by Arthur and Richmond Cavill [q.v.7] and Alick Wickham. Stedman switched in 1911 from what he called 'pure trudgen' to a two-beat version of the crawl, imitating Cecil Healy [q.v.9], the swimmer he admired most.

In 1912 Stedman won the 220-yards championship of Victoria, his first senior title, and joined the Melbourne Swimming Club. Respiratory troubles and a throat operation made him withdraw from a trial for fourth place in Australia's 4 × 200-metres freestyle relay team for the Olympic Games that year. After leaving school, he had taken a job with the tobacco merchant Joseph Kronheimer & Co., and 'flirted with Lady Nicotine'.

On 13 June 1916 Stedman enlisted in the Australian Imperial Force. He joined the 5th Field Artillery Brigade on the Western Front in August 1917, but was wounded at Passchendaele, Belgium, two months later when a shell burst in his gun-pit. Following a convalescence in England, he rejoined his unit in France in May 1918. For diving into the dark waters of the Hallue River on 23 June and rescuing a British soldier, he received an award from the Royal Humane Society, London. In September Stedman learned that his hero, Healy, had been killed at Mont St Quentin.

Discharged from the A.I.F. on 4 December 1919 in Melbourne, Stedman was chosen for the 1920 Olympics at Antwerp, Belgium. He led the Australian team in the procession at the opening ceremony. With (Sir) Frank Beaurepaire [q.v.7], Harry Hay and William Herald, he won a silver medal in the 4 × 200-metres relay. Back in Victoria, he took up a farming block at Red Cliffs under the soldier-settlement scheme. In 1921 he was victorious in 100- and 200-yards breast-stroke races at a carnival of champions in Hawaii. His Australian championships included the 100-yards freestyle (1920 and 1921), 220-yards breast-stroke (1921, 1924 and 1927) and 440-yards breast-stroke (1927). In 1924 he competed in freestyle and breast-stroke events at the Olympics in Paris.

From about 1927 to 1931 Stedman owned and managed a factory which processed dairy products at Lang Lang, Victoria. At Christ Church, Essendon, on 6 September 1930 he married with Anglican rites Violet Livingstone Jackson, an opera singer. He worked successively as a sales representative for B. Seppelt [q.v.6] & Sons Ltd, as a contracts officer with the Department of Supply and Development, and as office manager for Peter Isaacson Pty Ltd. Having turned to long-distance swimming, he won the three-mile (4.8 km) handicap along the Yarra River in 1946 (in record time) and in 1952. With his friend Percy Cerutty [q.v.13], he studied ways of delaying the process of ageing. Stedman died on 7 January 1979 at Prahran and was cremated. His wife and their son survived him.

H. Gordon, *Australia and the Olympic Games* (Brisb, 1994); *SMH*, 23 June 1921; Stedman collection (Aust Gallery of Sport and Olympic Museum, Melb); information from Mr J. A. Stedman, Ulladulla, NSW.   HARRY GORDON

STEELE, SIR CLIVE SELWYN (1892-1955), engineer and army officer, was born on 30 September 1892 at Canterbury, Melbourne, son of Victorian-born parents Herbert Selwyn Steele, warehouseman, and his wife Alice Lydia, née Sinclair. Clive was educated at Scotch College, where he was a prefect and captain of boats (1910), and at the University of Melbourne (B.C.E., 1919). Commissioned in the Militia in 1912, he was appointed second lieutenant, Royal Australian Engineers, Australian Imperial Force, on 8 October 1915. He sailed for Egypt in November with the 5th Field Company.

Transferred to the Western Front in March 1916, Steele rose to captain in September. On 6 January 1917 at the parish church, West Brompton, London, he married Annie Osland Bilson; they were to remain childless. At Péronne, France, in August 1918 he supervised repairs to bridges while under artillery and machine-gun fire. On the 31st he crawled some 200 yards (183 m) in front of the Australian lines and brought back details of damage to bridges across the River Somme and the Somme Canal. The information assisted planning to restore the crossings and he was awarded the Military Cross. In October he was promoted major. His A.I.F. appointment terminated in Melbourne on 1 August 1919.

Steele worked for the Australian Reinforced Concrete & Engineering Co. in 1919-21 and for James Hardie & Co. Pty Ltd in 1921-23. He set up in private practice as a consulting engineer in 1924. As designer and supervisor of structural works, he was involved in the construction of or alterations to the State Savings Bank of Victoria building in Melbourne, the members' stand at Flemington racecourse, the National Mutual Life Association of Australasia Ltd building in Brisbane, Her Majesty's

Theatre in Sydney and the Melbourne Town Hall. Meanwhile, he continued to serve in the Militia. Promoted lieutenant colonel (1926), he commanded the 4th Divisional Engineers (1926-31) and the 14th Infantry Battalion (1933-39).

On 13 October 1939 Steele was seconded to the A.I.F. and placed in command of the 6th Divisional Engineers. After the government decided to raise another division, he was promoted temporary brigadier and appointed chief engineer, I Corps, in April 1940. He sailed for the Middle East in September. During the campaign in Greece (April 1941) he was chief engineer of the Anzac Corps. At Fársala, on 18 April, a bomb crater in the road impeded the withdrawal of allied forces. Traffic came to a halt and vehicles were 'jammed head to tail for 10 miles' (16 km). Despite attacks by German aircraft, Steele took charge of a party which filled the crater, clearing the way for the convoy. He won the Distinguished Service Order and the Greek Military Cross.

Twice mentioned in dispatches for his service in the Middle East, Steele flew to Java, Netherlands East Indies, in January 1942. On 14 February he was sent to Sumatra, where he helped to organize the evacuation of allied troops from Oosthaven. He returned to Australia next month. Believing that General Sir Thomas Blamey [q.v.13] was to remain in the Middle East indefinitely, Steele, (Sir) Edmund Herring and G. A. Vasey [q.v.] asked Frank Forde, the minister for the army, to appoint (Sir) Horace Robertson [q.v.] commander-in-chief. They did not know that the government had already chosen Blamey. In April Steele was promoted temporary major general and appointed engineer-in-chief at Land Headquarters, Melbourne. Blamey learned of his part in the misnamed 'revolt of the generals' and treated him coolly until Steele assured him that no disloyalty had been intended.

To handle the influx of recruits needed for the war against Japan, Steele established the R.A.E. Training Centre at Kapooka, New South Wales, and increased the size of the School of Military Engineering at Liverpool. By 1945 there were 28 000 sappers in the Australian Military Forces. They cleared and disarmed mines, demolished obstacles, provided water supplies and other services to military camps, cut and milled timber, built huts, roads, bridges, railways, airfields and wharves, and operated the army's water-transport vessels. Steele travelled extensively in the South-West Pacific Area to inspect their activities. Finding that the 6th Divisional Engineers were languishing at Wondecla, North Queensland, in 1943, he set them research and development tasks. 'Some of the work was of doubtful usefulness but it kept the troops occupied'.

A reorganization at L.H.Q. in October 1943 added fortifications, works, engineer stores and transport to Steele's operational responsibilities. Although the consolidation of engineering functions increased efficiency, Brigadier Geoffrey Drake-Brockman [q.v.14] obliquely accused Steele of empire-building. Drake-Brockman was one of a number of people who found Steele's antipathy towards public servants, especially finance officers, excessive and unproductive. Steele was also criticized for meddling in design work, better left to his subordinates.

Despite his impatience with bureaucracy, Steele 'respected the need for paper-work, but would never let formalities stop him from gaining his ends'. He was admired throughout the army for his energy, drive and ability to get things done. Within the R.A.E., his humane leadership and loyalty to his officers and soldiers fostered *esprit de corps*. On 12 March 1946 he transferred to the Reserve of Officers. The University of Melbourne had awarded him the W. C. Kernot [q.v.5] medal for 1944. In 1953 he was appointed K.B.E. A council-member (1933 and 1946-50) of the Institution of Engineers, Australia, he chaired (1946) the Melbourne division and became an honorary member in 1954.

For recreation, Sir Clive played golf. He belonged to the Melbourne Club. Ebullient and personable, he moved comfortably among the city's professional élite. In 1945-46 he presided over the Old Scotch Collegians' Association and, from 1950, chaired the school council. He liked to proclaim the superiority of Scotch College over Melbourne Church of England Grammar School to provoke Herring and other friends who were old boys of Grammar. Survived by his wife, he died of myocardial infarction on 5 August 1955 at the Repatriation General Hospital, Heidelberg, and was cremated. His estate was sworn for probate at £46 131.

J. A. Hetherington, *Blamey* (Melb, 1954); G. Drake-Brockman, *The Turning Wheel* (Perth, 1960); L. J. Hartnett, *Big Wheels and Little Wheels* (Melb, 1964); R. McNicoll, *The Royal Australian Engineers 1902 to 1919* (Canb, 1979) and *The Royal Australian Engineers 1919 to 1945* (Canb, 1982); S. Sayers, *Ned Herring* (Melb, 1980); eminent members' records—Sir Clive Steele (Inst of Engineers, Aust, Canb).

DARRYL BENNET

STEIGRAD, JOSEPH (1902-1971), surgeon and soldier, was born on 28 January 1902 at Jaffa, Palestine (Israel), ninth and youngest child of Palestinian-born parents Samuel Steigrad, carter, and his wife Perl, née Grünstein, both of whom were Jewish. The family reached Melbourne in the *Bremen* on 20 February 1905. Five years later they settled at

Summer Hill, Sydney. With strong familial support, Joe gained a bursary to Sydney Boys' High School where he won an exhibition to study medicine at the University of Sydney (M.B., Ch.M., 1926). He was naturalized in 1926.

After working as a resident medical officer at Sydney Hospital, Steigrad—who had an affinity with children—was accepted in 1927 as a resident medical officer at the Royal Alexandra Hospital for Children, Camperdown. He was to serve the hospital as chief resident medical officer (1929-33), honorary surgeon (1933-61), consultant surgeon (1961-70) and a member of its board of management. He was also honorary surgeon at Royal South Sydney Hospital. From 1933 he practised in Macquarie Street. Highly skilled, he was noted for his gentle treatment of tissues. He became a fellow of the Royal Australasian College of Surgeons in 1933, lectured (from 1937) in paediatric surgery at the university and published in the *Medical Journal of Australia*.

At the district registrar's office, Paddington, on 19 May 1938 Steigrad married Isabel Heather Wilson (d.1982), a bank clerk. His engagement and marriage to a Gentile caused a rift between Steigrad and orthodox Jews of the Great Synagogue; he chose to worship at the Temple Emanuel, Woollahra, of which he was a founder. Heather was later converted to Judaism, and the couple remarried at the Temple Emanuel.

A lieutenant colonel in the Militia, Steigrad was seconded to the Australian Imperial Force on 13 October 1939, given command of the 2nd/1st Australian General Hospital and promoted colonel. Showing remarkable energy, he rapidly organized staff, equipment and stores, and sailed with the 6th Division for the Middle East in January 1940. The 600-bed tent hospital was established on the Gaza Ridge in Palestine. A firm, efficient, but kindly commanding officer, Steigrad was made assistant-director (1941-42) and deputy director (1942-43) of medical services. He was appointed C.B.E. (1942) and mentioned in dispatches. After returning to Australia in February 1943, he became D.D.M.S., III Corps, Western Australia (1943), and New Guinea Force (1944), and deputy director general, medical services, Land Headquarters (1944-45). He transferred to the Reserve of Officers on 18 December 1945 with the rank of honorary brigadier. Before returning to the Royal Alexandra, he drew up rehabilitation programmes for returning medical officers.

The war years were stressful ones for the family. Steigrad saw his elder son Stephen for the first time when the boy was 3 years old. Following his return, the family lived at Double Bay and later at Rose Bay. He said little about his war experiences, and rarely attended Anzac Day marches or unit re-

unions. As Australian Jewry's senior army officer of World War II, however, he was much in demand as a speaker on ceremonial occasions.

Steigrad led an extremely busy professional and social life. He was a member of Legacy, a Freemason, chairman of the board of governors of the New South Wales Association of Jewish Ex-Servicemen and Women's rehabilitation fund, a mentor of the Young Men's Hebrew Association, a member (1962-64) of the State council of the Australian Medical Association, deputy honorary director of the Children's Medical Research Foundation, chairman (from 1963) of the Advisory Committee for Training Speech Therapists, and a founder (1950) and president (1961-62) of the Australian Paediatric Association. A fine squash player and surf lifesaver in his youth, he remained lithe well into middle age. His pastimes included golf, orchid growing, and fishing holidays at Sussex Inlet. He was an honorary life member of the Imperial Service Club, and also belonged to Killara Golf, Monash Country and Tattersall's clubs.

In his later years Steigrad suffered from emphysema, a legacy of heavy smoking. He was appointed honorary director of the Postgraduate Committee in Medical Education of the University of New South Wales in 1964 and, later, warden of clinical studies at the Prince of Wales and Prince Henry hospitals.

Joe Steigrad was a calm, logical man, with a reputation as a superb chairman of committees. He died of myocardial infarction on 25 March 1971 at the Prince of Wales Hospital, Randwick, and was cremated. His wife and their two sons survived him. The first Steigrad memorial lecture, established by the Australian Academy of Forensic Sciences, was delivered by Dr Edgar Thomson [q.v.] in 1973.

R. Brasch, *Australian Jews of Today* (Syd, 1977); D. G. Hamilton, *Hand in Hand* (Syd, 1979); S. Simpson, *Medical Pathfinders* (Syd, 1990); *Aust Paediatric J*, 7, 1971, p 119; *MJA*, 26 Feb 1972, p 440; *Aust J of Forensic Sciences*, 5, Mar-June 1973, p 95; *Aust Jewish Times*, 1 Apr 1971; *SMH*, 9 Jan 1940, 26 Mar 1971; naturalization file, A1, item 1925/14495 (NAA, Canb); Royal A'sian College of Surgeons Archives, Melb; information from Dr S. Steigrad, Rose Bay, Syd.   G. T. FRANKI

STEINBERG, ISAAC NACHMAN (1888-1957), lawyer, politician and publicist, was born on 13 July 1888 at Dvinsk (Daugav'pils), Latvia, Russian Empire, son of Zerakh Steinberg, a Jewish merchant, and his wife Chiana, née Eliashev. Isaac spent most of his youth in Moscow, living in an environment characteristic of the Russian Jewish intelligentsia, but was educated at the gymnasium at Pernov (Pyarnu), Estonia. In 1906 he entered the Imperial Moscow University, where he studied law and joined the Socialist Revolutionary Party. Following his exile in 1907, he completed an LL.D. at the University of Heidelberg, Germany, in 1910. That year he returned to Russia. He worked as a lawyer, defending Jewish victims of the tsarist régime, and won endorsement for the Duma, the Russian parliament. In 1914 he married Nekhama Solomonovna Yeselson (d.1954); they were to have a son and two daughters. From December 1917 to March 1918 he was commissar of justice in Lenin's government during the Bolsheviks' short-lived coalition with the left wing of the S.R.P. After resigning from the government in protest at the Treaty of Brest-Litovsk, Steinberg campaigned against the Bolsheviks. Effectively banished in 1923, he moved to Germany.

When the Nazis came to power in 1933, Steinberg arranged for his wife and children to join him in London. There he helped to found the Freeland League for Jewish Territorial Colonization, a body which attempted to find a refuge for persecuted European Jews. The league selected the East Kimberley region in Australia's north-west, planned to buy an area of 7 million acres (28 000 km²), and hoped to settle 75 000 Jewish refugees to develop the pastoral and agricultural industries.

On 23 May 1939 Steinberg arrived in Perth. An indefatigable publicist for the Kimberley scheme, he appealed to people both on humanitarian grounds and by citing the officially declared need to populate northern Australia. He made a strong impression on all who met him. George Farwell [q.v.14] described him as having a 'thick, short body', a 'black beard bristling from a pale, fine-grained face' and 'quizzing eyes beneath that broad dome of forehead'. He 'talked with great passion, laughed explosively' and 'gave way to abrupt splurges of anger if his ideas were challenged'.

By early 1940 Steinberg had gained the support of the Western Australian government, the Australasian Council of Trade Unions, a number of leading public figures, and major newspapers such as the *Sydney Morning Herald*, the Melbourne *Argus* and the *West Australian*. He had also encountered opposition from the *Bulletin*, *Smith's Weekly*, some daily newspapers and several politicians, whose arguments ranged from the practical to the xenophobic and racist. For their part, many Australian Jews criticized the proposed settlement: some feared that it would provoke a wave of anti-Semitism in Australia, while others saw it as a threat to the Zionist cause.

Steinberg left Australia in June 1943 to rejoin his family in Canada. On 15 July 1944 he was informed by Prime Minister John Curtin [q.v.13] that the Australian government would not 'depart from the long-established policy in regard to alien settlement in Australia' and could not 'entertain the proposal for a group settlement of the exclusive type contemplated by the Freeland League'. Steinberg continued to wage a paper battle for the scheme. He approached successive prime ministers in 1945 and 1946, and published *Australia—The Unpromised Land* (London, 1948). It was to no avail.

After the State of Israel was established in 1948, Steinberg expressed concern at the idea of an exclusively Jewish—rather than a binational Jewish-Arab—nation. In the ensuing years he continued to be a proponent of Jewish settlement outside Israel. He died suddenly on 2 January 1957 in New York; his son and a daughter survived him. His close friend Erich Fromm wrote: 'Many people would have called Isaac Steinberg a dreamer, or a visionary, and yet, he was one of the true, and unfortunately few, realists of our time'.

B. J. Bialostotzky et al, *Yitshak Nahman Shtaynberg* (NY, 1961); G. Farwell, *Rejoice in Freedom* (Melb, 1976); B. Hooper, 'The Unpromised Land: A Jewish Refugee Settlement in the Kimberley?', in R. Bosworth and M. Melia (eds), *Aspects of Ethnicity* (Perth, 1991), *and* Australian Reactions to German Persecution of the Jews and Refugee Immigration, 1933-1947 (M.A. thesis, ANU, 1972); L. Gettler, *An Unpromised Land* (Fremantle, WA, 1993); *Aust Jewish Hist Soc J*, 5, no 4, 1961, p 170; *New York Times*, 3 Jan 1957.   BEVERLEY HOOPER

STEINER, LAJOS (1903-1975), engineer and international chess master, was born on 14 June 1903 at Nagyvárad (Oradea), Hungary (Romania), one of four children of Bernat Steiner, mathematics teacher, and his wife Cecilia, née Schwarz, both of whom were Jewish. Lajos was educated at the Technical High School, Budapest, and gained a diploma in mechanical engineering (1926) from the Technikum Mittweida, Germany. Both he and his elder brother Endre started playing in master chess events in Budapest while they were schoolboys. Lajos was granted the title of master at the age of 19. At the Kecskemet tournament in 1927 he tied for second with Aron Nimzovich (Nimzowitsch) behind Alexander Alekhine, a future world champion. In the late 1920s Steiner spent two years working as an engineer in the United States of America. Back in Europe, he turned professional, but made a precarious living from tournaments. Apart from two Hungarian championship wins (1931 and 1936), his best performances were at Mährisch Ostrau, Germany (1933, tied for second), Maribor, Yugoslavia (1934, tied for first), and Vienna (1935, tied for first).

In 1936 Steiner toured Australia. Although he played in the 1936-37 Australian championship in Perth, and won every game, he was ineligible for the title. He returned to Western Australia in the *Charon* on 11 March 1939, *en route* to settle in Sydney. His father and brother were to die in Nazi concentration camps. At the district registrar's office, Burwood, on 19 October 1939 Steiner married Augusta Edna Kingston, who had won the New South Wales women's chess championship six times; they were to remain childless. Unable to earn a living from tournament chess, he found work as a mechanical draughtsman, first with International Combustion Australasia Pty Ltd and then with Electricity Meter and Allied Industries Ltd. He was naturalized in 1944. In 1949 he was appointed a designing draughtsman at the Colonial Sugar Refining Co. Ltd's chemical factory at Lane Cove.

As a European chess master, Steiner greatly improved the standard of Australian chess simply by playing in tournaments over the next twenty-five years. He competed in six Australian championships and won four (1945, 1946-47, 1952-53 and 1958-59); he also won nine of his ten attempts at the New South Wales title (1940-41, 1943, 1944, 1945-46, 1953, 1955, 1958). Possessing total powers of concentration and a remarkable knowledge of uncommon variations of opening play, he impressed Cecil Purdy [q.v.] 'as one of the few thinking chess masters'. Fellow players appreciated his unruffled, courteous and cheerful demeanour.

A tower of strength in the Metropolitan Social Chess Club, Steiner contributed numerous articles to Purdy's chess magazine. He wrote an account, *Kings of the Chess Board, 1948* (1949), of his only return to Europe where he played in three tournaments, at Karlsbad (Karlovy Vary), Czechoslovakia, Budapest and Saltsjöbaden, Sweden. Due to his extended absence from the main chess centres of the world, the Fédération Internationale des Echecs never awarded him the title of grand master.

Steiner lived at Neutral Bay. Looking 'like a well-trained athlete', he was a keen amateur wrestler, and a good swimmer, tennis-player and sculler. He stopped competing in major tournaments in the early 1960s, but continued to play A-grade for Chatswood Chess Club and willingly helped young players. He died on 22 April 1975 at Castlecrag and was cremated. His wife survived him.

W. A. Foldeak, *Lajos Steiner* (Carlton, Eng, 1997); C. Chua, *Australian Chess at the Top* (Adel, 1998); *Chess World*, 1 Mar 1948, p 50, July 1954, p 157, May 1959, p 116; *SMH*, 31 July 1936, 29 May 1945, 25 Apr 1975; *Smith's Weekly* (Syd), 4 May 1946; naturalization file, A435, item 1944/4/3763.

JOHN S. PURDY

STELZER, EUNICE MINNIE (1880-1962), founder of the Happiness Club, was born on 13 December 1880 at Darlinghurst, Sydney, daughter of Alfred Sydney Carpenter, a native-born plasterer, and his wife Phoebe, née Parker, who came from New Zealand. Educated at Harvard College, Potts Point, Eunice was appointed a pupil-teacher at Crown Street Superior Public School in 1898 and promoted in 1900. She resigned in 1902 to teach music (stringed instruments) at a music warehouse. In 1903 she began to play at musicales held by the Theosophical Society in Australia.

At the Congregational Church, Pitt Street, on 20 April 1905 Eunice married William Jacob Stelzer, a manufacturing jeweller; they were to have five daughters, then a son. She performed in many charity concerts during World War I, and was thanked by the Belgian consul for her contributions to the Belgian Relief Fund.

A. E. Bennett [q.v.7] asked Mrs Stelzer in June 1927 to broadcast a musical item on the Theosophical Society's radio-station 2GB. She agreed to do so for one week only. An immediate success, she was encouraged by Bennett and joined the staff in 1929. From Monday to Friday she ran an afternoon session for women and soon began to receive letters from listeners, confiding their worries and seeking her advice. Although she attempted to answer them herself, she organized local suburban groups to assist her when the number of letters increased.

In October 1929 Stelzer launched the Happiness Club on 2GB to gather all the groups as branches. The club's motto was 'Others First'. She remained its president until 1950. Entirely staffed and run by volunteers, the club soon had thousands of members and raised money for a wide variety of charitable causes, such as Sydney and Royal Prince Alfred hospitals, the Far West Children's Health Scheme, the Smith Family, and the New South Wales Institution for the Deaf and Dumb and the Blind. It also supported individuals in need. In 1930, when the mayor of Rockdale telephoned to say he had found an empty house for a distressed family, but needed furniture, Stelzer appealed for help over the radio and furnished it in three minutes.

The Happiness Club expanded with younger sets and a boys' branch. It held balls, 'Queen' competitions, egg days, Christmas parties and afternoon teas. Hundreds of women were attracted to its functions, which came under vice-regal patronage in 1933. During World War II the club donated two mobile canteens, eight mobile food-trolleys and two ambulances, made 158 230 dressings and 9500 camouflage nets, knitted hundreds of garments for the Australian Comforts Fund and baked innumerable cakes for the troops.

Stelzer continued to broadcast on week-days until 1950, by which time the Happiness Club claimed more than 20 000 members; by 1954 it had raised and distributed £168 840, either in cash or as gifts of food or clothing. She became a life governor of five Sydney hospitals, and was awarded Queen Elizabeth II's coronation medal (1953). With her family's concurrence, she donated land at Newport to the club. Several cottages were built there to enable aged couples—many of whom were separated in homes for the elderly—to holiday together. Named the Eurobodalla Home, it was the forerunner of retirement villages.

An early admirer wrote of 'Mrs Stelzer's business ability, as well as her cheery, obliging disposition' which helped to bring a wider understanding 'of what mutual service … really means'. Survived by her husband and their children, Eunice Stelzer died on 4 June 1962 at Wahroonga and was cremated with Methodist forms. Her husband and daughter Joyce also worked for 2GB.

Wireless Weekly, 18 Sept, 4 Dec 1931, 9 Feb, 2, 16 Mar, 6 July, 28 Sept 1934; *ABC Weekly*, 20 Aug 1949, p 42; *Sunday Telegraph* (Syd), 22 June 1947; *SMH*, 2 June 1953, 5 June 1962; information from Mrs J. Whiteman, Wyoming, NSW.

RACHEL GRAHAME

STEPHENSON, HELEN ROSALIE; *see* BOWER

STEPHENSON, STUART (1867-1944), headmaster, was born on 19 December 1867 at Higher Buxton, Derbyshire, England, son of Robert Stephenson, Wesleyan minister, and his wife Mary, née Scott. From Kingswood School, Bath, Stuart won an open scholarship to Corpus Christi College, Oxford (B.A., 1889), where he read mathematics. In 1890 he sailed for Melbourne to assist his elder brother Arthur who had founded New College, Box Hill. He edited the school magazine, the *Tatler*, and continued his studies at the University of Melbourne (M.A., 1892). In 1896, when Arthur became headmaster of Wesley College, Stuart joined its staff as senior mathematics master. Appointed second master at Prince Albert College, Auckland, New Zealand, in 1898, he was to be made headmaster in 1906. On 25 January 1901 in her father's house at St Kilda, Melbourne, he married with Wesleyan forms Annie Emily, daughter of Robert McCutcheon [q.v.10]. He returned to New College as headmaster in 1907, but, despite his efforts, the number of pupils declined.

In 1910 Stephenson took up the post of second master at Brisbane Grammar School.

He began to rejuvenate the Old Boys' Association whose records and finances were in chaos after a fire at their rooms in 1909. Elected president (1911) of the association, he continued to be a member for the rest of his life. From 1916, as secretary of the school's war memorial committee, he worked tirelessly to obtain details about every past student who served in World War I. This information was entered in the 'Golden Book' which became the central feature of Grammar's War Memorial Library, opened in 1924. Drawing on the meticulous records he gathered, Stephenson compiled and edited an extensive register, *Annals of the Brisbane Grammar School 1869-1922* (1923). He 'possessed the rare gift of taking infinite pains. His capacity for work, thorough and unceasing, was amazing'. To mark its silver jubilee, the Old Boys' Association presented the book to the school.

Stephenson was appointed headmaster in June 1928. Following his wife's death in August that year, his daughter Jessie supervised the boarding-house and assumed the role of official hostess. He ran the school at a time of great financial stress when the Depression took its toll. The number of staff was continually reduced; those who remained were regularly dismissed at the end of the school year and re-employed on lower salaries. Led by Stephenson, the teachers made additional sacrifices so that many students could remain to complete their education. Stephenson's health began to fail. In 1935 the second master George Carson-Cooling [q.v.13] and his wife took over the boarding-house.

In 1940 Stephenson retired, intending to edit a second volume of the *Annals*, for which he had been collecting material since 1922. He served as secretary of another war memorial committee and involved himself with the unit of the Air Training Corps, formed at the school in 1943. Survived by his two daughters and two sons, he died on 31 December 1944 at Auchenflower and was cremated with Anglican rites. A school house at Grammar was named after him.

F. N. Bamford, *New College—Box Hill—Kingswood College* (Melb, 1966); G. Blainey et al, *Wesley College* (Melb, 1967); K. Willey, *The First Hundred Years* (Melb, 1968); D. Cotter, *Farmers, Ringmasters and Builders* (Melb, 1985); P. Barnett, *Images of a School* (Brisb, 1989); *Brisb Grammar School Mag*, June 1940; *Courier-Mail*, 1 Jan 1945; Brisb Grammar School, EDU/80 (QA); Brisb Grammar School archives.   P. J. BARNETT

STEVENS, DUNCAN HERBERT (1921-1964), naval officer, was born on 23 March 1921 at Fairfield, Melbourne, only child of (Sir) Jack Edwin Stawell Stevens [q.v.], a

Victorian-born public servant, and his wife Catherine McAllister, née Macdonald, who came from Scotland. Duncan attended Wesley College and entered the Royal Australian Naval College, Flinders Naval Depot, Westernport, on 1 January 1935. Graduating in 1939, he trained at sea and completed courses in England. During World War II he served in cruisers and destroyers, and was promoted lieutenant (1943). He remained at sea after the war, commanding four minor vessels, *Kangaroo* (1948-49), *Koala* (1949-50), *Reserve* (1950-51) and *Cowra* (1951-52). On 20 May 1949 at Dreger Harbour, near Finschhafen, Territory of Papua-New Guinea, he married Beatrice Louise Phippard.

Following a period (1952-54) ashore at H.M.A.S. *Tarangau*, Los Negros Island, Lieutenant Commander Stevens took command of the frigate *Quickmatch* in 1955. He was promoted commander and appointed training commander at F.N.D. in 1956. While executive-officer (1958-60) of the aircraft-carrier *Melbourne* he spent time in hospital suffering from a duodenal ulcer. In 1960 he attended the Royal Naval Staff College, Greenwich, England, and in 1960-62 worked in the Admiralty's Tactical and Weapons Policy Division.

Back in Australia, Stevens was promoted captain on 31 December 1962. Two days later he assumed command of the destroyer H.M.A.S. *Voyager*. Despite Rear Admiral (Sir) Alan McNicoll's judgement in January 1964 that Stevens had 'probably reached his ceiling', he had a good chance of attaining higher rank. Stevens was a friendly and gregarious man, but inclined to brood. He loved sport and, at the age of 42, still played in the ship's cricket team.

On the night of 10 February 1964 *Voyager* was operating with *Melbourne* off the south coast of New South Wales. It was the destroyer's responsibility to keep clear of the carrier. About 8.54 p.m. *Voyager* inexplicably turned towards *Melbourne*, as if to cross her path. Two minutes later the ships collided, 20 nautical miles (37 km) south-east of Jervis Bay. *Melbourne*'s bows struck *Voyager*'s port side and cut her in two. Both sections sank. Eighty-two men, all from *Voyager*, lost their lives, Stevens among them. Survived by his wife and their son, he was cremated.

The cause of the accident will never be known because all the key personnel on *Voyager*'s bridge were killed. Of several theories advanced to explain the destroyer's actions, two are plausible: that her officers had become confused and thought they were turning away from *Melbourne* rather than towards her; and that instructions—signalled from the carrier—changing the ships' course and *Voyager*'s station relative to *Melbourne* were misinterpreted aboard *Voyager*.

Sir John Spicer [q.v.], the royal commissioner who investigated the disaster, reported in August 1964. He concluded that the collision would not have occurred if a proper watch had been maintained in *Voyager*. Because he could not reconstruct events on the destroyer's bridge, he felt unable to determine the responsibility of any of her officers for what had occurred. In contrast, he criticized Captain R. J. Robertson and other officers in *Melbourne* for not questioning *Voyager*'s movements before a dangerous situation developed. Robertson was posted ashore.

Incensed by Spicer's and the navy's treatment of Robertson, Lieutenant Commander P. T. Cabban—who had been *Voyager*'s first lieutenant immediately before leaving the R.A.N. in January 1964—alleged that, in 1963, Stevens had been inconsistent in his ship-handling, frequently drunk when the ship was in harbour, and sometimes too ill to take command at sea. In 1967-68 a second royal commission, conducted by Sir Stanley Burbury, K. W. Asprey and G. A. G. Lucas, inquired into Cabban's statement.

The commissioners discounted evidence that Stevens had been volatile and impetuous on the bridge in favour of extensive testimony that he had been a competent seaman. They found that, in 1963-64, he had suffered 'intermittent recurrences' of his 'ulcer trouble' to which 'his drinking habits contributed'. Because of his medical condition, they held that he had been unfit to command *Voyager*. Exonerating *Melbourne*'s officers, the commissioners concluded that the collision resulted from a mistake on the bridge of *Voyager*. They claimed that Stevens' physical state helped to 'account for such an error'.

Yet, the commissioners had heard no evidence that Stevens was incapacitated on 10 February 1964. There is no reason to believe that his performance on the bridge that night was affected by illness, by alcohol, or by medication. In fairness, all that can be said is that, as *Voyager*'s commanding officer, he bore the ultimate responsibility for the tragedy.

T. Frame, *Where Fate Calls* (Syd, 1992), and for bib; information from Mr S. Stevens, Cannonvale, Qld.

DARRYL BENNET

STEVENS, GWENDOLYNE DAPHNE (1908-1974), hospital proprietress, sheep-breeder and mining entrepreneur, was born on 7 June 1908 at Quorn, South Australia, daughter of Hugo Albert Valentine Healey, painter and later publican, and his wife Jessie Gwendolyne, née Napier, both South Australian born. Gwendolyne attended several rural schools, including Innamincka Public, before proceeding to St Peter's Collegiate Girls' School, Adelaide.

Miss Healey trained at Burra public and (Royal) Adelaide hospitals, and was registered as a nurse on 11 July 1929. She then moved to Parkside Mental Hospital where she gained a certificate in psychiatric nursing in 1931 and became sister-in-charge. In 1934 she bought a large house at Payneham that had been built by James Marshall [q.v.5], converted it into a private psychiatric hospital and named it St Margaret's. As its owner and matron for eighteen years, she cared for patients suffering the early stages of nervous disorders, and provided them with a secure and restful setting, with aviaries amid beautiful gardens. That she took on such a task during the Depression, and succeeded in it, testified to her business acumen, organizing ability and compassion for those in need.

At the chapel of the Collegiate School of St Peter, Adelaide, on 12 April 1940 Healey married with Anglican rites George Dempster Stevens, a clerk employed by Dalgety [q.v.4] & Co. Ltd. They were to have two daughters. Pursuing her interest in community health, Mrs Stevens was founding president (1944-50) and a committee-member (until 1961) of the Payneham branch of the Mothers' and Babies' Health Association. After she sold her hospital in 1952, she set up Sterling Downs, a Poll Dorset stud on 2200 acres (890 ha) at Currency Creek, in 1957. She employed a manager to supervise the stud and visited it each week. In the 1960s she sold part of the land and moved the stud to Sterling Park, McLaren Vale. The stud was later sold and its sheep replaced with cattle.

Having noticed particular outcrops of rock at Sterling Park, Stevens arranged for drilling to be conducted, as a result of which she opened a quarry and sold building sands to the local council. In 1968 she became interested in the mining potential of the Northern Territory. She studied maps, obtained advice from geologists and concentrated on an area near Oenpelli, Arnhem Land. She received permission to prospect on 1282 square miles (3320 km^2) of Aboriginal reserve and negotiated an exploration programme with Queensland Mines Ltd. In 1970 that company discovered what was then described as the richest body of uranium ore in the world, at a site known to local Aborigines as Nabarlek. Newspapers referred to Stevens as 'probably the first woman in the world with a right to mine uranium'. She visited the area twice during the early stages of exploration and was staggered by the size of the find. In August 1971, however, Queensland Mines downgraded the ore reserves to about one-sixth of those announced a year earlier. Intending to use some of the proceeds of her investment to benefit the health of the Aborigines, Stevens

transferred the exploration licences to Queensland Mines in May 1973 and negotiated a royalty agreement. Mining at Nabarlek began in 1979.

Mrs Stevens both created and took advantage of opportunities in the areas of mental health, sheep-breeding and mining. Suffering from hypertension, she died of a cerebral haemorrhage on 3 March 1974 in her Kensington Park home and was cremated. She was survived by her husband and their daughters. Her estate was sworn for probate at $416 266.

SA Trained Nurses' Centenary Cte, *Nursing in South Australia* (Adel, 1939); T. Sykes, *The Money Miners* (Syd, 1978); J. W. Warburton, *Payneham, Garden Village to City* (Payneham, SA, 1983); J. W. Harris, *We Wish We'd Done More* (Adel, 1998); *Advertiser* (Adel), 2 Sept 1970, 5 Mar 1974; *SMH*, 2, 19 Sept 1970; Stevens family papers (held by Mrs P. N. Craven, Heathpool, Adel).   TONY BOTT

STEVENS, SIR JACK EDWIN STAWELL (1896-1969), army officer, public servant and businessman, was born on 7 September 1896 at Daylesford, Victoria, youngest of seven children of Melbourne-born parents Herbert Clarence Stevens, draper, and his wife Violet Ophelia, née Bury. Educated at Daylesford State School, Jack began work in a cigar factory at the age of 12. In 1915 he joined the Postmaster-General's Department as a clerk in the electrical engineers' branch. He enlisted in the Australian Imperial Force on 2 July, having served four years in the senior cadets and one in the Militia.

Following signals training, Stevens sailed for Egypt in November as a corporal. In March 1916 he was promoted sergeant and allotted to the 4th Divisional Signal Company. Three months later he was sent to France. For his 'devotion and keen sense of duty' during the fighting at Pozières and at the Ypres salient, Belgium, in August-October, he was awarded the Meritorious Service Medal. He was commissioned on 17 January 1917 and transferred next month to the 5th Divisional Signal Company. In April he was promoted lieutenant. He took part in operations at Polygon Wood (September) and in March 1918 was posted to the Australian Corps Signal Company. His A.I.F. appointment terminated in Melbourne on 28 October 1919.

Stevens resumed work with the P.M.G. At the Presbyterian Church, South Melbourne, on 26 April 1920 he married Catherine McAllister Macdonald. He rejoined the Militia in 1921. Promoted captain in 1922 and major in 1924, he commanded the 2nd Cavalry Divisional Signals (1923-26) and, as lieutenant colonel, the 4th Divisional Signals (1926-29), the 3rd Divisional Signals (1929-35) and the

57th/60th Infantry Battalion (1935-39). On 13 October 1939 he was seconded to the A.I.F. and given command of the 6th Divisional Signals. Short and slightly built, but 'waspishly aggressive and persistent', he was chosen by Major General (Sir) John Lavarack [q.v.15] in April 1940 to form and command the 21st Infantry Brigade, and was promoted colonel and temporary brigadier. He sailed for the Middle East in October.

Throughout the campaign against the Vichy French, in Syria in June-July 1941, Stevens handled his brigade with 'great skill'. His leadership, determination, courage and buoyant outlook were important factors in forcing an assault across the Litani River on 12 June when success seemed unlikely. Although wounded, he personally directed the operation. He won the Distinguished Service Order and was mentioned in dispatches. The actions of his brigade during the battle of Damour (5-9 July) further demonstrated his ability to carry out difficult missions.

The 21st Brigade returned to Australia in March 1942. Next month Stevens was promoted temporary major general and given command of the 4th Division. In August he was appointed commander of Northern Territory Force; four months later he was given additional command responsibilities for the 12th Division and the Northern Territory Lines of Communications Area. In April 1943 he took over the 6th Division, which was then undergoing training on the Atherton Tableland, Queensland. The division was deployed to New Guinea in late 1944 and saw action in the Aitape-Wewak area. Stevens's forces advanced along the coast to Wewak and cleared Japanese units from the Maprik area, inflicting heavy losses. For his 'gallant and distinguished service' and 'outstanding leadership in operations against the Japanese', he was appointed C.B. (1946). Against his wishes he relinquished his command in August 1945 to become assistant-commissioner of the Commonwealth Public Service Board. He was to continue his service in the Citizen Military Forces, commanding the 2nd Division in 1947-50 and serving as C.M.F. member of the Military Board for the two months prior to his transfer to the Reserve of Officers on 1 July 1950.

In September 1946 Stevens was made general manager and chief executive officer of the Overseas Telecommunications Commission. He was appointed secretary of the Department of National Development in 1950. As the Australian government developed an increasing interest in atomic energy, he was given responsibility for uranium mining at Rum Jungle, Northern Territory. In 1951 he became secretary of the newly restructured Department of Supply, which oversaw research and development of war matériel, in-cluding the procurement and use of uranium. 'Abrupt, tough and alert', he 'ran the department with a stern hand'. He negotiated agreements with Britain and the United States of America on atomic research issues, and helped the British to organize atomic tests in Australia. The minister for supply (Sir) Howard Beale was kept 'in the dark' about preparations for tests on the Monte Bello Islands, off Western Australia. Stevens felt uneasy that such information was withheld from the minister. Contrary to directions from Prime Minister (Sir) Robert Menzies [q.v.15], he secretly informed Beale of the plans.

Cabinet agreed to the creation of the Australian Atomic Energy Commission in September 1952 and appointed Stevens its first chairman. The A.A.E.C.'s role was to carry out research into atomic energy and earn Australia 'access to overseas technology during the Cold War'. Stevens led delegations to Washington and London to secure technical co-operation, and was closely involved in establishing the experimental reactor at Lucas Heights, Sydney. In 1955 he was appointed K.B.E.

Sir Jack retired from the public service in 1956. He became chairman of Australian Electrical Industries Ltd and of British Automotive Industries Pty Ltd, and a director of Commonwealth Industrial Gases Ltd, Custom Credit Corporation Ltd, Mount Isa Mines Ltd and the Trustees Executors & Agency Co. Ltd. Survived by his wife, he died of a coronary occlusion on 20 May 1969 in Sydney and was cremated with Anglican rites. A royal commission (1964) into the sinking of H.M.A.S. *Voyager* and another (1967-68) into the conduct of his only son Captain Duncan Stevens [q.v.] proved ordeals that probably contributed to his death.

G. Long, *Greece, Crete and Syria* (Canb, 1953) and *The Final Campaigns* (Canb, 1963); H. Beale, *This Inch of Time* (Melb, 1977); A. Cawte, *Atomic Australia 1944-1990* (Syd, 1992); *SMH*, 21 May 1969; J. Stevens, A Personal Story of the Service, as a Citizen Soldier, of Major-General Sir Jack Stevens, KBE, CB, DSO, ED (ms, AWM).

MICHAEL BOYLE

STEVENS, JOSEPH HANFORD (1906-1976), businessman, was born on 20 January 1906 at Wolverhampton, England, son of George Stevens, motor-works manager, and his wife Florence Sarah, née Capper. George and his three brothers produced the famous A.J.S. marque motorcycles, as well as four-wheel vehicles and radios. Educated at Wolverhampton Grammar School, Hanford joined the family firm and gained experience in all its sections. He rode A.J.S. motorcycles in Isle of Man Tourist-Trophy races, won the Belgian Grand Prix in 1925, and was said to be the first person to exceed 100 miles (161 km) per hour on a motorcycle on sand. In 1929 he obtained a flying licence.

By 1931 Stevens was the company's export sales manager. He met Kathleen Winifred Griffin, an 18-year-old stenographer, at Toronto, Canada, and married her a week later at Yonkers, New York, on 11 September 1931. On his return to England, he found that A.J.S. had gone into voluntary liquidation. A small screw-manufacturing business operated by the Stevens family survived and he worked there until 1937 when he joined the Bristol Aeroplane Co. In September 1939 that firm sent him to Australia to assist with the local production of Beaufort bombers. About six hundred sub-contractors in several States manufactured parts for the aircraft; these components were transported to Fishermens Bend, Melbourne, and Mascot, Sydney, for final assembly. Stevens held a succession of managerial posts in Melbourne and played a key role in the success of a project which delivered seven hundred Beauforts to the Royal Australian Air Force between August 1941 and August 1944.

Appointed to the Commonwealth Public Service on 6 May 1948, Stevens served at Canberra House, London, until 1953 as senior representative in Britain of the Department of Supply and the Department of Defence Production. He negotiated with the English Electric Co. Ltd to build the Canberra bomber in Australia. Back in Melbourne, he was assistant-secretary, aircraft production, Department of Defence Production. In 1954 he travelled abroad as a member of the R.A.A.F.'s re-equipment mission.

Stevens left the public service in 1956, having accepted an invitation from (Sir) Charles Hayward, chairman of Firth Cleveland Ltd in Britain, to become managing director of a subsidiary, Simmonds Aero-Accessories (Aerocessories) Pty Ltd, located at Ballarat, Victoria. Established in a former munitions factory, the business produced fasteners for the aviation and automotive industries. Stevens expanded operations, built a new factory and increased the number of employees to more than four hundred. He retired in 1973.

In the mid-1960s the Victorian government had appointed Stevens to the Decentralization Advisory Committee, which recommended various rural centres for accelerated development. He was active in the Victorian Chamber of Manufactures and in community work. Convivial and a good mixer, he was liked and respected by his colleagues and employees. He died of cancer on 25 September 1976 at Ballarat and was cremated with Anglican rites; his wife, and their daughter and son survived

him. The naming of the J. Hanford Stevens library at Sebastopol Secondary College acknowledged his term (1963-76) as president of the council of the former technical school.

D. P. Mellor, *The Role of Science and Industry* (Canb, 1958); S. J. Mills, *A.J.S. of Wolverhampton* (Sutton Coldfield, Eng, 1994); information from Mrs K. Stevens, Mrs C. Coltman and Mr A. Bell, Ballarat, Vic, and Mr B. Hodson, Murrumbeena, Melb.
                          FRANK HURLEY

STEVENSON, JOHN ROWLSTONE (1908-1971), parliamentary officer and soldier, was born on 7 October 1908 at Bondi, Sydney, son of John James Stevenson, a commercial traveller from the United States of America, and his Sydney-born wife Caroline Maude, née Rowlstone. Educated at Canterbury Boys' Intermediate High School, John took an office job, played hockey, and drove racing cars at Maroubra speedway. He was appointed third clerk on the staff of the Legislative Council in 1933 and second clerk in 1939.

After beginning compulsory military training in 1925, Stevenson had enlisted in the 45th Battalion, Citizen Military Forces, in 1927. Commissioned lieutenant (1929), he was promoted captain in 1934 and transferred to the artillery in 1937. On 13 October 1939 he was appointed major, 2nd/3rd Battalion, Australian Imperial Force. Five ft 10 ins (178 cm) tall and 11 st. 6 lb. (73 kg) in weight, he had a dark complexion and black hair. In January 1940 he sailed for the Middle East. He commanded the 16th Infantry Training Battalion from November before rejoining the 2nd/3rd in Palestine in May 1941. On 16 June that year at St George's Anglican Cathedral, Jerusalem, he married Rita Anne Hanscombe, the deputy-matron of the 2nd/1st Australian General Hospital. Two days later the 2nd/3rd moved to Syria to engage Vichy French forces.

Stevenson took command of the battalion on 21 June. He was promoted temporary lieutenant colonel on the 25th, twice mentioned in dispatches, and awarded the Distinguished Service Order for his leadership during the battle of Damour. After the armistice in July, his unit helped to garrison Syria and Lebanon. It sailed for Australia in March 1942, but was diverted to Ceylon (Sri Lanka) and did not disembark in Melbourne until August. By 21 September the 2nd/3rd had reached Papua.

On the Kokoda Track, Stevenson proved himself to be a confident leader and an adept tactician. He was wounded in his left ear on 22 October, but remained on duty until the 27th when he handed over his command. By then he had lost four stone (25 kg) in weight. On 25 November he rejoined the depleted 2nd/3rd on the Sanananda Track. The battalion was relieved on 19/20 December and returned to Australia in January 1943. Stevenson was promoted colonel and temporary brigadier on 31 March and given command of the 11th Infantry Brigade, which had been deployed for the defence of north-east Queensland and Merauke, Dutch New Guinea. Under its enterprising leader, the brigade fought on Bougainville from December 1944 until hostilities ceased in August 1945. Stevenson accepted the surrender of the Japanese forces on Nauru and Ocean islands, relinquished his command in December, came home in February 1946 and was transferred to the Reserve of Officers on 30 May. He was appointed a commander of the Order of Oranje-Nassau (1945) and C.B.E. (1947).

In 1946 Stevenson returned to the Legislative Council as usher of the Black Rod and first clerk; by 1954 he was clerk of the parliaments. Applying his knowledge of procedure and practice with common sense, he kept the council running smoothly. He was generous in his advice to members and a stickler for proper behaviour in the chamber. In 1954 he introduced the first of a series of consolidated indexes to supplement official parliamentary records. A man of decided opinions who supported the bicameral system, he openly advocated the (successful) 'No' vote in both the State referendum on the abolition of the council in 1961 and the Federal 'nexus' referendum in 1967. On issues of defence, he was prepared to criticize governments of any political persuasion.

Resuming part-time duty with the C.M.F., Stevenson commanded the 5th Brigade in 1948-51 and, as major general, the 2nd Division in 1957-59. He was honorary colonel of the 3rd Infantry Battalion (Werriwa Regiment) in 1957-60 and of the University of New South Wales Regiment in 1963-69, president (1962-66) of the United Service Institution of New South Wales, patron of the 2nd/3rd Battalion Association and president of Double Bay sub-branch of the Returned Services League of Australia.

During the Depression Stevenson had helped to run a boys' club at Christ Church St Laurence. He later worked to rehabilitate former prisoners. A Freemason and a Rotarian, he was a councillor (from 1958) of the National Roads and Motorists' Association and a member (from 1961) of the Archives Authority of New South Wales. He was also president (1963-65) of the Imperial Service Club, and a member of the Cruising Yacht Club of Australia and the Royal Australian Navy Sailing Association. Survived by his wife and their two daughters, he died suddenly of coronary vascular disease on 4 July 1971 in Fiji and was cremated in Sydney with Presbyterian forms and full military honours.

G. Long, *Greece, Crete and Syria* (Canb, 1953) and *The Final Campaigns* (Canb, 1963); D. McCarthy, *South-West Pacific Area—First Year* (Canb, 1959); D. Dexter, *The New Guinea Offensives* (Canb, 1961); *PD* (NSW), 4 Aug 1971, p 7; *Aust Lib J*, Aug 1969; *Open Road*, 1 Dec 1969; information from Mrs S. Dodds, Hurstville, Syd.   J. B. HOPLEY

STEWART, CHARLES JACKSON (1876-1954), hotelkeeper, was born on 22 March 1876 at Kangaroo Point, Brisbane, third of four children of Robert Stewart, a Scottish-born farmer, and his wife Mary, née North, who came from Ireland. Mary died in childbirth in 1878. Her two surviving children, Charles and William, were raised by their maternal grandmother and an aunt, while their father worked as a miner. Their grandmother's death in 1889 and their aunt's move to Cooktown obliged the boys to join the workforce.

Charles worked as an office-boy in the legal firm of Rees R. & Sydney Jones, Rockhampton, but lacked the money to be articled. Seeing no future in the law, he trained at night to become a tailor. He was initially employed by a Jewish master tailor, from whom he learned business acumen, before becoming shop manager at Charles Gilbert's large tailoring establishment in Queen Street, Brisbane. His first marketing coup came when he visited Sydney and obtained orders to supply suits to Queensland soldiers returning from the South African War.

In 1902 Stewart entered into partnership with E. J. Carroll [q.v.7] who was leasing unprofitable railway refreshment-rooms at Gympie, Landsborough and Ipswich. Despite his lack of catering experience, Stewart developed them into profitable businesses within three years. Both partners returned to Brisbane where they leased the Albion Hotel, as well as the Osbourne Hotel, Fortitude Valley, which Stewart managed. The Queensland Turf Club appointed him caterer at Eagle Farm racecourse in 1908, thereby beginning an association that was to continue until his death. In 1909 he moved to the Criterion Hotel, George Street. He and Carroll owned it by 1914. On 12 October that year at St Mary's Catholic Church, South Brisbane, Stewart married 26-year-old Jessie Dobbie.

By 1922 Stewart was sole owner of the Criterion and was offering a free delivery service in an unmarked van. A further innovation, Stewarts Home Supply, a bottle shop, opened the market to female customers. In 1926 he rebuilt the hotel. Rivalled in opulence only by Tattersall's Club, the Criterion featured marble throughout, and boasted Brisbane's largest cellar and first *en suite*. At various times Stewart also leased the Waterloo, Paddington and Boundary hotels.

Although he was an active anti-prohibitionist during the 1920s, Stewart never sought public office because he doubted his ability to address an audience. Essentially an entrepreneurial, hard-working businessman, he was extremely adept with figures and an astute negotiator. He was philanthropic, ethical and law-abiding, and firm but kind to his family, friends and staff alike. Passionate about football and cricket, he was vice-president of the Queensland Rugby Union, and a long-time member of the Queensland Turf and Tattersall's clubs.

Never physically robust, Stewart confined his activities to the Criterion and to Eagle Farm racecourse after his health deteriorated in the 1930s. A series of heart attacks left him an invalid for the last ten years of his life. Survived by his wife, and their daughter and son, he died on 24 October 1954 in his beloved Criterion and was buried in Toowong cemetery. In 1956 his son (Sir) Edward Stewart became chairman of Stewarts Hotels Pty Ltd.

J. M. Freeland, *The Australian Pub* (Melb, 1966); *Courier-Mail*, 26 Oct 1954; information from Sir Edward Stewart, Buderim, Qld, and Miss Mary Stewart, Hamilton, Brisb.　　MARGARET COOK

STEWART, FLORA SHAW (1886-1979), pioneer and hotelkeeper, was born on 28 August 1886 at Fountainbridge, Edinburgh, eldest of seven children of John Young, journey-man blacksmith, and his wife Catherine, née Christie. In 1888 the Youngs migrated to Australia and moved to the tablelands west of Cooktown, North Queensland, where Flora discovered a lifelong love of blood horses. John took his family to Papua in 1906 to investigate the possible purchase of an hotel. To obtain experience, Flora worked for five months as manageress of the Cosmopolitan Hotel, Samarai. She returned with her family to Queensland in 1909. At Charters Towers on 24 June that year Flora married with United Welsh Church forms Harry Gofton, an English-born horse-dealer.

The couple sailed to Papua and for three years grew rubber on Kanosia plantation; Flora visited nearby Port Moresby only once during that time, for the birth (1911) of her son Moresby. In 1913 Flora and Harry set off to mine gold on a tributary of the Vailala River. There Flora operated a trade store, kept fowls and pigs, shot deer and crocodiles for meat and skins, and made her own bread. She survived a number of illnesses and a miscarriage, without medical attention. After World War I broke out the Goftons came back to Australia. When Harry enlisted in the Australian Imperial Force on 21 March 1916, Flora returned to Port Moresby with her son and daughter. She worked in the drapery department of the Burns, Philp [qq.v.7,11] store before opening a guest-house. While serving with the 47th Battalion, Harry died of wounds in France on 27 March 1918. Flora went to Samarai in 1920 to help her sister to run the Cosmopolitan Hotel; she took it over in 1927.

On 17 March 1929 at St Paul's Church of England, Samarai, Flora married James Stewart, a 32-year-old building foreman; they were to have a daughter. They moved to Wau on the Morobe goldfield. Flora bought Harry Darby's old 'Kunai Pub' and transformed it into the Hotel Bulolo, the first regular hotel on the diggings. Her exploits became legendary. Known to all as 'Ma', she was the friend and confidante of countless miners and prospectors. She cut their hair, dressed their wounds and, in the absence of a bank, hid their gold under her bed—'the safest place in town'. 'Ma' had a robust sense of humour and was always ready to help those down on their luck, but she was a canny Scot and in no sense a 'soft touch'. Retaining her love of horses, she raced them with considerable success for years.

In March 1936 Mrs Stewart opened at Lae the famous Hotel Cecil. Her husband died in a motorcar accident in November 1937 and her son, a bomber pilot in the Royal Air Force, was killed in action in May 1940. In December 1941 Flora was evacuated to Australia with her two daughters. When she returned to Lae at the end of World War II, she took over the Australian Women's Army Service barracks and turned them into a temporary Hotel Cecil for the war-ravaged town. Following protracted battles with officials, she finally rebuilt the hotel on its pre-war site in 1951 and operated it until 1957. She and her daughters established Morobe Theatres Ltd in 1962; the firm constructed a modern picture theatre which opened in October 1963. A founding member of the Morobe Agricultural Society, she led the grand parades at annual shows until the end of her life. Survived by her daughters, she died on 13 May 1979 at Lae and was buried in the local cemetery.

J. Sinclair, *Golden Gateway* (Bathurst, 1998); *PIM*, July 1979; *SMH*, 26 July 1951; *Lae Nius*, 16, 18 May 1979; information from Mrs E. Birrell, Helensvale, Qld, and Mrs F. Bowman, East Melb; personal knowledge.　　JAMES SINCLAIR

STEWART, FRANCIS EUGENE (1923-1979), politician, was born on 20 February 1923 at Belmore, Sydney, second child of native-born parents Patrick Francis Stewart, railway clerk, and his wife Margaret Mary, née Donnellan. Frank was educated at St Joseph's convent school, Belmore, and by the

Christian Brothers at St Mary's Cathedral High School, Sydney. He began work in 1939 as a clerk in the office of the commissioner for road transport and tramways. On 3 November 1941 he enlisted in the Militia. He transferred to the Australian Imperial Force on 15 November 1943, served in New Guinea with the 39th Transport Platoon in 1944-45 and rose to sergeant. Discharged from the army on 11 December 1945, he returned to his civilian occupation. A keen sportsman, he held the Australian Army Service Corps' light-heavyweight boxing championship and played (1948-50) first-grade Rugby League football for Canterbury-Bankstown. At St Joseph's Catholic Church, Belmore, on 2 August 1952 he married Maureen Neagle Smith.

Following family tradition, Stewart had joined the Australian Labor Party in 1942. The Federal electorate of Lang contained his clan's home base, and, when the sitting member died in 1953, Stewart won the hotly contested pre-selection ballot. He was elected to the House of Representatives in a by-election on 29 August that year. In parliament, he made no secret of his right-wing Catholic views. He participated spiritedly in debates on defence and social security. In October 1954 a move was made in caucus against H. V. Evatt's [q.v.14] leadership: Stewart was one of eight New South Wales members who voted for a 'spill'. All of them were subsequently stigmatized as 'groupers'. In 1957 anti-grouper elements in Stewart's electorate tried unsuccessfully to deprive him of pre-selection. Later that year the A.L.P.'s federal executive received a complaint that he had breached party policy by advocating that the army be equipped with nuclear weapons. The executive unanimously exonerated him.

Stewart became Opposition spokesman on fuel and natural resources in April 1969. Given the new portfolio of tourism and recreation on 19 December 1972 in E. G. Whitlam's Labor ministry, he set up a wide-ranging programme of grants to sport, and arranged for the government to pay the full travel costs of Australian teams in the Commonwealth and Olympic games. Another of his initiatives was a bill, blocked in the Senate, to license travel agents and safeguard travellers' funds. In February 1973 Stewart was also appointed minister assisting the treasurer. W. G. Hayden found him 'a tremendously loyal colleague. He was always master of even the most complex economic documents, always ready strongly to support the Treasurer in a difficult Cabinet role'.

Following the general election in 1974, Stewart resumed his previous ministerial responsibilities, including those of vice-president of the Executive Council, a position he had held since November 1973 and one which was to embroil him in controversy. In May 1975, in the absence of the governor-general Sir John Kerr, he presided over an Executive Council meeting that revoked R. F. X. Connor's [q.v.13] authority to seek an overseas loan. Five months later Connor was forced to resign from the ministry for having misled the prime minister about his continued loan-raising activities. In December a report in the *Bulletin* claimed that Stewart had secretly told Kerr that Connor was entitled to believe he had Whitlam's approval to continue the search for loans. Stewart denied the assertion. The *Sydney Morning Herald* and the *Sun-Herald* later published allegations that the loans affair had so troubled Stewart's conscience that he had given confidential information to the Opposition about the matter. Both stories remain unproven.

Stewart did not hesitate to speak out on moral issues. A vigorous opponent of abortion and divorce, he led the opposition in parliament to the family law bill, which was passed on a free vote in 1975. Depressed and disillusioned, he contemplated retirement. The circumstances of the government's dismissal in November made him decide to stand again. He did not join Labor's shadow ministry. After his seat was abolished in 1977, he transferred to Grayndler.

Forthright and convivial, Stewart was solidly built, with the appearance of a front-row forward. He maintained his interest in sport throughout his life and was an excellent tennis player. While playing squash, he died suddenly of myocardial infarction on 16 April 1979 at Long Jetty, New South Wales; he was accorded a state funeral and was buried in Rookwood cemetery, Sydney. His wife, and their son and five daughters survived him. Stewart's younger brother, Kevin, held the seat of Canterbury in the Legislative Assembly in 1962-85 and was a minister in 1976-85.

PD (HR), 1 May 1979, p 1673; *PD* (Senate), 1 May 1979, p 1447; *Sun* (Syd), 3 Dec 1975; *Australian*, 4 Dec 1975, 17 Apr 1979; *Bulletin*, 6 Dec 1975; *SMH*, 6 Dec 1975, 17 Apr 1979, 11 Nov 1985; *Daily Telegraph* (Syd), 17 Apr 1979; *Sun-Herald* (Syd), 10 Nov 1985; information from Mr G. Freudenberg, Woollahra, and Mr R. Hall, Newtown, Syd.

DAVID CLUNE

STEWART, JAMES RIVERS BARRINGTON (1913-1962), archaeologist, numismatist and gentleman farmer, was born on 3 July 1913 at Elizabeth Bay, Sydney, only child of Albyn Athol Stewart, a native-born marine engineer and later company director, and his wife Frances Landseer, née Morris, who came from South Africa. Descended from Major General William Stewart [q.v.2] of Mount Pleasant, Bathurst, James attended (1927-30) The King's School, Parramatta, between his education in England at Pembroke House School, Richmond, and the Leys School, Cambridge. He read archaeology and anthropology at Trinity Hall, Cambridge (B.A., 1934; M.A., 1938). While an undergraduate, he took part in the last season of excavations conducted at Tell el-'Ajjul, Palestine, by Professor Sir Flinders Petrie. At All Saints parish church, Kingsdon, Somerset, England, on 1 July 1935 he married Eleanor Mary Neal; they were to have a son before being divorced in 1952.

After graduating, Stewart went to Turkey on a Wilkin studentship. In 1935 he visited Cyprus: thenceforward he devoted himself to exploring its Early Bronze Age civilization and its archaeological links with Anatolia, Turkey. He ran his first excavations (1937-38)—under the auspices of the British School at Athens—in the cemetery of Bellapais (Vounous) on the island's north coast. On 24 July 1940 Stewart was commissioned in the Cyprus Regiment, which garrisoned the Suez Canal. In April-May 1941 he fought successively in mainland Greece and on Crete where he was captured. His experiences as a prisoner of war heightened the bond he had formed with his Cypriot soldiers; his reliance on cats for warmth turned his fondness for them into a deep attachment. He also managed to do some research and acquire rare German books on archaeology.

Once liberated and demobilized, Stewart was encouraged to return to Australia by Professor A. D. Trendall and W. J. Beasley, founder of the Australian Institute of Archaeology, Melbourne. In 1947 he was appointed a teaching fellow in the department of history at the University of Sydney. He became senior lecturer (under Trendall) in the new department of archaeology in 1949, acting head of the department in 1954 and Edwin Cuthbert Hall professor of Middle Eastern archaeology in 1960. Meanwhile, he also worked as curator of the Nicholson [q.v.2] Museum. From 1951 he lived at Mount Pleasant, which he farmed and treated as an extension of the department of archaeology. He became a substantial property owner and a man of independent means. His students, stimulated by his enthusiasm for the archaeology of the Levant, were expected to spend time at 'the Mount' which housed his exceptional research library (ultimately bought by the Fisher [q.v.4] Library), rooms full of Bronze Age pottery and other antiquities, and 'upwards of twenty indoor and outdoor cats'. On 11 March 1952 at the registrar-general's office, Sydney, he married Dorothy Evelyn (Eve) Dray, a technical assistant.

Throughout his professional life, Stewart remained attached to northern Cyprus, not only because it faced Anatolia, but also because of its beauty and the friendliness of its inhabitants, Greek and Turkish Cypriot alike.

Eve's property at Tjiklos provided a local base for his archaeological explorations. As director of the Melbourne Cyprus expedition, he dug more cemeteries at Nicosia and Vasilia (1955), and around Karmi (1960-61). In addition to his excavation reports, he wrote extensively on Cypriot and Palestinian archaeology, notably in the second edition of the *Handbook to the Nicholson Museum* (1948), and on 'The Early Cypriote Bronze Age' in *The Swedish Cyprus Expedition* (Vol.IV, Part 1A, Lund, Sweden, 1962).

From his schooldays Stewart built up a large and outstanding collection of coins, particularly of Rome, Cyprus, Byzantium and the Crusades. He was a vice-president of the Numismatic Society of New South Wales and a fellow of the Royal Numismatic Society, London. His comprehensive work on the Lusignan history and coinage of medieval Cyprus remained unpublished until 2001.

Endowed with boyish good looks, Stewart was capable of much personal charm. He was accustomed to having his own way and had little patience with those who frustrated his ambitions. For all his efforts, he failed to establish an Australian archaeological school in Cyprus. No less galling was the refusal by Professor Einar Gjerstad, editor of *The Swedish Cyprus Expedition*, to publish the whole of Stewart's corpus of Early Bronze Age Cypriot antiquities.

A Presbyterian by upbringing, Stewart regularly stayed at St Andrew's College, University of Sydney. He belonged to the Australian Club. In November 1960 he was elected to the Australian Humanities Research Council. Suffering from hypertension, he died of cardiac failure on 6 February 1962 at Bathurst and was buried in the vegetable garden at Mount Pleasant. He was survived by his wife and by the son of his first marriage. His estate was sworn for probate at £262 066.

R. S. Merrillees, '"The Ordeal of Shaving in a Frozen Lake", Professor J. R. Stewart and the Swedish Cyprus Expedition', in P. Åström et al, *The Fantastic Years on Cyprus* (Jonsered, Sweden, 1994) and 'Professor James R. Stewart, Near Eastern Archaeologist', *Ancient Society: Resources for Teachers*, 14, no 1, 1984, p 17; J. M. Webb, *Cypriote Antiquities in Australian Collections* (Jonsered, 1997); Aust Humanities Research Council, *Annual Report*, 1961-62; Univ Syd Union, *Union Recorder*, 8 Mar 1962, p 15; *King's School Mag*, 1962, p 10; *SMH*, 30 Oct 1958, 6 June 1961, 7 Feb, 25 Sept 1962; *Sun-Herald* (Syd), 10 Sept 1962; information from Mrs D. E. Stewart, Wentworth Falls, NSW.

R. S. MERRILLEES

STEWART, MALCOLM CLARKE ('MAX') (1935-1977), racing motorist, was born on 14 March 1935 at Orange, New South Wales, youngest of three children of Malcolm Herbert Stewart, clerk, and his wife Isabella, née Clarke, both born in New South Wales. Educated at the local public school to Intermediate certificate level, 'Max' served an apprenticeship to a mechanic and became service manager for the area's Holden [q.v.9] dealer. At the Baptist Church, Orange, on 25 January 1958 he married a local girl Margaret Mary Allen, who was a shop-assistant. He acquired the Orange franchise for Triumph motorcars in 1964 and for Toyota cars and trucks in 1968.

Six ft 2 ins (188 cm) tall, lanky and fair haired, Stewart had no special sporting achievements at school. He began racing motorcycles about 1953. Claims that he was selected for an Australian motorcycle team to compete on the Isle of Man seem unlikely, as his road-race experience was limited. Pressure from his fiancée ended his two-wheel career in 1956. Although he contested interstate go-kart races in 1962-64, he won no State titles: he was simply too large for go-karts. Early in 1965 Stewart bought a two-year-old Rennmax-Ford, a road-racing car built in Sydney, which he drove in distinctive style—his jaw determined and his shoulders wedged into the narrow cockpit. With this car he won the 1½-litre Australian championship series in 1967. Next year, in a new Rennmax, he tied the series with Garrie Cooper. Late in 1968 Alec Mildren, a team-owner, offered Stewart a 1600cc Formula Two car. Using the Sydney-made Waggott engine, Stewart won the 1969 and 1970 F2 titles. He also raced as teammate to Kevin Bartlett in a 2-litre version of the same car in New Zealand, South East Asia and Japan. His attacking, full-throttle driving established him in the front rank.

Stewart's strong personal and financial base in an inland city was unusual for a leading racing driver. Some saw country-Australian character in his direct manner and his uncompromising, unpretentious approach to racing. A close friend recalled that, while Stewart carried an executive briefcase like the 'glossier' drivers, his contained engine parts, not contracts.

In 1971 Stewart narrowly won the Confederation of Australian Motor Sport's Gold Star championship for Australian drivers. After Mildren retired, Stewart switched to the newly introduced 5-litre Formula 5000. He broke his wrist—a rare accident for him—racing in the United States of America in 1973, but in 1974 dominated Australian Formula 5000 events, winning the Gold Star and the Australian Grand Prix in an English Lola T330. Securing sponsorship from the Sharp Corporation of Australia Pty Ltd, he moved with his family to Beacon Hill, Sydney, in 1975 to pursue racing full-time and again won the Australian Grand Prix that year.

At Calder Raceway on 19 March 1977 Stewart inexplicably hit a slower car during a practice session; he died from his injuries on the following day in Royal Melbourne Hospital and was cremated. His wife and their two daughters survived him. A non-smoker and non-drinker, he had made provision for his kidneys to be used as transplants. At Orange a park was named after him.

Aust Motor Racing Annual, 1975; *Racing Car News*, Sept 1967, p 49, Apr 1977, p 26; *Chequered Flag*, Dec 1975, p 59; *Aust Motoring News*, 26 Nov 1971; information from Mrs M. Stewart, Narraweena, Mr R. Young, Peakhurst, Syd, Mr A. Selmes, Orange, NSW, and Mr K. Bartlett, Maleny, Qld.

GRAHAM HOWARD

STEWART, NANCYE; *see* LYNTON

STIRLING, HAROLD VICTOR (1904-1968), politician, dairy-farmer and shire president, was born on 7 April 1904 at Carisbrook, Victoria, second child of Henry Stirling, dairy-farmer, and his wife Phillis, née Walker, both Victorian born. Harold's parents took advantage of the closer-settlement legislation and moved from Canary Island to Mead Estate, near Cohuna. Educated at Mead State and Kerang High schools, Harold joined the State Electricity Commission of Victoria and became a foreman. Although he had suffered ill health as a child, he was an enthusiastic sportsman—a runner, a cyclist, and 'clever' footballer for the Macorna and Union clubs. He also played in the Kerang and Mead brass bands. In later life he was president of the Union Football Club and a keen lawn bowler.

In 1929 Stirling took over his father's farm. On 11 September that year at the Anglican Church, Cohuna, he married Philippa Catherine Grills; they were to have three sons and a daughter. Involving himself in community affairs, he was a founder and president of the Young Farmers' Advisory Council and a member of the Cohuna Irrigators' Advisory Board. For nine years he chaired the committee of the Mead State School. He joined the Victorian Wheat and Woolgrowers' Association and served as State president (1949-52) of the Australian Primary Producers' Union, of which he was made a life member. A Cohuna shire councillor in 1944-59, he was shire president in 1956-57 and the council's delegate to the Murray Valley Development League.

Stirling joined the United Country Party in 1936 and was secretary of its Leitchville branch for eighteen years. He represented irrigators on the U.C.P.'s local district council and sat (1956-57) on the central council. In 1952 he won the seat of Swan Hill in the Legislative Assembly, a seat he was to hold until his death. During his political career he used his knowledge of local government to advance the interests of the municipalities in his electorate and vigorously sought new educational facilities for the children of his constituents. One of his proudest achievements was the establishment of Cohuna High School. As a politician who came from a district dependent on irrigation, he took a close interest in public works. He was a member (1955-64) and thrice chairman (1957, 1960 and 1963) of the parliamentary Public Works Committee and a member (1967-68) of the Meat Industry Committee.

In 1964 the Victorian Country Party rewarded Stirling for his services by appointing him its representative at Commonwealth Parliamentary Association conferences to be held in London, New Delhi and Ottawa. He died of cancer on 23 July 1968 at Kerang and was buried in the local cemetery with Methodist forms. His wife and their sons survived him. Politicians paid tribute to him, stressing his good humour and his close friendship with George Gibbs, the Australian Labor Party member (1955-67) for Portland, who had died in May: the comradeship of the two men, despite their political differences, reflected a mutual acknowledgment of each other's worth.

PD (Vic), 10 Sept 1968, p 22; *Age* (Melb) and *Bendigo Advertiser*, 24 July 1968; *Cohuna Farmers' Weekly* and *Kerang New Times*, 26 July 1968.
CHARLES FAHEY

STIRLING, HELEN DOROTHY (NELL) (1909-1951), radio actress, was born on 22 August 1909 at Summer Hill, Sydney, daughter of Henry James Malmgron, a New Zealand-born sharebroker's clerk of Danish-German descent, and his wife Mary Rose, née Lawrie, who came from South Australia. While still at school, Nell determined to go on the stage. After studying classical dancing under Frances Scully, she performed her own act at the Tivoli Theatre at the age of 16. Later, as a soubrette and tap dancer, she joined Jim Gerald's [q.v.14] company. In 1931 she danced in the Fullers' [qq.v.8] chorus line. Calling herself 'Nell Stirling', she was engaged by Harold Parks (an unsuccessful actor known as 'George Edwards' [q.v.8]) as his assistant in variety acts.

With striking red hair that 'curled into innumerable little anchovies around her oval face', Nell had long, shapely legs, 'unstoppable ambition and a steel-trap business brain'. In 1932 Edwards hesitated when radio-station 2UE offered him £75 to adapt *The Ghost Train*, engage and rehearse twelve actors, and bring the show live to air on Christmas Eve. Nell grasped the chance and engaged Maurice Francis, who wrote the first of thousands of scripts for them. To save money, she suggested that George could play six or seven different parts. The public loved him and dubbed him 'The Man with a Thousand Voices'.

By 1934 they had moved to radio 2GB. The George Edwards Players appeared in at least twenty-four live productions a week, starting with 'Darby and Joan at the Breakfast Table' at 7.40 a.m. (Monday to Friday). At night they broadcast four serials live to air in their 'melodramatic acting styles': 'David and Dawn' for children, an adventure adapted from a classic novel such as *Westward Ho!*, 'Inspector Scott of Scotland Yard', and 'Notable British Trials' —which provided the indefatigable George with the chance both to defend and prosecute himself. On 29 March 1934 George and Nell were married at St David's Presbyterian Church, Haberfield, where she had been christened. He was 47 years old and she was his third wife.

For a few years Nell's life was frenetic. In addition to playing the lead in almost every production, she marked all George's scripts, looked after the effects and properties (among them 'toy popguns for the popping of champagne corks'), edited scripts, cast and produced the plays, and chose the music. She became famous for her 'life-like screams of horror'. From May 1937 she played Mabel in the long-running serial, 'Dad and Dave of Snake Gully'. One year earlier the couple had signed a contract with Columbia Records which released them from their 'arduous evening schedule'. Radio-station 2UW and the Commonwealth Broadcasting Corporation Pty Ltd acquired sole broadcasting rights throughout Australasia to George Edwards Productions.

At an audition in 1934, Sumner Locke Elliott had thought that Nell Stirling 'looked like a barmaid who had won the Irish sweepstakes': covered with diamonds 'at ten o'clock in the morning', she wore 'rich glossy black satin', 'a wide-brimmed black velvet hat', and 'a great deal of mascara and lipstick'. Soon taken in hand by 'Andrea' (Dorothy Jenner, the newspaper columnist), Nell was to become noted for her smart clothes, hats, furs and jewellery.

Although they were known to their underpaid actors as 'Scrooge Edwards and Nell Pound Stirling', they spent their new found wealth recklessly. In 1937 they built their dream home, Darjoa, at Point Piper. 'The bathrooms were black with gold fittings imported from America, the furniture was light sycamore; wardrobes, sideboards and cocktail bars—one in each room—were all built in. There were cream walls throughout, and domed ceilings with concealed lighting'. In

1940 Miss Stirling provided the money to open the Women's All Services Canteen. She remained its patron until 1945. While George established a racing stable, she opened a nightclub; both enterprises lost money. Even worse, George bet on the horses and began drinking heavily. Nell brought him into line by having a baby in April 1941. Her listeners overwhelmed her with letters, hand-knitted garments and other gifts.

After World War II, Nell spent more time at her country house at Bowral. Late in the 1940s she called in a young accountant to take over the books from her ageing father. She divorced George in July 1948. At St Philip's Church of England, Sydney, on 9 November that year she married Alexander George Atwill, her accountant. The Atwills bought out Edwards. Nell Stirling died of an accidental overdose of carbitral capsules on 10 November 1951 at her Vaucluse home and was cremated with Anglican rites. Her husband and their daughter survived her, as did the daughter of her first marriage. She left her estate, sworn for probate at £15 840, to her daughters.

N. Bridges, *Wonderful Wireless* (Syd, 1983); R. Lane, *The Golden Age of Australian Radio Drama* (Melb, 1994); *Wireless Weekly*, 7 Dec 1934; *Radio Pictorial of Aust*, 1 June 1941, p 16, 1 Oct 1941, p 26, 1 May 1942, p 24; *Daily Telegraph* (Syd), 23 Aug 1945; *SMH*, 12 Nov 1951, 28 Feb 1952; *Bulletin*, 22 July 1980; N. Stirling photographs and recordings (ScreenSound Aust, Canb).   MARTHA RUTLEDGE

STIRLING, KENNETH GEORGE (1935-1973), accountant and benefactor, was born on 8 December 1935 in Adelaide, elder son of George Leonard Stirling, a railway engineman from Western Australia, and his South Australian-born wife Flora Elizabeth Joy, née Russell. Ken attended Quorn Public School and Scotch College, Adelaide, worked in an accountant's office, studied part time at the University of Adelaide (B.Ec., 1960) and qualified as an associate-member (1960) of the Australian Society of Accountants. At St Columba's Church of England, Hawthorn, on 28 April 1962 he married Bronte Stokes Gooden.

From 1960 Stirling was employed in accountancy and administration at Broken Hill Associated Smelters Pty Ltd, Port Pirie, and at Broken Hill South Ltd and P. G. Pak-Poy & Associates Pty Ltd in Adelaide. In 1969 he became secretary and a director of Samin Ltd, a reprocessor of copper residues. The firm had a considerable shareholding in Poseidon Ltd; when Samin shares were first traded on Australian stock exchanges in January 1970 they immediately rose to very high levels. The paper value of Stirling's interests in Samin

embarrassed him. According to his wife, 'he believed he hadn't earned the money the mining boom brought him' and 'his main concern was to use it for the good of the community'.

Stirling took a keen interest in the history of his mother's family property, Callanna, near Marree, and consulted records in the South Australian Archives. He joined the Nature Conservation Society of South Australia and contributed to its report on the Oraparinna area of the Flinders Ranges. His other interests included railway history, civil liberties, and the Adelaide University Graduates' Union, on which he served in 1970-73. After selling some of his Samin shares, he made several anonymous gifts in 1970: $50 000 to the Libraries Board of South Australia to accelerate the transfer of government and other records to the State archives, $200 000 to the Australian Conservation Foundation to establish national parks in South Australia, and $100 000 to the University of Adelaide to set up an educational radio station.

Assisted by Stirling's donation, the S.A.A. acquired important records from several government departments. The money he gave to the A.C.F. helped to establish national parks at Montacute and Mount Scott, both near Adelaide, and in the extension of existing reserves at Scott Creek, in the Mount Lofty Ranges, and Warrenben, on Yorke Peninsula. The University of Adelaide's radio-station 5UV, opened in 1972, became a model in the field of public broadcasting.

In 1971 Samin was taken over by Poseidon. Stirling regarded himself as a supernumerary, resigned in 1972 and found a job in a solicitor's office. Survived by his wife, and their daughter and son, he died suddenly of myocardial infarction on 8 November 1973 at the university oval and was cremated. His estate was sworn for probate at $289 903. In 1990 the State government acquired land in the Adelaide Hills for the Kenneth Stirling Conservation Park.

R. M. Gibbs, *Bulls, Bears and Wildcats* (Adel, 1988); Libraries Bd of SA, *Annual Report*, 1969/70, p 4, 1970/71, p 13, 1971/72, p 15; *N.C.S.S.A. Newsletter*, no 43, Nov 1973, p 27; information from Mrs C. H. Gooden, Millswood, Mrs B. Stirling, Mitcham, and Mr W. M. Rogers, Adel; personal knowledge.
COLIN LAWTON

STIRLING, LORNA MARY BELTON (1893-1956), musicologist, was born on 24 June 1893 at Hawthorn, Melbourne, eldest of three children of Victorian-born parents James Belton Stirling, draper, and his wife Mary Edith, née Smith. The family was involved in the arts and community service. Belton was an amateur musician, as was his brother

George, an organist, and their sister Mary, a pianist. Tall, fair-haired and attractive, Lorna attended Fintona school, Camberwell, and Methodist Ladies' College, Kew (dux 1910), and became a violin teacher. On entering the University Conservatorium of Music, she was awarded an exhibition in violin; additional studies included viola and piano, as well as theoretical subjects under Professor George Marshall-Hall [q.v.10]. She topped each year of her course for a diploma in music and at the end of her final year (1917) won an Ormond [q.v.5] exhibition.

Following the outbreak of World War I, Miss Stirling had performed in a string quartet which toured Victoria to raise money for the Australian Red Cross Society. She later performed as an accompanist in a series of concerts for children. From 1921 she wrote a regular children's page in the *Australian Musical News*. After studying in Germany for some months, she settled in London in 1922. She edited *Music and Youth and Panpipes*, contributed to the *Music Teacher*, the *Sackbut* and the *Manchester Guardian*, published a book, *Music through Games* (London, 1930), and lectured on music to school children. A series of her articles appeared in *Stead's Review* in 1931, demonstrating the insights she had gained into the modernist music she had heard in Europe. By 1932 she was back in Melbourne where, in the following year, she was appointed music critic for the *Star*.

In the mid-1930s Stirling toured Europe, the United States of America and South Africa. She became honorary secretary of the Victorian branch of the British Music Society and a member of the executive-committee of the Lyceum Club in 1936. During World War II she gave vital encouragement to her friend, the composer Margaret Sutherland. Together they inaugurated midday recitals in the Assembly Hall, Collins Street: the performances aided the Australian Red Cross Society's prisoner-of-war fund and provided a platform for works by Sutherland and other Melbourne composers.

Stirling and Sutherland began campaigning for an arts centre to be built on the site of the derelict Wirth's [q.v.12] Park. With John Lloyd, they launched the Combined Arts Centre Movement, enlisting the support of artists and arts societies. By November 1944 they had gathered 40 000 signatures to a petition seeking 'the erection of a Building or Buildings suitable for the use and presentation of [the] Arts for the benefit of the Public and under control of the State Authorities'. (The Victorian parliament finally passed the National Art Gallery and Cultural Centre Act in 1956.)

During the war Stirling also organized children's concerts on behalf of the B.M.S. and established a madrigal group, 'The Tudor Singers'. In 1942 she had been elected honorary secretary of the Lyceum Club, a role she apostrophized as 'Oil-Pourer, Back-patter, Exhorter, Consoler'. According to the club's history, she 'infused life and spirit into everything she did', and even composed songs and farces for club entertainments. She resigned in 1949 and travelled to Europe where she relished attending concerts, visiting galleries, and meeting composers and musicologists. In 1951 she was appointed temporary lecturer in music appreciation at the University of Melbourne, but serious illness led to her resignation at the end of 1954.

Stirling died of cancer on 9 February 1956 at her Hawthorn home and was cremated. She had destroyed the majority of her papers, including compositions, diaries and lectures. The bulk of her estate, sworn for probate at £29 386, was bequeathed to the University of Melbourne for the benefit of International House, and to found the Lorna Stirling Fund for international student exchange. From her art collection, she left Sir Arthur Streeton's [q.v.12] portrait of Marshall-Hall to the National Gallery of Victoria. Her university colleague Keith Macartney [q.v.15] recalled: 'Her knowledge of music, literature, painting, and the arts of the theatre was great, but her scholarship was carried lightly, and gifted as she was with vivid personality and a witty turn of phrase, she was able to get on terms with any audience, whether academic or not'.

A. T. Stirling, *Gang Forward* (Melb, 1972); *Univ Melb Gazette*, Aug 1956, p 32; *Age* (Melb), 11 Feb 1956; Stirling papers *and* Lyceum Club papers (LaTL).   SUZANNE ROBINSON

STOATE, THEODORE NORMAN (1895–1979), forester, was born on 13 January 1895 at Stepney, Adelaide, son of Alfred Thorne Stoate, draper, and his wife Bessie, née Haskins. 'Bill', as he was nicknamed, attended the Collegiate School of St Peter and studied forestry at the University of Adelaide (B.Sc., 1918; M.Sc., 1934; D.Sc., 1953). On 20 December 1915 he suspended his course and enlisted in the Australian Imperial Force. In March 1917 he was commissioned and posted to the 35th Battalion on the Western Front. He was gassed at Messines, Belgium, in June and invalided home; at this time his hair turned prematurely white. Lieutenant Stoate's A.I.F. appointment terminated in Adelaide on 14 January 1918.

After graduating, Stoate joined the Forestry Commission of New South Wales in 1919. Three years later he was seconded to the Forests Department, Western Australia, for six months. He was to stay there for thirty-one years. In 1923 he was appointed assistant working plans officer; by 1927 he was assistant-conservator to S. L. Kessell [q.v.15]. On 7 July 1924 at St Mary's Church of England, Busselton, he had married Marion Frances Josephine Brockman; they had two sons before she died in 1930. Awarded a (Sir) Russell Grimwade [q.v.9] scholarship that year, he sailed for England and entered the University of Oxford (Dip.For., 1931).

Back in Western Australia, Stoate investigated suspected nutrient deficiencies in *Pinus radiata* and *Pinus pinaster* plantations. When he observed trees near a wire fence thriving more than others, he deduced that they did so because zinc from the fence had leached into the soil. He subsequently found that 'irregular and abnormal' growth was due to a lack of superphosphate and minor elements. In 1939-40 he was seconded to the Woods and Forests Department, South Australia. Returning to Perth, he served as deputy-conservator (1941-45) and conservator (1946-53).

A solitary, academic widower, Stoate disliked the hurly-burly of political manoeuvring and detested what he called 'pannikin bosses'. He was happiest in the bush. Even there he always wore a neat suit and polished boots. Once, after a day's work, he helped to fight a karri wildfire. Removing his jacket and braces, and using his tie as a belt, he borrowed a shovel and toiled all night beside a bulldozer to build a fire-line. He returned to his office early in the morning. The bulldozer driver later asked: 'who was that old bugger swamping for me last night—he wasn't bad!'

The royal commission into forestry and timber matters reported in 1952 that 'the forest policy of the State is considered to be sound in principle, and soundly administered'. Nevertheless, after pressure from some timber merchants and a change of government, the new Labor minister and former forests department draftsman H. E. Graham did not renew Stoate's appointment in 1953.

Stoate became an international forestry consultant. Between 1963 and 1971 he held a series of research positions at the college of forestry, University of Washington, Seattle, United States of America. He encouraged young Australian foresters to undertake postgraduate study at the university, helped many with their research, and often treated them to a hearty steak and a pint. In Perth and at Seattle he lived in a sparse hotel room. At the age of 70 he still bounded joyfully up four flights of stairs to his office. Survived by one son, he died on 12 April 1979 at Busselton, Western Australia, and was buried in Karrakatta cemetery, Perth. *Eucalyptus stoatei* was named after him.

A. Rule, *Forests of Australia* (Syd, 1967); *50 Years of Forestry in Western Australia* (Perth, 1969); L. T. Carron, *A History of Forestry in Australia* (Canb, 1985); J. Mills, *The Timber People* (Perth, 1986); *Aust Forestry*, 42, no 2, 1979, p 61; family papers (held by Mr D. Stoate, West Leederville, Perth); information from Mr B. Beggs, Booragoon, Mr R. Underwood, Bicton, and Dr E. Hopkins, Como, Perth, and Mr J. Stoate, Anna Plains, near Broome, WA.
                                                                        JENNY MILLS

STOBIE, JAMES CYRIL (1895-1953), engineer and inventor, was born on 15 September 1895 at Parkside, Adelaide, only son and eldest of four children of South Australian-born parents James Stobie, grocer, and his wife Alice, née Ingleby. Known as Cyril or 'C', he attended Glenelg Public and Pulteney Street schools. A brilliant student, he won a scholarship to the Preparatory School, South Australian School of Mines and Industries. His education was made difficult by his father's business struggles and his untimely death in 1912. Cyril took over the family grocery shop at Mile End to support his mother and sisters. In 1915 he enrolled as an evening student at the School of Mines. He gained an associate diploma in mechanical and electrical engineering that year and a fellowship diploma in 1919. Fond of sport, he excelled at long-distance swimming and won the race from Grange to Henley Beach in 1922.

In 1916 Stobie had joined the staff of the Adelaide Electric Supply Co. Ltd. He continued his engineering studies part time at the University of Adelaide (B.E., 1921; M.E., 1932). Frederick Wheadon, A.E.S.Co.'s chief executive, became his mentor and the two formed a lifelong friendship. Stobie's career began to prosper. In 1923 he was appointed chief draftsman. At the Church of Christ, Unley, on 19 March 1924 he married Rita Muriel Maddern.

South Australia suffered from a scarcity of timber and an abundance of termites. Poles that were brought, at considerable expense, from other States were often destroyed by white ants. In 1924 Stobie invented the 'Stobie pole' to carry electricity cables and telegraph wires. It was constructed of two steel-I beams, held together by tie bolts; the space between them was filled with concrete. A.E.S.Co. paid him £500 for the patent rights. Although hopes of selling the design interstate and worldwide remained unfulfilled, the poles were used extensively in South Australia. In 1936 a Sterling coal truck was converted into a heavy pole-erector, designed by Stobie: it could install 70-ft (21 m) long, concrete-steel poles that weighed $8\frac{1}{2}$ tons.

Stobie was the founding editor (1926-40) of A.E.S.Co.'s in-house magazine, *Adelect*. Through this publication, he conveyed his vision of the company's future, interest in research, sense of fun and Christian values (he was a staunch Methodist). His face, with its full features, deep smile-lines and clear eyes, reflected his jovial disposition. Despite bouts of recurring illness, he became chief design engineer in 1946, when the Electricity Trust of South Australia took over from A.E.S.Co. In 1950 he was appointed assistant to the manager of engineering research. Survived by his wife, and their two daughters and two sons, he died of coronary thrombosis on 15 August 1953 at his Malvern home and was buried in Centennial Park cemetery. His estate was sworn for probate at £6092. The Stobie pole continues to be regarded with affection by many South Australians who consider it part of their heritage.

R. Linn, *ETSA* (Adel, 1996); *Adelect*, Dec 1953, July 1982; family information.   R. W. LINN

STOCKDILL, DONALD ALEXANDER (1923-1980), civil engineer, was born on 8 December 1923 at Claremont, Perth, only son and third of four children of Australian-born parents Herbert George Stockdill, schoolteacher, and his wife Evelyn Morrison, née McLennan. Don was educated at his father's school at Ravensthorpe and at Bunbury High School where he completed the Leaving certificate in 1940. After a year training to be a teacher, he entered the University of Western Australia (B.Sc., 1945; B.E., 1946); he studied civil engineering, rowed, and played hockey and jazz on the piano. Due to poor eyesight, he had been rejected for war service.

In 1946 Stockdill joined the new Commonwealth Department of Works and Housing (Department of Works from 1952) and tested materials for the construction of Essendon aerodrome, Melbourne. Next year he served as quality-control engineer for the aerodrome at Leigh Creek, South Australia. He went to the Northern Territory in 1948 as a design and construction engineer; in 1950 he was promoted district officer for civil works and housing. At St Luke's Church of England, Mosman Park, Perth, on 26 January 1951 he married Frona Cecile Carson, née Glaskin, a war widow with one child.

Posted to Adelaide in 1952, Stockdill became resident engineer for Adelaide airport in 1953. He worked at Woomera and at Edinburgh airfield before being appointed supervising engineer, roads and aerodromes, in 1957. That year he was employed on projects at the Weapons Research Establishment, Salisbury. Sent to London in 1959, he led a joint Australian-British team which was set up to design an underground launch complex for the Blue Streak ballistic missile.

Stockdill's appointment to Canberra in 1960 as principal engineer, major development section, with responsibility for the planning and design of major water- and sewerage-works, was indicative of the department's confidence in his abilities, but he had no experience in hydraulics and was regarded as an outsider. Moreover, he faced tense bureaucratic conflicts within the department and with the recently established National Capital Development Commission. He quickly proved his technical grasp, winning the respect of colleagues and clients alike for his quiet but insistent style in debating solutions to problems, and for his readiness to concede gracefully when the merits of the case warranted. An excellent manager, he defended his staff, gave them credit for their ideas, and made the section 'a good place to work'.

Visiting Paris in 1966 on a six-month scholarship awarded by the French government to study dams and allied structures with Coyne & Bellier, Stockdill returned to Australia a member of the Australian French Association of Professional and Technical Specialists, and a devotee of Peugeot motorcars and French cigarettes. He was also an active member of the Institution of Engineers, Australia, and chairman (1969) of its Canberra division. In addition to his work on major hydraulics infrastructure, he played a key role in fostering an inter-agency approach to the management of water in the Canberra region. His last major project was the technologically advanced Lower Molonglo Water Quality Control Centre, completed in August 1978. Survived by his wife, their son and two daughters, and his stepson, he died of cancer on 23 May 1980 at Woden Valley Hospital and was cremated.

A. Fitzgerald (ed), *Canberra's Engineering Heritage* (Canb, 1983); M. Higgins, *Dams on the Cotter* (Canb, 1998); *Canb Times*, 28 May 1980; information from Mr A. Fokkema, Queanbeyan, NSW, Mr C. Speldewinde, Campbell, and Mr J. Stockdill, Griffith, Canb.   IAN W. MORISON

STOKES, SIR HAROLD FREDERICK (1899-1977), engineer, company director and hospital president, was born on 7 January 1899 at Hawthorn, Melbourne, son of Victorian-born parents Frederick Percy Stokes, accountant, and his wife Nellie Henrietta Owen, née Wilcox. His grandfather Thomas Stokes had set up in Melbourne in 1856 as a die-sinker and manufacturer of medals and buttons. The business was to continue as Stokes & Sons Pty Ltd (from 1911) and Stokes (Australasia) Ltd (from 1962). Harold attended Melbourne Church of England Grammar School and entered Trinity College, University of Melbourne (B.Sc., 1921; B.E.E., 1924). He began work in 1924 as an assistant-engineer with William Adams & Co. Ltd; by 1927 he was head of its engineering department.

On 25 June 1936 at Christ Church, South Yarra, Stokes married with Anglican rites Ruth Alison Baird Good (d.1975), the 26-year-old daughter of a grazier. Appointed captain, Citizen Military Forces, on 20 May 1941, and promoted temporary major in October, he carried out ordnance engineering duties with Southern Command. His hopes of serving in Singapore were dashed when the island fell to the Japanese. In July 1942 he transferred to the Australian Imperial Force and in September rose to temporary lieutenant colonel (substantive March 1944). He was commander, electrical and mechanical engineers, Northern Territory Force, from June 1943 to May 1944, before becoming assistant-director of mechanical engineering, Land Headquarters, Melbourne. His A.I.F. appointment terminated on 8 November 1945.

Stokes retired from William Adams & Co. Ltd in 1951. A director (from 1936) of the family firm, he took on the role of its roving consultant. During World War II the company had produced munitions, including bomb casings and metal canteens. Subsequently, Stokes helped to turn the enterprise towards manufacturing components for Australia's automotive and domestic-appliance industries. After travelling abroad and seeing advances in technology, he modernized production methods and eventually introduced robotic welding. He sat on the boards of numerous other companies, among them Climatemaster Engineering Pty Ltd and Regent Insurance Ltd.

In 1952-74 Stokes was president of the Austin Hospital and chairman of the board of the Cancer Institute. His kindly and energetic leadership assisted the transition of the Austin from an institution for people with incurable diseases or conditions to a major general hospital with a university clinical school. For his services to the community, he was appointed C.B.E. (1966) and knighted (1974). He loved rural life, and took a hand in running the pastoral properties owned by his wife's family near Warrnambool and later near Lismore. Sir Harold was a member of the Royal Melbourne and Barwon Heads golf clubs, the Royal South Yarra Lawn Tennis Club, the Melbourne Club and the Naval and Military Club. When his children were young he kept a metal lathe in his garage to make model trains. Survived by his son and three daughters, he died on 4 August 1977 at Malvern and was cremated. A wing of the Austin Hospital was named after him.

E. W. Gault and A. Lucas, *A Century of Compassion* (Melb, 1982); *Age* (Melb), 1 Jan 1966, 15 June 1974; information from Mr W. Stokes, Hawthorn East, and Mrs A. Ringrose, Glen Iris, Melb.   JACQUELINE ABBOTT

STOKES, JOHN BRYANT (1925-1979), public servant, was born on 19 November 1925 at Marrickville, Sydney, eldest child of Reginald Bryant Stokes, surveyor, and his wife Edith, née Spiers, both of whom were born in New South Wales. John grew up at Cooma and attended the local public school until 1938 when he enrolled at Canberra High School. He gained the Leaving certificate in 1941 and in the following year took up a clerical position with the Commonwealth Treasury.

On 26 November 1943 Stokes enlisted in the Royal Australian Air Force. After he failed to qualify as a pilot at Narrandera, New South Wales, he undertook courses as a wireless operator and air gunner at Maryborough, Queensland, and as a telegraphist at Point Cook, Victoria. He was posted to a unit in Brisbane in March 1945, but injured himself while off duty and spent three months in hospital before being sent to Headquarters, Eastern Area, Sydney. Discharged from the R.A.A.F. on 5 October 1945, he returned to the Treasury. On 25 March 1950 at St Andrew's Presbyterian Church, Canberra, he married Christina Farquhar Smith, a stenographer from Scotland. He resumed part-time studies, begun before his enlistment, at Canberra University College (B.Com., 1953).

As chief finance officer (from 1968) in the Territories section of the Treasury, Stokes oversaw the finances of Canberra and of the Commonwealth's works programme, which included the National Capital Development Commission. He also held responsibility for the finances of the Northern Territory during the period which saw the rebuilding of Darwin in the wake of Cyclone Tracy. In 1976 he transferred to the new Department of Finance as assistant-secretary in charge of the works and mainland territories branch of the defence and works division. His major achievement was in negotiating financial arrangements for self-government in the Northern Territory. In 1979 he was acting-head of division.

Described as one who would have regretted that a candle could be burnt at two ends only, 'Stoker' enjoyed widespread popularity in Canberra's Rugby Union circles as a player and as an administrator. In 1969 he helped to found, and became first president of, Western Districts Rugby Union Football Club. A prominent Freemason, he had been initiated in 1951 into Lodge Canberra, of which he was worshipful master in 1959-60. He was a founder (1962) and office-bearer (1965-69) of Lodge Perfect, and was raised to grand lodge rank by the United Grand Lodge of New South Wales in 1975. In his spare time he helped 'hundreds' of non-English speaking immigrants with their income-tax returns at his O'Connor home. He later moved to Weetangera.

Stokes was an unconventional bureaucrat who did not always follow the rules. Regarded by some as 'wild' because he enjoyed a drink and the company of women, he was nevertheless respected for having overcome departmental resistance to financial autonomy for the Northern Territory. He died of cancer on 13 April 1979 at Canberra Hospital and was cremated; his wife, and their two daughters and two sons survived him.

List of Permanent Officers of the Commonwealth Public Service, 1948, 1951; *Government Gazette* (Cwlth), 1968; *Canb Times*, 17, 22 Apr 1979; information from Mr G. B. Stokes, Booragul, NSW, and the late Dr A. Heatley.   PETER ELDER

STOKES, SYDNEY WILLIAM (1887-1972), surveyor, was born on 17 March 1887 at Newcastle, New South Wales, tenth child of native-born parents Henry Edward Stokes, merchant, and his wife Clara Maude, daughter of J. F. Josephson [q.v.4]. Educated at Cooerwull Academy, Bowenfels, and at Sydney Grammar School, Syd passed first-year engineering at the University of Sydney. He sat the licensed surveyor's examination in 1912 before being articled to J. F. Foster of the Metropolitan Board of Water Supply and Sewerage. On 30 May 1914 at St Philip's Church of England, Sydney, he married Louisa Richards Cobcroft; they were to have a son and two daughters, and to live at Bellevue Hill for almost sixty years.

A man of conservative views, Stokes had been commissioned lieutenant, Australian Intelligence Corps, Militia, on 7 June 1910. He was promoted captain on 1 June 1914 and seconded for duty with the Intelligence Section, General Staff, in October. Appointed assistant-censor for New South Wales on 16 February 1915, he carried out 'confidential duties' for much of World War I as part of a large organization which scrutinized newspapers and intercepted correspondence, searching for evidence of espionage, labour militancy and trading with the enemy. He was mentioned in orders for his meritorious service. In October 1918 he was posted to the 17th Infantry Regiment. Transferred to the Reserve of Officers on 1 July 1921, he was placed on the Retired List five years later.

After the war, Stokes set up as a surveyor at 48 Elizabeth Street. From 1926 he practised in partnership with A. W. Miller. Their firm, S. W. Stokes & Miller, operated in Sydney's western suburbs, the northern beaches and central coast, and was increasingly involved in development projects in these areas. Stokes was business manager (1925-31), vice-president (1931-32) and president (1932-33) of the Institution of Surveyors, New South

Wales. While president, he tried to increase its public standing. By 1939 he was also a local government engineer. Although he personally adhered to solo-surveying, he advocated the amalgamation of surveyors in private practice and foresaw the use of calculating machines within the profession. His business affairs were diverse. He dabbled in the stock market and suffered severe financial strain when the Riviera Co-operative Country Club Ltd collapsed in 1935.

An active Freemason, Stokes was worshipful master (1926-27) of the Double Bay Lodge, and a founder (1930) and member (until 1955) of the Old Sydneians' Lodge. In World War II he resumed the duties he had performed in the previous conflict. Working in the office of the Department of the Army's district censor, Sydney, he took charge of a large staff responsible for cable censorship. The deputy district censor praised his 'ability to organise and direct' and his 'energy, trustworthiness, judgment and ability'. In the 1950s Stokes was interested in the Australian Decentralisation and New States Movement. A fellow of the Town and Country Planning Institution of New South Wales, he was elected a life-member (1955) of the Institution of Surveyors, Australia. He died on 9 August 1972 at the War Memorial Hospital, Waverley, and was cremated; his wife and their daughters survived him.

C. D. Coulthard-Clark, *The Citizen General Staff* (Canb, 1976); *Aust Surveyor*, Mar 1933, Mar 1973; *Newspaper News*, 2 Oct 1939; *Azimuth*, Apr 1999; *SMH*, 3 Feb, 9 June 1932; K. Fewster, Expression and Suppression: Aspects of Military Censorship in Australia during the Great War (Ph.D. thesis, UNSW, 1980); Stokes papers (ML); information from Mr J. Ruffels, Randwick, and Institution of Surveyors (NSW), Syd.   ANDREW MOORE

STONES, ELLIS ANDREW (1895-1975), garden designer, was born on 1 October 1895 at Wodonga, Victoria, only son and second of four children of Thomas James Stones, customs officer, and his wife Hannah May, née Downs, both Victorian born. Ellis grew up at Essendon, Melbourne. He attended Moonee Ponds West State School and served an apprenticeship to a carpenter with the Victorian Railways. Five ft 6 ins (168 cm) tall, with clear blue eyes and an infectious grin, he kept fit by boxing, and by playing cricket and football. He was energetic and modest, and had a strong artistic bent.

On 3 September 1914 Stones enlisted in the Australian Imperial Force and was posted to the 7th Battalion. During the landing at Gallipoli on 25 April 1915 he was wounded in the left leg. Invalided home, he was discharged from the A.I.F. on 27 March 1916.

After serving (1917-20) in the Australian Military Forces, he resumed work as a carpenter. His sunny nature helped him to endure hard physical labour despite constant pain from his shattered leg. At St John's Presbyterian Church, Essendon, on 14 March 1922 he married Olive Munro Doyle; they were to have a son (d.1923) and three daughters.

In 1923 Stones's health broke down and he moved to a sheep-station near Trangie, New South Wales, to recuperate. His sojourn in the outback reinforced his appreciation of the Australian landscape and was to influence his work in garden design. He later wrote that he wanted to make gardens that reminded people of nature and to bring a flavour of nature to the cities. From the mid-1920s he earned a living as a builder at Avenel, Victoria, and first worked with stone when he constructed two fireplaces. The Depression forced him to return to Melbourne, where he supported his family by doing odd jobs and patching fly-screens.

'Rocky' built a stone wall for Edna Walling [q.v.] in 1935. Recognizing his ability—which she called 'a rare thing this gift for placing stones'—she suggested that he abandon carpentry to work for her. She gave him a free hand to create walls, outcrops, pools and paths in her gardens at some of Melbourne's finest homes. Their best collaboration was seen in a free-form swimming pool and outcrop, built in 1939-40 for Edith Hughes-Jones [q.v.14] at Olinda. Stones soon had the confidence to undertake commissions on his own and established a following in the Ivanhoe-Heidelberg district, where he had settled in 1934.

Rejected for the A.I.F. in World War II, Stones worked as a carpenter in northern Australia with the Civil Constructional Corps before resuming his practice in 1944. Walling continued to give him jobs, and his own clients included (Sir) Russell Grimwade and Clive Disher [qq.v.9,14]. His relaxed style was characterized by rock-work which his contemporaries described as 'transcendental', and by a desire to relate house and garden. Like the American Thomas Church, he saw gardens as outdoor living places for people (he always included spots where children could play). He did much of his own construction work. His artist's eye and intuitive sense of space meant that he had no need to draw plans.

At the age of 70 Stones was appointed landscape architect to Merchant Builders Pty Ltd, a project-home company, through which he made the concept of landscape design more widely accessible. The firm named Elliston, a subdivision at Rosanna, after him. Appearances on television (1969-73), a column in the *Australian Home Beautiful* (1970-75) and his best-selling book, *Australian Garden Design* (1971), added to his reputation. He began designing landscapes for playgrounds, parks and other public spaces. Although he had given up construction in the mid-1960s, he continued to work long hours, often finishing with a free evening address to a community group. In the 1960s he was a popular lecturer in landscape design at the Royal Melbourne Institute of Technology and an adviser to the Town and Country Planning Board.

Stones supported the establishment of the Australian Institute of Landscape Architects (affiliate 1967, fellow 1975). A passionate conservationist, he campaigned against the pollution of the River Yarra. On 5 April 1975 he worked at Rosanna, landscaping Salt Creek. 'Oh, I've had a good day', he told Olive, 'There's a boy on the job who really understands what I'm talking about'. Stones died that evening at Ivanhoe and was cremated with Methodist forms; his wife and their daughters survived him. The Victorian chapter of the Royal Australian Institute of Architects posthumously awarded him its Robin Boyd [q.v.13] environmental medal for 1975. A prize for students of landscape architecture at the University of Melbourne was named after him.

A. Latreille, *The Natural Garden* (Melb, 1990), and for bib.   ANNE LATREILLE

STONHAM, ARTHUR ERNEST (1900-1966), magistrate, was born on 7 February 1900 at West Maitland, New South Wales, sixth child of native-born parents Alfred Ernest Albert Stonham, schoolteacher, and his wife Ada Sarah Grange, née Armstrong. His father's career took the family to Narellan, Goulburn and Deniliquin, and then to Sydney in 1908. Arthur knew what to expect when he was appointed a junior clerk in the Department of Attorney-General and Justice on 9 March 1916—country postings and, after a long apprenticeship, the distant prospect of promotion to the stipendiary magistracy.

On 4 May 1918 Stonham enlisted in the Australian Imperial Force, but only reached Durban, South Africa, by the time of the Armistice. At St Stephen's Anglican Church, Portland, New South Wales, on 30 April 1921 he married Elsie Gladys Lake. Sent to Kiama as clerk of petty sessions in 1925, he was transferred to Kurri Kurri in October 1926. The young and rather diminutive clerk carried out many extra duties and was an important contact between the government and local community: it was said that a C.P.S. had to be a cross between 'the Deity, a K.C., an actuary, a diplomat and Santa Claus'.

In 1930-33 Stonham was based in Sydney as senior information clerk. After serving at Windsor (1933-36), he returned to Sydney as first checking officer at the Children's Court in 1936 when maintenance work was especially heavy. He was admitted as a solicitor on 23 August 1940, shrewdly anticipating a later requirement that magistrates should have legal qualifications. As C.P.S. at Young (from 1940), he had to cope with staff shortages and the unpopularity of reduced services during World War II. In 1945 he was sent to Inverell.

Stonham was appointed stipendiary magistrate for Mudgee in 1947, Penrith in 1948 and Sydney in 1951. He continued to preside, and live, at Penrith, in the rapidly developing outer suburbs, and became involved with local welfare societies and youth clubs. Penrith court was noticeably strict about drink-driving, an offence that stemmed from postwar affluence. At the 1954 congress of the Australian Road Safety Council in Hobart, Stonham and F. S. Hansman [q.v.14] called for compulsory blood tests for drivers suspected of being under the influence of liquor. Stonham presided over the Magistrates' Institute, edited the *Stipendiary Magistrates' Bulletin* and joined the State government's Law Reform Committee. He was promoted to chief stipendiary magistrate in September 1962.

In organizing the overstretched city courts, Stonham confronted the contradictions of a public-service magistracy by trying to reconcile judicial independence with departmental demands for administrative accountability. Despite ill health, he was an energetic chairman, lobbying for more resources and even rostering himself to hear the controversial prosecution of R. S. Maher, the Speaker of the Legislative Assembly, who was charged with indecent exposure. Stockily built, with a down-to-earth manner, Stonham retired in February 1965. He had been admitted as a barrister on 29 May 1964.

Stonham continued to chair the Board of Official Visitors to Mental Asylums and joined the Australian Broadcasting Commission's disciplinary appeal board. Survived by his wife and their daughter, he died of myocardial infarction on 22 November 1966 at his Penrith home and was cremated. His unobtrusive efficiency had made him a model magistrate, but the public-service system which moulded him was coming into question.

Petty Sessions Chronicle, no 96, May 1934, p 3, no 340, Jan-Feb 1967, p 3; *SMH*, 18 Nov 1954, 11 Nov 1961, 26, 29 Jan, 6 Feb 1965; *Sun* (Syd), 4 Feb 1965; *Penrith Press*, 30 Nov, 7 Dec 1966; Attorney-General and Justice Dept, 7/7162.3, 12/12653 pt, *and* Public Service Bd, 8/2716 (NSWA).   HILARY GOLDER

STOREY, SIR JOHN STANLEY (1896-1955), industrialist, was born on 1 November 1896 at Balmain, Sydney, third of six children of native-born parents John Storey [q.v.12], boiler-maker, and his wife Elizabeth Merton, née Turnbull. Young John attended Fort Street Model (Boys' High) School. His father, uncles and brothers—all of whom had trained or were to train as tradesmen—were unimpressed by his decision to accept a scholarship to the University of Sydney (B.Sc., 1917) and were shocked by his lack of elementary workshop knowledge when he graduated. John's disappointment with the quality of university teaching made him favour technical education, albeit within a strong humanities context.

On 8 June 1917 Storey enlisted in the Australian Imperial Force; he was then 5 ft 10 ins (178 cm) tall and weighed 9 st. 10 lb. (62 kg). He qualified for a commission at the Engineer Officers' Training School, Roseville, but his father advised: 'Go away as a Private and learn to take orders before you give them, and get to know the thinking and habits of the Privates and N.C.O.'s before you try to lead them'. Embarking as a sapper in March 1918, he underwent further training in England and served in France after the Armistice. He later attributed what he knew about handling men to his experience in the ranks. During seven months leave in 1919, he worked for the Keighley Gas & Oil Engine Co. Ltd, in London and Yorkshire. Returning to Sydney, he was discharged from the A.I.F. on 8 March 1920, just before the election which made his father premier. The father's example of public service strongly influenced the son: '[he] drilled into us ... that we should devote 25% of our time ... to some national service for which there was no compensation and only blame for the job that you tried to do'. John inherited from his family a respect for manual work and for workers' legitimate aspirations to fair pay and conditions; he also inherited a distrust of political extremism, especially doctrinaire socialism.

In 1921 John and his brother Tasman established Storey Bros Ltd to make automotive accessories, but they had an uphill struggle against cheap imports. John founded (1925) the Automotive Manufacturers' Association of New South Wales, which advocated protection for the motor industry and the eventual manufacture of an Australian-made motorcar. The indifference of the Bruce-Page [qq.v.7, 11] government left him embittered. Returning from studying the motor industry in the United States of America in 1929, he established National Motor Springs Pty Ltd and Better Brakes Ltd. When the Scullin [q.v.11] government revised tariffs in 1930, Storey wrote the automotive section of the schedule, which he described as 'probably the most definite step so far taken by any Government towards the ultimate manufacture of an all-Australian car'.

At St Philip's Church of England, Sydney, on 7 July 1923 Storey had married Alma Doretta Leddin. (Sir) Edward Holden [q.v.9] recruited him in 1932 as manager of the troubled body-service division of General Motors-Holden's Ltd, Sydney. Within two years the division was returning substantial profits. In 1934 Storey became director of manufacturing, based in Melbourne, and joined the board. He investigated the layout of General Motors Corporation's plant at Detroit, U.S.A., in 1935, and supervised the erection of G.M.H. factories—on sites he selected at Fishermens Bend, Melbourne (completed 1936), and Pagewood, Sydney (1940)—and the refurbishment of plants in Brisbane and Perth. In 1936 G.M.H. joined the industrial syndicate formed by Essington Lewis [q.v.10] to prepare Australia for war. When the consortium set up Commonwealth Aircraft Corporation Pty Ltd, Storey was appointed alternate director to (Sir) Laurence Hartnett (managing director of G.M.H.) on the board of C.A.C.

In March 1940 the Menzies [q.v.15] government established the Aircraft Production Commission under (Sir) Harold Clapp [q.v.8] to produce the Bristol Aeroplane Co.'s Beaufort bomber for the British and Australian air forces. Hartnett, who had expected to lead the commission, churlishly refused to release Storey as Clapp's first assistant for the duration of the war. Storey resigned from G.M.H. Following the fall of France in June, the British government placed an embargo on the export of war materials and drastically reduced assistance to the Australian Beaufort programme. A decision was made to undertake complete local manufacture. Storey rose to the challenge of a lifetime: 'we decided to follow a good old Australian policy and give it a go'.

He accompanied Menzies on a tour of Britain and North America in January-May 1941. Menzies thought he and Storey made 'a good team'. Their mutual respect ripened into a warm friendship. The prime minister particularly admired Storey's plain speaking with Lord Beaverbrook, minister of aircraft production, to secure guarantees for delivery of materials from Britain and increased British orders for Australian-built aircraft. Storey inspected 21 aircraft factories and contacted 59 officials in Britain, visited 7 factories in the United States, and spoke with 37 officials there and in Canada. The progress of the aircraft industry astonished him, as did the pivotal role played by motorcar manufacturers. He admired the extent and skill of female labour, and found the overall efficiency of British administration impressive.

Confirming his belief in the superiority of British aircraft, Storey recommended Australian manufacture of the Beaufighter and the Lancaster bomber. He decided that both Britain and Australia needed urgently to extend the training of factory foremen and managers. To him, foremen were the vital link between management and workers, and foremanship was a stepping stone to management. In 1937 he had been one of a group of industrialists who requested the Victorian Education Department to initiate a course for foremen at the Melbourne Technical College. He established a course at G.M.H. in 1938, and the college adopted his curriculum in 1940. On his return to Australia in June 1941, he played a key role in establishing (August) the Institute of Industrial Management of Australia (Australian Institute of Management from 1949), of which he was foundation president, and national president in 1947-51.

The first Australian-built Beaufort took to the air in August 1941, the first was delivered to the Royal Australian Air Force in September, and the first equipped with Australian-built engines was ready in November, confounding the experts who had declared the project impossible. After Japan entered the war, the Curtin [q.v.13] government disbanded the A.P.C. and reorganized aircraft production under the director-generalship of Lewis. Confirmed as director of the Beaufort division, Storey faced a demanding production schedule.

On the basis of his knowledge of subcontracting in the automotive-parts industry, his acquaintance with car manufacturing in Britain and the U.S.A., his experience at G.M.H. and his conspectus of the aircraft industry in wartime Britain, and with the strong backing of Lewis, Storey sub-contracted to some six hundred firms across Australia the production of components which were fed into seven sub-assembly workshops and, finally, the main assembly factories at Fishermens Bend and at Mascot, Sydney. Harold Breen [q.v.13] remembered Storey in the war years as an inspirational leader, idolized by his co-workers: 'quick, smiling, bright-eyed . . . He talked well and a good deal . . . [and] was definite in his views'.

Storey's Beaufort division completed, on average, sixteen aircraft per month in 1942 and twenty-nine per month in 1943. A total of seven hundred were delivered, the last in August 1944. As the production of Beauforts tapered off, the division began constructing Beaufighters. In May 1944, surrounded by cheering workers, Storey handed over to the R.A.A.F. the first of an eventual 364 Australian-built Beaufighters, only six months after the start of production and fourteen months after receiving the drawings. He led a study team that visited Manchester, England, in 1944-45 to prepare for the manufacture of Lancasters in Australia. Redesigned as the Lincoln, the Australian aeroplane delivered to the R.A.A.F. in May 1946 was the first aircraft to be built in Australia while it was being developed in

Britain. It remains the biggest aircraft ever built in Australia.

The Beaufort project had been Australia's largest and most complex wartime industrial task. It inspired a superb team effort from some 10 000 workers, four-fifths of them with no previous factory experience, and one-third of them women. By 1945 Australia's sophisticated aircraft-manufacturing industry had introduced hundreds of companies to the skills and methods of modern mass production. 'Beaufort' Storey and his project had a profound impact on Australian social and industrial confidence.

Storey retired as director of the Beaufort division in October 1945. Proud as he was of the organization's achievements, he understood at first hand the sacrifices made by Australian service personnel and civilians. A devoted father, he was disturbed to discover that he had become a stranger to his family. The subsequent decision to remain in Melbourne, rather than return to Sydney, was a family one, made essentially by his four children, with whom he attempted to build metaphorical bridges on summer camping holidays. In 1946 he declined, on family grounds, (Sir) John Jensen's [q.v.14] request that he become Commonwealth coal commissioner. Personal tragedy struck when his adored elder son John was diagnosed with leukaemia. 'Why, oh why?', he asked, anguished by the young man's slow and agonizing decline and his death in 1947. Distraught, Storey threw himself into his work.

In 1945, with Hartnett still in command, Storey had no prospect of returning to G.M.H. That year he became chairman and joint managing director of Repco Ltd, one of Australia's principal makers and distributors of automotive parts. The stockbrokers J. B. Were [q.v.2] & Son had made his appointment—following the retirement of Repco's founder R. G. Russell [q.v.]—a condition of underwriting the sale of the Russell family shares. As chairman (and managing director until 1953), Storey transformed the enterprise. Cherubic and kindly in appearance, shy and yet sociable in manner, open-minded and tolerant in discussion, he was also razor sharp, given to robust debate and resolute in decision, qualities which he acknowledged had earned him a reputation for ruthlessness during the Beaufort years.

Anticipating a buoyant postwar economy, Storey shifted Repco's focus from replacement parts to manufacturing and supplying original equipment for the booming Australian-built motorcar industry. Change was effected only against opposition from some subordinates. Contracts with G.M.H., together with the development of markets in Asia and the Pacific, assured the company large, regular and standard orders that in turn guaranteed extended production runs. Storey reorganized management on the principles he had learned at G.M.H. and honed in the Beaufort division. He promoted from within, and often recruited from outside, as when he engaged proven personnel from the Department of Aircraft Production. In 1949 Repco was reconstituted as a holding company: its many subsidiary and associated firms became self-contained units within this structure. By 1955 Repco was a highly profitable, medium-sized operation, employing over 3000 people in ten specialized manufacturing plants and distribution centres.

Storey spent his afternoons at Repco, after a morning's work at Overseas Corporation (Australia) Ltd, a venture he had begun in 1945 (registered in 1946) with William Wasserman, chief of the American Lend-Lease Mission in Australia. The enterprise was part of an international chain designed to spread among non-communist countries new industrial technology, patent rights, manufacturing licences and retail franchises. Storey was managing director from the outset, and chairman from 1950. Having attracted key investors, he employed a core of specialists (in marketing, production planning and control, and cost accounting) to service subsidiary companies headed by carefully recruited managers skilled at handling labour and regulating production flows. Overseas Corporation's manufacturing and merchandising came to include steel furniture, truck brakes, sheet leather, aircraft parts and foodstuffs, but the most famous product was the Namco pressure-cooker. In 1948 Prime Minister Ben Chifley [q.v.13] sought one, thanked Storey for sending him this 'most desirable present for the wife', and insisted on being invoiced. Even the production of 25 000 cookers a month could not meet Australian demand.

Industrial relations in Storey's businesses remained amicable, even during industry-wide strikes. In his view, shop-floor unhappiness usually resulted from bad management. He blamed the industrial conflict of 1945-47 on poor government and weak management that had allowed communists to exploit the union movement's legitimate demands. Rejecting the notion of class war, he regarded society as being based on a harmony of interests. Unity of effort of managers and workers would produce what the Americans called synergism —'the dividends you get from teamwork'. Managers should eschew piece-work and incentive systems, accept the reality of Australia's high wage levels, shorter working week, and lower production runs and sales volumes, and remain competitive by becoming more efficient.

National and Imperial development and defence were Storey's major enthusiasms. Of English ancestry, he was by birth and upbringing a British Australian, and by experience between the wars an Australian industrial nationalist. His loyalties had blended as he contributed to Britain's and Australia's struggle against the might of Germany and Japan. He had marvelled at the morale of the English people under German bombing, and was thrilled with his fellow Australians' response in the great Pacific crisis. He saw postwar industrial development as producing a stronger and more self-reliant Australia that would in turn strengthen the Empire: 'This war has taught us that the preservation of the Empire is dependent on the strength of the individual units of which it is made up', he averred in an article in *Aircraft Production* (1945). Cultural and sentimental affinities with Britain would continue to be complemented by strong defence and technological links.

Storey believed that Australia had been imperilled by her unpreparedness, and that only an armed and self-reliant Australia would ensure her own security and win respect from Asian neighbours. Government and private enterprise must co-operate to preserve the nucleus of a defence industry that could rapidly expand aircraft and armament production in wartime. He saw Australian population increase as the key to industrial development, and industrial development as central to defence. There was safety, not so much in numbers, but in an expanding, skilled manufacturing workforce, notably for the motor vehicle industry which, he remained convinced, would again prove the backbone of defence production.

The Chifley government appointed Storey chairman of the Joint War Production Committee (May 1949) and of the Immigration Planning Council (October). The *raison d'être* of the production committee, within the Department of Defence, was to ensure that industrial capacity existed to meet the likely requirements of the armed forces; that of the planning council was to mesh immigration with economic development. Storey chose to serve these bodies without remuneration. Menzies' approval in Opposition—and quick confirmation in government—of the appointments demonstrated the strong political continuities in the major parties' approach to postwar development and defence.

Between May and August 1950 Storey travelled to Britain, Europe and North America to pursue his private business interests, to study war-production planning and to investigate European sources of immigrant labour. He was knighted that year, at Buckingham Palace, London. Although immensely impressed by the state of the manufacturing plant, management and workforce in northern Italy, he did not share long-standing Australian prejudices against southern Italians, and advocated a general assisted-immigration programme for Italian families. His extensive visit facilitated the first migration agreement (1951) between the Italian and Australian governments. While the Immigration Planning Council for a time favoured bringing bachelors from Europe to fill gaps in the labour force and to clear bottlenecks in production, under Storey's chairmanship the council argued persuasively for a balanced intake in the interests of social development and long-term population building.

In September 1950 Menzies issued his 'Defence Call to the Nation', declaring that Australia should prepare for the possibility of another world war within three years, and inaugurating an intense effort to co-ordinate the civil and military sectors of the economy. Storey had proposed the creation of national defence and resources councils, but a plethora of initiatives, planning bodies and committees led to overlap, confusion and frustration. The authority of the Joint War Production Committee was reduced by the National Security Resources Board. There was some public speculation late in 1951 that Storey would be given a co-ordinating role similar to that played by Lewis during World War II, but high inflation led to severe restrictions on credit and imports and the scaling back of immigration in 1951-52. Privately, Storey was critical of government timidity and public service indifference.

Another extended overseas trip in mid-1953, again combining private and government business, further convinced him of the necessity to integrate the industrial and defence sectors, such as was occurring in the United States. Storey's argument for an Australian industrial defence college on American lines found scant support among defence chiefs. Privately, he discussed the formation of a national preparedness association, and a defence league for youth, to arouse Australians to the danger from the 'Near North'.

For Storey, Asia's teeming population and pressure on resources, rather than communism, constituted the main threat. Sceptical that Asians would be assimilated, he opposed all but token immigration from that region. Discussions with political and community leaders during a 1954 trip to Singapore, Hong Kong, the Philippines and Japan convinced him, however, that the term 'White Australia' should be replaced by 'selective immigration', that both rhetoric and practice could and should avoid any suggestion of European racial superiority, and that offensive incidents had to be avoided. Administrative amendments to the Commonwealth's immigration policy followed. He favoured high rates of European immigration to build a population of twenty million within twenty-five years, and he pressed the government, with some success, to maintain immigration targets.

In the early 1950s, in addition to his public responsibilities, Sir John had oversight of twenty-two factories and was chairman or a director of eight other companies. He still found time for golf and tennis, entertaining and reading. Family and friends warned him to slow down. He attempted to resign from the Joint War Production Committee in 1952, and did retire from several boards in 1954-55. But his resolution to decline speaking engagements was no sooner made than broken, and he took on additional responsibilities. In January 1955 he was appointed to the Australian Atomic Energy Commission's industry advisory committee. Driven by his love of work and his patriotism, he simply could not rest.

Storey died of a coronary occlusion on 3 July 1955 in the Mercy Hospital, East Melbourne. He was accorded a state funeral and was cremated. His wife, and their two daughters and younger son survived him. Menzies honoured his loyal friendship, strength of character, leadership in industry, and, above all, his devotion to Australia's wartime defence: 'This is sad news for our country. John Storey was much more than a successful industrialist: he was a great Australian patriot'. Breen admired his acuity, originality and broad humanity, and his relentless pursuit of 'the vision of a great nation under the Southern Cross'.

Of Storey's estate, sworn for probate at £366 336, he bequeathed £100 000 for public education in management and £100 000 for the advancement of technical education in Victoria. He also left £100 to each working director and employee who had given more than ten years service to his private companies, National Motor Springs and National Industries; the residue was left to his widow and children. The Australian Institute of Management established a memorial lecture and medal. The Royal Melbourne Technical College, of whose governing council Storey had been vice-president, set up a memorial fund to provide scholarships, and named Storey Hall to honour Storey and his son John. (Sir) William Dargie's portrait (1954) of Storey is held by the family.

D. P. Mellor, *The Role of Science and Industry* (Canb, 1958); L. J. Hartnett, *Big Wheels and Little Wheels* (Melb, 1964); A. D. Storey, *Down the Corridors of Time* (Melb?, 1976); B. Carroll, *Australian Made* (Melb, 1987); S. Wilson, *Beaufort, Beaufighter and Mosquito in Australian Service* (Canb, 1990); J. Fogarty, *Leaders in Management* (Melb, 1991?); A. W. Martin and P. Hardy (eds), *Dark and Hurrying Days* (Canb, 1993); A. T. Ross, *Armed and Ready* (Syd, 1995); J. Rich, *Hartnett* (Syd, 1996); Repco papers *and* R. Murray and K. White, ms history of Repco, in R. Murray/K. White papers (Univ Melb Archives); H. P. Breen, autobiography (ms, extracts held by Mrs J. Cope-Williams, Lancefield, Vic); Menzies papers (NL); A439, item 1951/11/4323, A446, item 1954/41575, A816, item 37/301/279, A4556, item 51/1/3/2, A5954, especially items 54/10 and 617/5, A9790, item 1363,

A10875; information from Mrs J. Cope-Williams, Lancefield, Vic, and Mrs D. Richardson, Vaucluse, Syd.   JOHN LACK

STOTT, TOM CLEAVE (1899-1976), wheat-farmer and politician, was born on 6 June 1899 at St Peters, Adelaide, third of five children of South Australian-born parents Thomas Henry Stott, blacksmith, and his wife Ellen, née Watkins. Young Tom attended Norwood Public School and thereafter taught himself by reading. He claimed, with some licence, to have attended secondary school, as well as classes run by the Workers' Educational Association of South Australia and by a business college. In 1914 his father took up a selection at Peake, about 100 miles (160 km) south-east of Adelaide. The soil was unsuitable for cropping. Next year the family moved north to Mindarie, a desolate whistle-stop on the railway line running through the Murray Mallee to Paringa. The Stotts worked strenuously to carve a 5500-acre (2225 ha) farm out of virgin scrub, and knew continual hardship and poverty.

On 18 August 1926 at St Margaret's Church of England, Woodville, Adelaide, Stott married Linda Florence Verrall; they were childless. Clearing a farm for himself adjacent to his father's block, he became preoccupied with the problems that faced wheat-farmers, particularly low prices. By 1927 he saw the need for producers to organize themselves into pressure groups. Largely due to his efforts, the Farmers Protection Association was formed in 1929, with Stott its paid secretary. After several amalgamations and changes of name, the association eventually became the United Farmers and Graziers of South Australia in 1966; apart from a break in 1933-46, Stott was to remain secretary until 1969. When the Australian Wheatgrowers' Federation was established in 1931, he also became its energetic and dedicated general secretary, and was to hold that post until the same year, 1969. Having failed to gain Liberal and Country League pre-selection to contest the seat of Albert for the House of Assembly in 1933, he stood as an Independent and was one of two candidates elected. He sat in parliament for an unbroken thirty-seven years, representing Ridley from 1938 as an Independent.

Stott began his parliamentary career as an aggressive rebel who tried to secure advantages for primary producers. His persistence and resourcefulness led many to detest him. The premiers (Sir) Richard Butler [q.v.7] and (Sir) Thomas Playford worked hard to unseat him at subsequent elections. In 1939 Playford tried unsuccessfully to have him expelled from parliament on the ground of bankruptcy.

Yet, Playford and Stott both had tolerance for the infinite capacity of human folly. They gradually came to see the benefits of co-operation. From 1945 Stott developed a fervent admiration for Playford, and the two worked together to push through legislation to secure a stable price for wheat (1948) and to enable bulk handling of grain (1955).

Although Stott was prominent in bringing prosperity to the wheat industry, he rarely acknowledged the effort and commitment of the many other growers and officials who worked for similar objectives. He tried to create the impression that he alone achieved everything. This characteristic led him to make enemies, among them (Sir) John Teasdale [q.v.] and (Sir) John McEwen [q.v.15]. In 1946 he was elected to the West Torrens Council. He fulfilled his duties conscientiously, but his support for the proclamation of the district as a city lost him his seat in 1950—his only electoral defeat—and he regarded the years he spent in local government as the most difficult of his life.

Following the 1962 election, Stott held the balance of power in the House of Assembly and was elected Speaker. Consistently voting in favour of the Playford government, he saw his role as being to keep the Australian Labor Party out of office. He lost the speakership in 1965 when Labor won the election. Playford retired in 1966 and was succeeded as party leader by Raymond Steele Hall. When the Liberal and Country League was returned to government in 1968, Stott again held the balance of power and was again made Speaker. Hall was determined that a new dam should be built at Dartmouth, Victoria, rather than at Chowilla, in Stott's electorate. On 30 April 1970 Stott voted with the Opposition to defeat Hall's government. He claimed that he was too ill to contest the ensuing election, but Ridley had been altered in an electoral redistribution and he had little hope of retaining the seat. One year earlier he had resigned from his posts in the wheat industry.

A short, stout man, Stott was able to hide his personal animosity behind an open and friendly manner. He was vain and combative in nature, forceful and single-minded, and contemptuous of most of his political contemporaries. Politically astute, he proved to be a competent administrator and a deft critic, with an amazing ability for rapid analysis. A Freemason and a nominal Anglican, he hated cant and cared not a jot that some clergymen criticized him during election campaigns for smoking, drinking, and betting on racehorses. As Speaker he was exemplary—patient, tolerant, firm and unruffled; he never had to name or discipline a member, and even his opponents grudgingly admired him. Gregarious and gifted with a sense of humour, he enjoyed the affection and loyalty of his staff.

Above all, Stott possessed extraordinary energy. He was a shrewd investor who nurtured the investments made from his multiple sources of income. In 1954 he had been appointed C.B.E. Thereafter, he shamelessly and unsuccessfully sought a knighthood. The conservatives never forgave him for bringing down the Hall government; Labor considered it his only useful political achievement. Survived by his wife, he died on 21 October 1976 at Glenelg and was buried in Centennial Park cemetery.

R. I. Jennings, *Barnacles and Parasites* (Adel, 1992), *and* Independent Members of the South Australian Parliament, 1927-1970 (M.A. thesis, Univ Adel, 1982), and for bib; Stott papers (Mort L and held by author, Plympton, Adel).REECE JENNINGS

STOUT, JAMES VICTOR (1885-1964), trade union leader, was born on 10 August 1885 in Port Melbourne, fifth child of James Stout, a labourer from Scotland, and his English-born wife Agnes, née Lloyd. Vic grew up in the working-class suburb in which he was born, and attended Graham Street and Nott Street State schools in the depths of the 1890s depression. He worked in the boot trade and later in a draper's shop. An avid reader and amateur musician, he was a serious self-improver, non-smoker and temperance advocate. About 1906 he joined Tom Mann's [q.v.10] Victorian Socialist Party and the Political Labor Council of Victoria (Australian Labor Party). From 1907, when the drapers combined with other retail workers to form the Shop Assistants' Union of Victoria, he became more active in union affairs. On 17 September 1912 at the office of the government statist, Queen Street, Melbourne, he married 37-year-old Maud Mary Newton; they lived at Toorak and were to remain childless.

During World War I and the years immediately following, Stout was swept along by the tide of radicalism in the labour movement. In 1915 he was elected to the Melbourne Trades Hall Council as a delegate of the Shop Assistants' Union. In 1916-17 he staunchly opposed conscription for military service overseas. Although he was often sceptical of Labor's parliamentary wing, he agreed to contest the Victorian Legislative Assembly seat of Toorak in 1920, but lost to (Sir) Stanley Argyle [q.v.7]. After the Stouts moved to their own home at Black Rock, Vic began his career as a paid union official, becoming an organizer for the shop assistants in 1924. Despite his slightly high-pitched voice and unprepossessing appearance—he was about 5 ft 6 ins (168 cm) tall, of medium build and wore spectacles—he impressed colleagues with his resolute approach and his candid, occasionally abrupt, manner.

In the late 1920s Stout gradually assumed more prominent roles in the Victorian labour movement. In 1929 he again stood unsuccessfully against Argyle for Toorak. He was an active member of the Workers' Anti-Liquor Group that urged Victorians to embrace prohibition in 1930. He resolutely opposed the Premiers' Plan of 1931 and pressed for a 'clean out' of Labor Party members who accepted it. He contested the Legislative Assembly seat of Prahran in 1932, but was beaten by John Ellis, the United Australia Party candidate. In 1933 he was elected president of the Melbourne Trades Hall Council, for a one-year term.

After Albert Monk [q.v.15] relinquished the secretaryship of the T.H.C. in 1938, Stout won the post in a three-way contest. He was to retain it until his death. His ability to balance his private convictions and his public interests was immediately tested when the liquor issue arose once more: this time he moved that the T.H.C. adopt a neutral attitude. On most matters he took predictable positions. He believed that non-union, immigrant workers undercut industrial conditions and that wartime rationing threatened jobs. Throughout World War II he was at the centre of power in the Victorian labour movement. A long-time member of the central executive of the State A.L.P., he began the first of his five terms as president in 1942. He also served on the interstate executive of the Australasian (Australian) Council of Trade Unions. In addition, he sat (1938-43) on the General [Wages] Board and was appointed (1942) a member of the Industrial Appeals Court.

Stout was alarmed by increasing communist influence in unions affiliated with the T.H.C. From about 1942 he supported the A.L.P.'s industrial groups and, although he was a Protestant, began to co-operate secretly with the Catholic Social Studies Movement. By the end of the war the Victorian labour movement was bitterly divided. The State parliamentary party, led by John Cain [q.v.13], came under pressure from a faction dominated by 'the Movement'. Meetings of the T.H.C. often ended in bitter squabbles. With industrial issues increasingly complicated by ideological faction-fighting, Stout juggled unstable alliances at the Trades Hall and in the A.L.P. In 1948-49 he was criticized by left-wing unions and the Labor Party for reaching an agreement with the Hollway [q.v.14] government on the Essential Services Act (1948). In 1950 he resigned from the A.L.P.'s Victorian central executive in protest against a decision by the parliamentary party to support a Country Party government, a decision which reinforced his view that Labor politicians could not be trusted to represent workers' interests. Next year, however, he rejoined the central executive.

As right-wing elements became more stridently assertive, Stout changed tack about 1952 and looked to the left for support. Following H. V. Evatt's [q.v.14] denunciation of 'the Movement' in October 1954, the A.L.P.'s federal executive dismissed the Victorian central executive in November. A special State conference of the party elected Stout president of a new central executive in February 1955. He immediately turned on his former allies, declaring that the Victorian A.L.P. was 'almost in a state of fascism'. The federal Labor Party split at the Hobart conference in March and the Cain government in Victoria lost the election in May. Stout became a belligerent 'anti-grouper'—at the Trades Hall and on the A.C.T.U. and federal A.L.P. executives—periodically bemoaning the poor relations between labour's industrial and political wings.

In the midst of the turmoil, Stout's wife died on 8 July 1955. Never a gregarious man, he found occasional solace in playing the violin or listening to operatic recordings in private. As the labour movement slowly rebuilt its strength in the ensuing years, he went about his Trades Hall and other duties (including Sunday afternoon broadcasts on radio-station 3KZ) in his usual methodical manner. In 1961 he was elected federal president of the A.L.P.

On 12 March 1964 Stout collapsed at his desk in the Trades Hall. He died next day in St Vincent's Hospital, Fitzroy, and was cremated. Old comrades and adversaries paid him generous, if diplomatic, tributes.

L. J. Louis, *Trade Unions and the Depression* (Canb, 1968); R. Murray, *The Split* (Melb, 1970); P. Weller and B. Lloyd (eds), *Federal Executive Minutes, 1915-1955* (Melb, 1978); J. Hagan, *The History of the A.C.T.U.* (Melb, 1981); K. White, *John Cain & Victorian Labor 1917-1957* (Syd, 1982); T. Sheridan, *Division of Labour* (Melb, 1989); A. Best, *The History of the Liquor Trades Union in Victoria* (Melb, 1990); *Catholic Worker*, Apr 1964; *Outlook*, Apr 1964; Labour Hist, Melb, *Recorder*, Feb 1969, June 1977; *Age* (Melb) and *Sun News-Pictorial*, 14 Mar 1964; *Herald* (Melb), 18 Mar 1964.

PETER LOVE

STRACHAN, DAVID EDGAR (1919-1970), painter and printmaker, was born on 25 June 1919 at Salisbury, Wiltshire, England, eldest of four children of Major James Charles Power Strachan, Australian Army Medical Corps, Australian Imperial Force, and his wife Eleanor Margery Isobel, née Tapp, who came from Bath. The family moved to Adelaide in 1920 and to Creswick, Victoria, in the following year. David was sent to Creswick State and Geelong Church of England Grammar schools. By the age of 16 he wanted to be an artist. Accompanying his mother to London in 1936, he enrolled at the Slade School of Fine

Art, where he met Godfrey Miller [q.v.15]. In 1937 he attended the Académie de la Grande Chaumière, Paris, and painted at Cassis on the Mediterranean Sea. He returned to Australia in April 1938 and studied at the George Bell [q.v.7] School, Melbourne.

Strachan's earliest known paintings, such as 'Mother and Child' and 'Victorian Family' (both 1940), had an eerie, staged look which was to become characteristic of much of his work. His growing interest in classicism blended with a fascination for the dream-state and became reinforced in his work after he moved to Sydney in 1941. There he was befriended by Jean Bellette and her husband Paul Haefliger, who were to be driving forces behind the Sydney Art Group (founded 1945). He lived on the top floor of the Haefligers' house at Double Bay, and together the three artists drew from models whom the Haefligers hired. In this period Strachan painted and exhibited some of his most poetic works —mainly figurative and landscape subjects, and still-lifes of haunting beauty. His flowers, bowls of fruit, birds, and angelic figures glimmered out of the darkness as things not of this world, evoked faintly, like mythological personages in a gently spoken narrative. He 'spent an erratic war' painting camouflage at Bankstown aerodrome with other artists, among them (Sir) William Dobell [q.v.14], and dancing minor roles with Hélène Kirsova's [q.v.15] ballet company.

In 1948 Strachan settled in Paris. His paintings, included by Peter Bellew in an exhibition at the Musée National d'Art Moderne, had been well-received by French critics two years earlier. In 1950 he began tentative experiments in etching. These led to the formation of the Stramur-Presse, a business venture which published etchings and lithographs of leading French and English artists. His most important project was a series of twenty-two colour etchings illustrating Alister Kershaw's book of poems, *Accent & Hazard* (Paris, 1951).

Strachan continued to exhibit in Australia and maintained a lively social life with Australian friends. From Paris, he went for weekend painting trips with Moya Dyring [q.v.14] in her car and, after 1957, visited the Haefligers on Majorca. He lived in London in 1955-57. His paintings became progressively less soft in effect, his palette brightened, and his forms, especially the still-lifes, became spikier. In the late 1950s his attention drifted towards the study of Hindu philosophers and Jungian psychology. For most of 1957-58 he was enrolled at the C. G. Jung-Institut, Zürich, Switzerland. In 1959 he worked in Silvio Daneo's silkworm factory at Bricherasio, Italy.

In May 1960 Strachan returned to Sydney. He lived at Woolloomooloo before buying a house at Paddington in 1963. Having learned

in Paris, he was a remarkable cook, and introduced his friends 'to a style of kitchen-based living among scrubbed wooden furniture, tiles, handsome pots and pans, massed herbs and vegetables, fine cuisine, witty conversation, books and music'. Over the ensuing years he involved himself energetically with the art scene, exhibiting, teaching (1960-65) at East Sydney Technical College, fund-raising for memorials for Thea Proctor [q.v.11] and Dyring, and as the last president (1965) of the Society of Artists.

His paintings were out of harmony with the prevailing fashion for abstraction, but he won the Wynne prize for landscape painting in 1961 and 1964 (shared). Perhaps the most moving works of Strachan's last ten years were the mining landscapes, including those he painted near Hill End, leading up to his vast canvas, 'Lewers Freehold Mine'. This was a history picture, depicting the mine as it might have appeared in 1874. He presented it to the Creswick Historical Museum in 1970 in memory of his father.

Strachan died from injuries received in a motorcar accident on 23 November 1970 on the Hume Highway near Yass and was cremated. His family preserved the interior of his Sydney home much as he had left it, with the atmosphere of dusty, lived-in antiquity that he loved so much. As an artist, his closest affinity was probably with the French Symbolist Odilon Redon. Strachan's work is represented in public and private collections throughout Australia.

D. Thomas, *David Strachan, 1919-1970*, exhibition cat (Syd, 1973); L. Klepac, B. Pearce and J. McDonald, *David Strachan* (Syd, 1993); *Art and Aust*, 8, Mar 1971, p 330, 10, Apr 1973, p 332; *Hemisphere*, 20, Oct 1976, p 19; *SMH*, 9 June 1973; *SMH Good Weekend*, 3 Jan 1993; H. de Berg, David Strachan (taped interview, Nov 1962, NL); Strachan papers (Art Gallery of NSW Archives).

BARRY PEARCE

STRAHAN, FRANK (1886-1976), public servant, was born on 2 July 1886 at Fryerstown, Victoria, son of Richard Strahan, a schoolteacher from Ireland, and his second wife Sarah Jane, née Hardwick, who was born in Victoria. In 1894 the family moved to Bendigo. Frank was educated at a number of country schools. Entering the Commonwealth Public Service, he was appointed a clerk in the Treasury on 1 March 1906 and began to attend night-classes at the University of Melbourne (B.A., 1911; LL.B., 1915). At St Paul's Anglican Church, Bendigo, on 30 March 1914 he married Ella Mary Moore, a schoolteacher; they were childless.

In March 1913 Strahan had transferred to the Prime Minister's Department, which he later described as 'a letter-writing' office. As a senior clerk, he was involved in drafting correspondence and proclamations, and in decoding cables. In April 1921 he was promoted to assistant-secretary. Over the next fourteen years he was responsible for a wide range of activities, including parliamentary matters, correspondence with State governments, administrative arrangements and publicity. While a member of the Australian delegation to the Imperial Conference in London in 1923, he was treated by Prime Minister S. M. (Viscount) Bruce [q.v.7] as a well-paid messenger. Strahan's narrow conception of the role of a senior public servant was formed during the years that he worked for Bruce. In 1928 he was appointed C.B.E. Next year he served as secretary of a committee which organized the British, Australian and New Zealand Antarctic Research Expedition, led by Sir Douglas Mawson [q.v.10]. The Strahan Glacier in MacRobertson Land was named after him. In 1930 the government made him a director of Amalgamated Wireless (Australasia) Ltd. He was Australian secretary for the Duke of Gloucester's [q.v.14] tour in 1934 and that year was appointed C.V.O.

A small external affairs branch had been added to Strahan's responsibilities in 1930. Because he showed little interest in the creation of an Australian diplomatic service and was comparatively unfamiliar with foreign affairs, his relations with the branch's officers were strained. When Strahan was appointed secretary of the Prime Minister's Department in November 1935, a separate Department of External Affairs was established. Although he retained responsibility for Territories and for the High Commission in London, he headed a weakened department. Its standing slumped further with the approach of World War II and the ascendancy of the Department of Defence. Sir Paul Hasluck later described the secretary of that department, (Sir) Frederick Shedden [q.v.], as 'efficient, active and far-seeing', a contrast to Strahan whom he regarded as 'an easy-going old-style public servant'. Shedden began attending meetings of the War Cabinet in 1939, but it was only in July 1941 that, on the initiative of (Sir) Robert Menzies [q.v.15], Strahan became secretary of the full cabinet. He was, none the less, the first Commonwealth public servant to attend its meetings and the result was an immediate improvement in the organization of cabinet business.

Strahan described himself as 'just a clerk' who simply carried out the prime minister's directions. He was on good terms with the four prime ministers whom he served as secretary, but his influence on policy-making was limited. Although he attended the 1937 Imperial Conference with Joseph Lyons [q.v.10], he did not accompany Menzies, John Curtin

or J. B. Chifley [qq.v.13] on their overseas trips between 1941 and 1949. With the abolition of the War Cabinet, the work of the cabinet secretariat increased rapidly. Strahan and his deputies were hard-pressed. They resisted proposals that the department should extend its control to the large number of cabinet committees, and rejected suggestions that it should adopt a co-ordinating and advisory role similar to that of the Cabinet Office in Britain.

In August 1949 Strahan retired. He had lived in Canberra for more than twenty years, but shown little interest in local affairs. In 1950 he and his wife returned to Melbourne and settled at Box Hill. He continued to be a director of A.W.A. until 1962. After his wife died in 1965, Strahan lived alone, tending his garden, and occasionally meeting and reminiscing with former public-service colleagues. He died on 4 May 1976 at Camberwell and was cremated.

A. G. Price, *The Winning of Australian Antarctica* (Syd, 1962); P. Hasluck, *Diplomatic Witness* (Melb, 1980); P. G. Edwards, *Prime Ministers and Diplomats* (Melb, 1983); *Public Administration* (Syd), 26, 1967, p 32; J. S. Cumpston, Frank Strahan (taped interview, 1967, NL); John Farquharson, Hazel Craig (taped interview, 1997, NL); L. F. Crisp papers, box 39 (NL); A461, item U1/1/1 (NAA, Canb); personal knowledge.   GRAEME POWELL

STRATTON, JOHN PETER (1886-1966), trotting promoter, was born on 6 May 1886 at Mirboo North, Victoria, seventh of four teen children of Thomas Stratton, an illiterate farmer, and his wife Elizabeth, née Tainsh, both Victorian born. John was raised at Mooroopna and sent to the local primary school. Moving to Western Australia, he settled (about 1906) on a small farm at Benjaberring. On 9 March 1910 at the Church of Christ, Lake Street, Perth, he married Maud May East, a waitress; they were to have five children before separating in 1932. Stratton was injured in a farm accident in 1911 and lost the use of an arm. By 1920 he was living in Perth. He bought and sold real estate there, developed extensive farming and grazing holdings in Western Australia and Victoria, and in 1925 became treasurer of the Primary Producers' Association.

In 1929 Stratton and two lesser guarantors underwrote a loan to set up the Brennan Park trotting ground. In return, they were given three positions, and the right to nominate another member, giving them a majority on the Western Australian Trotting Association's committee of seven. Elected president of the W.A.T.A. in 1930, Stratton dominated his fellow committee-members by the strength of his personality and controlled the administration of trotting in Western Australia. Dynamic, egotistical, ruthless, and unrelenting in his pursuit of power, he engineered the exclusion of James Brennan, a former president and guarantor, from the committee.

Stratton was the moving force behind the establishment of the Inter-Dominion Trotting Conference in 1936 and its president until 1966. His horses ran in twenty-one consecutive Inter-Dominion Pacing championships and his wealth set him apart from the rest of the trotting fraternity. He served as president (1939-45) of the W.A. Sportsmen's Organizing Council for Patriotic Funds. In 1946 he established the Jane Brook horse stud at Midland, near Perth.

The guarantor system proved unpopular with many W.A.T.A. members, who frequently tried to abolish it and elect their committee democratically. In 1946 a royal commission into the administration, conduct and control of trotting found that Stratton had 'stacked' the W.A.T.A.'s membership, improperly changed the name of Brennan Park to Gloucester [q.v.14] Park in 1935, benefited financially from his presidency and forced the departure of the chairman of stewards who had disqualified one of his horses. It was also suspected that he had interfered in the handicapping of his horses. Although the commissioner thought that Stratton was 'not as frank in his evidence as he should have been', he acknowledged his strengths in managing and promoting trotting. The State government took control of trotting under the Western Australian Trotting Association Act (1946), but Stratton's power was left intact. Although the guarantors' liability ended in 1945, they were elected to the committee and Stratton retained the presidency until his death. He was a founding member (1961-66) of the Totalisator Agency Board of Western Australia.

Survived by his wife, and their two daughters and three sons, Stratton died on 26 July 1966 at his Nedlands home and was buried with Anglican rites in Karrakatta cemetery. His estate was sworn for probate at $842 606. He left relatively small bequests to his children and a pittance to his wife, and made generous provision for his long-time mistress —on the condition that she remained single. The bulk of his estate was used to set up a charitable trust from which funds were first distributed in 1974 to people suffering from physical or intellectual disabilities. The W.A.T.A. named the J. P. Stratton Cup after him.

WA Trotting Assn, *History of Trotting in the State of Western Australia* (Perth, 1970?); Roy Com ... into the administration, conduct and control of the sport of trotting in the state of WA, *V&P* (WA), 1946, 2; *West Australian*, 27 July, 25 Aug 1966, 10 May 1967, 4 Feb 1974; *Daily News* (Perth), 11 May 1967.

CHARLIE FOX

STREET, JESSIE MARY GREY (1889-1970), feminist, was born on 18 April 1889 at Ranchi, Bihar, India, eldest of three children of Charles Alfred Gordon Lillingston, civil servant, and his wife Mabel Harriet, sixth daughter of Edward David Stewart Ogilvie [q.v.5] of Yulgilbar station, near Grafton, New South Wales. When Mabel inherited Yulgilbar in 1896, Lillingston resigned from the Indian Civil Service to take up residence there. Jessie began her formal education with a governess. In 1904-06 she attended Wycombe Abbey School, Buckinghamshire, England. She matriculated by private study and enrolled in arts at the University of Sydney (B.A., 1911), where she lived at Women's College (1908) and also met her future husband.

Captain of the university women's hockey team, Jessie attended the inaugural meeting (1908) of the New South Wales Ladies' Hockey Association and played in its first interstate match (1909)—against Victoria. She was a founding member (1910) and president (1925-26) of Sydney University Women's Sports Association. With her parents, she visited Europe in 1911 and again in 1914. She worked in London as a volunteer at Bishop Creighton House, a Church of England settlement, and for the New York Protective and Probation Association at Waverley House, a reception centre for young women arrested as prostitutes. Back in Sydney, she married (Sir) Kenneth Street [q.v.] on 10 February 1916 at St John's Church of England, Darlinghurst; he was a barrister who subsequently became chief justice of New South Wales. They were to have four children, the youngest born in 1926.

In 1920 Jessie was secretary of the National Council of Women of New South Wales. She planned to liven up interest in the council's work by calling elections rather than co-opting office-bearers, but met opposition and resigned. From 1921 to 1950 she was a councillor of Women's College, as was her father-in-law in 1917-34. She became an executive-member of the Feminist Club and briefly its president (1929). When she invited the Women Voters Association, the Women's Service Guild and the Women's League to join with the Feminist Club to form the United Associations (later United Associations of Women) some club members objected and she resigned.

Street was elected president of the U.A. in 1930. She held that office on and off until 1950, standing down from time to time to allow other women the experience. The U.A. became the New South Wales branch of the Australian Federation of Women Voters, which had been founded by Bessie Rischbieth [q.v.11] in 1921 to give women a voice nationally and internationally. Rischbieth was Australia's leading feminist, and mentor to Street. She confided her plans for the A.F.W.V., suggested issues for action, used Street to interview ministers, and arranged for her to meet prominent overseas feminists. The A.F.W.V.'s journal, *Dawn*, was well established, and a useful medium for U.A. publicity.

The overriding objective of the A.F.W.W. and its affiliates was 'real equality' of status and opportunity—an end to discrimination against women in the workplace, in law, or in appointment to public office, as a consequence of marriage or motherhood. The welfare of children and the promotion of international peace were associated aims. The strategy of post-suffrage international feminism, which Rischbieth had helped to develop, was to mobilize nationally and internationally to bring pressure on government, both directly, and indirectly through the League of Nations.

In Geneva in 1930 Street linked up with the British Commonwealth League, joined a delegation seeking equal nationality rights for married women, addressed the Open Door International for the Economic Emancipation of the Woman Worker on the 'Iniquity of the Australian Basic Wage', and led a 'spontaneous' deputation to the director of the International Labour Organization. The Open Door worked for the repeal of all legislation and regulations that set special conditions for employing women, effectively excluding them from certain jobs and most trades. Street became vice-chairman of Equal Rights International. At home, she called on the government to respond positively to the League of Nations' resolution that had referred the Pan-American Equal Rights Treaty to member nations. She appealed (unsuccessfully) for the inclusion of an 'equal rights' clause in amendments to the Australian Constitution, put forward in 1944. Continuing to work with international feminism, she publicized its work when she was in Australia and renewed contact overseas in 1938, 1945 and later years.

The U.A. co-operated with other organizations in campaigns for equal guardianship rights, divorce law reform, the right of a married woman to retain her nationality and to establish separate domicile, the appointment of women to public office and to jury service, and the election of women to parliament. The methods were proven—public meetings, lectures, conferences, letters to editors and politicians, radio talks, deputations to ministers and public appeals. Throughout history, Street wrote, 'vital changes of policy have been brought about by moral pressure'.

The U.A. published numerous leaflets and pamphlets, including three written by Street —on equal pay, child endowment and woman as homemaker.

A woman's right to economic independence was the cause Street made especially her own. It encompassed a right to income for married women, a right to paid employment regardless of marital status, a right to compete alongside men in the labour market, equal pay, and just remuneration of skills. She ran a long and ultimately successful campaign against the Married Women Teachers' and Lecturers' Dismissal Act (1932, repealed 1947), protested strongly at the Trades and Labor Council of Queensland's proposal (1935) to deny work to married women, and objected to their dismissal by the Sydney County Council (1937) and the Commonwealth Public Service (postwar). She lobbied for child endowment to be paid to mothers (1941) and, without success, for a wife's right to an allowance: a wife who left an unsatisfactory husband could claim maintenance, so if she remained with him it was 'only fair' that she be 'legally entitled to the money for her maintenance'. In 1932 Street had devised an elaborate national insurance scheme, with provision for marriage endowment and child endowment.

Since slavery was abolished, all men were entitled to sell their labour at the highest price, but women were denied this right, which, Street stated, 'is the very foundation of human liberty'. Was it fair that a man with private income could claim a job while married women were refused employment? Regulations excluding women from certain work (for example with heavy machinery) were also unjust. Industrial safety was as much a concern for men as for women. To enjoy the right to work, women needed access to family planning. Street had started the short-lived Social Hygiene Association in 1916 to promote sex education. Later, through the Racial Hygiene Association of New South Wales, she was involved in setting up the first contraceptive clinic in Sydney (1933).

Street argued that equal pay was just, and would eliminate the pool of cheap female labour which 'continually menaces the employment of men and the standards of living of all workers'. This was especially so where technology was changing the nature of work. The U.A. briefed counsel to appear in equal-pay cases brought by the Federated Clerks' Union of Australia and the Shop Assistants' Union of New South Wales. As a foundation affiliate (1937) of the Council of Action for Equal Pay, the U.A. continued to co-operate with the unions, despite disagreement on the tactic of phasing in equal pay. In a major campaign in 1940, with support from twenty organizations, the U.A. briefed Nerida Cohen to intervene in the basic-wage inquiry. In the sequel, Street secured a commitment from a number of unions to make applications for equal pay, influencing the Australasian Council of Trade Unions' endorsement of equal pay in 1942. The substantial result was the creation of the Women's Employment Board that set wage rates for women war-workers at 60 to 100 per cent of male rates.

That women should be properly rewarded for skill was another of Street's concerns. In 1923 she had established the House Service Co. to supply casual domestic service to approved clients. An associated Home Training Institute (1927-35) contracted with employers to release full-time employees (untrained young women) for domestic science classes and for afternoon recreation. Street expected the conferral of diplomas to raise the status and remuneration of domestic servants, and she arranged afternoon recreation to counter loneliness. She helped other groups —a co-operative of unemployed women who produced vegetables, eggs and flowers (1932-34), a union which obtained the first industrial award for nurses (1936), and women contesting parliamentary elections. The conference on essential social services (1934) was intended to bring professionally trained social workers to the notice of potential employers. When only one woman was included in the team for the 1936 Olympic Games, Street ran a campaign for additional selections.

The Street family were foundation members of the New South Wales branch of the League of Nations Union. As the failures of the league became more apparent in the 1930s, the U.A. affiliated with the State branch of the International Peace Campaign. Jessie Street visited the Soviet Union, at the invitation of the Society for Cultural Relations with the U.S.S.R., when she took her younger daughter to Europe in 1938. After some weeks in the Soviet Union, she was satisfied that Russian women 'could enter any occupation under conditions of equality'. In Vienna she was deeply saddened by seeing the way that Nazis treated Jews. An advocate for the removal of restrictions on Jewish immigration to Palestine, and for an increased intake of Jewish refugees to Australia, she was to serve on the Aliens Classification and Advisory Committee in 1944 and later on the Commonwealth Immigration Advisory Council.

Jessie Street had joined the Australian Labor Party in 1939, convinced that the organized labour movement promoted much needed reforms. In 1943 she failed to obtain pre-selection for the House of Representatives seat of Eden-Monaro (which the A.L.P. won), but was endorsed for Wentworth, which she lost after distribution of preferences. In 1946 she was again defeated for Wentworth.

Three causes especially engaged her during World War II. One was the infringement of the civil liberties of women suspected of having sexual relations with servicemen and of women who were anonymously accused of suffering from venereal disease: under National Security Regulations, they were liable to summary arrest, compulsory examination and incarceration if found venereally infected. Another was aid for Russia. Street was president (from 1939) of the Sydney branch of the Society for Cultural Relations with the U.S.S.R. Following Germany's attack on the Soviet Union, she mobilized and chaired the high-powered Russian Medical Aid and Comforts Committee; when war with Japan shifted priorities for medicines, she organized the 'Sheepskins for Russia' Appeal. Her third wartime endeavour was to mobilize women behind a national programme for reconstruction. She convened the Australian Women's Conference for Victory in War and Victory in Peace which approved the Australian Woman's Charter (1943), a detailed programme of reforms for incorporation in government post-war planning. Over ninety organizations and all States were represented. To bring together so wide a body of support was an end she had in mind when she wrote in 1934 that women must organize. 'The vote is respected much more than justice and liberty'. By 1943 Jessie Street had become Australia's leading feminist. She financed the publication of the *Australian Women's Digest* (1944-47), a forum for discussion of charter reforms and the reporting of other news, and gave her money generously to good causes.

In 1945 Street was the only female adviser in the Australian delegation to the United Nations Conference on International Organization, held at San Francisco, United States of America. In co-operation with other women, she secured the insertion of the word 'sex' in the clause 'without distinction as to race, sex, language or religion' wherever it occurs in the Charter of the United Nations. The women canvassed widely for Article 8 which acknowledges the eligibility of 'men and women' to participate 'in any capacity and under conditions of equality' in the principal and subsidiary organs of the United Nations. 'Where the rules are silent', Street said, 'women are not usually considered'. She believed that the lobbying for Article 8 generated the favourable reception of Bertha Lutz's motion that the U.N. Economic and Social Council establish a commission on the status of women with a special charge to investigate discrimination. Street was Australia's first representative (1947-48) on this commission, and its vice-president. By then the Cold War had changed the climate for reform. Her intention had been for the commission to scrutinize the work of all U.N. bodies, but it was inadequately staffed and limited in its times of meetings. Her proposal for nationally based committees to support its work was endorsed, and she travelled around Australia to establish a network of committees.

Street was never attracted to, nor a member of, any communist party. After leaving San Francisco, she toured devastated Europe and was a guest of the Soviet Union, a nation which, she believed, had suffered too much destruction and loss of life to want another war. In working for better understanding of the Soviet Union, she saw herself as helping to promote peace. She was president (from 1946) of the Australian Russian Society. In Paris she clashed 'openly and bitterly' with Rischbieth at the congress of the International Alliance of Women for Suffrage and Equal Citizenship. In Sydney, she was labelled a 'Red' in a smear campaign. The second Australian Woman's Charter Conference (1946) became the occasion for sustained questioning of Street's claim to national leadership. The rift developing in the women's movement was the result in part of Street's abandonment of the strategy of non-party politics, but it was also profoundly influenced by Cold War fears.

Standing for the new Federal seat of Phillip in 1949 as an Independent Labour candidate, Street polled less than 6 per cent of the vote. She had been overseas for much of 1948, and come home via India and Japan. Seeing Hiroshima was among the 'most unforgettable' of her experiences. She became deeply committed to banning nuclear weapons. As president of the New South Wales Peace Council, she invited Dr Hewlett Johnson, the 'Red Dean' of Canterbury, to the first postwar Congress of the Australian Peace Council in 1950. Refused the use of Sydney Town Hall, she moved the conference to Melbourne. She went to England that year to help the British Peace Council to organize a world peace congress at Sheffield, but it was eventually held in Warsaw because of difficulties with visas.

On becoming an executive-member of the World Peace Council, Street established her residence in London. She travelled constantly, to peace meetings and conferences, to report on United Nations meetings for various Australian publications, and to visit old U.A. associates. She rejoined feminist friends in the British Commonwealth League, the Six Point Group, and the World Women's Party. The British Anti-Slavery Society appointed her to its executive and, at its request, she returned to Sydney in 1956 to report on the situation of Aboriginal Australians.

National responsibility for the 'care' of Aborigines had been A.F.W.V. policy from 1933. It was also the first plank in policy proposals for Aborigines in the Australian Woman's Charter. Responding to Aboriginal protest, the U.A. recommended the appointment of a woman and an Aborigine to the Aborigines Welfare Board. In 1956 Street urged Pearl

Gibbs to start the Aboriginal-Australian Fellowship. Street thought that the support of a national Aboriginal organization would 'help considerably' if her report were to be forwarded to the United Nations. Advised by Christian Jollie Smith [q.v.11], she drafted an amendment to the Australian Constitution to remove discriminatory references to Aborigines and suggested that the fellowship make it the focus of its first meeting in the Sydney Town Hall. As she travelled interstate collecting information for her report, she met Aboriginal leaders, to whom she explained the constitutional proposals and the importance of national organization. The Anti-Slavery Society decided against sending her report to the United Nations, but her visit had significant consequences. The Federal Council for Aboriginal Advancement (Federal Council for the Advancement of Aborigines and Torres Strait Islanders) was formed in 1958 and her suggested amendments to the Constitution were carried in the 1967 referendum.

Street resumed her work for peace. In 1960 she returned to Australia and began writing her memoirs. A first volume was published as *Truth or Repose* (1966), the second abandoned. When Jessie next travelled, it was mainly to see friends. Though often apart, husband and wife remained affectionate companions. He was a daily visitor in her final months in the Scottish Hospital. (Lady) Jessie Street (her preferred use of title) died on 2 July 1970 at Paddington and was cremated. Her husband, and their two daughters and two sons survived her. She bequeathed $10 000 to the Australia-Soviet Friendship Society and the bulk of her estate to her children.

Following celebrations for her centenary in 1989, the Jessie Street Trust was formed to provide financial assistance to projects in the areas of her main public activities. The Jessie Street National Women's Library was also established in Sydney. The library holds a portrait (1929) by Jerrold Nathan in which Jessie is bedecked in finery, but she commonly wore a tailored suit, simple blouse, cameo brooch and comfortable shoes. Of medium build, with her brown hair cut short for convenience, she had a warm, pleasant appearance and demeanour. Jessie could charm and cheer, and give and win loyalty. She had a talent for friendship and for persuading others to fight for justice.

P. Sekuless, *Jessie Street* (Brisb, 1978); W. Mitchell, *50 Years of Feminist Achievement* (Syd, 1979?); M. Bevege et al (eds), *Worth Her Salt* (Syd, 1982); H. Radi (ed), *Jessie Street* (Syd, 1990); M. Lake, *Getting Equal* (Syd, 1999); Street papers *and* Bessie Rischbieth papers (NL); United Assns of Women papers (ML); A6119, items 360-63 (NAA, Canb); information from Mrs P. Fingleton, Roseville, and Sir Laurence Street, Point Piper, Syd, and Mrs B. Mackay, Ballalaba, NSW.   HEATHER RADI

STREET, SIR KENNETH WHISTLER (1890-1972), chief justice and lieutenant-governor, was born on 28 January 1890 at Woollahra, Sydney, eldest son of (Sir) Philip Whistler Street [q.v.12], a Sydney-born barrister, and his wife Belinda Maud, née Poolman, who came from Melbourne. He attended Homebush and Sydney Grammar schools, entered St Paul's College, University of Sydney (B.A., 1911; LL.B., 1914), and won scholarships and prizes in law. World War I began while he was holidaying in England. He was commissioned on 29 September 1914 in the Duke of Cornwall's Light Infantry and sent to France, but an injury rendered him unfit for active service.

Returning to Sydney, Street was appointed lieutenant, 18th (North Sydney) Infantry Regiment, in December 1915. He served in the Adjutant General's Department, Army Headquarters, Melbourne, and was promoted temporary captain in September 1917. Although he had been admitted to the New South Wales Bar on 12 March 1915, he did not practise until he ceased full-time military duties in December 1919. At St John's Church of England, Darlinghurst, on 10 February 1916 he had married Jessie Mary Grey Lillingston [q.v. Street].

Between 1921 and 1927 Street lectured part time at the University of Sydney Law School. Meanwhile, he continued his career in the Militia as a legal staff officer (1922-28) and rose to the rank of lieutenant colonel. He was a considerable scholar in and beyond the law, being an authority on the writings of Pepys and an accomplished Latinist. Absorbed in his family's history, he privately published *Annals of the Street Family of Birtley* (1941), a book in which he demonstrated ancestral links to the English judiciary.

Street enjoyed a wide general practice and would have taken silk but for his appointment to serve on the reconstituted Industrial Commission of New South Wales from 16 December 1927. He was elevated as a judge of the Supreme Court on 7 October 1931. He thus joined the bench of which his father was then chief justice. In his eighteen years as a puisne judge he displayed industry, a deep sense of responsibility in performing his duties, and 'a personal charm which commended him to all who appeared in his court'. Street habitually used a monocle which augmented the impact of his exact, commanding and demanding figure in court. He once conceded that, 'I may have shown myself impatient, but never have I received discourtesy from any member of the profession'.

In 1949, as senior puisne judge, Street acted as chief justice when Sir Frederick Jordan [q.v.9] died. Confirmed in that office from 6 January 1950, he was sworn in on 7 February. He was assured that the legal profession's regard for him was 'based on its knowledge of him alone and not on any reflected glory of his ancestor'. The solicitor-general C. E. Weigall [q.v.12] acknowledged Street's 'talent for luminous exposition', his 'apt and felicitous language', and his ability to 'express himself with clarity and precision'.

Appointed K.C.M.G. (1956), and awarded an honorary LL.D. by the University of Sydney (1952), Sir Kenneth presided over a court trapped in antiquated procedure that stifled the expectations of an increasingly litigious community. Government expansion of the judicial bench made court administration more complex and imposed on the chief justice burdens of management largely foreign to his predecessors. He also personally superintended attempts to extract more efficient use of the limited space in the court's eccentric collection of buildings.

As chief justice, Sir Kenneth became lieutenant-governor and administered the State several times. Farewelled in court in December 1959, he retired from the bench on his seventieth birthday. He had few interests beyond the law, though he found recreation in gardening and cabinet-making, belonged to the Union and Royal Sydney Golf clubs, and supported organizations such as the Boy Scouts' Association. President of the St John Ambulance Association (1950-60) and of the St John Council (1965-72), he was appointed (1951) a knight of grace of the Order of St John of Jerusalem.

Street died on 15 February 1972 at his Darling Point home; he was accorded a state funeral and was buried in South Head cemetery. His two daughters and two sons survived him. The younger son (Sir) Laurence achieved in 1974 the rare distinction of occupying the same office of chief justice as had his father and grandfather. In public matters, Sir Kenneth and Lady Street seemed an improbable match, he being exceedingly conservative and formal, she being committed to radical movements, especially the furtherance of women's rights.

A portrait of Street by (Sir) William Dargie is held by the Supreme Court, Sydney.

J. M. Bennett, *Portraits of the Chief Justices of New South Wales* (Syd, 1977); J. and J. Mackinolty (eds), *A Century Down Town* (Syd, 1991); *State Reports* (NSW), 31, 1931, memoranda, 50, 1950, memoranda; *Aust Law J*, 23, 1950, pp 500, 526, 33, 1959, p 316, 46, 1972, p 96; *SMH*, 15 Dec 1959, 17 Feb 1972; *Sun-Herald* (Syd), 20 Feb 1972.

J. M. BENNETT

STREETEN, EDGAR ROBERT (1881-1943), Anglican clergyman and musician, was born on 21 November 1881 at Ealing, London, son of George Abbott Streeten, barrister, and his wife Anne Charlotte, née Kuhr. From the age of 10 Edgar was a chorister at King's College, Cambridge. He attended King's College Choir School and Aldenham Grammar School, Elstree, Hertfordshire, where he was awarded an exhibition. Entering King's College (B.A., 1904; M.A. 1910), he read classics and presided (1904) over the King's and 3rd Trinity Athletic Club. On 24 December 1905 he was made deacon and on 24 February 1907 he was ordained priest. In 1905-10 he served as curate at St Faith's Church, Brentford, Middlesex. He sailed for Queensland in 1910 to join St Andrew's Bush Brotherhood in the diocese of Rockhampton and ministered at Winton, Longreach, Emerald, Anakie and Barcaldine.

In 1912 Bishop George Halford [q.v.14] recalled Streeten to Rockhampton to be precentor at St Paul's Cathedral. On 3 November 1914 Streeten married Valentine Bayldon Allen at the cathedral. Returning to England in the following year, he held a curacy at St John the Baptist with All Saints Church, Windsor, Berkshire, before going to France in 1916 as chaplain with the 1st Cavalry Brigade, British Expeditionary Force. While there, he composed a musical setting for Psalm 124: 'If it had not been the Lord who was on our side, now may Israel say'.

Back at Rockhampton in 1919, Streeten rejoined the staff of St Paul's Cathedral. In 1921 he resigned to teach music privately, and was appointed cathedral organist. He retained his licence to officiate as a priest of the diocese, and sat on the diocesan board of missions (1922-25) and the diocesan council (1924-27). A teacher of instrumental music, singing and elocution, he also taught singing-in-unison as an art form quite separate from that of the soloist. By 1932 his students had won more than three hundred first prizes at Queensland eisteddfods; several of his pupils went on to study and perform in London and Europe.

From 1921 Streeten was honorary conductor of the Rockhampton Musical Union choir. By 1928 he had formed the Rockhampton Musical Union orchestra; he conducted it until 1936 when the orchestra was restructured as a separate part of the Musical Union. He was respected by students, choir and orchestra, not only for his dedication to musical accomplishment and his fine voice, but also for his ability to inspire discipline and practice until near perfection was achieved. In the 1920s and 1930s he produced, arranged and conducted Musical Union presentations that included the comic opera *Boccaccio*, the light opera *Les Cloches de Corneville* and a romantic musical play, *The Vagabond King*. His wife Valentine and their young son Edward were talented sopranos. She sang with the Musical Union choir and the family performed as a trio at Rockhampton recitals.

Survived by his wife and their son, Streeten died of a cerebral haemorrhage on 16 September 1943 at Barcaldine and was buried at Gracemere station, the home of the Archer family [qq.v.1]. A stained-glass window dedicated to his memory is in St Paul's Cathedral, Rockhampton.

L. McDonald, *Rockhampton* (Brisb, 1981); P. Wright, *The Music History of Rockhampton* (Rockhampton, Qld, 1990); Church of England, Diocese of Rockhampton Synod, *Procs*, 1920, 1922, 1924, 1927, 1942, 1943; information from Mr P. J. Marwedel, Yeppoon, and Dr T. A. Streeten, Toowoomba, Qld.
　　　　　　　　　　　　　　　　BETTY COSGROVE

STREHLOW, THEODOR GEORGE HENRY (1908-1978), linguist, was born on 6 June 1908 at Hermannsburg, Northern Territory, sixth and youngest child of German-born parents Carl Friedrich Theodor Strehlow [q.v.12], Lutheran missionary, and his wife Friedericke Johanna Henriette, née Keysser. In 1910-11 the family visited Germany where the five elder children were left with relations for formal schooling. Back at Hermannsburg, Theodor made friends with the Western Arrernte children. Their language became his, together with English and German.

Theodor received tuition on the mission, supplemented by his father's strictly administered instruction in Greek, Latin, music and Scripture. During World War I the boy was privy to his parents' anxious discussions about the fate of the mission, which perhaps contributed to his later propensity to locate blame beyond his immediate surroundings. In 1922 the close world of the mission collapsed as Carl succumbed to dropsy. Without ready access to medical attention, he was carried south in an improvised, horse-drawn vehicle via the Finke River to the Oodnadatta railhead. Theodor accompanied his parents and Arrernte helpers on the fateful journey which ended with his father's final torment at Horseshoe Bend.

Frieda took her son to Adelaide. Ted attended Immanuel College until 1927, then studied classics and English literature at the University of Adelaide (B.A. Hons, 1931; M.A., 1938; D.Litt., 1975). He excelled in Greek and Latin, winning the Barr Smith [q.v.6] and Andrew Scott prizes. After transferring to the English honours school, he won the John Howard Clark [q.v.3] prize. In 1931 his mother returned to Germany. With few prospects of employment at the height of the Depression, Strehlow was skilfully guided by his academic mentor, J. A. FitzHerbert, professor of classics. Familiar with Carl Strehlow's publications and aware of Theodor's unique qualifications as an Arrernte-speaking classicist, FitzHerbert trained him in phonetics and encouraged him to apply for an Australian National Research Council grant to study the Arrernte language.

Strehlow returned to Central Australia in March 1932. He began an intensive survey of the Arrernte dialects, travelling by camel with an Aboriginal guide. FitzHerbert recognized that Strehlow's project of 'salvage linguistics' had widened to include Aboriginal 'literature, history and antiquities, religion & philosophy', but continued to encourage his student and advocated an extension of his funding. Strehlow became accepted by Arrernte elders as a worthy recipient of spiritual knowledge. He filled his journals with transcriptions of sacred verses and maps of totemic centres, and began to receive ceremonial objects from ritual leaders who were facing the consequences of dispossession and acculturation.

By the end of 1933 Strehlow had completed a survey of the Northern, Western, Central and Southern Arrernte dialects. Within twelve months he had travelled almost three thousand miles (4800 km), collected more than thirty Arrernte and Loritja myths and a thousand song verses, and deciphered the arcane ceremonial language in which they were sung. FitzHerbert arranged for Strehlow to obtain a junior lecturer's post in the English department during 1934, enabling him to write up his results. The ensuing publications— 'Ankotarinja, An Aranda Myth' (*Oceania*, 1935), *Aranda Phonetics and Grammar* (Sydney, 1944) and *Aranda Traditions* (Melbourne, 1947)—were to establish Strehlow as a scholar for the next twenty-five years. If not the first of their kind, these publications amounted to a pioneering study of Aboriginal language and an incisive analysis of the connection between religious belief and Aboriginal landscape.

In 1935 Strehlow entered the field again, this time with a two-year fellowship from the A.N.R.C., on A. P. Elkin's [q.v.14] recommendation. The fellowship was extended to cover his participation that year in a Federal board of inquiry into the maltreatment of Aborigines in Central Australia. Strehlow returned briefly to Adelaide where, on 21 December 1935 at St Cuthbert's Church of England, Prospect, he married Bertha Gwendoline Alexandra James, a teacher. During their honeymoon, a research trip by camel to Macumba in the Northern Territory in mid-1936, she suffered a miscarriage. Later that year, through Elkin's influence, Strehlow was appointed patrol officer in Central Australia, the first full-time Commonwealth public servant dedicated to Aboriginal affairs. For the next six years he attended to Aboriginal social, political and material needs from the base which he and Bertha established at Jay Creek, west of Alice Springs.

Responding to reports of mistreatment, Strehlow continued to travel widely in Central Australia. Often in opposition to higher-ranking officials, he was responsible for increasing the rations distributed to needy Aboriginal people and the range of recipients. His recommendations and advocacy (in conjunction with his father's successor at Hermannsburg, Pastor F. W. Albrecht) contributed to the gazettal of Aboriginal reserves at Jay Creek and Haasts Bluff. Strehlow recommended that a number of European employers of Aboriginal labour be prosecuted for exploitation and physical abuse; despite his position as deputy-director of native affairs and his appointment as a justice of the peace, neither these nor other recommended reforms were pursued. He intervened in several cases to prevent the removal of 'half-caste' children from their mothers, terming the practice 'child robbery'.

Largely ostracized by White society, Strehlow became, as he put it, 'the most hated man in Central Australia'. He had little time for research, which resulted in additional frustration. FitzHerbert counselled patience: 'it is to be expected that you will gradually acquire authority, like moss or barnacles'. The outbreak of war with Germany placed additional pressure on Strehlow. With his commitment to Aboriginal literature and his own upbringing, he regarded himself as an Australian, but soon had to defend himself against charges of Nazism. On 26 May 1942 he was called up for full-time duty in the Militia; he regarded his abrupt release for military service as a betrayal by his superiors. After performing clerical work in a number of units, he was commissioned lieutenant on 8 February 1945 and posted to the Land Headquarters School of Civil Affairs, Canberra, where he trained servicemen to be colonial administrators.

Following his transfer to the Reserve of Officers on 20 March 1946, Strehlow was appointed research fellow in Australian linguistics and lecturer in English literature at the University of Adelaide. Conscious of the need to strengthen his academic base, he began writing a substantial work on Arrernte 'chants'. In 1949 he took up a two-year postgraduate fellowship at the Australian National University, Canberra, which enabled him to undertake further field-work: he made unique colour films of complete Arrernte ceremonial cycles, together with sound recordings, outstanding colour photographs and meticulously composed genealogies.

As president of the anthropology section at the conference of the Australian and New Zealand Association for the Advancement of Science, held in Perth in 1947, Strehlow had criticized the lack of linguistic training of anthropologists. In response, Elkin advised him to increase his own formal anthropological skills, suggesting that he study at the London School of Economics under Professor (Sir) Raymond Firth, an anthropologist.

Strehlow regarded his time in Britain from mid-1950 to early 1952 as wasted. Baulking at theoretical anthropology, he received little of the recognition he craved. He screened his four best ceremonial films and lectured at sixteen universities and scientific institutions across Europe, but the response was lukewarm until he crossed the English Channel. In Germany he met his elderly mother; she expressed disappointment at his failure to maintain contact with his sister and brothers.

Strehlow returned to Adelaide with a bitter sense of personal and professional alienation, convinced that he alone could interpret his data. The A.N.U.'s determination that he deposit research records and film—produced under its grant—led him to attempt to obtain support for a research department under his sole control. This action soured his long-standing friendship with FitzHerbert. Although Strehlow was appointed (1954) reader in Australian linguistics at the University of Adelaide, tensions developed in his relationship with the university hierarchy. His data-gathering continued unabated, and he became one of the country's most richly funded field-researchers during the 1950s and 1960s, but his publications in this period were mostly non-academic. A foreword to Rex Battarbee's [q.v.13] *Modern Australian Aboriginal Art* (Sydney, 1952), introductions to books on the work of the sculptor William Ricketts, and several published addresses endorsing a community obligation towards Aboriginal people and the value and social relevance of Aboriginal cosmology were all well received by a wider public.

Less popular was Strehlow's advocacy of the innocence of an Arrernte man, Rupert Max Stuart, who had been sentenced to death for brutal murder in 1959. He maintained, on linguistic grounds, that Stuart could not have furnished police with the confession which led to his conviction. His concern with such issues and with the fate of his research and artefact collection were major distractions. None the less, he completed three substantial, contrasting works in this period. Each contained his father's ghost, largely unacknowledged. The first, begun in 1939, was a meticulous revision (Sydney, 1956) of Carl Strehlow's translation of the New Testament into Arrernte. The second was his autobiographical narrative, *Journey to Horseshoe Bend* (Adelaide, 1969), which expressed the anguish of his father's death and his own revelation of the Arrernte landscape's sacred quality, while controversially sheeting home the blame for the tragedy to the Adelaide Lutheran hierarchy. The third was *Songs of Central Australia* (Sydney, 1971), his *magnum opus*. A dense, often bewilderingly literary work, with Greek and Norse mythological analogies, it seamlessly merged his own and his father's research into Arrernte sacred verse and totemic geography. *Songs* received mixed reviews. Subsequently, it has helped to elevate Aboriginal verse as literature, and to establish the Dreaming and the Aboriginal world-view as key concepts in an emerging Australian cultural identity.

During the 1960s the University of Adelaide continued to fund Strehlow's field-trips to Arrernte country. There he collaborated with failing elders to record their totemic ceremonies on film and tape. His poignant journal entries, describing the completion of those final, choreographed performances, increasingly evoked his own approaching nemesis. A lone field-worker, he operated as driver, mechanic and cook, as well as filming, photographing and constructing genealogies of his informants, and documenting the artefacts sold and given to him. His most successful field-trips placed an even greater burden on his abilities to process the information. Appointed to a personal chair at the university in 1970, he retired four years later. In 1978 he was awarded an honorary doctorate of philosophy by the University of Uppsala, Sweden.

Even as he became a more substantial and authoritative figure during the 1950s and 1960s, Strehlow was driven into an oppressive cycle of alienation by personal insecurity and by his growing suspicion of influential academics and policy advisers (such as Elkin, W. E. H. Stanner and H. C. Coombs). In 1973 he resigned from the Australian Institute of Aboriginal Affairs, of which he had been a founding member (1964). The wry sense of humour evident in his early correspondence and journals had left him. His personal life reflected this turmoil. Strehlow's relationship with two colleagues was destroyed when he accused them of theft of intellectual property. Finally, during the mid-1960s, his family life disintegrated. In 1968 he left Bertha and began living with his new secretary and research assistant, Kathleen Stuart, née Anderson, a 36-year-old divorcee. His marriage was dissolved on 6 September 1972. At the office of the principal registrar, Adelaide, on 25 September that year he married Kathleen, who had changed her surname by deed poll to Strehlow two months earlier. Strehlow's closest relationships had always been with those who accepted his views unquestioningly. Kathleen proved a fierce and dogged supporter. Their official correspondence was increasingly barbed with venom and directed at phantom conspiracies.

Strehlow's attempts to establish a viable research base at the university eventually foundered on one main sticking-point: his insistence that Kathleen be accorded full academic status. Unable to gain the university's agreement, he and Kathleen established the Strehlow Research Foundation at their home at Prospect in 1978. By this time the collection comprised 4500 Aboriginal song verses and more than 100 myths (all written in Arrernte and Loritja dialects and languages in his notebooks), 800 ceremonial acts captured on tape and 26 hours of film, maps of several hundred ceremonial and mythical sites, 8000 photographs, 150 detailed genealogies and, most controversially, a collection of 1200 sacred artefacts. Strehlow's public statements defending his proprietary right to pass this research collection and its intellectual property to his new wife breached undertakings made to Arrernte elders that their legacy would be protected according to Aboriginal custom. His sale in 1977 of restricted ceremonial photographs to the German magazine *Stern* led to unexpected syndicated publication in Australia during 1978, which incensed his critics and alienated old Arrernte friends. Strehlow's defence was unconvincing: he continued to assert his own historic relationship with his data and collections, a claim founded upon an incorrect assumption of cultural extinction.

Acutely ill in 1966, Strehlow suffered heart attacks in 1975 and 1976. The portentous rhetoric of his field journals, formerly focused on the final ceremonial acts of Arrernte ritual, turned in on his own dilemma. He died suddenly of hypertensive coronary artery disease on 3 October 1978 in Adelaide and was cremated. His wife and their son survived him, as did the daughter and two sons of his first marriage. The controversy over Strehlow's collection continued unabated. A decade later, negotiations between his widow and the Northern Territory government led to the purchase of most of the collection and the establishment of the Strehlow Research Centre at Alice Springs. Through that initiative, a part of Strehlow's vision for the preservation and use of his record of Arrernte culture was realized.

Aboriginal Hist, 3, no 1, 1979, p 85; *Oceania*, 49, no 3, 1979, p 230; Strehlow papers (Strehlow Research Centre, Alice Springs, NT); Stranks papers (Barr Smith L, Univ Adel); Univ Adel Archives; Anthropology Archives, SA Museum, Adel.

PHILIP JONES

STRETTON, LEONARD EDWARD BISHOP (1893-1967), judge and royal commissioner, was born on 10 October 1893 at Brunswick, Melbourne, fourth of five children of William John Stretton, a teetotal brewery clerk and compulsive gambler from England, and his Victorian-born wife Emma Lydia, née Pye. From the age of 6 he had a rural upbringing at Campbellfield, but the family returned to the northern suburbs when his father won Tattersall's Melbourne Cup sweepstake in 1902. Len was educated at Moreland State School, Thomas Palmer's [q.v.11] University High School, and at the University of Melbourne (LL.B., 1916) where he studied law and edited *Melbourne University Magazine*. He was twice prevented from volunteering for service during World War I because of a perceived heart murmur. At the Presbyterian manse, South Yarra, on 1 March 1919 he married Norah Helen Crawford, a teacher; they were to live in turn at Beaumaris, Hawthorn, Kew and Diamond Creek.

Stretton practised as a solicitor for ten years, signed the Bar roll in 1929 and, at the age of 43, was appointed a county court judge and chairman of general sessions. He was severe in punishing crimes of violence, but otherwise advocated leniency for young first offenders. In 1952 the Victorian cabinet rebuked him for his scathing comments on conditions at an emergency housing camp at Watsonia which, he believed, tended to turn its residents into criminals. The camp was closed soon afterwards. Although Stretton had served as an acting-justice (1951) of the Supreme Court of Victoria, he declined a permanent appointment, preferring to be involved in an impressive range of civil duties. A foundation member (1938) and chairman (1938-39 and 1940-64) of the State's Workers Compensation Board, he drafted the influential Workers' Compensation Act (1946) and the consolidating Act (1951). He was also a judge of the Court of Marine Inquiry and president of the Industrial Appeals Court.

On five occasions Stretton served as a Victorian royal commissioner. He investigated the causes of the devastating bushfires of January 1939 and the fires at Yallourn in February 1944, and inquired into forest grazing (1946), electricity supply (1947) and the bread industry (1949). His literary skills, moral vision and political audacity ensured that his reports would have an impact. Of Yallourn's impoverished civic culture, he thundered in 1944: 'Here indeed the townsman enjoys all that the heart of man may desire—except freedom, fresh air and independence'. He coined a conservation slogan in 1946 when he warned of 'an inseparable trinity—Forest, Soil, and Water'.

In 1939 Stretton's commission had sat within weeks of the bushfires, held hearings near incinerated townships in temperatures of 104°F. (40°C.), and constituted a wide-ranging investigation of the relationship of Australians to the bush. His report described the fires as 'the most disastrous forest calamity the State of Victoria has known' and declared with biblical gravity that they were 'lit by the hand of man'. The report was acknowledged for its literary qualities and anthologized in a collection of Australian nature writing, *Land of Wonder* (Sydney, 1964, edited by A. H. Chisholm [q.v.13]); passages from the report were set as a prescribed text for Victorian senior students of English. Stretton's recommendations officially sanctioned the common bush practice of controlled burning for fuel reduction, and led the government to broaden the responsibilities of the Forests Commission of Victoria and to form (1945) the Country Fire Authority.

In addition to his forthright pronouncements, Stretton was renowned for his wit and poetry. Some called him Victoria's 'judicial bard'. A staunch upholder of the dignity of the law, a fearless investigator and a humane judge, he was, as well, a champion of the underdog, an advocate of bush culture, a 'raconteur of high degree' and a lover of raffish literature. He treasured a set of the works of Charles Dickens [q.v.4] and had a particular liking for C. J. Dennis's [q.v.8] *The Songs of a Sentimental Bloke*, an epithet he might privately have given himself. He and (Sir) Robert Menzies [q.v.15] had become good friends at university, where they both admired Norah Crawford. Despite their political differences, the two men maintained an affectionate, sparring relationship throughout their careers.

In 1956 Stretton was appointed C.M.G. He retired from the bench in August 1964. President (1941-59) of the Victorian Association of Boys' Clubs and an associate of the Prisoners' Aid Society, he also belonged to the National Fitness Council of Victoria. For many years he maintained the daily discipline of a run and punching-bag practice before court. Survived by his wife, their daughter and two of their three sons, he died on 16 May 1967 in East Melbourne and was cremated. His reminiscences were published (1976) in the *La Trobe Library Journal*.

E. E. Hewitt, *Judges Through the Years* (Melb, 1984); K. Anderson, *Fossil in the Sandstone* (Melb, 1986); *Aust Law J*, 38, 30 Sept 1964, p 183; *Aust Bar Gazette*, 1, no 4, Dec 1964, p 22; *Law Inst J*, 41, no 9, Sept 1967, p 360; *Argus*, 15 Apr 1937, 27 Feb, 26 Mar 1952; *Sun News-Pictorial*, 1 Mar 1939, 15 Jan 1953; *Age* (Melb), 18 May 1939, 4 Aug 1964, 17 May 1967; family information.   TOM GRIFFITHS

STRUTT, CECIL WILLIAM (1902-1980), agricultural scientist and public servant, was born on 14 November 1902 at Wadhurst, Sussex, England, son of Alfred William Strutt, artist, and his wife Nellie Maria, née Ketchlee. William Strutt [q.v.6] was his grandfather. Young Bill wanted to be an artist, but was dissuaded by his father. He attended Taunton School, Somerset, where he developed a love of cricket and was later employed as sportsmaster. Winning a scholarship in 1925 to the University of London (B.Sc.Agric., 1928), he studied at the South-Eastern Agricultural College, Wye, Kent; after graduating, he joined the college's staff for a year. At the parish church, Tenterden, on 31 December 1932 he married Catherine Alice Burke.

In 1931 Strutt had become a technical adviser to R. Silcock & Sons Ltd, a firm of animal-fodder manufacturers with which he remained until 1945. During World War II his work was classified as a reserved occupation which excluded him from military service. Joining the Ministry of Agriculture's national agricultural advisory service in 1946, he visited Australia that year and was involved in negotiating the Anglo-Australian meat agreement (1947). He was appointed to the British High Commission, Canberra, in 1948 as agricultural attaché. In 1953 he returned to England.

(Sir) John Crawford, secretary of the Department of Commerce and Agriculture, persuaded Strutt in 1954 to join the Commonwealth Public Service. He held the post of assistant-secretary (1955-66) in the division of agricultural production, Department of Primary Industry. In 1955 he was appointed Commonwealth deputy wool adviser; from 1957 he also chaired the Wool Research Committee and the Wheat Industry Research Council. He resigned in 1966 to manage a United Nations project aimed at improving the cattle and sheep industries in Uruguay.

Back in Canberra in 1968, Strutt was appointed executive-officer of the Australian-Asian Universities Co-operation Scheme and of the Australian Vice-Chancellors' Committee. He also worked for the Australian Farmers' Federation, and was secretary (1973-77) of the scholarship programme run by the Australian Nuffield Farming Scholars' Association. In 1977 he was made a fellow of the Australian Institute of Agricultural Science. Retirement from the public service also allowed him to devote more time to community affairs. A parish councillor (from 1959) of the Church of St John the Baptist, Reid, he played a notable part in saving from demolition the historic schoolhouse in the church grounds and restoring it as a museum (opened 1969). He was a member (1970-80), acting secretary (1975-76) and president (1977-80) of its board of management. His 'tenacity, meticulous methods', 'powers of persuasion' and 'thoughtfulness' inspired all who worked with him.

Strutt continued to love cricket, played golf and enjoyed gardening. A 'wide-shouldered, good-looking' man with a 'crinkly smile', he usually had a pipe clenched firmly between his teeth. He died on 1 May 1980 in Woden Valley Hospital and was buried with Anglican rites in Gungahlin cemetery; his wife and their two daughters survived him.

Canb and District Hist Soc, *Newsletter*, June/July 1980; St John's Church, Canb, *Parish Notes*, 38, no 5, 1980; Wye College Agricola Club, *J*, 11, no 2, 1980/81, p 67; *Canb Times*, 13 Aug 1977; information from Mrs S. McColl, Toronto, Canada.

P. G. F. HENDERSON

STUART, JOHN ANDREW (1940-1979), criminal, was born on 15 September 1940 in Brisbane, fifth child of Queensland-born parents David James Cochrane Stuart (d.1956), invalid pensioner, and his wife Edna Ruby Rita, née Morgan. John left school at the age of 13. In 1955 he was charged with stabbing a youth during a brawl at Fortitude Valley. Over the next ten years he received a number of convictions, in New South Wales and Queensland, for burglary, car theft, dangerous driving and escaping from custody. In 1966 he was found guilty of malicious wounding. Although he was considered to be highly intelligent, he had spent twelve years in detention by 1972, including several periods in mental institutions.

On 8 March 1973 fifteen people died in the fire-bombing of the Whiskey Au Go Go nightclub at Fortitude Valley. Two days later, acting on information from Stuart's elder brother, police arrested Stuart and his alleged accomplice James Finch and charged them with murder. Stuart had paid Finch's air-fare from England and he had arrived ten days before the fire. Both of them maintained their innocence during their trial, which began on 10 September that year. Stuart claimed that, after he had been approached by members of a Sydney-based crime syndicate who wanted him to extort money from managers of Brisbane nightclubs, he tried to warn the police about plans to set fire to the Whiskey Au Go Go. The police alleged that Finch had lit the fire, but that Stuart was the chief instigator, and that he had spread rumours about the Sydney syndicate to intimidate nightclub owners and to avoid blame. Having dismissed his counsel early in the trial, Stuart thrice swallowed pieces of wire: he was absent from court much of the time while recovering from operations in Royal Brisbane Hospital. The two men were convicted, largely on the basis of a typewritten record of a police interview with Finch, unsigned by the suspect. On 22 October they were sentenced to imprisonment for life.

Detained in the maximum security wing of Brisbane (Boggo Road) gaol, Stuart went on a hunger strike, continued to swallow wire, and staged a roof-top protest in 1977, pulling bricks and guttering from the roof to form the words 'innocent—victim of police verbal'. He died of idiopathic myocarditis on 1 January 1979 in Brisbane gaol and was buried with Salvation Army forms in Lutwyche cemetery.

Controversy over the verdict and the cause of Stuart's death continued for a decade. In 1985 an international authority on 'stylometry' (the analysis of speech patterns) testified that it was extremely unlikely that Finch's confession was recorded verbatim and that it had probably been composed by the police. On 22 November 1988 the *Bulletin* published an interview with one of the six officers involved in the case who claimed that Finch's confession had been fabricated. Stuart's mother Edna Watts asserted that, before her son's death, she had received phone calls alleging that prison officials planned to poison Stuart. The Prisoners' Action Group maintained that Stuart had been a paid informer in investigations into police corruption, and that he may have been bashed by guards several days before his death. In 1988 Finch was paroled from prison and deported to England where he admitted that he, Stuart and four others were responsible for the murders. Told that he could be extradited to Brisbane to face further charges, he again proclaimed his innocence.

M. Browne (ed), *Australian Crime* (Syd, 1993); *Jail News*, 3 Feb 1979; *Sunday Mail* (Brisb), 7 Jan 1979; *Telegraph* (Brisb), 24 Feb 1986; *Bulletin*, 23 Feb, 15 and 22 Nov 1988; *Sun* (Brisb), 21 Mar 1988, 10 Jan 1989.

TIM PRENZLER

STUART JONES, REGINALD; *see* JONES

STUCKEY, REGINALD ROBERT (1881-1948), public servant, was born on 25 February 1881 in Adelaide, fifth of nine children of South Australian-born parents Joseph James Stuckey, solicitor and actuary, and his wife Alice, daughter of Charles Mann [q.v.2]. Like his father, Reginald was interested in mathematics. He attended the Collegiate School of St Peter, Adelaide, topped the senior examination in 1896 and won (but did not take up) a scholarship to the University of Adelaide. Choosing to follow a career in insurance, he obtained a post with the Australian Mutual Provident Society in 1897. He studied by correspondence and qualified as an associate (1905) of the Institute of Actuaries, London. On 14 February 1911 at Stow [q.v.2] Memorial Church, Adelaide, he married Jessie Bridgman (d.1942) with Congregational forms.

In 1914 Stuckey left the A.M.P. to become public actuary. Nine years later he was made under-treasurer for South Australia. He chaired the State Bank of South Australia (1926-48) and the State's Public Debt Commission (1926-46), and presided (1927-48) over the South Australian Superannuation Fund Board. Lionel Hill [q.v.9], the premier, appointed him in 1927 to a royal commission which was to inquire into the financial effects of Federation on South Australia, but on 31 August that year (Sir) Richard Butler's [q.v.7] newly elected government revoked the royal commission. A committee, chaired by Stuckey, completed the commission's work in December, drawing attention to the 'disabilities sustained' by the State since 1901 and outlining the reasons that justified a claim for extra assistance from the Federal government. As the Depression deepened, the State's finances deteriorated further. In 1932 Stuckey chaired another committee which prepared a case for South Australia to receive a special grant from the Commonwealth. That year he was appointed C.M.G.

A member (from 1930) of the advisory committee on State finance, Stuckey assisted the Federal government in 1931 with the Australian conversion loan, which dealt with the nation's internal debt. He served (1932-33) on the South Australian committee on debt adjustment in regard to the agricultural and pastoral industries, and was a member (1933-39) of the Farmers' Assistance Board. In February 1946 he retired from the public service. He was a man of ability, integrity and dedication who had helped to guide South Australia through the difficult years of the Depression and World War II.

At St Theodore's Church of England, Rose Park, on 26 October 1946 Stuckey married Mary Hazel Kenney, a 38-year-old civil servant. They lived in the suburb of Highgate. The only club he belonged to was the Commercial Travellers Association of South Australia. Suffering from high blood pressure, he died of retroperitoneal haemorrhage on 5 July 1948 in Adelaide and was buried in North Road cemetery. His wife survived him, as did the son and two daughters of his first marriage. In expressing his condolences, Premier (Sir) Thomas Playford said that Stuckey had achieved a nationwide reputation for his management of the State's accounts and been complimented many times by parliamentary commissions.

Chronicle (Adel), 26 June 1930, 8 July 1948; *SMH*, 3 June 1932, 8 Dec 1933; *Advertiser* (Adel), 6 July 1948.   TONY BOTT

STUMP,   CLAUDE   WITHERINGTON (1891-1971), army officer and professor of histology and embryology, was born on 28 October 1891 at Malvern, Adelaide, second of four children of Alfred Augustus Stump, a Tasmanian-born photographer, and his second wife Rosa Ada, née Potter, who was born in South Australia. After attending Kyre College, Unley, Claude enrolled (1910) at the University of Edinburgh (M.B., Ch.B., 1917; M.D., 1923; D.Sc., 1924). He interrupted his medical studies to serve with a unit of the British Red Cross Society attached to the Serbian army in the Balkan war of 1912-13. After World War I broke out, he was commissioned on 14 December 1914 in the 8th Battalion, King's Own Scottish Borderers, and fought on the Western Front at Loos, France, and on the Somme. At the end of 1916 he returned to Edinburgh to complete his degree. Back in Adelaide, he was appointed captain, Australian Army Medical Corps, Australian Imperial Force, on 4 October 1917 and served in France with the 11th Field Ambulance. He specialized in operating on the most gravely wounded and was to remember this period as the most satisfying of his career. His appointment terminated in Adelaide on 22 November 1919.

From 1920 to 1922 Stump held a Crichton research scholarship in anatomy in Edinburgh. He worked (1920-21) as house physician and then as house surgeon in the Royal Infirmary, and as a demonstrator and lecturer in anatomy at the university. On 30 November 1920 he married Christina Margaret Calder Urquhart (d.1965) at the North British Station Hotel, Edinburgh, with the forms of the Church of Scotland. Late in 1922 he was appointed a Carnegie research fellow. In the following year he was awarded the Gunning Victoria jubilee prize for his M.D. thesis, 'Histogenesis of Bone'.

Sailing for Bangkok with his wife and young family in 1924, Stump took up the chair of anatomy (which was partly funded by the Rockefeller Foundation) at Chulalongkorn University. To gain access to better research facilities, he contacted Arthur Burkitt [q.v.13] at the University of Sydney. Stump was appointed associate-professor in the department of anatomy at that university in 1926. He greatly assisted the development of his discipline and faculty by attracting two major endowments. One, offered in 1928 by the Sydney businessman George Henry Bosch [q.v.7], was used to establish chairs in histology and embryology, medicine, surgery, and bacteriology. Stump was Bosch professor of histology and embryology from 1928 until he retired in 1956. The other endowment, a large grant that stemmed from Stump's and Bosch's visit to the Rockefeller Foundation in New York, enabled the building of a new medical school (now known as the Blackburn [q.v.7] Building) at the university. These benefactions made Stump an important figure in the growth of the university's faculty of medicine.

Despite his early brilliance as a student and young medical scientist, Stump's scholarly output was limited. In the second half of the 1920s he published substantial studies on myelinogenesis, the morphology of a human blastocyst (an embryo in a very early stage) and the embryology of whales. He was also credited with assembling unique collections of material in mammalian and marsupial embryology. His own account, written in the mid-1930s, of the genesis of the new medical school at the university made clear that he still held the view that 'academic medicine requires the whole time service of a staff trained in the scientific method and enjoying (proper) laboratory facilities and equipment'.

In 1930 Stump was elected a fellow of the Royal Society of Edinburgh, an honour warranted by his scholarly record and appointment. Thereafter he was virtually silent as a scholar, his voice stilled perhaps by the exigencies of the Depression and World War II. Nevertheless, the drive which took him from Adelaide to Edinburgh, to brilliance in his studies and early research, and to service in two wars before he reached the age of 30, remained evident. He was a demanding teacher who was strict with his students. He was also a demanding colleague, arguing fiercely for the academic independence of his subject and for the establishment of histology and embryology as a separate department.

Stump enjoyed gardening at his Gordon home and later lived at Palm Beach. He died on 23 December 1971 at Mona Vale and was cremated without a religious service. His daughter and two sons survived him.

J. A. Young et al (eds), *Centenary Book of the University of Sydney Faculty of Medicine* (Syd, 1984); *SMH*, 13 Apr 1926; Stump papers (Univ Syd Archives and Shellshear Museum, Dept Anatomy, Univ Syd).   JONATHAN STONE

STURDEE, SIR VERNON ASHTON HOBART (1890-1966), army officer, was born on 16 April 1890 at Frankston, Victoria, son of Alfred Hobart Sturdee, a medical practitioner from England, and his Victorian-born wife Laura Isabell, née Merrett. Lieutenant (Sir) Doveton Sturdee, Royal Navy (later admiral of the fleet), and (Sir) Charles Merrett [q.v.10] were his uncles. His father was to command the 2nd Field Ambulance, Australian Imperial Force, at Gallipoli.

Educated at Melbourne Church of England Grammar School, Vernon was apprenticed to an engineer at Jaques Bros, Richmond. He spent nine months as a sapper in the Corps of Australian Engineers, Militia, before being commissioned in 1908. On 1 February 1911 he was appointed lieutenant on probation, Royal Australian Engineers, Permanent Military Forces. In the following year he was posted to Brisbane for staff duties in the 1st Military District. At St Luke's Church of England, North Fitzroy, Melbourne, on 4 February 1913 he married Edith Georgina Robins.

In March 1913 Sturdee was posted back to Melbourne. Transferring to the A.I.F. on 25 August 1914, he was promoted captain in October, the month he embarked for Egypt. On 25 April 1915 he landed at Gallipoli as adjutant, 1st Divisional Engineers. Suffering from influenza, he was evacuated in July, but returned in September as a major, commanding the 5th Field Company, 2nd Divisional Engineers. For the next three months he controlled the engineering and mining work at Steele's, Quinn's and Courtney's posts. From January 1916 he supervised the building of huts at Tel el Kebir camp, Egypt. After the 5th Division was raised, his field company was transferred to that formation and renumbered the 8th. In March he took charge of the construction of defences at Ferry Post and showed 'marked ability'.

Sent to France in June 1916, Sturdee was commended for the 'skill and energy' with which he prepared for major operations in July in the Cordonnerie sector, near Armentières. He acted as commander, Royal Engineers, Franks Force, in September-October, and led a party which repaired the road between Albert and Montauban in November. For his work in 1915-16 he was awarded the Distinguished Service Order. On 13 February 1917 he was promoted temporary lieutenant colonel and given command of the 4th Pioneer Battalion. Over the next nine months the unit maintained roads, constructed camps, laid cables and dug communication trenches.

In November 1917 Sturdee was appointed commander, Royal Australian Engineers, 5th Division. In what was an exceptional case for an officer from the dominions, he was seconded in March 1918 to British General Headquarters, France, as a general staff officer, 2nd grade. The secondment gave him invaluable experience and an insight into the conduct of large-scale operations. Returning to the 5th Division in October, he sailed for Australia next month and disembarked in Sydney in January 1919. He was appointed O.B.E. (1919) and twice mentioned in dispatches for his service in World War I.

After Sturdee's A.I.F. appointment terminated on 14 March, he carried out staff duties in Melbourne. In 1922-23 he completed the course at the Staff College, Quetta, India. A year as instructor in engineering and surveying at the Royal Military College, Duntroon, Federal Capital Territory, was followed by a term (from 1925) on the staff of the 4th Division. Sent to London in May 1929, he served on exchange at the War Office with the Directorate of Military Operations and Intelligence, attended the Imperial Defence College in 1931 and then held the post of military representative at the Australian High Commission.

Home once more in February 1933, Sturdee was appointed director of military operations and intelligence at Army Headquarters, Melbourne. In May 1935 he was given the added duties of assistant-secretary (military) to the Council of Defence. Two months later he was promoted brevet colonel (substantive July 1937). He was primarily concerned with the operational aspects of plans to mobilize forces to defend Australia and to raise other formations to serve overseas. In March 1938 he became the inaugural director of staff duties. He was appointed C.B.E. in 1939. At the request of the Australian government a British officer, Lieutenant General E. K. Squires [q.v.12], reviewed the Australian Military Forces in 1938-39. Sturdee supported his proposals for reform.

Following the outbreak of World War II, Squires (then chief of the General Staff) promoted Sturdee temporary lieutenant general in September 1939 and appointed him head of the new Eastern Command, Sydney, from 13 October. Next month Sturdee was also given the duties of commander, 2nd Military District. He took charge of raising, accommodating, training and equipping A.I.F. units in New South Wales at the same time as he prepared local defences. On 1 July 1940 he readily accepted demotion to major general on his appointment as commander of the 8th Division. His pleasure in having been given an operational command was to be brief. Squires had died in March and his successor as C.G.S., Sir Brudenell White [q.v.12], was killed in an aeroplane crash on 13 August. Seventeen days later Sturdee was promoted lieutenant general and appointed C.G.S., first military member of the Military Board and head of the Australian Section of the Imperial General Staff.

A 'gifted officer', Sturdee was well qualified by education and experience for his role as principal military adviser to the government. He oversaw the expansion of the A.I.F. and the Militia, encouraged the local production of munitions, formulated plans to meet a southward thrust by the Japanese, developed coastal and anti-aircraft defences, and initiated a vast works programme. Despite his efforts, Australia remained relatively unprepared, even vulnerable, when Japan entered the war in December 1941. Sturdee found himself obliged to deploy inadequate forces to outposts north of Australia, only to see them lost in futile and costly operations. None the less, he correctly advocated that Port Moresby be held as the base for a counter-attack in Papua and New Guinea.

In the 1920s and 1930s Sturdee had questioned the wisdom of relying on the British base in Singapore for Australia's security. On 15 February 1942, the day Singapore fell, he submitted a paper that dealt with the future employment of the A.I.F. Observing that, in the war against Japan, 'we have violated the principle of the concentration of forces in our efforts to hold numerous small localities', he concluded that Australia was the only suitable strategic base where the Allies could build up their strength and take the offensive against the Japanese. The immediate problem was to protect Australia from invasion. To that end, the 7th Division—which was *en route* to the Far East—and the remainder of the A.I.F. in the Middle East should be brought home. He threatened to resign if the government rejected his advice, but Prime Minister Curtin [q.v.13] agreed with him. While Curtin took on (Sir) Winston Churchill and Franklin D. Roosevelt to prevent the 7th Division from being sent to Burma, Sturdee firmly maintained his position against the views of the chiefs of staff in London and Washington.

The appointments, in March and April 1942, of Sir Thomas Blamey [q.v.13] as commander-in-chief, Australian Military Forces, and General Douglas MacArthur [q.v.15] as supreme commander, South-West Pacific Area, diminished the importance of the office of C.G.S. Recognizing that all major decisions affecting the conduct of the war would thereafter be made in the United States of America, Curtin and Blamey sought a senior and experienced officer to head the Australian Military Mission to Washington. They chose Sturdee. He took up the post in September, having extracted a promise from Blamey that, after one year, he would return to an operational command. In Washington, he forcefully brought Australia's requirements to the attention of the Combined Chiefs of Staff and established the right of direct access to General George Marshall, chief of the U.S. Army. Sturdee was appointed C.B. in 1943.

Blamey honoured his promise, albeit six months late, and in March 1944 Sturdee took command of the First Australian Army. From his headquarters at Lae, New Guinea, he directed the operations of 110 000 personnel engaged in fighting the Japanese between the Solomon Islands in the east and the border with the Netherlands New Guinea in the west. Those who served under him found him to be 'a wise and tolerant commander who gave clear orders' and left his subordinates 'to get on with the job whilst he did his utmost to see that they were adequately supported'. At a ceremony on board H.M.S. *Glory* at Rabaul, New Britain, on 6 September 1945 he accepted the surrender of Japanese forces in his area. Blamey recommended him for a knighthood, and he was mentioned in dispatches for his services in the South-West Pacific Area.

On 1 December 1945 Sturdee was appointed acting commander-in-chief, Australian Military Forces, based in Melbourne. Four months later he resumed the duties of C.G.S., first military member of the Military Board and chief of the Australian Section of the

Imperial General Staff. He had to oversee the repatriation and demobilization of the wartime army, and to organize the Australian contingent for service with the British Commonwealth Occupation Force, Japan; he was also responsible for the establishment of the Australian Regular Army and of the reconstituted Citizen Military Forces. To meet future requirements of the armed services, he strongly supported efforts to retain the industrial capacity that Australia had developed during the war.

Sir Sydney Rowell [q.v.] described Sturdee as 'a kindly, humble and simple man who carried out his work with the minimum of fuss'. Sturdee's sheer professionalism earned him the trust of politicians of all parties. His steadfastness in the anxious months that followed Japan's entry into the war had won him widespread admiration, and he was described as 'the rock on which the army, and indeed the government rested during the weeks of panic in early 1942'. His resolute insistence that the A.I.F. divisions intended for operations in the Far East should return to Australia helped to ensure that troops were available to halt the Japanese advance in Papua. On 17 April 1950 he was placed on the Retired List. In 1951 he was appointed K.B.E. He burnt his private papers, commenting, 'I have done the job. It is over'.

Sir Vernon was 5 ft 10½ ins (179 cm) tall and slimly built. Uninterested in sport, he liked pottering about his garden and making things in his well-equipped workshop. In retirement, he continued to live at Kooyong, Melbourne. He was a director of Standard Telephones & Cables Pty Ltd and honorary colonel (1951-56) of the Royal Corps of Australian Electrical and Mechanical Engineers. Survived by his wife, their daughter and one of their two sons, he died on 25 May 1966 at the Repatriation General Hospital, Heidelberg; he was accorded a full military funeral and was cremated. Murray Griffin's portrait of Sturdee is held by the family.

L. Wigmore, *The Japanese Thrust* (Canb, 1957); S. F. Rowell, *Full Circle* (Melb, 1974); D. M. Horner, *Crisis of Command* (Canb, 1978); D. M. Horner (ed), *The Commanders* (Syd, 1984); *Defence Force J*, no 41, July/Aug 1983, no 81, Mar/Apr 1990; information from Mrs M. Buckley, Toorak, Melb.

JAMES WOOD

SUGERMAN, SIR BERNARD (1904-1976), judge, was born on 5 July 1904 at Rockdale, Sydney, son of Solomon Ruben Sugerman (d.1922), a commercial traveller from Scotland, and his native-born wife Florrie, née Green (d.1905). Solomon remarried in 1907. Bernie (as his name was registered and as he was known to his friends throughout life)

excelled at Sydney Boys' High School, gaining an exhibition to the University of Sydney (LL.B., 1925); he graduated with first-class honours and shared the university medal in law with L. J. Pilkington. He was admitted to the Bar on 12 March 1926 and set up practice in Chancery Chambers with his friends E. D. Roper and (Sir) Alan Taylor [qq.v.]. Although Sugerman had a retiring nature and lacked gifts of advocacy, he managed 'to survive those early difficult years'. At the Great Synagogue, Sydney, on 4 January 1928 he married Sarah Rosenblum, a schoolteacher from South Africa.

Editorial work and writing augmented Sugerman's earnings and helped him to establish a reputation for erudition. He lectured (1926-43) on contracts, mercantile law and torts at the university. In addition, he founded and was first editor (1927-46) of the *Australian Law Journal*; he was also editor in chief (1934-39) of the *Australian Digest*, an invaluable source of reference for the published decisions of the courts. From 1942 to 1946 he edited the *Commonwealth Law Reports*. He was a council-member (1939-43) of the New South Wales Bar Association and deputy-president (1941-43) of the Solicitors Admission Board.

Sugerman gradually acquired a sound practice. In October 1943 he was appointed K.C. He began to appear before the High Court of Australia in important appeals in constitutional cases. On 15 April 1946 he was appointed to the bench of the Commonwealth Court of Conciliation and Arbitration to hear the application by fifty-three trade unions for a standard working week of forty hours. Following a protracted hearing, he was one of the three judges who unanimously upheld the unions' claim.

Resigning from the arbitration court, Sugerman was elevated to the Supreme Court of New South Wales on 10 September 1947. He presided over the Land and Valuation Court from that year until 1961. Much of the litigation related to resumption of property by the Crown and issues of compensation. Claims resulting from untested town and country planning schemes often proved difficult for the court to resolve. In disposing of numerous matters arising under the various provisions of the Crown Lands Acts, Sugerman took into account the public interest as well as the demands of justice.

Sugerman sat mainly in the Equity jurisdiction. Later he became a more regular member of the Full Court and of the Court of Appeal. He was objective, courteous and attentive, and his judgements clarified legal principles relevant to the case. In 1960 he sat on the Full Court that dismissed an application for an injunction sought by (Sir) Hector Clayton [q.v.13] to prevent the government proceeding with an enabling bill to hold a referendum on the abolition of the Legislative Council. That he was not appointed first president of the new Court of Appeal in 1965 caused him pain and displeasure, but he became its second president on 22 January 1970, the year in which he was knighted. He was twice acting chief justice between 1971 and 1972, and administrator of the State, briefly, in 1970. Ill health obliged him to retire on 29 September 1972.

Within the Sydney Jewish community, Sugerman was involved with the Australian Friends of the Israel Philharmonic Orchestra, the Friends of the Hebrew University of Jerusalem, and the Australian Jewish Historical Society. A Freemason, he was a life-governor (1962) of the Benevolent Society of New South Wales and president (1969-70) of the Australian Academy of Forensic Sciences. He belonged to the Australian Elizabethan Theatre Trust, the Kabeiroi dining club of the University of Sydney, the University Club and the Selden Society, London. In June 1976 the University of Sydney conferred on him the degree of doctor of laws. Sir Bernard died on 3 November that year at Bellevue Hill and was buried in Rookwood cemetery; his wife and their two sons survived him. Sugerman's judgements reflected his scholarship and a wisdom broadened by his wide jurisprudential approach to the law and society.

Aust Law J, 20, 1946, p 16, 46, 1972, p 481, 50, 1976, p 613; *NSW Reports*, 1960, p 572; Aust Jewish Hist Soc, *J*, 8, 1977, p 143, *and* M. Forbes, 'The Most Distinguished Life of Sir Bernard Sugerman', 14, 1999, p 614; *SMH*, 15 Apr 1925, 15 Oct 1943, 31 Oct 1946, 9, 11 Sept 1947, 28 Dec 1961, 13 June 1970, 27 Aug 1971, 5 Nov 1976; *Aust Jewish Times*, 11 Nov 1976; Sugerman papers (ML). M. Z. FORBES

SULLIVAN, CORNELIUS; *see* COLLEANO

SULLIVAN, JEREMIAH (1877-1960), Jesuit priest and philosopher, was born on 31 December 1877 at Preston, Melbourne, tenth of fourteen children of Irish-born parents Eugene Sullivan, farmer, and his wife Mary, née Doran. Jeremiah attended the convent school at Heidelberg and St Patrick's College, Melbourne. He entered the Society of Jesus on 8 September 1894 at Loyola, Greenwich, Sydney, and was a novice under Fr Aloysius Sturzo. After studying literature and classics, he taught (1899-1905) at St Ignatius' College, Riverview, where he was prefect of discipline, debating and rowing.

In 1905 Sullivan sailed via Ireland to England to read philosophy (1905-08) at Stonyhurst College, Lancashire. He proceeded to theology, first at Milltown Park, Dublin (1908-

09), then at Innsbruck, Austria (1909-11)—where he was ordained priest on 26 July 1911 —and finally at Posillipo, near Naples, Italy. 'Spot' (as he was nicknamed) was back in Ireland, at Tullabeg College, for his tertianship (1912-13). Returning to Sydney and Riverview, he was prefect of studies (from 1913). In 1917-23 he was rector of Xavier College, Melbourne, where he was also prefect of studies (from 1919). During this period the college acquired Burke Hall in Studley Park Road, Kew.

In 1923 Sullivan became the first native-born superior of the Jesuits' 'Irish Mission' in Australia. He visited Rome and Ireland several times. As a superior, he consistently showed good judgement; he was mild and generous, but could be firm when necessary. The last superior before Australia was raised to the rank of a Jesuit vice-province at Easter 1931, Sullivan was better liked by his men than either his predecessor Fr William Lockington or his successor Fr John Fahy. He again spent some months at Xavier, as headmaster in 1931, and was the sole Catholic member of the fledgling Headmasters' Conference of Australia, which was founded that year. In 1931-34 he served as superior at the parish of Hawthorn. From 1935 to 1946 he lived at the regional seminary, Corpus Christi Ecclesiastical College, Werribee, as administrator, consultor, and professor of pastoral theology and philosophy. His students regarded him as a genuinely humane Australian priest. While rector (1946-52) of Loyola College, Watsonia, he continued to teach and became a father-figure to the many young men in training.

A handsome and striking-looking man in his prime, with a stately walk and a sonorous voice, Sullivan was all his life a prodigious reader. He was hampered from early manhood by indifferent health. His great power and breadth of mind, his joy in work and his capacity for doing almost anything well, drove him in his earlier years to attempt too much and do too many things. Spot was never narrow or petty in any of his actions, but kind, understanding and sincere. His peers and subjects respected him as a good leader. He was very reserved, a gentleman in every sense of the word, and deeply spiritual. Sullivan died on 17 February 1960 at St Vincent's Hospital, Fitzroy, and was buried in Boroondara cemetery.

D. Strong, *The Australian Dictionary of Jesuit Biography, 1848-1998* (Syd, 1999); Society of Jesus Archives, Hawthorn, Melb. J. EDDY

SULLIVAN, MICHAEL JOSEPH (1894-1974), bridge player, publicist and administrator, was born on 9 August 1894 at Christmas

Creek, near Beaudesert, Queensland, elder son of Irish-born parents Martin Sullivan (d.1904), farmer, and his wife Mary, née Smith. Educated at Christmas Creek State School and St Joseph's College, Nudgee, Brisbane, Mick topped the senior commercial class in 1908 and gained first place in the Queensland shorthand examination. He then worked on the family farm. At St Joseph's Catholic Church, Christmas Creek, on 25 June 1919 he married Catherine Honora Cahill. In 1922 the farm was sold. He opened a furniture and sports store at Southport in partnership with his brother and became president (1924) of the local chamber of commerce. An able administrator, he helped to found the United South Coast Rugby League competition and the district tennis association.

Sullivan's wife died in 1930, leaving him with four children to raise. His business failed during the Depression and he moved to Brisbane. Unable to find permanent employment, he took a string of odd jobs. To sustain his spirit, he began to play auction bridge, and then contract bridge. In 1932 he and W. F. R. Boyce formed the Brisbane Bridge Club. A strong player, Sullivan won many State and national championships, including the Australia and New Zealand Olympiad (1937 and 1939) and—with Harold Hiley—the Australian open pairs championship (1943, 1950 and 1956). His articles in Brisbane and provincial newspapers, and his weekly radio programme with Boyce in 1941, helped to promote the game at the local level, and to provide him with a small income. He also ran a café in Brisbane for some years.

Tournament director of the Queensland Bridge Association in 1938-52, Sullivan aimed to bring Australia into international competition. Although 'world championships' were occasionally held, participation was confined to a few select countries. Sullivan was convinced that Australian players could compete at international level. His articles in the American *Bridge World*, the British *Bridge Magazine* and the *European Bridge Review* urged the establishment of a genuinely international bridge organization and a genuinely open world championship. To demonstrate the level of skill of Australian players he organized a world par contest in 1951 in conjunction with the fiftieth anniversary of Australian Federation. Prepared in advance with particular problems to be solved, hands were sent to venues in Australia and overseas to be played simultaneously. The standard of hands came as a revelation to foreign contestants, though typical of those used locally. Australian players won first, second and fourth places.

In 1958 Sullivan represented the Australian Bridge Council at a meeting in Oslo that led to the formation of the World Bridge Federation. Appointed to its inaugural council, he chaired the constitution committee. In 1960 he helped to set up, and played in, the international bridge Olympiad at Turin, Italy. He was involved in planning the W.B.F. par championships in 1961 and 1963, and was joint-formulator (1963) of the rules of par point contract bridge. In July 1974 he was made an honorary life member of the Australian Bridge Federation. Survived by his son and two of his three daughters, he died on 29 December 1974 at Beaudesert and was buried in Christmas Creek cemetery.

Golden Jubilee of St Joseph's College, Nudgee, 1891-1941 (Brisb, 1941); C. Chua, *The History of Australian Bridge 1930-1990* (Canb, 1993); C. Masters (ed), *Mind Games* (Brisb, 1999); *Aust Bridge*, 6, no 1, Feb 1975, p 2; *Northern Star* (Lismore, NSW), 1 May 1939; information from Mrs M. Brown, Beaudesert, Qld, and Dr J. Sullivan, Indooroopilly, Brisb.   CATHY CHUA

SUMMERVILLE, SIR WILLIAM ALAN THOMPSON (1904-1980), agricultural scientist and public servant, was born on 6 February 1904 at Ipswich, Queensland, seventh of eight children of Ipswich-born parents William Henry Summerville, solicitor, and his wife Annie Agnes, née Herbert. Alan enjoyed cricket at Ipswich Grammar School (1917-21) and was a determined, short, compact figure on the Rugby field. In 1922 he was appointed a 'learner in entomology' under Henry Tryon [q.v.12] in the Department of Agriculture and Stock, Brisbane. He studied part time at the University of Queensland (B.Sc., 1929; M.Sc., 1933; D.Sc., 1944).

In 1929 Summerville was promoted to assistant-entomologist and posted to Nambour to work on horticultural crops. At the Methodist Church, Sherwood, on 3 September 1930 he married Ethel May Barker. His early research, reported in the *Queensland Agricultural Journal* (1934), was on the scale insects of citrus and the spiny and bronze bugs of orange-trees. He found that oil sprays were a more effective means of control than the growers' hazardous method of fumigating with cyanide. As senior research officer from 1937, he investigated the physiology of the banana plant. He found that the area of leaves available to light interception was a controlling factor in crop growth and inflorescence development. His work earned him his doctorate.

Transferred to Brisbane in 1942 to assist the wartime organization of vegetable production, Summerville was made director of horticulture in 1945. Two years later he was appointed director of plant industry: his division embraced agriculture, horticulture, agricultural chemistry, entomology, plant pathology and botany. He advanced applied research in horticulture and pastures, and built up soil conservation teams. In 1957 he was elected president of the Australian Institute of Agricultural Science. He became under-secretary of the department in 1958 and its director-general in 1959.

A decisive, quick-witted and articulate administrator, Summerville helped to transform the role of the department from one of regulation to one of providing landholders with effective advice based on sound research. The number of staff increased. Several laboratories and research stations were established to deal with the needs of specific industries. New branches broadened the scope of the department's work in plant, soil and animal science, in economics and in agricultural education.

Summerville's special contribution lay in his staffing policies. Recruiting men and women from interstate and from British Commonwealth countries, he encouraged them to gain further education and experience overseas, and provided them with opportunities for promotion. His tough and incisive manner concealed a warm-hearted and sensitive concern for individuals' difficulties. He once arranged for a plant-breeder working at Biloela to attend an extension course in Brisbane where his wife was in hospital. Afterwards, the scientist suggested he should return to Biloela to plant his experimental crop. Summerville responded: 'Marriott, there are more important things in life than bloody cotton!' On another occasion a scientist presented with some trepidation his proposed overseas itinerary; Summerville insisted that he spend more time in London for his cultural enrichment.

From 1962 Summerville oversaw the development of 360 holdings in Central Queensland on brigalow scrub land. He had good rapport with landholders. When criticized by a farmer over the operation of a pasture-improvement scheme, he persuaded the farmer to serve on its executive-committee. Summerville forged strong links with other government departments and agencies, such as the Irrigation and Water Supply Commission, and gave robust, independent advice to his ministers. He also served (1956-64) on the senate of the University of Queensland, which granted him an honorary LL.D. in 1963.

As agent-general in London in 1964-70, Summerville proved a buoyant, convivial advocate of his State's interests. In 1968 he was knighted. Back in Queensland, he chaired (1970-73) the Sugar Board. Sir Alan possessed a fine sense of humour, laughed a great deal, and was passionate in the honesty of his dealings with people and in his enthusiasm for the vocation of agricultural science. He had wide cultural and sporting interests, and was fond

of early Australian poetry. Survived by his wife and their two daughters, he died on 20 December 1980 at Auchenflower and was cremated with Anglican rites.

P. J. Skerman et al, *Guiding Queensland Agriculture, 1887-1987* (Brisb, 1988); P. J. Skerman, *The First 100 Years* (Brisb, 1998); *J of the Aust Inst of Agr Science*, 47, 1981, p 88; information from Sir Theodor Bray, St Lucia, Ms P. Ganly, Bulimba, Ms I. Harrison, Chermside, Mr T. A. Laidlaw and Dr J. K. Leslie, Taringa, Ms A. Summerville, Indooroopilly, Brisb, Mr K. C. Leverington, Beechmont, Ms S. Welch, Stafford, Qld, and the late Mr S. Marriott.

L. R. HUMPHREYS

SUNDERLAND, HARRY (1889-1964), football administrator and journalist, was born on 23 November 1889 at Gympie, Queensland, eldest of three children of Joseph Sunderland, an English-born engine driver, and his wife Sarah, née Lidgard, who came from New South Wales. Educated at two state schools at Toowoomba, Harry became a journalist on the *Toowoomba Chronicle*. On 6 June 1910 he married 17-year-old Annie Smith with the forms of the Joyful News Mission in her parents' home at Kelvin Grove, Brisbane.

In 1913-22 Sunderland was secretary of the Queensland Rugby League. For the first few years of his appointment he stood as guarantor for the league's financial dealings and helped to make the Q.R.L. financially viable. The league's action in continuing its competition throughout World War I struck a number of people as being unpatriotic. Sunderland countered the ensuing criticism by donating proceeds of football carnivals to the Queensland Patriotic Fund and by arranging games between representative sides and Brisbane-based servicemen. Many Rugby Union players and supporters, and sometimes entire clubs, transferred their allegiance to Rugby League.

Sunderland accompanied the Australian Kangaroo tour of England for the Sydney *Sun* in 1921-22. His journalistic activities and his position as secretary of the Q.R.L. gave rise to accusations of a conflict of interest. In 1918 the Brisbane *Truth* had revealed that Sunderland received as secretary of the league 'in the vicinity of £300. This, for about twelve weeks' work, pans out at £25 per week'. His salary, when added to his earnings from articles written for the Brisbane *Daily Standard* and *Daily Mail*, and his income from his part-ownership of a sports magazine, *Pink-un*, antagonized those involved in what was predominantly a working-class sport. Officials and players resented his administrative style and called him the 'little dictator' (he was a short man with a pot-belly). In 1922 the discontent led to a players' strike. Brisbane players broke away from the Q.R.L. to form the Brisbane Rugby League.

That year Sunderland moved to Melbourne to work on the *Sun News-Pictorial*. He tried, unsuccessfully, to promote Rugby League in Victoria. Persuaded to return to the Q.R.L. in 1925, he was its secretary (1925-38), a Queensland selector and coach, and a member (1925-39) of the Australian Rugby League Board of Control. He managed the Kangaroo teams on their tours of England in 1929-30, 1933-34 and 1937-38, and did much to establish the game in France, particularly through a demonstration match between Australia and England, held in Paris in 1933. An avid follower of sport in general, he attended the Olympic Games (1932) at Los Angeles and several baseball matches in the United States of America. He was sometime secretary of the Queensland Cricket Association, the Queensland Amateur Boxing Association and the Queensland Wrestling Union.

Following a dispute with the Australian Board of Control during the 1937-38 Kangaroo tour, Sunderland left for England in 1939 to become manager of the Wigan Rugby League Football Club. He covered Rugby League for the northern edition of the London *Daily Mail* and worked as a broadcaster. Survived by his wife and one of their three sons, he died on 15 January 1964 at Chorlton upon Medlock, Manchester. The Sunderland medal, awarded to the best Australian player in each home Rugby League series against England, was named (1964) after him. His son (Sir) Sydney Sunderland was dean (1953-71) of the faculty of medicine, University of Melbourne.

J. Pollard (ed), *Rugby League the Australian Way* (Syd, 1981); *Truth* (Brisb), 6 Oct 1918; *Telegraph* (Syd), 7 June 1929; *SMH*, 30 May 1938; E. J. Scott, Rugby League in Brisbane: From the Genesis to the Formation of the Brisbane Rugby League (M.Qual. thesis, Human Movement Studies, Univ Qld, 1989); Scott papers (held by author, Rainworth, Brisb); information from the late Messrs M. and P. Scott.

EDMOND SCOTT

SUNNERS, ERNEST FRANCIS EDWARD (1884-1948), chairman of the Queensland Meat Industry Board, was born on 8 December 1884 at East Bundaberg, Queensland, third of six children of Edward James Sunners, an engineer from New South Wales, and his English-born wife Mary Ann, née Shaw. Educated at state schools and at Brisbane Grammar School, Ernest was employed as an accountant in North Queensland. In 1913 he took up a post in the Townsville office of the Australian Meat Export Co. Ltd (later Swift Australian Co. Ltd). At St Andrew's Church of England, Lutwyche, Brisbane, on

1 December 1914 he married Mary Sutherland. He worked for some time in the offices of Swift & Co. at Chicago, Illinois, and St Paul, Minnesota, United States of America. Returning to Brisbane about 1925, he became treasurer, secretary and a director of Swift's Australian branch, and manager of its meatworks at Cannon Hill. He served (1927 28) as a member of a commission on the Queensland beef cattle industry which recommended the establishment of public abattoirs in Brisbane.

In 1931 the Queensland government bought Swift's Cannon Hill facilities and converted them to a public abattoir. That year Sunners was appointed founding chairman of the Queensland Meat Industry Board (set up to administer the meatworks and sale-yards) and general manager of the abattoir. He was to hold both posts until his death. Australian processors struggled to find a means of exporting chilled (as distinct from frozen) meat to European markets. During the early 1930s the Q.M.I.B. co-operated with the Council for Scientific and Industrial Research in its experiments on the preparation and storage of chilled beef. In 1934, in conjunction with the C.S.I.R., Sunners helped to organize the first shipment of chilled beef from Brisbane in the *Idomeneus*.

A founding member (1936-46) of the Australian Meat Board, Sunners assisted in regulating the flow of meat to overseas markets and in exercising control over the vessels in which it was shipped. He sat on the A.M.B.'s executive-committee, beef committee and wartime meat supplies technical committee, and on the chilled beef shipping sub-committee. Deputy-controller of meat supplies in Queensland (1943-46), he also served on Commonwealth and State meat canning committees. H. H. Collins [q.v.13], Queensland's secretary for agriculture and stock, described him as 'one of the most competent authorities in Australia on the meat industry' and praised him for carrying out the Meat Board's operation 'with distinction'.

In 1945 Sunners chaired a royal commission which inquired into the construction of public abattoirs in towns outside Brisbane. At the University of Queensland, he served on the boards of the faculties of veterinary science (1936-47) and commerce (1937-47), and on the appointments board (1937-45). He enjoyed playing golf and belonged to the Royal Queensland Golf Club. Survived by his wife, and their son and daughter, he died of a coronary occlusion on 26 May 1948 at Woolloongabba and was cremated. The government accepted the recommendation of his commission and amended legislation in 1949 to allow for the establishment of public abattoirs at regional centres, using Cannon Hill as a model.

Queensland and Queenslanders (Brisb, 1936); *PD* (Qld), 1948-49, p 2084; *Brisb Courier*, 27 May 1948.

DAWN MAY

SUTCLIFFE, GEORGE GRIBBON (1895-1964), public servant, was born on 2 February 1895 at Coburg, Melbourne, second son of John Sutcliffe, a Victorian-born prison warder, and his wife Mary, née Perryman, who came from England. Educated at state schools, George joined the Commonwealth Public Service in December 1909 and was employed as a telegraph messenger with the Postmaster-General's Department, Ballarat. On 3 August 1915 he enlisted in the Australian Imperial Force. He served (from 1916) with the Australian Army Postal Corps in England and France, and rose to company sergeant major. Discharged from the A.I.F. in Melbourne on 10 October 1919, he returned to the P.M.G. and worked in its accounts branch. At the Methodist Church, Elsternwick, on 20 November 1920 he married Beatrice Isobel Fricker; their only child, a daughter (b.1940), was to die in 1962.

A quietly ambitious man, Sutcliffe studied part time at the University of Melbourne (B.Com., 1931). He was general president (1938-43) and a life member (1943) of the Commonwealth Public Service Clerical Association. In 1946 he was promoted to assistant-secretary in the Department of Supply and Shipping. After World War II he represented the Commonwealth on the Stevedoring Industry Commission, and served on the Australian Shipping and the Australian Shipbuilding boards. He briefly held the position of permanent head of the Department of Shipping and Fuel before he was appointed commissioner of the Commonwealth Public Service Board on 23 November 1948. Moving with his family to Canberra, he became the 'human face' of the board in what was essentially a public-service town.

Sutcliffe settled easily into the role of community leader. A 'splendid public speaker with a delicate sense of humour', he was foundation president (1953) and first freeman (1957) of Canberra Rostrum Club No.1, and a life member (1959) of the Australian Capital Territory dais of Australian Rostrum. He was also a warden (1955-61) of the Anglican Church of St John the Baptist, Reid, a councillor (1961-64) of the Diocese of Canberra and Goulburn, and president (1951-54) of the Royal Canberra Golf Club. In 1956 he was appointed C.B.E.

Representing the public service board, Sutcliffe had attended the inaugural meeting of the A.C.T. Good Neighbour Council in March 1950. The government-supported Good Neighbour movement co-ordinated the efforts of voluntary organizations and individuals in 'extending the hand of friendship' to postwar immigrants. It offered practical help to new settlers and encouraged their assimilation. Sutcliffe chaired the A.C.T. council in 1951-54. His contacts, organizational skill, and calm demeanour proved invaluable in establishing the council and reconciling the competing interests of its constituents. On his retirement from the public service in 1960, he was appointed Commonwealth co-ordinator of Good Neighbour councils. He secured government and community support for the movement at a time when the speed and scale of immigration stimulated debate over integration and the nature of Australian citizenship.

Above average height, with an open face and receding hair, Sutcliffe was a sincere, unassuming, conservative and widely respected man. He died of a coronary occlusion on 10 December 1964 at Goulburn, New South Wales, and was buried in Canberra cemetery. His wife survived him.

C. I. Fleming, *A History of the Good Neighbour Council of the Australian Capital Territory Inc.* (Canb, 1975); *Royal Canberra Golf Club Jubilee History, 1926-1976* (Canb, 1977); R. Ayrton and T. Trebilco, *History of A.C.T. Rostrum* (Canb, 1978); A. H. Body, *Firm Still You Stand* (Canb, 1986); *Canb Viewpoint*, Feb 1965; *Canb Times*, 15 Dec 1964; ACT Good Neighbour Council, series AA1980/254 (NAA, Canb); J. T. Massey papers (NL).　　HILARY KENT

SUTHERLAND, KEITH LEONARD (1916-1980), industrial chemist, was born on 17 January 1916 at North Carlton, Melbourne, son of Victorian-born parents Alexander Philip Sutherland, a clerk in the public service, and his wife Irene Bertha, née Barker. Educated at Melbourne High School and the University of Melbourne (B.Sc., 1937; M.Sc., 1941; D.Sc., 1948), Keith joined (Sir) Ian Wark's research group in the chemistry department. Helped by sponsorship from mining companies, he carried out research into mineral flotation. In 1940 he trained civilians to deal with unexploded bombs. At the Methodist Church, Caulfield, on 7 December that year he married Marjory Evelyn O'Connor, a typiste; their marriage was to end in divorce.

When Wark moved to the Council for Scientific and Industrial Research in 1941 as director of the division of industrial chemistry, Sutherland was appointed head of the division's physical chemistry section. War-related research allowed him to demonstrate his versatility. In 1942, with John Stuart Anderson, he undertook to supply zinc arsenide for testing the efficiency of gas masks. The chemical was prepared on the roof of the university's chemistry building by the hazardous process of stirring arsenic into molten zinc. Both men suffered rashes and hair loss, taking more than a year to recover. Sutherland also worked with Enid Plante on the separation of medicinally useful ergot from rye to overcome the limited supply of the drug occasioned by World War II. In 1943 they built a pilot flotation plant and separated much of that year's crop. Sutherland was awarded his doctorate and the David Syme [q.v.6] prize by the University of Melbourne in 1948 for his thesis, 'Physics and Chemistry of the Flotation Process'.

Although versatile, Sutherland had a special talent for the more difficult aspects of the theory of flotation systems and surface chemistry. Awarded a Davy-Faraday fellowship, he went to London in 1947 to pursue research with (Sir) Eric Rideal at the Royal Institution of Great Britain (Ph.D., 1950, University of London). Sutherland did his most fundamental work during those years. His 1948 paper on the kinetics of flotation processes, published in the American *Journal of Physical and Colloid Chemistry* (1948), continues to be cited.

In 1950 Sutherland was induced to return to Australia to resume his former post at the Commonwealth Scientific and Industrial Research Organization. He was to become head of the new division of physical chemistry in 1958. His flotation work culminated in his co-authorship with Wark of the revised and enlarged edition of *Principles of Flotation* (Melbourne, 1955), first published by Wark in 1938. The Royal Australian Chemical Institute bestowed on Sutherland the H. G. Smith [q.v.11] memorial medal in 1957. He was elected a fellow of the Australian Academy of Science in 1959.

That year he was appointed director of research in Sydney for the Colonial Sugar Refining Co. Ltd, a position which he held until he retired in 1978. The major events of his tenure were the establishment in 1960 of the David North Plant Research Centre in Brisbane (where a phytotron was operated for plant-breeding research into sugar cane) and the construction in 1962 of C.S.R.'s industrial research laboratory at Roseville, Sydney. He generated new projects, helped to found (1965) the Australian Industrial Research Group and encouraged his scientists to join learned societies.

In the 1960s, while involved in the management of Lizard Island Research Station on the Great Barrier Reef, Sutherland became interested in malacology and accumulated an important shell collection. His interest involved him with the Australian Museum, Sydney: he was an honorary curator in the malacology department, a trustee (from 1966) and president of the trustees (1972-74). He enjoyed playing squash and tennis. On 14 February 1968 at the registrar general's office, Sydney, he married Mary Bickart, née Lindley, a secretary and a divorcee who had previously changed her surname to Sutherland by deed poll.

A part-time member (1965-71) of the C.S.I.R.O. executive, Sutherland served in Indonesia as a consultant with the United Nations Educational, Scientific and Cultural Organization, an experience which gave him an abiding interest in using science and technology to assist developing countries. He delivered the Liversidge [q.v.5] lecture at the Australian and New Zealand Association for the Advancement of Science's congress in 1970 and served as the association's president in 1978. He was also a fellow (1974) of the R.A.C.I., president (1975) of its New South Wales branch and a founding member (1974) of the Australian Academy of Technological Sciences. In 1977 he was appointed O.B.E. Although gravely ill, he chaired a committee in 1979 that reported to the Australian government on lead tetraethyl in urban pollution, writing most of the report himself.

Sutherland died of cancer on 26 January 1980 at Wahroonga and was cremated with the forms of the Uniting Church. His wife survived him, as did the daughter and three sons of his first marriage.

Records of the Aust Academy of Science, 4, no 2, 1979, p 7; *Chemistry in Aust*, 47, no 5, May 1980, p 211; *Hist Records of Aust Science*, 5, no 2, 1981, p 79; *SMH*, 11 June 1977, 30 Jan 1980; R. I. Nicholson, Research in CSR (ts, file note 1345, CSR L, Syd); Wark papers (Basser L, Aust Academy of Science, Canb); CSIRO files, A8520, items PH/SUT004 pts 1 & 2, PH/SUT004B and PH/SUT00E (NAA, Canb).   DAVID PHILIP MILLER

SUTTON, DORIS MANNERS-; see GENTILE

SVERJENSKY, ALEXANDER (1901-1971), musician and pianoforte teacher, was born on 26 March 1901 at Riga, Russia (Latvia), son of Boris Sverjensky, railway commissioner, and his wife Sophie, née Mironoff. Alexander attended the Aleksandra Gimnazija, Riga, and began piano lessons at the age of 12. He studied under Alexander Glazunov at the Petrograd (St Petersburg) Conservatory from 1915 and also worked with the Imperial Opera soprano Lydia Lipkovska. Later, he attended the University of Tomsk where he read some law.

Following difficult years in Siberia and Moscow, Sverjensky grew so disenchanted with the new Bolshevik régime that he fled across Russia to China in 1922. He spent eleven months there and contacted Madame Lipkovska, by then an émigré. In 1923-24 he was her accompanist on a tour of China, Japan, the Philippines, Australia and New Zealand. After more concerts in Europe, Sverjensky returned to Sydney on 22 June 1925 in the *Ville de Strassbourg* to settle permanently. On 20 October 1927 at St Stephen's Presbyterian Church, Phillip Street, he married Mary Beryl Hartley Murdoch; they were to have a son before she divorced him in April 1943. Sverjensky was naturalized on 17 September 1930. At the registrar-general's office, Sydney, on 24 June 1943 he married Enith Clarke, a teacher of piano.

Sverjensky's well-attended chamber-music concerts made a notable impact in the 1920s and 1930s. He was a passionate proponent of Russian music: his expressive and informed performances of works by Stravinsky, Scriabin, Medtner, Balakirev, Glazunov and Rachmaninov encouraged audiences to move beyond an often-stereotyped appreciation of Russian composition. In 1926 he introduced the music of Prokofiev to Australia. From 1933 he played with the Australian Broadcasting Commission's Sydney orchestra. He founded his own trio in 1936, with Albert Cazabon (violin) and George Elwood (cello). In an environment where the approach to music was often deadeningly conservative, Sverjensky's concerts were memorable for their imaginative programming, especially in the juxtaposition of works drawn from widely disparate musical periods.

Appraisals of Sverjensky's talents as a concert pianist were mixed, but he was nationally recognized as one of the greatest piano teachers of his generation. Working at first from a private studio, he went on to teach at the New South Wales State Conservatorium of Music from 1938 to 1969. The doyen of the conservatorium's piano professors, he was also the best paid. Students found him extremely intimidating. He was a highly prescriptive instructor whose lessons were notoriously expensive and demanding. Nonetheless, his stern perfectionism, commitment to his pupils' musical development, and great understanding of pianoforte technique shaped the lives of legions of young pianists. His pupils spanned several generations of Australia's leading exponents of pianoforte and included Richard Farrell, Romola Costantino, Roger Woodward and Malcolm Williamson. Such students helped to spread his reputation abroad.

Although Sverjensky was a forthright spokesman for the conservatorium staff on many industrial issues, he was zealous in defending his untrammelled entrepreneurial freedom and opposed to the conversion of conservatorium teaching positions from a casual to a full-time basis. Always an enigmatic figure, he was also influential in numerous music organizations. He served as chairman of the National Council of Musical Associations of Australia, president of the Musical Association of New South Wales and a federal examiner for the Australian Music Examinations Board. His involvement with general music education led him to lecture for the A.B.C.

In June 1951 Sverjensky divorced his wife. On 5 July that year he married 22-year-old Isla Lilian Draper at the registrar-general's office. Affectionately known as 'Sver', he was slightly built, bespectacled, and balding from an early age. His hands were large and his high domed forehead helped to create an aura of intensity and intellectualism. He was widely regarded as a gifted linguist, and as a ladies' man. A member of the Royal Automobile Club of Australia, he played tennis and bridge, and enjoyed gardening. He died of heart disease on 3 October 1971 at his home at Bondi Beach and was cremated without a religious service; his wife and their son survived him, as did the son of his first marriage. A special memorial concert was held that month at the conservatorium, featuring his colleague Robert Pikler and former students.

Theatre, Society and Home, 1 Apr 1924; *Aust Musical News*, 1 Feb 1929, 1 Nov 1932, 1 Nov 1933, 1 Aug 1936, 1 Jan 1938, 1 Dec 1944; *SMH*, 13 Nov 1937, 13 Dec 1943, 27 Apr 1945, 1, 2, 8 Dec 1950, 6 Oct 1971; *Sun-Herald* (Syd), 10 Oct 1971; naturalization file, A1, item 1930/7103 (NAA, Canb).

DIANE COLLINS

SWAIN, EDITH MURIEL MAITLAND (1880-1964), public servant and physical-fitness advocate, was born on 15 March 1880 at Balmain, Sydney, eldest child of Edward Plant Swain, a merchant from England, and his Tasmanian-born wife Annie Maria, née Dodd. Educated at Parramatta by the Sisters of Mercy, Muriel passed the senior public examination in 1899, the year in which the clerical division of the New South Wales Public Service was opened to women. On 21 March 1900 she was appointed compiler in the Registry of Friendly Societies and Trade Unions. She studied part time at the University of Sydney (B.A., 1909; B.Ec., 1914), and in 1914 became a professional officer and sub-editor of the *New South Wales Industrial Gazette*, Department of Labour and Industry. Then her career stalled. In 1928 she accepted a transfer to clerical duties and a drop in salary. She was on loan to the Family Endowment Office in 1931-33.

No distinction had existed between the terms of appointment for male and female clerks when Swain entered the public service. As the industrial courts developed the concept of male wages notionally tied to family needs, the Public Service Board began to discriminate against women, reducing the number and range of increments offered to them. In 1912 Swain was elected to the council of the Public

Service Association of New South Wales in opposition to these moves. In 1915 the board introduced separate entry examinations and lower starting salaries for female clerks, and also restricted the kind of work they would be permitted to perform. After the association's leaders abandoned the women, they formed their own section, with Swain as president, but were unable to prevent further erosion of their conditions.

An attractive woman who dressed smartly, Swain lived with her parents and siblings. Her family was comparatively well-to-do. Free from domestic responsibilities and experienced in administration, she proved a willing recruit to the circle of university-educated, leisured and professionally employed office-holders in the National Council of Women of New South Wales and its affiliates. She and Grace Scobie [q.v.11] prepared a detailed report on prenatal and postnatal care of infants for an N.C.W. sub-committee in 1922.

Miss Swain joined the Vocational Guidance Council and the governing body of the girls' department of the Young Women's Christian Association, Sydney. The national Y.W.C.A. nominated her as a delegate to the first Pan-Pacific Women's Conference, held in Honolulu, Hawaii, in 1928. At the request of Jessie Street [q.v.], she co-ordinated the work of committees that gathered information on discriminatory laws and practices for the United Associations (of Women). She attended the fourth conference of the Institute of Pacific Relations, at Hangchow and Shanghai, China, in 1931, then travelled on to Mukden and Tokyo.

Healthy recreation had become the focus of Swain's activities. She presided over a Y.W.C.A. hockey team and, in 1930-31, the City Girls' Amateur Sports Association. At a meeting called by the Parks and Playgrounds Movement of New South Wales, she was the unanimous nominee of the women's organizations to join a consultative committee which examined recreational facilities in Sydney and reported in 1932. That year she attended the International Recreation Congress, at Los Angeles, United States of America, representing the Workers' Sports Federation of Australia, the Town Planning Association of New South Wales and the Parks and Playgrounds Movement.

Having recognized a need to educate voluntary workers, Swain became a foundation member of the Council for Recreation and Leadership (Recreation and Leadership Movement) and director of its training programme. In 1937 a campaign for fitness and good citizenship was endorsed at the national Conference on Recreational Policy. With Zoe Benjamin [q.v.7], Swain ran the Recreation and Leadership Movement's summer school (1939) on 'Education for a Leisured Citizen-

ship'. She contributed to both the formation and the work of the Australian Youth Council. Her aims throughout were to develop the skills that flow from games, to raise health standards and to produce co-operative citizens. The formation of the New South Wales State Council for Physical Fitness in 1939 and the provision of Federal funding for physical education marked a transition from volunteer initiative to professional control.

About 1940 Swain retired from the public service. Save for a brief period as director of training for the Women's Union of Service in the early years of World War II, she took no further part in public life. She died on 11 November 1964 at Mosman and was cremated with Anglican rites.

Pan-Pacific Union, *Women of the Pacific* (Honolulu, US, 1928); Official Consultative Committee of the Parks and Playgrounds Movement of New South Wales, in conjunction with the Surveyor-General, *Basic Report on the Present and Future Requirements of the Parks and Playgrounds in the Sydney Metropolitan District* (Syd, 1932); D. Deacon, *Managing Gender* (Melb, 1989); Recreation and Leadership Movement, *Annual Report*, 1936/37-1939/40; *Harmony* (Syd), 25 Sept 1935.

HEATHER RADI

SWAN, ANDREW DAVID (1896-1980), air force officer, was born on 19 November 1896 at Perth, Scotland, son of David Swan, a sergeant in the British Army, and his wife Lillias McAinsh, née Young. Andrew joined the Army Ordnance Corps as a clerk in December 1910. Within five years he gained third- and second-class army educational certificates. In February 1913 he transferred to the 1st Battalion, the Black Watch (Royal Highland Regiment). He served (from 1915) on the Western Front and was twice mentioned in dispatches.

In November 1918 Swan was posted to the records section, Army Headquarters, Bombay, India. He proceeded with the Waziristan Field Force to the North-West Frontier, and was discharged from the British Army on 29 December 1923 with the rank of sergeant. Migrating to Australia, he worked as a railway-construction labourer in Melbourne. On 21 July 1925 he enlisted in the Royal Australian Air Force and was sent as an aircraftman to No.1 Flying Training School, Point Cook. At the Baptist Church, Collins Street, Melbourne, on 16 July 1927 he married Sylvia Irene Lane, a librarian.

Promoted sergeant in October 1929, Swan became disciplinary sergeant major at No.1 F.T.S. in January 1931 and sergeant major, first class, in August 1933. He was commissioned flying officer on 1 September 1938. After World War II began he served as adjutant at station headquarters, Laverton, and (from March 1940) at No.1 Engineering School, Melbourne. He was made honorary flight lieutenant in September 1940. For his work in training new ground-staff he was appointed M.B.E. in 1941. In October that year he was promoted temporary squadron leader. Two months later he was transferred to Darwin as senior administrative officer.

On 19 February 1942 Japanese aircraft attacked the town. Amid the chaos Swan helped to operate a Lewis-gun before leading a party of men into a burning hangar to recover ammunition. He was mentioned in dispatches. When the raids ended that day, the commander of the R.A.A.F. station, Group Captain Sturt Griffith [q.v.14], told Swan to direct all personnel to move a short distance inland, away from the base. Passed on by word of mouth, this imprecise order was misinterpreted by many as an instruction to abandon their positions and evacuate the town. (Sir) Charles Lowe [q.v.15], who inquired into the circumstances of the Japanese attacks, commended Swan's conduct, both during and after the raids.

From 4 March 1942 Swan commanded the R.A.A.F. station in Darwin. In October he was posted to the air force establishment at Ascot Vale, Melbourne, as S.A.O. and officer commanding. Promoted acting wing commander in August 1943 (substantive September 1948), he joined R.A.A.F. Overseas Headquarters, London, that month. He returned to Melbourne in November 1944 and took charge of the Aircrew School at Watsonia. In February 1946 he became S.A.O. of No.81 Wing, which formed part of the British Commonwealth Occupation Force, Japan. Back home in April 1947, he was appointed S.A.O., R.A.A.F. station, Point Cook; he also acted (August-September) as temporary commandant of the newly formed R.A.A.F. College. Following his retirement on 19 November 1949, he lived at Seaford. He died on 22 May 1980 at Frankston and was cremated with Presbyterian forms; his wife and their son survived him.

D. Gillison, *Royal Australian Air Force 1939-1942* (Canb, 1962); R. E. Frost, *RAAF College & Academy 1947-86* (Canb, 1991); N. C. Smith, *One Thousand Airmen* (Melb, 1995); *Commission of Inquiry Concerning the Circumstances Connected with the Attack made by Japanese Aircraft at Darwin on 19th February, 1942* (Canb, 1945); Darwin documents, box file (RAAF Museum, Point Cook, Vic).
                                    PETER HELSON

SWANN, ISABEL; see LONGWORTH

SWANSON, VICTOR GEORGE (1910-1972), engineer, was born on 9 October 1910 at Maryborough, Victoria, son of Australian-born parents George Swanson, engine driver, and his wife Clementina Victoria, née Pearce. Educated at Kyneton High School, Vic began his career in 1927 as an engineering cadet with the Victorian Department of Public Works. After surveying roads for three years, he entered the University of Melbourne (B.C.E., 1934), where he won *Argus* and Stawell [q.v.6] scholarships. In 1934 he joined the State Rivers and Water Supply Commission. His duties involved him, successively, in hydraulic research, design work and hydraulic modelling. At Scots Church, Melbourne, on 8 February 1941 he married with Presbyterian forms Phyllis Jean Heron, a clerk.

In 1935 Swanson had been commissioned in the Citizen Military Forces. Called up for full-time duty on 30 July 1941 as a temporary major (substantive August 1943), he served in the Northern Territory with the Royal Australian Engineers and transferred to the Australian Imperial Force on 21 July 1942. From October 1943 he commanded the 20th Field Company, R.A.E., in New Guinea. The company helped to build the 2nd/7th Australian General Hospital at Lae and provided a reticulated water supply to its 1000-bed hospital. Swanson was mentioned in dispatches for his work. In May 1945 he was posted to the staff of Major General (Sir) Clive Steele [q.v.], engineer-in-chief at Army Headquarters, Melbourne. His A.I.F. appointment terminated on 24 August. Active in the C.M.F. in 1950-56, he commanded (from 1954) the 22nd Construction Regiment as a temporary lieutenant colonel.

When World War II ended, Swanson had returned to the State Rivers and Water Supply Commission. In 1946-50 he was resident engineer with the Cairn Curran Dam project, on the Loddon River. For the next five years he was assistant-engineer, supervision, engaged in enlarging the Eildon Reservoir and building the associated township. Located on the Goulburn River, the dam was one of Victoria's major water conservation and hydro-electric undertakings. With a storage capacity of 2.75 million acre feet (3.39 million Ml), it was the largest dam in Australia, providing water for irrigation to northern Victoria and peak-load electricity to Melbourne. Swanson was promoted assistant chief construction engineer before transferring in 1956 to the Department of Public Works as chief civil engineer and chief engineer, ports and harbours.

On 4 March 1960 Swanson was appointed chairman of the Melbourne Harbor Trust commissioners, becoming, in effect, general manager 'of Australia's largest general cargo port'. His twelve-year tenure witnessed 'an unprecedented period of major development'. The throughput of cargo rose from 9.4 million tons in 1960 to 17 million in 1972, and the capital value of the port doubled. As a result of his recommendations, it was decided in 1965 'to prepare for the entry of container and unit ships'. He ensured that specialized facilities and equipment were provided for these vessels at a separate dock, which was named after him. The first container berth for overseas trade was opened in 1969 and the fourth began handling ships in 1972.

Swanson was an associate-member (1938), member (1953) and fellow (1968) of the Institution of Engineers, Australia, a member (1936) of the American Society of Civil Engineers, a director and president (1969-71) of the International Association of Ports and Harbors, and president (from 1971) of the Association of Australian Port and Marine Authorities. In 1970 he was appointed C.B.E. Five ft 9 ins (175 cm) tall, with blue eyes, brown hair and a fair complexion, he was modest and quietly spoken. He suffered from renal failure for some years. During the last six months of his working life he was only able to continue with the aid of a dialysis machine. Survived by his wife, and their son and daughter, he died of acute coronary insufficiency on 14 September 1972 at his Mont Albert home and was cremated.

O. Ruhen, *Port of Melbourne 1835-1976* (Syd, 1976); *Port of Melbourne Q*, Apr-June 1969, p 13, Oct-Dec 1972, p 13; *Cargo Handling and Shipbuilding Q*, 11, no 4, Dec 1972, p 26; *Age* (Melb), 15 Sept 1972.

J. S. HARDY

SWANTON, CEDRIC HOWELL (1899-1970), psychiatrist, was born on 23 March 1899 at Kew, Melbourne, third child of Victorian-born parents William Howell Swanton, shipping manager, and his wife Lucy Freeman, née Kitchen. Cedric attended Scotch College and the University of Melbourne (M.B., B.S., 1924). At Scots Church, Melbourne, on 27 March 1926 he married Ethel May Tovell. He then undertook postgraduate work in surgery in Edinburgh and London, and became a fellow (1926) of the Royal College of Surgeons, Edinburgh.

On his return to Australia, Swanton defied expectations that he would embark on a career as a surgeon, and established a general practice at Merrylands, Sydney, in 1929. Four years later he again abruptly changed course, returning to London to train in psychiatry at the Tavistock Clinic. He gained a diploma of psychiatric medicine (University of London, 1935). In 1937 he set up as a consultant psychiatrist in Macquarie Street, Sydney, and was appointed to the honorary staff at the new psychiatric clinic at Royal Prince Alfred Hospital, where he remained until he retired in 1959. He also held appointments at the Women's Hospital, Crown Street, the Eastern Suburbs Hospital and the Northcott [q.v.15] Neurological Centre. His reputation grew: he was president (1958) of the Australasian Association of Psychiatrists, a fellow (1962) of the Royal Australasian College of Physicians, and a foundation member (1963) and fellow (1965) of the Australian and New Zealand College of Psychiatrists. In addition, he acted as an adviser to a number of journals, including *Modern Medicine*.

Despite his training in psychotherapy and psychoanalysis, Swanton became an enthusiastic advocate of physical treatment. One of the first Australian psychiatrists to use electroconvulsive therapy, he continually modified his own apparatus to improve its efficiency. He remained a proponent of this method throughout his career and instructed some younger psychiatrists in its intricacies, including Harry Bailey, later notorious for his mistreatment of patients at the Chelmsford Private Hospital. Psychosurgery (leucotomy) was also one of Swanton's favourite therapies, but he remained sceptical about the effectiveness of the new psychotropic drugs that revolutionized psychiatric practice in the late 1950s—perhaps reflecting the influence of his earliest medical interests.

Swanton was a highly regarded teacher, factual rather than fanciful in diagnosis, though prone to aphorism and didacticism. He took a great interest in university matters, generally preferring local to overseas candidates for academic positions. In 1962 he helped to secure the appointment of David Maddison to the chair of psychiatry at the University of Sydney.

A dour, laconic, thin-lipped, bespectacled man, of rather severe but distinguished appearance, Swanton belonged to the University and Royal Sydney Golf clubs. He was noted for his integrity, sense of justice and generosity. Deeply sentimental, he endeared himself to many of his colleagues. Following one of his regular fishing expeditions, he died suddenly on 11 September 1970 at his Elizabeth Bay home and was cremated without a religious service. His wife, and their two sons and two daughters survived him.

G. L. McDonald (ed), *Roll of the Royal Australasian College of Physicians*, 1 (Syd, 1988); *Aust and NZ J of Psychiatry*, 4 Dec 1970; *MJA*, 14 Aug 1971.

STEPHEN GARTON

SWIFT, SIR BRIAN HERBERT (1893-1969), obstetrician and gynaecologist, and NEVILLE CROPLEY (1895-1918), soldier, were born on 2 February 1893 and 19 September 1895 in Adelaide, second and youngest of three sons of Harry Swift, a medical practitioner from England, and his South Australian-born wife

Kate Marion Lilian, née Peacock. Their father, the first to describe erythrœdema ('the pink disease'), became dean of the faculty of medicine, University of Adelaide, in 1924. His sons attended the Collegiate School of St Peter. Brian studied elementary science for a year at the University of Adelaide before proceeding to Gonville and Caius College, Cambridge (B.A., 1914; M.B., B.Ch., 1916; M.A., M.D., 1936). On 2 August 1916 he was commissioned lieutenant, Royal Army Medical Corps. Twelve months later he was promoted captain. He served briefly in hospitals at Leith, near Edinburgh, and then on the Western Front. In 1918 he won the Military Cross for his 'splendid example of courage and determination' under enemy fire. He transferred to the Royal Air Force in September 1918.

After being demobilized from the air force on 23 October 1919, Swift returned to Adelaide where he entered general practice and set his sights on an appointment to the honorary staff of a public hospital. He worked as anaesthetist (from 1920) at the Adelaide Children's Hospital, as senior obstetrician (from 1922) at the Queen's Home (Queen Victoria Maternity Hospital) and as tutor (from 1924) in obstetrics at the University of Adelaide. In 1925 he travelled to Britain for further obstetric training and obtained a fellowship (1926) of the Royal College of Surgeons, Edinburgh. He also studied in Vienna, a 'Mecca' for gynaecologists in the 1920s. Back in Adelaide in 1928, he moved into specialist practice in obstetrics and gynaecology. Honorary senior obstetrician at the Queen's Home, he also held the posts of honorary assistant gynaecologist (1929-39) and honorary gynaecologist (1940-53) at (Royal) Adelaide Hospital. He convened the postgraduate medical committee of the South Australian branch of the British Medical Association and was elected (1931) a fellow of the Royal Australasian College of Surgeons.

At St Peter's College chapel on 5 April 1934 Swift married with Anglican rites Joan Royal Tennant, the grand-daughter of Andrew Tennant [q.v.6]; they were to have a son and daughter. He visited Cambridge in 1936 to present his doctoral thesis: it was based on a series of cases from which he had deduced a connection between vitamin deficiency in the diet and a form of irritation of the vulva. His search for recent advances in his field took him again to Vienna, and to Paris, Stockholm, London and New York. In 1937 he was elected a fellow of the Royal College of Obstetrics and Gynaecology, London.

On 1 November 1940 Swift was appointed major, Australian Army Medical Corps, Australian Imperial Force. He served (1941-42) in the Middle East, initially with the 2nd/9th Australian General Hospital and later with the 2nd/2nd A.G.H. In March 1942 he came home

to Adelaide and was based at the 101st A.G.H. until he transferred to the Reserve of Officers on 24 July 1943. He was a consultant gynaecologist to the Royal Australian Air Force in 1943-45.

Highly regarded by his colleagues for his skill, Swift introduced a number of techniques in gynaecological surgery to Australia. In 1945 he set up a sterility clinic at the Royal Adelaide Hospital. He pioneered the use of the Papanicolaou smear. In treating cancer of the cervix his surgery made a virtue of 'respect for human tissue' at a time when operations were usually 'more heroic' and some of his peers were dabbling in fierce radiotherapies. He presided (1945-46) over the State branch of the B.M.A., and was a founder (1947) and chairman (1953-56) of the Australian regional council of the Royal College of Obstetricians and Gynaecologists. From 1948 to 1952 he lectured in gynaecology at the university. He was knighted in 1954.

Sir Brian held interests in rural properties. Winner of the South Australian Amateur Golf Championship in 1924, he was captain (1950 and 1956) and president (1961-66) of the Royal Adelaide Golf Club. He enjoyed cricket and casting for salmon. Survived by his wife and their daughter, he died on 19 May 1969 at his Medindie home and was buried in North Road cemetery. His estate was sworn for probate at $438 551.

Neville Swift sailed for Britain after the outbreak of World War I and was commissioned in the East Lancashire Regiment on 26 June 1915. He served (from October) in France, but was wounded near Pozières in August 1916 and invalided to Britain. Two months later he returned to the Western Front. Wounded again in January 1917, he recovered in England and by October was back with his unit as an acting captain and company commander. During the fighting in December, his part of the front line came under heavy shelling: he dug out buried men, reorganized the line and established new posts while the enemy bombardment continued. He was awarded the Military Cross.

In January 1918 Swift led his company in a relief operation, carried out under a sustained barrage. He achieved his objective, won a Bar to his M.C. and was promoted acting major. Two months later the Germans mounted an offensive on the Somme. Attached to the King's Own Royal Lancaster Regiment, Swift commanded his battalion in a successful counter-attack, but was wounded on 27 March and died next day. He was awarded the Distinguished Service Order and mentioned in dispatches.

J. Peel (comp), *The Lives of the Fellows of the Royal College of Obstetricians and Gynaecologists 1929-1969* (Lond, 1976); I. A. McDonald et al, *Super*

Ardua (Melb, 1981); *MJA*, 20 Sept 1969; *Sabretache*, 26, July/Sept 1985; *Observer* (Adel), 23 Aug 1924; *Advertiser* (Adel), 14 Sept 1968, 20 May 1969.

NEVILLE HICKS
JANE HARFORD

SYKES, STEPHEN JOSEPH (1920-1957), air force officer and grazier, was born on 21 April 1920 at Goulburn, New South Wales, son of native-born parents Charles Ignatius Sykes, grazier, and his wife Mona Mary, née Purcell. The family had been on the land since George Sykes, the son of a convict, was granted 100 acres (40 ha) in the early years of local settlement. Educated at Currawang Public School and St Patrick's College, Goulburn, Steve studied woolclassing, worked on the family property, served (1940-41) in a troop of the 7th Light Horse Regiment (Militia), and played tennis.

On 23 May 1942 Sykes enlisted in the Royal Australian Air Force. He trained in New South Wales, embarked for Canada, topped his pilot's course in May 1943 and was commissioned. Promoted flying officer in November, he reached Britain next month. In May 1944 he was posted to No.455 Squadron, R.A.A.F., successively based at Langham, Norfolk, and at Dallachy, Scotland. The twin-engined Bristol Beaufighters, with which the squadron attacked enemy shipping and shore defences, suited his ability and aggressive flying. He was 'a skilled pilot and remarkable shot who forced home all his attacks with the utmost determination and effect'.

Sykes was popular and respected. In the air he was cool and resolute; on the ground he was 'a quiet and thoughtful man who kept largely to himself'. He flew forty-two sorties in one year of operational duty, attacking twenty-eight enemy ships, as well as gun-emplacements and a radar-station. His aircraft was often damaged. On 12 September 1944 he took part in a raid on shipping near Den Helder harbour, the Netherlands. In spite of 'fierce fire from the enemy defences', he came in so low that part of a trawler's mast was embedded in the nose of his Beaufighter. Undeterred, he then engaged enemy shore positions. With his compass shot out and other damage to his plane, he followed another aircraft to base and made a crash-landing. He won the Distinguished Flying Cross.

On 4 April 1945, during a series of attacks on heavily defended shipping in Norwegian waters, Sykes led eight aircraft against a merchantman in Aardals Fiord. His Beaufighter was hit on its approach, but he remained in formation. Closer to the target, a shell burst in front of his cockpit, blowing out the pilot's window: he received thirteen wounds, including a fractured arm and injuries to his leg.

When he managed to pull the plane from its dive, his navigator Flying Officer H. W. Pearson dressed his wounds, administered morphia, and assisted at the controls. Despite the extreme cold, Sykes flew the aircraft 400 nautical miles (740 km) and made a one-handed emergency landing at Sumburgh, Shetland Islands. He was awarded the Distinguished Service Order for his 'courage, fortitude and devotion to duty'. Sent to a rehabilitation centre, he soon recovered, but did not fly operationally again. In May he was promoted flight lieutenant. On 3 January 1946 he returned to Australia.

Back in the district in which he had been raised, Sykes took up a soldier-settlement property, named it Dallachy, and established himself as a progressive grazier. At the Cathedral of St Peter and St Paul, Goulburn, on 8 September 1948 he married with Catholic rites Kathleen Anne McGrath; they were to have a daughter and four sons. He took part in returned servicemen's activities, retained his interest in flying and played golf. In 1953 he became foundation president of the Goulburn Aero Club. On 19 January 1957, while was instructing a pupil in the club's newly delivered Chipmunk trainer, the machine spun into the ground, killing both of them. Survived by his wife and their sons, Sykes was buried in Spring Valley cemetery, near Goulburn.

Victory Roll (Canb, 1945); F. Johnson (ed), *R.A.A.F. Over Europe* (Lond, 1946); J. Herington, *Air Power Over Europe, 1944-1945* (Canb, 1963); I. Gordon, *Strike and Strike Again* (Canb, 1995); *Goulburn Evening Penny Post*, 21 Jan 1957; RAAF biog records, AWM 65 (AWM); information from Mrs K. Sykes, Waitara, Syd.   PETER BURNESS

SYME, EVELINE WINIFRED (1888-1961), painter and printmaker, was born on 26 October 1888 at Thames Ditton, Surrey, England, daughter of Joseph Cowen Syme, newspaper proprietor, and his wife Laura, née Blair. Ebenezer Syme [q.v.6] was her grandfather. Eveline was raised in the family mansion at St Kilda, Melbourne. After leaving the Church of England Girls' Grammar School, Melbourne, she voyaged to England and studied classics in 1907-10 at Newnham College, Cambridge (B.A., M.A., 1930). Because the University of Cambridge did not then award degrees to women, she applied to the University of Melbourne for accreditation, but was only granted admission to third-year classics. She chose instead to complete a diploma of education (1914).

Syme's artistic career was enhanced by her close friendship with Ethel Spowers [q.v.]. She studied painting at art schools in Paris in the early 1920s, notably under Maurice Denis and André Lhote, and held a solo exhibition, mainly of water-colours, at Queen's Hall, Melbourne, in 1925. Her one-woman shows, at the Athenaeum Gallery (1928) and Everyman's Library and Bookshop (1931), included linocuts and wood-engravings. While many of her water-colours and prints drew on her travels through England, Provence, France, and Tuscany, Italy, she also responded to the Australian landscape, particularly the countryside around Melbourne and Sydney, and at Port Arthur, Tasmania. Syme's chance discovery of Claude Flight's textbook, *Lino-Cuts* (London, 1927), inspired her to enrol (with Spowers) in his classes at the Grosvenor School of Modern Art, London, in January 1929. In keeping with Flight's modernist conception of the linocut, she began to produce prints incorporating bold colour and rhythmic design.

Returning to Melbourne in 1929 with an exhibition of contemporary wood-engravings from the Redfern Gallery, London, Syme became a cautious advocate of modern art. She published a perceptive account of Flight and his teaching in the *Recorder* (1929) and spoke on the radio about wood-engraving; she also wrote a pioneering essay on women artists in Victoria from 1857, which was published in the *Centenary Gift Book* (1934), edited by Frances Fraser and Nettie Palmer [q.v.11]. Syme was a founding member (1932-38) of George Bell's [q.v.7] Contemporary Group. She regularly exhibited with the Melbourne Society of Women Painters and Sculptors and with the Independent Group of Artists. Her linocuts, perhaps her most significant achievement, owed much to her collaboration with Spowers.

During the mid-1930s Syme was prominent in moves to establish a women's residential college at the University of Melbourne. In 1936, as vice-president of the appeal committee, she donated the proceeds of her print retrospective (held at the gallery of the Arts and Crafts Society of Victoria) to the building fund. A foundation member (1936-61) of the council of University Women's College, she served as its president (1940-47) and as a member of its finance committee. She was appointed to the first council of the National Gallery Society of Victoria in 1947 and sat on its executive-committee in 1948-53. In addition, she was a member (1919) and president (1950-51) of the Lyceum Club.

A tall, elegant and reserved woman, Syme had a 'crisp, quick voice' and a 'rather abrupt manner'. She died on 6 June 1961 at Richmond and was buried with Presbyterian forms in Brighton cemetery. In her will she left her books and £5000 to University Women's College. Edith Alsop's portrait (1932) of Syme is held by University College. Syme's work is represented in the National Gallery of Aus-

tralia, Canberra, State galleries in Melbourne, Sydney and Adelaide, and the Ballarat Fine Art Gallery, Victoria.

C. Deutsher and R. Butler (comp), *A Survey of Australian Relief Prints 1900/1950*, exhibition cat (Melb, 1978); J. Burke, *Australian Women Artists 1840-1940* (Melb, 1980); S. Coppel, *Linocuts of the Machine Age* (Aldershot, Eng, 1995); *Herald* (Melb), 21 Sept 1925, 5 Mar 1928, 9 June 1961; *Age* (Melb), 22 Sept 1925, 6 Mar 1928, 8 June 1961; *Argus*, 22 Sept 1925, 23 Nov 1927, 18 Aug 1931, 5 May 1936; *Sun News-Pictorial*, 6 Mar 1928, 18 Aug 1931, 5 May 1936.   STEPHEN COPPEL

SYME, HUGH RANDALL (1903-1965), naval officer, bomb disarmer and newspaper proprietor, was born on 20 February 1903 at Kew, Melbourne, third child of Australian-born parents John Herbert Syme, journalist, and his wife Ethel Maud, née King. David Syme [q.v.6] was his grandfather. Educated at Scotch College and the University of Melbourne, Hugh rose to become assistant-manager of the family business, which published the *Age*. At St George's Church of England, Malvern, on 12 May 1931 he married Olive Alyson Clark; they were childless and divorced in 1940.

A keen yachtsman and part-owner of the 82-footer (25 m) *Westwind*, Syme was appointed probationary sub-lieutenant, Royal Australian Naval Volunteer Reserve, on 1 September 1940. He was mobilized sixteen days later and sent to England for training at H.M.S. *King Alfred*. With John Mould [q.v.15], H. D. Reid and J. H. H. Kessack, he was one of the first Australians chosen to serve in the Royal Navy's Rendering Mines Safe section which had been established to disarm unexploded (and often booby-trapped) bombs and mines scattered across Britain by German aircraft.

Syme was promoted lieutenant on 17 December 1940 and posted to the naval base H.M.S. *Vernon*, where he quickly gained a reputation for courage and initiative. He was awarded the George Medal in June 1941 for his coolness in dealing with ten mines. In June 1942 he was awarded a Bar to his G.M. for disarming a mine that had lodged deep in clay in a reservoir embankment at Primrose Hill, London. After tunnelling to the mine, he found that the fuse was on the other side, and had to tunnel around it. His action in disarming the weapon in extraordinarily difficult and dangerous conditions saved the neighbourhood from possible flooding.

On 3 March 1943 Syme was awarded the George Cross for carrying out nineteen mine-recovery operations. The most important had taken place in November 1942 at Weston-super-Mare, Somerset, where he defused a new mine known as a Type T. He endured painful electric shocks while insulating the detonator wires and at one stage hung upside down in a mud hole. Other clearance officers found the information he had gained from the Type T invaluable. The award of his G.C. made Syme the most highly decorated officer in the R.A.N. at that time. His expertise was such that, despite the scepticism of the scientists who devised it, he defused a new British magnetic mine, much to their chagrin. Some of them refused to speak to him for months.

Following the deaths of his father and of his uncle Sir Geoffrey Syme [q.v.12], Hugh sailed for Australia in January 1943 and became a trustee of the family company. On 12 March 1943 at the Presbyterian Church, West Hawthorn, he married Joan, the 26-year-old daughter of Delamore McCay [q.v.10]. He attempted to return to England, but the R.A.N. decided to avail itself of his experience, and in April 1943 he set up a bomb-disposal section at H.M.A.S. *Cerberus*, Westernport. The organization was never operationally required because the United States Navy's Mobile Explosive Investigation Unit jealously guarded its control over bomb disposal in the Pacific. Seeing no useful role to play, Syme returned to civilian life in December 1944.

In 1946 he was appointed general manager of the *Age*. Two years later a public company, David Syme & Co. Ltd, was formed. After overseeing the firm's entry into television in 1956, he continued as general manager until 1963 and as a director until his death. He immersed himself in business matters, becoming a director of the Victorian Broadcasting Network Ltd and Anti-Friction Bearings Ltd, president (1959) of the Australian Newspapers Council and chairman of the Newspaper Proprietors' Association of Melbourne.

A member of the Athenaeum and Yorick clubs, Syme enjoyed motor racing, fishing and shooting. He was also a keen gardener who cultivated rare specimens of orchids. Survived by his wife and their three daughters, he died of a cerebral tumour on 7 November 1965 at Epworth Hospital, Richmond, and was cremated with Anglican rites and full naval honours. His estate was sworn for probate at £106 914.

J. F. Turner, *Service Most Silent* (Syd, 1955); I. Southall, *Softly Tread the Brave* (Syd, 1960); G. H. Gill, *Royal Australian Navy 1942-1945* (Canb, 1968); P. Firkins, *Of Nautilis and Eagles* (Syd, 1975); L. Wigmore (ed), *They Dared Mightily*, 2nd edn, revised and condensed by J. Williams and A. Staunton (Canb, 1986); *SMH*, 13 June 1941, 8 Nov 1965; *Age* (Melb), 8, 11 Nov 1965.

RICHARD REFSHAUGE

SYME, KATHLEEN ALICE (1896-1977), journalist, company director and welfare worker, was born on 15 February 1896 at Lilydale, Victoria, eldest of four daughters of Arthur Edward Syme, physician and surgeon, and his wife Amy, née Horne, both Victorian born. Educated at Lauriston Girls' School and the University of Melbourne (B.A., 1919; M.A., 1921; LL.B., 1923), Kathleen became in turn a journalist and editor with the *Age*, founded by her grandfather David Syme [q.v.6]. In 1943 she retired from editing to take her father's place as a trustee of the David Syme and the David Syme Charitable trusts (she chaired both from 1967). She became a director of David Syme & Co. Ltd in 1948. Regarded with respect and affection by the staff of the *Age*, she remained an active member of the board until 1971.

To the end of her life Miss Syme was proud to call herself a journalist, but she devoted her later years to institutions catering for the welfare of others, principally women. While she was an undergraduate she had signed a petition calling for a residential college for female students. Her 'persuasive advocacy' helped make University Women's College a reality two decades later. As a member of its council in 1943-74 and president in 1947-54, she gained the committee experience that was to underpin her second career. She was also a foundation member of the Victorian Women Graduates' Association, which named (1967) a research scholarship after her in acknowledgement of her endeavours to advance educational opportunities for women.

Syme had joined the board of the (Royal) Women's Hospital in 1949 and served as president in 1956-59. In addition, she was a trustee of the Vera Scantlebury Brown [q.v.11] Child Welfare Memorial Trust, a body which provided money to enable doctors, nurses and welfare workers to study overseas. Attracted by the idea of helping people at every stage of life, 'from their infancy to their twilight', she next turned her attention to the elderly. She joined the board of Greenvale Village for the Aged on its inception in 1954 and held office as vice-president in 1961-75. An 'astute and effective executive', she believed that the voluntary committees on which she served represented 'nearly every human value that is worth while'. She was appointed O.B.E. in 1968.

A handsome, stylish woman who remained 'young in outlook', Syme maintained a close association with her nieces and nephews, and their families. She loved literature, the theatre and ballet. In 1952-54 she was president of the Lyceum Club. Another of her pleasures was breeding and racing horses. It was a passion and talent she had inherited from her father. Her thoroughbred mares, kept on a property near Dandenong, produced a number of successful hunters and racehorses, including Conservatory, Williamstown and Good Prince.

She died on 3 September 1977 in East Melbourne and was cremated with Anglican rites. Her estate was sworn for probate at $634 002. The education centre at the Royal Women's Hospital was named after her.

Your Hospitals, 1, no 6, Dec 1964; *Age* (Melb), 8 June 1968, 16 Feb 1971, 5, 6 Sept 1977; *Australian*, 5-6 Nov 1983; information from Mrs J. Adams, Hawthorn East, Melb.   CAROLYN RASMUSSEN

SYMES, GEORGE WILLIAM (1896-1980), army officer and governor's secretary, was born on 12 January 1896 at Minterne Magna, Dorset, England, son of George Symes, sergeant major, Royal Artillery, and his wife Eliza, née Paulley. On leaving Bridport Secondary School, George enlisted in the British Army. Tall and athletic, he showed qualities of leadership and was commissioned in the Durham Light Infantry on 14 June 1915. While serving in the Machine Gun Corps in World War I, he won the Military Cross (1916) for capturing twenty Germans single-handed in a communications trench. In 1918 he was awarded a Bar to his M.C.

After the war, Symes performed staff duties in Britain and India, and rose to major (1938). At St John's Anglican Church, Colaba, Bombay, on 11 December 1939 he married Katherine Bellairs Lucas (d.1961), a South Australian. The outbreak of World War II led to his rapid promotion: by November 1940 he was in England as an acting brigadier. On 11 February 1942 he was promoted acting major general (substantive July 1944) and given command of the 70th Division, which was sent from the Middle East to India. In 1943 the division was broken up in order to provide manpower for Major General Orde Wingate's Special Force, operating behind Japanese lines in Burma. Symes was appointed Wingate's second-in-command.

When Wingate was killed in an air crash in March 1944, Symes was astonished to be passed over as his successor, but bore the setback with public equanimity. He remained in Burma until December 1945 and was twice mentioned in dispatches. In 1946 he was appointed C.B. and colonel of the York and Lancaster Regiment. Following two commands in England and a career that was distinguished rather than brilliant, he retired from the army in April 1949 and settled in Adelaide.

Symes cut an imposing figure as private secretary (1956-64) in turn to governors Sir Robert George and Sir Edric Bastyan [qq.v.14,13], the latter an old army colleague. A staunch Anglican, a synodsman and a member (1953-80) of the diocesan council, Symes presided (1952-72) over the charitable institution, the Cottage Homes. He was president (1954-57) of the Royal Geographical Society of Australasia, South Australian branch; he contributed articles on South Australian history to its *Proceedings* and wrote four articles for the *Australian Dictionary of Biography*. His full-scale life of Sir Charles Todd [q.v.6] remained unfinished. A principal founder (1956) of the National Trust of South Australia, he was also an inaugural director (1954-78) of Santos Ltd.

On 30 March 1967 at St Peter's Church of England, Box Hill, Melbourne, Symes married a widow, Kathleen Cavenagh Champion de Crespigny, née Cudmore, grand-daughter of J. F. Cudmore [q.v.8]. They lived at Tennyson, Adelaide. Survived by his wife, he died on 26 August 1980 at St Andrew's Presbyterian Hospital, South Terrace, and was buried in Centennial Park cemetery. He bequeathed money to the State branch of the R.G.S.A. for an award for historical research. In 1982 a memorial to George and Katherine Symes was dedicated in the chapel of the York and Lancaster Regiment, Sheffield Cathedral, England.

Collected Papers of George W. Symes 1896-1980 (Adel, 1981); *PRGSSA*, 1979; National Trust of SA, *Annual Report*, 1980, and *Newsletter*, Oct 1980; *Adel Church Guardian*, Oct 1980; *Advertiser* (Adel), 28 Aug, 1 Sept 1980; *The Times*, 4, 9, 13 Sept 1980; Symes papers (Mort L); Symes diaries (Imperial War Museum, Lond); information from Mrs K. Symes, Tennyson, Adel.   ROGER ANDRÉ

SYMES, PHILIP JAMES (1866-1957), businessman, was born on 7 October 1866 at Bristol, England, son of James Symes, linen draper, and his wife Fanny Leonard, née Crouch. Educated at Dr Nunn's College, Weston-super-Mare, Somerset, Philip migrated to Queensland at the age of 17. In 1890, with Digby Denham [q.v.8] and his brother Edward, he founded Denham Bros, produce merchants of Sydney and Brisbane. Symes visited Central Queensland in 1895 and recommended that a new branch of the company be opened at Rockhampton. Next year a store was established there, with Symes as managing partner. He extended its operations in 1902 to include a wholesale grocery and a hide-and-skins department.

In 1904 Symes returned to Brisbane. On 29 October that year at St Peter's Church of England, Melbourne, he married Lilian Brayshay, a teacher; they were childless. After farming and breeding horses at Warwick, Queensland, and in Tasmania, he re-entered the world of business in Brisbane. When Denham Bros (Rockhampton) Ltd was formed in 1912, he was appointed chairman, a position he held until his death. The firm became a proprietary company in 1932. Convinced that a cement company could operate profitably in

Queensland and compete with cement from New South Wales and with that imported from Europe and New Zealand, Symes was an inaugural director (1914-57) and chairman (1929-55) of Queensland Cement & Lime Co. Ltd, based at Darra, Ipswich. He also sat (1934-57) on the board of the construction company Hornibrook [q.v.14] Highway Ltd.

A successful and prudent businessman, Symes exploited opportunities for expansion and innovation. He strongly advocated that Denham Bros move into soft-drink manufacturing in the 1940s, and persuaded Queensland Cement & Lime to replace jute bags with cheaper, heavy-gauge paper ones. Denham Bros directors held him in such esteem that his offer to resign as chairman, in his eighty-fifth year, was declined.

Symes was a council-member (1913-57), a vice-president (1937-38 and 1940-56) and a trustee (1941-57) of the (Royal) National Agricultural and Industrial Association of Queensland; he served on its ring committee (1916-55) and as chief ring steward (1930-40). He had presided over the Hamilton company of the Boy Scouts' Association and become a foundation member (1920) of the (Royal) Queensland Golf Club. His other recreations as a young man included hunting and polo.

Survived by his wife, Symes died on 25 March 1957 at Turrawan Private Hospital, Clayfield, and was cremated. (Sir) Albert Axon [q.v.13], who succeeded Symes as chairman of Queensland Cement & Lime, described him as the 'grand old man of the cement industry'. Symes's estate was sworn for probate at £131 815. He bequeathed £11 250 to twenty-six religious, charitable and public organizations. Most of the money from the sale of his Denham Bros shares went, at his request, to the Church of England, which used it to build two homes for the aged: Symes Thorpe at Toowoomba, and Symes Grove at Taigum, Brisbane.

T. B. Macaulay (comp), *The Denham Story* (Rockhampton, Qld, 1986); J. Anderson, *A History of QCL's Darra Cement Plant 1914-1998* (Brisb, 1997); *Courier-Mail*, 26 Mar, 9 July 1957; *Bulletin*, 3 Apr 1957; W. Browne, History of the Queensland Cement & Lime Company Limited (ts, held by Qld Cement Ltd, Brisb); Denham Bros (Rockhampton) Ltd papers, Capricornia collection (Central Qld Univ L, Rockhampton campus); Qld Cement Ltd papers (OL).   P. A. DANAHER

SZABADOS, MIKLOS (1912-1962), table-tennis player, was born on 7 March 1912 in Budapest, younger son of Sandor Szabados, flour-mill manager, and his wife Rose, née Schwartz, a professor of languages and history. After receiving a table-tennis set from his mother for his thirteenth birthday, Miklos developed a passion for the game. He won his first major tournament in Hungary in 1927. Attributing his success to hard work and concentration, he defeated his friend Victor Barna for the world championship singles title in 1931. He teamed with Barna to win the doubles title six times, and also won the mixed doubles three times. Szabados played for the Hungarian team that won the Swaythling Cup five times between 1928 and 1935. His outstanding year was 1931: he won all four world events—the singles, doubles and mixed-doubles titles, and the Swaythling Cup. He began studying engineering at the University of Berlin, but, being of part-Jewish descent, fled to Paris in 1933. He coached table-tennis players in that city before moving to Britain in 1936.

With Istvan (Stephen) Kelen, Szabados reached Adelaide in August 1937 on a world tour. Sponsored by the New South Wales Table Tennis Association, they played exhibition games in Adelaide and Melbourne, then competed in the Australian championships in Sydney. The Hungarian pair won every match: Szabados defeated Kelen in four sets in the singles title, and they won the doubles in straight sets. Large crowds admired Szabados's clever footwork, good defence, fierce forehand and effective long game. Their tour eventually took them to China, Japan, South Africa, South America, India, Malaya and Java.

Returning to Australia in August 1939, Szabados settled in Sydney. By 1941 he owned a table-tennis club in Pitt Street. At Elizabeth Bay, on 26 December that year, he married with Presbyterian forms Marie Alice Bracher, a saleswoman; they had one child before being divorced in 1954. He was called up by the Allied Works Council and served as a mess orderly at Alice Springs, Northern Territory, in 1943-44. Naturalized in 1944, he was also known as Nicholas or Michael.

Of middle height, with wide brown eyes, Szabados was strong and muscular. He won the Australian Table Tennis Championship singles (1950 and 1952), doubles (1950) and mixed doubles (1955). Operating table-tennis academies in the city (in the 1940s), Petersham (in the 1950s) and Bondi Junction (from the late 1950s), he was prominent in coaching younger players and in staging exhibitions to popularize the game. Two of his protégés became Australian singles champions—Cliff McDonald (1959, 1964 and 1966) and Michael Wilcox (1963 and 1967). Szabados and his pupils gave many exhibition matches around the State, during which he played with two or three balls at the same time, hit shots from behind his legs, and even returned the ball with his bald head; he developed his own unique stroke, a backhand forehand (hitting with a backhand action on the forehand side).

He also played matches with celebrities such as the tennis player Bobby Riggs (1948) and the concert pianist Julius Katchen (1955).

Szabados was a gregarious man who enjoyed cooking, playing cards until late at night and drinking coffee. Survived by his son, he died of pneumonia on 12 February 1962 at Ashfield and was cremated with Anglican rites. In 1987 his name was listed in the International Jewish Sports Hall of Fame, Netanya, Israel.

S. Schiff, *Table Tennis Comes of Age* (Lond, 1949); J. M. Siegman, *The International Jewish Sports Hall of Fame* (NY, 1992); *Sports Novels*, July 1950, p 26; *People*, 3 Jan 1951, p 22; *SMH*, 18, 26 Aug, 10 Sept 1937, 14, 16 Dec 1948, 13 Aug 1949, 11 July 1955, 13 Feb 1962; N. Szabados, naturalization file, A435, item 1944/4/2857 (NAA, Canb). R. I. CASHMAN

T

TALBOT SMITH, SYDNEY; *see* SMITH, SYDNEY TALBOT

TANCRED, HENRY EUGENE (1897-1961), Rugby footballer, meat wholesaler and exporter, and horse-racing administrator, was born on 25 May 1897 at Balmain, Sydney, sixth of ten children of Thomas Tancred, a butcher from California, United States of America, and his Victorian-born wife Anna, née O'Connor. Harry was educated at the Christian Brothers' St Joseph's School, Rozelle, before his family moved to Wellington, New Zealand, to pursue further opportunities in the meat trade. Leaving school at the age of 13, he worked as a drover and then as a slaughterman.

Harry Tancred played for the Petone Rugby (Union) Football Club's first-grade side from 1914 and represented New Zealand on Rugby League tours to Australia in 1919 and 1921 (captain). Six ft 2 ins (188 cm) tall and 15 stone (95 kg) in weight, he was 'strong, burly and fast for a man of his build'. Resettling in Sydney, he played in the forwards for the State Rugby Union side against the visiting New Zealand Maoris in 1923. For his contributions as a player and as an administrator with the Randwick and Drummoyne clubs, he was to be made a life member of the New South Wales Rugby Union. At the Church of Mary Immaculate, Waverley, on 1 June 1929 he married Myra Kathleen Bresnahan with Catholic rites.

Tancred gave up football to concentrate on the family's growing meat business, Tancred Bros, which he had started 'on a shoestring' in 1922. He was founding chairman and managing director of Tancred Bros Pty Ltd in 1932, and of its successor, Tancred Bros Industries Ltd, which was registered as a public company in 1956. Tancred Bros became one of the country's largest wholesale butchering firms. It owned meatworks at Tenterfield and Bourke, and at Beaudesert, Queensland, and had grazing interests throughout Australia. President (1929) of the Wholesale Meat Traders' Protective Association, Tancred was a member of the Meat Industry Advisory Committee during World War II and of the Australian Meat Board (1946-61). He travelled extensively overseas.

His work involved stock deals with men connected with the turf, whose conversation stimulated his interest in horse-racing. Tancred bought his first horse, Thornleigh, for 100 guineas in 1929. Trained by Jack Jamieson, it won a dozen races, mostly in the Grafton area. Tancred subsequently owned a series of moderately performed horses until he acquired a bay colt named High Caste in 1937 for 7000 guineas. Known as 'The Strawberry Bull', because of the fleck in his red coat, High Caste won the Australian Jockey Club's Epsom Handicap in 1940. Maurice McCarten [q.v.15] later trained Tancred's horses.

In 1943 the State Labor government established the Sydney Turf Club and empowered it to stage race meetings and wind up the proprietary racing clubs. Whereas the A.J.C. committee was dominated by wealthy graziers, many with Country Party affiliations, the first S.T.C. directors—Tancred among them—tended to be lawyers or self-made, wealthy businessmen, less likely to be aligned with conservative political parties.

Impressed by the amenities at American racecourses during his visit in 1946, Tancred was receptive to innovations. While he was vice-chairman (1945-53), the S.T.C. introduced the photo-finish camera in 1946 and replaced the wire starting system with barrier stalls in 1947. As chairman (from 1953), Tancred continued to push for the modernization of racing. Electrical timing devices and patrol films were introduced, and the first Golden Slipper Stakes, for two-year-olds, was run at Rosehill in 1957. Less successful were the trials of totalizator-only betting meetings held early in 1959: attendances and turnover both dropped, a sign that bookmakers were still a racing drawcard. Although Tancred was not a good mixer, he was willing to listen to criticism.

After suffering a severe stroke, Tancred resigned as chairman in 1959. He was appointed C.B.E. in 1960. Survived by his wife, and their son and daughter, he died of a coronary occlusion on 15 November 1961 at his Bellevue Hill home and was buried in Waverley cemetery.

His youngest brother ARNOLD JOSEPH (1904-1963) was born on 30 October 1904 at Leichhardt and educated at St Patrick's College, Wellington. He returned to Sydney in the mid-1920s and played Rugby Union for Glebe-Balmain. With another brother, James, he toured Britain, France and Canada with the New South Wales Waratahs in 1927-28. A 'tall, vigorous back row forward', he was 'a fearsome tackler, but lacked pace'. He managed the Australian Wallaby team that toured Britain and France in 1947-48, and was president of the New South Wales Rugby Union in 1959.

Arnold succeeded his brother Harry as chairman and managing director of Tancred

Bros and was a member (1961-63) of the Meat Board. He pioneered the export of meat to the U.S.A. Keen on horse-racing, he owned Putoko, which won the Brisbane Cup in 1952. He died of a coronary occlusion on 22 September 1963 at his Drummoyne home and was buried in Northern Suburbs cemetery. His wife Mary Esther, née Brett, whom he had married on 9 May 1935 at St Mary's Catholic Cathedral, Sydney, and their two daughters and two sons survived him.

R. Boulter, *Forty Years On, the Sydney Turf Club* (Syd, 1984); N. Penton, *A Racing Heart* (Syd, 1987); M. Painter and R. Waterhouse, *The Principal Club* (Syd, 1992); *People* (Syd), 16 Nov 1955; *Meat Producer and Exporter*, Nov 1961, p 2; Oct 1963, p 2; *Pastoral Review*, 19 Dec 1961, p 1411; *Referee*, 11 June 1919; *SMH*, 5 June 1929, 17 Aug 1943, 20 Apr 1945, 2 Nov, 30 Dec 1946, 4 Jan, 9 June, 15 Oct 1947, 1 Nov 1952, 22 Jan 1953, 26 Feb, 14 July 1959, 1 Jan 1960, 16 Nov 1961, 6 Apr 1962, 23 Sept 1963, 22 Mar 1986.

RICHARD WATERHOUSE

TANNER, SIR EDGAR STEPHEN (1904-1979), sports administrator and politician, was born on 10 August 1904 at Albany, Western Australia, eldest of four children of Edgar Tanner, a Victorian-born labourer and later a hotelkeeper, and his wife Emily, née Prosser, from England. Young Edgar attended All Saints Grammar School, St Kilda, Melbourne (school captain 1922). He joined the advertising staff of the Herald and Weekly Times Ltd and studied commerce at the University of Melbourne where he won a Blue for boxing. Of the more than one hundred amateur bouts that he contested as a featherweight, he lost only a handful. In the 1930s he was secretary of the Victorian Amateur Boxing and Wrestling Association. He managed Australia's boxing and wrestling team at the 1938 British Empire Games, Sydney. On 11 June 1938 at Holy Trinity Church of England, Balaclava, Melbourne, he married Edna May Ponsonby.

In 1929 Tanner had been commissioned in the Militia. He was appointed temporary captain, Australian Imperial Force, on 11 November 1941 and posted as intelligence officer of 'Gull Force' which was sent to Ambon, Netherlands East Indies, in January 1942. Superior numbers of Japanese troops overwhelmed the Australians next month. Tanner was imprisoned on Ambon and later on the Chinese island of Hainan. His zeal for organizing sporting competitions remained unbounded. On one occasion, he arranged a foot-race meeting between Japanese guards and Dutch and Australian prisoners desperate to win the prize of eggs. Defeated in the early races, the Japanese withdrew from the remainder. Only three weeks after Tanner's

return to Melbourne in October 1945, he began organizing an amateur boxing tournament. His A.I.F. appointment terminated on 3 January 1946.

Although Tanner resumed his position with the Herald and Weekly Times Ltd, the Olympic movement became his life's work. In June 1946 he convened a meeting of the Victorian Olympic Council—at which he was elected secretary-treasurer—and began a campaign for the games to be held in Melbourne. He and the V.O.C.'s chairman, Bill Uren, lobbied businessmen and State political leaders and attracted the vigorous support of the lord mayor of Melbourne, (Sir) Raymond Connelly, and an Olympian and previous lord mayor, Sir Frank Beaurepaire [qq.v.13,7]. Tanner was appointed secretary-treasurer of the Australian Olympic Federation in 1947 and next year managed the national team at the games in London. Postwar austerity was such that he often had to thumb lifts to the stadiums for his team-members in lorries, wagons and private cars; one group of athletes reached Wembley Stadium in a garbage truck.

Tanner served as secretary of the organizing committee for the Melbourne Olympic Games, held in 1956. Despite international tensions and boycotts by seven countries, the Olympics proved a popular success and were dubbed the 'Friendly Games'. He was appointed C.B.E. (1957) for his work. In 1968 he was knighted. A member (1952-76) of the Australian delegations to six Olympiads, he also headed the Australian British Empire (and Commonwealth) Games Association and numerous national and State sporting bodies. In May 1955 he had won for the Liberal and Country Party the seat of Ripponlea in the Victorian Legislative Assembly, defeating T. T. Hollway [q.v.14]. He held Ripponlea until 1967, then Caulfield. Sir Edgar was chairman of committees and deputy-speaker (1970-73) before retiring from parliament in February 1976.

Of stocky build, 5 ft 7 ins (170 cm) tall, with brown hair and light-brown eyes, Tanner had sharp features which contrasted with his gentle, measured manner. He was a highly organized and decisive administrator but not officious. Although he expressed himself cautiously in public, he was not afraid to speak his mind. Perhaps because his background was in a sport that keenly differentiated between amateur and professional status, he maintained an uncompromising view that Baron de Coubertin's Olympics should not be tainted by professionalism. In 1952 he had refused to exempt the cyclist E. R. Mockridge [q.v.15] from a fidelity bond to remain amateur for two years after the Helsinki Games. A majority of the A.O.F. overruled him and accepted a compromise that allowed Mockridge to take part.

In March 1973 Tanner succeeded Sir Harold Alderson [q.v.13] as president of the A.O.F. but by then much younger men such as David McKenzie, Kevan Gosper and Phil Coles were emerging as Olympic administrators with new ideas and their own ambitions. After thirty-one uninterrupted years of executive service in the A.O.F., Tanner was defeated in ballots for president and vice-president in 1977. He died on 21 November 1979 at North Caulfield and was buried in New Cheltenham cemetery. His wife and their daughter survived him, as did their son Ted who became the Liberal member for Caulfield in 1979. Two amateur boxing trophies were established in Sir Edgar's name.

Archie Lionel Tanner (1908-1975), Edgar's brother, was Victorian lightweight amateur boxing champion as a young man, and a referee of that sport at Olympic Games in 1956-68 and at British Empire and Commonwealth Games in 1962-66. He had served as a clerk in the Royal Australian Air Force in 1940-45. After twice unsuccessfully contesting Gippsland in the Victorian Legislative Council, he was Liberal member for Morwell in the Legislative Assembly in 1967-70.

H. Gordon, *Australia and the Olympic Games* (Brisb, 1994); *Herald* (Melb), 2 Aug 1972; information from Mr E. M. P. Tanner, Caulfield, Melb, and Mr H. Gordon, Main Beach, Qld.

MARK MCGINNESS

TATE, JOHN PERCIVAL (1894-1977), architect, town planner and politician, was born on 21 March 1894 in Wellington, New Zealand, son of Robert Gillies Tate, merchant, and his wife Frances Lilian, née Gumley. On leaving school, John served his articles with Panton & Son, civil engineers and architects at Timaru, and completed his training in 1914. He migrated to Sydney where he established a practice, John P. Tate & Young, architects and consulting engineers. At the Scots Church, Church Hill, on 31 December 1920 he married with Presbyterian forms Gladys Woodland, née Farquharson, a widow.

Tate's early commissions included the Manchester Unity building in Elizabeth Street (designed 1921, completed 1924), one of the first high-rise buildings in the city. His planning skill was evident in the building's structural detail and in the use of reinforced concrete. In the 1920s Tate also supervised construction of steelworks at Port Kembla. Following the outbreak of World War II, he joined the Commonwealth Department of the Interior in 1940 as superintending architect, New South Wales, responsible for the defence works programme in that State. In 1942 he became State construction manager

for the Allied Works Council. Towards the end of the war, Tate met Walter Bunning [q.v.13], executive-officer of the Commonwealth Housing Commission and a leading advocate of urban planning. Tate was elected an associate of the Royal Australian Institute of Architects in 1945 and joined the Town and Country Planning Institute of New South Wales in August 1946.

After winning a seat on the Ryde Municipal Council in 1944, Tate had become inaugural chairman of the Cumberland County Council in 1945. Its primary task was to create and complete a planning scheme within three years. From the outset, the County Council was in a precarious position, particularly with its constituent councils, who were uneasy about its new powers. Moreover, anticipated Commonwealth funding never eventuated. In partnership with the council's chief planner Sidney Luker [q.v.15], Tate brought the scheme together within the allotted time and presented it to J. J. Cahill [q.v.13], the minister for local government, in July 1948. The County of Cumberland Planning Scheme advocated decentralization, zoning, green belts, open spaces, and improved road and rail systems.

The State government's delay in gazetting the scheme eroded its potential. Land necessary for its success began to be privately developed. In January 1951 Tate refused to stand again as chairman: he declared that the plan had been betrayed and blamed the 'inertia of Government' for what he saw as the greatest 'civic tragedy' since Federation.

Tate was an executive-member (1947-49) of the Local Government Association of New South Wales. He represented Gipps (1947-51) and City (1953-56) wards on Sydney City Council, where he led those aldermen who belonged to the Civic Reform Association. A founding member of the Liberal Party, he was elected to the Senate in December 1949. He won a second term in April 1951 and chaired the Standing Committee on Regulations and Ordinances. Dropped from the Liberal Senate team for the 1953 election, he retired from Federal politics in June.

Although the County of Cumberland scheme was never fully realized, Tate's peers recognized his contribution to town planning in Australia. He was elected a fellow (1950) of the Royal Australian Institute of Architects, a fellow (1962) of the Town and Country Planning Institute of Australia and a life-fellow (1974) of its successor, the Royal Australian Planning Institute. A widower, he moved to Canberra in 1976. On 7 June that year he married 63-year-old Bernice Ida Cheetham at the local registry office. He died on 21 January 1977 at Canberra Hospital and was cremated. His wife survived him, as did the four sons of his first marriage.

Building (Syd), 12 May 1921, p 56, 12 May 1923, p 67; *Roy Aust Planning Inst J*, 15, no 2, May 1977, p 49; *SMH*, 6 Dec 1947, 15 Dec 1949, 15 Mar 1950, 15, 16 Jan 1951, 21, 22 Mar 1953, 27 Jan 1977; *Canb Times*, 25 Jan 1977; Roy Aust Planning Inst records (NL).
SARAH-JANE RENNIE

TATE, NEVA JOSEPHINE; *see* CARR-GLYN

TAYLOR, SIR ALAN RUSSELL (1901-1969), judge, was born on 25 November 1901 at Newcastle, New South Wales, fifth son of Walter Durham Taylor, a customs officer from England, and his native-born wife Lilias Martha, née Hewitt. The family moved to Sydney about 1911. Alan attended Fort Street Boys' High School until he was 14. In 1917 he joined the Commonwealth Public Service as a clerk in the Postmaster-General's Department. While studying law at the University of Sydney (LL.B., 1926), he worked in the Commonwealth Crown Solicitor's Office until January 1924. He graduated with second-class honours, and was admitted to the Bar on 2 June 1926. Although he was to practise mainly in common law and company law, he also built up a 'considerable practice in Admiralty'. Based in Chancery Chambers from 1926, he moved with his friends (Sir) Bernard Sugerman and E. D. Roper [qq.v.] to University Chambers in 1939. Three years later he took rooms in Chalfont Chambers.

At St Philip's Church of England, Sydney, on 25 July 1933 Taylor had married Ceinwen Gertrude Williams, a public servant. In 1936-42, at the university, he was Challis [q.v.3] lecturer in legal interpretation. Regularly briefed by the Crown, he increasingly appeared as a junior before the High Court of Australia in leading constitutional litigation, such as the Uniform Tax case (1942). He took silk in October 1943 and presided over the New South Wales Bar Association in 1948-49. Taylor appeared in the High Court for the English-controlled Bank of Australasia as a member of the legal team led by (Sir) Garfield Barwick that successfully challenged the validity of the Chifley [q.v.13] government's legislation to nationalize the trading banks in 1949.

'One of the great appellate advocates', Taylor had an incisive mind. He knew where his genial questions were heading—the first seemed harmless, but the last was often unanswerable. In 1950 the Commonwealth briefed him to defend High Court decisions in three cases (*Nelungaloo Pty Ltd* v. *The Commonwealth*, *Grace Bros Pty Ltd* v. *The Commonwealth*, and *Bonython and others* v. *The Commonwealth*) before the Privy Council in London. He won them all—Nelungaloo on a technicality, to the displeasure of Barwick,

the opposing counsel. While in London Taylor also appeared before the Privy Council to oppose leave to appeal in the 'Whose Baby' case (*Morrison* v. *Jenkins*) and won that, too. Back home, with other leading barristers he suffered a rare defeat in 1951 after attempting to defend the validity of the Communist Party Dissolution Act (1950) in the High Court.

When Taylor was elevated to the Supreme Court bench on 5 May 1952, (Sir) Norman Cowper, a Sydney solicitor, in congratulating him, reflected on their long association and lamented the loss to the Bar of the 'quiet persuasiveness' of his advocacy: 'the effortless flow, the apt phrase, the pleasant voice and manner, the patience, ready wit and genial humour, the ability to draw a fine distinction with convincing lucidity, the wealth of learning at immediate command'.

After Sir Owen Dixon [q.v.14] became chief justice, Taylor was appointed to the High Court on 3 September 1952 at the behest of (Sir) Robert Menzies [q.v.15]. In the 1950s the States' efforts to protect the railways by imposing charges and taxes on interstate road carriers led to a series of transport cases in the High Court which frequently deemed such legislation unconstitutional. An adherent of free-enterprise doctrines, Taylor believed (with Dixon) that section 92 of the Constitution guaranteed that each individual had a constitutional right to engage in interstate trade: 'it seems clear to me that any impost or tax, or so-called charge, whether levied upon a limited class for special purposes or by way of contribution to a tax for general purposes, which is made payable as a condition of engaging in or carrying on inter-State trade, must offend against s. 92'.

A down-to-earth, no-nonsense man, Taylor was robust in manner and had little time for excessive legalism. Lacking the intellectual approach of Dixon, he preferred to 'decide the case in hand according to accepted principles and was not greatly interested in the organic development of the law'. He was an indefatigable worker who liked to write his judgements on the day that the case closed and in Barwick's court 'undertook more than his share of the burdensome task of producing' the many joint judgements of the court. His colleagues appreciated his wide general knowledge, experience of the law, and 'mastery of constitutional principle and precedent'. As a K.C. he had taken extreme care in preparing his arguments. On the bench, he expected the same standards from counsel appearing before him. When faced with what he considered to be 'a plethora of irrelevancies', he was forthright, and at times impatient and curt with counsel.

Taylor was big, bluff and 'craggy', a good tennis-player in his youth and later a keen golfer. He belonged to the Australian, Royal

Sydney Golf and Elanora Country clubs, and enjoyed playing snooker at the University Club. In 1955 he was appointed K.B.E. Sworn of the Privy Council by Queen Elizabeth II at Government House, Canberra, on 19 February 1963, he sat on its judicial committee in London for three months in 1967, hearing and disposing of appeals.

Suffering from coronary sclerosis, Sir Alan died of myocardial infarction on 3 August 1969 at his Vaucluse home and was cremated. His wife, and their daughter and son survived him. Barwick considered Taylor to have been 'a most distinguished judge, one of the ablest this country has produced'. He recalled 'the warmth of his friendship, his unfailing good humour, and his ready turn of wit and phrase on all occasions [which made] our daily association with him pleasant and memorable ... Indeed he was a companionable man—kind, loyal and generous in his friendship'. Brian Blanchard's portrait of Taylor is held by the family.

J. M. Bennett, *Keystone of the Federal Arch* (Canb, 1980); D. Marr, *Barwick* (Syd, 1980); G. Fricke, *Judges of the High Court* (Melb, 1986); *Management Newsletter*, Oct 1968, p 6; *Cwlth Law Reports*, 118, 1968-69, p vii; *Aust Law J*, 43, 29 Aug 1969, p 352; *Law Council Newsletter*, 4, 1969, p 3; *SMH*, 18 Sept 1951, 30 Apr 1952, 5 Aug 1969; information from Mrs M. Ostinga, Potts Point, Mr Justice R. G. Reynolds, Woollahra, Syd, Mr D. Taylor, City Beach, Perth, and Mr Justice R. Else-Mitchell, Duffy, Canb.

MARTHA RUTLEDGE

TAYLOR, DAVID PHILLIPS FOULKES (1929-1966), furniture designer, was born on 23 June 1929 in Perth, eldest of five children of Douglas Charles Foulkes Taylor, an English-born pastoralist, and his wife Helen Rosemary Dorothy Blake, née Taylor, who was born in India. David was educated at Christ Church Grammar School, Perth, and Geelong Church of England Grammar School, Victoria, where he was exposed to the ideas of modernism by the art teacher Ludwig Hirschfeld-Mack [q.v.14]. While still at school he longed to travel, to live a Bohemian life in Paris, to mix with architects and to collect art, antiques and modern furniture.

In 1947 David Foulkes Taylor enrolled in architecture at Perth Technical College, but after a year left for London to study at the Central School of Arts and Crafts, Holborn. Holidays were spent hitchhiking on the Continent. He gained experience with Norman Potter, a furniture craftsman at Corsham, Wiltshire, before moving on to New York. Back in Perth in 1954, he began to design furniture. Three years later he visited Japan where, on 4 July 1957, he married Mary Attaway Lee, an American playwright and musician known as 'Maryat' Lee, whom he had met in London. After the wedding he returned to Perth, and his wife to the United States of America; they remained childless. The marriage was unconventional as they were to pursue their careers on different continents.

A promoter of modern design, Foulkes Taylor, as he was known, opened a showroom at his Crawley home in 1957. He displayed furniture made by noted European craftsmen, and also ceramics, glassware, pictures and imported fabrics. The Triangle Gallery, which he established at the same address in 1960, soon became a gathering spot for people interested in the arts. He commissioned the modernist architect Julius Elischer to design a purpose-built gallery at Nedlands. The new building, occupied in 1965, created a sculptural setting for imported pieces and the work of local artists and craftsmen.

Foulkes Taylor's own designs, while in the modernist tradition, were eclectic. Influenced by Scandinavian and English work, he was also interested in Japanese arts and crafts and American Shaker decorative arts. He collected early colonial furniture of Western Australia. Receiving commissions from individual clients and from architects to design or supply modern furniture, he was reliant on the ability of craftsmen to understand his concepts. He encouraged them to use jarrah, a local timber. His enthusiasm for the wood was shared by Joseph Pietrocola and Charles and Roy Catt, who made his later designs.

A committee-member (1955-57) of the Art Gallery Society, Foulkes Taylor was a member of the Weld Club, the Royal Freshwater Bay Yacht Club, the Fabian Society and the Australian Labor Party. He died of the effects of injuries received in a motorcar accident on 19 September 1966 at Woodside, Victoria, and was cremated with Baptist forms. His wife survived him. Robert Bell described him as having had 'a pervasive influence on the design of the "new" Perth of the 1960s'. In 1982 the Western Australian Institute of Technology staged an exhibition of modern design, The Foulkes Taylor Years.

P. Duffy (ed), *The Foulkes Taylor Years*, exhibition cat (Perth, 1982); *Corian*, Dec 1945; *Craftwest*, no 4, 1995, p 23; *West Australian*, 20 Sept, 14 Oct 1966.

DOROTHY ERICKSON

TAYLOR, DORIS IRENE (1901-1968), founder of Meals on Wheels, was born on 25 July 1901 at Norwood, Adelaide, eldest of four children of Thomas Simpkin Taylor, bricklayer, and his wife Angelina, née Williams, late Pulford. Doris spent her childhood first at Mount Gambier and then at Norwood. A fall at the age of 7 caused her to limp quite badly. In 1912 she sustained a spinal injury from another fall and was permanently paralysed. After several operations and years of extended stays in hospital, it was suggested that she should live in the Home for Incurables. Doris and her mother strongly resisted this proposal: Doris went home and remained 'independent' for the rest of her life.

Little is known of Miss Taylor's education, save that she was well read. She was confined to a wheelchair, and her condition was compounded by rheumatoid arthritis so severe that she was completely dependent upon others for her physical needs. Her mobility only extended to her head and shoulders, and, to a limited extent, her arms. Although her hands were twisted and stiff, and she could not raise her arms high enough to brush her hair, she devised her own method of putting on lipstick, making telephone calls and doing embroidery.

Taylor's character and determination led her to find ways to participate in society. During the Depression she became secretary of a local kindergarten mothers' club and helped to create schemes to raise funds. Her work in promoting a soup kitchen heightened her awareness of social injustice. As secretary of the West Norwood sub-branch of the Australian Labor Party, she was credited with pesuading Donald Dunstan to join the party and to seek pre-selection for the House of Assembly seat of Norwood in 1952. She successfully managed his first election campaign. In the early 1950s she also acted as public relations officer for the South Australian division of the Australian Pensioners' League and helped to reorganize the Authorised Newsagents' Association of South Australia Ltd.

About this time Taylor began to campaign for improvements to social services for the aged, the infirm, the underprivileged and those most vulnerable in the community. She saw that political action was essential and thought that 'good legislation could ensure security and protection for everybody'. While conscious that the elderly required greater levels of help, she clearly understood their need for independence and their wish to be looked after in their own homes.

In 1953 Taylor founded Meals on Wheels. The first kitchen opened at Port Adelaide in August 1954; others soon followed in different Adelaide suburbs. Operated by volunteers, Meals on Wheels delivered five hot meals each week to those who were unable to cook for themselves. For many recipients, the daily visits also provided an important social contact with the outside world. The organization grew into a State-wide body and served as a model for other States and countries to follow. Meals on Wheels began operating in Tasmania in 1955, Queensland in 1956 and New

South Wales in 1957. Taylor's vision embraced supplementary activities: home help, hair care, laundry, library and chiropody services, the supply of frozen meals, and a hospital-based meal service. In 1965 an adviser in geriatrics for the World Health Organization commented that Taylor had built up 'the best, most complete and most effectively integrated system of preventive medicine for old folk operating anywhere in the world'.

Described as courageous, determined and indefatigable, Taylor believed that each individual had the right to be treated with dignity. From its inception, she was the inspiration and driving force behind Meals on Wheels: she travelled extensively in South Australia and other States, urged governments and local authorities to provide support, and took the lead in negotiating expansion of the service. From 1958 to 1968 Meals on Wheels in South Australia employed her as its paid organizer. In 1967 twenty-one kitchens in the State supplied a total of 336 581 meals; by that year more than two million meals had been delivered.

In 1959 Taylor had been appointed M.B.E. Fond of A. A. Milne's *Winnie the Pooh*, she entertained her nieces and nephews with stories, and pictures and poems about animals in clothes. She died of bronchopneumonia on 23 May 1968 in Royal Adelaide Hospital and was cremated with Methodist forms.

D. Dunstan, *Felicia* (Melb, 1981); S. Baldwin (ed), *Unsung Heroes & Heroines of Australia* (Melb, 1988); M. Cudmore, *A Meal a Day* (Adel, 1996); Meals on Wheels (SA), *Annual Report*, 1968; information from Mrs J. Pegler, Athelstone, Adel.

GREG CRAFTER

TAYLOR, DOUGLAS ROY (1903-1968), labourer and soldier, was born on 14 August 1903 at Portlethen, Kincardineshire, Scotland, son of David Taylor, master blacksmith, and his wife Elizabeth, née Watson. By 1939 'Jock' was working as a labourer in Melbourne. Six feet (183 cm) tall, with hazel eyes and auburn hair, he enlisted in the Australian Imperial Force on 23 October; he was posted to the 2nd/7th Battalion in November and promoted corporal in the following month. On 9 March 1940 at the Methodist Church, Seymour, he married Lesley May Heeps, a 22-year-old nurse. He embarked for the Middle East on 15 April.

When operations in Libya began in January 1941, Taylor quickly stood out as a fearless soldier who relished being in the thick of battle. At Bardia, he disrupted the Italian supply-line with accurate rifle-fire until enemy guns retaliated with a direct hit on the post he was occupying. He emerged unscathed, shrugging off 'bits of concrete and saying with a giggle: "See, the bastards don't like it"'.

On 17 April at Lárisa, Greece, Taylor and some of his section manned a train abandoned by its Greek crew during a prolonged air-attack and took the widely dispersed 2nd/7th Battalion to Domokos, some 80 miles (130 km) away. Two days later he led an attempt to retrieve a train-load of valuable fuel, ammunition and explosives. German aircraft attacked while he was alone in the engine and blew up the trucks' contents. His hair was singed but he was otherwise unharmed. Evacuated via Crete to Egypt, he rejoined his battalion in Palestine. In August he was promoted acting sergeant.

The 2nd/7th sailed to Colombo in March 1942 and spent three months garrisoning Ceylon (Sri Lanka). Following a term in Australia, the battalion was sent to Milne Bay, Papua, in October. At Buna, on 5 December, Taylor had command of a Bren-gun carrier which, with four others, led American infantry against entrenched Japanese positions. Peppered by enemy fire, all five vehicles were abandoned within half an hour and most of the men killed, including the platoon commander. Taylor found himself in charge. He and his crew succeeded in silencing two strong-posts: one of his men was killed and all of the remainder wounded. Taylor's left arm was shattered by machine-gun bullets. Bleeding profusely, he crawled to the rear of the third strong-post and destroyed it with grenades. He lost and regained consciousness, then made his way back to the American lines. For his 'inspiring example' he was awarded the Distinguished Conduct Medal.

Following a lengthy stay in hospitals and convalescent units, Taylor rejoined his battalion in November 1943. Promoted acting warrant officer, class two, in January 1944, he served in the Aitape-Wewak campaign (1944-45) in New Guinea. He was discharged from the army, medically unfit, on 5 October 1945. After he returned home, he spent five years as licensee of the Prince Patrick Hotel, Collingwood, before working for the Essendon City Council. A widower, he married an 80-year-old divorcee Victoria Emily Crossey, née Jenyns, on 19 February 1968 at the office of the government statist, Melbourne. He committed suicide by inhaling carbon monoxide gas on 19 September that year at his Caulfield home. Survived by his wife, he was cremated. Geoffrey Mainwaring's portrait of Taylor is held by the Australian War Memorial, Canberra.

G. Long, *To Benghazi* (Canb, 1952) and *Greece, Crete and Syria* (Canb, 1953); D. McCarthy, *South-West Pacific Area—First Year* (Canb, 1959); W. P. Bolger and J. G. Littlewood, *The Fiery Phoenix* (Melb, 1983); *Collingwood and Fitzroy Courier*, 31 July 1958.   A. J. SWEETING

TAYLOR, GEORGE FRANCIS (1903-1979), secret service officer and banker, was born on 13 January 1903 at Prahran, Melbourne, son of George Arthur Taylor, merchant, and his wife Annie Mary, née Ryan, both Melbourne born. George was educated at Xavier College (dux 1921) and at the University of Melbourne (B.A. Hons, 1925; M.A., 1927; LL.B., 1928) where he won prizes for debating. He freelanced as a journalist and occasionally wrote on foreign affairs before joining the Shell Co. of Australia Ltd in 1930.

Business, and his ambition to write a book on British foreign policy, took Taylor to London in the mid-1930s. At the Church of the Oratory, Kensington, on 17 June 1937 he married with Catholic rites 21-year-old Judith Vivian Rose Price. In July 1939 he was employed by Major Laurence Grand in section D (for 'Destruction') of the Secret Intelligence Service. The section had been established (1938) to investigate the potential of sabotage and subversion in time of war. Early in 1940 Taylor was appointed head of its Balkan network—which had the task of staunching the flow of Romanian oil to Germany—but his contribution lay as much in defining strategy and tactics as it did in conducting operations. Before the fall of France, he advocated sabotage of communications by local patriots under British direction; after June, he was an architect of the 'secret army' strategy, by which Britain hoped to foment uprisings in occupied Europe.

The Special Operations Executive, created in July 1940, incorporated section D. Taylor became chief of staff to Sir Frank Nelson, S.O.E.'s first executive head. Finding that Taylor's Balkan organization was the only functional asset inherited from the section, Nelson sent him to the region in January 1941 to oversee measures to counter the Germans' expected offensive. When the Yugoslav government succumbed to Nazi coercion on 25 March, S.O.E. agents promoted the military coup which toppled it thirty-six hours later. After the Germans invaded, Taylor and most of his colleagues were captured by the Italians while trying to escape from the Adriatic coast. Mistakenly assumed to be a diplomat, he was held for two months before being released. Back in London, he was made director of overseas groups and missions in March 1942. In mid-1943 he briefly served as chief of staff to Sir Charles Hambro, who replaced Nelson. Taylor saw out the war as director of S.O.E.'s Far East group, which entailed extensive travel. He had been given the honorary rank of colonel and been appointed C.B.E. (1943).

A short, dark man with sharp features and methodical habits, Taylor had impressed Julian Amery in 1940 by eating identical meals in the same restaurant on three successive evenings. He was invariably described by admirers and detractors as utterly ruthless, though his friends added 'but brilliant'. The last chief under whom he served, Major General (Sir) Colin Gubbins, regarded him as 'a very able, quick-thinking officer, of great energy and persistence, who at times presses his points too hard'. Taylor became a director (1950), deputy-chairman (1966) and chairman (1970) of the Bank of London & South America Ltd, and helped to implement its merger (1971) with Lloyds Bank Europe Ltd. He returned to Australia in the mid-1970s and settled in Perth. Survived by his wife, and their son and two daughters, he died on 17 January 1979 at Nedlands and was buried in Karrakatta cemetery.

B. Sweet-Escott, *Baker Street Irregular* (Lond, 1965); J. Amery, *Approach March* (Lond, 1973); P. Auty and R. Clogg (eds), *British Policy towards Wartime Resistance in Yugoslavia and Greece* (NY, 1975); D. Stafford, *Britain and European Resistance, 1940-1945* (Lond, 1980); C. Cruickshank, *SOE in the Far East* (Oxford, 1983); Xavier College, *Xaverian*, 1921-22 and 1925-29; Bank of London & South America Ltd, *Report & Accounts*, 1970; SOE papers (PRO, Lond); G. Taylor personal file (Foreign and Cwlth Office, Lond).　　MARK WHEELER

TAYLOR, HAROLD BURFIELD (1890-1966), chemist and army officer, was born on 10 August 1890 at Enfield, Sydney, third child of Ernest Burfield Taylor, a civil servant from England, and his native-born wife Louisa Henrietta, née Chowne. Harold was educated at Sydney Boys' High School and the University of Sydney (B.Sc., 1912; D.Sc., 1925). From his undergraduate years he retained two abiding interests—'the pursuit of chemistry and military science'. He served in the Sydney University Scouts (Militia) and was commissioned on 16 February 1913. In June 1915 he became assistant government analyst in the New South Wales Department of Public Health.

Appointed second lieutenant, Australian Imperial Force, on 16 September that year, Taylor joined the 19th Battalion in Egypt in January 1916. In March he was sent to France, where he proved a brave and resourceful leader. He was promoted lieutenant in June and captain in February 1917. On 15 April his company helped to stem a German attack at Lagnicourt. While under heavy machine-gun fire, he 'moved up and down' the position, encouraging his men. He was awarded the Military Cross. With a small party, he captured Daisy Wood, east of Ypres, Belgium, on 9 October; for his example, courage and initiative, he won a Bar to his M.C.

When Taylor's A.I.F. appointment terminated in Sydney on 30 April 1919, he returned to his work as an analyst. In 1927 he was elected a fellow of the (Royal) Australian Chemical Institute. He came to public notice for his research on the preservation of milk, and in 1930 was promoted second government analyst. After resuming his Militia service in 1920, he rose to lieutenant colonel in 1927 and commanded a number of battalions from 1926 until the outbreak of World War II. In October 1939 he was promoted temporary brigadier and given the 5th Brigade. Seconded to the A.I.F. on 1 July 1940, he was placed in command of the 22nd Brigade, 8th Division. At St Matthew's Church of England, Manly, on 23 October that year he married Nellie Birkenhead Starling; they had no children.

Arriving in Singapore ahead of his brigade on 7 February 1941, Taylor soon fell out with his divisional commander, Major General H. G. Bennett [q.v.13]. Both were men of strong opinions and obstinate temperament. Much of the burden of the 8th Division's resistance to the Japanese advance in Malaya and Singapore fell on Taylor's brigade. As the Japanese swept across Singapore Island in early February 1942, Bennett made 'disparaging remarks' about the way Taylor handled the defence of his sector and about the men in the 22nd. By 12 February Taylor was exhausted and Bennett relieved him of command. Taylor later wrote bitterly of his relations with Bennett, and considered him prey to vanity and personal ambition. Others thought that Taylor's removal from command reflected no official discredit on the 'thorny brigadier'.

Following the surrender of Singapore on 15 February 1942, Taylor spent his initial period of captivity at Changi, where he helped to set up classes in basic education and advanced courses in languages, science and law. The scheme collapsed when most of the prisoners of war were dispatched to work-camps in Asia. Taylor was later described, somewhat grandiloquently, as the 'Chancellor of Changi'. In August the Japanese sent him and other senior officers to Formosa (Taiwan), whence he was removed to Mukden camp, Manchuria. There he remained until the war ended. Imprisonment took its toll: he was not deemed fit to transfer to the Retired List until 9 January 1946.

Back in Sydney Taylor was appointed government analyst in March 1946. The work of his laboratory staff was wide-ranging: they analysed adulterated food, checked that water was fit for human consumption and even monitored the quality of ink used in post offices. Taylor sat on several committees, one of which set the standard quality for a regular loaf of bread. It was his testimony at trials involving poisoning that brought him greatest prominence. Newspapers relished accounts of how he personally tasted liquids for evidence that they contained strychnine or cyanide. As one account put it, he 'lives as next-door neighbour to death'. Taylor retired from the public service in September 1954, but continued to work as a consultant. His recreations included fishing, golf and tennis. Survived by his wife, he died on 15 March 1966 at the Repatriation General Hospital, Concord, and was cremated. Alec Hill, who had served under him in the Militia, remembered him as 'quiet, unflappable and firm, with a fine bearing and a sense of humour'.

C. E. W. Bean, *The A.I.F. in France, 1917* (Syd, 1933); L. Wigmore, *The Japanese Thrust* (Canb, 1957); *People* (Syd), 22 Nov 1950; Roy Aust Chemical Inst, *Procs*, 33, no 8, Aug 1966, p 200; *Stand–To* (Canb), 10, no 6, Oct-Dec 1966, p 37; *SMH*, 12 Apr 1928, 26 May 1949, 9 Sept 1951; H. B. Taylor diary, 1 July 1940-30 Nov 1941 (AWM).

RICHARD E. REID

TAYLOR, HERBERT (1885-1970), accountant and company director, was born on 11 May 1885 at Malmsbury, Victoria, eldest of five children of Ralph Herbert William Taylor, schoolteacher, and his wife Alice Ann, née French, both Victorian born. His father was headmaster (1882-94) of Nhill State School and then of a succession of suburban schools in Melbourne. From 1896 the family lived at Ormond. Leaving Caulfield Grammar School in 1902, Herbert began work as a clerk with W. J. Bush & Co. Ltd, chemical manufacturers. Three years later he joined the accountants Flack & Flack [q.v.8] who sent him in 1907 to open their Perth office. In 1913 he became senior audit clerk with a Melbourne firm of accountants, Young & Outhwaite. Founded in 1909, the firm built its reputation on prudence, sound accounting practice and professional education. Taylor secured his permanent career with a partnership in 1917; he was to become senior partner on A. H. Outhwaite's retirement in 1947.

On 8 May 1919 at the Congregational Church, Brighton, Taylor married Doris Madeline Brock (d.1966). A founding (1928) fellow of the Institute of Chartered Accountants in Australia, he was (from 1933) one of two inaugural vice-presidents of the offshoot Chartered Accountants (Aust.) Research Society of Victoria. Its object was to bring members of the institute together, 'professionally, socially and in various forms of sport'. Under the society's auspices, Taylor published two booklets, *The Organisation of a Chartered Accountant's Office* (1933) and *The Audit of Sharebrokers' Accounts* (1937). His third publication, *The Business Man and His Investments*, appeared in 1945.

A man of 'exceptional energy and conscientiousness', Taylor was elected junior vice-president of the Melbourne Chamber of Commerce in 1941 and president in 1943. He joined the Institute of Public Affairs and was to serve on its council in 1945-66. From June to September 1944, as an I.P.A. nominee, he chaired several meetings of Victorian political groups opposed to the Australian Labor Party and reported the outcome to (Sir) Robert Menzies [q.v.15]. These meetings preceded Menzies' conventions—in Canberra in October and at Albury, New South Wales, in December—which led to the formation of the Liberal Party of Australia.

One of twenty-two appointees to the party's provisional Victorian executive, Taylor was its interim chairman before handing over in June 1945 to (Sir) William Anderson [q.v.13], a fellow resident of East Malvern. Taylor withdrew from the political front line, in accordance with the policy of the Victorian I.P.A. He served on the Liberal Party's finance committee and became a trustee of the State branch. After two years as president of the Associated Chambers of Commerce of Australia, he voiced in April 1947 the Liberal stance against the rise of 'autocratic Socialism', deploring worker intimidation by an extremist minority of union leaders and calling on Australians to restore 'the desire to do good work'.

Company boards that sought Taylor's financial expertise included the Argus & Australasian Ltd and A. V. Jennings Industries (Australia) Ltd. He chaired Sargood Gardiner Ltd, William Drummond & Co. Ltd, Griffiths Bros Ltd and Aberfoyle Holdings Ltd. A councillor (1945-55) of the University of Melbourne, he was chairman (1950-54) of its finance committee. In addition, he was treasurer (1950-55), vice-president (1956-61) and president (1961-65) of the Royal Automobile Club of Victoria. He became a fellow of the Institute of Directors, London. In 1959 he was appointed C.M.G.

Taylor belonged to the Melbourne and Athenaeum clubs. His youthful interest in cricket and tennis gave way to golf, which he played at the Metropolitan club at Oakleigh (member 1919) and later at the Portsea club. One of the reformist 'Metropolitan Bolsheviks' of the early 1920s, he joined the committee in 1928, and was treasurer (1933-35), club captain (1941-43), president (1952-54) and a life member (from 1956). During World War II he wrote a much-appreciated newsletter of club doings, spiced with 'salty humour' and a 'pinch of sentiment', for the eighty members on active service. By invitation, he joined the international Senior Golfers' Society and the Royal and Ancient Golf Club of St Andrews, Scotland. He also enjoyed fly-fishing, bowls and horse-racing. The Royal Victorian Institute for the Blind and the Freemasons' Hospital both made him a life governor. Survived by his three sons, he died on 24 July 1970 in East Melbourne and was cremated. His eldest son Grahame joined Young & Outhwaite.

J. Kissling, *Seventy Years* (Melb, 1973); P. Aimer, *Politics, Power and Persuasion* (Melb, 1974); N. J. Marshall, *A Jubilee History 1928-1978* (Melb, 1978); D. Garden, *Builders to the Nation* (Melb, 1992); I. Hancock, *National and Permanent?* (Melb, 2000); *IPA Review*, July/Sept 1970; *Royalauto*, Sept 1970; *Argus*, 29 May 1943, 30 Dec 1944, 23, 24 Apr 1947; information from Mr A. G. Taylor, Toorak, Melb.

SUSAN PRIESTLEY

TAYLOR, JOSEPH PATRICK (1908-1976), casino-operator and gambler, was born on 24 November 1908 in Sydney, son of native-born parents Edmund Barton Taylor, hotel cellarman, and his wife Norah Catherine, née Killalea. As a young man, Joe took up boxing and played Rugby League football; he later managed League teams and boxers, before working as a billposter. On 15 August 1932 at St Pius's Catholic Church, Enmore, he married Edith Anne May Johnson. They had a son before he divorced her on 7 September 1944. At the district registrar's office, Waverley, on 29 September that year he married Elizabeth Watson. By that stage he described himself as a bookmaker and shipwright.

During World War II Taylor became involved with 'Thommo's' two-up school, a series of 'floating' games begun in 1910 by George Joseph Guest, which operated illegally in inner Sydney for decades. In 1949 Taylor reopened Rose's Restaurant, 105 York Street, as the Celebrity Restaurant Club and brought American entertainers to Sydney. His nightclub flourished and in 1954 he opened the Carlisle Club in Kellett Street, Kings Cross, which was similarly successful. He provided illicit casino facilities, mainly for games like baccarat. The clubs were predominantly decorated in red, his favourite colour (he regarded red presents such as ties or socks as lucky). In 1954, when Guest died, Taylor took control of Thommo's.

A 'magnificent, if unflamboyant, gambler at cards, horses or greyhounds', Taylor lived by his belief that 'money is nothing but betting ammunition, and it's not worth having if you can't get the pleasure of giving it to your friends'. He owned racehorses and served on the committee of City Tattersall's Club for more than ten years. In 1962 he had his most famous win when his horse Birthday Card won the Sydney Turf Club's Golden Slipper Stakes. He gave away most of his winnings and lost the rest on another of his horses which ran last in the last race of the day. Bill Waterhouse, the bookmaker, said that Taylor was 'one of the few men in the world who completely doesn't give a damn about money'.

Nicknamed 'The Boss', Taylor was well known to many people, including the radio personality Jack Davey [q.v.13], the State premier Robin (Sir Robert) Askin and the newspaper publisher Ezra Norton [q.v.15]. He also associated with major illegal gambling operators, among them Perce Galea [q.v.14], and with more notorious individuals, such as Frederick Charles Anderson and Len McPherson. Police spasmodically raided Thommo's, but many suspected that the raids were staged. In the late 1960s, while Askin was premier and Norman Allan [q.v.13] his police commissioner, Sydney's gambling clubs were transformed into fully-fledged casinos.

A widower, Taylor married Patricia Mary Moffit, née Kessey, on 29 September 1971 at the registrar general's office, Sydney. She was a 46-year-old secretary and a divorcee; he gave his occupation as restaurateur. He died of myocardial infarction on 17 August 1976 in Sydney Hospital and was cremated. His wife survived him, as did the son of his first marriage and the two daughters of his second.

D. Hickie, *The Prince and the Premier* (Syd, 1985); G. Freeman, *George Freeman, an Autobiography* (Syd, 1988); *Daily Mirror* (Syd), 19, 20 Aug 1976; *Sun* (Syd), 20 Aug 1976; *SMH*, 23 Mar 1985.

MALCOLM BROWN

TAYLOR, LYRA VERONICA ESMERALDA (1894-1979), social worker and public servant, was born on 11 July 1894 at Ngaire (Stratford), New Zealand, one of four children of Robert Taylor, a farmer from England, and his New Zealand-born wife Mary, née Morrison. After her father died, scholarships enabled Lyra to remain at school and to attend Victoria University College (LL.B., N.Z., 1918). In 1918 she became the first woman to be admitted to the Bar in Wellington; within seven years she was made a partner in a law firm.

Interested in the social implications of the law, Miss Taylor attended the conference of the International Council of Women, held in Washington, D.C., in 1925. She entered Johns Hopkins University, Baltimore (M.A., 1927), and carried out research at the Juvenile Court, Boston, Massachusetts. Meanwhile, she also engaged in social work for the Family Welfare Agency of Baltimore. Leaving the United States in 1929, she worked as district secretary, Family Welfare Association, Montreal, Canada, and taught at the Montreal School of Social Work. As director (1934-39) of an education programme in social work, run by the local branch of the Young Women's Christian Association, she found her role 'interesting but not congenial'.

In 1940 Taylor was appointed general secretary of the Y.W.C.A., Sydney. She introduced more liberal policies, encouraged self-reliance, tolerated smoking and drinking (in moderation), and invited servicemen to the Y for 'Open House'. The board of directors did not embrace her ideas and in December 1942 she declined to renew her contract. A committee-member (1940-42) of the New South Wales Council of Social Service, she served (1940-44) on the board of social studies, University of Sydney, and lectured part time (1941) in the university's department of social sciences. She usually dressed in black, and wore her hair in an old-fashioned bun.

Taylor returned to Canada in 1943. Next year she was invited by the Commonwealth Department of Social Services to establish its social work section in Melbourne and to advise on social-services legislation. She initiated a programme to train social workers under the Colombo Plan, and encouraged Australians to take up United Nations scholarships in this field in the United States. In 1946 she became a founding member of the Australian Association of Social Workers. From 1947 to 1952 she served as a member of the board of social studies, University of Melbourne. A key figure in raising the status of social work, she frequently travelled abroad to undertake research, attend conferences and gain fresh ideas.

In 1959 Taylor retired from the public service. Appointed O.B.E. that year, she joined the Old People's Welfare Council of Victoria as assistant-director. She was director (1965-69) of the National Old People's Welfare Council of Australia (Australian Council on the Ageing from 1968). In 1969 she spent six months in Perth as acting-director, Western Australian Council on the Ageing. Lyra Taylor died on 23 March 1979 at Richmond, Melbourne, and was buried with Anglican rites in Fawkner cemetery.

G. Gatfield, *Without Prejudice* (Wellington, NZ, 1996); *Aust Social Work*, 32, 3 Sept 1979, p 49; *SMH*, 30 Nov 1939, 29 Aug 1942, 28 Oct 1944; *Smith's Weekly* (Syd), 4 Oct 1941; M. Glasson, Lyra Taylor (taped interview, 1972, NL); information from Mrs E. McGuire, Yarralumla, Canb.

ANTHEA BUNDOCK

TAYLOR, RONALD (1918-1942), sailor, was born on 29 April 1918 at Carlton, Melbourne, fourth of ten children of Collingwood-born parents George Taylor, ironworker, and his wife Elsie, née Davey. Raised at Carlton and Port Melbourne, Ron was a typical boy of the time: he played cricket and Australian Rules football, went fishing and rode billycarts. He developed an interest in the Royal Australian Navy through watching warships entering port and from talking to sailors about life in the service. At the age of 7 he became the mascot of the sloop H.M.A.S. *Marguerite* and was given his own uniform to wear on special occasions.

In 1930, in the Depression, George Taylor abandoned his family. The two eldest boys went to Queensland to work on a sugar-cane plantation and the eldest girl found a job on a farm; Ron and his brother Ray stayed at home; the five youngest children were placed in institutions. Ron left school at the end of Grade 8 to work as a labourer. On 12 June 1935 he joined the R.A.N. as an ordinary seaman. He was then 5 ft 6¼ ins (168 cm) tall, with dark brown hair, brown eyes and a fresh complexion; within twelve months he had gained almost 2 ins (5 cm) in height and had an anchor tattooed in red and blue on his right forearm.

Taylor began his training at Flinders Naval Depot, Westernport. In April 1936 he was posted to the cruiser H.M.A.S. *Australia*. After undertaking a course in gunnery (April-September 1938) at Flinders, he served in the destroyer H.M.A.S. *Vampire* and in the cruiser H.M.A.S. *Adelaide* before transferring to the sloop H.M.A.S. *Yarra*, in August 1939.

Yarra remained in Australian waters until August 1940 when she was dispatched to Aden to join the Red Sea Force. The ship took part in operations against Iraq in May 1941 and against Persia in August. 'Buck' Taylor was promoted acting leading seaman and given command of one of *Yarra*'s four-inch (100 mm) guns. *Yarra* was in the Mediterranean in November-December, escorting convoys which ferried supplies and troops to the allied garrison at Tobruk, Libya. On each of the four trips the sloop made, Taylor's gun was active in beating off enemy air-attacks.

By early 1942 *Yarra* was employed on escort duties between Java and Singapore. On 5 February she rescued 1804 people from the burning troop-ship *Empress of Asia* which had been crippled by an air-attack near Singapore. (Sir) Hastings Harrington [q.v.14] later reported that Taylor had controlled his gun 'on this occasion, as on many others', with 'judgment and determination', and added that his 'keenness and courage' set a good example to those around him.

On 27 February 1942 *Yarra* was ordered to escort three auxiliary vessels from Java to Fremantle, Western Australia. Five Japanese warships intercepted the convoy on 4 March. Despite *Yarra*'s gallant defence, all four allied vessels were destroyed, with the sloop the last to be sunk. Taylor ignored the order to abandon ship and stayed alone at his gun, firing slowly and defiantly at the enemy until he was killed shortly before the ship went down.

T. M. Jones and I. L. Idriess, *The Silent Service* (Syd, 1944); A. F. Parry, *H.M.A.S. Yarra* (Syd, 1944);

G. H. Gill, *Royal Australian Navy 1939-1942* (Canb, 1957); S. Baldwin (ed), *Unsung Heroes and Heroines of Australia* (Melb, 1988); family papers held by, and information from, Mrs D. Pezzi, Frankston, Vic.

GREG SWINDEN

TEAKLE, LAURENCE JOHN HARTLEY (1901-1979), professor of agriculture, was born on 2 August 1901 at Hawker, South Australia, eldest of seven children of David John Teakle, farmer, and his wife Bertha, née Bridgeman, both South Australian born. In 1903 the family moved to Western Australia and settled on a farm in the Northampton district, north of Geraldton. Hartley was educated at a small one-teacher school at Isseka siding, at Perth Modern School and at the University of Western Australia (B.Sc.Agric., 1923) where he won the Amy Saw scholarship. Joining the Department of Agriculture as an agricultural adviser in 1923, he travelled to the United States of America to study plant nutrition at the University of California, Berkeley (M.S., 1924; Ph.D., 1927). On 7 June 1927 at Berkeley he married with Methodist Episcopal forms Beatrice Elizabeth Inch, a schoolteacher.

Returning to Western Australia, Teakle was appointed research officer and adviser in plant nutrition in the Department of Agriculture in 1928. For the next nineteen years he investigated soils and plant nutrition from Esperance to the Ord River. He also lectured at the university on 'Soil Science and Fertilizers'. His numerous reports and research papers (over sixty as senior author) made major contributions to the understanding of soil salinity and agricultural development through their analysis of soils, examination of phosphate fertilizer experiments and identification of micro-nutrient deficiencies in crops. In his presidential address to the Royal Society of Western Australia in 1938, he offered a description of Western Australian soils and their properties which has served as a standard for all subsequent work. He was gazetted commissioner of soil conservation in July 1946.

Next year Teakle was appointed professor of agriculture at the University of Queensland. Developing broad interests in the agricultural and pastoral industries, he promoted research into many of the problems that affected them. In 1951 he was awarded the Farrer [q.v.8] medal. He chaired (1957-63) the Queensland Wheat Industry Research Committee and published (with R. A. Boyle) *Fertilizers for the Farm and Garden* (Sydney, c.1958). Becoming increasingly involved in university administration, he served as president (1960-62) of the professorial board, deputy vice-chancellor (1963-70) and acting

vice-chancellor (1967 and 1969). These difficult years saw a rapid growth in enrolments, student unrest, and an increasingly antagonistic government and press. The university conferred an honorary LL.D. on Teakle in 1969. He retired in December 1970, the year in which he was appointed C.M.G.

An associate (1929) of the (Royal) Australian Chemical Institute and an honorary member of the Australian Society of Soil Science, Teakle was a fellow of the Australian Institute of Agricultural Science (1962) and of the Australian College of Education (1970). A building at the university was named after him in 1971. He was a staunch Methodist, a devoted family man, and a person of 'boundless mental and physical energy'. In his retirement he wrote *The David Teakle Saga* (1979), a 290-page family history. Survived by his wife, and their daughter and three sons, he died on 8 December 1979 at Auchenflower and was buried in Pinaroo lawn cemetery, Aspley.

G. H. Burvill (ed), *Agriculture in Western Australia* (Perth, 1979); M. I. Thomis, *A Place of Light and Learning* (Brisb, 1985); *J of Roy Soc of WA*, 63, 1980, p 63; *Soil News*, no 48, 1981, p 12; G. H. Burvill, information on L. J. H. Teakle (WA Dept Agriculture L, Perth).

JACK F. LONERAGAN

TEARLE, WILLIAM (1911-1979), educationist, was born on 11 September 1911 at Hillgrove, New South Wales, son of native-born parents William Tearle, goldminer, and his wife Stella Malvena Margaret, née Moore. Bill junior was educated at Lithgow Intermediate High School, and at the University of Sydney (B.Sc.Agr., 1933) while at Teachers' College. In 1933 the Department of Education sent him to Wagga Wagga High School as science and agriculture teacher, overseer of the school's farm and supervisor of its junior farmers' club. Some three hundred of these clubs were established throughout the State to promote the use of science in agriculture and other rural industries, retain young people on the land, foster citizenship and leadership skills, and provide opportunities for social functions and travel.

On 15 May 1939 at St Mary's Catholic Cathedral, Sydney, Tearle married Sheila Eileen Byrne, a teacher. Throughout his postings at Hurlstone Agricultural High School (1936-39 and 1947-48) and at high schools at Temora (1940 and 1948-53) and Griffith (1941-46), he continued his work with junior farmers. While at Griffith, he rode his bicycle to inspect club projects at centres such as Yenda and Yoogali (for which the department allowed him $1\frac{1}{2}$d. per mile) and mobilized members to assist the Council for Scientific and Industrial Research in studies of soils and irrigation. He also contributed articles to the local press on junior-farming activities, and conducted a weekly programme on radio-station 2RG.

In September 1953 Tearle was transferred to the department's head office in Sydney and appointed State organizer of junior farmers' clubs. The movement for which he was responsible was highly regarded in educational circles. The junior farmers were required (with some adult supervision) to undertake and document projects, a number of which were entered in club competitions. State championships at the Royal Easter Show marked the climax of the year's work. Junior farmers participated in other show activities, learning to become judges and officials, as well as competitors. Tearle set up annual conferences for junior farmers: the first was held at Dungog in 1957. These events, with field-days, residential schools, and a programme of interstate and overseas visits and exchanges, enabled young people to broaden their horizons and to meet others with similar interests.

By the 1950s the gender imbalance in the clubs had become a matter of concern. That girls made up only about 35 per cent of the members inhibited the clubs' social attractiveness. Tearle secured the appointment of a woman supervisor and expanded the range of projects to include home-making subjects (girls had previously engaged in the same activities as boys—such as keeping poultry, raising calves or growing vegetables). In 1966 the movement was renamed the Rural Youth Organisation of New South Wales. Helped by his wife, Tearle established and edited a bi-monthly journal, *Rural Youth* (1966-72), which conveyed information to the clubs and provided a forum for their members.

Tearle saw the value of forging links with government departments and commercial corporations, among them the Rural Bank of New South Wales, which sponsored the clubs generously. He retired in February 1976. Survived by his wife and their son, he died of cerebrovascular disease on 25 June 1979 at Kogarah and was buried in Woronora lawn cemetery.

Bank Notes (Syd), 19, Sept 1937, p 34; *Area News* (Griffith, NSW), 27 June 1979; *Daily Advertiser* (Wagga Wagga, NSW), 25 July 1979; Tearle papers (ML); teachers' records, Dept of Education (NSW) Archives, Syd.   BEVERLEY KINGSTON

TEASDALE, SIR JOHN SMITH (1881-1962), wheat-farmer and administrator, was born on 28 June 1881 at Alston, Cumberland, England, son of James Teasdale, stonemason, and his wife Jane, née Maughan. Educated locally, John worked for Robert Stephenson & Co. Ltd at Darlington, Durham, and as a grain merchant. In 1911 he migrated to Western Australia with at least three of his brothers; they settled in the Bruce Rock district, at Belka and Totadgin. Drought destroyed their first crop in 1914. Local farmers met with John to discuss ways of improving their lot. By 1916 he was an executive-member of the Farmers and Settlers' Association of Western Australia. He supported orderly marketing and helped to found a co-operative, the Wheat Pool of Western Australia, in 1922. During the 1920s he visited Britain and the United States of America several times on the co-operative's behalf.

On 22 August 1929 at the district registrar's office, Perth, Teasdale married 23-year-old Luita Christina Waldeck. A staunch member of the Country Party, he lobbied the government for the Farmers' Debts Adjustment Act (1930). That year he advised wheat-growers throughout the State to 'concentrate their resources' by employing 'better methods of cultivation on smaller areas of first-class land'. President (1932-40) of the Primary Producers' Association of Western Australia, he intensified his commitment to controlled marketing when world wheat prices fell during the Depression. In 1932 he proposed that Prime Minister Lyons [q.v.10] should call for a 20 per cent reduction in the acreage of all major wheat-producing countries. In December that year the radical Wheatgrowers' Union of Western Australia led a movement to withhold the delivery of wheat in an effort to force the establishment of a compulsory national pool. Teasdale opposed the proposal and pushed through the farmers' picket lines at Belka to ensure that his wheat was delivered. His wheat bags were slashed by the picketers. He became a founding director of Co-operative Bulk Handling Ltd in 1933.

In 1939 Teasdale was appointed a growers' representative on the Australian Wheat Board. He chaired (1947) the Western Australian royal commission on wheat marketing and stabilization. In July 1950 (Sir) John McEwen [q.v.15] dismissed the A.W.B.'s chairman and replaced him with Teasdale; justifying his action, he praised Teasdale's practical farming experience, commitment, negotiating skills, and understanding of the rural economy and international trade. Teasdale moved to Melbourne and remained chairman until his death. He supported research into new strains of wheat and endeavoured to develop new markets, but he opposed selling wheat to China on extended credit, an issue on which he was out-voted by the board.

Teasdale was appointed C.B.E. in 1948 and knighted in 1951. He advocated government support for the primary sector, but maintained that 'the produce of the land belongs in its entirety to the producer, subject only to the fulfilment of his lawful obligations'. Survived by his wife and their daughter, Sir John died on 2 July 1962 in his home at Kew and was cremated with Anglican rites.

F. R. Mercer, *On Farmers' Service* (Perth, 1955); J. Sandford, *Walter Harper and the Wheat Farmers* (Perth, 1955); J. K. Ewers, *Bruce Rock* (Perth, 1959); C. Ayris, *A Heritage Ingrained* (Perth, 1999); *West Australian*, 22 July 1950, 3 July 1962; *SMH*, 3 July 1962; personal information. CLEMENT MULCAHY

TELFER, ALBERT HAROLD (1900-1979), public servant, was born on 23 August 1900 at Collie, Western Australia, fourth child of Victorian-born parents James Gibson Telfer, carpenter, and his wife Sarah Ann, née Armstrong. Educated locally and at Perth Boys' School, Bert joined the Department of Mines as a clerk in January 1916. By the age of 26 he was acting principal registrar. At St George's Cathedral, Perth, on 1 December 1926 he married with Anglican rites Emily Tasker (d.1969), a typiste. Appointed assistant under-secretary for mines in 1936, he gave particular support to the gold-mining industry, and advocated that the government increase its financial assistance to prospectors and small-scale operators. In 1937 he was seconded to the Commonwealth Department of the Interior to inquire into mining administration and ordinances in the Northern Territory. He was promoted to under-secretary for mines in July 1938 and was to retain that post until he retired in 1965, a record term of twenty-seven years.

During World War II Telfer also served as deputy Commonwealth controller of minerals in Western Australia and under-secretary for civil defence. In 1946 he was appointed I.S.O. Anticipating an increased demand for minerals in the postwar period, he argued that the state should have a central role in the search for, and development of, new deposits. In the 1940s he extended the roles of the government geologist and the geological survey. Championing his department's work in regard to the coal resources near Collie, he helped to promote policies that led to open-cut mining there. He backed the expansion of his chemical branch, and defended the department for retaining control of the Western Australian School of Mines at a time when there was pressure to transfer the school to the University of Western Australia.

By the 1960s Western Australia had become one of the world's leading producers of iron ore, bauxite, mineral sands and nickel. Telfer enjoyed good relations with development-minded governments, especially that of (Sir) David Brand which came to office in 1959. The role of the Department of Mines did not extend to promoting the foreign investment or establishing the infrastructure that was central to the mineral 'boom' of the 1960s and 1970s: this work fell to the Department of Industrial Development and its minister (Sir) Charles Court.

In 1965 Telfer was appointed chairman of the Mining Advisory Committee. Next year he was made an honorary member of the Australasian Institute of Mining and Metallurgy. On 15 December 1969 at St Matthew's Church of England, Guildford, he married Catherine Frances Magnus; she was the widowed sister of J. E. Macartney [q.v.15]. A member of the committee that inquired (1970-71) into the operation of the Mining Act (1904-70), Telfer recommended new legislation to reflect the change from 'pick and shovel' methods to mechanization. In 1970 he was appointed O.B.E. Gardening, motoring, tennis and golf enabled him to relax from the stresses of his work. He died on 4 August 1979 in Royal Perth Hospital and was cremated; his wife survived him, as did the daughter of his first marriage. The Telfer Dome, in the Paterson Range south-east of Port Hedland, was named (1975) after him.

K. Spillman, *A Rich Endowment* (Perth, 1993); M. and A. Webb, *Golden Destiny* (Boulder, WA, 1993); Mines Dept (WA), *Annual Report*, 1949; *West Australian*, 11 Sept 1937, 6 Aug 1979; P. Bertola, Kalgoorlie, Gold and the World Economy, 1893-1972 (Ph.D. thesis, Curtin Univ, 1994); B. Sheppard, unpublished notes on Bert Telfer and the Telfer Gold Mine (held by Mr B. Sheppard, Perth). PATRICK BERTOLA

TELFER, MARGARET ALISON (1904-1974), university registrar, was born on 21 October 1904 at Lismore, New South Wales, second child of James Barnet Telfer, a native-born schoolteacher, and his wife Margaret Augusta, née Craig, who came from England. Peg attended Tamworth and Newcastle High schools, and entered Women's College, University of Sydney (B.A., 1925; Dip.Ed., 1926). Involved in student societies, she held office in the university women's sports association and enjoyed skiing.

After serving as secretary (from 1926) of the Sydney University Women's Union, Miss Telfer was appointed adviser to women students in 1939. Encouraged by the vice-chancellor Sir Robert Wallace [q.v.12], she became deputy assistant registrar in 1944. She was promoted to assistant registrar in 1947 and deputy registrar in 1950. During her early years in the registrar's department she interviewed numerous ex-servicemen and women seeking war-service matriculation, meticulously reviewed all cases, and showed continuing interest in their welfare.

When Margaret Telfer accepted the university senate's offer of the position of registrar in August 1955, she was the first woman to hold a top administrative post in any Commonwealth university. A travel grant from the Carnegie Corporation of New York in 1956 enabled her to study administration and student services in British and North American universities. On her return she faced challenges arising from increased student numbers (both undergraduate and postgraduate), demands from departments and faculties, and pressures that flowed from the implementation of Sir Keith Murray's report (1957) on Australian universities. She tried to keep a balance between the senate, the administration, the professorial and nonprofessorial staff, and the students. Confronted with complex problems, she quite often calmly provided a simple solution.

A member (1940-55) of the Board of Social Studies, Telfer was appointed (1953) to the committee, chaired by (Sir) Harold Wyndham, that surveyed secondary education in New South Wales. She was a council-member (1940-59 and 1963-69) of Women's College, a trustee (1966-69) and council-member (1969-74) of the Public Library of New South Wales, president of the Sydney University Women Graduates' Association (1945-47) and of the Australian Federation of University Women (1958-60), and a member (1967-74) of the Parole Board, New South Wales. In 1960 she was appointed O.B.E. The University of Sydney conferred on her an honorary Litt.D. in 1969.

Dignified, efficient, courteous, patient and sympathetic, Telfer was readily available to staff and students who sought her help, advice, and knowledge of 'university rules, procedures, precedents and lore'. In May 1967, at the time of her retirement, Professor W. M. O'Neil wrote of her as a 'traditionalist' in a period of change, 'constantly reminding us whence we came and where we originally set out to go'. He further pointed out 'she has of course not been able to please everyone. That was not possible and she knew it. That, indeed, is why she has made her way to the top'.

Miss Telfer was a slender, dark-haired, elegant woman. Colleagues affectionately remembered her 'gentle wit and humour and the quiet authority with which she expressed her views'. She died of a coronary occlusion on 24 May 1974 at her Wollstonecraft home and was cremated.

S. Lilienthal, *Newtown Tarts* (Syd, 1997); Univ Syd, *Gazette*, 2, no 13, 1967, p 202; U. Bygott, 'The Office of Registrar', Univ Syd, *Record*, no 1, Mar 1992, p 18; *Report of the Council of the Library of NSW*, 1973/74; *SMH*, 9 Mar 1939, 8 Feb 1950, 10 Aug 1955, 11 June 1960, 10 May, 22 Dec 1967, 1 May 1969, 27 May 1974; file G3/158 (Univ Syd Archives).   URSULA BYGOTT

THATCHER, THOMAS (1886-1948), educationist, was born on 13 November 1886 at Laidley, Queensland, eighth and youngest child of Thomas Thatcher, a Primitive Methodist minister from England, and his Irish-born wife Jane, née Carson. Young Tom attended state schools, and Brisbane Grammar School where he won Lilley [q.v.5] silver medals in both the lower and upper schools. After two years as an assistant probationer at Richmond Hill State School, Charters Towers, he qualified as a teacher in 1907. He then returned to Laidley and farmed for four years. A foundation student (1911) of the University of Queensland (B.A., 1917), he graduated with first-class honours in philosophy, winning the Archibald [q.v.7] scholarship and a government gold medal. While an undergraduate, he tutored in philosophy at Women's College, served as a temporary lecturer in logic and worked for a few months as an assistant to the director of correspondence studies.

In 1915 Thatcher was appointed private secretary to Governor Sir Hamilton Goold-Adams [q.v.9]. Four years later he was employed as parliamentary reporter for the *Daily Mail* and leader-writer for the *Sunday Mail*. He turned to fruit-growing at Glen Aplin and became a member of the Stanthorpe Shire Council. In her father's house at Fortitude Valley on 31 December 1920 he married with Presbyterian forms Olive Adam, a 24-year-old schoolteacher; they were to have eight children. Representing the Country and Progressive National Party, he stood unsuccessfully for the Legislative Assembly seat of Brisbane in 1929. From that year until 1932 he was private secretary to H. E. Sizer [q.v.11], the minister for labour and industry. Thatcher helped to reorganize the system of relief work, set up the Queensland Social Service League and held the post of secretary to the Unemployment Council. Defeated for the seat of Ithaca in the 1932 election, he resumed teaching, first at Brisbane State High School and then at Toowoomba State High School and Technical College.

Thatcher was appointed director of external studies, University of Queensland, on 11 December 1937. In addition to his regular duties, he edited the *Calendar of the University of Queensland* and the *Manual of Public Examinations*. He was also secretary of the public lectures committee, the appointments board and the standing committee of council. During World War II external-studies courses were offered to military personnel; after it ended, ex-servicemen and women swelled the ranks of external students. Securing the support of an assistant-director, Thatcher introduced a vacation study school in 1947, established a lending library for external students and stipulated that graduate assistants provide tutorials for them. In 1948, aided by Commonwealth funds, the university agreed to his request to set up study circles in regional centres.

Intelligent, focused and resourceful, Thatcher proved an outstanding administrator, gifted with tact and thoughtfulness, loyalty and trustworthiness. He died of cancer on 23 May 1948 in a private hospital at Vaucluse, Sydney, and was buried with Anglican rites in Toowong cemetery, Brisbane. His wife, their three sons and four of their five daughters survived him. The university's new external-studies library was named after him.

R. D. Kitchen, *Men of Vision* (Brisb, 1985); M. I. Thomis, *A Place of Light and Learning* (Brisb, 1985); Univ Qld Archives.   JOHN LAVERTY

THEODOSY, ARCHBISHOP; *see* PUTILIN

THEOPHYLACTOS;   *see*   PAPATHANA-SOPOULOS

THOM, WILLIAM CUMMING (1898-1979), Presbyterian minister and college principal, was born on 6 July 1898 at Aberdeen, Scotland, son of Charles Lumsden Thom, nurseryman's carter, and his wife Jane Ann, née Forsyth. William was educated at Gordon's College and the University of Aberdeen (M.A., 1917; B.D., 1920; Ph.D., 1924; D.D., 1948). Enlisting in the Royal Field Artillery on 6 August 1916, he served in France and was commissioned on 9 April 1918 in the Royal Garrison Artillery. He was Hugh Black resident fellow (from 1920) at the Union Theological Seminary, New York, where he graduated master of sacred theology in 1922. Ordained minister in 1923 by the United Free Church of Scotland, Thom was called to Carnoustie. At King's College chapel, Aberdeen, on 15 March 1923 he married Helen Allan Sorley (d.1965). He ministered at Wellpark Church, Glasgow, from 1927 and transferred to Lauriston Church, Edinburgh, in 1931.

In June 1938 Thom took up appointments as principal of St Andrew's College, University of Sydney, and, at the Theological Hall, as Hunter-Baillie professor of Oriental and Polynesian languages and professor of Hebrew and exegetical theology of the Old Testament. His plans for a new building to house more students had to be postponed due to World War II. The Presbyterian women's college, of which he had dreamed, gave way to a sportsfield in St Andrew's grounds, but he drew satisfaction from creating a chapel.

Thom took a firm line, expelling students for unsatisfactory behaviour and reimposing fines for missing daily prayers. His commendable attempts to reform the college's entrenched fresher practices (which ranged from minor duties to humiliation and a degree of violence) caused resentment and offended growing demands for student autonomy. The presence of ex-servicemen not only made the student body more complex, but also led to a challenge to the college's inadequate system of discipline. Perceived as authoritarian and tactless, Thom contributed to a crisis which climaxed at the notorious meeting in August 1947 when some students fused the lights and threw eggs at him. Thereafter, he struggled to maintain his position. During leave of absence in 1948, he attended ecumenical conferences in Amsterdam and Geneva. On his return to Sydney it was clear that he had lost the confidence of the college council and he resigned in 1949.

In June 1951 Cumming Thom (as he by then styled his surname) accepted a call to St David's, Haberfield. It had a strong middle-class congregation to which he gave vigorous, well-regarded leadership. A forceful preacher and a liberal theologian, he encouraged inter-denominational links at Haberfield.

The Presbyterian Church in Sydney welcomed Thom as a scholar and a Scot. Familiar as a preacher, broadcaster and contributor to the *New South Wales Presbyterian*, he was active in the General Assembly of the Presbyterian Church and its committees, and was also a church trustee. In 1955 he was elected moderator. As convenor of the assembly's Christian unity committee, he was deeply committed to the organic union of the Congregational, Methodist and Presbyterian churches. Although his work on a basis of union was superseded, he regarded his support for Christian unity as his most valuable contribution to the life of the Church and Christianity in Australia. By 1965 his health was declining. He retired from St David's at the end of 1968. After several years he returned to Aberdeen, where he died on 25 March 1979. His two sons survived him.

R. I. Jack, *The Andrew's Book* (Syd, 1989); *Minutes of Procs of the General Assembly of the Presbyterian Church of Aust in the State of NSW*, 1938-69; *NSW Presbyterian*, 13 July 1938, 14 June 1939, 1 May 1940, 27 July 1951, 20 May 1955; St David's Church, Haberfield, *St David's Review*, June 1952, Apr 1954, Jan 1956, Jan 1958, Feb 1962, June 1965; *SMH*, 19 Mar 1938, 4 Jan 1955; F. Chisholm, St Andrew's College—A Three-Cornered Conflict 1938-50 (B.A. Hons thesis, Univ Syd, 1983); St David's Church, Haberfield, Minutes of Sessions, 1951-68 (Uniting Church Archives, North Parramatta, Syd).

JOAN MANSFIELD

THOMAS, BESSIE MARGARET (1892-1968), librarian, was born on 14 March 1892 in Sydney, third child of Henry Charles Thomas, a clerk from England, and his native-born wife Gertrude Augusta, née Hillyer. In the mid-1890s the family moved to Canada, where Bess was educated and trained as a secretary and as a librarian. Living at Toronto from 1922, she worked as an assistant-librarian at the local university in 1927-28. She was impressed by the free library services in North America, particularly the Boys and Girls House of the Toronto Public Library. Persuaded by her cousin Mrs Edith Allworth to return to Sydney, she had arrived there by 1931. She was strongly influenced by Ralph Munn's and Ernest Pitt's [q.v.11] critical report (1934) on Australian libraries.

Bess Thomas 'had that magical touch: she drew people to her'. At a meeting chaired by Professor E. R. Holme [q.v.9] in September 1934, it was agreed that she and Edith Allworth, as honorary librarians, should establish a children's library at Mosman, which would allow free access to books for children of every age 'to inculcate and develop in them an understanding and love of good literature'. In December 1934 the Mosman Children's Library opened in the garage of the Allworths' home in Parriwi Road, with 350 books collected 'door-to-door' by Bess and Edith. The library soon outgrew its premises and was moved to a building behind Killarney School. In 1943 it found a new home in a building provided by the Department of Education, on the corner of Military and Belmont roads.

Committed to administering the library so as to fit it for inclusion in a municipal public library, Thomas imposed a fine of one penny if a book was overdue without good reason. She encouraged other activities—story hours, book-reviewing, a weekly chess group and play readings. Rosemary Dobson conducted a poetry group. Edith looked after the younger children and repaired the books, helped by the Friends of the Mosman Children's Library.

In 1945 the local council adopted the Library Act (1939) and the Mosman Municipal Library was opened with Thomas as chief librarian, the first woman in New South Wales to be appointed to such a position. The stock of 7000 books belonging to the children's library was incorporated into the Municipal Library. At that time there were 1700 borrowers. In 1952, when the library moved to Boronia, at 624 Military Road, the stock had risen to over 18 000 volumes; there were nearly 6500 borrowers. In 1949 Thomas had formed discussion groups to study English and Australian literature. Visiting librarians from other States and overseas used Mosman Municipal Library as a benchmark for children's library services. Thomas was also involved in the education of children's librarians and used the children's section of the library at Mosman to run various training courses.

Miss Thomas retired as chief librarian on 15 March 1962. She died on 7 March 1968 at the Sacred Heart Hospice, Darlinghurst, and was cremated with Anglican rites. In 1977 the children's libraries section of the Library Association of Australia established the Bess Thomas award to encourage excellence in children's librarianship.

G. Souter, *Mosman* (Melb, 1994); *A'sian Book News and Lib J*, 1, Nov 1946, p 179; *Aust Lib J*, Dec 1975, p 482; *Orana*, 14, no 3, Aug 1978, p 70; *SMH*, 29 Dec 1934, 24 Sept 1959; H. M. Hicks, Dip.Lib. assignment (ms, 1966, Mosman Municipal L).

ALAN VENTRESS

THOMAS, DAVID EVAN (1902-1978), geologist, was born on 4 August 1902 at Ammanford, Carmarthenshire, Wales, third son of Thomas Thomas, railway signalman, and his wife Margaret, née Roderick. David attended the Amman Valley County School and the University College of Wales, Aberystwyth (B.Sc. Hons, University of Wales, 1924). His education had been facilitated by scholarships during his secondary schooling, by part-time employment as a coalminer in his university years, and by a Rudler exhibition in geology at Aberystwyth in 1924. After graduating, he worked as an underground surveyor at the Blaenau colliery. This experience engendered a love of geological surveying, structural geology and graptolite biostratigraphy, and reinforced his predilection for precision.

In 1925 Thomas migrated to Australia. A seamen's strike compelled him to travel the last leg of his journey by train from Fremantle to Melbourne. Joining the Victorian Education Department in November, he taught in schools at Kennedys Creek and Nhill, but clashed with a district inspector over teaching methods and transferred to the Department of Mines in April 1927 as an assistant field geologist. He undertook surveys in the Western District, Gippsland and central Victoria. On 20 October 1932 at Lancefield he married with Catholic rites Mary Scanlon (d.1977); two of their three sons died in infancy. In 1939-42 Thomas was head of the department's office at Castlemaine. With A. R. Keble [q.v.14] and later W. J. Harris, he surveyed the geological structure of central Victoria, making particular use of graptolite biostratigraphy. For this work the University of Melbourne awarded him a D.Sc. (1940).

Appointed government geologist of Tasmania in February 1942, Thomas undertook research on graptolites, dendroids and hydroids, interspersed with investigations of strategic minerals required during wartime. In February 1944 he returned to Victoria and took a post with the State Rivers and Water

Supply Commission. His meticulous geological mapping for the enlargement of the Eildon Reservoir brought him into daily contact with engineers. Thomas's monograph, *Geology of the Eildon Dam Project* (1947), stamped him as arguably the best structural geologist in Australia.

In May 1945 Thomas rejoined the Department of Mines and in February 1946 became Victoria's chief government geologist (director of geological survey from 1960). Field geology continued to be his passion, despite the administrative chores that governed much of his time, and he often devoted his weekends to field-work with his young geologists. Overcoming the resistance of a succession of cabinet ministers and departmental secretaries, he managed to increase the number of geologists on his staff from three to twenty. They benefited from his leadership and relentless efforts on their behalf. He encouraged them to carry out both detailed and broad-based research, insisted that they publish their results and persuaded the government to allow them to undertake doctoral studies. Three of his major initiatives were to create an energetic groundwater group, to develop engineering geology, and to foster biostratigraphy as a means of obtaining fine-scale correlations of the times of deposit of rock sequences to illuminate regional geological relationships.

Thomas published voluminously on the geology of Victoria and, to a lesser extent, Tasmania. He produced over one hundred scientific papers, fourteen geological maps, and more than 120 unpublished reports on almost all aspects of the earth sciences. His papers encompassed economic geology, structural and stratigraphic studies, graptolite and hydroid investigations, and regional geology. He had an admirable command of earth-science literature in French and German, and a commendable ability to embrace new ideas.

On regular trout-fishing expeditions in eastern Victoria, Thomas and Harris made observations of rock formations and collected graptolites. Their work led to radical reinterpretations of the geological structure of the State. Thomas achieved international recognition for his research on graptolites, work that had been largely done as a hobby. Thomas and Harris used Victoria's graptolite faunas to elaborate the scheme for dividing the sedimentary rock sequences of the Ordovician period into a succession of biostrophic zones. In 1963 Thomas was elected a fellow of the Australian Academy of Science.

Thomas was a councillor and life member of the Royal Society of Victoria. He served on the State committee of the Council for Scientific and Industrial Research (Commonwealth Scientific and Industrial Research Organiz-

ation) and many other scientific and governmental bodies. On leave in 1963-64, he led a United Nations team to investigate the underground water and mineral resources of Cyprus, but civil war crippled the project. After his formal retirement in 1967, he was an honorary geological consultant to the department for several years.

As a boy, Thomas had an excellent soprano voice. He played the piano and enjoyed classical music, especially opera and choral singing. At the Amman Valley County School he had captained the Rugby Union football and cricket teams; at Aberystwyth he gained a Blue for boxing. In Australia he took up golf and earned a low handicap. He continued to play cricket, prided himself on his accuracy as a spin bowler, and had an encyclopaedic knowledge of the game. It was his custom to hold court in the Windsor Hotel, Spring Street, Melbourne, where—in conversations liberal with anecdote, wry humour and gentle repartee—he acquainted many of the geological fraternity with recondite and at times bizarre aspects of the scientific and commercial worlds, with the taxonomy and biostratigraphy of his beloved graptolites, and with the technical minutiae and history of various sports.

Thomas had a commanding presence that some initially found intimidating and that belied his graciousness, affability, loyalty and unswerving intellectual honesty. Survived by his son, he died on 27 November 1978 at Camberwell and was buried in Templestowe cemetery. The Victorian division of the Geological Society of Australia instituted the D. E. Thomas medal which is awarded to university students who excel in field-work.

Mining and Geological J, 6, no 6, 1970; Aust Academy of Science, *Year Book*, 1980; *Hist Records of Aust Science*, 5, no 2, 1981, p 90; family information.   JOHN A. TALENT

THOMAS, ERNEST AMBROSE (1886-1958), farmer and managing director of a milling co-operative, was born on 20 May 1886 at Lithgow, New South Wales, ninth of ten children of David Thomas, a miner from Wales, and his English-born wife Susanna, née Frith. Educated locally, Ernie worked as a coalminer at Lithgow and in the Illawarra district before moving to Queensland about 1904. He took jobs in a foundry and a brickworks, and as a railway fettler in the Toowoomba area. In 1910 he joined his elder brothers in selecting a small property in the Hunterton district, near Roma. With his earnings from employment off the farm for part of each year, he soon bought out his brothers.

On 13 September 1915 in her father's house at Roma he married Florence Ethel Salisbury with the forms of the Churches of Christ.

Acquiring additional land, Thomas consolidated his grain, wool and beef-cattle properties as the Gwenbrook Farming & Pastoral Co. He also experimented with cotton growing, and developed an interest in closer settlement and the co-operative movement. Elected to various local government and farmers' organizations, he not only helped to obtain extensions to the nearby railway but also promoted immunization against diphtheria. While chairman of the graziers' sub-committee of the Queensland Council of Agriculture, he initiated a meat stabilization scheme and was appointed to the State Meat Advisory Board. He was a member (1930-36) of the Bungil Shire Council. In 1932 he unsuccessfully contested the Legislative Assembly seat of Maranoa for the Country and Progressive National Party.

As chairman (1932-38) of the State Wheat Board, Thomas grew frustrated by decreasing world prices, the failure of the 'grow more wheat' campaign, the 'dumping' in Queensland of cheaper wheat from New South Wales, and attempts by the Queensland government and millers to lower prices further. He and others responded to wheat-growers' protests by establishing the Queensland Co-operative Milling Association. The group acquired, through vendor finance, the Brisbane and Toowoomba mills of the Dominion Milling Co. Ltd for £541 161 and began operations in March 1938.

Prevented by legislation from holding positions simultaneously on the boards of the S.W.B. and Q.C.M.A., Thomas chose to serve (1939-54) as chairman of the latter organization. In 1947 having settled his sons on family and neighbouring properties, he moved to Toowoomba as managing director (from 1948) of the Q.C.M.A. Under his guidance, the co-operative introduced Queensland's first cereal laboratory, modernized both mills, repaid vendor finance (1945), established six regional depots, acquired produce and transport operations (1947), and set up a merchandizing department (1949). In 1952-54 it ran a facility at Gladstone to export sorghum. On 25 May 1954 Thomas resigned as chairman after a disagreement over the means of raising additional shareholder capital. He relinquished his post as managing director on 30 November that year.

Thomas was a forceful, eloquent advocate for the co-operative movement and 'the man on the land'. In 1937 he was awarded King George VI's coronation medal. He enjoyed gardening, photography and sketching caricatures of his fellow members during board-meetings. Survived by his wife, their five sons and one of their two daughters, he died on 29 December 1958 at Toowoomba and was cremated with Methodist forms.

Queensland Co-operative Milling Association, *Record of Achievement* (Toowoomba, Qld, 1950) and *Annual Report*, 1966; M. Rafferty, *The History of Flourmilling in Queensland to 1988* (Toowoomba, Qld, 1988); R. S. Marriott and G. McLean, *Going with the Grain* (Toowoomba, Qld, 1991); *Brish Courier*, 31 May 1932; *Daily Mail* (Brisb), 9 June 1932; *Clifton Courier*, 13 Sept 1932; *Chronicle* (Toowoomba), 30 Dec 1958, 3 Jan 1959; A History of the Thomas Family (ts, undated, held by Mrs G. Fluck, Toowoomba, Qld).   M. FRENCH

THOMAS, KATHLEEN KYFFIN (1891-1973), community worker, was born on 7 February 1891 in Adelaide, sixth of seven children of South Australian-born parents (Sir) Robert Kyffin Thomas [q.v.6], newspaper proprietor, and his wife Amelia, née Bowen. Esther (Stella) Bowen [q.v.7] was her cousin. Educated at Miss Martin's school, Kathleen worked as a governess and in 1908 studied English at the University of Adelaide—she later regretted not completing a degree—and played hockey. In 1909 she accompanied her parents to the Imperial Press Conference in London.

Inspired by Lady Galway [q.v.14] at the inaugural meeting of the South Australian division of the British Red Cross Society on 14 August 1914, Miss Kyffin Thomas volunteered to work in the central stores depot, located in the Government House stables; she sorted clothing and packed comforts for soldiers overseas. Soon becoming Lady Galway's secretary for Red Cross, she was elected (1915) to the general committee, which she served as honorary assistant-secretary. In 1918 she was made honorary secretary of the Australian Red Cross Society, South Australian division. That year she was appointed O.B.E. Following Lady Galway's departure in January 1919 and the return of sick and wounded servicemen, she worked more intensively; in 1920 she resigned the secretaryship for health reasons, but remained on the executive committee. In 1930 she represented South Australia at the British Empire Red Cross Conference in London.

Kyffin Thomas had been secretary (1916-21) of the newspaper branch of the Victoria League for Commonwealth Friendship, which dispatched local newspapers, books, and magazines to soldiers in Australian and overseas hospitals. She was the league's honorary secretary from 1922 to 1947. A founding member (1935) of the Pioneers' Association of South Australia, she was on the executive (1935-36) of the Women's Centenary Council of South Australia.

During World War II Kyffin Thomas's experience proved invaluable. In December 1938 she had helped to establish the Red Cross's emergency service which trained women in non-combatant roles. Visiting far-flung Red Cross branches in South Australia and at Broken Hill, New South Wales, she recruited volunteers for instruction in first aid, home nursing and air-raid precautions. By October next year 10 000 women had joined the service in South Australia. From April 1939 she organized the Red Cross transport service, which trained and allocated female drivers and mechanics. In uniform as divisional commandant (1941-51) of Red Cross women personnel, she led her well-trained, disciplined group of volunteers 'with a rod of iron—and was kind'. She gave radio talks on Red Cross activities for the Australian Broadcasting Commission and, as director of Red Cross hospital visiting (1941-47), supervised one hundred volunteers.

Definite, but co-operative and friendly, Kyffin Thomas inspired respect and affection. She was devoted to her family. In 1946 she was appointed (officer) to the Order of St John of Jerusalem. She chaired (1947-55) the Junior Red Cross Society, and presided (1951-53) over the Adelaide Lyceum Club. Awarded honorary life membership of the Red Cross, she became vice-president in 1955. After receiving the Red Cross's fifty years' service medal in 1964, she retired. She died on 15 March 1973 at the Helping Hand Centre, North Adelaide, and was cremated.

Greater than their Knowing (Adel, 1986); Aust Red Cross Soc (SA), *Annual Report*, 1973, p 55; *Register* (Adel), 21 June 1918; *Advertiser* (Adel), 16 Apr 1947, 27 Oct 1964; K. Kyffin Thomas, autobiographical notes (ts, 1972, held by family members); Aust Red Cross Soc, records (North Adel).

HELEN JONES

THOMAS, LAURENCE NICHOLAS BARRETT (1915-1974), art gallery director and critic, was born on 19 January 1915 at St Kilda, Melbourne, second son of Nicholas Thomas, a printer from South Australia, and his Victorian-born wife, Annie Amelia, née Barrett. As a child, Laurie enjoyed drawing, reading and writing. He left school torn between attending the National Gallery schools and taking up a scholarship at the university. The effect of the Depression on his family denied him either course. After trudging the streets for months door-knocking for employment, he worked for three years as a clerk and rent collector with the Small Arms Co. Pty Ltd. He gave most of his wages to his mother and spent what remained on building up a small library to educate himself.

Contemplating a clerical career, Thomas entered Queen's College, University of Melbourne (B.A., Hons, 1938; Dip.Ed., 1940), with the support of the Methodist Church. He joined the university's Tin Alley Players, tutored (1938) in English and became a resident tutor at the college. In 1939 he went to Perth as an assistant temporary lecturer in English under (Sir) Walter Murdoch [q.v.10] at the University of Western Australia.

On 1 May 1941 Thomas was commissioned paymaster sub-lieutenant in the Royal Australian Naval Volunteer Reserve. Promoted lieutenant (1942), he carried out intelligence duties in the Northern Territory, New Guinea, Queensland and Victoria. His naval appointment terminated in Melbourne on 24 May 1946. At Queen's College chapel on 27 June 1942 he had married Jessie Enid Weate, a laboratory assistant; they had three children before being divorced.

Thomas took up a Gowrie [q.v.9] postgraduate research scholarship for ex-servicemen and travelled to Britain in 1946. At King's College, Cambridge, he began a thesis on poetry. Disliking the prevailing reductionist-analytic approach in English studies, he informally attended the sessions of the Austrian philosopher Ludwig Wittgenstein. Back in Melbourne, he was employed as art critic (1949-50) with the *Herald* before being made assistant-director (1950-52) of the National Gallery of Victoria under (Sir) Daryl Lindsay [q.v.10]. He organized and wrote part of the catalogue for the Jubilee Exhibition of Australian Art, which toured all State galleries and was notable for its inclusion of Aboriginal art.

In 1952 Thomas became director of the Western Australian Art Gallery. A dispute with the trustees led him to leave for Sydney in 1956. Following a brief period as theatre reviewer for the *Sun* newspaper in 1957, he was its leader-writer until 1961. He also produced theatre, film and art reviews, and feature articles on various topics. In 1961 he was appointed director of the Queensland Art Gallery. He again came into conflict with parochial attitudes and resigned in 1967. As a gallery director in Perth and Brisbane, he had pioneered the exhibition and cataloguing of Aboriginal art as *art* rather than 'artefacture', acquired work by young painters for public collections, and flown exhibitions of paintings to remote areas of Western Australia and Queensland. On 1 April 1966 at the general registry office, Brisbane, he had married Dorothy Jean Bronwyn Yeates, née Tricks, an artist and a divorcee.

Returning to Sydney, Thomas was arts editor and feature writer for the *Australian* from 1968 until about 1973. He had appeared regularly on the Australian Broadcasting Commission's television programme 'The Critics' in the early 1960s, and in other programmes on art and painters. His reviews, feature articles and tributes in the *Australian* revealed his joyful commitment to the arts—though they were not without occasional pungent comment. In 1969 the interim council of the Australian National Gallery recommended that Thomas be appointed foundation director of the gallery. Prime Minister (Sir) John Gorton vetoed that recommendation, causing Lindsay to resign as chairman of the interim council and provoking considerable public controversy.

Thomas never quite recovered from the rebuff. He helped to produce various exhibition catalogues and edited *200 Years of Australian Painting* (Sydney, 1971). His last major project was selecting illustrations and writing the foreword for *Arthur Boyd Drawings, 1934-1970* (London, 1973). Awarded a grant by the Australian Council for the Arts in 1973, he began accumulating notes for a book on the history of Australian art. He died of cancer on 20 August 1974 at his Paddington home and was cremated; his wife survived him, as did the son and two daughters of his first marriage. Charles Blackman and John Olsen, two of his closest friends, published a selection of his writings from the *Australian* as *The Most Noble Art of Them All* (Brisbane, 1976) and paid homage to his eloquence, generosity of spirit and love of life. Ivor Hele's portrait of Thomas is held by the Art Gallery of New South Wales.

Art and Aust, Oct-Dec 1974; *SMH*, 1 Mar 1971, 21 Aug 1974; Hazel de Berg, Laurie Thomas (taped interview, 1963, NL); Thomas papers (NL); information from Dr R. Smith, Highton, Vic, and the late Mrs B. Thomas.   BARRY PEARCE

THOMAS, MARY BERTHA RAINE; *see* RAINE

THOMPSON, FRANCIS WEBSTER (1913-1974), horse-breeder, was born on 13 April 1913 at Neutral Bay, Sydney, fourth child and only son of native-born parents Alfred Webster Thompson (d.1945), grazier, and his wife Sarah Daisy, née Brecht. The family was descended from John Thompson, an assisted immigrant (1832) who managed Edward Cox's [q.v.3] Rylstone property, Rawdon, and took up land in the district. By the mid-1850s the Thompsons had moved north across the Great Dividing Range into the Widden Valley. There, two brothers from the third generation, John (1844-1914) and James (1851-1911), at Widden and Oakleigh respectively,

established an ascendancy in horse-breeding that was virtually unchallenged between the end of the nineteenth century and World War II. Alfred and his cousin Herbert (1879-1955) sustained this success against the competition of breeders operating from Scone, in a more accessible part of the Upper Hunter Valley.

Educated at The King's School, Parramatta, Frank joined his father at the family stud, Widden. His training included working on leading studs in England, France and Ireland in 1936; he also bought the successful sire, Brueghel, at Milan, Italy. On 30 November 1937 he married with Anglican rites Margaret May Gore Merewether at All Saints Church, Woollahra, Sydney. After serving in the Militia in the 1930s, Thompson was appointed lieutenant, Armoured Corps, Australian Imperial Force, on 1 February 1941. In September he joined the 2nd/6th Armoured Regiment, with which he served in Papua (September 1942-February 1943) and then in Australia. He held the rank of major for twenty-one months before his A.I.F. appointment terminated on 20 July 1944.

Thompson was a committee-member (1945-74) and president (1948-50) of the State division of the Bloodhorse Breeders' Association of Australia and foundation federal president in 1945-53. Like his father, he was a committee-member (1951-74) of the Australian Jockey Club. He raced a few of the horses he had bred, including Lady Pirouette (dam of Indian Summer) and Tornado.

In a calling where luck, as well as skill, in choosing the right stallions was (and is) important, Thompson developed at Widden a basis for survival in the new capital-intensive world of breeding. From the late 1940s, an airstrip brought a remote valley deep in the Wollemi National Park into contact with racing centres. When the American cattle-breeder Robert Kleberg of King Ranch, Texas, purchased a neighbouring property, Thompson bought Santa Gertrudis bulls from him to cross with his Shorthorn cows. He later established a Santa Gertrudis stud and promoted the breed in Australia.

Divorced on 9 April 1963, next day at St Andrew's Scots Church, Rose Bay, Sydney, Thompson married Valda Merlyn Martin, née Ridley. He belonged to the New South Wales, Australian, Union and Athenaeum clubs. Survived by his wife, and by the son and two daughters of his first marriage, he died of myocardial infarction on 27 August 1974 in his flat at Darling Point and was buried at Widden. Although the stud was influential between 1946 and 1974—not least through Brueghel and Edmundo—triumphs comparable to those of the pre-1939 period were not to return until the 1970s and 1980s with the progeny of Vain and Bletchingly.

D. M. Barric, *Valley of Champions* (Melb, 1967); P. Taylor, *Thoroughbred Studs of Australia & New Zealand* (Syd, 1986); M. Painter and R. Waterhouse, *The Principal Club* (Syd, 1992); *King's School Mag*, no 292, Dec 1974, p 74; *SMH*, 14 Feb, 9 Apr 1948, 12 Feb, 17 Sept 1949, 22 Dec 1951, 28 Aug 1974.

WALLACE KIRSOP

THOMPSON, FREDA MARY (1906-1980), aviatrix, was born on 5 April 1906 at South Yarra, Melbourne, elder daughter of Victorian-born parents Frederick Henry Thompson, gentleman, and his wife Martha, née Hollins. Educated (1911-23) at Toorak College, Freda travelled to Europe with the family in 1926. After flying in a passenger-aircraft from Paris to London, she wrote in her diary, 'Jolly fine fly. Would go again if I could'. She took her first flying lesson in May 1930 at Essendon, Melbourne. Replacing music classes with regular flying training, she received an 'A' (private) pilot's licence (number 596) on 16 September that year. In 1932 she gained a 'B' (commercial) pilot's licence (number 390) and became the fifth woman in Australia to attain it.

In 1933 Thompson qualified as a flying instructor, but she was never to be employed as one. Contemporary newspaper reports acclaimed her as the first woman in the British Empire to hold an instructor's certificate. She sailed for England in April 1934 to take delivery of a new de Havilland Moth Major with long-range fuel tanks. By this time she had over 250 hours flying experience. On 28 September she left Lympne, Kent, for Australia, flying solo. At Mégara, Greece, her aircraft, G-ACUC (VH-UUC), was damaged in a precautionary landing. Despite being delayed in Athens for twenty days while the plane was repaired, she arrived in Darwin on 6 November.

At the beginning of World War II, Thompson sold her beloved Moth Major which she had named *Christopher Robin*. In 1940-42 she was commandant for Victoria of the Women's Air Training Corps. When she received no reply to her application to join the Women's Auxiliary Australian Air Force, she enlisted in the Australian Women's Army Service on 5 March 1942. Her enlistment papers described her as being 5 ft 4¾ ins (164 cm) tall, with blue eyes and auburn hair, and gave her religious affiliation as Anglican. She served as an ambulance driver and was promoted acting sergeant before being discharged from the A.W.A.S. on 25 August 1944.

After the war Thompson bought a de Havilland Hornet Moth, VH-UYO, from Nancy Lyle and named it *Christopher Robin II*. She flew the aircraft extensively within Australia, and in 1952 co-piloted it to the Territory of Papua and New Guinea and back. Competing in air races and formation-flying events, she won forty-seven trophies, and was president (1948) and thrice open champion of the Royal Victorian Aero Club. She did not seek a career in aviation, but supported women who did, arguing that, for any pilot, solid nerve was more important than brute strength. By 1980 she had logged 3330 hours.

Although Miss Thompson was a perfectionist in her flying, she was modest about her achievements and 'could charm with a smile'. Forthright in manner, she had a mind of her own and a sound business sense. She was awarded King George VI's (1937) and Queen Elizabeth II's (1953) coronation medals. In 1972 she was appointed O.B.E. The Australian Women Pilots' Association, of which she was a foundation member (1950), honoured her in 1973 by inaugurating the Freda Thompson Aerial Derby, a race around Port Phillip Bay for women pilots. She died on 11 December 1980 at Malvern and was cremated.

J. A. Palmer, *Goggles and God Help You* (Maryborough, Vic, 1986); N. M. Parnell and T. Boughton, *Flypast* (Canb, 1988); Aust Women Pilots' Assn records *and* Thompson papers (NL); information from Mrs C. Embling, Benalla, Vic.

VAL DENNIS

THOMPSON, JAMES TUSON (1879-1954), insurance manager, was born on 17 August 1879 at Ararat, Victoria, second child of Florance Thompson, a draper from England, and his wife Ann, née Tuson, who was born at Ararat. Educated at a state school and privately at Geelong, James began work in the office of a Melbourne solicitor. He found that he was temperamentally unsuited to law and moved to New South Wales where, in 1899, he became an agent of the Australasian Temperance & General Mutual Life Assurance Society Ltd. T. & G. was the first insurance company in Australia to offer industrial assurance, by which many who could not afford ordinary life insurance received coverage in return for the regular payment of small premiums.

Industrial assurance, which relied on agents making frequent home visits, was ideally suited to Thompson's energy and natural flair for salesmanship. His early success in New South Wales led to posts as a superintendent, both in that State and in Victoria. In 1907 he was appointed manager of the Western Australian branch. Instructed soon after his arrival to close the branch, he ignored orders, recruited and personally trained more agents, and put the operation on a secure footing. In September 1908 he was made inspector of branches for Victoria and Tasmania. He continued to promote industrial assurance and in 1909 was given charge of a new four-man group, known as the field special staff (later interstate inspectorial staff). These agents, experts in industrial policies, went from State to State soliciting extra premiums from existing policy-holders. The members of the F.S.S. proved extremely proficient in gaining new business.

On his rounds in the bush, Thompson welcomed overnight stays on farms. He used the opportunities to 'convert' farmers to life assurance and to learn of others who might be similarly persuaded. On one occasion, however, he 'slept the night under his trap when his commission failed to come through and he had no money'. In 1912 he took charge of all branch organization. Constant travel—involving visits to the society's offices in Australia and New Zealand—remained an integral part of his job. At St Paul's Cathedral, Melbourne, on 1 April 1916 he married with Anglican rites Lina May Butcher (d.1940).

In 1917 Thompson was appointed acting general manager of T. & G. He was confirmed in the post in the following year. From 1922 he was managing director and chairman. For years afterwards he believed that he had been 'unjustly treated' as acting general manager and inadequately remunerated in comparison with his predecessor. In 1939 he threatened to resign, but, after negotiations with the board, was persuaded to stay.

The thirty-seven years of Thompson's leadership of T. & G. saw a continuing focus on industrial assurance and the society's steady growth. In 1917 funds stood at £2.5 million; by 1949 the figure was £63.6 million. Accident assurance (introduced in 1929) succeeded, despite the Depression. During the 1930s a popular, low-interest, home-loan scheme was developed. The losses sustained in the Depression by American life assurance firms which had invested freely on the stock market convinced Thompson that T. & G. should never invest in shares: only gilt-edged government or semi-government securities, and commercial and housing mortgages, were acceptable. Security was paramount, and the society was not to be tempted by high rates of interest.

In the 1920s Thompson had embarked on a building programme that left a striking physical legacy. Distinctive T. & G. buildings were erected in major Australasian cities. All were constructed in a neo-Renaissance style and were part of his deliberate strategy to exhibit the society. He chose their locations with the same intent, moving, for example, the head office in Melbourne to the fashionable eastern end of Collins Street in 1928.

Thompson had a chauffeur-driven car, a home at Toorak and a holiday house at Portsea. Although he would not countenance T. & G. doing likewise, he invested in the share market, transacting much of his business during office hours. He was a member of the Athenaeum and Savage clubs, and a devotee of horse-racing, golf and tennis. To motivate his staff, he made them compete, 'setting one against another, or one division or branch against another'. Fair haired and solidly built, he spoke and moved quickly. He had a 'distinctive walk peculiar to sergeant-majors on parade', and, when occasion demanded it, 'could roar like a bull'. At the annual meeting of winning divisions, he set a three-minute limit on all speeches—other than his own: a staff member enforced the edict by using a ruler to tap the legs of wordy speakers. During his term of office, T. & G. was said to stand for 'Thompson and God'.

Despite his ready adoption of the trappings of authority, Thompson remained primarily a salesman and motivator. He never lost his passion for travel and for keeping in personal touch with the various branches. If he could inspire fear, he was also respected for his straightforwardness. As one of his executives put it, he was 'a little Hitler', but 'also quite a friendly old bloke'. The society was his life and he remained in harness until his death. Survived by his adopted daughter, he died on 19 November 1954 at his Toorak home and was buried in Box Hill cemetery. His estate was sworn for probate at £93 078. In his will he bequeathed £1000 to his chauffeur.

Thompson had stayed on too long and refused to countenance the retirement of his senior colleagues. By 1954 T. & G. was being run by 'a small coterie of elderly people, with little idea of training or grooming successors'. The costs of administering industrial assurance were steadily increasing, and insufficient attention was paid to the development of ordinary business and broader investment strategies. Yet, by his tireless promotion of industrial assurance over several decades, Thompson had achieved a significant social good. Many households of limited means were given access to life assurance for the first time. In 1983 T. & G. merged with a larger competitor, the National Mutual Life Association of Australasia Ltd.

S. Thomas, *Yours for Life* (Melb, 1976); *A'sian Insurance and Banking Record*, 21 Dec 1954; *Herald* (Melb), 20 Nov 1954; Geoff Browne papers (Univ Melb Archives).   GEOFF BROWNE

THOMPSON, JOHN CHRISTOPHER (1893-1958), Catholic priest and educationist, was born on 1 June 1893 at Drumcondra, Dublin, son of James Thompson, saddler, and his wife Mary Jane, née Clery. Educated at the Christian Brothers' O'Connell School in Richmond Street, St Vincent's College, Castleknock, and University College, Dublin (B.A. Hons, 1913; M.A., 1922, National University of

Ireland), John began his novitiate in the community of the Vincentian priests on 19 October 1913 and was ordained priest on 16 March 1919 at Holy Cross College, Clonliffe. Following a short period at Castleknock, he taught philosophy at the Irish College, Paris. In 1922 he became lecturer in English and history at St Mary's College, Hammersmith, London (relocated at Strawberry Hill, Twickenham, from 1923); the college became the exemplary teacher-training establishment for the Catholic Church in England. He also obtained a diploma in education (1929) from the University of Oxford.

In June 1929 Thompson was appointed the first director of Catholic education in New South Wales. The creation of the post was largely due to Dr Michael Sheehan, the coadjutor archbishop, who had eventually convinced Archbishop Michael Kelly [q.v.9] and other bishops of a crisis in educational standards. After visiting France and Germany to review teaching methods, Thompson arrived in Sydney in late November. He never returned to Britain or Ireland. In March 1930 he was appointed to the additional post of resident vice-rector at St John's College, University of Sydney, under Maurice O'Reilly [q.v.11]; he was to become rector on O'Reilly's death in 1933.

Catholic schools were staffed mainly by nuns and brothers, whose formal teacher-training was brief, perfunctory and uncoordinated. Thompson consulted bishops, clergy, religious superiors and school principals. He developed training courses, examinations and texts, insofar as his limited resources permitted. The Catholic community, emerging from the Depression, had little to offer. C. J. Duffy, his successor, said that Thompson had no office, no staff and no finance. He attended State and national conferences, pressing the need for a liberal, as distinct from a specialist, education. In 1946 he vigorously opposed C. E. Martin's [q.v.15] proposal that there should be a 'core curriculum' of compulsory subjects. By the 1950s, when the religious Orders had, with Thompson's encouragement, improved the quality of their teachers, and a strong diocesan administration of education had emerged, his role gradually diminished.

As rector of St John's College, Thompson was well respected, but he was extremely shy in contrast to his fiery predecessor. He was spiritual director to the Sydney University Newman Society as well as to the superior council of the Society of St Vincent de Paul in Australia. In 1940 he had been a foundation councillor of the Australian Catholic Historical Society. Despite his reserve and gentle demeanour, he was an able controversialist. He jousted with Professor John Anderson [q.v.7] with voice and pen, conducted weekly sessions on Catholic doctrine on radio-station 2UE (and later 2SM), and published articles, including a treatise on medical and legal ethics.

For some years Thompson suffered from heart disease. He died of a coronary occlusion on 6 June 1958 at Rockhampton, Queensland, and was buried in Rookwood cemetery, Sydney. William Pidgeon's portrait of Fr Thompson is held by St John's College.

J of the Aust Catholic Hist Soc, 7, no 1, 1981, p 28; *Catholic Weekly* (Syd), 12 June, 11 Sept 1958; Vincentian Provincial Office archives, Raheny, Dublin.

BRIAN MAHER

THOMPSON, JOHN JOSEPH MEAGHER (1907-1968), poet and broadcaster, was born on 20 December 1907 at Kew, Melbourne, elder son of Victorian-born parents John Grattan Thompson, dentist, and his wife Nora Catherine, née Meagher. Young John was educated at Melbourne Church of England Grammar School and the University of Melbourne (B.A., 1929). In 1931 his grandfather paid his fare to London where, on an allowance of £2 a week, he endeavoured to make a name as a poet and novelist. Although he was unable to sell any of his novels, he published a collection of romantic lyrics, *Three Dawns Ago* (1935). After some time on a farm at Affpuddle, Dorset, he returned to London in 1937 and met Patricia Drakeford Cole; they were married at the register office, Westminster, on 4 June 1938. The couple moved in leftist circles—Patricia worked at Victor Gollancz's Left Book Club—and John supplemented his allowance by work as a film extra and photographic model.

With war looming, the Thompsons travelled to Perth early in 1939. John was employed as an announcer with the Australian Broadcasting Commission. He and Patricia joined the Communist Party of Australia: John later described Marxism as 'probably the last Christian heresy'. *Sesame and Other Poems* (Sydney, 1944) marked a shift from his earlier verse and included some political and Australian themes. Enlisting in the Australian Imperial Force on 12 December 1942, Thompson qualified as a radio mechanic and performed educational duties in Australia before being discharged from the army on 2 August 1945 to work as an A.B.C. war correspondent. He reported the Japanese surrender at Rabaul and wrote an account of the Indonesian struggle for independence, *Hubbub in Java* (Sydney, 1946).

Thompson settled in Sydney, and became senior feature writer and producer at the A.B.C. In 1946 he devised the popular literary programme, 'Quality Street', and in 1949 accompanied A. P. Elkin [q.v.14] on an anthropological expedition to Arnhem Land. He spent six months in London in 1951, working under Laurence Gilliam at the British Broadcasting Corporation. Over the years, Thompson wrote, produced and narrated many radio documentaries, mostly on literary and historical subjects. He also reported on his travels in Australia, South Africa, India, and the Pacific islands. In 1961 he ran a course on broadcasting at Radio Malaya. He edited selections of his radio portraits of famous Australians, *On Lips of Living Men* (Melbourne, 1962) and *Five to Remember* (1965). His *Bill Harney's War* (1983) was published posthumously.

Tall, fair, blue-eyed and handsome, Thompson was a generous, self-effacing man who spoke with the patrician tones then favoured by the A.B.C. His career in radio overshadowed his poetry—which his wife called 'the guiding spirit of his entire life'—and he regretted not writing more. Largely traditional in form and characterized by reasoned clarity, Thompson's best work was shaped by his experience with the spoken word. His third collection, *Thirty Poems* (Sydney, 1954), won the Grace Leven prize. He collected many of his poems in *I Hate and I Love* (Melbourne, 1964). With Kenneth Slessor [q.v.] and R. G. Howarth [q.v.14], he edited *The Penguin Book of Australian Verse* (London, 1958). Assistant-editor (1959-61) of *Southerly*, he also edited *Australian Poetry 1965* (Sydney).

In 1964 the Thompsons founded the Paddington Society to protect the Victorian character of the suburb in which they had lived since 1951. John was its president. Early in 1968 he retired from the A.B.C. Following an operation for a duodenal ulcer, he died on 19 July that year at St Luke's Hospital, Darlinghurst, and was cremated; his wife, and their son and adopted son survived him. A small fountain opposite Paddington Town Hall commemorates him. Colin Colahan's portrait of Thompson is held by the family.

K. S. Inglis, *This is the ABC* (Melb, 1983); P. Thompson, *Accidental Chords* (Melb, 1988); D. Foster (ed), *Self Portraits* (Canb, 1991); *Meanjin Q*, 28, 1969, p 132; *SMH*, 6 July 1955, 9 Aug 1964, 20 July 1968, 28 June 1977; Thompson papers (ML); information from Mr P. Thompson, Bellevue Hill, Syd.   PETER KIRKPATRICK

THOMPSON, LESLIE MUIR (1885-1975), Methodist clergyman, was born on 1 December 1885 at Geelong, Victoria, second son of William Thompson, produce merchant, and his wife Annie, née Brennan, both Victorian born. After the family moved to Melbourne, his parents were associated with the Wesleyan Methodist Church, Prahran. Educated at state primary schools, at Wesley College and at Queen's College, University of Melbourne (B.A., Dip.Ed., 1913; M.A., 1916), Les showed a keen mind, devotion to the Church, contempt for formality, and an enduring ecumenical vision. He began training as a home mission assistant in 1911 and was ordained in 1912.

In 1914 Thompson was appointed to the Methodist mission to the Indians in Fiji. As part of his training, he spent two years in India studying languages. On 18 March 1915 at the Wesleyan Methodist Church, Benares (Varanasi), he married Grace Elizabeth Foster Waitt. In 1916 he took charge of the mission at Navua, on the south coast of Viti Levu, Fiji, where he witnessed the end of the sugar industry's indentured-labour system, under which Indians led a life of 'virtual serfdom'. The Methodists taught many non-Europeans in the colony and Thompson oversaw several small schools for Indian children. Transferred in 1918 to Nausori, he again supervised a number of schools for Indians.

As the mission's secretary for education and its representative on the Fijian Board of Education, Thompson formed a united front with his Catholic counterpart in opposing the new educational policies of the governor, Sir Bickham Sweet-Escott. With quiet perseverance, Thompson and his Methodist colleagues overcame the objections of their superiors in Sydney and acquired land at Navuso on which they established a successful agricultural training school. He sat on the Fijian Education Commission in 1926 and persuaded Governor Sir Eyre Hutson to appoint Frank Tate [q.v.12] as its adviser.

In 1927 Thompson represented Fiji at the Imperial Education Conference, held in London. He attended the first ecumenical World Conference on Faith and Order at Lausanne, Switzerland, as a delegate of the Methodist Church in Australia and the South Pacific. His final missionary appointment was to Suva. There, among other duties, he superintended a large school in which 'Fijian and Indian boys studied and did practical work side by side'. He thought that both 'races' could 'without disadvantage be educated together'. In 1931 he returned to Victoria. His reminiscences were to be published in *Melbourne Studies in Education 1966* (1967), edited by E. L. French.

Thompson was a circuit minister in 1931-48, serving first at Kyneton and then in Melbourne. His ministries were characterized by liturgical order and pastoral fidelity. While stationed at Williamstown in World War II, he was a naval reserve chaplain (1942-45). He also worked as secretary (1938-49) of the Victorian Council of Churches, a role in which he promoted Life and Work weeks, lecture visits by church leaders from overseas, and measures to assist the postwar relief and rehabilitation of European churches.

Seeing 'religious education as an influential field for ecumenical endeavour', Thompson contributed to the implementation of graded lessons in state schools and helped to prepare an agreed syllabus. In 1949 he was appointed director of the Council for Christian Education in Schools. His diplomacy was important in negotiations which led to the Victorian Education (Religious Instruction) Act (1950) allowing religious instruction to be given in state schools during school hours. Thompson obtained Commonwealth government recognition of the council as a charitable organization, an important step in securing financial support from corporations and individuals for secondary-school chaplaincies. His success in obtaining concessions from politicians disturbed some of his clerical brethren who saw him as a schemer.

Following his retirement in 1957, Thompson continued to foster support for Christian education as convenor of the Australian Council of Churches' education commission, and as a member of the Methodist standing commission on education and of the Wesley College council. He died on 30 October 1975 at Canterbury and was cremated; his wife, their three sons and two of their three daughters survived him. W. H. Frederick [q.v.14] praised his gifts and his multifaceted ministry.

Methodist Church (Vic and Tas), *Minutes of the Annual Conference*, 1911-76; Methodist ministers' records (Uniting Church in Aust, Synod of Vic Archives, Elsternwick, Vic); Council for Christian Education in Schools records (SLV).

T. M. O'CONNOR

THOMSON, DONALD FINLAY FERGUSSON (1901-1970), anthropologist and zoologist, was born on 26 June 1901 at Brighton, Melbourne, second child of Harry Alexander Fergusson Thomson, a Scottish-born musician, and his wife Isabelle Alice, née Davies, who came from England. Donald had a childhood passion for natural history and went on forays to collect birds' eggs. Inspired by Sir Robert Scott, he dreamed of joining polar expeditions. The 'born adventurer' initially proceeded from Scotch College to the University of Melbourne (B.Sc., 1925; D.Sc., 1934). While there, he asked Sir Baldwin Spencer to obtain him a place on (Sir) Hubert Wilkins's [qq.v.12] expedition to northern Australia. Persuaded to complete his degree first, he prepared himself for future field-work by learning photography. After graduating he was employed as a journalist on the *Herald*.

On 30 December 1925, in the memorial hall of his old school, Thomson married with Presbyterian forms Gladys Winifred Coleman;

they were to have two sons. In 1927 he studied at the University of Sydney for a diploma in anthropology (1928). His teacher, A. R. Radcliffe-Brown [q.v.11], supported his application to the Australian National Research Council for funds to conduct anthropological and zoological field-work on Cape York Peninsula, Queensland.

Granted £600 by the A.N.R.C., Thomson set out in April 1928. He covered thousands of miles on horseback, took many glass-plate negatives and collected zoological specimens and ethnographic objects. In January 1929 he returned to Melbourne. The A.N.R.C. awarded him a grant for a second expedition, but he became involved in a dispute with its treasurer H. G. Chapman [q.v.7] who refused to provide the funds until he handed over material he had previously gathered. Thomson surrendered his grant. Accompanied by his wife, he left for Queensland, determined to support himself by journalism. Chapman, who falsely insinuated dishonesty on Thomson's part, was later found to have embezzled council money. The episode made Thomson deeply suspicious of the A.N.R.C. and may have turned Sydney's academic establishment against him.

By the end of his first period of field-work he had lost the support of Radcliffe-Brown who felt that Thomson, despite his scientific background, was 'not whole-heartedly a scientist'. The judgement reflected Radcliffe-Brown's narrow, structural-functionalist conception of anthropology. Thomson had a broader view of the discipline, an interest in art and material culture, and scant concern for new developments in social theory.

Back in Melbourne in late 1929, Thomson joined the staff of the Walter and Eliza Hall [qq.v.9] Institute of Research in Pathology and Medicine and worked on antivenenes. In 1932 he became a research fellow in the department of anatomy, University of Melbourne, which financed his last expedition (1932-33) to Cape York Peninsula. The publications resulting from his field-work included *Birds of Cape York Peninsula* (1935). He was to be attached to the university for most of the remainder of his career, as a research fellow (1932-37 and 1945-53), senior research fellow (1953-64) and professor of anthropology (1964-68).

Thomson supported Aboriginal rights. Appalled by conditions on W. F. MacKenzie's [q.v.15] Presbyterian mission at Aurukun, Queensland, he offered to address Church leaders behind closed doors, but they refused him a hearing. This experience may have coloured his attitude to missionaries in general. In 1932-33 Aborigines killed five Japanese and three Europeans near Caledon Bay and Blue Mud Bay, Northern Territory. The news led to talk of a punitive expedition. Thomson volunteered to investigate the conditions and concerns of the Aboriginal people, and to make policy recommendations. He received considerable support in Melbourne from academics and the press, particularly the *Herald*. His proposal was eventually accepted. In March 1935 he left for eastern Arnhem Land as a representative of the Commonwealth government.

Apart from a break in January-June 1936, Thomson remained in Arnhem Land until September 1937, acting as an investigator, an advocate and a mediator. He facilitated the establishment of peaceful relations between the Yolngu people and the Commonwealth government, and befriended Wonggu [q.v.], leader of the Djapu clan from the Caledon Bay region. Thomson organized the release of Mau, Natjelma and Narkaya, three of Wonggu's sons who had been imprisoned in Darwin for the killing of the Japanese, and personally returned them to their homeland in 1936. He sought to protect the integrity and inviolability of the Arnhem Land reserve by excluding non-Aboriginal people, and he recommended that European administrators should have a detailed understanding of the laws and practices of Aboriginal society.

In early 1938 Thomson sailed for England to take up a Rockefeller Foundation fellowship at Christ's College, Cambridge (Ph.D., 1950). His research was supervised by A. C. Haddon, one of the founders of evolutionary anthropology. Although there was never a trace of evolutionism in Thomson's writings, his association with Haddon may have further distanced him from the Radcliffe-Brown school. The Royal Anthropological Society of Great Britain and Ireland awarded him the Wellcome medal (1939) for his pioneering work in applied anthropology.

Thomson returned to Australia when World War II began. On 8 January 1940 he was commissioned flying officer, Royal Australian Air Force. Attached to No.11 Squadron, Port Moresby, as an intelligence officer, he helped to establish the coastwatching system in the Solomon Islands. By April 1941 he was serving at Air Force Headquarters, Melbourne. Seconded to the Australian Military Forces in June, he was sent to the Northern Territory to raise and command the 7th Military District's Special Reconnaissance Unit. In 1942-43 Squadron Leader Thomson and his men, most of them Aborigines, patrolled the coast of Arnhem Land and trained to fight as guerrillas in the event of a Japanese invasion. He left the unit in mid-1943. As a temporary wing commander, he had charge of two expeditions which explored the south-eastern part of Japanese-occupied Netherlands New Guinea. Natives attacked his party during the second journey and he was severely wounded. For his leadership of these operations he was appointed O.B.E. (1945). His R.A.A.F. appoint-

ment was terminated on medical grounds on 13 October 1944.

After the war Thomson was offered a lectureship at Cambridge, but he remained in Melbourne where he published his major work, *Economic Structure and the Ceremonial Exchange Cycle in Arnhem Land* (1949). He won the patron's medal of the Royal Geographical Society, London, in 1951 and the Rivers memorial medal of the Royal Anthropological Institute of Great Britain and Ireland in 1952. It was, however, a difficult time for him. In 1944 he had been diagnosed as suffering from diabetes, and his health never fully recovered from the hardships of his field-work and war service. His long absences from home strained his marriage; he and Gladys were to be divorced in 1954. A fire in 1946 at premises controlled by the Department of Information destroyed the 20 000 ft (6096 m) of film he had shot in Arnhem Land. He regarded those films as perhaps the best record he had made of Aboriginal life.

In 1946-47 Thomson published a series of articles in the *Herald* on justice for the Aborigines. The articles brought into the open his underlying disagreement with Professor A. P. Elkin [q.v.14], who had greater sympathy with the policy of assimilation. Thomson campaigned vigorously in 1947 against the establishment of a rocket range at Woomera, South Australia, because of the threat it posed to desert-dwelling Aborigines. Again, he was opposed by Elkin. Serving on the Victorian Aborigines Welfare Board from 1957, Thomson found that little notice was taken of his advice. He resigned in frustration in 1967.

At the Presbyterian Church, Warragul, on 7 May 1955 Thomson had married Dorita Maria McColl, a 25-year-old technical assistant. Between 1957 and 1965 he mounted three expeditions to study the Pintupi people of the Gibson and Great Sandy deserts. In this research he concentrated on the Aborigines' hunting and gathering practices; the results were less significant than his earlier work on Cape York Peninsula and in Arnhem Land. *Bindibu Country* (1975) provided an account of two of his trips. Thomson became increasingly removed from academic life and from mainstream developments in anthropology. A number of circumstances contributed to his isolation: the fact that he was the only anthropologist at the University of Melbourne, Elkin's constant and tiring opposition to his work and to the policies he advocated, and his tendency to work best alone.

On Thomson's retirement from the university in 1968, members of the professorial board praised him as 'a man of action and a distinguished scholar'. They thought that his work for Aborigines and his controversial personality merited his being described as 'Australia's Lawrence of Arabia'. Yet in many respects his life was tragic. He failed to gain the recognition as a scientist that he felt he deserved, and he failed to alter government policy towards Aboriginal people. Ironically, near the end of his life, events seemed to be catching up with him. Anthropologists were shifting towards the kinds of research that he had carried out and the movement to grant land rights to Aborigines was strengthening. But, by that time, Thomson had long been disillusioned with politicians and become alienated from most of his anthropological colleagues. He died of coronary artery sclerosis on 12 May 1970 at his Eltham farm and was cremated; his wife and their son and three daughters survived him, as did the sons of his first marriage.

The destruction of Thomson's films had made him determined to keep personal control of the other material he had acquired through his field-work. It was only after his death that the full richness of his achievement became apparent. The collection of more than 7000 artefacts, comprehensive in its scope and scrupulously described, together with 11 000 photographs documenting every aspect of Aboriginal daily and ritual life, enables the viewer to recapture the Aboriginal world of Cape York and Arnhem Land in the 1930s and 1940s. Thomson also left about 7500 pages of field-notes, 25 000 ft (7620 m) of film from later expeditions, and 2500 natural science specimens.

He had recorded in immense detail the cultural dimensions of Aboriginal society—its material culture, art, ceremonial performances, burial practices, and hunting-and-gathering economy. Moreover, Thomson wrote powerful evocations of the aesthetics of Arnhem Land life, and was sensitive to the poetics of Yolngu art and language. A meticulous ethnographer, he used his command of the language to identify central concepts that revealed the workings of Yolngu society from within, concepts such as 'marr' or ancestral power.

N. Peterson, 'Donald Thomson: A Biographical Sketch', in N. Peterson (comp), *Donald Thomson in Arnhem Land* (Melb, 1983); D. Carment (et al), *Northern Territory Dictionary of Biography*, 1 (Darwin, 1990); 'The Big Picture: Thomson of Arnhem Land', ABC TV, 29 June 2000 (ABC Archives, Syd); Donald Thomson collection (National Museum of Vic); information from Mrs D. Thomson, Melb.

HOWARD MORPHY

THOMSON, EDGAR FREDERICK (1903-1977), pathologist and army officer, was born on 4 April 1903 at Invercargill, New Zealand, son of New Zealand-born parents Frederick Augustus Thomson, carriage-painter, and his wife Ada, née Neal. Educated at Southland Boys' High School and the University of Otago, Dunedin (M.B., Ch.B., N.Z., 1926), Edgar worked (from 1927) for the professors of pathology and bacteriology at the Otago medical school before becoming assistant-pathologist at Christchurch Hospital in 1929. On 10 December that year at the Presbyterian Church, Owaka, he married Ellen Doris Latta. In 1933 he was appointed bacteriologist at Royal Prince Alfred Hospital, Sydney. He resumed his former post at Christchurch in 1937, but returned to R.P.A.H. in 1939 and that year began lecturing part time at the University of Sydney.

In December 1939 Thomson organized the blood-grouping of all members of the 16th Brigade, Australian Imperial Force. The task was completed in three weeks and with such precision that no soldier was subsequently reported to have received incompatible blood. On 22 May 1940 Thomson was appointed major, Australian Army Medical Corps, A.I.F. He sailed for the Middle East in October as pathologist to the 2nd/5th Australian General Hospital. After briefly commanding a British mobile bacteriological laboratory, he embarked for Greece with the 2nd/5th A.G.H. in April 1941. During the campaign his vigilant concern for the health and welfare of members of his unit endeared him to them. He assisted Matron K. A. L. Best [q.v.13] to evacuate the nursing staff to Crete without loss of life.

Thomson returned to Australia in March 1942 and commanded the 2nd/3rd Mobile Bacteriological Laboratory from October. In May 1943 he was appointed assistant-director of pathology at Land Headquarters, Melbourne. Promoted lieutenant colonel in October 1944, he visited army medical units in the field and helped his chief E. V. Keogh [q.v.15] to make arrangements for manufacturing penicillin in Australia. Thomson transferred to the Reserve of Officers on 8 March 1946. Active in the Citizen Military Forces as commander of the 1st General Hospital (1952-57) and as deputy-director of medical services, Eastern Command (1957-62), he retired with the rank of honorary colonel.

Back at R.P.A.H., Thomson had become director of the Fairfax [qq.v.4,8,14] Institute of Pathology in 1947. He was the hospital's general superintendent in 1958-66. As chairman (1947-68) of the Australian Red Cross Society's national transfusion committee, he encouraged co-operation between State directors of the Blood Transfusion Service. In 1963 he was appointed C.M.G. He chaired (1963-66) the Australian Drug Evaluation Committee and the National Health and Medical Research Council's antibiotics advisory committee; his long experience with antibiotics proved invaluable in guiding national policy on their use.

Thomson was founding president (1956-57) of the (Royal) College of Pathologists of Australia and the first recipient (1977) of its gold medal for outstanding service. He was a council-member and president (1956-57) of the New South Wales branch of the British (Australian) Medical Association, and a councillor of the federal organization. As the A.M.A.'s full-time secretary-general in 1967-72, he was frequently involved in negotiations with the Commonwealth government. Survived by his wife and their two sons, he died on 4 September 1977 at R.P.A.H. and was cremated. Graeme Inson's portrait of Thomson is held by the Australian Red Cross, Melbourne.

A. S. Walker, *Clinical Problems of War* (Canb, 1952); *AMA Gazette*, 15 Sept 1977, 19 Jan, 8 June 1978; *British Medical J*, 26 Nov 1977, p 1422; *MJA*, 22 Apr 1978, p 440; information from Miss N. Minogue, Balwyn, Melb, Dr E. Shaw, Yeronga, Brisb, and Dr N. Thomson, Riverview, Syd.

W. D. REFSHAUGE
JAMES C. MCALLESTER

THORNTON, ALEXANDER GEORGE (1914-1942), soldier, was born on 29 June 1914 at Paddington, Sydney, second child of Percy George Thornton (d.1932), an Australian-born clerk, and his wife Nellie, née Maidment (d.1926), who came from New Zealand. Owing to the illness and deaths of their parents, George and his siblings spent a number of years in the foster care of relations and friends. During the Depression he worked intermittently as a labourer. In March 1939 he stowed away in a ship bound for Fremantle, Western Australia, where he was arrested and gaoled for fifteen days under an assumed name, 'George Maidment'.

On 15 June 1940 Thornton enlisted in the Australian Imperial Force, again using his alias. Five ft 9 ins (175 cm) tall, with brown eyes and light brown hair, he was posted to the 2nd/16th Battalion at Northam. With his unit, he embarked for the Middle East on 25 October 1940 and reached Palestine on 26 November. He spent most of 1941 attached to a training battalion and in hospital with minor ailments, but fought in the battle of Damour on 5-9 July during the Syrian campaign. Returning to Australia in March 1942, he was sent to Queensland for jungle-warfare training in May and to Port Moresby in August.

The men of the 2nd/16th Battalion were quickly thrown into action on the Kokoda Track. Reaching Eora Creek on 27 August 1942, 'A' and 'B' companies made their way via Alola to the Abuari area, where the advancing Japanese were entrenched in camouflaged, carefully prepared positions on a ridge. Late on the morning of 30 August the two companies attacked up a steep, wooded slope.

Maidment's platoon was halted, with heavy casualties. His section leader, Corporal M. T. Clarke, was killed.

Maidment snatched grenades from Clarke's pouches, dashed up the slope, destroyed the foremost enemy machine-gun posts and sustained a severe wound to his chest. With his grenades expended and the enemy pressing forward, he ran back to Clarke's body, seized his Tommy-gun, stood in the middle of the track and held the enemy with accurate fire until his ammunition was exhausted. His actions inflicted severe casualties on the Japanese, prevented further losses among his comrades, and allowed his platoon to fight clear and re-form. The recommendation that he be awarded the Victoria Cross stated that his 'unsurpassed courage, fortitude and devotion to duty' set an 'inspiring example'.

Although exhausted and suffering from loss of blood, Maidment refused every offer of assistance. On his arrival at the regimental aid-post, he collapsed. He was evacuated (on a stretcher) along the track and was reported to have reached Templeton's Crossing *en route* to Myola. In December 1943 an inquiry into his whereabouts proved inconclusive. He was officially registered as missing and was believed to have died from his wounds. His body was never found.

Maidment had always been a controversial character during his army service. Unruly, especially when affected by alcohol, and resentful of authority, he had incurred several punishments (including periods of military confinement) for insubordinate language, disobedience and absence without leave. As one of his officers reported, with some respect, 'Maidment was a very strong character who could be coached but not ruled'. The recommendation that he receive the Victoria Cross was endorsed at higher levels, but finally downgraded to the award of the Distinguished Conduct Medal. He is commemorated, in his correct name, on the memorial at Port Moresby to Australian servicemen who gave their lives in Papua and have no known graves.

M. Uren, *A Thousand Men at War* (Melb, 1959); H. D. Steward, *Recollections of a Regimental Medical Officer* (Melb, 1983); B. Edgar, *Warrior of Kokoda* (Syd, 1999); AWM 52, item 8/3/16, and AWM 88, item AMF I/4 (AWM); WAS 672, consignment 4173, item 24 (WAA); information from Lt Col F. H. Sublet, Mt Eliza, Vic, Mrs L. and Mr M. Thornton, Camp Hill, Brisb, Mr J. Blythe, Floreat, Mrs J. Fraser, Waterman, and Messrs D. K. Norrish, J. Moir, and R. Wiseman, 2/16th Battalion Assn, Perth.

KEITH D. HOWARD

THORNTON, ERNEST (1907-1969), trade-union leader, was born on 13 March 1907 at Huddersfield, Yorkshire, England, son of

Lewis Thornton, tram driver, and his wife Selina, née Kerry. Ernie's mother, a domestic servant from Ireland, left when he was 2, and he was raised by his father. After taking factory and building jobs, he was brought to Sydney by the Dreadnought Trust. Arriving in the *Demosthenes* on 12 June 1924, he was sent to the Government Training Farm at Scheyville, near Windsor. He soon left to work in the construction industry and became a militant unionist. Unemployed in the Depression, he joined the communist-led Militant Minority Movement and, through it, the Communist Party of Australia. In a civil ceremony at 157 Collins Street, Melbourne, on 9 August 1934 he married Alice Mary ('Lila') Felstead, née Curtis, a divorcee with two sons.

Using rigid discipline and a national network of members, the C.P.A. campaigned to take over the trade-union movement as a base for revolution. Thornton led a drive to capture the Federated Ironworkers' Association of Australia, which covered steelworkers, tradesmen's assistants and other semi-skilled metal workers. Young, vigorous and confident in his cause (unlike some F.I.A. officials), he was elected as an organizer in the Melbourne office in 1935. Within a year he was part-time general secretary. From 1937 he was a member of the central committee of the C.P.A.

The recovery in industry in the late 1930s boosted union membership and funds. Thornton's post was made full time and he moved to the national office in Sydney in mid-1939. Despite the embarrassment of the Hitler-Stalin pact and Communist coolness during the early stages of World War II, Thornton and his 'red' colleagues cemented party control over the F.I.A. Communists held most of the paid jobs, and amalgamated the F.I.A. with unions covering wiremakers and munitions workers.

This success was due partly to the dynamism and ruthless militancy of Thornton and his team, but it also owed much to the erratically buoyant wartime economic conditions which persisted into the postwar years. Thornton published numerous propaganda pamphlets, including *Stronger Trade Unions* (1943). Working with its allies, the Communist Party was almost able to control the Australasian Council of Trade Unions congress in 1945. Like other communist leaders, Thornton proclaimed his allegiance to the Soviet Union and his ardent admiration of Josef Stalin. He frequently travelled to conferences overseas and in 1950 held three valid passports.

In 1946 Thornton's control of the F.I.A. was challenged by a dissident group in the Balmain branch on Sydney's waterfront and by the Australian Labor Party's Industrial Groups. Laurie Short, a Balmain dissident, led a well-organized 'grouper ticket' against Thornton at the 1949 F.I.A. elections. The returns showed that the 'Thornton ticket' had won, but Short challenged the ballot. Following a long, sensational inquiry in the Commonwealth Court of Conciliation and Arbitration, Judge E. A. Dunphy found that 'persons unknown' had rigged the ballot (with 1800 or more forged votes) and declared Short elected national secretary. Short's team won most F.I.A. positions in the ensuing national elections (1951 and 1952).

In 1950, however, Thornton had resigned to become Australasian representative at the liaison bureau of the World Federation of Trade Unions, in Peking (Beijing). The A.C.T.U. withdrew recognition of the W.F.T.U. and Thornton returned, jobless, to Australia three years later. The new F.I.A. leaders, fearing a comeback, refused to accept him in any F.I.A. industries. In 1957-67 he was a full-time employee of the Communist Party. With the decline in party finances, he returned, at the age of 60, to manual work, qualified as a crane driver, and became honorary Sydney president of the Federated Engine Drivers' and Firemen's Association of Australasia.

Energetic, fluent, domineering, dogmatic and at times a bully, Thornton was also intensely loyal, warm hearted and committed to the working-class cause. People either loved or hated him. He was of middle height and strongly built, and retained a trace of his Yorkshire accent. Steel-rimmed spectacles and a stubborn 'five-o'clock shadow' made him look more sinister than he was. Thornton remained a communist to the core, but increasingly took the less immoderate side in internal debates. Survived by his wife and two stepsons, he died of myocardial infarction on 29 June 1969 at his Lidcombe home and was cremated.

J. Sendy, *Comrades Come Rally* (Melb, 1978); R. Murray and K. White, *The Ironworkers* (Syd, 1982); S. Short, *Laurie Short* (Syd, 1992); *People* (Syd), 19 May 1954, p 16; *SMH*, 30 June 1969; *Tribune* (Syd), 2 July 1969; ASIO file, A6119, items 397 and 398 (NAA, Canb); information from Mr L. Short, Mosman, Mrs L. Thornton, Lidcombe, and Mr J. McPhillips, Syd.   ROBERT MURRAY

THORPE, DANIEL WRIXON (1889-1976), publisher, was born on 16 March 1889 at Macorna, Victoria, third of nine children of James Thorpe, farmer, and his wife Dorothy, née Angus, both Victorian born. (Sir) Fred Thorpe [q.v.] was his younger brother. Daniel was educated at Macorna until the family moved to Melbourne in 1899. He then attended North Fitzroy State School. Having gained his Merit certificate and worked part time in a newsagency, he left school in 1903 to serve an apprenticeship with George Robertson [q.v.6] & Co. Ltd, stationers, and was also introduced to bookselling. He transferred to James Spicer & Sons Ltd, paper merchants, in 1909 and rose from counterhand to assistant general manager. At the Baptist Church, Kew, on 18 November 1911 he married Miriam Schenk (d.1959); they were to have a son and two daughters.

When World War I began, Thorpe was a member of the Fitzroy Rifle Club. He was called up for coastal-defence service, but was declared medically unfit. His duties at Spicer's grew more onerous as others enlisted and war conditions affected the availability, quality and cost of imports. In 1915 he became president of the Wholesale and Manufacturing Stationers' Association, formed to settle pricing disputes. Peace brought further anxiety with a slump in prices and fluctuating exchange rates.

Long aware of the lack of a trade periodical for stationers, booksellers and newsagents, and seeking independence from the competitive business world, Thorpe left Spicer's in 1921 to start the *Australian Stationery and Fancy Goods Journal*. It soon included bookselling news and in 1926 was retitled the *Booksellers Stationers and Fancy Goods Journal of Australia and New Zealand*. Lacking capital, Thorpe worked from one room with a typist and had some 'trying' years. He travelled Australia, seeking ideas, subscribers and advertising, and joined trade associations. His journal discussed foreign competition, salesmanship, market conditions and ideas for the Christmas trade, advised on new shop-fittings, and reported association news. In the 1930s Thorpe wrote successful booklets on the game of bridge, under the pen-name 'Ace High'.

From December 1928 Thorpe had published *All About Books for Australian and New Zealand Readers*, which carried reports from literary societies, as well as news of books and authors. He gave prominence to Australian publications, especially through the regular contributions of Nettie Palmer and later Fred Macartney [qq.v.11,15]. In 1931 children's book notes appeared, written by Thorpe's elder daughter Joyce, who began aged 12 what would soon be a significant connexion with the business. *All About Books* ceased publication in March 1938 for want of support. It was briefly revived in 1961.

Well known and knowledgeable, but no trade competitor, Thorpe was secretary (1925-49) of the Associated Booksellers of Australia and New Zealand (Australian Booksellers' Association). In 1928 the A.B.A. included him in its overseas mission to persuade British publishers to give Australian booksellers better terms. Due to increasing association work, he employed a second assistant and moved to a larger office in 1933. By the outbreak of World War II he was honorary secretary to five trade associations: he accepted an honorarium, only to preserve 'reasonable independence'. He also joined the Paper Trade Advisory Committee and was appointed honorary technical adviser to the Commonwealth controller of paper, whom he accompanied in 1944 to the United States of America and Britain to discuss supplies.

After the war Thorpe's trade journal for stationers, booksellers and newsagents prospered and grew (its cumbersome title had been simplified in 1937 to *Ideas*). He relinquished A.B.A. commitments and in 1948 formed his business into a family company, D. W. Thorpe Pty Ltd. In 1956 it introduced *Australian Books in Print*, and divided *Ideas* into two journals, one to serve newsagents and stationers, and the other, booksellers. The firm purchased its own premises, at 384 Spencer Street, in 1959. In semi-retirement Thorpe continued to write and contribute ideas, leaving the running of the company to a business manager. The arrangement proved unfortunate and the business declined. It was only restored and expanded when his daughter Joyce Nicholson was appointed managing director in 1968. At his behest she published a new journal, *Educational Books and Equipment*.

Interested in the firm to the end, Thorpe was a kindly and peaceable man, a Methodist lay preacher, and a keen golfer. He died on 29 June 1976 at Southport, Queensland, and was cremated. His daughters survived him.

R. J. Thorpe, *Daniel Thorpe's Family* (Melb, 1996); J. T. Nicholson and D. W. Thorpe, *A Life of Books* (Melb, 2000); D. W. Thorpe Pty Ltd records (Univ Melb Archives).   CECILY CLOSE

THORPE, FRANK GORDON (1885-1967), public servant, was born on 15 February 1885 at Kooreh, Victoria, second child of William Jabez Thorpe, schoolteacher, and his wife Kate, née Mann, both Victorian born. Educated at St Arnaud and Warrnambool State schools, Frank entered the Post and Telegraph Department in 1898 as a telegraph messenger. He transferred to the Commonwealth Public Service in 1901 and became personal clerk to the deputy postmaster-general. Seconded to the Department of Defence during World War I, he rose to be head of the army pay office in Melbourne with the honorary rank of lieutenant colonel. On 24 January 1917 at the Methodist Church, Brighton, he married Elsie Rebecca Leake; they had one child, a son, before she died in 1921.

That year Thorpe joined the Prime Minister's Department as a senior clerk. In 1923 he was appointed an assistant-inspector with the Commonwealth Public Service Board. His responsibility for industrial arbitration involved him in negotiations with staff associations. At Holy Trinity Church, Surrey Hills, on 21 August 1926 he married with Anglican rites Vera Hope Donaldson, a typist. The board moved to Canberra in 1928. When Thorpe was promoted to be its secretary next year, he retained his role in industrial relations.

By 1931, due to the exigencies of the Depression, the Federal government had allowed the number of public service commissioners on the board to decline from three to one. To reduce the burden on (Sir) William Clemens [q.v.8], who was handling retrenchments and reductions in salaries, Thorpe was chosen for the new position of assistant-commissioner in September 1932. Appointed M.B.E. in 1936, he succeeded Clemens as commissioner on 27 March 1937. Although he was hamstrung by having insufficient staff, he managed to deal with the more important issues. In 1939 he was appointed C.M.G. Throughout World War II he worked under increased pressure that stemmed from the creation of additional departments and the recruitment of larger numbers of public servants (including many women), but he had little time for analysing the needs of individual departments in regard to staff and training.

In 1940-43 Thorpe argued against full preference for returned servicemen to gain employment in the public service on the grounds that such a practice had denied young people the opportunity to enter the third division after World War I. The government overruled him. His major achievement lay in his harmonious negotiations with staff associations following the implementation of the Commonwealth Public Service Act (No.2, 1945), legislation which modified the promotions system and provided for greater staff involvement in decision-making. He retired on 26 March 1947.

A skilful negotiator, Thorpe had been popular with staff-association officials. His 'conciliatory attitude' had saved the public-service arbitration system from collapse, but, in Gerald Caiden's view, his kindness and courtesy had 'allowed the more unscrupulous to take advantage of him'. Thorpe's recreations were motoring, bowls, golf and gardening. Survived by his wife, he died on 30 March 1967 at Canberra Community Hospital and was cremated with Presbyterian forms. His only child Harold had been killed in India in 1943 while serving with the Royal Australian Air Force.

G. E. Caiden, *Career Service* (Melb, 1965); Public Service Bd, *Annual Report*, 1923-47; information from Mr R. Hyslop, Yarralumla, Canb.

MATTHEW CALABY

THORPE, SIR FRED GARNER (1893-1970), engineer and army officer, was born on Christmas Day 1893 at Macorna, Victoria, fifth of nine children of James Thorpe, store-manager, and his wife Dorothy, née Angus, both Victorian born. Daniel Wrixon Thorpe [q.v.] was his elder brother. Fred attended state schools at Macorna and North Fitzroy, Melbourne, before being apprenticed (1910) to the Victorian Railways as a fitter and turner in the rolling-stock division. He won a scholarship to the Working Men's College, where he obtained diplomas in mechanical and electrical engineering in 1915.

On 15 July that year Thorpe enlisted in the Australian Imperial Force. He served in Egypt with the 5th Field Company, Australian Engineers. In March 1916 his unit was sent to France. Commissioned on 20 October, he was transferred to the 6th Field Company in December and promoted lieutenant in April 1917. Near Bullecourt, on 3-6 May, he 'set a splendid example' in charge of parties that worked in communication and support trenches while under heavy fire. He won the Military Cross. At Trinity Chapel, Paddington, London, on 11 December 1918 he married with Wesleyan Methodist forms Myrtle Mary Amelia Bishop. His A.I.F. appointment terminated on 7 December 1919.

Leaving the railways in 1920, Thorpe joined Gibson, Battle (Melbourne) Pty Ltd as a sales engineer. In 1925 he moved to Bevan & Edwards Pty Ltd (later E. P. Bevan & Son Pty Ltd) which amalgamated in 1938 with the machine-tool division of McPherson's [q.v.10] Ltd to form Associated Machine Tools Australia Pty Ltd. Thorpe was appointed a director of the new company. The merger reflected a fear that war would disrupt overseas supplies of 'machines used to make other machines'; it was therefore essential that Australia become self-sufficient in lathes and forging presses, and in equipment 'for planing, boring, sawing, grinding, milling, filing and reaming'. Associated Machine Tools Australia was licensed to manufacture any product of Associated British Machine Tool Makers Ltd, a group of eight leading British manufacturers.

Thorpe was sent to England in 1939 to gain a more thorough understanding of the manufacture of machine tools. On his return in September, he took charge of McPherson's works at Kensington. By this time he was acknowledged as Australia's leading authority in his field. Having served in the Militia (from 1921) and risen to the rank of lieutenant colonel (1934), he was appointed on 1 April 1939 to the part-time post of chief engineer, 3rd District Base, Melbourne, as a temporary colonel. In July 1940 he relinquished his military appointment to become director of machine tools and gauges, Department of Munitions. The directorate had been established to 'control the production, reconditioning, acquisition, disposal and distribution of machine tools, ball bearings, electrical equipment, gauges, factory equipment, transmission gears and hand tools'.

Under Thorpe's supervision, tool-making expanded dramatically. He later recalled the important contribution of firms which had taken the opportunity during the 'phoney war' to obtain British designs of 'high production, high quality machines' previously not made in Australia. The experience gained in manufacturing this equipment proved invaluable in increasing the number, variety and complexity of machine tools built in Australia. In 1943 some two hundred manufacturers, employing 12 000 staff, produced 14 000 such items, ranging from a lathe weighing 132 tons to intricate precision instruments. Local firms made 37 000 of the 63 000 machine tools supplied to the armed forces and industry in 1940-45.

Thorpe's 'drive and energy' were crucial to his directorate's achievement, but there were deficiencies in his administration. Other sections of the department complained about long delays in the supply of machine tools. Thorpe never established clear procedures for charting and scheduling: after naming a delivery date, he had no system for monitoring production or advising changes to that date.

There were additional problems. Thorpe's close association with McPherson's led in 1941 to claims by New South Wales manufacturers of favouritism in the letting of war contracts. Moreover, the directorate experienced constant difficulty in recovering machine tools that had been assigned to manufacturers for specific jobs and were later required elsewhere. These manufacturers had a considerable hold over Thorpe and his colleagues; as potential customers for machine tools after the war, they could threaten to boycott their businesses. Coming from a small firm, Thorpe lacked the power of big businessmen in the department, such as Sir Colin Fraser and Essington Lewis [qq.v.8,10], to resist such intimidatory tactics.

In June 1945 Thorpe returned to McPherson's as manager of the machinery department. Three years later he was promoted to technical director. Following his retirement in 1953, he set up as a chartered engineer. One of his commissions was to advise Broken Hill Proprietary Co. Ltd on its machine-tool requirements. From 1952 he chaired the Federal minister for supply's advisory committee on machine tools and gauges for industry and government munitions establishments. He claimed that a machine-tool industry was essential to the nation's security and that the Commonwealth government should protect local manufacturers from overseas competitors.

Thorpe was a director of Renold Chains (Australia) Pty Ltd, Vickers Australia Pty Ltd,

Bermid Auto Castings Pty Ltd and N. F. Thorpe Pty Ltd (his son's engineering venture at Briar Hill). He was a trustee (1945-63) of the National Museum of Victoria and chairman (1950-54 and 1964-65) of the Museum of Applied Science of Victoria. In 1952 he was knighted. In 1962 he received the Jack Finlay award from the Institution of Production Engineers. He belonged to the Naval and Military Club, and enjoyed gardening in his later years. Sir Fred died on 29 March 1970 at Rosanna and was cremated; his wife and their son survived him.

D. P. Mellor, *The Role of Science and Industry* (Canb, 1958); A. T. Ross, *Armed & Ready* (Syd, 1995); *Aust Machinery and Production Engineering*, Apr 1969; *SMH*, 13 Sept 1952, 11 May 1959; *Age* (Melb), 31 Mar 1970.   CHARLES FAHEY

THYER, JAMES HERVEY (1897-1977), army officer, was born on 30 September 1897 at Natimuk, Victoria, fifth of seven children of South Australian-born parents James Thyer, police constable, and his wife Isabella, née Hervey. Educated at Perth Modern School, Jim entered the Royal Military College, Duntroon, Federal Capital Territory, in February 1915. He graduated in 1917 and was commissioned lieutenant, Australian Imperial Force, on 1 January 1918. In April-November he trained in Britain; following the Armistice, he served with signals units in France. Returning to Australia in December 1919, he transferred to the Staff Corps in October 1920. He held a series of staff and regimental appointments, and rose to captain (1926) and major (1936). At St George's Church of England, Queenscliff, Victoria, on 7 November 1928 he had married Marjorie Chalk Firth.

Five ft 8½ ins (174 cm) tall, with a florid complexion, hazel eyes, brown hair and a calm disposition, Thyer was seconded to the A.I.F. on 4 April 1940. Within three months he was promoted lieutenant colonel and given command of the 8th Divisional Signals. He reached Singapore in February 1941. In July Major General H. G. Bennett [q.v.13] chose him to be the division's general staff officer, 1st grade, and promoted him colonel. Bennett's headquarters was riven by personal and professional feuds. His relationship with Thyer steadily deteriorated.

In mid-January 1942 the soldiers of the 8th Division came into contact with the Japanese who were advancing through southern Malaya. Following the retreat to Singapore on 31 January, the division was sent to defend a vulnerable sector in the island's north-west. When Thyer urged Bennett to consider preparing a reserve line across a narrow neck of land, Bennett accused him of having a 'withdrawal complex'. The Australian force was swamped by the Japanese assault on the night of 8/9 February. Singapore fell on the 15th. Thyer was awarded the Distinguished Service Order for his planning and supervision throughout the campaign.

Initially held in captivity at Changi, Thyer refused to tell the Japanese about Australia's defence capabilities, despite their threats to shoot him. He was taken to Formosa (Taiwan) in August 1942, and then to Mukden, Manchuria, where he acted as a spokesman for the prisoners of war. With Lieutenant Colonel C. H. Kappe, he compiled a report on operations in Malaya and Singapore: it concluded that, although units fought 'reasonably well', the A.I.F. 'did not measure up to the task required of it'. In September 1945 Thyer was released and repatriated. For his leadership and courage as a prisoner of war, he was appointed C.B.E. (1947).

Thyer strongly disapproved of Bennett's escape from Singapore on the night of the surrender. Late in 1945 he told a military court of inquiry and a royal commission that the general's conduct was 'unethical'. He transferred to the Retired List on 3 November 1947. Promoted honorary brigadier in 1955, he was colonel commandant, Royal Australian Corps of Signals, in 1957-67. Settling in Adelaide, he completed in 1974 the first volume of a history of that corps. He died on 9 January 1977 in the Repatriation General Hospital, Daw Park, and was cremated. His wife survived him; they had no children.

L. Wigmore, *The Japanese Thrust* (Canb, 1957); F. Legg, *The Gordon Bennett Story* (Syd, 1965); A. B. Lodge, *The Fall of General Gordon Bennett* (Syd, 1986); P. Elphick, *Singapore* (Lond, 1995); J. Wyett, *Staff Wallah* (Syd, 1996); M. H. Murfett et al, *Between Two Oceans* (Lond, 1999); J. H. Thyer and C. H. Kappe, Report on Operations of 8th Australian Division AIF in Malaya (AWM); Official History 1939-45 War: Records of Lionel Wigmore (AWM).

ALAN WARREN

TIEGS, OSCAR WERNER (1897-1956), professor of zoology, was born on 12 March 1897 at Kangaroo Point, Brisbane, only son and eldest child of Otto Theodor Carl Tiegs, a Prussian-born merchant, and his wife Helene Caroline Ottilie, née Meyer, who came from Hanover. Sent to Brisbane Grammar School, Oscar gained a scholarship to the University of Queensland (B.Sc., 1919; M.Sc., 1921) and specialized in biology. In 1920-21 he held a Walter and Eliza Hall [qq.v.9] fellowship in economic biology. He joined scientists studying the control of the blowfly and prickly pear, and took part in the campaign to eradicate hookworm.

Accompanying Professor T. H. Johnston [q.v.9] to the University of Adelaide in 1922, Tiegs helped to establish the new department of zoology and acted as head in Johnston's absence that year. He also completed a thesis 'on the histology of metamorphosis of a Chalcid wasp, *Nasonia*', for which he was awarded a D.Sc. (1922) at the age of 25. The observations he made in the course of this work formed the foundation of most of his later research.

In 1925 Tiegs was appointed to a lectureship in the zoology department under Professor W. E. Agar [q.v.7] at the University of Melbourne. At the Presbyterian Church, Hawthorn, on 14 August 1926 he married Ethel Mary Hamilton, a telephonist. He won the university's David Syme [q.v.6] research prize in 1928. With the aid of a Rockefeller travelling fellowship, he spent a year at the universities of Cambridge, England, and Utrecht, the Netherlands, before returning to Melbourne. He was promoted to associate-professor in 1931 and professor of zoology in 1948.

Fascinated by insects since his childhood, Tiegs was an outstanding morphologist who devoted a lifetime to meticulous microscopic observation of invertebrates, principally insects and myriapods. His investigations ranged from 'physiological analysis of nervous and muscular action to studies in classical invertebrate embryology comparable to the very best work of the last century'. He illustrated his papers with beautiful diagrams. The microscopical examinations he made of the structure of muscle fibre and the nature of the nerve connections within it created a base upon which others could build. His findings on the embryology of insects and myriapods led to the division of the phylum Arthropoda into two distinct parts: one comprising the insects, myriapods, and the genus *Peripatus*; the other consisting of the Trilobites, Crustacea and arachnids. Shortly before his death he completed a comprehensive review of arthropod evolution which his colleagues prepared for publication.

Tiegs was a master of technique, with a 'shrewd perception of relationships in multitudinous detail'. He was elected a fellow (1944) of the Royal Society, London, and a foundation fellow (1954) of the Australian Academy of Science. In 1956 he was awarded the (W. B.) Clarke [q.v.3] medal by the Royal Society of New South Wales. He travelled overseas for a second time, in 1954, to consult with his peers, few of whom had both the skill and the time to address the fundamental problems that absorbed him. Significant as his contribution was to zoology, his geographical isolation and his own diffidence probably prevented him from realizing his maximum potential.

Although Tiegs served as dean of the faculty of science in 1950-52, he much preferred the laboratory, the departmental museum—which he extended and improved—and the lecture theatre to the committee-room. His lectures, given mostly to first-year students, were 'models of presentation and clarity' that drew on his easy command of English and 'natural artistic ability'. To his staff he offered the freedom and encouragement that nurtured world-class research. A man for whom the line between work and recreation was blurred, he often took the classes of a staff-member on leave so as to lighten the burden on his colleagues.

Slightly built, with a laugh 'appropriate to a more robust physique', 'Sandy' Tiegs was a modest, warm and unassuming man whose friendships were deep and lasting. He was a shrewd judge of character and refreshingly direct in his dealings. Ethel shared his interests in art, literature and music. Suffering from aortic stenosis, he died of a coronary occlusion on 5 November 1956 in his home at Hawthorn and was cremated with Methodist forms. His wife survived him; they had no children.

Biog Memoirs of Fellows of Roy Soc (Lond), 3, 1957, p 247; *Aust J of Science*, 19, no 4, 21 Feb 1957, p 151; *Univ Melb Gazette*, 13, no 1, 11 Apr 1957; *Argus*, 15 Mar 1944; *Age* (Melb), 5 June 1947, 6 Apr 1956; *Herald* (Melb), 5 Nov 1956.

CAROLYN RASMUSSEN

TIER, BERNARD JOHN PATRICK (1916-1973), newspaper editor, was born on 18 March 1916 at Woollahra, Sydney, third of five children of native-born parents James George Tier, clerk, and his wife Nellie, née Latimer. After completing his schooling at Christian Brothers' College, Manly, at the height of the Depression, Jack found it difficult to obtain regular employment. He picked up casual work, reporting on sport for the daily *Sun*, where his father was a respected clerk.

On 2 July 1940 Tier enlisted in the Australian Imperial Force. Within five weeks he was made acting sergeant in the 2nd/3rd Pioneer Battalion. He served in the Northern Territory before embarking for the Middle East in November 1941. His unit saw action in North Africa in 1942. Promoted acting warrant officer, class two, in September, he was mentioned in dispatches for his gallant service. The 2nd/3rd returned to Australia in February 1943 and he was posted to the 31st Infantry Training Battalion. Six ft 1 in. (185 cm) tall, a lanky, long-legged and swift-striding man with an easy grin, Tier was, and remained, the archetypal digger. While on leave in Sydney, he married with Catholic rites Kathleen Leah Clements, a typist, on 26 January 1944 at the Church of Mary Immaculate, Manly. Three months later he rejoined the 2nd/3rd and in May 1945 took part in the invasion of Tarakan Island, Borneo. He was discharged in Sydney on 9 January 1946 as an acting warrant officer, class one.

That year Tier joined the *Sun* as a sports writer. Following John Fairfax & Sons [qq.v.4, 8] Pty Ltd's purchase of the *Sun* in 1953, Tier became part of a dedicated production team around Lindsay Clinch, its new executive-editor. The *Sun* exulted in bold and brash stories and layouts. It passed the rival *Daily Mirror*'s circulation in 1955 and held its lead for the next decade. When Tier was named editor in August 1959, Fairfax had recently acquired the *Mirror* and put Clinch in editorial charge of it. Tier relished competing, successfully, against the admired chief who had shaped his style. By October 1961 Clinch was back at the *Sun* as executive-editor. Tier succeeded him in May 1965, but used the title of editor until his death.

An energetic, hard-working, hands-on editor, Tier had flair, cheerful enthusiasm and an easy informality that generated team spirit. He enjoyed warm support from the Fairfax board and senior executives, who gave him full control at a time when the *Mirror*'s renewal under Rupert Murdoch was causing anxiety. The *Sun* remained aggressively competitive, but was less sensational and more community-oriented, and at times came close to recovering its circulation lead. Tier encouraged good relations with government and city leaders. In 1971 he initiated the *Sun* Sydney-to-Surf race, an annual fun run in which thousands took part.

Tier was known for his love of sailing and Rugby League football. Suffering from coronary atherosclerosis, he died of myocardial infarction on 9 November 1973 at his Turramurra home and was buried in Frenchs Forest cemetery; his wife, and their two sons and three daughters survived him. The Jack Tier marathon for sailing skiffs was named after him.

G. Souter, *Company of Heralds* (Melb, 1981); *Sun* (Syd), 9, 13, 14 Nov 1973; *SMH*, 13 Nov 1973; information from, and correspondence held by, Mrs K. Tier, Turramurra, Syd; information from Mr A. J. Tier, Balgowlah, Syd, and Mr I. Arnold, Calamvale, Brisb; personal knowledge.   STUART INDER

TIERNEY, JOHN LAWRENCE (1892-1972), schoolteacher and author, was born on 17 June 1892 on the family farm at Eurunderee, near Mudgee, New South Wales, youngest of eleven children of John Tierney (d.1891), a schoolteacher from Ireland, and his German-born wife Elizabeth, née Rheinberger. Young John attended Eurunderee Public School (where his father had taught Henry Lawson [q.v.10]) and Mudgee District School. He entered Teachers' College, Sydney, in 1911 and began to teach in 1913. As an evening student, he studied English at the University of Sydney (B.A., 1914; M.A., 1922) and wrote his thesis on Australian literature. He spent 1923 in Britain, teaching at St George's College, Weybridge, and studying for a diploma of education (awarded in 1925) at the University of Oxford. Between various short postings, he taught at Sydney Technical High School (1918-24) and Fort Street (1924-39). He was at Homebush High School from 1944 until he retired in 1951.

On 6 September 1932, at Wollstonecraft, Tierney had married with Catholic rites Effie Isabelle Brodie, a clerk and an Anglican. They lived at Pennant Hills before moving in 1939 to Beecroft where they remained for most of their lives. Tierney's bush-lore approach to his garden and orchard led him to dig a deep trench (through sandstone in some places) around his Beecroft garden to prevent the roots of bush trees from feeding on his soil. His children long remembered the joys and dangers of 'Dad's trench'.

Effie and her friend Marjorie Barnard (with whom she had worked at Sydney Technical College library) encouraged Tierney to write down some of the stories that he told them about his largely unrewarded efforts to become a commercially successful orchardist at Glenorie. Barnard advised him to send them to the *Bulletin*. He met Douglas Stewart, editor of the 'Red Page', and Norman Lindsay [q.v.10] who became a close friend. Both were enthusiastic about his writing. Stewart described Tierney as 'long and stooping, with a sharp inquisitive nose and small bright darting blue eyes. He had a genial, sympathetic manner and, with his reddish, weather-tanned face, looked like a farmer or the priest of a country parish'. Lindsay commended his love of the earth and its produce, and his characteristic modesty.

Tierney's first of many short stories, 'Uncle's Career', appeared in the *Bulletin* on 17 June 1942 under his pen-name, 'Brian James'. He published four collections of short stories, *First Furrow* (1944), *Cookabundy Bridge* (1946, awarded the S. H. Prior [q.v.11] memorial prize), *The Bunyip of Barney's Elbow* (1956) and *The Big Burn* (1965). As Brian James, he also edited *Selected Australian Stories* (Melbourne, 1959) and *Australian Short Stories* (London, 1963). His two novels, *The Advancement of Spencer Button* (1950) and *Hopeton High* (1963), drew on his experiences and observations as a schoolteacher.

In all his work, Tierney conveyed the comic aspects of character and situation by means of dry understatement; gifted with a sense of place, he also portrayed the physical sur-

roundings of his characters. He wrote rapidly in exercise books, and rewrote little. His unpublished pieces include reminiscences of his childhood at Eurunderee. Survived by his wife, their daughter and two of their three sons, he died on 11 February 1972 at Burwood and was buried in North Rocks cemetery. Brian James belonged to the same *Bulletin* tradition as A. H. Davis ('Steele Rudd'), Frank Dalby Davison [qq.v.8,13] and Eric Schlunke [q.v.]. He shared with them a sardonic sense of humour and a capacity for satire, realism and stylistic economy.

N. Lindsay, 'Introduction', in B. James, *The Big Burn* (Syd, 1965); D. Stewart, *Norman Lindsay* (Melb, 1975); H. de Berg, J. Tierney (taped interview, 1967, NL); Tierney papers, *and* Norman Lindsay papers, *and* Angus & Robertson correspondence (ML); teachers' records (NSW Dept of Education, Syd); information from Mr A. Tierney, Goulburn, NSW.   MARY MCPHERSON

TILL, PETER LEONARD (1937-1976), public servant, was born on 9 February 1937 at Portsmouth, England, only child of Leonard Alfred Till, chemist's assistant, and his wife Dorothy Mary, née Starling. Peter attended Hambledon County Primary and Portsmouth Grammar schools. In 1955 he entered Jesus College, Oxford (B.A., 1959), where he read classics, and philosophy, politics and economics. At the register office, Oxford, on 18 June 1959 he married Tjitske Dani Noppen, a nurse; they had no children and later divorced. After a year teaching at Trinity College, Dublin, he was recruited to the Commonwealth Treasury and arrived in Canberra in 1960. Characteristically untidy and energetic, he was prominent in debates among policy officers in the back bar of the Hotel Canberra —once challenging John Stone, then a rising Treasury officer, to a foot race of 20 miles (32 km) to Lake George. Stone won.

Leaving the Treasury for Paris in 1965, Till joined the Organization for Economic Cooperation and Development. He specialized in macro-economic policy. On 12 May 1967 at the consular section of the British Embassy, Paris, he married Carol Elizabeth Morris, a secretary. The ideal of social and economic reconstruction in Europe inspired him, but in the early 1970s he grew disillusioned and resigned his post. Encouraged by Australian contacts, Michael Keating and Patrick Troy, he returned to Canberra in 1973 to become one of the senior contract executives around whom the Department of Urban and Regional Development, created by the new Labor government, took shape. He was appointed first assistant secretary and headed successively the resource allocation, strategy, and land divisions.

Till and Troy advised the minister Tom Uren during intense negotiations with Treasury about priorities in public expenditure and new practices of functional budgeting. As an economist, Till was sharp in identifying inefficiencies and subsidies to privileged groups. As a reformer, he was keen to push an agenda of state intervention. Although sometimes combative and abrasive, he won respect for his basic compassion and moral sense, tempered by keen economic understanding. He was pivotal to efforts—often under the pressures of achieving consensus and managing controversy—to bring coherence to the department's activities.

The negotiations over the Albury-Wodonga growth centre were an important part of Till's work, as was the rehabilitation of Darwin after the 1974 cyclone. His travels fostered a strong attachment to the country and provided a ready store of anecdotes about the outback. An emotional restlessness was central to his nature, and possibly a reason for his professional mobility. His second marriage, also childless, ended in divorce, and he formed several close relationships that eventually became strained.

Following the dismissal and defeat of the Whitlam government, D.U.R.D. was incorporated in the Department of Environment, Housing and Community Development in December 1975. Till retained his post, but the political mood had changed and he spoke of returning to Paris. He died of meningitis on 21 May 1976 in Canberra Hospital and was cremated. A memorial trust funded the restoration of huts in Kosciusko National Park, New South Wales, and in the French Alps, reflecting his passion for walking. In August 1980 the Peter Till Environmental Laboratory was opened at Albury.

P. N. Troy (ed), *Federal Power in Australia's Cities* (Syd, 1978); C. J. Lloyd and P. N. Troy, *Innovation and Reaction* (Syd, 1981); T. Uren, *Straight Left* (Syd, 1994); *Canb Times*, 22, 27 May 1976; information from Dr M. S. Keating, Isaacs, Prof P. N. Troy, Reid, Canb, and Mr J. Stone, East Melb.

NICHOLAS BROWN

TILLEY, CECIL EDGAR (1894-1973), petrologist and mineralogist, was born on 14 May 1894 at Unley, Adelaide, youngest of five children of John Thomas Edward Tilley, a civil engineer from London, and his South Australian-born wife Catherine Jane, née Nicholas. Cecil attended Adelaide High School and the University of Adelaide (B.Sc., 1914). He then followed his teacher W. R. Browne [q.v.13] to the University of Sydney (B.Sc., 1916), where he studied chemistry and geology, and became a junior demonstrator in geology and mineralogy. In late 1916

he travelled to England to work in the munitions industry. After the Armistice he returned to Australia. Awarded an 1851 Exhibition scholarship in 1919, he went back to England to study petrology under Alfred Harker at the University of Cambridge (Ph.D., 1922). There he was appointed demonstrator (1923) and lecturer (1929) in petrology, and professor of mineralogy and petrology (1931). At Holy Trinity Church, Kingsway, London, on 21 June 1928 he had married Irene Doris Marshall with Anglican rites.

In his early years at Cambridge, Tilley based his work on a suite of metamorphic rocks from Eyre Peninsula, South Australia. The focus of his research turned specifically to contact metamorphism, and he set about unravelling reactions associated with the steep thermal gradients at the contacts between magmas and chalks and limestones. In the process, he discovered and described a number of new minerals. He also worked on regional metamorphism in the Scottish Highlands, pioneered the mapping of metamorphic zones and introduced the concept of the isogradic surface. From about 1950 he concentrated on igneous rocks, in particular the nature and classification of basalts. After his retirement in 1961, he divided his time between his home base at Cambridge and the Carnegie Institution's geophysical laboratory in Washington, D.C., where he continued his research on basaltic rocks in collaboration with experimental petrologists. During his career he published 122 papers, only 35 of which were written with co-authors.

Tilley was a dominant figure in modern metamorphic and igneous petrology. A fellow (1938) and vice-president (1949-50) of the Royal Society, he was awarded a Royal medal in 1967. He was president of the Mineralogical Society (1948-51 and 1957-60), the International Mineralogical Association (1964-70) and the Geological Society of London (1949-50). Tilley won the Mineralogical Society of America's Roebling medal (1954) and the G.S.L.'s Wollaston medal (1960). He also received honorary doctorates from the Victoria University of Manchester (1956) and the University of Sydney (1964), and honorary fellowships from numerous scientific societies.

A tall, broad-shouldered and solidly built man, Tilley had large hands and penetrating eyes that gave no hint of his shyness and modesty. He possessed acute powers of observation, both in the field and with a microscope. His passion for examining rocks in thin-section, on which he spent much time, was driven by what he called the 'supreme exhilaration of the chase'. He brought to petrology a systematic and rigorous working method—exhaustive collection in the field, painstaking petrographic examination, mineral separation and chemical analysis, and complete command of the literature—which he instilled in his research students.

Tilley had spent a year in Australia in 1938-39. After World War II, he made three other extended visits. Encouraged by him, a succession of young Australians went to Cambridge to undertake postgraduate study and returned to hold academic positions in Australian universities. Through them, Tilley influenced the teaching of geology in his native land. He died on 24 January 1973 in his Cambridge home and was cremated; his wife and their daughter survived him.

DNB, 1971-80; *Biog Memoirs of Fellows of Roy Soc* (Lond), 20, 1974, p 381; *American Mineralogist*, 59, 1974, p 427; *Mineralogical Mag*, 39, no 305, Mar 1974, p 493; *SMH*, 12 Aug 1931, 26 May 1938, 31 Jan 1964; *Daily Telegraph* (Syd), 31 Jan 1964; *The Times*, 26 Jan 1973.   ALLAN PRING

TILLEY, FRANK EDWARD (1883-1954), stockbroker, was born on 22 October 1883 at Charters Towers, Queensland, second son of Tasmanian-born parents William Henry Tilley (d.1928), a carrier who became a stockbroker and company director, and his wife Mary Ann, née Jordan. Frank attended Charters Towers State School and, after the family moved to Sydney in 1900, Sydney Grammar School. He entered his father's stockbroking firm, William Tilley & Co., in 1902 and was taken into partnership in 1911, the same year as he joined the Sydney Stock Exchange. At St Stephen's Presbyterian Church, Sydney, on 16 March 1915 he married Evelyn May Perdriau, a niece of Henry Perdriau [q.v.11].

Frank Tilley succeeded his father as director of the Australia Hotel Co. Ltd (chairman from 1943), the Hotel Metropole Ltd and Joe Gardiner Ltd. A committee-member (1921-22 and 1939-52) of the Sydney Stock Exchange, he was elected chairman in 1941. Although F. O. Steel resigned from the committee in protest against the chairman continuing to hold directorships in listed companies, Tilley was to be re-elected annually until 1952. The Stock Exchange was a small institution in 1941, with a hundred members and a staff of twenty-four. Its chairman was a figure of authority who managed the organization and presided over sharetraders in the call room, sometimes an unruly gathering which needed firm control.

During World War II the Stock Exchange was reduced in several ways: many brokers and staff left to serve in the armed forces, the volume of business declined, and government regulations threatened the very existence of the stockmarket. In 1942 Tilley convinced R. A. Rowe, chairman of the Stock Exchange of Melbourne, that co-operation with J. B. Chifley [q.v.13], the Federal treasurer, was

in their best interests, despite their political and philosophical differences with the Labor government. The three men met regularly to negotiate controls on the price of shares and developed a friendly working relationship based on mutual respect. A few stockbrokers, however, criticized the two chairmen for acting without consultation and for acquiescing in unnecessary regulation.

With the support of a largely conservative membership, Tilley discouraged proposals in 1947 (when price controls were lifted) and 1950 which would have changed the rules of an expanding Sydney Stock Exchange to allow advertising, the establishment of branch offices, and the introduction of continuous dealing (post trading) instead of the regular call system. Disapproving of the entry of institutions into equity investment, he forecast that they would take over the market. He favoured the continuation of small family firms, ideally where son learned from father.

Tilley was of middle height and fair complexion, with neat hair and horn-rimmed spectacles. In his public role he was inclined to be short-tempered, aloof and autocratic, but in private he was genial. His friends were fellow stockbrokers; social life consisted of bridge evenings and dinner-parties at one another's homes on the North Shore. A keen golfer, he belonged to the Killara (captain 1932-33) and Australian golf clubs.

After suffering a stroke, Tilley resigned as chairman in 1952. He died on 23 October 1954 at his Killara home and, although an Anglican, was cremated with Presbyterian forms. Tilley was survived by his wife, and their daughter and son William John who became a committee-member of the Sydney Stock Exchange and built the family firm into a large organization.

S. Salsbury and K. Sweeney, *The Bull, the Bear and the Kangaroo* (Syd, 1988) and *Sydney Stockbrokers* (Syd, 1992); *SMH*, 13 Feb 1941, 23 July 1952, 26 Oct 1954; Sydney Stock Exchange records; information from Messrs W. J. Tilley, Darling Point, A. H. Urquhart, Point Piper, B. Todhunter, Vaucluse, and Miss J. Kerr, Willoughby, Syd.   KAY SWEENEY

TINDALE, GEORGE BARRAND (1903-1977), agricultural scientist and horticulturist, was born on 20 October 1903 at Hawthorn, Melbourne, second child of Victorian-born parents George Tindale, accountant, and his wife Letitia, née Pierce. Sent to Melbourne High School, George gained a free place at the University of Melbourne (B.Ag.Sc., 1926), where he won a Wrixon [q.v.6] exhibition in agriculture and agricultural engineering. On 22 March 1926 he joined the Victorian Department of Agriculture as research officer at the Government Cool Stores, Victoria Dock, West Melbourne. Although pathologists in several States had previously carried out cool-storage investigations, he was the first full-time researcher in the field in Australia.

Working mostly on his own, Tindale devised experiments, obtained essential scientific equipment and established contact with the horticultural industry. In his first year he conducted trials with several fruits. He published a paper on the cool storage of Washington navel oranges (*Journal of the Department of Agriculture of Victoria*, 1927) to assist the fledgling export trade in that product. His tests with grapes led to a consignment being shipped to Britain in 1928. Granted study leave in England that year, he worked at the East Malling Research Station, Kent, and visited numerous other establishments, including the Low Temperature Research Station, Cambridge. This experience influenced his approach to storage research, especially into the effects of maturity, cultural conditions, temperature and atmosphere. He also gained an appreciation of fruit quality—its aroma, flavour and texture—as distinct from mere marketability.

In 1931 Tindale was joined by S. A. Trout, a biochemist with the Council for Scientific and Industrial Research, and next year by F. E. Huelin, a C.S.I.R. chemist. The three formed an excellent team, with Tindale providing the horticultural knowledge, and his A-model Ford for transport. Their report on the storage, ripening and respiration of pears (*Journal of Agriculture, Victoria,* 1938) laid the foundation for a large increase in Victoria's export of the fruit. Another joint paper dealt with the popular but difficult-to-store Jonathan apple. Tindale worked alone for much of the 1940s, conducting storage experiments on a wide range of fruit, and publishing the results in the *Journal of Agriculture, Victoria*. He was an excellent adviser, assisting growers of numerous horticultural products to adopt new storage practices and develop export trades.

Temperature control in many early cold stores by means of wall coils or battery systems proved adequate for frozen meat, but not for fruit. Experimenting with ceiling-mounted coils and brine recirculation, Tindale achieved precise temperature control and high humidity conditions. His methods were adopted in numerous Victorian cool stores with excellent results. In 1956 he moved to the Horticultural Research Station, Scoresby, as leader of the post-harvest section. New facilities at the establishment allowed larger and more complex experiments which suited his philosophy: 'If you put enough questions to nature she will give you the answer'. He published *Apple and Pear Cool Storage in Victoria* (Melbourne, 1966).

Tindale devoted his weekends to his 400-acre (160 ha) sheep-farm at Woori Yallock. His love of ornamental horticulture led him in 1958 to buy Pallants Hill, an 8.4-acre (3.4 ha) property at Sherbrooke in the Dandenong Ranges. The many large mountain ashes remaining on the holding had been underplanted with exotic trees and shrubs, especially rhododendrons, azaleas and camellias. He developed the garden into one of the finest in the district. In 1960 the third conference of Australasian technical officers engaged on research into fruit and vegetable storage was held at the property's homestead. On 25 March 1961 at St Columba's Presbyterian Church, Balwyn, Tindale married Margaret Ruth Adams, a 42-year-old artist. She added several of her sculptures to the grounds, and helped to design the extensive rockery plantings and the layout of the walks.

After his retirement in 1968, Tindale continued to improve his garden and served as secretary of the Ferny Creek Horticultural Society. He died on 21 May 1977 at Pallants Hill and was cremated. His wife survived him and managed the property until 1980 when she gave it to the Victorian Conservation Trust. The Department of Conservation and Environment opened the George Tindale Memorial Garden to the public.

ABC, *Gardens of Victoria, 1991/92* (Syd, 1991); I. D. Peggie, 'Postharvest Horticulture in Australia —A History from 1880 to 1945', in *Proceedings of the Australasian Postharvest Conference . . . 1993* (Lawes, Qld, 1993); *Food Technology in Aust*, 22, no 5, May 1970, p 216.   IAN D. PEGGIE

TIPPAKLIPPA; *see* LAMPUNGMEIUA

TIPPER, ALFRED HENRY (1867-1944), cyclist and showman, was born on 12 July 1867 at Sale, Victoria, second son of Thomas Tipper, a grocer from England, and his Irish-born wife Catherine, née Chadwick. Alfred claimed to have been abandoned by his parents at the age of 2 and brought up as a ward of the state. In his youth he worked on a dairy farm and also acquired a considerable knowledge of mechanics. He took up competitive cycling in the 1880s, during the early stages of the boom in that sport.

Following the trend for undertaking long distances, Tipper rode from Sydney to Melbourne in 1896, carrying a 70-lb. (32 kg) swag. He built an enduring career by combining cycling with showmanship and mechanical ingenuity. In 1904-24 he produced a series of miniature bicycles, ranging from 4½ ins (11.4 cm) to 10 ins (25.4 cm) in height. In 1908 he set out to work and ride his way around the world. He began his journey with just one penny in his pocket and returned, after six years and 85 000 miles (136 790 km), with four shillings and sixpence. While in Britain and the United States of America, he perfected his 'singing and comedy cycling act' which sustained him for years to come in his travels around Australia.

By the 1930s Tipper was part-owner of a bicycle shop at Richmond, Melbourne. He lived in a horse-drawn caravan, constructed from the body of an old Ford motorcar. Known as 'Professor' Tipper, he cultivated a flowing white beard and advocated simple diet and 'rational dress'. His 6 ft 3 ins (191 cm) frame remained supple in his seventies, and he often wore only a thin shirt and 'little short pants'. The 'professor's' gift for publicity was undimmed. In summer months he toured with a selection of his seventy bicycles, performing trick cycling and teaching children to ride. He was presumably the first person to ride a five-inch (12.7 cm) bicycle while singing *Highlands and Lowlands*.

Tipper produced postcards documenting his achievements and worked at developing a pedal-powered aeroplane. He died on 2 April 1944 in Royal Melbourne Hospital and was buried in Fawkner cemetery. His death certificate stated that he was married, but when, where and to whom remain unknown. The sale of his effects realized £4 5s. His possessions included five works of art—signed 'H. D.' but possibly painted by him—which were later displayed in the window of a bicycle shop in the city. The paintings, showing Tipper and his bicycles set against backdrops of Australian towns and countryside, caught the eye of Albert Tucker, and featured on the cover of *Angry Penguins* in December 1944. Tucker acclaimed the works as those of a 'natural artist', possessing a 'startling sense of life expressed through an unfaltering sense of form, pattern, texture and color'. He asserted that 'problems of style and technique' mattered little for the 'primitive' painter; 'the sustained intensity of his vision' solved them for him.

R. Haese, *Rebels and Precursors* (Melb, 1981); *Copping it Sweet: Shared Memories of Richmond* (Melb, 1988); *Sun News-Pictorial*, 2 Dec 1939, 3 Apr 1944; *Herald* (Melb), 28 Aug 1945.

GEOFF BROWNE

TIPPER, JOHN DUNCAN (1886-1970), conservationist and electrical engineer, was born on 4 August 1886 at West Maitland, New South Wales, elder child of Edwin Tipper, an English-born printer and later a journalist, and his native-born second wife Elizabeth, née McInnes. On his retirement, Edwin established apiaries at Willow Tree. John and his sister Elizabeth spent much of their childhood studying birds and animals in the Liverpool Ranges. He developed an appreciation of indigenous culture through his contact with Aborigines near the Barrington River.

Schooled at West Maitland, Tipper joined the electrical tramways branch of the New South Wales Government Railways and Tramways on 13 December 1910 and worked as a tracer. At St James's Church of England, Sydney, on 5 December 1912 he married Florence Wynn Clarke. He studied fitting and turning (1912-13) and electrical engineering (1914-17) part time at Sydney Technical College and qualified as an associate (1920). Promoted to draftsman in 1917, Tipper was an assistant-engineer from 1929 until he retired as engineer (third class) in October 1952. He was an associate-member of the Institution of Engineers, Australia.

Tipper belonged to the Wild Life Preservation Society of Australia. In 1928 he became founding president of the Rangers' League of New South Wales—a volunteer group dedicated to preserving natural bushland and preventing bushfires. In 1932 he helped to found the Australian Bushland Conservation Association, but his preservation ideals were constantly frustrated by continuing damage to Sydney's national parks. His desire for a region protected from fires and illegal trafficking in native flowers led him in 1933 to obtain a lease of some 2000 acres (800 ha) around Muogamarra Ridge (overlooking the Hawkesbury River) from the Department of Lands.

The reserve was established in 1934 and opened to the public in the following year. Called the Muogamarra Sanctuary, its name came from the Awabakal Aboriginal dialect and meant 'preserve for the future'. Tipper worked tirelessly to protect the native flora: he set up a volunteer bush fire brigade and, eventually, an environmental study centre and museum. Public access was limited during the six-week wildflower blooming season from mid-August to the end of September.

In 1953 Tipper surrendered his lease. Supported by the State government, Muogamarra Sanctuary was administered by trustees from 1954, with Tipper their president and resident curator. In 1967 the newly established National Parks and Wildlife Service assumed control of Muogamarra. Tipper grew increasingly angered by its management practices. Disagreements over the level of protection afforded to Aboriginal relics within Muogamarra combined with his own ill health to end his association with the sanctuary in 1968.

'J.D.' (as Tipper was known to his friends) was a passionate naturalist who believed that conservation was a calling 'as exacting, responsible and individualistic as any of the senior professions'. A widower, he married

Enid Constance Monaghan at St Margaret's Presbyterian Church, Turramurra, on 22 August 1966. He died on 8 September 1970 at Wahroonga and was cremated with Anglican rites; his wife survived him, as did the son of his first marriage.

Muogamarra Nature Reserve (NSW National Parks and Wildlife Service leaflet, nd); Rangers' League of NSW, *Bulletin*, no 2, 1930; *SMH*, 2 Feb, 29 June, 3 Dec 1929, 7 Feb, 5 Nov, 3 Dec 1930, 9 May 1931, 12 July 1932, 7 Dec 1935, 14 Mar 1950, 26 June, 18 July 1953, 1, 22 Feb, 1 Sept 1955; Tipper papers (Dixson L, Syd); Railway service personal history card: J. D. Tipper (NSWA).

RICHARD GOWERS

TIPPING, EDMOND WILLIAM (1915-1970), journalist, was born on 27 August 1915 at Moonee Ponds, Melbourne, second child of Victorian-born parents James Gregory Tipping, schoolteacher, and his wife Mary Ellen, née Walsh. Bill was educated at St Kevin's College, Toorak, where he became school captain (1933), and at the University of Melbourne, where he studied law, excelled as a debater, edited the student newspaper *Farrago* and became university correspondent for the *Herald*. His interview with Percy Grainger [q.v.9] caught the attention of Sir Keith Murdoch [q.v.10] who in November 1939 offered him a position on the *Herald*. A Catholic of radical and independent outlook, Tipping had been one of those who opposed the conservative group led by B. A. Santamaria in the battle for control of the *Catholic Worker*.

At St Patrick's Catholic Cathedral, Melbourne, on 28 February 1942 Tipping married a former fellow student Marjorie Jean McCredie, a public servant and a non-Catholic. Called up for full-time service in the Militia that month, he transferred to the Australian Imperial Force in November and joined the 3rd Division's headquarters. He reached Port Moresby in March 1943, but was repatriated next month with suspected tuberculosis. Discharged from the army on 28 March 1944, he was commissioned in the Royal Australian Air Force in July as a public relations officer. He covered the war in the South-West Pacific Area for the service magazine *Wings* before being demobilized in November 1945.

That year Tipping returned to the *Herald*. His perceptive, even-handed reports on the 1946 coal strikes won praise and he rapidly rose to be chief of staff by 1950. 'You are in the direct line of succession', Murdoch told him. In 1951 Tipping was the first Australian to win a Nieman fellowship in journalism at Harvard University, United States of America. There he observed American styles of reporting and made enduring friendships. He would later

work as Australian correspondent for *Time* magazine and the *New York Times*. Boston offered expert medical care for the Tippings' third child, Peter, the severity of whose intellectual disablement was confirmed.

In May 1952 Murdoch urgently recalled Tipping to Melbourne. He had been hand-picked to write a new American-style column. The *Herald*'s circulation soared, and Tipping's column, 'In Black and White', became a fixture. His wry humour, common touch and pithy conversational style made him, as fellow journalist Keith Dunstan noted, the 'Mr Melbourne' of his time. Publicly apolitical, he was a confidant of both Labor and Liberal politicians. On Sunday mornings his family debated whether (Sir) Henry Bolte or Arthur Calwell [q.v.13] would be first to ring after 'Tip' returned from Mass. With Marjorie, he was a friend and convivial host to many of Melbourne's liberal elite, the Zelman Cowens, Robin Boyds [q.v.13] and Hector Crawfords.

Tipping was a passionate advocate for the underdog. In 1953 he described the plight of an intellectually disabled boy, 'Michael', whose parents tied him to a stake in the backyard rather than admit him to the government's run-down Kew Cottages. The story aroused widespread sympathy among readers unaware how closely the issue touched the columnist's own family. With support from the *Herald* and his friend Cunningham Dax, chairman of Victoria's Mental Hygiene Authority, Tipping became a vigorous campaigner for the mentally handicapped.

His relaxed style belied the stresses of a punishing workload. A self-confessed 'fifty cigarettes-a-day-man', Tipping often worked into the small hours. In addition to writing his daily column, he was a regular commentator on radio 3DB, a member of the popular 'Meet the Press' panel on television-station HSV-7, a lecturer in journalism at the University of Melbourne, an official of the Australian Journalists' Association and correspondent for a string of overseas papers. By the early 1960s the limitations of being 'Mr Melbourne' were beginning to chafe. He wanted 'to get out and report and investigate as much as possible'. Tipping's angry accounts of conditions in South Africa in the wake of the Sharpeville massacre (1960) won him a Walkley [q.v.] award. By 1968 he was back in the United States as the *Herald*'s Washington correspondent, writing an acclaimed article on the riots outside the Democratic Party's convention at Chicago. After covering the launch of *Apollo 11* in July 1969, he fell gravely ill and returned to Melbourne.

Friends rallied to the family's support, and established the E. W. Tipping Foundation to assist intellectually handicapped children. Tipping died of cancer on 29 April 1970 in East Melbourne and was buried in Burwood cemetery. His wife and two of their three sons survived him.

J. Tipping, *Bush Teachers of Victoria* (Adel, 1991); C. Sampford and C.-A. Bois (eds), *Sir Zelman Cowen* (Syd, 1997); *Herald* (Melb), 29 Apr, 1, 2 May 1970; *Sun News-Pictorial*, 30 Apr 1970; *Washington Post*, 3 May 1970; Tipping papers (SLV); information from and papers held by Mrs M. Tipping, Melb.

GRAEME DAVISON

TOLIMAN, MATTHIAS TUTANAVA (1925-1973), schoolteacher and politician, was born on 25 August 1925 in Bitakapuk hamlet, Paparatava village, New Britain, Mandated Territory of New Guinea, son of To Liman, a traditional Tolai village leader, and his wife Ia Kabu. Matt attended a village school then boarded at St John's De La Salle School, Kinagunan. He entered St Mary's Seminary, Vunapope, to train for the priesthood, but the Japanese occupation of New Britain interrupted his studies from 1942.

When World War II ended, Toliman decided to become a teacher. He taught in mission schools, completed his secondary education and gained a teacher's certificate in 1957. Soon after, he married Matilda, a fellow graduate. Successfully treated for tuberculosis in 1958, he was appointed headmaster of a Catholic school near his home next year. He stood as a candidate in Papua and New Guinea's first common-roll elections in 1964 and won the Rabaul open seat in the new House of Assembly. Toliman served as under-secretary to the Department of the Administrator (1964-66) and to the departments of Education and Local Government (1966-68). As ministerial member for education (1968-72) in the second House—to which he was returned by the Gazelle open electorate—he brought together government and church schools in a National Teaching Service. A member (1964-72) of the Administrator's Executive Council, he travelled abroad and twice joined the Australian delegation to the United Nations Trusteeship Council. In 1971 he was appointed C.B.E.

As political parties took shape in the late 1960s, Toliman was one of the founders and leaders of what became the United Party. Its conservative policy included gradual progress towards independence for the Territory of Papua and New Guinea (in keeping with the Australian government's programme) and contrasted with the policy of the Pangu Pati, led by (Sir) Michael Somare, which called for more rapid progress towards that goal. Toliman won unanimous support for his resolution on 2 September 1964 that Papuans and New Guineans alone should determine 'when the time is ripe for self-government . . .

and the form that government should take'. During a crisis in New Britain in 1969-72, he strongly supported the Gazelle Peninsula Local Government Council and clashed verbally, and even physically, with the breakaway Mataungan Association's supporters. These political tensions added to the strain of his additional parliamentary duties.

After the 1972 elections the House of Assembly was empowered to choose a chief minister as a step towards self-government. Although the United Party, led by Toliman, was the largest single party in the House, the Pangu Pati formed a coalition and obtained a majority, whereupon Somare became chief minister and Toliman leader of the Opposition. Tall, good-looking and an impressive speaker, Toliman was an outstanding political leader, liked and respected by his allies and his opponents. Members of all parties were shocked when he collapsed in the House of Assembly on 6 September 1973. He died of heart disease later that day and was buried with Catholic rites in Bitakapuk cemetery. His wife and their seven children survived him.

D. G. Bettison et al (eds), *The Papua-New Guinea Elections 1964* (Canb, 1965); L. W. Johnson, *Colonial Sunset* (Brisb, 1983); *Aust External Territories*, 9, no 3, 1969, p 24; *SMH*, 7, 8 Sept 1973; *Post-Courier* (PNG), 7, 10 Sept 1973; personal knowledge.

NEVILLE THRELFALL

TOMLINSON, ERNEST WILLIAM (1871-1947), engineer, was born on 5 December 1871 at Old Radford, Nottinghamshire, England, son of Edwin Tomlinson, iron-turner, and his wife Esther, née Pearson. In 1884 the Tomlinsons migrated with their eight children in the *Lady Douglas* to Perth, where Edwin established the Phoenix foundry. After serving an apprenticeship (1885-92) to a fitter and turner with the family firm, Ernest spent a few months in New Zealand, studying at Wellington Technical School. From 1892 he worked at the Western Australian Government Railways locomotive workshops. With his brother Edward, he established in 1896 the engineering firm of Tomlinson Bros. At St Brigid's Catholic Church, West Perth, on 15 October 1902 he married Charlotte Robinson.

The firm soon became Western Australia's largest engineering works. A major project was to manufacture iron for the William Street (Horseshoe) bridge, constructed in 1903-04. Ernest Tomlinson spent seven months on the Pilbara coast in 1908, attempting to salvage the wrecked steamer *Mildura*; once, when supplies ran short, he sailed alone to Onslow for provisions, taking two days and two nights. During World War I he wanted to secure a share of the munitions industry for

Western Australia. From designs communicated from England, he manufactured a prototype eighteen-pound (8.2 kg) shell and is said to have taken it to Essington Lewis [q.v.10] in Melbourne. Asked whether his company could produce the shell at reasonable cost, the fiery Tomlinson retorted: 'look, I made the damn thing'. He secured the contract. Acquiring the site of a vegetable market at the eastern edge of Perth's central business district, he persuaded other firms to lend their machine tools for the duration of the war, and replaced them or returned them in good order afterwards. He was also responsible for selecting munitions workers for service in England, and acted as a consultant to the wartime minister for defence, Senator (Sir) George Pearce [q.v.11]. In 1920 he was appointed O.B.E.

Tomlinson was a leader of the local business community in the interwar years. A founding member of the Perth division of the Institution of Engineers, Australia, he was chairman of Plaimar Ltd and A. T. Brine & Sons, and a director of Plaistowe & Co. Ltd and Hadfields (W.A.) Ltd. Edward retired from Tomlinsons in 1929, but Ernest remained governing director until his death. Tomlinsons began to manufacture steel products. Assisted by his two sons, Ernest was respected as a strict but fair employer. His main recreations were yachting and motorboating. A trim, white-moustached figure in blazer and whites, he was commodore (1926-46) of the Perth Flying Squadron.

During World War II Tomlinson served on the State board of management for munitions production. With the East Perth site restricted from growing, he reluctantly accepted his sons' proposal that the firm purchase 16 acres (6.5 ha) at Welshpool, adjoining the Commonwealth government's munitions works. The move to the new site was in the planning stage when Tomlinson died on 12 January 1947 at Subiaco. He was buried in Karrakatta cemetery. His wife, and their two sons and three daughters survived him.

V. H. Colless, *Men of Western Australia* (Perth, 1937); *West Australian*, 14 Mar 1904, 14 Jan 1947; information from Mr E. E. Tomlinson, Dalkeith, Perth.   G. C. BOLTON

TONKIN, JOHN ANDREW (1900-1952), public servant, was born on 3 February 1900 at Maryborough, Victoria, fourth child of Richard Edwards Tonkin, blacksmith, and his wife Nora, née O'Brien, both Victorian born. Educated at the local Brigidine convent school, John began work as a clerk in the Commonwealth Auditor-General's Office, Melbourne, in 1916. At St Francis's Catholic

Church, Lonsdale Street, on 26 November 1921 he married Janet Glenleith Nesbitt, a saleswoman. He studied accountancy part time before enrolling at the University of Melbourne (B.Com., 1931).

In 1930 Tonkin transferred to the Department of Markets (Department of Commerce from 1932, Department of Commerce and Agriculture from 1942), beginning an involvement with trade policy that was to last for the rest of his career. He developed a specialized interest in extending Australia's economic links with Asia, and became officer-in-charge of the department's Eastern trade section. In 1933 he went on a promotional tour through the Netherlands East Indies and Malaya to Hong Kong, where he represented the Commonwealth government at the British Empire Fair. Posted to Japan in 1935 as assistant trade commissioner, he returned in 1938 and joined the external trade section.

World War II created huge challenges for the Department of Commerce. Its staff played an important part in ensuring that, despite chronic problems with manpower and transport, agriculture provided maximum support for the war effort. In pursuing this objective, Tonkin showed an extraordinary capacity for hard work. Based in Canberra, he held the substantive position of chief investigation officer (from 1939) in the department's trade section. He was also chairman of the Australian Tobacco Board, secretary of both the Australian Agricultural Council and the Wheat Industry Stabilization Board, and Commonwealth representative on the Australian Wine Board and the Federal Citrus Council.

Late in 1942 Tonkin was made controller of meat supplies and chairman of the Meat Industry Commission (Meat Industry Advisory Committee from March 1943). With demand exceeding supply, he was responsible for planning and co-ordinating the production and distribution of meat for the armed forces and the civilian population, as well as for American service personnel and the traditional British market. Following the introduction of meat rationing and guaranteed prices early in 1944, he concentrated on improving the movement of stock to abattoirs.

Appointed an assistant secretary of the department in 1946, Tonkin returned to work in external trade and took part in discussions with representatives of foreign countries. In October 1948 he attended the Commonwealth prime ministers' conference in London, helping to negotiate long-term, fixed-price contracts for the export of primary products to Britain. He cautiously opposed granting Japan the status of most favoured nation. Tonkin played a leading role in Australia's activities as a contracting party (from 1947) to the General Agreement on Tariffs and Trade, led successive Australian delegations to G.A.T.T.

sessions and served as vice-chairman (from April 1951) of G.A.T.T. He was also chairman of the Federal Export Advisory Committee and a member of the Commonwealth Film Board.

Tonkin was promoted first assistant secretary in 1949 and director of marketing in 1950. He acted as secretary for extended periods, and was doing so at the time of his death. A gifted administrator and planner, he enjoyed the confidence and respect of primary producers and of ministers from both sides of politics. Although mild mannered and softly spoken, he proved a tenacious and effective advocate of Australia's interests. He pioneered the organized promotion of Australian exports, appreciating the potential importance of Asia as a market. For recreation, he swam and played golf. He died of a coronary occlusion on 17 December 1952 in his home at Forrest and was buried in Canberra cemetery. His wife and their three daughters survived him.

S. J. Butlin and C. B. Schedvin, *War Economy 1942-45* (Canb, 1977); P. Dorling (ed), *Documents on Australian Foreign Policy 1937-49*, 11 (Canb, 1994); *The Australia-Japan Agreement on Commerce, 1957* (Canb, 1997); P. Andre (ed), *Documents on Australian Foreign Policy 1937-49*, 14 (Canb, 1998); *SMH*, 5, 8 June 1935, 23 Dec 1946, 1 Apr 1950, 8 Apr 1951, 18 Dec 1952; *Smith's Weekly* (Syd), 3 April 1943; *Canb Times*, 18-20 Dec 1952.

LLOYD BRODRICK

TOOTH, SIR EDWIN MARSDEN (1886-1957), businessman and philanthropist, was born on 9 October 1886 at Sherwood, Brisbane, fourth of five children of Sidney Herbert Tooth, grazier, and his wife Emily Isabella, née Hassall, both of whom came from New South Wales. His grandfather was W. B. Tooth, his great-grandfather was Rev. Thomas Hassall, and his great-great-grandfather was Rev. Samuel Marsden [qq.v.6,1,2]. Educated at Brisbane Central School, Edwin spent a year with the South Australian Land Mortgage & Agency Co. Ltd as a salesman before joining the Canada Cycle & Motor Co. Ltd.

Enlisting in the Australian Imperial Force on 5 July 1915, Tooth was commissioned in October and promoted lieutenant in January 1916. He reached the Middle East in April and in the following month was sent to the Western Front where he served with the 2nd Tunnelling Company. In June 1918 he was gassed. From 29 September to 3 October that year he took charge of roadwork near Bellincourt, France, while under heavy fire and won the Military Cross. He was also mentioned in dispatches (1919). His A.I.F. appointment terminated in England on 10 June 1919. On his way home to Brisbane, he studied the motor industry in the United States of America.

In 1923 Tooth obtained the dealership for Dodge Bros motorcars to distribute its vehicles throughout northern New South Wales, Queensland and the Northern Territory. He formed Austral Motors Pty Ltd in 1924 and established his business in Boundary Street, Spring Hill. Queensland motorists readily accepted Dodge cars because they were solid enough to withstand long distances on outback roads. From 1928 Tooth's company expanded to include De Soto, Chrysler, Plymouth and Standard Motor Co. vehicles, making him a leader of the motorcar industry in Brisbane.

At St John's Cathedral, Brisbane, on 24 April 1935 Tooth married with Anglican rites Elsie Marguerite Fuller. The couple settled into a large house in Eldernell Avenue, Hamilton, built in 1869 for William Hemmant [q.v.4]. They renamed it Farsley, after Samuel Marsden's birthplace in Yorkshire. Tooth formed several other companies—Stradbroke Motors Pty Ltd (1928), British Tractor & Implements Pty Ltd (1948) and Farsley Motors Pty Ltd (1952). Business boomed after World War II and he opened new showrooms in the suburbs. In 1956 Austral Motors was converted into a public company, with Tooth its chairman.

Towards the end of his life, Tooth became involved in philanthropy. He gave generously to medical, educational and charitable institutions. In 1956 he contributed £35 000 to the Brisbane Hospitals Board for the construction of the Edwin M. Tooth Lecture Theatre and the Edwin M. Tooth Laboratories for Research in Medicine at (Royal) Brisbane Hospital. Although the new facilities belonged to the board, they were made available to the University of Queensland's medical school. He subsequently endowed the Edwin Tooth scholarship for postgraduate study in medicine. In addition, he provided £20 000 for a visiting professorship at Brisbane Hospital to enable an eminent teacher of medicine, surgery, or obstetrics and gynaecology to work there each year.

A member of the Brisbane, Tattersall's and United Service clubs, Tooth enjoyed fishing, shooting and golf. He was knighted in 1957. In April that year he donated £5000 to the Legacy Club of Brisbane. Suffering from cirrhosis of the liver, he died of chronic nephritis on 27 May 1957 at his Hamilton home and was cremated. His wife survived him; they had no children. His estate was sworn for probate at £719 852. From this sum he bequeathed about £500 000 to charities and educational institutions run by the Anglican diocese of Brisbane, including provision to establish the Edwin Marsden Tooth Memorial Home for the aged. Further money was left to the University of

Queensland for an institute of agricultural research. In 1962 the diocese purchased Farsley as a residence for the archbishop.

North Brisbane Hospitals Board, *The Royal Brisbane Hospital Centenary* (Brisb, 1967); R. L. Doherty (ed), *A Medical School for Queensland* (Brisb, 1986); J. H. Tyrer, *History of the Brisbane Hospital and its Affiliates* (Brisb, 1993); C of E, Diocese of Brisb, *Church Chronicle*, 1 Apr 1962, p 8; Austral Motors Holding Ltd, *Annual Report*, 1972/73; *Courier-Mail*, 1 Jan, 13 Apr, 28 May, 16 Oct 1957.

ELIZABETH DAVIES

TO ROT, PETER (1912?-1945), martyr, was born probably in 1912 at Rakunai, New Pomerania (New Britain), New Guinea, third of six children of Angelo Tu Puia, a Tolai village chief, and his wife Maria Ia Tumul, both of whom had been received into the Catholic Church in 1898. Peter was baptized soon after his birth. He had an unremarkable childhood and adolescence, closely attached to his family, the Church and the mission school. Pleasant in nature, and gentle and helpful in disposition, he was enrolled in 1930 at St Paul's College, Taliligap, which was founded by the Missionaries of the Sacred Heart for the formation of lay catechists. Three years later he was appointed catechist to the parish of Rakunai. On 11 November 1936 he married Paula Ia Varpit.

The Japanese occupation of New Britain in January 1942 marked a turning-point in To Rot's life. When the European missionaries were interned, he found himself responsible for the mission. He gathered the people for prayer, baptized and catechized adults and children, officiated at marriages, visited the sick, taught school children and catechists, and carried food to the interned missionaries and prisoners of war. Towards the end of 1943 Japanese tolerance of the Christian faith changed to confrontation. Peter was summoned to a meeting, questioned about his activities and ordered to restrict them on the grounds of 'wartime security'. About March 1944 he was forbidden to engage in any form of religious observance. Although he exercised more prudence, he refused to cease doing what he regarded as his duty. He built an underground shelter on his property at Taogo and continued to bring people there for prayer and the Sacraments. The Japanese had already imprisoned and executed those who broke their regulations, and he was aware of the risks involved.

To Rot faced a moral dilemma when the Japanese legalized polygamy with the declared intention of winning the collaboration of the village chiefs and local population. Because he spoke strongly against the practice, he was declared 'a malign and uncooperative'

antagonist, not only of the Japanese, but also of local collaborators. To Metapa—a native policeman serving the Japanese—who wanted to take a Catholic woman as his second wife, reported him for officiating at the marriage of two Catholic couples. To Rot was arrested in April or May 1945 and sentenced to two months detention. In June or July that year, as the time for his release approached, he was murdered by two officers of the Japanese military police, Yoshinori Machida and Gunto, assisted by an army doctor who administered a lethal injection. The people of Rakunai buried him in the mission cemetery. His wife, and their son and daughter survived him; a second son, born after To Rot's execution, died in infancy.

On 2 April 1993, in the presence of Pope John Paul II, a decree was promulgated regarding the martyrdom of Peter To Rot, killed '*in odium fidei*'. He was beatified by the pontiff on 17 January 1995 in Port Moresby. The cause of his canonization proceeds.

J. Dempsey, *Peter To Rot, Martyr* (Toowoomba, Qld, 1989) and for documents; *Catholic Voice*, Oct 1992; *Post-Courier*, 17, 18 Jan 1995; MP742/1, item 336/1/1955 (NAA, Melb).

JOHN CORNELIUS DEMPSEY

TORR, ALEXANDER GEORGE (1907-1952), army officer and engineer, was born on 8 April 1907 at Newtown, Sydney, third child of John Alexander Torr, an engineer from England, and his Sydney-born wife Emily Jane, née Williams. Educated at Randwick High School and Sydney Technical College, Alex was employed as a mechanical engineer, first with the British Tobacco Co. (Australia) Ltd and then with the British-Australasian Tobacco Co. Pty Ltd. After serving in the cadets, he was commissioned in January 1926 in the 19th Battalion (Militia). At St Luke's Church of England, Concord, on 24 February 1931 he married Nola Harris West. In April 1932 he transferred to the (Royal) Australian Engineers (Militia). He was promoted captain in May 1937.

Seconded to the 6th Divisional Engineers, Australian Imperial Force, on 13 October 1939, Major Torr embarked for the Middle East in January 1940 as officer commanding the 2nd/1st Field Company. He remained a citizen-soldier in outlook. His informal style proved popular with his men, but led to criticism in some quarters about the standard of discipline in his company.

The 2nd/1st Field Company went into action at Bardia, Libya, on 3 January 1941 and at Tobruk on 21 January. Torr led from the front during both battles. At Tobruk he personally disarmed anti-tank mines and removed wire entanglements. For his leadership he was awarded the Distinguished Service Order and mentioned in dispatches. He led his unit during the ill-fated campaigns (April-May) in Greece and Crete. On Crete he was the senior Australian engineer officer, but there was a shortage of plant and equipment, and he had little opportunity to employ his men in their intended role.

After the evacuation of Crete, Torr became liaison officer to the engineer-in-chief at General Headquarters, Middle East. He was made temporary lieutenant colonel on 2 September and appointed general staff officer, grade 1, at A.I.F. Headquarters, Middle East. In December he was again mentioned in dispatches. Torr excelled as an engineer staff officer, displaying great ability as a planner and organizer. Returning to Australia in May 1942, he was chief engineer of New Guinea Force (January-September 1943 and May-July 1944), of I Corps (September 1943-April 1944), of II Corps (April-May 1944) and of the First Army (August 1944-May 1945). He was promoted temporary brigadier on 1 January 1943. Energetic and technically gifted, he showed efficiency in overcoming numerous engineering challenges presented in difficult terrain. His most acclaimed work was with N.G.F. when he oversaw complex engineering planning for the Huon Peninsula operations (September-October 1943). He was appointed C.B.E. (1945) for his work in the South-West Pacific Area and twice more mentioned in dispatches (1944 and 1946).

Torr saw out World War II as deputy engineer-in-chief, Australian Military Forces. Placed on the Reserve of Officers on 22 February 1946, he returned to British-Australasian Tobacco as chief engineer and moved to Melbourne. Later he became general manager of Gibson Battle & Co. Ltd. He died of lung cancer on 9 August 1952 at the Repatriation General Hospital, Heidelberg, and was cremated. His wife and two sons survived him.

The Corps of Royal Australian Engineers in the Second World War 1939-45 (Melb, 1946); G. Long, *To Benghazi* (Canb, 1952) and *Greece, Crete and Syria* (Canb, 1953); R. McNicoll, *The Royal Australian Engineers 1919 to 1945* (Canb, 1982); *Sunday Herald*, 10 Aug 1952; AWM 168 (AWM).

GARTH PRATTEN

TOVELL, RAYMOND WALTER (1890-1966), accountant, army officer and politician, was born on 9 March 1890 at Brighton, Melbourne, fourth child of Victorian-born parents Charles Edward Tovell, solicitor, and his wife Mary Annie, née Mitchell. Educated at Brighton Grammar School, where he joined the cadets, Ray qualified as an accountant in 1911, continued his studies in London in 1912-

13 and began work as an auditor in Melbourne. He enlisted in the Australian Imperial Force on 28 April 1915. Unbeknown to him, his elder brother John had been killed in action at Gallipoli three days previously. Five ft 8½ ins (174 cm) tall, with dark hair, brown eyes and a bronzed complexion, Tovell showed leadership qualities which impressed his superiors and led to his selection for officer-training. On 6 July he was commissioned. He sailed for Egypt in October and was posted to the 4th Pioneer Battalion in March 1916.

Sent to France in June, Captain Tovell took part in battles at Pozières and suffered shell-shock near Delville Wood in December. He served with the 1st Anzac Light Railways before becoming a trainee staff officer with the 4th Infantry Brigade in July 1917. Promoted major in October, he was appointed brigade major in February 1918. He was awarded the Distinguished Service Order for his deeds at Hebuterne (March-April), Villers Bretonneux (May) and Hamel (June-July), and for his 'energy, cheerfulness and all-round knowledge' which assisted the commanding officers within the brigade during the August offensive. Transferred to transport duties in London in March 1919, he was granted six months leave from April to gain further experience in accountancy in England. His A.I.F. appointment terminated in Melbourne on 12 December 1919. He was thrice mentioned in dispatches.

Resuming work as a public accountant, he set up a partnership, Tovell & Lucas. At All Saints Church, St Kilda, on 10 June 1924 he married 21-year-old Madeleine Eliza Dubrelle Guthrie with Anglican rites. He served as a Brighton city councillor (1924-26) and as president (1928-35) of the local branch of the Returned Sailors' and Soldiers' Imperial League of Australia. In 1921 he had joined the Militia. Promoted lieutenant colonel (1926), he commanded the 14th Battalion (Prahran Regiment) in 1924-29 and the 46th Battalion (Brighton Rifles) in 1932-38. From October 1939 he led the 10th Brigade as a temporary brigadier.

On 1 July 1940 Tovell was seconded to the A.I.F. and appointed commander of the 26th Brigade. By December he was in the Middle East. He won a Bar to his D.S.O. for his part in the successful withdrawal to Tobruk, Libya, in April 1941, and for the manner in which his men subsequently resisted strong attacks and conducted raids on the enemy. Throughout the operations Tovell displayed 'ability, resourcefulness, thoroughness and keenness of the highest order'. After being relieved in October, his brigade prepared defences in Syria, then moved to Egypt where it was engaged in heavy fighting at Tel el Eisa in July 1942. Tovell was appointed C.B.E. (1943) for his service in the Middle East, including his temporary command of the 9th Division for periods totalling three months.

Back in Australia in November 1942, Tovell was posted to II Corps headquarters. He commanded the Southern Training Reinforcement Centre (from April 1943) and the Moresby Base Sub-Area (from January 1944). Attached to Land Headquarters in March 1944, he was appointed deputy adjutant-general two months later. In Melbourne, on 20 December 1945, he transferred to the Reserve of Officers as an honorary brigadier. He was twice mentioned in dispatches during World War II. Although he had been a hard-working commander 'with a sense of humour', who had taken 'a friendly interest in his officers and men', he 'lacked the streak of ruthlessness' common among his peers.

In 1945 Tovell entered the Legislative Assembly as the Liberal Party member for Brighton. While minister of public instruction (7 December 1948 to 27 June 1950) in the Hollway [q.v.14] government, he endeavoured to overcome a shortage of teachers, staff accommodation and classrooms. He held this portfolio again, and that of electrical undertakings, in Hollway's three-day administration in October 1952. Tovell was one of six Hollway supporters who were expelled from the Liberal and Country Party in August 1953. He was defeated in the 1955 election. A prominent Freemason, he belonged to the United Grand Lodge of Victoria. Rifle-shooting was his favourite pastime. He died on 18 June 1966 at Brighton and was cremated; his wife and their two daughters survived him.

K. West, *Power in the Liberal Party* (Melb, 1965); B. Maughan, *Tobruk and El Alamein* (Canb, 1966); Education Dept (Vic), *Vision and Realisation*, 1, L. J. Blake ed (Melb, 1973); *SMH*, 7 Dec 1948, 14 Aug 1953; *Age* (Melb), 14 Aug 1953; *Canb Times*, 20 June 1966; AWM 43, item A879 (AWM).   NEIL SMITH

TOWNLEY, ATHOL GORDON (1905-1963), pharmacist and politician, was born on 3 October 1905 in Hobart, younger son and fourth child of Tasmanian-born parents Reginald George Townley (d.1906), accountant, and his wife Susan, née Bickford. After Reginald's death, Susan and her three surviving children lived with her sister Rebecca and brother-in-law Harry Sidwell. Educated at Elizabeth Street State and Hobart High schools, and at Hobart Technical College, Athol qualified as a pharmaceutical chemist in 1928. He served his apprenticeship in his uncle's company Ash, Sidwell & Co.

About 1930 Athol and his elder brother Rex moved to Sydney seeking employment. Athol joined Gartrell White [q.v. C. A. White] Ltd,

bakers, where he was placed in charge of the laboratory responsible for quality control. At the Baptist Church, Dulwich Hill, on 26 December 1931 he married Hazel Florence Greenwood. The couple moved to Hobart, and in 1935 Athol joined Rex in partnership in Sidwell & Townley. He eventually became general manager of the firm, which was to own three pharmacies in Hobart, the main one being at 26 Elizabeth Street opposite the General Post Office.

Townley developed a wide network of acquaintances due to his activity in many voluntary organizations, including the Baptist Church. An active sportsman, he played Australian Rules football for North Hobart and cricket for New Town. His church and community work gave him an understanding of the disadvantaged, and he was never as rigid in his attitude to trade unions as were many of his future Liberal Party colleagues. In a notable political speech (1950) he reminded employers that in their drive for profit they should remember that their employees were 'human beings' who possessed 'human dignity'.

On 15 September 1940 Townley was appointed probationary sub-lieutenant, Royal Australian Naval Volunteer Reserve. Mobilized eight days later, he was promoted provisional lieutenant in February 1941 and sent to England, where he trained and was briefly involved in bomb- and mine-disposal work. Back in Australia, he commanded the patrol boat *Steady Hour* which assisted in destroying a Japanese midget submarine in Sydney Harbour on 1 June 1942. He took command of Fairmile Motor Launch No.817 in January 1943 and was promoted acting lieutenant commander on 31 March. His boat was the first of its class to go to Papua, where it conducted anti-submarine patrols, escorted convoys, and took part in coastal surveillance and general harassment of Japanese small-boat traffic. M.L.817 was assigned to the United States' VII Amphibious Force for the assault on Lae, New Guinea, but came under bombing attack at Morobe on 3 September. Townley nursed the craft to safety, enabling it to be towed to Sydney for repairs. He later commanded a flotilla of Fairmiles. Demobilized on 25 June 1945, he remained in the naval reserve until 1955.

The Townley brothers saw their pharmacies as an important part of the Hobart community. They were highly regarded for their willingness to give discounts, or even free medicines, to the needy. When they began to involve themselves in Hobart politics, their benevolence had enabled them to build up a great deal of community support. Although Athol's early political views were sympathetic to Labor, he became interested in the recently formed Liberal Party, largely because of his opposition to bank national-ization. Unexpectedly invited to stand as a Liberal candidate in the Federal election on 10 December 1949, he won the House of Representatives seat of Denison; he was to hold it until his death. In 1946 Rex had been elected to the House of Assembly for Denison as an Independent although he was to lead the State Liberal Party in 1950-56. Neither brother ever lost a parliamentary election contest.

Townley was a popular member of parlia-ment. Don Whitington [q.v.] described him as 'a bluff, friendly, robust man', who mixed easily, and called most people 'mate'. (Sir) John McEwen was endlessly tolerant of Town-ley's habit of appearing in his office to recount his latest joke, while (Sir) Robert Menzies [qq.v.15] enjoyed his cricket yarns, although others found that his wartime stories could start to pall. Townley disliked the abrasive-ness of the House of Representatives, and always endeavoured to treat his opponents with courtesy. Arthur Calwell [q.v.13] later acknowledged that Townley 'could enter into debate, take all the barbs that were hurled at him and, in replying, not seem to wound', while (Sir) Paul Hasluck noted that he was not the type of politician who plotted against his colleagues.

Menzies plucked Townley from the back-bench on 11 May 1951 to become minister for social services. He was successively given the portfolios of air and civil aviation (9 July 1954), immigration (24 October 1956), and supply and defence production (11 February 1958). He was a safe, if unspectacular, junior minis-ter, whose most notable achievements were the introduction of non-means-tested pen-sions for the blind, and the 'Bring out a Briton' scheme. Townley was appointed minister for defence on 10 December 1958. His advance-ment reflected the patronage of Menzies, who seemed to see something of a larrikin son in the brash Tasmanian.

Townley's charitable view of his fellows and of society excluded communists: 'I find it dif-ficult to see how we can extend the orthodox and normal processes of the law to Com-munists'. In 1959 and 1962 he oversaw in-creases in defence spending designed to enable Australia to act effectively with Western allies in South-East Asia. On 24 May 1962 he announced that Australia would be sending thirty army advisers to the Republic of Viet-nam (South Vietnam). His justification was that if communism succeeded in Vietnam, it would affect South-East Asian security and ultimately threaten Australia—a view that be-came known as the 'domino' theory. Townley claimed that, in accordance with Australia's obligations to the South-East Asia Treaty Organization, the advisers were being sent in response to a South Vietnamese invitation and would have no combat role. A critic, John

Murphy, later noted that each of these asser-tions 'was, at best, a half-truth'. Townley was thus the agent for ushering in 'one of the most divisive, bitter and controversial eras of con-flict in Australia's history'.

In the early 1960s Townley endured a long period of ill health, suffering a heart attack and recurring bouts of pneumonia. In May 1963 Menzies relieved him of ministerial duties for two months to enable him to re-cuperate. Despite continuing poor health, Townley travelled to Washington in October to sign an agreement for the purchase of new strike aircraft (later known as the F-111). Menzies used this initiative in the 1963 elec-tion campaign, but as the cost of the aircraft increased it became clear that the contract had been poorly executed.

During the negotiations, Sir Howard Beale, the Australian ambassador to the United States of America, had been concerned about Townley's physical well-being. When he fare-welled the minister he advised a less frenetic journey home: 'take a slow boat to China'. On 17 December Menzies announced that Town-ley would succeed Beale, but Townley died of myocardial infarction seven days later, on 24 December 1963, at the Mercy Hospital, East Melbourne. He was accorded a state funeral and was cremated. His wife and their son sur-vived him. The loss to the prime minister was great: 'I cannot permit myself to say all that one should say. This touches me too closely'.

The ease with which Townley had risen in the ranks had antagonized many Liberals. Hasluck, who described him as a 'teacher's pet', characteristically dismissed his 'slight' administrative abilities, claimed that no cabi-net colleagues rated him highly (except for Menzies), and alleged that senior depart-mental officers had complained of his 'lack of courage' in making hard decisions. Peter Howson disliked this 'complete extrovert', whose speeches in the House were 'lament-able', and who 'never expressed an opinion but those the PM wanted to hear'. By contrast, the retired public servant Sir John Bunting, who had been present at many cabinet meet-ings, noted that Townley was one of a small number of colleagues on whom Menzies relied for their 'general experience and wis-dom, including political wisdom'. Bunting believed that their true value lay not so much in their control of particular portfolios, as in their 'matter-of-fact' political judgement and advice. Townley, for example, dealt with the controversy over nuclear tests at Maralinga, South Australia, by focusing on the need to minimize the political impact caused by safety fears, rather than on the issue of the tests themselves.

Townley was a man who scorned the theor-etical, preferring 'plain down-to-earth com-mon sense', and it seems that for Menzies this trait was worth a great deal. Hasluck conceded that Townley had 'brought a warmth into human relations generally in the Cabinet circle', and marvelled at the high regard for him that many Hobart citizens displayed at his funeral; they recognized the humanity of the man who had earned so respected a place among them.

K. West, *Power in the Liberal Party* (Melb, 1965); G. Greenwood and N. Harper (eds), *Australia in World Affairs 1961-1965* (Vancouver, 1968); T. H. Kewley, *Social Security in Australia, 1900-72* (Syd, 1973); H. Beale, *This Inch of Time* (Melb, 1977); P. Howson, *The Howson Diaries* (Melb, 1984); P. Edwards, *Crises and Commitments* (Syd, 1992); P. Hasluck, *The Chance of Politics* (Melb, 1997); A. Crowe, *The Battle after the War* (Syd, 1999); *PD* (Cwlth), 15 Mar 1950, p 801, 16 May 1950, p 2675, 2 Nov 1950, p 1870, (HR), 25 Feb 1964, p 16; *Mercury* (Hob), 26 Dec 1963, 11 Sept 1985; Townley papers (NL); information from Mr A. Townley, Hob.

SCOTT BENNETT

TOWNSEND, ALBERT RINDER (1891-1944) and HARRY ORTON (1892-1942), public servants, were born on 3 March 1891 and 8 October 1892 at Brunswick, Melbourne, first and second of four children of Victorian-born parents Harry Orton Townsend, clerk, and his wife Frances Mary, née Eastwood. Educated at Moreland State School and at Thomas Palmer's [q.v.11] University High School, Albert joined the Victorian Railways in 1907. Later that year he entered the Commonwealth Public Service as a clerk in the accounts branch of the Department of Trade and Customs, a department in which he was to spend the rest of his career. He held clerical positions in the Long Room, in the correspondence and records branch, and on the central staff before being appointed accountant in 1924. At the Baptist Church, Brunswick, on 4 September 1915 he had married Daisy Gay, a clerk.

In 1917-21 Townsend filled the additional role of secretary of the Commonwealth Film Censorship Board. From 1922 he played an important part in the government's administration of the sugar industry. Based in Canberra, he served (1930-31) on the Sugar Inquiry Committee and chaired (from 1931) the Fruit Industry Sugar Concession Committee. In 1935 he represented the Commonwealth at a conference of sugar technologists, held in Brisbane. He was official adviser to R. G. (Baron) Casey [q.v.13], leader of the Australian delegation to the International Sugar Conference in London, in 1937.

Townsend's involvement in primary industry was not confined to sugar. In 1930 he was appointed chairman of the Cotton Development Advisory Committee which investigated production levels, experimental work and marketing. He subsequently chaired the Cotton Supplies Committee and the Tobacco Inquiry Committee, and prepared (1940) a departmental report on the building of merchant ships in Australia.

In 1933 Townsend was appointed O.B.E. He was promoted to chief investigation officer in November 1935. His pastimes were reading and playing golf. In March 1944 he retired due to ill health. He died of a ruptured duodenal ulcer on 24 April that year at Allawah Private Hospital and was buried in Canberra cemetery. His wife, and their daughter and two sons survived him. Described as 'one of the most brilliant men in the Public Service', he exemplified the dedicated, hard-working and apolitical public servant.

Orton Townsend was educated at Wesley College, Melbourne. In 1909 he began work as a clerk on the central staff of the Postmaster-General's Department. On 29 May 1915 he enlisted in the Australian Imperial Force. He embarked for Egypt in July and performed clerical duties (from October) at 1st Division headquarters, Gallipoli. Promoted staff sergeant in January 1916, he reached France in March and was attached to I Anzac Corps headquarters. In 1916 he was awarded the Meritorious Service Medal. He was commissioned quartermaster and honorary lieutenant in May 1917, and promoted captain in August 1918. Transferred to London, he became assistant military secretary to the general officer commanding, A.I.F., in June 1919. That year he was appointed O.B.E. and mentioned in dispatches. His A.I.F. appointment terminated in Melbourne on 4 June 1920.

Returning to his former department, Townsend worked in the chief accountant's office. In 1922 he transferred (for two years) to the public service of the Mandated Territory of New Guinea in the post of temporary treasurer, based in Rabaul. After several extensions to the time of his transfer, he resigned from the Commonwealth Public Service and was appointed treasurer on 12 January 1929. Visiting Brisbane, he had married 21-year-old Annie Clare Dennis on 27 November 1925 at St Joseph's Catholic Church, Corinda. They were to remain childless and she returned from New Guinea to Australia in 1935. Townsend became chairman of the Territory's Purchase Board in 1932. In the following year he was appointed by the Commonwealth government to New Guinea's first Legislative Council, on which he served until 1942. He was made acting collector of customs in 1936 and commissioner of employees' compensation in 1939. During this time his duties included investigating the feasibility of combining the administrations of the territories of New Guinea and Papua.

In January 1942 the Japanese invaded New Guinea. Townsend was captured while assisting in the evacuation of expatriates from Rabaul. Although his wife received a letter from him while he was a prisoner of war in New Guinea, it was later rumoured that he and more than a thousand other prisoners had been taken on board the Japanese transport *Montevideo Maru*. On 1 July 1942 that vessel was torpedoed by an American submarine and sunk off Luzon in the Philippines. Unaware of Townsend's fate, James Halligan [q.v.14] short-listed him for the position of administrator of the Territory. In 1945, when Japanese records became available, it was confirmed that Townsend and his fellow prisoners had perished. His wife survived him. From humble beginnings, the pipe-smoking Orton Townsend had risen rapidly in both the military and civil services. Like his brother, he typified the conscientious public servant for whom duty was paramount.

PP (Cwlth), 1929-31, 3, p 39, 1932-34, 4, p 2299, 1935-37, 3, p 1610; *PD* (Cwlth), 24 Aug 1937, p 39; *Canb Times*, 18 Mar, 25, 26 Apr 1944, 5 Nov 1945; A452, item 1959/5892 (NAA, Canb).

BRIAN WIMBORNE

TRIBOLET, DONALD HAMILTON (1897-1980), educationist, was born on 4 November 1897 at South Bridgewater (Granton), Tasmania, third child of Walter Tribolet, a fruit-grower from Victoria, and his wife Isabella, née Walker. Educated at Bridgewater State School, Donald began his career at the Philip Smith Training College, Hobart, in 1912 and was subsequently posted as a demonstration teacher to Wellington Square Practising School, Launceston. He enlisted in the Australian Imperial Force on 7 December 1917, joined the 1st Divisional Signal company in France four days before the Armistice, and was discharged from the army on 30 June 1919 in Hobart. Resuming teaching, at Charles Street State School, Launceston, he studied part time at the University of Tasmania (B.A., 1924). On 20 December 1924 he married Marjorie Ethel Smith at St Luke's Church of England, Campbell Town.

Head teacher at Glenorchy (1925) and Branxholm (1925-27) State schools, Tribolet became assistant-master of method at the Training College, Hobart, in 1927. He was head teacher at Macquarie Street State School (1930-34), and master of method at the practising schools at Devonport (1935-40) and Elizabeth Street, Hobart (1941). On 23 August 1941 he was commissioned in the Royal Australian Air Force and appointed to the Administrative and Special Duties Branch. He served with Royal Air Force units in the Middle East, carrying out administrative and educational

duties, and rising to temporary squadron leader (1943). His R.A.A.F. appointment terminated in Australia on 13 November 1944. Back in Tasmania, he returned to his former department as an education officer.

In 1946, when the State government extended the compulsory school leaving age from 14 to 16, Tribolet was seconded to 'organize and arrange details'. The change led to a large increase in enrolments and a shortage of teachers. In 1947 Tribolet set up an emergency training centre at Launceston to provide one-year courses for primary and infant teachers. He was appointed acting-secretary for education in 1950, deputy-director of education in 1951 and director of education in 1952.

Tribolet toured Britain and the United States of America in 1955 to study secondary education. His report recommended the establishment of experimental comprehensive high schools and he oversaw their introduction, beginning in 1956. His concern for the professional standing and welfare of teachers resulted in improvements in their salaries and conditions. In 1960 the Federal government's Office of Education selected him to lead a mission to Commonwealth countries in East Africa and to advise how Australia could best assist education there. Tribolet retired in 1962. The State minister for education, W. E. Neilson, observed that his direction of Tasmanian education had shown 'foresight, energy and skill that could only be described as brilliant'. That year Tribolet was elected a fellow of the Australian College of Education. In 1962-70 he served as secretary of the Tasmanian branch of the Liberal Party of Australia. Survived by his wife and their three daughters, he died on 7 October 1980 in Hobart and was cremated.

E. Fist, *Gladly Teach* (Hob, 1993); *Educational Record*, 15 Aug 1946; *Tas Education*, Dec 1955; *Mercury* (Hob), 15 Sept 1960, 23 Dec 1961, 17 Feb 1962, 9 Oct 1980; Dept of Education (Tas), staff file, ED 190/58 (TA).

DAVID DILGER

TRITTON, LYDIA ELLEN (1899-1946), journalist and public speaker, was born on 19 September 1899 in East Brisbane, fourth of six children of Frederick William Tritton, a furniture warehouseman from Jersey, Channel Islands, who became a wealthy retailer, and his English-born wife Eliza Ellen, née Worrall. Educated at the Brisbane High School for Girls (Somerville House from 1920), Lydia insisted on the *faux* French name of 'Nellé', preferring to be 'hated [rather] than ignored'. After leaving school, she made several public appearances as an elocutionist, and published privately an anthology of verse, *Poems* (c.1920). She moved to Sydney in the early 1920s and worked as a journalist.

In 1925 Miss Tritton sailed for London. She toured the Continent and gained a reputation as an authority on international affairs. In Italy she read the *Journal* (Paris, 1887) of Marie Bashkirtseff, a nineteenth-century Russian émigré who had lived in France. It inspired her to meet and mix with expatriate Russians. At the register office, Kensington, London, on 11 December 1928 she married Nicholas Alexander Nadejine, a 43-year-old professional singer and former officer in the White Russian Army. They were childless. While visiting Brisbane, Nadejine gave a recital; Nell (as she by then styled her Christian name) took private lessons in Russian from Nina Maximoff (later Christesen), who was to found the department of Russian language and literature at the University of Melbourne. Back in London, Nadejine unsuccessfully tried to join the Covent Garden opera company. Thereafter he reputedly deceived his wife with 'some crazy elderly Englishwomen who were rich and idle'. Nicholas and Nell were divorced in 1936.

In the early 1930s, possibly in Paris, Mrs Nadejine had met the exiled Alexander Kerensky and begun working as his secretary. Kerensky, a lawyer, had been a member of the Russian duma, minister for war, and prime minister of Russia for three months from July 1917. After the October revolution he lived in Paris, but spent some time in the United States of America raising money for the anti-Bolshevik cause. Nell fell in love with him. Kerensky did not at first reciprocate her affections. In March-June 1939 she visited Brisbane, where she lectured to various organizations on international politics and continued her Russian lessons, with M. I. Maximoff, Nina's father. Kerensky enticed her to come to the United States by suggesting they might soon be married. His divorce from his wife Olga became absolute on 29 June. Alexander and Nell were married at Martins Creek, Pennsylvania, on 20 August that year. The justice of the peace in whose home the ceremony took place, reported that 'a man wearing a monocle and carrying a cane arrived accompanied by a pretty blonde'.

M. and Mme Kerensky left New York at the end of September 1939 and took up residence in Paris. The self-exiled Russian author Nina Berberova, whom they visited frequently, described Nell as 'beautiful, calm, and intelligent', with 'shoulders and a bosom like Anna Karenina'. On 11 June 1940, shortly before the fall of France, the couple left Paris by motor-car. After a harrowing trip, they reached the Spanish border eighteen days later. Kerensky, as a Russian refugee, was not permitted to cross. They both turned back, and drove to St Jean-de-Luz whence they made their way to England in a British naval vessel. Travelling in a trans-Atlantic liner, they arrived in New York on 12 August 1940 and received a triumphal welcome from the *New York Times*. They lived in a small, rented apartment on Park Avenue until 1942 when they acquired a large wooden farmhouse near the New York-Connecticut border. Kerensky's lecture tours provided their main source of income. Their life, when they were together, was idyllic, with numerous visitors and games of croquet.

During her husband's absences, Mrs Kerensky sometimes thought of returning to Australia to undertake war-work. They moved to a smaller house closer to New York city and in October 1945 travelled to Brisbane. In February 1946, while staying with her parents at Clayfield, Nell suffered a stroke. Survived by her husband, she died of chronic nephritis on 10 April that year and was cremated with Anglican rites. On his return to Paris in 1949, Kerensky read to Berberova his 'History of the Illness and Death of Nell'.

N. Berberova, *The Italics are Mine* (NY, 1969); R. Abraham, *Alexander Kerensky* (NY, 1987); J. Armstrong, *The Christesen Romance* (Melb, 1996); *Courier-Mail*, 23 Aug 1939, 11 Apr 1946.

JUDITH ARMSTRONG

TROUT, SIR HERBERT LEON (1906-1978), solicitor, businessman and benefactor, was born on 12 February 1906 at Red Hill, Brisbane, seventh child of Queensland-born parents Walter John Trout, butcher, and his wife Margaret Alice, née Storie. Leon attended Kelvin Grove State School and won a scholarship to Brisbane Grammar School. An average student, he excelled at gymnastics and was senior champion in 1922. Boxing and golf were his other sporting interests. He was articled to C. B. Fox and on 2 May 1928 admitted as a solicitor of the Supreme Court of Queensland. After difficult years as a sole legal practitioner he entered into partnership in 1932 with an established solicitor, M. M. Edwards. He gained accountancy qualifications, becoming an associate (1932) and fellow (1948) of the Federal Institute of Accountants.

On 16 October 1936 at St John's Cathedral, Brisbane, Trout married with Anglican rites 20-year-old Peggy Elaine Hyland; they were childless. Enlisting in the Royal Australian Air Force on 4 May 1942, he was commissioned next month in the Administrative and Special Duties Branch. He was posted in October 1942 as adjutant of No.75 Squadron at Milne Bay, Papua, then in March 1943 of No.77 Squadron in Darwin. Flying Officer Trout's R.A.A.F. appointment was terminated at his request on 4 January 1944.

Back in Brisbane, Trout practised law on his own until he formed a partnership with P. C. Bernays in 1950. The practice was expanded in 1959 to include Arthur Tingle and subsequently developed into one of Brisbane's leading law firms. Although not politically ambitious, Trout was president (1953-57) of the Liberal Party of Australia, Queensland division. Dedicated to party loyalty and unity, he was discerning about candidate pre-selection and effective as a fund-raiser, but his strength lay in his determination to 'get things done'. His notable bluntness and impatience with time-wasters was offset by an engaging charm and compassion for disadvantaged people. He attracted like-minded individuals to the party and his significant contribution to the win by the coalition of the Country and Liberal parties at the State election in 1957 was widely acknowledged.

After three years (1953-56) as president of the Brisbane Chamber of Commerce, Trout realized a long-held ambition when he became the second Queenslander to serve as president (1957-59) of the Associated Chambers of Commerce of Australia. An outspoken advocate of private enterprise and individual endeavour, he championed industrial expansion, the formation of a development-oriented northern Australian commission, and the abolition of probate and succession duties. He was chairman of Barnes Engineering Pty Ltd, Queensland Battery Smelting Works Pty Ltd and Queensland Metal Co. Pty Ltd, and a director of Chevron Queensland Ltd (1957-77) and the Norwich Union Life Insurance Society.

With his wife Trout became well known as an art collector and patron; he had made his first purchase, an Impressionist print, while still at school. Founding president (1951-54) of the Queensland National Gallery Society, he donated the first of many works to the Queensland National Art Gallery in 1953. The Trouts' home, Everton House, described in 1953 as a 'spectacular country homestead', was the centrepiece of his successful suburban estate development at Everton Park. It provided a lively social venue for arts enthusiasts and housed the couple's extensive collection, including portraits painted in 1959 of Trout by (Sir) William Dobell [q.v.14] and of his wife by (Sir) William Dargie. Trout was knighted in 1959.

Appointed a trustee of the Q.A.G. that year, Sir Leon presided (1965-78) over the board. In the 1960s the gallery shared a sub-standard building with the Queensland Museum. Trout initiated and forcefully advocated the plan to include an art gallery in the proposed Queensland cultural centre in South Brisbane. He was credited with achieving economic stability and a vision for the gallery, but his amateur enthusiasm and business orientation often did not impress arts professionals. Board meetings could become volatile, especially when Sir Leon eschewed diplomacy in favour of directness.

During their frequent overseas travels the Trouts bought works for their collection. They visited numerous galleries and returned home with knowledge of the latest international trends. At the Q.A.G. clashes occurred when Sir Leon tried to introduce what other trustees considered inappropriate ideas for the gallery's exhibitions and its overall administration. When president (1956-57) of the Brisbane Club, he introduced an art collection programme and annoyed some members by replacing the portraits of former presidents with expensive traditional paintings. He resigned from the artworks committee after it installed a modernist painting, Sam Fullbrook's 'The Jockey', which was not to his taste.

Trout was president of the Queensland Society of Blind Citizens (1938-47), the Royal Automobile Club of Queensland (1945-47), the Australian Automobile Association (1946-47) and the Australia Britain Society. He was a board-member of the Salvation Army and a patron of gymnastics. Survived by his wife, he died on 6 March 1978 in Brisbane and was cremated with Presbyterian forms. His estate was sworn for probate at $2 293 274. The new art gallery building was opened in 1982, largely due to 'Sir Leon's vision, tenacity and persistence', according to the president of trustees, Peter Botsman.

M. I. Thomis, *The Brisbane Club* (Brisb, 1980); Queensland Art Gallery, *Gifts from the Collection of Sir Leon & Lady Trout* (Brisb, 1984); *The Trout Collection in Profile* (Brisb, 1993); P. L. Ryan, *Friends for Forty Years* (Brisb, 1993); S. Keays, *Firm Foundations* (Brisb, 2000); *Nth Aust Mthly*, Dec 1954; *Qld Law Soc J*, Apr 1978; *Courier-Mail*, 14 Nov 1953, 8 Aug 1975, 8 Mar 1978; information from Mr R. Mellish, Ascot, Mrs P. Barnett, Mr G. Deeb, the Hon Sir James Killen, and Mr I. Hiley, Brisb, and the late Sir William Knox.   KAY COHEN

TROY, PATRICK LAURENCE (1908-1978), trade unionist, was born on 17 January 1908 in South Melbourne, second of ten children of Patrick William Troy, a marine officer from Ireland, and his Victorian-born wife Hilda Winifred, née Ainsworth. The family moved to Fremantle, Western Australia, during World War I. Educated at the local Christian Brothers' College, Paddy left school in 1921 and worked in a variety of manual occupations until 1924 when he signed on as a seaman in the State Shipping Service.

In 1926 the Troys settled at Geraldton. Paddy's employment as a dredgehand ended with the onset of the Depression. As his father's health declined, he assumed responsibility for his younger siblings. The experience of prolonged unemployment, punctuated by occasional relief work and casual labouring, proved formative: he broke with the Catholic

Church, left the Australian Labor Party, turned to political action on behalf of the unemployed and in 1934 joined the Communist Party of Australia. In this capacity he led a strike in 1936 at the Youanmi gold-mine, where he worked as a rigger and safety officer. At St John's Church of England, Fremantle, on 14 September 1935 he had married Mabel Grace Nielsen (d.1975).

Imprisoned for three months after the Communist Party was banned in May 1940, Troy returned to the maritime industry at the port of Fremantle and obtained a master's certificate. In 1944 he was elected an official of the Coastal Dock, Rivers and Harbour Works Union of Workers. The union covered harbour construction workers, the crews of harbour vessels, tradesmen's assistants and general port labourers, who were mostly employed as casual workers for meagre wages. As its secretary from 1948, Troy was a particularly effective militant who improved members' pay and conditions. When the Court of Arbitration of Western Australia deregistered the union in 1952, and the Australian Workers' Union poached the harbour construction workers, he set about rebuilding the Maritime Services Union and became its full-time secretary. He also helped to establish (1955) the State branch of the Federated Miscellaneous Workers' Union. Thwarted in his efforts to amalgamate the State's maritime unions, he helped to form the new Western Australian Trades and Labor Council in 1963.

Troy used the morning pick-up of his members to drive home the need for working-class unity. He was especially active in the peace movement and in supporting Aboriginal emancipation. While unsuccessful in his repeated candidature for State and Federal parliaments, he nevertheless commanded the trust and affection of the port workforce, and the respect of employers. Of average height, small framed, widely read, articulate and fiery, he was Western Australia's best-known communist. He was both compassionate and demanding, and lived out his socialist principles in open-handed generosity and constant activity.

In 1973 Troy retired. At Attadale, on 5 December 1976 he married with Congregational forms Evelyn May Henderson, a widow. Following cardiac surgery, he died of cerebral infarction on 19 April 1978 in Royal Perth Hospital and was cremated; his wife survived him, as did the three sons and two daughters of his first marriage. A pilot boat was named after him. The Perth branch of the Australian Society for the Study of Labour History commemorates him with an essay competition.

S. Macintyre, *Militant* (Syd, 1984), and for bib; M. Hess, *From Fragmentation to Unity* (Perth, 1989).   STUART MACINTYRE

TRUCHANAS, OLEGAS (1923-1972), wilderness photographer and conservationist, was born on 22 September 1923 at Siauliai, Lithuania, son of Eduard Truchan, civil servant, and his wife Tatjana, née Bronovickaja-Baronenko. During World War II Oleg was active in the Lithuanian resistance. He went to Germany in 1944, and began law studies at the University of Munich. After the university closed temporarily in May 1945 he moved to the Baltic displaced persons camp at Garmisch. On 23 February 1949 he arrived in Melbourne in the *Nea Hellas*. Sent initially to the Bonegilla migrant reception centre in Victoria, he chose to go to Tasmania where he was assigned to manual labour for the Electrolytic Zinc Co. of Australasia Ltd, Risdon. In 1951 he joined the Hydro-Electric Commission, Hobart, as a meter-reader. Becoming an engineering clerk two years later, he was to work in the area of statistical analysis until 1971.

Deeply attracted to Tasmania's wilderness areas, Truchanas undertook many solitary excursions, on foot and by canoe, into the island's south-west. Black and white and, later, colour photography became the medium through which he expressed his considerable artistic talents; he won prizes in overseas and Australian competitions. In 1952, climbing alone and without support, he reached the summit of Federation Peak. Twice, in December 1954 and February 1958, he travelled down the Serpentine and Gordon rivers from Lake Pedder to Macquarie Harbour in a self-designed kayak, a feat never before accomplished. On 21 January 1956 at Chalmers Church, Launceston, he married with Presbyterian forms Melva Janet Stocks, a clerical typist.

In October 1963 the Tasmanian government decided that the State's south-west was to be opened up to hydro-electric development. The fears of conservationists were realized in 1965 when the premier Eric Reece announced that there would be 'some modification of Lake Pedder National Park', and that the water level of the lake would be raised. Truchanas, placing himself in a difficult position with his employer, gave a series of audiovisual lectures in the Hobart Town Hall and elsewhere in Tasmania, aimed at publicizing the environmental losses that would follow the flooding of the lake. The project went ahead despite the protests. In February 1967 Truchanas's collection of photographs was burnt in the Hobart bushfires that destroyed his home; he immediately set about replacing the lost pictures.

From 1961 Truchanas was a leader and instructor at adventure camps run by the National Fitness Council of Tasmania. A founding member (1968) of the Tasmanian Conservation Trust, he campaigned with other members for the preservation of the Huon pine, which was threatened with extinction by logging; on 5 August 1970 one thousand acres [405 ha] of Huon pine forest on the Denison River were gazetted for protection under the Scenery Preservation Act (1915). In 1971 Truchanas was elected to the council of the Australian Conservation Foundation. At the end of that year he resigned from the H.E.C. and set out to re-visit 'The Splits' on the Gordon River, which he had previously navigated and photographed. On 6 January 1972, while attempting to retrieve his canoe, he slipped on wet rocks and disappeared. His body was found three days later, wedged against a submerged tree. After cremation, his ashes were spread over Lake Pedder. He was survived by his wife, and their two daughters and son.

The artist Max Angus said in a tribute that Truchanas's 'physical, mental and spiritual powers, his passionate love for this island, combined to make him . . . our chief guide and conscience in times of threat to our national environment, and prime source of revelation of the grandeur of our wilderness through the mastery of his camera'. He included a selection of Truchanas's best photographs in his book *The World of Olegas Truchanas* (1975). Mount Truchanas, in the Hamersley Range, Western Australia (1975) and the Truchanas Huon Pine Forest (1990), were named after the conservationist. In 1998 the Queen Victoria Museum and Art Gallery, Launceston, acquired a collection of his photographs; the National Museum of Australia holds a canvas-covered canoe made by him.

Tas Tramp, no 24, 1982-83; *Mercury* (Hob), 10, 12-14, 17 Jan 1972; Dept Immigration file, A11925, item 1105 (NAA, Canb). DAN SPROD

TRUEBRIDGE, BENJAMIN ARTHUR (1882-1955), poet, was born on 23 September 1882 at Carlton, Melbourne, eldest of six children of Victorian-born parents William Molish Truebridge, composer, and his wife Irene, née Greenslade. Educated at Middle Park State School and then privately, he became a music teacher. In 1915 he taught violin at the Conservatorium of Music, University of Melbourne. At St Silas's Church of England, Albert Park, on 26 October 1910 he had married Edith Annie Luther, a nurse. They lived for a time at Camberwell and were later divorced.

Leaving Melbourne about 1920, Truebridge worked his way around Australia and New Zealand for the next decade as fruit-picker, gold fossicker, music teacher, and masseur. During these years several of his light lyrics appeared in the *Bulletin,* under the pseudonym 'Brian Vrepont', a Frenchified version of Truebridge. Settling in Brisbane in the early 1930s, he published his first book, *Plays and Flower Verses for Youth* (1934). He was by then writing prolifically, mainly for the Brisbane *Telegraph* which printed nearly seventy of his poems and a large number of his reviews. In 1939 he won the C. J. Dennis [q.v.8] memorial prize for *The Miracle* (Melbourne, 1939), a long philosophical poem. Colin Bingham, the *Telegraph*'s literary editor, described it as 'a powerful . . . and moving indictment of Man's shameful misuse of his priceless heritage, the soil'. On 29 September 1939 at the general registry office, Brisbane, Truebridge married 26-year-old Elma Helene Stehn.

In 1940 Vrepont, Clem Christesen, James Picot [q.v.15] and Paul Grano [q.v.9] founded *Meanjin Papers*. Vrepont's 'The Apple Tree' —later referred to by Douglas Stewart as 'perhaps the most beautiful lyric ever written in Australia'—was the first item in the inaugural issue. Most of his poems were passionate responses to nature, underpinned by a form of 'pagan' pantheism and extending, politically, to a form of revolutionary pacifism. Quick-tempered and acerbic, he was also fervently anti-Catholic (which brought him into conflict with Grano, a Catholic), and contemptuous of the traditionalism of the Brisbane literary establishment. His most radically experimental work (prose poems and a variety of musically influenced forms) appeared in the early 1940s in *Angry Penguins* and the avant-garde Melbourne magazine *Comment*.

Vrepont's second book of poetry, *Beyond the Claw* (Sydney, 1943), received mixed reviews. Soon afterwards he moved to Sydney where he was employed as a salesman by the booksellers Angus & Robertson [qq.v.7,11] Ltd. In 1945 he received a Commonwealth Literary Fund grant to write a novel, 'The Time has Come', which he completed but never published. About 1950 he and his wife moved to Perth. He continued to write poems and reviews, and taught music. In appearance and lifestyle he was the typical 'decadent' of the 1920s: slim and over six feet (183 cm) tall, with a thin, suntanned face, deep-set eyes and grey-silver hair brushed back from a fine forehead. Although he was something of a loner, his relationships with women were intense, and complicated. In 1952 his marriage broke down. Truebridge died on 10 March 1955 in Royal Perth Hospital and was cremated. His wife survived him. He had no children.

C. Bingham, *The Beckoning Horizon* (Melb, 1983); L. Strahan, *Just City and the Mirrors* (Melb, 1984); Rex Ingamells papers (LaTL); Meanjin Archives (Baillieu L, Univ Melb); Cwlth Literary Fund—B. Vrepont, A463, item 1958/568 (NAA, Canb). PATRICK BUCKRIDGE

TRUMBLE, HUGH COMPSON (1894-1962), surgeon, was born on 29 May 1894 at Nhill, Victoria, fourth child of Australian-born parents John William Trumble, solicitor, and his wife Susan Compson, née Davies. John and his brother Hugh Trumble [q.v.12] played Test cricket for Australia. The family moved to Brighton, Melbourne, where young Hugh attended Brighton Grammar School (dux 1911). His medical course at the University of Melbourne (M.B., B.S., 1916) was shortened because of World War I. Without undertaking a residency, he immediately applied for a commission in the Australian Imperial Force.

On 12 September 1916 Trumble was appointed captain, Australian Army Medical Corps, A.I.F. He served on the Western Front from April 1917, chiefly as medical officer of the 14th Battalion. Over three days and nights from 4 July 1918, at Vaire Wood, near Corbie, France, he worked in the open, treating casualties while under enemy fire. For this and earlier work, he was awarded the Military Cross. In February he had been gassed; in August he suffered a wound in the back. Following the Armistice, he and (Sir) Hugh Cairns [q.v.7] travelled on the Continent. Cairns thought that Trumble was 'extraordinarily brainy in a practical way'. The two men were to remain lifelong friends. Trumble's A.I.F. appointment terminated in England on 7 June 1920. By then he had begun postgraduate work in London. In 1921 he qualified as a fellow of the Royal College of Surgeons, England.

Returning to Melbourne, Trumble was appointed to the staff of the Alfred Hospital in March 1922. That year he also joined the Austin Hospital, which treated patients with pulmonary and bone tuberculosis and other conditions considered incurable. He worked as a general surgeon, but his interests were wide and he was to make a considerable contribution to orthopaedics, thoracic surgery and the surgery of the autonomic nervous system. In 1924 he published a paper, 'The Treatment of Tuberculosis Abscesses'. At that time the accepted remedy was incision and drainage. This procedure inevitably led to a chronic sinus and long-term problems of management. Trumble advocated aspiration of the 'cold abscess' using a relatively small-bore needle into which was introduced a corkscrew-like spiral of fine wire which could be used to clear the needle of 'debris', so often the cause of blockages. He argued that patience was necessary because it could take an hour to empty a large collection, and that later aspirations would probably drain off the pus without trouble.

In 1926 and 1928 Trumble published papers on the treatment of tuberculosis of the spine. His 'Note on the Position of the Patient in the Performance of Thoracoplasty and certain other Operations' (1940) recommended that the patient be positioned with the healthy lung uppermost. He designed especially long rib-scrapers to make the operation feasible. A master in the use of plaster of Paris and the fabrication of beds and splints, he invented an ingenious 'saddle appliance' to relieve a lower limb from the strain of bearing weight. In the management of tuberculosis of the hip, he reasoned that it was unwise 'to resort to operative measures whilst the inflammatory process is still active'. Using an extra-articular bone graft, he devised a means of fixation of the hip. His procedure was widely adopted by orthopaedic surgeons, but not with his name attached to it.

Trumble grew increasingly dissatisfied with varying descriptions in anatomical texts and complained that 'the nomenclature of the anatomists is chaotic'. To rectify the problem, he dissected 'dogs, cats, guinea-pigs, rabbits, opossums, monkeys, and human beings' over a long period and produced a number of papers illustrated by beautiful diagrams. The practical side of this work was seen in his papers (1937, 1947 and 1954) on the relief of pain in the legs of people suffering from peripheral vascular disease, on the control of cardiac pain and on sympathectomy in the treatment of high blood pressure.

At St John's Church of England, Toorak, on 17 December 1930 Trumble had married Uira Irwin Kathrine Pyatt Law. When his brother-in-law Leonard Cox [q.v.13] established a neurology clinic at the Alfred in 1934, the need for a neurosurgeon was soon apparent. Trumble set up Australia's first neurosurgical unit at the hospital, and began a close and productive collaboration with Cox. He read the literature on operations, adapted procedures to his own style, and became remarkably skilful; he also invented a craniotome, and so involved himself in the new discipline that he dropped virtually all other professional activities. By 1939 special neurosurgical facilities were provided in a new block where his unit remained until his retirement. His appointment as neurosurgeon in 1946 merely formalized a role he had made his own.

To demonstrate his own techniques and to view the work of other surgeons, Trumble arranged to travel abroad in 1940, but the war in Europe made him turn back after he reached New Zealand. He took up additional duties as consultant neurosurgeon to the Australian Military Forces in Victoria. In this role, he had considerable influence on (Sir) Sydney Sunderland. The Society of Australasian Neurosurgeons (Neurosurgical Society of Australasia) was formed in 1940: Trumble was one of eight foundation members.

Few surgeons of the first half of the twentieth century could match Trumble's talents. He displayed breadth of knowledge, original thought in finding solutions to problems that confronted him, skill in inventing instruments or making appliances to suit his purpose, and masterly operative technique. In the theatre he was unhurried, but never wasted movement or moment. Many of his instruments were home-made and he had to be persuaded to have them electroplated. He had around him a devoted team of nurses and doctors. A number of the latter went on to be leaders in neurosurgery.

A brilliant but essentially shy man, Trumble avoided all forms of public recognition. He was very much an individual, enterprising and ingenious, but also self-willed and contrary. After retiring in 1954, he held interests in a farm and a pine plantation. The Alfred Hospital published *The Collected Papers of Hugh Trumble* in 1957. Inheriting his family's aptitude for ball games, he played tennis and golf well into his sixties. A cerebrovascular seizure crippled his right side in 1960. He died of myocardial infarction on 16 October 1962 in the Alfred and was cremated; his wife, and their son and daughter survived him.

Lives of the Fellows of the Royal College of Surgeons of England 1952-1964 (Edinb, 1970); A. M. Mitchell, *The Hospital South of the Yarra* (Melb, 1977); *Alfred Hospital: Faces and Places*, 1, 2 (Melb, 1996, 1999); *MJA*, 1, 1963, p 406.   J. S. GUEST

TRUNDLE, JEAN AMALIE (1905-1965), teacher, actress and theatre director, was born on 24 March 1905 in South Brisbane, elder daughter of Frank John Trundle, a Queensland-born plumber, and his wife Jemima Jane, née Archibald, who came from Scotland. Jean studied speech and drama in Brisbane with Barbara Sisley, and qualified as an associate (1922) and licentiate (1924) in elocution of Trinity College of Music, London. By 1925 she was running her own speech-training school in the city. A talented actress, she appeared in plays directed by Sisley and Rhoda Felgate for the Brisbane Repertory Theatre Society. She and her pupils formed the Jean Trundle Players; they presented stage productions to benefit charities in the suburbs and various country towns.

As a speech and drama teacher, Miss Trundle showed skill in preparing young people for performance, particularly in dialogue recitals, and achieved continuing success at eisteddfods. She also trained verse-speaking choirs that were hailed by adjudicators in the 1930s as 'deserving the highest possible praise'. On 5 January 1935 at St Andrew's Presbyterian Church, Brisbane, she married Victor James Hardgraves, a commercial traveller who was also secretary of the Dickens [q.v.4] Fellowship, an actor, and

business manager of the Jean Trundle Players. Jean and Vic were childless. In February 1936 they launched a new body, Brisbane Amateur Theatres, to present plays with 'popular appeal'. Trundle directed their first production, Leslie Howard's *Tell Me the Truth*, in which she took the leading role. It was followed by an adaptation of Charles Dickens's *Oliver Twist*, starring her husband. As B.A.T.'s leading figure, she continued to direct and produce plays regularly until 1965.

Trundle's first Shakespearian production was *The Merchant of Venice* in 1943. From that year until 1965 B.A.T. presented, annually, the Shakespearian play set for the schools' junior public examination; Trundle directed ten of the twenty-two productions. In 1947 B.A.T. was renamed the Brisbane Arts Theatre. Rehearsals, set construction and planning-meetings took place at the Hardgraves' home. Performances were held in the Albert Hall. The group's increasing professionalism and successful touring ventures, as well as the excitement generated by the production of modern works such as Tennessee Williams's *A Streetcar Named Desire*, led B.A.T. to acquire its own playhouse. In 1959 the company bought a former second-hand shop on Petrie Terrace. After much fund-raising, the building was converted into a theatre. For its opening in September 1961, Trundle directed *The Multi-Coloured Umbrella* by Barbara Vernon [q.v.].

A flamboyant and stylish woman, Trundle grew more eccentric as she aged. Her last production for B.A.T., in June 1965, was her favourite, *The Merchant of Venice*. A Toowoomba critic wrote that 'the co-producers, Jean Trundle and Vic Hardgraves, threw tradition to the winds and set forth the gayest, most colourful and robust interpretation of Shakespeare's classic tragi-comedy ever to gladden a reviewer's heart'. Survived by her husband, Jean Trundle died of lobar pneumonia on 23 July 1965 at Ashgrove and was cremated. She had dedicated her life to encouraging young people to love literature and the theatre. A drama competition for Queensland secondary school students was named (1966) after her.

Brisbane Arts Theatre, the First Fifty Years 1936-1986 (Brisb, 1987); *Toowoomba Chronicle* and *Darling Downs Gazette*, 12 July 1965; J. Radbourne, Little Theatre: its development, since World War II, in Australia, with particular reference to Queensland (M.A. thesis, Univ Qld, 1978); V. Hardgraves, scrapbooks (Fryer L, Univ Qld).

JENNIFER RADBOURNE

TRUSCOTT, KEITH WILLIAM (1916-1943), Australian Rules footballer and air force officer, was born on 17 May 1916 at Prahran, Melbourne, second child of William Edward Truscott, wickerworker, and his wife Maude Mabel, née Powell, both Victorian born. Keith was educated at Melbourne High School, where he captained the first XI and the first XVIII, and proved a good scholar. He practised as a student-teacher at Spensley Street State School, Clifton Hill, in 1935-36 before working as a clerk with W. Angliss [q.v.7] & Co. Pty Ltd, at Footscray. A powerfully built man, 5 ft 9 ins (175 cm) tall and 12 st. 13 lb. (82 kg) in weight, he had auburn hair and dark grey eyes.

From 1937 'Bluey' Truscott played for the Melbourne Football Club. A half-forward flanker in Melbourne's premiership team in 1939, he kicked two goals and was among the best players. His decision to enlist in the Royal Australian Air Force on 21 July 1940 attracted much publicity. Curiously, for someone of his mental and physical ability, he struggled with flying lessons; had he not been a prominent sportsman he would have been suspended from pilot training. Given extra time denied to others, he began to demonstrate the qualities of co-ordination, anticipation, judgement and determination which had made him a champion footballer. Yet he never fully came to terms with landing and persistently levelled out about 20 ft (6 m) too high. Granted leave by the air force in September 1940, he again played in Melbourne's winning grand-final side.

In November that year Truscott reached Canada under the Empire Air Training Scheme. He was commissioned in February 1941 and sent to England where he joined No.452 Squadron in May. Flying Spitfires, he took part in offensive patrols and escorted bombers. He was promoted acting flight lieutenant in September. Next month he won the Distinguished Flying Cross for destroying six enemy aircraft. In January 1942 he rose to acting squadron leader (substantive October) and became commanding officer of No.452. By March, when he was awarded a Bar to his D.F.C., he had shot down eleven German aircraft, probably destroyed another three, and damaged two. He was, by then, the best-known pilot in the R.A.A.F., with a reputation that rested as much on his appealing personality as it did on his considerable achievements. Such was his popularity in England that the Marquess of Donegall organized a public fund to which red-headed Britons paid £5000 to 'buy' Bluey his own Spitfire.

Returning to Australia on leave in May 1942, Truscott turned out one last time for the Melbourne Football Club. He was unfit and out of touch, and struggled to keep up with the play, but he was given a hero's reception by thousands of supporters. Several days later he encountered his former teacher, Bill Woodfull

[q.v.12], who asked him how he had enjoyed his return to football. 'Not for me. Too dangerous', Truscott answered.

Truscott's talent for being in the thick of the action saw him posted to No.76 Squadron. Its members reached Papua in July 1942, only weeks before a Japanese force landed at Milne Bay. The Kittyhawk fighter-bombers of No.75 and No.76 squadrons played a decisive role in driving back the enemy: for the first time in World War II a Japanese land offensive was defeated. On 27 August, when No.76 Squadron's commanding officer was killed at a critical stage of the battle, Truscott took command. For several days, while the outcome hung in the balance, he led from the front as the Kittyhawk pilots strafed and bombed enemy land and sea forces, and repelled occasional air-attacks. Conditions were appalling, with near-constant rain, mist and low cloud, a perilously slippery airstrip, and often intense anti-aircraft fire. Truscott was mentioned in dispatches (1943).

After the battle of Milne Bay, No.76 Squadron performed a relatively routine, sometimes tedious, garrison role in northwest Australia, though Truscott did manage to shoot down a Japanese bomber, increasing his tally to fourteen enemy aircraft destroyed, three probables and three damaged. On 28 March 1943, while carrying out mock attacks over Exmouth Gulf, Western Australia, he misjudged his height, struck the water and was killed. He was buried with Anglican rites and full air force honours in Karrakatta cemetery, Perth. Alfred Cook's portrait of Truscott is held by the Australian War Memorial, Canberra.

J. Herington, *Air War Against Germany and Italy 1939-1943* (Canb, 1954); I. Southall, *Bluey Truscott* (Syd, 1958); D. Gillison, *Royal Australian Air Force 1939-1942* (Canb, 1962); C. Shores and C. Williams, *Aces High* (Lond, 1994); A. Stephens, *High Fliers* (Canb, 1996); A. D. Garrison, *Australian Fighter Aces 1914-1953* (Canb, 1999).   ALAN STEPHENS

TUCKER, GRAHAM SHARDALOW LEE (1924-1980), economic historian, was born on 19 August 1924 at Moonee Ponds, Melbourne, second child of Victorian-born parents Charles Victor Lee Tucker, bank manager, and his wife Vera Winifred, née Simpson. Educated at Trinity Grammar School, Kew, Graham began work as a clerk with the Vacuum Oil Co. Pty Ltd. He enlisted in the Royal Australian Air Force on 27 August 1942 and served as a radio operator at bases in Australia. Commissioned in January 1944 as a radio operator, aircrew, he was posted to No.1 Aircraft Depot, Laverton, Victoria, and took part in test flights.

His R.A.A.F. appointment was terminated on medical grounds on 19 May 1945.

In 1946 Tucker entered the University of Melbourne (B.Com. Hons, 1950) under the Commonwealth Reconstruction Training Scheme. At Christ Church, Hawthorn, on 7 February 1948 he married with Anglican rites Lois Flora Monger, a stenographer. Graduating with first-class honours, he was keen to become an academic. In 1950 he was appointed senior tutor in the university's department of economic history.

Encouraged by Professor John La Nauze to pursue his interest in the history of economic thought, Tucker proceeded to Christ's College, Cambridge (Ph.D., 1954). His supervisor was Piero Sraffa, who was then editing the works and correspondence of David Ricardo. Tucker examined the theories of pre-classical and classical economists. His close study of the literature from a quasi-Keynesian viewpoint yielded new insights, particularly on the debates between Ricardo and Thomas Malthus on aggregate demand. Awarded (1955) the Ellen McArthur prize, his thesis was later published as *Progress and Profits in British Economic Thought, 1650-1850* (Cambridge, 1960).

Tucker returned to the University of Melbourne in 1954. He became lecturer (1954), senior lecturer (1956) and reader (1959) in economic history. In January 1961 he was appointed to the chair of economic history in the School of General Studies, Australian National University, Canberra. Although he carried a heavy administrative load, he built a reputation as a committed teacher and meticulous scholar. Further study of classical theories—particularly on the long-term relationships between land use, capital accumulation and trends in profits, wages and population growth—led him to demographic history. His article 'English Pre-Industrial Population Trends' (*Economic History Review*, 1963) increased scholarly understanding of the effects of industrialization on population growth. A collaborative monograph with Colin Forster, *Economic Opportunity and White American Fertility Ratios, 1800-1860* (New Haven, 1972), defended, refined and extended Yasukichi Yasuba's proposition that the availability of land was a major determinant of fertility. Tucker was particularly pleased to identify the British politician William Huskisson as the author of the well-known, but anonymously published, *Essays on Political Economy* (London, 1830).

Tall and lean, with aquiline features, Tucker was an unassuming and fastidious man with a dry sense of humour. Trout-fishing was his favourite recreation. He became withdrawn as his health slowly deteriorated. Following surgery for the removal of a non-malignant brain tumour, he died of a cerebral haemorrhage on 29 May 1980 in Royal Canberra Hospital and was cremated. His wife and their daughter survived him.

Economic J, 72, no 286, June 1962, p 374; *ANU Reporter*, 13 June 1980; *Economic Record*, 56, no 154, Sept 1980, p 278; *Aust Economic Hist Review*, 21, no 1, Sept 1981, p 1.   MARJORIE HARPER

TUCKER, PERCY JOHN ROBERT (1919-1980), public servant, politician and mayor, was born on 5 December 1919 at Rockhampton, Queensland, son of Percy Clifford Tucker, an artist and furniture salesman, and his wife Beatrice, née Guthrie, both Queensland born. Educated at Rockhampton State High School and Rockhampton Technical College, Perc began work in 1937 as a clerk in the Department of Public Works, Brisbane. Next year he returned to Rockhampton to the office of the Deputy Registrar of Titles, in which he became a draftsman. He joined the Royal Australian Air Force on 6 December 1940, but failed aircrew training and was discharged in January 1941. Enlisting in the Citizen Military Forces on 5 November that year, he transferred to the Australian Imperial Force in March 1943. A corporal in the 42nd Infantry Battalion, he carried out intelligence duties in Papua (1942-43) and New Guinea (1943), and on Bougainville (1944-45).

At Holy Trinity Church, Mackay, on 10 June 1944 Tucker married with Anglican rites Isabel May Campbell, a hairdresser. Following his discharge from the A.I.F. on 5 November 1945, he resumed his job at Rockhampton. In 1948-55 he served part time with his old battalion and rose to temporary captain (1954) in the C.M.F. He transferred to the Townsville branch of the titles office in 1955 and was soon promoted to second-in-charge. In 1956 he joined the Australian Labor Party. Four years later he won the seat of Townsville North in the Legislative Assembly. He was elected deputy-leader of the parliamentary party in 1966 and leader on 1 July 1974. In opposition to (Sir) Johannes Bjelke-Petersen's government, Tucker performed well and earned respect as a hard-working politician. On 23 October 1974 he challenged Bjelke-Petersen to go to the polls; at the ensuing election, on 7 December, Tucker lost his seat.

In 1976 Tucker was elected mayor of Townsville. The A.L.P. team won an 8-3 majority on the City Council. In the 1979 election 'Tucker's Ten' secured every council position, with Tucker capturing 60 per cent of the popular vote for mayor. Under his leadership, projects related to roads, drains, sewerage and water-reticulation were undertaken, and work began on the second stage of the Ross River dam. The council was responsible for the design and building of the Townsville Civic Theatre, the development of the Flinders Mall and the planning of an art gallery. Despite his heavy workload, Tucker involved himself in a wide range of community affairs. No event 'was too small to be favoured by his mayoral attendance'.

Although he was regarded as a reliable 'party' man, Tucker retained his independence. When Sir John Kerr visited Townsville in July 1976, Tucker welcomed him officially, despite widespread Labor Party hostility towards the governor-general. On a later occasion he resigned (briefly) as leader of the municipal wing of the Labor caucus in protest at the decision to disallow the loading of coal at the local port. He died of myocardial infarction on 20 August 1980 at Townsville and was cremated with Presbyterian forms. His wife, their daughter and two of their three sons survived him. The Perc Tucker Regional Gallery was named (1981) after him.

PD (Qld), 17 Apr 1968, p 3058, 19 Aug 1969, p 37, 5 Sept 1972, p 359, 23 Oct 1974, p 1546, 26 Aug 1980, p 152; *Townsville Daily Bulletin*, 29 Mar, 8 July 1976, 2 Apr 1979, 21, 25 Aug 1980; information from Mr M. Reynolds, Townsville, Qld, Mrs I. M. Tucker, Brisb, and Dr P. Tucker, Brisb.   ANNE SMITH

TUCKSON, JOHN ANTHONY (1921-1973), artist and art-gallery administrator, was born on 18 January 1921 at Port Said, Egypt, second child of William Tuckson, a Suez Canal pilot (and amateur painter), and his wife Eléonore, née Pegler. From the age of 8 Tony was a boarder, first at Gresham's School, Holt, Norfolk, and then at Christ's College, Finchley, London. He visited the Canal during holidays. After studying painting for two years at the Hornsey School of Art, London, he began work in a furniture store at Kingston-upon-Thames in 1939 and attended night-classes at the Kingston School of Art.

Enlisting in the Royal Air Force on 10 June 1940, Tuckson trained as a pilot at Edmonton, Canada, and flew Spitfires over Britain and Europe. In May 1941 he was commissioned. He arrived in Darwin in August 1942 with No.54 Squadron, R.A.F., and saw action against the Japanese. On leave in Sydney, he married Dorothea Margaret Bisset, a munitions worker and former design student, on 23 November 1943 at St James's Church of England, Turramurra. He served in a training unit as an instructor in Wirraway aircraft, and continued sketching throughout the war. Back in London in 1945, he admired the paintings of Picasso, Matisse, Klee and Cézanne.

Tuckson was demobilized from the R.A.F. with the rank of flight lieutenant on 10 August 1946 in Sydney. He studied at East Sydney Technical College for three years under the Commonwealth Reconstruction Training Scheme, qualified in December 1949, and began exhibiting with the Society of Artists and the Contemporary Art Society of Australia. Appointed assistant-director of the National Art Gallery of New South Wales under Hal Missingham in October 1950, he was reclassified as deputy-director in 1957.

In 1949 Tuckson had been 'bowled over' by an exhibition in Sydney of R. M. Berndt's collection of Aboriginal art from Arnhem Land. He accompanied Stuart Scougall, an orthopaedic surgeon and art patron, to Melville Island and Arnhem Land in 1958 and 1959 on collecting expeditions for the gallery. Most spectacular in the Scougall gift was a group of carved and painted *pukamani* burial-ceremony poles: Tuckson installed them near the entrance to the gallery in June 1959. He prepared a large exhibition of Aboriginal bark paintings, carved figures, and sacred and secular objects, which toured (1960-61) all State galleries. It gave rise to a book edited by Berndt, *Australian Aboriginal Art* (New York, 1964). Tuckson shifted Australia's perception of Aboriginal art. Whereas it had been exhibited as ethnographica in natural-history museums, he gave it the status of fine art.

Other curatorial innovations for which he was responsible included the introduction of Melanesian art to the gallery's collection in 1962, the major exhibition, Melanesian Art, in 1966, and the collection-display, Aboriginal and Melanesian Art, that opened in 1973. Following Tuckson's overseas study tour in 1967-68, the architect Andrew Anderson was engaged to upgrade and extend the run-down, nineteenth-century gallery. The Art Gallery of New South Wales, reopened in March 1972, is Tuckson's great museological achievement.

Tuckson exhibited a mere nine of his own paintings between 1954 and 1962, and claimed that he was 'only a Sunday painter'. Until 1958 he had been a 'School of Paris' painter of figure compositions, nudes, heads, and occasional still lifes and interiors. The derivative style obscured the merits of this work. Tuckson always painted at home—from May 1949 in a house at Gordon, designed for the Tucksons by W. R. Richardson, and from 1962 in another new house at Wahroonga by Russell Jack.

In 1970 Tuckson's first solo exhibition, at Watters Gallery, presented one new painting, with sixty-four from 1958-65. His next and last exhibition, of twenty-two large, new works, was held in 1973. Tuckson's late abstract paintings were a kind of self-portraiture, emphasizing an inner, subjective world. He was promptly recognized as probably Australia's best Abstract Expressionist.

Tuckson died of cancer on 24 November 1973 at Wahroonga, and was cremated. His wife and their son survived him. The

A.G.N.S.W. held a memorial exhibition in 1976. His paintings, displayed in an international context at the National Gallery of Australia, can seem as good as, or better than, those by Jackson Pollock.

P. Sutton (ed), *Dreamings* (Melb, 1988); D. Thomas et al, *Tony Tuckson* (Syd, 1989); T. Maloon, *Tony Tuckson, Themes and Variations* (Melb, 1989); S. Rainbird et al, *Guide to the Papers of Tony Tuckson (1921-1973) in the Archive of the Art Gallery of New South Wales* (Syd, 1999); 'Tuckson' (video, Syd, 1988); information from Mrs M. Tuckson, Wahroonga, Syd; personal knowledge.

DANIEL THOMAS

TUDAWALI, ROBERT (c.1929-1967), actor and advocate of Aboriginal rights, was born about 1929 on Melville Island, Northern Territory, son of Tiwi parents. He later said of his childhood: 'I hunted, fought, sang like all my people. No clothes. No worries. The country I ran in was my own—every rock, tree meant something to me'. In the late 1930s he went to Darwin by canoe with his parents and took the name Bobby Wilson (using the surname of his father's employer). Despite only a rudimentary education at the Native Affairs Branch school at Kahlin compound, he acquired a rich English vocabulary, and learned to speak in the beautifully modulated tones for which he was often mocked as 'Gentleman Bobbie'.

Late in 1941 Tudawali became an orderly in a Royal Australian Air Force medical aid-post. After the first two Japanese air-raids on Darwin on 19 February 1942, he was among a group of Aborigines who were moved to Mataranka. Employed in an army store and then in a mechanical workshop, he learned to drive. Towards the end of the war he was transferred back to Darwin, where he worked as a waiter at Larrakeyah Barracks. For him to gain this 'inside' position, one of the highest to which a 'full-blood' Aborigine could then aspire, his style and self-assurance must have been evident.

Various menial jobs followed. Tudawali married Peggy, a Wadyigini (Wogait) woman, in 1948; they lived at the Bagot Native Settlement, Darwin. He was a good boxer and an outstanding Australian Rules football player. An opponent, Ted Egan, recalled that he once unsuccessfully tried to get past Tudawali. As Egan picked himself up from the tackle, Tudawali said encouragingly, 'Well played, old chap'.

In 1952 Charles Chauvel [q.v.7] and his wife Elsa chose Tudawali for the leading male role in *Jedda* (1955), a full-length colour motion picture filmed in the Territory and in Sydney. He became Marbuck, an outlawed traditional Aborigine who challenged the White world when he stole the part-Aboriginal heroine.

Tudawali was a sensation and the film a success. Its gloomy conclusion, that tensions created by the Aboriginal transition from the traditional to the contemporary could be resolved only by violent death, was mirrored by Tudawali's own life.

Back in Darwin, Tudawali was allocated a house in a White suburb. After a few months, however, he moved back to Bagot at his own request. He worked as a groundsman at Government House, where his affable and direct (but never 'cheeky') manner won forgiveness for his indifferent work performance, until he told the administrator, 'My education did not teach me how to rake leaves. My education has taught me how to drink, smoke, and mix with white women'. In March 1956 national newspapers claimed that he was destitute and suffering from tuberculosis. The minister for territories (Sir) Paul Hasluck came under heavy fire in the Commonwealth parliament for the alleged failure of the Territory's Welfare Branch to protect Tudawali's interests. Although he received further roles in an undistinguished film, *Dust in the Sun* (1958), and in the early television series 'Whiplash', he drifted in and out of hospital, where he was treated for tuberculosis, and in and out of gaol for repeated offences against liquor laws. In 1963 the Welfare Branch banished him to Melville Island for nine months, and his health improved, but he regressed on his return to Darwin.

Tudawali's life gained new purpose when he was elected vice-president (1966) of the Northern Territory Council for Aboriginal Rights. He joined a handful of Darwin people who were quick to extend tangible and moral support to the Aboriginal stockmen who had walked off Wave Hill cattle station. Advocating equality and self-determination for his people, he planned to travel south on a fundraising and community education tour early in 1967. He was too ill to make the trip, however, and had to be readmitted to hospital.

His first marriage having disintegrated, Tudawali married a woman named Nancy. He began drinking even more heavily and regularly came under adverse notice by the authorities. In July 1967 he was involved in a drinking session at Bagot. He claimed that an argument broke out because he refused to surrender his 11-year-old daughter Christine in marriage, and that some men either threw him on a fire or lit a fire around him while he lay drunk and ill on the ground. Survived by his wife, and by the two daughters of his first marriage, he died of severe burns and tuberculosis on 26 July that year in Darwin Hospital and was buried in Darwin cemetery. A film of his life, *Tudawali*, was made in 1987.

F. Hardy, *The Unlucky Australians* (Melb, 1968); *People* (Syd), 21 Apr 1954, p 23; *NT News*, 6 Jan

1955, 20, 22 Mar, 5 Apr 1956, 26 July 1967; *Examiner* (Launc), 27 July 1967; *SMH*, 27 July, 11 Nov 1967; F1, item 1952/998 pt 1 (NAA, Darwin) and A452, item 1955/579 (NAA, Canb); information from Mr B. T. Manning, Stuart Park, Mrs L. Pascoe, Winnellie, and Br J. Pye, Nightcliff, Darwin, Mr C. Lovegrove, Howard Springs, Mr E. J. Egan, Alice Springs, and Mr L. N. Penhall, McMinns Lagoon, NT, and Dr J. Morris, Creswick, Vic.   PETER FORREST

TULLIPAN, RONALD WILLIAM (1917-1975), author, was born on 10 October 1917 at Murwillumbah, New South Wales, fourth son of native-born parents Edgar William Tullipan, a travelling showman, and his wife Vera Hilda, née Gumsffres. Ron's schooling was erratic; his parents divorced in 1929 and for some time he was a State ward, living in St Vincent's Orphanage, Brisbane. As a young man, short and slightly built, he did farmwork in the Warwick district and found it extremely hard. During the Depression he went on the road, but later found employment as a builder's labourer. On 23 October 1937 at St Ita's Church, Dutton Park, Brisbane, he married with Catholic rites 14-year-old Kathrine Mary Power. Two of their four daughters died in infancy.

Enlisting in the Australian Imperial Force on 13 July 1941, Tullipan was posted to the 5th Armoured Regiment. He became 'a bit rebellious about not being sent abroad' and suffered numerous periods of detention for disobedience and absence without leave. In November 1944 he was posted to the 58th/59th Battalion and next month arrived in Bougainville. After being wounded in action in May 1945, he was discharged from the A.I.F. in Brisbane on 22 November.

During his army service Tullipan developed a 'fever to write', teaching himself by dissecting the work of others. Divorcing his wife in 1947, he went to Sydney, hoping to establish himself as a writer. He lived with Florence Vivienne (Vi) Murray, née James; she and her son adopted his surname. In the early 1950s they moved to Cairns where he worked on the wharfs loading sugar and becoming involved in union affairs. His experiences reinforced his strong sympathies for the workingman. Continuing his efforts to improve his writing skills, he had some short stories published in popular magazines such as *Australian Journal*, sometimes under the nom-de-plume 'Nudgee'. He also earned money as a commercial artist. The couple travelled overseas in 1955 and again towards the end of the decade, when they visited the Soviet Union. In 1958-60 they ran a confectionery shop in London, and Tullipan took art lessons.

On their return to Sydney, the Australasian Book Society published Tullipan's first novel,

Follow the Sun (1960), which was based on his observations of the waterfront. He developed a style which was honest and realistic. His work displayed a sense of form, though it was often naive in character portrayal. His autobiographical novels *Rear Vision* (1961) and *March into Morning* (1962) both won Dame Mary Gilmore [q.v.9] awards. For about six years from 1962 he lived in the Blue Mountains at Springwood, but maintained his literary connexions in Sydney and lectured for the Australasian Book Society. A member of the Sydney Realist Writers' Group, he became president (1967) of the national council and served (1967-70) on the editorial board of the *Realist*. Although a bushfire in November 1968 destroyed his house and possessions, he completed his last novel, *Daylight Robbery* (1970), a story reflecting his knowledge of bushranger history, particularly the Ned Kelly [q.v.5] story.

In 1970 Tullipan was awarded a Commonwealth Literary Fund fellowship of $3000. His writing and art were not selling, and after living in Sydney for a while the couple moved in 1973 to Brisbane where he became vice-president of the Queensland branch of the Artists' Guild of Australia. He died of a cerebral haemorrhage on 24 November 1975 in Brisbane and was buried in Dutton Park cemetery. His two daughters and Vi Tullipan, who had steadfastly supported him in his literary endeavours, survived him. His estate was valued at $1237. A self-portrait (1951) is held by the University of Queensland.

H. de Berg, Ron Tullipan (taped interview, NL); Tullipan papers (Fryer L, Univ Qld, and NL); information from Mrs G. L. Tullipan, Mount Warren Park, and Mr J. P. Penberthy, West End, Brisb.

NANCY BONNIN

TULLY, JOAN (1907-1973), agricultural scientist, was born on 9 September 1907 at Mortlake, Surrey, England, elder child of Walter Edgar Hearman, motor engineer, and his wife Minnie, née Merrifield. The family migrated to Western Australia in the *Afric* in 1913 and settled on a farm at Donnybrook. Educated by her mother for several years, Joan attended Presbyterian Ladies' College, Perth, and the University of Western Australia (B.Sc., 1932). She went on to study horticulture at the East Malling Research Station, University of London (Ph.D., 1936). Back in Western Australia in 1936, she joined the Forests Department as a research officer. In 1938 she was appointed plant physiologist at the Council for Scientific and Industrial Research's irrigation research station, Griffith, New South Wales.

On 2 March 1944, at the local Presbyterian Church, Joan married Archie Scott Tully, a valuer and a widower with four children. She resigned from her post in February 1945 only to be widowed two months later. Responsible for the care and upbringing of her step-children, one of whom was handicapped, she returned to work for the C.S.I.R. in 1946. She was seconded to the Department of Agriculture's Murrumbidgee Irrigation Area agricultural service to provide on-farm advice, mainly to Italian immigrants. Her accounts of this work appeared in the *Journal of the Australian Institute of Agricultural Science* (1951) and the *Australian Journal of Social Issues* (1962). She also developed an interest in country women, their families, and their needs. Prompted by her experiences in the M.I.A., she turned her attention to the behavioural sciences, won a Fulbright scholarship and studied extension education at Cornell University, Ithaca, New York, in 1952-53.

In 1956 Tully transferred to the Commonwealth Scientific and Industrial Research Organization's agricultural research liaison section, Melbourne. She was seconded to the department of psychology at the University of Melbourne in 1957 to work with Oscar Oeser and F. E. Emery on factors that affected farmers' decision-making. Moving to the university's faculty of agriculture in 1959, she completed a major research project on dairy-farmers in the Rochester district. In 1961 she took up a lectureship in the department of adult education, University of New England, Armidale, New South Wales.

Next year Tully was appointed senior lecturer in the department of agriculture, University of Queensland. She introduced the first postgraduate diploma course in agricultural extension in Australia, supervised research students and taught undergraduates. Her publications emphasized that the behavioural sciences were the cornerstones of extension teaching and crucial when working with client communities. Tully was promoted to reader in 1971 and elected a fellow of the Australian Institute of Agricultural Science in 1972. She formally retired that year, but continued to teach on a temporary basis.

An independent and determined woman, Tully succeeded in what was predominantly a masculine world. Having confronted sexist attitudes of male colleagues throughout her career, she was adamant that women should not expect privileges because of their gender, but should obtain professional recognition on their merits. She died of myocardial infarction on 11 June 1973 at Chermside Hospital, Brisbane, and was cremated with Methodist forms; her stepson and two of her three stepdaughters survived her. John Hearman, her brother, was Speaker of the Western Australian Legislative Assembly in 1959-68.

Aust J of Adult Education, 13, no 3, Nov 1973, p 146; *Courier-Mail*, 13 June 1973; Tully papers (held by the family); CSIRO files, A9778, items D30/5/23/5 and D30/5/23/11A, A8520, item PH/TUL/001, pt 1 (NAA, Canb); personal knowledge.

BRUCE CROUCH

TURNBULL, KEITH HECTOR (1907-1978), farmer and politician, was born on 28 December 1907 at Bendigo, Victoria, youngest of ten children of Walter Turnbull, farmer, and his wife Margaret, née Gunning, both Victorian born. Educated at Wedderburn State School, Keith worked on his father's nearby property. On 24 July 1940 he married Olive Jean Mellis at Bendigo with Presbyterian forms; she was a saleswoman. He enlisted in the Citizen Military Forces on 20 January 1942, served in Victoria and Western Australia as a gunner and cook, and was promoted acting corporal. Discharged from the army on 13 October 1944, he joined two of his brothers in establishing at Wedderburn a Corriedale stud, said to be one of the best in Victoria.

On 13 May 1950 Turnbull won the Legislative Assembly seat of Korong for the Liberal and Country Party. He held it until 1955. Following an electoral redistribution, he was returned for Kara Kara in 1955, 1958 and 1961. In (Sir) Henry Bolte's government he served as commissioner of Crown Lands and Survey, president of the Board of Land and Works, and minister of soldier settlement (June 1955-July 1964), and as minister for conservation (July 1961-July 1964), roles in which he fostered rural development.

In 1946-55 the Victorian government had acquired 1 010 967 acres (409 128 ha) of freehold land for the soldier-settlement scheme. A further 195 693 acres (79 195 ha) was purchased in the first four years of Turnbull's term as minister. By 1959 the scheme had placed some six thousand returned servicemen on the land. When the number of war veterans seeking assistance declined, Turnbull established a general settlement scheme which extended similar benefits to civilians. Under the Land Settlement Act (1959), the Soldier Settlement Commission was empowered to purchase and subdivide land for sale to any male British subject, over the age of 21, provided he had sufficient experience and prospects of success. The project aroused strong interest. By 1963 nearly seven thousand applications had been received for the designated 197 farms.

Turnbull had introduced the Vermin and Noxious Weeds Act (1957) which gave the Department of Crown Lands and Survey wide powers to compel landholders to destroy pests. This legislation aimed to eradicate rabbits by the myxoma virus, by poisoning and by the fumigation and destruction of burrows. The Act also required landholders to exterminate noxious weeds. In addition to providing staff to destroy weeds on crown land, the department helped private land-owners by charging moderate rates for the hire of its plant and equipment.

At places such as Ballarat and Bendigo, extensive work was undertaken during Turn-bull's term as minister to rehabilitate aban-doned mining sites. In 1962 he sponsored legislation which encouraged rural land-holders to nominate their combined prop-erties as group conservation areas, in each of which measures would be taken to control erosion. Two years earlier, with his support, the co-operative Eppalock Catchment Project had begun. Involving the government and farmers throughout an 800-square-mile (2070 km²) region, the project aimed not only to conserve soil, but to protect the catchment area of Victoria's fourth largest reservoir.

Although Turnbull was defeated by Wil-liam Phelan [q.v.15], the Country Party candi-date, at the general election on 27 June 1964, the Bolte government continued to make use of his knowledge of rural industries. In 1965 he was appointed chairman of the Grain Elev-ators Board: responsible for the bulk-handling of the State's wheat and barley harvests, he was to retain that office until 1977. He was a trustee (1960-78) of the Melbourne Cricket Ground. As a young man, he had raced a pacer, Brandy Scott, without success. As an older one, he served (1969-78) on the Trot-ting Control Board, and represented it on the committee of the Victoria Trotting Club and the Totalizator Agency Board.

In his retirement Turnbull maintained a keen interest in the affairs of the Rural Finance and Settlement Commission. He was remem-bered in parliament for his friendliness and sense of fun, and for the wise counsel he had offered young back-benchers. Turnbull was gifted with a fine singing voice, and played the piano at social, sporting and even some politi-cal occasions. Predeceased by his wife, and survived by his son and four daughters, he died of myocardial infarction on 4 Septem-ber 1978 at Ascot Vale, Melbourne; he was accorded a state funeral and was buried in the New Cheltenham cemetery. His estate was sworn for probate at $269 620.

R. Smallwood, *Hard to go Bung* (Melb, 1992); *PD* (Vic), 12 Sept 1978, p 3501; *Herald* (Melb), 6 July 1964; *Sun News-Pictorial*, 5 Sept 1978.

CHARLES FAHEY

TURNBULL, STANLEY CLIVE PERRY (1906-1975), journalist, author, poet and critic, was born on 22 December 1906 at Glenorchy,

Tasmania, son of James Arthur Perry Turn-bull, a Tasmanian-born orchardist, and his wife Isabella Urquhart, née Holt, who came from Canada. The family traced its ancestry to colonial gentry in Van Diemen's Land, to Boston loyalists who migrated to Quebec during the American Revolution, and, farther back, to marauders on the Scottish borders.

Clive was educated in Hobart at Leslie House School, The Hutchins School and Christ College. He became a reporter on the *Mercury* in 1922, moved to the *Argus* (Mel-bourne) in 1926, and in 1932 began his associ-ation with the Melbourne *Herald* and its chief, (Sir) Keith Murdoch [q.v.10]. The association —briefly interrupted by wartime duties as press officer (1940) to Essington Lewis [q.v.10] and as Far Eastern representative (1940-41) of Australian Associated Press Pty Ltd—was to last until 1949. He had a term as the *Herald*'s man in London and toured Europe for the newspaper in 1936.

Turnbull lived for a time in the old 'Paris end' of Collins Street, frequenting the fringes of its mild bohemia. He was friendly with the family of John Wren [q.v.12], especially with Wren's daughter Mary. On 16 June 1938 at the office of the government statist, Melbourne, he married Joyce Ellen Hammond; they lived at Hawthorn, in a graceful Victorian-period house beside the Yarra River.

In some sense Melbourne's journalistic doyen, Turnbull was a respected writer of special articles which sustained the *Herald*'s high reputation as a quality broadsheet. He produced, however, a great body of work far transcending journalism—books of history, biography, art criticism and poetry. In 1933 he had published *Outside Looking In*, an elegant volume of fifteen poems, but no further verse appeared until *14 Poems* in 1944. This tiny *oeuvre* sufficed for one critic to say (as it had been written of A. E. Housman) that 'though he may have had few strings to his lyre, those he had were of pure gold'.

Black War (1948) was an indignant but scholarly exposure of White atrocity in Turn-bull's home island. An engaging series of six 'bijou' biographies, published in 1945-48, in-cluded lives of Francis Adams, Peter Lalor and Paddy Hannan [qq.v.3,5,9]. A keen sub-scriber to the Ned Kelly [q.v.5] myth, Turn-bull produced the bibliography *Kellyana* in 1943. He wrote numerous books, pamphlets and articles on Australian painters and paint-ing, notably *Art Here, from Buvelot to Nolan* (1947); he contributed to *The Art of Rupert Bunny* (Sydney, 1948) and to a larger survey, *Antipodean Vision* (1962); and he published an elegantly illustrated *Concise History of Aus-tralia* (1965). These works are only a small selection from his large output.

Murdoch had given Turnbull the role of art critic (1942) at the *Herald*, in addition to his duties as a staff writer. To friends, Turnbull disclosed a hearty dislike of Murdoch, and in a man so shrewd as Sir Keith it is impossible that the antipathy remained undetected. Yet his new art critic was given scope and support over many years, and was consulted on Murdoch's own art purchases. Turnbull's appreciation of the Australian modern art movement was warm, but he was no undiscriminating 'Angry Penguin'. Although he praised, for example, (Sir) Sidney Nolan's 'Ned Kelly' series, he thought that much of the art boom during and after World War II was meretricious. He believed that (Sir) Ivor Hele's drawings and paintings constituted the finest artistic expression of the direct experience of battle.

In 1949 the London *Daily Mirror* group of companies bought the *Argus*, with Turnbull's crucial help in their purchase of a controlling block of shares. He joined the *Argus* as editorial adviser and was acting-editor in 1951. The new English owners failed to cope with the unfamiliar Australian *milieu*, and Turnbull left in 1952. Thereafter he undertook occasional journalism, wrote book reviews for the *Age* and attended to his private business interests, among them a public relations consultancy whose clients included the Broken Hill Proprietary Co. Ltd and the University of Melbourne. The latter engagement was short-lived, and his comment on resigning it illustrated his famous vein of comic irascibility: 'I'll never work for a university again until they abolish the long vacation; it gives academics too much spare time to plot the undoing of sensible reforms'.

Turnbull's opinions in general were of liberal-radical bent, and his Saturday 'Free Speech' column in the *Herald* was widely read. Despite the tensions of the Cold War, and the sharply different views of Murdoch, it was never interrupted. Joyce Turnbull had active communist associations, and partly for that reason Clive was summonsed before the (Petrov) royal commission on espionage on 18 January 1955. He felt keenly the absurdity and indignity of having to appear. Always the scholar, he accumulated a library of Australiana which brought nearly $300 000 at auction in 1981. Late in life he acquired a retreat on Victoria's wild south coast near Port Campbell, explaining the move to a friend characteristically: 'It had a windmill, buddy. It didn't work, but it creaked. It seemed so Australian'.

In any gathering, Turnbull was a 'presence'. Substantial of build, pale of complexion, with rather prominent eyes and a striking black moustache, he thought that he 'looked like a Frenchman'. While he was convivial in newspapermen's bars and in restaurants, there lay not far beneath the surface a sombre melancholy. His deeply complex character arose partly from his passion for ancient tradition

and the values of a gentleman; both were at odds with industrial society—generator, as he saw it, of little but vulgarity, unemployment and war. In his own lines:

Metal does not mate with flesh.
No mirror's dimmer for our breath.
I would have lived in the world's morning
instead of at the world's death!

This insightful Australian, author of countless acts of private generosity and understanding, died of cancer on 25 May 1975 at Hawthorn and was cremated with Anglican rites. His wife, their two sons and one of their two daughters survived him. Noel Counihan's portrait of Turnbull is held by the family.

SMH, 8 Aug 1958, 18 Sept 1965; *Age* (Melb), 26 May 1975; *Mercury* (Hob), 26 May 1975, 2 Oct 1981; personal knowledge.   PETER RYAN

TURNBULL, SIR WINTON GEORGE (1899–1980), auctioneer and politician, was born on 13 December 1899 at Hamilton, Victoria, youngest of three children of Adam Beverly Turnbull (d.1922), farmer, and his wife Georgina Agnes, née Drummond (d.1934), both Victorian born. A compulsive chronicler of family milestones, Winton was proud of his great-grandfather, Rev. Adam Turnbull [q.v.2], and of his grandfather, another Adam, who held Winninburn station and helped to establish St Andrew's Presbyterian Church, Coleraine. He seldom mentioned his father. His parents' only surviving son, he attended local schools for short periods, but was educated mainly by his mother.

After farming near Horsham, Turnbull and his mother settled at Warracknabeal. In 1922-32 he was employed by Young Bros as an auctioneer of livestock. With his mother's encouragement, he took part in debates and eisteddfods, winning in the open impromptu-speech category at Ballarat's South Street competitions. They moved to Essendon in 1933. Turnbull worked for Macarthur & Macleod Pty Ltd at the Newmarket saleyards and claimed to have made the first wireless broadcasts of livestock-marketing reports from there in 1936. A regular visitor to the Mallee and Wimmera districts, he failed to win Country Party pre-selection for the House of Representatives seat of Bendigo in 1937, but, at the State general election in March 1940, finished a respectable runner-up in the poll for the Legislative Assembly seat of Lowan. On 9 July he enlisted in the Australian Imperial Force. In April 1941 he was sent to Malaya with the 2nd/2nd Convalescence Depot. Captured at the fall of Singapore in February 1942, Staff Sergeant Turnbull was incarcerated for three and a half years at Changi; he helped to maintain morale by organizing debates and giving talks on his saleyard experiences.

Turnbull returned to Australia in October 1945. Next month he unsuccessfully contested the Victorian Legislative Assembly seat of Borung. In January 1946 he was endorsed as a Country Party candidate for a by-election for Wimmera in the House of Representatives. He cut a striking figure on the hustings. Still in uniform, 5 ft 11 ins (180 cm) tall and gaunt, with hazel eyes, receding hair, and a slouch hat tilted rakishly over his forehead, he gently badgered listeners in a 'rapid, high-pitched voice'. Judged 'a first-class platform speaker', he was decisively elected on 9 February. He was discharged from the army on 26 February and took his place in parliament on 6 March. On the following day he made a stylish, conventionally country-minded maiden speech, prompting one member on his own side to declare that 'Wimmera has at last found a man'.

At the manse of St John's Presbyterian Church, Essendon, on 22 December 1947 Turnbull married Beryl Bradley, a 32-year-old tailoress. They lived at St Arnaud for about ten years before moving to Boort. A regular churchgoer, Winton enjoyed a flutter at the races, but eschewed parliamentary 'perks', having 'not the slightest doubt' that trips abroad could be 'overdone'. Beryl gardened, preserved fruit, and entertained visiting journalists by holding paper spills which her husband cut into strips with a stockwhip.

Appointed Country Party whip in February 1956, Turnbull never missed a single day's sitting during his twenty-six years and eight months in the House of Representatives. In his opinion, that constituted an 'unchallenged world record'. From 1949 he represented Mallee, part of his original Wimmera electorate. While members accustomed to hearing him champion rural malapportionment jeered that he wanted votes for rabbits and kangaroos, he exulted in having 'burned out' seven Holden [q.v.9] motorcars in travelling around his 18 500 sq. mile (48 000 km²) constituency. As spokesman for '80 per cent of the dry fruits area of Australia', he shamelessly manned the 'parish pump'. In 1968 he was appointed C.B.E.

Turnbull measured his performance at question time against Eddie Ward [q.v.], who asked fewer questions but scored more points. When Turnbull repeatedly brandished a bunch of skeleton weed, Ward suggested that he indicate which was the weed. Good humoured and generous amid the rough and tumble of debate, though increasingly given to speeches as rotund as his ageing figure, Turnbull once asked rhetorically, 'What is life's greatest gift?' He ignored shouts of

'raisins and currants', and patiently explained that it was 'the will to serve, not the capacity'.

In 1972 Turnbull was knighted. He retired from parliament that year. Well liked on both sides of the chamber, he was respected for his probity and 'undiminished ardour in everything pertaining to his duties'. Sir Winton died on 15 January 1980 at Bendigo and was cremated. His wife survived him; there were no children.

J. Killen, *Killen* (Syd, 1985); P. de Serville, *Pounds and Pedigrees* (Melb, 1991); *St Arnaud Mercury*, 8 Feb 1957; *SMH*, 11 May 1963; *Herald* (Melb), 18 June 1968; Turnbull family papers (RHSV); information from Mrs J. Dietrich, Wagga Wagga, NSW, Mr P. S. Fisher, Horsham, and Mrs M. Kennedy, Warracknabeal, Vic.   DONALD BOADLE

TURNER, IAN ALEXANDER HAMILTON (1922-1978), political activist and historian, was born on 10 March 1922 at East Malvern, Melbourne, son of Australian-born parents Francis Herbert Blackley Turner, wheat-farmer, and his wife Nina Florence, née Lang. Ian was educated at Nhill State School, Geelong College (on a scholarship) and the University of Melbourne (LL.B., 1948; B.A., 1949). At school and university he cut his political teeth in debates about the Spanish Civil War, fascism and communism.

On 23 October 1941 Turner was called up for full-time service in the Militia. In August 1942 he transferred to the Australian Imperial Force. Next year he joined the Communist Party of Australia. He served as a driver with headquarters staff in Queensland (1942-43) and in New Guinea (1943-44) where he was reduced in rank from lance corporal to private for insubordination. While attached to headquarters, I Corps, on the Atherton Tableland, Queensland, he became an acting corporal in the Australian Army Education Service. He was discharged from the A.I.F. on 7 February 1945 in Melbourne.

Returning to the university, Turner was co-editor of *Farrago*, joint-secretary of the Labor Club and president of the Students' Representative Council. His study of history and politics under Max Crawford, Percy Partridge and Manning Clark deepened his love for his country, and its art, literature and landscape. Marxism proved 'the deepest influence on his thought'. He embraced the radical nationalist tradition and began his lifelong exploration of the left in Australian history and society. At a civil ceremony in Melbourne on 28 February 1948 he married Amirah Gust, an assistant-librarian and fellow communist; they had three children before being divorced.

In 1949 Turner was made secretary of the Australian Peace Council. He organized anti-war conferences in Australia and attended similar congresses in Europe. The Communist Party then directed him to gain 'proletarian industrial experience'. Obtaining a job as a railway cleaner, he was elected an official in the Australian Railways Union, but felt that his expectations were 'absurdly romantic'. When the railways sacked him in 1952, he stood unsuccessfully for the Legislative Assembly seat of Glen Iris as a communist candidate and worked as secretary of the Australasian Book Society. His opposition to the Soviet Union's suppression of the Hungarian uprising in 1956 led to his expulsion from the C.P.A. in 1958.

Turner studied at the Research School of Social Sciences, Australian National University (Ph.D., 1963). His thesis examined the dynamics of the labour movement in eastern Australia in 1900-21 and provided the foundation for his most substantial book, *Industrial Labour and Politics* (Canberra, 1965), and its offshoot, *Sydney's Burning* (Melbourne, 1967). After lecturing in history at the University of Adelaide from 1962, he moved in 1964 to Monash University, Melbourne, where he distinguished himself as an original, brilliant and inspiring teacher of Australian history and as an outstanding supervisor of honours and postgraduate students. In 1969 he was promoted to associate-professor. He wrote *In Union is Strength* (1976), edited *The Great Depression* (with L. J. Louis, 1968) and *The Australian Dream* (1968), and published numerous articles.

On 27 April 1968, at Richmond, Turner married with Methodist forms Ann Barnard, a schoolteacher and a divorcee. After they separated, he lived with Leonie Sandercock. By 1970 he was a leader of the Labor Unity faction in the Victorian branch of the Australian Labor Party. He used his skills to help prevent a split in the State party following federal intervention that year. The Whitlam government appointed him to the Australia Council. His transition from communist to social democrat worried and confused some of his radical associates.

Turner maintained a long association with Stephen Murray-Smith and the journal *Overland*. Despite his introspective and often despondent commentaries on 'an age of sterile materialism' in Australia, he revelled in his country's popular culture. He wrote seminal essays for *Cinderella Dressed in Yella* (1969) —a collection of 'Australian children's play rhymes', which he edited with June Factor and Wendy Lowenstein—and for *Australian Graffiti* (1975), which he produced with Rennie Ellis. In 1966-78 he delivered his annual Barassi memorial lecture on Australian Rules football, equipped with a Richmond 'beanie', a can of beer, and a pie and sauce.

A lover of jazz and modern art, Turner conducted a salon at his Richmond home where artists (such as Clifton Pugh, Noel Counihan and Fred Williams), writers (among them David Williamson), folk-musicians, students and politicians gathered to enjoy the company of this outgoing, yet sometimes enigmatic, 'everyman's academic', with his barrel chest, twinkling eyes, grizzled hair and beard, and intense pronouncements. He was attracted to women and attractive to them. While playing beach cricket, he died of a coronary occlusion on 27 December 1978 on Erith Island, Bass Strait, and was cremated. His wife survived him, as did the son and two daughters of his first marriage. Portraits of Turner by Counihan, Williams and Pugh are held privately. Sandercock and Murray-Smith edited a selection of his writings, *Room for Manoeuvre* (1982).

A. Inglis, *Amirah* (Melb, 1983) and *The Hammer & Sickle and the Washing Up* (Melb, 1995); *Monash Reporter*, Mar 1979; *Overland*, no 76/77, Oct 1979; *Age* (Melb), 28, 29 Dec 1978; *National Times*, 12-18 Sept 1982; 'An Evening with ... Ian Turner', ABC TV, 2 Feb 1976 (ABC Archives, Syd); personal knowledge.   D. B. WATERSON

TURNER, WILLIAM TERRY (1887-1959), public servant, was born on 1 December 1887 at Woolloomooloo, Sydney, youngest of four children of Fred Turner [q.v.12], an English-born botanist, and his wife Jane Isabella, née George, who came from Wales. Educated at St John's Parochial School, Darlinghurst, and Fort Street Model School, Bill entered the Commonwealth Public Service on 13 June 1905 as a clerk in the Department of Trade and Customs.

On 11 October 1916 Turner enlisted in the Australian Imperial Force. In December 1917 he joined the 56th Infantry Battalion in France. There he 'took his share of the infantryman's tasks—holding the line, carrying, digging, wiring, patrolling, and attacking' in the often desperate fighting at Villers Bretonneux (April 1918), Morlancourt (July), Amiens (August) and Péronne (August-September). Promoted temporary sergeant in December 1918, he returned to Sydney in August 1919 and was discharged from the army on 15 September. He was modest about his World War I service, later describing his contribution as 'nothing really outstanding' and his survival as 'fortunate'.

At St Paul's Church of England, Chatswood, on 13 April 1920 Turner married Annie Isabella Griffiths, a 43-year-old nurse; they were childless. Annie had served in England with Queen Alexandra's Imperial Medical Nursing Service from July 1915 to June 1916. She enlisted in the Australian Army Nursing Service on 31 May 1917. Sent to Hortiach and

Salonica (Thessaloniki), Greece, she was promoted sister and worked in British hospitals from August 1917 to December 1918. The nurses were 'housed in tents or huts in a barbed-wire enclosure to keep out prowlers'. For the most part, conditions were deplorable.

After the war Bill was placed in charge of the activities of the Commonwealth public trustee and then those of the Clearing Office in New South Wales. In 1932-36 he was based in New York as Australian customs representative for the United States of America and Canada. Returning home, he worked at the department's central office in Canberra. During World War II he administered economic warfare measures, restrictions on merchant shipping, and the control of exports and contraband. He became collector of customs for South Australia in September 1944 and assistant comptroller-general in July 1945. In addition, he was chairman (1944-48) of the Newsprint Pool Committee, in which capacity he advised the government on the rationing of paper.

Turner was appointed comptroller-general of customs on 7 February 1949. He was admired for his organizational abilities, capacity for hard work and 'attractive and likeable personality'. Following his formal retirement on 30 December 1952, he continued to work as a consultant. In 1953 he was appointed I.S.O. A prominent member of the Barton sub-branch of the Returned Sailors', Soldiers' and Airmen's Imperial League of Australia, he had been president of both the Canberra City Bowling Club (1948) and the Rotary Club of Canberra (1951). He died on 26 January 1959 at Canberra Community Hospital and was cremated. His wife (d.1973) survived him.

D. Day, *Contraband and Controversy* (Canb, 1996); *Stand-To* (Canb), 4, no 3, May-June 1954, p 47; *Canb Times*, 27 Jan 1959; 1DRL/0586 (AWM).

RICHARD GORRELL

TYRRELL, EDWARD GEORGE YOUNG ('DAN') (1871-1959), vigneron, was born on 9 July 1871 at Owlpen, near Maitland, New South Wales, second of ten children of Edward Tyrrell, a vigneron from England, and his native-born wife Susan, née Hungerford. Edward senior had come to Australia in 1850 on the advice of his uncle William Tyrrell [q.v.6], the Anglican bishop of Newcastle. In 1858 Edward occupied Ashmans, 330 acres (134 ha) of limestone country at Pokolbin, where he built a slab hut. He planted vines in 1861. The cuttings were drawn from the collection planted by James Busby [q.v.1] at

Kirkton, a nearby property, in 1832. Edward had his first vintage in 1864. His eldest daughter Susan married William MacDonald who planted the Ben Ean vineyard. Only two of Edward's children stayed on Ashmans: young Edward, known as 'Dan', and Avery (b.1891).

Dan made his first wine in 1885 when he was 14 years of age and his last in 1959—seventy-four consecutive vintages. After his father died in 1909, he ran the winery while Avery cared for the vineyards. He continued the simple winemaking practices taught to him by his father, believed that earth floors helped wine to mature, and distrusted gadgets such as thermometers. When wine was fermenting during vintage, he tested its temperature by plunging his arm into the vat and relying on his judgement.

Philobert Terrier, who worked the Kaludah Winery and later St Helena, both at Lochinvar, exerted an early influence on Dan. For some years Dan ran the Kaludah Winery and vineyards as well as the Tyrrell Winery. He bought high quality grapes from other local growers for blending with his own, and sold most of his wine to merchants and other vignerons (particularly Maurice O'Shea [q.v.15]) who retailed it under their own labels. When Avery's son Murray joined him at the winery in the 1950s, he tried to persuade Dan to bottle some wine under a Tyrrell label. The old man would not listen. He believed in doing things the way they had always been done.

Tyrrell, a bachelor, was 6 ft 5 ins (196 cm) tall and spare in build, with aquiline features. He had been a fine athlete in his youth and a crack shot. If he felt off colour, he took a hoe and worked in the vineyard 'to shake my liver up'. 'Hard work—it never hurt anybody', he often said, but 'work and worry . . . would kill anyone'. Another of his sayings was 'I want to wear out, not rust out'. He worked until the day he died. Although he refused to have a radio set or a refrigerator in his home, he made one concession to progress by owning a motor car. On 13 April 1959, at the age of 87, he drove ten miles to the police station at Branxton, renewed his driving licence and returned in the afternoon. He died that evening in his kitchen and was buried with Anglican rites in Rothbury cemetery.

Dr Max Lake wrote that 'his wines were simple, honest, great big reds and whites. His name is revered in Pokolbin. Dan Tyrrell spared no effort to help a battler'.

M. Lake, *Hunter Winemakers* (Brisb, 1970); J. Halliday and R. Jarratt, *The Wines & History of the Hunter Valley* (Syd, 1979); D. Paterson, *Tyrrell's 125 Years of Traditional Wine Making* (Syd, 1983); *SMH*, 15 Apr 1959, 25 Feb 1967.

GIL WAHLQUIST

U

UHR, Sir CLIVE WENTWORTH (1903-1974), radiologist and racing administrator, was born on New Year's Day 1903 in Brisbane, only child of Wentworth Charles Henry Uhr, a Queensland-born bank manager, and his wife Margaret, née Cleary, who came from Ireland. Clive's grandfather was Wentworth D'Arcy Uhr [q.v.6]. He was educated at Gatton State High School and St John's College, University of Sydney (M.B., Ch.M., 1926). Tall, rangy and active, he represented his college at cricket, shooting and tennis.

Back in Queensland, Uhr was appointed resident medical officer (1927), surgical registrar (1928) and radium registrar (1929) at (Royal) Brisbane Hospital. Entering private practice in 1932 as a diagnostic radiologist, he continued at the hospital as assistant-radiologist (1932), assistant radium therapist (1933), and senior radiologist (1938). On 24 August 1933 at St Stephen's Cathedral, Brisbane, he had married with Catholic rites Marie Josephine Barry.

On 31 December 1940 Uhr was appointed captain, Australian Army Medical Corps, Australian Imperial Force. Next day he was promoted major and posted as radiologist to the 2nd/10th Australian General Hospital. The unit was sent to Singapore in February and stationed at Malacca, Malaya, in support of the 22nd Brigade. Following the Japanese invasion, the 2nd/10th withdrew to Singapore in mid-January 1942. Uhr worked as anaesthetist as well as radiologist during the campaign. Taken prisoner in February, he was in charge of all X-ray work for the A.I.F. at Changi from August, relying on fluoroscopy when supplies of film ran out. He conducted a survey of men, including survivors from 'F' Force, diagnosed with cardiac beriberi, and established that most had no radiological evidence of damage to the heart. In addition, he was given clinical duties. Private Douglas McLaggan saw him as a good medical officer and 'a man you could talk to'. He returned to Brisbane in September 1945 and transferred to the Reserve of Officers on 6 November.

After the war Uhr was always available to the men with whom he had served in Malaya. Admiring their stubborn courage, he often used the phrase 'as hard to shift as the 22nd Brigade'. Every Anzac Day he marched at the head of the Catholic War Veterans' Association, bringing together his passions for the 8th Division and the Catholic Church. He was a member of the Medical Board of Queensland (1955-74) and the council of the Queensland Radium Institute (1955-74), and had been a founder (1939) of the local branch of the Australian and New Zealand Association of Radiology (Royal Australasian College of Radiologists). Uhr was visiting radiologist at the Repatriation General Hospital, Greenslopes, and honorary radiologist at Mt Olivet Hospital for the Incurably Sick and Dying, Kangaroo Point. After he retired from his medical practice in 1963, he was on the relieving list of Chermside and Redcliffe hospitals.

Elected to the committee of the Brisbane Amateur Turf Club in 1947, Uhr helped to persuade John Wren [q.v.12] to sell Doomben racecourse to the B.A.T.C. in 1953. As chairman (1954-74) he built up the Queensland winter racing carnival, particularly the Doomben Ten Thousand and the Doomben Cup. He believed that the ordinary race-goer deserved the best: each race day 'the Doc' would walk from the Flat through the St Leger enclosure to the Paddock, open always to comments and suggestions from punters. Although he preferred flat racing, he was the driving force behind the launch of the Albion Park Trotting Club which staged its first meeting in September 1968. He was chairman of the club in 1968-74.

Uhr had a wide range of community interests. President of Past Brothers Leagues Club and the Brisbane Rugby League, he was a member of the Rothmans National Sports Foundation. He was president (1953-74) of the Xavier Society, a group of Catholic laymen who raised funds for Mt Olivet hospital and the Xavier Home for Crippled Children, and was involved with Duchesne and St Leo's colleges, University of Queensland. He was concerned about justice and good government and was in great demand as a public speaker. Interested in the work of B. A. Santamaria, in 1957 he unsuccessfully stood for the Legislative Assembly seat of Kedron, representing the newly formed Queensland Labor Party.

In 1960 Uhr helped to set up the Boys Town foundation which raised funds for a home at Beaudesert. That year he was named Queensland's 'Father of the Year'. He was appointed C.B.E. in 1961 and knighted in 1972. Sir Clive was an intensely private man, passionately Australian, a steadfast friend and a devoted husband. He died on 19 September 1974 at his Ascot home and was buried in Nudgee cemetery. His wife, their four sons and two of their three daughters survived him.

A. S. Walker, *Clinical Problems of War* (Canb, 1952); O. B. Steele, *Altars & Artillery* (Brisb, 1980); K. Noud, *Courses for Horses* (Brisb, 1989); D. McLaggan, *The Will to Survive* (Syd, 1995); J. Ryan et al, *Australasian Radiology* (Syd, 1996); Xavier

Society, *Annual Report*, 1953; *Memoirs of the Qld Museum*, 27, 1989, p 567; *Qld Trotter and Pacer*, Oct 1974; *MJA*, 25 Jan 1975; *Australian*, 21 Sept 1974; *Catholic Leader*, 13 Oct 1974.   MICHAEL UHR

UMBAGAI, ELKIN (1921-1980), Aboriginal leader, was born on 19 February 1921 at the Presbyterian Mission to the Aborigines at Kunmunya, Western Australia, daughter of Aboriginal parents Ernest Nyimandooma and his wife Ruby Marutja. Nyimandooma had walked to the mission from Prince Regent River about 1912; Marutja came from the Glenelg River region. Elkin's name was an Anglicized version of the Worora word for a type of shell, nyalikanya.

Rev. J. R. B. Love [q.v.10] and his wife, who were at Kunmunya in 1927-40, had a profound impact on Elkin and her people. Elkin's mother became the Loves' house-worker and her father helped Love to translate parts of the Bible into Worora. Her parents mediated between Aborigines and missionaries, and informed Europeans about the Wororas' language and culture. Educated at the mission school, Elkin was reputed to be the first Australian to receive the interpreter's badge of the Girl Guides Association for being able to read and write in an indigenous language and English. She corresponded with Love after he left Kunmunya. As a young woman she was married according to traditional custom. When her husband died she was married successively to two others, both of whom also died. In the late 1940s she became Sambo Umbagai's wife; they were to have seven children between 1951 and 1965. On 4 February 1969, Elkin and Sam Umbagai married in a Christian ceremony at the Mowanjum Presbyterian Church.

After Kunmunya had closed in 1956, the Umbagai family and others established the Mowanjum Aboriginal community 6 miles (10 km) from the township of Derby, outside their traditional country. Teaching in the local school and working at the Native Hospital, Elkin Umbagai helped to formulate a vision for the community, embracing employment, housing and schooling. Later she expressed her disappointment that her plans did not eventuate. The Mowanjum people continued to struggle for respect and respectability.

Elkin Umbagai's storytelling and writing skills were renowned: she instructed researchers in the fields of linguistics, anthropology and archaeology; she prepared historical notes for Maisie McKenzie's history of the mission, *Road to Mowanjum* (Sydney, 1969); and she collected material for *Visions of Mowanjum* (Adelaide, 1980) and Peter Lucich's collection, *Children's Stories from the Worora* (Canberra, 1969). Deeply spiritual,

she believed that Christianity and her own laws and customs could be intertwined; she took advantage of opportunities to travel with Christian groups. She was fascinated by changing technology and new ideas that might improve her people's way of life. In 1967 she was made Kimberley 'grandmother of the year'. Suffering from diabetes mellitus, she died of cerebrovascular haemorrhage on 24 January 1980 at Derby and was buried with Uniting Church forms in the local cemetery. Her husband, and their five daughters and two sons survived her.

M. McKenzie, *The Road to Mowanjum* (Syd, 1969); D. Popham (ed), *Reflections* (Perth, 1978); *Visions of Mowanjum* (Adel, 1980); *West Australian*, 1 Dec 1978, 25 Jan 1980; J. R. B. Love papers (SLSA); Presbyterian Church of Aust, Board of Missions, correspondence to Rev. C. Mathew, MSS 1893, box 1 (2502), 5/10/1943 (ML); information from Mrs P. Barunga, Ms H. Umbagai, and Mr P. Neoworra, Derby, WA.   MARY ANNE JEBB
VALDA J. BLUNDELL

UNDERWOOD, ERIC JOHN (1905-1980), professor of agriculture, was born on 7 September 1905 at Harlington, Middlesex, England, youngest of three children of James Underwood, master harness-maker, and his wife Elizabeth Gilbert, née Lowe. When his wife died in 1907, James left their children with relations and migrated to Western Australia. He settled at Mount Barker. After a long period of correspondence, he persuaded Kate Taysom, a friend in England, to chaperon the children to Australia. They reached Fremantle on Eric's eighth birthday. James and Kate were married next day. Eric attended Mount Barker State, North Perth State and Perth Modern schools. In 1920 his father took up a block near Coorow, about 155 miles (250 km) north of Perth; Eric worked on the 1850-acre (750 ha) property during school holidays.

While serving a cadetship (from 1924) with the Department of Agriculture, Underwood studied at the University of Western Australia (B.Sc.Agric., 1928). He won the Norman Albert prize and the Amy Saw scholarship, came under the supervision of Professor J. W. Paterson [q.v.11] in his final year and graduated with first-class honours. His thesis, a botanical and chemical study of Western Australian pastures, was published in 1929. Taking up a Hackett [q.v.9] research studentship at Gonville and Caius College, Cambridge (Ph.D., 1931), he continued investigating pasture growth, at the university's Animal Nutrition Institute. In 1931 he returned to the Department of Agriculture in Perth.

Appointed animal nutrition officer in 1933, Underwood engaged in research on 'Denmark wasting disease', a disorder that affected cattle and sheep. The cause of the disease was thought to be iron deficiency. Working with J. F. Filmer, a veterinary scientist skilled in pathology and haematology, Underwood concluded that the wasting disease was due to a lack of cobalt. Other researchers in South Australia, led by Hedley Marston [q.v.15], were investigating the same problem: in January 1935 they named cobalt as the deficient element. Underwood and Filmer reported their findings two months later.

At St Andrew's Presbyterian Church, Perth, on 23 June 1934 Underwood had married Erica Reid Chandler, a schoolteacher. With colleagues in the Department of Agriculture, he embarked on an examination of the poor pastures in the south-west and the wheat-belt of Western Australia, analysing the associated problems of low productivity, poor lambing percentages, pregnancy toxaemia and other symptoms of malnutrition in sheep. He also maintained his interest in trace elements, particularly cobalt, copper and manganese. After spending two years (from June 1936) at the University of Wisconsin, United States of America, on a Commonwealth Fund fellowship, he was invited to work at the University of Western Australia's institute of agriculture. There, with access to better facilities than in the Department of Agriculture, he began a series of experiments designed to increase the fertility of ewes.

From the 1930s farmers had planted subterranean clover to improve the quality of their soil and the nutritive value of their pastures. By 1943 a severe breeding problem was evident in sheep that grazed on clover-dominated pastures. Underwood chaired a committee—comprising scientists from the university, the Department of Agriculture, and the Council for Scientific and Industrial Research—to co-ordinate research. With H. W. Bennetts [q.v.13] and F. L. Shier, he showed that the cause of the problem lay in naturally occurring oestrogens in the pastures. This work led to further investigations into the chemistry and biology of phyto-oestrogens, and their potency and metabolic effects.

In 1946 Underwood was appointed Hackett professor of agriculture, dean of the faculty and director of the university's institute of agriculture. The research and teaching activities of the institute gradually outstripped available resources. Underwood sought external funding. He gained support from the Commonwealth Scientific and Industrial Research Organization, the Wool Research Trust Fund and local industry, and helped to set up the Soil Fertility Research Fund (1954) and the Wheat Industry Research Committee of Western Australia (1958). His paper, 'New Deal for Agriculture', which he presented to the university's administrators, resulted in additional

staffing that benefited research and increased postgraduate numbers.

Underwood was an excellent lecturer whose logical manner of presentation made even the most complex material easily understood. In 1940 he had published a review on the significance of trace elements in nutrition (*Nutrition Abstracts and Reviews*, 9) which established him as a leader in the field. He expanded this article into a book, *Trace Elements in Human and Animal Nutrition* (New York, 1956), and revised it in 1962, 1971 and 1977. Another book, *The Mineral Nutrition of Livestock* (Aberdeen, Scotland, 1966), followed. In part, his success sprang from his capacity to concentrate totally on the task of the moment, and to be undisturbed by any interruption. He never wrote drafts in double spacing because his writing was so precise that he needed little room for corrections. With the exception of a few minor alterations, his first draft was usually his last.

Underwood had chaired (1946-59) the Tuberculosis Association of Western Australia and been federal president (1956-58) of the National Association for the Prevention of Tuberculosis. In 1963 he was appointed C.B.E. In 1966 he was awarded the Farrer [q.v.8] medal. After retiring from the university in 1970, he continued to serve (1966-75) on the executive of the C.S.I.R.O., wrote a number of chapters and papers, and lectured on a wide variety of subjects. He was a fellow of the Royal Society, London (1970), the Australian Academy of Science (1954), the Australian Institute of Agricultural Science (1958), the Australian Society of Animal Production (1970) and the Australian Academy of Technological Sciences (1975). Honorary degrees were conferred on him by the universities of New England (D.Rur.Sc., 1967), Western Australia (D.Sc.Agric., 1969) and Wisconsin (D.Sc., 1980). He was appointed A.O. in 1976. Survived by his wife, and their two daughters and two sons, he died on 19 August 1980 in Royal Perth Hospital and was cremated.

F. Alexander, *Campus at Crawley* (Melb, 1963); Univ of WA, *Univ News*, Dec 1970, p 1, Sept 1980, p 3; *Biog Memoirs of Fellows of Roy Soc* (Lond), 27, 1981, p 579; *West Australian*, 4 Jan 1971, 8 Aug 1979; Underwood papers (NL).　　　　　　　R. J. MOIR

UPJOHN, Sir WILLAM GEORGE DISMORE (1888-1979), surgeon, was born on 16 March 1888 at Narrabri, New South Wales, son of Australian-born parents George Dismore Upjohn, watchmaker, and his wife Jane, née McKenzie. William was educated locally, then in Victoria at Wesley College and the University of Melbourne (M.B., 1909; B.S., 1910;

M.D., 1912; M.S., 1913). He and his contemporaries at the medical school, (Sir) Alan Newton and (Sir) Victor Hurley [qq.v.11,14], were to dominate surgery in Melbourne. Following residencies at the (Royal) Melbourne and (Royal) Children's hospitals, Upjohn took the part-time post of Stewart lecturer in anatomy and entered private practice as assistant to Frank Cole [q.v.8].

Having served in the Militia, Upjohn was appointed major, Australian Army Medical Corps, Australian Imperial Force, on 1 May 1915. He served as pathologist to the 3rd Australian General Hospital, Lemnos, during the latter part of the Gallipoli campaign. Under the leadership of (Sir) Charles Martin [q.v.10], the director of the Lister Institute of Preventive Medicine, he investigated a dysentery epidemic that ravaged the Australian troops. In April 1916 he moved to France with the 2nd A.G.H. Six months later he was promoted temporary lieutenant colonel (substantive February 1917). As the hospital's senior surgeon, he was a member of surgical teams detached to the 2nd Australian Casualty Clearing Station and the 11th A.C.C.S. He was twice mentioned in dispatches (1918) and was appointed O.B.E. (1919). After the Armistice he studied at the London and Middlesex hospitals, and qualified as a fellow (1919) of the Royal College of Surgeons, England. His A.I.F. appointment terminated on 13 February 1920 in Melbourne.

That year Upjohn was appointed surgeon to out-patients at both the Melbourne and Children's hospitals. He resigned from the latter in 1927 on his promotion to in-patient surgeon at the Melbourne, a position he was to retain until he retired in 1948. At St John's Church of England, Toorak, on 16 March 1927 he married Norma Sarah Gregory Withers. A foundation member (1927) of the (Royal) Australasian College of Surgeons, he presided over the Victorian branch of the British Medical Association in 1933-34. During World War II he succeeded (1942) Newton as deputy-chairman of the Central Medical Co-ordination Committee, which controlled the allocation of medical manpower to meet military and civilian needs. He was also a visiting surgeon at the 115th Australian General Hospital, Heidelberg.

Never one to advise surgery unless it was absolutely necessary, Upjohn regarded himself as a 'physician who operates'. He was an extremely skilled general surgeon. His war experiences and his work at the Children's, where bone disease was common, gave him a special interest in orthopaedics. He taught by example rather than precept, and enlivened his rather dry delivery with ironic humour. In his later years he criticized his own lack of initiative and that of his colleagues who, he claimed, had 'maintained surgery at a high standard' without contributing 'any original discovery or procedure'. He published 'Forty Years of Surgery at the Royal Melbourne Hospital' (*Royal Melbourne Hospital Clinical Reports*, 1948); he also gave the ninth (Sir George) Syme [q.v.12] memorial lecture, 'Since Syme: Transformation and Dislocation' (*Medical Journal of Australia*, 1953), and the 1960 Sir Richard Stawell [q.v.12] oration, 'Infectious Enthusiasm' (*M.J.A.*, 1960).

Upjohn chaired Victoria's Consultative Council on Poliomyelitis and the advisory committee to the Hospitals and Charities Commission. In 1958 he was knighted. He joined the committee of management of Royal Melbourne Hospital in 1959 and served as president from 1960 until he retired on his eightieth birthday. Elected (1959) to the council of the University of Melbourne, he had terms as deputy-chancellor (1962-66 and 1970-73) and chancellor (1966-67). In 1962 the university conferred on him an LL.D. (*honoris causa*).

A man of few words, he insisted on being addressed as Dr Upjohn (because of his M.D.), commonly wore the short black coat and striped trousers of a London consultant, and drove the same black Rolls-Royce motorcar (not always slowly) for fifty years. He appeared at first meeting to be an extreme and rigid conservative. The reverse was the case, and many knew him to be kindly and compassionate. Apart from medicine, his interests lay in the humanities, especially English literature and history. From this reading and his vast medical experience, he gave advice, laced with common sense and wisdom, to all who sought his help. In committee he usually said little, but what he said was always to the point. At one faculty meeting a heated debate took place over a proposal to name a new building after a recently retired member. Upjohn's single query, 'Was any other name considered?', abruptly ended the discussion.

Late in life Sir William claimed that his greatest contribution to the Children's Hospital had been to insist that (Dame) Jean Macnamara [q.v.10] and (Dame) Kate Campbell be appointed to its staff. Long before any changes were proposed, he condemned the honorary system in public hospitals as archaic. Moreover, he deplored the increasing length and specialization of university medical courses, and regretted the absence of general practitioners from their staff. In his view, the nationalization of medicine was inevitable. He died on 18 January 1979 at Toorak and was cremated; his wife, their two daughters and their elder son survived him. Peter Zageris's portrait (1973) of Upjohn is held by the University of Melbourne, which established (1974) the Upjohn medal for distinguished service to medicine in Australia.

A. G. Butler (ed), *Official History of the Australian Army Medical Services in the War of 1914-1918*, 1-2 (Melb, 1930, Canb, 1940); K. F. Russell, *The Melbourne Medical School 1862-1962* (Melb, 1977); A. Gregory, *The Ever Open Door* (Melb, 1998); P. Yule, *The Royal Children's Hospital* (Syd, 1999); information from Mr J. Upjohn, Malvern, Melb; personal knowledge.   JOHN V. HURLEY*

UPTON, THOMAS HAYNES (1889-1956), civil engineer and public servant, was born on 2 June 1889 at Collingwood, Melbourne, eldest of three children of Victorian-born parents Thomas Upton, civil servant, and his second wife Mary Sophia, née Haynes. Sent to Hawthorn State School, young Thomas won a scholarship to Wesley College where he also won a Draper [q.v.1] scholarship. He played hockey at school and later with the Hawthorn club. Awarded an exhibition, he entered Ormond [q.v.5] College in 1906 and studied civil engineering at the University of Melbourne (B.Sc., 1910; M.Sc., 1912; B.C.E., 1912; M.C.E., 1919). He graduated (1910) with first-class honours and the Dixson scholarship, and won the Stawell [q.v.6] scholarship (1912). In 1912-13 he gained practical experience working for (Sir) John Monash [q.v.10].

In 1913 Upton travelled to Britain via Africa and Europe. He worked for about eight months for a consulting engineer in England, designing structural steelwork for bridges and buildings and checking calculations for designs in reinforced concrete. In 1914 he was appointed assistant-engineer to the Victorian Country Roads Board and instructed to brief himself on modern road-making practices and materials in Britain and the United States of America.

When World War I broke out, Upton was granted leave. Enlisting in the British Army in September 1914, he was posted to the Royal Naval Division as a sapper. On 6 December he was appointed temporary lieutenant, Royal Engineers. He served on the Western Front with its 130th Field Company until he was wounded in February 1916 and evacuated to England. Back in action with the 74th Field Company, R.E., from August, he was again wounded, in March 1917, and brought to England to recover. He was attached to the R.E. Bridging School, Aire (later Monchy Cayeux), France, in December as acting captain. From March 1918 he performed staff duties at General Headquarters; his responsibilities, still related to bridging, encompassed the wider field of route selection and the design of special structures. In October 1918 he returned to the Bridging School as chief instructor. He was thrice mentioned in dispatches (1916, 1918 and 1919). Demobilized from the army in April 1919, he was appointed O.B.E. that year.

Having rejoined the C.R.B., Upton completed his assignment, which had been interrupted by the war, by returning to Australia via the U.S.A. From September 1919 to February 1922 he was engaged in work associated with major roads in Victoria. A significant bridge over the Barwon River at Moorabool Street, Geelong, was designed and built under his supervision. In early 1920, with William Calder, chairman of the C.R.B., and Professor Henry Payne [qq.v.7,11], he sat on a committee that judged designs for a bridge over the River Yarra at Church Street, Richmond. On 26 October 1921 he married Jessie Toon Smith (d.1922) with Methodist forms at her home at Kew. While senior lecturer (from 1922) in civil engineering at the university, he undertook a survey of the State's road-making materials and established a road-materials testing laboratory.

In February 1925 Upton was appointed to the statutory Main Roads Board in New South Wales. Shortly before moving to Sydney, he married Irene Dodgshun, a clerk, on 18 February at the Presbyterian Church, Surrey Hills. During the next seven years, under Upton's guidance, the board organized the design and construction of a State-wide system of roads. On 22 March 1932 Premier J. T. Lang [q.v.9] abolished the board. During the remainder of that year Upton was retained by the Department of Transport in an advisory capacity, and as a member of a committee inquiring into motor omnibus transport in Sydney and Newcastle. Late in 1932 the new premier, (Sir) Bertram Stevens [q.v.12], created the Department of Main Roads. Upton was gazetted assistant commissioner.

On 30 April 1935 Upton was transferred to the Metropolitan Water, Sewerage and Drainage Board as president. Although the Depression had begun to ease, an eight-year drought was to accentuate the board's problems. Under Upton's direction, the board was well on the way to eliminating a backlog of works when World War II broke out. Thereafter, many of its design and construction resources were diverted to the war effort. The largest of these works was the Captain Cook [q.v.1] Graving Dock at Garden Island for the Royal Australian Navy. After 1945 the water board reverted to its statutory responsibilities. Its major task—to augment Sydney's water supply—was effected by the construction of Warragamba Dam on the Nepean River, which was progressing satisfactorily when Upton retired in April 1955.

A founding associate (1919) and member (1922) of the Institution of Engineers, Australia, Upton joined its board of examiners in 1932. Representing (1939-54) the Sydney division on the council, he was elected a vice-president in 1944 and president in 1946. He chaired (1948-56) the Standards Association of Australia. Upton was awarded the Kernot and (Sir) Peter Nicol Russell [qq.v.5,6] medals, respectively by the University of Melbourne in 1947 and by the I.E.A. in 1949. The University of Western Australia conferred on him an honorary doctorate of engineering in 1949.

For his work over many decades for Killara Congregational Church, Upton was appointed a life deacon. He held offices in the Congregational Union of New South Wales and the World Council of Churches, and was a councillor of Sydney City Mission. Retaining the moustache and bearing that reflected his military experience, he was a warm-hearted man, deeply interested in his fellows and in the team he gathered about him. He belonged to the Rotary Club of Sydney and Killara Bowling Club. Upton died of a coronary occlusion on 25 October 1956 in his home at Killara and was cremated with Congregational forms. His wife, and their three daughters and two sons survived him.

A. H. Corbett, *The Institution of Engineers, Australia* (Syd, 1973); Inst of Engineers, Aust, *J*, 20, 1948, p 71, 21, 1949, p 183, 28, 1956, p 298; *Syd Water Bd J*, 5, Apr 1955, p 3; 6, Jan 1957, p 100; *Reticulator*, Apr/May 1955, p 12; Inst of Mercantile and Industrial Administration, *Nexus*, Oct 1956, p 18; *SMH*, 16 Feb 1925, 6, 28 Apr 1955, 27 Oct 1956; *Sun-Herald* (Syd), 17 Apr 1955; Upton family papers (held by Mrs M. Pulsford, Northbridge, Syd); information from Uniting Church Records and Historical Society, North Parramatta, Syd.

T. F. C. LAWRENCE

UREN, MALCOLM JOHN LEGGOE (1900-1973), journalist, was born on 7 January 1900 at West Hindmarsh, Adelaide, son of Malcolm Francis Uren, schoolteacher, and his wife Millicent Jane, née Leggoe. The family moved to Perth where young Malcolm attended primary school and Perth Modern School. After trying life as a dental student and a boundary rider, he joined the *West Australian* as a cadet journalist in 1920. He was to remain with West Australian Newspapers Ltd until he retired in 1965. At Wesley Church, Perth, on 25 August 1923 he married Lenora Emily Olive Klenk who used her stepfather's surname, Stradwick. In 1930 Uren's local experience helped the touring British musicologist Dr Thomas Wood; their travels featured in Wood's book, *Cobbers* (London, 1934). Wood paid tribute to Uren as a 'good friend ... who made half this book possible ... who was defeated by no question and who made every courtesy his own'.

In 1941 Uren was appointed editor-in-chief of West Australian Newspapers' associate publications, among them the rural weekly *Western Mail* and the radio-guide *Broadcaster*,

in which capacity he gave generous encouragement to young Western Australian short-story writers and poets. Wood returned to Australia in 1944, ostensibly on a propaganda mission about British morale, but also for intelligence purposes. He enlisted Uren as an aide, under the guise of a war correspondent in the South-West Pacific. Returning to civilian life, Uren added (1948) a women's magazine, *Milady*, to his responsibilities.

The gregarious Uren became a prominent figure in Perth. In his earlier years he captained the pressmen against parliament in their annual cricket match. He was a Freemason, a member of Wesley Church and a noted raconteur. Following a major reorganization, he worked as assistant to the managing editor James Macartney [q.v.15] in 1953-56. Although Uren was a very moderate drinker and Macartney a stalwart toper, they formed a strong partnership. Uren led several parties of journalists, politicians and businessmen to assess the developmental prospects of the North-West. In 1962 he served as media consultant to the British Empire and Commonwealth Games in Perth.

Keenly interested in Western Australian history, Uren published several works which found an appreciative public. *Sailormen's Ghosts* (Melbourne, 1940), based on a reconnoitring journey to the Abrolhos Islands, provided a lively account of seventeenth-century Dutch shipwrecks. He collaborated with Robert Stephens on *Waterless Horizons* (Melbourne, 1941), a study of Edward John Eyre [q.v.1]. Uren's *Land Looking West* (London, 1948), a biography of Governor Sir James Stirling [q.v.2], remained unsupplanted fifty years later; his *Glint of Gold* (Melbourne, 1948), an account of the 1890s goldrushes, drew on oral histories from veterans of that period. He published several later works, some of them dutiful commissioned histories which lacked the narrative zest of his earlier publications. Like a number of Western Australian writers of his generation, he was disadvantaged by isolation. In 1965 he was appointed O.B.E. He died on 22 July 1973 in Perth and was cremated. His wife and their son Malcolm ('Bon'), a respected journalist with West Australian Newspapers, survived him.

Newspaper House News, Oct 1973; *West Australian*, 23 July 1973; Thomas Wood papers (NL); information from, and notebooks held by, Mr M. C. Uren, South Perth.

G. C. BOLTON

UTZ, STANLEY FREDERICK (1898-1974), sharebroker, businessman and Liberal Party official, was born on 17 May 1898 in Sydney, eighth child of John Frederick Utz, a storekeeper from Germany, and his native-born wife Ellen, née Bruhn. John had established the Sunlight Flour Mill at Glen Innes in 1881 and was mayor of the municipality in 1883. Stan was educated at Sydney Grammar School. He enlisted in the Australian Imperial Force on 28 October 1918, shortly before the Armistice, and was discharged on 11 March 1919. Over the next eight years he worked his way up to become manager of MacRae Knitting Mills Ltd.

Turning to stockbroking, Utz went into partnership with L. G. I. Bode, son of his old schoolmaster. Utz & Bode began trading in 1927. After Sam Hordern [q.v.14] joined the partnership in 1938, Hordern, Utz & Bode developed into one of Sydney's leading stock-broking firms. Utz travelled extensively and established worldwide contacts. At the Congregational Church, Pitt Street, Sydney, on 19 September 1935 he married Janet Cuthbertson Saxton (d.1952).

From the 1930s Utz was a director of various tin-mining and dredging operations in Siam (Thailand) and Malaya, including Burma-Malay Tin Ltd, until local interests bought out the Australian and other foreign shareholders in the early 1950s. A founder and councillor of the State branch of the Institute of Directors in Australia, Utz chaired several companies in the 1960s, among them Babcock & Wilcox Australia Ltd, Hannam's Pty Ltd and Wright [q.v.6] Heaton & Co. Ltd. He was also a director of Bailey Meters & Controls Pty Ltd. In 1967, with the Rothschilds, he helped to establish the investment and merchant banking house International Pacific Corporation Ltd, of which he was a foundation director.

As Federal treasurer (1956-62) of the Liberal Party of Australia, Utz used his wide-ranging business connexions to raise money for the party, particularly during Federal election campaigns. Involved in various charities, he served (1967-73) on the New South Wales State Cancer Council, and, privately, gave generously to cancer research. He belonged to the Australian, American National and New South Wales clubs, the Sydney Cricket Ground, and the Australian Jockey, Australian Golf and Elanora Country clubs.

A keen golfer, Utz often brought his own gardener with him when he played at Elanora. While he was on the links, the gardener changed the flowerbeds to ensure that the borders were colourful—all at Utz's expense. In 1964 Utz presented Elanora with the gateway which now forms a striking entrance to the club. A plaque was later placed on one of the pillars in memory of his generosity. In later life he lived with his two sisters at Bellevue Hill and remained active on the Sydney Stock Exchange. He died on 6 May 1974 at St Vincent's Hospital, Darlinghurst, and was cremated with Anglican rites. Childless, he left the bulk of his estate, sworn for probate at $725 706, to the State Cancer Council.

S. H. Barry, *Elanora* (Syd, 1977); S. Salsbury and K. Sweeney, *Sydney Stockbrokers* (Syd, 1992); *Aust Director*, Aug 1974, p 68; *SMH*, 13 Jan, 25 Mar, 21 Dec 1948, 20 Oct 1967, 8 May, 17 Oct 1974; information from Mr J. Utz, Seaforth, and Mr R. Utz, Mosman, Syd.   JIM BAIN

V

VALE, MARGARET MILDRED (1893-1972), public servant, was born on 27 February 1893 at Glebe, Sydney, third daughter of Stephen Wills Vale, a South Australian-born assayer, and his wife Margaret, née Rorison, who came from England. Educated at Sydney Girls' High School, Millie obtained four 'A' passes in the junior public examination in 1909. She entered the Commonwealth Public Service on 22 January 1912 as a typist in the office of the public service inspector for New South Wales and was to spend her entire career there. Since she never married, she was able to retain permanent status.

After three years as a typist, Miss Vale responded to an advertisement for a post as a clerical officer. Her application to sit the examination was initially rejected, as the intention was to recruit male clerks. Persevering with her claim that there was no indication of this restriction in the advertisement, she sat the examination and passed easily. On 1 March 1915 she was transferred from the general to the clerical division and appointed clerk, class 5, at an annual salary of £132.

The public service inspector's office undertook, in each State, the administrative functions of the Commonwealth Public Service Board. One of its duties was to promulgate, within Commonwealth departments and instrumentalities, the terms and conditions of employment of staff. Following the passage of the Arbitration (Public Service) Act (1920), Vale developed a reputation as an expert on the arbitrator's determinations made under the Act.

Her acute mind, mastery of her work and ability to give context to decisions intimidated a number of her junior (and even senior) colleagues, as did her manner. Vale's formality, and air of obvious efficiency, belied her kindly nature. She generously shared her knowledge with junior staff and went out of her way to support them in unusual circumstances. On one occasion a pay officer's pistol accidentally discharged and the bullet ricocheted off the walls of the office: no one was injured and the incident remained unreported.

In her later years Vale was slightly stooped and wore her grey hair in a bun. Her intensity was occasionally softened by a high-pitched laugh. Neither her age nor her stoop detracted from her skill as a tennis-player. She enjoyed the game throughout her life and still played at A-grade level in her sixty-fifth year. In 1949 she was classified as clerk (female) on a salary of £603 per annum. On 26 February 1958 she retired from the public service. In an era when female public servants did not receive the same opportunities as their male counterparts, she had been obliged to perform better than many of her male colleagues in order to be regarded as their equal. Those who worked with her knew her real worth. She died on 10 February 1972 at Chatswood and was cremated with Methodist forms.

Aust Women's Weekly, 19 Feb 1958; *SMH*, 15 Jan 1958; information from Mr W. J. Harris, Braddon, Canb, and Dr G. R. Curnow, Hampton, NSW.

GREG CURNOW

VALE, MARY (1887-1968), Sister of Mercy, was born on 30 September 1887 at Mudgee, New South Wales, younger of twin daughters and second of nine children of Australian-born parents Maurice Vale, draper, and his wife Mary, née McMahon. Mary was educated by the Sisters of Mercy at Mudgee. Like others in her family, she was musically inclined and learned to play the piano. When her mother died in 1909, Mary looked after her siblings, who called her 'Mim'. In 1914 she joined the Sisters of Mercy, entering St Michael's Central Novitiate and Scholasticate, Goulburn. Professed on 21 September 1916, she took the religious name of Mary Alphonsus Liguori and made her final vows on 18 January 1922. Having trained as an infants' schoolteacher, she taught at the parish school and gave music lessons after hours.

In 1930 Sister Liguori took charge of St John's Orphanage for Boys, where she was assisted by four other Sisters who taught in the attached school. Although the resources of the home were strained by some eighty boys (rising to about 140 during World War II), she could not turn away a needy child. On several occasions she took in whole families until they could be accommodated elsewhere. She managed to see that the boys were warm and reasonably fed, and tried to ensure that the older ones were well dressed when they attended the Christian Brothers' school. Endeavouring to augment the limited funds, she continued to give music lessons to outside pupils and was responsible for a dairy. The boys, under supervision, milked the cows and distributed milk to the townspeople.

Compassionate and warm hearted, Sister Liguori was short in stature and inclined to be stout. Her complexion was florid, and, as she aged, she carried her head a little to the side. Her voice was soft. She tried to create a feeling of security and to give each boy a sense of his own dignity. In an effort to maintain family

434

ties, she arranged for those boys who had sisters at the girls' orphanage to spend time with them. When she saw her charges had a special need, she tried to meet it. In 1927 she had established St John's Hostel for working orphan boys who were unable to pay boarding-house fees. Two of her aunts cared for them to provide elements of home life.

Mother Liguori (by 1942) took a keen interest in and maintained contact with her old boys. To promote a sense of solidarity, she organized reunions, at which a Redemptorist Father conducted a retreat. The reunions were to continue until the home closed in 1978, by which year almost two thousand boys had been cared for at St John's. In 1945 Mother Liguori was transferred to St Joseph's Orphanage for Girls. She returned to St John's home for three years in 1952. In semi-retirement, she taught music at Stockinbingal, and then at Crookwell until about 1962. A woman of faith, hope, love and prayer, she died on 3 February 1968 at Mount St Joseph's Home, Young, and was buried in the local cemetery.

B. Maher, *Planting the Celtic Cross* (Canb, 1997); E. M. Casey, *Held in Our Hearts* (Canb, 2000); Sisters of Mercy (Goulburn) Archives (Canb); information from Sr E. M. Casey, Braddon, ACT, and Fr G. Lloyd, Sr G. Cummins and Sr N. Galvin, Young, NSW.   SOPHIE MCGRATH

VALLIS, ROBERT ELIAH (1887-1954), naturalist, and ELIAH CLOSE (1890-1965), entomologist, were born on 17 June 1887 at Emerald, Queensland, and 19 February 1890 at Westwood, third and fourth of five children of English-born parents Eliah Close Vallis, railway inspector, and his second wife Amy Edith, née Hansom, late Edwards. Both of their parents had children by previous marriages. The brothers attended North Rockhampton State School. Fond of the bush, they continued to educate themselves in natural history. They collected birds' eggs as school-boys before progressing to butterflies and beetles. Bob and Close began collecting insects in the nearby Berserker Range, on North Keppel Island and in the central coastal areas, and learned the skills required to preserve and mount their specimens. In time they extended their endeavours to the rain-forests of North Queensland.

Bob worked as a labourer. On 26 January 1916 he enlisted in the Australian Imperial Force. He served (from November) on the Western Front with the 3rd Pioneer Battalion. After losing the second, third and fourth fingers of his right hand in an accident in August 1917, he was sent home and discharged from the A.I.F. on 23 January 1918. At St Barnabas's Church of England, North Rockhampton, on 16 June 1919 he married Mildred Honor Bainbridge; they were to remain childless. Bob took a job with the railways, but suffered chronic ill health and was unable to make arduous bush treks in his later life. He set aside a room in his North Rockhampton home as a natural history museum. He also collected artefacts from North America and from New Guinea. In 1948, with his brother Close, he helped to found the Rockhampton and District Field Naturalists Club. They rarely missed a meeting or an excursion, and taught young people about nature. That they lived only a few doors from one another enabled them to compare their entomological specimens. Bob Vallis died of a coronary occlusion on 17 October 1954 at North Rockhampton and was buried in the local cemetery. His wife survived him.

Close worked for the Lakes Creek meatworks as a maintenance carpenter. On 7 January 1929 at St Barnabas's he married Agnes Elizabeth Bainbridge, Mildred's sister. Claiming that the State had some of the finest butterflies in the world, he spent his annual holidays collecting in North Queensland. He believed that the best way to obtain perfect specimens was to propagate them: 'capture the caterpillar and feed him till he pupates into [a] chrysalis'. Beetles and dragonflies proved less troublesome. Two new species that he discovered were named after him: a dragonfly, *Phasmosticta vallisi* (1955), and a beetle, *Stigmodera (Castiarina) vallisii* (1964).

Survived by his wife and their daughter, Close Vallis died on 26 May 1965 in his home and was cremated. That year Livingstone Shire Council named a park on Bluff Hill, Yeppoon, after him. The butterflies and beetles from the brothers' collections were donated to the Queensland Museum and the Rockhampton Botanic Gardens.

Entomologist's Monthly Mag, 91, Sept 1955; Linnean Soc NSW, *Procs*, 89, 1964, p 128; *Morning Bulletin*, 20 Oct 1954, 19 July 1989; papers held by and information from Mrs D. Pearson, North Rockhampton, Qld.   LORNA MCDONALD

VAN DE VELDE, HENRI (1878-1947), merchant and felt manufacturer, was born on 13 July 1878 in Brussels, son of Clement Van de Velde, civil engineer, and his wife Maria, née Bruteyn. With his parents and sister, he reached Sydney in the *Salazie* on 11 December 1884. Clement was vice-consul (consul 1891-94) for Belgium. Henri was later sent home to continue his education before returning in the *Polynesien* in March 1892; he attended Sydney Grammar School until September 1893 and began working as a woolclasser. When his father went back to Belgium, Henri defied his parents' wishes and remained in Australia.

In 1900 Van de Velde established himself as a hide exporter in Brisbane. At the general registry office on 5 October 1901 he married Jeannette Davison Ffoulkes, née Smith, a divorcee; they had three children before divorcing. The couple enjoyed music—Van de Velde played the violin accompanied by his wife on the piano. Declared insolvent in July 1902, he was discharged in October. Two years later he advertised as an importer and exporter of hides and skins, a wine and spirit merchant and a sugar-buyer. On 5 January 1905 he was naturalized; he later served as a justice of the peace for Queensland. Unable to find his certificate, he was again naturalized in 1932.

By 1913 Van de Velde was established in Sydney. During World War I he won a contract to supply woollen blankets to the army. The business was registered in 1921 as Sydney Felt and Textiles Ltd; from 1924 he was managing director. Under his leadership, the company grew rapidly and changed its name to Felt and Textiles of Australia Ltd next year. It was to become widely known for manufacturing the ubiquitous floor covering Feltex. At the registry office, Manly, on 3 September 1926 he married 35-year-old Una Ethel Maitland; their only child Paul died in 1930.

Van de Velde travelled extensively to expand Felt and Textiles' interests. He started a subsidiary company to manufacture felt slippers in Wellington, New Zealand, in 1929 and in 1932 oversaw the establishment of a factory at Durban, South Africa. In 1937 the firm was registered as a public company. Two years later Van de Velde joined the board of Bradford Cotton Mills Ltd. He also acquired grazing properties in New Zealand. Following the slump during World War II, he travelled to England and the United States of America in 1946 to re-establish his export markets. One of 'the major industrial undertakings in the Commonwealth', the firm had interests in sixty-five factories in five States, as well as subsidiaries in South Africa and New Zealand. In order to meet demand for its range of textile products, which encompassed footwear, carpet and saddle felts, the company was a substantial purchaser of the Australian wool clip.

The Blue Mountains became Van de Velde's passion and solace. Encouraged by his friend R. J. Wilson, he was leasing Everglades at Leura by 1933. Van de Velde purchased the property in lots in 1935 and 1938 and asked Eric Langton Apperly to design a house. He employed Paul Sorensen, a local nurseryman, as one of a team who contributed to the creation of a terraced garden. Van de Velde spent most weekends at Leura guiding its progress. He acquired rare trees and shrubs and, while on business trips overseas, bought sculptures for the garden. During World War II he raised £1200 annually for the Australian Red Cross

Society by opening Everglades to the public twice a year.

Powerfully built and 6 ft 3 ins (191 cm) tall, Van de Velde was 'almost fanatical about physical fitness'. A keen sportsman in his youth, he was said to have marked W. J. Wallace during the All Blacks Rugby Union tour of Australia in 1903 and to have sparred with American heavyweight boxer Jack Johnson before his 1907 championship fight in Sydney. He looked after the health of his employees. At the firm's Botany Road factory he included a clinic to provide free physiotherapy and medical treatment. In 1939 he commissioned a rooftop garden for his staff at the company headquarters, Feltex House, George Street.

Survived by his wife, and by the two daughters and son of his first marriage, Van de Velde died on 8 June 1947 in New York and was cremated. His ashes were flown back to Sydney. He left most of his estate, sworn for probate at £378 390, to his wife and children. Everglades was sold by the family soon after his death, and was acquired by the State branch of the National Trust of Australia in 1962.

Felt and Textiles of Australia Limited (Melb, 1950); R. Ratcliffe, *Everglades Gardens* (Syd, 1995); Felt and Textiles of Australia Ltd, *Annual Report* and *Address of Chairman*, 1937-47; *Aust Women's Weekly*, 15 Nov 1961; *SMH*, 24 Apr 1924, 27 Feb 1929, 22 Oct 1932, 21 Mar, 22 June 1939, 20 Feb 1940, 10 June, 1, 6 Nov 1947, 8 June 1948, 7 Oct 1950, 9 Mar 1962; naturalization file, A1, item 1932/8450, *and* Dept External Affairs files, A4311, item 549/31, and A1067, item T46/157 (NAA, Canb); bankruptcy file, PRV11576/1/1104 1902/5585 (QA); information from Mr P. Van de Velde, Clontarf, Syd.

N. T. McLennan

VAN OTTERLOO, JAN WILLIAM (WILLEM) (1907-1978), orchestra conductor, was born on 27 December 1907 at Winterswijk, the Netherlands, son of William Frederik van Otterloo, railways inspector, and his wife Anna Catharina, née Enderlé. He qualified to study medicine at the University of Utrecht but subsequently switched to cello and composition at the Amsterdam Conservatory. Awarded a prize by the Concertgebouw Orchestra for his *Suite No.3*, he conducted its first performance in 1932. He was appointed assistant-conductor of the Utrecht Municipal Orchestra (in which he had played the cello) in 1933, and four years later became joint chief conductor.

From 1949 until 1973 Willem van Otterloo was chief conductor of The Hague Residentie-Orkest. He made many recordings with the orchestra, especially in the 1950s, and toured widely with it in Europe and the United States of America, as well as conducting the leading orchestras of many countries. His own compositions included a symphony, three suites and a string quartet and trio. In recognition of his outstanding contribution to European music van Otterloo was, among other honours, appointed to the orders of Oranje-Nassau and the Lion of the Netherlands, and the Dannebrog (Denmark), and to the Légion d'honneur (France).

After successful tours of Australia for the Australian Broadcasting Commission in 1962 and 1965, van Otterloo was chief conductor (1967-68) of the Melbourne Symphony Orchestra. In 1967 he took the orchestra on its first overseas tour, to North America, where it performed twice at the World Exhibition (Expo 67) at Montreal. As principal guest conductor, in 1970 he again toured with the orchestra. The quality of its thirty performances in Washington, New York and other cities of the U.S.A. established Australia's musical reputation. In 1973 van Otterloo became chief conductor of the Sydney Symphony Orchestra (while remaining conductor of the Dusseldorf Symphony Orchestra, Germany). He led the S.S.O. on its 1974 tour of Britain and Europe. Sympathetic to contemporary music, he incorporated new works of such Australian composers as Peter Sculthorpe, Don Banks, John Anthill and Robert Hughes into the concerts overseas.

Australian musicians revered van Otterloo for his vast musical knowledge, genuineness, empathetic musicality and strong discipline. His ability to train orchestras to professional standards and to aspire to world-class performance was a special gift. As a conductor he was one of the 'dry-stick' school, but his reputation in Australia was as a musician capable of great emotion, who elicited the best from his players, even if he was reserved and punctilious. His style exacted a fine orchestral sound which avoided the spectacular.

Blue-eyed, silver-haired and handsome, his bearing 'courtly and gracious', van Otterloo looked 'like an elderly European statesman'. He loved the music of Bach as well as Bruckner and was an authority on the traditional orchestral repertoire of the nineteenth and early twentieth centuries. In private he enjoyed listening to jazz. Other passions were fast cars, fine food and beautiful women. He had been married twice in the Netherlands, both marriages ending in divorce. On 12 August 1970 he married Carola Gertie Ludewig, a 25-year-old German-born air hostess, at the office of the government statist, Melbourne. He died from the effects of injuries received in a motorcar accident on 27 July 1978 at East St Kilda, Melbourne. His body was flown to The Hague for cremation. He was survived by his wife, and by two sons and a daughter of his first marriage and two daughters of his second.

C. Buttrose, *Playing for Australia* (Syd, 1982); E. Duyker, *The Dutch in Australia* (Melb, 1987); *Age* (Melb), 2 Aug, 21 Dec 1965, 23 May 1967, 1 July 1970, 6 Mar 1971, 28 July 1978; *SMH* and *Australian*, 25, 28 July 1978; *The Times*, 28 July 1978; information from Prof J. Hopkins, South Melb.

R. E. NORTHEY

VANTHOFF, PERCIVAL EVERT RUSSELL (1894-1967), public servant, was born on 12 January 1894 at Cobram, Victoria, elder surviving son of Isaac Vanthoff (d.1901), saddler, and his wife Mary Jane, née Russell, both Victorian born. The family moved to Rushworth in 1901. Educated at the local state school, Percy joined the Postmaster-General's Department on 13 February 1908 as a telegraph messenger. He transferred to Melbourne as a letter carrier in 1911 and became a clerk in 1913. His rise through the department's administration was interrupted only by his service with the Australian Naval and Military Expeditionary Force in World War I. At Brunswick, Melbourne, on 22 November 1924 he married with Methodist forms Ruby Ella Shanks, a machinist. In 1929 he was promoted inspector (commercial) in the telephone branch. For his work as the P.M.G.'s liaison officer during the Duke of Gloucester's [q.v.14] Australian tour, he was appointed M.V.O. in 1934.

'Van', as he was known to friends and colleagues, overcame the many obstacles in his path with determination and hard work. His father's death had left him with early responsibilities to his mother and younger brother. While serving in New Guinea in the war he contracted malaria, which affected his health for some years. In his thirties he developed diabetes mellitus and lost almost half of his imposing 15 st. (95 kg) before his condition was correctly diagnosed. Although successfully controlled with insulin, the disease left him with little energy for activities outside his work.

In 1942 Vanthoff rose to superintendent in the telephone branch. He was chief inspector of telephones from 1944 and of postal services from 1945. Promoted director (planning and organization) in 1948, he became deputy director-general of posts and telegraphs next year. In 1949-56 he represented the P.M.G. on the Australian Broadcasting Commission. Vanthoff was appointed O.B.E. in 1955. On 21 May 1958 he succeeded Sir Giles Chippindall [q.v.13] as director-general of posts and telegraphs. At a time of rapid expansion for the department, Vanthoff oversaw the development of an automatic teleprinter switching system to create a more efficient telegraph service, and worked towards the provision of a six-tube coaxial cable between Sydney and Melbourne.

Retiring on 31 December 1958, Vanthoff had embodied the finest traditions of the Commonwealth Public Service. He observed strict political neutrality, enjoyed good relations with his ministers, took great pride in his department's contribution to the nation's advancement, and attached little importance to personal enrichment or social status. Accordingly, he declined offers of highly paid work in private industry and steadfastly refused to move from working-class Coburg to a more expensive suburb. An open, kindly man with deep, brown eyes and dark, curly hair, he was equally at ease with the Duke of Gloucester as with the most junior members of his own office staff. For recreation he enjoyed reading and gardening. His final years were devoted largely to caring for his wife, who was suffering from dementia. Five months after her death, he died on 30 July 1967 at Richmond and was cremated with Anglican rites. His son and daughter survived him.

G. C. Bolton, *Dick Boyer* (Canb, 1967); K. S. Inglis, *This is the ABC* (Melb, 1983); A. Moyal, *Clear Across Australia* (Melb, 1984); *SMH*, 30 June 1958; *Age* (Melb), 1 Aug 1967; information from Mr G. N. Vanthoff, Doncaster, and Mrs M. J. Outen, Templestowe, Melb.   D. P. BLAAZER

VANZETTI, FRANCESCO CESARE LUIGI STEFANO (1878-1967), public servant and university lecturer, was born on 29 April 1878 at Padua, Italy, eldest child of Domenico Vanzetti, clerk, and his wife Malvina, née Ricca. Francesco, intending to become an architect, began studies at the Accademia di Belle Arti, Florence, but was orphaned at 17. His uncle Eugenio Vanzetti [q.v.12] brought him to Western Australia; they arrived at Albany in the *Ormuz* on 3 January 1896. Other members of his family were to follow. Francesco settled in Perth and was employed from 1900 as a clerk in the statistical branch, Department of Mines. Tall, handsome and personable, he joined the Western Australian Society of Arts, serving as honorary secretary from 1901, and treasurer in 1903-06. He designed bookplates, catalogue covers, fountains, furniture, jewellery and a leadlight panel for H.M.S. *Commonwealth*, and taught drawing at the Fremantle Evening School.

On 26 February 1903 at St Bartholomew's Church of England, East Perth, Vanzetti married Evelyn Baxter (d.1960). Naturalized on 30 September that year, he was to Anglicize his name to Francis. With J. W. R. Linton [q.v.10] he won a national competition in 1909 to design and make a challenge shield for the Commonwealth Council of the Rifle Associations of Australia. The two men did not work well together and fell out shortly after. In 1912 Vanzetti selected land at Marchagee, north of Moora. To fund the venture he sold his house at South Perth and its contents, including all his art works and his wife's jewellery. Drought, flood and wheat rust dogged the family's farming efforts and they were in danger of losing the property until his wife borrowed money and purchased it in her own right.

In 1919 Vanzetti joined the Department of Agriculture in Perth as a clerk while his wife worked the farm with the help of their two sons. He became assistant to G. L. Sutton [q.v.12], and in 1922 was appointed wheat experimentalist at the Merredin Experiment Farm. As part of his duties he lectured to farmers and wrote on agricultural matters for the *Western Mail*. When he was not promoted in 1924, he resigned and returned to the farm for four years. He called this period his 'dishwashing years', although he continued to write articles on agriculture for the *West Australian* until 1930.

Vanzetti met Professor (Sir) Walter Murdoch [q.v.10] about 1928. At Murdoch's suggestion the University of Western Australia established an Italian course, and Vanzetti began lecturing part time in 1929. Joining the University Art Club, he exhibited his old designs for jewellery and became an art critic for the *West Australian*. In 1933 he wrote: 'culture alone can liberate us from the slavery and incubus of our modern materialistic existence'. When Mrs Vanzetti returned to Perth in 1952 the couple bought a house at Claremont. Founding president (1952-55) of the Dante Alighieri Society in Western Australia, he was awarded the society's gold medal in 1956. In 1962 the university conferred an honorary M.A. on him. He continued lecturing for one more year, retiring at the age of 85. Survived by his sons, he died on 10 September 1967 at Claremont and was cremated. Since 1987 the department of Italian at the University of Western Australia has commemorated him with the Vanzetti memorial lecture.

J. Gentilli, *The Unbent Poplar* (Perth, 1988); *Gazette of Univ WA*, 17, no 3, Sept 1967, p 34; *Western Mail* (Perth), 26 Sept 1903, 3 Dec 1904; *West Australian*, 9 Feb 1909, 15 Sept 1967.

DOROTHY ERICKSON

VARLEY, ARTHUR LESLIE (1893-1944), army officer and stock-and-station agent, was born on 13 October 1893 at Rookwood, Sydney, third child of native-born parents William Ashton Varley, telegraph operator, and his wife Elizabeth Ellen, née Stubbin. Educated in the New England region, Arthur began work as a clerk. On 24 August 1915 he enlisted in the Australian Imperial Force. Sailing for Egypt in October, he was posted to the 45th Battalion and commissioned in March 1916.

Three months later Varley arrived in France. In August he took part in the fighting at Pozières and was promoted lieutenant. He became adjutant in September. His battalion commander, Lieutenant Colonel S. C. E. Herring [q.v.9], was to remember his actions at Messines, Belgium, in June 1917, when he guided the medical officer, a few signallers and Herring himself to an advanced battle station through a desolate landscape swept by fire—'a magnificent feat'. During that battle he also went forward to take control of two companies at Owl Trench and organized a counter-attack. He was awarded the Military Cross for 'his coolness under fire and utter disregard of personal danger' and next month promoted captain. Appointed staff captain, 12th Brigade, in January 1918, he won a Bar to his M.C. for supervising the resupply of a battalion while under heavy fire in operations east of Hamel, France, in August. His A.I.F. appointment terminated in Sydney on 4 October 1919. He was mentioned in dispatches.

At St Peter's Cathedral, Armidale, on 17 December 1919 Varley married with Anglican rites Linda Adelaide Middleton; they had three children before Linda died in 1925. On 22 September 1926 at St Jude's Church of England, Randwick, Sydney, Varley married a 40-year-old divorcee Ethel Stevens, née Parker; they were childless. With Ethel's brother he ran a stock-and-station agency at Inverell. He also owned a grazing property named Kahmoo. A fine sportsman, he had played Rugby Union football for New England and tennis for Armidale. As a cricketer he was a consistent number-three batsman and a fast bowler. Alan Kippax [q.v.9], giving an exhibition in 1924, asked that he be taken off: 'It's impossible for me to give a demonstration when he's bowling like that'.

Active in the Militia from February 1939, Varley was given command of the 35th Battalion in September and promoted temporary lieutenant colonel in December. He had 'keen blue eyes and a sparsely-built frame which accentuated his military bearing'. Seconded to the A.I.F. on 1 July 1940, he was placed in command of the 2nd/18th Battalion, which reached Malaya in February as part of the 22nd Brigade. Varley's battalion did not go into action until the night of 26/27 January 1942, when it mounted an effective ambush at the Nithsdale rubber estate, south of Mersing. He continued to lead from the front when the Japanese landed on Singapore Island on 8 February. Four days later Major General H. G. Bennett [q.v.13] relieved H. B. Taylor [q.v.] of command of the 22nd Brigade, replacing him with Varley, whom he promoted temporary brigadier. Singapore fell on 15 February.

In May Varley took command of 'A' Force, a working party of 3000 Australian prisoners of war drawn mainly from the 22nd Brigade.

The force was sent to Burma to work on the Burma-Thailand Railway, and was joined there by prisoners from the Netherlands East Indies; from October Varley commanded some 9000 men. Lieutenant Colonel C. G. W. Anderson was to write of Varley's 'strong personality [and] his vigorous and fearless championship of the troops'. Varley recorded in his diary the conditions (the hospital was 'about equal to a fowl shed . . . on a very poor farm'), his efforts to obtain necessities for the men ('Must keep plugging. This is a battle for life'), and the names of the dead (the Japanese 'do not mind if the line is dotted with crosses'). With the railway completed, Varley was sent to Thailand in January 1944 then back to Singapore where a British gunner remembered him as 'a lonely rather majestic figure still with his faded red tabs, and an air of battered dignity'.

On 6 September 1944 Varley embarked for Formosa (Taiwan) in the Japanese transport *Rakuyo Maru*. Early on 12 September the vessel was torpedoed by an American submarine. Varley was last seen in command of a group of seven lifeboats, reportedly 'heading north-west'. Others in the water thought they heard machine-gun fire from that direction, possibly from Japanese frigates which might have killed Varley and his party. The date of his death, though probably 14 September, was formally given as 13 September 1944. He was survived by his wife and by the daughter and two sons of his first marriage. His elder son Jack had won the M.C. in Malaya; his younger son Robert was killed in action in New Guinea in April 1945. Arthur Varley's name is inscribed on the Labuan Memorial, Sabah, Malaysia, for servicemen with no known graves.

J. E. Lee, *The Chronicle of the 45th Battalion, A.I.F.* (Syd, 1924); L. Wigmore, *The Japanese Thrust* (Canb, 1957); J. Burfitt, *Against All Odds* (Syd, 1991); D. Wall, *Heroes at Sea* (Syd, 1991); J. Uhr, *Against the Sun* (Syd, 1998); *Reveille* (Syd), 1 Dec 1944; *Inverell Times*, 20 Jan 1941, 26 Feb 1999; War Diary, 2/18th Battalion, AWM 52, item 8/3/18, Report on POW Conditions, AWM 54, item 554/2/4, and A. L. Varley Diary, AWM 3DRL, item 2691 (AWM).   JANET UHR

VARLEY, GWENDOLINE (1896-1975), sports organizer and broadcaster, was born on 8 November 1896 at Kew, Melbourne, eldest child of English-born parents Charles Edward Varley, printer, and his wife Elizabeth, née Purves. Gwen was educated at Melbourne Church of England Girls' Grammar School, where she distinguished herself as an athlete. She then spent two years as sports mistress at Geelong Church of England Girls' Grammar School (the Hermitage) before taking up welfare work. Moving to Sydney in the early 1920s, she became organizing secretary of the City Girls' Amateur Sports Association in 1925 and inaugurated Girls' Week to raise funds. Her efforts brought her to 'the notice of the studios' and by 1928 she was broadcasting with radio-station 2BL.

As founding secretary (from 1928) of the 2BL Women's Amateur Sports Association (later the Australian Broadcasting Co. Women's Association), Miss Varley used the wireless to co-ordinate activities, which included golf, tennis, 'motor picnics', bridge, handicrafts and social functions. By 1930 the association had five hundred members. In May 1933, ten months after the Australian Broadcasting Commission was established, she began the women's sporting session on radio 2FC. Hundreds of clubs in the city and country sent her news and results. She interviewed prominent sportswomen, and also directed 2FC's health session.

Varley captained an A-grade tennis team and served on the women's executive of the New South Wales Lawn Tennis Association. She was a committee-member of the New South Wales Women's Hockey Association, secretary and president of the New South Wales Women's Basketball Association and a member of the committee of the New South Wales Women's Cricket Association. She also swam, rowed, ran, fenced and skated, played golf, hockey and croquet, and drove her own car.

Returning to Melbourne in 1935, Varley joined radio 3AW and, in the following year, began its Women's Association to run sporting and social activities. Membership began at 750 and grew to seven thousand by August 1937. Her sister Joyce had joined her at 3AW in 1936 and taken charge of a similar project for 'the Younger Set'. Flying to Sydney, Gwen helped to set up the Australian Women's League, attached to 2CH. She arranged competitions between the association and the league in golf, tennis, bridge and dancing. In October 1937 she organized celebrations to mark the association's second birthday: a garden party, attended by Dame Enid Lyons, highlighted a 'gala Carnival Week' of social functions and sporting events.

Gwen Varley was described as a 'Sport Who is a Sport' and as 'typical of what an out-of-doors, sports-loving Australian girl should be'. Both in broadcasting and in organizing, she was a leader in what her contemporaries saw as 'the golden age of women's sport'. At the Presbyterian Church, St Kilda, on 21 June 1938 she married Hector Maximus Greig, an importer and a widower with two sons. Thereafter, although she continued to be active in numerous organizations, especially the Young Women's Christian Association, she gave her first priority to family life. Survived by her husband and stepsons, she died on 24 May 1975 at North Balwyn and was cremated.

M. K. Stell, *Half the Race* (Syd, 1991); *Wireless Weekly*, 19 Jan 1934; *Listener In*, 7, 28 Apr 1934, 12 Sept, 17 Oct 1936, 21-27 Aug, 2-8 Oct 1937, 25 June-1 July 1938; *Smith's Weekly* (Syd), 21 Jan 1928; Aust Tennis Museum Archives (Syd); ABC Document Archives (Syd); information from Mr R. Greig, Balwyn, Melb.   MARION CONSANDINE

VASEY, GEORGE ALAN (1895-1945), army officer, was born on 29 March 1895 at East Malvern, Melbourne, third of six children of Victorian-born parents George Brinsden Vasey and his wife Alice Isabel, née McCutcheon. His father, a relatively unsuccessful barrister and solicitor, edited the *Argus Law Reports*. Alan, as he was known within his family, was educated at Wesley College. In March 1913 he entered the Royal Military College, Duntroon, Federal Capital Territory. Following the outbreak of World War I, Vasey's class graduated early and he was commissioned lieutenant in the Permanent Military Forces on 29 June 1915. He joined the Australian Imperial Force next month, arrived in France in March 1916, held various regimental posts in the 2nd Divisional Artillery and saw action in the Somme campaign. Promoted captain in August, he became commander of the 13th Field Battery in November.

In February 1917 Vasey was appointed trainee staff captain on the 11th Infantry Brigade's headquarters. The brigade took part in the battles of Messines (June) and Ypres (October) in Belgium. Vasey, who had been made brigade major in August, developed a strong friendship with his commander Brigadier General James Cannan [q.v.13], who described him as 'hard-working, meticulous, alert, convincing and courageous—yet somewhat shy and bashful'. Except for a short break, Major Vasey held that appointment until the war ended, taking part in the defence of Amiens (March 1918), the allied offensive (August) and the attack on the Hindenburg Line (September-October). He was awarded the Distinguished Service Order (1918) and twice mentioned in dispatches.

Vasey returned to Australia in September 1919. When his A.I.F. appointment terminated in Melbourne on 6 November, he went back to the P.M.F. as a lieutenant and honorary major. He was not promoted to substantive major until 1 March 1935. In the meantime, he endured a series of discouraging postings as adjutant, quartermaster and brigade major of artillery and infantry units in the Militia. The Vasey who had been so confident and outgoing during the latter fighting on the Western Front gradually withdrew into himself. Studying at night, he qualified as an accountant. At St Matthew's Church of England, Glenroy, Melbourne, on 17 May 1921 he married Jessie Mary Halbert [q.v. Vasey]. He attended the

Staff College, Quetta, India, in 1928-29. Back in Australia in 1930, he accepted more Militia appointments, but contemplated leaving the army. In 1934, however, he returned to India on exchange as brigade major of the 8th Indian Brigade. From 1936 he served at the headquarters of the Rawalpindi District on the North-West Frontier where there were minor operations against local tribesmen.

In April 1937 Vasey joined Army Headquarters, Melbourne, and in December 1938 became general staff officer, 1st grade (training). He was promoted substantive lieutenant colonel on 2 November 1939. Apart from the two years at Quetta, he had spent twenty years as a brigade major or in a similar posting while citizen-officers who had joined the Militia after World War I had risen to the rank of lieutenant colonel by the mid-1930s.

Following the outbreak of World War II, Lieutenant General Sir Thomas Blamey [q.v.13], commander of the 6th Division, A.I.F., selected Vasey as his assistant-adjutant and quartermaster general. On 15 December 1939 the 6th Division's advance party, headed by Colonel Vasey, embarked for Palestine. He was still the division's senior administrative staff officer during the capture of Bardia in January 1941, but was head of the operational staff when the division advanced to Benghazi. Promoted temporary brigadier in March, he was given command of the 19th Brigade and appointed C.B.E. (1941).

In bitter fighting in Greece in April 1941 Vasey revealed outstanding ability as a leader. His brigade took the first shock of the German assault and fought a determined rearguard action at Vevi, near the Greek-Yugoslav border. Later, it held the vital Brallos Pass. Vasey's tall, gaunt frame, with his head of wiry black hair parted in the middle, could always be found in the forward areas. He talked to his soldiers in colourful language that soon became legendary but never seemed to offend. As commander of the Australian forces on Crete in May 1941, he faced a series of desperate situations and was among the last to be evacuated. He was awarded a Bar to his D.S.O. (1941) and the Greek Military Cross (1944).

Returning to Australia in December 1941, Vasey was promoted temporary major general (substantive 1 September 1942), initially as chief of staff, Home Forces, and then—after Blamey became commander-in-chief, Australian Military Forces—as deputy-chief of the General Staff. In September 1942 he was sent to Port Moresby to command the 6th Division. Next month he took over the 7th Division, then fighting its way north along the Kokoda Trail. His leading soldiers entered Kokoda on 2 November. Boldly sending troops through the jungle, he trapped the Japanese at Gorari. Between mid-November and mid-January 1943 Vasey's division fought the grim battles for Sanananda and Gona on the north coast of Papua. The American general Robert Eichelberger remarked that, even after many weeks in the jungle, Vasey 'looked like a commander'. He was appointed C.B. (1943) and awarded the United States' Distinguished Service Cross (1944).

For much of 1943 Vasey trained the 7th Division on the Atherton Tableland, Queensland, before leading it throughout the successful Lae-Nadzab campaign in New Guinea. On 5 September, the day after the 9th Division landed by sea near Lae, elements of the 7th Division landed by air at Nadzab. The 25th Brigade advanced rapidly and captured Lae on 16 September. Often near the front line, Vasey had a strong rapport with his soldiers. '[T]hese fellows of mine are in marvellous form', he wrote, 'I have never seen a body of men so physically and mentally fit'. They nicknamed him 'Bloody George'.

Vasey moved quickly. Reversing his axis, he sent his troops up the Markham Valley and into the Ramu Valley. In a daring attack the 2nd/6th Independent Company seized Kaiapit, and Vasey reinforced it by flying in the 21st Brigade. The 2nd/16th Battalion stormed Shaggy Ridge on 27 December and the division continued the offensive towards Madang. Major W. B. Russell recalled providing a platoon to escort Vasey to Shaggy Ridge: 'They cleaned and tried to polish their sodden boots and equipment as though it was a ceremonial parade. Whenever General Vasey appeared, either on foot or in a jeep, it was all the troops could do to avoid calling out "How are you George?", such a sense of comradeship prevailed between the General and his men'. In February 1944 Vasey was evacuated sick, shortly before his division was relieved by the 11th. He was twice more mentioned in dispatches.

Sent home to recuperate, Vasey was disappointed to find that Blamey preferred Major General (Sir) Stanley Savige [q.v.] for corps command. In June 1944 Vasey was stricken with polyneuritis and forced to relinquish his command. He was determined to lead a division in battle again, although it was to be months before he began to regain his strength. Blamey feared for Vasey's health, but the latter's immense popularity and the intervention of Frank Forde, minister for the army, assisted Vasey's cause. There were suggestions that the government was grooming him to replace Blamey. Early in 1945 he was given the 6th Division, which was fighting around Wewak in New Guinea. He flew north to assume command, but on 5 March 1945 the Hudson aircraft in which he was travelling crashed into the sea off Cairns killing all on board. Survived by his wife and their two sons, he was buried with full military honours in Cairns cemetery.

Blamey described Vasey as 'a well loved friend ... brave ... resourceful ... destined by training and capacity to rise to the very top of his profession'. Prime Minister John Curtin [q.v.13] thought that Vasey was 'a brilliant soldier' and that Australia owed him 'a very great debt of gratitude'. General Douglas MacArthur [q.v.15] regarded him 'as a superior division commander'. Major Russell wrote: 'No soldier or general could have been so loved and worshipped by his men. I think most of our heroic dreams were associated with some hope of special service or sacrifice for him'.

Another unnamed senior officer passed the following judgement on Vasey:

He could be ruthless and kindly, tolerant of human weakness in the doers and triers, fiercely intolerant of conniving, laziness and inefficiency. He hated importance and was quick to deflate it. He could throw away the book when the occasion required, and he could produce it and use it when it served his ends. Like many apparently tough characters, Vasey was at bottom sentimental, and that was one of his most loveable traits.

It was a 'fair estimate', with the qualification that, as a commander, 'Vasey never let sentiment transcend logic; in military matters his head always ruled his heart'.

Shortly before his last flight, he had told his wife to 'look after the war widows because the bloody government won't'. Alice Bale's [q.v.7] portrait of Vasey is held by the Australian War Memorial, Canberra.

J. Hetherington, *Australians* (Melb, 1960); S. F. Rowell, *Full Circle* (Melb, 1974); M. T. Clark, *No Mean Destiny* (Melb, 1986); D. M. Horner, *General Vasey's War* (Melb, 1992); Vasey papers (NL).

DAVID HORNER

VASEY, JESSIE MARY (1897-1966), founder of the War Widows' Guild of Australia, was born on 19 October 1897 at Roma, Queensland, eldest of three daughters of Australian-born parents Joseph Halbert, farmer and grazier, and his wife Jessie, née Dobbin. Young Jessie attended Moreton Bay Girls' High School, Brisbane. After the family moved to Melbourne in 1911, she was sent to Lauriston Girls' School and Methodist Ladies' College. While studying at the University of Melbourne (B.A. Hons, 1921), she lived at Trinity College Hostel (later Janet Clarke [q.v.3] Hall).

On 17 May 1921 at St Matthew's Church of England, Glenroy, Jessie married George Alan Vasey [q.v.], an army officer; they were to have two sons. An outspoken woman, she loved literature and archaeology, and earned a reputation as a bluestocking. She assumed her role as a soldier's wife with confidence and ease, and became an accomplished hostess. George's service entailed frequent moves; in 1928-29 and 1934-37 the family was based in India. By the eve of World War II they were back in Victoria, where they bought a property at Wantirna, in the foothills of the Dandenong Ranges.

When George sailed for the Middle East in December 1939, Jessie threw her energies into the war effort. Having become involved in the Australian Comforts Fund, she served as secretary of the Australian Imperial Force Women's Association, a body which sought to help soldiers' wives and widows. Her work made her familiar with war widows' financial and emotional burdens, and moved her to ameliorate their plight. She had a keen sense of the particular anguish of women whose husbands had been killed accidentally rather than in action. In a twist of cruel irony, her own husband was killed in an aeroplane crash in March 1945. On their last evening together, he had told her: 'Stick to the war widows and when I come back you shall have every atom of help I can give you'. Their cause became her crusade.

In October 1945 Mrs Vasey wrote to all Victorian war widows, urging them to attend a meeting to form a craft guild. About three hundred did so. On 22 May 1946 the War Widows' Craft Guild held its first meeting, with Vasey as president. She set about making the guild a national organization and travelled extensively. Branches were formed in New South Wales, South Australia and Western Australia in 1946, in Tasmania and Queensland in 1947, and in the Australian Capital Territory in 1951. In November 1947 Vasey had convened a national conference which adopted a federal constitution and formed the War Widows' Guild of Australia. She was elected its president.

Vasey drew inspiration from the efforts of war widows beyond Australia and went abroad to contact her French and British counterparts. Open to widows from both world wars, the guild aimed to benefit its members materially, and to uphold the memories of their men. It is 'no mean destiny to be called upon to go on for a man who has laid down his life', she declared. The guild organized classes in weaving—which drew women together in a supportive environment—and established a cottage industry through which they could supplement their incomes by selling their wares.

Once the W.W.G.A. was running smoothly, Vasey campaigned for an increase in the war widows' pension. The pensions payable to former soldiers and their dependants had remained the same from 1920 to 1943. In the latter year war pensioners were granted an increase, but the amount paid to widows remained little more than half the basic wage. With the onset of postwar inflation, war widows suffered financial distress. In 1947 the pensions were increased, largely due to her efforts. She lobbied politicians, and organized rallies, to have the war widows' pension tied to the basic wage. Tensions arose between Legacy and the W.W.G.A.: Legacy aimed to supplement the widows' incomes rather than to promote their economic independence, which was Vasey's ultimate goal.

The next project that Vasey embarked upon was her most ambitious. Aware that many war widows, elderly and ill, were unable to find adequate accommodation, she decided to provide housing for them. In the 1950s the guild proposed a national housing scheme to build self-contained flats for aged widows. (Sir) Robert Menzies' [q.v.15] government passed the Aged Persons Homes Act in 1954, whereby the Commonwealth matched funds raised by voluntary agencies. The guild formed a company, the Vasey Housing Auxiliary, with Jessie as its managing director. Despite being diagnosed with leukaemia in the early 1960s, she was determined to continue her work. By 1965, in Victoria alone, 250 war widows were being accommodated under the scheme. Twenty years later the guild's nationwide housing estate would be valued at $60 million.

An inspiring, energetic and passionate leader, Vasey had lively blue eyes, a sharp wit, and a regal bearing which was accentuated by the large, eye-catching hats she wore. Her compelling character commanded respect. She was appointed O.B.E. (1950) and C.B.E. (1963) for her services to war widows. In 1953 she was sponsored by the Australian government to attend the coronation of Queen Elizabeth II. Although she did not always succeed in her efforts, Vasey established the guild as a powerful bloc, well able to represent the interests of its members. Survived by her younger son, she died of cerebral thrombosis on 22 September 1966 at Grafton, New South Wales, and was buried with Presbyterian forms in Lilydale cemetery, Melbourne.

M. T. Clark, *No Mean Destiny* (Melb, 1986); J. Damousi, *The Labour of Loss* (Melb, 1999); *J of the AWM*, no 5, Oct 1984, p 9; *Age*, 23 Sept 1966, 13 Oct 1995; Vasey papers (NL).   JOY DAMOUSI

VASSILIEFF, DANILA (DANIEL) IVAN-OVICH (1897-1958), painter and sculptor, was born on 16 December 1897 at Kagalnitskaya, near Rostov-na-Donu, Russia, son of Ivan Ivanovich Vassilieff and his wife Eudoxia, née Perepelitsina. His father was a Cossack and his mother a Ukrainian. Educated at a technical school at Novocherkassk and at a military academy in St Petersburg, Danila specialized in mechanical engineering. From mid-1917 he served on the Eastern Front with a Don Cossack cavalry regiment. He saw action with the White forces in the Russian Civil War and claimed to have risen to the rank of lieutenant colonel. After being captured by the Reds at Baku in April 1920, he escaped and made his way via Persia and India to China. At the Shanghai Russian Church on 13 May 1923 he married Anisia Nicolaevna; they separated in 1929 and were divorced in 1947. Convinced that he was sterile as a result of his wartime sexual exploits, he continued to be a womanizer.

In July 1923 Vassilieff and his wife had arrived in Queensland where they bought a sugar-farm at Yurunga, near Ingham. By 1928 he was employed on railway construction at Mataranka, Northern Territory. Although he was naturalized in 1929, he left Australia that year. He studied art under Dimitri Ismailovitch in Brazil (1930-31) and exhibited in the West Indies and South America (1932-33), and in England, Spain and Portugal (1933-35). While living in England, he mixed in White Russian circles, befriended Vladimir Polunin, and began to see a relationship between the modernist movement and Russian decorative art.

Vassilieff returned to Australia in October 1935 and settled in Sydney. Combining an iconic style with immediate experience, he painted turbulent street scenes of inner-city areas. He also produced still lifes, such as 'Red Roses', unflattering portraits, and lively landscapes of the windswept Woronora area. His expressionist paintings impressed Basil Burdett, Sydney Ure Smith, Gavin Long [qq.v.7,11,15] and John Young [q.v.], and he exhibited twice at the Macquarie Galleries. In 1937 he eloped with Helen Macdonald. They lived at Biloela, Queensland, and then in Melbourne. Enthusiastic reviews of his paintings —often of children playing in the streets of Collingwood, Fitzroy and East Melbourne— established his reputation.

Welcomed into the city's artistic circles, particularly by George Bell, Adrian Lawlor, Vance and Nettie Palmer [qq.v.7,10,11], and John and Sunday Reed, Vassilieff joined the Contemporary Art Society. His confident attack on 'fine art', and his insistence that 'gut' response and 'message' mattered more than intellect and aesthetics, influenced younger artists, among them Albert Tucker, Lina Bryans, Joy Hester [q.v.14] and (Sir) Sidney Nolan. In 1939 he oversaw the building of, and became foundation art teacher at, Clive and Janet Nield's experimental Koornong School, Warrandyte. Nearby, he built Stonygrad, a house of stone and logs. He sang bass in the choir of a Russian Orthodox Church, and mixed with members of the Covent Garden Russian Ballet during its Melbourne seasons.

For Connie Smith, Vassilieff painted a four-part screen, 'Expulsion from Paradise'. Its theme of the fall of man had a lasting impact on Arthur Boyd and John Perceval, both of whom visited him to learn to paint quickly. Vassilieff, however, regarded religious subjects as suitable only for the decorative arts. His rejection of all dogma—religious, political and aesthetic—annoyed the social realists. In 1944 he helped to defeat the communist attempt to take over the Contemporary Art Society. Helen's departure that year provided a catalyst for a series of cryptic and costumed allegorical pictures, including 'Firebird from Drummoyne', which triggered Nolan's blending of iconic and folk traditions in his Ned Kelly [q.v.5] paintings. Vassilieff's 'Peter and the Wolf' gouaches (1948) responded, perhaps jealously, to the success of Nolan's Kelly paintings.

At Wesley Church, Melbourne, on 20 March 1947 Vassilieff married Elizabeth Orme Hamill, née Sutton, a 31-year-old lecturer and a divorcee, who had bought Stonygrad from him. After a number of paintings on the theme of marriage, he transferred his energies to sculpture, using limestone from Lilydale; power tools enabled him to work faster and to respond spontaneously to the grain. Vassilieff reconciled the formal language of European iconic art with the lively shapes of folk art in his vigorous standing figures, such as 'Petit Bourgeois', 'Mechanical Man' and 'Stenka Razin'. The aesthetic elements—which he sometimes sacrificed to the more urgent need for expression in his paintings—were achieved through the brilliant finish which revealed the metamorphic pattern of the marble. In the early 1950s the titles of his paintings and sculpture assumed an aggressively anti-imperialist mood, due in part to his wife's political activity. In 1953 he became vice-president of the Contemporary Art Society.

As his relationship with Elizabeth deteriorated, Vassilieff explored the theme of conflict between the sexes in a series of paintings and sculptures. The couple separated in 1954. In May he obtained a post with the Education Department as art teacher at Mildura High School. He painted portraits of the school's staff, expressed his reaction to provincial society in a number of 'psychological' paintings, and fished in the Murray River. Transferred to Swan Hill High School in 1955, he carved some small pieces, and painted mildly satirical water-colours of the local population. He exhibited at the Gallery of Contemporary Art, Melbourne, in 1956, but his work was barely noticed. A retrospective exhibition of his sculpture at the same gallery in 1957 was disparaged by the critics. The Education Department sent him to Eltham High School that year and then dismissed him on the grounds of unsatisfactory performance.

Keen-eyed, sallow and lean, Vassilieff spoke broken English in a low, resonant voice. He spent his final months in a shack near Mildura painting water-colours that suggest the fragmentation and absurdity of life. Survived by his wife, he died of a coronary occlusion on 22 March 1958 at Heide, the Reeds' property at Bulleen, and was cremated. A memorial exhibition of his *oeuvre* was held at the Museum of Modern Art of Australia, Melbourne, in 1959. His work is represented in major Australian galleries.

K. Scarlett, *Australian Sculptors* (Melb, 1980); F. St J. Moore, *Vassilieff and his Art* (Melb, 1982), and *Vassilieff*, exhibition cat (Melb, 1985), *and* 'Vassilieff's "Expulsion" Screen and Melbourne Expressionism', *Art and Aust*, Autumn 1986, p 358, *and* 'Force of Nature: Danila Vassilieff's, *Stenka Razin, 1953*' in D. Thomas (ed), *Creating Australia* (Syd, 1988); *Art in Aust*, series 3, no 62, 15 Feb 1936, p 70; *Angry Penguins*, Sept 1943; *Meanjin*, 17, no 1, Apr 1958, p 83; *Art and Aust*, 4, no 2, Sept 1966, p 113.
                                              FELICITY ST J. MOORE

VAUGHAN, HUBERT (1888-1976), insurance manager and actuary, was born on 8 July 1888 at Alexandria, Sydney, third son of native-born parents Kelson Sydney James Vaughan, clerk, and his wife Gertrude, née Skinner. Educated at the Marist Brothers' High School, Darlinghurst, Hubert joined the Mutual Life & Citizens' Assurance Co. Ltd in 1906. He qualified as a fellow of the Institute of Actuaries, London, in 1912 and lectured part time on actuarial mathematics at the University of Sydney in 1914. Vaughan sailed for Britain in July 1915, intending to join the British Army. Commissioned in the artillery on 29 October, he served on the Western Front with a heavy howitzer battery and held the rank of lieutenant (from July 1917). He took part in the fierce fighting during the German offensive in March 1918 and was wounded in September. After being demobilized from the army, he visited Canada.

Back in Sydney, Vaughan returned to the M.L.C. and was appointed assistant actuary (1921) and associate actuary (1927). At the Church of Our Lady of Dolours, Chatswood, on 24 June 1921 he married with Catholic rites Eileen Charlotte Appleton (d.1953); they were childless. He was one of three advisers to the Commonwealth royal commission on national insurance (1923-27) and helped to draft the State's Local Government (Superannuation) Act (1927). From 1938 he was a member of the committee that advised the Commonwealth government on the Life Insurance Act which was eventually passed in 1945. At the M.L.C. he had been promoted to actuary in 1935, secretary in 1939, and general secretary and actuary in 1941, a post from which he retired in 1954. A director of the company (from 1951), he was deputy-chairman in 1961-68.

Much of Vaughan's energy was devoted to actuarial education. He firmly believed that promotion should be based on merit, not on seniority 'which is a tenet of the Australian religion'. As joint secretary with Milton Alder [q.v.13], he had been a founder in 1925 of the State branch of the Economic Society of Australia and New Zealand. President of the Actuarial Society of Australia and New Zealand in 1933 and 1947, he published widely in a number of journals. He wrote mainly on the theories of interpolation, graduation, valuation, endowment assurance and summation formulae. In 1947 he was awarded the Messenger and Brown prize for his contributions to the *Journal of the Institute of Actuaries*.

Work was Vaughan's greatest passion, although he sometimes relaxed by swimming and playing golf. He belonged to the Chatswood Golf Club and owned a modest home at Chatswood in which he lived for fifty-five years. A member of the University Club, he had a wide general knowledge, and special interests in physics and Shakespeare. His shy and reserved manner, dry humour, slow speech and several mild eccentricities gave credence to an assertion, popular at the time, that one had to be slightly odd to be an actuary. Vaughan died on 22 February 1976 at his Chatswood home and was cremated. He left $10 000 to the Institute of Actuaries, London. Macquarie University named a prize for actuarial studies after him.

G. E. Hall and A. Cousins (eds), *Book of Remembrance of the University of Sydney in the Great War, 1914-1918* (Syd, 1939); A. C. Gray, *Life Insurance in Australia* (Melb, 1977); C. Bellis, *The Future-Managers* (Syd, 1997); *Inst of Actuaries Year Book* (UK), 1975-76, p 134; *Inst of Actuaries of Aust and NZ, Trans*, 1976; information from Mr D. Wood, North Sydney, and the late Prof A. Pollard.

RAYMOND NOBBS

VEALE, WILLIAM CHARLES DOUGLAS (1895-1971), soldier, engineer and town clerk, was born on 16 May 1895 at Bendigo, Victoria, tenth and youngest child of John Veale, a Cornish-born mining manager, and his wife Mary Jane, née Christian, who came from the Isle of Man. Educated at St Andrew's College and the School of Mines, Bendigo, Bill was apprenticed to an engineer with the Whittlesea Shire Council at Morang.

On 14 February 1916 Veale enlisted in the Australian Imperial Force and in August he joined the 5th Field Company, Royal Australian Engineers, on the Western Front. Over a period of twenty-six hours at Broodseinde, Belgium, beginning on 9 October 1917, he helped to lay 'jumping off' tapes while under fire and then moved wounded members of his party to safety. He was awarded the Distinguished Conduct Medal. Commissioned in February 1918, he was posted to the 7th Field Company, R.A.E., in April and promoted lieutenant in May. Near Péronne, France, on the night of 28/29 August he supervised, at short notice and without alerting the enemy, the construction of two bridges needed by the infantry next morning. For this work he won the Military Cross.

After gaining engineering experience (March-October 1919) in England with the municipality of Stoke-on-Trent, Staffordshire, and the Ministry of Transport, London, Veale arrived in Melbourne where his A.I.F. appointment terminated on 2 March 1920. He joined the Kowree Shire Council, Edenhope, as engineer. On 12 February 1923 at All Saints' Church of England, Bright, he married Eileen Guest. In October that year he was appointed assistant city engineer and surveyor with the Adelaide City Council; he became deputy city engineer three years later. Although offered the new post of director of public works in Tasmania in 1929, he was persuaded to remain in Adelaide when the council promoted him city engineer and building surveyor. He supervised construction of the new Adelaide Bridge, completed in 1931, and landscaping along the River Torrens. The council's programme of civil engineering works was curtailed first by the Depression, and then by World War II.

Active in the Militia, Veale rose to lieutenant colonel in 1936. On 2 July 1940 he was appointed to command the 2nd/3rd Pioneer Battalion, A.I.F. Twelve months later he became chief engineer, 7th Military District, Darwin. Promoted temporary brigadier, he flew to Timor in February to take command of Sparrow Force. Later that month the main body of his troops was overwhelmed by superior numbers of Japanese and forced to surrender. An officer of his rank was not needed to lead the remainder who fought on as commandos and he was evacuated in May. In 1942-44 he commanded the R.A.E. Training Centre, Kapooka, New South Wales. He spent lengthy periods in Papua and New Guinea as chief engineer of the Second Army (1944-45) and the First Army (1945-46), and was mentioned in dispatches. On 25 April 1946 in Adelaide he transferred to the Reserve of Officers, and resumed duty with the council.

In January 1947 Veale was appointed town clerk. He was to hold the post for nearly nineteen years, overseeing much of Adelaide's postwar development. Underground drainage was upgraded to overcome problems of flooding, streets were widened to improve traffic flow, and car parking difficulties were eased by the introduction of on-street parking meters and the provision of more off-street parking spaces. In 1957 Veale was sent overseas by the council for five months to gather new ideas. Having visited some forty cities in Europe and North America, he made numerous recommendations for improving Adelaide, most of which were implemented. He initiated an extensive programme of landscaping and beautification, and created new parks and gardens, boating lakes and picnic grounds. After years of shabby neglect, the city's parklands were transformed.

Veale represented the council on a number of town-planning organizations, including the Local Government Act Advisory Committee (1934-48) and the Building Act Inquiry Committee (1937-40). He was deputy-chairman (1956-67) of the State planning committee which produced the metropolitan Adelaide development plan. President (1948-54) of the Planning Institute of South Australia, he was federal president (1954-55) of the (Royal) Australian Planning Institute, and was elected a fellow of the Institute of Municipal Administration. A member of the Institution of Engineers, Australia, from 1926, he had been chairman of the Adelaide division in 1932. He was involved with the Adelaide Festival of Arts from its inception in 1959.

Short and solid, Veale was a shy man who shunned the limelight. He was a prodigious worker, arriving at the Town Hall at dawn each day and working long into the night. A meticulous administrator, he frequently drove around the city to see for himself exactly what was going on. His authoritarian style of management made him difficult to work with; he was blunt and abrupt with a violent temper, and was hard on his staff. Relations with lord mayors and councillors were not always harmonious. He was appointed C.B.E. in 1954.

On Veale's retirement in November 1965, the *Advertiser* summed up his forty-two years of service: 'no one man since Col. Light [q.v.2] has left his imprint so ineffacably [sic] on the City of Adelaide, or so transformed its character'. Gardens, laid out in Adelaide's south parklands, were named after Veale in 1964. He spent his later years gardening at his North Adelaide home and strolling through the parks he had created. A member of the Naval Military & Air Force Club, he had presided (1930) over the Legacy Club of Adelaide. He died on 17 August 1971 in North Adelaide and was cremated; his wife and their two daughters survived him.

R. McNicoll, *The Royal Australian Engineers 1902 to 1919* (Melb, 1979) and *The Royal Australian Engineers 1919 to 1945* (Canb 1982); *Advertiser* (Adel) and *News* (Adel), 23 Nov 1965, 18 Aug 1971; *Aust Municipal J*, Nov 1971, p 133; Town Clerk's and City Engineer's Depts, records (Adel City Council Archives); information from Mr R. A. Harris, Tranmere, and Mr D. J. Williams, Tusmore, Adel.

ROBERT THORNTON

VEITCH, ROBERT (1890-1972), entomologist, was born on 15 August 1890 in Edinburgh, son of John Veitch, solicitor, and his wife Ann Campbell, née Sinclair. Robert was educated at Daniel Stewart's College, the Royal High School and the University of Edinburgh (B.Sc.Agr., 1911; B.Sc.For., 1912). He worked for a year at the Imperial Institute of Entomology, British Museum, London, before joining the Colonial Sugar Refining Co. Ltd at Suva, Fiji, in July 1914. Engaged in field studies as an entomologist in Fiji, New South Wales and Queensland, he also visited and worked at experiment stations in the United States of America and Hawaii. On 1 March 1919 at Lautoka, Fiji, he married Alice Esmee Berry (d.1964).

In July 1925, after Henry Tryon's [q.v.12] retirement, Veitch was appointed chief entomologist with the Queensland Department of Agriculture and Stock, Brisbane. An able administrator, he oversaw the expansion and decentralization of entomological research in Queensland, assigning his subordinates to the major cropping areas of the State. He encouraged local insect collecting expeditions; in 1932 a new species of 'moss bug', *Hemiodoecus veitchi* (*Hackeriella veitchi*), was named after him. Contributing thirty-six articles on agricultural pest control to the *Queensland Agricultural Journal* between 1926 and 1941, he also produced three handbooks. With J. H. Simmonds he wrote *Pests and Diseases of Queensland Fruit and Vegetables* (1929).

A fellow (1914-60) of the Royal Entomological Society of London, and of the Linnean Society of New South Wales (from 1917), Veitch was active in Brisbane scientific societies, serving as president of the Entomological Society of Queensland (1932) and the Royal Society of Queensland (1935-36). He was founding vice-president (1935), and president (1936), of the Queensland branch of the Australian Institute of Agricultural Science. Officially sponsored consultations in 1936 between Veitch and Professor E. J. Goddard [q.v.9] led to the establishment of the division of plant industry (research) within the department. With Veitch as director, the division's activities expanded to include advisory and regulatory services. In 1947 he was appointed assistant under-secretary (technical) to Arthur Bell [q.v.13].

Veitch's official retirement was postponed until 31 December 1956. He was dedicated to his work and the department was reluctant to lose his expertise. Recalled as a part-time consultant for three days a week after Bell's death in 1958, he ceased working on 30 June 1960. A man of medium height and solid build, he appeared on first meeting to be a dour, hard-headed, canny Scot. Once his confidence had been won, however, he turned out to be warm, kindly and approachable, with a puckish sense of humour. He died on 22 September 1972 at Clayfield, and was cremated with Presbyterian forms. His estate was sworn for probate at $105 497; childless, he made bequests to family members and Scottish charities, and left the residue to the Presbyterian Church for St Andrew's War Memorial Hospital, Brisbane, and to the Library Board of Queensland.

Changing Patterns in Entomology (Brisb, 1974); *Qld Agr J*, 25, no 2, 1926, p 104, 37, no 5, 1932, p 262; Entomological Soc of Qld, *News Bulletin*, no 90, 1972, p 21; J. C. Gill, 'Robert Veitch 1890-1972', *Qld Heritage*, 3, no 10, 1979, p 4; Veitch personal file, RS14417/1/277, A/54249 PSB 7883 (QA).

J. C. H. GILL*
PETER L. LLOYD

VENNING, FRANK OSMOND (1876-1968), organizer of lifesaving, was born on 29 July 1876 at Shoreditch, London, son of Frank Venning, cigar-dealer, and his wife Frances Ann, née Strawson. Educated locally, Frank won numerous swimming and diving competitions. He and a friend rescued a couple from a boating accident on the River Lea, a tributary of the Thames. After meeting William Henry, founder of the (Royal) Life Saving Society, Frank joined his squad of six which toured England in 1894 giving displays of diving, lifesaving and scientific swimming. He worked in a government office for six months, then resigned to go to sea; in 1895 he reputedly saved a sailor who had fallen overboard.

On 24 April 1899 at St Bartholomew's Church of England, Dalston, London, Venning married Henrietta Smith. They travelled to Western Australia, arriving at Albany in the *Orient* on 2 June that year. After a failed business venture they returned to England, and Venning was employed as a gas-fitter. He was persuaded by Frank Springfield of Queensland and (Sir) Frank Beaurepaire [q.v.7], whom he met at the London Olympic Games in 1908, to migrate again to Australia. The Vennings and their three children reached Brisbane in the *Orotava* on 31 December 1908; three more children were born in Queensland. Manager (1909-15) of the Booroodabin baths, Fortitude Valley, he introduced water polo, diving and lifesaving.

In 1910 Venning helped to reorganize the defunct Queensland head centre of the Royal Life Saving Society; he was to serve (1910-15, 1920-47) as secretary. In 1912 he obtained his R.L.S.S. bronze medal, instructor's certificate and award of merit. After three young men drowned at Southport that year, a reel, line and belt were installed on the beach; Venning arranged a demonstration of the equipment and helped to train teams in its use. He tried cane-farming (1915-17) on the Maroochy

River, and established (1915) a branch of the R.L.S.S. at Maroochydore. By the early 1920s he was lessee of the Ithaca baths, Brisbane. He and others launched lifesaving branches at Mooloolaba (1923) and Alexandra Headland (1924); with Joe Betts he formed clubs from the south coast to Cairns.

In 1930 Venning was a founder of the Queensland State centre of the Surf Life Saving Association of Australia; the new group and the R.L.S.S. agreed that year that the S.L.S.A.A. would supervise the patrolling of surf beaches and the R.L.S.S. would control lifesaving activities in inland waters, bays and estuaries. Venning served as Queensland secretary (1930-34), chief examiner (1930-31) and vice-president (1934-46, 1953-55) of the S.L.S.A.A. As an instructor he introduced lifesaving into state primary and secondary schools. He convened meetings, prepared demonstrations, arranged examinations, allocated instructors for classes and judges for competitions, reviewed and investigated new methods of resuscitation, and selected teams for interstate competitions. In World War II he trained service personnel in swimming and lifesaving, and lectured part time in the department of physical education, University of Queensland.

Venning retired as manager of the Ithaca baths, and by 1947 had moved to Mooloolaba. President (1954-57) of the Mooloolaba Surf Life Saving Club, he was awarded (1961) life membership of the S.L.S.A.A., and was appointed M.B.E. in 1963. During his lifetime he had received all the awards of the R.L.S.S. including the distinguished service medal with bronze and silver bars. He was a life governor of its London and Queensland centres. Survived by his wife, their three daughters and two of their three sons, he died on 26 July 1968 in Brisbane and was cremated.

J. R. Winders, *Surf Life Saving in Queensland* (Brisb, 1970); J. Downes, *Royal Life* (Syd, 1993); R. Longhurst, *Mooloolaba Surf Lifesaving Club* (Mooloolaba, Qld, 1997), and *Preserving Lives, Preserving Values* (Brisb, 2000); Surf Life Saving Assn of Aust (Qld), *Annual Report*, 1979-80; State Govt Insurance Office, *Insurance Lines*, 63, no 2, Dec 1981, p 17; *Courier-Mail*, 27 Oct, 14 Dec 1910.

TED TURNER

VERCO, DAVID JAMES ARMOUR (1913-1972), educationist, was born on 22 December 1913 at Dulwich Hill, Sydney, son of Australian-born parents Clement Armour Verco, medical practitioner, and his wife Isabel Scott, née Hunter. David was educated at Stanmore Public and Fort Street Boys' High schools, at Teachers College and at the University of Sydney (B.A., 1934; Dip.Ed., 1935; M.A., 1937). In 1935 he was seconded for two years from the Department of Education to the Australian Council for Educational Research (founded 1930), based in Melbourne. Next year he played a significant role in developing and standardizing group-intelligence tests on a large representative sample of students from Australian state schools and in collecting information on the training of teachers in Australia.

On his return to Sydney in 1937, Verco was sent to Fort Street Boys' High School to undertake counselling and teaching duties. After a few months he was seconded as assistant to the research officer (Sir) Harold Wyndham in the Department of Education. At Canterbury, Melbourne, on 29 March 1938 Verco married Marjory Irene Gordon Hare with the forms of the Churches of Christ. He was promoted acting research officer in 1943 and principal research and guidance officer in 1947. Assistant (from 1953) to Wyndham, the new director-general of education, he was appointed director of teacher training (1958), deputy director-general of education (1963), associate director-general (1968) and director-general (1969).

A committed and far-sighted reformer, Verco exerted considerable influence on the school system in New South Wales through his liberal views on the function of education. He expanded the system of educational guidance that Wyndham had brought to public schools and introduced procedures for the formal training of school counsellors. His high ideals for teachers were revealed in his chapter on the profession in *The Foundations of Education* (1962). He oversaw the extension of pre-service training and the establishment of in-service courses for teachers. The broadly based Education Advisory Commission of New South Wales was established in 1970, and curriculum development was enhanced with the establishment of a directorate of studies in 1971.

Verco served a four-year term on the Australian Council for Educational Research and established two educational research centres within the Department of Education. In 1970 he was appointed to the Commonwealth government's newly established Australian Advisory Committee on Research and Development in Education. An accomplished public speaker, he published several significant articles, including 'Psychological Services in Education Departments' (*Australian Journal of Psychology*, 1958). He lectured part time (1960-72) in the department of education at the University of Sydney, and was a member (from 1966) of the board of governors of the New South Wales State Conservatorium of Music, a fellow (1969-72) of the senate of the University of Sydney and a councillor (1969-72) of Macquarie University.

At a national level, Verco received many requests for his services. Travel grants enabled him to study educational administration and the training and accreditation of teachers in North America and Britain in 1958 and 1963. He reviewed educational services in the Territory of Papua and New Guinea in 1966 for the Commonwealth government, and represented Australia at the United Nations Educational, Scientific and Cultural Organization's conference (1958) and its International Conference on Educational Planning (1968), both held in Paris.

Verco enjoyed golf, tennis and walking, and had an absorbing interest in music. He was an active churchgoer, an elder and organist at the North Turramurra Church of Christ. Suffering from coronary arteriosclerosis, he retired early in 1972, but continued to work on governing bodies involved in research and higher education. He died on 18 August that year at his Mosman home and was cremated; his wife, and their two daughters and two sons survived him. Progressive and constructive in his educational views, and courteous and dignified in manner, Verco was highly respected among Australian educationists for his intellect and his administrative ability. (Sir) Charles Cutler, the State's minister for education, praised his 'capacity for precise analysis and decision, and his respect for opposing points of view'.

W. M. O'Neil, *A Century of Psychology in Australia* (Syd, 1987); *Fortian*, 1972, p 10; *SMH*, 8 Jan 1969, 6 Aug 1971, 6 Jan, 3, 19 Aug 1972; W. L. J. O'Reilly, A Study of the Development of Guidance in New South Wales State Schools (M.Ed. thesis, Univ Syd, 1964); J. Lewis, A History of the Development of the Division of Guidance and Special Education, in the Education Department in New South Wales (M.Ed. long essay, Univ Syd, 1978); staff records (NSW Dept of Education, Syd); information from Mrs M. Verco, Cherrybrook, NSW; personal knowledge.

DON SPEARRITT

VERNON, BARBARA MARY (1916-1978), playwright, was born on 25 July 1916 at Inverell, New South Wales, fourth and youngest child of native-born parents Murray Menzies Vernon, medical practitioner, and his wife Constance Emma Elliott, née Barling. Barbara was educated at the New England Girls' School, Armidale. A 'voracious reader', she worked in the Inverell Municipal Library before joining the Women's Auxiliary Australian Air Force on 18 February 1943. She served in the Directorate of Training, Air Force Headquarters, Melbourne, and rose to temporary corporal before her discharge on 12 April 1946.

Returning to Inverell, Vernon became an announcer with Northern Broadcasters Ltd's radio station 2NZ. Her wish to broadcast local drama led her to form the 2NZ Dramatic Club.

As the club could not afford to pay royalties to authors, necessity drove her to write plays herself. Her energy kept Inverell theatre vigorous for more than a decade, although she recorded, with mild exasperation, perennial artistic disputes among the company.

In September 1956 (Dame) Doris Fitton staged Vernon's play *Naked Possum*, set in the Malayan jungle, at the Independent Theatre, Sydney. Next year Vernon gained attention when *The Multi-Coloured Umbrella* won second prize in the Sydney Journalists' Club's competition for new Australian works. It was produced at the Little Theatre, Melbourne, and by J. C. Williamson [q.v.6] Ltd at the Theatre Royal, Sydney, that year. The play explored tensions over money and sex within a happy-go-lucky family of bookmakers in the showy, robust suburbia of the *nouveau riche*. In January 1958 a member of the New South Wales Legislative Assembly protested that its subject matter was unsuitable for general viewing after the Australian Broadcasting Commission had presented the play on television.

Publicity photographs from the late 1950s show Barbara Vernon with firm, even features below arched brows and a high forehead. In her notebooks she recorded sharp, satiric observations on people encountered by chance. Her formula for a successful play included a good title and 'an upper middle class country town setting'. Among her other works were *The Passionate Pianist* (Hobart, 1958) and the radio serial 'The Questing Heart'. For relaxation, she wrote 'swashbuckling plays with lots of action' for children: at least five were staged at the Independent.

In 1959 Barbara and her widowed mother moved to Cremorne, Sydney. After working as a freelance writer, in 1961 she gained employment with the A.B.C. as a play reader (script editor from 1965) with the drama and features department. In addition to duties as reader and editor, she wrote hundreds of scripts for both television and radio. She was script editor for the television serial (1973) of Ethel Turner's [q.v.12] *Seven Little Australians* and she contributed to a television serial in the mid-1970s, 'Certain Women'.

Vernon achieved her greatest acclaim when she wrote the early scripts for 'Bellbird', a television serial about life in a rural community, which ran (1967-77) four nights per week, for fifteen minutes before the evening news. Described by one critic as 'not so much a drama as a reassuring habit', 'Bellbird' nonetheless had an audience of nearly two million by 1972. Vernon published two novels, *Bellbird* (1970) and *A Big Day at Bellbird* (1972). The film *Country Town* (1971) was based on *Bellbird*. Residents of Inverell assumed, with varying emotions, that their own lives and foibles could be found in the denizens of Bellbird, an accusation that she always denied.

Although she chronicled in her notes a series of passionate entanglements, Barbara Vernon never married. She retired from the A.B.C. in 1976 and purchased the Old Parsonage at Cassilis. While visiting Sydney she died of cardiomyopathy on 16 April 1978 at St Vincent's Hospital, Darlinghurst. She was buried with Anglican rites in Northern Suburbs cemetery.

L. Rees, *The Making of Australian Drama* (Syd, 1973); K. S. Inglis, *This is the ABC* (Melb, 1983); H. Radi (ed), *200 Australian Women* (Syd, 1988); E. Wiedemann, *Holding its Own* (Inverell, NSW, 1998); *ABC Weekly*, 13 Nov 1957; *SMH*, 9 Sept 1956, 19 Feb, 6, 11 Nov 1957, 31 Jan 1958, 2 Oct 1967; *Sun* (Syd), 22 Nov 1967; *Inverell Times*, 18 Apr 1978; Vernon papers (ML); staff record (ABC Archives, Syd).

JANE CONNORS

VIAL, LEIGH GRANT (1909-1943), patrol officer and coastwatcher, was born on 28 February 1909 at Camberwell, Melbourne, eldest of four sons of Victorian-born parents Stanley Browning Vial, school proprietor, and his wife Mary, née Smith. Educated at Wesley College, Leigh worked in retail stores before beginning a commerce degree at the University of Melbourne in 1932. In November that year he applied to be a cadet patrol officer in the Mandated Territory of New Guinea. Stocky, self-reliant, quiet and earnest, he was one of ten chosen from 1659 applicants, and in June 1933 was sent to Morobe District.

In August-October 1934 Vial accompanied assistant district officer Gerry Keogh in chasing the murderer Ludwig Schmidt through unexplored country between the Lai and Sau rivers in the western Highlands. Vial attended a patrol officers' course at the University of Sydney in February-August 1935. Judged 'very solid and thoughtful', he was promoted patrol officer on 7 June. He returned to Morobe and was posted first to Otibanda then in July 1936 to Buki, south of Finschhafen.

At Salamaua on 26 November 1936 he married Marjorie Kathleen Strangward in a civil ceremony. They went to Buki, but Leigh was rarely at home, patrolling for months in the mountains. He was transferred to Salamaua in late 1937 and Madang in June 1938, and on 31 August 1940 was made assistant district officer, Rabaul. On 15 August 1938 he had become the first European to climb Mount Wilhelm, the Territory's highest peak, and during his town postings he wrote fifteen articles on the peoples of Morobe and the Highlands, most for *Walkabout* or *Oceania*.

A day before the Japanese occupied Rabaul on 23 January 1942, Vial led one hundred ground crew of No.24 Squadron, Royal Australian Air Force, to Put Put on the east coast of New Britain, where two flying boats took them to Townsville, Queensland. He was appointed pilot officer, R.A.A.F., on 28 January and assigned to coastwatching in New Guinea. Reaching Salamaua on 20 February, he took his cumbersome teleradio inland, and on 28 February, his thirty-third birthday, he and two New Guineans set up an observation post looking north-east over Salamaua and Lae. He wrote later that O.P.s should be positioned in terrain that confused radio direction-finders, and have well-concealed lines of withdrawal, cloud-free views and a water supply.

New Guineans pronounced Vial's name 'Well'; his post became 'Well's O-Pip'. From it his clear, calm voice sent as many as nine messages a day on the weather and on Japanese aircraft, ship and troop movements. He was nicknamed 'Golden Voice', and an American pilot was to recall, 'we all felt a closeness to him'. In the dank jungle, constantly wet, beset by leeches and mosquitoes, he suffered tinea so badly that he had to crawl to send reports. The Japanese attempted to bribe local people to betray him, and two patrols passed under the tree in which he was hiding, but he remained until 12 June, when he moved closer to Salamaua to get under cloud. The new post was extremely dangerous, and on 24 June Vial suspected that a Japanese aeroplane had located it. He moved to what became known as Vial's O.P., and later admitted to a 'bad scare' once a week on average. On 28 July he was promoted flying officer, but poor food, privation and the constant use of binoculars were blinding him, and he was relieved on 11 August. He walked to Wau in two days, then flew to Port Moresby. His intelligence officer reported that 'not on any single occasion did he neglect to get his messages through'. For his 'extraordinary heroism' he was awarded (1942) the United States' Distinguished Service Cross, that country's second highest bravery decoration and its highest for non-citizens.

On leave in August-November 1942, Vial wrote a handbook on jungle survival. He then took command of the Port Moresby section of the Far East Liaison Office, which made propaganda broadcasts, dropped leaflets—some of which Vial wrote—and supplied allied patrols in Japanese-occupied territory. In January 1943 he was promoted flight lieutenant, but on 30 April, on a supply drop, the Liberator carrying him crashed near Bena Bena in the Highlands. All twelve on board were killed. Their bodies were recovered and buried in Lae war cemetery. Vial's wife, and their son and two daughters, who had been evacuated to Melbourne, survived him.

D. Dexter, *The New Guinea Offensives* (Canb, 1961); D. Gillison, *Royal Australian Air Force 1939-1942* (Canb, 1962); R. Piper, *The Hidden Chapters* (Melb, 1995); J. Sinclair, *Golden Gateway* (Bathurst, NSW, 1998); *Stand-To* (Canb), 6, no 6, Nov 1958-Jan 1959, p 3; *SMH*, 15 Apr 1944; J. R. Black papers, MS 8346, series 2, folder 2 (NL); A518, item E852/1/5 (NAA, Canb); information from Mrs L. Gilham, Brighton, Melb, Mr R. K. Piper, Higgins, Canb, and Mr J. Sinclair, Alexandra Headland, Qld.

BILL GAMMAGE

VICKERS, PATRICK JOHN (1935-1968), naval officer, was born on 28 June 1935 in Brisbane. At the age of 8 he was adopted by Frank Vickers, foreman, and his wife Annie Agnes, née Cornhill, both Queenslanders. Pat was a good student at Nambour High School, and also at Gatton Agricultural High School and College where he obtained diplomas in agriculture (1952), animal husbandry (1953) and horticulture (1954). After attending the Teachers' Training College, Brisbane, he taught at Gatton (1953-54) then at Warwick High School (1955). He also studied part time at the University of Queensland (B.Com., 1964). On 6 January 1956 he joined the Royal Australian Navy for aircrew training. Achieving a 'special distinction in ground subjects', he graduated as a pilot in May 1957. That month he was promoted acting sub-lieutenant and granted a short-service commission. Following operational flying training at the Naval Air Station, Nowra, New South Wales, he qualified on 20 December 1957 as a fighter-pilot in Sea Fury aircraft.

In March 1959 Vickers was promoted lieutenant. Having learned to fly jet aircraft in all weathers, he was posted in July to No.805 Squadron which operated Sea Venoms from the Naval Air Station and periodically from the aircraft-carrier H.M.A.S. *Melbourne*. Vickers accepted a permanent commission in 1961. Switching to helicopters, he was sent to Britain where he completed a helicopter flying-instructor's course then spent two years (1962-64) on exchange with the Royal Navy, gaining experience and training other pilots. He became very proficient at both flying and teaching.

Returning to Australia, Vickers served at Nowra and at sea in *Melbourne*. He made frequent rescue flights from the naval air station. On the night of 20/21 May 1966 he searched fruitlessly for survivors after the dredge *W. D. Atlas* sank off Jervis Bay. Next morning he tried again and plucked from huge seas two of only four crewmen saved; thirteen others died. On 22 March 1967 he was promoted lieutenant commander. Later that year he helped to form the R.A.N. Helicopter Flight Vietnam. Consisting of eight pilots, four observers and support staff, the R.A.N.H.F.V. joined the United States Army's 135th Assault Helicopter Company at Vung Tau, Republic of Vietnam (South Vietnam), in October.

Vickers was assigned as commander of the company's 1st Platoon, responsible for twenty-two pilots and eleven new Iroquois UH-1H aircraft. He was also appointed senior instructor-pilot of the 222nd Combat Aviation Battalion, of which the 135th A.H.C. formed part. The company began operational flying at an intense rate. On 19 December 1967 Vickers led his platoon, with U.S. Army troops on board, against a battalion of the People's Liberation Armed Forces (Viet Cong) which was well dug in, near Long Binh. The action continued late into the night and featured Vickers' platoon flying in and out of the contact zone, landing reinforcements and recovering the wounded. Artillery units and helicopter gunships gave covering fire but the troop-carriers still faced grave risks. For his leadership throughout the engagement, Vickers was recommended for both American and Australian bravery awards.

The 135th A.H.C. moved to the American Black Horse base, south of Xuan Loc, in December 1967. While Vickers' helicopters were landing soldiers near My Tho on 8 February 1968, they met a hail of fire from the ground at the critical moment of troop-disembarkation. One aircraft was destroyed and seven of the remaining eight were damaged. Again, Vickers displayed courage and determination as platoon commander. On 22 February 1968 he was descending to land near Xuan Loc when his aircraft, leading the fleet of eleven helicopters, came under small-arms fire and he was hit in the head. His co-pilot immediately flew to the hospital pad at Black Horse, but Vickers died that day and was cremated. One of the R.A.N.'s most accomplished aviators and widely respected, he was posthumously mentioned in dispatches.

S. Eather, *Get the Bloody Job Done* (Syd, 1998); J. Grey, *Up Top* (Syd, 1998); *Sun-Herald* (Syd), 22 May 1966; *Courier-Mail*, 24 Feb, 17 Sept 1968; *Gatton Star*, 7 Mar 1968; personal knowledge.

NEIL RALPH

VICKERY, EBENEZER FRANK (1880-1970), solicitor and philanthropist, was born on 12 January 1880 at Burburgate, near Gunnedah, New South Wales, son of Ebenezer Vickery, a general manager from Sydney, and his wife Ellen Jane, née Firth, who was born at Vava'u, Friendly Islands (Tonga), the daughter of missionaries. Ebenezer Vickery [q.v.6] was his grandfather and Joyce Vickery [q.v.] his cousin.

Educated at Sydney Grammar School and the University of Sydney (B.A., 1901; LL.B., 1904), Frank was articled to Arthur Wigram Allen of Allen, Allen [qq.v.1,3] & Hemsley and admitted as a solicitor on 19 November 1904.

He belonged to the Sydney Rowing Club in the early 1900s and played for Waverley Cricket Club's second XI in 1908-09. At the Methodist Church, Bondi, on 2 July 1908 he married Ethel Agnes Rabbitts (d.1956); they were to have three children. In 1910-13 he was a member of Woollahra Municipal Council.

By 1908 Vickery had established his own firm in Vickery's Chambers. He later practised with various partners (including G. H. Wilson and R. J. B. Parkhill), operating from the Australasia Chambers, Martin Place. A shareholder (1902-39) in the public company, E. Vickery & Sons Ltd, merchants, colliery proprietors and graziers, he was appointed a director of the Alliance Assurance Co. Ltd in 1938.

Like his father and grandfather, and many other family members, Vickery was committed to Methodism. For forty years he was superintendent of the Sunday school at the Bondi Wesleyan Church. In 1910 he joined the committee of the Young Men's Christian Association. While serving on the general (from 1913) and executive (from 1921) committees of the Central Methodist Mission, he took part in the wider work of the Methodist Connexion in New South Wales. He was a councillor (1915-69) and benefactor of Wesley College, honorary solicitor to the C.M.M. and a member of the Lyceum Trust.

Vickery's share of his family's wealth enabled him to continue the generous benefactions to the Methodist Church begun by his grandfather. He donated Edina, the family home at Waverley, for use as a hospital; it was opened as the War Memorial Hospital in 1921 and Vickery was, at times, its honorary secretary. In 1941 he bought eleven acres (4.5 ha) at Sylvania on which the C.M.M. established a retirement village; it was re-named the Frank Vickery Village in 1962. He claimed to have been motivated in his work, both in the law and in the Church, by the 'desire for common justice for the greatest number and by Christian idealism'.

Frugal in his personal habits, Vickery reputedly had an allowance of 2s. 6d. a week while he was an articled clerk. He belonged to the University Club (from 1909) and enjoyed gardening. His family life was marked by tragedy: his younger son, Major Ian Vickery, Australian Army Medical Corps, was killed in action on 27 November 1942 in Papua and his daughter Mary died of a blood clot in 1947. Survived by his elder son, Vickery died on (or about) 9 July 1970 at his Bellevue Hill home and was buried in South Head cemetery.

W. C. O'Reilly, *Wesley College (within the University of Sydney)* (Syd, 1956); D. Wright, *Mantle of Christ* (Brisb, 1984); D. Wright and E. G. Clancy, *The Methodists* (Syd, 1993); Central Methodist Mission (Syd), *Annual Report*, 1906-57; *Methodist* (Syd),

11 Jan, 26 July 1919, 12 Feb 1921, 25 Nov 1922, 8 Mar 1924, 20 Apr 1935; *SMH*, 12 Jan 1970; Vickery papers (ML).   PATRICIA CURTHOYS

VICKERY, JOYCE WINIFRED (1908-1979), botanist and conservationist, was born on 15 December 1908 at Strathfield, Sydney, youngest of four children of native-born parents George Begg Vickery, merchant, and his wife Elizabeth Alice Adeline, née Rossbach (d.1923). Her father was an amateur microscopist and a member of the Royal Society of New South Wales. Ebenezer Vickery [q.v.6] was her grandfather and Frank Vickery [q.v.] her cousin. Joyce was educated at the Methodist Ladies' College, Burwood, and the University of Sydney (B.Sc., 1931; M.Sc., 1933; D.Sc., 1959). In 1931 she was appointed demonstrator in botany. While at university, she held (1931-36) a science research scholarship, joined the Linnean (1930) and Royal (1935) societies of New South Wales, and was a founder (1930) and president (1934) of the Sydney University Biology Society.

Miss Vickery enjoyed camping and outdoor life, and spent much of her holidays engaged in field-work with her colleagues. In 1931 she and her close friend in the Department of Agriculture, Lilian Ross Fraser, bought a second-hand 1926 Chevrolet Tourer and explored the upper Williams River and Barrington Tops. From these trips, they published a series of pioneering ecological papers. Vickery was offered the post of assistant botanist at the National Herbarium of New South Wales in August 1936: she refused £188 a year, insisted on being paid according to her qualifications, and negotiated a salary of £251. Thereafter she conducted long-running battles with the Public Service Board over equal pay.

Believing systematics to be fundamental to all botanical work, Vickery led a revival of taxonomic research. In 1937-38 she spent a year (largely self-funded) at the Royal Botanic Gardens, Kew, London. Following her return, she trained a new generation of professional systematists. In 1939 she persuaded Robert Anderson [q.v.13] to publish a journal, *Contributions from the New South Wales National Herbarium*. As its editor, she displayed a 'gift for lucid expression' and carried out her duties 'with studied diplomacy', but sometimes felt it necessary 'almost to rewrite another's work'. During World War II she joined the National Emergency Services as an ambulance driver.

Vickery's major research interest centred on the revision of Australian grass species, the *Gramineae*, that were notoriously difficult to classify. Her work was meticulous and painstaking, characterized by fine attention to detail, rigorous pursuit of historical information and a careful, even-handed approach to opposing arguments. Her methods were conservative and empirical: she saw morphology as the primary basis for taxonomy, but respected new theoretical and technical approaches.

At the herbarium Vickery gave generously of her time in identifying specimens for a wide range of clients. Sometimes she came to public notice for her forensic services. Her identification of plant fragments on the suspect's car and clothing led to the conviction in 1961 of Stephen Leslie Bradley [q.v.13] for the kidnapping and murder of Graeme Thorne. She worked tirelessly to reconstruct the herbarium as a modern scientific research institution, to raise standards, to organize and extend its library and specimen collections, and to initiate and edit its publications, including a new *Flora of New South Wales* (1971-84).

Acutely conscious of the need for conservation, Vickery supported John Tipper's [q.v.] Muogamarra Sanctuary, served as a trustee of the Elouera Bushland Reserve and campaigned in the 1960s for the preservation of the fragile ecology of Kosciusko State Park, for which she produced (at her own expense) an extensive report on grazing and erosion. In 1959 she gained a doctorate of science for her revision of the genus *Poa* in Australia. She was appointed M.B.E. in 1962 and awarded the (W. B.) Clarke [q.v.3] medal by the local Royal Society in 1964. Promoted to senior botanist that year, she retired in 1968, but continued her research. In 1973-79 she was honorary research fellow at the herbarium. As honorary treasurer (1971-78) of the Linnean Society, she tried to improve its finances.

Reserved and formal in her personal style and conservative in her values, Dr Vickery was good humoured, modest, tolerant of others and an independent thinker. She abandoned religious belief early in her career. Imbued with her family's ethics of self-discipline, loyalty and public service, she was generous in her professional and financial support of others, and, although wealthy, chose to live within her earned income. When she felt herself to be right, she was blunt and outspoken. Declaring in childhood that 'she didn't want any man hanging on to *her* coat-tails', she never married and lived sustained by a few deep friendships. She died of cancer on 29 May 1979 at her Cheltenham home and was cremated. The Linnean Society, which benefited from her generosity, named its research fund after her.

H. Radi (ed), *200 Australian Women* (Syd, 1988); Roy Soc of NSW, *J and Procs*, 97, 1964, p 227, 113, 1980, p 104; NSW Dept Agriculture, *Telopea*, 2, no 1, 1980, p 1; *SMH*, 27 July 1934, 2 Sept 1936, 18 Feb, 24 May 1958, 26 Apr 1959, 2 June 1962, 16 Jan 1963,

17 May 1966, 4 Jan 1968, 8 June 1979; Vickery papers (National Herbarium of NSW Archives, Syd); information from Mrs V. Jones, North Epping, and Dr B. Briggs, Syd.   CLAIRE HOOKER

VOSS, HARRIETTE MARTHA (1887-1951), medical practitioner and community worker, was born on 10 October 1887 at Fortitude Valley, Brisbane, youngest of five children of Robert Skerritt Exton, an artist from England, and his Irish-born wife Rose, née Robinson. Rose was a cousin of Sir Hercules Robinson [q.v.6]. Ettie studied at Brisbane Girls' Grammar School and the University of Sydney (M.B., Ch.M, 1915). She was appointed resident medical officer at the Royal Alexandra Hospital for Children, Camperdown, in March 1915 and promoted chief R.M.O. next year. On 8 July 1919 at Holy Trinity Church, Fortitude Valley, she married with Anglican rites Paul Ernest Voss, a medical practitioner. They had one child.

In partnership with his father Francis Voss [q.v.12], Paul practised at Penmaen, Bolsover Street, Rockhampton, and also treated patients at Hillcrest, a private hospital owned by the family. His wife did not practise medicine after her marriage. Living at Penmaen and later at another family home, Securus, on the coast at Tanby Point, Emu Park, she involved herself in community activities. After being patroness (1920) of the Rockhampton Young Women's Christian Association, she served as its honorary treasurer (1922-25) and president (1933-51). Under her direction, the local Y.W.C.A. provided accommodation for, at times, an average of twenty-five servicewomen a week during World War II and formed a club for the wives of servicemen from the United States of America. Rest and refreshment facilities at the association's rooms were open to working women and girls, and to families of Australian armed-services personnel and civilians.

Throughout the war years Mrs Voss worked for the Australian Red Cross Society at Rockhampton. In 1942-45 she presided over the entertainment committee of the local branch of the American National Red Cross, staging concerts and acting as hostess at dances. She helped to form the women's auxiliary of the Rockhampton and District Patriotic Fund and held the office of organizing secretary. The auxiliary raised money for comforts for those serving overseas, dispatching nine thousand parcels in a single year. It also provided supplementary income to their families, if they were in need. At the Patriotic Fund depot women provided regular farewell luncheons for drafts of more than one hundred soldiers about to embark on active service. They organized entertainment for American and other allied troops, and operated a free canteen at the aerodrome for travelling personnel. As a representative of 'local patriotic bodies', Voss was introduced to Mrs Eleanor Roosevelt, wife of the president of the United States, who visited American troops stationed at Rockhampton in September 1943.

After her husband died in 1948, Voss became manager of Hillcrest hospital. In 1951 ill health forced her to resign that post, as well as her presidency of the Y.W.C.A. She died of cancer on 20 December that year at Emu Park and was cremated; her son survived her. According to her wish, Hillcrest was acquired by St Andrew's Presbyterian Church. The Harriette M. Voss clubrooms, in a new Y.W.C.A. building in Bolsover Street, were opened in 1955.

L. McDonald, *Rockhampton* (Brisb, 1981) and *A Ministry of Caring* (Rockhampton, Qld, 1992); *Morning Bulletin*, 21 Sept 1945, 26 Dec 1951; Voss family papers *and* YWCA (Rockhampton) papers (Capricornia Collection, Central Qld Univ L).

BETTY COSGROVE

VREPONT, BRIAN; *see* TRUEBRIDGE, BENJAMIN ARTHUR

VROLAND, ANTON WILLIAM RUTHERFORD (1874-1957), educationist, and ANNA FELLOWES (1902-1978), schoolteacher and human-rights advocate, were husband and wife. Anton was born on 12 September 1874 at Gledefield, near Ararat, Victoria, eldest of at least nine children of Carl Häkam Ferdinand Vroland, a schoolteacher from Sweden, and his Victorian-born wife Janet Huntley, née Scott. Educated at the rural schools where his father taught and at Trinity Grammar School, Maldon, he became a student teacher at Daylesford State School in 1892. He gained his certificate at the Melbourne Training College next year. Beginning at small country schools, he was a head teacher of primary schools for the whole of his career, except while studying for a diploma of education at the University of Melbourne in 1910-11.

Bingomunjie (1894-98) and Dales Creek (1898-1900) were Vroland's first two schools. Influenced by his reading, the views of his father, demonstrations he witnessed of 'discovery' teaching, and his reactions to rigid practice-classes at college, he investigated the methods of the 'new education'. His pedagogical thinking was based on the concepts of the integrated primary school syllabus, and the pupil as the centre of all engagement in and beyond the classroom. A 'visionary [with] a hard practical core', he believed that teaching should create 'a climate of delight' in a classroom, and, if this were accomplished, education would not need to be compulsory. Such views, consistent with progressive practices in Europe and the United States of America, were novel in Victoria.

At Strathbogie North (1901-06) and Allambee East (1906-10), Vroland experimented with 'practical' arithmetic, spelling and reading reforms, and nature lessons in the bush. Not all inspectors and parents approved of his methods, though at Allambee East the inspector was so enthralled by his teaching that he dispatched long reports to Frank Tate [q.v.12], the director of education. Tate encouraged Vroland to write a series of graded texts, the Austral Grammars, which made extensive use of Australian examples and applied, possibly for the first time, the inductive method to language development. The textbooks were published in 1908-13 and later revised. In her mother's home at Toorak, Melbourne, on 3 January 1906 Vroland had married with Methodist forms Marion Ellen Bryant (d.1932), a schoolteacher; they had no children.

Vroland then taught at Elmore (1912-17), Dimboola (1918-23) and Elsternwick, Melbourne (1923-39). A Rechabite and a Freemason, he was also a member of the Australian Natives' Association, and a supporter of mechanics' institutes and free libraries. While at Dimboola, he campaigned for improved living conditions of Aborigines. President (1919) and a long-serving councillor of the Victorian State Schools Teachers' Union, he was a member (1921) of the first national council of the Australian Teachers' Federation. From 1917 he published privately the *Program* as a practical aid for teachers. The periodical (retitled the *Teachers' Journal* in 1924) became the official organ of the Victorian Teachers' Union, which he helped to form in 1926. He also championed fairer inspectorial methods and equal pay for women teachers. As the union's representative he served on the State Schools' Horticultural Society, the State Schools' Relief Committee and the curriculum revision committees of 1920 and 1932. In 1938 he was a founder of the Education Reform Association.

Transforming Elsternwick State School into a beacon of progressive education, Vroland instituted an opportunity class, pioneered the use of film as a teaching aid, set up a central library, taught foreign languages, and—as he had done in the bush—divided the school's grounds into sections for playground, cultivated garden and natural habitat. Inspectors' reports recognized the 'vitality' of his initiatives. Former students recalled that 'we were always happy'. As secretary (1936-55) of Charles Strong's [q.v.6] Australian Church, Vroland was involved in the peace movement and in penal and child-welfare reform. His executive-membership of the Vic-

torian chapter of the New Education Fellowship reactivated his interest in Aboriginal advancement. Retiring from the Education Department in September 1939, he returned to the classroom as a 'wartime retread'.

In 1941 Vroland formulated the Victorian Labor Party's platform on education. He popularized his curriculum reforms at public meetings, in lectures and in the press. When young, he had been a good sportsman. At Bingomunjie he had broken horses, and in his sixties he rode with a party from Briagalong to Omeo. He was tall and slim with a long face, strong jaw, thick brown hair (later a distinguished grey) and dense moustache. Pupils and student-teachers had regarded him with awe, but never feared him, and came to appreciate his wry sense of humour and passion for teaching. To those who lamented his lack of public recognition, he said: 'Never mind. My work is of the future'. On 11 January 1947 at the Australian Church, Russell Street, Melbourne, he married Anna Fellowes White. He died on 19 August 1957 at his Box Hill home and was cremated. His estate was sworn for probate at £300.

Anna was born on 7 May 1902 at Ascot Vale, Melbourne, third child of Australian-born parents John White, farmer, and his wife Jane, née Butler. Educated at home by an aunt and at Methodist Ladies' College, Kew, she began teaching at private girls' schools. The most rewarding five years of her life were spent at an experimental primary school at Belgrave. She later taught intermittently in the state school system, and in 1954 at Methodist Ladies' College. In 1961 she was appointed headmistress of Woodstock Girls' School, Albury, New South Wales, but she was dismissed only six months later because of her progressive teaching methods. At the time there were unfounded rumours that she had communist connexions. She finished her teaching career in Melbourne, at Box Hill Girls' Technical School, in 1964.

Miss White's approach to teaching and learning did not always endear her to principals and colleagues. Believing that the purpose of education was to 'lead out from the deeply hidden self whatever potentially is there', she applied this philosophy to all aspects of her life. She was passionate about peace, justice and human rights; her radio talks on international affairs were published as *Who Goes Where?* (Mildura, 1938). Her main concern, however, was the plight of Australia's Aborigines, especially those living in Victoria, most of whom were of mixed descent and so officially considered non-Aboriginal.

From the 1930s White kept in regular contact with many Victorian Aborigines and listened to their views. In 1951 she published, as Vroland, *Their Music Has Roots*, an anthropological analysis of ten songs. She sought to promote a broader definition of Aboriginality, reliant on self-identification rather than physical appearance or the retention of 'traditional' culture. Disheartened by the slow pace of change, she withdrew from her causes in 1957. Her criticism of government assimilation policies and her advocacy of Aboriginal rights anticipated the move towards self-determination in the late 1960s.

Although Mrs Vroland had joined the Women's International League for Peace and Freedom, and the New Education Fellowship, she had little tolerance of people whose ideas differed from her own, and frequently worked alone. She died on 23 April 1978 at Box Hill and was buried in Templestowe cemetery; she had no children.

S. Kerin, *An Attitude of Respect* (Melb, 1999); Vic Teachers' Union (Melb), *Teachers' J*, 51, no 2, Apr 1968; *Educational Magazine*, 31, no 6, 1974; *Sun* (Syd), 11, 14 Aug 1961; *Age* (Melb), 12 Aug 1961; *SMH*, 14, 15 Aug 1961; *Sun News-Pictorial*, 15 Aug 1961; H. J. Lawry, Anton Vroland: His Life and Work (M.Ed. thesis, Monash Univ, 1981); Vroland papers (NL).

ANDREW SPAULL
SITARANI KERIN

W

WADE, HARRIE WALTER (1905-1964), farmer and politician, was born on 10 January 1905 at Clear Lake, Victoria, second child of Harrie Walter Wade, farmer, and his wife Ada Louisa, née Edmonds, both Victorian born. Educated at Horsham State and High schools, young Harrie worked as a schoolteacher and a clerk before moving to Goroke and becoming an accountant. At St John's Church of England, Horsham, on 15 October 1932 he married Olive May Newton, a book-keeper. The couple took up farming on the banks of Natimuk Lake. Wade became active in politics and in 1934 joined the United Country Party. He successfully stood for the Arapiles Shire Council in August 1941 and was elected shire president in 1948 and 1951.

In October 1941 Wade had been appointed president of the newly formed Natimuk Bush Fire Brigade. When a disastrous fire swept through parts of the Wimmera district in 1944, he organized the fire-fighting and clean-up. He was to serve as president of the Victorian Rural Fire Brigades' Association in 1954-58. Keenly interested in land settlement, he unsuccessfully proposed in 1945 the development of an irrigation scheme around Natimuk Lake for returned soldiers.

At the 1949 Federal election Wade stood as the Country Party candidate for the House of Representatives seat of Wimmera. Although defeated by W. R. Lawrence, the Liberal Party candidate, Wade, a staunch opponent of communism and socialism, remarked that he was happy about the election result because the 'main objective was to defeat the Chifley [q.v.13] government'. He was chief president of the Victorian Country Party in 1952-54.

Selling his property at Natimuk Lake in 1954, Wade moved to Horsham and bought a farm nearby. He was president of the Wimmera Band Group, and of the Central Wimmera Football League, vice-president of the Natimuk Agricultural and Pastoral Society and of the Wimmera Trotting Club, and a member of the Horsham State School committee. In 1955-61 he was a Horsham city councillor.

On 10 December 1955 Wade was elected to the Senate; he took his seat on 1 July 1956. He spoke with authority on matters such as the wool and wheat industries, the state of country roads, and the importance of promoting Australian products and developing overseas markets. Aware of the need for Australian producers to be efficient and competitive, he stated that whether 'we produce motor cars, butter, textiles or anything else, the whole world to-day is fighting for markets, and as a young and great trading nation we have to do all we can to meet the situation'. He acknowledged that credit should be made readily available to primary producers and strongly supported the establishment of the Commonwealth Development Bank of Australia, particularly for its potential role in encouraging young men to settle on the land.

Regarding Australia as 'a western outpost of democracy in an Asian area', Wade endorsed the Colombo Plan. He advocated the Agreement on Commerce between Australia and Japan (1957) and in January 1958 joined a parliamentary delegation to Japan which helped to promote understanding and co-operation between the two countries. He stressed the need for Australia to train specialists to represent its interests in Asia.

Wade was appointed successively minister for air on 29 December 1960 and minister for health on 22 December 1961. He believed that a voluntary health insurance scheme based on self-help was 'the most appropriate to our Australian needs and way of life', though he recognized that those less able to help themselves required assistance. He initiated a number of amendments to the National Health Act (1953) to extend hospital benefits. Leader of the Country Party in the Senate from March 1961, he was promoted to the inner cabinet in December 1963.

A 'shrewd, calculating politician' with 'a dry wit' and a 'wry smile', Wade could 'grasp a situation with the alacrity of a panther'. Forceful and sincere, he 'detested intrigue and slyness in every shape and form'. In October 1964 Wade suffered a heart attack while mustering sheep on his property. He died of myocardial infarction on 18 November that year at his Horsham home; he was accorded a state funeral and was buried in the local cemetery. His wife and their son survived him.

A. Lockwood, *Nine Around the Table* (Natimuk, Vic, 1988); PD (Senate), 2 Oct 1957, p 306, 26 Mar 1958, p 375, 21 Oct 1959, p 1100, 23, 24 Aug 1960, pp 161, 171, 15 May 1963, p 460, 14 May 1964, p 1147; *Horsham Times*, 21 Sept 1948, 8 Nov 1949, 14 Sept 1951; *Warracknabeal Herald*, 16 Dec 1949, 11 Nov 1955; *Countryman* (Melb), 11 Nov 1955, 13 Jan, 6 July 1956, 3 Dec 1964.

KATHLEEN DERMODY

WADHAM, SIR SAMUEL MACMAHON (1891-1972), professor of agriculture, was born on 31 October 1891 at Ealing, Middlesex, England, second child of Samuel Thomas Wadham (d.1906), railway agent, and his wife

Mary Louisa Amy, née MacMahon. Aged 69 when his son was born, Wadham senior retired during Samuel's childhood and took his family to Eastbourne, Sussex. From the Boys' Municipal Secondary School, young Samuel won a scholarship to Merchant Taylors' School and the family moved to London in 1904.

Maintaining high scholastic standards, Wadham displayed 'scientific interest and enterprise', and won prizes in history, divinity and English, despite being 'too sententious' and 'fond of moralizing'. He gained colours for cricket, bowling to the great W. G. Grace in a match against the Marylebone Cricket Club in 1910. His coach commented variously that he: 'Has an enormous leg-break and uses his brains well'; cannot 'keep still when batting'; and needs to be 'rather more silent'. Awarded an open entrance scholarship at Christ's College, Cambridge (B.A., 1913; Agr.Dip., 1913; M.A., 1917), he achieved first-class honours in both parts of the natural sciences tripos and participated in the college's debating society, usually taking radical stances. He went to Germany in 1914 to study clover at the University of Hamburg, but returned prematurely, crossing the frontier on 2 August, the day before Germany declared war on France.

That month Wadham enlisted in the British Army. Commissioned in the Durham Light Infantry on 26 February 1915 and promoted temporary captain in September, he was sent to the Wireless Training Centre, near Worcester. From September 1917 he served in the Middle East as a signals officer. He was mentioned in dispatches, modestly fancying that the award was for 'putting an electric light in the Corps Commandant's tent'. At the Catholic Apostolic Church, Gordon Square, London, on 12 April 1919 he married Dorothy Fanny Baylis, a schoolmistress and childhood friend.

The Wadhams moved to Cambridge where Samuel became junior then senior demonstrator in botany. Dorothy ran the Deric House Home School at their residence. Wadham was among young academics, including J. M. (Baron) Keynes, who, wishing to reform university governance, made submissions to the 1920 royal commission on the universities of Oxford and Cambridge. In addition to his teaching, Wadham pursued mycological studies with F. T. Brooks, carried out seminal research on the ecology of the Fens, and collaborated with (Sir) Frank Engledow in establishing the basis of yield variation in cereals. The latter work exhibited a rigorous mathematical approach at a time when the application of statistical method to biology was in its infancy.

In 1925 the University of Melbourne advertised its chair of agriculture. George Swinburne, a member of the university's council, and Sir John MacFarland [qq.v.12,10], the chancellor, were in London in July. On (Sir) Roland Biffen's advice, Swinburne travelled to Cambridge and interviewed Wadham who was loath to let his name go forward unless there was a high chance of success. Swinburne and MacFarland indicated their strong support, and Wadham made an application which was then rejected outright by the selection committee in Melbourne; he was perceived as lacking practical experience. After MacFarland and Swinburne returned to Melbourne, Wadham was unanimously appointed. No Australian professor of agriculture was to understand farmers as well as this Cambridge 'laboratory man'. Wadham stated his plans: 'The production side of agriculture ought to be taught from the biological point of view'. It is 'the economics of agricultural practice ... so badly represented in Cambridge, which I propose to emphasize in Melbourne. I fully realize that for the first year or two I must be more a student there'.

Wadham arrived in Melbourne in September 1926 without his family. He had a five-year appointment only, and Dorothy was attached to Cambridge, her school, and her aged parents. He lived in Queen's College where E. H. Sugden [q.v.12] became his friend and mentor. A. W. Jessep was appointed for 1927 to assist Wadham but otherwise Wadham was the sole academic in the faculty of agriculture; its courses were taught mainly by part-time lecturers from the Victorian Department of Agriculture. He inherited a generalist curriculum which exposed students to a range of disciplines and technologies. The basic structure of the course, with minor changes, was to be maintained over the next thirty years. Wadham travelled the countryside assiduously and soon gained recognition in the farming community. At the request of ex-servicemen, in 1929 he sat as their representative on a State government board dealing with settlement in the Mallee region; he was successful in having the sizes of farms increased.

For some time Wadham had been urging Dorothy to join him in Australia, and she agreed to visit late in 1930. On 19 October, however, her car overturned in a ditch, near Stevenage, Hertfordshire. The Wadhams' daughter and elder son died but their younger son, Ben, survived. Wadham sailed for England, the pain of his slow journey exacerbated by poor health and the absence of any direct word from his wife.

Dorothy and Ben spent most of 1931 in Australia with Wadham who, after a fierce battle, secured university tenure that year. Following another visit to Melbourne in 1934, she decided to make her home in Australia. The Wadhams bought a comfortable house at Parkville where Dorothy engaged in passionate but 'destructive' gardening.

Wadham had considerable influence as an educator. He was highly articulate; in *Who's Who* 'talking' appeared as his sole recreational interest, although in the Australian version he added 'and sleeping'. Usually lecturing extempore, he illustrated his themes with anecdotes and ironic humour. He had an 'inimitable and whimsical style' but spoke with passion, communicating his enthusiasm. Much of his material was informed by a 'dry cynicism'. Students from the country, such as F. J. R. Hird, later recalled the impact of encountering for the first time a teacher whose treatment of questions was open and inquiring. Wadham's mission was to educate students in science as applied to agriculture; his approach was eclectic, thematic, philosophical, and with some biological science woven into the economic and sociological context of agricultural practice. His social conscience, his concern for environmental conservation, and his emphasis on the development of problem-solving skills were explicit.

Conceiving popular education as a primary aspect of his vocation, Wadham was an inveterate journalist and public commentator from his early years in Australia until his old age. Agricultural issues, in the widest sense of the term, were his central preoccupation but he engaged in controversies on other social and philosophical questions. His regular broadcasts led to an immense popular following. Brought up an Anglican, he turned to Methodism in mid-life and became a lay preacher but later returned to Anglicanism.

Wadham gradually attained a high place in university affairs. In 1933 he mediated successfully in a quarrel between the students of Trinity College and their warden (Sir) John Behan [q.v.7]. He conducted a successful campaign to secure the appointment in 1935 of his Cambridge friend (Sir) Raymond Priestley [q.v.11] as the University of Melbourne's first paid vice-chancellor. That year Wadham was elected to the university's council. Acting-chairman of the professorial board in 1936, he was vice-chairman in 1940 and chairman in 1941-43. He became a close friend of (Sir) John Medley [q.v.15] who succeeded Priestley in 1938.

Active on the major committees of the university, Wadham advocated the introduction of examination boards and in World War II facilitated the necessary adjustments to many procedures. When difficult questions arose, he was not usually prominent in debate, reserving his intervention until he could propose a generally acceptable outcome. He was involved in two major controversies: the appointment of J. S. Turner (rather than Ethel McLennan) to the chair of botany, and the council's acceptance of the resignation of T. H. Laby [q.v.9] from the chair of natural philosophy; Laby had resigned as a ploy but Wadham and the council, whose patience had been greatly tested, refused to let him withdraw.

By 1951 the academic staff of the school of agriculture had increased to six. During Wadham's deanship 427 students graduated with bachelors' degrees, 81 with masters' degrees and 4 with doctorates of philosophy. The school building was enlarged in 1956, aided by a substantial donation from Wadham's friend V. Y. Kimpton, a flour-miller. Managing his research funds skilfully, Wadham maintained a small group of research students in a well-run, happy school known for its regional surveys: the basaltic country at Mount Gellibrand, near Colac; the infertile, sandy lands about Berwick; and the rural area of Whittlesea on the fringes of suburban Melbourne. Wadham's emphasis on improving the amenities and circumstances of rural life was to be influential. A social analysis of the country towns of Victoria and a study of living and working conditions on wheat farms were carried out. These were followed by a major investigation of the sheep industry in the west of the State. The production of dried fruit and the marketing of fruit and vegetables also received attention.

Wadham did not make a major contribution to the advancement of any discipline within agricultural science; his achievement was in intellectual synthesis, exemplified by the four editions (1939-64) of *Land Utilization in Australia* which he wrote with G. L. Wood [q.v.]. Land utilization was not a well-established subject in 1939 when the book first appeared. No one had attempted a synoptic account of the factors that determined the evolution of land settlement and a description of its present condition. Wadham and Wood dwelt not only on biological productive capacity but also on economic opportunity: the profitability of rural industry, as compared with the secondary sector and as affected by the terms of world trade. Moreover, they looked forward to the possibilities that might be created by new scientific discoveries. Their book widened perceptions about the diversity of landscapes and farming systems in the country, and heightened a sense of national identity.

An inquiry in 1928 into the dairy industry in the eastern States, on behalf of the Council for Scientific and Industrial Research, had begun Wadham's long record of service on government bodies. He was a member in 1934-35 of Sir Herbert Gepp's [q.v.8] royal commission on the wheat, flour and bread industries, and in 1943-46 of the Commonwealth Rural Reconstruction Commission. The period of the latter assignment was the most strenuous of his life, as he wrestled with the whole gamut of rural problems in Australia; the nature of soldier settlement after the war was one significant outcome. Much of the commission's work fell on Wadham and C. R. Lambert [q.v.15], and the two wrote most of the ten substantial reports.

These reports included a general survey of rural conditions and provided a detailed consideration of the issues involved in land settlement: farm size and suitability, training of settlers, land tenure and valuation. They proposed commercial policies for rural credit, debt adjustment, wages and agricultural marketing. Although they treated the expansion of irrigation with caution, they endorsed the Snowy Mountains scheme. Education figured strongly in their treatment of rural life and amenities, and they noted that advances in agricultural research were crucial to rural progress. The reports had a careful analytical character, based on historical perspectives and statistical data. They stressed above all the need for efficiency in farm production; the extent of the rural population, and even the level of production, were secondary.

Membership of the Commonwealth Immigration Planning Council occupied some of Wadham's time in 1949-62. His signal achievement was the part he played in the defeat of the programme of B. A. Santamaria and the National Catholic Rural Movement to foster Italian peasant migration for small-holder, subsistence settlement.

Wadham was knighted in 1956 and awarded an honorary doctorate of laws at the university's centenary celebrations that year. Retiring in February 1957, he remained active, continuing his journalism and giving his time to such bodies as the Citizens Welfare Service of Victoria, the University of Melbourne's schools board, the Royal Botanic Gardens, the Australian Institute of Agricultural Science, committees of the Commonwealth Scientific and Industrial Research Organization and, in 1961-65, (Sir) Leslie Martin's committee on the future of tertiary education in Australia. Wadham became a lay canon of St Paul's Cathedral in 1959. He presided (1961) over the Australian and New Zealand Association for the Advancement of Science and published *Australian Farming 1788-1965* (1967).

In the early 1960s Wadham made a brief return to biological research, working on the structure of silica in plants. Concurrently, he was much involved in the controversy regarding the reopening of the University of Melbourne's veterinary school. He and Professor D. E. Tribe unsuccessfully opposed the plan because it would reduce the income of other university departments. Wadham's major accomplishment in retirement was his chairmanship (1959-69) of the council of International House, which he developed into a well-funded hall of residence accommodating more than 240 students from overseas and Australia. The house's great decade of expansion was made possible by his persistence,

sagacity and ability to deal with the university's administration.

After 1931 Wadham visited Britain only twice. He was frequently dismissive of that country's agriculture, with its attitude of dependency on government subsidies, and of the selfishness of British trade policies. His modesty and informality made him effective in the Australian community. He was clever, diligent, articulate and determined. In contrast with his choleric expressions of 'contempt for the illogical, the pretentious and trivial', he always adopted a gentle, kindly approach to those in need of his sympathy. All his life he used his social skills to amuse his companions. Sir Samuel was a member of the Wallaby, Rotary and Beefsteak clubs.

Wadham exerted a profound influence on the agricultural policies that sustained Australian rural communities, both through direct intervention and through the work of his graduates. In 1955 he and his wife moved to Brunswick. For many years, he suffered from arthritis and a gastric ulcer. Survived by his wife and their son, he died on 18 September 1972 at Parkville and was cremated. The Institute of Land and Food Resources at the University of Melbourne holds a portrait of him by Jack Carington Smith (1956), and International House has one by Clifton Pugh (1964).

L. R. Humphreys, *Wadham: Scientist for Land and People* (Melb, 2000), and for sources.

L. R. HUMPHREYS

WAGNER, CHARLES ARTHUR (1916-1943), army officer, was born on 12 August 1916 at Bondi, Sydney, seventh child of native-born parents Edward Wagner, pipe-layer, and his wife Annie Eliza, née Thies. Educated locally, Charlie became a Boy Scout, gaining his King's Scout award and later becoming a scoutmaster. While working as a pump hand for a boot-making firm, he served in the Militia, specializing in intelligence. At the district registrar's office, Paddington, on 30 January 1936 he married Audrey Thurza Blackburn.

On 3 June 1940 Wagner enlisted in the Australian Imperial Force. Posted to the 2nd/18th Battalion, he was appointed its intelligence sergeant in September. The battalion moved to Malaya in February 1941 as part of the 22nd Brigade. Wagner immediately set about getting to know the country, gathering information and learning Malay. When the Japanese attacked in December, the 22nd Brigade was defending the Mersing area on the east coast. The 2nd/18th Battalion, under Lieutenant Colonel A. L. Varley [q.v.], first went into action on the night of 26/27 January 1942, when it ambushed a large enemy force near the Nithsdale rubber estate. At a critical time in the battle, Wagner moved forward through enemy lines and accurately ascertained the Japanese positions; this action allowed supporting artillery fire to land 'with pin-point accuracy amongst the Japanese, causing severe casualties'. He later went into the area a second time bearing withdrawal orders for the survivors of the 2nd/18th's forward companies. For his 'coolness, courage and devotion to duty' he was awarded the Distinguished Conduct Medal.

Commissioned lieutenant on 14 February 1942, Wagner became a prisoner of war when Singapore fell next day. At first he was incarcerated at Changi, but passive acceptance of this fate was not in his nature. Shipped to Borneo in March 1943 as a member of 'E' Force, he escaped from Berhala Island on 4 June with seven companions, among them R. K. McLaren [q.v.15], and the eight made a hazardous journey to the island of Tawitawi. There the Australians joined the Filipino guerrillas and were attached to the 125th Infantry Regiment, United States Forces in the Philippines. A 'truly aggressive character with evidently some high leadership ability', Wagner was 'short, dark and tough with a ready smile'. He led the first offensive action with the guerrillas in August, when his party ambushed a Japanese submarine chaser as it left the wharf on the island of Bongao. At least eleven of the crew, including the captain, were reportedly killed.

In late October 1943 the Australians were ordered to report to guerrilla headquarters at Liangan on Mindanao. After a dangerous voyage by boat and an arduous trek across the mountains of western Mindanao, they reached their destination in December. While helping to repel a Japanese attack, Wagner was killed by a sniper's bullet on 21 December 1943. Survived by his wife and their two sons, he was buried locally. After the war his remains were reinterred in Sai Wan war cemetery, Hong Kong. He was posthumously mentioned in dispatches.

O. L. Ziegler (ed), *Men May Smoke* (Syd, 1948); H. Richardson, *One-Man War* (Syd, 1957); W. Wallace, *Escape from Hell* (Lond, 1958); S. Ross, *And Tomorrow Freedom* (Syd, 1989); J. Burfitt, *Against All Odds* (Syd, 1991); A. Powell, *War by Stealth* (Melb, 1996); *Salute* (Syd), 9, no 3, Apr-May 1997, p 35; information from Mrs A. T. Elliott, Kincumber, NSW.   PETER SINFIELD

WAGSTAFF, ERNEST EDWARD (1870-1965), petroleum executive, was born on 13 May 1870 at Stifford, Essex, England, son of Thomas Wagstaff, farmer, and his wife Ann Jane Jardine, née Guiver. Educated at Grays and Stratford, young Wagstaff began work as an office junior in London in 1886. Three years later he entered the petroleum industry, rising quickly in the Anglo-American Oil Co. Ltd (a subsidiary of Standard Oil), and then in the Anglo-Caucasian Oil Co. Ltd and the Consolidated Petroleum Co. Ltd (both belonging to the Rothschild group). He made his name by efficiently organizing the construction of terminal facilities for imported kerosene, then the main oil product. On 10 October 1894 at the parish church, Woodford, Essex, he had married Florence Emilie Clerc (d.1952).

In 1903 Consolidated joined the 'Shell' Transport & Trading Co. Ltd and the Royal Dutch Petroleum Co. in forming the Asiatic Petroleum Co. Ltd to distribute the products of the three parent firms in Asia, Australasia and parts of Africa. Wagstaff was sent to Melbourne in 1904 to head Asiatic's Australasian subsidiary. He named the enterprise the British Imperial Oil Co. Ltd, hoping to appeal to the imperial patriotism of his customers, and fearing that the word 'Asiatic' might be poorly received in Australia. The business was to be retitled the Shell Co. of Australia Ltd in 1927.

Wagstaff arrived in Australia just as the motorcar was about to become practical and popular. After World War I he oversaw the introduction of bulk-handling of motor spirit. His company was the biggest supplier of the commodity in Australia for most of the twentieth century. The principal reason for this success was that the crude oil which the Royal Dutch/Shell Group produced in the Netherlands East Indies and British Borneo was particularly suitable for refining into fuel for early automobile engines. As an employer, Wagstaff shared the conglomerate's paternal, gentlemanly, public-spirited values, which the colossal expansion of a profitable industry made practicable. He worked both co-operatively and competitively with other leaders of the local oil industry such as H. C. Cornforth of the Vacuum Oil Co. Pty Ltd, the chief Standard Oil outlet in Australia.

A pioneer motorist, Wagstaff helped to expand the market for his products. On an earlier trip to Australia in 1901, he had driven from Melbourne to Sydney—then a hazardous undertaking, over rough roads that deteriorated into tracks, and without roadside fuel and repair facilities. In 1908 he drove a 28-horse-power Daimler through the Ninety Mile Desert in South Australia, the extremely sandy stretch that inhibited motoring between Melbourne and Adelaide. He was an early member (life member 1958) of the (Royal) Automobile Club of Victoria.

Made wealthy by the commission basis of his remuneration, Wagstaff retired in 1927 and built up a notable collection of antiques in his home at Toorak. He died on 16 September

1965 at Kew and was cremated. Having had no children of his own, he directed in his will that the bulk of his estate, sworn for probate at £506 736, was to be used to provide incomes for his nieces and nephews in England until their deaths; the principal was then to be shared between the (Royal) Victorian Eye and Ear Hospital and the Royal Victorian Institute for the Blind. The last surviving niece turned the estate over to the institutions in 1996, when its value was approximately $11 million.

R. Murray, *Go Well: One Hundred Years of Shell in Australia* (Melb, 2001); *Shell House J,* June 1951; *Herald* (Melb), 8, 21 Feb 1966; information from Mrs J. Bintcliffe, Romford, Essex, Eng.
ROBERT MURRAY

WAINE, CECIL SCOTT *see* SCOTT WAINE

WAKEFIELD, NORMAN ARTHUR (1918-1972), naturalist, was born on 28 November 1918 at Romsey, Victoria, second of four children of Harold Richard Wakefield, saddler, and his wife Agnes Jane, née Gardner, both of whom were born in Victoria. Norman's early education at Orbost State and Higher Elementary schools was complemented by bush excursions with his father. He spent two years at Scotch College, Melbourne, before returning as a student-teacher to his old primary school. In 1937 at Melbourne Teachers' College, he was inspired by his lecturer in nature study, H. W. Wilson [q.v.12]. Wakefield used his early postings to schools at Combienbar (1938-39), Bindi (1939) and Genoa (1940-41) to conduct extensive field-trips in Gippsland. He was an enthusiastic and energetic fieldworker, with a particular interest in botany. Having been nominated by W. H. Nicholls [q.v.11], he joined the Field Naturalists' Club of Victoria in 1938.

On 13 October 1941 Wakefield was mobilized in the Militia. He joined the 2nd Field Regiment, Royal Australian Artillery, in May 1942, and transferred to the Australian Imperial Force in November. After serving as a bombardier in Papua and New Guinea (1943-44), and on Bougainville (1944-45), he returned to Australia with a collection of ferns dried in the ovens of army kitchens and now housed in the British Museum, London, and the National Herbarium of Victoria, Melbourne. Discharged from the army on 7 September 1945, he continued teaching, principally at Cann River (1946-50) and Prahran (1951-55). On 17 November 1951 at the Methodist Church, Cheltenham, he married Eileen Mary Holdsworth, née Connley, a post-

mistress, and a divorcee; the marriage later ended in divorce.

In 1955 Wakefield consolidated his work by publishing *Ferns of Victoria and Tasmania,* and took up a lectureship in nature study at Melbourne Teachers' College. By 1957 he had described thirty-nine previously unknown plant species. He edited the F.N.C.V.'s journal, *Victorian Naturalist,* in 1952-57 and 1958-64, as well as contributing 126 articles—on subjects ranging from ornithology and botany to history—to its pages. The club awarded him honorary membership (1956) and the Australian natural history medallion (1962). Although he studied botany at the University of Melbourne (B.Sc., 1960), he moved into zoological research and founded the F.N.C.V.'s fauna group. He was also a member of the Royal Society of Victoria. Beginning research at Monash University (M.Sc., 1969) into the sub-fossil deposits in caves, he wrote his thesis on 'late Pleistocene and recent cave-deposits in south-eastern Australia'. This expertise enabled him to identify in 1966 a living mountain pygmy possum, *Burramys parvus,* a species previously known only from fossils.

From 1966 Wakefield lectured in biology at Monash Teachers' College. He published widely in both international and local journals. In 1972 his work received international attention in *Nature,* when he reported the discovery of the oldest known fossil footprints (355 million years old) near the Genoa River. He reached an even wider public audience with his regular columns in the *Age* in 1963-71, some of which were published as *A Naturalist's Diary* (1967). Additionally, he broadcast on the study of nature for schools. His commitment to the public aspects of biology was demonstrated by the time he devoted to the committees of management of the Mallacoota Inlet National Park and the Lakes National Park, and the Victorian National Parks Association.

Wakefield was a gifted teacher and communicator. His somewhat imposing and solemn appearance belied a nature which his colleague J. W. Willis described as 'gentle, cheerful, helpful, open-hearted, honourable, meticulous and tidy'. Courageous and tenacious, he inspired confidence and was 'loyal and stalwart'. At the Cairns [q.v.3] Memorial Church, East Melbourne, on 10 September 1968 he had married with Presbyterian forms Audrey Isobel Wilson, a 34-year-old lecturer. On 23 September 1972, while lopping branches from a tree at his Sherbrooke home, he fell and was killed. Survived by his wife, he was cremated. He left a lasting legacy to both amateur and professional biology in Victoria.

Vic Naturalist, 81, Nov 1964, p 192, 89, Oct 1972, p 2, 90, Apr 1973, p 103; *Age* (Melb), 25 Sept 1972; Keith Dempster papers (LaTL). DANIELLE CLODE

WAKEHURST, JOHN DE VERE LODER, 2nd BARON (1895-1970), governor, was born on 5 February 1895 at Cadogan Square, London, only son and eldest of five children of Gerald Walter Erskine Loder, later 1st Baron Wakehurst of Ardingly, and his wife Lady Louise de Vere Beauclerk, daughter of the 10th Duke of St Albans. A barrister and railway company chairman, Gerald was Conservative member of the House of Commons for Brighton (1889-1905). John attended St Aubyn's preparatory school, Rottingdean, and Eton College. He excelled at French, German and history, enjoyed acting, and visited Germany several times. His mother, believing him to be the incarnation of Pharaoh Thotmes (Thutmose) III, encouraged his interest in Egyptology. Destined for Trinity College, Cambridge, instead he was commissioned in the 4th Battalion, Royal Sussex Regiment, on 6 October 1914. After service at Gallipoli, and in the Intelligence Corps in Egypt and Palestine, Captain Loder was mentioned in dispatches and demobilized in 1919.

Loder worked in the Foreign Office (1919-22), and with the League of Nations (1922-24). On 3 June 1920, at Holy Trinity parish church, Chelsea, London, he had married MARGARET (1899-1994), daughter of Sir Charles Tennant, baronet, and his second wife Marguerite, née Miles. Born on 4 November 1899 at The Glen, Innerleithen, Peeblesshire, Scotland, Peggy was a half-sister of Margot Asquith (Lady Oxford). The Loders, both possessing private means, visited Australia in 1924 during a world tour. John was Unionist (Conservative) member in the Commons for East Leicester (1924-29) and for Lewes, East Sussex (1931-36). Succeeding to the barony in 1936, next year he was appointed governor of New South Wales and K.C.M.G. On 8 April 1937 the family arrived in Sydney, and Lord Wakehurst was sworn in. Tall, red-haired and blue-eyed, with a slight stammer, he was 'active, ruddy-complexioned, and companionable . . . an outdoor man', interested in travel. His wife, in her memoirs, *In a Lifetime Full* (Milldale, England, 1989), described him as 'not demonstrative' but 'loyal and kind'. She was tall, brown-haired and brown-eyed, with a 'clipped English manner of speech', but with 'all the Tennant vitality' and 'ebullience'; she adored sailing.

Both proved popular vice-regal representatives, enthusiastically entering into local activities. Their three sons attended school in Australia—the eldest joined the Royal Australian Navy and served in H.M.A.S. *Australia* —and their daughter trained as a social worker. Wakehurst handled sensibly a sudden constitutional crisis when (Sir) Bertram Stevens [q.v.12] resigned in August 1939 after a censure motion was carried against him, by commissioning his treasurer Alexander Mair [q.v.10] as premier. In January 1940 the governor and his wife helped to fight bushfires near Moss Vale. World War II entailed extra duties and each participated vigorously. In June 1940 Lady Wakehurst convened a conference which formed the Women's Australian National Services, of which she became president and commander-in-chief. Active in the normal duties of a governor's consort, such as the Australian Red Cross Society and the Girl Guides' Association, she won praise for her 'competence, dignity, and charm'.

Despite the *Labor Daily*'s charge that his politics were 'akin to Fascism', and J. T. Lang's [q.v.9] demand for his recall over the Mair appointment, Wakehurst was a moderate, even left-wing Tory and was close to (Sir) William McKell who became Labor premier in May 1941. In 1942-45 the governor promoted Australian inter-denominational church co-operation. The Wakehursts accompanied General Sir Thomas Blamey [q.v.13] and his wife in 1945 on a visit to troops in the South-West Pacific Area, and departed from Sydney on leave on 6 June. The governor's extended appointment ended on 8 January 1946—then a record term. Succeeded by (Sir) John Northcott [q.v.15], he was the last 'imported' governor of New South Wales.

Back in Britain, Wakehurst gave illustrated lectures on Australia's war effort, using his own colour movies. Governor of Northern Ireland in 1952-64, he was appointed to the Order of the Garter in 1962. He wrote many articles and six books, including *Bolshevism in Perspective* (1931)—after visits to the Soviet Union where he met Stalin's mother—and, with Hilary St George Saunders, thrillers under the pen-name 'Cornelius Cofyn'. His recreations were fishing, tennis and golf (his handicap was eight). He loved theatre, opera and ballet and was a trustee of the Royal Opera House, Covent Garden, a governor of the Royal Ballet and lord prior (1948-69) of the Order of St John of Jerusalem. Wakehurst died on 30 October 1970 at his home at Chelsea, London. His portrait, by (Sir) William Dobell [q.v.14], is held in Government House, Sydney. Lady Wakehurst, appointed D.B.E. in 1964, was active in British charitable organizations and president of the National Schizophrenia Fellowship until 1984. Survived by their daughter and three sons, she died on 19 August 1994.

History of the Women's Australian National Services, 1940-1946 (Syd, 1947); D. Aitkin, *The Colonel* (Canb, 1969); C. Cunneen, *William John McKell* (Syd, 2000); *SMH*, 7 Jan, 5, 9 Apr 1937, 29 Jan, 19, 26 June 1940, 26 May 1945; *Labor Daily*, 8 Jan 1937; *Smith's Weekly* (Syd), 2 June 1945; *The Times*, 31 Oct, 30 Nov 1970, 23 Aug 1994; *Sun-Herald* (Syd), 1 Nov 1970; Wakehurst papers (ML); information from Miss B. McKell, Bowral, NSW.

CHRIS CUNNEEN

WALDOCK, ARTHUR JOHN ALFRED (1898-1950), professor of English, was born on 26 January 1898 at Hinton, New South Wales, only son of Rev. Arthur John Waldock [q.v.l2], a Baptist minister from Victoria, and his native-born wife Charlotte, née Godfrey. His father moved to Sydney in 1899. John attended Sydney Boys' High School and the University of Sydney (B.A., 1918; M.A., 1925). He graduated with first-class honours in English literature and history, having been greatly influenced by (Sir) Mungo MacCallum and George Arnold Wood [qq.v.10,12].

After briefly teaching at Sydney Church of England Grammar School (Shore) and the Royal Australian Naval College, Jervis Bay, Waldock was appointed lecturer in English at the university in 1919. He remained at Sydney for the rest of his life, apart from a year at the University of London in 1924 and some study leave abroad.

Backed by a strong testimonial from the university librarian H. M. Green [q.v.14], who was himself a candidate, Waldock succeeded J. Le Gay Brereton in the Challis [qq.v.7,3] chair of English literature in 1934. His own range of literary interests was catholic. He soon introduced courses in modern English and American literature. Steeped in European culture and, to some observers, reminiscent of an 'Oxbridge don', Waldock gave an international flavour to his Sydney department. While a patron of Australian writers (and assistant-secretary of the Australian English Association from 1923), he could not believe that what they produced merited separate and distinct study.

Waldock had gained acclaim in Britain with *Hamlet: a Study in Critical Method* (Cambridge, 1931). Its sensitivity to characterization and acute analysis of dramatic technique, succinctly presented, were to be his critical hallmarks. The breadth of his lectures was shown in the collection of studies, *James, Joyce and Others* (London, 1937). He returned to the classical field with *Paradise Lost and its Critics* (Cambridge, 1947). His most controversial work, the study of Milton, was criticized for undervaluing the character of epic poetry; it was also alleged that Waldock's 'intelligent secularism' exposed him to historical error. F. R. Leavis (with whom Waldock had little in common) defended the distinction of the book. Waldock's reputation overseas was enhanced by his work on *Paradise Lost*.

A humble man of retiring disposition, Waldock lived modestly, for some years at a Young Men's Christian Association hostel. But he gathered great affection and friendship. He ran an effective department which coped competently with the pressures of the postwar university expansion. Yet he was averse to leadership and administration, and

succeeded through the loyalty that his gentle and humorous personality elicited: 'he would ask as a favour what he was entitled to command'. He was a stimulating teacher of small groups and, for all his diffidence, was a superb lecturer to large classes: 'every lecture he gave was a finished piece of art'.

Waldock had moved on from Milton to Sophocles. His study of the Greek dramatist was due to be published by Cambridge University Press. He was planning a work on Euripides and thinking about further work on Shakespeare. At the beginning of 1950, intending to marry Brydie Kelsall and travel with her to see his English publishers, he was taken ill. He died of acute pancreatitis on 14 January after an operation at St Luke's Hospital, Sydney. Survived by his father, he was buried with Baptist forms in Northern Suburbs cemetery. *Sophocles the Dramatist* (Cambridge, 1951) appeared posthumously and his three major publications were subsequently reprinted.

C. Turney et al, *Australia's First*, 1 (Syd, 1991); W. F. Connell et al, *Australia's First*, 2 (Syd, 1995); B. H. Fletcher, *History and Achievement* (Syd, 1999); Univ Syd Union, *Union Recorder*, 16 Mar 1950; *Southerly*, 12, no 1, 1951, 35, no 1, 1974, *SMH*, 21 June 1934, 12 June 1936, 15 Jan 1950; *The Times Literary Supp*, 27 Nov 1947; *Sunday Herald*, 15 Jan 1950; *Bulletin*, 25 Jan 1950.   K. J. CABLE

WALKER, BERTHA MAY (1912-1975), labour activist, was born on 8 July 1912 at Richmond, Melbourne, elder child of Victorian-born parents Thomas Percival Laidler [q.v.9], bookseller's assistant and socialist, and his wife Christiane Alicia, née Gross. For most of Bertha's childhood the family lived above Will Andrade's [q.v.7] bookshop in Bourke Street. Known as 'Bubbles', she retained memories of meetings on the Yarra Bank and in the rooms of the Industrial Workers of the World. Her teddy bear was ripped apart by police during a raid on the Laidlers' living quarters. She went to Queensberry Street State School, Carlton, which she called 'a school of poor children'. At the age of 8 she attended her first lectures on communism and meetings of the Socialist Sunday School. On 5 May 1924 she headed the eight-hour-day procession as the May queen.

After leaving Stott's Business College, Laidler entered the Victorian Public Service and worked in the motor registration branch. She attended classes run by the Communist Party of Australia and took charge of the Young Comrades Club. In 1928 she began what was to be an intermittent relationship with the communist writer Judah Waten; they sailed for Europe in March 1931. Settling in London, they found jobs with the National

Unemployed Workers' Movement. She joined the Communist Party of Great Britain and was on the N.U.W.M.'s national women's committee. Returning to Melbourne in May 1933, Laidler was active in the C.P.A., the Shop Assistants' Union of Victoria and the Spanish Relief Committee, as well as being one of the few women associated with the Swanston Family Hotel group of left-wing artists and intellectuals.

Laidler worked for the Federated Ironworkers Association of Australia in Melbourne, Sydney and Newcastle, before following Waten and Noel Counihan to New Zealand in 1939. She was employed in the office of the Motor Transport Workers' Union in Wellington and for six months edited the illegal newspaper of the Communist Party of New Zealand. Back in Melbourne from late 1940, she was a member of the C.P.A.'s State committee during the period in which the party was proscribed, and soon became a full-time worker for the party and chairman of its eastern district, based at Richmond. In June 1943 she stood as C.P.A. candidate for the Legislative Assembly seat of Richmond, winning 32 per cent of votes.

From 7 May 1945 to 15 May 1946 Laidler served in Melbourne with the Women's Auxiliary Australian Air Force. She moved to Darwin in October as a bookkeeper-typist and journalist with the North Australian Workers' Union. There, on 17 December 1946 at Melville Church, she married with Presbyterian forms Joseph Walker, the union's secretary; they moved to Melbourne next year. Busy starting a family and earning a living as a shorthand-typist—mainly for legal firms—and somewhat tired of C.P.A. bureaucracy, she stopped most of her political involvement, although her views remained close to those of the party.

In 1956 Bertha Walker began collaborating with her father on his reminiscences. A founder (1962) of the Melbourne branch of the Australian Society for the Study of Labour History, she became a regular contributor to its newsletter, *Recorder*. In 1966 she formed the Anti-Conscription Jubilee Committee to honour veterans of the 1916-17 campaigns. Conscious of the relevance of history to current struggles, she published a pamphlet, *How to Defeat Conscription* (1968), which sold nearly two thousand copies.

Walker's book on her father's life and times, *Solidarity Forever*, appeared in 1972. Many of its vivid descriptions of incidents, including the 1923 police strike and the protests in 1924 against the execution of Angus Murray, were drawn from her own memory. Part memoir and part history, the work is an invaluable resource; its thoroughness, good humour, commitment and lack of pretension reflected her personality. She returned to a manuscript she had begun earlier, dealing with the Depression; it combined her own research with accounts by participants in the events, but was not published. Predeceased by her husband and survived by her son, she died of liver disease on 24 May 1975 at Carlton and, after a secular service conducted by John Arrowsmith, was cremated.

Aust Soc for the Study of Labour Hist (Melb), *Recorder*, no 58, June 1972, no 76, June 1975, no 77, Aug 1975; Walker papers (LaTL); information from Ms P. Counihan and Mr A. Walker, Melb.

DAVID HUDSON

WALKER, CLIFTON REGINALD ('RICHARD DIXON') (1905-1976), Communist Party official, was born on 26 May 1905 at Forbes, New South Wales, fourth child of native-born parents Henry Kidd Walker, miner, and his wife Emily, née Wilmott. The Walkers eventually moved to Lithgow, where Emily ran a boarding house to supplement the family income. Reginald left school at the age of 14 and, after some time unemployed, gained his first job in a bicycle shop. He then worked at the post office before joining the New South Wales Government Railways and Tramways in 1925.

His unemployment and early experiences at work politicized him. Briefly a member of the Australian Labor Party, he was drawn to the Communist Party of Australia. He moved to Sydney in 1928 to work at the railway parcels office. Early in 1929 he became secretary of his sub-branch of the Australian Railways Union and the Sydney branch of the C.P.A.

In December 1929 Walker was elected to the central executive committee of the Communist Party as part of a successful push led by L. L. Sharkey [q.v.] and J. B. Miles [q.v.15] against 'right deviation' and towards a stance independent of the A.L.P. He was to serve on the central (later national) committee until 1974. In January 1931 he left for the Soviet Union, where he attended the International Lenin School in Moscow and briefly worked on a collective farm in the summer of 1932. When he returned to Australia in March 1933 he had changed his name to 'Richard Dixon', vainly hoping to avoid recognition from the security service which regarded him as 'a dangerous revolutionary'. Appointed a full-time paid C.P.A. employee, he rose to assistant general secretary in 1937 and national president in 1948, a position he held until he retired in 1972. As Walker, he had married Dorothy Jean Button on 25 March 1939 at the North Sydney registry office.

Dixon was a prolific writer and pamphleteer, and in the late 1930s editor of the *Com-*

munist Review. In one notable publication in 1945, he attacked the White Australia policy as another version of Hitler's racist theories and offensive to such wartime allies as China and India. He unsuccessfully stood for the Senate as a Communist Party candidate in 1951 and 1953, and appeared on behalf of the party before the (Petrov) royal commission on espionage in October 1954.

Known to his colleagues as Dick, he remained an ardent supporter of the Soviet Union and made frequent visits there and to Eastern Europe. Nevertheless, he accepted the shift by the C.P.A. in the 1960s to an independent approach and protested against the Soviet invasion of Czechoslovakia in August 1968. Dixon was described in an intelligence report (1953) as a 'slightly built figure with a prim, "school-masterish" manner'; he was 'nevertheless, a forceful character by virtue of his capacity for hard work and his organising ability'. In 'a quiet but effective manner' he insisted on 'strict attention to detail and observance of Party discipline—a reprimand from DIXON is evidently to be feared'.

Walker had a strong commitment to his family and also became a keen golfer. He died of hypertensive cardiovascular disease on 7 March 1976 at his home at Bankstown, and was cremated. His wife and their daughter survived him.

E. Aarons, *What's Left?* (Melb, 1993); B. Symons et al, *Communism in Australia* (Canb, 1994); S. Macintyre, *The Reds* (Syd, 1998); *Tribune* (Syd), 10 Mar 1976; Communist Party of Aust records (ML); Richard Dixon papers (NL); ASIO file, A6119, item 1477 (NAA, Canb); information from Mrs T. Baxter, Bankstown, Mr E. Aarons, Minto, Mr L. Aarons, Maianbar, Syd, and Mrs B. Lewis, Woonona, NSW.   GREG PATMORE

WALKER, THEODORE GORDON (1900-1971), army officer and businessman, was born on 14 October 1900 at Richmond, Melbourne, eldest of five children of Victorian-born parents Arthur Walker, commercial traveller, and his wife Elizabeth Georgiana, née Gordon. After attending Surrey Hills State School and Wesley College, Theo passed the examination of the Commonwealth Institute of Accountants and studied at the University of Melbourne (B.Com., 1935). He worked for the State Savings Bank of Victoria until the outbreak of World War II. At St Paul's Cathedral, Melbourne, on 27 January 1931 he had married with Anglican rites Ida Fairfax Richardson, a kindergarten mistress.

In 1914 Walker had joined the 48th Battalion, Militia, as a junior cadet. Commissioned lieutenant in 1921, he rose to lieutenant colonel and commanding officer of the battalion (which had become the 24th) in 1935, taking over from his friend (Sir) Stanley Savige [q.v.]. He briefly commanded the combined 24th/39th Battalion in 1939 before being chosen to lead the 2nd/7th Battalion, Australian Imperial Force, on 13 October. The 2nd/7th sailed for the Middle East in April 1940 and was sent to Libya in December. Savige believed that Walker's sound planning, leadership under fire and execution of orders were 'the chief contributing factors in the success' of the 17th Brigade in the battle of Bardia (3-5 January 1941). He was awarded the Distinguished Service Order. The 2nd/7th also took part in the capture of Tobruk (21-22 January). Walker was selected to attend the Senior Officers' Tactical Course that might have led to his promotion, but he deferred his nomination so that he could continue his command in the Greek campaign.

The 2nd/7th Battalion embarked in April 1941 and deployed via Athens to Lárisa. Under considerable pressure, it withdrew until it was evacuated from the port of Kalámai (Kalamáta). Arriving in Crete on 27 April, the battalion became involved in the ultimately unsuccessful defence of the island. It gained the battle honour '42nd Street' for a bayonet charge on 27 May that forced the Germans back more than a mile (1.6 km). Almost all the survivors of the 2nd/7th were taken prisoner on 1 June. Walker is said to have stepped off an evacuation vessel at the last moment when he realized that most of his men would be left behind. He was captured but escaped for several days until retaken and transferred to a series of prisoner-of-war camps in Greece and Germany. Released in April 1945, he returned to Australia where his A.I.F. appointment terminated on 24 August. He had been mentioned in dispatches (1941).

Walker was a short, quiet and self-assured man who was considered fearless by his soldiers. After the war he joined Richardson Gears Pty Ltd, a family company, as its sales manager and advanced to become managing director of Sonnerdale Richardson David Brown (Vic.) Pty Ltd. In 1955 he purchased a dairy farm at Coldstream, Victoria, and later grazing properties near Kyneton. He was active in the Australian Red Cross Society, Legacy and the Returned Sailors', Soldiers' and Airmen's Imperial League of Australia. A vestryman at Christ Church, Hawthorn, and a Freemason, he was also a member of the Melbourne Cricket, Naval and Military, Sandringham Yacht and Banks Rowing clubs. In his youth he had been a strong middle-distance swimmer for the Surrey Park Swimming Club. Survived by his wife, and their two daughters and son, he died on 25 October 1971 at Kyneton and was cremated.

G. Long, *To Benghazi* (Canb, 1952) and *Greece, Crete and Syria* (Canb, 1953); W. P. Bolger and J. G.

Littlewood, *The Fiery Phoenix* (Melb, 1983); J. G. Littlewood, The 2/7th Australian Infantry Battalion, 1939-1946 (ms, AWM); T. G. Walker, Diary, AWM 67, item 3/410 (AWM); family papers (held by Mr R. G. Walker, Kyneton, Vic).   MICHAEL O'BRIEN

WALKER, WILLIAM ALEXANDER GEORGE (1889-1969), orchardist and nurseryman, was born on New Year's Day 1889 at Prospect, near Launceston, Tasmania, fourth of eight children of Frank Walker, a seedsman and florist who came from England, and his wife Anne Fortune, née Bryans. Frank had established (1876) a nursery at Launceston, and in 1902 acquired 50 acres (20 ha) at Lalla, 17 miles (28 km) north-east of the city, where he planted fruit trees. Educated at Scotch College, Launceston, Will began work at his father's orchard, and helped to develop and manage both it and the nursery. In 1908 they sent their first shipment of apples to England and Germany. On 22 March 1913 at St Stephen's Hall, Underwood, Walker married with Anglican rites Mary Orr (d.1968).

At the nursery the Walkers grew large quantities of trees to supply the expanding fruit-growing industry in Tasmania, and for export to mainland States and overseas. Will worked hard to improve the quality of his apples. One of his selections in the 1920s produced the famous Lalla Red Delicious apple. Lalla apples have since been extensively grown in Tasmania, throughout Australia, and in other countries including the United States of America, Argentina, South Africa and New Zealand. Walker introduced many new varieties of fruit, vegetables and flowers into Tasmania, and produced pears, peaches, plums, strawberries, cherries and tomatoes for sale. He propagated and sold garden plants: ericas, rhododendrons, azaleas, roses, Japanese maples and other ornamental trees. The forty-eight pear trees he trained to arch over the driveway at Lalla became a well-known tourist attraction.

Although Walker left Lalla in 1925 to help run the family's florist business at Launceston, he continued to supervise activities at the orchard. Successful at fruit shows, he won (1936) a Hogg silver medal, presented by the Royal Horticultural Society, London, for an exhibit of apples packed for market. He was a director of Ash Plantations Ltd, formed in 1933 to supply timber from English ash trees for the manufacture of tennis racquets at Launceston. His nursery supplied the young trees for the company's plantation at Hollybank, in the Underwood district. The business failed due to the slow growth of the trees.

In 1937 Walker developed a new apple orchard and nursery at Cormiston, in the West Tamar district. His apple-case label retained the Lalla brand name. Around this time he and (Sir) Ivan Holyman [q.v.14] of Australian National Airways Pty Ltd pioneered transport by air of fresh strawberries to the mainland and South East Asian markets. Walker profitably exported cymbidium orchids to the United States of America, entailing visits there in 1948 and 1953.

Tall, well built and fit, Walker had been a sprinter in his youth. He was a quiet, shy man who enjoyed his work and liked to create beautiful gardens. Advising freely on the cultivation of plants and on landscaping, he also gave exotic trees and shrubs to numerous institutions. From 1935 his firm, F. Walker & Sons, donated 8500 young trees that were planted along the Midland Highway (between Launceston and Hobart) to commemorate Tasmanian pioneers. An authority on rhododendrons, he was a founding member and benefactor of the Tasmanian Rhododendron Trust, which developed the gardens at the Punch Bowl Reserve at Launceston in 1962.

Walker was an active member of the Launceston Rotary Club, and at one time was involved with the Boy Scouts' Association. He supported the Northern Tasmanian Home for Boys, and was a life member of the Society for the Care of Crippled Children. His hobby was photography. He died on 7 September 1969 at Launceston and was cremated. His four sons and two daughters, all of whom were engaged in horticulture, survived him. The garden at Lalla, leased by his family to the Tasmanian government, was named the W. A. G. Walker Rhododendron Reserve in 1982.

Tas J of Agriculture, 40, no 4, Nov 1969; *Daily Telegraph* (Launc), 1 Feb 1909; *Examiner* (Launc), 8 Sept 1969, 30 Sept 1976, 8 Nov 1982; Walker family file, Tassell papers (Queen Vic Museum and Art Gallery, Launc); family information.
                                 BARBARA VALENTINE
                                 MARGARET TASSELL

WALKLEY, SIR WILLIAM GASTON (1896-1976), businessman, was born on 1 November 1896 at Otaki, New Zealand, son of London-born parents Herbert Walkley, draper, and his wife Jessie Annie, née Gaston. William attended several schools as the family moved from town to town in an arc surrounding Palmerston North. In middle age he rose at 4 o'clock and went to bed about 8 p.m., a habit formed in the dairying country of his youth.

On 12 April 1917 Walkley enlisted in the New Zealand Expeditionary Force. He trained in England from February 1918, but had two spells in hospital and did not see action. In January 1919 he was promoted temporary warrant officer. At the register office, Andover, Hampshire, on 21 July that year he married Marjory Ponting, a schoolteacher; the marriage was to end in divorce. Returning to New Zealand, he was discharged from the army on 2 February 1920.

In February 1921 Walkley was admitted as an associate of the New Zealand Society of Accountants. About 1922 he opened an accountancy practice at Hawera, the centre of a rich farming district. He sat on the local borough council between 1925 and 1935. At Hawera he met William Arthur O'Callaghan, an accountant and motorcar-dealer twenty years his senior. By the end of the 1920s O'Callaghan presided over the North Island Motor Union. He recruited Walkley as its secretary. Motorists complained that foreign oil companies set the price of petrol. Ostensibly to bring down prices, O'Callaghan and Walkley helped to form the Associated Motorists' Petrol Co. Ltd in 1931, selling under the Europa brand-name. Walkley had little capital to invest, but earned commissions by hawking shares.

The price of petrol, and alleged transfer pricing to limit the tax foreign oil companies paid, were also bitter issues in Australia. In 1935 a consortium of New Zealand businessmen backed O'Callaghan, Walkley and George Hutchison of the Automobile Association (Auckland) when they approached the National Roads and Motorists' Association in Sydney offering to repeat the New Zealand experiment. The N.R.M.A. council decided not to sponsor an oil company officially, but its president, J. C. Watson [q.v.12], and its secretary, treasurer and solicitors sought investors. Early in 1936 the *Open Road*, the N.R.M.A.'s periodical, publicized the float of the Australian Motorists Petroleum Co. Ltd.

During the summer of 1935-36 Walkley sold his practice at Hawera and settled in Sydney as the A.M.P.Co.'s general manager. He recruited staff, sold shares, arranged pump-space at service stations and supervised the excavation at Bald Rock, Balmain, to make room for tanks and offices beside White Bay on Sydney Harbour. The first tanker from the Richfield Oil Corporation, United States of America, arrived at White Bay in December 1937. By that time the company had substantial capital and bank credit, storage tanks, drivers, and sufficient pumps at service stations to begin trading. Walkley, gregarious, ebullient and audacious, had bustled many diverse people into co-operation. He joined the board as managing director in August 1939.

During World War II Walkley served on the Oil Advisory Committee and the board of Pool Petroleum Pty Ltd, both of which supervised the distribution of petrol. He came in touch with Federal politicians, bureaucrats and industrialists, particularly with Sir George Wales of the Alba Petroleum Co. of Australia Ltd, a Melbourne-based firm with a small market in Tasmania and South Australia. In 1943 Walkley and Wales travelled to the U.S.A. to arrange for supplies of cheap Middle East oil through the California Texas Oil Co. Ltd. The A.M.P.Co. bought out Alba amicably in 1945. The company changed its name to Ampol Petroleum Ltd in 1949.

At St Stephen's Presbyterian Church, Sydney, on 19 December 1945 Walkley had married Theresa May Stevens, née Fisher, a 36-year-old divorcee who had been his private secretary since 1937. They lived at Manly. On their many overseas journeys, by luxury liner more often than by aeroplane, she carried a stenographer's pad and typewriter, and helped to compose the cables, submissions, memoranda and reports that arose from business transacted. Tess answered telephone calls at night, decided whether Walkley needed to be woken, and typed his notes. She was as bustling and decisive as her husband.

The Chifley [q.v.13] government persisted with petrol rationing postwar because of the worldwide shortage of American dollars. By 1948 Walkley was openly campaigning against rationing and instigating searches across Europe for cargoes that might be bought for pounds sterling. He provided (Sir) Arthur Fadden [q.v.14] with a thick file of calculations, plans and opinions to enable the coalition parties to make petrol rationing a central issue at the 1949 election. Fadden in particular presented Ampol as a gallant Australian company battling against foreign oil monopolies. Walkley was careful to cultivate politicians on both sides in State politics, but, as the Liberal and Country parties were to remain in office for the rest of his working life, he had little to do with Labor at the Federal level.

Australia was totally dependent on oil imports until the late 1960s. Walkley's visits to oil-rich North America during his nation's wartime stringency had impressed him with the need for domestic self-sufficiency. He had used the diplomatic pouch in 1943 to send geological data to Frank Morgan, Richfield's vice-president and chief geologist. After the war he consulted (Sir) Harold Raggatt [q.v.], founding director of the Bureau of Mineral Resources, Geology and Geophysics. Morgan and Walkley flew over the Exmouth Gulf region of Western Australia in April 1947. Two months later Walkley obtained from the State government exclusive exploratory rights over 'about 325,000 square miles [841 750 km^2] of country'. Richfield, rather than Ampol, paid the early expenses of the search for oil because the Ampol board feared its uncertainty and cost.

Richfield withdrew in 1948, but Walkley cajoled Caltex—which had become Ampol's main supplier of oil by the late 1940s—to send its leading geologists to Australia in 1950 and six members of its board to Western Australia in 1951. The Western Australian government responded by substantially reducing the royalties it would demand and by re-amending (1951) the State Petroleum Act (1936) in ways congenial to Caltex, and to Walkley. West Australian Petroleum Pty Ltd (Wapet), formed in 1952, was four-fifths owned by Caltex and one-fifth by Ampol. The Western Australian government sanctioned the transfer to Wapet of the exploration zone. In the following year Ampol established Ampol Exploration Ltd and offered 30 per cent of stock to the public. The new company took over Ampol's minority holding in Wapet. Walkley's lone efforts were recognized when he was appointed chairman of Ampol Exploration.

Walkley was jubilant when the first well (drilled at Rough Range, beside Exmouth Gulf) struck oil at the end of 1953, triggering stock market frenzy in oil-exploration stocks. Although Wapet's later discoveries were scanty, the unused portions of its zone were parcelled out by the government to other companies. Raggatt and Morgan, among many others, believed that subsequent deployment of foreign and domestic capital in oil exploration owed much to Walkley's pioneering example. In the 1950s Walkley took the lead in lobbying to secure tax breaks and trade-offs that would make the expensive risks of mineral exploration acceptable to investors.

An enthusiast for resource development generally, Walkley was a foundation council-member (1954) of Professor Harry Messel's Nuclear Research Foundation within the University of Sydney, to which Ampol made annual donations. In 1962 Walkley brought (Sir) Roderick Miller [q.v.15] on to Ampol's board, and in return became a director of R. W. Miller (Holdings) Ltd. When Miller bought an oil tanker in 1963, their interests came into open conflict. Each man resigned from the other's board. Walkley was also a director (from 1963) and chairman (1966-67) of Thiess Holdings Ltd. Messel, Miller, (Sir) Leslie Thiess and Sir Frank Packer [q.v.15] were all grandstanding empire-builders who were drawn to Walkley, as he was to them.

Inspired by what he saw on regular visits to the United States (to California above all), Walkley dreamed of an Australian continent holding 150 million people, especially if the government built highways for settlement and defence, and diverted coastal rivers inland. The Snowy Mountains Hydro-Electric Scheme provided a triumphant example of publicly funded infrastructure, creating the conditions for private investment, both large and small. In 1961 Walkley contributed an article to the *Sydney Morning Herald* series, 'If I ran this country'. He began by saying that, 'under-populated' and 'under-developed', Australia 'will cease to be a white man's country

. . . Australians are but a drop of white in a sea of colour that teems with more than 1,200 million land-hungry Asiatics'. Immigration made sense to him on a personal level: he was a migrant (and the son of migrants) who returned regularly to London, the city that his parents had left in hope of betterment. Moreover, immigration made sense for his core business, the sale of motor oils.

Ampol targeted the sporting public by sponsoring contests that ranged from polocrosse to fishing. O'Callaghan and Walkley, both ardent golfers, established the Ampol tournament in 1947. By the mid-1950s it was the richest tournament outside the United States. The company paid leading American and other foreign golfers to play in Australia. As Australian representative (1957) on the International Golf Association, Walkley arranged for the seventh annual Canada Cup to be held at Royal Melbourne Golf Club in 1959. The company put up half the money and he chaired the organizing committee, of which the governor of Victoria was honorary president.

A member of Manly Surf Club, Walkley took a personal interest in lifesaving. In 1953 he accompanied the president of the Surf Life Saving Association of Australia and a group of champion lifesavers whom the company sent to Hawaii to start clubs there. Other endowments followed, including assistance that brought six overseas teams to compete at surf carnivals to coincide with the Melbourne Olympic Games in 1956.

Walkley had first become interested in soccer when he 'realised that so many people from overseas were making their homes in Australia'. From 1958 Ampol donated the winner's cup and prize-money for the pre-season competition in New South Wales and arranged for pre-season interstate champions to meet in a national knock-out competition. While president (1963-70) of the Australian Soccer Federation, he negotiated Australia's reaffiliation with the Fédération Internationale de Football Association in July 1963. Australia could again campaign for the World Cup, welcome international teams, and send its own national team abroad. Walkley became inaugural president of the Oceania conference of F.I.F.A in 1965, a post he relinquished in March 1970.

To be successful, sponsorship required publicists. Walkley courted the media and used charter flights to ferry journalists around the nation to special business and sporting occasions. He enjoyed the conviviality of these gatherings, and the goodwill that flowed from them. Announcing, shrewdly, that 'in all my experience with journalists I have never had a confidence broken', he had endowed the annual Walkley awards for journalism in 1956, to be administered by the Australian Journalists' Association. He always presented the awards himself and bequeathed $10 000 to the A.J.A. to perpetuate them.

Just as Walkley worked on forming a mutually advantageous relationship with the media, he believed that a successful enterprise flourished through loyalty given as well as received. When he retired as managing director of Ampol in March 1963, the then chairman of the board had been the accountant for the company's float in 1936, the deputy-chairman had been Alba's chairman in 1945, and three other board-members had begun as company employees. Whenever he spoke about management, Walkley emphasized that subordinates should be rewarded, materially and with public praise, for useful ideas and criticisms.

Walkley thrived on conversation and on informality. He loved talking, but not into microphones or camera lenses because his manner of speaking was vernacular and jocular. Among navy-clad businessmen he was the one in the powder-blue suit and matching bow-tie. Among a crowd of sportsmen he was the one with the most alarming tan, burnished by sunlight reflected from salt water—on Manly beach at daybreak, on his ocean cruiser *Serena*, and on the stateroom-deck of liners.

In 1960 Walkley joined the board of the Royal New South Wales Institution for Deaf and Blind Children and chaired a fund-raising committee of Sydney businessmen to help it build schools for the deaf and the blind at North Rocks, near Parramatta. In 1965 he became president of the institution. Two years later he visited every premier, minister of education and State director of education in an attempt to obtain endorsement and funding for a national school for the deaf-blind. Despite chronic illness, he remained president until his death.

Appointed C.B.E. in 1961, Walkley was knighted in 1967. Soon after, he retired from his directorships in Ampol, Ampol Exploration and Thiess. He died on 12 April 1976 at Manly District Hospital and was cremated with Anglican rites; his wife survived him. Walkley had told a journalist three years earlier, 'I've done everything I wanted to and enjoyed doing it too'. Childless, he left his wife $100 000 and a life interest in the residue of his estate. On her death, the money would establish the Sir William Walkley Trust for the benefit of the Royal New South Wales Institution for Deaf and Blind Children.

C. Simpson, *Show Me a Mountain* (Syd, 1961); H. G. Raggatt, *Mountains of Ore* (Melb, 1968); *Ampol News Bulletin*, May, July 1953, July, Dec 1954, Mar 1955, July, Sept, Dec 1956, Jan, Sept, Nov 1957, Apr 1958, Feb, Oct 1959, Mar, Apr, May 1960, Dec 1962; *People* (Syd), 13 Jan 1954, p 40; *Woman's Day*, 27 Oct 1958; *Ampol Staff News*, July 1963, May-June 1976; *SMH*, 3 June, 26, 27 Oct, 11, 29 Nov 1949, 8 Feb 1950, 7 May 1951, 5, 7, 12 Sept, 5, 22 Dec 1953, 4 Sept 1957, 12 Apr 1961, 31 July, 25, 26 Oct, 2 Nov 1963, 23 Sept, 3, 17 Nov 1967, 6 Sept 1973; *Sun-Herald* (Syd), 6 Dec 1953; *Sun* (Syd), 28 Nov 1958, 5 Mar 1970; A. Wilkinson, *The NRMA Story, 1920-21 to 1963-64* (ts, 1964, held by NRMA Archives, Syd); Walkley papers *and* Ampol papers (ML).

BARRIE DYSTER

WALKOM, ARTHUR BACHE (1889-1976), palaeobotanist and museum director, was born on 8 February 1889 at Grafton, New South Wales, son of Archibald John Walkom, a native-born telegraph operator, and his wife Annie Elizabeth, née Bache, who came from England. Following the family's move to Sydney, Arthur attended Petersham Public and Fort Street Model schools. His father (who was interested in shells and fossils) took him to meetings of the Field Naturalists' Club.

Walkom graduated from the University of Sydney (B.Sc., 1910; D.Sc., 1918) with first-class honours in geology and shared the university medal with W. R. Browne [q.v.13]. He worked under Professor (Sir) Edgeworth David [q.v.8] as a junior demonstrator. Appointed Linnean Macleay [q.v.5] fellow in geology in April 1912, he studied the stratigraphical relations of the permo-carboniferous (now permian) area of Australia, starting in the Maitland-Singleton district. His early research involved investigating the volcanic rocks of the Pokolbin area with Browne and reporting on the pyroxene granulites collected by David on (Sir) Ernest Shackleton's Antarctic expedition of 1907-09.

At St Andrew's Presbyterian Church, Chatswood, on 8 February 1913 Walkom married Constance Mary McLean (d.1975), a former fellow student. They were to have a son and a daughter, and to live at Killara for many years. In March 1913 he became assistant-lecturer in geology at the University of Queensland, under H. C. Richards [q.v.11]. Walkom was honorary palaeobotanist (1915-17) at the Queensland Museum, as well as honorary secretary (1916-18) and president (1918-19) of the Royal Society of Queensland, and editor (1914-18) of its *Proceedings*. He researched the Mesozoic and upper Palaeozoic fossil floras of Eastern Australia and received his doctorate from the University of Sydney in 1918 for his work on the geology of the lower Mesozoic rocks of Queensland.

Back in Sydney, in 1919 Walkom succeeded J. J. Fletcher [q.v.8] as secretary of the Linnean Society of New South Wales and held the post until 1940. His duties involved general administration and editing the society's *Proceedings*. In addition to some fifty scientific articles, he wrote the society's *Jubilee History* (1925) and compiled an index to the first fifty years of the *Proceedings* (1929). In 1926, on a Rockefeller Foundation scholarship, Walkom studied for a year at Cambridge under an eminent palaeobotanist, Professor (Sir) Albert Seward. While travelling on the Continent, Walkom visited the home of Linnaeus at Uppsala, Sweden. He attended meetings of the International Geological Congress in South Africa in 1929 and in Washington in 1933.

Elected a trustee of the Australian Museum in April 1939, Walkom resigned when he was appointed director in November 1940, following the retirement of Dr Charles Anderson [q.v.7]. The museum's trustees saw Walkom as a capable administrator, although staff found him formal, conservative and aloof. As director, he brought little change or innovation. He served (1947-54) on the United Nations Educational, Scientific and Cultural Organization's Australian committee for museums, and on its Australian national advisory committee. In 1948 he attended the third General Conference of U.N.E.S.C.O. in Beirut; he was a delegate at science congresses in New Zealand (1949) and at Bangalore, India (1951).

Walkom retired from the museum in November 1954. He had continued his long association with the Linnean Society, as editor (1919-66) of the *Proceedings*, president (1941-42), treasurer (1942-70) and joint honorary secretary with Browne (1952-66). Resigning from the council in 1972, after fifty-three years of continuous service, Walkom was made councillor emeritus. As his honorary work for scientific societies grew, his own scientific writings virtually ceased from the late 1940s. Walkom was general secretary (1926-47), president (1949-51) and life member (1955) of the Australasian (Australian and New Zealand) Association for the Advancement of Science; his presidential address was on 'Gondwanaland: a problem in palaeogeography'. He edited (1922-29) the Australian National Research Council's *Australian Science Abstracts*, and served as its secretary (1937-40). Having joined the Royal Society of New South Wales in 1911, he was a life-member from 1919 and president in 1943. He was awarded the society's (W. B.) Clarke [q.v.3] medal in 1948 for his researches in palaeobotany and its bronze medal in 1953 for his contribution to the organization of Australian science; he received the A.N.Z.A.A.S. medal in 1970.

As a young man Walkom had enjoyed playing tennis; he was a member of Killara Lawn Tennis Club and the council (1924-35) of the New South Wales Lawn Tennis Association. Later he took up bowls and keenly followed televised cricket Tests. He belonged to the University Club. Survived by his daughter, he died on 2 July 1976 at Hornsby and was cremated. A fossil conifer genus, *Walkomiella*, was named after him.

R. Strahan et el (eds), *Rare and Curious Specimens* (Syd, 1979); *Aust Museum Mag*, June 1948, p 234, Dec 1954, p 241; Roy Soc NSW, *J and Procs*, 1978, p 59; Linnean Soc NSW, *Procs*, 102, 1978, p 148; *SMH*, 6 Aug, 7 Oct 1929, 4 Oct 1940, 17 Apr 1954, 16 Sept 1970; Linnean Soc of NSW records (ML).
                                                          JAN BRAZIER

WALLACE, GEORGE LEONARD (1918-1968), comedian, was born on 16 May 1918 at Walkerston, near Mackay, Queensland, only child of native-born George Stevenson Wallace [q.v.12], actor, and his wife Margarita Edith Emma, née Nicholas, who came from New Zealand. George Stevenson Wallace was then working as a canecutter. Young George was born into a family of comedians; his grandfather George 'Broncho' Wallace was a black-faced corner-man in minstrel shows, and his great-grandfather was the Irish comic 'Pipeclay' Wallace. Soon after his birth, the family moved to Brisbane where his father worked as a stage hand before winning an amateur theatrical contest which launched his professional career as a comedian.

As an infant George was transported around the Queensland and New South Wales vaudeville circuits in a theatre basket. In Sydney, at the age of 3, he made his first on-stage appearance when his father carried him from the audience and introduced him as 'Wee Georgie Wallace—a chip off the old bloke'. Wallace later recounted that, balanced upon his father's hand, he sang a verse of the only song he knew: '*Go Wash an Elephant (if you want to do something big)*'. Between the ages of 5 and 14, he performed pantomime in Brisbane and Sydney during school holidays as one of the 'Sunshine Kiddies'. He clowned, danced, and sang the music-hall 'tear-jerker' *Mother, Speak to Ethel*. As a child, however, he never warmed to the theatre.

In 1932 Wallace began to study commercial art at the Darlinghurst branch of the Sydney Technical College. Joining the Bohemian set, he grew his hair long and made a thirty-five minute film—a 'horror/sci-fi spoof', *The Corpse Goes West*. 'We were the Beatniks of our day', he later wrote, 'people said we were idiotic'. At 19 he opened his own commercial art studio. On 1 October 1941 Wallace began full-time service in the Militia with the 1st Survey Regiment. In July 1942 he was posted to the 2nd Division Concert Party. He transferred to the Australian Imperial Force in September and toured Australia, New Guinea and New Britain with the concert party, as producer and comedian. Commissioned lieutenant in January 1946, he prided himself on being the only officer in the army whom no one saluted and everyone called George. His A.I.F. appointment terminated in Sydney on 3 April 1946.

Following three broken engagements to Marjorie Bruce-Clarke, a stenographer, Wallace married her on 10 January 1945 at St Philip's Church of England, Sydney. After the war, twenty-five members of the concert party re-formed as the 'Kangaroosters' (later 'Kangaroos') which worked the Tivoli circuit in Australia and New Zealand. On 27 December 1948 the 'Kangaroos' opened in *Meet the Girls* at the Theatre Royal in Brisbane; for Wallace a ten-week engagement extended to a decade. His four thousand or so performances at the Royal in revue and pantomime in one straight run were considered at the time to be 'easily a world record for a comedian'. Surrounded by a bevy of scantily-clad showgirls, known by various names including the 'Nudie Cuties', he perfected his rubber-faced caricatures of judges and drunks, as well as stock characters such as 'Georgie the Sissy' and 'Lieutenant Wallace, the harshest disciplinarian in the army'. His favourite props were a lighted cigarette and a battered old hat.

Driven by the example of his more famous father, and living to a degree in his professional shadow, George Wallace junior struggled constantly to excel. He was considered 'a villain for work'; he arranged scores, painted scenery, wrote scripts and regularly performed. At an emotional Theatre Royal farewell performance on Christmas Eve 1958, he introduced his ailing father as replacement resident comedian and then left to work for the entrepreneur Harry Wren at the Empire Theatre, Sydney.

As television increasingly supplanted vaudeville, Wallace began making guest appearances on the Sydney programmes ATN-7's 'Curtain Call' and TCN-9's Joe Martin's 'Late Show'. He felt uncomfortable with the new medium and initially expressed himself as 'shockingly disappointed' with his performances. Groomed for television by Alec Kellaway, and using the actor Guy Doleman as straight man, he was by 1959 hosting a late show on TCN-9 which ran for fifty-four weeks. On 15 September 1960 he appeared on BTQ-7's 'Late Show' and immediately felt at home with the Brisbane audience.

In February next year Wallace headed the cast of 'Theatre Royal' on BTQ-7, which reproduced the old stage of the defunct vaudeville house, complete with curtains, footlights, stage props, dancing girls, and camera shots over the heads of a darkened audience in order to replicate the ambience of a bygone era. With another concert-hall stalwart Eddie Edwards, and television stars Dick McCann and Jackie Ellison, Wallace devoted the rest of his life to making 'Theatre Royal' a success. In 1962-63 it won him Logie awards as the State's most outstanding actor; the show was voted by viewers the most popular for six consecutive years (1962-67). By 1967 he had written around 2500 comedy sketches for television. He also performed on Melbourne HSV-7's 'Variety 7' and continued to appear in BTQ-7's 'Revue 7' and 'Late Show'. 'You're never off the chain', he complained, 'A man must be mad . . . You're more whacked than a three-legged kangaroo dog walking home from Bourke'. In 1962 the Wallace family settled at the Gold Coast.

George Wallace junior observed in 1965 that 'most people in show business have short-contracted lives'. His own hard-working one was ample testament to this. A shy, gentle and generous perfectionist, he was a natural and instinctively funny comedian. With a forte for timing, for playing situation comedy and for taking spectacular 'pratfalls', as well as revelling in the power of the ad lib, he carved out his own unique niche as the last of the real Australian music-hall entertainers.

Overwork led increasingly to health problems. In 1961 Wallace collapsed from nervous exhaustion and in 1965 spent time in hospital with a haemorrhaging ulcer. During 1967 he suffered a mild stroke, followed in August 1968 by a severe stroke which paralysed him. He died of cerebrovascular disease on 30 September that year at Southport, Queensland, and was cremated. His wife, and their daughter and son survived him.

J. West, *Theatre in Australia* (Syd, 1978); M. Pate, *An Entertaining War* (Syd, 1986); *TV Week*, 12 Oct 1968; *Outdoor Showman*, Nov 1968, p 8; *Courier-Mail*, 1 Oct 1968.   RAYMOND EVANS

WALLACE, VICTOR HUGO (1893-1977), medical practitioner, eugenicist and sexologist, was born on 17 November 1893 at Boorhaman, Victoria, third of eight children of Victorian-born parents John Murray Wallace, schoolteacher and later farmer, and his wife Harriet Udy, née Grigg. Victor boarded at Wesley College and won a scholarship to the University of Melbourne (M.B., B.S., 1918; M.D., 1920). In 1918-19 he was a resident at the Melbourne Hospital and in 1919-20 at the Queen's Memorial Infectious Diseases Hospital. Having sailed to Britain in 1921, he held a number of hospital appointments there, worked as a locum tenens and obtained a fellowship (1924) of the Royal College of Surgeons, Edinburgh. He travelled extensively in Britain and Europe, and in 1923 voyaged to Singapore, Hong Kong, China and Malaya then back to Britain as a ship's surgeon. Returning to Australia in 1926, he served as government medical officer in Port Moresby for eight months in 1926-27 before leasing a practice at Charlton, Victoria.

In 1928 Wallace settled at Hughesdale, Melbourne, and established a general practice which he was to maintain until his death. From 1932 until the late 1960s he also kept consulting rooms as a gynaecologist in Collins Street, Melbourne. On 22 March 1933 at Queen's College, University of Melbourne, he married with Methodist forms Ethelwyn Iris Woolford, a 21-year-old clerk. They were to have five children between 1934 and 1940.

Wallace's experiences of travel in Asia and Europe, together with the suffering he witnessed in Australia during the Depression, fuelled his desire to alleviate social problems, especially the hardships and crowded living conditions of the poor. He developed interests in birth control and the social dimensions of sexual behaviour. In October 1934 he, Dr George Simpson [q.v.] and Dr (Dame) Mary Herring established a birth-control centre, the Women's Welfare Clinic, under the auspices of the Melbourne District Nursing Society. The clinic was intended to assist overburdened working-class mothers. It opened at Collingwood with no publicity and thus avoided controversy.

Associating with intellectual and professional people who shared his interests in selective breeding and population policies, Wallace was a founding member (1936) of the Eugenics Society of Victoria and was to serve as the association's honorary secretary until its activities ceased in 1961. He hoped that the society would attract financial benefactors willing to help in the founding of additional birth-control clinics. In 1939 the organization publicly announced its intention to establish a new centre. The proposal generated heated criticism, including condemnation in parliament and denunciation by church leaders, and was shelved.

In 1940 Wallace and a small group of sympathizers formed the Social Hygiene Society, with the aim of starting a clinic dispensing 'scientific instruction on matters pertaining to marital relations'. With funding from Janie Butler, a philanthropist and eugenicist, the society quietly opened a clinic in Collins Street in February 1941. The facility provided patients with rubber pessaries and spermicidal jelly. As World War II continued, supplies of rubber dwindled. The clinic was obliged to close in September 1942 because pessaries had become unobtainable.

From the late 1930s to the mid-1950s, Wallace lectured on 'Sex, Marriage and Family' for the Workers' Educational Association of Victoria and its successor the Council of Adult Education, Victoria. A founding member (1948) of the Melbourne Marriage Guidance Council (Marriage Guidance Council of Victoria), he served on the executive and acted as chief lecturer. He informed his audiences that instruction in 'the technique of sexual intercourse' and in remedies for sexual dysfunction would be invaluable to married couples and to society at large. As well as promoting the health and well-being of the partners, marital satisfaction would help to improve the quality and quantity of the next generation.

In his clinical work, Wallace specialized in counselling people with sexual problems. Patients were attracted by word of mouth, and by his reputation as a lecturer and writer in the field. He gave advice on such matters as hormone therapy, copulatory techniques, contraceptive methods, and the use of mechanical and pneumatic devices. In 1947-55 he was the Australian editor of the journal *Marriage Hygiene* (later the *International Journal of Sexology*).

Wallace's book, *Women and Children First* (1946), outlined a population policy for Australia. A survey of 530 of his patients had revealed eighteen major reasons why people were practising family planning. Financial, psychological, marital and health-related factors all played a part. To increase the birth rate, Wallace recommended marriage loans, larger maternity allowances and child endowment payments, birth-control clinics (in the interests of maternal health), crèches, free education, liberalized divorce laws, and marriage guidance counselling.

Since the death in action of his younger brother John in World War I, Wallace had been interested in the causes of war and the means of its prevention. He published a collection of essays by authors from various disciplines—including economics, education, medicine, theology and physics—as *Paths to Peace* (1957). Prime Minister Jawaharlal Nehru of India contributed a foreword to the book, and Wallace a chapter entitled 'A World Population Policy as a Factor in Maintaining Peace'. In his later years he edited a guide to preventive medicine, *Good Health* (1968). He also published a family history, *The Wallace Story* (1973). Immediately before his death, he was working on a book about drug addiction. He died on 9 April 1977 at Hughesdale and was buried in Springvale cemetery. His wife, their two sons and two of their three daughters survived him.

MJA, 11 Feb 1978, p 155; *Argus*, 24 Apr, 8-10 May 1939; G. McBurnie, Constructing Sexuality in Victoria 1930-1950: Sex Reformers Associated with the Victorian Eugenics Society (Ph.D. thesis, Monash Univ, 1989); Wallace papers (Univ Melb Archives).   GRANT MCBURNIE

WALLER, CHRISTIAN MARJORY EMILY CARLYLE (1894-1954), artist, was born on 2 August 1894 at Castlemaine, Victoria, fifth daughter and youngest of seven children of William Edward Yandell (d.1899), a Victorian-born plasterer, and his wife Emily, née James, who came from England. Christian began her art studies in 1905 under Carl Steiner at the Castlemaine School of Mines and was later taught by Hugh Fegan at the Bendigo School of Mines. She exhibited her work at the Bendigo Art Gallery and the local Masonic Hall in 1909, and in Melbourne next year.

The family moved in 1910 to Melbourne where Christian attended the National Gallery schools. She studied under Frederick McCubbin and Bernard Hall [qq.v.10,9], won several student prizes, exhibited (1913-22) with the Victorian Artists Society and illustrated publications, such as *Melba's Gift Book of Australian Art and Literature* (1915), edited by Franklin Peterson, and E. J. Brady's [q.v.11,7] *Australia Unlimited* (1918). On 21 October 1915 at the manse of St Andrew's Presbyterian Church, Carlton, she married her former fellow-student Mervyn Napier Waller [q.v.12]; they were childless. Napier lost his right arm while serving on the Western Front in 1916. After he returned to Australia in 1917, she supported him briefly by working as a commercial artist.

During the 1920s Christian Waller became a leading book illustrator, winning acclaim as the first Australian artist to illustrate *Alice in Wonderland* (1924). Her work reflected Classical, Medieval, Pre-Raphaelite and Art Nouveau influences. She also produced woodcuts and linocuts, including fine bookplates. From about 1928 she designed stained-glass windows. The Wallers travelled to London in 1929 to investigate the manufacture of stained glass at Whall & Whall Ltd's premises. They also visited Ireland to meet the mystic writers Lord Edward Dunsany and 'A.E.' (G. W. Russell). Returning to Australia via Italy, they studied the mosaics at Ravenna and Venice. Christian signed and exhibited her work under her maiden name until 1930, but thereafter used her married name.

In the 1930s Waller produced her finest prints, book designs and stained glass, her work being more Art Deco in style and showing her interest in theosophy. Her art and writing featured in *Manuscripts*, edited and published by H. T. Miller. Using the 1849 press she owned with her husband, in 1932 she designed, cut, and hand printed *The Great Breath: a book of seven designs*, her best printed work. A copy, purchased by the National Gallery of Victoria in the year it was published, was her first work to enter a public collection. Her illustrated fairy tale, *The Gates of Dawn*, also appeared in 1932. She created stained-glass windows for a number of churches—especially for those designed by Louis Williams—in Melbourne, Geelong, and rural centres in New South Wales. Sometimes she collaborated with her husband, both being recognized as among Australia's leading stained-glass artists.

Estranged from Napier, Christian went to New York in 1939. She joined one of the communes established by the religious leader Father Devine, and completed several murals. In 1940 she returned to the home she shared with her husband at Ivanhoe, Melbourne. She immersed herself in her work and became increasingly reclusive. In 1942 she painted a large mural for Christ Church, Geelong; by 1948 she had completed more than fifty stained-glass windows.

Christian's early interest in subjects from classical antiquity had broadened to include Celtic romance and Arthurian legend. Her literary leanings dwindled as her mystical beliefs deepened; her later prints, murals and stained glass reflected the change. Stylistically, her art changed from Art Nouveau with its love of the curvilinear, to Art Deco with its sunrays, zig-zags and angular forms. Survived by her husband, she died of hypertensive heart failure on 25 May 1954 at Ivanhoe and was cremated. The Bendigo Art Gallery holds her self-portrait (1915); Napier Waller's portrait (1932) of his wife is held by the National Gallery of Australia, Canberra. Her work is represented in major Australian galleries.

D. Thomas (ed), *The Art of Christian Waller*, exhibition cat (Bendigo, Vic, 1992), and for bib.

DAVID THOMAS

WALLER, HECTOR MACDONALD LAWS (1900-1942), naval officer, was born on 4 April 1900 at Benalla, Victoria, youngest of ten children of William Frederick Waller, storekeeper, and his wife Helen, née Duncan, both Victorian born. Hec was educated at the Benalla Higher Elementary School and was appointed cadet midshipman in the Royal Australian Navy on 31 December 1913. He entered the R.A.N. College, Osborne House, Geelong (relocated at Jervis Bay, Federal Capital Territory, in 1915). Chief cadet captain in his final year, he was awarded the King's medal on graduating in 1917. On 1 January 1918 he was promoted midshipman.

Sent to Britain, Waller was appointed to the battleship H.M.S. *Agincourt* in the Grand Fleet in April. He transferred to the cruiser H.M.A.S. *Melbourne* in February 1919 and returned to Australia in April. Made acting sub-lieutenant in September that year and lieutenant in March 1921, he went to sea as a watch-keeper and undertook professional courses in Britain before joining the staff of the R.A.N.C. in March 1923. At the Methodist Church, Lewisham, Sydney, on 7 April that year he married Nancy Bowes.

Waller began training as a signals officer in England in 1924. He topped the advanced course and in May 1926 took charge of the

Signals and Wireless-Telegraphy School at Flinders Naval Depot, Westernport, Victoria. In 1928-30 he served with the Royal Navy as signals officer in the destroyer leader H.M.S. *Broke*. A lieutenant commander from 1929, he was posted to the flagship of the Australian Squadron, H.M.A.S. *Australia*, as squadron signals officer in July 1930. He continued to specialize in communications, developing an impressive reputation. Promoted commander in 1934, he was appointed executive officer of the R.A.N.C., which had been moved to Flinders Naval Depot.

In 1936-37 Waller spent six months with the British Admiralty's Naval Intelligence Division before taking up an exchange posting as executive officer of the repair ship H.M.S. *Resource*. More importantly, in 1937-39 he commanded the destroyer H.M.S. *Brazen*. This was a learning experience for Waller, who found—as did many other specialists in their first seagoing command—that he needed to develop his shiphandling skills. In a busy fourteen months which included monitoring the Spanish Civil War, he learned his trade well.

After a short stint at Navy Office, Melbourne, in September 1939 Waller was given command of the destroyer leader H.M.A.S. *Stuart*. In December she and her four consorts arrived in the Mediterranean. Derisively nicknamed the 'Scrap-Iron Flotilla' by German propaganda, the Australian ships rapidly made their mark. Waller gained the respect of both the commander-in-chief, Admiral Sir Andrew (Viscount) Cunningham, and the vice admiral (destroyers), John (Baron) Tovey. The seamanship he displayed in the salvage of the disabled tanker *Trocas* confirmed their initial impressions. He was appointed to command the 10th Destroyer Flotilla (incorporating the Australian ships) in May 1940 and promoted captain on 30 June.

By this time Italy had entered the war. The flotilla took part in the battle of Calabria in July. For his 'courage, enterprise and devotion to duty', Waller was awarded the Distinguished Service Order in September. He won a Bar to his D.S.O. for the role played by *Stuart* in the battle of Matapan in March 1941. The flotilla continued to be prominent in operations off Greece and Crete, and along the North African coast, particularly in the 'Tobruk Ferry' which supplied the besieged fortress. When Prime Minister (Sir) Robert Menzies [q.v.15] visited the Middle East that year, Cunningham introduced Waller to him as 'one of the greatest captains who ever sailed the seas'.

Twice mentioned in dispatches, Waller returned to Australia in September and next month took command of the cruiser H.M.A.S. *Perth*. In January 1942 the ship was sent to the American-British-Dutch-Australian area to help defend the Netherlands East Indies.

The hastily assembled allied naval forces proved no match for the Japanese, and suffered severe losses in the battle of the Java Sea on 27 February. That night Waller withdrew *Perth* and her sole remaining consort, U.S.S. *Houston*. This action was later criticized by Waller's Dutch superior, Admiral C. E. L. Helfrich, because it contravened his instruction to fight to the last ship. But Waller, of all people, knew the difference between gallantry and suicide and had both the combat experience and the moral courage to make the distinction. There can be no doubt that his action was correct. The following day *Perth* and *Houston* attempted to break out of the archipelago but encountered a Japanese invasion convoy and its escort at the entrance to the Sunda Strait. The allied cruisers destroyed at least four transports and a minesweeper, but both were eventually sunk in the early hours of 1 March 1942.

Waller was listed as missing, presumed killed. Survived by his wife and their two sons, he was posthumously mentioned in dispatches. Cunningham wrote that Waller's death was 'a heavy deprivation for the young Navy of Australia'. He had been the outstanding officer of his generation. A Collins-class submarine, launched in 1997, was named after him. Joshua Smith's posthumous portrait of him is held by the Australian War Memorial, Canberra.

L. E. Clifford, *The Leader of the Crocks* (Melb, 1945); F. B. Eldridge, *A History of the Royal Australian Naval College* (Melb, 1949); A. B. Cunningham, *A Sailor's Odyssey* (Lond, 1951); R. McKie, *Proud Echo* (Syd, 1953); G. H. Gill, *Royal Australian Navy 1939-1942* (Canb, 1957); L. J. Lind and A. Payne, *Scrap Iron Destroyers* (Syd, 1976); A. Payne, *H.M.A.S. Perth* (Syd, 1978); *Naval Hist Review*, Aug 1972, p 5; *SMH*, 14 Sept 1940, 5 Feb, 14 Mar 1942; information from Mr M. Waller, Oklahoma, and Dr J. Waller, Texas, U.S.A.   J. V. P. GOLDRICK

WALLING, EDNA MARGARET (1895-1973), garden designer, was born on 4 December 1895 at York, England, second daughter of William Walling, furniture dealer's clerk, and his wife Harriet Margaret, née Goff. Edna attended school at the Convent of Notre Dame, Plymouth, Devon. She later recalled her fondness for the English countryside which she had enjoyed exploring with her father. He also steered her towards the practical arts. Arriving in New Zealand in 1912 with her family, she worked for a short time as a maid on a property in the country and began a nursing course at Christchurch. About 1914 the Wallings moved to Melbourne where William became warehouse director with Toledo-Berkel Pty Ltd.

Encouraged by her mother, Edna studied at the School of Horticulture, Burnley, gaining her government certificate in December 1917. She then began work as a jobbing gardener around Melbourne. Asked by an architect to plan a garden, she jumped at the opportunity. More commissions followed and by the early 1920s she had built a flourishing practice in garden design. She developed a sophisticated style, which attracted an equally sophisticated clientele, and rapidly became the leading exponent of the art in Victoria. Soon her reputation spread to other States. Her regular gardening columns (1926-46) in *Australian Home Beautiful* enhanced her reputation and extended her influence. She also contributed articles to other magazines.

Walling's design idiom matured in the mid-1920s and changed little during her career. To some extent, she emulated the styles of Spanish and Italian gardens and the work of Sir Edwin Lutyens and Gertrude Jekyll in Britain. The gardens she created typically exhibited a strong architectural character. For clients in the wealthy suburbs of Melbourne and on country estates, her designs included grand architectural features—walls, pergolas, stairs, parterres, pools and colonnades—woven into a formal geometry; but she always found a space for a 'wild' (unstructured) section. As her standing increased, she took up commissions in South Australia and New South Wales.

For clients with more modest means, Walling's approach was more relaxed, relying on curving lawns and garden beds to give the illusion of greater space. But rarely were there no stone walls or other structural features. Whether the garden was big or small, she created a succession of 'pictures'. Her handling of space, contour, level and vista was brilliant. Equally impressive was her mastery of plants and their visual and ecological relationships. Her gardens, no matter how formal, were clothed by a soft and consistent palette of plants. She favoured greens and used other colours sparingly, mostly in pastel tones or white. For many clients she produced an exquisite water-colour plan of the garden as a means of conveying her proposals. Most of her gardens were constructed by Eric Hammond. Walling often provided the plants from her own nursery and was frequently on site giving instructions and helping with the physical labour.

In the early 1920s Walling had acquired land at Mooroolbark where she built a house for herself, known as Sonning. Here she lived and worked, establishing her nursery and gathering around her a group of like-minded people for whom she designed picturesque 'English' cottages and gardens. She named the area Bickleigh Vale village. Some people, rather unkindly, called it Trouser Lane because of the dress of its predominantly female residents. The village was, and remains, an extraordinary experiment in urban development. In Walling's lifetime, and beyond, it has become a place of pilgrimage for her many followers. She designed several other group-housing estates. One, at Mount Kembla in New South Wales, was built for Broken Hill Associated Smelters Pty Ltd. Others remained on paper.

By the 1940s Walling's was a household name and she capitalized on her popularity by publishing four successful books: *Gardens in Australia* (1943); *Cottage and Garden in Australia* (1947); *A Gardener's Log* (1948); and *The Australian Roadside* (1952). A further monograph, *On the Trail of Australian Wildflowers,* appeared posthumously in 1984. Several more manuscripts were unpublished. Her influence on twentieth century gardening in Australia was enormous. The visual impact of the hundreds of gardens she created, her extensive writing, and the respect she commanded from those with whom she worked, including Glen Wilson, Ellis Stones [q.v.] and Eric Hammond, had a considerable effect on the next generation. In the 1980s and 1990s she was to become almost a cult figure for many Australian gardeners and a number of books were published about her work.

In the mid-1940s Walling had developed a particular interest in native plants; she had begun using them in domestic gardens in the 1920s. An early and active conservationist, she joined battles to protect the natural environment and crusaded for the preservation of indigenous roadside vegetation. She was an outstanding photographer who always took her camera on her extensive travels. Classical music was another of her passions.

Miss Walling was not a person to be taken lightly. On site, dressed in her customary jodhpur, jacket and tie, with strong, handsome features, she was energetic, determined and very demanding. These character traits often provoked conflict, especially with some of her wealthy male clients. Yet she was also generous, fun loving and good company, attracting many loyal admirers and friends. By 1967, tiring of the characterless suburbs advancing towards Bickleigh Vale, she moved to Buderim, Queensland, to be in a warmer climate and near to her niece Barbara Barnes. Walling never married. She maintained a close relationship with Lorna Fielden, a teacher for whom she had designed a house and garden, Lynton Lee, at Bickleigh Vale. Fielden also moved to Buderim. Walling died on 8 August 1973 at Nambour and was cremated with Christian Scientist forms.

P. Watts, *The Gardens of Edna Walling* (Melb, 1981); B. Hall and J. Mather, *Australian Women Photographers 1840-1960* (Melb, 1986); T. Dixon and J. Churchill, *Gardens in Time* (Syd, 1988) and *The Vision of Edna Walling* (Melb, 1998); Walling papers (LaTL).   PETER WATTS

WALLIS, JOSEPH JOHN (1888-1952), boxing referee, was born on 3 December 1888 at St Peters, Sydney, eldest child of Sydney-born parents Joseph Newton, brickmaker, and his wife Georgina Jane, née Calf. Like many working-class youths, Joe boxed for money and masculine honour. After substituting in a bout for a friend called Wallis, he assumed that surname. He fought as a featherweight at the Gaiety Athletic Club, Castlereagh Street, but soon turned welterweight. By 1910 he was also a produce merchant. On 2 July that year at the Methodist Church, Newtown, he married Alice Gertrude Makin.

From 1914 Wallis refereed at the Olympia Athletic Club, Newtown (to 1916), the Hippodrome and (from 1919) the Stadium, Rushcutters Bay. Referees in his day controlled and scored fights unaided by judges. Wallis used a five-point system devised at a conference in 1914 of managers, referees, trainers, and representatives of Stadiums Ltd. His longevity as 'third man' in the ring revealed his skill and toughness, given the hooting, abuse and sackings meted out to incompetent or unpopular referees. He habitually left the ring promptly after each decision. On 16 February 1927 his alacrity did not save him from an irate loser, Johnny Reisler, who attacked him. Wallis fought back and a mêlée ensued. The rigour of refereeing five fights on a card, at several venues, most weeks of the year, was mitigated when bouts were reduced from 20 rounds to 15 in 1927.

Of middle height, Wallis steadily put on weight until he was a portly fifteen stone (95 kg). Photographs of him officiating in his middle age show him in white shirt and trousers and black and white patterned shoes, with hands clasped behind his back, accentuating his ample stomach. Peter Corris has claimed that he used his weight as an asset to 'rough up' lighter boxers 'spelling in a clinch'. Wallis's contemporaries generally admired him, however. In 1940 Archie Moore, a first-class American middleweight who fought seven times in Australia, declared him 'one of the greatest referees in the world'. Merv Williams [q.v.] later asserted that 'nothing ruffled' him, that his 'judgement was respected', and that he 'seldom put his hands on the contestants'.

In 1941 Wallis opposed calls for a boxing commission, mirroring the views of his employer, Stadiums Ltd. He prolonged some unequal bouts. In the hard-hitting, 1949 Australian lightweight title-fight, in which Archie Kemp died after an eleventh-round knockout

by Jack Hassen, neither the police officers supervising the event nor Wallis had intervened. He claimed that, although both boxers had been 'a bit dazed', a 'referee has to decide these things in the ring, and at the moment . . . If a referee stops a contest prematurely he comes in for hot criticism'. In June 1950 the police ordered him to stop a fight in which Freddie Dawson had knocked Hassen down three times. It was Wallis's last time as third man. Ill health and some controversial decisions caused his retirement.

Wallis ran a gymnasium and owned the Cricketers' Arms Hotel, Moore Park. Survived by his wife, and two of their three sons, he died of cancer on 30 October 1952 at Camperdown and was buried in Woronora cemetery.

P. Corris, *Lords of the Ring* (Syd, 1980); *Sporting Judge*, 25 Jan 1919; *Sporting Globe*, 31 Oct, 7 Nov 1952; *SMH*, 24 July 1940, 5 Dec 1944, 14 Sept 1946, 21 Sept 1949, 28 July 1950, 31 Oct 1952.

RICHARD BROOME

WALLWORK, WILLIAM JOHN (1903-1971), magistrate, was born on 5 September 1903 at Fremantle, Western Australia, younger son of Henry Charles Wallwork (d.1911), a London-born clerk, and his wife Margaret, née Lowry, who came from Victoria. Raised in financial hardship by his mother, Bill was educated at the local state school and at Christian Brothers' College, Fremantle. A brilliant student, he first passed the Leaving certificate examination at the age of 13. In 1921 he joined the State Treasury in Perth as a junior clerk and five years later transferred to the Crown Law Department, gaining experience as a clerk of courts at Fremantle. Having qualified as a licentiate (1925), and later as an associate, of the Commonwealth Institute of Accountants, he returned to Treasury in 1932. On 9 September 1933 at St Patrick's Catholic Church, Fremantle, he married Margaret Mary Mulcahy (d.1955); later that month he took up the post of resident magistrate at Broome.

In 1935 Wallwork moved to Bunbury, where he served as magistrate for six years, combining traditional police-court work with responsibility for industrial disputes. He forged a long-standing association with the State's coal industry based at nearby Collie. Believing that he should tackle disputes at the coalface, on many occasions he donned overalls and miner's hat and, with lamp in hand, went underground to investigate a situation first hand. His ability to cut through the maze of conflicting evidence, and his cheerful and outspoken manner, earned the confidence of both miners and managers. He quickly gained a reputation as one of the State's most successful industrial arbitrators.

Wallwork returned to Perth in 1940 as senior police magistrate. His status in legal circles was enhanced in 1945 when the High Court of Australia, in *Gratwick* v. *Johnson*, upheld his decision in *R.* v. *Johnson*, which declared invalid and unconstitutional an order under the National Security Regulations forbidding interstate rail travel except by Commonwealth permit. He served as chairman of the Local Coal Reference Board (1941-43, 1946-52), and of its successor, the Western Australian Coal Industry Tribunal (1952-68). In 1946-47 he was royal commissioner inquiring into the coal-mining industry of Western Australia; his report paid particular attention to the social and industrial conditions of miners. On the tribunal he tackled some of the biggest disputes in the history of Western Australian mining. When the companies were pressed by the State government to produce cheaper coal using more efficient open-cut methods, the miners feared a rise in unemployment. Under Wallwork's direction the tribunal facilitated the introduction of new production contracts between mining companies and government.

In 1957 Wallwork was appointed unfair trading control commissioner. His controversial decision next year, declaring Cockburn Cement Pty Ltd guilty of unfair trading because of its monopolistic practices, showed his unflinching concern for the public interest. On 31 October 1959 at St Thomas's Church, Claremont, he married with Catholic rites Rita Kathleen McMullan, a 37-year-old nurse. Becoming chief stipendiary magistrate in 1960, he conducted State royal commissions into allegations of bribery of members of parliament in relation to the totalisator agency board betting bill 1960 (1960-61) and into safety of ships (1964). He retired in 1968.

Despite his heavy workload, Wallwork cultivated many private pursuits—in particular sailing and fishing—and was noted for his love of poetry, operatic arias and history. In the early 1930s he had played for the Perth Rugby Union Football Club in the first-grade competition. At Bunbury he was founding president (1936-37) of the town's Apex club. Gregarious and generous, he was most content in the company of his family. He died of myocardial infarction on 12 February 1971 at Subiaco and was buried in Karrakatta cemetery. His wife and their two sons, and the three sons and two daughters of his first marriage survived him.

C. Stedman, *100 Years of Collie Coal* (Perth, 1988); *Daily News* (Perth), 5 Mar 1945, 6 Jan 1958, 20 Sept 1968; *Collie Miner*, 18 Feb 1971; L. Marchewka, The Collie Coal Industry 1945-1963 (B.Ed. thesis, Claremont Teachers College, Perth, 1964); information from Mr W. Wallwork, Nedlands, Perth, and Ms S. Cooper, Perth.

QUENTIN BERESFORD

WALSH, AGNES MARION McLEAN (1884-1967), hospital matron, was born on 10 June 1884 at Mount McKinlay, near Dungog, New South Wales, youngest of fifteen children of Richard McQueen Gibson, a labourer from Scotland, and his native-born wife Kate, née Cameron. Educated at Dungog and in Sydney, Agnes became a saleswoman. On 25 October 1910 at the Sacred Heart Church, Murwillumbah, she married with Catholic rites 46-year-old Edmond John Walsh, a railway employee. Widowed four years later, she trained in obstetric nursing at the Royal Hospital for Women, Paddington, Sydney. She passed her final examination in June 1916 and then worked in the city slums as a district midwife.

In 1917 Walsh travelled to Western Australia on holiday and, hoping to serve in World War I, stayed to enrol as a probationer at (Royal) Perth Hospital. Registered as a general nurse on 8 June 1920, she joined the staff of King Edward Memorial Hospital for Women, Subiaco. She was appointed matron in 1922, shortly before qualifying at the Tresillian Mothercraft Training Centre, Sydney. As the administrator of K.E.M.H. she answered directly to the commissioner of public health. She was adept at assessing the strengths of her staff and delegating responsibilities. The hospital ran within its operating budget, and acquired new wards, nurses' quarters and ante-natal facilities. In 1946 she oversaw one of the first full Rh-factor blood transfusions carried out in Australia.

Walsh had firm views on single motherhood. She considered that the paramount issues were the pregnant woman's well-being and her right to choose to keep or adopt out her baby. Encountering many agitated and scandalized parents, she was to say later that the young mothers' relations usually were 'too full of self-pity because of the coming social stigma, and too pre-occupied with their own broken hearts, to spare a sympathetic thought for the central figure in the drama'. She encouraged her staff to serve as witnesses at marriages performed in the hospital.

A council-member of the West Australian branch of the Australasian Trained Nurses' Association from the late 1920s, Walsh served (1936-59) as State president of the Florence Nightingale Committee. In 1937 she was a delegate to the International Council of Nurses congress in London, and in 1943 was seconded to a medical survey committee which was associated with the Commonwealth parliamentary joint committee on social security. The only woman member (from 1946) of the National Health and Medical Research Council, she travelled to Britain in 1948 to study the latest developments in midwifery. She was a founder and second president (1950) of the College of Nursing, Australia.

Awarded King George VI's coronation medal in 1937, Walsh was appointed O.B.E. in 1949. After retiring in 1954 she shared a house at Subiaco with Mary Carson, her long-time deputy-matron and friend. She served (1954-67) on the board of management of the hospital and, with Ruth Allen's help, published her autobiography, *Life in her Hands* (Melbourne, 1955). Musically gifted, she had a fine contralto voice; she also enjoyed horse-racing. She died on 12 August 1967 at Shenton Park and was cremated with Presbyterian forms. The nurses' home at K.E.M.H. was named after her in 1953.

V. Hobbs, *But Westward Look* (Perth, 1980); B. C. Cohen and R. L. Hutchinson, A History of the King Edward Memorial Hospital for Women: The First Fifty Years, 1916 to 1966 (ts, 1966, BL); V. Hobbs, Dorothy Wiley and Miss Taylor, 1971, *and* R. Bottle, 1975 (taped interviews, BL); King Edward Memorial Hospital for Women records (BL).

PHILIPPA MARTYR

WALSH, SIR CYRIL AMBROSE (1909-1973), judge, was born on 15 June 1909 in Sydney, sixth child and fourth son of native-born parents of Irish descent Michael John Walsh, labourer, and his wife Mary Ellen, née Murphy. Despite their humble origins, at least three of the children achieved distinction in their chosen careers. Cyril grew up at Werrington on the western outskirts of Sydney, where his father had acquired a small dairy farm. He attended the convent school run by the Sisters of St Joseph of the Sacred Heart, St Marys, and Parramatta High School. While at St John's College, University of Sydney (B.A., 1930; LL.B., 1934), he was secretary then president of the college's students club. Having won sundry prizes and scholarships, he graduated in 1930 with first-class honours and the university medal in both English and philosophy, first-class honours in Latin and the James Coutts scholarship for English. He also gained first-class honours and the university medal in law, and shared the John George Dalley prize.

On 25 May 1934 Walsh was admitted to the New South Wales Bar and, shortly after, entered Chalfont Chambers, Phillip Street, where his colleagues included W. F. Sheahan [q.v.] and (Sir) Garfield Barwick. Although Walsh developed a substantial practice, especially in the Equity jurisdiction, an innate diffidence and reluctance for self-promotion precluded him from attaining public recognition. On 28 November 1942 he married Mary Agnes Smyth at St Joseph's Catholic Church, Enfield.

His colleagues at the Bar never doubted that his professional competence entitled Walsh to judicial office. At the relatively early age of 44 and although he had not taken silk, he was elevated to the bench of the Supreme Court of New South Wales on 8 February 1954. As a trial judge, he was outstanding. He was courteous, patient and fair; his judgements and charges to juries were models of lucidity. From 1958 he was the judge in charge of a separate commercial causes list and a judge in admiralty. He also heard appeals to the Full Court and sat on the Law Reform Committee. In 1962 he represented Australia at a meeting in Bangkok of the working party of the United Nations Economic Commission for Asia and the Far East which discussed international commercial arbitration.

On the establishment of the Court of Appeal in New South Wales, Walsh was named one of the original judges of appeal on 1 January 1966. His membership enhanced the reputation of that court. Barwick noted his 'calm and incisive analysis of the facts of a case and his percipience in identifying the legal principles which were apposite to the case'. On 3 October 1969 he became a justice of the High Court of Australia (filling the vacancy occasioned by the death of Sir Alan Taylor [q.v.]). He was appointed K.B.E. the same month and, on 1 January 1971, to the Privy Council. Walsh assumed new judicial duties, especially in the field of constitutional law. Chosen for the Supreme Court by a Labor premier and for the High Court by a Liberal prime minister, he never divulged his private political views. As an appellate judge, he was scholarly and painstaking, 'ever anxious to understand the submissions of counsel'.

Walsh maintained a close connexion with St John's College; he was a fellow (1955-73) and deputy-chairman (1969-72) of its council. A foundation member (1945) of the St Thomas More Society, he was involved with it for the remainder of his life, as a councillor and as president (1955-58 and 1962-64). He frequented the University Club in Phillip Street and enjoyed attending conventions of the Law Council of Australia.

Although by nature gentle and unassuming, Walsh delighted in social occasions with family, friends and colleagues. He derived the utmost pleasure from a close-knit family life and from the professional and academic achievements of his three sons, of whom he was intensely proud. He was tall (6 ft 3 ins, 191 cm), and lanky with a broad and lofty forehead, dark hair and hazel eyes.

Walsh died of cancer, in office, on 29 November 1973 at Sydney Hospital and was buried in Northern Suburbs cemetery. His wife and their sons survived him. At the time of his death he and his wife were living at Mosman, but for most of their married life they had resided at Summer Hill. At the special sitting of the High Court, Chief Justice Barwick, who admired Walsh as a lawyer and as a judge, said that he 'had not reached his zenith. The Court has lost a Justice from whom increasingly distinguished service was confidently expected'. D. B. Wilson's portrait (1976) of Walsh is held by St John's College.

E. Neumann, *The High Court of Australia* (Syd, 1971); G. Fricke, *Judges of the High Court* (Melb, 1986); *Oxford Companion to the High Court* (Melb, 2001); *Aust Law J*, 27, 1954, p 607, 43, 1969, p 636, 47, 1973, p 752; *Cwlth Law Reports*, 128, 1972-73; *SMH*, 30 Nov, 1 Dec 1973; St John's College records (Univ Syd Archives); information from Lady Walsh, Mosman, Syd, and the Hon C. J. Bannon, Syd.

JOHN KENNEDY MCLAUGHLIN

WALSH, EDWARD JOSEPH (1894-1976), cane-farmer and politician, was born on 30 June 1894 at Mackay, Queensland, youngest of five children of Irish-born parents Michael Walsh, publican, and his wife Margaret, née Barrett. Raised in a Catholic children's home, Ted suffered from severe trachoma which required several long stays in hospital; he received only a rudimentary education. He began work as a rural labourer and railway fettler, and was active in the Australian Workers' Union. On 24 May 1922 at the Church of the Holy Spirit, Capella, he married with Anglican rites Jessie Winifred Bailey (d.1951), a schoolteacher. By 1925 he had acquired a cane-farm at Sarina. A member of the Plane Creek mill suppliers' committee, he was appointed to the Mackay district cane-growers' executive in 1932.

Persuaded by William Forgan Smith and Clarrie Fallon [qq.v.11,14] to enter State politics, in 1935 Walsh defeated (Sir) Arthur Fadden [q.v.14] to take the seat of Mirani for the Australian Labor Party. He was secretary for public lands (1940-44) and minister for transport (1944-47). Losing his seat in 1947, he became a full-time organizer for the A.L.P.; his salary was paid by the A.W.U. He retained his place on the Queensland central executive of the Labor Party and was appointed with R. J. J. Bukowski [q.v.13] and T. W. Rasey to the industrial groups committee. In 1950 he captured Bundaberg for the A.L.P. from J. F. Barnes [q.v.13]. His pamphlet *What Frank Barnes has done for Bundaberg* comprised a caption and six blank pages. Walsh's motto 'think big for Bundaberg', combined with parish-pump largesse and a prosperous sugar industry, enabled him to retain the seat until his retirement in 1969.

Treasurer (1951-57) in E. M. Hanlon's and V. C. Gair's [qq.v.14] governments, Walsh was cautious and competent. In the 1950s he coped with the effects of the Commonwealth's assumption (1942) of uniform income tax powers and its reduction to Queensland's share of financial disbursements. Walsh found it difficult to fund the free hospital scheme and a number of development projects; his last budget in 1956 showed a deficit of £1.75 million. This factor was one cause of Labor's disastrous election result the following year.

A strong anti-communist, Walsh nevertheless at first opposed banning the Communist Party of Australia, but in 1951 surreptitiously supported the 'Yes' case in the Federal referendum. He sought closer relations with B. A. Santamaria's National Civic Council. While never wholeheartedly accepting the philosophies of the National Catholic Rural Movement as articulated by Santamaria and Colin Clark, he was sympathetic to rural development through State investment. On 8 January 1955 at Archbishop (Sir) James Duhig's [q.v.8] residence Wynberg at New Farm, Brisbane, he married with Catholic rites Ellen Virena Curnow.

Walsh was caught up in the growing conflict between the A.L.P. organization and the parliamentary party over policy implementation. When the Labor-in-Politics convention at Mackay in March 1956 instructed the government to introduce three weeks annual leave for public servants, he supported Gair in refusing to 'surrender' to the demand. Gair was expelled from the party on 24 April 1957 and the A.L.P. lost office four months later. The extent to which Walsh was responsible for the disaster has been the subject of debate. (Sir) John Egerton believed that Walsh had pushed Gair to the limit in order to displace him, and should bear a substantial portion of the blame. Walsh's refusal to capitalize on the impasse, however, demonstrated his continuing loyalty to Gair. This, with his insistence on treasury's financial rectitude, worked to his own ultimate political disadvantage. Expelled from the A.L.P. on 4 May 1957, he joined the new Queensland Labor Party and was re-elected to parliament in August that year. In 1962 he refused to support the amalgamation of the Q.L.P. with the Democratic Labor Party. He won as an Independent at the elections in 1963 and 1966.

When young, Walsh was a handsome, tall man with keen but hooded eyes, slicked black hair, and a drooping moustache. As he aged his weight increased to over twenty stone (127 kg). His recipe for longevity was pure Queensland: 'Mow your own lawn, eat T-bone steaks and adulterate the milk—and a drop of Bundy is the only way to do that'. A master of parliamentary procedure, he was a forthright debater. He was intensely loyal to his friends and implacably hostile to his enemies—of whom there were many—and was willing to resort to fisticuffs. It was alleged that Walsh had a 'little black book' in which parliamentarians' peccadilloes were kept for use in times of 'trouble' and 'difficulties'. Nor was he averse to using his position to bestow gifts in the form of Golden Casket art union franchises.

Torn between loyalties to his party and the Catholic church, and concerned for small-scale rural enterprises, he was a victim of ideological currents he could not master, and personal attachments that were often misplaced. Because he was not prepared to abandon old ties, his power and political creativity were essentially finished by the 'split'. Nevertheless, his energy, financial competence and grass-roots ability to 'deliver the goods' in a hostile political environment, marked him as larger than just a typical figure of his State and time. Survived by his wife, and by the two sons and daughter of his first marriage, he died on 26 February 1976 in South Brisbane and was buried in Hemmant cemetery.

C. Lack (comp), *Three Decades of Queensland Political History, 1929-1960* (Brisb, 1962); D. J. Murphy et al (eds), *Labor in Power* (Brisb, 1980); R. Fitzgerald and H. Thornton, *Labor in Queensland* (Brisb, 1989); *PD* (Qld), 1975-76, p 2601; *Worker* (Brisb), 23 Apr 1935; *SMH*, 3 May 1957; *Bundaberg News-Mail*, 11, 16 Jan 1969, 27 Feb 1976; *Courier-Mail*, 27 Feb 1976; information from the Hon T. J. Burns, Churchill, Mr M. Cross, Mount Gravatt, Brisb, and the late Mr J. E. Duggan.

D. B. WATERSON

WALSH, FRANCIS HENRY (1897-1968), stonemason and premier, was born on 6 July 1897 at O'Halloran Hill, Adelaide, one of eight children of Irish-born parents Thomas Walsh, labourer, and his wife Ellen, née McDonough. Educated at state schools and at Christian Brothers' College, Adelaide, Frank left school at 15 and worked as a messenger-boy before being apprenticed to a stonemason. He followed his trade for many years, and from 1923 served on the executive of the South Australian branch of the Operative Stonemasons' Society of Australia. On 29 December 1925 at St Anacletus's Church, Peterborough, he married with Catholic rites Hilda Mary Cave. They lived at Black Forest in a modest but neat home which had a freestone frontage cut by Walsh.

In 1924, as State president of the stonemasons' society, Walsh began a thirty-eight-year career of leadership of the State and federal bodies. Employed in 1938 on the project to complete Parliament House in Adelaide, he followed in the footsteps of Labor premier Thomas Price [q.v.11], who had worked as a stonemason on the first stage of the building fifty years before. Walsh said of his political aspirations that, having worked *on* parliament, there was every reason why he should work *in* parliament. In the March election he contested the safe Liberal and Country League House of Assembly seat of Mitcham for the A.L.P. Although unsuccessful, his vigorous campaign was noticed and he was endorsed at the next general election for the adjoining seat of Goodwood. He entered the House of Assembly in March 1941; he was to hold Goodwood (renamed Edwardstown in 1956) continuously, until he retired in 1968.

On the Opposition back-benches Walsh's aggressive style of debate resulted in his election in 1949 as deputy to the avuncular Mick O'Halloran [q.v.15]. During the split of the 1950s he supported O'Halloran's refusal to condone the industrial groups, and resisted the element that became the Democratic Labor Party. A practising Catholic in a Protestant-dominated Labor caucus, Walsh had no time for the mixing of church and politics. In his maiden speech in 1941 he had recounted how he had rejected 'a reverend gentleman's' offer of a preferred place on a sectarian how-to-vote ticket. He asserted that such tickets should only be issued by political parties: 'I think it would be for the best for persons connected with churches to look after their own religious matters and leave politics alone'.

Walsh's years as deputy-leader did not guarantee him the leadership on O'Halloran's death in 1960. With Labor needing to shake itself out of the torpor of apparent permanent Opposition, he was challenged by two candidates, one of whom was the dynamic young Donald Dunstan. Walsh managed to win the contest, declaring that he was determined to achieve government. His attacks on the premier (Sir) Thomas Playford were energetic but marred by his habit of uttering malapropisms and using complex words in the wrong context.

In the 1962 election Labor gained a substantial majority of votes over the incumbent L.C.L. but failed to win government. For the next three years Playford depended on the casting vote of the Speaker Tom Stott [q.v.], an Independent, to stay in power. With a determined sense of grievance, Walsh refused to recognize Playford by the courtesy title of 'premier', and referred to him as 'treasurer', deriving from his main portfolio. Industrial development and demographic change were eroding the advantage which the L.C.L. gained from existing electoral boundaries. A redistribution, which would have entrenched the imbalance, was blocked by Labor.

At the election in March 1965 Walsh became the first Labor premier in South Australia in thirty-two years—and the first Catholic. On gaining office he underlined his legitimacy by creating the portfolio and department of the premier, and was the first person to be officially designated 'premier'. Already aged 67, Walsh was required under party rules to retire from parliament at the next election. He was thus seen as a stop-gap leader, but surprised his critics with an ability to sustain the role for the next two years. Apart from active support for gambling law reform (which resulted in a State lottery and the establishment of the Totalisator Agency Board), and more liberal licensing laws, his policies followed those of Playford, emphasizing industrialization and resource development. Quick to recognize the value of natural gas discoveries at Moomba in the north of the State, he obtained Commonwealth government assistance to build a pipeline to Adelaide.

Enjoying the role of premier, Walsh was reluctant to step down to allow a successor to be groomed, and suggested that the retiring age might be lifted for him. His colleagues disagreed and moves to induce him to resign culminated in a motion to the State council of the party congratulating him on his 'three achievements': leading Labor from the political wilderness of Opposition; bringing natural gas to Adelaide; and selflessly stepping down so that a new leader could establish himself before the next election. Although somewhat bemused, he accepted with good grace the overwhelming reception accorded to him on this occasion, and resigned as leader on 1 June 1967. He continued in cabinet as minister of social welfare in Dunstan's first government until March 1968.

Of medium height, with hair cut short at the back and sides and neatly parted in the middle, Walsh was a speaker of the old school with a loud, stump-thumping technique and high-velocity delivery which was ill-adapted to the emerging medium of television. His and Playford's retirements, at the same time, marked the end of a century-old political style. The incoming L.C.L. government of R. Steele Hall appointed Walsh to the State Forestry Board. Two days later, on 18 May 1968, he died of a coronary occlusion at Parkside and was buried in Centennial Park cemetery after a state funeral. His wife and their two sons survived him.

N. Blewett and D. Jaensch, *Playford to Dunstan* (Melb, 1971); D. Jaensch, *The Government of South Australia* (Brisb, 1977); D. Dunstan, *Felicia* (Melb, 1981); A. Parkin and J. Warhurst (eds), *Machine Politics in the Australian Labor Party* (Syd, 1983); D. Jaensch (ed), *The Flinders History of South Australia* (Adel, 1986); *PD* (SA), 17 July 1941, p 144, 25 June 1968, p 5; *Advertiser* (Adel), 8 Mar 1965, 23 Mar 1966, 21 Jan 1967, 17, 20 May 1968; *News* (Adel), 8 Mar 1965; *Sunday Mail* (Adel), 20 May 1967.   J. C. BANNON

WALSH, HERBERT FITZGERALD (1905-1972), solicitor and company director, was born on 16 September 1905 at Brighton

Beach, Melbourne, sixth child of Tasmanian-born parents John Aloysius Walsh, hotel-keeper, and his wife Caroline Pauline, née Kelly. Educated in Tasmania at Launceston Church Grammar School, 'Gerry' became a bank officer and moved to Melbourne. He rose to branch manager and studied at the University of Melbourne (LL.B., 1934). On 3 January 1935 at the Church of the Good Shepherd, Upper Macedon, he married with Anglican rites Brenda Alice Gordon Guest (d.1968). Her family were well-known biscuit manufacturers.

Articled in 1935 to E. J. Hamilton of the Melbourne law firm of Malleson, Stewart, Stawell & Nankivell, Walsh was admitted to practice as a barrister and solicitor on 2 March 1936. The firm made him a partner in 1937. In the late 1930s he began a long association with (Sir) Ivan Holyman [q.v.14], head of Australian National Airways Pty Ltd, the country's major internal carrier. After serving from August 1940 as a gunner in the Royal Australian Artillery, Citizen Military Forces, Walsh was discharged in February 1941 because of a toxic goitre, from which he had recovered by 1942.

In addition to his legal work, he assisted Holyman to run A.N.A. As general manager, Walsh organized aircraft which provided logistic support to Australian troops in the South-West Pacific Area during and after World War II. In 1945 J. B. Chifley's [q.v.13] Australian Labor Party government attempted to nationalize the airlines. Walsh remained a partner in Malleson, Stewart & Co. and guided A.N.A. in its successful challenge to the legislation in the High Court of Australia. As a result, litigants in other High Court cases instructed the practice to act for them. Walsh became pre-eminent in the law of the air and in constitutional law.

One of the founders of the Liberal Party of Australia, he spoke on radio during the 1949 Federal election campaign in support of his friend (Sir) Robert Menzies [q.v.15]. Walsh resumed full-time legal work in 1952, becoming senior partner of his firm in 1963. Involved with more than fifty companies, he was chairman of a substantial number, including Red Tulip Pty Ltd, Hooker (Chemical) Australia Pty Ltd and Silverton Transport & General Industries Ltd, and a director of many more, among them Moulded Products (Australasia) Ltd. He was a friend of Lang Hancock whom he helped to set up trade and mining connections in Japan.

Walsh retired from his partnership and was appointed a consultant to Mallesons on 1 July 1970. Described as 'a very clever, good-looking man' who wore a rose in his buttonhole, he was 6 ft 3 ins (191 cm) tall, 'energetic, friendly, at ease in any company ... a beach-lover, a golfer, and eminently likeable'. With his

flamboyant personality, he was 'almost a buc-
caneering type'. He was a member of the
Melbourne, Australian, Broken Hill and (in
Canberra) Commonwealth clubs; and the
Royal Sydney, Royal Melbourne, Peninsula
Country, and Frankston golf clubs. Survived
by his son and two daughters, he died of cancer on 18 March 1972 at Mornington and was
cremated.

R. Campbell, *Mallesons* (Melb, 1989); *Age* (Melb),
22 Mar 1972; information from Ms A. Walsh, South
Yarra, Melb.   ROWAN SMITH

WALTERS, ALLAN LESLIE (1905-1968),
air force officer, was born on 2 November
1905 at Ascot Vale, Melbourne, second child
of Victorian-born parents Arthur Ferdinand
Walters, schoolteacher, and his wife Edith
Mary, née Russell. Allan moved with his
parents to Perth at an early age and was educated at Perth Modern School. He spent four
years in the senior cadets and eight months in
the Citizen Military Forces before entering
(in February 1924) the Royal Military College, Duntroon, Federal Capital Territory. In
December 1927 he graduated as lieutenant,
but he transferred to the Royal Australian Air
Force on 1 February 1928.

Promoted flying officer in February 1929,
'Wally' Walters completed his initial pilot
training next month. He undertook a number
of specialist courses with particular emphasis
on flying instruction, at which he excelled,
eventually achieving the seldom-awarded
grading of 'A1'. A member of No.3 Squadron
based at Richmond, New South Wales, he
earned a reputation as an aerobatics pilot,
participating in the air shows that were such
a feature of aviation in the 1930s. Fair, slim
and blue-eyed, he cut a dashing figure. While
courting his future wife Jean Grace Belford,
daughter of Rev. G. F. B. Manning, rector of
All Saints Church, North Parramatta, he performed stunts over the church. Manning
married Wally and Jean with Anglican rites at
that church on 30 June 1930.

In 1936 Flight Lieutenant Walters graduated from the Royal Air Force Staff College,
Andover, England. Promoted squadron leader
in March 1937, he returned to Australia in
June and was appointed commanding officer
of No.22 Squadron at Richmond, where he
flew Hawker Demon and Avro Anson aircraft.
He commanded No.3 Squadron in 1938-39
before serving at Air Force Headquarters,
Melbourne, as director of staff duties.

To counter the emerging Japanese threat in
South East Asia, Australia began deploying
forces to support the British in Malaya. In
July 1940 Walters took No.1 Squadron, newly
equipped with Lockheed Hudson aircraft, to

Singapore. Commanding the squadron as a
temporary wing commander, he led it until
May 1941, when he became commanding
officer, R.A.A.F. Station, Laverton, Victoria.
For training No.1 Squadron 'to a particularly
high standard' and himself taking 'a very
active part in all operations', he was awarded
the Air Force Cross. He was promoted temporary group captain in April 1942.

The remainder of Walters' war service
alternated between staff appointments and
operational commands. His commands were
No.1 (Fighter) Wing, Darwin (1942-43), No.72
Wing, Merauke, Netherlands New Guinea
(1943-44), and Northern Command (1945-46).
He was mentioned in dispatches and, for his
'leadership and resource' during operations in
New Guinea, New Britain and Bougainville,
was appointed C.B.E. (1946). In his flying
appointments he proclaimed himself to be
Australia's oldest fighter pilot. Although probably inaccurate, the claim illustrated his eager-
ness to be as personally involved in the action
as any of the pilots under his command. For
example, on 20 June 1943 he had taken part in
a major engagement over Darwin between his
three Spitfire squadrons and a force of Japanese bombers and fighters, shooting down
one enemy fighter. Promoted acting air commodore in February 1945, he represented the
R.A.A.F. at the Japanese surrender at Wewak,
New Guinea, in September.

After serving at Air Force Headquarters as
director of air staff plans and policy, Walters
attended the 1947 course at the Imperial Defence College, London. Promoted acting air
vice marshal in October 1952 (substantive
in January 1954), he held three major commands: Southern Area (1948-50), Home
Command (1954-57) and Support Command
(1959-62). He also occupied key overseas posts
as air officer commanding, R.A.A.F. Overseas
Headquarters, London (1951-52), and head of
the Australian Joint Services Staff in Washington (1952-53). From 1957 to 1959 he was air
member for personnel on the Air Board. In
May-June 1956 he took a flight of five Canberra bombers on a goodwill visit to the United
States of America. He was appointed C.B. that
year.

Walters retired from the R.A.A.F. on 16 May
1962 in Melbourne. He was one of a small
group of air force officers who had trained at
R.M.C. in the 1920s and subsequently led the
R.A.A.F. from the late 1930s to the early 1960s
through successive periods of major expansion, great operational demand, demobilization
and contraction, and finally reconstruction
and modernization. In retirement he enjoyed
horse-racing and maintained his membership
of the Melbourne Club. He died of cardiorenal failure on 19 October 1968 at Heidelberg
and was cremated with full air force honours.
His wife and their daughter survived him.

G. Odgers, *Air War Against Japan 1943-1945* (Canb, 1957); D. Gillison, *Royal Australian Air Force 1939-1942* (Canb, 1962); C. D. Coulthard-Clark, *The Third Brother* (Syd, 1991); A. Stephens, *Going Solo* (Canb, 1995); *Herald* (Melb), 17 May, 2 June 1962; information from Air Chief Marshal Sir Neville McNamara, Bowral, Air Vice Marshal F. Barnes, Tweed Heads, NSW, Air Marshals J. Newham, Church Point, Syd, D. Evans, Aranda, and B. Gration, Kambah, and Sir Richard Kingsland, Campbell, Canb; personal knowledge.

RAY FUNNELL

WALTON, GERTRUDE MARY (1881-1951), headmistress, was born on 1 April 1881 at Derby, England, daughter of James Pollitt Walton, schoolmaster, and his wife Margaret Ellen, née Hanesworth. Gertrude, her mother, two brothers and two sisters migrated to Western Australia in 1891; her father, recently appointed inspector of schools, had arrived the previous year. Educated privately, she passed the South Australian senior public examination in 1898. She attended the University of Adelaide (B.A., 1904) and the Sorbonnne, Paris (diplôme d'études Françaises, 1908), and taught for a year in the École Primaire Supérieure at Guise.

Returning to Perth, Miss Walton joined the staff of the newly established Methodist Ladies' College in 1909 as first mistress. In 1913 she was appointed headmistress. Although restrained by an all-male and rigidly Methodist school council—in 1914 she had to obtain permission to read her own report on speech day—she succeeded in establishing herself as a leader in education. She travelled to England and Europe in 1920, visiting schools and observing advances in education. Next year she introduced a modified version of the Dalton plan, which encouraged students to work at their own pace; it remained in operation at the school until 1945. At much the same time Margaret Bailey [q.v.7] introduced a similar version of the Dalton plan at Ascham, Sydney.

Affectionately known as 'Wal', Walton taught English, history, religious studies and, for a short time, French. She was respected for her enthusiasm and her scholarship. Always interested in developments in education, she attended New Education Fellowship conferences in England (1936) and in Perth (1937). After retiring in 1945, she wrote a history of M.L.C., *The Building of a Tradition* (1949). She used extracts from her speech night reports to encapsulate the principal elements of her educational philosophy: delaying specialization as long as possible, acquiring self-discipline, and learning to face and conquer personal difficulties. Stressing the importance of preparing for an occupation (other than marriage), and of pursuing worthwhile leisure activities, she aimed to foster in her pupils 'a well-balanced character and enthusiastic devotion to some worthy aim in life'.

An independent woman, Walton travelled overseas alone. At home she drove (less than perfectly) her own car. Friends and pupils remembered her series of little terriers, always named Ferdinand. A keen theatre-goer, she read widely, particularly enjoying crime fiction, and wrote an unpublished dissertation: 'The vogue of the detective novel'. She considered that acquiring a love of good books was more important than academic success. Of middle height and conservatively dressed, she had dark hair, a slightly olive complexion, a loud, fruity laugh, and large, luminous eyes which her great-nephew Storry Walton remembered as 'cool and appraising, observant: terrible in reproval, kind and serene at other times'. She died of coronary vascular disease on 20 February 1951 at Blackpool, England, and was cremated. Walton bequeathed £500 to M.L.C. for the library; it was named after her in 1957.

J. Lang, *A Living Tradition* (Perth, 1980); J. Shepherd, *The Quiet Revolution* (1997, copy held MLC Archives, Perth); *West Australian*, 22 Feb 1951; Walton family papers (MLC Archives, Perth); family information.

JULIET LUDBROOK

WANG, DAVID NENG HWAN (1920-1978), merchant, was born on 12 February 1920 near San Chang, Haimen county, Kiangsu (Jiangsu) province, China, fourth of six children of Wang De Xiu, peasant farmer, and his wife, a member of the Jiang family who was known after her marriage as Wang Jiang Shi. Wang Neng Hwan attended school from the age of 9, and at 18 went to nearby Shanghai to study radio communications. In 1939 he entered a military academy in Chungking (Chongqing). Promoted lieutenant in 1941 in the Nationalist Chinese army, he served in the intelligence section of the general headquarters. He was posted to Singapore, but the Japanese invasion of Malaya saw him diverted to Australia in 1942 as a captain with the Chinese military mission.

In Melbourne Wang met Mabel Chen, the Australian-born daughter of George Wing Dann Chen, a leading Chinese businessman. From 1944 Wang served as a liaison officer in India and Burma. On being demobilized, he returned to Shanghai where Mabel joined him in 1946 and where they were married. China's political turmoil caused them to leave for Melbourne in early 1948. Supported by Arthur Calwell [q.v.13], a long-time friend of the Chen family, Wang entered Australia on a business permit, renewable but requiring a minimum annual turnover of £500.

Mabel chose the name David for him. Their business was registered as David Wang & Co. and they bought the goodwill of a small gift shop at South Yarra. Anticipating a growing taste for oriental wares, they prospered almost immediately, obtaining Chinese goods through a Hong Kong agent, and later importing from Taiwan, Japan, the Philippines, Malaysia, Thailand and the Pacific Islands, and, after 1972, mainland China. The Wangs largely pioneered the trade in Chinese caneware, bamboo blinds, camphorwood chests, and arts and crafts. Fireworks were among their most lucrative earners. In 1962, wishing to make his first overseas business trip on an Australian passport, David applied for naturalization six months before he had completed the required fifteen years residence, and succeeded on appeal. He purchased and demolished the 'Canton Building 1888' in Little Bourke Street, erecting in its place a modern emporium, opened in 1964 by Calwell.

By the mid-1960s David and Mabel Wang were business and social successes. Their import operation was flourishing, with four shops and showrooms, a factory and a bulk warehouse. Handsome and personable, and noted for his Chinese New Year hospitality at his home at Toorak, Wang was poised to enter Melbourne's staid civic and business Establishment. On Calwell's nomination he was appointed a justice of the peace in February 1964.

Campaigning for a brighter city with more street-entertainment and night-life, and an international flavour to appeal to tourists, Wang was elected in August 1969 to the Melbourne City Council; he was Melbourne's first Chinese-born councillor. He joined the council's dominant Civic Group, and served on the finance and the parks, gardens and recreation sub-committees, among others. As founder and chairman of the Keep Melbourne Beautiful citizens' committee and of the Make Melbourne Brighter committee, he advocated a cleaner city, extended shopping hours and liberalized liquor laws: 'Part of Melbourne's problem', he observed, 'is its social rigidity'. He achieved some success in rejuvenating the central business district.

When Wang won his seat for a third time, in 1975, some observers predicted his election as mayor. Having experienced little personal prejudice in the business and professional *milieux*, he saw his advance as demonstrating the fairness of the Australian people, as distinct from the sometimes overbearing behaviour of the country's officialdom. Cautious and a gradualist, he condemned examples of racism in public life, welcomed the replacement of the White Australia policy by selective immigration, forecast a multi-racial nation,

and supported an Asian immigration quota. In 1977 he described Australia as a cosmopolitan community and endorsed racial integration, including mixed marriages, arguing that the Australian Chinese should serve as a bridge of friendship between the two countries. The tolerance displayed by Australian youth made him optimistic about the future.

Wang had initiated Melbourne's Chinatown project in 1960, and he revived it in the 1970s as a city councillor and as a founder of the Chinese Professional and Businessmen's Association of Victoria. He wished to transform the declining Chinese quarter of Little Bourke Street with authentic imported pagodas, archways and lighting. Critics asserted that the scheme would make Melbourne's Chinese community a curiosity, and that some Chinese found the very term 'Chinatown' offensive. Wang replied that it would promote China's five-thousand-year-old culture. As president of the Little Bourke Street Traders, he wanted to attract Melbourne shoppers and tourists. The launch of Chinatown in the spring of 1976 coincided with the press announcement of Wang's candidacy for the mayoralty, but in the event he did not seek nomination.

When political opposition delayed the completion of Chinatown, Wang sought a fresh challenge. He decided to establish in Melbourne the largest Chinese emporium outside Hong Kong, as a showcase for the culture of the land of his birth. The press now dubbed him the 'King of Chinatown', but the project was barely started when Wang suffered a heart attack at a function on 31 December 1977. He died in the early hours of 1 January 1978 at St Vincent's Hospital, Fitzroy, and was buried with Anglican rites in Boroondara cemetery, Kew. His wife and their two sons and two daughters survived him. A 1966 portrait by Paul Fitzgerald is held by his family, who completed the David Wang Emporium and opened it in 1979. Melbourne's Moomba procession that year featured, as have Chinese New Year celebrations ever since, a spectacular Dai Loong ceremonial dragon bought with the proceeds of an appeal David Wang had launched shortly before his death.

Age (Melb), 5 Jan, 1 Feb 1960, 5 Feb 1964, 28 July 1969, 16 Feb, 23 July 1970, 11 May 1971, 20 Jan, 4, 26 Aug 1976, 14 Feb 1977, 2 Jan, 22 June 1978, 20, 31 Jan 1979; *Australian*, 23 Jan 1967, 1 Sept 1969, 10 Oct 1971, 9 Feb 1972, 17 June 1977, 4 Jan 1978; *Sun News-Pictorial*, 29 July, 30 Aug, 1 Sept 1969, 20 Jan, 3 Feb, 10 Apr, 4 Aug 1976, 14 Feb, 17 June, 13 Dec 1977, 2 Jan, 23 June 1978; *Herald* (Melb), 24 Apr, 10 May 1971, 3 Apr 1973, 19 Jan, 9 Apr, 22 May, 6 July 1976, 20 June 1981, 10 Feb 1983; *A'sian*, Feb 1978; *Aust Financial Review*, 2 Feb 1978; 'Reunion', SBS TV, 1 Oct 1998 (ScreenSound Aust, Canb); information from Mrs M. Wang, Malvern, Melb.

JOHN LACK

WANGANEEN, ROBERT McKENZIE (1896-1975), Aboriginal community leader, was born on 23 February 1896 at Point Pearce Mission Station, Yorke Peninsula, South Australia, fifth of ten children of Aboriginal parents Robert Wanganeen, labourer, and his wife Susan, née Hughes. Young Robert's grandfather James Wanganeen, a Maraura man from the Upper Murray, had been sent to the Poonindie Mission Station, near Port Lincoln, in the early 1850s after attending the Native School Establishment in Adelaide. Robert senior was born at Poonindie in 1868 but, as a youth, had moved to Point Pearce where he met and married in 1886 Susan, a Narrunga woman.

Educated at the Point Pearce mission school, young Robert was, like his father, keen on sport; during the 1920s and 1930s he was captain and coach of the local Australian Rules football team and also a skilful cricketer. He lived with Dulcie Lena Sansbury who bore him a son in 1920. In 1922, at the age of 17, Dulcie died of tuberculosis. On 7 January 1924 at the Methodist manse at nearby Maitland, Wanganeen married Dulcie's cousin, 17-year-old Doreen Violet Sansbury (d.1944), an Adnyamathanha woman from the Flinders Ranges. They were to have eleven children. By the 1930s he was a respected community leader and spokesman, known as 'the chief' by the residents of Point Pearce. In 1933 he was elected president of the local branch of the newly formed Australian Aborigines' Union which lobbied the South Australian government for improved conditions at the station, and advocated land grants for Aboriginal people so that they could become independent of government rations and assistance.

Frustrated by the continuing lack of opportunities at the mission, Wanganeen organized in the 1940s and 1950s a number of petitions seeking improved wages and conditions for the residents. When members of the Aborigines Protection Board visited Point Pearce in 1953-54, he acted as spokesman, debating publicly with (Sir) John Cleland [q.v.8], the board's deputy-chairman, on the need for higher wages and better medical and educational facilities, and an end to inequalities in social service payments for Aboriginal people. In 1958 Wanganeen and Percy Rigney, a Ngarrindjeri man from the Point McLeay mission, were invited to address the anthropological section at the Adelaide meeting of the Australian and New Zealand Association for the Advancement of Science. According to the annual report of the Aborigines' Friends' Association, both spoke eloquently on the problems then confronting Aboriginal people and were commended by the delegates for their valuable contribution.

Survived by four sons and two daughters, Wanganeen died on 13 December 1975 in Adelaide and was buried in Point Pearce cemetery. He was greatly respected by the wider non-Aboriginal community as well as by his Aboriginal relations and friends; his funeral was one of the largest seen on Yorke Peninsula to that time.

D. Kartinyeri, *The Wanganeen Family Genealogy* (Adel, 1985); Aborigines' Friends' Assn, *Annual Report*, 1958, p 9; Aborigines Dept, correspondence files, 1941-55 (SRSA).   TOM GARA

WARD, CHARLES MELBOURNE (1903-1966), actor, naturalist and marine collector, was born on 6 October 1903 in Melbourne, younger son of American-born parents Hugh Joseph Ward [q.v.12], theatrical manager, and his wife Grace, née Miller, a concert singer. As a child 'Mel' travelled with his parents: his schooling was erratic and included a year (1917) at a private school in New York, and some years at the Marist Brothers' High School, Darlinghurst, Sydney. In 1919 he left school to go on the stage mainly as an acrobatic and eccentric dancer and comedian, making his début in *The Bing Boys on Broadway*. He played the saxophone and clarinet (claiming to have performed with the first jazz band to appear on the Sydney stage), toured with his father's productions and frequently visited the United States of America.

From early childhood Ward had been fascinated by the crabs he found on beaches and in rock pools; as a schoolboy he haunted the American Museum of Natural History. After a small red crab that he discovered on a Queensland beach was named (1926) *Cleistostoma wardi* after him, he abandoned the stage for marine zoology. By the late 1920s, he had collected not only in Australia, but also in Samoa, Fiji and Hawaii, along the Atlantic and Californian coasts of the U.S.A., and in Cuba, Panama and Mexico. By using his athletic skills he managed to catch a particular crab that lived in quicksand in Cuba. He was a member (1926), fellow (1936) and life-member (1947) of the Royal Zoological Society of New South Wales. In 1929 he was elected a fellow of the Zoological Society, London, and appointed honorary zoologist at the Australian Museum, Sydney, where his friends Tom Iredale [q.v.9] and G. P. Whitley [q.v.] worked. Ward also belonged to the Royal Australian Historical Society, the Royal, Linnean and Anthropological societies of New South Wales and the Art Galleries and Museums Association of Australia and New Zealand. He published in Australian and international scientific journals.

Possessing independent means, in 1930-31 Ward embarked on a scientific 'Grand Tour': he worked with Dr Mary Rathbun at the

Smithsonian Institution, Washington, lectured at the British Museum, London, studied in museums in Berlin and Paris, and collected in the Mediterranean. Back in Sydney, he married Halley Kate Foster on 27 October 1931 at the district registry office, Randwick. Accompanying American film-makers to New Guinea in 1932, he became interested in the people and collected artefacts and zoological specimens. In December 1933 the Wards went to Lindeman Island on the Great Barrier Reef as entertainers, playing duets on the clarinet and guitar for tourists. They combed the reef at every low tide. He found turtle-riding 'a fascinating sport, as exciting as anything I know'. Mel set up a museum and laboratory. In the 1930s he collected for the Australian Museum, carried out research for the Raffles Museum, Singapore, and the Mauritius Institute, and exchanged specimens with other museums and collectors. Sun-browned and stocky, he had big blue eyes and 'a mass of curly dark hair'; later he was 'grey-maned'.

They returned to Sydney in 1935, lived at Double Bay, and spent many months on camping trips, collecting and learning Aboriginal lore, as Mel took an increasing interest in indigenous people and their relationship with the local fauna and flora. During World War II Ward, rejected for military service on physical grounds, offered himself as an honorary entertainer, and lecturer to the Australian Army Education Service. Soon he was teaching Australian jungle fighters tropical hygiene and how to live off the land in the Dorrigo rainforest.

In 1943 Ward moved to the Blue Mountains and opened his Gallery of Natural History and Native Art in a long, narrow fibro building at the Hydro Majestic Hotel, Medlow Bath. As well as his own natural history collections, including 25 000 crabs, he had inherited from his father 'old Japanese armour, weapons, and valuable relics from many foreign lands as well as souvenirs of stage productions'. Ward also acquired convict relics, historical documents and rare Australian books. The museum incongruously combined 'old curiosity shop and scientific exhibits'. He delighted in expounding the minutest detail to visitors. In the late 1950s he appeared on television in Channel 9's 'Mickey Mouse Club' and 'Ninepins' show. He wrote for *Outdoors and Fishing* and lectured to many groups.

Childless, Ward 'adopted' Blackheath Public School: he talked to the boys, taught them bushcraft, let them loose among his collections and helped with the school plays, 'putting on make-up and lending stage props'. He suffered from diabetes mellitus and died of a coronary occlusion on 6 October 1966 at his Medlow Bath home; he was buried with Anglican rites in Blackheath cemetery. His wife survived him. He left his scientific collec-

tions and library to the Australian Museum. At least sixteen species or sub-species were named after him.

J. Devanney, *Bird of Paradise* (Syd, 1945); *People* (Syd), 17 Jan 1951, p 26; *TV Times*, 21 Oct 1961, p 16; Roy Zoological Soc of NSW, *Procs*, 24 Feb 1967, p 15; *SMH*, 20 July 1929, 7 Aug 1930, 16 Jan, 9 May 1931, 24 Apr 1933, 23 Dec 1937, 16 Sept 1942, 25 May 1943; *Sun* (Syd), 19 Oct 1966, p 50; V. Mauldon, Melbourne Ward's Gallery of Natural History and Native Art (Dip. Museum Studies, Univ Syd, 1989); Ward papers (Aust Museum, Syd).

MARTHA RUTLEDGE

WARD, EDWARD JOHN (1899-1963), politician, was born on 21 March 1899 at Darlington, Sydney, fourth child and elder son of native-born parents Edward James Ward, tramway labourer, and his wife Mary Ann, née Maher. Known to his family as Ned, he grew up in a Catholic working-class family at Surry Hills. He began his education at the convent school of St Francis de Sales, but the small fees were beyond the family budget; he was transferred to Cleveland Street then Crown Street Superior Public schools. His militancy was already apparent: he organized a snap strike against school 'conditions' (which failed when classmates deserted him). Leaving school at 14, he had a succession of jobs—fruit-picker, printer's devil, hardware-store clerk and tarpaulin-maker.

World War I reinforced Ward's radical instincts. He joined the local branch of the Political Labor League at 16, the earliest possible age, and his active involvement in the 1917 general strike cost him his job at the Eveleigh railway workshops. Itinerant employment ensued. A non-smoking teetotaller, he busied himself with boxing and athletics, educational reading (a lifelong priority) and the pursuit of his future wife Edith Martha May Bishop, a packer from Parramatta. Six feet (183 cm) tall and solidly built, he was strong and fit; he boxed professionally to supplement his erratic income but was frequently broke—sometimes after visiting Edith he walked some 16 miles (26 km) home to Surry Hills.

On 27 September 1924 Ward married Edith at St Patrick's Church, Parramatta. He toiled as a labourer and chainman on the tramways, and consolidated his reputation as a fiery orator and pugnacious class warrior. Capable and committed, he became a prominent militant in his union, president of the Surry Hills branch of the Australian Labor Party and an alderman (1930-34) on the Sydney Municipal Council. His advancement in the strife-torn State labour movement was accelerated by his admiration for J. T. Lang and friendship with J. A. Beasley [qq.v.9,13]. He was Beasley's campaign director in the 1929 Federal election, which ushered in the Scullin [q.v.11] government.

Ward gained pre-selection for a Federal by-election in the Labor stronghold of East Sydney, which he won on 7 March 1931. His arrival in Canberra as an uncompromising Lang supporter increased tensions in the government. On 12 March, at his first caucus meeting, he joined Beasley and four other Langites in a walk-out, and eight months later they voted with the Opposition to bring down the government. In the ensuing landslide on 19 December even East Sydney was captured by the United Australia Party. Ward, however, was reprieved: J. J. Clasby, who unseated him, died within a month. In the fiercely contested by-election on 6 February 1932—L. L. Cunningham [q.v.13] stood on behalf of federal Labor (the 'official' A.L.P.)—Ward narrowly beat W. V. McCall [q.v.15] to regain his seat. The 'Firebrand of East Sydney' was to hold it until his death.

With his machine-gun oratory and hard-hitting style most suited to Opposition, Eddie Ward (as he was publicly known) established himself as a formidable parliamentary 'bomb-thrower'. He gradually distanced himself from Lang as the ex-premier's influence waned and the Langites rejoined (1936) the federal A.L.P., now led by John Curtin [q.v.13]. In the face of disturbing international developments, Ward maintained his iconoclastic isolationism and exacerbated the complex challenges confronting Curtin. Renewed upheaval in New South Wales resulted in 1940 in another A.L.P. split, but this time Ward did not join Lang and Beasley in breaking away.

Minister for labour and national service from 7 October 1941, Ward openly opposed and frequently unsettled Prime Minister Curtin. He and Arthur Calwell [q.v.13] became known as the 'terrible twins'. Amid searing exchanges on conscription, Curtin broke down after Ward accused him of 'putting young men into the slaughterhouse, although thirty years ago you would not go into it yourself'.

Although he was a generally competent administrator, what Ward accomplished as a minister was overshadowed by his notorious agitation concerning the 'Brisbane Line'. In pursuing sensational allegations with characteristic vindictiveness, he was evidently prompted by information he believed genuine. Curtin abetted him for political reasons, then suspended him from the ministry while an abortive royal commission evaluated an aspect of the controversy. Ward's campaign enraged the Opposition and helped Labor to win the 1943 general election, but he was demoted to the portfolios of transport and external territories on 21 September; Curtin observed that the 'Japs have got the external territories and the army's got the transport'.

Ward had a more amiable relationship with J. B. Chifley [q.v.13], but maintained his hostility to policy initiatives he found unpalatable, most notably, during the Chifley government, the ratification (1947) of the Bretton Woods international monetary agreement and the 'monstrous' measures to quash the 1949 coal-miners' strike. In 1948 he again stood down temporarily as a minister after an old Langite friend, J. S. Garden [q.v.8], implicated him in corruption. Garden, exposed as a liar and forger, was gaoled; Ward was exonerated by a royal commission.

Following Labor's defeat on 10 December 1949, Ward spent the remainder of his career in Opposition. Prime Minister (Sir) Robert Menzies [q.v.15] was a favourite target; observers enjoyed their jousts. Ward described Menzies as a 'posturing individual with the scowl of Mussolini, the bombast of Hitler, and the physical proportions of Goering', and was fond of saying that Menzies' burgeoning military career had been halted by the outbreak of World War I.

Les Haylen [q.v.14] regarded Ward as an unusual 'Labor ranter', being 'meticulously dressed, his iron grey hair swept back from his forehead ... He looked like a dentist ready to drill. He had a rocket take-off—not for him, the preamble, the body of the speech, the lead off and the peroration. He was airborne from the time his hand hit the table'. An opponent, Sir Percy Spender, found him 'a formidable antagonist, a supremely confident demagogue, and an outstanding rabble-rouser' who 'spat out his vituperations as lava erupts from a volcano'. To Ward's colleague Gil Duthie, he was a 'devastating verbal swordsman' whose 'whole life was wrapped up in politics'. The journalist Edgar Holt discerned an 'air of an East Sydney Robespierre, a pea-green incorruptible with an Australian accent'.

Ward shunned vulgar anecdotes, did not swear and refused to wear a dinner suit. In private he could be amiable and amusing, but not with Labor's opponents—to him they were 'enemies inside the House and enemies outside'. He was a successful litigant in libel cases, receiving lucrative damages. His dramatic exposés were a product of careful preparation and an unrivalled intelligence network. Even friends were wary of him; he had a dossier on every Liberal and, Clyde Cameron suspected, 'on most of his colleagues as well'.

During Labor's internecine strife in the 1950s Ward was a predictably fierce adversary. His prominence in fighting Menzies' Communist Party dissolution bill (1950) was followed by conduct that inflamed the Labor caucus ructions. More than once during this tumultuous period he involved himself in fisticuffs with colleagues. His unforgiving hostility to Labor 'rats' was underlined when he refused to attend a function honouring

W. M. Hughes's [q.v.9] fifty consecutive years as a parliamentarian, explaining that he did not eat cheese.

Ward's bids for the deputy leadership in 1946, 1950, 1951 (twice) and 1956 were unsuccessful, as was his challenge to H. V. Evatt's [q.v.14] leadership after the 1958 election. His narrow defeat by E. G. Whitlam in 1960 when he had been expected to become Calwell's deputy rankled most of all. Embittered, he remained assiduous as ever in his parliamentary duties, but was sidelined with heart disease and diabetes mellitus for months in 1960-61. He joked that his first inkling of ill health came when he 'took a swing at Gough Whitlam—and missed'.

By 1962 Ward had been a member of the House of Representatives for three decades, a longer uninterrupted span than anyone else then serving; no member since Federation had matched his fourteen suspensions. In May 1963, on the last sitting day before the winter recess, he was again suspended; he never returned. Survived by his wife, and their daughter and son, he died of myocardial infarction on 31 July that year at St Vincent's Hospital, Sydney; he was accorded a state funeral and was buried with Catholic rites in Randwick cemetery.

Heartfelt eulogies underlined how much rank-and-file 'true believers' relished his implacable combativeness. Calwell later described him as an irrepressible fighter and unrelenting hater. Curtin had dismissed him as a 'bloody ratbag'. Some commentators highlighted his limited horizons and achievements. On the other hand Arthur Hoyle believed that many of Ward's generation revered 'the most authentic voice that the working class in Australia has had'.

E. Spratt, *Eddie Ward* (Adel, 1965); L. Haylen, *Twenty Years' Hard Labor* (Melb, 1969); E. Holt, *Politics is People* (Syd, 1969); G. Duthie, *I Had 50,000 Bosses* (Syd, 1984); D. Connell, *The Confessions of Clyde Cameron 1913-1990* (Syd, 1990); R. McMullin, *The Light on the Hill* (Melb, 1991); A. Hoyle, *Eddie Ward* (Canb, 1994); P. Burns, *The Brisbane Line Controversy* (Syd, 1998); *SMH*, 1 Aug 1963; Ward papers (NL).   Ross McMullin

WARD, HUGH KINGSLEY (1887-1972), bacteriologist, was born on 17 September 1887 at Petersham, Sydney, youngest of eight children of New Zealand-born Frederick William Ward [q.v.12], editor of the *Daily Telegraph*, and his wife Amy Ada, née Cooke, from New South Wales. L. K. Ward [q.v.] was his brother. Hugh was educated at Sydney Grammar School and the University of Sydney (M.B., 1910) where he graduated with first-class honours. Awarded the 1911 Rhodes scholarship for New South Wales, he pro-

ceeded to New College, Oxford. There he experimented with serological tests for syphilis and in 1913 gained diplomas in anthropology and public health. He rowed in the Australian VIII at the 1912 Olympic Games in Stockholm and for Oxford in 1913 and 1914.

Appointed lieutenant, Royal Army Medical Corps Special Reserve, on 5 August 1914, Ward arrived in France a week later. He became regimental medical officer of the 2nd Battalion, King's Royal Rifle Corps. In April 1915 he was promoted captain. He was wounded in action several times and in 1916 won the Military Cross for showing 'an utter contempt for danger' while attending to wounded men. Taken prisoner at Nieuport, Belgium, in June 1917, he was released in March next year. He was gassed at Arras, France, but continued to serve. For his repeated acts of gallantry he was awarded two Bars to his M.C. and twice mentioned in dispatches.

On demobilization, Ward resumed his experimental work at Oxford. He was awarded a Rockefeller Foundation fellowship (1923-24) to conduct research in the department of bacteriology and immunology at Harvard University in the United States of America, then headed by Hans Zinsser. He returned to Oxford then in 1926 joined the staff of Harvard at Zinsser's invitation. There he studied streptococci and persuaded a young John F. Enders to research infectious diseases; Enders was later to win a Nobel prize for culturing poliomyelitis viruses. At St George's Church, Montreal, Canada, on 9 May 1927 Ward married with Anglican rites Constance Isabella Brougham (d.1971), a librarian and daughter of Ernest Brougham Docker [q.v.8].

In 1935 Ward became Bosch [q.v.7] professor of bacteriology at the University of Sydney. He gave undergraduate teaching a high priority, designing a course that took clinical disease as a starting point rather than micro-organisms. His opportunities for personal research were constrained by World War II and its aftermath of large student numbers, but he inspired students to take a B.Sc. (Med.) degree in bacteriology; they included Donald Metcalf, J. F. A. P. Miller and (Sir) Gustav Nossal, three major figures in medical research in postwar Australia.

A man of vision, personal integrity and charm, Ward did not seek recognition and was embarrassed by praise. He played a major role in local and national medical and scientific affairs, and, at the University of Sydney, in sport (the gymnasium was named in his honour) as well as academic matters. With his close friends (Sir) Macfarlane Burnet and E. V. Keogh [q.v.15], he formed a powerful trio of microbiologists who greatly influenced medical research in Australia. He was a founding member (1936) of the National

Health and Medical Research Council. As chairman (1952-53) of the Australian National Research Council, he prepared the way for the smooth transfer in 1954 of many of its functions and awards to the newly formed Australian Academy of Science. He served on the interim council (1948-51) and the council (1951-53) of the Australian National University.

Retiring in 1952, Ward resigned from over thirty committees. From 1952 to 1969 he was a medical officer with the Red Cross Blood Transfusion Service, publishing (with R. J. Walsh) his only book, *A Guide to Blood Transfusion*, in 1957. In his later years he read widely on the arts, current affairs and history. Survived by his son and daughter, he died on 22 November 1972 in Sydney Hospital and was cremated.

G. E. Hall and A. Cousins (eds), *Book of Remembrance of the University of Sydney in the Great War 1914-1918* (Syd, 1939); J. A. Young et al (eds), *Centenary Book of the University of Sydney Faculty of Medicine* (Syd, 1984); G. L. McDonald (ed), *Roll of the Royal Australasian College of Physicians*, 1, 1938-75 (Syd, 1988); F. Fenner (ed), *History of Microbiology in Australia* (Canb, 1990); *Aust J of Experimental Biology and Medical Science*, 41, Aug 1963, p 381; *SMH*, 23 Nov 1972.   FRANK FENNER
P. M. DE BURGH

WARD, LEONARD KEITH (1879-1964), geologist and public servant, was born on 17 February 1879 at Petersham, Sydney, fourth of eight children of Frederick William Ward [q.v.12], a journalist from New Zealand, and his Australian-born wife Amy Ada, née Cooke. One of his brothers was Hugh Kingsley Ward [q.v.]. After attending Sydney and Brisbane Grammar schools and winning a Queensland university exhibition, Keith studied arts and then mining and metallurgy at the University of Sydney (B.A., 1900; B.E., 1903). Taught geology by (Sir) Edgeworth David [q.v.8], he gained experience with Broken Hill Proprietary Co. Ltd before joining the staff of the Western Australian School of Mines, Kalgoorlie, in 1903.

On 7 December 1907 at St Patrick's Cathedral, Melbourne, Ward married with Catholic rites Estella Jane Hockin (d.1957). In 1907-11 he was assistant government geologist and inspector of mines in Tasmania. On 1 January 1912 he succeeded H. Y. L. Brown [q.v.7] as government geologist in South Australia. From 1916 he had additional duties as director of mines and supervisor of boring. When the Geological Survey and the Department of Mines were combined into the one organization in 1917, he was appointed head of department; in 1919 he also became secretary to the minister of mines.

From the beginning Ward worked to integrate the mining industry with the South Australian economy. He regarded the State's mineral resources as public property to be used and regulated in the best interests of the community: increased production of minerals would foster the expansion of local industries, and thereby boost employment. In 1914 (and 1928) he was responsible for revisions of Brown's geological map of South Australia. Under his direction a department of chemistry was established in 1915 to conduct systematic chemical industrial research on South Australia's natural resources. He was appointed a member of the Leigh Creek coal committee (1916) and of the advisory committee (1943). In 1918 he became chairman of the mineral industry committee set up by the Commonwealth Advisory Council of Science and Industry in South Australia. His concern for industrial safety and employees' health resulted in greater protection for workers; in the 1920s he oversaw the implementation of new regulations to prevent lead and gas poisoning, and to cover the use of electricity in mines, works and quarries. In 1926 the University of Adelaide conferred a doctorate of science on Ward for a thesis on the geological history of Central Australia.

Ward stressed the value of having a national geological survey in addition to the State enterprises. As a consultant to the Commonwealth government he investigated water supplies in the Northern Territory and Central Australia (1923-31), and chaired the fifth interstate conference on artesian water (1928). He advised on mining in the Northern Territory (1927-30) and on the establishment of an ore-treatment plant at the Tennant Creek goldfield (1937). A member (1929-30) of the Federal and New South Wales governments' royal commission on the coal industry, he was appointed (1934) to the Commonwealth committee which investigated the construction of a plant to produce oil by the hydrogenation of coal. In 1935 he joined the geological advisory committee formed to assist Anglo-Persian Oil Co. geologists who were investigating sites in Australia for Commonwealth Oil Refineries Ltd. He served on the State advisory committee of the Council for Scientific and Industrial Research (1926-44), the executive committee of the Imperial Geophysical Experimental Survey (1928-31) and the Commonwealth Oil Advisory Committee (1936-40).

A member of the Australasian Institute of Mining and Metallurgy from 1918, the Australian National Research Council, and the council (1917-43) of the South Australian School of Mines and Industries, Ward was also a fellow of the Geological Society of America. He presided over the geology and mineralogy section of the sixteenth meeting (1923) of the Australasian Association for the

Advancement of Science, held in Wellington, New Zealand, the Royal Society of South Australia (1928-30) and the State branch of the Royal Geographical Society of Australasia (1930-31).

Honest, unassuming, modest and kind, Ward 'took quiet delight in cutting the self-important down to size, and in bringing to light the true facts of any situation'. He was an easy-going, congenial and humorous person who was renowned for his 'cheery laugh' and fondness for telling amusing stories. Appointed I.S.O. in 1943, he was awarded the (W. B.) Clarke [q.v.3] and (Sir Joseph) Verco [q.v.12] medals by the Royal societies of New South Wales (1930) and South Australia (1955) respectively. After retiring in 1944 as director of mines and government geologist, he was a consultant to the department for five years until forced to resign because of continuing ill health. Survived by two of his three sons and his three daughters, he died on 30 September 1964 at Toorak Gardens, Adelaide, and was cremated with Anglican rites.

B. O'Neil, *In Search of Mineral Wealth* (Adel, 1982) and *Above and Below* (Adel, 1995); Roy Soc SA, *Trans*, 89, 1965, p 291; *Daily Herald* (Adel), 28 Nov 1911; *Register* (Adel), 24 Jan 1928; Ward biog file (Mort L).   BERNARD O'NEIL

WARD, MARY ALICE (1896-1972), teacher and pastoralist, was born on 1 September 1896 at Kooringa, Burra, South Australia, eldest of eight children of John McEntyre, an engineer from Victor Harbor, and his wife Margaret Anne, née Kelleher. By 1904 the family had moved to the Western Australian goldfields, living first at Kalgoorlie and then Coolgardie. Mary began teaching at Tunneys State School in June 1915, and gained her junior cadet training certificate in September next year. In 1918-24 she taught at Kalgoorlie, Boulder and Carlisle. Promoted to head teacher in 1924, she moved often—to Parkfield, Pingrup, Cottesloe, Wyering, Keysbrook and Latham —before transferring to Wyndham in 1932. On 27 December that year at the office of the district registrar, Wyndham, she married Philip ('Ted') Ward, a stockman.

For two years the Wards lived at Jack Kilfoyle's [q.v.15] Rosewood station, 120 miles (193 km) south-east of Wyndham. With Mary's brother Stuart they joined the gold-rush at Tennant Creek, Northern Territory, in 1935. Prospecting at a mine site that they called Blue Moon they struck gold, reputedly worth £80 000. In 1941 the Wards bought the cattle station Banka Banka, a property of almost two thousand sq. miles (5180 km²) located 60 miles (97 km) north of Tennant Creek. Mary supervised the development of

an extensive garden, and during World War II Banka Banka supplied the army (which had a staging camp nearby) with meat, eggs, fruit and vegetables. The homestead, close to the Stuart Highway, was a regular stopping place for travellers and Mrs Ward's hospitality became legendary. In 1945 Ted Ward was among the first to truck cattle by road, and in the early 1950s the Wards acquired Lilleyvale in western Queensland (soon replaced with Fermoy, near Longreach) for use as a fattening station.

Having no children of her own, Mrs Ward cared for the babies of her Warumungu employees. In the 1950s a native affairs branch inspector wrote that 'youngsters on this station look the picture of health, and this is entirely due to the unremitting personal care and attention given by Mrs Ward'. She and her husband did not agree with the policy of removing part-Aborigines from their mothers. They sent children to school at Alice Springs at their own expense until 1961, when due to her efforts a government school opened at Banka Banka.

After her husband's death in 1959 Mrs Ward ran the stations. Known as 'the missus of Banka Banka', she also owned a butcher shop at Tennant Creek, supplying it from an abattoir on the property. One of her cattle managers recalled that she spent money on the welfare of her Aboriginal staff—many of whom she trained in domestic and station duties—while economizing on repairs and improvements, and eschewing new management methods. She was known to have dismissed White employees because of their ill treatment of Aborigines. She acquired five houses at Tennant Creek for her old retainers and, despite objections from the local town management board, arranged for construction in 1968-69 of a large red-brick building to house former employees and their relations. The 'Mary Ward Hostel' (also known as the 'Pink Palace') was later used for a range of community purposes. She was appointed M.B.E. in 1968.

Mrs Ward was short, with a 'ready smile'. Her delicate appearance belied her strength of character and confidence. In 1970, suffering ill health, she sold Banka Banka—she had already disposed of Fermoy—and moved to Adelaide. She died on 27 July 1972 at her North Adelaide home, and was buried with Catholic rites in Centennial Park cemetery.

H. Tuxworth, *Tennant Creek Yesterday and Today* (Tennant Creek, NT, 1978); T. Cole, *Spears & Smoke Signals* (Darwin, 1986); A. Smith, *Convoys up the Track* (Adel, 1991); 'A Big Country—Missus of Banka Banka', ABC TV, 6 Nov 1969 (ABC Archives); Liz Evans, taped interview with Albert Hooker (c1981, NT Archives); Banka Banka station journals in H. Tuxworth collection, boxes 6 and 7 (Fryer L, Univ Qld); Lilleyvale, Fermoy and Banka Banka station journals in Tuxworth-Fullwood collection (National Trust Museum, Tennant Creek, NT).

DAVID NASH

WARDLE, ROBERT NORMAN (1895-1979), veterinarian and public servant, was born on 1 July 1895 at Ballarat, Victoria, youngest of seven children of Henry Thomas Wardle, timber merchant, and his wife Isabella, née Allan, both Victorian born. Bob was educated at Humffray Street and Dana Street State schools, Ballarat Agricultural High School and the University of Melbourne (B.V.Sc., 1916). On 6 March 1917 he was appointed captain, Australian Army Veterinary Corps, Australian Imperial Force. Arriving in Egypt in June, he served with the Australian Mounted Division and from November 1918 commanded the 8th Australian Mobile Veterinary Section in Palestine. He returned to Melbourne where his A.I.F. appointment terminated on 3 October 1919.

While in private practice (1920-26) at Geelong, Wardle was honorary veterinary surgeon to the Geelong Agricultural and Pastoral Society, the Geelong Racing, Geelong Trotting and Victoria Coursing clubs, and the Gordon Wool Advisory Committee. At the Collins Street Baptist Church, Melbourne, on 25 April 1922 he married Dorothy Evelyn Rule (d.1953); they were to have two sons. As veterinary officer (1926-39) with the Victorian Department of Agriculture, he cared for Clydesdale horses especially and toured Victoria with the Better Farming Train, which advised farmers on good agricultural practice.

Moving to Canberra in 1939 as director of the division of veterinary hygiene, Commonwealth Department of Health, Wardle concentrated on animal quarantine to keep out foot-and-mouth and other exotic diseases. He was chairman of the Cattle Tick Commission, a member of the standing committee of the Australian Agricultural Council, and permanent Australian delegate to the Office International des Epizooties, Paris. In 1949 he led the Australian contingent to the International Veterinary Congress in London. During his term as director, horses were refused entry for the 1956 Olympic Games in Melbourne, resulting in the equestrian events being held in Stockholm. Retiring on 30 June 1960, he had done much to protect Australia from the 'incursion of serious diseases of animals'. He was a member of the Australian Veterinary Association and a life member (1971) of the Australian College of Veterinary Scientists.

On 12 April 1955 at the Church of St John the Baptist, Reid, Wardle had married with Anglican rites Patience Australie, daughter of Robin and Pattie Tillyard [qq.v.12]. The couple bred ponies and fattened steers on Maitai, their 40-acre (16 ha) property near Murrumbateman, New South Wales. Bob was an expert rider who loved horses and specialized in their treatment. He tipped winners but was never known to bet. A strict Methodist, he was a keen student of Bible and Middle East history, and a trustee of the National Memorial Church, Forrest.

Wardle was president of the Horticultural Society of Canberra (1954-56), the Rotary Club of Canberra (1948-49) and the local division of the Australian Red Cross Society (1950-52), and a member of the Melbourne Cricket Club and the Canberra and District Historical Society. He was a man of middle height, with a moustache and confident bearing. Combining passionate involvement with stubbornness and a sometimes disarming directness, he adhered to 'proper procedure'. His dry wit was accompanied by a twinkle in his eye. Survived by his wife, and by a son of his first marriage, he died on 21 July 1979 at his Forrest home and was buried in Canberra cemetery.

I. M. Parsonson, *The Australian Ark* (Melb, 2000); *J of the Aust Veterinary Assn*, 55, no 9, Sept 1979, p 453; Canb and District Hist Soc, *Newsletter*, no 207, Sept 1979, p 7; Geelong Hist Soc, *Investigator*, 21, no 2, June 1986, p 51; *Canb Times*, 24 July 1979; funeral address by Rev I. S. Williams (copy on ADB file); information from and papers held by Mr D. Wardle, Lyons, Canb.   BARBARA DAWSON

WARFE, GEORGE RADFORD (1912-1975), army officer, was born on 27 July 1912 at Leongatha, Victoria, third child of Melbourne-born parents George Henry Warfe, carrier, and his wife Ethel Charlotte, née Armstrong. Educated locally and at the Working Men's College, Melbourne, young George was employed as a builder and cabinet-maker. At St Peter's Church, Leongatha, on 11 June 1938 he married with Anglican rites Ola Grace Dysart, a shop assistant; they had no children. Having enlisted in the 29th/22nd Battalion, Militia, in March 1937, he was appointed probationary lieutenant in February 1939. He was seconded to the Australian Imperial Force on 13 October 1939 and posted to the 2nd/6th Battalion.

Arriving in the Middle East in May 1940, Warfe commanded the battalion's Bren-gun carrier platoon in the battle of Bardia, Libya, on 3-5 January 1941. The carrier platoon seized Post 13 and helped to capture Post 11 of the Italian defences, and Warfe established a reputation for aggressiveness, pugnacity and professionalism. Five ft 9½ ins (177 cm) tall and broad-shouldered, with strong features, black hair and a steady gaze, he was known for his trenchant use of the Australian vernacular. He was appointed second-in-command of 'D' Company before the capture of Tobruk (21-22 January) and the subsequent advance on Benghazi. Promoted temporary captain in March (substantive in August), he further revealed his toughness in the ill-fated Greek campaign in April. After retraining in Palestine and Syria, he returned to Australia in August 1942. He had been mentioned in dispatches.

Later that month Warfe attended the Guerrilla Warfare School, Wilsons Promontory, Victoria. He was promoted temporary major and given command of the 2nd/3rd Independent Company in September. The unit trained in Queensland before deploying to New Guinea in January 1943. There the 'Mad Major', as Peter Pinney described him, conducted operations in the offensive leading to the capture of Salamaua. For his 'determined leadership and inspiring personal example', in the fighting at Goodview Junction and Ambush Knoll in July, he was awarded the Military Cross. He was again mentioned in dispatches.

Warfe assumed administrative command of the 58th/59th Battalion in August. Promoted temporary lieutenant colonel next month, he led the battalion until the end of the Salamaua campaign. Back in Australia in October, he was attached to the 2nd/7th Cavalry (Commando) Regiment, but was in hospital with malaria from December to March 1944. He returned to the 58th/59th Battalion in April, commanding the unit in New Guinea until July, in Queensland while it re-formed, and on Bougainville from December 1944. He was the ideal commander for this relatively inexperienced Militia battalion—its history recorded that 'Warfe's dynamic personality and ruthless drive had quickly welded the unit into an aggressive and confident band of jungle fighters'.

In January 1945 Warfe took over the 2nd/24th Battalion, which he commanded in the bitter fighting on Tarakan Island, Borneo, from May. He won the Distinguished Service Order for his role in the capture of the airfield. On 28 February 1946 his A.I.F. appointment terminated in Melbourne. Divorced in March, he married Elvie Clark Ross (d.1971), a secretary, on 13 April that year at the Methodist Church, St Kilda.

Warfe returned to building but was soon soldiering again part-time, commanding (1948-50) the 5th Battalion (Victorian Scottish Regiment), Citizen Military Forces. In July-August 1950 he was a member of (Sir) William Bridgeford's [q.v.13] mission which went to Malaya to advise on the Emergency. He resumed full-time duty in December and commanded (1951-53) the 15th National Service Training Battalion, being confirmed as sub-

stantive lieutenant colonel, Australian Regular Army, in October 1951.

In 1953 Warfe attended staff college. Next year he commanded the 20th National Service Training Battalion before serving with the Australian Observer Unit in Malaya in August-December. He returned to Australia to become chief instructor at the Jungle Training Centre, Canungra, Queensland. With Colonel F. P. Serong, he instituted a tough and realistic training régime that would influence generations of soldiers and help to develop the army's remarkable proficiency in jungle warfare. From February 1957 he served as a senior staff officer in Melbourne, first in the directorate of military training, Army Headquarters, and then (from February 1959) at 3rd Division headquarters. He retired from the A.R.A. on 27 July 1962.

Promoted colonel, C.M.F., two days later, Warfe commanded (1962-65) the 1st Battalion, Royal Victoria Regiment. During this period he was employed as training officer at B.X. Plastics (Aust.) Pty Ltd. As a senior adviser to the United States Mission, he supervised instruction at the Vietnamese National Police Field Force Training Centre at Trai Mat, Republic of Vietnam (South Vietnam), in 1966-67.

Back in Melbourne, Warfe worked as personnel manager with Clark Rubber Stores Ltd. He served as co-ordinator of civil defence, Victoria, in 1969-75. For recreation he enjoyed hunting, shooting and fishing. He died of cancer on 5 November 1975 at Brighton and was cremated. The three sons of his second marriage, all of whom also became colonels, survived him. Portraits of him by (Sir) Ivor Hele (1943) and Geoffrey Mainwaring (1957) are held by the Australian War Memorial, Canberra.

R. Mathews, *Militia Battalion at War* (Syd, 1961); R. P. Serle (ed), *The Second Twenty-Fourth* (Brisb, 1963); H. Gullett, *Not as a Duty Only* (Melb, 1976); D. Hay, *Nothing Over Us* (Canb, 1984); I. McNeill, *The Team* (Canb, 1984); P. Pinney, *The Barbarians* (Brisb, 1988); R. Garland, *Nothing is Forever* (Syd, 1997); information from Col P. Warfe, Garran, Canb.   ALAN RYAN

WARING, HORACE (1910-1980), zoologist, was born on 17 December 1910 at Toxteth Park, Liverpool, England, son of Frank Waring, hosier and glover, and his wife Emma Hender, née Macdonald. Educated at Holt Secondary School and the University of Liverpool (B.Sc., 1931; M.Sc., 1933), Harry won an Edward Forbes exhibition tenable at the university and its marine biological station, Port Erin, Isle of Man. In 1937 he joined the zoology department of the University of Aberdeen (D.Sc., 1939). At the Sefton parish church, Lancashire, on 3 September 1938, he married

Doreen Dickinson (d.1976). From 1941 he was an entomologist with the Ministry of Agriculture & Fisheries, working in Scotland on control of parasites in farm animals. In 1946 he took up the post of head of the zoology department, University of Birmingham.

On 1 May 1948 Waring was appointed professor of zoology at the University of Western Australia. As an experimental zoologist he brought a new approach to a department whose work had been largely taxonomic. He determined to undertake research on marsupials. Warned that obtaining funds for research would be difficult, he responded by establishing an extensive network of people and organizations to help him. (Sir) Ian Clunies Ross [q.v.13] of the Commonwealth Scientific and Industrial Research Organization arranged for an annual grant, and Francis Ratcliffe [q.v.], officer-in-charge of the C.S.I.R.O. wildlife survey section, fostered co-operation between his staff and Waring's group. The Broken Hill Proprietory Co. Ltd provided transport to islands off the Kimberley coast, and the Department of Defence authorized the use of facilities on Garden Island. The Western Australian Department of Fisheries and Fauna assisted in various ways; later its minister, Graham MacKinnon, helped to achieve the vesting (1970) of the Jandakot reserve, near Rockingham, for the establishment of a breeding colony of marsupials.

Starting with quokkas, Waring's field of research was reproductive physiology, in particular the immunological competence, endocrine function and other aspects of development of the pouched embryo. He also developed an interest in nutritional physiology, and studied with R. J. Moir the ruminant-like function of the enlarged foregut of marsupials. With Moir and C. H. Tyndale-Biscoe he wrote a major review of the comparative physiology of marsupials in *Advances in Comparative Physiology and Biochemistry* (1966). The publication of his monograph *Color Change Mechanisms of Cold-Blooded Vertebrates* in 1963 was the culmination of work begun when he was a student. Chairman (1958-59) of the professorial board and acting vice-chancellor in 1958, he disliked administration but regarded it as a necessary evil to be tolerated so that he could pursue his research. Loud and boisterous, and unwilling to suffer fools, he took his teaching duties seriously and remained interested in his students and their careers. In 1970 the university awarded him an honorary doctorate of science.

After retiring in December 1975 Waring stayed on as honorary research fellow, continuing to publish papers on the immunology of marsupials and hormones of marsupials and monotremes. On 11 May 1979 at their home at North Beach he married in a civil ceremony Muriel Naomi Crapp, née McIlwraith,

a widow. Elected (1954) a fellow of the Australian Academy of Science, he was awarded (1962) the Royal Society of New South Wales's (W. B.) Clarke [q.v.3] medal, and shared (1970) with A. R. Main the Britannica Australia award for science. In 1980 he was awarded the Mueller [q.v.5] medal by the Australian and New Zealand Association for the Advancement of Science. Having suffered for some years from cardiorenal failure, he died on 9 August 1980 at Nedlands and was cremated. His wife, and the son and daughter of his first marriage survived him. The marsupial reserve at Jandakot was named after him in 1982.

F. Alexander, *Campus at Crawley* (Melb, 1963); Univ WA, *Univ News*, Dec 1970, p 6, Dec 1975, p 3, Sept 1980, p 4, 5 Oct 1982, p 17; *Hist Records of Aust Science*, 5, no 2, 1981, p 116; staff file (Univ WA Archives).
A. R. MAIN

WARLOW-DAVIES, ERIC JOHN (1910-1964), aircraft engineer, was born on 4 January 1910 at Broken Hill, New South Wales, son of native-born parents Harry Warlow Davies, mining engineer, and his wife Muriel Winifred Julie, née Bate, great-granddaughter of Samuel Bate [q.v.1]. After World War I Harry was appointed chief engineer of the Electrolytic Zinc Co. of Australasia Ltd, Risdon, Tasmania. Eric attended The Hutchins School, Hobart, where he won numerous prizes and scholarships. In 1928 he entered the University of Tasmania (B.Sc., 1931). He read physics, mathematics and engineering, served as secretary (1929) and later president of the university union, co-edited the university magazine, and enjoyed rifle-shooting, rowing and soccer.

Selected as Rhodes scholar for Tasmania in 1932, Warlow-Davies proceeded to Corpus Christi College, Oxford (B.A., 1934; D.Phil., 1939), and graduated with first-class honours in engineering science. Warlow, as he was known to his friends, worked at the Royal Aircraft Establishment, Farnborough, from 1936 and at the London, Midland & Scottish Railway Co.'s research laboratory, Derby, from 1938. He contributed several papers to scientific and engineering journals reporting on his own or collaborative research into such matters as the 'impact strength' and 'fatigue strength' of materials, problems of repeatability and standardization, the effects of 'fretting corrosion' on fatigue strength and the 'dielectric breakdown strength' of lubricating materials.

In 1942, persuaded by (Sir) Stanley Hooker (assistant chief engineer of Rolls-Royce Ltd), Warlow-Davies joined the firm; he was appointed quality engineer at the plant near

Glasgow where Merlin engines were being made for British fighter aircraft. Hooker said of him: 'No scratch or frettage was too microscopic to escape his attention, and he possessed the sixth sense of being able instantly to recognise whether such a mark would lead to a dangerous failure'. In 1946 Warlow-Davies was sent to Montreal, Canada, to oversee the development and manufacture of Merlin engines for DC-4M civil airliners. Next year he published a paper concerning the advantages of liquid-cooling systems for aircraft engines, in comparison with air-cooling systems. Back in Britain in 1948, he was technical-services and quality engineer at Rolls-Royce's works near Derby, becoming chief development engineer for the Nene and Derwent engines the following year. He returned to Montreal in 1951 as general manager and chief engineer of Rolls-Royce of Canada Ltd, with responsibility for the Nene engines which the company was supplying for T-33A Silver Star jet trainers. He was unhappy in this work, for the senior management position cut him off from his first love, engineering.

With the help of Hooker, then chief engineer at the Bristol Aeroplane Co. Ltd's engine division (Bristol Aero-Engines Ltd from 1956), Warlow-Davies left Canada and Rolls-Royce in July 1953. He was welcomed to Filton, England, by Bristol's new managing director, Air Chief Marshal Sir Alec Coryton, as chief engineer for current-production jet engines, the Proteus and the Olympus. Coryton and Warlow-Davies became firm friends. Together they purchased a 1904 Humberette which they entered in many vintage motorcar rallies. In 1959 Bristol Aero-Engines Ltd merged with Armstrong Siddeley Motors Ltd to form Bristol Siddeley Engines Ltd. Warlow-Davies was appointed chief engineer (aero); by 1963 he was managing director.

In 1962 the French and British governments agreed to combine in their attempts to build a supersonic airliner. The aircraft, eventually called the Concorde, was to be powered by four Olympus engines, constructed by Bristol Siddeley and the Société Nationale d'Étude et de Construction de Moteurs d'Aviation. Warlow-Davies led a team which designed a more powerful variant of the Olympus 301 (capable of a thrust of 20 000 lb.). The development of the Olympus 593 (capable of a thrust of 38 000 lb.) for the Concorde is a measure of Warlow-Davies' achievement. From January 1964 he was also a member of the British Air Registration Board.

Warlow-Davies never married. Tall and spare, he was said to have been feared by younger entrants to his profession as an uncompromising stickler for accuracy in all their calculations, and for the fullest necessary detail in engineering drawings. An associate, Professor Martyn Farley, wrote that his 'con-

tribution was immense and many of his colleagues acquired reputations by learning from him and living in the culture that he created'. On holiday in Corsica with friends, Warlow-Davies collapsed on 28 June 1964 while swimming at a beach between the towns of L'Ile-Rousse and Calvi. A local doctor pronounced him dead, certifying that he had died of a stroke complicated by a heart attack. His body was brought back to Derby, England, where he was cremated. He was named a 'Hutchins Lion' by his old school in Hobart.

C. Burnet, *Three Centuries to Concorde* (Lond, 1979); S. Hooker, *Not Much of an Engineer* (Shrewsbury, Eng, 1984); *The Times* and *Nice-matin* (France), 30 June 1964; information from Mrs P. Lukins, Bristol, and Mrs D. Russell, Derby, Eng.

R. C. SHARMAN

WARNER, SIR ARTHUR GEORGE (1899-1966), businessman and politician, was born on 31 July 1899 at Lower Clapton, London, son of Arthur Warner, electrical engineer and later manager, and his wife Emily, née Cheesman. Young Arthur attended Sir George Monoux Grammar School, Chingford, Essex, and began a science degree at the University of London. Abandoning his studies, he was appointed temporary flight officer, Royal Naval Air Service, on 13 August 1917. He transferred to the Royal Air Force as a kite-balloon officer and rose to the rank of lieutenant. In 1920 he migrated to Australia and became an orchardist at Scottsdale, Tasmania. On 14 August that year at Wesley Church, Melbourne, he married with Methodist forms Ethel Wakefield. Finding the life of a farmer uncongenial and unremunerative, he studied accountancy by correspondence, moved to Melbourne and set up as a consulting accountant.

In 1922, in partnership with Louis Abrahams, Warner established a small basement store, stocking imported telephone equipment and radio parts. The outlet was the beginning of what was to become a vast industrial and commercial empire. As chairman and managing director, Warner headed (from 1939) Electronic Industries Ltd, manufacturer of the Astor range of products, especially radios and later television sets. Progressively, he became owner or chairman of numerous companies, including Australian & International Insurances Ltd and Radio Corporation Pty Ltd. He also chaired (to 1961) General Television Corporation Pty Ltd which in 1955 obtained one of the first two licences issued to commercial operators in Melbourne.

Warner was active in a variety of industry associations and other bodies, such as the Melbourne Chamber of Commerce, the Victorian Chamber of Manufactures, the Economic Society of Australia and New Zealand, and the Institute of Industrial Management of Australia. He was an original member of the council of the Institute of Public Affairs which was launched in 1943. During World War II the Federal government appointed him controller of finance in the Department of Munitions.

An obsessive worker, Warner entered the Victorian parliament on 15 June 1946 as an Independent (Progressive Liberal), defeating (Sir) James Disney [q.v.14], the sitting Liberal Party member for Higinbotham in the Legislative Council. The Australian Labor Party leader John Cain [q.v.13] accused him of spending up to £10 000 to win the seat. Warner replied that, while his 'friends' did not spend that much, he was 'prepared to admit the campaign was well organised'.

Joining the Liberal Party, Warner assumed office as minister in charge of materials and of housing in the coalition government (November 1947-December 1948) of T. T. Hollway and (Sir) John McDonald [qq.v.14,15]. In the succeeding Hollway administration, he held the same portfolios, with that of State development. He refused to divest himself of his business interests. After public criticism by two Liberal and Country Party back-benchers, F. L. Edmunds and J. S. Lechte, in September 1949, Hollway agreed to establish an inquiry into the administration of housing. In December Hollway took State development from Warner and made him responsible for electrical undertakings instead; he remained in cabinet until the government fell in June 1950.

Despairing of Hollway's idiosyncratic leadership, Warner was a leading figure in the campaign to expel him from the L.C.P. in 1952. Seven of Hollway's supporters followed him out of the party, causing questions to be asked about Warner's political judgement. Warner strongly endorsed the new leader Leslie Norman but Norman lost his seat to Hollway at the general election that year. When Norman's replacement Trevor Oldham [q.v.15] was killed in a plane crash in May 1953, Warner used his considerable influence to secure the leadership for (Sir) Henry Bolte, against (Sir) Arthur Rylah [q.v.]. Warner's reputation as Bolte's kingmaker was later used by the Labor Party to embarrass the inexperienced premier after he gained power on 7 June 1955. Only after he refreshed his mandate at the 1958 election was he able to throw off the perception that he was Warner's puppet.

As minister of transport and a vice-president of the Board of Land and Works in Bolte's government, Warner ranked third in cabinet. He also acted as leader of the government in the Legislative Council, charged with the carriage of a heavy legislative agenda. His task was made more demanding by the government's lack of a majority in the Upper House,

where the Country Party held the balance of power. He developed into an adroit parliamentary tactician and his jousts with the Labor leader Jack Galbally became renowned, yet the two remained friends. In 1956 Warner was knighted; he was to be appointed K.B.E. in 1962.

Warner was determined to reform the railways and stem their financial losses but his business interests caused further controversy. On 19 November 1958 the Opposition initiated a motion of no confidence in the government, one of the grounds being that a company contracted to install vending-machines on railway stations was a subsidiary of Electronic Industries Ltd. The Opposition raised a second issue involving conflict of interest on 3 March 1959, alleging that a public drinking-fountain had been removed from Ringwood railway station and replaced by a soft drink vending-machine supplied by Warner's company. On 22 March 1960 the minister was the target of yet another no confidence motion when it was revealed that an engineering company in which he held an interest had received a government loan of £27 500. Bolte's arguments in his defence were, according to Katherine West, 'evasively feeble', but Warner survived.

Described as 'never bored' and 'never boring', the 'suave and softly-spoken' Warner was a keen member of the Royal Brighton Yacht Club. He sailed his yawl *Winston Churchill* to victory in the Queenscliff to Sydney yacht race in 1956, and from that year competed regularly in the Sydney to Hobart race. On 6 April 1959 during a storm in Bass Strait, the *Winston Churchill* began to take water. Warner managed to beach her near Wonthaggi. While struggling ashore, he was thrown from the yacht's dinghy and almost drowned.

Following a heart attack in 1960 Warner reduced his considerable ministerial duties and, in September 1962, resigned from cabinet. Another reason for his resignation may have been his vehement opposition to Bolte's decision (later thwarted by the High Court of Australia) to execute the convicted murderer Robert Tait. On 20 June 1964 Sir Arthur retired from parliament. He had a house at Brighton and a grazing property at Yea. Survived by his wife and their two sons, he died of myocardial infarction on 3 April 1966 at Seymour; after a state funeral with Anglican rites, he was cremated. His estate was sworn for probate at $557 815.

K. West, *Power in the Liberal Party* (Melb, 1965); M. Davis, *Australian Ocean Racing* (Syd, 1967); P. Aimer, *Politics, Power and Persuasion* (Melb, 1974); P. Blazey, *Bolte* (Melb, 1990); *PD* (Vic), 19 Nov 1958, p 1803, 3 Mar 1959, p 2406, 30 Apr 1964, p 4263, 5 Apr 1966, p 3142; *Nation* (Syd), 22 Nov 1958; *Sun-Herald* (Syd), 12 Apr 1959.   B. J. COSTAR

WARNES, CATHERINE ANNE (1949-1969), entertainer, was born on 7 December 1949 at Arncliffe, Sydney, second of three children of George Alfred Warnes, an English-born motor mechanic, and his wife Nancy Starnes, née Buck, from Sydney. Cathy attended Athelstane Public and Arncliffe Girls' High schools. She showed an early interest in the performing arts and, while in primary school, began taking singing and dancing lessons.

By the age of 12 Warnes was appearing on stage in local community and school concerts. Spotted by a talent scout, she was offered a permanent spot, dancing on television station TCN-9's programme 'Opportunity Knocks'. At 16 she won second prize for singing in the Starflight talent quest. This competition was conducted by another popular Channel 9 show, 'Bandstand', on which she became a regular performer. She began entertaining in clubs, even though she was under the legal age to enter these premises, and recorded advertising jingles for radio and television. Later she joined the 'pop' singer 'Col Joye' on several concert tours around Australia. Warnes used the stage name 'Cathy Wayne'.

In the first half of 1967 she travelled with other entertainers to the Republic of Vietnam (South Vietnam) on a wartime concert tour sponsored by the Australian Forces Advisory Committee on Entertainment. Because she was not yet 18, it had been necessary for Bruce Webber, the organizer of the tour, to obtain the approval of her parents for her to take part. He recalled that she had 'leapt at the chance' to go to South Vietnam. Members of F.A.C.E. concert parties were not paid for their services but were given a daily living allowance and a security guarantee.

In mid-1969 Warnes returned to South Vietnam as the lead singer in an Australian pop group, 'Sweethearts on Parade'. The tour was privately arranged by Ingrid Hart, a promoter and performer, and was not under the auspices of the Australian government. On 20 July that year at Da Nang, Warnes was on stage in a club for non-commissioned officers of the United States Marine Corps when a bullet, fired from outside the club, passed through the insect-screen of an open window and hit her in the chest, killing her. Her body was returned to Australia and cremated with Anglican rites.

Sergeant J. W. Killen, U.S. Marines, was convicted of the unpremeditated murder of Warnes, allegedly while attempting to shoot his commanding officer, Major R. E. Simons, who had been in the audience. Nancy Warnes was reported as saying that she and her husband had not been in favour of their daughter's second trip to Vietnam but that 'she wanted to go—Cathy had a will of her own'.

Her father told journalists that she had hoped to '"save a few dollars" to help her singing career on return to Sydney'. Catherine Warnes was one of three Australian women killed in Vietnam during the war. The other two, Lee Makk and Margaret Moses [q.v.15], were welfare workers who died in an aeroplane crash in 1975.

S. McHugh, *Minefields and Miniskirts* (Syd, 1993); *SMH*, 23 July 1969; *Australian*, 18 Aug 1988; A4531, item 62/2/3/2 (NAA, Canb); information from Mr B. Webber, Manly, Ms E. Burton, Darlinghurst, and Mr P. Powler, Coogee, Syd.

MICHELLE RAYNER

WARNE-SMITH, IVOR PHILLIP SCHARRER (1897-1960), Australian Rules footballer, was born on 29 October 1897 in North Sydney, third of four sons of Victorian-born parents Charles Warne-Smith (previously Smith), journalist, and his wife Naomi, née Scharrer. The family later moved to Brighton, Melbourne. Ivor was educated at Wesley College where he excelled at football, cricket, athletics and tennis; he was public schools' cricket champion in 1914. Claiming to be aged 18, on 14 May 1915 he enlisted in the Australian Imperial Force. He served at Gallipoli (1915) with the 7th Battalion and on the Western Front (1916-18) with the 15th Machine-Gun Company and the 5th Machine-Gun Battalion. In December 1917 he was commissioned and in March 1918 promoted lieutenant. Gassed in April, he was wounded in the head and leg in September. Both his elder brothers were killed in action in France. His A.I.F. appointment terminated in Melbourne on 2 July 1919.

That year Warne-Smith began his career with the Victorian Football League, playing eight games with the Melbourne club. In 1920 he moved to Latrobe, Tasmania, to grow apples. Appointed captain-coach (1922) of the town's football team, he led it to premierships in 1922 and 1924. He also captained the North-Western Football Union's representative team and won the 1924 Cheel medal as the union's best and fairest player. On 18 January 1922 at a civil ceremony in Melbourne he had married Marjorie Clements.

In 1925 Warne-Smith returned to Victoria. Richmond attempted to bring him back to the V.F.L. but Melbourne insisted that he was still their player. Resuming with his old club that year, he was to take the field in 146 games and kick 110 goals. In 1926 Melbourne won the premiership and Warne-Smith the Brownlow medal, the V.F.L.'s award for best and fairest player. Two years later he won a second Brownlow, the first man to do so. He was captain-coach in 1928-31 and non-playing coach in 1932 though he briefly came out of retirement as a player during the season. Additionally, he represented Victoria on six occasions, several as State captain.

Warne-Smith was 5 ft 11½ ins (182 cm) tall and weighed 12 st. 7 lb. (79 kg). He performed well in almost any position, including the ruck, but many of his best games were as a centre-man. An intelligent player, he could kick with either foot, take high marks and change the direction of the game with his handball. After he stopped playing he wrote regularly on football for the *Argus*. His main source of income was his job with the Vacuum Oil Co. Pty Ltd. Having joined the company in 1926, he was superintendent of its Yarraville terminal for many years then executive-assistant to the Victorian operations manager.

On 1 August 1940 Warne-Smith was commissioned lieutenant, Australian Army Service Corps, A.I.F. He served in the Middle East (1941-42) with I Corps Petrol Park and in the Northern Territory (1942-43) with the Bulk Issue Petrol and Oil Depot. Promoted major, he commanded the 1st Bulk Petroleum Storage Company in New Guinea (1943-44) and the 4th B.P.S.C. in New Guinea and Borneo (1944-45). For his leadership during the Borneo operations, he was mentioned in dispatches. He transferred to the Reserve of Officers on 3 October 1945 in Melbourne.

From 1949 until his death Warne-Smith served as chairman of selectors for Melbourne and helped Norm Smith [q.v.] steer the club to premierships in 1955, 1956, 1957 and 1959. Warne-Smith sat on the committee of the Melbourne Cricket Club and played with M.C.C. teams, hitting a century at the age of 58. Ill health forced him to retire from Vacuum Oil in 1959. The Warne-Smiths lived at Brighton and Armadale before moving to Mount Martha. Survived by his wife, and their daughter and son, he died of coronary vascular disease on 4 March 1960 at Newport and was cremated. His friends remembered him as a gentlemanly, charming and unassuming man who never boasted of his achievements.

J. Donnelly, *Football Guide: 1947* (Launc, Tas, 1947); E. C. H. Taylor, *100 Years of Football* (Melb, 1957); K. Pinchin, *A Century of Tasmanian Football 1879-1979* (Hob, 1979); G. Hobbs, *125 Yrs of the Melbourne Demons* (Melb, 1984); R. Holmesby and J. Main, *The Encyclopedia of AFL Footballers* (Melb, 1998); L. Carroll, *The Grand Old Flag* (Melb, 1999); *Argus*, 7 Mar 1918; *Age* (Melb), 30 Jan 1959, 7 Mar 1960; *Herald* (Melb), 8 Mar 1960; information from and papers held by Mr M. Warne-Smith, Melb.

DAVE NADEL

WARREN, JOHN ROGER HOGARTH (1905-1960), winemaker, was born on 18 March 1905 at Busselton, Western Australia, third child of South Australian-born parents Thomas Hogarth Warren, farmer, and his wife Fanny Maud, née Woolfitt. Shortly after his birth the family moved to Kadina, South Australia. Roger attended the Collegiate School of St Peter, Adelaide, and Roseworthy Agricultural College (R.D.A., 1924), where he obtained honours in chemistry and surveying. He became a woolclasser, but in 1929 a former fellow student Colin Haselgrove, a winemaker and manager with Thomas Hardy [q.v.4] & Sons, persuaded him to join the firm. Devoting two hours a night three times a week to instructing him about the business, Hazelgrove trained Warren as a winemaker and arranged for him to become his 'understudy' at Hardy's.

On 14 September 1935 at St Peter's College chapel Warren married with Anglican rites Helen Josephine Verco, a great-niece of Sir Joseph Verco [q.v.12]. At Hardy's he was promoted senior technical officer in 1938. Based at the Mile End Cellars in Adelaide, in 1953 Warren joined the Hardy's board and succeeded Hazelgrove as technical director, becoming in effect chief winemaker.

Warren's skill, and the relative lack of interest in table wines on the part of the industry and the public generally, gave him opportunities to specialize. Well known for his excellent palate and memory for wines—and his appropriately large nose—he developed outstanding Hardy styles. Some were elite wines made in small amounts. He was noted, however, for his table wine blends such as Cabinet Claret, St Thomas Burgundy and Old Castle Riesling, which he produced in large quantities. These wines helped to change Australian drinking habits in the 1950s. With privileged access to different suppliers of grapes, he travelled regularly to the Hunter Valley of New South Wales, northern Victoria and the wine-growing districts of South Australia, to purchase wine for these blends. Also an expert spirit maker, he nurtured Hardy's best brandies.

With Maurice O'Shea [q.v.15] and Colin Preece [q.v.], Roger Warren is generally placed among the outstanding Australian winemakers of his generation. John Fornachon [q.v.14] was another friend and associate. Photographs taken of Warren at industry functions show a tall and bespectacled man, enjoying himself in company. Normally reserved, unassuming and easy to get along with, he could be candid and outgoing to a degree which was disconcerting to some. According to his fellow workers he had no sense of time and was always late for meetings. He was an active member of two wine and food societies —the Bacchus Club of Adelaide and the Lockleys Beefsteak and Burgundy Club. In 1949 he joined the Kooyonga Golf Club. Survived by his wife and their three sons, he died of myocardial infarction on 17 March 1960 at Norwood and was cremated.

M. Lake, *Classic Wines of Australia* (Brisb, 1966); R. Burden, *A Family Tradition in Fine Winemaking* (Adel, 1978); G. C. Bishop, *Australian Winemaking, the Roseworthy Influence* (Adel, 1980); *Wine and Spirit News and Aust Vigneron*, Apr 1960; *Advertiser* (Adel), 18 Mar 1960; information from Mr R. Heath and Dr B. Rankine, Adel.   DAVID DUNSTAN

WATERHOUSE, LESLIE VICKERY (1886-1945), mining engineer, was born on 18 March 1886 at Waverley, Sydney, third son and fifth child of Gustavus John Waterhouse, a Tasmanian-born merchant, and his wife Mary Jane, daughter of Ebenezer Vickery [q.v.6], from Sydney. Rev. Jabez Waterhouse was his grandfather, and Gustavus Athol and Eben Gowrie Waterhouse [qq.v.6,12] were his brothers. Educated at Sydney Grammar School, Les studied mining and metallurgy at the University of Sydney (B.E., 1910).

After three years with the Broken Hill Proprietary Co. Ltd, Waterhouse worked for the Mount Lyell Mining & Railway Co. at Queenstown, Tasmania, where he designed, erected and operated a copper-flotation plant. In Sydney, on 18 February 1915, he married Dorothy Edna, daughter of Rev. William Taylor [q.v.12], at the Methodist Church, Lindfield. Following his departure from Mount Lyell in 1919, Waterhouse's varied experiences included salvaging blistered copper from the *Karitane*, wrecked in Bass Strait, and zinc from the *Yarra*, wrecked in the Solomon Islands.

Having joined W. A. Freeman [q.v.8] on the board of the Canadian mining company Placer Development Ltd in 1928, Waterhouse was largely responsible for co-ordinating and guiding exploitation of the company's option over alluvial gold leases at Bulolo, Mandated Territory of New Guinea. He and another director, a dredge-design expert, decided that the most economical approach to mining would be to use two electrically driven dredges. However, the difficult terrain and absence of roads made it impractical to use land transport to bring in from Lae the dredges, machinery and materials to build a hydro-electric power station and new township. The solution was air transport.

Bulolo Gold Dredging Ltd was established in 1930 by Placer Development, with Waterhouse a director and executive engineer. Advised by Ernest Mustar [q.v.10], the company acquired two G.31 Junkers passenger aircraft, named *Peter* and *Paul*, which were modified to enable them to carry up to 7000 lb. (3175 kg) in freight. As a director of Guinea Airways Ltd which operated the aeroplanes, Waterhouse did much to ensure their successful deploy-

ment. The 2300-ton dredges were transported in sections so that no single piece weighed more than three and a half tons. Over eighteen months from March 1931, *Peter* and *Paul* made 1370 flights and carried 3657 short tons. An air lift of such magnitude had never been attempted anywhere in the world. The first dredge began operations in March 1932. With Waterhouse's direction and support, the scale of operations expanded dramatically; components for six more dredges and a second hydro-electric plant were flown into Bulolo. By 1942, when Japanese aircraft attacks halted mining operations, the leases had produced 1.3 million oz. (36 854 kg) of gold and 575 000 oz. (16 301 kg) of silver.

From 1929 Waterhouse had been a councilmember of the Australasian Institute of Mining and Metallurgy. As president in 1938 he tried to strengthen ties with the institute's far-flung membership. In the 1930s Waterhouse expanded Placer Development's Australian operations. He was managing director of its subsidiaries, Clutha Development Ltd, Rutherglen Gold Dumps Ltd and Gold Dumps Pty Ltd.

Waterhouse was a reserved, modest man, who was convivial in familiar surroundings. A quick thinker, he had confidence in his ability and judgement, was direct in his dealings with others and had an acute business sense. He enjoyed fishing and playing golf, and belonged to the Royal Society of New South Wales, the Australian and New South Wales clubs, Royal Sydney Yacht Squadron, Royal Sydney Golf and Elanora Country clubs and the Rabaul Club, New Guinea. Survived by his wife and their two daughters, Waterhouse died of cancer on 27 November 1945 at his Bellevue Hill home and was cremated with Anglican rites.

A. M. Healy, *Bulolo* (Canb, 1967); J. Sinclair, *Wings of Gold* (Syd, 1978); A. W. John, *Fortune Favoured Me* (Melb, 1999); A'sian Inst of Mining and Metallurgy, *Procs*, 1946, p 49; Roy Soc NSW, *J and Procs*, 81, 1947, p 299; *PIM*, Dec 1945; *Chemical Engineering and Mining Review*, 10 Feb 1950; *Rabaul Times*, 17 Jan 1930, 15 Apr 1932; *SMH*, 30 Mar, 29 Oct 1932, 5 June 1933, 16 Aug 1938; History of Placer Development (ms, 1970, held by author).

MICHAEL WATERHOUSE

WATERS, DONALD EDWARD (1922-1974), Aboriginal soldier and shearer, was born on 20 July 1922 at the Euraba Aboriginal Station, near Boomi, New South Wales, third child of Donald Waters, labourer, and his wife Grace, née Bennett, both born in New South Wales. His parents were of mixed Aboriginal and European descent. The boy was always known in the family as 'Jim', possibly to avoid confusion with his father. He attended Toomelah Aboriginal School until 1932 when the family moved to Nindigully, south-east of St George, Queensland, and he completed his education at the local one-teacher school.

At age 14 Waters started work with his father, ringbarking, fencing and yard building. He was later employed on Balagna station as a general labourer earning twelve shillings and six pence for a six-day week. To increase his income, he turned to contract shearing. On 9 July 1942 he was mobilized in the Militia, the authorities ignoring his Aboriginal features because of the extreme manpower shortage. Attached to the 4th Infantry Training Battalion, based at Warwick, in April 1943 he was removed from a jungle-warfare course as unsuitable. He immediately asked for a transfer to the Australian Imperial Force; his request was granted on 24 April.

While recovering from a fractured right hand suffered in May 1943, Waters volunteered to join a group of soldiers who were to be deliberately infected with malaria, under experimental conditions, in order to test the efficacy of different drugs in treating the disease. Volunteers were required to be physically fit, mentally stable, and free from venereal disease, asthma, jaundice and previous exposure to malaria. Clinical trials at Cairns and on the Atherton Tableland demonstrated the suppressive and curative powers of Atebrin, and led to measures that dramatically reduced the incidence of malaria among allied servicemen. Waters and his fellow human 'guinea-pigs' were formally commended (1945) by the commander-in-chief, General Sir Thomas Blamey [q.v.13], 'for distinguished services in the South-West Pacific Area'.

In March 1944 Waters was fit enough to reattempt, and pass, jungle-warfare training. He was posted to the 2nd/23rd Battalion in May. Sailing from Cairns in April 1945, the unit took part in the landing on Tarakan Island, Borneo, on 1 May. The 2nd/23rd was involved in periods of heavy fighting to mid-June, and then in mopping-up operations until hostilities ceased on 15 August. Donald's younger brother Leonard (d.1993) flew Kittyhawks with No.78 Squadron, Royal Australian Air Force, in support of the troops on the ground in Borneo. From February 1946 to January 1947 Private Waters served in the 122nd Transport Platoon with the British Commonwealth Occupation Force, Japan. He was discharged from the army on 18 February in Sydney.

Waters returned to northern New South Wales and resumed work as a shearer. At the Aboriginal Station, Boggabilla, on 23 May 1949 he married with Anglican rites 18-year-old Ruby Orcher. They later lived at Tamworth. Survived by his wife, and their two daughters and four sons, he died of respiratory failure on 16 September 1974 at Tamworth and was buried in the lawn cemetery.

A. S. Walker, *Clinical Problems of War* (Canb, 1952); *Chronicle* (Toowoomba), 2 Dec 1981; War Diary, 2/23rd Battalion, AWM 52, item 8/3/23, and Recognition Malaria Experiment Volunteers, AWM 119, item 77 (AWM).   DAVID HUGGONSON

WATERS, WILLIAM FRANCIS (1897-1968), public servant and bushwalker, was born on 22 August 1897 at Traralgon, Victoria, only child of Victorian-born parents Francis William Waters, railway employee, and his wife Eva, née Hillard. Educated at country and suburban state schools and at Melbourne High School, Bill joined the Department of Defence on 16 November 1914 as a naval staff clerk. In 1926 he transferred to the Department of Trade and Customs (Customs and Excise from 1956). He served as an examining officer before rising to supervisor (1948), investigation officer (1951) and senior investigation officer (1957). On 21 August 1962 he retired.

While Waters enjoyed moderate success in his working life, he excelled in his leisure pursuits. In 1908 he had joined the Boy Scouts Association. As a youth he took an avid interest in his health and fitness, and aged about 18 he enrolled in a school of physical culture. He represented Victoria at lacrosse (1925) and boxed as an amateur heavyweight. But he most enjoyed the nascent pastime of bushwalking. When living in western Gippsland as a child, he had been inspired by the sight of Mount Baw Baw. Victoria's alpine regions 'exercised a strong fascination' for him and in 1917 he undertook his 'first serious walking trip'—along the Baw Baw tourist track. In 1922 he became a rover scout.

Next year Waters joined the Melbourne Amateur Walking and Touring Club and thereafter devoted enormous energy and enthusiasm to its administration and activities. He was a committee-member (1925-27), secretary (1928-34), chief leader (1934-67) and president (1967-68). On bushwalks he preferred to get off the beaten track and, with a small group of committed members, undertook a number of long-distance hikes through remote wilderness regions. He and his companions were forced to design and make most of their equipment as suitable gear was not then available commercially; Waters introduced the practice of wearing shorts. A member of the committee which had instigated (1928) the club's magazine, the *Melbourne Walker*, he was a prolific contributor. He wrote articles on his walking trips and keenly researched the history of the areas through which he trekked. In 1947 the club rewarded his dedication with life membership. His enthusiasm for outdoor activity extended to skiing and he tirelessly promoted the sport, particularly its cross-country form.

Committed to the scouting movement, Waters took two extended periods of unpaid leave (1929-30 and 1953-54) to attend international gatherings. In 1930-65 he was headquarters commissioner for rover scouts in Victoria. He made bushwalking and skiing part of the training of rovers and helped to introduce thousands of young people to these two forms of recreation. According to his friend Harry Stephenson, to be trained by Waters 'really meant *trained*'. For his efforts he was awarded (1961) the Silver Wolf, the highest scouting honour. He was chairman of the Kinglake National Park committee of management, a member of the Royal Historical Society of Victoria and a Freemason; just before his death he was elected to the council of the National Parks Association. Waters never married. He died on 8 October 1968 at Fitzroy and was cremated.

H. Stephenson, *W. F. 'Bill' Waters* (Melb, 1982); A. D. Budge, *No End to Walking* (Melb, 1992); *Melb Walker*, 31, 1960, p 76, 40, 1969, p 39.

MELISSA HARPER

WATKIN, SIR HERBERT GEORGE (1898-1966), educationist, was born on 8 October 1898 at East Bundaberg, Queensland, second of five children of English-born parents Richard Frederick Watkin, labourer, and his wife Alice Maud, née Croucher. Herbert attended the local state school and, for a few months, Bundaberg State High School. Having trained as a pupil-teacher (1912-16) at Bundaberg East State School, he joined the staff at Bundaberg North State School in 1917. He enlisted in the Australian Imperial Force on 15 May 1918 and served in Britain and, after the Armistice, in France. Discharged in Brisbane on 23 July 1920, he resumed teaching at Bundaberg North and transferred to Bundaberg South two years later.

On 16 December 1927 in her home at South Bundaberg, Watkin married with Presbyterian forms Ettie Winning Cairns, a clerk. That year he had enrolled as an external student at the University of Queensland (B.A., 1936; Dip.Ed., 1938). He spent periods as relieving head teacher at district schools; as he was the proud owner of a Harley-Davidson motorcycle, transport presented no problem. Moving to Brisbane in 1928, he taught for eight years at Ascot State School, with a year's break in 1931 when he was an exchange teacher in London. He lectured at Queensland Teachers' Training College in 1937-38, and was acting-principal (1939-40) of Rock-

hampton State High School and Technical College. After serving as inspector of schools for several years in the Cairns and Mackay districts, he was appointed principal of Brisbane State High School in 1947.

On 17 January 1952 Watkin became director-general of education. He inherited a system with a rigid inspectorial system, too few teachers, a teachers' college housed in makeshift buildings, and an inadequate one-year training course. His problems were exacerbated by a rapid increase in population in the early 1950s that led to large classes and over-crowded schools, and by the Labor government of Vince Gair [q.v.14], which gave education a low priority. Educationists, including (Sir) Fred Schonell [q.v.] and the Queensland Teachers' Union, criticized the State scholarship examination, because of its cramping influence on primary education; Watkin, proud of his success as a 'scholarship teacher', defended it at first. There were some reforms: in 1952 a new primary syllabus was introduced into schools, and from 1957 the locally prepared and outmoded Queensland school readers were phased out and replaced (to Watkin's chagrin) by Schonell's *Happy Venture* (Edinburgh, 1939-50) and *Wide Range* (Edinburgh, 1948-53) readers.

In 1957 Jack Pizzey [q.v.], whom Watkin had known since 1927 when he was a pupil teacher at Bundaberg, became minister of education in the new Country Party-Liberal government led by (Sir) Frank Nicklin [q.v.15]; he was ranked third in cabinet and was determined to improve education in Queensland. Watkin was appointed in 1960 chairman of a committee to inquire into secondary education in Queensland. Swept along by Pizzey's reforming zeal, he presented in September next year a four-page interim report recommending abolition of the State scholarship examination, entry to high school after seven rather than eight years of primary schooling, a new secondary curriculum devised to suit individual aptitudes and interests, and an increase in the minimum school leaving age to 15 years. The government moved quickly to implement the changes.

Watkin was considered aloof, authoritarian and conservative by his senior officers and teachers. While he was chairman (from 1956) of the new Queensland Conservatorium of Music's advisory council, his interference led to the resignation of the director William Lovelock in 1958. Outside the department Watkin was seen as hail-fellow-well-met. Deputy-chancellor (1953-66) of the University of Queensland, he received an honorary doctorate of laws in 1960. He was a founding fellow (1961) of the Australian College of Education.

Chairman (1959) of the National Fitness Council of Queensland, Watkin was a trustee

(1959-66) of the Queensland Art Gallery. In 1964 he was knighted. When he retired that year Pizzey wrote to him: 'little did we know when teaching together we would be occupying today the positions we do. We shall both have the happiest of memories of a long association which has produced the greatest expansion of educational facilities ever effected in the history of this state'. Sir Herbert was appointed (1965) chairman of the Institute of Higher Technical Education, Territory of Papua and New Guinea. Survived by his wife and their daughter, he died of myocardial infarction on 20 August 1966 in Brisbane and was cremated with Congregational forms.

R. Goodman, *Secondary Education in Queensland, 1860-1960* (Canb, 1968); Annual Report of the Director-General of Education, *PP* (Qld), 1952-66; *Qld Teachers' J*, Feb 1952; *Courier-Mail*, 13 June 1964, 22 Aug 1966; Watkin personal file and staff card (QA).   GEOFFREY SWAN

WATSON, ALAN CAMERON (1900-1976), Presbyterian minister, was born on 16 March 1900 at Feilding, New Zealand, youngest of four children of Thomas Watson, an auctioneer from Scotland, and his wife Marion, née Thomson, a New Zealander. After attending Feilding District High School, Alan entered the University of Otago (B.A., N.Z., 1923; M.A., 1924; Dip.Soc.Sc., 1924), Dunedin, where he studied philosophy, represented the university at hockey, served on the executive of the Students' Association, and became active in the New Zealand Student Christian Movement. At Knox College—which profoundly shaped him—he edited the *Collegian* (1921-22), held office as president (1924), and tutored in philosophy (1922-27). Influenced by William Hewitson, the Victorian-born master of Knox, Watson developed a passionate interest in a new world order. He shared informal discussions with Walter Nash and other future leaders of the New Zealand Labour Party, and lectured for the Workers' Educational Association.

On completion of theological studies, Watson was ordained in December 1925. He was assistant at First Church, Dunedin, before being called to East Taieri in 1927. His gifted preaching, pastoral care and compassion for the poor endeared him to his parishioners. He persuaded the Dunedin City Council to set up a camp for the unemployed at Deep Creek. The teaching of the Bible came alive for him as he ministered to these people. At St Andrew's Presbyterian Church, New Plymouth, on 17 January 1928, he married Eileen Margaret Ballantyne (1902-1969), a schoolteacher and fellow-graduate of the University of Otago. Her practical wisdom and keen mind made her an invaluable partner in her husband's ministry.

The Watsons moved to St Paul's, Christchurch, in May 1932. In this large central parish, Watson ran innovative educational courses. He also encouraged his congregation to be active in civic life, setting an example through his membership of Rotary, support for the unemployed, and involvement with the Nurse Maude District Nursing Association. Impressed by the work of Toyohiko Kagawa in Japanese slums, he invited him to Christchurch in 1935. Watson's commitment to social justice and ecumenism were reinforced when he attended two conferences in Britain in 1937: that on Life and Work at Oxford, and that on Faith and Order in Edinburgh. He worked closely with Campbell West-Watson, the Anglican bishop of Christchurch, and became known, jocularly, as 'Bishop East-Watson'.

On 31 March 1942 Watson began a notable term as minister at Toorak Presbyterian Church, Melbourne. In 1959-76 he wrote weekly articles—entitled 'A Saturday Reflection' from 1966—that appeared anonymously in the *Age*. The essays discussed personal, cultural and philosophical topics, and the usages of language, and revealed his humane view of the world. A respected Rotarian, a well-known broadcaster, a fine preacher and pastor to people in all walks of life, he was sensitive to the joys and tragedies of living in God's creation. Throughout his ministry, he read widely in literature and theology, believing that preaching was a sacred trust demanding the most careful preparation and a steady growth in discernment. He served on many committees of the Victorian Presbyterian Assembly, including one concerned with theological education, and advocated state aid to schools. His standing in the Church was reflected in his election to terms as moderator (1953-54) of the General Assembly of Victoria and moderator-general (1959-62) of Australia. He was a fair-minded chairman, an excellent debater, and a master of judicious public statements.

Watson worked tirelessly for Christian unity and fostered closer relations with Asian churches, especially through Inter-Church Aid. He was a vice-president (1954-60) of the World Presbyterian Alliance, and a member of the central committee of the World Council of Churches. Lewis and Clark College, Portland, Oregon, United States of America, awarded him an honorary doctorate of divinity (1954) for his international leadership. In 1961-63 he chaired the Australian Council of Churches. An influential member (from 1956) of the Joint Commission on Church Union set up by the Presbyterians, Methodists and Congregationalists, he wrote the dissenting report which led to the rejection of a proposal to

introduce bishops into the Uniting Church in
Australia. He retired on 30 June 1967 and was
appointed C.M.G. next year.

Craggily handsome, Watson was tall and
lithe. Presence and eloquence balanced his
Scottish reserve. He loved sport, gardening
and reading, and could laugh uproariously.
Survived by his daughter and two sons, he
died on 15 January 1976 in his home at
Mornington and was cremated.

The Knox College Register 1909-1973 (Dunedin,
NZ, 1973); D. Watson, 'Foreword', in D. Watson and
N. Watson (eds), *Alan Watson's Saturday Reflections*
(Melb, 1976); *Age* (Melb), 1 July 1967, 16 Jan 1976;
information from Mrs M. St John, Malvern, Melb,
and Dr D. Watson, Kallista, Vic.   IAN BREWARD

WATSON, GEORGE HERBERT (1894-
1963), mining dredge designer, was born on
2 April 1894 in Port Melbourne, eldest of four
children of Henry Edward Watson, a carpenter from New Zealand, and his Victorian-born
wife Charlesena Mary, née Cuthill. George
began work in 1911 as an apprentice in the
Victorian Railways' workshop at Newport,
spending more than a year on a training
course at the Working Men's College in the
city. In 1915 he was a draftsman living in Port
Melbourne. On 5 May that year he married
Gertrude Maud Agar, a furniture saleswoman,
at the Presbyterian Church, Albert and Middle
Park.

By 1927 Watson was working in the
Malayan tinfields for Alluvial Tin (Malaya)
Ltd. His technical ability was recognized by
the company, which sent him to Holland to
buy suitable dredges, then supervise their
construction. In the 1930s Watson became
closely involved with Ambrose Pratt [q.v.11]
in Peninsula Tin N.L. and with E. H. and F. G.
Pratten as a fellow director of Alluvial Gold
Ltd and associated companies which operated
in Asia, New Guinea and New Zealand. In 1937
Watson assigned to Alluvial Mining Equipment Ltd his copyright for the Newstead
dredge and bucket dredges he had designed
for the Victoria Gold Dredging Co. N.L.

Watson, working from Sydney, designed
and constructed gold dredges for use in Victoria and New Zealand. He was managing
director of Peninsula Tin N.L. and others of
the group's companies operating in Malaya
and New Zealand by 1937. Walter Burley
Griffin's [q.v.9] associate E. M. Nicholls designed a house for him at Point Piper. After
World War II ended, Watson was appointed to
the first inspection party organized by the
British government to visit the Malayan tinfields to consider rehabilitation of working
equipment and compensation for individual
companies. He began to diversify his activities.
Retaining his directorships in the Malayan

companies, he joined (1949) the board of
Burma-Malay Tin Ltd. As chairman of Tableland Tin Dredging N.L., he complained in
1951 that price fixing was detrimental to the
Australian tin industry.

From 1945 to 1952 Watson was part-time
chairman of the Australian Aluminium Production Commission, a statutory authority
attached to the Commonwealth Department
of Munitions. The Commonwealth parliament's Joint Committee of Public Accounts
investigated the commission in 1955 and found
that Watson could not 'escape blame for the
conditions that developed', namely 'waste,
inefficiency, misjudgment and chaos' at the
aluminium works at Bell Bay, Tasmania. He
and his fellow commissioners were also criticized for granting contracts to companies
with which he was involved. Watson denied
that he had been involved in improper practice, and pointed out that he had only been a
part-time chairman, and that the government
should have appointed a full-time one if it
wished for a tighter rein on its affairs.

Watson had been managing director of
Commonwealth Engineering Co. Ltd since
1947. His previous connexions may have
influenced the sale of the company's diesel-
hydraulic rail cars to Malaya in 1957. He also
visited South Africa to promote sales in 1959.
George Watson died of cancer on 27 May
1963 at his Darling Point home and was cremated. His wife and their two sons and daughter survived him.

PP (Cwlth), 1954-55, nos 69 and 69A; *PD* (HR), 14
Oct 1954, p 1983, 1985; *Industrial Aust and Mining
Standard*, 1 June 1937, p 149; *SMH*, 28 Apr, 28 Aug
1945, 11 Oct 1946, 25 Oct, 9 Nov 1949, 28 Nov 1951,
15 Oct, 10 Dec 1954, 22, 23 Feb, 3 June 1955, 28 May
1963; Newport Apprentice Training Scheme (RMIT
Univ Archives); Copyright files, A1336, items 29501
and 29502 *and* Dept External Affairs file, A2937,
item 255 (NAA, Canb).   D. F. BRANAGAN

WATSON, SIR HENRY KEITH (1900-1973),
businessman and politician, was born on
22 August 1900 at Southern Cross, Western
Australia, son of William Henry Watson, a
Victorian-born storekeeper, and his wife
Martha Elizabeth, née Smith, who came from
South Australia. Educated at Cottesloe and
Claremont State schools, Perth, Keith joined
the taxation branch of the Commonwealth
Treasury as a clerk in 1915. He left in 1922
to establish a business in Perth as a taxation
consultant and public accountant. On 17
November 1926 at the Hardey Memorial
Methodist Church, Cottesloe, he married
Edith Wilson Symonds.

Vice-president of the State National Party
in 1933, Watson had stood three times for the

House of Representatives seat of Fremantle as an Independent (1928 and 1931) and a Nationalist (1929). In 1929 he was elected an associate and in 1946 a fellow of the Institute of Incorporated Secretaries. A director (1932-72) and chairman (1951-71) of the Perth Building Society, he was president (1951-68) of the Western Australian Permanent Building Societies' Association.

As a co-founder (1930) and later chairman of the Dominion League of Western Australia, Watson helped to prepare the State's case for secession. He was a central figure in the 1933 referendum campaign that resulted in a clear majority of electors voting to withdraw from the Commonwealth. In 1934-35 he was a member of the delegation that presented the petition for secession to the British parliament in London, where it was rejected. Remaining vehemently committed to States rights, he labelled the Commonwealth Grants Commission (founded in 1933) 'an anti-secessionist committee'. He rallied opposition against referenda to increase Federal government powers over marketing, aviation, rents and prices and criticized the High Court of Australia for its expansive interpretation of Commonwealth powers exemplified in the Uniform Tax case (1942).

In 1941 at a by-election, Watson contested the Legislative Council seat of Metropolitan Province for the National Party, losing by one vote. He won the seat at another by-election in May 1948. By then he was vice-president of the State Liberal Party. Quickly becoming adept at using standing orders, he challenged virtually every form of government regulation which had been established during World War II, even measures supported by his own party. He opposed government ownership of industry, because it 'completely [sapped] the fibre of our national life' and led to 'inefficiency'. As the leader of a ginger group of Liberal Party 'no-controllers', he often forced the government to engage in protracted debates. He defended the restrictive franchise of the Legislative Council. When universal franchise was introduced for that chamber before the 1964 election, he argued that the State's constitution should be amended to give the Upper House equal power with the Legislative Assembly in respect of all money bills.

Chairman (1959-68) of W. Thomas & Co. (W.A.) Ltd, Watson held directorships with Western Australian Insurance Co. Ltd (1949-60), Western Press Ltd (1951-55) and George Weston Foods Ltd (1967-70). He was a member of the Nedlands Golf and Dalkeith Bowling clubs. In 1968, the year in which he retired from parliament, he was knighted. Survived by his wife and their son, Sir Keith died on 13 January 1973 at Bentley, Perth, and was cremated. Their two daughters had predeceased him.

R. Pervan and C. Sharman (eds), *Essays on Western Australian Politics* (Perth, 1979); C. T. Stannage (ed), *A New History of Western Australia* (Perth, 1981); B. Moore, *A Superior Kind of Savings Bank* (Perth, 1989); D. Black (ed), *The House on the Hill* (Perth, 1991); *PD* (WA), 10 Aug 1948, p 282, 5 Aug 1964, p 60; *Univ Studies in WA Hist*, 111, no 2, 1958; *West Australian*, 28 May 1935, 15 Jan 1973.

HARRY C. J. PHILLIPS

WATSON, JAMES CALEXTE (1903-1962), wine-saloon proprietor, was born on 18 October 1903 at Carlton, Melbourne, son of James Watson, a Tasmanian-born coalminer and former fossicker, and his Italian-born wife Giselda, née Panelli. The couple was related to an extensive network of owners of Melbourne wine-bars and cafés, including members of the Denat, Virgona and Massoni families. Jimmy's second name honoured his uncle Calexte Denat, a noted French-Swiss restaurateur. The boy attended suburban state schools and, at age 14, took flute lessons from John Amadio [q.v.7]. He played professionally in theatre and cinema orchestras and assisted in the bars and restaurants of his parents and other relations. On 22 April 1931 at St Augustine's Church, Moreland, he married with Anglican rites Esther (Essie) Helena Mary Grenfell, a stenographer. When 'talkies' reduced opportunities for professional musicians in cinemas, he turned to the only other livelihood he knew. In 1935 he purchased a wine-saloon in Lygon Street, Carlton, moving into rooms above the two shops that formed the business.

Trading as J. C. Watson, wine merchant, he was permitted to sell only Australian wine, and no beer or spirits, under the terms of his licence. At the time, wine-saloons were the haunts of mainly elderly people known as 'plonkos' who drank glasses of cheap fortified wine called 'fourpenny darks'. Seeking to improve his business, Watson introduced better varieties of fortified and table wines (which he bottled himself from hogsheads), kept a collection of aged vintages for discerning customers, organized excursions to wineries, and welcomed international visitors. Meanwhile, he attended to the needs of his inherited clientele with special prices for pensioners, and card games and fishing trips for 'regulars'. In 1947 the family moved to Ascot House at Ascot Vale; Essie ran its reception rooms as a complementary enterprise; food from Ascot House also raised the quality of catering at the wine-saloon.

Watson's gregarious and humane personality gave the wine-bar its character. Dressed in a leather apron, he was an ever-present but democratically minded host. Physically robust, quick-witted and very much in charge, he did not tolerate pretentiousness or drunkenness and would eject people when necessary. Unlike most licensed premises of the period, Watson's was an environment where women could feel comfortable. The business grew, especially after 1945. A new generation, including staff and students at the nearby University of Melbourne, came to enjoy the inexpensive wine, as well as the food (from Ascot House or the local shops) and cheerful banter. Watson would give impoverished students a free meal as he reasoned rightly that they would come back as paying regulars. By the late 1950s the bar had become a Melbourne institution.

About 1960 Watson decided to renovate the saloon. (Sir) Roy Grounds failed to complete the subsequent commission; after his father's death Allan Watson accepted a design by Robin Boyd [q.v.13]. Having suffered from diabetes mellitus for several years, Jimmy died of a coronary occlusion on 22 February 1962 in East Melbourne and was cremated. His wife and their son survived him. Several hundred people attended his funeral and fellow traders lined both sides of Lygon Street. His friends instituted the Jimmy Watson memorial trophy at the annual Royal Melbourne Wine Show for the best one-year-old red, a style of wine that he had stocked for his customers to buy and cellar. A posthumous portrait of him by (Sir) William Dargie hangs in the bar at Jimmy Watson's. Allan continued the business.

G. Poliness, *Jimmy Watson's Wine Bar* (Melb, 1989); *Sun News-Pictorial*, 23 Feb 1962; *Age* (Melb), 18 Aug 1981; information from Mr A. and Mrs J. Watson, Kew, Melb.   DAVID DUNSTAN

WATSON, JAMES KINGSTON (1908-1978), newspaper editor, was born on 1 September 1908 at Broken Hill, New South Wales, son of Leonard James Percival Watson, a South Australian-born journalist, and his wife Lily Alicia, née Fanning, from Dublin. Dux of University High School, Melbourne, 'King' joined the Melbourne *Herald* as a cadet in 1927. He specialized in sports reporting then became police roundsman for the *Sun News-Pictorial*.

In 1933 Watson was one of the talented young journalists recruited to the *Star*. When it closed in 1936, he returned to the *Herald*. On 18 June 1938 he married with Presbyterian forms Eleanor Armstrong Macfarlane, director of the *Sun News-Pictorial*'s children's supplement, at Cairns [q.v.3] Memorial Church, East Melbourne. Moving to Sydney that year, he joined many of his former *Star* colleagues on the *Daily Telegraph*, revitalized by Consolidated Press Ltd. In 1939 he was appointed news editor of the new *Sunday Telegraph*,

edited by Cyril Pearl. A former vice-president of the Victorian district of the Australian Journalists' Association, Watson was active in the formation of the Journalists' Club, Sydney.

Watson became deputy-editor at Consolidated Press's London bureau in 1943. He served as a war correspondent at Supreme Headquarters, Allied Expeditionary Force. On the liberation of France, he opened Consolidated Press's office in Paris, returning to London in 1946. Back in Sydney in 1948, Watson became deputy news editor of the *Daily Telegraph* and news editor in 1951. Following an interregnum on the death of Brian Penton [q.v.15], he was appointed acting editor in 1953 (confirmed 1954).

A sparkling luncheon companion, Watson was passionate about literature and classical music. In 1950 he and Eleanor had acquired Kyarra, a run-down mansion built at Hunters Hill in 1886, which they lovingly restored. After a consortium headed by Consolidated Press obtained one of Sydney's first television licences, he became a regular interviewer on the panel show, 'Meet the Press'.

Watson, who was fiercely loyal to (Sir) Frank Packer [q.v.15], was unlucky to occupy the editorial chair at the time when he became increasingly interventionist, particularly in support of the Liberal Party. In 1967 Watson failed to dissuade Packer from running a crude editorial about race riots at Detroit, which attracted widespread condemnation. Although David McNicoll described Watson as 'one of the best newspapermen Australia ever produced', he lacked the mercurial brilliance of such predecessors as Penton and Pearl. The columnist Robert ('Buzz') Kennedy believed that the *Telegraph* lost some of its 'zing' under Watson's long editorship.

In 1970, after leading the Australian delegation to the Commonwealth Press Union conference in England, Watson retired as editor. He remained associated with special projects and television, and in 1971 took charge of the *Sunday Telegraph* after the editor suddenly quit. When the *Telegraph*s were sold to News Ltd in 1972, he edited the combined *Sunday Telegraph* and *Sunday Australian*. After 'retiring' from News Ltd in 1974, Watson was recalled to Australian Consolidated Press as head of the London bureau. He died suddenly on 14 September 1978 in New York and was cremated; a memorial service was held at St Bride's parish church, Fleet Street, London. His wife and their daughter survived him. A portrait of Watson by W. E. Pidgeon is held by the family.

D. McNicoll, *Luck's a Fortune* (Syd, 1979); B. Kennedy, *It was Bloody Marvellous* (Syd, 1996); B. Griffen-Foley, *The House of Packer* (Syd, 1999); *Journalist*, 30 Sept 1933; *Newspaper News*, 1 May 1945, 1 Oct 1951; *Daily Telegraph* (Syd), 31 Oct

1970, 16 Sept 1978; Watson papers (ML); information from Mrs E. Watson, Fig Tree Pocket, Brisb.

BRIDGET GRIFFEN-FOLEY

WATSON, JOHN ALEXANDER (1891-1980), grocer, insurance agent and army officer, was born on 25 June 1891 at Ballarat, Victoria, only son and youngest of four surviving children of Alexander Watson, a miner from Scotland, and his Victorian-born wife Susan Harriet, née Moizer. His father died when he was young, and John moved with his mother to West Brunswick when she remarried. After leaving school, he entered the grocery trade.

On 19 June 1915 Watson enlisted as a driver in the Australian Army Service Corps, Australian Imperial Force. He was then 5 ft 9 ins (175 cm) tall, with a sallow complexion, hazel eyes and dark brown hair. In 1916-18 he served with the 5th Divisional Train in Egypt and on the Western Front, attaining the rank of corporal. Discharged in Melbourne on 15 July 1919, he went into business as a grocer. At the Methodist Church, Coburg, on 6 December 1924 he married Florence Grace Kendall Francis. He lost his business during the Depression and was employed by the Australian Mutual Provident Society as a collector.

Having joined the Citizen Military Forces, Watson was commissioned lieutenant in the 4th Divisional Train in June 1926. He rose to captain in 1929 and major in 1934. As part of a new wave of Militia commanders, he was promoted lieutenant colonel and appointed to head the 4th Divisional A.A.S.C. in March 1939. On 1 May 1940 he transferred to the A.I.F. as the commander of I Corps Troops Supply Column. Arriving in the Middle East in February 1941, he was given command of the 9th Divisional A A S C in March. During the siege of Tobruk, Libya (April-October), he led the logistic-support organization, comprising nearly 2500 troops and a thousand vehicles, with 'energy and resourcefulness' and was appointed O.B.E. (1942). For his zeal and efficiency at the battle of El Alamein (October-November 1942), he won the Distinguished Service Order. He was twice mentioned in dispatches. His soldiers knew him as 'Dadda', a father figure who was both uncompromising in the standards he set and always mindful of their welfare.

Back in Australia in February 1943, Watson was promoted temporary colonel next month. He was successively deputy-director of supply and transport, II Corps and (from April 1944) I Corps in New Guinea and on the Atherton Tableland, Queensland. In June he became D.D.S.T. at Advanced Land Headquarters, which moved from Brisbane to Hollandia, Netherlands New Guinea, in November and to Morotai, Netherlands East Indies, in March 1945. Evacuated ill in May, he was appointed temporary D.D.S.T., Victoria Lines of Communication Area (later Southern Command), in July. From August 1946 he worked with the executive officer of the Committee of Review of Interim Army Strengths. His appointment terminated on 5 February 1948.

Watson returned to the A.M.P. as an insurance agent. After retiring, he and his wife played golf, wintered in Queensland and maintained their long connexion with the Coburg Methodist Church. He was also an active Freemason. Remembered by his family as a 'dapper little gentleman', he was fastidious about his appearance, and a stickler for good manners and correct speech. He died on 1 March 1980 at Heidelberg and was cremated; his wife and their two daughters survived him.

H. Fairclough, *Equal to the Task* (Melb, 1962); N. Lindsay, *Equal to the Task*, 1 (Brisb, 1992); information from Mrs J. Fotheringham, Launc, Tas, and Mrs M. Knight, Balwyn, Melb.   NEVILLE LINDSAY

WATSON, JOHN ANDREW (1879-1953), insurance commissioner, was born on 14 December 1879 in South Brisbane, eldest of three children of English-born parents Andrew Hendry Watson, clerk, and his wife Hannah Harriett Louisa, née Priest. John attended Kelvin Grove and Petrie Terrace State schools before entering Brisbane Grammar School in 1893 on a scholarship. He left next year, with a report containing the parting assessment: 'school career spoilt by irregular attendance'. From 1897 he worked for a firm of insurance agents, Holmes & Church, moving in 1904 to the Yorkshire Insurance Co. Ltd as chief clerk and accountant. In 1912 he was admitted as a fellow of the Queensland (Commonwealth from 1921) Institute of Accountants. That year he opened a local branch of the Australian Mutual Fire Insurance Society Ltd; he managed the office for four years. On 8 August 1914 at Wesley Methodist Church, Kangaroo Point, he married Minna Pauline Maurice, a typiste.

In 1916 Watson was elected president of the Insurance Institute of Queensland and was appointed deputy insurance commissioner of the new State Accident Insurance Office, established to handle workers' compensation. In February 1917 the office was authorized to transact all classes of insurance business; it became known as the State Government Insurance Office. Watson succeeded John Goodwyn as State insurance commissioner in 1920. The very antithesis of his more brilliant and flamboyant predecessor, he was short of stature, blunt and direct in manner, respected rather than loved. Most of his years in office were times of severe financial stringency, encompassing the Depression and World War II. He was subjected to the close scrutiny of his ministers, first the attorney-general, and later the treasurer. Additionally, A. E. Moore's [q.v.10] Country and Progressive National Party's government of 1929-32 had severe ideological reservations about the very existence of the S.G.I.O. The private insurance companies were also antagonistic as, under Watson's direction, the office became a substantial competitor for business.

In June 1945 the *Australasian Insurance and Banking Record* observed that a less cautious administrator than Watson might have captured more than a 13.5 per cent share of the fire, accident and marine insurance market. He retired on 31 December that year. Although he had been unwilling to take risks, he left a strong, decentralized organization that had survived the political traumas of its early decades and was poised for major expansion in postwar years. Retirement gifts of a watch, and silver and china teasets, were somewhat at variance with his outdoor hobbies of motoring, gardening, and bushcraft. Elected (1935) a fellow of the Incorporated Australian Insurance Institute, he was also a trustee (1939-46) of Brisbane Grammar School and a founding member and president of the Coorparoo Bowling Club. He died on 12 January 1953 in Brisbane and was buried in Bulimba cemetery. His wife had died twelve days earlier. He was survived by his daughter and three of his four sons; his son John had died on active service with the Royal Australian Air Force in 1944.

M. I. Thomis and M. Wales, *From SGIO to Suncorp* (Brisb, 1986); *SGIO Official J*, Jan 1931, Nov 1945, Jan 1946; *A'sian Insurance and Banking Record*, 21 June 1945, p 273; *Courier-Mail*, 14 Jan 1953; A/54106, item F3361 (QA).

MALCOLM I. THOMIS

WATTS, ARTHUR FREDERICK (1897-1970), lawyer and politician, was born on 26 May 1897 at Islington, London, son of Arthur Joseph Watts, dentist, and his wife Martha Kathleen, née Bradfield. In 1906 the family migrated to Perth, and then settled at Katanning, in the wheat-belt. After attending Thomas Street (Perth) and Katanning State schools, Arthur was sent to Guildford Grammar School, Perth, as a boarder. Articled in 1915 to G. A. Cooper at Katanning, and in 1919 to Harry Keall of the Perth law firm Villeneuve Smith & Keall, he was admitted to the Supreme Court of Western Australia on 20 December 1920 as a barrister and solicitor. He practised at Katanning with Cooper, later

acquiring the practice in partnership with T. A. Gee. On 21 April 1924 at St George's Cathedral, Perth, he married with Anglican rites Dorothy Furness Thomson, a music teacher.

A member (1926-36) of the Katanning Road Board, Watts was vice-chairman from 1930. He unsuccessfully contested the Legislative Assembly seat of Katanning for the Country Party at the 1933 State election. At a by-election on 31 August 1935 he narrowly won the seat. Succeeding (Sir) Charles Latham [q.v.10] as State party leader and leader of the Opposition on 7 October 1942, he chaired the royal commission on the Vermin Act (1945) and two select committees—on the Commonwealth powers bill (1943), and the handling of wool at appraisement centres (1945)—and served on several others. The coalition of the Liberal Party and the Country and Democratic League won office in March 1947, with the Liberals securing one more seat than the Country Party. Watts became deputy-premier to (Sir) Ross McLarty [q.v.15] and was appointed minister of education and industrial development. His wife died that year, and on 18 June 1948 at St Andrew's Church of England, Katanning, he married Ida Gladys O'Halloran, née Connolly, a widowed secretary.

From 1950 Watts represented the electorate of Stirling. In 1947-53 he earned a reputation as a capable and energetic minister—he also held the portfolios of housing (from 1949) and child welfare (from 1950)—and successfully maintained harmonious relations between the coalition partners. Back in Opposition (1953-59), he chaired the 1957 honorary royal commission on restrictive trade practices and legislation. From April 1959, during (Sir) David Brand's [q.v.13] first term as premier, he was again deputy-premier. He was attorney-general and minister for education and electricity until 31 January 1962 when he resigned from parliament to take up a post as chairman of the State Licensing Courts. Apart from the political nature of his appointment (which was for three years), it was controversial because of the attendant increase in remuneration. Reappointed for a second term in 1965, he retired in 1968.

In the 1930s Watts had served as chairman of the Katanning branch of the St John Ambulance Association in Western Australia and as president of the Katanning Cricket Board. A founding member and patron (1951-70) of the Spastic Welfare Association of Western Australia, and patron of the Katanning branch of the Maternal and Infant Health Association, he chaired (1947-52, 1959-61) the National Fitness Council of Western Australia. He was appointed a commander brother of the Order of St John (1945) and C.M.G. (1949). One of Western Australia's most effective rural politicians, he had a particular interest in agricultural education and rural and industrial development. In his spare time he enjoyed reading and motoring. Survived by his wife, and the son and daughter of his first marriage, he died on 8 June 1970 in his home at Dalkeith, Perth, and was buried in Karrakatta cemetery.

Great Southern Herald, 7, 14, 17 Aug, 4 Sept 1935; *West Australian*, 8 Oct 1942, 9 June 1949, 10 Jan 1962, 26 Feb 1968, 9 June 1970; *Countryman* (Perth), 11 Jan 1962; *Bulletin*, 3 Feb 1962.
DAVID BLACK

WATTS, ERNEST ALFRED (1893-1979), builder, was born on 20 April 1893 in West Melbourne, second son of Henry Watts, an English-born stone-sawyer, and his wife Emily, née Cook, from Victoria. Following a state school education, Ernie was indentured to a builder, Clements Langford. On 23 October 1915 at Northcote Watts married with Anglican rites Mabel Courtis (d.1971), a trimmer. He studied building and contracting with International Correspondence Schools Ltd. Having saved £400, at age 24 he went into business for himself; at first he concentrated on houses.

In the mid-1920s Watts gained three major construction contracts in the city: a store in Bourke Street for G. J. Coles [q.v.13] & Co. Pty Ltd, premises for Debenhams (Australia) Pty Ltd and additions to the National Gallery of Victoria. Weathering the Depression, he built many large structures, including the Chevron Hotel (1934), the southern stand at the Melbourne Cricket Ground (1936) and the Hotel Australia (1939). His election, unopposed, as president (1938-39) of the Master Builders Association of Victoria reflected his prominence in the industry. In 1940 he went into partnership with his younger brothers Frank and Frederick and with Lewis Milne and Ralph Stout.

Commercial and industrial building slowed in World War II but the Watts organization secured numerous government orders to construct defence facilities in Victoria, New South Wales and Tasmania. It carried out extensive work at Fishermens Bend, Melbourne, for the Department of Aircraft Production. Flourishing after the war, the firm completed office buildings in the city for a number of corporations, among them the Bank of Adelaide and Ansett Transport Industries Ltd. Major works commissioned by industrial undertakings included an assembly plant at Broadmeadows for the Ford Motor Co. of Australia Ltd. Among other Watts constructions were the Footscray and Traralgon district hospitals. In Sydney the firm built the regional shopping centres Miranda Fair, at Miranda, and Roselands, at

Wiley Park. The value of its new work in the years 1960-64 was £37 152 376.

The business had been incorporated on 30 November 1953 as E. A. Watts Pty Ltd; each of the five partners became a director, with Ernie as chairman. A subsidiary of the Watts organization (which had also operated as a partnership) was incorporated on the same date, as Collingwood Timber Joinery & Trading Co. Pty Ltd. In 1958 the Australian Institute of Builders, of which Watts was a fellow (1951), awarded him its medal for overcoming building problems associated with the geological strata beneath Melbourne. On 6 August 1964 he and his colleagues floated a public company, E. A. Watts Holdings Ltd.

Patrick Tennison had described Watts in 1963 as 'impressively agile and forceful', and quoted one of his employees as saying that 'he never asks [his men] to do anything he couldn't do himself'. Needing little sleep, Watts was usually at his huge desk in the company's Collingwood headquarters by 7.45 a.m. and was likely to have risen three hours earlier in summer to water his garden. Golf was his other principal form of recreation. On 28 April 1966 he announced his retirement. He was a life governor of the Royal Victorian Institute for the Blind and the Austin, Freemasons' and Royal Children's hospitals. Survived by his five daughters, he died on 4 January 1979 at his East Ivanhoe home and was cremated.

Building Achievement in Australia (Melb, 1965?); W. R. H. Keast, *Building Victoria* (Melb, 1994); *Aust Builder*, Feb 1979; *SMH*, 13 May 1958, 5 Jan 1979; *Sun News-Pictorial*, 11 Jan 1963; *Age* (Melb), 5 Jan 1979; E. A. Watts Holdings Ltd records, Stock Exchange of Melb Ltd collection (Univ Melb Archives).
FRANK STRAHAN

WATTS, MARGARET STURGE (1892-1978), welfare worker, was born on 12 June 1892 at Everton, Liverpool, England, fourth of five children of James Herbert Thorp, medical practitioner, and his wife Anne Sturge, née Eliott. The family traced its Quaker membership back to the seventeenth century. Margaret attended South Liverpool Corporation School, the Mount School, York, and Woodbrooke College, Birmingham; known as Peg, she was a tall girl with light-brown hair and dark-blue eyes. In 1911 she accompanied her parents when they were sent by the Society of Friends in England to advise Tasmanian Quakers about the consequences of the Australian Defence Act of 1909. They decided to remain; her father practised as a locum in Queensland and her two brothers also settled in Australia.

Like her co-religionists, Margaret Thorp was a pacifist. During World War I she helped Cecilia John and Adela Pankhurst [qq.v.9,

12 Walsh] to found (1916) a branch of the Women's Peace Army in Queensland, becoming its honorary secretary; she was also busy with the Children's Peace Army. Unusually articulate, she held open-air meetings from Rockhampton to Mount Morgan. She showed 'much courage in the fight against conscription': at one rally she was knocked down, kicked and thrown out, before returning by another door. Increasingly she was drawn to the 'Revolutionary Pacifists'. Under surveillance by military intelligence from 1917, she was seen as 'a full-blown Red Ragger and revolutionary'.

To 'gain more knowledge about factory conditions', in 1916 Margaret Thorp had worked for three months in Johnson & Sons' boot factory, Brisbane, and conscientiously tried to live on 12s. 6d. a week, 'but often on a Friday would call myself a fraud and have a good meal in town'. In November 1918 she was appointed an inspector of factories and shops. She went to Britain in March 1920. Fluent in French and German, she was accepted by the Friends' War Victims Relief Committee. She served (1920-21) with Quaker teams under the British Red Cross Society in Berlin and in 1921 reported on the famine in the Volga provinces of Russia where an Englishman, Arthur Watts, was in charge of the Quaker relief until he contracted typhus. Returning to Australia in October, she lectured in every State for Lady Forster's Fund for Stricken Europe.

Appointed welfare superintendent at Anthony Hordern & Sons [qq.v.4] Ltd's department store in mid-1923, Margaret Thorp organized physical culture, music and dramatic societies. While an executive-member of the Young Women's Christian Association for two years, she was a founder (with Eleanor Hinder [q.v.9]) and president (1923-28) of the City Girls' Amateur Sports Association. She represented the C.G.A.S.A. on the National Council of Women of New South Wales and was convener (1923-26) of the council's standing committee on trades and professions for women.

Having raised the money to bring Watts to Sydney, Margaret nursed him back to health. She married him with Quaker forms on 10 October 1925 at Killara: 'He seemed to have been entrusted into my care and I admired his singleness of mind and utter sincerity'. In 1931 Arthur returned permanently to the Soviet Union. She did not share her husband's fascination with things Russian, especially 'changing revolutionary conditions', and remained in Sydney; they were childless and divorced in 1936. In 1930 she had been appointed welfare officer for the New South Wales Society for Crippled Children and, in 1931, executive secretary of its central council of the women's auxiliaries. She visited Britain and the United States of America in 1935 to see the latest methods of treatment and rehabilitation.

In response to an urgent plea for help from the Friends in England, Watts resigned and sailed for Europe in February 1946. In Berlin she chaired the co-ordinated British relief teams charged with maintaining public health and child welfare. Compassionate and practical, she worked among the destitute and the displaced: 'Life was tiring and depressing—I often cried myself to sleep feeling utterly inadequate'. In 1947 she returned to Australia seeking supplies and money. Next year, at the request of (Sir) Richard Boyer [q.v.13], she toured the country for the United Nations Appeal for Children.

With first-hand knowledge of what many immigrants had suffered, in October 1949 Margaret Watts was appointed State executive secretary of the New Settlers' League of Australia (Good Neighbour Council of New South Wales from 1956). She and her staff helped immigrants to find work, provided interpreters, organized experts to advise and protect them when buying property, and arranged friendly visitors to lonely people in homes and hospitals. A justice of the peace (1955), she was appointed M.B.E. in 1957.

Following her retirement in 1962, the Quaker 'Meeting for Worship' at Devonshire Street, Surry Hills, remained the centre of her existence. Watts chaired (1966) the Quaker Service Council. Strongly critical of the futility of the Vietnam War, she tried to help Vietnamese orphans by arranging for their adoption in Australia. To the end of her life, she entertained—immigrants, Friends, Asian students—at her flat in Greenknowe Avenue, Potts Point, which was filled with seventeenth-century carved, wooden furniture. She enjoyed music and sketching. In 1975 the Council on the Ageing named her senior woman citizen of the year. Margaret Watts died on 5 May 1978 at St Vincent's Hospital, Darlinghurst, and was cremated. Her sister-in-law later confessed: Margaret 'had such abounding energy & dedication to & for whatever she was doing that very few people could stand the strain!'

A'sian Friend, 30 Oct 1916, p 1022, 6 June 1917, p 1071, 20 Aug 1917, p 1099, 21 Apr 1919, p 1275, June 1921, p 1506, Dec 1921, p 1553, June 1922, p 1601, June 1923, p 1706; *Friend* (Lond), 59, 1919, p 455, 137, 1979, p 208; National Council of Women (NSW), *Biennial Report*, 1923-24, 1924-26; *SMH*, 5 July 1926, 27 Sept 1935, 13 Oct 1945, 15 Oct 1966, 24 July 1967, 20 Apr 1972, 11 Jan, 6 May, 28 June 1978; *Mirror* (Syd), 13 June 1957; *Sunday Telegraph* (Syd), 23 Aug 1959; *Sun-Herald* (Syd), 21 Oct 1962; M. and W. Oates, Dictionary of Australian Quaker Biography (NL); B. Marsden-Smedley, Australian Quakers and the 1914-1918 War (M.Phil. thesis, Univ Syd, 1992); Testimony to the Grace of God in the Life of Margaret Watts (ts, 1979, copy on ADB file); Religious Society of Friends (Quakers) in

Australia, papers concerning M. Watts (ML); Investigation Branch file, A402, item W245 (NAA, Canb).

MARTHA RUTLEDGE

WAUGH, KEITH CAMERON (1886-1974), Commonwealth crown solicitor, was born on 24 March 1886 at Wollongong, New South Wales, eldest child of native-born parents Rev. Robert Hope Waugh, Presbyterian minister, and his wife Annie Eliza, daughter of Rev. James Cameron [q.v.3]. In 1893 the family moved to Neutral Bay, Sydney. Keith attended Sydney Grammar School and studied mining and metallurgy at the University of Sydney (B.E., 1908). His interest switched to the law, and he was articled to Aubrey Halloran and later to J. S. Cargill. On 19 February 1914 he was admitted as a solicitor of the Supreme Court of New South Wales.

Enlisting in the Australian Imperial Force on 28 September that year, Waugh served with the 13th Battalion at Gallipoli from April 1915. He was severely wounded in the shoulder on 18 August and evacuated to Egypt. Becoming a storeman, he served there until September 1916 when he was sent to England. In November he was attached to the A.I.F. Kit Store, London, rising to staff sergeant in December 1917. He returned to Australia in April 1918 and was discharged on 17 May because of asthma.

Waugh joined the New South Wales branch of the Commonwealth Crown Solicitor's Office as a clerk in the professional division on 17 March 1919. At the Holy Trinity Church, Kew, Melbourne, on 7 December 1925 he married with Anglican rites Bertha Winifred Simm, a clerk; they were childless. He was in charge of the Canberra office from November 1926 until the crown solicitor moved there from Melbourne the following year.

On his friend H. F. E. Whitlam's [q.v.] appointment as crown solicitor, Waugh succeeded him as assistant crown solicitor on 4 February 1937. Acute staff shortages occurred during World War II and, with only four officers holding substantive positions in the office, Waugh supervised all legal work arising in the Australian Capital Territory. In the immediate postwar period he gave most of the office's formal opinions. He was appointed crown solicitor on 10 November 1949, holding the position until his retirement on 23 March 1951.

Except for a period spent at Manly, Sydney, Waugh lived at Forrest, Canberra. His pastimes included growing and grafting fruit trees, weaving, golf and, late in life, walking for exercise. Vice-president (1938-48) and a life member (1947) of the A.C.T. Rugby Union, he was the first life member of the Eastern Suburbs Rugby Union Football Club. He was

a respected member of the Barton sub-branch of the Returned Services League of Australia. A foundation member of St Andrew's Presbyterian Church, Forrest, he was secretary of the board of management for about twenty years. Of strong, stocky build with a shock of white hair, he was a kindly man who enjoyed the company of children and played popular tunes on the piano by ear. Survived by his wife, he died on 9 March 1974 at the Allambee Nursing Home, Aranda, and was cremated.

H. E. Renfree, *History of the Crown Solicitor's Office* (Canb, 1970); *Echo* (Canb), no 175, Apr 1974; Canb and District Hist Soc, *Newsletter*, no 153, May 1974, p 10; *Canb Times*, 11 Mar 1974; information from Mrs C. Haslam, Hawthorn, Melb, Mr P. MacNicol, Curtin, Mr J. Cassell, Barton, and Mr B. May, Duffy, Canb.   C. C. CRESWELL

WAYNE, CATHY; *see* WARNES

WEARNE, MARGARET (1893-1967), trade unionist, was born on 9 February 1893 at Eaglehawk, near Bendigo, Victoria, eighth child of Joseph Wearne, a Cornish-born miner, and his wife Mary Ann, née Smith, from Victoria. In 1913 Margaret began work in the confectionery trade. A foundation member of the Female Confectioners' Union in 1916, she was employed in the MacRobertson [q.v.11 Robertson] complex at Fitzroy. Miss Wearne held a number of leading positions in the union, including that of president of the Victorian branch and first general secretary. In addition, she was a delegate on the Melbourne Trades Hall Council. She represented her co-workers on the Confectioners [Wages] Board of Victoria from 1920 and in 1928 appeared as an advocate for her union before the Commonwealth Court of Conciliation and Arbitration; she was said to be the first woman to present a case to the tribunal.

One forum for Wearne was the *Woman's Clarion*, which described itself as 'the first journal published by a Woman's Trades Union in Australia'. As founding editor in 1921, she promoted the union's central demands which included an eight-hour day, a 40-hour week, holiday pay and equal pay for women. She worked tirelessly and energetically, travelling throughout Victoria and Tasmania to negotiate with firms for better wages and conditions for women in confectionery factories. An efficient and effective organizer, she was reported in 1921 to have enrolled with the union 95 per cent of the staff in the department of MacRobertsons in which she worked.

In the 1920s Wearne fought vigorously against efforts by the (male) Confectioners' Industrial Union of Australia to recruit female members, on the grounds that a separate female union was needed to safeguard the conditions of women workers. In no uncertain terms she claimed that she would 'resist most strenuously any attempt to rob women and girls of the rights conferred upon this Union'. Despite her efforts, the union amalgamated in 1945 with the Federated Confectioners Association of Australia. The merger diminished her influence; in the new union she was assistant-secretary of the Victorian branch.

Wearne had been a member of the Australian Labor Party from 1919 and a delegate at every State conference between 1928 and 1952. She was secretary of the Women's Central Organising Committee from 1944 until 1959. Described as having 'an absolute devotion to duty [and] an unselfish mind', and as being 'clear and quick to grapple with the difficulties that arise from day to day', she made the labour movement her life project. On her retirement in 1952, she believed that 'girls in the industry today do not appreciate the work done by the union in improving their wages and conditions and take too much for granted'.

'Reserved, generous and gentle', with a 'quiet, steady personality', Wearne remained a staunch advocate of female workers' industrial and political rights. On 25 September 1954 at Christmas Hills she married with Presbyterian forms Thomas James Copeland, a 74-year-old estate agent and widower. Predeceased by her husband, she died on 31 August 1967 at Preston, Melbourne, and was buried in Preston cemetery.

F. Fraser and N. Palmer (eds), *Centenary Gift Book* (Melb, 1934); *Woman's Clarion*, 7 Nov 1921, 20 Mar 1922, 20 Sept 1923, 20 Mar 1924, July 1926; *Herald* (Melb), 23 July 1952; *Age* (Melb), 31 July 1952; *Sun News-Pictorial*, 1 Aug 1952.

JOY DAMOUSI

WEBB, ARCHIBALD BERTRAM (1887-1944), artist, was born on 4 March 1887 at Kennington, Kent, England, eldest son of Thomas Waters Webb, newspaper reporter, and his wife Emily, née Tubb. Archibald studied under W. P. Robins at St Martin's School of Art, London, and also took night classes at the City and Guilds of London Art School. He was a freelance illustrator and commercial artist in 1905-14 for such periodicals as the *Critic*, of which his father was editor, the *Pall Mall Magazine*, *Photography and Focus*, *John Bull* and *Sketch*. On 31 March 1915 he married Ada Olive Barrett at the register office, West Ham, London. Suffering from the effects of rheumatic fever, he was advised that the English climate was detrimental to his health. He and his wife migrated to Western Australia in the *Osterley*, reaching Fremantle on 11 May 1915.

For two years Webb worked as a commercial artist, and as a teaching assistant at Perth Technical School. In 1917-21 he was employed by the Department of Agriculture as a clerk in the Agricultural Bank of Western Australia, at Narrogin. On his return to Perth he was appointed assistant art master at the technical school, on the recommendation of J. W. R. Linton [q.v.10]. Among his students were Hal Missingham, Ivor Hunt, Edith Trethowan and Beatrice Darbyshire.

Webb lived at Nedlands, close to the Swan River, a favourite subject for his prints and water-colours. Reputedly a reserved and rather private man, with a stern and somewhat arrogant mien, he worked largely in isolation. Influenced by English art of the 1880s, he was unimpressed with most modernist developments, which he termed the 'Continental movement'. He adopted variations of the style and techniques used in Japanese woodcuts. His interest in Art Nouveau was also evident in the design of many of his works. While preferring persimmon wood, he experimented with easier-to-find local hardwoods, working on the plank grain. His woodcuts were favourably reviewed in *Art in Australia* (1924) and the London magazine *Studio* (1926).

In 1927 and 1930 Webb was commissioned by the Empire Marketing Board to produce posters advertising Australian primary industries, for display in Britain. He helped to teach a course in fine arts (1927-32) at the University of Western Australia, and succeeded Linton as head of the art department at Perth Technical School in 1932. After diagnosis of Parkinson's disease in 1934, he resigned his post and travelled with his wife and family to England in search of a cure. That year fifty-eight of his best water-colours, lithographs and woodcuts were exhibited at the Fine Art Society, London. He produced posters for the Great Western Railway Co. and designed wallpapers for John Line & Sons Ltd.

His health failing to improve, Webb returned to Perth in 1937; he opened an art school, where he continued to teach and show his work until his death. He also exhibited with the Perth Society of Artists. In 1938 his work was included in exhibitions in Sydney, organized by the Australian Academy of Art and the National Art Gallery of New South Wales. Survived by his wife and their three daughters, he died of a cerebral haemorrhage on 11 June 1944 in Perth and was buried with Anglican rites in Karrakatta cemetery. Examples of his work are held by the Art Gallery of Western Australia, the National Gallery of Victoria and the British Museum, London.

Westralia Gift Book (Perth, 1916); J. P. Dunne and J. H. MacKell, *'I Will Arise'* (Perth, 1980); *A. B. Webb, Edith Trethowan and Beatrice Darbyshire,* exhibition cat (Perth, 1980); *Art in Aust*, no 8, June 1924; *Studio* (Lond), 92, Nov 1926; *Art and Aust*, 16, no 4, June 1979, p 380; *West Australian*, 1 Oct 1929, 19 Jan 1937, 4 Oct 1977; Holmes à Court Collection archives, Perth; Art Gallery of WA archives.

BELINDA CARRIGAN

WEBB, FRANCIS CHARLES (1925-1973), poet, was born on 8 February 1925 at Rose Park, Adelaide, third of four children and only son of Claude Webb-Wagg, a professional musician from Sydney, and his English-born wife Hazel Leonie, daughter of Francis Foy [q.v.8] who had established Mark Foy's [q.v.4] Ltd's store in Sydney. In 1927 Hazel died suddenly. Soon after, Claude (who seems to have had a prior history of mental illness) lapsed into chronic depression and in 1931 had himself admitted to Callan Park Mental Hospital in Sydney, where he died in 1945. He had placed his children in the care of their paternal grandparents, Charles and Amy Webb-Wagg, who lived in North Sydney. Although Charles was not a Catholic, Amy was, and the children were brought up in that faith. A profound and intense Catholicism was to occupy a central place in Francis's verse.

Educated at several Catholic schools on the North Shore, Frank manifested an early talent for poetry; one piece, 'The Hero of the Plains', survives from a set of seven poems that he wrote at the age of 7 for his grandmother's birthday. After attending the Christian Brothers' High School, Lewisham, for two years, he gained first-class honours and second place in the State in the Leaving certificate English examination for 1942. He deferred taking up an exhibition at the University of Sydney. On 10 June that year, as F. Webb, he published a poem, 'Palace of Dreams', in the *Bulletin*; both Douglas Stewart, its literary editor, and Norman Lindsay [q.v.10] encouraged him.

In 1943 Webb started corresponding with Clem Christesen, founding editor of *Meanjin Papers*. In later years he felt more at home with *Meanjin* and the Melbourne literary community than with Stewart, Lindsay, and the *Bulletin* school. On 11 May 1943 Webb enlisted in the Royal Australian Air Force. He trained as a wireless air gunner in Australia and Canada but did not see action. Returning to Sydney, he was demobilized on 5 March 1946 as a flight sergeant. He enrolled in arts at the university but failed to complete the year, withdrawing apparently to devote himself to his own thought and creative writing.

In the immediate postwar years, Webb's career flourished. Individual pieces appeared in the *Bulletin*, and in 1948 his book of poems, *A Drum for Ben Boyd*, was published, with illustrations by Lindsay. By then Webb had left for Canada, where he worked for two years, as a farm hand and as a publisher's reader and editor. He seems to have had, for the only time in his life, girlfriends, to one of whom he dedicated the poem 'For Ethel'. In 1949, wishing to return to his native land, he travelled by way of England, where he succumbed to the first of many distressing episodes that psychiatrists diagnosed as acute manifestations of chronic schizophrenia.

Reaching Australia in 1950 in the care of his sister Leonie and a special nurse, for the next few years he led an itinerant life, moving mainly between Sydney, Melbourne and Adelaide, and publishing two collections of poems—*Leichhardt in Theatre* (1952) and *Birthday* (Adelaide, 1953). The title piece of the latter, a verse play for radio dealing with the final days of Hitler, was produced (1955) by the British Broadcasting Corporation.

In 1953 Webb flew to Vancouver, Canada, where he experienced electro-convulsive therapy. Back in Sydney, he travelled almost immediately to Britain. Crossing to Dublin, he was again taken to a mental hospital but released on condition that he return to England. There, after deliberately breaking a store window, he was committed to Winson Green, near Birmingham. He was later moved to Hellesdon and then David Rice hospitals, Norwich. The landscape and religious associations of Norfolk, the region of his forebears, gave him material for many poems.

Due to the intervention of David Campbell [q.v.13], Webb received a Commonwealth Literary Fund grant of £1000 in 1958. Late in 1960 he returned to Sydney. On 10 November he was admitted to Parramatta Psychiatric Hospital. The rest of his life was passed almost entirely in institutions, with brief respites when he was released on licence or, occasionally, absconded. *Socrates and Other Poems* was published in 1961. His *Collected Poems*, prepared for the press under his supervision, appeared in 1969. He died of a coronary occlusion on 23 November 1973 at Rydalmere Hospital, and was buried in Northern Suburbs cemetery.

Webb contrived to make major poetry out of his often desperate institutional experiences—the 'Ward Two' sequence, or from his English years, 'A Death at Winson Green'. After the early 1950s his interests moved to such personalities as St Francis of Assisi (in 'The Canticle', 1953), Socrates and the explorer Edward John Eyre [q.v.1]. 'Eyre All Alone' (1961) became a vehicle for Webb's own spiritual pilgrimage. Other works displayed a fascination with landscapes and seascapes, and a passionate love of music. His verse is densely metaphoric, technically inventive, sometimes lyrical, always erudite, and often 'difficult'.

Questions about the relation between the condition psychiatrists described as schizophrenia, the sources of artistic creativity, and the nature of religious experience permeated Webb's entire output. Outside his work, he rarely achieved happiness. Yet he had the gift of friendship, attracting the lasting affection of fellow writers such as Stewart, Campbell, Christesen, Nan McDonald [q.v.15], Rosemary Dobson, Vincent Buckley, Chris Wallace-Crabbe, Craig Powell and Alec Hope. Sir Herbert Read described him as 'one of the greatest poets of our time ... the most unjustly neglected poet of this century'. In his preface to the *Collected Poems* he quoted Webb's lines depicting the Norfolk painter Anthony Sandys as an equally exact description of the poet's own achievement:

Fullness, shadow: what to tell again
But the so tender voyaging line of truth.
Time shuffles a timid foot, will linger
While the tired cockcrow of your lifted finger
Opens dawn and a worn album of love and
    pain.
Brown eyes and hair flow humbly from the
    earth.

M. Griffith, *God's Fool* (Syd, 1991); B. Ashcroft, *The Gimbals of Unease* (Perth, 1996); H. P. Heseltine, 'Francis Webb, 1925-1973: A Tribute', *Meanjin Q*, 33, Mar 1974, p 5; *Poetry Aust*, no 56, Sept 1975, p 5; PM's Dept, series A3211, item 1969/3169 pt 2.

H. P. HESELTINE

WEBB, LEICESTER CHISHOLM (1905-1962), political scientist, public servant and journalist, was born on 17 May 1905 at Leicester, England, son of New Zealand-born parents Leonard Francis Webb, land surveyor, and his wife Jessie, née Chisholm, a nursing sister. The family home was at Invercargill, New Zealand. Leicester was educated at Waitaki Boys' High School, Oamaru, and Canterbury College (B.A., 1928, N.Z.; M.A., 1929), Christchurch, where he graduated with first-class honours in history.

Employed as a political journalist with the *Press*, Christchurch, Webb worked in the press gallery in Wellington and as a leaderwriter. He studied for two years at Gonville and Caius College, Cambridge, for a time under the distinguished theorist (Sir) Ernest Barker, and then briefly at the Graduate Institute of International Studies, Geneva. Back at Christchurch, he married with Anglican rites Caroline Mabel West, daughter of Bishop C. W. West-Watson, on 29 December 1932 at Christ Church Cathedral. He returned to his position on the *Press* and to part-time lecturing in political science in the history department at Canterbury College. During this period he wrote *The Control of Education in New Zealand* (Wellington, 1937) and began research on the colonial history of Canterbury. He also produced a booklet entitled *Government in New Zealand* (1940).

Webb became director of current affairs in the Army Education and Welfare Service in 1942. He was 'soon helping, quite unofficially, to draft Ministerial statements on wartime economic policy'. By 1943 he had joined the Economic Stabilization Commission; he was director of stabilization in 1944-50. He was also head of New Zealand's Marketing Department in 1948-50. These positions involved him in international trade negotiations which brought him into contact with leading Australians such as the economist (Sir) Douglas Copland [q.v.13]. Webb was president of the New Zealand Institute of Public Administration. When he informed the government in 1950 that he was resigning, the prime minister (Sir) Sidney Holland personally intervened to delay his departure so that he could complete a major project, *The New Zealand Economy 1939-1951* (1952).

In May 1951 Webb was appointed reader in political science, a discipline still in its infancy, at the Research School of Social Sciences, Australian National University, Canberra; he was also head of department. He quickly established his Australian credentials with a study of the 1951 referendum on the banning of the Communist Party of Australia. This was published to general acclaim as *Communism and Democracy in Australia* (Melbourne, 1954). In 1956 Webb was made professor of political science. He was also acting head of the department of international relations in the Research School of Pacific Studies in 1958-60.

Webb's personal academic pursuits were broad. He maintained his interest in public administration and public broadcasting. Initially concerned with political ideas, especially liberalism, his research ranged widely over Australian politics, international relations and comparative politics. Under his guidance, the department's major theme was the actions of corporate groups, such as political parties, pressure groups and business organizations in pluralist democracy. He was sceptical of the growing influence of American behaviourism on the study of politics. In 1958 he edited *Legal Personality and Political Pluralism*. Next year he sketched his ideas in an inaugural lecture, *Politics and Polity* (Canberra, 1960). His absorption in church and state issues extended to Italian politics: he published *Church and State in Italy, 1947-1957* (1958). He also wrote about the politics of Pakistan and coordinated a study of the South-East Asia Treaty Organization.

President of the Australian Political Studies Association and the Canberra branch of the Australian Institute of International Affairs, Webb was active in the Australian Institute of Political Science and regularly wrote the 'Political Review' in its journal, *Australian Quarterly*. He was a valued member of committees for both the Australian Broadcasting

Commission and the Australian Broadcasting Control Board. In 1955 he had used his experience in applied economics to conduct, for the minister of the interior, an inquiry into milk supplies in the Australian Capital Territory.

Webb stood 5 ft 10½ ins (179 cm) tall, with auburn hair and a slight build. He was a private and reserved man, 'totally unostentatious', and wholly devoted to his family. He had played Rugby Union football in his youth and later coached at Canberra Grammar School, but his 'real love and joy' was his regular weekend trout fishing. A lay preacher at St Paul's Church of England, Manuka, he was a member of the diocesan and general synods. Just before his death he was elected chairman of the Australian Commission of the Churches on International Affairs. While some of his university colleagues queried his performance as a departmental head, he was an unfailingly generous man and 'his support and affection for his protégés was unlimited'.

Caroline Webb shared in her husband's research. Prominent in women's organizations, she was national president (1961-62) of the Pan-Pacific and South East Asia Women's Association. She and Leicester died together from injuries received as passengers in a motorcar accident on 23 June 1962 on the Midland Highway, near Ross, Tasmania. Survived by their two sons and two daughters, they were buried in Canberra cemetery.

Aust Q, 34, no 3, Sept 1962, p 7; *Aust J of Politics and Hist*, 8, no 2, Nov 1962, p 224; *Canb Times*, *SMH*, *Mercury* (Hob) and *The Times*, 25 June 1962; *Press* (Christchurch, NZ), 26 June 1962; R. S. Parker papers (NL); Webb personal file (ANU Archives, Canb); information from and papers held by Mrs R. Miller, McMahons Point, Syd, and Mrs D. Webb, Yarralumla, Canb; information from Mr J. Webb, Ascot, Brisb, Profs J. Rydon, Kew, R. Martin, La Trobe Univ, Melb, R. Wettenhall, Deakin, Canb, and B. Graham, Hove, Sussex, Eng.

JOHN WARHURST

WEBB, THOMAS THEODOR (1885-1948), Methodist missionary, was born on 11 April 1885 at Lyndoch, South Australia, third of five children of Alfred Walter Webb, an Adelaide-born miller, and his wife Martha Ann, née Baker, who came from London. Theodor spent his early childhood in the farming community of Perry Bridge, Gippsland, Victoria. At the nearby Ramahyuck mission he first encountered Aboriginal people and gained knowledge of their relations with White settlers.

Accepted as a candidate for the Methodist ministry in 1909, Webb studied at Queen's College, University of Melbourne, before being posted as a probationary minister to Wentworth, New South Wales, in 1911 and Ballarat, Victoria, in 1913. From 1914 he was a chaplain for workers constructing the transcontinental railway. On 5 March 1915 he was ordained. Commissioned chaplain in the Australian Imperial Force on 19 September 1916, he served on the Western Front in 1917-18 and rose to chaplain, 3rd class (major). After his A.I.F. appointment terminated in Melbourne on 4 October 1919, he preached in the Brunswick, Wonthaggi and Ararat circuits. At All Saints Pro-Cathedral, Bendigo, on 5 April 1923 he married with Anglican rites Eva Mary Ranson (d.1947), a schoolteacher.

The Methodist Missionary Society of Australasia made Webb superintendent of Milingimbi station, Crocodile Islands, Northern Territory, and chairman of the North Australia District in 1926. His appointment coincided with the election of a new general secretary of the M.M.S.A., John Burton [q.v.7], who visited the mission in 1927. Both men brought fresh insights to mission work and wrote on a wide range of missiological, historical and anthropological subjects. Webb was able to diagnose difficulties and appraise situations rapidly. He made a number of significant changes, abolishing the 'open-house' policy of feeding Aborigines, and in 1932 replacing the dormitory with a cottage system so that Aboriginal families could settle on the mission station.

In 1939 Webb produced the district's first clearly articulated policy statement, giving directives for mission work and imparting positive regard for the Aborigines and their culture. He initiated language study, contributed articles to *Oceania* and the *Missionary Review*, and published two informative booklets, *The Aborigines of East Arnhem Land* (Melbourne, 1934) and *Spears to Spades* (Sydney, 1938). The most profound thinker of the mission in his era, and the most anthropologically informed, he was encouraged by Professor A. P. Elkin [q.v.14]. He gave the mission an intellectual leadership that was previously lacking, but was often frustrated by the apparent indifference of the Mission Board in Sydney.

Webb was 5 ft 9½ ins (177 cm) tall, with a heavy build and strong physique. A photograph portrayed him as stern, but he had a quick sense of humour, appreciated music and enjoyed singing. Forthright in expressing his opinions, he vigorously defended the rights and well-being of Aborigines. In 1939, in poor health and wishing to be reunited with his children who were at school in Victoria, he and his wife retired to Melbourne. However, he undertook deputation and translating work, and continued to preach in suburban churches. Survived by his son and daughter, he died of cardiorenal failure on 14 November 1948 at Richmond, and was cremated.

M. McKenzie, *Mission to Arnhem Land* (Adel, 1976); A. Grant, *Aliens in Arnhem Land* (Syd, 1995);

D. Carment and H. J. Wilson (eds), *Northern Territory Dictionary of Biography*, 3 (Darwin, 1996); J. Kadiba, 'Methodist Mission Policies and Aboriginal Church Leadership in Arnhem Land', in M. Hutchinson and G. Treloar (eds), *This Gospel Shall be Preached* (Syd, 1998); *Missionary Review*, 5 Feb 1940, Dec 1948; Milingimbi Mission Review Reports, A431, item 1951/1397 (NAA, Canb); Methodist Overseas Mission papers (ML); information from Mrs A. Lawrence, Ringwood, Melb.

JOHN KADIBA

WEBB, SIR WILLIAM FLOOD (1887-1972), judge, was born on 21 January 1887 in South Brisbane, third of five children of William Webb, an English-born storekeeper, and his wife Catherine Mary, née Geaney, from Ireland. William's three brothers died in infancy and his mother in 1891. Next year his father married her sister Bridget; they had three children. In 1894-97 William attended St Kilian's school, South Brisbane. After William Webb senior died in 1898, Bridget took the children to the home of her sister Margaret and her husband Martin Crane on their sheep-property near Warwick. William attended St Mary's convent school, Warwick, conducted by the Sisters of Mercy. Recognizing his ability, his teachers, notably Mother Kevin and Sister Mary Vincent, encouraged him and gave him extra tuition; he won a State scholarship. Having gained second place in the Queensland Public Service examination, he began work in the Home Secretary's Department on 3 February 1904.

Acting on T. W. McCawley's [q.v.10] advice, Webb studied law as a means of advancement in the public service. He passed his final Bar examination on 20 May 1913 with the exceptionally high average of 71.5 per cent and on 4 June was admitted to the Bar. Rising rapidly, he was appointed chief legal assistant in the Crown Solicitor's Office in September 1914 and official solicitor to the public curator in February 1916; the role of public defender was added to his duties two months later. On 1 June 1917 he succeeded McCawley as crown solicitor and secretary of the Attorney-General's Department.

When young, Webb was a tall, slim man of serious mien. Over the years he developed into an imposing figure, with a smooth face, a Roman nose, steady brown eyes, black hair and a deliberate, though kindly, manner. As a young man, he enjoyed tennis and golf. He hosted tennis parties at his home—living first at Highgate Hill then Greenslopes and later Holland Park—and always played in long whites and a tie. A devout Catholic, he remained attentive to the duties and teachings of his faith. On 17 March 1917 at the Sacred Heart Church, Sandgate, he had married Beatrice Agnew (d.1970). Her infectious laugh

and high spirits provided a fitting foil to his gravity.

One of a group of young lawyers whom Premier T. J. Ryan [q.v.11] gathered around him, Webb was appointed solicitor-general of Queensland in April 1922. Under the supervision of the attorney-general, he conducted crown cases in the courts and controlled the crown legal work. He carried out his duties with vigour and enthusiasm, gaining notable successes in the Full Court and the Court of Criminal Appeal with cases involving divorce, income tax, stamp duty, succession duty, and compulsory acquisition and compensation, and with criminal prosecutions and appeals. From the beginning of his term as crown solicitor, he had been involved in the heavy litigation between the Labor government and those opposed to or affected by its actions. One example was a six-day special case resulting from the government's compulsory purchase of the Brisbane tramways; an appeal was lodged with the Privy Council but the case was settled before a hearing took place.

In 1925 Webb was appointed a judge of the Supreme Court of Queensland and president of the Court of Industrial Arbitration. Next year he began the first of five terms as chairman of the Central Sugar Cane Prices Board. David Marr described Webb as 'cautious' and 'colourless' on the bench—excellent judicial qualities in which he would have taken pride. He was an exemplar of Viscount Radcliffe's prescription for judges: weighty but not ponderous, and learned but reticent. B. H. McPherson noted the moral courage Webb displayed when, sitting in the Full Court, he did not hesitate to reverse decisions by H. D. Macrossan [q.v.10], whom he succeeded in 1940 as senior puisne judge and chief justice. He was knighted in 1942. Ross Johnston depicted his demeanour in court as:

the model of polite, courteous behaviour; he was patient and understanding; he did not easily ruffle, but would sit coolly, unconcernedly through the heated argument, smiling gently, his brown eyes alert and at the end of the proceedings, give a calm reasoned answer to the problem, an answer freed from the temperamental, emotional involvement of the parties concerned.

Like other judges, Sir William took extra-judicial appointments in World War II. He refused the deputy-chairmanship of the Australian Industrial Relations Council, however, because he would have been subject to the direction of a Federal government minister and he believed that his judicial independence would have been compromised. When the government decided in 1942 to establish the council as an independent body, he accepted the post of chairman. In 1943 the government commissioned him to inquire into atrocities committed by Japanese forces in Papua and New Guinea. Next year he reported on the operation of postal, telegraphic and telephonic censorship.

From 29 April 1946 Webb presided over the sittings in Tokyo of the International Military Tribunal for the Far East. The tribunal consisted of nine, later eleven, judges from the same number of allied nations. Twenty-eight major war criminals were indicted, four more than the number at Nuremberg, Germany. Oral testimony was heard from 419 witnesses but the bulk of the evidence was given in 779 affidavits and 4336 documents. The proceedings took two and a half years and were recorded in a transcript 49 858 pages long. Webb's personal burden was increased by the convention that he alone should speak on behalf of the judges.

Before the I.M.T.F.E. had begun its hearings, Webb called it the most 'important criminal trial in all history'. John Pritchard noted that it developed 'into an enormous affair which dwarfed the activities of its more famous sister-tribunal sitting at Nuremberg'. After Webb and his colleagues handed down their judgement in 1948, seven of the accused applied to the Supreme Court of the United States of America for leave to file petitions for writs of habeas corpus. The court refused the application. In giving his reasons, Justice W. O. Douglas quoted with approval from the separate opinion of Webb and his analysis of the basis of the tribunal and system of law it applied. Pritchard assessed Webb's performance ambivalently: 'To his credit, he was hard-working and endeavoured to be conscientious'. He was 'softly-spoken' yet he intimidated witnesses, attorneys 'and even his colleagues on the bench'. Despite his 'abrasiveness', he could be 'courteous' and there were occasions when 'he displayed considerable sensitivity, particularly in chambers'.

On 16 May 1946 Webb had been appointed to the High Court of Australia. His first case was *Nelungaloo Pty Ltd* v. *Commonwealth*, for which he interrupted his sittings in Tokyo and which was heard in the Full High Court in June-July 1947. After returning to the court in 1949, Webb sat in more than fifty important constitutional cases, including the succession of transport cases involving section 92 of the Constitution, the second pharmaceutical benefits case (1949) in which he ruled against the Federal Labor government's legislation, and the Australian Communist Party case (1951) in which he held that an Act by the coalition government of (Sir) Robert Menzies [q.v.15] to proscribe the party was invalid. Webb had been accused in 1942 of pro-Labor sympathies but, according to Geoffrey Sawer, they 'never showed in his judgments'.

Appointed K.B.E. in 1954, Webb retired from the High Court on 16 May 1958. He accepted the chairmanship of Electric Power Transmission Pty Ltd and came out of retirement to sit on a number of remuneration tribunals established by the Queensland government. The University of Queensland conferred an honorary doctorate of laws on him in 1967. He died on 11 August 1972 in South Brisbane and was buried in Nudgee cemetery. His four daughters and two sons survived him. Sir William's portrait by Archibald Colquhoun hangs in the High Court building, Canberra.

G. Sawer, *Australian Federal Politics and Law 1929-1949* (Melb, 1963); B. V. A. Röling and C. F. Rüter (eds), *The Tokyo Judgment* (Amsterdam, Netherlands, 1977); R. Johnston, *History of the Queensland Bar* (Brisb, 1979); D. Marr, *Barwick* (Syd, 1980); G. Fricke, *Judges of the High Court* (Melb, 1986); J. Pritchard, *An Overview of the Historical Importance of the Tokyo War Trial* (Oxford, 1987); B. H. McPherson, *The Supreme Court of Queensland, 1859-1960* (Syd, 1989); *Cwlth Law Reports*, 127, 1971-72; *Catholic Leader*, 3 Sept 1972.
H. A. WELD

WEDGWOOD, CAMILLA HILDEGARDE (1901-1955), anthropologist and educationist, was born on 25 March 1901 at Newcastle-upon-Tyne, England, fifth of seven children of Josiah Clement Wedgwood, a naval architect, and his wife Ethel Kate, daughter of Charles (Lord) Bowen, a lord of appeal in ordinary. Descended from Josiah Wedgwood (1730-1795), the master potter, the Wedgwood and Darwin [q.v.1] families were intertwined; Ralph Vaughan Williams, Gwen Raverat, and C. V. Wedgwood were cousins. Josiah Clement fought in the Boer War then spent some years in South Africa; Camilla passed her early childhood with her maternal grandmother at Halsteads in the Lake District and, after 1906, with her parents at The Ark, Moddershall, near the family kilns in Staffordshire.

Aided by her famous name and the financial stability that flowed from the sale of Wedgwood pottery, Camilla was free to express her inherited independence, strong social conscience and streak of individualism. After attending the Orme Girls' School, Newcastle-under-Lyme, Staffordshire, she followed her two brothers to Bedales School in Hampshire. At the age of 17 she entered Bedford College for Women, University of London. Here, she developed lifelong interests in debating and drama, Icelandic studies and Old Norse, and early English sagas such as *Beowulf*. Her rugged, independent bearing, as well as her sympathy for 'primitive' peoples, earned her the sobriquet of 'The Ancient Briton'.

Her parents separated in 1914 and divorced five years later; her mother migrated to Switzerland with her two youngest daughters.

Camilla and the four elder children were thrown closer together. In 1920 she followed her mother's example and attended Newnham College, Cambridge, where she studied anthropology under W. E. Armstrong and A. C. Haddon. She passed with first-class honours the English tripos in 1922 and the anthropology tripos in 1924 but the university did not award degrees to women until 1948. At Newnham she held the Arthur Hugh Clough (1923) and Bathurst (1924) scholarships, and qualified as M.A. in 1927. She joined the Society of Friends in 1925 and taught (1926-27) at Bedford College.

In 1928 Professor A. R. Radcliffe-Brown [q.v.11] appointed Wedgwood temporary lecturer in anthropology at the University of Sydney, to replace Bernard Deacon, who had died at Malekula, New Hebrides. Instead of pursuing her own research, she accepted the self-effacing task of editing Raymond Firth's *Primitive Economics of the New Zealand Maori* (London, 1929) and Deacon's *Malekula* (London, l934). Wedgwood lectured (1930) at the University of Capetown, South Africa, and was assistant lecturer (1931-32) under Bronislaw Malinowski at the London School of Economics and Political Science. She was a fellow (1924) and council-member (1931-32) of the Royal Anthropological Institute of Great Britain and Ireland.

Granted a fellowship by the Australian National Research Council, Wedgwood was encouraged by Professor A. P. Elkin [q.v.14] and Firth to carry out field-work. In 1932-34 she studied the lives of women and children on Manam, a volcanic island of 4000 inhabitants off the northern coast of New Guinea. She investigated methods of reviving native arts and crafts on Nauru in 1935.

In her publications Wedgwood took a Durkheimian view of religion and warfare as fortifying social cohesion, an emphasis she inherited through Malinowski. Adopting her own version of the 'participant-observation' method of field-work, she immersed herself in social activity on Manam, to such effect that Manam women recollected twenty years later: 'she knew how to plant taro. She dug the hole. She cooked the taro just as we do. She cut away the scrub with a bush knife as we do. If a man died she sat in the middle with all the other women and grieved for him. She was not like white people, she was just like us black-skinned folk'. It was clear from her research on Manam and Nauru that she saw a subordinate role for women in marriage and the wider society as part of the natural order. This was in spite of her own unmarried independence and the personal singularity which reflected her fine intellect.

A member of the early cohort of women field-workers who included Audrey Richards, Ruth Benedict and Margaret Mead, Wedg-

wood established her scholarly reputation with her Manam research. The publishers of her monumental edition of *Malekula* had been threatened with litigation because, faced with Deacon's disorderly notes, she unwittingly ascribed material in her text to him instead of to the anthropologist John Layard. By the mid-1930s she had been passed over for tenured positions both in Sydney and at the L.S.E.

In June 1935 Miss Wedgwood was appointed principal of Women's College within the University of Sydney. During a distinguished eight years in the post she stressed the importance of interaction between the college and the university (she herself was honorary lecturer in anthropology) and cultural links with the older universities in Britain. She presided over the construction in 1937 of the (S. J.) Williams [q.v.12] wing, providing accommodation for fourteen additional students and paid for out of housekeeping savings, and the remodelling in 1938 of the kitchens and staff quarters. Despite her commanding manner, 'she could mix with her students informally without any loss of dignity'. Although she was best known for her involvement in their dramatic productions and her love of poetry, her students were impressed by her skill as a public speaker and her 'complete disregard for the conventions of fashion'. Her deep, confident voice and gracious manners gave an impression of the serenity sometimes possessed by English county families with an unquestioning acceptance of their own worth.

Wedgwood's Fabian and Quaker social conscience led her to accept many responsibilities. From 1937 she was secretary of the German Emergency Fellowship Committee, which included Max Lemberg and Sydney Morris [qq.v.15]. She pleaded the cause of Jewish and non-Aryan Christian victims of Nazi persecution before (Sir) John McEwen [q.v.15], minister for the interior. In close contact with her father, she raised money for refugee passages to Australia, but confided to her sister Helen that she felt like 'a mouse nibbling at a mountain'. She publicly protested against the treatment of the internees in the *Dunera* and the refugees in the *Strouma* which sank in the Black Sea.

As a college principal and daughter of a well-known British Labour politician (raised to the peerage in 1942), Wedgwood was a public figure in Sydney, prominent in charitable causes as well as a member of the strongly pacifist Sydney Meeting of Quakers. Among other organizations, she was involved with the Rachel Forster Hospital for Women and Children, the Anthropological Society of New South Wales, the Australian Federation of University Women and the Australian Institute of International Affairs. In her social reformist interests as a member of the Australian

Student Christian Movement, she retained her Quaker concerns. Increasingly drawn to Anglicanism, she was much influenced by C. S. Lewis and Dorothy L. Sayers; in December 1943 she acted in May Hollinworth's [q.v.14] production of T. S. Eliot's *Murder in the Cathedral*. Her attraction to Anglicanism was closely linked with her understanding of visible symbols and rituals as the binding elements of any society. The solemnity of the Anglo-Catholic feast day opened a new world to her, accustomed as she was to the simplicity of the Quaker meeting. As a disciple of Malinowski, she well understood that the vehicle of authentic religious experience lay in the rites and spells, artefacts and ceremonial feasting of most societies. Early in 1944 she renounced the unqualified pacifism of the Sydney Meeting of Quakers and became an Anglican.

On 11 January 1944 Wedgwood was commissioned acting lieutenant colonel, Australian Army Medical Women's Service. Serving as a research officer (anthropology) in Alf Conlon's [q.v.13] Directorate of Research (and Civil Affairs), she developed policies for postwar educational reconstruction in Papua and New Guinea where she served intermittently in 1944-45. She had a strong dash of egalitarianism. On army bivouacs, when offered a cigarette by her young cadets her reply was: 'No thanks, I roll my own'.

From January 1945 Wedgwood was an outstandingly popular lecturer at the Land Headquarters School of Civil Affairs, Duntroon, Canberra, and, following her demobilization on 16 January 1946, at the Australian School of Pacific Administration, Mosman, Sydney. Her greatest written accomplishments were her pioneering surveys of mission schools in Papua and New Guinea (1944-47), compiled as a prelude to establishing a government education scheme. In England for family reasons in 1947-48, she taught at the Institute of Education, University of London. Back in Sydney, she was senior lecturer in native administration at A.S.O.P.A.

'Behind her apparent self-confidence', Elkin found her 'somewhat retiring and lonely'. She kept in close touch by correspondence with her distant family, especially her sister Helen, and relied on old Sydney friends Theresa Britton and her family, Clare Stevenson and Stella James. Camilla Wedgwood died of cancer on 17 May 1955 at Royal North Shore Hospital, St Leonards, and was cremated. A girls' secondary school at Goroka in the New Guinea Highlands and a memorial lecture in Port Moresby were named after her; her friend James McAuley [q.v.15] dedicated to her his poem 'Winter Nightfall'.

W. V. Hole and A. H. Treweeke, *The History of the Women's College within the University of Sydney* (Syd, 1953); D. Wetherell and C. Carr-Gregg, *Camilla* (Syd, 1990), and for bib; *South Pacific*, 8, no 6, July 1955, p 110; *Oceania*, 26, no 3, Mar 1956, p 172.

DAVID WETHERELL

WEDGWOOD, DAME IVY EVELYN ANNIE (1896-1975), politician, was born on 18 October 1896 at Malvern, Melbourne, daughter of Victorian-born parents Albert Drury, farmer, and his wife Elizabeth, née Evans. Educated in Melbourne, Ivy worked as a clerk and later an accountant with a firm of importers. At St Thomas's Church, Essendon, on 7 October 1921 she married with Anglican rites Jack Kearns Wedgwood, a Woodend motor mechanic, war veteran and descendant of Josiah Wedgwood (1730-1795), the master potter. Although they were to have no children, and Jack's wartime injuries added to the demands of marriage, the Wedgwoods were to remain a devoted couple for over fifty-three years.

As a result of her employment as private secretary to Prime Minister S. M. (Viscount) Bruce [q.v.7], Wedgwood became interested in politics. She joined the Australian Women's National League through the influence of her neighbour, and senior league member, Edith Haynes. Formed in 1904 to oppose socialism, support the monarchy, protect the interests of women and children, and educate women in politics, it was, at its peak, the largest women's political organization in Australia. It provided valuable electoral backing for selected candidates of the National, United Australia and Liberal parties. Wedgwood rose rapidly through its ranks to become a member of the executive committee.

Like (Dame) Elizabeth (May) Couchman, who led the A.W.N.L. from 1927 to 1945 and who was a close political ally, Wedgwood concluded that the heyday of separate women's political organizations such as the A.W.N.L. had passed, and that conservatively inclined women would do better to join mainstream non-Labor bodies. With Couchman and Haynes, Wedgwood was a delegate to the conferences convened by (Sir) Robert Menzies [q.v.15] in Canberra and at Albury, New South Wales, in 1944 to revive the waning forces of Australian conservatism. She supported Menzies' efforts to found a new party which would subsume the league, and was an important champion of the merger in the often acrimonious league meetings that eventually endorsed the proposal.

Wedgwood, with other former A.W.N.L. members, was prominent in the Liberal Party of Australia. A vice-president of the party's Victorian division, she chaired the central committee of the women's section in 1948-50, presided over the Australian Women's Liberal

Club for many years, and sat on the State and federal executives. On 10 December 1949 she was elected to the Senate, the third woman to enter the chamber and the first from Victoria.

Short, with 'greying hair always immaculately waved', Wedgwood impressed her fellow senators as having a 'compassionate concern for causes, for the handicapped and for people in whom she was interested' and 'sound common sense' which frequently 'put quite pompous politicians in their place'. She presented her arguments 'logically and persistently, but without fireworks'. Although she never achieved ministerial office, she played an important part in the formulation of government policy in the areas of health and welfare. She was a member of the House Committee (1950-55, 1965-68), the Joint Committee of Public Accounts (1955-71), and the joint select committees on the new and permanent parliament house (1965-71), and the Australian Capital Territory (1968). As a temporary chairman of committees in 1962-71, and thus the second woman to preside over the Senate, she headed its Select Committee on Medical and Hospital Costs (1968-70), and its Legislative and General Purpose Standing Committee on Health and Welfare (1970-71) which reported on the health needs of people with mental and physical disabilities.

At various times, Wedgwood was president of the Australian Council of Domiciliary Nursing, honorary treasurer of the Royal District Nursing Service and president of the After-Care Hospital in Melbourne. She was a former president of the Women Justices' Association and had been a special magistrate in the Children's Court, Melbourne. A keen advocate of the interests of middle-class working women, she served on the executive of the National Council of Women of Victoria and was a member of the Business and Professional Women's Club and the Soroptimist Club of Melbourne. She also belonged to the Australian Institute of International Affairs and the Lyceum Club, and enjoyed gardening and the theatre. In 1967 she was appointed D.B.E.

Wedgwood believed that women had a duty to prepare themselves for an informed entry into the public realm by self-education on political and social questions. Despite her support for the integration of the A.W.N.L. into the Liberal Party, she acknowledged the importance of women forming autonomous associations within which they could realize their own concerns. In an article in *Woman's Day* in 1969 she urged: 'Get into your women's organisations and train yourself for Parliament. It is a specialised existence which requires work and study'. Her own career demonstrated the profound shift in the expectations and opportunities of middle-class Australian women during the twentieth century.

After Prime Minister (Sir) John Gorton failed to persuade cabinet to enable a husband to receive benefits from his deceased wife's parliamentary superannuation, Dame Ivy became a principal plotter in his demise in March 1971. She retired from the Senate on 30 June. Survived by her husband, she died on 24 July 1975 at Toorak and was cremated. Prime Minister Gough Whitlam described her as 'a gracious and esteemed colleague' who would be fondly remembered by all Victorians. Malcolm Fraser, the leader of the Opposition, referred to her as 'a great Australian' who had provided much useful advice throughout his political career. The Liberal senator Margaret Guilfoyle observed: 'She knew that women needed to be integrated into the political system if they were to have the influence that we believe Australian women should have in political life'.

A. Millar, *Trust the Women* (Canb, 1993); D. Sydenham, *Women of Influence* (Melb, 1996); G. Henderson, *Menzies' Child* (Syd, 1998); *PD* (Senate), 12 May 1971, pp 1707, 1711, 19 Aug 1975, p 1; *Woman's Day*, 21 July 1969, p 21; *Herald* (Melb), 6 June 1970; *Age* (Melb), 26 July 1975; Wedgwood papers (NL). DOUG SCOBIE

WEEKS, LEWIS GEORGE (1893-1977), geologist, was born on 22 May 1893 near Chilton, Wisconsin, United States of America, second of six children of George Weeks, an American-born farmer, and his wife Katherine, née Schneider, who came from Switzerland. Lewis attended Chilton High School and worked as a schoolteacher before studying geology at the University of Wisconsin (B.A., 1917; D.Sc., 1970). In 1917-18 he served as an aviator in the United States Navy. Following brief periods as a geologist and mining engineer in Mexico, and as a teacher at Cornell University, Ithaca, New York, he was recruited in 1920 by a British company searching for oil in India. At All Saints Pro-Cathedral, Shillong, Assam, on 12 October 1921 he married Alice Una Austin with Anglican rites.

Joining the Standard Oil Co. of New Jersey (Esso, later Exxon) in 1924, Weeks travelled extensively in South America on field-work. In 1938 he moved to New York as a research geologist. He was credited with discovering (1947) huge oil reserves at Leduc, Alberta, Canada. In 1958 he retired as the company's chief geologist and set up as an independent consultant. One of his first clients, Broken Hill Proprietary Co. Ltd, sought his services as the 'best petroleum geologist in America' to assist its efforts to find oil in Australia. Visiting Australia in 1960, he asked for (and was granted) a 2.5 per cent royalty on any commercial discovery. He then recommended that B.H.P. begin exploration off the south-eastern coast of Victoria. It was critical timing, as the technology for drilling in rough seas was then being developed in California.

Geologists had known from the 1920s that there might be major oil accumulations in the offshore Gippsland Basin. A huge investment in capital, skill and new technology would be required to find them: Weeks's great advantages were his reputation, knowledge and contacts. With his backing, B.H.P. took up permits over most of the region and started preliminary investigations. The results were sufficiently encouraging for the company to seek an international oil company as a partner. Weeks's involvement was one factor that led Esso to agree to continue the exploration programme in return for 50 per cent of the profits. Drilling by Esso in the 1960s revealed the largest oil and natural-gas province found in Australia to that time. By the early 1970s the wells supplied two-thirds of Australia's crude-oil needs and had the capacity to provide more natural gas than Victorians could consume.

Wiry in build, Weeks was nervous, individualistic, strong willed, health conscious, financially careful, and a committed Christian. He used much of his new wealth to establish an oil-exploration company and to endow his favourite institutions, among them the University of Wisconsin. Although he often returned to Australia, he never warmed to it. After his wife died, he married with Episcopalian rites her widowed friend Anne Sutton, née Newman, on 14 December 1957 at Salt Lake City. He died on 4 March 1977 in his home at Westport, Connecticut, and was buried in the cemetery of St James the Less, Scarsdale, New York. His wife survived him, as did the son of his first marriage. Weeks's memoirs, *A Lifelong Love Affair*, were published in 1978.

R. Murray, *Fuels Rush In* (Melb, 1972) and The Bass Strait Story (ms, 1986, Univ Melb Archives), *Herald* (Melb), 3 May 1969; information from Mr B. Foster, Elwood, Mr J. Norgard, Toorak, Melb, and the late Mr B. Hopkins.   ROBERT MURRAY

WELCH, LESLIE ST VINCENT (1879-1947), medical practitioner, was born on 7 February 1879 at Bondi, Sydney, eldest of four sons of English-born parents John St Vincent Welch, insurance manager, and his wife Emily, née Thackeray. After attending Sydney Church of England Grammar School (Shore) and studying engineering for two years at the University of Sydney, Leslie decided to enter medicine. He trained in London, mainly at St Bartholomew's Hospital, qualifying in 1907 as a licentiate of the Royal College of Physicians and a member of the Royal College of Surgeons. Returning to New South

Wales, he was registered to practise on 11 November 1908. On 12 June 1909 at St Paul's Church of England, Byron Bay, he married Beatrice Emily Sparrow, a nurse.

Before World War I Welch worked at Bangalow and Bombala, in Sydney at Neutral Bay and Manly, and at Narrandera and Abermain. On 14 July 1915 he was appointed captain, Australian Army Medical Corps, Australian Imperial Force. He served in Egypt, where he was mentioned in dispatches, and with the 2nd Divisional Ammunition Column on the Western Front. His A.I.F. appointment terminated in Australia on 17 January 1917 and he returned to Abermain. In 1920 he moved to Kempsey. He was divorced on 13 June 1922. At the district registrar's office, St Leonards, Sydney, on 29 July that year he married May Winston Reeve, née Anderson, an American-born widow.

On 1 June 1926 Welch became chief medical officer of the medical branch, Queensland Department of Public Instruction. Next year he visited outback schools investigating trachoma ('sandy blight'), an eye disease then affecting 20 per cent of western Queensland pupils. He arranged for the appointment of a full-time ophthalmologist, and enlisted local doctors and school nursing sisters to examine and treat affected children. In 1928 he helped to establish the (Thomas) Wilson Ophthalmic School Hostel, a sanatorium in Brisbane for more serious cases. Under his supervision hygiene lessons aimed at preventing the condition were incorporated into the school curriculum.

From 1930 Welch, with (Sir) Raphael Cilento, director of the division of tropical hygiene, Commonwealth Department of Health, and Dr John Coffey, Queensland commissioner of public health, directed a joint Federal and State campaign to reduce the incidence of hookworm in children. Welch also tried to eliminate contagious infestations in schools, such as scabies and head lice, and set up travelling rail dental clinics. A member of the State Nutritional Advisory Board, he arranged for free (or very cheap) milk at schools and promoted the nutritious Oslo lunch. Appointed (1938) an honorary lecturer in the department of social and tropical medicine, University of Queensland, he wrote articles (under a nom de plume) for the popular press.

A strong and uncompromising advocate for children, Welch served (1938-47) on the executive of the Queensland Bush Children's Health Scheme, which brought country children to the city for medical treatment or to camps at the beach for holidays. Charming and courteous, he was an accomplished cellist and a keen photographer who used many of his own images in official reports and publications. Welch, who suffered from diabetes, retired on 9 June 1947. Survived by his wife, he died of myocardial infarction on 20 August that year in Brisbane and was buried in Brookfield cemetery. He had been childless. His brother Kenyon was Australia's first flying doctor.

J. H. Pearn, *Focus and Innovation* (Brisb, 1986); R. Patrick, *A History of Health & Medicine in Queensland 1824-1960* (Brisb, 1987); *MJA*, 6 Dec 1947, p 707.   M. D. COBCROFT

WELLS, SIR HENRY (1898-1973), army officer, was born on 22 March 1898 at Kyneton, Victoria, youngest of seven children of Arthur Wells, draper, and his wife Elizabeth, née Carter, both Victorian born. Educated at Kyneton High School, 'Bill', as he was known to his family, entered the Royal Military College, Duntroon, Federal Capital Territory, in February 1916. A notable sportsman, he graduated in December 1919 and was appointed lieutenant, Permanent Military Forces. He trained in England before becoming adjutant and quartermaster of the 8th (1921) and 9th (1922) Light Horse regiments. Appointed brigade major of the 6th Cavalry Brigade in February 1926, he was made instructor at the Small Arms School, Sydney, in July. At St John's Church of England, Cessnock, on 14 December that year he married Lorna Irene Skippen.

Returning to the R.M.C. as a company commander in 1927, Wells rose to captain in December. He again taught at the Small Arms School (from 1931) and in 1934-35 attended the Staff College, Camberley, England. Back in Australia in 1936, he was adjutant and quartermaster of the 4th/3rd Battalion, then brigade major of the 1st Infantry Brigade. In 1938 he was appointed lecturer in tactics at the R.M.C.

Wells transferred to the Australian Imperial Force in April 1940 as a major and was posted to 7th Division headquarters. Arriving in the Middle East in December, he was promoted lieutenant colonel and seconded to headquarters, I Corps, as senior liaison officer. He was appointed O.B.E. for his work in the disastrous Greek campaign of April 1941, during which he travelled extensively between the headquarters and co-ordinated the withdrawal of Imperial and Greek troops from the Veria Pass. Evacuated, he became a general staff officer, 2nd grade, at headquarters, I Corps, in June. Five months later he was promoted colonel and posted as general staff officer, 1st grade, of the 9th Division under Major General (Sir) Leslie Morshead [q.v.15]. For the 'ability, keen perception and anticipation, and sound knowledge' he displayed during the battle of El Alamein, Egypt, in October-November 1942, Wells was awarded the Distinguished

Service Order (1943). He had been twice mentioned in dispatches.

By February 1943 Wells was back in Australia. Next month he was appointed brigadier, general staff, on the headquarters of II Corps. Promoted temporary brigadier in April, he served in New Guinea from October 1943 to February 1944. He was elevated to C.B.E. (1945) for his 'tireless energy and ready adaptability' during the successful operations in the Ramu Valley which culminated in the capture of Madang. Again mentioned in dispatches, he transferred in April 1944 to I Corps which moved to Hollandia, Netherlands New Guinea, in October.

Attached to Army Headquarters, Melbourne, from September 1945, Wells was appointed director of military operations in March 1946. Four months later he became deputy chief of the General Staff as a temporary major general. In 1947 he attended the Imperial Defence College, London, and in 1949-51 commanded R.M.C., Duntroon. Promoted temporary lieutenant general in February 1951 (substantive 12 April 1954), he was given Southern Command. In 1953-54 he was commander-in-chief, British Commonwealth Forces, Korea. He was appointed C.B. and to the United States of America's Legion of Merit in 1954.

Wells was made chief of the General Staff in December 1954. He presided over the deployment of Australian troops to Malaya during the Emergency and the creation of the first regular brigade group. Elevated to K.B.E. in 1956, he made official visits to Britain, the U.S.A., Canada, Thailand and the Philippines. He became the first chairman of the Chiefs of Staff Committee in March 1958. An extremely competent staff officer, he retired on 22 March 1959 and was appointed honorary colonel of the Royal Victoria Regiment in April 1961.

Five ft 7 ins (170 cm) tall and stocky, Wells had a dark complexion, brown eyes and bushy eyebrows; he was balding from an early age. His friends nicknamed him 'Bomba'. He had a clear speaking voice, with a good turn of phrase, but was somewhat reserved and taciturn. Keen on physical fitness, he played golf in his later years. He was frugal: even during the Depression, he told his officers, he had invested 10 per cent of his income in shares. In retirement he was a director of a number of companies, among them Broken Hill South Ltd, Metal Manufactures Ltd, Navcot Australia Pty Ltd and Sitmar Line (Australia) Pty Ltd. Survived by his wife and their two sons, Sir Henry died on 20 October 1973 at Yarrawonga, Victoria, and, following a funeral conducted with full military honours at Toorak Presbyterian Church, he was cremated. He bequeathed a large part of his estate, sworn for probate at $161 543, to Junior Legacy, Melbourne.

G. Long, *Greece, Crete and Syria* (Canb, 1953); B. Maughan, *Tobruk and El Alamein* (Canb, 1966); J. Hetherington, *Blamey, Controversial Soldier* (Canb, 1973); R. O'Neill, *Australia in the Korean War 1950-53*, 1 and 2 (Canb, 1981, 1985); P. Dennis and J. Grey, *Emergency and Confrontation* (Syd, 1996); information from Lieut Gen H. J. Coates, Griffith, Canb.   E. M. ANDREWS*

WELLS, THOMAS ALEXANDER (1888-1954), judge, was born on 10 February 1888 at Wallacetown, near Wagga Wagga, New South Wales, twelfth child of Ezekiel Wells, a native-born farmer, and his wife Rose Ann, née Toland, who came from England. Educated at Wagga Grammar School, Tommy worked as a correspondence clerk in Sydney. At St David's Presbyterian Church, Ashfield, on 2 March 1910 he married Martha May Doris Myers. In 1913 he joined the reporting staff of the Supreme Court of New South Wales.

On 17 February 1917 Wells enlisted in the Australian Imperial Force. Serving in France with the Australian Corps Heavy Trench Mortar Battery from April 1918, he was gassed in July and was in hospital for three months. He returned to Australia in August 1919 as a corporal and was discharged on 3 September. Back at his old job, he studied part time at the University of Sydney (LL.B., 1924). Admitted to the New South Wales Bar on 31 July 1924, he practised until 1933. On 28 August that year he was sworn in as judge of the Supreme Court of the Northern Territory, a thankless posting but a welcome relief to a 'briefless barrister'.

Wells had a formidable presence. The curl to his mouth and a wen on his upper lip conveyed an impression of contempt which was bolstered by his often offensive *obiter dicta*. He repeatedly refused to believe the evidence of Aboriginal witnesses, his bias being reinforced by the shortcomings of the court's interpreting service. When an Aborigine called Tuckiar was found guilty and sentenced to death in August 1934 for killing Constable A. S. McColl at Woodah Island, Professor A. P. Elkin [q.v.14] and the Association for the Protection of Native Races led moves to have the conviction overturned. The High Court of Australia upheld the appeal on the grounds that Wells should not have rejected the evidence of an Aboriginal witness as fabricated. During the trials of several Aboriginal men for sexual offences in 1937-38, Wells regretted that he could not order corporal punishment. He believed flogging to be a more effective punishment for Aborigines than custodial sentences.

In 1938 Wells ruled in favour of Japanese plaintiffs who had sued the administrator of the Northern Territory, C. L. A. Abbott [q.v.13], and the captain of the patrol boat *Larrakia* for the unlawful seizure of pearling luggers alleged to have trespassed into the offshore area of an Aboriginal reserve. The antagonism between Abbott and Wells erupted in 1941 when the judge publicly denounced the administrator for neglecting to issue an ordinance to establish the legal status of the Air Raid Precautions organization.

Immediately after the bombing of Darwin on 19 February 1942, Wells arranged for the release of all prisoners from the Darwin Gaol and Labour Prison and urged the Aboriginal inmates to kill as many Japanese as they could. He also took charge of the evacuation by train of hundreds of survivors of the raids. When Abbott left for Alice Springs on 2 March 1942, Wells remained in Darwin and carried on with the civil administration of the 'Top End' of the Northern Territory in a characteristically unconventional way until Abbott's return in July 1945.

Wells continued to preside over the Supreme Court in Darwin and in 1946 condemned the belief that Aborigines should not be subject to the White man's law as 'sloppy sentimentality'. He formally retired in 1952, having suffered a stroke two years earlier. Survived by his wife, and their daughter and two sons, he died on 13 September 1954 in Darwin Hospital and was buried in Darwin general cemetery with Catholic rites.

T. Wise, *The Self-Made Anthropologist* (Syd, 1985); D. Carment and B. James (eds), *Northern Territory Dictionary of Biography*, 2 (Darwin, 1992); T. Egan, *Justice All Their Own* (Melb, 1996); *Cwlth Law Reports*, 52, 1934-35, p 335; Assn for the Protection of Native Races, *Annual Report*, 1933-34; *SMH*, 22 Aug 1933, 14 Sept 1954; *Northern Standard* (Darwin), 30 Dec 1941; Darwin air raid, A431, item 1949/687, and A816, item 37/301/293 (NAA, Canb); History J. Wells, E475 (NAA, Darwin).

PETER ELDER

WENTCHER, TINA (1887-1974), sculptor, was born on 17 December 1887 in Constantinople (Istanbul), daughter of Jewish parents David Leon Haim, a Serbian-born merchant, and his wife Rebecca, née Mondolfo, who was born in Italy. The family moved to Vienna then Berlin. Tina later claimed to have lived in Berlin from 1904 but other sources suggest that she spent her childhood and adolescence there. She entered a private art school where her teachers, including Levin Funke, encouraged her to set up her own studio. A limestone bust she made of one of her sisters was accepted by the Berlin *Sezession*. This remarkable achievement resulted in a commission to carve authorized copies of sculptures in the city's Egyptian Museum.

In 1913-14 Haim studied in Paris, her work earning praise from Rodin. On 8 August 1914 in Berlin she married Julius Wentscher, a painter then serving in the artillery. Exhibiting as Tina Haim-Wentscher and joining the *Sezession*, she became a member of the Wilhelmine and Weimar *avant-garde*. Numerous galleries and museums in Berlin acquired examples of her work, including a head of the artist and sculptor Käthe Kollwitz (Nationalgalerie). The Wentschers made artistic tours of Greece and Egypt in the 1920s.

From 1931 the couple travelled in the Far East. Social and artistic success, followed by warnings from Kollwitz and Julius's Jewish mother about the worsening position of Jews in Germany, convinced the Wentschers to postpone their return to Berlin. They held exhibitions, collected curios and accepted commissions in the Netherlands East Indies (Indonesia) (1931-32 and 1933-34), China (1932-33), Siam (Thailand) (1935-36), Singapore (1936-37) and Malaya (Malaysia) (1936-40). Their works were bought for public and private collections but many did not survive World War II. Tina and Julius collaborated in executing highly praised, life-size dioramas representing Malayan industries for the British Empire Exhibition, Glasgow, 1938.

After being sent to Australia as enemy aliens and interned (1940-42) at Tatura, Victoria, the Wentschers settled in Melbourne and Anglicized their name to Wentcher. Tina adapted quickly. In the 1940s and 1950s she sent sculptures to the major art societies, exhibited regularly and won two prizes. Among her early Australian works was a bust of Hephzibah Menuhin (held by Haileybury College, East Brighton). Her participation in charitable work for the Royal Children's Hospital led to a close friendship with Dame Elisabeth Murdoch.

Despite her eminence among early modernist sculptors, Wentcher never developed as an artist beyond what she had achieved in her Asian work, which was radical to Australian eyes. The distinct personality and presence of these pieces forged her reputation, as did her connexion with famous people such as Käthe Kollwitz. While praised for their delicacy and subtlety, Wentcher's creations reflect the monumental sharpness and clarity of line and expression—derived from ancient Egyptian and Greek sculpture—that fascinated early twentieth-century dissident German artists. Her commissions in Australia were generally small-scale plaques and busts. Unlike male modernist sculptors, she did not receive public validation through government teaching positions, though she found many advocates among her peers.

Childless and predeceased by her husband, Wentcher died on 21 April 1974 at St Kilda and was cremated. The Association of Sculptors of Victoria (of which she had been a member) named a prize in her memory. Her work is represented in the National Gallery of Australia, Canberra, and other major collections; the McClelland Gallery, Langwarrin, Melbourne, holds a number of key pieces.

K. Scarlett, *Australian Sculptors* (Melb, 1980); *Tina Wentcher 1887-1974: A Centennial Exhibition*, exhibition cat (Melb, 1987); A367, item C57073 (NAA, Canb); Wentcher files (McClelland Gallery, Langwarrin, Vic, and Aust Art and Artists Collection, Arts L, SLV).   JULIET PEERS

WEST, EVELYN MAUDE (1888-1969), accountant, shire secretary and community worker, was born on 14 September 1888 at Traralgon, Victoria, second of five children of Walter West, blacksmith, and his wife Susan, née Barrett, both Victorian born. Two of her siblings died in infancy. Educated locally, Eva passed the municipal clerk's examination in 1914. She briefly worked for the Shire of Poowong and Jeetho until 1915 when she joined the Country Roads Board, Melbourne. In 1918 she, Mary Humble and Irene Bourne were the first women to be admitted to the Incorporated Institute of Accountants, Victoria (Commonwealth Institute of Accountants from 1921, Australian Society of Accountants from 1952).

Miss West was employed by the Young Men's Christian Association and by Holmes & McCrindle, public accountants, before returning to Traralgon where she began her own practice as an accountant and auditor. Her father had been secretary (from 1907) of the Traralgon Shire Council. During the years that he was a member (1922-29) of the Legislative Assembly, Eva worked as the shire's assistant-secretary, with responsibility for day-to-day administration. Appointed acting-secretary in 1934, she was said to be 'one of [only] three women occupying important municipal positions in Victoria'.

In January 1935 West was confirmed in the post of shire secretary. She also became secretary of the Traralgon Waterworks Trust and later the Traralgon Sewerage Authority. While she was shire secretary, Traralgon's population increased and the shire's economy developed. The council undertook major infrastructure works, particularly when the Australian Paper Manufacturers Ltd's Maryvale Mill commenced operations and most of its workers decided to live at Traralgon. West earned respect as an effective administrator. Her meticulous attention to the accounts won praise from the shire's auditors. In World War II she was the driving force behind the Traralgon Salvage Committee, which raised money for benevolent purposes. A testimonial letter from councillors on her retirement in

1946 described her as genial, obliging and courteous.

Devoted to the community and compassionate towards the needy, West held honorary positions on more than twenty associations and committees. She took a special interest in the education and advancement of young women: she founded a local company of the Girl Guides' Association, served on the council of St Anne's Church of England Girls' Grammar School, Sale, and sponsored a bursary to pay for the schooling of a clergyman's daughter. West and her two sisters cared for the illegitimate child of a single woman, and Eva met the cost of the girl's education at a boarding-school. In 1958 Miss West was appointed M.B.E. A woman of presence and humility, she lived simply, sleeping on the verandah of the small, weatherboard home which she shared with her sisters. She died on 20 June 1969 at Traralgon and was buried with Anglican rites in the local cemetery. In her memory, the Traralgon Business and Professional Women's Club instituted an annual scholarship for a female student.

J. Hammett, 'Eva West (1888-1969)', in *Five Gippsland Women* (Churchill, Vic, 1991) and 'Eva West: A Citizen in the Community' (copy held by ADB), and for bib.   JENNY HAMMETT

WEST, RAYMOND (1897-1968), town clerk, was born on 5 May 1897 at Shepparton, Victoria, sixth child of Victorian-born parents William Payne West, clerk, and his wife Florence, née Nightingale. John West [q.v.12] was his uncle. Educated at Shepparton Agricultural High School, Ray enlisted in the Australian Imperial Force on 8 April 1915. He served with the 5th Battalion at Gallipoli (November-December) and on the Western Front (March-July 1916) where he was promoted sergeant. A wound he suffered at Pozières, France, in July resulted in the loss of his right eye. After treatment in England, he was repatriated and discharged from the A.I.F. on 26 December 1917. Commissioned in the Australian Military Forces in July 1918, he performed training duties in Victoria before resigning in 1921 as a lieutenant.

In 1922 West joined the staff of the Coburg City Council, Melbourne, where he gained his municipal clerk's certificate. At St Ambrose's Catholic Church, Brunswick, on 20 October 1923, he married Ethel Eileen Davis. By 1926 he was secretary to the Yea Shire Council. On 27 September 1927 he was appointed town clerk for the newly established Borough of Shepparton. An exemplary servant of local government, he combined a commitment to order and proper procedures with an imagin-

ative approach to civic improvement. He advocated town planning, oversaw the building of the council offices and art gallery, prepared a scheme for financing the construction of new streets and urged the council to proceed with a sewerage system. Shepparton was proclaimed a city in 1949. Its swimming pool, named after him, was opened in 1955. Retiring in 1960, he was appointed M.B.E. in 1961.

West had been the force behind the establishment in Victoria of the Institute of Municipal Administration (later Victorian division of the Institute of Municipal Administration, Australia), the purpose of which was to increase the status of local government clerical staff and improve the standard of their work. He believed that administrators needed to be as well qualified and learned as professional and technical staff. Elected foundation president in 1936, he held office for two years and saw the institute grow into a national body in 1949.

When not occupied with his official duties, West endeavoured to improve the cultural life of Shepparton by encouraging the public appreciation of history, art and music. A member of the Royal Historical Society of Victoria, he published numerous works of local history, including *Those Were the Days* (1962). In retirement he busied himself preserving the city's historical records and cataloguing its art collection. He was active in the Returned Sailors', Soldiers' and Airmen's Imperial League of Australia and a trustee of the Shepparton War Memorial. During World War II he had commanded (as lieutenant colonel) the 22nd Battalion, Volunteer Defence Corps, with headquarters at Benalla. He was a member of Shepparton's bowling and Rotary clubs. Towards the end of his life he suffered from cerebral atherosclerosis. He died of bronchopneumonia on 28 February 1968 at Numurkah and was buried with Anglican rites in Shepparton cemetery. His wife and their daughter survived him. The Shepparton Art Gallery holds Ernest Buckmaster's [q.v.13] portrait of him.

Local Govt Administration, Dec 1960/Feb 1961; *Aust Municipal J*, Mar 1968; *Shepparton News*, 1 Mar 1968; information from Local Government Professionals Inc., South Melb.   R. KISS

WEST, REGINALD ARTHUR (1883-1964), headmaster, was born on 11 July 1883 at Woodville, Adelaide, eldest of nine children of Australian born parents William Arthur West, schoolteacher, and his wife Emilie, née Burnard. From Norwood Public School Reg won a scholarship to Prince Alfred College, where he was a contemporary of J. F. Ward [q.v.12] and came under the influence of the headmaster Frederic Chapple [q.v.7]. At the University of Adelaide (B.A., 1902; M.A., 1905) he majored in mathematics and philosophy and was awarded the William Roby Fletcher [q.v.4] prize for psychology and logic. Determined to become a schoolteacher rather than an academic, in 1903 he joined the staff of the Pupil Teachers' School in Grote Street. Five years later it was absorbed into the new Adelaide High School, on the same site, with W. J. Adey [q.v.7] as headmaster. At the Parkside Methodist Church on 21 December 1912 West married Eva Beatrice Annie Claughton (d.1947), also a schoolteacher; they had a son and two daughters.

Promoted to second master at A.H.S. in 1912 and appointed headmaster in 1920, West inherited a well-organized school with a strong academic curriculum oriented to preparing pupils for tertiary studies. Under his direction A.H.S. became a worthy rival to the long-established private secondary schools and developed a vigorous sporting tradition. His pupils included (Sir) Hugh Cairns, J. P. Cartledge, (Sir) George Ligertwood [qq.v.7,13, 15], and (Sir) Marcus Oliphant; at least five were Rhodes scholars. Although the school was not in any sense selective, it was to retain its status as a special senior high school for almost forty years. It was never fully co-educational (except at upper levels), and the girls' and boys' premises were separated by a wall. In the 1920s A.H.S. faced a serious crisis in accommodation on a site which had been too small from the beginning. Rooms were hired in nearby church halls, factories and elsewhere to relieve the congestion. From 1929 it took over a primary school in distant Currie Street to house junior-school boys; it remained in use until the new boys' school opened on West Terrace in 1951.

Walking every day between the main school and Currie Street, West maintained a continuous presence in his widely scattered school of over one thousand pupils. He counselled prospective students on their courses and did the bulk of the timetabling. At A.H.S. pupils were called by their first names. West was particularly concerned about children from country areas, who travelled each day to the school by train; he enjoyed hearing news from them about ex-students from the same district.

His office was next to the main entrance to the central girls' building, and the door was usually open; women teachers came and went as often as the men to confer with the headmaster. The school's extra-curricular activities were voluntary for both pupils and staff, but they were encouraged and promoted, almost imperceptibly, by West. His deputy, C. M. Ward, said in 1948: 'No one could show more consideration for the individuality of both teachers and students ... In a happy atmosphere free from repression, with no absurd barriers between staff and students, and with flourishing extra-school activities managed to a great extent by the students themselves, self-discipline has thrived along with sound work'. Although West was not an eloquent man, his school assemblies in the (Thomas) Price [q.v.11] Memorial Hall made a lasting impact. He moved easily among the distinguished visiting speakers; where these were also old scholars the affection in which they held him was obvious to all present.

Thrice elected president (1928, 1931, 1939) of the South Australian Public Teachers' Union, West was a member (1933-53) of the council of the University of Adelaide. He was appointed O.B.E. in 1947, and retired next year after twenty-eight years as headmaster. In his later years he was content to enjoy time with his family, attend adult education classes, and work in his garden. Retaining his remarkable memory for names and faces into old age, he occasionally attended school functions. He was a staunch Methodist. Survived by his daughters, he died on 6 October 1964 at Hindmarsh and was buried in Dudley Park cemetery. A portrait of West by Douglas Roberts is held by Adelaide High School.

C. Thiele, *Grains of Mustard Seed* (Adel, 1975); *Adelaide High School Mag*, Sept 1947, Sept 1948; *SA Teachers' J*, Nov 1964; *Black and White Rag*, Dec 1964; *Advertiser* (Adel), 16 Apr 1958, 7 Oct 1964; *SA Methodist*, 23 Oct 1964; information from Mrs J. Jacobs, Glenside, and Mrs N. Pryor, West Beach, Adel.
                                                    J. H. PASH

WESTACOTT, GODFREY (1888-1977), journalist, was born on 21 August 1888 at Fortitude Valley, Brisbane, third of eight children of William Westacott, an English-born joiner, and his wife Alice, née Jones, who came from Wales. 'George' spent his childhood and youth at Mount Morgan and was educated at the local state school. As a paper-boy he delivered the Rockhampton afternoon newspaper, the *Daily Record*, to Mount Morgan homes after dark. The round was long and he was glad to give it up when he was apprenticed to a printer on the *Mount Morgan Herald*. He was paid five shillings a week and taught shorthand by one of the paper's part-owners. Laid off after the *Herald* struck financial difficulties, he continued his apprenticeship with the *Mount Morgan Chronicle*.

After standing uncomfortably for hours by the bedside of the acting-editor of the *Chronicle*, Paul de Montalk (who was suffering from rheumatism), using a tray as a desk and scribbling page after page of copy, Westacott concluded that journalism might be 'a good way of earning a living without having to get out of bed'. He then joined the staff of the

Daily Record as a local correspondent. His reports of the mine accidents at Mount Morgan in 1908 led to a full-time position at Rockhampton on the *Record*; he rose to become sub-editor under W. S. Buzacott, son of C. H. Buzacott [q.v.3].

In 1922 the *Record* became the *Evening News*; seven years later it was bought by the Dunn [qq.v.8] family, and Westacott was appointed editor. When that paper closed in July 1941 he shifted to the *Morning Bulletin*, as assistant to the managing editor Andrew Dunn and the associate-editor, Captain Fred Rhodes. Taking over as editor in 1954, he aimed to produce a first-class newspaper with good circulation which would attract advertisers. He fostered the correspondence page as a forum for discussion. Providing his cadet journalists with wise counsel and encouragement, he often quoted C. P. Scott of the *Manchester Guardian*: 'Comment is free, but facts are sacred'.

Westacott was best remembered by Central Queensland readers for his whimsical weekly articles on current affairs. In 1922 he had introduced a column, generally called 'Topics of the Day', and wrote it, or variations of it, until his death. In his light, mildly satirical style he poked fun at local authorities, politicians and pompous individuals, usually disguising his sting with subtle humour. His popular commentary on Rockhampton City Council meetings, appearing under the heading 'Guildhall Gallery Notes', provided a quirky, affectionate look at the council. One of his protégés was A. T. ('Bert') Hinchliffe, later editor of the Toowoomba *Chronicle*, who recalled that 'Topics' was always the best-read part of the paper and 'prominent citizens rated it an honour to get a mention in the column'. Another colleague, Denis Butler, chief leader-writer for the *Newcastle Morning Herald* in the 1970s, said that 'if ever there was a bloke who managed to touch the funnybone of a whole city, it was George Westacott'.

Active in promoting district affairs, Westacott helped to form the Central Queensland Advancement League. In 1949, on behalf of the league, he compiled a book outlining the pastoral, agricultural and mining resources of Central Queensland and its tourist attractions. A life member of the Rockhampton Club, the Rockhampton Jockey, Rotary and Leagues clubs, and the Rockhampton Agricultural Society, he was closely involved with the local School of Arts and president (1956-58) of the Rockhampton and District Historical Society. He wrote two booklets, *Revised History of the Port of Rockhampton* (1970) and, with A. Gill, *Chronological History of the Lakes Creek Meat Works* (1971). Appointed O.B.E. in 1962, he retired as editor in 1964.

Westacott was highly regarded by political leaders. At a reception in Sydney for news-paper editors from around Australia, the prime minister (Sir) Robert Menzies [q.v.15] spotted him on the other side of the room, ignored everyone else and walked across, grasped his hand and greeted him warmly. A gentle and courteous man, Westacott never married. He died on 9 January 1977 in the North Rockhampton home he shared with his sister Dorothy; his last column had appeared in the *Morning Bulletin* the day before. He was buried with Baptist forms in the local cemetery.

L. McDonald, *Rockhampton* (Brisb, 1981); *Central Qld Herald*, 16 July 1936; *Morning Bulletin*, 1 Jan 1962, 11 Jan 1977; R. Kirkpatrick, Ghost of Caution Haunts House of Dunn (Ph.D. thesis, Univ Qld, 1995); G. Westacott, Autobiographical Notes *and* A. T. Hinchliffe's notes (copies held by author, Middle Park, Brisb); information from the late Mr D. Butler.   ROD KIRKPATRICK

WESTON, JACK KEITH (1912-1963), soldier, was born on 7 January 1912 in North Adelaide, tenth child of Australian-born parents Alfred Leonard Weston, railway ganger, and his wife Mabel Annie, née Brumby. Educated at Woodside and Parilla Public schools, Jack worked as a stockman and labourer. At St Martin's Church, Campbelltown, on 4 February 1931 he married with Anglican rites Naomi Florence Usher, a waitress. He was employed as a tractor driver at Appila when he enlisted in the Australian Imperial Force on 25 June 1940. Posted to the 2nd/48th Battalion, he embarked for the Middle East in November as a corporal.

In North Africa 'Tex' Weston emerged as an outstanding member of an equally outstanding battalion. From April 1941 the 2nd/48th was besieged at Tobruk, Libya. Weston took part in and led numerous night patrols, displaying an extraordinary ability to navigate by the stars through no man's land, often travelling long distances outside the Australian lines to reconnoitre German and Italian positions. In engagements with the enemy he displayed courage, aggression and a cool head. For his work on twenty-three patrols up to 31 July he was awarded the Distinguished Conduct Medal. Confirmed in the rank of sergeant on 19 October, he left Tobruk with his battalion three days later.

Following a period of training and garrison duty in Palestine, Syria and Lebanon, in June 1942 the 2nd/48th Battalion moved to Egypt with the 9th Division. Weston was again active in patrolling enemy positions at night. On 10 July 1942 during the division's assault on Tel el Eisa, his platoon was ordered to silence a battery of German field-guns that were firing on the advancing Australians. As platoon sergeant, he led the attack, seizing the battery and then single-handedly capturing the crews of a further four guns that he had observed. Later that day he kept the platoon intact when it was overrun by tanks, and took some German tank crews prisoner. For his 'determination and courage' he was awarded the Military Medal, becoming the only Australian to be awarded both the D.C.M. and M.M. in the Middle East in World War II.

On 31 October 1942 in the battle of El Alamein Weston was badly wounded in his left arm and right leg. In spite of his injuries he carried another wounded soldier a mile (1.6 km) back to the dressing station. He rejoined the 2nd/48th Battalion from hospital on 8 January 1943, less than a month before it embarked for Australia. After home leave and several months of jungle-warfare training, he arrived at Milne Bay, Papua, on 6 August 1943. For seven weeks he served in Papua and around Lae, New Guinea, before spending almost five months in hospital with malaria and dysentery. He rejoined his battalion on 1 March 1944 but ten days later was again in hospital with malaria. Medically downgraded, he served with a number of units in South Australia before being discharged on 7 March 1945.

Weston was six feet (183 cm) tall and well built. He had been a tough soldier who was admired by his men and respected by his superiors. Softly spoken and described as a 'real bushman', he enjoyed a drink and a joke, and 'taking the mickey' out of officers. In 1946 he joined the Australian contingent for the Victory March in London. He managed pastoral stations in New South Wales and South Australia, and hotels at Cleve and Cowell. Survived by his wife, their daughter and one of their two sons, he died of cancer on 13 December 1963 at the Repatriation General Hospital, Daw Park, Adelaide, and was cremated.

J. G. Glenn, *Tobruk to Tarakan* (Adel, 1960); B. Maughan, *Tobruk and El Alamein* (Canb, 1966); G. A. Mackinlay, *True Courage* (Syd, 1992); *Advertiser* (Adel), 14 Dec 1963; information from Mr D. Adams, Cumberland Park, Adel.

LLOYD BRODRICK

WESTON, NORA KATE (1880-1965), woodcarver, was born on 18 June 1880 at Parramatta, Sydney, eighth of nine children of native-born parents Frederick Weston, draftsman, and his wife Mary Ann, née Elliott. Lieutenant George Johnston [q.v.2] was Nora's great-grandfather. Her education at home had a practical, outdoor emphasis. She matured into a tall, physically active woman who possessed a sense of humour and freely used slang and Australianisms.

By 1902 Nora was living in Alexandra House, a residence for colonial students in London, while she studied at the School of Art Wood-Carving, South Kensington. She formed a lifelong friendship with fellow Australian, Eirene Mort [q.v.10]. On their return to Sydney in 1906, they rented a studio in the city. Weston, known as 'Chips', described herself as a cabinet-maker and taught woodcarving, carpentry and leatherwork. The pair set up as interior decorators, creating dados, ornaments and furnishings with an Australian flavour. In a complementary working relationship, Weston executed Mort's designs for such objects as a chair made of silky oak and Australian leather, and copper boxes. To further their aims, in 1906 they founded the short-lived Australian Guild of Handicraft for women, which hoped to produce articles for 'household use and decoration'. The group staged an exhibition in December.

Joining the Society of Arts and Crafts of New South Wales (founded 1906) in March 1908, Weston was briefly custodian of its rooms. At the society's exhibition in 1910, she and Mort included cushions, blotters and leatherwork as well as larger displays and panels. In 1911, before an extended visit to England, Weston acted as honorary secretary. On her return she resumed her association with the society, serving on its selection committee (1917-19) and its general committee (1918, 1929-32). She taught at a studio in Rowe Street in the 1920s.

Weston developed friendships with Thea Proctor, Margaret Preston [qq.v.11] and many others, and arranged nature study picnics in the bush. She attended and provided scenery and costumes for the Artists' Ball from 1922. Relying on the sale of her wood, metal and leather products for an income, she usually produced small items suitable for gifts. From about 1920 she and Mort lived together at Vaucluse until moving to Greenhayes, Mittagong, in 1937 and to Bowral in 1960.

As they had in World War I, Weston and Mort taught crafts to wounded and convalescent soldiers in various hospitals in World War II; they continued to visit returned soldiers after the war. Miss Weston remained a constant companion to Eirene Mort. Her health declined slowly over many years. She died on 16 August 1965 at Berrima and was cremated with Anglican rites. A well-attended memorial exhibition was held in their Bowral home.

A History of the Society of Arts & Crafts of New South Wales 1906-1991 (Syd, 1991); P. Starr, Wielding the Waratah—Eirene Mort. A study of an artist/craftswoman's training and working experiences from the period 1879 to 1910 (B.A. Hons thesis, Univ Syd, 1980); Soc of Arts and Crafts of NSW *and* Mort family papers (ML); information from Miss M. Mort, Adamstown Heights, Syd.

JANE E. HUNT

WHEARE, Sir KENNETH CLINTON (1907-1979), professor of government and vice-chancellor, was born on 26 March 1907 at Warragul, Victoria, eldest of three children of Australian-born parents Eustace Leonard Wheare, grocer's assistant, and his wife Kathleen Frances, née Kinahan. Leonard bettered himself in 1914 by becoming an insurance agent. The family settled in Melbourne in 1922. Kenneth had attended state and high schools at Stawell and Maryborough. In 1923 he entered Scotch College, Melbourne, where he became a prefect and ran the debating club. Winning a scholarship to Ormond [q.v.5] College, he took first-class honours in Greek and philosophy at the University of Melbourne (B.A. Hons, 1929). Slight and frail, he played no sport, but was an outstanding president of the Students' Representative Council, and his selection as Victorian Rhodes scholar for 1929 was popular.

At Oriel College, Oxford (B.A., 1932; M.A., 1935; D.Litt., 1957), Wheare's tutors mistook his unassuming demeanour for lack of ability, but he won a first in philosophy, politics and economics and was awarded the Cecil peace prize. Oxford suited him and after a succession of appointments he became Gladstone professor of government and public administration in 1944. He also suffered a personal tragedy: on 22 March 1934 at St Columba's Presbyterian Chapel, Oxford, he had married Helen Mary, daughter of Stella Allan [q.v.7]; after the birth of a son she became incurably ill and they were divorced. At the register office, Oxford, on 5 January 1943 he married 26-year-old Joan Randell; they had two sons and two daughters.

Wheare's first research won him the Beit prize in colonial history. Published as *The Statute of Westminster, 1931* (Oxford, 1933), it dealt with the Act which restructured the British Empire and offered Australia an independence its governments were reluctant to accept. The constitution of the Empire and Commonwealth, then a fertile field, became Wheare's main subject. After 1945 he was much called on as a constitutional adviser, notably to the National Convention of Newfoundland (1946-47) and to conferences (1951-53) on the Central African Federation. 'I see they've torn up another of my constitutions', he is reputed to have said over one breakfast newspaper. His monographs *The Statute of Westminster and Dominion Status* (five editions, 1938-53) and *The Constitutional Structure of the Commonwealth* (1960) record authoritatively the evolution of the colonies into independent states.

As teacher and speaker, Wheare displayed brisk common sense spiced with wit; satirical but never malicious, he was sometimes earthy in private. His writings—concise, deceptively simple, apparently innocent of theory but in-

formed by it—ranged over government and administration at all levels. Four editions of *Federal Government* (1946-63) confirmed his mastery of that subject. His inaugural lecture had analysed Britain's government as 'a parliamentary bureaucracy', 'the ideally best form of government for a modern industrial state'. *Government by Committee* (1955) was enlivened by his experience on the Oxford City Council (1940-57), the Departmental Committee on Children and the Cinema (chairman 1947-50), and many university and other committees, where his skills were superb. Unobtrusive, with a habit of 'backing into the limelight and quietly disappearing again', he was nevertheless decisive: 'Over my dead body, Mr Vice-Chancellor', he once objected, 'if I may take up a moderate position in this matter'.

In 1956 Wheare became rector of Exeter College, an old establishment in need of improvement, which he achieved by reducing the intake, strengthening the fellowship and extending the buildings. He had served on the important Committee on Administrative Tribunals and Inquiries (1955-57) headed by Sir Oliver (Lord) Franks. To Franks's later commission of inquiry into the University of Oxford, he submitted 'a classic statement of the principles and virtues of academic self-government'. As Oxford's first Australian vice-chancellor (1964-66), he guided the university to adopt some of Franks's reforms.

Wheare had been appointed C.M.G. (1953) and was knighted in 1966. He chaired (1962-69) the Rhodes Trust and presided (1967-71) over the British Academy. In 1972 when he retired early as rector of Exeter, he became chancellor of the University of Liverpool, a role he took seriously, though characteristically delighted to be made honorary admiral of the Isle of Man herring fishery fleet. He was awarded honorary fellowships of five Oxford colleges and honorary doctorates from the universities of Cambridge, Exeter, Liverpool and Manchester, and Columbia, New York.

In retirement Wheare delivered the 1973 Hamlyn lectures; his topic, *Maladministration and its Remedies* (London, 1973), broke more new ground. One of his last writings was a review article on the 1975 constitutional crisis in Australia; he knew more about his homeland than it did of him. He died on 7 September 1979 at Oxford. It was said that nobody in Oxford had more friends and fewer enemies. Portraits of him are held by Exeter College and Rhodes House, Oxford, the University of Liverpool, and his family. His likeness is also preserved as a gargoyle on the Bodleian Library, between an emu and a kangaroo.

H. V. Hodson (ed), *The Annual Register: A Record of World Events* (Lond, 1980); *DNB*, 1971-80; *Political Studies*, 28, 1980; *Proceedings of the British*

Academy, 67, 1981; *Daily Telegraph* (Lond), 8 Sept 1979; *The Times*, 19 Nov 1979; C. Santamaria, K. C. Wheare (taped interview, 5 Feb 1975, NL); Rhodes Trust archives (Rhodes House, Oxford, Eng, and Univ Melb Archives).   J. R. POYNTER

WHEATLEY, KEVIN ARTHUR (1937-1965), soldier, was born on 13 March 1937 at Surry Hills, Sydney, third child of Raymond George Wheatley, labourer, and his wife Ivy Sarah Ann, née Newman, both born in Sydney. Educated at Maroubra Junction Junior Technical School, Kevin worked as a milk carter, food sterilizer, machine operator and brick burner. At the registrar-general's office, Sydney, on 20 July 1954 he married a 14-year-old milk-bar assistant Edna Aileen Davis, who used her stepfather's surname, Gimson.

On 12 June 1956 Wheatley enlisted in the Australian Regular Army. Following recruit training he joined the 4th Battalion, Royal Australian Regiment, in September 1956 and transferred to the 3rd Battalion in March 1957. He served in the Malayan Emergency from September that year to July 1959, before transferring in August to the 2nd Battalion and in June 1961 to the 1st Battalion. In January 1964 he was promoted sergeant and in August, temporary warrant officer, class two. Short and stocky, he was a highly respected and well-liked non-commissioned officer with a reputation as a rough, wild man who was a good soldier. He was known as 'Dasher' for his Rugby Union football prowess.

Arriving in the Republic of Vietnam (South Vietnam) in March 1965, Wheatley joined the Australian Army Training Team Vietnam. He distinguished himself on 28 May by risking heavy fire to rescue a 3-year-old girl. On 18 August, when South Vietnamese troops ceased advancing during an assault, he took the lead and inspired them to continue charging up a hill. His men routed some fifty People's Liberation Armed Forces (Viet Cong) soldiers.

Wheatley and another Australian, Warrant Officer R. J. Swanton, were on a search and destroy mission in the Tra Bong valley, Quang Ngai province, with a platoon of the Civil Irregular Defence Group on 13 November 1965 when it was attacked by the Viet Cong. The platoon broke in the face of heavy fire and began to scatter. Swanton was shot in the chest. Although told that Swanton was dying, Wheatley refused to leave him. Under heavy machine-gun and rifle fire, he half-dragged and half-carried Swanton out of open rice paddies into the comparative safety of nearby jungle. He refused a second request to withdraw, pulled the pins from his two grenades and waited with his motionless colleague while the enemy approached. Two grenade explosions were heard, followed by several bursts of fire. Wheatley and Swanton were found at first light next morning, dead from gunshot wounds.

The Australian policy at the time was to bury war dead overseas but Wheatley's body was returned to Australia after funds were raised privately. Survived by his wife, and their son and three daughters, he was buried with full military honours in Pine Grove cemetery, Eastern Creek, Sydney. A public outcry resulted in the government announcing on 21 January 1966 that the remains of service personnel who died overseas would in future be returned to Australia at public expense if their families desired.

For refusing to abandon a wounded comrade in the face of overwhelming odds Wheatley was posthumously awarded the Victoria Cross. He had also been awarded the United States of America's Silver Star. The Republic of Vietnam had appointed him a knight of its National Order and awarded him its Military Merit Medal and Cross of Gallantry with Palm. In 1993 Wheatley's V.C. and other medals were presented to the Australian War Memorial, Canberra.

I. McNeill, *The Team* (Brisb, 1984) and *To Long Tan* (Syd, 1993); L. Wigmore, *They Dared Mightily*, 2nd edn revised and condensed by J. Williams and A. Staunton (Canb, 1986); B. Breen, *First to Fight* (Syd, 1988); M. Adkin, *The Last Eleven?* (Lond, 1991); I. Walters, *Dasher Wheatley and Australia in Vietnam* (Darwin, 1998); A. Staunton, 'Blaming Buckingham Palace', *Sabretache*, 38, no 3, July-Sept 1997, p 14; A4393, item 66/W/14, and A2880, item 5/5/21 (NAA, Canb).   ANTHONY STAUNTON

WHELLER, HAROLD MANUEL (1882-1979), Methodist minister, was born on 26 January 1882 at Tarlee, South Australia, third of five children of James Manuel Wheller, a South Australian-born machinist, and his wife Mary Jane, née Gullidge. Educated at Stanley Grammar School, Watervale, Harold worked as a clerk at Norwood, Adelaide, before entering Queen's College, University of Melbourne, in 1905. He moved to Queensland and in March 1906 was ordained in Brisbane. His first appointment was at Paddington. On 10 May 1910 at Kennedy Terrace Methodist Church, Red Hill, he married Edith May Stack (d.1963), a schoolteacher. They were to have two sons and a daughter.

For twenty-one years Wheller ministered in several Brisbane parishes, and at Cairns, Ipswich, Stanthorpe and Warwick. He was secretary (1923-25) and president (1926) of the Queensland Methodist Conference. In 1927 he was appointed superintendent of the Brisbane Central Mission. His twenty-five year ministry there was characterized by forthright preaching and practical social service. During the Depression he provided the unemployed and destitute with physical and spiritual assistance, while encouraging the recipients to maintain self-respect. He established two hostels for the homeless, and arranged for the mission (under the leadership of Mrs Wheller) to supply daily meals to over four hundred men. Clothing was distributed to those in need. For a decade from 1931 he conducted a weekly worship service for unemployed men. He helped to administer the Queensland Book Depot, the William Powell home for discharged prisoners and St Helen's Hospital. In 1936 he founded the Garden Settlement for Aged People at Chermside, Brisbane, on land donated by George Marchant [q.v.10].

A constant advocate of ecumenism, Wheller presided over the Queensland Council of Churches and the State committee of the World Council of Churches. In 1937 he had advocated union between Methodists and Congregationalists, arguing that it would bring greater 'impact and effectiveness' in the community. He was a dynamic speaker who claimed to 'always put the pulpit first'. Rev. George Nash observed that, when preaching, Wheller blended theological insight with 'evangelical ardour and Christlike compassion'. In 1933 he had published a collection of his sermons, *Our Quest for God*. A man of deep spirituality, he viewed the Methodist hymn book as an excellent devotional resource. He was president-general of the Methodist Church of Australasia in 1941-45.

Wheller was appointed O.B.E. in 1952. That year he retired from active ministry but he continued to administer the Garden Settlement until 1976, when there were over six hundred residents living in self-contained cottages, hostel accommodation or nursing homes. He was a member of the University of Queensland senate in 1936-56, and a founding member (1918), chairman (1965-70) and life member (1970) of the Queensland Temperance League. Of slight build and dour expression, he had great energy, compassion and capacity for enduring friendship. 'H.M.', as he was affectionately known, enjoyed watching cricket, but his work was his hobby. Survived by his daughter, he died on 17 November 1979 at Auchenflower and was cremated. The Garden Settlement was named after him in 1980.

R. S. C. Dingle, *The Garden Settlement* (Brisb, 1967?); D. L. Tucker, *50 Years of Caring* (Brisb, 1986); Methodist Church of A'sia (Qld), *Conference Minutes* (1926, 1927, 1952); Central Methodist Mission (Brisb), *Annual Report*, 1930-31, 1932-33; Uniting Church in Aust, Qld Synod, *Minutes and Supplementary Reports*, 1980; *Methodist Times*, 28 Feb, 10 Apr, 1 May 1952, 3 Feb 1972, 25 Nov 1976; *Life and Times*, 23 Jan 1980; information from Miss D. Wheller, Bardon, and Rev G. Nash, Oxley, Brisb.

JENNIFER NOBLE

WHITE, SIR ALFRED EDWARD ROWDEN (1874-1963) and EDWARD ROWDEN (1881-1958), medical practitioners, were born on 5 November 1874 and 14 November 1881 in Hobart, fifth and seventh of seven children of a Tasmanian-born servant Susannah Mary Gooding (d.1888). Although their father was not named when their births were registered, there is evidence proving beyond reasonable doubt that they were the sons of (Sir) Samuel James Way [q.v.12], chief justice of South Australia. Way and Gooding never married. Their relationship was kept secret presumably because Susannah's background—her mother and paternal grandparents had been transported to Australia as convicts—would have been socially unacceptable for the wife of an ambitious lawyer. Way looked after Gooding and her children with diligence and affection, and in the 1880s moved them to Melbourne. By that time they were using the surname of White.

Alfred progressed from Alexander Sutherland's [q.v.6] Carlton College (dux 1893) to the University of Melbourne (M.B., 1899; B.S., 1900; M.D., 1906), where he lived at Ormond [q.v.5] College. In the early years of the new century he held posts as senior medical officer at the Alfred and Children's hospitals, and for six years acted as assistant to (Sir) Richard Stawell [q.v.12]. This experience enabled him to establish himself in private practice as a physician. His reputation grew rapidly and he took up honorary appointments at the Children's and St Vincent's hospitals, and the Victorian Foundling Hospital and Infants' Home. He was also a clinical instructor and lecturer to medical students.

Appointed major, Australian Army Medical Corps, Australian Imperial Force, on 6 June 1917, White served in France with the 2nd Australian General Hospital. His A.I.F. appointment terminated on 6 December 1919 and he resumed practice in Melbourne. In 1930 he helped to found the Association of Physicians of Australasia and in 1938 its successor the Royal Australasian College of Physicians; he was a councillor of both and vice-president (1944-46) of the R.A.C.P. He chaired the medical staffs of both the Children's and St Vincent's hospitals before retiring in 1938.

Made wealthy by prudent investments, White was a generous benefactor of medical, cultural and charitable organizations, including the Royal Australasian College of Surgeons, the Victorian branch of the British Medical Association (to endow the Sir Richard Stawell oration), the R.A.C.P., the Royal

College of Obstetricians and Gynaecologists, the Rio Vista Gallery, Mildura, the National Theatre Movement of Australia, the National Trust of Australia and the Operation Youth Appeal of the Young Men's Christian Association. Always a strong supporter of the University of Melbourne, he gave money towards the establishment of a chair of medicine and the Rowden White Library in Union House. He and Edward remained close. In 1955 Alfred set up the A. E. Rowden White and Edward R. White Foundation for Medical Research at the Royal Women's Hospital.

Appointed C.M.G. in 1953, White was knighted in 1961. Sir Rowden (as he styled himself) was below average height and solidly built. He displayed a controlled and alert manner, his modulated speaking voice conveying a reluctance to express emotion. Unmarried, he lived for many years with a couple named Kilburn; their daughter Doris, whom he treated as his niece, later kept house and cared for him. He died on 15 January 1963 in his home at Toorak and was cremated. His will directed that the income from the bulk of his estate, sworn for probate at £835 639, be used to finance medical and scientific research at the University of Melbourne under the name of the A. E. Rowden White Foundation. A portrait of him by W. B. McInnes [q.v.10] is held by the university.

Edward attended Geelong Church of England Grammar School (senior prefect 1900) and Trinity College, University of Melbourne (M.B., B.S., 1907; M.D., 1911), excelling at cricket and tennis. He was a resident at the Melbourne, Children's (where he became the medical superintendent) and Women's hospitals before commencing practice as an obstetrician and gynaecologist, initially as assistant to Rothwell Adam [q.v.7]. In 1914 White was appointed honorary obstetrician to the Women's Hospital. Commissioned as captain, A.A.M.C., A.I.F., on 2 October that year, and posted to the 3rd Light Horse Field Ambulance, he served at Gallipoli and in Sinai and Palestine. In February 1917 he was promoted temporary lieutenant colonel and placed in command of the 2nd L.H.F.A. Having been mentioned in dispatches, he was demobilized in Melbourne on 12 October that year. Four days later at St John's Church of England, Toorak, he married Gladys Mary Northcote (d.1955).

During a visit to the United States of America in 1928, White reputedly performed —at H. S. Crossen's clinic, St Louis—the first 'Manchester operation' for uterine prolapse undertaken in that country. From 1918 he had been active in the Militia; he was promoted colonel in 1936. Joining the A.I.F. on 1 January 1941, he sailed for Malaya in February as commanding officer of the 2nd/10th Australian General Hospital. The hospital was based at

Malacca until January 1942 when it withdrew to Singapore just ahead of the advancing Japanese. White remained composed and in control, though the hospital was virtually in the front line; he was mentioned in dispatches. Taken prisoner next month, he was moved to Formosa (Taiwan) in August and to Manchuria in November 1944. He endured the ordeal with dignity and strength of character, despite his age and news of the death (1942) of his only son, James. Repatriated in October 1945, he transferred to the Reserve of Officers on 5 February 1946.

That year White retired from the honorary staff of the Women's Hospital. He had played a leading role in the early development and activities in Australia of the Royal College of Obstetricians and Gynaecologists. In 1947 he took charge of fund-raising to establish the Arthur Wilson [q.v.12] Foundation which, among other activities, acquired premises in Melbourne for the Australian regional council of the college. White was 5 ft 7 ins (170 cm) tall, had a trim, athletic figure and was always well groomed. Less reserved than his brother, he had a welcoming smile and a warm, cheerful personality. He died on 31 July 1958 in his home at Toorak and was cremated. His only daughter survived him.

G. L. McDonald (ed), *Roll of the Royal Australasian College of Physicians*, 1, 1938-75 (Syd, 1988); J. J. Corfield and M. Collins Persse (comps), *Geelong Grammarians*, 1 (Geelong, Vic, 1996); *Corian*, Aug 1958; *MJA*, 13 Dec 1958, p 811, 3 Aug 1963, p 202; *Aust J of Legal Hist*, 1, no 2, 1995; family papers (copies held by ADB); information from Mrs E. Moran, Toorak, Melb.   STEPHEN JAMES

WHITE, ALFRED SPURGEON (1890-1977), accountant, was born on 2 October 1890 at his parents' home, Yarrawonga, Stanmore, Sydney, youngest of five children of English-born parents William White, a baker from the Isle of Grain, Kent, and his wife Anna Maria, née King. William's Great Southern Bakeries at Redfern and Newtown had flourished. He served (1893-94) as president of the Baptist Union of New South Wales as did his son-in-law, the evangelist Rev. C. James Tinsley (1912-13), long-time pastor at Stanmore, and Alfred's elder brother William (1913-14, 1930-31).

Alfred was educated at Stanmore Superior Public School and Newington College. By 1915 he had qualified as an associate of the Federal Institute of Accountants and by 1929 as a fellow of the Institute of Chartered Accountants in Australia. He established 'a reputable firm of chartered accountants' with A. T. Iliffe; other partners over the years included H. Thew, C. A. Fox and S. C. Gillmore. The firm provided accounting facilities to the

Baptist Church. Both White and Iliffe served as treasurer for various church committees; White for over fifty years was honorary treasurer of the New South Wales Baptist Union's Trust Funds. On 14 April 1915 at the Baptist Mission, Blackheath, he had married Dorothy Maud Mary Field.

By his 'diligence and competence', White prospered and 'promoted and established many thriving and financially successful companies'. He was secretary to the bakers and millers Gartrell White Ltd (run by his brothers William and Clarence [q.v.]), and to Australian Cash Orders Ltd, a retail credit scheme pioneered by William Buckingham, a fellow Baptist. White was a founder and managing secretary of the Employers' Mutual Indemnity Association Ltd. From 1929 to 1972 he chaired Whitefields Ltd, a housing development and rental firm. He gradually acquired associated interests as chairman of Ormonoid Roofing & Asphalts Co. and Motor Discounts Ltd, and as director of Australian Home Furnishers Ltd, Sylvatone Ltd, Poole & Steel Ltd and other companies. In 1949 he joined the board of Federal Mutual Insurance Co. of Australia Ltd (which immediately began to advertise in the *Australian Baptist*).

White's success in housing finance carried over into his church activities: he was treasurer of the New South Wales Homes for Incurables at Ryde, of the Loan and Building Fund, and of the Aged and Infirm Ministers' Fund. In February 1972 he announced the gift of $400 000 to the New South Wales Baptist Homes Trust to provide for underprivileged children.

By the 1940s the Whites were living at a new Yarrawonga, in Woodland Avenue, Pymble, where he pursued his interest in gardening and music. They also maintained a holiday house, Thorington, at Blackheath. In 1976 after the death of their unmarried daughter Dorothy who had lived with them at Pymble, White and his wife moved to Canberra to live with another daughter, Jean Price. He died on 31 March 1977 in Canberra Hospital and was cremated. His wife and their two remaining daughters survived him.

A. C. Prior, *Some Fell on Good Ground* (Syd, 1966); *SMH*, 3 Mar 1930, 28 June 1933, 23 July 1937, 24 Feb 1972; *Aust Baptist*, 8 Mar 1972, 20 Apr 1977.
BEVERLEY KINGSTON

WHITE, ANNA FELLOWES; *see* VROLAND

WHITE, CLARENCE ARTHUR (1886-1956), baker, flour-miller and company director, was born on 10 December 1886 at Redfern, Sydney, fourth of five children of English-born parents William White, a prominent Sydney baker, and his wife Anna Maria, née King. Like his brothers William and Alfred [q.v.], Clarrie was educated at Stanmore Superior Public School and Newington College. He was only 17 when his father died in 1903, leaving a large enterprise, the Great Southern Bakeries, Redfern and Newtown. A fast bowler, he played first-grade cricket for Redfern, in the same team as Arthur Mailey [q.v.10]. On 2 February 1910 he married with Baptist forms Marian Grace Holmes at the School of Arts, Glen Oak.

The firm came under the control of William junior and Clarence. They relied on technical expertise provided by their managers at Redfern and Newtown. Like other bakers in Australia, they suffered from the inability of millers to blend different grades of wheat to provide for long and uniform runs of flour. Bread quality was, at best, mediocre, because flour varied from day to day. Clarence tried to remedy this situation by using large silo complexes to allow blending.

In 1917 the Whites, Francis Gartrell and Abel & Co. Ltd amalgamated. Next year the firm was re-registered as Gartrell White Ltd, bread and cake manufacturers; William was chairman and Clarence a director and general manager. In the 1930s Clarence advocated a scientific approach to bread making. Technological innovations included the application of column chromatography and of the chlorination process for cake flours. He was also interested in the new managerial techniques pioneered in Australia by Sir Herbert Gepp [q.v.8], who in 1934-36 chaired the royal commission on the wheat, flour and bread industries; its third report criticized the inefficiency of the bread industry.

White spent much time trying to discourage new entrants to the market and agitating for government policies favourable to the industry—stable markets through government bread zoning and protection of manufacturers. The links between bakers and flour-millers ensured that there was little open price competition; he was particularly close to Gillespie [q.v.9] Bros Ltd. He used his father's connexions in business, in the Baptist Church and in local politics to build up a powerful interest.

In 1940 White became managing director of Gartrell White and chairman of the Namoi Milling Co., Gunnedah. An executive-member, he was a dominating force in the Master Bakers' Association of New South Wales. The concentration of the baking industry accelerated in 1946 when the association became the Bread Manufacturers of New South Wales. White supported these moves and he also campaigned tirelessly against government regulation of prices, which the industry blamed for low profits. Gartrell White was acquired by the Canadian company George

Weston Ltd in 1948: White was a director (1948-56) and chairman (1948-50) of George Weston (Australia) Pty Ltd and a director (1949) of Green's Products Ltd.

A committed Baptist, White was president of the Sydney Missionary and Bible College (1939-56), and of the Sydney battalion of the Boys' Brigade (1941-47). Although he devoted most of his time to business, he also presided over Bankstown Golf Club (1937-39) and later enjoyed playing bowls. Retiring in 1953, he died of a coronary occlusion on 31 August 1956 at his residence at Enfield and was cremated. His wife and their two daughters and three sons survived him. None of the children was involved in manufacturing.

Official Journal of Bread Manufacturers of NSW, Dec 1953, Sept 1956; *Daily Telegraph* (Syd), 8 Sept 1903; *SMH*, 8 Sept 1903, 13 Mar 1911, 29 Dec 1934, 9, 14 Oct 1943, 10 Oct 1946, 3 Nov 1947, 4 Sept 1956.

GEORGE PARSONS

WHITE, ERIC; *see* EDGLEY

WHITE, JOHN MENZIES (1911-1971), accountant, was born on 28 May 1911 at Elsternwick, Melbourne, eldest son of Stanley McKellar White (1883-1949), a Victorian-born Commonwealth public servant, and his wife Florence Amy, née Menzies, who came from Queensland. He spent his early childhood in Brisbane, where his father was deputy-commissioner of taxation. In 1920 Stanley established a consulting accountancy practice in Sydney. The family lived at Gordon. After attending North Sydney Boys' High School, John joined his father's firm.

In reaction to new taxes imposed by the Scullin [q.v.11] government, Stanley White had helped to establish the Taxpayers' Association of New South Wales in 1930 and served as president. John became secretary and editor of its monthly (*Taxpayers'*) *Bulletin* and wrote books of advice for taxpayers. He campaigned for the abolition of 'the burdensome Wages Tax and Special Income Tax, the iniquitous Federal Property Tax, the uneconomic Land Tax and the harassing Sales Tax'. On 7 July 1934 he married Helen Mitchell McLean, a nurse, at the Presbyterian Church, Lindfield.

White used his administrative skills to benefit several conservative political causes, usually involving his father. In 1934 he became secretary of the Australian branch of the Bribery and Secret Commissions Prevention League charged with exposing corrupt practices in government and private enterprise. The Constitutional Reform Association also worked from the family office, with Stanley on its executive and John as secretary. Backed by prominent citizens, including Sir Robert Garran and Sir George Julius [qq.v.8,9], the association campaigned for more efficient government through abolition of the States.

In the 1930s John White had supported the halting moves towards uniform taxation and attacked the inefficiency of overlapping State and Commonwealth income tax systems. He enthusiastically endorsed the Curtin [q.v.13] government's uniform tax scheme, although he remained concerned that 'a fair share of the extra revenue should be provided by the lower income earners'. To this end he became an early advocate of 'pay-as-you-go income tax', devising a policy for the United Australia Party for the 1943 election. White hailed a similar scheme that Curtin implemented next year.

By 1944 White was an associate of the Commonwealth Institute of Accountants; later he was a fellow of the Australian Society of Accountants and of the Institute of Taxation, England. By 1952 the family firm had become S. McKellar White & Associates. After the war, working with Eric Risstrom in Melbourne, John broadened the advisory functions of the Taxpayers' Association, using radio and public lectures. He continued to publish practical guides for taxpayers and income tax ready-reckoners, while campaigning for tax reductions, especially for those on higher rates. After 1949 he criticized some tax policies of the Liberal Party and Country Party coalition, particularly their treatment of business.

White was a tall, thin man with an erect carriage, and a fair complexion—a legacy of his Scottish ancestry, of which he was proud. For much of his married life, he lived on the North Shore, played golf, tennis and billiards, and belonged to Killara Golf Club, the Australasian Pioneers' and Millions clubs and the Royal Automobile Club of Australia. He sometimes styled himself McKellar White. A Presbyterian, he was an elder of St Stephen's, Macquarie Street, and involved with the Australian Inland Mission. He died of cancer on 10 February 1971 at his home at Woollahra. His wife and their two daughters and son survived him.

Constitutional Reform Assn, *The Abolition of State Parliaments* (Syd, 1939); *Taxpayers' Bulletin*, Jan 1934, Apr 1944, 25 Oct 1951; *Bribery*, no 1, Oct 1935; *SMH*, 28 Jan, 24 Aug 1943, 12 Feb 1971; Bribery and Secret Commissions Prevention League, Minutes of 2nd annual meeting, 21 May 1936 (ML); information from Mrs M. Fenner, Edgecliff and Mrs H. J. Scott, Paddington, Syd, and Mr E. Risstrom, Melb.

JAMES GILLESPIE

WHITE, MONTGOMERY (1905-1955), agricultural chemist, was born on 8 August

1905 at Fischerton, Tate Tin Mines, near Chillagoe, Queensland, fourth of five children of Ernest White, a storekeeper from Cornwall, and his Queensland-born wife Caroline Ann, née Montgomery. Monty attended several state schools in North Queensland and Townsville Grammar School. In 1924 he won an open scholarship to the University of Queensland (B.Sc., 1927; M.Sc., 1929). He was awarded research scholarships in 1928 and 1930, and in 1929-30 had a part-time post in the chemistry department. On 18 July 1930 at the university's King's College, Kangaroo Point, Brisbane, he married with Methodist forms Jessie Isabella Smart, a schoolteacher. That year he won an 1851 Exhibition scholarship. He took it up at University College, London (Ph.D., 1933) and pursued a chemical investigation of vitamin B2.

Employed by the Queensland Meat Industry Board as an expert in animal nutrition, White was sent from England to the United States of America to inspect production facilities run by some of the large meat companies. On his return to Queensland he became biochemist at the board's abattoir at Cannon Hill, Brisbane, managed by Ernest Sunners [q.v.]. At the same time he tutored in science at King's College. In 1936 he joined the Queensland Department of Agriculture and Stock as an animal nutrition officer; he worked on the drought-feeding of sheep. Five years later he was appointed the department's agricultural chemist. He travelled widely in the State, and developed a detailed knowledge of the livestock industries. Under his leadership there were significant advances in the understanding and treatment of animal-nutrition problems in Queensland, such as copper and cobalt deficiencies in sheep and cattle, and fluorosis in sheep. In 1939 he was a specialist lecturer in agriculture at the University of Queensland. He was a member (1947-53) of the university senate and the faculty of agriculture.

White was active in the Royal Australian Chemical Institute, serving as vice-president (1951-53) and president (1953-55) of the Queensland branch, and national vice-president in 1955. That year he was elected a fellow of the institute. He helped to introduce a technical college diploma in Queensland which acted as an acceptable qualification for admittance to the R.A.C.I.

Warm-hearted and loyal, White had many friends. With his wide range of scientific interests and encyclopaedic knowledge, he inspired and encouraged all who associated with him. He regularly gave practical advice to farmers and graziers, and strongly influenced the development of the pastoral and agricultural industries of Queensland. Despite serious illness he continued to work as the State's chief agricultural chemist until three weeks before his death. Survived by his wife, three sons and two daughters, he died of cancer on 22 September 1955 at his Hawthorne home and was cremated.

P. J. Skerman et al, *Guiding Queensland Agriculture, 1887-1987* (Brisb, 1988); P. J. Skerman, *The First One Hundred Years* (Brisb, 1998); Royal Aust Chemical Inst, *Procs*, 11, 1955, p 206; *Univ Qld Gazette*, no 33, 1955, p 10; *Livestock Bulletin*, 49, 1956, p 136.   ROBIN BRUCE

WHITE, SIR THOMAS WALTER (1888-1957), airman, businessman and politician, was born on 26 April 1888 at Hotham (North Melbourne), third child of Charles James White, a London-born brass-finisher and later hardware merchant, and his Victorian-born wife Emily Jane, née Jenkins. Thomas attended Moreland State School and it is said that family circumstances prevented him from taking up a scholarship to Scotch College. At an early age he joined the Citizen Military Forces as a bugler. In 1911 he was commissioned in the 5th Australian Regiment. He prided himself as an athlete, competing in running, cycling and boxing events.

By 1914 White was also interested in aviation. Selected for the Australian Flying Corps, in August he became one of the first batch of officers to train at Point Cook, where he helped found the Australian Aero Club. On 1 April 1915 he was appointed captain, Australian Imperial Force, and adjutant of a small unit, known as the Half-Flight, which was sent to Basra, Mesopotamia, for service with the Indian Army. He survived several incidents which involved landing behind enemy lines but on 13 November, while on a mission to cut telegraph wires near Baghdad, was captured by Arabs and Turks. Imprisoned in Turkey, he escaped from a train in Constantinople (Istanbul) in July 1918, sailed to Odessa, Ukraine, Russia, as a stowaway in a cargo ship and reached London on 22 December. He was awarded the Distinguished Flying Cross and twice mentioned in dispatches for his exploits.

White was to describe his adventures in *Guests of the Unspeakable* (London, 1928). He was critical of the Australian tendency, in the wake of Gallipoli, to regard the Turks as honourable foes, pointing instead to the thousands of British and Indian prisoners who had died on long marches. After the war he closely identified with ex-servicemen's causes, and his war experience was fundamental to the shaping of his political persona. He also claimed that his encounter with Bolshevism at Odessa laid the foundations of his later vigorous anti-communism.

In London White met Vera [q.v. White], daughter of the former Australian prime minister Alfred Deakin [q.v.8]. Within a few weeks they were engaged. Thomas left England in September 1919 and spent almost three months in the United States of America on the way home, making business contacts for his father's firm. His A.I.F. appointment terminated in Sydney on 6 January 1920. Overcoming resistance from some of the Deakin family, Vera and Tom were married on 22 March 1920 at St John's Church of England, Toorak, Melbourne.

From 1920 to 1932 White was managing director of C. J. White & Sons Pty Ltd. Beginning his political apprenticeship, in 1925 he stood unsuccessfully as Nationalist candidate for the seat of Maribynong in the House of Representatives; two years later he contested the Legislative Assembly seat of Prahran. In 1928 he failed in a bid to gain Nationalist preselection for the Senate. His opportunity came in 1929 when he won pre-selection, and on 3 August a by-election, for Balaclava, the safe seat that he was to hold in Federal parliament for twenty-two years.

White devoted his maiden speech to a subject he considered 'almost sacred', the building of the Australian War Memorial in Canberra. In October he found himself part of the Opposition to the Scullin [q.v.11] government, which was, as he put it, 'unique, because it is 100 percent. a non-soldier ministry'. He soon made his mark as a pugnacious parliamentarian and on 14 January 1933 gained a place in the Lyons [q.v.10] government, taking over from Sir Henry Gullett [q.v.9] as minister for trade and customs.

Despite being a dedicated protectionist, White was required to continue his predecessor's work of reducing and consolidating the tariff. He saw himself as presiding over the greatest period of industrial expansion Australia had yet known. Although he was responsible for the implementation (from 1936) of the controversial and ultimately unsuccessful trade-diversion policy, which endeavoured to reassert the Imperial connection by increasing trade with Britain at the expense of Japan and the U.S.A., the policy itself owed more to Lyons and Gullett.

White was a strong supporter of the book and film censorship which his department administered. Nevertheless, he attempted to place himself at arm's length from the decisions involved, appointing an advisory board of 'scholarly and enlightened men', chaired by Sir Robert Garran [q.v.8], to make recommendations concerning books. White conceded that censorship, whether for indecency or sedition, had increased, but put this down to 'a greater production of books'. He privately expressed the view that James Joyce's *Ulysses* was 'the foulest novel yet in spite of the author's much vaunted new technique'.

In 1937 White came close to resigning as a minister in protest against the government's failure to introduce universal service. Lyons reconstructed the ministry in November 1938. On learning that R. G. (Baron) Casey [q.v.13] had been advanced in seniority over him, White made his displeasure clear during the swearing in on 7 November. Next day, when he discovered that he had also been excluded from the inner cabinet that Lyons had established, he angrily resigned, condemning 'the control of the Government of Australia by a small coterie of Ministers'. One of that 'coterie' was the ambitious (Sir) Robert Menzies [q.v.15] whom White had long disliked, partly because of his failure to serve in World War I. After Lyons's death in 1939, White nominated for the leadership contest ultimately won by Menzies, but in a field of four was the first eliminated.

White had travelled to England in 1938 with Menzies and Sir Earle Page [q.v.11] to represent Australia in trade negotiations and, like Menzies, visited Germany. In July White was Australia's delegate at the inter-governmental conference on refugees held at Evian, France. He chaired a sub-committee which interviewed representatives of organizations involved in the reception of political refugees, most of them Jewish, from Germany and Austria. Much moved by the stories told, he affirmed that Australia would play its part, but also said that, having 'no real racial problem, we are not desirous of importing one by encouraging any scheme of large-scale foreign migration'. In 1929-38 he was, as his father-in-law had been, an occasional anonymous correspondent for the London *Morning Post* (*Daily Telegraph and Morning Post*).

On his return from Europe, and even more so after his resignation, White urged the importance of defence. As a lieutenant colonel in the C.M.F., he had commanded the 6th Battalion in 1926-31. On 9 April 1940 he transferred to the Citizen Air Force as a temporary squadron leader. Taking leave from parliament, he commanded a training school at Somers then in 1941 went to England where he administered Australian aircrew and acted as liaison officer with the Royal Air Force. He still longed to fly, and on several occasions surreptitiously took part in operations as a second pilot. From the outset, he had been a strong supporter of the Empire Air Training Scheme. His 'story in verse', *Sky Saga* (London, 1943), saluted the Imperial heroes of the air.

Returning to Melbourne in 1943, White served at the Royal Australian Air Force Staff School before being demobilized as honorary group captain on 9 December 1944. He resumed parliamentary duties and took part in the October 1944 conference in Canberra that led to the founding of the Liberal Party of Australia. Old rivalries were put to one side and, when Menzies led the Liberal Party and Country Party coalition to victory in the 1949 general election, he invited White to take the portfolios of air and civil aviation. On 21 June 1951 White resigned from parliament to become Australian high commissioner in Britain, a post that he filled with his customary energy and good humour. Next year he was appointed K.B.E. After his term expired in 1956, he lived in Melbourne.

Throughout his career White was active in a range of organizations including Legacy, the (Royal) Flying Doctor Service of Australia and the Royal Empire Society; in particular he had a long involvement with the Royal Life Saving Society (Australian chairman 1934-51). He shared an interest in the arts with his wife and while high commissioner in London sponsored the Society of Australian Writers there. Sir Thomas suffered from emphysema. Survived by his wife and their four daughters, he died of myocardial infarction on 13 October 1957 at his South Yarra home and was buried in Point Lonsdale cemetery.

Well dressed and debonair, White had been friendly and approachable but as a politician his style was vigorous and combative. He was a loyal imperialist, insisting (*Australian Statesman*, January 1944) that 'the magnificent work of the British Empire must go on'. His sense of duty had led him to volunteer as a special constable during the 1923 Melbourne police strike, and in the Depression he saw the New Guard and 'other loyal organisations' as having 'created a feeling of security among the law abiding'. He retained many of the values of the self-made man, and was attuned to the interests of small rather than big business. In a family dispute he once described his brother-in-law Herbert Brookes [q.v.7] as employing the technique of 'the business bully—the coward who skulks behind all the social privileges and the protection of capital'. He was devoted to his wife and depended much on her for advice and support; she may also have been useful in bringing him into contact with social networks able to assist his career. Through his loyalty and generosity White won the respect of friends and associates. In a remarkable tribute (Sir) Edward Dunlop described him as 'perhaps the best loved man of his generation'.

A. W. Martin, *Robert Menzies*, 1 (Melb, 1993); *PD* (Cwlth), 22 Aug 1929, p 261, 29 Nov 1929, p 520; *People* (Syd), 23 May 1951; *Argus*, 9 Nov 1938; White papers (NL); information from and papers held by Mrs J. Harley, Melb.   JOHN RICKARD

WHITE, VERA DEAKIN (1891-1978), Red Cross worker, was born on 25 December 1891 at South Yarra, Melbourne, third and youngest daughter of Victorian-born parents Alfred Deakin [q.v.8], barrister and later prime min-

ister, and his wife Elizabeth Martha Anne ('Pattie'), née Browne. Like her sisters Ivy and Stella, Vera was educated for some years by her aunt Catherine (Katie) Deakin, before attending Melbourne Church of England Girls' Grammar School. She attended lectures in English literature at the University of Melbourne but her foremost interest at this time was music. Encouraged by Katie, she learned cello and singing, performing for the first time at a concert associated with the Australian Exhibition of Women's Work in 1907. Six years later she journeyed to Europe, chaperoned by Katie, to pursue her musical studies in Berlin and Budapest. Although Vera's teacher believed that she had a future as a concert artist, her parents opposed this choice of a career.

Vera and Katie were in London when World War I broke out; within a few days Vera was organizing a meeting of 'Melbourne girls' to undertake war work. Nevertheless, the travellers soon returned to Australia where Vera joined the fledgling Australian branch of the British Red Cross Society and completed a course in home nursing. In 1915 she accompanied her parents to San Francisco, United States of America. On their return to Melbourne, she was eager to play some part in the war abroad, but her parents wanted her to stay home. Undaunted, she contacted (Sir) Norman Brookes [q.v.7] who was with the Red Cross in Cairo, asking if there were opportunities for war work there. Brookes encouraged her to come at once. Accompanied by her friend Winifred Johnson, Vera reached Port Said on 20 October 1915. The day after her arrival in Cairo, she opened the Australian Wounded and Missing Inquiry Bureau.

The bureau sought to garner information about the fate of Australian soldiers in the Gallipoli campaign on behalf of relations seeking news of them. With the movement of the Australians to the Western Front in 1916, the bureau shifted its headquarters to London. Vera's dealings with the army were frequently testing: as she later recalled, 'we were often met with suspicion and eventually jealousy, as we had made ourselves felt as a court of appeal for relatives who were unsuccessful in obtaining satisfaction from the military authorities'. In mobilizing a large body of volunteers, Vera developed considerable managerial skills. The organization dispatched more than 25 000 answers to inquiries from relations in one year alone. For her work, the 25-year-old was appointed O.B.E. in 1917. She was to reactivate the bureau during World War II.

In December 1918 Vera met at the bureau a young officer, (Sir) Thomas White [q.v.], who had recently escaped from Turkey where he had been a prisoner of war. In about three weeks they were engaged. She returned to Melbourne in April 1919 to be with her dying father. Her mother was initially unenthusiastic about her match with White, and her brother-in-law Herbert Brookes [q.v.7] played some part in attempting to discourage the marriage, but Vera was determined. She and Tom were married on 22 March 1920 at St John's Church of England, Toorak.

Vera encouraged and helped Tom in his political career; she was also occupied in raising four daughters. But in the 1930s her own philanthropic activities began to flower. Among numerous offices, she served (from 1931) on the management committee of the (Royal) Children's Hospital, becoming a life governor in 1949, and presided (1961-65) over the Victorian Society for Crippled Children and Adults. Her overriding commitment was always to the Red Cross, of which she was made an honorary life member in 1945. She was Victorian divisional commandant in 1938-45 and national vice-chairman in 1945-50 and 1964-66, and in 1950 was appointed chairman of the music therapy service.

According to one authority, Lady White—her husband was appointed K.B.E. in 1952—'probably had a greater influence than any other single person on the development of the Australian Red Cross'. A portrait of her by Robert Hofmann, which hangs at the family's holiday home, Ballara, at Point Lonsdale, shows her in her Red Cross uniform. Her work was interrupted by her departure for London in 1951 with her husband, and also by her intermittent ill health, but on returning to Australia in 1956, and following Tom's death in 1957, she resumed her daunting schedule. She was a capable organizer and an eloquent speaker, and knew how to run a meeting. One of her co-workers remembered her as being 'strict' but 'also gentle'. The daughter of Alfred Deakin, who had found her mission in the Great War, always maintained a sense of moral commitment. Survived by her daughters, she died on 9 August 1978 at South Yarra and was cremated. Her estate was sworn for probate at $300 278.

J. Rickard, *A Family Romance* (Melb, 1996); *VHJ*, 47, no 1, Feb 1976; Red Cross Soc (Vic), *Newsnotes*, Sept 1978; C. Deakin *and* T. W. White papers (NL); information from and papers held by Mrs J. Harley, Melb.   JOHN RICKARD

WHITE-HANEY, ROSE ETHEL JANET (1877-1953), botanist, was born on 11 March 1877 at the Melbourne Observatory, South Yarra, seventh of eight children of English-born parents Edward John White, astronomer, and his wife Sarah Susanna Catharine, née L'Oste. 'Jean' was educated privately until the age of 15, and then at Presbyterian Ladies' College, and the University of Melbourne (B.Sc., 1904; M.Sc., 1906; D.Sc., 1909). She taught science at P.L.C. After sharing (1906) the MacBain [q.v.5] research scholarship in biology she was awarded, two years later, a Victorian government scholarship. Under the direction of A. J. Ewart [q.v.8] she investigated the enzymes and latent life of seeds. The work was published (1910) in *Proceedings of the Royal Society of London*. She was elected (1908) a member of the Royal Society of Victoria, and in 1908-11 her research papers on bitter pit in apples and the formation of red wood in conifers appeared in its proceedings.

In 1912 the Queensland Board of Advice on Prickly Pear Destruction appointed White officer-in-charge of its experimental station at Dulacca, about 261 miles (420 km) west of Brisbane. She arrived at the undeveloped site in July, and immediately began studies on the control of Dulacca pear (*Opuntia inermis*), working in a tent until the laboratory building was completed several months later. During the next four years she conducted more than ten thousand chemical poisoning experiments and tested fungal cultures imported from overseas by T. H. Johnston and Henry Tryon [qq.v.9,12]. She also demonstrated the efficacy of the cochineal insect *Coccus indicus* (Green) as a controlling agent for *Opuntia monacantha*, a species of prickly pear that was widespread in North Queensland.

On 22 February 1915 at Holy Advent Church of England, Malvern, Melbourne, White married Victor William Haney, an American-born agricultural chemist. Her marriage did not affect her employment, but the station at Dulacca closed in 1916. In her final report she concluded that arsenic pentoxide was superior to other chemicals in destroying the pear, but that, given the cost of poisoning, the only real solution lay in discovering 'some parasitic insects or organisms capable of bringing about the destruction of the different species of prickly-pear as completely as the *Coccus indicus* (Green) has done for the *monacantha* species in North Queensland'. Eventually the moth *Cactoblastis cactorum*, introduced to Queensland in 1926, controlled prickly pear.

White-Haney lived for a short time in Western Queensland before moving to Brisbane. She was a founding member (1919) of the Lyceum Club (secretary 1922-24, president 1924-26), a committee-member (1925-26) of the Queensland Bush Book Club, and a fund-raiser (1924-29) for Women's College, University of Queensland. She attended the 1926 Pan-Pacific Science Congress in Tokyo, and two years later was employed on a short-term contract by the Council for Scientific and Industrial Research to study the pasture weeds Noogoora and Bathurst burrs. This was her last scientific project. In 1930 she joined her husband who had returned to the

United States of America some years earlier. She visited Australia in 1936. Survived by her husband and their two sons, she died on 21 October 1953 at Camarillo, California, and was buried in Inglewood Park cemetery.

F. Kelly, *Degrees of Liberation* (Melb, 1985); *Aust J of Science*, 17, no 1, 1954, p 24; *Nature* (Lond), 9 Oct 1954, p 676; *Queenslander*, 24 Nov 1927, 29 May 1930; *Courier-Mail*, 6 Nov 1953; *Argus*, 12 Nov 1953.

H. TREVOR CLIFFORD

WHITEHEAD, DOROTHY ELEANOR (1908-1976), headmistress, was born on 9 August 1908 at Geelong, Victoria, elder child of James Whitehead, clerk, and his wife Jessie, née Brown, both Victorian born. Educated privately until the age of 10, Dorothy then attended Alexandra College, Hamilton. She completed her schooling at the Church of England Girls' Grammar School, Ballarat, where she appreciated the staff's attentiveness to the needs of individual students. Inspired to become a teacher, she took the course at the Associated Teachers' Training Institution, but, after studying at the University of Melbourne (B.A. Hons, 1932; M.A., 1945), worked as secretary to the manager of a woolbroking and pastoral company.

On 19 January 1942 Whitehead enlisted in the Australian Women's Army Service as a stenographer. Commissioned lieutenant in April, she performed staff duties at the headquarters of the Victorian (1942-43) and New South Wales (1943-44) Lines of Communication areas, and at Land Headquarters, Melbourne. In May 1945 she was promoted temporary major and appointed assistant-controller, A.W.A.S., at L.H.Q. She transferred to the Reserve of Officers on 11 December.

Miss Whitehead taught English and history at Toorak College, Mount Eliza, before spending a year in Britain, visiting schools and doing a little teaching. In 1949 she was appointed headmistress of Ascham School, Sydney. Instead of the overbearing major they had anticipated, the staff found a quiet, dignified woman who 'could be strict but also humane'. She proved herself an excellent administrator. Under her supervision, an extensive building and renovation programme was completed. A new science block enabled the school to add physics and chemistry to the curriculum. With her abiding commitment to an education which met individual needs, she wholeheartedly supported the Dalton plan, introduced to the school by her predecessor Margaret Bailey [q.v.7].

While at Ascham, Miss Whitehead was a member of the Teachers' Guild of New South Wales, State president of the Association of Headmistresses of Independent Schools of Australia, a founder (1959) of the Australian College of Education, and a member of the education committee of the Australian National Advisory Committee for the United Nations Educational, Scientific and Cultural Organization. In 1961 she was appointed headmistress of Firbank Church of England Girls' Grammar School, Brighton, Melbourne.

At Firbank she showed the same administrative ability as at Ascham. During her term a new boarding school and physical education centre were constructed. In accordance with her own philosophy of education, she abolished streamed classes, introduced a flexible choice of subjects, replaced examinations with tests, encouraged innovatory teaching methods and initiated a counselling and remedial service. She defended the value of independent schools as providing choice and diversity, and applauded the increasing number of bursaries and scholarships available to prospective students. In 1964 she was the sole woman member of the Advisory Committee on Educational Television Services, chaired by W. J. Weeden. Continuing to serve the Headmistresses Association (as State secretary), she also sat on the Victorian Curriculum Advisory Board. She was a delegate to the National Council of Women, and a member of the Lyceum Club, Melbourne, and the Macquarie Club, Sydney.

Although only 5 ft 1 in. (155 cm) tall, Miss Whitehead had presence and could be intimidating. She was always immaculately groomed and conservatively dressed, often in shades of blue to match her cornflower-blue eyes. An exceptionally private woman, reserved and perhaps shy, she was nevertheless approachable to students and staff, who appreciated her support and incisive advice. They respected her efficiency and firmness of purpose, and admired the serenity that weathered crises and instilled confidence. Her teachers valued her trust in them, her willingness to delegate and her insistence on their professionalism. If she lacked the pedagogic passion of some of the State's pioneering headmistresses, her cool-headed, practical approach was well suited to the consolidation and growth of established schools. Retiring from Firbank in 1970, she taught for short periods in two girls' schools and maintained her interest in theatre, music, art and literature. She died of cancer on 1 July 1976 at Malvern and was cremated.

C. F. Simpson et al (eds), *Ascham Remembered 1886-1986* (Syd, 1986); *Firbank Log*, 1962-64, 1970, 1976; *Pride*, Nov 1969; Aust College of Education, *Unicorn*, 3, no 1, Mar 1977; *SMH*, 10 Mar 1949, 15 Aug 1955; *Age* (Melb), 3, 5 July 1976; information from Mrs E. Warne, Hawthorn, Mrs E. Boston, Cheltenham, Mrs M. Arcaro, North Balwyn, and Mrs F. Berry, Beaumaris, Melb.

DIANE LANGMORE

WHITEHOUSE, FREDERICK WILLIAM (1900-1973), geologist, was born on 20 December 1900 at Ipswich, Queensland, eldest of five children of Queensland-born Frederick William Whitehouse, baker, and his wife Florence Amelia, née Terrey, from New South Wales. After boarding at Ipswich Grammar School, Fred graduated with first-class honours in geology and mineralogy from the University of Queensland (B.Sc., 1922; M.Sc., 1924; D.Sc., 1939), and won a government gold medal for outstanding merit. Taking up a university foundation travelling scholarship at St John's College, Cambridge (Ph.D., 1925), he wrote a thesis on marine Cretaceous sequences of Australia.

On his return to Queensland in 1925, Whitehouse was appointed government geologist. Next year he began lecturing in geology at the University of Queensland; over three decades he was to alternate between working for the State government and the university. He helped to map the geology of western Queensland while studying the region's fossil fauna. In 1941 he was awarded the Royal Society of New South Wales's Walter Burfitt [q.v.7] prize and medal for his work on the stratigraphy of the Great Artesian Basin. On 7 July that year he enlisted in the Australian Imperial Force. Commissioned lieutenant, Royal Australian Engineers, in January 1942, he applied his geological knowledge to road-building in Queensland and New Guinea in 1942-43, and to formulating procedures for amphibious assaults across coral reefs in 1944-45. He travelled extensively in the South-West Pacific Area and in September 1945 rose to temporary lieutenant colonel. Mentioned in dispatches for his work, he was demobilized on 21 December.

In 1946-47 Whitehouse was seconded to the Department of the Co-ordinator-General of Public Works; he was a member of the committee on postwar reconstruction and was involved with the northern Australia development project. He resumed lecturing at the university in 1948, and was promoted to associate-professor next year. Continuing his studies on the stratigraphy of the artesian basin, he described the natural leakage from the system, particularly the mound springs. This was probably his most significant contribution to geology, and was published as an appendix, 'The Geology of the Queensland Portion of the Great Australian Artesian Basin', in the report, *Artesian Water Supplies in Queensland* (1954). He was also interested in quaternary geomorphology.

With his energy and outstanding wit, Whitehouse inspired both colleagues and students. A governor of Cromwell College, University of Queensland, he was active in the university's rowing club and dramatic society. He was president of the Queensland Naturalists'

Club and Nature-Lovers' League (1929) and the Royal Society of Queensland (1940-41). In the Boy Scouts' Association, he rose from rover leader in 1932 to deputy chief commissioner in 1954-55. He was leading eight hundred senior scouts on a hike across Fraser Island in 1951 when one contracted poliomyelitis and the camp was quarantined for a week. Rations were in short supply and he supervised the boys as they used their scouting skills to live partly off the land.

Whitehouse toured Queensland in 1953, visiting schools and showing a film to publicize the university. Two years later he was dismissed from his teaching post after receiving a three-month suspended sentence for committing an act of 'gross indecency' with a young man. There was no suggestion that the charge had any connection with his public activities. He then worked as a geological consultant. Continuing to participate in the work of scientific organizations, he was president (1972-73) of the Anthropological Society of Queensland. Unmarried, he died on 22 March 1973 in Brisbane and was cremated with Anglican rites.

D. Hill, *The First Fifty Years of the Department of Geology of the University of Queensland* (Brisb, 1981); R. Fones, *In the Light of all the Years* (Brisb, 1992); *Qld Naturalist*, 21, Jan 1974; *SMH*, 17 Apr 1955; *Courier-Mail*, 13 May, 17 Aug 1955; Univ Qld Archives; personal file, A/54231, item 7153 (QA); information from Dr R. Fairbridge, New York, and Mr S. Routh, Bardon, Qld.   RICHARD E. CHAPMAN

WHITELAW, JOHN STEWART (1894-1964), soldier, was born on 26 August 1894 at Hawthorn, Melbourne, only son and eldest of three children of Victorian-born parents Thomas Smiley Whitelaw, ironmonger, and his wife Margaret Lawson, née Hunter. Educated at Wesley College, John entered the Royal Military College, Duntroon, Federal Capital Territory, in June 1911. He was appointed lieutenant, Australian Imperial Force, in August 1914 and posted to the 7th Battalion. Two months later he embarked for Egypt. At Gallipoli on 25 April 1915 he suffered a severe bullet-wound to the foot. After recovering in hospitals in Egypt and England, he returned to Melbourne in December 1915. His A.I.F. appointment terminated on 25 July 1916 and he was assigned to the Administrative and Instructional Staff of the 3rd Military District. On 27 December that year at St Mark's Church of England, Camberwell, he married Esther Augusta Norman.

Transferring to the Royal Australian Garrison Artillery in September 1917, Whitelaw performed staff and regimental duties in New South Wales, Queensland and Victoria. In

October 1920 he was allocated to the newly formed Staff Corps as a captain. A student at the School of Gunnery (reorganized as the Artillery Schools of Instruction), Sydney, in 1921, he returned as an instructor in 1927. He completed further gunnery training in England in 1928-30. Becoming chief instructor at the A.S.I. (renamed the School of Artillery) in January 1931, he was promoted major in October. From 1935 he served on the General Staff at Army Headquarters, Melbourne, rising to substantive lieutenant colonel in July 1937.

Following the outbreak of World War II, in November 1939 Whitelaw was promoted colonel and appointed commander, coast defences, Eastern Command (New South Wales). It was an important and demanding position, and during this period Whitelaw made what was probably his most significant contribution to Australian artillery work. The use of radar equipment in target-location and gunlaying was then in its infancy. Both the navy and air force hoped to acquire this new technology from Britain, but Whitelaw pushed hard for the development and domestic manufacture of the equipment. The first coast-watching, or shore defence, radar sets were constructed by the Postmaster-General's Department. This marked the beginning of the serious study of the military application of radar in Australia. Whitelaw travelled to the Netherlands East Indies and Singapore in 1941 to observe trials of coastal artillery. In 1940-42 he was also an aide-de-camp to the governor-general Baron (Earl) Gowrie [q.v.9]. Made temporary brigadier in February 1941, he was appointed C.B.E. in 1942.

In April 1942, as the Pacific war reached crisis point, Whitelaw was promoted temporary major general (substantive 1 September) and appointed major general, royal artillery, with responsibility for all gunnery matters within the Australian army. Based at Land Headquarters, Melbourne, he dealt with the technological and supply problems in Australia and visited forward areas in Papua and New Guinea. He approved the development and introduction of a shortened 25-pounder (11 kg) field-gun that could be broken down into relatively light units and deployed in remote jungle or mountainous terrain. As the Japanese advance was first halted, then driven back, his sphere of activity spread across the South-West Pacific Area.

Whitelaw assumed command of the Victoria Lines of Communication Area in June 1945 and of Western Command in March 1946. In March-June 1947 he left his headquarters in Perth to serve as president of the war crimes tribunal at Rabaul, Territory of Papua-New Guinea, where he heard painful accounts of the mistreatment of Australian prisoners of war by the Japanese. On 27

August 1951 he retired from the army. He had been appointed C.B. that year.

Five ft 9 ins (175 cm) tall, Whitelaw had a 'trim, soldierly figure' and black hair. His work had been marked by careful preparation, but he recognized that risks must be taken in time of war. He had a 'fertile mind' and was 'alert to new ideas and possibilities'. Although forthright and stern, he 'showed sympathy and kindness to those in difficulty or trouble'. In retirement he lived at Upper Beaconsfield, Victoria. He was active in Legacy, the Victorian Country Fire Authority and his church, and interested in history, gardening and carpentry. Retaining his links with his old regiment, he was colonel commandant, Royal Australian Artillery, in 1955-61. He died of cardiac infarction on 21 April 1964 at Berwick and was cremated; his wife survived him, as did their three sons, all of whom became artillery officers.

D. P. Mellor, *The Role of Science and Industry* (Canb, 1958); C. B. Schedvin, *Shaping Science and Industry* (Syd, 1987); D. Horner, *The Gunners* (Syd, 1995); *Cannonball*, no 31, Dec 1997, p 16; information from Brig F. T. Whitelaw, Ashmore, Qld, and Maj Gen J. Whitelaw, Kingston, Canb.

JACKSON HUGHES

WHITINGTON, BERTRAM LINDON (1911-1977), political journalist, was born on 31 January 1911 at Ballarat, Victoria, third child of Australian-born parents Bertram Whitington, metallurgist, and his wife Hilda Eleigh, née Carkeet. 'Don', as he was always known, grew up in Tasmania and was educated at the Friends' High School, Hobart. He completed a two-year woolclassing course at the Gordon Institute of Technology, Geelong, Victoria, which involved some work as a rouseabout at shearing sheds in New South Wales and Tasmania. In the Depression he did odd jobs before he was taken on by H. R. Munro [q.v.10] as a jackeroo, assistant book-keeper and chauffeur at Keera station near Bingara, New South Wales. He began contributing articles to the *Bingara Telegraph*, *Northern Daily Leader*, *Bulletin* and *Walkabout*, and in December 1933, with £5 in the bank, set out for Sydney determined to become a journalist. The wool-shed ethos—a strong sense of mateship and solidarity with fellow workers—would nonetheless remain with him for the rest of his life.

After working as a casual reporter for the Melbourne *Star* and other newspapers, Whitington accepted a cadetship on (Sir) Frank Packer's [q.v.15] *Daily Telegraph* in September 1936. At St Matthew's Church, Manly, on 5 November that year he married with Anglican rites Victorie Daphne Teasdale, a sales-assistant who used her stepfather's surname, Stansfield; separated in 1961, they were later divorced. Following brief stints on the *Labor Daily* and the Brisbane *Courier-Mail*, he was appointed head of the *Telegraph*'s Canberra bureau in 1941. His career thereafter centred on Federal politics and he became one of Australia's best known political journalists. In 1944 he was selected to join a government-sponsored press delegation to study the war effort in Canada and the United States of America. On his return, he supported the striking printers and journalists involved in the Sydney newspaper dispute of October. He was removed from his Canberra post, despite his reputation as a discerning and clear-eyed political correspondent.

For the next three years Whitington worked as a feature writer on the *Sunday Telegraph*. Quitting daily-newspaper journalism, he formed a partnership with Eric White, a Liberal Party publicity officer, and in January 1948 launched the subscription newsletter *Inside Canberra*. After a shaky start, *Inside Canberra* increased steadily in circulation and prestige. Two other newsletters followed— *Money Matters* and *Canberra Survey*. A few years later Whitington and White founded the *Northern Territory News* and the *Mount Isa Mail*. The sale of both papers to Rupert Murdoch saw the partners end their association in 1957. That year Whitington established Australian Press Services Pty Ltd with *Inside Canberra* as the principal operation.

Politics had become a consuming passion for Whitington and he wrote a series of books on the subject, most notably *The House Will Divide* (1954), *Ring the Bells* (1956), *The Rulers* (1964), *Twelfth Man?* (1972) and *The Witless Men* (1975). He also wrote several novels, including *Treasure Upon the Earth* (1957) and *Miles Pegs* (1963), and a play, *God Bless the Browns*. His unfinished autobiography was to appear in 1978 as *Strive To Be Fair*.

Prime Minister Gough Whitlam described Whitington as 'one of the ablest and most honourable men in Australian journalism', while a colleague, Bob Walker, suggested he had been born with the '3-H Factor'—humour, humanity and humility. He had a craggy face, crooked grin, jaunty air, twinkling eye, and lifelong stutter. Ever ambivalent about his political allegiances, he recognized the shortcomings of both sides. Politicians of all persuasions respected him. The touchstone of his journalism was fairness, coupled with astute political judgement.

Whitington listed his recreations as birdwatching, carousing and Australian Rules football. On 26 February 1974 at Inverloch, Victoria, he married with Presbyterian forms Helen Elizabeth Scott, a 29-year-old secretary. Survived by his wife, and by the two sons and daughter of his first marriage, he died of a cerebral embolism on 5 May 1977 in Canberra Hospital and was buried with Anglican rites in Canberra cemetery.

C. J. Lloyd, *Profession: Journalist* (Syd, 1985) and *Parliament and the Press* (Melb, 1988); D. Bowman, *The Captive Press* (Melb, 1988); P. Buckridge, *The Scandalous Penton* (Brisb, 1994); H. Myers, *The Whispering Gallery* (Syd, 1999); *Journalist*, July 1977; *SMH*, 20 Apr 1967; Whitington papers (NL); information from Mrs H. Parkes, Deakin, Mr R. Chalmers, Chifley, Canb, and Mr R. Whitington, Pymble, Syd.   JOHN FARQUHARSON

WHITLAM, HARRY FREDERICK ERNEST (1884-1961), Commonwealth crown solicitor, was born on 3 April 1884 at Prahran, Melbourne, eldest of five children of Victorian-born parents Henry Hugh Gough Whitlam, clerk, and his wife Janet Turnbull, née Steele. Educated at Armadale State School and, on a scholarship, at Wesley College, Fred took first place in the Victorian Public Service clerical examination in December 1900 and entered the Department of Lands and Survey on 8 July 1901. He transferred to the Crown Solicitor's Office and in 1911 joined the Commonwealth Public Service in the land tax branch of the Treasury. Having gained accountancy qualifications and studied at the University of Melbourne (LL.B., 1914), he was appointed to a professional position in the Commonwealth Crown Solicitor's Office in 1913. At the Collins Street Baptist Church on 10 September 1914 he married Martha Maddocks (d.1958). Their daughter Freda was to become principal of Presbyterian Ladies' College, Croydon, Sydney, and later moderator of the New South Wales Synod of the Uniting Church in Australia; their son Gough was to become prime minister.

Promoted to senior clerk in 1917, Whitlam transferred to the Sydney office next year. On 12 April 1920 he was admitted as a barrister and solicitor of the High Court of Australia on the motion of his chief and mentor Sir Robert Garran [q.v.8]. He rose to deputy crown solicitor in 1921. Moving to Canberra as assistant crown solicitor in 1927, he succeeded W. H. Sharwood [q.v.11] as crown solicitor on 29 December 1936.

In the small Canberra community, the successive Whitlam family homes were notable for well-stocked libraries, the hospitality of their imposing hostess, and the scholarship and kindly courtesy of her husband. Whitlam contributed widely to civic life. He lectured in commercial law at Canberra University College, served on the college council and became president of the University Association of Canberra. President of the Young Men's Christian Association of Canberra, he was also a member of the Canberra Grammar School council. (Sir) Paul Hasluck recalled: 'Any educational or cultural activity in those days in Canberra depended a good deal on Fred Whitlam'. Gough Whitlam recorded that until wartime pressures made it impossible, his father 'was the virtual ombudsman and legal aid officer for the people of Canberra'. In retirement, while negotiating on behalf of the solicitor-general (Sir) Kenneth Bailey [q.v.13], he was to give sympathetic consideration to the complex land-lease needs of the infant Australian National University.

Whitlam's influence as a senior legal adviser to the government for over twelve years was extensive and significant. On the Lyons [q.v.10] government's controversial national insurance initiative, for example, he drafted legislation for the National Insurance Commission, recommended the appointment of J. B. Brigden [q.v.7] as chairman, and drew up the agreement between the commission and the Australian branch of the British Medical Association. He also briefed W. R. Dovey [q.v.14], his son's future father-in-law, as counsel assisting the subsequent royal commission. Closer in political sentiment to John Curtin and J. B. Chifley [qq.v.13] than to their predecessors, Whitlam was largely responsible for preparing the documentation for the 1944 referendum on Commonwealth powers and, with the solicitor-general, for advising H. V. Evatt [q.v.14] during the bank nationalization litigation (1947-49).

Accompanying the Australian delegation to the Paris Peace Conference in 1946, Whitlam put the case for Evatt's 'very ambitious' proposal for an international human-rights court. Instructed by Evatt not to compromise, he reported to his wife that he had 'stiffened the sinews and summoned up the blood', but to no avail. Early drafts of Article 18 of the 1948 Universal Declaration of Human Rights reflected his advocacy of freedom to change religion or belief as well as to manifest and teach them. He retired as crown solicitor on 2 April 1949, but continued to be closely involved in United Nations matters as an adviser to the Department of External Affairs and Australian representative at sessions (1950, 1954) of the U.N. Commission on Human Rights.

Chairman of the Australian Commission of the Churches on International Affairs and a good friend of the Australian Student Christian Movement in its postwar immigration and international concerns, Whitlam was enlisted to draft a constitution for the Australian Council of Churches. He had an abiding interest in theology, generally attending with his family whatever church was most convenient. In latter years he was in the Presbyterian fold, becoming an elder of St Andrew's Church, Forrest, Canberra. Survived by his two children, he died on 8 December 1961 in Canberra Community Hospital and was cremated. Greatly respected, and especially popular with younger generations of public servants, Whitlam had, according to H. C. Coombs, 'a memorable command of the English language' and 'a gentle, softly spoken style but as deep a commitment to social reform as his son'. Many, like Hasluck, remembered 'a public-spirited, meticulous and dutiful man with an inquiring but cautious mind'.

H. E. Renfree, *History of the Crown Solicitor's Office* (Canb, 1970); H. C. Coombs, *Trial Balance* (Melb, 1981); P. Hasluck, *The Chance of Politics* (Melb, 1997); M1505, item 1383 (NAA, Canb); information from and papers held by the Hon E. G. Whitlam, Syd, and Dr F. L. Whitlam, Penrith, NSW.

CAMERON HAZLEHURST

WHITLEY, CUTHBERT CLAUDE MORTIER (1886-1942), architect and public servant, was born on 30 July 1886 at Rutherglen, Victoria, second surviving child of Charles Herbert Whitley, a schoolteacher from England, and his Victorian-born wife Elizabeth, née Horrocks. Cuthbert trained in design and building with the Victorian Public Works Department. In 1912 he joined the Commonwealth Public Service as a draughtsman in the public works branch of the Department of Home Affairs. At St John's Church of England, Camberwell, on 25 January 1913 he married Mabel Violet Tudor, a hair-frame maker.

In 1920 Whitley was appointed architect in the Department of Works and Railways. Soon after, he was admitted as an associate of the Royal Victorian Institute of Architects and the Royal Institute of British Architects. A protégé of the chief architect J. S. Murdoch [q.v.10], he prepared preliminary drawings for the Commonwealth Bank of Australia building in Brisbane and later contributed to the design of the adjacent Commonwealth offices.

Whitley was transferred in 1929 to Canberra, where he worked under the principal designing architect (later chief architect) E. H. Henderson. In 1935 Whitley was promoted to senior architect in the Department of the Interior. His first major project was a new building for the Patent Office on Kings Avenue, for which he chose a formal axial composition with sandstone facings and restrained Art Deco embellishment.

In 1936 Whitley designed Ainslie Public School (1938). His plans were both functional and elegant, with carefully articulated facades and creative treatment of conventional materials internally and externally. Art Deco motifs such as chevrons and vertical flutes suggested a fresh and forward-looking view of education. He followed this building with a dramatic design for Canberra High School (1939) at Acton, with a lofty clock tower marking the high ground overlooking the city centre and long symmetrical wings of classrooms terminating in bold semicircular ends. He enlivened the formality of the composition with decorative elements integrated into the overall design. Featuring many technological innovations, it was described at the time as 'the most modern school in Australia'.

Following Henderson's death in 1939, Whitley was acting chief architect for some six months. His ambitions for a truly modern Canberra were also realized in smaller projects, including houses, and the city's first fire station, at Forrest. The flat roofs, crisp steel-framed windows and unrelieved brick walls of these buildings were early expressions in Canberra of the Inter-War Functionalist style.

Whitley lived with his family at Reid and walked each day to work in the city centre. A quiet, unassuming man and a Freemason, he had played Australian Rules football with the Hawthorn Football Club in Melbourne and won several trophies for golf in Canberra. He travelled only for work and, despite his appreciation of contemporary architectural movements, never went overseas. After suffering the first of several strokes in 1941, he retired on 19 September 1942. He died of a cerebral haemorrhage on 23 October that year in Canberra Community Hospital and was buried in Canberra cemetery. His wife, and their daughter and son survived him.

K. Charlton, *Federal Capital Architecture* (Canb, 1984) and The Career of C. C. M. Whitley A.R.V.I.A., A.R.I.B.A. (ts, 2000, copy on ADB file); Pegrum & Associates, *The Old Patent Office, Canberra* (Canb, 1998); Daryl Jackson Alastair Swayn Pty Ltd, *Canberra School of Art: Conservation Management Plan* (Canb, 2000); *Canb Times*, 18 Sept 1939, 28 Oct 1942; information from Mrs J. Nicholls, Reid, Canb.

ROGER PEGRUM

WHITLEY, GILBERT PERCY (1903-1975), ichthyologist and author, was born on 9 June 1903 at Swaythling, near Southampton, England, eldest of three children of Percy Nathan Whitley, drapery buyer, and his wife Clara Minnie, née Moass. Gilbert was educated at King Edward VI School, Southampton, and at Osborne House school, Romsey, Hampshire. With his parents and two sisters, he migrated to Sydney in 1921. On 18 April 1922 he joined the staff of the Australian Museum and worked under Allan McCulloch [q.v.10]. He studied zoology at Sydney Technical College (1922) and the University of Sydney (1924). Following McCulloch's death, on 2 October 1925 Whitley was appointed ichthyologist (later curator of fishes).

In 1923 he had published his first article, 'The Praying Mantis', in the *Australian Museum Magazine*. Whitley's prodigious output was to include over 550 papers and five books

on his ichthyological interests—the fish (from seahorses to sharks) of Australia, New Zealand, New Guinea and the South Pacific. He described hundreds of new genera and species and studied most aspects of Australian marine and freshwater fishes, including ecology, fisheries and taxonomy. His taxonomy revealed confidence and something of his impish nature: his 'little regard for rules of nomenclature' provoked disagreement and displeasure from international colleagues on more than one occasion. Keenly interested in history, especially that of biology and zoology, and the lives of early Australian naturalists, he delighted 'in digging up historical details' for colleagues. One major disappointment for Whitley was the trustees' decision not to publish his history of the Australian Museum. The manuscript was essentially a collector's history, strong on detail but lacking explanation and analysis.

During World War II, Whitley was rejected by the Royal Australian Air Force, despite his stated qualifications of 'drawing and languages'. Instead, he was seconded (1942-46) to the division of fisheries of the Council for Scientific and Industrial Research. He conducted investigations, including one into shark capture, to assess potential national food supplies. Well suited to such activity, Whitley was photographed (and remembered) with sleeves rolled up, looking into a microscope in the fisheries department, wading in tropical oceans or searching through a carpet of sea grass. He was a man engrossed in his work.

Throughout his curatorship, Whitley enhanced and expanded museum material, becoming well known for his enthusiasm. He particularly enjoyed foreign travel (usually at his own expense) and collecting expeditions with his friends Tom Iredale and Anthony Musgrave [qq.v.9,10]. His term of office was notable for the registration (involving identification and tagging) of some 37 000 specimens, which almost doubled the collection. His growing reputation impressed and inspired such donors as Melbourne Ward [q.v.].

Whitley was president (1940-41, 1959-60 and 1973-74) and a fellow (1934) of the Royal Zoological Society of New South Wales; he edited its publications in 1947-71. He served on the councils of the Royal Australian Historical Society and the Anthropological Society of New South Wales, on the Great Barrier Reef Committee and as president (1963-64) of the Linnean Society of New South Wales; he was also involved with the Australian and New Zealand Association for the Advancement of Science. Whitley was awarded the Natural History Medallion for 1967 by the Field Naturalists Club of Victoria and the (W. B.) Clarke [q.v.3] medal for 1970 by the Royal Society of New South Wales. In 1971 he funded the Whitley awards by the zoological society for outstanding publications containing significant information on Australasian fauna.

Known for his sense of humour, wit and outgoing nature, Whitley was warmly regarded by colleagues. One recalled his entering 'Genius and diligence' under 'Qualifications' in a Public Service Board survey; the incident also suggested his occasional impatience with authority. The Whitley papers held in the Australian Museum include the endearingly named 'Whitleyana'. One item, the 'Song of the Ichthyologist', an affectionate parody, contained the following lines:

Although it surely wasn't Gilbert's 'dearest
  wish',
He's been appointed nursemaid to a lot of
  stinking fish

Whitley retired in September 1964. His passion for work never waned; he continued his research throughout his retirement, just as he had on holidays and long service leave. Nevertheless, he was interested in all the arts. He played the piano, frequently attended concerts and the theatre and rarely missed a good film or art exhibition. Gilbert Whitley died on 18 July 1975 at his Mosman home and was cremated. He was unmarried.

Aust Natural Hist, 14, Dec 1964, p 383; Aust Museum, *Museum Newsheet*, 10, no 1, 23 July 1975, p 1; *Copeia*, 4, Dec 1975, p 792; *Aust Zoologist*, 19, no 1, 1976, p 111; Linnean Soc NSW, *Procs*, 101, 1977, p 256; Whitley papers (ML and Basser L, Canb); Whitley bib reference file, Aust Museum, Syd.
MAREE MURRAY
JOHN ROACH

WHITTA, CLIFFORD NICHOLLS (1903-1956), radio entertainer, was born on 24 September 1903 at North Carlton, Melbourne, second son of Victorian-born parents John Whitta, decorator, and his wife Lydia, née Nicholls. The family was thrifty and religious, and Cliff's childhood was ordered, secure, uneventful and happy. He attended the Methodist Church in Nicholson Street, Fitzroy, three times each Sunday. Educated at Princes Hill State School, he served as an apprentice to a jeweller then tried poultry-farming at Eltham before deciding to become a wireless announcer. The taunts of his brother and friends spurred him on.

Learning guitar from Oreste Manzoni at (G. L.) Allan's [q.v.3] music store, Whitta was taken on by the Australian Broadcasting Co. as an instrumentalist in the dance band of radio-station 3AR. From about 1931 he worked on the children's session at 3LO. Dropping his surname, he styled himself Cliff, or 'Nicky', Nicholls. He sang in a number of J. C. Williamson [q.v.6] Ltd musicals, including *The Chocolate Soldier* which starred Gladys Mon-

crieff [q.v.10]. Lack of work in the Depression prompted him to move to Sydney where he found a job with the retailers Anthony Hordern [qq.v.4,9] & Sons Ltd.

In 1932 Nicholls joined Melbourne radio-station 3AW. He performed on the children's programme and teamed with Fred Tupper as 'Nicky and Tuppy' to provide the station's popular breakfast entertainment. In 1933 3AW employed Kathleen Mavourneen Lindgren as Nicholls's co-host of the children's show; she took the professional name, 'Nancy Lee'. The two developed 'Chatterbox Corner' which, with its theme song, *Being a Chum is Fun*, was said to be 'the best children's session in Australia'. Clifford and Kathleen were married on 31 August 1935 at the Methodist Church, Richmond. In 1944 she withdrew from radio and public life to care for their two sons.

Nicholls's decision to leave 3AW in 1946 caused an outcry among his listeners. Moving to Sydney, he worked for radio 2CH. Next year he returned to Melbourne and briefly resumed jewellery making but in 1948 accepted a position with 3KZ as compere of the breakfast session. He introduced a segment, 'Junior Stars of the Air', to which a number of notable Australian announcers and entertainers were to trace their professional beginnings. In 1950 he transferred to 3UZ where he presented the morning session and formed his most celebrated 'on air' relationship—with the young Graham Kennedy, who acknowledged him as his mentor.

Though seemingly a master of spontaneous witticisms, Nicholls spent hours preparing for each show, aided by scrapbooks of jokes and 'gags' which he meticulously collected. In front of the microphone he was sincere and personal, giving the impression that he was addressing himself 'to that one person out there whom he liked, understood and felt for'. At its most popular, his programme on 3UZ attracted 73 per cent of listeners. In 1956 he was contracted to appear on television. He died of a coronary occlusion on 8 September that year in his home at Ivanhoe and was cremated. More than 100 000 people watched the funeral procession. His wife and their sons survived him.

N. Lee and D. Messenger, *Being a Chum was Fun* (Melb, 1979); *Listener In*, 28 Aug-3 Sept 1954; *Argus*, 10, 11, 12, 15 Sept 1956.
DALLY MESSENGER

WICKS, TORY MARCELLA (1900-1977), hockey player and administrator, was born on 13 May 1900 at Waverley, Sydney, third daughter and middle child of Leslie Fletcher Wicks, a native-born schoolteacher, and his wife Annie Louise, née McCullagh, who came from Victoria. Named Pretoria, she was always known as Tory. Educated at Fort Street Girls' High School, she worked as a typiste and then as a secretary. She and her sisters Nancie and Mildred founded the Gumnuts Hockey Club, a team of ex-students from Fort Street, in 1920.

Selected for the New South Wales team in 1923, Wicks was chosen for the All Australia Women's Hockey Team two years later. She remained a member of both teams almost continuously until 1935. When an English touring team visited in 1927, she was Australian vice-captain. In 1930 Wicks led the Australian team as captain on its first international tour, to South Africa, Britain and Europe. A physically fit and reliable player, she used her keen sense of anticipation to direct the team from her position at full-back. Although the primary purpose of the tour was to absorb 'technique and tactics' rather than to win, Australia recorded its first international victory—against Ireland. Wicks remained in Europe until 1931 on an extended holiday as guest of her many hockey friends. Later in her life she declared: 'I know of no better passport around the world than a hockey stick'.

In 1935 Wicks captained Australia against New Zealand before retiring from international hockey. She earned (1936) the All Australia badge in hockey umpiring; with Mollie Dive and Kate Ogilvie she set and maintained high standards. Over many years she travelled to country centres to coach players and umpires. Wicks held senior administrative positions within the Sydney, New South Wales and Australian women's hockey associations. In 1953 she was elected secretary of the International Federation of Women's Hockey Associations. Her contacts proved invaluable. With her co-delegate and friend, Dr Marie Hamilton [q.v.14], she successfully lobbied to hold the triennial international tournament in Sydney in May 1956. For three years she worked tirelessly, often until 2 a.m., to co-ordinate the tour, turning her family home at Bondi into the hub of hockey administration.

In an era of strictly amateur sport, she raised the £30 000 necessary to host nine international teams for a fortnight's matches followed by a three-month goodwill tour of country centres and cities across Australia. Wicks was made a vice-president of the I.F.W.H.A. and a life-member of both the New South Wales and All Australia Women's Hockey associations. She never retired from promoting the game she loved. A stylish, neat woman with piercing, blue eyes, she drew companionship from those she met through hockey.

Tory Wicks died on 8 February 1977 at St Vincent's Hospital, Darlinghurst, and was cremated with Anglican rites. The naming of the Tory Wicks Memorial Playing Field at Ryde was a tribute to her tenacity of purpose and ideals. Her sister Nancie Wicks (1898-1981) also served the game of hockey, as an international player and administrator; she was appointed M.B.E. (1977) for her services to hockey and her charity work with the Rachel Forster Hospital for Women and Children.

L. Hodges, *A History of the New South Wales Women's Hockey Association 1908-1983* (Syd, 1984); *Aust Women's Weekly*, 6 June 1956; *SMH*, 20 Feb 1931, 11 July 1954, 11, 20, 23 May 1956.

MARION K. STELL

WIGGINS, CARN SCARLETT (1898-1969), air force officer and public servant, was born on 6 October 1898 at Mudgee, New South Wales, second child of John Scarlett Wiggins, a draper from Ireland, and his Victorian-born wife Florence Elizabeth, née Smith. Educated in Hobart at Battery Point State School and The Hutchins School, Carn entered the Royal Military College, Duntroon, Federal Capital Territory, in February 1916. He graduated as lieutenant in December 1920 and trained as a signals officer in England. On his return to Australia, he was posted to the 3rd Divisional Signals in Melbourne (1922) and the 11th Mixed Brigade in Brisbane (1923). At Kangaroo Point on 9 February 1924 he married with Presbyterian forms Jean de Belle Graham; they had eleven children before being divorced in 1949. He resigned from the army on 31 May 1924.

Joining the Royal Australian Air Force as a flying officer on 2 July 1925, Wiggins specialized in signals. He was promoted flight lieutenant in 1928 and squadron leader in 1936. Competent, knowledgeable and energetic, in the 1930s he was one of Australia's small band of experts in the rapidly emerging field of radio communications. In May 1937 he was seconded to the civil aviation branch, Department of Defence, Melbourne. Having risen to wing commander in March 1939, he transferred to the R.A.A.F. Reserve on 20 July and was appointed chief electrical engineer in the new Department of Civil Aviation.

On 25 July 1940 Wiggins was recalled to the Active List as director of signals, Air Force Headquarters, Melbourne. Promoted temporary group captain on 1 September, he was responsible for the organization and supervision of all types of service communications. His first priority was to establish a reliable long-range radio network to support R.A.A.F. operations in Australia and the region. Radar was now extensively used and electronic warfare was also increasingly important. Signals intelligence, in particular, would play a major role in the war in the Pacific. As the R.A.A.F.'s senior expert in these diverse and arcane fields, Wiggins worked to ensure that R.A.A.F. equipment, procedures and knowledge met operational needs despite rapid technological progress.

Wiggins soon acquired a reputation for 'getting things done'. His 'captain of the team' approach gave his staff wide responsibility and empowered them to make decisions. This drew the best out of competent people who displayed initiative, and many of his wartime staff regarded him highly both as a man and a manager. Very sociable, he was able to build a strong rapport with both his superiors and opposite numbers in the other services.

Early in 1942 the Japanese advance through the Netherlands East Indies and attack on Darwin placed especially heavy demands on Australia's signals systems. Communications between the air officer commanding at Darwin and the central war rooms at Bandung, N.E.I., and in Melbourne were, however, maintained. This achievement was largely due to 'good initial planning and installation work' under Wiggins' direction. He was appointed C.B.E. (1942) for his 'outstanding technical ability coupled with his initiative and administrative skill'. Despite 'long and arduous hours of duty', he displayed 'resourcefulness' and 'outstanding foresight' which enabled the signals system to operate 'in a high state of efficiency'.

Wiggins was appointed director of communications, Allied Air Forces Headquarters, South-West Pacific Area, in July 1942, and then director of communications at Headquarters, R.A.A.F. Command, in March 1943. In each post his experience, personal drive and ability to create 'teams' enhanced his effectiveness. During this period he travelled to New Guinea and the South-West Pacific to obtain first-hand knowledge, but by 1944 the war was moving further north. He was made director of radio services, Air Force Headquarters, in August 1944. From January 1945 he was director of telecommunications and radar, a title more closely reflecting his wartime duties.

On 10 October 1945 Wiggins was placed on the R.A.A.F. Reserve. Returning to the Department of Civil Aviation, he was director of air navigation and safety in 1946-48 and assistant director (operations) from 1948 until his retirement in 1963. He died on 5 December 1969 while travelling between Frankston and Prahran and was cremated with Anglican rites. Seven of his eight sons and two of his three daughters survived him.

D. P. Mellor, *The Role of Science and Industry* (Canb, 1958); D. Gillison, *Royal Australian Air Force 1939-1942* (Canb, 1962); E. R. Hall, *A Saga of Achievement* (Melb, 1978); R. C. Meyer, *Aeradio in Australia* (Canb, 1985); C. D. Coulthard-Clark, *The Third Brother* (Syd, 1991); *Age* (Melb), 8 Dec 1969; information from Mr A. Skimin, Weetangera, Mr J. A. Weddell, Red Hill, Canb, and Mr B. Cooper, Robina, Qld.   DOUG HURST

WILDING, WINIFRED DORIS (1909-1978), community worker, was born on 3 January 1909 at Portswood, Southampton, England, daughter of Job Henry Harman, army pensioner, and his wife Sarah Florence, née Minty. Orphaned at the age of 11, 'Joyce' was sent to a convent. On 18 July 1932 at St Colman's Catholic Church, Cosham, Portsmouth, she married Francis James Wilding, a milk roundsman. She had met Frank when he delivered milk to the convent at which she was employed as housemaid. Next year their first child was born at Portsmouth and, shortly after, the family migrated to Australia, taking with them the proceeds of the sale of a Wilding family inheritance. They broke their journey in Burma, where they were joined by Frank's brother Harry. Reaching North Queensland, the brothers leased land on Long Island, near Proserpine, and invested all their funds in a banana-growing venture. In 1936 the business failed and they lost their money.

The Wildings lived for a time in a tent at Kingaroy while Frank worked on peanut-farms, earning 'government relief'. The family moved to Brisbane and three more children were born. By 1953 Mrs Wilding was running a boarding house for young men in the family's home at West End. She responded to a public appeal from the Anglican bishop of North Queensland, Ian Shevill, who was seeking accommodation in Brisbane for an Aboriginal youth from Townsville, Tennyson Kynuna; he had been offered an apprenticeship in Brisbane with Evans, Deakin & Co. Pty Ltd, shipbuilders. The Queensland Department of Native Affairs then requested her to take two Aboriginal trainee schoolteachers. Their arrival triggered an exodus of her twenty White guests, whose families objected to their 'living . . . with the Blacks'.

Facing what she later described as her 'first real experience of racial hatred', Wilding opened her doors to homeless Aborigines. Dependent on Frank's wage, supplemented by public donations, she refused to turn anyone away. Despite angry protests and threats to her life, the residence became over-crowded. She campaigned for a guaranteed source of food, shelter, medical care and legal representation for people in need, and in 1961 helped to form the One People of Australia League. Next year, O.P.A.L. appointed her matron of Brisbane's first purpose-designed hostel for homeless Aborigines and Torres Strait Islanders (O.P.A.L. House), in South Brisbane. When

O.P.A.L. opened the Joyce Wilding Home, a refuge for widows, deserted mothers and children, at Eight Mile Plains in June 1970, Wilding became matron. The following year, disheartened by the policies of the new O.P.A.L. board, she resigned.

Wilding was a brown-haired, hazel-eyed woman of middle height, whose determination to help the underprivileged hid an innate shyness. A practising Catholic of wide ecumenical sympathies, she was driven by a strong urge to 'care for the needy'. She championed multiculturalism, race and gender equality, and support for unmarried mothers, but was criticized for her 'paternalism' and her 'tame-cat' endorsement of government policies, and was called a 'do-gooder'. In her diary in 1973 she expressed anguish about the bigotry of the 1950s and 1960s, and observed that 'prejudice is the curse of us all, for we are all guilty of it sometime in our lives'. She was appointed M.B.E. in 1964, and in 1966 was made the Quota Club of Brisbane's 'Woman of the Year' and the Senior Citizens' 'Gracious Lady of the Year'.

A founding member (1957) of the St Veronica Welfare Committee, Wilding visited India and East Pakistan (Bangladesh) three times between 1957 and 1975. Her daughter was living at the Anand Milk Union Ltd's dairy colony, in Gujarat, India. After one trip she founded a relief society and organized shipments from Brisbane of blankets and clothing, and health equipment, for Dr R. R. Doshi's tuberculosis clinic at Anand. In 1976 she collected goods to send to people in India suffering from Hansen's bacillus (leprosy). She was presented with a humanitarian award by the Rosicrucian Order, Grand Lodge of San José, California, United States of America, in 1977. Survived by her three daughters and son, she died of cancer on 3 December 1978 in South Brisbane, two months after her husband, and was buried with Uniting Church forms in Cleveland cemetery.

S. Baldwin (ed), *Unsung Heroes & Heroines of Australia* (Melb, 1988); E. Darling, *They Spoke Out Pretty Good* (Melb, 1998); *Aboriginal and Islanders Advancement News*, 4, no 1, 1979, p 3; *Courier-Mail*, 4 Dec 1978; Wilding diaries (held by author); family information.   ELAINE DARLING

WILHELM, DONALD LANCELOT (1919-1977), professor of pathology, was born on 20 August 1919 at Woodside, South Australia, eldest of six children of Berthold Benjamin Wilhelm, dairy-farmer, and his wife Clara Melvina, née Pfeiffer. His parents were from German-speaking, Lutheran families who had arrived in Australia in the late 1830s. They were hard-working dairy-farmers in the Adelaide Hills for whom money was in short supply. Don attended Mount Torrens Public and Birdwood High schools. He showed strong determination and an adventurous spirit. His boyhood interests included stamp and birds' egg collecting, card games, chess, rabbit-shooting and cricket. He was opening batsman at Birdwood High and later played district cricket. Five ft 9 ins (175 cm) tall, he was fair haired with green eyes.

From an early age, encouraged by his mother, Wilhelm wanted to be a doctor. At the University of Adelaide (M.B., B.S., 1942; M.D., 1951) he was a top student, enjoying a good relationship with (Sir) John Cleland [q.v.8], professor of pathology, whom he admired. He won the mile race at a university sports day, followed horse-racing and, a small-time gambler, ran a book on the Melbourne Cup. As a student he played snooker for money; he was also a very good bridge player, but preferred poker. In 1943 he was a resident at Royal Adelaide Hospital. On 6 April 1944 at St Augustine's Church of England, Unley, he married Eileen Vimy Klopper, a senior nurse at R.A.H.

After serving part time in the Citizen Military Forces from April 1943, Wilhelm was called up for full-time duty as captain, Australian Army Medical Corps, Australian Imperial Force, on 1 February 1944 and posted to the 2nd/13th Field Ambulance. He served in Darwin and North Queensland then took part in the invasion of Brunei, Borneo, in June 1945. Helping to restore hospital facilities in the town of Brunei, he treated soldiers and local inhabitants, many of whom had been mistreated by the Japanese. He attended to patients with tropical ulcers, yaws, venereal disease, malaria and tuberculosis, and amputated the hands and limbs of children injured by Japanese booby traps. A senior officer of the British Borneo Civil Affairs Unit praised him 'for his devotion to duty and his untiring efforts'. Wilhelm was a caring and skilled doctor who demonstrated fine surgical skills.

In January 1946 he was transferred to the 121st Australian General Hospital, Katherine, Northern Territory, but, diagnosed with tuberculosis, became a patient there next month. Moved in August to the 105th Australian Military Hospital, Daws Road, Adelaide, he was discharged in September. His A.I.F. appointment terminated on 11 October. He accepted his condition philosophically and found his way back to health, with the help of his wife. His choice of a career in pathology was the result of the need to curtail his activities during his convalescence. He joined the University of Adelaide department of pathology in 1947 as a demonstrator and, appointed lecturer in 1949, directed (1950-51) the pathology department of the Repatriation General Hospital, Springbank. During this time he completed a thesis on lung cancer for his doctorate.

Although not guaranteed financial support, Wilhelm went to London in 1951 to gain experience in experimental pathology. He was appointed research assistant in the department of morbid anatomy, University College Hospital medical school, headed by (Sir) Roy Cameron who stimulated his interest in fundamental issues in pathology. Next year he joined the scientific staff of the Lister Institute of Preventive Medicine, working with (Sir) Ashley Miles in the department of experimental pathology. This period of research was his most productive.

Wilhelm accepted the foundation chair of pathology at the University of New South Wales in 1960. He built up a vigorous department and attracted good staff to enhance the university and hospital diagnostic, research and teaching programmes. He held practical classes in experimental pathology in which students were able to undertake basic experiments in such areas as inflammation, healing and necrosis. They appreciated Wilhelm as a teacher; one found him 'approachable, tolerant, interesting, humorous and nice'. He also developed an active research group and supervised their doctoral projects. The themes were Wilhelm's central interests—inflammation, healing and regeneration, vascular problems and later mast cells. He meticulously supervised his students, held frequent discussions of ongoing work, critically reviewed experiments and edited papers with his red biro.

Outside the department, Wilhelm was director of pathology at the laboratories of Prince Henry, Prince of Wales and Eastern Suburbs hospitals as well as consultant pathologist at the Royal Hospital for Women, and at St George, Sutherland and Bankstown hospitals. He was on the board of St George Hospital and adviser in pathology to the regional director of health of the Southern Metropolitan Health Region. Having steered the development of the Australian Society for Experimental Pathology, he was its first president (1969-71). He was a fellow of the (Royal) College of Pathologists of Australia and associate editor of *Pathology* for eight years.

A member of many committees, including advisory committees of the National Health and Medical Research Council, the New South Wales State Cancer Council, and the National Heart Foundation of Australia, Wilhelm was a director (1964-72) of the Asthma Foundation of New South Wales. The last held a particular appeal for him because of his interest in inflammation; in 1973 he was elected a life governor of the foundation. He strongly supported Vimy in her work for the Family Planning Association and the International Planned Parenthood Federation, and also served on the State committee of the United Nations International Children's Emergency Fund.

Wilhelm's research interests were recorded in some fifty-six papers and seven chapters of books. He made three lasting contributions to understanding of the inflammatory response. First, he analysed the dynamics of vascular permeability changes (vessel leakage), brought about by injury. He stressed the use of mild stimuli to cause minimal damage so the detailed cellular events could be readily defined. Secondly, he and Miles, in analysing chemical mediators of inflammation, characterized globulin permeability factor, now recognized as a trigger for bradykinin production. Thirdly, they defined criteria for characterizing chemical mediators from tissues.

As an investigator Wilhelm was methodical, industrious and persistent. His friend Trevor Dinning stated that he was 'always a well organised and committed person', who appreciated elegant techniques in the experimental setting where tissue reactions could be manipulated. He liked the clean-cut, well defined experiment illustrated in many of his own studies on vascular permeability changes in inflammation. He was exacting in writing up his papers and those of his students.

Wilhelm enjoyed family life. He was a gracious man with a good sense of humour who welcomed students and friends to his home. Following a cholecystectomy in the 1970s, Wilhelm's tuberculosis was reactivated. He died suddenly on 24 July 1977 at São Paulo, Brazil, where he was undertaking research. He was cremated. His wife and their son and daughter survived him.

B. W. Zweifach et al (eds), *The Inflammatory Process* (NY, 1965); L. McCarthy, *Medics at War* (Perth, 1995); *MJA*, 17 June 1978, p 654; information from Dr T. A. R. Dinning, Mylor, SA, Dr R. A. Hayes, Syd, Mrs V. Wilhelm, Syd, Dr C. D. Swaine, Georgetown, Qld, and Mr W. Wilhelm, Warburton, Vic.

H. KONRAD MULLER

WILKINSON, HERBERT JOHN (1891-1963), anatomist, was born on 15 December 1891 at Norwood, Adelaide, fifth of six children of South Australian-born parents Frank Wilkinson, accountant, and his wife Amelia, née Smith. Herbert spent his early childhood in the north of the State, before moving with his family back to Adelaide where he attended Flinders Street Public School. In 1907 he was accepted on probation at the Pupil Teachers' School; he taught (1909-10) at Flinders Street and in 1911 entered University Training College. In 1913 he taught at Adelaide High School while studying part time at the University of Adelaide (B.A., 1914). On 29 April 1915 at St Martin's Church of England, Kensington,

Sydney, he married Elsie Butler Hughes; next month he took up a post as teacher of chemistry at Brisbane Grammar School.

In 1916 Wilkinson joined the staff of Sydney Grammar School. Four years later he enrolled in medicine at the University of Sydney (M.B., Ch.M., 1925; M.D., 1930). During his course he demonstrated in histology and on graduation was appointed lecturer in anatomy and histology. Influenced by Professor J. I. Hunter [q.v.9], he began his research on the innervation of skeletal muscle. He also investigated the nervous mechanism responsible for changes in size of the pupil of the eye; this work was published in 1927 in the *Medical Journal of Australia*. That year he won the Peter Bancroft prize for research in medicine and was promoted to senior lecturer. Awarded a Rockefeller Foundation fellowship, he travelled to Europe and the United States of America and continued (1928-30) his inquiry into the innervation of striated muscle. His main interest was the alleged 'double innervation' of the muscle fibres peculiar to skeletal muscle by nerve fibres originating from two different sites, the spinal cord and the sympathetic nervous system. He demonstrated that the muscle fibres were innervated solely by nerve fibres from the cord, and that the nerve fibres from the sympathetic nervous system were concerned only with the innervation of intramuscular blood-vessels. His findings, published in the *M.J.A.* in 1929, disproved Hunter's interpretation of the role of sympathetic nerve fibres and excited considerable controversy. After further experiments, he confirmed his conclusions in an article that appeared in the *Journal of Comparative Neurology* in 1934.

With a developing international reputation in neuromuscular research, Wilkinson was appointed (Sir Thomas) Elder [q.v.4] professor of anatomy and histology at the University of Adelaide in 1930. He was awarded an M.D. by that university in 1934. In 1936 he moved to Brisbane to become foundation professor of anatomy and dean of the faculty of medicine at the University of Queensland's new medical school. He played a vital part in setting up the school and designing the buildings. After writing the foreword to Elizabeth Kenny's [q.v.9] contentious book *Infantile Paralysis and Cerebral Diplegia* (Sydney, 1937), he lost the support of those in the medical profession who were opposed to Kenny's methods of treating poliomyelitis.

In February 1938 members of the medical faculty were upset when a newspaper reported —without Wilkinson's prior knowledge—his suggestion that the university employ full-time clinicians to take charge of hospital departments concerned with teaching medical students. The proposal was intended as a compromise between the views of the doctors, who preferred to retain the honorary system, and of C. E. Chuter [q.v.13], under-secretary of the Department of Health and Home Affairs, who wanted full-time salaried specialist staff in public hospitals. Unable to convince the medical faculty that he had not 'leaked' his report to the press, he was replaced as dean. In 1944 the university conferred on him his third M.D. He served as dean again in 1954-57 and, after retiring in 1959 due to ill health, was made professor emeritus.

Of medium build and fair complexion, Wilkinson had an urbane and agreeable manner and a distinct presence. In 1945 he was president of the Royal Society of Queensland. A man of wide cultural interests, including music and the history of medicine, he constantly encouraged his students to take an interest in other disciplines. Known as 'Wilkie', he was celebrated in the students' song book as 'the cultured professor'. Since his school days he had been interested in Aboriginal culture: he was founding president (1948-50), vice-president (1951-55) and council-member (1956-60) of the Anthropological Society of Queensland. With L. P. Winterbotham [q.v.], he helped to found (1948) the ethnological museum at the university. Predeceased by his wife and son, he died on 15 February 1963 at Herston, Brisbane, and was cremated.

R. Kelly (ed), *The University of Queensland Union Song Book* (Brisb, 1947); R. L. Doherty (ed), *A Medical School for Queensland* (Brisb, 1986); H. Gregory, *Vivant Professores* (Brisb, 1987); G. Kenny, 'H. J. Wilkinson—the travail of a pioneer with muscle', in J. Pearn (ed), *Pioneer Medicine in Australia* (Brisb, 1988); M. J. Eadie, *The Flowering of a Waratah* (Syd, 2000); *MJA*, 8 June 1963, p 869; *Telegraph* (Brisb), 28 Feb 1938; Wilkinson personal file (Univ Qld Archives); information from Miss M. Wilkinson, Melb; personal information.

GEOFFREY KENNY

WILKINSON, HEYWOOD (1906-1977), coalmining engineer, was born on 22 June 1906 at East Greta, New South Wales, third of five sons of English-born parents Robert Bertram Wilkinson, an engine driver, and his wife Emma, née Higginson. After attending Greta Public and East Maitland Boys' High schools, in 1921 Heywood began work underground at the East Greta colliery. In 1929 he became a contract miner working for his father, then under-manager in the Broken Hill Proprietary Co. Ltd's John Darling colliery. Meanwhile, he attended night classes on coalmining and mine surveying at Cessnock, and at Newcastle Technical College. At St John's Church, Cessnock, on 2 December 1933 he married with Anglican rites Alma Irene Gibson, a typiste. They were to live at New Lambton.

After gaining wide practical experience in several mines, Wilkinson became under-manager in B.H.P.'s Burwood colliery, near Newcastle, in February 1935 and, in 1937, manager. He was awarded medals for his role in fighting the major 1938 underground fire at Waratah, a neighbouring colliery, and for eleven years service as a member of the New-castle Mines Rescue Committee. Appointed assistant superintendent of collieries for B.H.P. in 1945, he was promoted to super-intendent in 1954. Five years later, in August 1959, he became general superintendent of collieries for B.H.P. when the south coast coal-mines of Australian Iron and Steel Ltd were added to his responsibilities.

A leader in the modernization of coalmin-ing in Australia, Wilkinson backed the con-version from tracked to trackless mechanized methods. In 1947, 1957 and 1964 he travelled extensively overseas to study modern prac-tices, visiting the United States of America, Britain and Germany. He introduced inno-vative mechanization including an inclined conveyor drift at the Burwood colliery and oversaw the first successful longwall mining system in Australia at the Kemira colliery. Under his leadership, production and working conditions on both the north and south coal-fields improved enormously. In 1950 the out-put of coal in New South Wales was 13 million tons from 18 000 employees; by 1966 it had risen to over 25 million tons from 12 000 employees. While he was proud of his part in this achievement, he gave credit to his com-pany and many others.

Sponsored by Essington Lewis [q.v.10], Wil-kinson had joined the Australasian Institute of Mining and Metallurgy in 1945; he was a councillor (1957-66) and vice-president (1964-65), and was awarded the institute's medal for 1966 for 'his services to the coal industry, including his work in the introduction of mechanized mining practices and his great contribution to the development of human relations'. He served on advisory committees of the University of New South Wales and of the Department of Technical Education, and as an adviser to the State Mines Control Authority, the Goldfields Coal Syndicate's mine at Collie, Western Australia, and the Blair Athol Opencut Collieries Ltd, Queens-land. In addition, he was a director of Corrimal Coke Pty Ltd and Pacific Coal Co. Pty Ltd. He retired from B.H.P. in 1966 and was a member (1968-72) of the Joint Coal Board.

In private life Wilkinson's affability and earthy sense of humour led to warm friend-ships and close family ties. A straightforward man of strong character, tough, determined and willing to make courageous decisions, he was autocratic in his management style and a hard negotiator. He was respected by all, feared by some and trusted as a man of his

word by both trade union leaders and busi-ness colleagues. Money and position left him unaffected; he always retained his practical approach to life.

Of average height, Wilkinson was strongly built. He had a fair complexion, blue eyes—bespectacled in later life—and reddish, sandy hair. A founder and patron of the Burwood Colliery Bowling Club, he played bowls, dominoes (a game with him was obligatory for his colliery managers), golf (rarely) and an occasional game of cards. In particular, he loved fishing, usually in the estuary at Forster. On 23 December 1977, he set out with two other men from Taree in a powered dinghy to fish on the Manning River but was drowned when their boat capsized at Old Bar; he was cremated. His wife, and their son and daugh-ter survived him.

BHP Review, June 1947, Oct 1966; *Newcastle Morning Herald*, 17 Oct 1938, 26 Dec 1977; A'sian Inst of Mining and Metallurgy records (Melb); information from Mr J. Wasson, Syd, Mr W. Bris-bane, Mount Ousley, Mr S. R. Wilkinson, Ashton Field, Mr B. Duncan, Swansea Heads, NSW, and Mr J. Carthew, Urrbrae, Adel; family information.

D. F. FAIRWEATHER

WILLIAMS, CLIVE ANDREW (1915?-1980), Aboriginal leader, was born probably on 22 February 1915 at Casino, New South Wales, second of five children of Walter Williams, an Aboriginal tracker, and his wife Violet, née Joseph, from Queensland. Clive attended the public school and was one of few Aborigines accepted at Casino Intermediate High School. At the age of 15 he began work on the railways at Coonabarabran. He re-turned to Casino where he was employed in the butter factory. While still a young man, Williams planned to travel to Bellbrook on the Macleay River to participate in an initiation ceremony. He found, to his disappointment, that the ceremonies had recently been discon-tinued, as they had among his own Bundjalung people on the Richmond and Clarence rivers.

At St John's Presbyterian Church, Coraki, on 26 April 1941 Williams married Ida Drew, who had been taken from her parents by the Aborigines Protection Board. He built a rough dwelling and continued to work in the Casino butter factory. The family then lived for a time on the Aboriginal reserve, but in 1962 moved to a cottage in the town. In the mid-1960s Williams accepted accommodation at Tranby Co-operative College for Aborigines at Glebe, Sydney, where his work with Rev. Alfred Clint [q.v.13] and the Co-operative for Aborigines Ltd was highly regarded. He gained employ-ment with the Department of Main Roads and brought his growing family to their new home at Rozelle.

Having joined the Aboriginal-Australian Fellowship, Williams attended the annual conferences of the Federal Council for the Advancement of Aborigines and Torres Strait Islanders. Before the 1967 referendum, he helped in the successful campaign for the removal of the two offensive clauses in the Constitution relating to Aborigines. A member of the executive committee of the Aboriginal Education Council, he was involved with the early leadership training schools and other community development programmes. His wise counsel was appreciated.

In the 1960s the Commonwealth government was promoting the doctrine of 'assimilation', while Aboriginal organizations, especially F.C.A.A.T.S.I., wanted increased recognition of Aboriginal identity. Caught between two worlds, Williams was fiercely proud of his Aboriginal heritage but remained gentle and non-aggressive. In 1967 he took the leading role in a film, *One Man's Road*, produced by the Commonwealth Film Unit for the Department of Interior; in it he and Ida told of their life and struggles. He was dismayed to discover that the Department of Territories used the film as propaganda to promote assimilation.

Williams and his family returned to the North Coast where he quickly became involved with the community. He was a leader among a group of Aboriginal elders who worked with the administrators of the Northern Rivers College of Advanced Education towards the recognition of the interests of the Bundjalung and other Aboriginal communities in the area. Suffering from hypertension, Clive Williams died of myocardial infarction on 1 December 1980 at his Lismore home and was buried in Goonellabah cemetery. His wife, and their three sons and six daughters survived him.

Armidale and District Hist Soc, *J and Procs*, Oct 1962, p 28; *Identity*, July 1971, p 26; personal knowledge.   ALAN T. DUNCAN

WILLIAMS, SIR DUDLEY (1889-1963), judge, was born on 7 December 1889 at Milsons Point, Sydney, third child of Prosper Orleans Williams, solicitor, and his wife Florence Mary, née Milson, both born in Sydney. Dudley was a grandson of J. H. Williams [q.v.6] and a great-grandson of James Milson [q.v.2]. Educated at Sydney Church of England Grammar School (Shore) and the University of Sydney (B.A., 1912; LL.B., 1915), he gained awards for tennis and rowing at both institutions. He sailed to England in 1915 intending to join the British Army. On 31 August he was commissioned in the Royal Field Artillery Special Reserve. While serving on the Western Front, he rose to acting captain and won the Military Cross; he was also twice mentioned in dispatches. At All Souls Church of England, St Marylebone, London, on 15 March 1919 he married Catherine Agnes Rua Mackenzie Webster; she was a descendant of John Fairfax [q.v.4].

Returning to Sydney in mid-1919, Williams, who had been admitted to the Bar on 2 July 1915, was appointed associate to Sir William Cullen [q.v.8], chief justice of New South Wales. Two years later he began practising at the Bar. His career was to follow a pattern set by (Sir) George Rich [q.v.11] several decades earlier. Williams worked mainly in the Equity jurisdiction but also handled cases involving companies, wills, intellectual property and taxation. Gazetted K.C. on 1 March 1935, he was made an acting-judge of the Supreme Court of New South Wales on 17 November 1939; the appointment was confirmed in June 1940. On 15 October that year he was appointed to the High Court of Australia.

Williams was the first of eight High Court judges nominated by Prime Minister (Sir) Robert Menzies [q.v.15]. He and most of those whom Menzies chose after him conformed to a pattern: career lawyers, they were conservative by disposition but free from overt party political involvement, and were inclined to construe the Constitution in a legalistic fashion. In personality, background and interests, Williams was probably closer to Menzies' subsequent appointments—including those of the four who were to sit with him, (Sir) Wilfred Fullagar [q.v.14], (Sir) Frank Kitto, (Sir) Alan Taylor [q.v.] and (Sir) Douglas Menzies [q.v.15]—than he was to the judges whom he joined in 1940. Nevertheless, he shared the conservative approach of senior colleagues such as Rich and Sir Hayden Starke [q.v.12] and fitted in with the life of the court. Continuing to follow the example of Rich, he avoided publicity but he proved to be much more conscientious than the older man in writing judgements.

Like other members of the court, Williams supported a wide construction of the defence power during World War II. He joined his brethren in rejecting attempts by Prime Minister J. B. Chifley's [q.v.13] Australian Labor Party government to nationalize aviation (1945) and banking (1947). At the outset of the bank nationalization case (1948), he announced that he and his family had shareholdings in two private banks. Nevertheless, he refused to disqualify himself from hearing the challenge to the legislation, on the ground that he had no pecuniary interest in the shares which he held as trustee for his sister.

Williams enjoyed the camaraderie of the High Court. The work was arduous, the more so because the court was required to manage its business with only six members. A seventh justice, (Sir) William Webb [q.v.], was appointed in 1946. Four years later Fullagar and Kitto joined the court in place of the elderly Starke and Rich. Although Chief Justice Sir Owen Dixon [q.v.14] set the tone from 1952, Williams, with his equable temperament, helped to maintain the prestige of the court and its reputation as a civilized institution. He was a polite, kind man with a ready smile and a down-to-earth attitude. His thoughtful posture on the bench masked his love of sport, entertaining and dancing, and his fondness for popular musicals. He had studied Latin but not Greek. Often sitting in court between Dixon and Fullagar, who were both classical Greek scholars, he was not impressed by their practice of passing notes across him in Greek.

When dealing with constitutional cases— which in his time largely concerned the powers over defence, industrial disputes and interstate trade and commerce—Williams applied analytical techniques then commonly used by Equity lawyers; logic and precision were the hallmarks. Dixon was to eulogize the 'energy and unremitting application' which characterized his work and 'the careful, methodical and thorough investigation' he made of each case, no matter how complex. But these techniques did not necessarily foster the broader needs of a 'living' Constitution. Williams relished Equity appeals and those involving intellectual property, in which he and his peers sat as a single judge in the first instance. His experience in valuation law was widely recognized by his colleagues. Otherwise, he found his work demanding and uncongenial and towards the end of his career regretted that he had left the New South Wales Equity Court.

In 1952 Williams presided as acting chief justice for three months. Two years later he was appointed K.B.E. About 1957 his health began to fail and on 31 July 1958 he retired in Sydney. A conscientious craftsman, he had set himself modest targets on his appointment to the High Court, and he had met these aims. (Sir) Victor Windeyer who took his place on the bench praised him for his courtesy and learning. Sir Dudley had extensive pastoral interests. He was a keen gardener. Predeceased by his wife and survived by his son and four daughters, he died on 8 January 1963 at Paddington and was cremated.

G. Fricke, *Judges of the High Court* (Melb, 1986), and for sources; *Cwlth Law Reports*, 107, 1961-62; family information.　　　　GRAHAM FRICKE
　　　　　　　　　　　　　　SIMON SHELLER

WILLIAMS, GEORGE KENNETH (1896-1974), metallurgist, was born on 21 February 1896 at Tarnagulla, Victoria, third child of Victorian-born parents William Williams, schoolteacher, and his wife Laura, née Heyward. The family moved to Bacchus Marsh, where he attended state school and won a scholarship to Wesley College, Melbourne. Awarded a major scholarship to Queen's College, he studied mining engineering at the University of Melbourne (B.M.E., 1920; M.M.E., 1925; D.Eng., 1934).

In March 1919 Williams began work with Broken Hill Associated Smelters Pty Ltd, at the company's research station in South Melbourne. The facility investigated methods of improving the treatment of lead at B.H.A.S.'s smelting works, Port Pirie, South Australia. Gilbert Rigg, the technical director, instructed Williams to examine the Parkes refining process. This procedure, which used zinc to help separate gold and silver from lead bullion, was employed throughout the world. Involving a sequence of intricate heating and cooling operations, the process was inefficient and resulted in 'a great waste of fuel and loss of time'. Williams heated numerous mixtures of silver, lead and zinc to liquefaction then observed the behaviour of the metals as they cooled.

Transferred to Port Pirie in 1921, he applied his laboratory results in a series of trials. He worked under O. H. Woodward [q.v.12] who next year made him superintendent of the research department. Williams's new crust enrichment process, which markedly reduced the cost of producing silver, was patented and put into operation in 1923. He described his work in a paper published (1925) in the *Proceedings of the Australasian Institute of Mining and Metallurgy*, and submitted an expanded dissertation for his master's degree. On 26 May 1926 at St Paul's Church of England, Port Pirie, he married Phyllis Marion Bensley.

Williams set out to change the total lead-refining process from forty-eight episodic batch operations—carried out by large crews and requiring an extensive area—to a continuous flow process. After successful trials in late 1925, a semi-commercial de-silverizing plant was constructed. Extensive tests from August 1927 to the end of 1928 indicated the need for a larger, but still semi-commercial plant, with bigger kettles providing more space to allow the de-silvering crusts to form and be removed. A new series of tests began on 2 January 1929.

Although the costs were very high, both Woodward and (Sir) Colin Fraser [q.v.8], the chairman of the board, supported Williams. Work went on at a 'frantic' pace, spurred by Williams's enthusiasm and his rapport with his foremen and labouring staff. He discussed plant problems freely with his subordinates, explained the steps he was trying to achieve, and always listened to their ideas and suggestions. As a result, they became personally committed to the project. Frank Green recalled that he 'could be a hard driver, but the technical men received an unforgettable lesson in concentrated analytical thinking, persistence in the face of reverses and, above all, the will to succeed'. 'G.K.' had an ability to focus on the work needed to achieve results, and not to be diverted by peripheral issues.

Consistent commercial grades of lead were finally attained in August 1930 when Williams and his team began operating a large, three-section kettle successfully. An even larger, four-section kettle came into use in October. The timing was fortunate as the Depression soon reduced the amount of money available for research. Other stages of the continuous-flow refinery—the prior removal of arsenic, antimony and tin and the extraction of zinc after de-silverizing—were quickly implemented. During the subsequent preparations for commercial operations, the high-quality iron and steel castings required for the kettles were built by the Sydney firm of Bradford [q.v.13] Kendall Ltd. The cordial relations established between Williams and the managing director Jim Kendall were strengthened by their mutual love of horse-racing.

The big kettle was the vital unit in the continuous refining train. It was 'a monument to the genius' of Williams and 'one of the great achievements in modern non-ferrous metallurgy'. Patented, the process was 'duplicated in most of the large lead-producing areas of the world'. Williams ensured that royalty payments were divided equally among the staff and workmen involved in its development, and among the widows of those who had died. He published a description of his work in the *Proceedings* of the A.I.M.M. in 1932 and in a book, *The Development and Application of the Continuous Lead Refining Process* (Melbourne, undated), which established his international reputation as a leader in the field. The University of Melbourne awarded him the W. C. Kernot [q.v.5] medal for 1931. Additionally, he won the medal of the Australasian Institute of Mining and Metallurgy in 1942 and the gold medal of the Institution of Mining and Metallurgy (London) in 1951.

Williams was responsible (from 1930) for advances in the design of blast-furnaces used in the treatment of lead, and (from 1934) for improvements in the sintering process. He was appointed chief metallurgist in 1933, assistant general superintendent of B.H.A.S. in 1935 and works manager in 1942. Moving to Britain in 1948, he was metallurgical consultant to Consolidated Zinc Corporation Ltd and to Imperial Smelting Corporation Ltd in the development of its blast-furnace for the production of zinc at Avonmouth, Bristol. In 1957 he returned to Melbourne as a consultant to Consolidated Zinc Pty Ltd (Conzinc Riotinto of Australia Ltd from 1962). Retiring in 1966,

he lived in Adelaide. Queen's College, University of Melbourne, elected him a fellow in 1967, and the university established the G. K. Williams laboratory for extractive metallurgy. He died on 6 April 1974 in Adelaide, and was cremated. His wife and their two sons survived him.

F. A. Green, *The Port Pirie Smelters* (Melb, 1977); A'sian Inst of Mining and Metallurgy, *Procs*, no 129, 31 Mar 1943; Inst of Mining and Metallurgy, *Bulletin*, no 548, July 1952; *Age* (Melb), 9 Apr 1974.

D. F. BRANAGAN

WILLIAMS, IDRIS (1895-1960), coalminer and trade unionist, was born on 21 June 1895 at Mountain Ash, Glamorgan, Wales, son of David Williams, miner, and his wife Elizabeth, née Morgan. In the class-conscious Welsh mining valleys, Idris entered the pits aged 13 and began his lifelong involvement with unionism by joining the committee of the Powell Duffryn miners' lodge. He served in France with the Royal Field Artillery in World War I and lost his right leg in the battle of the Somme (1916). Disillusioned with the 'land fit for heroes', he left for Australia in 1920.

Soon after his arrival, Williams began mining black coal at Wonthaggi, Victoria. He became deeply involved in the cultural and sporting life of the town as a leading choral singer, conductor of the brass band, chairman of the miners' union theatre and secretary of the East Wonthaggi football club. His role in the historic five-month coal strike of 1934 was significant. As vice-president of the Victorian district of the Miners' Federation and a prominent member of the Minority Movement (an auxiliary of the Communist Party of Australia), he helped to pioneer new strike tactics and to gain for the town the dubious title of 'Red Wonthaggi'. His local popularity was immense. After the successful strike, he held office as president of the Wonthaggi District Trades and Labor Council, and State president (1934-46) and secretary (1946-47) of his union; he was also the first communist to serve (1944-47) on the Wonthaggi Borough Council.

On 18 August 1934 at Wonthaggi Williams married with Methodist forms his landlady Emily Amelia Matthews, née Barry (d.1950), a widow with three children. Idris and Emily were to have two children. Although he was very close to his family, none of them embraced his left-wing views. Honoured as Wonthaggi's 'finest citizen' and 'favourite son', he moved to Sydney in 1947 on his election as general president of the Miners' Federation, the first from outside New South Wales. He had stood as a communist candidate and had defeated his Labor opponent by a hefty majority of 1800 votes. His weekly salary was now

£12. In 1949 the foreign affairs sub-committee of the American House of Representatives absurdly named him as one of seven Australians who were 'ruthless directors of the Communist offensive in Europe and the Orient'. Williams was a loyal communist but a poor ideologue. He spoke the practical idiom of the pits more fluently than the theoretical language of the well-read Marxist.

Williams was obliged, however, to inject ideology into the industrial struggle in the winter of 1949. A general coal strike brought the union into direct conflict with the Chifley [q.v.13] government which, convinced that the stoppage had been engineered by the communists, responded savagely. Williams and other union officials were sentenced to twelve months gaol for contempt of court after they refused to reveal the whereabouts of £15 000 of union funds that emergency legislation had tried to 'freeze'; they were incarcerated for six weeks. Williams achieved a measure of martyrdom when, due to his imprisonment, the Department of Repatriation temporarily stopped his £9 weekly war-disability pension which it administered for the British government. Despite the collapse of the strike and the increasing chilliness of the Cold War, he was re-elected the following year with a record majority. Most coalminers believed, correctly, that he was a unionist first and a communist second.

From 1952 Williams's physical condition, already undermined by his war service and work in the mines, deteriorated further. He began to moderate his great fondness for tobacco (he was a chain-smoker) and alcohol (he was 'severely reprimanded' in January 1950 by party officials for 'excessive drinking') —but not his capacity for singing Welsh ballads at union functions. In February 1955 he resigned from the union leadership on grounds of ill health. For the last five years of his life, he was active in the retired mineworkers' association and the Illawarra branch of the C.P.A. He underwent major heart surgery in 1958.

At the district registrar's office, Hurstville, on 19 December 1958 Williams married Lilian Frances Perry, née Binskin, a widow. Suffering from cancer, he died of cerebrovascular disease on 9 October 1960 in Sydney and was cremated. His wife survived him, as did the son and daughter of his first marriage. Throughout the coal industry and the wider labour movement he had been regarded as a union official of integrity and sincerity. A communist colleague eulogized his 'devotion to his ideals', and 'the warmth of his personality, the kindness of his disposition', and 'the essential humanity of his approach to life'.

E. Ross, *A History of the Miners' Federation of Australia* (Syd, 1970); *Common Cause*, 22 Jan, 12 Mar 1955, 15, 22 Oct 1960; *Tribune* (Syd), 4 Apr 1947, 23 July, 10 Aug 1949, 12 Oct 1960; *Daily Telegraph* (Syd), 24 June 1949; *Express* (Wonthaggi, Vic), 13 Oct 1960; P. Cochrane, The Wonthaggi Coal Strike 1934 (B.A. Hons thesis, La Trobe Univ, 1973); A6119, items 890, 902 and 903, and M1509, item 36 (NAA, Canb).

PHILLIP DEERY

WILLIAMS, KATHERINE MARY ISABEL (1895-1975), unionist, was born on 23 April 1895 at Lara, Victoria, second of five children of Edward Crombie Chambers, an articled law clerk from Queensland, and his locally born wife Jane Miriam, née Harding. After attending Melbourne University High School, Kath graduated from the Melbourne College of Domestic Economy in 1915 and commenced teaching at Daylesford the next year. Reports on her teaching described her as bright, hard-working and reliable. On 31 March 1917 at Box Hill she married, with the forms of the Churches of Christ, Percy James Clarey [q.v.13], a young trade union leader. Kath supported and encouraged his political ambitions.

Devoted to the Australian Labor Party, Mrs Clarey became secretary of its Caulfield branch, president of the Women's Organising Committee and a member of the State executive. She stood as Labor candidate for the seat of Caulfield in the Legislative Assembly election of 1935 but withdrew before the poll. In December, with Maurice Blackburn [q.v.7] and others, she was excluded from the A.L.P., having spoken at a rally organized by the Victorian Council against War and Fascism; contrary to the party's policy, she advocated that sanctions be imposed against Italy, after its invasion of Abyssinia. She was reinstated the following year. Her developing radical views and activities had strained the marriage; in 1936 she joined the Communist Party of Australia and she and Clarey were divorced in December. She was granted custody of their younger son.

Returning to teaching in 1938, at Portland, Kath transferred in 1942 to Wonthaggi, where she threw herself into local activities and supported the miners. On 11 August 1945 at the office of the government statist, Melbourne, she married an English-born coalminer, Anthony ('Andy') Williams. The marriage was unsuccessful; she returned to Melbourne in 1948 and became an organizer for the Liquor Trades Union. She immediately took up the issue of equal pay for women. Her position on the State committee of the Communist Party (from 1948) enabled her to apply pressure on her trade union comrades. She presented the case for equal pay as union delegate to the Melbourne Trades Hall Council and, after the Australian Council of Trade Unions' congress of 1953 agreed to establish equal pay committees in each State, Mrs Williams was elected secretary of the Victorian committee. She also became a delegate to A.C.T.U. conferences. An observer at the first World Conference of Working Women, held in Budapest in 1956, she presented a paper on the campaign in Australia. When she returned, she wrote a booklet about the struggle, *Equality Will Be Won* (1956).

Kath Williams was the dynamic force behind the equal pay campaign in Victoria during the 1950s and 1960s. She organized meetings, conferences and street demonstrations, addressed gatherings, participated in deputations, and produced leaflets and circulars to be distributed to all unions. In 1963 she resigned from the C.P.A. and joined the new Communist Party of Australia (Marxist-Leninist). Williams retired from her position as union organizer in 1967. Having seen equal pay become a reality for Australian women, she died on 17 April 1975 at Oakleigh and was buried in Springvale cemetery. The two sons of her first marriage survived her.

A. Best, *The History of the Liquor Trades Union in Victoria* (Melb, 1990); Z. D'Aprano, *Kath Williams* (Melb, 2001); Labour Hist, Melb, *Recorder*, no 76, June 1975, p 16; *Argus*, 16 Mar 1939, 12 Jan 1953; *Sun News-Pictorial*, 5 July 1963.

ZELDA D'APRANO

WILLIAMS, MERVYN LOUIS (1902-1980), boxer and sports writer, was born on 12 March 1902 at Aramac, Queensland, son of Charles Williams, station overseer, and his wife Delia Isabella, née Phillips, both Queensland born. Educated at Ipswich Grammar School, Merv was State amateur middleweight boxing champion at age 17 and undefeated when he turned professional at 18. He worked as a blacksmith's hand, miner and breadcarter to harden his medium build.

In 1922 Williams defeated Max Gornik for the Queensland middleweight title, the first of his three State championships. Williams never gained a national title, losing at his last attempt to George Thompson, the Australian heavyweight champion, in April 1930. A skilful combatant with a formidable right cross, by then Williams had competed tenaciously with a damaged hand for six years, regaining the State middleweight title against Harry Casey, a spoiler, in July. A bored crowd booed them, one man hurling a bottle. Lured from retirement by a purse of £100 in December 1931, Williams was pounded to the canvas seven times by Fred Henneberry at Leichhardt Stadium, Sydney.

To supplement his income, Williams sold cars in Sydney, and then managed hotels 'where I had more fights than I ever had in the ring'. In 1932 he moved to Melbourne. At the Preston Presbyterian Church on 21 May that year he married Floris Elizabeth (Betty) McAlley, a photographic employee. For the next six years he refereed at the Fitzroy and West Melbourne stadiums. After a close contest in May 1938, he ruled that an overseas boxer, Claude Varner, had defeated the heavily backed Australian featherweight champion Mickey Miller. Williams's decision caused a riot and his employers, Stadiums Ltd, promptly sacked him. Because the fight was close, he could have followed the wishes of the spectators and crowned Miller but he stated that 'a referee who gives decisions to suit the crowds is true neither to himself nor to the fighters'.

The *Sporting Globe* immediately hired Williams to report the rematch. In his article he fearlessly suggested foul play; Varner's aggression and superb in-fighting skills were strangely absent causing him to lose. Thereafter, Williams covered all sports for the newspaper, as well as producing a weekly report on boxing. He wrote and spoke flamboyantly, one article in 1939 describing a boxer as being 'as cool as the tip of an Eskimo's nose'. The cigar-smoking, joke-cracking Williams, whose black-rimmed glasses were pinned by ears thickened from boxing, broadcast his 'Mervisms' on radio 3DB's 'Sports Forum', and later on HSV7's 'TV Ringside'. Tired and beaten boxers 'couldn't run out of sight on a dark night', 'swayed like a jelly in a wind', or 'had less chance than a crippled prawn in a flock of seagulls'.

Williams's integrity and his fatherly advice to boxers were notable and were informed by his view that pugilists did not enjoy fighting; to them it was a job. As a fighter, referee and journalist, he was known as 'Mr Boxing'. He raised funds for the Royal Children's Hospital, describing his involvement as 'one of the greatest and most rewarding of all life's tasks'; from 1960 to 1964, when he suffered a heart attack, he carried out the strenuous, year-round duties of director of the *Sporting Globe*-3DB-HSV7 Good Friday Appeal. Predeceased by his wife and survived by his only daughter, he died on 6 January 1980 at Heidelberg and was cremated with Anglican rites.

Brisb Courier, 15 Feb, 5 Apr, 5 May, 21 July 1930; *SMH*, 24 Aug, 5 Dec 1931, 9 Jan 1980; *Sporting Globe*, 18 May, 1 June 1938, 22 Jan 1980; *Herald* (Melb), 5 Mar 1960, 13 Apr 1963; *Sun News-Pictorial*, 8 Jan 1980; Williams papers (NL).

RICHARD BROOME

WILLIAMS, REES DAVID ('BARNEY') (1910-1979), bank clerk and trade unionist, was born on 15 June 1910 at Moonee Ponds, Melbourne, third child of Victorian-born parents David Williams, teacher, and his wife Martha Amy Olivia, née Etheridge. 'Barney' attended state schools at Ascot Vale and Essendon before proceeding to Scotch College. He joined the Moonee Ponds branch of the State Savings Bank of Victoria in 1925, transferred to head office six months later, studied part time at the University of Melbourne and obtained a diploma of commerce (1948). At St James's Catholic Church, Elsternwick, on 11 December 1940 he married Ellenor Sheila O'Brien, a clerk, with whom he moved to Sandringham. Sheila's brother-in-law was Francis Field, an Australian Labor Party member (from 1937) of the Legislative Assembly. Influenced by Field and the O'Brien family, Williams had joined the A.L.P. shortly before his marriage. In 1941 he was elected secretary of its Sandringham branch.

On 23 February 1942 Williams enlisted in the Australian Imperial Force. He performed pay and accounts duties in Victoria, rose to staff sergeant and was discharged from the army on 21 November 1945. After returning to his job with the bank, he invested in a biscuit-factory which he managed in his spare time with his brother-in-law John O'Brien. They lost about £4000 in the venture. On 25 February 1947 the Cain [q.v.13] government, in which Field was deputy-premier, appointed Williams a commissioner of the State Savings Bank; his seven-year term was subsequently renewed. The Opposition, the press and Williams's former workmates regarded the appointment as nepotism. Williams supplemented his commissioner's stipend of £500 per annum by practising privately as an accountant.

When the government was defeated in November 1947, Williams sought a paid trade-union position. By April 1950 he had won a campaign to become secretary of both the State and federal branches of the Australian Bank Officials' Association (Australian Bank Employees Union from 1978). He held these posts until 1973, played a critical role in fostering increased militancy and led the A.B.O.A. in its first industrial action (1968). During this period organizations that represented white-collar workers ceased to be 'gentlemen's clubs' and became trade unions. As federal secretary (from 1956) of the Australian Council of Salaried and Professional Associations, Williams dreamed of uniting its constituent bodies and 'delivering them in a wheelbarrow' to the Australian Council of Trade Unions.

Williams had been converted to Catholicism in 1949. Within the A.L.P. he was regarded as a 'numbers man' and a moderate. In the years that preceded the party's split in the mid-1950s, he paid a heavy personal price for his commitment to mainstream Labor: supporters of both the right and left wings often vilified him, as did members of the Catholic community. From 1965 he led a largely right-wing group, the Participants, who sought to

make the party more attractive to a broader section of the electorate. He established an influential network of friends, among them John Button, R. J. L. Hawke and Gough Whitlam, and tried to build bridges between the A.L.P. and white-collar unions.

In March 1973 the Whitlam government appointed Williams a director of the Commonwealth Banking Corporation. He resigned in November to become (from 3 December) a deputy-president of the Commonwealth Conciliation and Arbitration Commission. Unhappy on the bench, he stepped down in January 1975 and returned to the board of the Commonwealth Bank. Although he was a public figure, he kept his personal life private. Loyal to his friends, he could be fierce towards his opponents. He was unwavering in his commitment to radicalizing the white-collar unions and to reforming the A.L.P. in order to make it a party of government. Hawke described him as 'the most selfless man I ever met in the trade union movement and the A.L.P.'. Williams suffered from hypertension. Survived by his wife, and their daughter and two sons, he died of a coronary occlusion on 28 July 1979 at Sandringham and was buried in New Cheltenham cemetery.

K. White, *Barney, the Story of Rees D. Williams, Architect of the White-Collar Union Movement* (Melb, 1989), and for bib.   KATE WHITE

WILLIAMSON, ADA JEAN HOUNSELL (1891-1977), journalist, was born on 31 October 1891 at Belmont, New South Wales, eldest of five children of native-born parents John Alexander Williamson, contractor, and his wife Ada Mary Theobald, née Hannell. Known as Jean, to distinguish her from her mother, she was privately educated at Newcastle. She began her career as a freelance contributor to the *Australian Town and Country Journal*, *Evening News* and *Sunday Sun*. In 1916 she joined the staff of the Sydney-based *Farmer and Settler* newspaper, where for two years she conducted the women's page. John Fairfax & Sons [qq.v.4,8] Ltd offered her a cadetship on the *Sydney Morning Herald* in 1918. She soon succeeded Florence Baverstock as social editor, working in a tiny corner of the *Herald* building, which she maintained was the office broom-cupboard.

Baverstock's daughter Dolly, who worked with Williamson, remembered her as 'a big, lazy, sweet-natured woman' who never seemed flustered. She was easy going, forthright, sometimes bawdy, and jovial with her fellow workers. Often absent from work, due to illness, she was dismissed in November 1919. In a letter begging for reinstatement, she explained that 'last year was an abnormal year for me. The week I joined the staff, my fiancé, Lt Atkinson, died as a result of disease contracted while on active service. Then sickness was rampant in my own home, so that the loss I sustained and general worries all brought about my breakdown, rather than the strenuousness of my duties'. Allowed to continue, she was promoted to 'senior grade' in 1926 and A grade by 1929. She was a staunch member of the Australian Journalists' Association. In 1927 she covered the opening of Parliament House in Canberra by the Duke of York, receiving a special dress allowance of £20.

Williamson joined the staff of (Sir) Frank Packer and E. G. Theodore's [qq.v.15,12] new magazine, the *Australian Women's Weekly*, in June 1933. Expecting to be an administrative editor, she was surprised when asked to take charge of fiction. By 1934, she edited a page entitled 'New Books'. She recalled: 'I didn't like it at first but there came an upsurge of excitement when country women began writing such intimate letters saying how The Weekly enriched their lives—revealing unconsciously their loneliness. I began to think of the shortage of lighter-type reading matter in my family home in the country and my ideas changed'.

In 1936 Packer and Theodore established Consolidated Press Ltd, which took over the *Weekly*, and in March launched the revamped *Daily Telegraph*. They appointed Williamson as one of its 'Ten Brilliant Editors', describing her as combining 'a rare understanding of women's interests with a polished newspaper technique'. After organizing the enlarged women's section, she soon returned to the *Weekly* as fiction editor. She selected weekly serials by such well-known authors as Dornford Yates (1934), Agatha Christie (1943), Duff Cooper (1949) and Georgette Heyer (1954), as well as three or four short stories per issue. Few writers were Australian, although she did include works by Dorothy Cottrell [q.v.8] and Nevil Shute [q.v.15 Norway] in the 1950s.

By the time Jean Williamson retired in 1959 the formula had scarcely changed. Her hobby was breeding prize-winning poultry. She died on 14 January 1977 at the Masonic Hospital, Ashfield, and was cremated. She had never married.

D. McNicoll, *Luck's a Fortune* (Syd, 1979); D. O'Brien, *The Weekly* (Melb, 1982); V. Lawson, *Connie Sweetheart* (Melb, 1990); *Newspaper News*, 2 Mar 1936, p 15, 10 July 1959, p 1; *Journalist*, Mar 1977, p 5; *Daily Telegraph* (Syd), 17 Mar 1936, p 5; John Fairfax Group Pty Ltd Archives, Syd.

VALERIE LAWSON

WILLIAMSON, WILLIAM JAMES (1922-1979), jockey, was born on 19 December 1922 at Williamstown, Melbourne, son of Victorian-born parents William James Williamson, machinist, and his wife Euphemia Agnes, née Whitehead. Fascinated early by horses, Bill left Mordialloc-Chelsea High School at age 14 and was apprenticed to the trainer F. H. Lewis; he and his brother the jockey Robert Lewis [q.v.10] were Bill's great-uncles. Williamson's first winning ride was in 1937 on Lilirene, coincidentally the last winner that Bobby Lewis had ridden. On 5 January 1942 Williamson was mobilized for full-time duty in the Militia. He served in Melbourne as a driver with the 119th General Transport Company and as a clerk at the Bulk Stationery Store. Discharged from the army on 30 October 1944, he returned to the racetrack.

On one occasion in 1946 Williamson missed his train and had to hitchhike to a race-meeting at Albury, New South Wales. Engaged for five events at the meeting, he triumphed in all of them. On 17 January 1949 at St Paul's Church of England, Caulfield, Melbourne, he married Zelma Ava Dickman, a hairdresser. His first Victorian jockeys' premiership came in the 1951-52 season. He rode Dalray to victory in the 1952 Melbourne Cup.

Williamson won five more Victorian jockeys' premierships. Horses ridden by him took first place in the W. S. Cox Plate and Brisbane Cup (Hydrogen in 1953), the Duke of Edinburgh Australian Cup (Sunish in 1954), the Caulfield Cup (Rising Fast in 1955 and Ilumquh in 1960) and many other major events. He set a Victorian record in the 1953-54 season, securing the jockeys' premiership with sixty-seven and a half winners. In October 1954 he suffered life-threatening injuries in a fall during the running of the One Thousand Guineas and was out of racing for about nine months.

After riding successfully in Malaya in 1959, Williamson moved to Europe in 1960. Based first in Ireland then in England, he enjoyed wins in numerous important races, often in the company of three other expatriate Australian jockeys: George Moore, Neville Sellwood [q.v.] and A. E. 'Scobie' Breasley. Williamson was victorious in the Prix de l'Arc de Triomphe at Longchamp, Paris, in 1968 and 1969. The second of these rides, on Levmoss at 50/1, drew from Lester Piggott the compliment that Williamson was 'the best big-race jockey in the world'.

Sleepy-eyed and laconic, Williamson was known to racegoers as 'Weary Willie' because of his impassive appearance, whether his races ended in victory, defeat or controversy. His outstanding qualities as a rider were his ability to judge a horse's pace, his patience and his sense of timing. In 1971 he rode in France for the Aga Khan. On his retirement in 1973 he was appointed racing manager for the Indian shipping magnate Ravi Tikkoo. Williamson returned to Melbourne in 1977 and took a position as assistant-starter with the

Victoria Racing Club. He died of cancer on 28 January 1979 at South Caulfield and was buried in New Cheltenham cemetery. His wife and their two sons survived him.

M. Cavanough, *The Melbourne Cup* (Syd, 1978); J. Pollard, *Australian Horse Racing* (Syd, 1988); G. Hutchinson (ed), *They're Racing* (Melb, 1999); *People* (Syd), 21 Oct 1953; *Daily Mirror* (Syd), 8 Feb 1974; *Age* (Melb), 29 Jan 1979.   BRIAN STODDART

WILLIS, RUPERT ALLAN (1898-1980), pathologist, was born on 24 December 1898 at Yarram, Victoria, elder son of Australian-born parents Benjamin James Willis, bank accountant, and his wife Mary Elizabeth Giles, née James. Educated at Yarram State and Melbourne High schools, and the University of Melbourne (M.B., B.S., 1922; M.D., 1929; D.Sc., 1932), he spent two years as a resident medical officer at the Alfred Hospital, Melbourne. On 14 February 1924 at Warrandyte he married with Presbyterian forms Alice Margaret Tolhurst (d.1962), a nurse. The couple moved to Lilydale, Tasmania, where Rupert entered general practice and carried out histological research in a backyard laboratory, studying diseased tissue from animals.

Returning to Melbourne in 1927, Willis was appointed medical superintendent of the Austin Hospital for Incurable and Chronic Diseases, Heidelberg. One reform he instituted was to remove the word 'Incurable' from the institution's title. His studies resulting from the hundreds of post-mortem examinations he performed there, many on cancer victims, led to the award of his doctorates.

Willis became hospital pathologist at the Alfred Hospital in 1930. His first monograph, *The Spread of Tumours in the Human Body* (London, 1934), was based on his work, for which he was to be awarded the David Syme [q.v.6] research prize (1935). Granted a Rockefeller Foundation fellowship in 1933, he conducted research on the transplantation of embryonic tissues at the Buckston Browne Research Farm at Downe, Kent, England, under Sir Arthur Keith. Back at the Alfred in 1935, he demonstrated post-mortem examinations for medical students and lectured at the university. Under his guidance the hospital's output in pathological testing trebled by 1940.

In 1945 Willis was appointed Collins professor of human and comparative pathology at the Hunterian Museum of the Royal College of Surgeons, London. He published *Pathology of Tumours* in 1948. That year he transferred to the Royal Cancer Hospital, Fulham, as director of pathology, his work resulting in *Principles of Pathology* (1950). In 1950 he moved to the University of Leeds as professor of pathology. The duties included research,

teaching, administration and consultation with regional medical practitioners. His personal research was to culminate in *The Borderland of Embryology and Pathology* (1958). Retiring and unassuming by nature, he found university politics and committee work a stressful distraction from scholarship. Recurring illness eventually prompted his early retirement to Nancledra, Cornwall, in 1955.

At his cottage, Riverside, Willis developed a private laboratory supported by Medical Research Council grants. The University of Leeds allowed doctoral students to work with him there. Assessing the effects of cigarette smoke on the lung tissue of rats was a major project of the laboratory from 1959. Next year he and Margaret revisited Australia; he was keynote speaker at the first Victorian Cancer Congress. He occupied the Macfarlane chair of experimental medicine at the University of Glasgow, Scotland, in 1963-64, and returned to Australia for three extended working holidays in 1964-65, 1973-74 and 1975-76. In 1969 he had moved to Heswall, Cheshire, to live in semi-retirement with his daughter and her family.

Five ft 4 ins (163 cm) tall and wiry, Willis was dark-haired, of ruddy-brown complexion and meticulously neat in dress and personal habits. A generous friend, he enjoyed warm relationships with his colleagues, staff and students. He had diverse talents and interests —acrobatics, juggling, Chinese porcelain, classical music, gardening and mineralogy. Proud of his origins, he always travelled on an Australian passport. As well as fellowships in the Royal colleges of Physicians, Surgeons and Pathologists, England, the Royal Australasian College of Physicians and the Royal College of Pathologists of Australia (Australasia), he received honorary doctorates from the universities of Perugia, Italy, and Glasgow. He died on 26 March 1980 at Birkenhead, Merseyside, and was cremated with Anglican rites; his daughter and son survived him. Harley Griffiths' portrait of him is held by the Austin & Repatriation Medical Centre.

Dept of Pathology, Univ Melb, *The Melbourne School of Pathology* (Melb, 1962); A. M. Mitchell, *The Hospital South of the Yarra* (Melb, 1977); E. W. Gault and A. Lucas, *A Century of Compassion* (Melb, 1982); G. L. McDonald (ed), *Roll of the Royal Australasian College of Physicians*, 2, 1976-1990 (Syd, 1994); *MJA*, 13 Jan 1979, p 15, 9 Aug 1980, p 166; *American J of Surgical Pathology*, 4, no 5, Oct 1980, p 511; *Pathology*, 12, Oct 1980, p 649; Joint Autobiography of Margaret and Rupert Willis (ms, LaTL).

IAN HOWIE-WILLIS

WILLMORE, GEORGE MALCOLM (1895-1978), real-estate developer, was born on 24 September 1895 at Islington, London, son of

George John Willmore, assurance agent, and his wife Daisy Annie Julia, née Holmes. G. J. Willmore was later a Salvation Army missionary. After migrating to Australia as an adolescent, young George became a salesman. On 1 November 1914 he enlisted in the Australian Imperial Force and in April 1915 landed at Gallipoli with the 4th Battalion. Suffering from shock, he was evacuated in August to England where he performed staff duties and rose to warrant officer (1919). On 23 September 1916 he married Annie Jane Helena Hall at the register office, West Ham, London. He was discharged from the A.I.F. in Sydney on 23 May 1920.

Employed briefly by the Bureau of Meteorology at Narrabri, New South Wales, Willmore returned to Sydney where he worked in advertising and met a salesman, Reginald Randell. Becoming business partners, the pair first manufactured non-slip floor polish which they sold to the Myer [qq.v.10,15] retail business. In 1925, having acquired an office in Bligh Street and a motorcycle with side-car, they established a real-estate agency, Willmore & Randell Ltd. They proclaimed the firm to be 'Sydney's largest and most progressive organisation specialising in the management and control of subdivisions', and claimed to have sold over £1 million worth of Sydney real estate in 1927-28.

Newspaper advertisements solicited business, offering to realize estates for landowners quickly. Willmore personally wrote the detailed marketing material which touted high capital growth at terms as low as a shilling a day, covenants to prevent 'the encroachment of undesirable buildings', and 'glorious breeze-cooled positions . . . of rare charm'. Free train fares or inspections by motorcar offered further incentive to prospective clients. The business expanded until there were almost fifty offices in South Australia, Victoria, New South Wales and Queensland. The Willmore family lived at Vaucluse, in a home which boasted housemaids and gardeners, and a Buick motorcar in the garage.

The onset of the Depression in 1929 damaged business; within a year all offices had closed and Willmore & Randell was in liquidation. Willmore sold the Vaucluse property, and the family lived for a time in a house at Randwick; (Sir) Leslie Hooker [q.v.14] personally collected the rent. Prospects remained poor until 1935 when Willmore and others formed a new real-estate company, and the Willmore & Randell name once again appeared in Sydney and Melbourne. The Willmores moved to Rose Bay. Property markets were sluggish after World War II because of government controls over land sales, but activity picked up about 1950. The firm began to specialize in subdividing large tracts of land outside cities, developing new suburbs with hundreds or even thousands of building blocks, and providing infrastructure and community facilities, ranging from halls and kindergartens to American-influenced resort-style features. During the mid-1950s the partnership was divided in all but name; Randell took over the Victorian and South Australian operations and Willmore controlled the business in New South Wales and Queensland. Willmore aimed to be the 'Woolworths of real estate'; eventually the company became one of the largest broad-acre subdivision firms in Australia.

In 1965 Willmore and his wife obtained a Mexican divorce, and on 11 March 1969 at Las Vegas, Nevada, United States of America, he married Gertrude Elizabeth Gardiner, a 37-year-old widow. In 1974 the company's major financier, Cambridge Credit Corporation Ltd, was placed in receivership. During the ensuing crisis, most of the firm's numerous subsidiaries received wind-up notices but the parent company survived. Next year Willmore moved to Queensland and managed the Brisbane office. In April 1978 his wife announced that she proposed to begin divorce proceedings.

Described by his son Ian as fiery-tempered, and a 'very complex man, full of ideas, impatient, commanding, and not at all pleased if anyone else seemed to be outclassing him even in a small way', Willmore was dynamic, autocratic and somewhat intimidating. Real-estate colleagues recalled an extravagant host, a natural risk-taker with breadth of vision, imagination, and a daring and ruthless approach to business. He had 'a remarkable ability to make money, and an equal ability to spend it'. A small dapper man, he was fond of fine suits, Rolls Royces and the bright lights of Sydney, New York and Hollywood. He 'tipped his manicurist and hairdresser with blocks of land, [and] spent lavishly in Sydney's night spots and on five-star travel overseas'. Particularly generous to his grandchildren, he was a dominant presence in family life. He died on 26 July 1978 at Buderim, Queensland, and was cremated with Christian Science forms. His wife, and the three daughters and three sons of his first marriage, survived him.

I. Willmore and E. Warburton, *Willmore & Randell* (Syd, 1994); *Brisb Courier*, 8 Jan, 6 Nov 1929, 5 July 1930; *Courier-Mail*, 1 Aug 1978; *SMH*, 5 Aug 1978; information from Mr I. G. V. and Mrs B. Willmore, Bellevue Hill, Syd, and Mr L. Willmore, Sunnybank Hills, Dr C. Jones, Camp Hill, and Mrs M. Welch, Arana Hills, Brisb.   JUDITH A. NISSEN

WILLOUGHBY, JOHN EDWARD (1908-1962), public servant, was born on 22 August 1908 at Guildford, Sydney, eldest child of

Charles Anthony Willoughby, painter and later mayor of Granville, and his wife Edith Roslyn, née Evans, both born in New South Wales. Educated at Guildford Public and Parramatta Boys' Intermediate High schools, John (also known as Jack) began work on 2 February 1925 as a clerk with the Metropolitan Water, Sewerage and Drainage Board. In his spare time he served in the Militia (1926-32), held various positions in the Boy Scouts' Association (until 1935) and rowed for Drummoyne; he was a member of the VIII which won the lightweight State championship in 1931 and 1932. At St Stephen's Church, Chatswood, on 8 September 1934 he married with Anglican rites Anna Christina Grace Finlay, a comptometrist.

Having taken a succession of Workers' Educational Association and University Extension Board courses in 1934-38, Willoughby matriculated in 1940. He studied at the University of Sydney (B.Ec., 1944), graduating with second-class honours. While at university he had won (1943) the Sir George Murray [q.v.10] essay competition run by the South Australian branch of the Institute of Public Administration. In April 1944 he was lent to the Commonwealth Department of Post-war Reconstruction as a temporary senior investigation officer, based in Canberra. There he was closely involved in policy planning by the re-establishment division. He also acted as secretary and executive officer of a number of inter-departmental committees. In 1945 he moved his family to Canberra and in December next year was permanently appointed to the Commonwealth Public Service as senior research officer in the division of economic policy.

In May 1947 Willoughby was promoted senior project officer in the office of the Public Service Board, Prime Minister's Department, where he worked on staff-training and recruitment policies, including the establishment of cadetship schemes. He lectured part time in public administration and political science at Canberra University College in 1948-50. Promoted assistant-inspector in July 1949, he was appointed assistant-secretary (research and development, later industries and commerce) in the Department of External Territories (Department of Territories from 1951) in March 1950. He headed the division which formulated policy advice to the minister on matters of economic development. A key issue for Papua and New Guinea with which he contended was the tension between the need for rapid development of the economic and revenue base by capital and entrepreneurship from outside, and the fundamental need, recognized by the minister, (Sir) Paul Hasluck, to ensure that adequate resources were kept unalienated to meet the future needs of the indigenous people.

Promoted to first assistant secretary in July 1956, Willoughby deputized for the secretary in all of the department's activities, with particular responsibility for budgetary and public-service matters. The building up of fiscal self-reliance in Papua and New Guinea, including the very unpopular introduction of income tax, and the beginning of a programme to replace expatriate with local officers in the Territory's public service, were examples of significant measures which required his sound and far-sighted thinking. Within Australia, substantial action was taken to counter the health, educational and economic disadvantages of the Northern Territory's Aborigines. For Nauru, attention focused on the future of the small population when the phosphate deposits there were worked out towards the end of the century.

In 1961 Willoughby chaired a committee, consisting of representatives of the Prime Minister's Department, the Papua and New Guinea administration, and the Australian School of Pacific Administration, which examined all aspects of tertiary education and higher training in Papua and New Guinea. The committee's recommendations set the pattern for the development of tertiary institutions, including the Administrative College, the Institute of Higher Technical Education, teacher- and medical-training colleges, and eventually the University of Papua and New Guinea.

Of middle height, with dark, wavy hair, Willoughby had a restrained but confident manner, and a marked ability to develop the talents of his subordinates and delegate policy-advising work to them, while still making his own capable contribution. He listed his recreations as reading and colour photography. Survived by his wife, and their two daughters and two sons, he died of a coronary occlusion on 23 June 1962 while playing golf at the Royal Canberra Golf Club and was buried with Methodist forms in Canberra cemetery.

P. Hasluck, *A Time for Building* (Melb, 1976); *Canb Times*, 25 June 1962; Willoughby papers (NL); personal file, CP268/3, item Willoughby J E, applications for positions, A1361, item 34/1/12 pt 1894 (NAA, Canb); information from Mrs D. Carroll, Red Hill, Canb; personal knowledge.

ROBERT S. SWIFT

WILLS, SIR KENNETH AGNEW (1896-1977), army officer and businessman, was born on 3 March 1896 at Kent Town, Adelaide, youngest of four children of Richard John Henry Wills, a South Australian-born merchant, and his wife Caroline Agnew, née Fedden, who came from Scotland. A year after her husband's death in 1901, Caroline Wills took the family back to Britain. Ken was educated at University College School, London.

He hoped to become a doctor, but at the start of World War I volunteered for military service. Commissioned on 26 August 1914 in the Prince of Wales's Own Civil Service Rifles, he saw action on the Western Front (1916 and 1918) and in Greece (1916-17) and Palestine (1917-18), and rose to temporary captain. In 1918 he was awarded the Military Cross and, suffering from the effects of mustard gas, invalided to England.

After the war Wills was employed in London by his family's company, George Wills & Sons Ltd, shipping and forwarding agents. He worked at the Baltic Mercantile & Shipping Exchange Ltd, canvassing for cargoes between London and Australia. On 1 September 1920 at All Saints Church of England, Fulham, he married Viola Ethel Crossland (d.1956). Next year the firm sent him to South Australia. Appointed a director (1924) and managing director (1928), he restructured the company and set up headquarters in Adelaide. Under his management it flourished as a wholesale distributor of clothing, textiles and fancy goods. He guided the firm through the Depression, acquiring substantial holdings in cement, hardware and other manufacturing companies; by 1936 the company was again making a profit.

On 3 September 1939 Wills was mobilized for full-time service in the Citizen Military Forces and on 1 June 1940 was appointed major, Australian Imperial Force. In September he joined the headquarters of I Corps in the Middle East. He took part in the campaigns in Libya (January-February 1941), Greece (April-May) and Syria (June-July), and for his work was appointed O.B.E. (1941). Promoted lieutenant colonel in June, he returned to Australia in March 1942. Next month he was made temporary colonel (substantive October 1944) and posted as general staff officer, grade one (intelligence), at First Army headquarters. He was deputy-director of military intelligence at Advanced Land Headquarters, Brisbane (January-August 1943 and March-October 1944), and at headquarters, New Guinea Force (September 1943-March 1944). His clerk Sid Jordan described him as a good soldier, sharp, tough and fair, a man who 'took the shortest route to an object'. Wills was mentioned in dispatches for his services in New Guinea.

Made temporary brigadier, on 17 October 1944 he was appointed controller, Allied Intelligence Bureau, responsible to Douglas MacArthur's [q.v.15] General Headquarters, South-West Pacific Area. The A.I.B. was located in Brisbane then Hollandia, Netherlands New Guinea. It directed and co-ordinated all espionage, sabotage, information-gathering, guerrilla-warfare and propaganda operations in the region. The controller had to reconcile the interests of five allied powers: the United States of America, Australia, Britain, the Netherlands and New Zealand.

Wills clarified the A.I.B.'s chain of command and asserted his authority over its affiliated organizations, especially the Services Reconnaissance Department. He arranged for aircraft to be provided specifically for A.I.B. activities. Additionally, he persuaded MacArthur's chief of staff, Lieutenant General R. K. Sutherland, to streamline procedures for approving the bureau's operations; proposals for future projects were to be submitted directly to Sutherland, via Major General C. A. Willoughby, the chief of intelligence. Once projects moved from the realm of the strategic to that of the tactical, operational control was to pass to the local task force commander. Wills dealt diplomatically with both Sutherland and Willoughby and, in contrast to his predecessor, C. G. Roberts [q.v.], earned high praise from them. His practical and firm leadership has been credited with reducing casualties among A.I.B. operatives and with contributing to the success of the Borneo campaign which was spearheaded by the S.R.D. Transferring to the Reserve of Officers on 23 October 1945, he was elevated to C.B.E. (1947).

Back in Adelaide, Wills resumed work with G. & R. Wills & Co. He floated it as a public company in 1946, and saw its five-shilling shares trading at over a pound within six months. Chairman of the company until 1976, he was also a board-member (1950-71) and chairman (1968-71) of Advertiser Newspapers Ltd. He sat on the University of Adelaide council (1945-68), chaired the university's finance committee (1954-60), and served as deputy-chancellor (1961-65) and chancellor (1966-68). Years later it was revealed that he was the 'anonymous benefactor' who had made possible the opening of the staff club in 1950. He persuaded his sister Kathleen Lumley to fund a new college for postgraduate students. His successful fund-raising allowed, among other things, the construction in 1958 of a new university union and the purchase of land for staff housing and a gymnasium. He supported the vice-chancellor A. P. Rowe [q.v.] in his reforms: defined salary scales, annual review for promotions and study leave for staff.

On 14 January 1959 at St Peter's Church of England, Glenelg, Wills married Mavis Catherine Gilfillan, née Marsh, a widow. He served on the Australian Universities Commission in 1959-65. Knighted in 1960, he was elected deputy-chairman of the local council of the Order of St John of Jerusalem and appointed K.St.J. in 1963. Sir Kenneth had been a member of the Adelaide Club since 1924. Survived by his wife and the son and daughter of his first marriage, he died on 13 May 1977 in Adelaide and was cremated. His estate was sworn for probate at $399 918. The Wills building and the Wills refectory at the University of Adelaide were named after him; the university holds two portraits of him by (Sir) Ivor Hele, painted in 1953 and 1968.

H. N. Huffadine, *These Hundred Years* (Adel, 1949); W. G. K. Duncan and R. A. Leonard, *The University of Adelaide, 1874-1974* (Adel, 1973); A. Powell, *War by Stealth* (Melb, 1996); *Advertiser* (Adel), 14 May 1977; information from Mr W. J. A. Wills, Walkerville, Adel.   DAVID PALMER

WILMOT, REGINALD WILLIAM WIN-CHESTER (1911-1954), broadcaster, war correspondent and historian, was born on 21 June 1911 at Brighton, Melbourne, fourth and youngest child of Victorian-born parents Reginald William Ernest Wilmot, journalist, and his wife Jane Marian, née Tracy. After attending Melbourne Church of England Grammar School which he captained in 1930, Chester entered the University of Melbourne (B.A., 1935; LL.B., 1936) and majored in history and politics for his arts degree. He was a member of Melbourne's Inter-Varsity Debating Team in 1932-33 and 1935. As president of the Students' Representative Council next year, he was a close ally of the vice-chancellor (Sir) Raymond Priestley [q.v.11]. Wilmot took a leading part in the formation of the National Union of Australian University Students. He also wrote for the *Star* newspaper and gave talks for the Australian Broadcasting Commission.

In 1937 Wilmot and Alan Benjamin embarked on an international debating tour, visiting universities in the Philippines, Japan, the United States of America, Canada and Britain. They travelled around Europe and, while in Germany during the Munich crisis (September 1938), Wilmot observed a Nazi Party rally at Nuremberg. Back in Australia in January 1939, he yielded to pressure from his family and next month started work as an articled law clerk. He continued his radio talks and was elected to the council of the University of Melbourne.

After the outbreak of World War II, Wilmot was appointed a correspondent with the A.B.C.'s field unit, which sailed for the Middle East in September 1940. He soon proved himself an outstanding broadcaster and reporter, providing masterly descriptions of action and brilliant analyses of strategy. Recognized as one of the best correspondents in the Middle East, he pioneered interviews at a time when a report read by an announcer was considered sufficient. Wilmot's 'articulate, powerfully spoken accounts' of the soldiers' experiences were often accompanied by the sounds of battle behind his voice. In 1941 he covered the see-sawing campaigns in North Africa and the fighting in Greece and Syria. His story

of the battle of Beda Fomm, Libya, was a scoop but he allowed other correspondents to base their accounts on his briefing. He spent several months at Tobruk during the siege then reported the British offensive, Operation Crusader, in which he was slightly wounded on 25 November.

With the entry of Japan into the war, Wilmot returned to Australia and became the A.B.C.'s principal war correspondent in the Pacific. On Anzac Day 1942 at the chapel of the Collegiate School of St Peter, Adelaide, he married Edith French Irwin, a student. He was sent to Port Moresby to cover the Papuan campaign. In August Wilmot, his friend Damien Parer [q.v.15] and a journalist, Osmar White, struggled along the Kokoda Track with the 21st Brigade, Australian Imperial Force, led by Brigadier A. W. Potts [q.v.]. During the brigade's fighting withdrawal, the three newsmen became very critical of the high command for failing to provide Potts and his men with proper equipment, suitably camouflaged uniforms and adequate supplies. Wilmot attempted to broadcast his views but his scripts were censored.

Back in Port Moresby, Wilmot was caught up in the clash between the commander-in-chief, General Sir Thomas Blamey [q.v.13], and the commander of New Guinea Force, Lieutenant General (Sir) Sydney Rowell [q.v.]. When Blamey sacked Rowell, Wilmot protested to Prime Minister John Curtin [q.v.13]. His representations failed and in November Blamey cancelled his accreditation as a war correspondent. The stated reason was that Wilmot was undermining the authority of the commander-in-chief by continuing to express in public his suspicions that Blamey had engaged in corrupt conduct in the Middle East. It is more likely, however, that Wilmot was removed from Papua because a report on the campaign that he had written for Rowell (who included it in his dispatch) implied inefficiency on the part of Blamey's headquarters. The A.B.C. supported Wilmot throughout the dispute.

Based in Sydney, Wilmot broadcast regularly for the A.B.C., published a book, *Tobruk 1941* (1944), and scripted and partly narrated a documentary film, *Sons of the Anzacs* (1943), for the Australian War Memorial. *Tobruk* combined a series of vivid impressions of life during the siege with a description of the campaign based on interviews with participants. Largely due to his efforts, the narrative in *Sons of the Anzacs* accurately complemented the footage of soldiers in action; he had been present when many of the sequences were filmed.

Rumours circulated that Blamey planned to have Wilmot conscripted into the army. Offered a position with the British Broadcasting Corporation's programme, 'War

Report', he started work in London in May 1944. He landed in Normandy by glider with the British 6th Airborne Division on D-Day (6 June) and soon became one of the most famous of the correspondents reporting from Europe. After covering many of the major British operations, he recorded the ceremony at Luneberg on 4 May 1945 in which German forces surrendered to Field Marshal Sir Bernard (Viscount) Montgomery.

Living in England after the war, Wilmot wrote and presented radio and television documentaries dealing with the war and with current affairs. He chaired the first live television coverage of a British general election in 1950. In his book *The Struggle for Europe* (London, 1952), a history of the period 1940-45, he argued that, although the Western Allies had succeeded militarily and freed parts of Europe from one tyranny, they had failed politically and left the eastern states in the grip of another. The book was an instant best seller. Its blend of lucid narrative, close analysis and judicious character studies gave it authority, but its eloquent defence of Montgomery's strategy and of British policy provoked debate. Inevitably, as Wilmot himself conceded, some of his conclusions required revision but his honesty and integrity made the book a classic.

Wilmot was 'a heavy-shouldered man' with a 'strong-boned face and deep-set, restlessly questing eyes'. Intense, argumentative, often dogmatic but never personal in debate, he fearlessly sought the truth. In late 1953 he travelled to Australia to take part in the B.B.C.'s round-the-world Christmas Day broadcast which that year was conducted from Sydney. On 10 January 1954 the Comet airliner in which he was flying back to England crashed into the Mediterranean Sea killing all on board. Wilmot's body was recovered and buried at Porto Azzurro, on nearby Elba. His wife and their son and two daughters survived him.

J. Hetherington, *Australians* (Melb, 1960); K. S. Inglis, *This is the ABC* (Melb, 1983); Wilmot papers (NL); Wilmot files (NAA).   NEIL MCDONALD

WILSON, ALEXANDER (1889-1954), farmer and politician, was born on 7 June 1889 at Whitespots, near Newtownards, County Down, Ireland, second son of Alexander Wilson, farmer and builder, and his wife Anna, née McGowan. Educated at the Clifton Street National School, Belfast, and Belfast Technical College, Alex migrated alone to Victoria in 1908. He worked for his cousin Hugh McClelland [q.v.10] on his property in the Mallee then from 1914 grew wheat on his own farm at Speed. At the Presbyterian Church, Birchip,

on 16 August 1922 he married 21-year-old Ivy Isabella Gould.

From 1928 Wilson worked diligently to build up the Victorian Wheatgrowers' (later Wheat and Woolgrowers') Association which sought to attain 'a stable and profitable price for wheat'. He was elected president of the organization and vice-president of the Australian Wheatgrowers' Federation in 1937. With the support of the V.W.G.A., he stood that year as Victorian United Country Party candidate for the seat of Wimmera in the House of Representatives. His principal opponent was McClelland, the sitting member who was endorsed by the federal Australian Country Party. The federal party's participation in the Lyons [q.v.10] government angered the Victorian party. Wilson won the seat on 23 October.

Considered by the V.W.G.A.'s newspaper to be the 'only friend of the Wheatgrower in federal parliament', Wilson advocated an orderly marketing scheme for the commodity in the bad seasons of 1938-39. He defeated McClelland again in the 1940 election which left him and another Victorian Independent, (Sir) Arthur Coles, holding the balance of power in the House of Representatives. They kept successive prime ministers (Sir) Robert Menzies and (Sir) Arthur Fadden [qq.v.15,14] in power until 3 October 1941 when Coles announced that he would vote to bring down the government. Wilson, who had often voted with the Australian Labor Party and who had been assiduously cultivated by H. V. Evatt [q.v.14], followed suit.

In explaining why he intended to cross the floor, Wilson said in parliament that he had always had some sympathy for the A.L.P. and that the platform of his party in Victoria was similar to that of Labor. He believed that the government had provided too little relief for primary producers, and that its financial policy for prosecuting World War II would increase public indebtedness and risk a postwar depression. In his view, all credit should be created through the Commonwealth Bank of Australia, 'the people's bank'. He looked to Labor for 'stable and safe government' during and after the war. With his support and that of Coles, the A.L.P. under John Curtin [q.v.13] gained power on 7 October.

Backing W. J. Scully's [q.v.] wheat stabilization plan, Wilson won comfortably in the 1943 election. He resigned from parliament on 31 December 1945 and next day assumed office as administrator of Norfolk Island. Opposition politicians criticized the appointment as payment for 'services rendered' to the A.L.P. After returning to Victoria in 1952, he bought a farm at Ultima. He was an inactive Presbyterian and a lapsed Freemason with a keen interest in music. Survived by his wife and their four daughters and two sons, he died of cancer on 26 January 1954 at Richmond, Melbourne, and was cremated.

PD (Cwlth), 3 Oct 1941, p 713, 6 Mar 1946, p 37, 11 Apr 1946, p 1481; *Age* (Melb), 18 Oct 1937; R. F. I. Smith, 'Organise or be Damned': Australian Wheatgrowers' Organisations and Wheat Marketing, 1927-1948 (Ph.D. thesis, ANU, 1969); information from Mrs M. Davies, Swan Hill, and Mr J. Alexander, Blairgowrie, Vic.   BARRY O. JONES
                       TONY LAMB

WILSON, BOBBY; *see* TUDAWALI

WILSON, EDWARD JAMES GREGORY (1897-1972), banker, was born on 22 October 1897 at Terang, Victoria, third child of Arthur Edward Wilson, hairdresser, and his wife Mary Jane, née Bran, both Victorian born. Greg spent most of his childhood near Lilydale. Qualifying at a Melbourne business college, he took a job as a junior bank clerk in 1914. Folklore has it that this red-headed youth quarrelled with his general manager and left after a week. He joined the English, Scottish & Australian Bank Ltd, where he worked in the general manager's department from 1917.

At the Methodist Church, Auburn, on 6 September 1922 Wilson married Hazel Janet Feore; they were childless. In 1925 he was promoted to general manager's accountant. He became a fellow (president 1947-55) of the Bankers' Institute of Australasia, and an accredited accountant and company secretary. After some months in London at the head offices of the E.S.& A. and the Westminster Bank Ltd, he was appointed manager of the Royal Bank branch of the E.S.& A., Melbourne, in 1938. He was promoted the E.S.& A.'s chief inspector in 1939 and its general manager in 1946.

Wilson's elevation occurred at a time of deteriorating relations between the banks and the Commonwealth government that culminated in J. B. Chifley's [q.v.13] attempt to nationalize the industry through the Banking Act (1947). With (Sir) Leslie McConnan [q.v.15], Wilson was a member of the executive-committee of the Associated Banks (Victoria) which campaigned against the measure until the Federal election in 1949. Having won the war against nationalization, he lost the peace in his dealings with a central bank whose authority he never accepted. In an attempt to build market share and profitability, he engaged in brinkmanship with the authorities by making more loans than his holdings of liquid assets permitted.

Equally bold in handling the E.S.& A.'s internal affairs, Wilson pioneered modern personnel-management practices in Australian banking. E.S.& A. staff, who addressed one another on a first name basis, were better trained and paid than their peers. While all the banks were beginning to mechanize, the E.S.& A. led the way, using a closed-circuit television link to centralize functions in its two largest city branches. The E.S.& A. introduced the country's first drive-in branches, adopted a modern style of architecture for its buildings, and became the first private bank to start a hire-purchase business. Wilson's innovations to balance-sheet management, aborted in his own day, anticipated the ingenious 'financial engineering' of the 1980s.

Although Wilson chaired the A.B.V. in 1953, by the following year he was losing the support of his board in London. Its directors had, until then, been largely ignorant of his failure to conform to the dictates of Australia's central bank. Under increasing pressure from without and within, Wilson resigned unexpectedly on the grounds of ill health in May 1955. He had been Australia's most daring and innovative banker of his generation. In his retirement he continued to be involved with Rotary, the Junior Chamber of Commerce and the Australian Elizabethan Theatre Trust; for his community service he was appointed C.M.G. (1957). Survived by his wife, he died on 30 June 1972 at Hawthorn and was cremated. His estate was sworn for probate at $36 906.

A. L. May, *The Battle for the Banks* (Syd, 1968); D. T. Merrett, *ANZ Bank* (Syd, 1985); *A'sian Insurance and Banking Record*, 21 Oct 1946, p 582, June 1955, p 253; *ANZ Newslink*, Aug 1972.
                       D. T. MERRETT

WILSON, ELLA (1870-1959), Sister of Charity, was born on 21 August 1870 at East Maitland, New South Wales, second daughter of Frederick Alfred Adolphus Wilson, a bank accountant from Victoria, and his locally born wife Jemima Duncan, née Thomson. Ella matriculated in 1889 and entered the University of Sydney (B.A., 1892; M.A., 1895). She taught in turn at several grammar schools in Queensland, including Ipswich Girls' Grammar School (1897-98), where she also instructed the girls in swimming. Introduced to the youthful Father (Sir) James Duhig [q.v.8], she was converted to Catholicism in 1900. On 15 January 1903 she sought admission into the Sisters of Charity in Sydney. Having taken the religious name Mary Dunstan, she was professed on 21 October 1905. After a few years of teaching, she was sent to the University of Melbourne (Dip.Ed., 1908).

At the Mother House in Sydney, the Congregation in 1905 established formally St

Vincent's Training School. Connected with the Novitiate, it used St Mary's Cathedral Girls' School for practice teaching. In 1915 Sister Dunstan, who had been teaching at the training school since her return from Melbourne, was appointed mistress of method, a post she held for twenty-seven years.

Sister Dunstan wrote books, lectures, articles for periodicals, and numerous issues of the *Catholic School Paper*. Her introduction to psychology, *How our Minds Work* (1925), was highly regarded as a textbook for student teachers; the Victorian school inspectors J. A. Seitz and Julia T. Flynn [qq.v.11,8] praised it in 1929. The Sisters of Charity took part in conferences on education during the summer holidays. At the Catholic Education Association's conference in Sydney in May 1927, Sister Dunstan lectured on 'Geography for Third Class', using a three-dimensional model of Sydney Harbour, and on 'How to Use the *School Paper*'. In the late 1930s, as radical groups were gaining a foothold in the community, she wrote *The Child and the Communist* (1937) which sold more than 22 000 copies. She published *The Junior Bible and Church History* in 1941 and *Keep in Step with the Church*, echoing Chesterton and Belloc, in 1949. For nine set English classics she compiled books of notes, questions and exercises. Her *Social Studies for Secondary School Pupils and those at Home* had appeared in 1939.

In 1942 Mother Dunstan was elected general councillor and assistant (1942-48) to the superior general, whom she advised on educational matters. Her devotion to the sick was outstanding. Small and slightly built, she showed a ready wit, radiated kindness and peace, loved her Congregation, admired nature, and had a most charitable spirit. She died on 29 March 1959 at the Sacred Heart Hospice, Darlinghurst, and was buried in Rookwood cemetery.

Freeman's J, 2 June 1927; Ipswich Girls' Grammar archives, Qld; Sisters of Charity archives, Potts Point, Syd.   CATHERINE O'CARRIGAN

WILSON, ELLEN MARY; *see* KENT HUGHES

WILSON, JACK (1905-1972), engineer and manufacturer, was born on 16 May 1905 at Batley, Yorkshire, England, only child of Dan Wilson, manager of the local co-operative society grocery shop, and his wife Susan Gertrude, née Colbeck. Educated at Purlwell Council and Batley Grammar schools, Jack was apprenticed in 1920 to Ward & Co., electrical and mechanical engineers and contractors; he also attended nearby technical colleges. He became a draftsman in 1924, and later a designer, with the Yorkshire Electric Transformer Co.

Determined to better himself by emigrating, Wilson arrived in Victoria in 1929 and joined the British Electric Transformer Co. (Australia), South Melbourne. He went into business for himself in 1933, manufacturing small transformers in South Melbourne's 'Galvo Country', and moving several times before settling at Port Melbourne in 1938. Expansion was financed by his savings and by loans from friends. Primitive buildings and plant put a premium on improvization and hard labour, but the Wilson Electric Transformer Co. Pty Ltd, formed in 1937 with Jack as managing director, built a reputation for stability and reliability. The 'Chief' commanded the loyalty of his workers by force of personality (he had a fearsome temper and was given to colourful language); they also appreciated his concern for their personal welfare, and his policies of promoting from within, encouraging apprenticeships and providing superannuation.

On 17 June 1939 at All Saints Church of England, St Kilda, Wilson married Dulcie Dorothy Ann Howard, a receptionist; they were childless and divorced in 1946. Commissioned lieutenant, Militia, in December 1940, he transferred to the Australian Imperial Force on 7 August 1942 and next month was promoted major, Australian Army Ordnance Corps (later Australian Electrical and Mechanical Engineers). He served in the Middle East with the (British) 1st Armoured Division (May-December 1943) and performed staff and training duties in Australia before transferring to the Reserve of Officers on 20 June 1945. At the Collins Street Independent Church, Melbourne, on 3 September 1946, he married with Congregational forms 26-year-old Betty Evelyn Webster; they had two sons and a daughter.

Seeking increased capital and larger premises to cope with his obligations to demobilized employees, Wilson extended the firm's British agency work and accepted low profits in order to win large contracts. In 1950 the Wilsons moved to Glen Waverley, where Jack had purchased an 11-acre (4 ha) site to which he transferred the factory and office in 1950-53. For the cramped, inner-city industrial world of second-hand premises, and of close social relations with hard-drinking employees for whom the corner pub was an after-hours annexe, he substituted a purpose-built factory amid market gardens then yielding to raw outer suburbia. Observing his guiding principles—'Specialize, Standardize, Simplify'—the company prospered.

Travelling frequently in the 1950s and 1960s to keep abreast of new technology, Wilson forged strong co-operative relationships with firms in England, New Zealand and Canada.

An arrangement with Ferranti Ltd of England enabled Wilson's company to make large-capacity transformers for power utilities and mining and manufacturing enterprises. In 1963 he opened a plant at Clovelly Park, South Australia.

Wilson played a leading role in many peak manufacturing, professional and governmental bodies, including the Australian Electrical Manufacturers' Association; the Standards Association of Australia; the National Association of Testing Authorities, Australia; the Institution of Engineers, Australia; the electrical advisory committee to the minister for supply; the Electrical Research Board; the International Electrotechnical Commission (Australian national committee); and the council of the Institution of Electrical Engineers (Britain). He was also a member of the Australian committee of the Conférence Internationale des Grands Réseaux Electriques.

Locally, Wilson was a councillor (1954-57) and president (1956-57) of Mulgrave Shire and a member of the councils of Jordanville and Syndal technical schools. He was a supporter of the department of electrical engineering at Monash University, for which he supplied equipment and funded prizes, and where he was to be honoured posthumously by the Jack Wilson high voltage laboratory.

Committed to maintaining Australian ownership in the face of global rationalization, mergers and takeovers in the electrical industy, Wilson deplored as a form of financial totalitarianism 'the colonization of good, sound, profitable Australian industries by overseas and particularly U.S.A. interests'. In declining health from 1966 and concerned by the question of his succession (his elder son Robert was only 18 that year), he contemplated selling the business, but resolved instead that the enterprise would continue and remain independent. Survived by his wife and their two sons, Wilson died of a coronary occlusion on 30 March 1972 at Glen Waverley and was cremated with Methodist forms. His flourishing company, then employing three hundred people, has remained (as Wilson Transformer Co. Pty Ltd, under Robert's management from 1979) the largest Australian-owned manufacturer of power and distribution transformers. A 1970 portrait of Jack Wilson by Paul Fitzgerald hangs in the Glen Waverley office.

R. S. McNaught, *Wilson Transformer* (Melb, 1983); information from Mr L. D. Kemp, Balwyn, Mrs B. E. Wilson, Hawthorn, and Mr R. J. C. Wilson, Glen Waverley, Mclb.   JOHN LACK

WILSON, LAWRENCE GEORGE (1920-1980), photographer, was born on 17 August 1920 at Geelong West, Victoria, second and only surviving child of Australian-born parents George Alfred Wilson, labourer, and his wife Lilian May, née Oldaker. Leaving Newtown State School at age 14, Laurie first worked as a farm hand. He was to live all his life at and around Geelong West and probably never journeyed beyond Victoria. In World War II he was exempted from military service. Interested in photography, he spent ten months in 1941 assisting at Lockwood's Studios, Geelong, but the pay was poor and he took a job at the Corio Picture Theatre as a projectionist. On 11 December 1943 at St Giles' Presbyterian Church, Geelong, he married Lorna Gwendoline Thomas (d.1979), a machinist and an usher at the cinema. Gwen was an accomplished ballroom dancer and, with customary dispatch, Laurie took lessons so that he could partner her.

In 1945 the Wilsons opened a photographic studio in Moorabool Street. Much of their living came from photographing wedding parties and formal groups of débutantes, posed in accordance with the custom of the day. Gwen, who had no children, became a skilled hand-colourist in the business. Crisply bearded, tallish and wiry, Laurie suffered from delicate health throughout his life. In 1962 he underwent an operation for cancer. He and Gwen sold their studio and lived on a pension. They sent their files of negatives to the municipal tip. Laurie kept only one camera. Later he wrote:

I cannot draw, paint, or sculpt and technology has given me a means of expression otherwise denied. I am no 'words' man. I have been photographing people, to please them, for thirty years. After illness forced me to retire, I began to work with landscape as a kind of occupational therapy. The relief was immense.

Becoming a successful member of the local camera club, Wilson used his skills to express the urgency of his response to nature. In 1971 he was elected a fellow of the Royal Photographic Society of Great Britain. But his work at this time seemed constrained, and was often burdened with 'meaningful' titles. Then suddenly he freed himself creatively. A suite of prints, 'Dog Rocks', made near Fyansford in 1974, was the watershed. One of these images was the only Australian photograph selected in 1975 for the international exhibition, The Land, at the Victoria and Albert Museum, London. That year Wilson received a major grant from the Australia Council.

That an ordinary photographer should in his last years unleash such an outpouring of the imagination was remarkable. Photographs of subtle delicacy and passion gave way to imagery ever more enigmatic as death approached. Lyric harmony of mist and pale moon yielded to harsh tonalities of ocean tumult and stark wasteland. There emerged finally a sense of confrontation and doom. Wilson died of cancer on 8 September 1980 at Geelong and was cremated. He bequeathed money to the National Gallery of Victoria for the production (1982) of a book on his work, to be presented to educational and cultural institutions. His photographs are held in collections in Australia and overseas.

J. Boddington, *Laurie Wilson* (Melb, 1982); information from Mr B. Ketchen, Geelong, Vic; personal information.   JENNIE BODDINGTON

WILSON, NORAH MAGDALENE (1901-1971), Aboriginal community leader, was born on 12 August 1901 at Bookabie, South Australia, daughter of Jack Boxer, an Englishman, and an Aboriginal mother of Kukata descent, who subsequently married Steve Hart, an Aborigine. Norah took his surname. As a child she spent some time in the bush with her family, learning traditional stories and food-gathering skills.

Koonibba Mission, established near Ceduna by the Lutheran Church in 1901, provided a base for local Aboriginal families. While many of the adults worked on nearby farms their children, including Norah, lived at the mission in the children's home. At school she learned to read and write, became proficient at needlework and crochet, and played the organ. She was baptized on 12 September 1915 at Koonibba, and confirmed on 26 May 1918. On 8 June 1921 at the Evangelical Lutheran Church of Our Redeemer, Koonibba, she married Ernest Roy Wilson, a labourer, who was of Wirrangu and Irish descent.

In the early years of married life, Norah moved around with Ernest who was working on stations. After he found employment with South Australian Railways as a fettler, the growing family spent happy years at small coastal settlements—Kyancutta, Warramboo, Yantanabie and Minnipa—in the western region of South Australia. Ernest was a noted Australian Rules footballer in country leagues. In 1942 the Wilsons, keen for their ten children to have a good secondary education, moved to Adelaide where Ernest continued to work for the railways. The family lived with other Aboriginal people in rented accommodation at Goodwood, before buying a house in the city. Their home was a centre for Aborigines visiting from the west coast and other outback areas. Young men who had enlisted or worked in the defence forces were welcomed; Pastor C. V. Eckermann described '12 to 20 men "camping" there, men asleep on every square inch of floor, and in every room'. The family attended Bethlehem Lutheran Church in Flinders Street. When a worship centre for Aboriginal people opened in Franklin Street, Norah became a leader of its community activities, played the organ, and worked for the Aboriginal Lutheran Fellowship.

After seven years in Adelaide the Wilsons moved to Largs Bay and Ernest worked on the Port Adelaide wharfs. Norah continued her involvement in community and church life. A much-respected matriarch, she provided open house for Aboriginal guests from rural areas, and also conducted meetings for women. To keep in touch with aspects of traditional life, she stayed from time to time with relations at Port Augusta and occasionally participated in ceremonies. She visited Aborigines in hospital and children living in the United Aborigines' Mission's Colebrook Home, supplying a link between people in rural areas and their families in Adelaide. Government workers sought her guidance in cross-cultural matters and her assistance as an interpreter.

Ernest and Norah moved again, to their own house at Cheltenham, and attended the local Lutheran Church. In 1962 they gained certificates of exemption from the provisions of the Aborigines Act (1934-39). Suffering from diabetes, hypertension and heart disease, Norah Wilson died on 7 July 1971 at Woodville and was buried in Cheltenham cemetery. Her husband, three of their four sons and their six daughters survived her.

E. Harms and C. Hoff (eds), *Second Koonibba Jubilee Booklet, 1901-1951* (Adel, 1951?); C. Mattingley and K. Hampton (eds), *Survival in Our Own Land* (Adel, 1988); information from Ms G. Wilson, Alberton, and Ms N. Wilson, Seaton, Adel.
                                            W. H. EDWARDS

WILSON, RONALD MARTIN (1886-1967), architect and engineer, was born on 14 July 1886 at Yeronga, Brisbane, eldest of three children of ALEXANDER BROWN WILSON (1857-1938), architect, and his London-born wife Ellen Mary Watt, née Martin. Alex was born on 5 June 1857 at Glasgow, Scotland, fifth son of George Wilson, silk merchant, and his wife Margaret, née Watson. After the family migrated to Brisbane in 1864 he attended the Normal School. He began work with the Department of Public Works in 1875 and joined the architect F. D. G. Stanley as principal draftsman in 1882. Next year Wilson was admitted as an associate of the Royal Institute of British Architects. In 1884 he established his own practice. A founding fellow (1888) of the Queensland Institute of Architects, he served four times (1899-1900, 1910-12, 1914-16, 1920-23) as president. Survived by his wife, daughter and three sons, he died on 5 May 1938 at his Kangaroo Point home and was cremated with Presbyterian forms.

Ron, who attended Brisbane Normal and Grammar schools, passed the New South

Wales junior public examination in 1902 and won a silver medal for physiology. He went to work in his father's office, becoming chief architectural assistant in 1908. While working, he graduated in civil engineering from the University of Queensland (B.E. Hons, 1915; M.E., 1921). Awarded a Walter and Eliza Hall [qq.v.9] travelling scholarship, he spent two years (1915-17) in the United States of America investigating structural steel and reinforced concrete construction. In Britain he joined (1917) the Ministry of Munitions and later the Ministry of Food, overseeing planning and construction of factories and cold stores. Before returning to Queensland in 1919 he studied town planning at the Architectural Association, London.

Entering into partnership with Alex Wilson in 1920, he practised alone after his father retired eight years later. On 21 December 1929 in the chapel of the Glennie [q.v.4] Memorial School, Toowoomba, he married with Anglican rites 26-year-old Olga Esme Mansfield Wallis. His work included the Ithaca and St Lucia Presbyterian churches, Birt & Co. Pty Ltd's wharves at Newstead, the Cliffside Flats at South Brisbane, and butter factories and industrial buildings. A founding associate (1919) of the Institution of Engineers, Australia, and inaugural fellow (1930) of the Royal Australian Institute of Architects, he was a strong advocate of town planning.

Wilson was a member of the State government's university design select committee (1921) which recommended a permanent site for the institution, and the Greater Brisbane City Council's cross-river commission (1925) which proposed construction of the bridge which was named after J. D. Story [q.v.12] in 1937. During World War II he was employed by the Commonwealth government to design sewerage plants for military establishments. In 1955 his son Blair joined the practice. Among the buildings for which the firm was responsible over the next twelve years were the Greek Orthodox Church of St George, South Brisbane, the Stanthorpe Civic Centre, extensions to the university's school of veterinary science and the Albany Creek crematorium.

Like his father, Ron Wilson was honorary architect to the Presbyterian Church, and a yachtsman. His interest in learning never waned and in his later years he attended lectures on anthropology and on topics such as the matrix theory for the design of indeterminate structures. He died on 19 July 1967 at his St Lucia home and was cremated with Presbyterian forms. Predeceased by a son and a daughter, he was survived by his wife and their other son and daughter.

D. Watson and J. McKay, *Queensland Architects of the 19th Century* (Brisb, 1994); Royal Aust Inst of Architects (Qld), *Centreline*, July 1967, p 5; A. B. and R. M. Wilson collection (Fryer L, Univ Qld).

DON WATSON
BLAIR WILSON

WILSON, SIR THOMAS GEORGE (1876-1958), obstetrician and gynaecologist, was born on 27 March 1876 at Armidale, New South Wales, fourth of six children of Irish-born parents Charles Graham Wilson, council clerk, and his wife Annie Jane, née McBride. George was educated at New England Grammar School and the University of Sydney (M.B., Ch.M., 1899; M.D., 1904). He qualified as a fellow of the Royal College of Surgeons, Edinburgh, in 1901 and undertook postgraduate work in London, Dublin and Vienna.

Settling in Adelaide, Wilson practised first as a physician and then as a surgeon. On 4 June 1902 at Christ Church, Adelaide, he married with Anglican rites Alice May, daughter of (Sir) George Brookman [q.v.7]. They had no children and were later divorced. He was an honorary gynaecologist (1902-27) at the (Royal) Adelaide Hospital and honorary obstetrician (1903-46) at the Queen's Home (Queen Victoria Maternity Hospital). In 1909 he helped to found the Ru Rua private hospital. Believing that routine examination of all pregnant women would reduce the occurrence of complications, he established a pioneering ante-natal clinic at the Adelaide Hospital in 1910. Two years later he was appointed tutor in obstetrics at the University of Adelaide.

On 19 October 1914 Wilson was commissioned major, Australian Army Medical Corps, Australian Imperial Force. He served in Egypt and on Lemnos (January-July 1915) with the 1st Australian Stationary Hospital before being repatriated because of illness. His A.I.F. appointment was terminated in January 1916. He returned to his medical practice and academic duties. On 15 May he was reappointed to the A.I.F. as lieutenant colonel and officer commanding troops in the hospital ship *Karoola*. In March-August 1918 he accompanied Major General R. H. J. Fetherston [q.v.8], director general of medical services, Australian Military Forces, on a tour of North America, Britain and Europe. From September Wilson was attached to the 1st Australian General Hospital in France then in England. His military service ended in Adelaide on 4 August 1919.

Resuming his practice, Wilson revived the ante-natal clinic which had lapsed in his absence. It was transferred to the Queen's Home in 1927, and named after him in 1932. Exerting a strong influence on the hospital's policy and development, Wilson was a member of the committee of management from

1908 and president in 1935-50. New accommodation for nurses, opened in 1949, was named after him. At the university he had become lecturer in gynaecology in 1920, and in obstetrics in 1924. On 1 February 1923 at Holy Trinity Church of England, Adelaide, he married Elsa May Cuzens, a nurse.

While overseas in 1935 Wilson investigated ways of reducing maternal mortality; he reported that this could best be achieved by improved medical training. His recommendations led to the appointment of a full-time director in obstetrics at the university in 1940, and ultimately to the establishment of a chair in obstetrics and gynaecology. Having retired in January 1940, Wilson returned in September, on the resignation of the first director, to fill the vacancy until April 1942. He then continued in an advisory capacity until December 1943. Although no longer lecturing, he continued to examine in obstetrics until 1947.

Never occupying a full-time university position, and receiving no payment as a hospital honorary, Wilson derived virtually all his income from private practice. In both practice and teaching he concentrated on the essentials, while insisting on adequate practical obstetrical experience for students. Recognizing the importance of nurses' education, he strove, in conflict with the State government, to maintain the high midwifery standards of the Australasian Trained Nurses' Association. He was a founder (1905) of its South Australian branch and later president then patron. As an inaugural member (1920) of the State Nurses Registration Board, he helped to draw up regulations for training nurses in midwifery and served as an examiner for the board for many years.

A founding fellow of the (Royal) Australasian College of Surgeons (1927) and the Royal College of Obstetricians and Gynaecologists, London (1929), Wilson was elected (1924) a fellow of the American College of Surgeons. He was president of the South Australian branch of the British Medical Association (1922) and of the Mothers and Babies' Health Association (1935). He gave money and equipment to the Queen Victoria Maternity Hospital, endowed (1938) a travelling scholarship in obstetrics at the university and contributed in 1940 to the salary of the new director of obstetrics. Appointed C.M.G. in 1942, he was knighted in 1950.

A big man, deaf in later years, Sir George was impressive and dominant, arousing both gratitude and ire. Known generally as 'T.G.' (or 'Tin Guts' to some irreverent young men), he was highly regarded by nurses and students, who found him considerate and fair, despite his gruff manner. He was a member of the Adelaide Club from 1905. A keen sportsman, he had played tennis for New South Wales, rowed for the University of Sydney,

and served as captain (1931-33) and president (1941-50) of the Royal Adelaide Golf Club. He played golf and tennis into his seventies. Survived by his wife and their two sons, he died on 15 March 1958 in his North Adelaide home and was cremated.

Proceedings at the Opening of the T. G. Wilson Wing by His Excellency the Governor, Sir Willoughby Norrie (Adel, 1949); J. E. Hughes, *A History of the Royal Adelaide Hospital* (Adel, 1982); P. Kenny (ed), *The Founders of the Royal Australasian College of Surgeons* (Melb, 1984); I. L. D. Forbes, *The Queen Victoria Hospital, Rose Park, South Australia, 1901-1987* (Adel, 1988); *MJA*, 28 June 1958, p 19; *Advertiser* (Adel), 1 Jan 1942, 2 Jan 1950, 17 Mar 1958; Univ Adel Archives; information from Drs C. G. Wilson, Walkerville, G. H. Jones, Burnside, and R. Beard, Kensington Gardens, Adel.

J. H. LOVE

WINNING, NORMAN ISAAC (1906-1950), army officer and planter, was born on 27 May 1906 at Oban, Argyllshire, Scotland, second child of Isaac Winning, schoolteacher, and his wife Eliza Clark, née Greenlees. Probably educated at a local school at Troon, Ayrshire, Norman worked briefly as an apprentice in a shipping company. Before World War II he was employed by an Anglo-Dutch firm, Pamanoekan en Tjiasemlanden, as a planter in Java, Netherlands East Indies. He married Georgie Nell Morris Taylor; they had no children.

Having travelled to Sydney, Winning enlisted in the Australian Imperial Force on 2 September 1940 and was posted to the 1st Cavalry Training Squadron. He rose to temporary warrant officer and in December 1941 was commissioned lieutenant and transferred to the 4th Independent Company. Promoted captain in March 1942, he embarked for Port Moresby next month with the 5th (2nd/5th) Independent Company which was later renamed the 2nd/5th Cavalry (Commando) Squadron. The company flew to Wau, New Guinea, in May and, as part of Kanga Force, began to patrol the tracks leading into the Bulolo Valley and to harass the Japanese forces.

On 29 June Winning led a highly successful raid on Salamaua. At least one hundred Japanese soldiers were killed, buildings were destroyed, and enemy equipment and documents were captured. It was the first offensive action on land against the Japanese in World War II. Winning continued to display inspiring leadership. He earned considerable respect from his troops for his outstanding planning skills, boundless energy, resourcefulness and concern for their welfare in adverse climatic conditions and rugged terrain. The unit's war diary described him as 'not only their leader but their friend—a man among men'. He was twice mentioned in dispatches.

The 2nd/5th returned to Australia in May 1943 for further training in Queensland. In November Winning was transferred to the 2nd/4th Cavalry (Commando) Squadron as second-in-command and sent to New Guinea, where the unit was deployed in operations near Finschhafen. Back in Australia in February 1944, he was seconded to the Far Eastern Liaison Office in April. On 8 July he was promoted major and given command of the 2nd/8th Commando Squadron which trained at Lae, New Guinea, before arriving on Bougainville in October-November. The squadron was primarily employed in patrolling. Winning's men took part in a number of engagements with the enemy near the Jaba River and in the area north of the Buin Road. Following the cessation of hostilities, Winning came home to Australia where his A.I.F. appointment terminated on 26 September 1945. He was recommended for the Distinguished Service Order for his exploits in Bougainville but, for reasons which are unclear, the award was downgraded to M.B.E. (1947).

Despite an outward appearance of severity, Winning had been enormously popular with his troops. His red hair earned him the nickname 'Red Steer'. Tough, active, unorthodox, enterprising and shrewd, he gained the confidence and co-operation of the men he commanded. The 2nd/5th was often heard singing the ballad 'When the "Red Steer's" eyes are gleaming, Sure it looks like trouble ahead' to the tune of 'When Irish Eyes are Smiling'. After briefly working as a clerk in Sydney, he returned to Java to manage Sumurbarang estate for P. & T. He was shot dead by terrorists on 2 or 3 December 1950 near Subang and was buried in the local cemetery. His wife survived him.

D. McCarthy, *South-West Pacific Area—First Year* (Canb, 1959); G. Long, *The Final Campaigns* (Canb, 1963); A. A. Pirie, *Commando—Double Black* (Syd, 1993); D. Astill, *Commando White Diamond* (Syd, 1996); War Diaries, 2/5 Independent Company, AWM 52, item 25/3/5, and 2/8 Cavalry Commando Squadron, AWM 52, item 2/2/60 (AWM).

DARRYL MCINTYRE

WINNING, ROBERT EMMETT (1906-1971), pharmacist and army officer, was born on 9 April 1906 at Hurstville, Sydney, second of five children of Robert Wilfred Winning, an ironmonger from the United States of America, and his English-born second wife Elizabeth, née Lund. Young Bob attended Sydney Boys' High School. Having passed botany (1925), chemistry (1926) and materia medica (1930) at the University of Sydney, and the required examinations under the Pharmacy Act (1897), he was registered as a pharmacist on 12 January 1932.

Commissioned lieutenant in the Militia in December 1927, Winning was promoted captain in February 1936. He was seconded to the Australian Imperial Force on 13 October 1939 and posted to the 2nd/4th Battalion as a major. At this time he was 5 ft 9 ins (175 cm) tall and slim in build, with brown eyes and dark brown hair. In February 1940 the battalion arrived in the Middle East. Winning's competence as a company commander impressed the commanding officer, Lieutenant Colonel (Sir) Ivan Dougherty, who made him his second-in-command. As part of the attack on Derna, Libya, in January 1941, Winning organized a deception plan which led the Italians to believe that the 2nd/4th's position was stronger than it was, and to shell unoccupied ground.

At the beginning of the disastrous Greek campaign in April 1941, Dougherty entrusted the battalion to Winning, who stayed and planned its defensive lines while Dougherty went forward to make sense of the rapidly deteriorating situation. In Crete in May the battalion caused heavy casualties among German airborne troops before withdrawing to Palestine. Mentioned in dispatches, Winning was promoted lieutenant colonel in July and appointed to command the 2nd/8th Battalion. He rebuilt the unit after its losses in Greece and Crete, and introduced a training regimen which stressed realistic exercises and the importance of clear orders. In October the battalion was sent to Syria on garrison duty.

Back in Australia in March 1942, the 2nd/8th formed part of Northern Territory Force. Winning was appointed O.B.E. in 1943. He was promoted temporary brigadier in February that year and given command of the 3rd Brigade, then (in April 1944) the 12th Brigade. In May 1945 he took over the 13th Brigade in New Britain. On 14 July he responded to unrest in a company of the 1st New Guinea Battalion by ordering it to be disarmed and marched to the rear. His superiors later accepted the validity of complaints made by native soldiers, increasing their wages and providing them with army-issue shirts and shorts. He was awarded the Distinguished Service Order (1947) for his skilful handling of the brigade in operations against the Japanese.

Winning embarked for Australia in March 1946. On 24 April he transferred to the Reserve of Officers. He worked at his brother-in-law's factory at Rushcutters Bay, Sydney, before becoming head pharmacist at St Luke's Hospital, Darlinghurst, in 1948. At the Church of Our Lady of the Rosary, Kensington, on 1 October 1955 he married with Catholic rites Valerie Joan-Ann Green, a 31-year-old chemist's assistant; they were childless.

Strong-minded and sometimes sarcastic, Winning led a very private life. On or about 21 November 1971 he died from injuries sustained when he fell from the cliff-top at The Gap, Watsons Bay. The coroner was unable to say whether the fall was accidental or otherwise. Survived by his wife, he was cremated with Anglican rites.

G. Long, *Greece, Crete and Syria* (Canb, 1953) and *The Final Campaigns* (Canb, 1963); 2/4th Battalion Assn, *White Over Green* (Syd, 1963); 2/8th Battalion Assn, *The Second Eighth* (Melb, 1984); War Diaries, 2/4th Battalion, AWM 52, item 8/3/4, and 2/8th Battalion, AWM 52, item 8/3/8 (AWM); information from Mrs L. Toll, Coogee, Syd, and Mr B. Winning, Cairo, Egypt.   JOHN CONNOR

WINSOR, REGINALD (1891-1963), railway commissioner, was born on 5 July 1891 at Singleton, New South Wales, fourth child of native-born parents Richard Winsor, fireman, and his wife Mary, née Gordon. Educated locally, Reg joined the New South Wales Government Railways and Tramways as a probationer at Singleton on 3 November 1906 at five shillings a week. He took advantage of the classes offered by the Railway Institute to acquire skills in accounting, becoming coaching clerk with the institute in 1911. Subsequently he rose to the positions of clerk, night officer, station master and station accounts inspector in various parts of the State. At St Alban's Church of England, Belmore, Sydney, he married Hilda May McDonagh on 15 March 1920.

In 1929 Winsor successfully sued the commissioners of railways over a disputed appointment and was made chief clerk in the locomotive accounts branch. He was appointed assistant locomotive accountant in 1933 and was transferred to the mechanical branch in 1936. As president (1931-40) of the Railways and Tramways Officers' Association, he was unhappy with the inflexible structure of the railway administration and argued strongly for reform and promotion on merit. He clashed bitterly with Premier (Sir) Bertram Stevens over salary cuts and openly upheld his predecessor J. T. Lang [qq.v.12,9] as 'the most vigorous champion of workers' rights'. Later he supported the Australian Labor Party. Staff shortages during World War II caused serious industrial difficulties; in 1942 the commissioner T. J. Hartigan [q.v.14] appointed him acting chief staff superintendent (confirmed 1945). The appointment was controversial: the railways were strongly divided on political and sectarian grounds and the choice was seen (probably without justification) as favouring Labor and the Catholic elements. Impatient with bureaucratic 'red tape', Winsor preferred to rely on 'the telephone or personal contact over a glass of beer to get results'. He kept the railways working—without strikes.

In 1948 F. C. Garside [q.v.14] replaced Hartigan; Winsor was promoted to assistant-commissioner for railways. He found it increasingly difficult to work with Garside, with whom he clashed on numerous issues. During the floods and the coal strike in the winter of 1949, he was appointed emergency transport co-ordinator with almost unlimited powers. His 'energy, unconventionality and ability to make split-second decisions' enabled him to 'shine in times of crisis'. In September 1949 he became commissioner for road transport and tramways. Under the Transport and Highways Act (1950), he was named director of transport and highways for five years. These moves strengthened his relations with the State Labor government, but many in the railways saw him as a turncoat who had become 'the government's man'. He courted publicity and did not flinch from controversy.

Unable to stem the losses incurred by the railways, Garside retired in poor health on 5 February 1952 and was replaced by K. A. Fraser [q.v.14], an engineer who died in April. Winsor accepted the post of chief commissioner in September, on the condition of greater independence from government control. Within the upper echelons of the railways, the appointment angered the conservative faction. He compounded the antagonism by introducing major cost-saving measures, including staff reductions and the suspension of the Eastern Suburbs railway. At the same time, he endeavoured to generate new business by using diesel locomotives, air-conditioned trains, freight containers and streamlined procedures.

These measures lessened but did not prevent deficits, nor did they smooth relations within the railways themselves. In December 1954 Winsor took extended sick leave. He returned to duty in April 1955, and gained major publicity through the railway centenary in September, but found it harder to handle the government on the one side, and factional fighting inside the railways on the other. In July 1955 Neil McCusker was appointed senior executive officer, a move strongly opposed by Winsor. The resulting internal disputes within the department caused serious damage, not simply to the administration, but to the morale of the railways as a whole. Losses continued, and a series of delays and accidents in the metropolitan area in 1955-56 made a mockery of Winsor's slogan, 'The Rail Way is the Safe Way', and brought matters to a head. Requested to resign by the State government, he did so and his service ended on 31 July 1956; McCusker replaced him. Winsor had been willing to take a stand against the government when he felt it to be in the best interest of the railways. The service changed beyond recognition once he was gone.

Winsor maintained contact with former colleagues from his home at Belmore. He was 'something of a pint-sized Falstaff' with 'a rollicking sense of humour and a magnificent command of Australian colloquialisms'. A member of the Royal Automobile Club of Australia, he enjoyed boating, fishing and playing bowls. He died on 21 October 1963 at Royal Prince Alfred Hospital, Camperdown, and was buried with Methodist forms in Woronora cemetery. His wife and their daughter survived him.

SMH, 24 Sept 1934, 16 May, 9 July 1950, 26 July 1956, 22 Oct 1963; railway service record (NSWA).

R. M. AUDLEY

WINSTON, ARTHUR DENIS (1908-1980), architect and town planner, was born on 27 July 1908 at Liverpool, England, only surviving son of Edward Michael Winston, dentist, and his wife Maria Linda, née Holt. Denis attended Montessori and private schools then, displaying an aptitude for art and drawing, entered the school of architecture, University of Liverpool (B.Arch., 1931) and graduated with first-class honours. Walking daily to university through the congested Jewish quarter he became interested in city planning and, awarded a scholarship, began a postgraduate diploma in civic design (1936). In 1932 he took up a Commonwealth Fund fellowship to study city and landscape planning at Harvard University (A.M., 1933), United States of America. He travelled extensively and gained experience with short placements in architectural offices, twice with Corbett, Harrison & MacMurray, New York. On his return to Liverpool he completed his diploma with a thesis on park systems, which was much influenced by his American visit.

In October 1934 Winston had accepted a lectureship in architecture at Armstrong (later King's) College, Newcastle upon Tyne, a college of the University of Durham. Two years later he returned to Liverpool as a senior lecturer, and was involved in planning work for the Merseyside Civic Society. In 1937 he co-produced a prize-winning design for the proposed satellite town of Kincorth near Aberdeen, Scotland. He became senior architect with the Northern Ireland Ministry of Home Affairs in 1942 and was a member of its planning commission. In 1945 he was awarded the Royal Institute of British Architects' distinction in town planning. That year he moved to Southampton as borough architect and chief planning officer.

New planning laws passed in New South Wales in 1945 created a demand for trained town planners. The faculty of architecture at the University of Sydney decided to introduce a two-year postgraduate diploma course to begin in 1949. Winston was appointed to the foundation chair in town and country planning—the first in Australia. Sailing into Sydney Harbour on New Year's Eve, 1948, he plunged immediately into numerous meetings bringing together public servants, academics, architects and planners as he prepared for his first group of students. He wrote to his mother: 'I get the impression I have come here at the right time and have a good chance of becoming influential'. On 28 December 1956 at the registrar-general's office, Sydney, he married Joan May Elliott, née Kelly, an almoner and divorcee with a son. There were no children of the marriage.

The University of Sydney had a monopoly on the education of town planners in the city until the late 1960s. Under Winston's direction it introduced a master's degree in town and country planning in 1956 and conferred its first doctorate in the field in 1965. Winston established the Planning Research Centre in 1964 to promote contacts between 'town and gown'. His life revolved around the university: he lived, with his wife, at St Andrew's College for many years, served on numerous university committees and was dean of the faculty in 1964-65.

Providing strategic planning advice to the Department of Local Government was part of his professorial duties until 1959. Winston soon established himself as an influential consultant to government authorities and private clients. He was a site consultant (1954-70) to the Australian National University, Canberra, planner of the new towns of Adaminaby and Jindabyne for the Snowy Mountains Hydro-electric Authority, and a member of several government committees, including the technical advisory panel for construction of the Sydney Opera House (1958-66) and the National Capital Planning Committee (1964-70). In 1955-56 he had visited Egypt for the United Nations Technical Assistance Administration.

Over the years Winston's interests had expanded from the design of structures into the improvement of the broader physical environment. He represented a direct link to heroes of British urban planning such as Sir Patrick Abercrombie and Sir Raymond Unwin. His major preoccupations were good civic design and decentralization. He corresponded frequently with the American urban sociologist Lewis Mumford. Winston was a compelling and eloquent speaker; most of his published papers resulted from a heavy schedule of public lectures and conference addresses. His book, *Sydney's Great Experiment* (1957), was a comprehensive account of the 1948 County of Cumberland Planning Scheme.

In 1951 Winston had led the move to amalgamate several State-based organizations into the (Royal) Australian Planning Institute. As president (1951-53) he assumed a vital, unifying leadership role for the emerging profession. Concentrating on the 'big picture', he was content to leave implementation to others. He was awarded the Sidney Luker [q.v.15] memorial medal by the Sydney division of the institute in 1956 and the (Sir James) Barrett [q.v.7] medal of the Town and Country Planning Authority of Victoria in 1970. Following his retirement in 1973, he kept professionally active and in 1977 was appointed honorary visiting professor in the school of housing, building and planning, Universiti Sains Malaysia, Penang.

Short and bespectacled, with dark curly hair, Winston was sprightly, energetic, thoughtful and urbane. He was a keen traveller, and had wide interests ranging from ancient history to tennis. Highly respected yet modest, he not only built up the national and international reputation of the department of town and country planning, but also did much to raise awareness of planning issues in the community. According to Sir John Overall he was 'undoubtedly the most important influence in planning in Australia in the post-war period'. In 1978 he was appointed C.B.E. Survived by his wife, he died suddenly on 19 May 1980 at Penang, while on his third visit to Malaysia, and was cremated. His work was commemorated in various prizes and memorial lectures; the architecture library at the University of Sydney was named after him.

R. Freestone, *Denis Winston, an Annotated Bibliography, 1949-1976* (Syd, 1983); P. Ashton (comp), *Planning Sydney* (Syd, 1992); *Aust Planner*, 18, no 3, 1980, p 90, 20, no 2, 1982, p 93; Royal Aust Inst of Architects (NSW), *Bulletin*, July 1980, p 2; *SMH*, 11 June 1980; Winston papers (Univ Syd Archives); information from Mr W. Abraham, Jamberoo, NSW, and Mrs J. Winston, Syd.

ROBERT FREESTONE

WINTER, TERENCE CECIL (1906-1980), trade union official and conciliation and arbitration commissioner, was born on 21 April 1906 at Granville, Sydney, eldest of three children of Silas Winter, bricklayer, and his wife Lizzie, née McGregor, both born in New South Wales. Silas suffered intermittent unemployment and his experiences no doubt influenced his son. Terry sang in the choir of the local Methodist Church. Later he was to be sceptical of dogma, whether religious or political. Educated at public schools and Sydney Technical High School, he began work in 1922 as a junior clerk with Elliott Bros Ltd, chemical manufacturers.

On 4 July 1923 Winter was appointed a junior clerk with the Sydney Municipal Council. He joined the Federated Municipal and Shire Council Employees' Union of Australia in 1927. At St Stephen's Church, Newtown, on 26 April 1930 he married with Anglican rites Fannie Hazel Vermeesch; they were childless and later divorced. In 1935 he was transferred to the Sydney County Council. Active in his union, he served as president (1938) and secretary (1939-45 and 1946-47) of the Town Hall branch. He spent two years from November 1944 in Perth as secretary of the Western Australian Municipal, Road Boards, Parks and Racecourse Employees' Union of Workers and the West Australian Local Governing Bodies Officers' Association Union of Workers. On 23 May 1947 at the district registrar's office, Paddington, Sydney, he married Beryl Ellen Lewis, a 27-year-old stenographer who helped him with his union work.

Elected federal secretary of the M.E.U. in 1947, Winter displayed extensive knowledge of the industrial relations system. In 1949-50 he and W. P. Evans represented the Australian Council of Trade Unions in the basic wage case before the Commonwealth Court of Conciliation and Arbitration. Winter was a lifelong member of the Australian Labor Party and a leading opponent of the industrial groups in the State branch. In 1952 he spent six months overseas on a Commonwealth Bank of Australia scholarship to study industrial management. Elected to the A.C.T.U. executive in 1957, he formed close relationships with R. J. L. Hawke and with Ray Gietzelt of the Federated Miscellaneous Workers Union of Australia. Winter visited the People's Republic of China (1958) and the Soviet Union (1959) as an A.C.T.U. delegate, and also toured Israel (1959). In 1962 he led the Australian workers' delegation to the forty-sixth session of the International Labour Conference at Geneva and the seventh congress of the International Confederation of Free Trade Unions in Berlin.

On 16 April 1963 Winter was appointed a commissioner on the Commonwealth Conciliation and Arbitration Commission. His primary responsibility was for the metal trades industry. He kept up a tenacious programme of workshop inspections despite serious injuries, sustained in a motorcar accident, to his right leg. Among the more able of the tribunal's members, he conducted (1966-67) a major work value inquiry into the metal trades. In 1970 he awarded equal pay to women in the industry. He retired from the commission on 21 April 1971 and was appointed O.B.E. that year. After working as a research officer with the F.M.W.U., he set up in 1973 as a consultant in industrial relations; his reports to the Federal government included *Power over Prices and Incomes* (Canberra, 1973).

Winter was a 'man's man' who behaved towards women with grace and consideration. An avid reader, he enjoyed the classics—especially works by Marvell and Shakespeare—humorous publications, and literature dealing with life and politics beyond Australia. His tastes in music ranged from the compositions of Beethoven, Mozart and Gershwin to jazz and musicals. He was a talented, self-taught carpenter and cabinet-maker. Keen on football, cricket and bushwalking, he was physically adventurous, once attempting to cross a flooded creek by motorcar and having to be rescued by a bulldozer. He died on 14 August 1980 at Manly and, after a large, non-religious funeral, was cremated. His wife and their younger daughter survived him. Hawke paid tribute to his learning, intellect, internationalism, commitment to the ideals of democratic socialism, and generosity of spirit.

R. Murray, *The Split* (Melb, 1970); J. Hutson, *Six Wage Concepts* (Syd, 1971); B. D'Alpuget, *Mediator* (Melb, 1977); *Counsellor* (NSW), Aug 1947, June 1963; *Federation News*, Aug-Sept 1971; G. B. Kitay, Federal Conciliation and Arbitration in Australia 1967-1981 (Ph.D. thesis, ANU, 1984); Winter papers (NL); information from and papers held by Mrs B. Winter, Marrickville, Syd. SUZANNE JAMIESON

WINTERBOTHAM, LINDSEY PAGE (1887-1960), medical practitioner and anthropologist, was born on 14 April 1887 in North Adelaide, eldest of three children of Lindsey Percy Winterbotham, a wool-scourer from England, and his South Australian-born wife Fanny, née de Mole. After attending the Collegiate School of St Peter, Lindsey studied medicine at the University of Adelaide for two years then transferred to the University of Melbourne (M.B., B.S., 1908). Moving to Queensland, he spent eighteen months as a resident medical officer at the Brisbane General Hospital. He held brief locum tenencies at several country towns before establishing his own practice at Lowood, west of Brisbane, in 1909. On 20 February 1912 at St Andrew's Church, South Brisbane, he married with Anglican rites Constance Mary Moore, a nurse. Next year he bought a practice on Ipswich Road at Annerley, Brisbane; he was to live there for the rest of his life.

On 1 January 1914 Winterbotham was appointed captain, Australian (Army) Medical Corps, Militia. During World War I, he served in training areas around Brisbane. He was honorary surgeon (1920-25) at the Mater Misericordiae Hospital, South Brisbane, and for many years a visiting medical officer to the Blind, Deaf and Dumb Institution of Queensland. Active in the Queensland branch of the British Medical Association, he helped to organize the general practitioners' group of the association in 1939, serving as chairman until 1949; as president in 1944 he sought pay rises for R.M.O.s. He sat on many committees including one concerned with wartime petrol rationing, lectured in medical ethics at the University of Queensland and was patron (1943-44) of the university's medical society.

Inspired by a patient, Winterbotham became deeply interested in anthropology. He interviewed and corresponded with many Aborigines, among them William McKenzie, from the Kilcoy district. Developing a substantial oral history collection, he published the information in journals such as *Mankind*. Among his contributions were details of cultural practices of Aborigines from Cape York Peninsula (1948) and songs of the Jinibara people (1954). In 1951 his (E. Sandford) Jackson [q.v.9] lecture, 'Primitive Medical Art and Primitive Medicine-Men of Australia', appeared in the *Medical Journal of Australia*. With H. J. Wilkinson [q.v.] and F. S. Colliver, he had established the Anthropological Society of Queensland in 1948. The society aimed to preserve the indigenous cultures of Australia, New Zealand, Papua and New Guinea. At the first meeting Wilkinson delivered a paper, 'An Introduction to Anthropology'. He was honorary secretary for the first two years and president in 1954-55.

In 1948 Winterbotham had donated his collection of artefacts to the University of Queensland, to encourage the formation of a museum to facilitate the teaching of anthropology. The university set up an ethnological museum with Winterbotham as honorary curator. After the State government provided a grant of £1000 for the museum in 1950, he wrote to station owners, medical practitioners and others around the country, and placed advertisements in local and national newspapers, outlining the types of material objects the museum wished to collect. Shire councils in Australia and missionaries in Papua and New Guinea acted as receiving agents. Five hundred individuals and organizations donated ten thousand objects. He remained honorary curator for the rest of his life.

Winterbotham was a deeply religious man. Sport was a passion: he was a lacrosse Blue, a president of the Annerley Bowling Club, a keen fisherman and an excellent shot. Stamp collecting and reading—especially the poetry of Rudyard Kipling—were other interests. He was active in the South Brisbane Rotary Club. Survived by his wife, and their five sons and only daughter, he died on 26 February 1960 in South Brisbane and was buried with Anglican rites in Hemmant cemetery.

J. Pearn (ed), *Some Milestones of Australian Medicine* (Brisb, 1994); *MJA*, 4 June 1960, p 908; *Mankind*, 5, no 10, June 1961, p 438; Winterbotham papers (Anthropology Museum, Univ Qld); information from Mr J. Winterbotham, Alexandra Hills, Brisb, and Dr G. Kenny, Glen Iris, Melb.

KATHRYN FRANKLAND

WISEWOULD, GWENETH (1884-1972), medical practitioner, was born on 30 August 1884 at Brighton, Melbourne, only child of Australian-born parents Francis Wisewould, solicitor, and his wife Isabel Alice, née Field. Privately tutored at home, Gweneth graduated from the University of Melbourne (M.B., B.S., 1915). She was a resident at the Melbourne (1915-16) and Alfred (1916) hospitals, and senior resident (1917) at the Queen's Memorial Infectious Diseases Hospital, before engaging in private practice at St Kilda and Elsternwick and in the city. Holding a number of honorary posts, she performed ear, nose and throat work and general surgery (1918-36) at the Queen Victoria Memorial Hospital for Women and Children; she also instructed medical students in anaesthetics (1918-29) at the Alfred Hospital.

Unconventional, artistic and mildly bohemian in outlook, Wisewould suffered from baseless allegations of professional incapacity and sexual impropriety with patients. Her practice declined and she decided to move to the country where she would be able to treat 'the patient as a whole individual'. In 1938 she set up at Trentham, 59 miles (95 km) north-west of Melbourne. She proceeded 'to make the little town my home and its people my heritage', serving as its doctor until the day of her death at the age of 87. Conditions in the small settlements of the region, and on the roads over the hilly terrain between them, demanded physical courage and resourcefulness. Her considerable surgical skills enabled her to deal with emergencies, whether she was obliged to operate in isolated cottages or in Trentham's tiny hospital she called her 'home from home'. She explained the singularity of her masculine apparel: 'you cannot do this work looking pretty'. Sturdily built and wrapped in an ancient greatcoat, she worked long hours and travelled tirelessly.

In 1971 Wisewould published a minor medico-social classic, *Outpost*, an account of her life and work in the country. She wrote with compassion, sensitivity and humour of her patients: townspeople, foundry-workers, timber-getters, farmers, graziers and itinerant potato diggers. 'Dirt never degraded here. Of class distinction there was none', she claimed, praising the community's strong work ethic. Her acute observation of social and environmental conditions and of local personalities, as well as her first-hand experience of the practical application of changing medical knowledge after World War II, gave the book enduring value as a social history of rural Victoria.

Wisewould lived alone after the death in 1953 of her lifelong friend Isabella Bell ('Ellabelle'), who had accompanied her to Trentham and who had required intensive nursing for advanced rheumatoid arthritis. Wisewould's nearest relations were a cousin and his daughter, and an 'adopted sister' Dorothy Bethune. Personally frugal but generous to others, she often omitted to charge for her services. In 1968 she donated $20 000 to the University of Melbourne to provide 'Truganini Scholarships' for Aboriginal students. She died on 20 January 1972 at Trentham and was buried, with Anglican rites, in the local cemetery, much mourned by the community she had served with 'gritty dedication' for so long. Her estate was sworn for probate at $93 462.

S. Priestley, *Bush Nursing in Victoria* (Melb, 1986); I. Braybrook, *Gweneth Wisewould Outpost Doctor* (Harcourt, Vic, 1993); *Age* (Melb) and *Sun News-Pictorial*, 27 June 1968, 21 Jan 1972; *Advertiser* (Adel), 21 Jan 1972; *SMH*, 26 Feb 1972; 'Night Cap', ABC TV, 13 July 1971 (ABC Archives, Syd); Wisewould papers (NL).   FARLEY KELLY

WITT, SIDNEY HERBERT (1892-1973), electrical engineer, was born on 12 March 1892 at Windsor, Melbourne, son of Australian-born parents Herbert Horatio Witt, broker, and his wife Mathilde Laura Ida, née Schultze. Educated in Melbourne, he joined the Commonwealth Postmaster-General's Department as a junior instrument fitter, electrical engineer's branch, on 10 February 1910. By completing training courses and displaying innovative skills, he became an assistant-engineer in December 1913.

In 1921-22 Witt accompanied the chief electrical engineer Frederick Golding on a study tour of the United States of America, Britain and Europe to investigate the latest developments in telegraphy, telephony and radio communication. On his return he played a leading part in the planning for an Australian trunk telephone network. At the instigation of (Sir) Harry Brown [q.v.7], Witt was appointed in June 1923 to found a research section at the department's headquarters building; next year he was promoted supervising engineer. In 1925 his team of five became the staff of the P.M.G. 'Research Laboratories', charged with monitoring developments in electrical communication, undertaking experimental work, formulating standards for telephone transmission and linking new research discoveries to the work of the department's engineers.

At Holy Trinity Church, Kew, on 18 August 1923 Witt had married with Anglican rites Viola Phoebe Jackson. A slim, spry and highly active man, he had a creative and wide-ranging grasp of telecommunication science. From 1924 he contributed to the introduction of voice frequency repeaters and 3-channel carrier systems into the trunk network. In 1927 he was prominent in planning and setting up a national broadcasting service. He promoted studies of new telegraphy and telephony systems, established national frequency standards and initiated scientific research programmes for the quality control of telecommunications equipment. Under his direction the small P.M.G. research laboratories became the focus of advanced telecommunication studies in Australia.

During World War II the P.M.G. laboratories carried out telecommunications research, design and development for the armed services and contributed to the establishment of an emergency telegraph system. In collaboration with the radiophysics laboratory of the Council for Scientific and Industrial Research, they embarked on some twenty secret radar projects based on information brought back from Britain in 1939 by David Martyn [q.v.15]. While the C.S.I.R. radiophysics research team prepared the prototype for Australia's radar equipment, the P.M.G. laboratories shaped specifications and production design, and advised the Department of Munitions on the large-scale manufacture of the radar apparatus. This complex developmental work was crucial in bringing radar into operation in Australia and earned Witt the in-house title of 'the father of radar'.

In 1941 Witt had designed and helped to set up the short-wave transmitting station at Shepparton for broadcasts to the South Pacific and South-East Asia regions, a service which was to become Radio Australia. He retired from the laboratories in June 1945 to undertake a series of assignments as Australian delegate to meetings of the International Telecommunications Union concerned with formulating an international plan of frequency allocations for radio communication. These discussions led in 1947 to the establishment of the International Frequency Registration Board, to which Witt was elected as Australia's representative.

Witt moved with his family to Geneva in January 1948 to assume full-time duties on the I.F.R.B. Chairman in 1949, he remained there until his retirement in 1957. He was an active member of the Institution of Engineers, Australia, the Postal Electrical Society, the Institution of Radio Engineers, Australia, and other professional bodies. For recreation he played golf. Survived by his wife and their son, he died on 28 June 1973 at Glen Iris, Melbourne, and was cremated.

A. Moyal, *Clear Across Australia* (Melb, 1984); J. F. Ross, *Radio Broadcasting Technology* (Port Macquarie, NSW, 1998); *Procs of the IREE*, 34, no 7, Aug 1973, p 287; Aust Post Office Research Laboratories, *Review of Activities*, 1973, p 10; Telstra Research Laboratories, *New Horizons*, 1998, p 47; personal information.   ANN MOYAL

WITTRUP, ELLEN; see KIRSOVA

WOLINSKI, NAOMI (1881-1969), lawn bowls champion and administrator, was born on 26 March 1881 at Sandhurst (Bendigo), Victoria, eighth of twelve children of Solomon Herman, accountant, and his London-born wife Elizabeth, née Oxlade. Solomon had migrated to Victoria in 1864 from Konin, Poland. The family moved to Perth in 1894. There, at the Synagogue, on 1 July 1903 Naomi married Ury Wolinski (d.1963), a Polish-born civil servant; their only son was born in 1904. In 1910 they moved to Sydney. Soon after the death of her infant daughter in 1911, Naomi, confined to bed with sand-bag weights to correct spine damage, went back to Perth for eighteen months to be nursed by her family. After she returned to Sydney, the Wolinskis settled at Neutral Bay.

Ury, a member of North Sydney Bowling Club, won his first club championship in 1917. When Naomi took up the game in the late 1920s she played at Wollstonecraft Bowling Club. She was a founder (1930), inaugural vice-president, honorary secretary (1931-32), president (1933-58) and life-member (1938) of the New South Wales Ladies' (Women's) Bowling Association. Under her leadership the association rapidly expanded; by 1957 it had affiliated 261 women's clubs with some 12 000 members. She travelled widely to attend the openings of many new clubs and to organize a zone structure for inter-club play and district championships. A founder of the association's journal, (*Women's*) *Bowls News*, she chaired (1949-58) its editorial committee.

Mrs Wolinski was an ardent patriot, and an even more ardent organizer. In 1940 she had served on a panel to further the sale of war savings certificates. She was a justice of the peace from 1941 and later a warden with first-aid qualifications under the National Emergency Services. As an executive-member of the Lord Mayor's Patriotic and War Fund of New South Wales (Australian Comforts Fund) from 1942, she organized a band of women bowlers to produce items of clothing for the armed services overseas; her group made over 65 000 garments and raised thousands of pounds to provide comforts for servicemen and women.

In 1946 the N.S.W.W.B.A. subscribed for the Wolinski Shield, to be competed for annually by affiliated clubs; entrance fees were given to charity. In 1947 Mrs Wolinski was elected foundation president of the Australian Women's Bowling Council; she remained New South Wales delegate until she retired in 1958. She was a vice-president (1938-50) and president (1950-64) of the National Council of Amateur Sports Women of New South Wales. In 1950, with Dr Marie Hamilton [q.v.14] and the journalist Ruth Preddy, she persuaded the secretary for lands to provide grounds dedicated to women's sport: 20 acres (8 ha) at Matraville and 30 acres (12 ha) at Terrey Hills were gazetted 'as a memorial to women of the services and women war workers'.

'Wol', as she was known, was an enthusiastic and talented lawn bowler who had won twelve club championships and four interstate 'Test Matches' (1947, 1954, 1955 and 1958). For many years she taught bowls to women patients at Parramatta Mental Hospital. In 1953 she was awarded Queen Elizabeth II's coronation medal and in 1960 was appointed M.B.E. Survived by her son, she died on 14 September 1969 at Mosman, and was cremated with Jewish rites.

Bowls News (Syd), Oct 1969, p 20; *SMH*, 2 Apr 1936, 1 Jan 1960; *Sunday Mirror* (Syd), 8 Feb 1959; NSW Women's Bowling Assn Archives, Syd; Honours, A463, item 1958/2218 (NAA, Canb); information from Mrs R. Galbraith, Dural, NSW.

LOUELLA MCCARTHY

WONGGU (c.1880-1959), Aboriginal leader, was born into the Djapu clan from Caledon Bay, north-east Arnhem Land, Northern Territory. The Djapu are part of a larger group of the indigenous inhabitants of north-east Arnhem Land who call themselves Yolngu (the people), and others Balanda (outsiders). In the past non-Aborigines often but incorrectly referred to the Yolngu as the Balamumu. Wonggu's name has been spelt in various ways, including Wongo, Ongoo and Wongu. When Donald Thomson [q.v.] met him in the mid-1930s, he judged him to be over 50 years of age. By then he was the senior elder of the Djapu, with more than twenty wives and at least sixty children.

In August 1932 Wonggu and his large clan began collecting and processing trepang in Caledon Bay for Frederick Gray, captain of the lugger *Northam*. Next month two similar vessels, *Myrtle Olga* and *Raff*, crewed by six Japanese and eight Aborigines, sailed into the bay to gather trepang. On the morning of 17 September the Djapu attacked the Japanese, five of whom were killed (the other escaped). Historians have suggested various motives for the killings: a protest against non-Aboriginal incursion into Arnhem Land; anger over the exploitation of Aboriginal labour in the trepang industry; revenge for insults and verbal abuse;

punishment for the sexual mistreatment of Aboriginal women; and the protection of nearby sacred sites from possible desecration.

Gray and his men immediately departed in the three luggers for Darwin, reporting the occurrence to the administration by telegram from Milingimbi *en route*. Efforts by the police in 1932-33 to apprehend the perpetrators were unsuccessful. The press erroneously linked the killing of three Europeans in the region in 1933 to the massacre at Caledon Bay and the incidents became known as the 'Black War'. Three of Wonggu's sons, Mau (Mow), Natjelma (Natchelma, Watchelma) and Narkaya (Narkaia), were implicated as leaders of the assault on the Japanese trepangers. In 1934 Gray persuaded them to accompany him and Hubert Warren's [q.v.12] 'peace party' to Darwin. They stood trial for murder and on 1 August T. A. Wells [q.v.] sentenced them to twenty years imprisonment. After lobbying by groups and individuals concerned about Aboriginal welfare, the three men were released in June 1936; they were repatriated by Donald Thomson, who had been commissioned by the Commonwealth government to establish good relations with the Yolngu.

In 1937-38 Wonggu and his family left the Caledon Bay area and settled at Yirrkala, a mission station on the Gove Peninsula established by the Methodists in 1935 in response to the Caledon Bay massacre. The drawing together of different groups created tensions and Wonggu's family was involved in a period of lethal conflict. He provided scouts and guides to assist Thomson's Special Reconnaissance Unit in World War II.

'Wonggu, King of the Balamumu', had caught the imagination of the popular press in the 1930s and his name was prominent in sensational reports of the incidents in Arnhem Land. Ion Idriess [q.v.9] and Victor Hall characterized him as an evil genius in their accounts of the Caledon Bay massacre. Thomson disagreed, respecting him as a 'gallant warrior', 'frank and completely fearless'. He described Wonggu as 'a tall, powerful man with [an] intelligent face, deep set eyes and a heavy beard, trimmed almost in Van Dyck style'. Fred Gray was to remember him as an impressive man in whose company he spent the happiest time of his life. Wonggu died on 7 June 1959 at Yirrkala. A man of influence, authority and charisma, he represented a romantic and little known aspect of Northern Territory history. More importantly, the events in which he was involved drew attention to the issues of Aboriginal justice and rights to land.

I. L. Idriess, *Man Tracks* (Syd, 1935); V. C. Hall, *Dreamtime Justice* (Adel, 1962); M. Dewar, *The 'Black War' in Arnhem Land* (Darwin, 1992); J. Kadiba, *An Account of the Fijian Missionaries in*

Arnhem Land 1916-1988 (Darwin, 1994); T. Egan, *Justice All Their Own* (Melb, 1996); *Northern Standard* (Darwin), 1 June 1934; F. Gray papers (Aust Inst of Aboriginal and Torres Strait Islander Studies, Canb); A1, item 1938/6715 (NAA, Canb); F1, item 1936/386 (NAA, Darwin); information from the late Mr F. Gray (notes held by author).

MICKEY DEWAR

WOOD, EDWARD JAMES FERGUSON (1904-1972), marine microbiologist, was born on 23 June 1904 at Eagle Junction, Brisbane, son of Australian-born parents James Boyne Wood, engineer, and his wife Maud, née Barrymore. 'Fergie' attended Eagle Junction State School and Brisbane Grammar School where he won the Lilley [q.v.5] silver medal and the Russell Walker Grant memorial medal. At the University of Queensland (B.Sc., 1927; M.Sc., 1929; B.A., 1935; D.Sc., 1966), he gained first-class honours in botany (plant pathology) with a thesis on Fiji disease in sugar-cane. From 1925 he had held a cadetship with the Department of Agriculture and Stock. He remained with the department as an assistant-pathologist in the Queensland Bureau of Sugar Experiment Stations. In 1929-34 he studied English and philosophy at the university in the evenings. At St James's Church of England, Yeppoon, on 29 April 1931 he married Hazel Jessie Fisher.

In 1933 Wood joined the Commonwealth Department of Health, Melbourne, as a technical assistant but he resigned to take up a lectureship in bacteriology at the University of Melbourne in April 1934. On 1 September 1937 he was appointed an assistant research officer in the Council for Scientific and Industrial Research's new fisheries investigations section, located in the bacteriology department of the university. In June 1938 he moved to Sydney when the section was transferred to Cronulla. He was promoted in 1958 to principal research scientist in the Commonwealth Scientific and Industrial Research Organization's division of fisheries and oceanography.

As a marine scientist, Wood carried out his earliest work on the processing and bacterial spoilage of fish. After the Japanese supply of agar—necessary for biomedical research—ceased in World War II, he analysed the properties of this algal product and explored possible local sources of the substance; his investigations included a survey of Australian seaweeds. Under the influence of the Dutch microbiologist Baas Becking, Wood then turned to the study of bacterial activity in oceans and estuaries, undertaking important work on seagrasses, marine pollution and underwater fouling. Next, he concentrated on ground-breaking, fundamental research into phytoplankton organisms, particularly diatoms and dinoflagellates in Australian and New Zealand waters. While with the C.S.I.R. and C.S.I.R.O., he published some seventy papers and held two visiting appointments in the United States of America.

Wood's difficult personality led to some alienation from his colleagues. In 1963, anticipating that he was about to be retired from C.S.I.R.O., he accepted the post of professor of marine microbiology and deputy-chairman of the Institute of Marine Science, University of Miami, U.S.A. He wrote *Studies in Microbial Ecology of the Australasian Region* (Weinheim, Germany, 1964)—which was accepted for his doctorate—*Marine Microbial Ecology* (London, 1965), *Microbiology of Oceans and Estuaries* (Amsterdam, 1967), *Dinoflagellates of the Caribbean Sea and Adjacent Areas* (Coral Gables, Florida, U.S.A., c.1968) and *The Living Ocean* (London, 1975); he also co-edited two books. His colleague R. E. Johannes described him as a pioneer in 'the emergence of marine microbiology as a recognized scientific discipline', and praised him for 'continually generating novel and stimulating hypotheses'.

In 1970 Wood returned to Sydney. The United Nations invited him to act as an adviser on harvesting the sea to provide food for people in developing countries but ill health intervened. He died of cancer on 15 May 1972 at Caringbah, and was cremated. His wife and their three daughters survived him.

Coresearch, no 55, Oct 1963, no 160, July 1972; *Aust Marine Science Bulletin*, July 1972; *Search* (Syd), 3, no 9, Sept 1972; Wood personal file (CSIRO Archives, Canb); S50, Minutes of meeting of Science Executive Cte, 9 Dec 1964 (Univ Qld Archives).

JOHN JENKIN
SOPHIE C. DUCKER

WOOD, GORDON LESLIE (1890-1953), economist, was born on 29 August 1890 at Launceston, Tasmania, eldest child of Tasmanian-born parents Walter Leslie Wood, compositor, and his wife Emily, née Porter. Educated at the Charles Street State School and the University of Tasmania (B.A., 1914; M.A., 1922), Gordon trained as a teacher and in 1913 was posted to Hobart High School. At Chalmers Church, Launceston, on 1 July 1914 he married with Presbyterian forms Adeline Grieve. He transferred in 1919 to the Collegiate School of St Peter, Adelaide.

In 1923 Wood published *The Tasmanian Environment*, a human and economic geography of the State. He investigated the flow of rivers in parts of the Australian Alps, and the ecological threat to mountainous regions from deforestation, land clearance and cattle grazing. Additionally, he studied Australia's balance of payments, a task that employed his considerable mathematical skills. This diversified output probably influenced (Sir) Douglas Copland [q.v.13] to choose Wood in 1924 as his first academic subordinate in the faculty of commerce at the University of Melbourne. He was appointed senior lecturer in economics and economic geography.

'With his enthusiasm, sound judgment and vigorous personality', Wood successfully acted as head of the faculty during Copland's numerous absences. Copland, Wood and Frank Mauldon [q.v.15], the third full-time member of staff, bore a heavy teaching load and also lectured to university extension classes. Wood wrote papers on subjects such as conservation in the catchment areas of Australian rivers, the geographical distribution of the country's population, and the development of the Northern Territory. His survey for the Institute of Pacific Relations, *The Pacific Basin*, was published in 1930. The previous year he had taken up a Rockefeller Foundation fellowship in England to work on *Borrowing and Business in Australia* (London, 1930). In part an analysis of economic fluctuations to that date, the book won for its author the Harbison-Higinbotham [q.v.4] research scholarship (1930).

The university awarded Wood a doctorate of letters in 1930 and promoted him to associate-professor in 1931. His grasp of current economic problems was supported by an ability to synthesize and co-ordinate, as testified by his numerous joint publications. In 1932 he began the labour that was to result in a major work with (Sir) Samuel Wadham [q.v.], *Land Utilization in Australia* (1939). Wood became a regular broadcaster on current affairs. Newspapers, trade unions and business and professional associations asked him for analyses and addresses on the Depression. He went out of his way to enlighten and sometimes reassure these interest groups, though he worried privately at the possibility of endless and 'unjust' deflation, the injustice stemming from the fact that continuing deflation meant more working people being thrown out of work while *rentiers* resisted any reduction in their incomes.

Wood gave devoted service as secretary (1925-53) of the Economic Society of Australia and New Zealand and as a member (1936-53) of the Commonwealth Grants Commission. He was active on many university boards and committees. In 1944 he was appointed to the Sidney Myer [q.v.10] chair of commerce. After suffering a cerebral thrombosis, he died suddenly on 29 June 1953 in Royal Melbourne Hospital and was cremated with Methodist forms. His wife and their two daughters survived him.

Economic Record, 30, no 58, May 1954, p 1; Wood papers (Univ Melb Archives *and* NL); personal information.   ROBERT WILSON

WOOD, JOSEPH GARNETT (1900-1959), botanist, was born on 2 September 1900 at Mitcham, Adelaide, eldest of four children of John Wood, baker's assistant, and his wife Susanna, née Garnett. From early childhood Joe enjoyed rambles on the Fleurieu Peninsula and, with Aborigines from Point McLeay mission, in the Coorong region; later he was to explore farther afield. He attended Unley High School and the South Australian School of Mines and Industries. At the University of Adelaide (B.Sc., 1922; M.Sc., 1928; D.Sc., 1933), he won a John Bagot medal for first-year botany and a John L. Young [q.v.6] research scholarship. After graduating with honours in chemistry, he became a demonstrator in botany in 1923, simultaneously taking advanced courses in the subject and lecturing to senior students in plant physiology.

Influenced by Professor T. G. B. Osborn [q.v.11], Wood became interested in the mechanisms which enabled the survival of the semi-succulent chenopod vegetation in the parched inland and the sclerophyllous vegetation on the nutrient-poor soils in the Adelaide Hills. Awarded an 1851 Exhibition scholarship, in 1925-27 he carried out research at Gonville and Caius College, Cambridge (Ph.D., 1933), on photosynthesis. He returned to the University of Adelaide in October 1927. Osborn co-opted him and T. B. Paltridge, from the Council of Scientific and Industrial Research, to establish experimental plots at the Koonamore Vegetation Reserve. The research area, 240 miles (386 km) north-east of the city, had been set up by the university in 1926 in one of the most overgrazed portions of South Australia, to investigate regenerating arid-zone flora. The two men continued recording changes in plant life there for eleven years. Until the early 1950s, Wood's research was to focus on stomatal physiology and the biochemistry of native plants under water stress.

In 1928 Wood had been appointed lecturer-in-charge of the university's botany department. Using data from J. M. Black's [q.v.7] *The Flora of South Australia* (1922-29), he compiled a description of the floristics and ecology of the mallee, which appeared in *Transactions of the Royal Society of South Australia* in 1929. He was fascinated by the meeting of western and eastern Australian floras on Kangaroo Island, and published next year an analysis of the island's vegetation in *Transactions*. On 7 February 1931 at Christ Church, Yankalilla, he married with Anglican rites 18-year-old Joan Hazel.

Promoted to professor of botany on 1 January 1935, Wood was dean (1937-40, 1946-48) of the faculty of science and chairman (1956-59) of the board of research studies. He published his handbook *The Vegetation of South Australia* in 1937. The sharp disjunctions between savanna and sclerophyll vegetations on soils of contrasting nutrient levels, seen in the Mount Lofty Ranges, focused his attention on mineral nutrition of native plant communities. Interested in nitrogen metabolism of *Atriplex* (saltbush) in the arid zone, he collaborated with the plant biochemist A. H. K. Petrie, of the (Peter) Waite [q.v.6] Agricultural Research Institute, to investigate nitrogen metabolism of agricultural plants. Although the work was truncated by Petrie's death in 1942, Wood contributed reviews to three international journals—*Chronica Botanica* (1942), *Annual Review of Biochemistry* (1945) and *Annual Review of Plant Physiology* (1953)—on the biochemistry of nitrogen and sulphur metabolism in pasture plants. He attracted the best minds from Australia and abroad to address the major factors affecting Australian vegetation—aridity and mineral nutrition. Under his direction postgraduate students tackled the metabolism of copper and zinc, and the role of molybdenum in nitrogen fixation in legumes.

Early in the 1940s Wood argued for the inclusion of biology in the high school science syllabus. To assist in the training of secondary science teachers he mounted a week's refresher course in biology in 1942, and presented a first-year course in the subject at night. Botany students at the university studied the South Australian vegetation in detail during field excursions. Second-year students, working alone or in pairs, were expected to produce both a species study and a small ecological survey. In their third year, they learned about the physico-chemical processes which operate within native plants in the field. 'Lateral thinking' was fostered in all undergraduate courses, and formed the basis for postgraduate research.

President (1942) of the Royal Society of South Australia, Wood was awarded its Sir Joseph Verco [q.v.12] medal in 1944. The Royal Society of New South Wales gave him in 1952 the (W. B.) Clarke [q.v.3] medal. He was a member of the (interim) council (1948-59) of the Australian National University, Canberra, of the Commonwealth Scientific and Industrial Research Organization's advisory council (1950-56, 1959), and of the United Nations Educational, Scientific and Cultural Organization's advisory committee on arid-zone research (1952-59). Elected (1954) a fellow of the Australian Academy of Science, he was founding president (1958) of the Australian Society of Plant Physiologists.

Despite the recognition Wood received as a result of his exceptional intellect and enthusiasm, he was an extremely anxious man and a chain-smoker. Before he delivered a lecture, to undergraduates or to scientific colleagues, his nervousness tormented him. Although his approach to staff and students appeared formal, students appreciated his constant interest, evident during his daily circuit of the department, and his challenging questions both in discussions and in examinations.

Wood conveyed his love of both nature and literature to his three daughters; the eldest recalled him reading to her (with appropriate voices) Shakespeare as well as *Winnie the Pooh*. He appreciated good conversation, food and wine, and developed a beautiful garden. As supporters of contemporary Australian art, he and his wife frequented Adelaide exhibitions and purchased many fine paintings. Survived by his wife and their daughters, he died of a coronary occlusion on 8 December 1959 at his home at Beaumont and was cremated.

R. L. Specht, 'Australia', in E. J. Kormondy and J. F. McCormick (eds), *Handbook of Contemporary Developments in World Ecology* (Westport, Connecticut, 1981); *Nature* (Lond), 185, no 4709, 30 Jan 1960, p 282; Aust Academy of Science, *Year Book*, 1960, p 29; Roy Soc SA, *Trans*, 84, 1961, p 1.

RAY SPECHT

WOOD, PAUL HAMILTON (1907-1962), cardiologist, was born on 16 August 1907 at Coonoor, India, third of four children of Richard Boardman Wood, civil servant, and his wife Geraldine, née Tomson. Paul was educated at Yardley Court Preparatory School, Kent, England, and, after his family migrated to Tasmania in 1920, at Launceston Church Grammar School. Following in the professional footsteps of his grandfather and great-grandfather, he enrolled in medicine at the University of Melbourne (M.B., B.S., 1931; M.D., 1941). He excelled at sport, gaining a Blue for Rugby Union football and being selected for the combined Australian universities' team, and winning several awards for skiing. Academically, his fortunes were mixed: he passed surgery and obstetrics in his final-year examinations, but failed medicine. Although he was successful in the supplementary examination, he missed out on a hospital appointment in Melbourne. He went instead to Christchurch General Hospital, New Zealand.

In 1933 Wood returned to Britain to commence his specialist training. He qualified as a member (fellow 1940) of the Royal College of Physicians, London, and accepted a position at the Hospital for Consumption and Diseases of the Chest, Brompton. Next year he was appointed resident medical officer at the National Hospital for Diseases of the Heart. There he established a reputation based on his wide knowledge and exceptional clinical judgement. At the parish church, St Marylebone, on 29 December 1934 he married Elizabeth Josephine Guthrie. In 1935 he was recruited by Professor (Sir) Francis Fraser to join the staff of the recently established British Postgraduate Medical School at Hammersmith Hospital. Wood carried out clinical investigations of cardiac patients and taught medical students. From 1937 he was also a physician to outpatients at the National Hospital for Diseases of the Heart, where he worked with such outstanding cardiologists as (Sir) John Parkinson, Maurice Campbell, Evan Bedford and William Evans.

With the outbreak of World War II, Wood joined the Emergency Medical Service in 1940 and was attached to the 'effort syndrome' unit where he established that condition as a functional or psychiatric disorder. His findings and conclusions were the subject of his Goulstonian lecture to the R.C.P. in 1941. On 21 February 1942 he was commissioned in the Royal Army Medical Corps. Promoted temporary major in June and acting lieutenant colonel in August, he served in North Africa and Italy. He was mentioned in dispatches, appointed O.B.E. (1945) and elevated to the local rank of brigadier in December 1945.

After his demobilization in 1946, Wood threw his restless and limitless energies into the pursuit of investigative cardiology. Early in 1947 he began performing cardiac catheterizations at Hammersmith Hospital. He measured intravascular pressures and oxygen saturation in patients with congenital and valvular heart disease, providing a sound scientific basis for surgical correction. Dean of the Institute of Cardiology at the National Hospital for Diseases of the Heart from 1947, he was appointed director in 1950. He was also in charge of the cardiac department at the Brompton Hospital. During the war years he had written the first draft of his monumental textbook, *Diseases of the Heart and Circulation* (London, 1950). Largely based on personal experiences, and enriched by his work in the cardiac catheterization laboratory and operating theatre of Russell (Baron) Brock, it was an instant success.

Much sought after around the world as a lecturer and teacher in cardiology, Wood revisited Australia in 1951. He made a significant impact, even though his opinions of local cardiac practices were not entirely flattering. His somewhat scornful remarks were directed especially towards senior colleagues, who were not accustomed to having their diagnoses and opinions challenged. The younger generation of cardiologists remained his disciples to the last. In 1961, as Sir Arthur Sims Commonwealth travelling professor, he toured Canada.

Wood was the most stimulating and inspiring cardiologist in the English-speaking world during the middle of the twentieth century. He questioned existing concepts and attempted to base every aspect of clinical diagnosis and treatment on verifiable physiological facts. A 'pale, wiry man of ascetic appearance', he was intense, direct and occasionally sarcastic in medical discussions, but could be warm and charming to his close friends. He had a keen interest in gardening. Survived by his wife, and their two sons and a daughter, he died of myocardial infarction on 13 July 1962 in Middlesex Hospital, London.

Lives of the Fellows of the Royal College of Physicians of London, 5 (Lond, 1968); *British Medical J*, 28 July 1962, p 262; *MJA*, 27 Oct 1962, p 683; *British Heart J*, 24, no 5, 1962, p 661; G. Bauer, 'Paul Wood Remembered', in *On the Pulse*, 8, no 2, June 1996, p 2; *American J of Cardiology*, 85, 1 Jan 2000, p 75.

GASTON BAUER

WOODBURY, AUSTIN MALONEY (1899-1979), priest, philosopher and theologian, was born on 2 March 1899 at Lower Mangrove (Spencer), New South Wales, fifth son of native-born parents Austin Herbert Woodbury, orchardist, and his wife Margaret, née Maloney. His great-grandfather, Richard Woodbury, sentenced to transportation for seven years in 1803, had arrived in the colony in 1806 and become district constable of the Lower Hawkesbury in 1820; his descendants still farm in the area. After leaving the local public school, young Austin studied by correspondence while helping on the farm. As a boy, he showed 'a reflectiveness and concern beyond his age'.

Belonging to a devout Catholic family—four of his sisters were to join religious Orders—Woodbury entered the Society of Mary (Marist Fathers) in 1918 and completed secondary studies at the juniorate, in Sydney and at Mittagong (1919-20). From 1921 he was at Mount St Mary's Seminary, Greenmeadows, Hawkes Bay, New Zealand; he took his first vows on 2 February 1923. He studied (1926-28) in Rome at the Dominican Ponteficio Ateneo 'Angelicum' where he was influenced by Fr Reginald Garrigou-Lagrange, who was prominent in the revival of Thomistic studies. Ordained in Rome on 31 July 1927, Woodbury gained doctorates in theology and philosophy. Back in New Zealand, he taught at St Patrick's College, Wellington, then at Greenmeadows (1930-36). From 1938 to 1943 he was founding rector of Blessed Peter Chanel's Seminary, Toongabbie, New South Wales. There, in 1941, he started an Australian Illawarra Shorthorn stud, Meadowstream.

In 1945 Woodbury established the Aquinas Academy in Gloucester Street, Sydney, to fulfil his ambition of sharing philosophical and theological insights with the Catholic laity. Concentrating on the original texts of Aquinas, he showed remarkable penetration as an interpreter of Thomist metaphysical principles. His incisive and entertaining expository style made philosophy's subtleties intelligible to the uninitiated. Communicating his own enthusiasm, he inspired several of his students to obtain doctorates abroad. He made a great impact upon the narrow outlook of Sydney Catholicism. His students came from all walks of life, including the professions and the universities. By 1963 the second Vatican Council was bringing an end to the closed world of Counter-Reformation Catholicism. The analytical approach of the medieval scholastics gave way to a renewal movement seeking a more inclusive synthesis of Christian thought: the academy struggled for relevance.

Tall, impressive and authoritarian, Woodbury scorned non-philosophers. He and his associates in the academy stood aloof from the political controversies of their day. Although sensitive, he lacked the capacity to engage with those holding contrary views; he had been nicknamed 'Bismarck' as a seminarian. His belligerent essays in controversy had little impact outside Catholic circles. He retired to Hunters Hill in 1974.

Woodbury had maintained close links with the Australian Illawarra Shorthorn Society and became an acknowledged authority on the breed, regularly visiting the Royal Easter Show. In the 1950s, as well as running the Aquinas Academy, he managed Collisdun stud at St Michael's Orphanage, Baulkham Hills. Troubled by bronchial illness throughout his life, Woodbury died on 3 February 1979 at St Vincent's Hospital, Darlinghurst, and was buried in the Marist cemetery, Toongabbie; he was later reinterred beside his parents at Spencer.

C. J. Baxter (ed), *General Musters of New South Wales, Norfolk Island and Van Diemen's Land 1811* (Syd, 1987); *A'sian Catholic Record*, 55, 1978, p 142; *Sydney Gazette*, 20 May 1820, 29 Jan 1829, *SMH*, 6 Feb 1979; information from Fr P. McMurrich, Marist Fathers' Archives, Hunters Hill, Syd.

JOHN THORNHILL

WOODGER, WILLIAM GEORGE (1887-1979), real-estate and stock-and-station agent, valuer and auctioneer, was born on 12 December 1887 at Garryowen, near Queanbeyan, New South Wales, youngest of eleven children of native-born parents Robert Woodger, labourer, and his wife Keturah, née Hilder. After completing his primary schooling at Queanbeyan, he was employed in the local stock-and-station agency of Thomas P. Maxwell, in which his elder brother Thomas Ernest (1872-1961) was a silent partner. Bill became a junior partner on his eighteenth birthday.

In 1910 Woodger moved to Sydney to work for a pastoral firm, Warden Harry Graves Ltd. With A. E. Robinson he compiled two editions of *The Australian Stock and Property Code*, a listing of telegraphic codes used by stock-and-station agents throughout Australia. On 27 September 1913 at Holy Cross Church, Woollahra, he married with Catholic rites Elsie Barton Dawkins (d.1965), a secretary in the same company, who was to compile a third edition of the list while her husband was overseas in World War I. Enlisting in the Australian Imperial Force on 30 October 1916, Woodger was posted to the 4th Battalion. He served on the Western Front from March 1918 until October, when he was sent to England to attend an officer-training course. Commissioned in January 1919, he was promoted lieutenant in April. His A.I.F. appointment terminated in Sydney on 19 September.

Next year he and his brother Tom entered into partnership as auctioneers and stock-and-station agents at Queanbeyan. They were joined by John Henry Calthorpe, a Gallipoli veteran, and on 10 March 1920 the firm became Woodgers & Calthorpe. On 12 December 1924 Bill Woodger represented the company in the joint auction, with the Sydney firm of Richardson & Wrench, of the first group of Canberra business and residential leases. Woodgers & Calthorpe, which was registered as a limited company in 1927, continued acting for the Commonwealth in the sale of Canberra leases for the next thirty-five years. The firm struck bad times during the Depression when the development of Canberra virtually ceased. Woodger was a member of a small group named the Kangaroo Club which aimed to 'keep Canberra hopping'. Both he and Calthorpe invested in Canberra businesses and, through the Canberra Building & Investment Co. Ltd, were active in the development of the Sydney and Melbourne buildings, the nucleus of the future city centre.

Woodger was president of the New South Wales division of the Commonwealth Institute of Valuers in 1949-52 and a vice-president of the general council of the institute in 1955-57. Following Calthorpe's death in 1950, the firm continued expanding under Woodger until 1959 when it merged with L. J. Hooker [q.v.14] Ltd. As chairman of L. J. Hooker Ltd & Woodgers & Calthorpe Ltd, he was appointed to the board of L. J. Hooker Investment Corporation Ltd and Hooker Pastoral Co. Pty Ltd. In 1960 he was entrusted with the acquisition of W. L. Buckland's [q.v.13] huge sheep and cattle properties which included Victoria River Downs, Northern Territory, and stud properties in four States—said to be the largest pastoral purchase in Australia's history. He retired in 1964, regretful that he was not twenty years younger to take advantage of the great future he foresaw for Canberra.

A strongly built man with a good speaking voice, Woodger took a leading place in Canberra business, sporting and public life. In his early years in Canberra he had been chairman of the Canberra City Area Lessees' Association, the original body representing crown lessees. He was president of the Canberra Chamber of Commerce, a director of the Canberra Tourist Bureau, and a founder and director of a number of Canberra businesses including Canberra Steam Laundry Ltd, Canberra Shops Ltd, Federal Meat Purveyors Pty Ltd and Federal Finance Co. Ltd. He was also a director of Australian Landtrusts Pty Ltd and Television Australia Ltd.

Foundation president (1930-31) of the Canberra Amateur Swimming Club and president (1939-45) of the Australian Capital Territory Rugby Union, Woodger also held various offices in the Royal Canberra Golf Club. During World War II he was the commander of No.43 Squadron, Air Training Corps, chairman of the local recruiting committee and a member of bodies controlling land sales and petrol distribution. He was president of the Canberra City sub-branch of the Returned Sailors', Soldiers' and Airmen's Imperial League of Australia. Survived by his four daughters, he died on 25 January 1979 at Lane Cove, Sydney, and was cremated.

J. Gibbney, *Canberra 1913-1953* (Canb, 1988); *Country Life Stock & Station J*, 10 Dec 1954, p 6, 'Agents Supp', 8 July 1960, p 30; *Canb Times*, 9, 13 Dec 1954, 5 Nov 1960, 12 Mar 1963, 10 Dec 1964, 1 Feb 1979; information from Miss H. Woodger, Chifley, Canb.   PATRICIA CLARKE

WOODS, JOHN GRIEVE (1900-1980), medical practitioner, was born on 17 January 1900 at Albury, New South Wales, eighth child of William Cleaver Woods, a physician from Liverpool, England, and his native-born wife Margaret, née Grieve. John was educated at Albury, then at Scotch College, Melbourne. Having completed first-year medicine at the University of Melbourne (M.B., B.S., 1923), he enlisted on 27 March 1918 in the Australian Imperial Force. Arriving in England on 14 November as a reinforcement for the 14th Battalion, he returned to Melbourne where he was discharged from the A.I.F. on 24 March 1919.

Woods resumed his studies at the university and was a resident medical officer at the Alfred Hospital. On 24 March 1925 he married Lucie Edith Munro (d.1985) at Scots Church. He practised at Corowa, New South Wales (1925-27) and, from 1928, at Urana. Seeking 'a varied and adventurous life', on 15 June 1939 he entered the Australian Aerial Medical Services (Flying Doctor Service of Australia from 1942), started by Rev. John Flynn [q.v.8]. The authorities refused to permit Woods to join the Australian Army Medical Corps in World War II.

Based at Broken Hill, he originally flew in Fox Moth aeroplanes on charter from Australian National Airways Pty Ltd. Later the F.D.S. bought a Dragon Moth. From 1939 to 1942 his pilot was Hugh Bond, a colourful character. Woods never interfered in flying matters, accepting his pilot's dictum: 'render unto Bond, the things that are Bond's'. As no nursing sisters were available, the pilot became his clinical assistant on calls. They communicated by passing notes through a trapdoor; the noise made even shouted conversation impossible. In his first year he made 45 medical flights and flew 17 129 miles (27 566 km). In the year ending 30 June 1943 he made 72 flights and covered 32 549 miles (52 382 km).

During his service, Woods survived a crash and a number of forced landings. As well as carrying out mercy flights, and directing surgery by radio, he paid regular monthly visits to such isolated centres as Tibooburra, Pooncarie and Menindee where he introduced the immunization of children and was often called on to act as a dentist and veterinary surgeon. The 'tall, rather lean, sunburnt doctor, with his surprisingly youthful appearance and reticent manner', entered into the lives of his patients. He wrote of his experiences in the magazine, the *Flying Doctor*.

In 1948 Woods visited Britain and the United States of America to study medical developments and to investigate the possible prevention and cure of airsickness. On resigning from the F.D.S. in 1949, he entered general practice: first at Malvern, Melbourne, in 1949-63, and then at Newcastle, New South Wales, from 1963 until he retired in 1975. John Woods was a kindly, compassionate and humorous man who understood country people. Music-making was 'something of a passion with him': he played the piano well, built himself an electronic organ and provided music for country dances on his piano accordion. Carrying the necessary equipment with him on his flights, he tuned many a piano on isolated stations. A keen cricketer in his youth, he played tennis and later golf. Survived by his wife, and their son and daughter, he died on 27 April 1980 at Royal Newcastle Hospital and was cremated. Three of his brothers and his son became medical practitioners.

J. Bilton, *The Royal Flying Doctor Service of Australia* (Syd, 1961); M. Page, *The Flying Doctor Story, 1928-78* (Adel, 1977); *Royal Flying Doctor Service of Australia* (Syd, 1990); *Flying Doctor*, 1 Oct 1941, 1 July 1942, 1 Apr 1948; *SMH*, 2 Aug 1940, 12 Aug 1943, 12 Feb 1949; *New York Times*, 20 June 1946; information from Dr J. C. Woods, Gisborne, Vic.   G. T. FRANKI

WOODWARD, SIR ERIC WINSLOW (1899-1967), army officer and governor, was born on 21 July 1899 at Hay, New South Wales, third son of Victorian-born parents Albert William Woodward (d.1911), manager of Toms Lake station (near Booligal), and his wife Marie Caldwell, née Reid. Bert Woodward later managed two properties in Queensland: Biddenham, north of Charleville, and Ellangowan, near Clifton. Eric attended Toowoomba Grammar School, where he did well academically, captained the swimming team, played in the first XV, and 'proved himself industrious and gentlemanly and a boy of sterling character'. His mother's reduced means after her husband's death prevented him from going to university. In 1917 he entered the Royal Military College, Duntroon, Federal Capital Territory. He graduated close to the top of his class and was commissioned lieutenant on 16 December 1920.

In 1921-22 Woodward served for twelve months with the 7th Queen's Own Hussars in India. Returning to Australia, he gained further experience as adjutant and quartermaster of light horse regiments in New South Wales. In 1925 he transferred to the Royal Australian Air Force and qualified as a pilot at No.1 Flying Training School, Point Cook, Victoria. He was made adjutant of the school and developed a reputation as an excellent pilot. On 7 February 1927 at St Stephen's Presbyterian Church, West Caulfield, he married his cousin Amy Freame Weller. Her distress at the high death rate of R.A.A.F. aircrew in flying accidents may have influenced his decision to revert to the army in 1928.

Promoted captain in December, Woodward became adjutant and quartermaster of the 19th Light Horse Regiment, at Ballarat (1928-29), and of the 4th L.H.R., at Warrnambool (1929-34), before being posted to the Directorate of Military Training, Army Headquarters, Melbourne. In January 1937 he was sent to the Staff College, Camberley, England. Next year he gained his majority. Back in Australia, he joined the Australian Imperial Force on 13 October 1939 as deputy assistant quartermaster general, 6th Division, responsible for logistical matters: accommodation, transport, and the supply of food, clothing and ammunition. He sailed for the Middle East in April 1940.

For 'devotion to duty', especially in the operations in North Africa (December 1940-January 1941), Woodward was appointed O.B.E. (1941). He served in Greece (March-April) as a lieutenant colonel on General Sir Thomas Blamey's [q.v.13] staff. Promoted temporary colonel in May, he was assistant adjutant and quartermaster general, I Corps, in the Syrian campaign (June-July). Following a series of short appointments, he was posted as A.A. & Q.M.G., 9th Division, in May 1942.

Sir Leslie Morshead [q.v.15] praised his efforts before and during the battle of El Alamein, Egypt (23 October-4 November), describing him as 'one of the finest staff officers I have ever known'. Woodward was awarded the Distinguished Service Order. He was twice mentioned in dispatches for his work in the Middle East.

Arriving in Australia in February 1943, Woodward held the post of brigadier, general staff, at headquarters, Northern Territory Force (March-December), and then that of director of staff duties at Land Headquarters, Melbourne. In July 1945-March 1946 he was D.A. & Q.M.G., and sometime senior officer, at headquarters, Morotai Force. After a term at A.H.Q., Melbourne, in 1946-47, he attended the Imperial Defence College (1948), and remained in London as Australian army representative. From December 1949 he was at A.H.Q., Melbourne, as deputy adjutant general. He implemented the new national service scheme, and fought for improvements in soldiers' pay and conditions. For several months in 1950-51 he reported directly to Prime Minister (Sir) Robert Menzies [q.v.15] as head of a special staff which planned counter-measures should the government's attempt to proscribe the Communist Party of Australia lead to widespread industrial unrest.

On 20 February 1951 Woodward was promoted temporary major general and made deputy chief of the General Staff. Seven months later he became adjutant general. In 1952 he was elevated to C.B.E. Although he was seen as a candidate for appointment as chief of the General Staff, he was 'tired of dealing with bureaucrats and politicians' and requested that his name should not be put forward. He moved to Sydney in May as general officer commanding, Eastern Command. His new role as senior army officer in New South Wales—which his great-grandfather Charles William Wall had filled in 1823-25—made him a public figure. In speeches and interviews with journalists he avoided controversy. Promoted temporary lieutenant general and substantive major general in December 1953, he was appointed C.B. in 1956.

When Sir John Northcott's [q.v.15] successful term as governor of New South Wales drew to a close, Premier J. J. Cahill [q.v.13] sought another Australian-born military officer to succeed him. He chose Woodward, who assumed office on 1 August 1957. The thirty-first governor of New South Wales, he was the first to have been born there. Appointed K.C.M.G. (1958) and K.C.V.O. (1963), he was awarded honorary doctorates by the universities of New South Wales (1958), Sydney (1959) and New England (1961). His term was free from serious constitutional problems, and he came to like and respect Cahill and his successors R. J. Heffron [q.v.14] and J. B. Renshaw.

Sir Eric and Lady Woodward carried out their duties assiduously, travelling throughout the State, supporting charitable, community and religious organizations, and hosting the many official visitors who stayed at Government House. Democratically minded, they endeavoured to meet a cross-section of the community and to be 'a unifying force' in society. They were understandably annoyed when (Sir) Roden Cutler announced in 1965 (as governor-designate) that he intended to make the office less stuffy and bring it closer to the people. Woodward retired on 31 July that year. Thereafter, he and his wife lived at Wahroonga.

Woodward was six feet (183 cm) tall, handsome and athletic. Driven 'by conscience and a sense of duty', he was an intelligent and hard-working man, always attentive to detail. He found it difficult to delegate responsibility and could sometimes be 'excessively censorious' of the work of others. Sir Eric died of myocardial infarction on 29 December 1967 at Royal Prince Alfred Hospital, Camperdown; he was accorded a state funeral with full military honours and was cremated. His wife survived him, as did their daughter and their son (Sir) Edward who became a judge. W. E. Pidgeon's portrait of Woodward is held by Government House, Sydney.

SMH, 28 July 1965, 30 Dec 1967; information from and papers held by Sir Edward Woodward, South Yarra, Melb.   DARRYL BENNET

WOOLACOTT, FRANCIS PROSSER (1903-1968), structural engineer and architect, was born on 11 June 1903 at Annandale, Sydney, eldest of three children of Henry Lovel Woolacott, a native-born general agent, and his second wife Jane Kate, née Wilmott, from Melbourne. Esmé Fenston [q.v.14] was his sister. At Drummoyne Public School, Frank was frustrated by the absence of science teaching and left with the Intermediate certificate. Articled to an elderly architect, he was released to study part time at Sydney Technical College. He was employed as a draughtsman in various architectural offices, cycling to and from work each day and studying at night. While still a student he undertook much of the structural engineering design at Henry Budden's office. Mastery of the aesthetic components of his profession did not come easily to him, but he understood 'bending moments, deflections, reinforced concrete and trusses'.

Registered to practise on 5 November 1928, Woolacott was admitted as an associate of the Royal Australian Institute of Architects in 1932. At Henry White's [q.v.12] practice, he designed the first theatre dress circles unsupported by thick columns in the stalls. His engineering and architectural practice began in 1933 with a loan of £100 from his future wife. Next year he opened an office in King Street. At St Peter's Church, Neutral Bay, on 15 January 1935 he married with Anglican rites Beatrice Joan Holland, a nurse. Terence Hale, who joined him in 1937, worked on local defence projects during World War II when Woolacott was attached (1943-46) to the United States Army as an engineer.

After the war Woolacott & Hale prospered and acted as structural consultants to many of Sydney's architects, all levels of government, and public companies. In some instances, such as the commissions for Nestlé factories in New South Wales and interstate, Woolacott acted as both architect and engineer. In the 1960s the practice extended its activities from multi-storeyed city buildings, schools, churches and industrial constructions to hydraulic services, waste and water treatment, roads, bridges and aircraft hangars. With the admission of new partners the firm underwent various name changes, but eventually reverted to its origins with the name Woolacotts.

From 1936 Woolacott was a member (vice-president 1938-39, president 1941-42) of the Association of Consulting Structural Engineers of New South Wales, founded in 1933 to establish structural engineering as a profession distinct from architecture. He served on several of its committees and, in 1960-68, on the Cumberland, Newcastle and Wollongong Board of Appeal Panel of the Department of Local Government. A member of the Institution of Engineers, Australia, from 1961, he spent much time transmitting the importance of professional standards and integrity to younger colleagues. He stressed the obligations of architects to design buildings that met the functional needs of clients, to supervise meticulously the construction, and to check and re-check their calculations.

Music was Woolacott's other main interest; when young he had won medals for piano playing. One of his earliest purchases was a phonograph. An unassuming and modest man, short in stature, with a ready smile, he took little interest in entertaining clients. His motorcar—a baby Fiat—contrasted sharply with the Mercedes of one of his partners. Troubled with misdiagnosed illnesses during the last fifteen years of his life, he died of hypertensive heart disease on 30 March 1968 at his Mosman home, and was cremated. His wife and their daughter survived him.

The History of the Association of Consulting Structural Engineers of New South Wales (Syd, 1983); J. E. Corlett, speech at 50th anniversary celebration of Royal Sydney Yacht Squadron, 13 Dec 1982 (copy on ADB file); Assn of Consulting Structural Engineers of NSW Archives, Syd; information from Woolacotts Consulting Engineers, Artarmon, Syd, Mrs J. Curnow, Hampton, NSW, and the late Mrs J. Woolacott; personal knowledge.

ROSS CURNOW

WOOLCOCK, JAMES GILBERT (1874-1957), mining engineer and metallurgist, was born on 7 November 1874 at Alma, South Australia, third of ten children of Richard Woolcock, a schoolmaster from Cornwall, and his South Australian-born wife Caroline, née Bottrill. Richard became a Church of Christ (later Baptist) minister and the family moved often. James was educated at Unley High School, Adelaide, and the South Australian School of Mines and Industries where in 1892 he completed a course in assaying and metallurgy taught by E. H. Rennie [q.v.11]. In 1894 he joined the Department of Mines. Employed at the State government's gold treatment plant at Mount Torrens in the Adelaide Hills, he became battery manager two years later.

In December 1896 the South Australian government sent Woolcock, as leader of a team of twelve men, to construct a gold-treatment plant in the Macdonnell Ranges at Arltunga, 60 miles (100 km) east of Alice Springs. Some seventy gold prospectors had been reported to be active there in what was thought to be a potentially rich goldfield. The decision to build the battery apparently owed much to the lobbying of F. J. Gillen [q.v.9]. Under Woolcock's direction, the heavy equipment was transported by rail to the terminus at Oodnadatta, thence some 404 miles (650 km) by camel and horse-drawn wagon to Alice Springs, and finally another 60 miles (100 km) to Arltunga. Heat, drought, remoteness, a shortage of food and water, a fire in the goods shed at Oodnadatta, and recalcitrant camels were obstacles overcome on the journey.

When the site for the works, selected earlier by the government geologist H. Y. L. Brown [q.v.7], proved to be unsuitable because of insufficient water, Woolcock chose a new one 8 miles (13 km) away. Gillen eventually opened the plant in February 1898. With a fifty-five tons per week capacity and employing about thirty men, it comprised a ten-head stamp battery to crush the hard quartzite ore, amalgamation plates to catch the gold, a cyanide plant to treat the tailings, a large boiler and some buildings. Woolcock was appointed a commissioner of the peace on 8 June that year. As magistrate at Arltunga, he took an interest in the welfare of local Aborigines.

In November 1898 Woolcock resigned and returned to Adelaide. On 13 September 1899 at the Christian Chapel, Norwood, he married,

with the forms of the Churches of Christ, Jane Johnston. He sluiced for gold in Victoria, worked as assayer on the Princess Royal mine at Norseman, Western Australia, and managed two small mines in South Australia, at Tarcoola and Deloraine. From about 1915 he was a mining consultant. After his wife died in 1938 he moved to Reynella. A director (1946-57) of South Australian Barytes Ltd, he helped to develop its mine near Blinman and the treatment plant at Quorn. Woolcock was a good-looking man of average height, with swept-back dark hair and a large moustache. In later years he participated in community affairs. Survived by three of his four sons, he died on 14 March 1957 at Reynella and was buried in Mitcham cemetery, Adelaide.

B. Woolcock, *A Family Who's Who* (Adel, 1981); B. O'Neil, *In Search of Mineral Wealth* (Adel, 1982); J. Mulvaney et al (eds), 'My Dear Spencer' (Melb, 1997); *Register* (Adel), 12 Feb 1898; J. Banks, James Gilbert Woolcock, ts of radio talk, 5CL, 1970 (Mort L); M. B. Woolcock, A Family Review, 1960, in M. S. Fisher papers (Mort L). D. F. FAIRWEATHER

WOOLLACOTT, ERNEST HENRY (1888-1977), Methodist minister, was born on 20 November 1888 at Aberdeen, Burra, South Australia, sixth of thirteen children of Thomas Henry Woollacott, a native-born contractor, and his wife Catherine Frances Carnatic, née Young, who had been born at sea. Raised in a staunchly Methodist home, Ernest was educated at Burra Public School. He preached locally from 1909 and was received as a candidate for the ministry by the South Australian Methodist Conference in 1913. In 1913-14 he attended Prince Alfred College, Adelaide; he then continued his theological studies at the Methodist Training Home, Brighton, while serving as a probationer at Morgan, Lamcroo, North Adelaide and Waikerie. On 6 March 1918 he was ordained at Kent Town, and on 3 April that year at the Glenelg Methodist Church he married Selma Beatrice White (d.1936).

Ministerial appointments followed at Saddleworth (1918), Orroroo (1921), Broken Hill, New South Wales (1924), Parkside, Adelaide (1928), Port Wakefield (1931) and Woodville (1935). On 26 July 1938 at the Marion Methodist Church, Woollacott married Edith Mary Parsons (d.1967), a 35-year-old nurse. In 1937 he had been 'set apart' for one year by the Methodist conference, as organizer of the church's social service department; he continued next year as secretary while serving at Maitland. He was appointed full-time superintendent of the department in 1939.

Woollacott brought to this role a strong commitment to social righteousness, a sharp mind and tactical skill. He was impatient with the view that religion and politics should be kept separate, and worked to secure pre-selection for parliamentary candidates who would stand firm on moral issues. A strong supporter of the temperance movement and an opponent of all forms of gambling, he tried to persuade politicians to adopt his views. He was founding director (1939) of the United Churches Social Reform Board, an alliance of Nonconformist churches which made well-informed contributions to public debate, and to parliamentary inquiries into liquor licensing, hotel opening hours, lotteries and off-course betting. With Woollacott as its chief strategist, the board successfully campaigned for the closing of betting shops during World War II and prevented their reopening afterwards.

The work of the social service department extended beyond the maintenance of 'unswerving hostility' to alcohol and gambling. Woollacott presided over an increasingly complex agenda that included postwar reconstruction, housing, promotion of community centres, monitoring of standards of radio and films, marriage guidance, international understanding, immigration, Aboriginal welfare, and industrial chaplaincy. In 1955, largely due to his efforts, the State government agreed to subsidize church homes for the aged. He was president (1949-50) of the State committee of the World Council of Churches.

In the 1950s Woollacott helped to establish Westminster School at Marion. Retiring in 1959 after twenty-two years as director of the social service department, he held office as secretary of the school council (1959-70) and chaplain (1961-63). In 1971 he published a history of the school's first decade. Always interested in sport, he played competitive bowls in his later years, and was a passionate supporter of the Sturt Football Club, Unley. Although he never moderated his position on alcohol or gambling, and regretted the weakening of the church's stance on these issues, he mixed easily with those who held different views. Survived by the son of his second marriage, he died on 18 April 1977 at Marion and was cremated. A boarding house at Westminster was named after him.

A. D. Hunt, *This Side of Heaven* (Adel, 1985); Methodist Church of A'sia (SA), *Conference Minutes*, 1937-60; T. R. Hayward, The Methodist Church and Social Problems in South Australia, 1900-1952 (B.A. Hons thesis, Univ Adel, 1952); J. Raftery, Till Every Foe is Vanquished: Churches and Social Issues in South Australia, 1919-1939 (Ph.D. thesis, Flinders Univ, 1988).   JUDITH RAFTERY

WOOTTEN, SIR GEORGE FREDERICK (1893-1970), soldier, solicitor and administrator, was born on 1 May 1893 at Marrickville,

Sydney, seventh child of London-born parents William Frederick Wootten, carpenter and later civil engineer, and his wife Louisa, née Old. He attended Fort Street Model School and, encouraged by his father, entered the Royal Military College, Duntroon, Federal Capital Territory, in 1911. Graduating in August 1914, Lieutenant Wootten was posted to the 1st Battalion, Australian Imperial Force. He went ashore at Gallipoli on 25 April 1915, became adjutant of his battalion next day and quickly won a reputation for courage. In May he was promoted captain. By the time of the evacuation in December he was a major.

When (Sir) John Monash [q.v.10] was forming the 3rd Australian Division in England in 1916, Wootten served briefly on his staff, but he made his name at the infantry brigade level in 1916-17. He was brigade major first to James Cannan of the 11th Brigade, then to (Sir) Charles Rosenthal [qq.v.13,11] of the 9th Brigade, both outstanding commanders. Wootten was awarded the Distinguished Service Order in October 1917 for excellent staff work. Two months later he was transferred to the headquarters of the 5th Division where he worked in the operations branch. In October 1918 he joined the General Staff at Field Marshal Sir Douglas (Earl) Haig's headquarters. His six months there completed a remarkable wartime experience as a staff officer. He was four times mentioned in dispatches. Only 25 years old, he was posted to the Staff College, Camberley, England, in March 1919. At St Joseph's Catholic Church, Roehampton, London, on 3 January 1920 he married Muriel Anna Frances Bisgood, a nurse.

That month Wootten sailed home to an Australia tired of war and with little interest in its army which was about to be reorganized and sharply reduced. Junior staff appointments in Adelaide then Hobart had no allure for Wootten who, as a brevet major, was on captain's pay. In 1923 he resigned his commission. His father-in-law in England came to the rescue, obtaining for him the managership of a clothing factory. He went back to England where he made a success of his job and enjoyed playing Rugby Union football. His children did not flourish, however; advised to move them to a warmer climate, he returned to Australia in 1926 with little prospect of work.

Perhaps Wootten recalled the advice of his headmaster at Fort Street that he should become a lawyer. As assistance was available from the Repatriation Commission, he opted for the law and was articled to J. E. Harcourt at West Wyalong. This was a period of poverty for the Woottens, whose fourth child was born in 1930, although their vegetable garden and poultry enabled them to eat well. Like many former officers, Wootten joined one of the anti-communist organizations, the Old

Guard; by 1931 he was employed as an organizer in Sydney. On 30 July that year, having completed his articles, he was admitted as a solicitor. He practised in a number of centres including Singleton, then went back to West Wyalong in 1936 to join a firm which became known as G. P. Evans, Englert & Wootten, but there was not much work in so small a town. His army pension, with money and parcels from England, kept the family going.

Developments in the army, made in response to events in Europe and East Asia, gave Wootten his chance. He was given command of the 21st Light Horse Regiment, Citizen Military Forces, in 1937 and promoted lieutenant colonel. By this time he was, in one respect, a changed man. Having given up smoking in 1930, he had begun to put on weight; he was over fifteen stone (95 kg) when he took command. By 1941 he would weigh twenty stone (127 kg). He was 5 ft 9 ins (175 cm) tall.

On 13 October 1939 Wootten was seconded to the A.I.F. and appointed to command the 2nd/2nd Infantry Battalion, despite doubts about his physical fitness for such a post. When the A.I.F. Reinforcement Depot was set up in Palestine late in 1940, he was promoted temporary brigadier and made its commander. In February 1941 he was given the well trained and equipped 18th Brigade.

As part of the 7th Division which was earmarked for the expedition to Greece, Wootten was instructed in March 1941 to capture the minor Italian fortress at Giarabub, Libya. This done, he was suddenly ordered on 4 April to move his brigade forthwith to Tobruk because the German *Afrika Korps* was transforming the situation in the Western Desert. Nine days later he came under the command of Major General (Sir) Leslie Morshead [q.v.15] who had raised and trained the 18th Brigade. After nearly five months besieged, Wootten's was the first brigade to be relieved. It rejoined the 7th Division, but only after the 7th's successful campaign in Syria. He was awarded a Bar to his D.S.O. for his leadership at Tobruk.

In March 1942 Wootten returned to Australia. When belatedly the 7th Division was sent to Papua to intervene in the crisis on the Kokoda Track in August 1942, his brigade was detached to bolster the defence of the Milne Bay airstrips. Having helped Milne Force to crush the Japanese, he took part in the worst fighting of the Pacific war—Buna and Sanananda, where pressure from General Douglas MacArthur's [q.v.15] ignorant General Headquarters for quick results in impossible situations caused unnecessary casualties. In March 1943, as temporary major general, Wootten succeeded Morshead as commander of the 9th Division, which was training on the Atherton Tableland, Queensland. He was appointed C.B.E. in May.

Wootten's massive frame attracted irreverent nicknames, but he won the respect of his division. If he was not as close to his soldiers as Morshead, he left lasting impressions of his mental power and tactical skill on officers of great distinction. MacArthur rated him as 'the best soldier in the Australian army who had it in him to reach the highest position' and Lieutenant General Robert Eichelberger, who commanded the Americans at Buna and Sanananda, wrote: 'He was always one of the best'. Brigadier Sir Frederick Chilton saw him as 'a formidable man indeed—I have never met another man of stronger will and personality'. Although his anger could be frightening, it was usually brief; his sense of humour extended even to himself. To the officer discreetly watching him test a wooden bench he remarked: 'When you are my size, Hill, you sit with circumspection'. It was probably his bulk that accounted for the rarity of his visits to forward troops during battle. His children were to remember him for his gentleness and the fun they had with him, but this was also the man who was to dismiss Brigadier Bernard Evans at Finschhafen, New Guinea.

The task of training his division for jungle warfare and amphibious operations was not lightened for Wootten by the death of his elder son George in an aircraft accident in May 1943 while he was on active service with the Royal Australian Air Force. From September that year to January 1944 he led his division to victories in New Guinea at Lae, Finschhafen and Sattelberg. A year of rest and training in Australia was followed by the pointless but successful operations of June-July 1945 in Borneo around Brunei and Labuan. Wootten worked to re-establish civil order in the former British territories, supporting the British Borneo Civil Affairs Unit attached to his headquarters. He was appointed C.B. (1945), General Sir Thomas Blamey [q.v.13] twice recommended him and other generals in vain for appointment as K.B.E. In 1944 he had received the United States of America's Distinguished Service Cross. One of his brigadiers, Selwyn Porter [q.v.], remembered him as 'the shrewdest Divisional Commander whom I have encountered . . . He was sound, sure and careful'.

Wootten left Labuan for Sydney on 22 September 1945 and transferred to the Reserve of Officers on 14 October, but Blamey appointed him to the military court of inquiry into Major General Gordon Bennett's [q.v.13] escape from Singapore. Another task, more to his liking, was the chairmanship (1945-58) of the Repatriation Commission in Melbourne; he devoted himself strenuously to the welfare of veterans. Yet the army still called: he commanded the 3rd Division, C.M.F., in 1947-50 and was the C.M.F. member of the Military Board in 1948-50.

Elevated to K.B.E. in 1958, Wootten returned to Sydney on his retirement that year from the Repatriation Commission. He was exhausted by the intensity of the work, after two world wars and the difficult years between them. 'Even the zest for sailing had gone', but he watched tennis and Test cricket. Although Sir George lived for a time in nursing homes, his wife and family cared for him. He died at the Repatriation General Hospital, Concord, on 31 March 1970 and was buried with full military honours and Anglican rites in Northern Suburbs cemetery; his wife, and their two daughters and younger son survived him. A portrait (1956) by (Sir) William Dargie is held by the Australian War Memorial, Canberra.

G. Long, *To Benghazi* (Canb, 1952) and *The Final Campaigns* (Canb, 1963); D. McCarthy, *South-West Pacific Area—First Year* (Canb, 1959); D. Dexter, *The New Guinea Offensives* (Canb, 1961); B. Maughan, *Tobruk and El Alamein* (Canb, 1966); D. M. Horner, *Crisis of Command* (Canb, 1978); A. Moore, *The Secret Army and the Premier* (Syd, 1989); P. Brune, *The Spell Broken* (Syd, 1997); J. Coates, *Bravery Above Blunder* (Melb, 1999); Wootten papers (AWM); information from Lieut Gen Sir Thomas Daly, Bellevue Hill, Syd, and Dr W. J. Wootten, Wingham, NSW.   A. J. HILL

WORRALL, DAVID THOMAS (1894-1968), journalist and radio-station manager, was born on 18 June 1894 at Castle Hill, New South Wales, son of Thomas Hirst Worrall, an English-born orchardist and artist, and his wife Emily Jane, née Barker, from New South Wales. Dave attended public schools in the Hunter River region and spent most of his childhood at West Maitland. He moved to Sydney as a youth, and took a junior position at the *Sun* newspaper, later joining the reporting staff.

Enlisting in the Australian Imperial Force on 14 October 1915, Worrall sailed for Egypt in December. He was wounded in the head while serving as a gunner with the 21st Field Artillery Brigade at Pozières, France, in August 1916. After recovering in England, he saw further action with the 2nd F.A.B. Returning to Sydney, he was discharged from the A.I.F. on 29 July 1919. He spent time on the staff of the *Newcastle Morning Herald* then in 1922 joined (Sir) Hugh Denison's [q.v.8] *Sun News-Pictorial* in Melbourne. Three years later he was in New York, reporting for the *World* and 'stringing' for (Sir) Keith Murdoch's [q.v.10] Melbourne *Herald* and Denison's Sydney *Sun*. Worrall came to regard the United States of America as the benchmark for innovation, design and good practice.

In 1928 Worrall returned to Melbourne and began a lifelong association with Murdoch media interests. He organized the *Herald*'s Learn-to-Swim campaign and the 'Ideal Town' competition. On 18 April 1929 at the Independent Church, Collins Street, he married with Congregational forms Kathleen Zoe Norris who later became well known as the radio personality 'Martha Gardener'. In July 1929 Murdoch appointed Worrall manager of his fledgling radio-station 3DB with a brief to sell sponsorship by the hour and transmit 'news flashes from the resources of the Herald and Weekly Times'. Worrall was partly responsible for the first commercial 'synthetic' broadcast of Test cricket, when 3DB carried studio-produced commentaries on the 1930 Australian tour of England. From 1942 he played a key role in organizing the annual *Sporting Globe*-3DB Good Friday Appeal for the (Royal) Children's Hospital.

Worrall gradually moved 3DB's programming away from vaudeville, pantomime, stunts and amateurism, replacing them with big-budget music, quiz and sports productions sponsored by national advertisers and relayed to other cities. He introduced to Australia breakfast sessions, hit parades and sponsored programmes. By 1949 he had lured the Colgate and Lever shows away from his rivals and 3DB was enjoying an immense following with more than a third of Melbourne's licence-holders regularly 'tuning-in'. The station produced outstanding broadcasts of horse-racing, called by Eric Welch [q.v.12]. An astute judge of popular culture and an able manager, Worrall kept abreast of developments in new media, including television, through correspondence and frequent overseas trips. He supported the construction of the Sidney Myer [q.v.10] Music Bowl, and ensured its popularity by staging Music for the People concerts.

Radio 3DB had been a founder of the Australian Federation of Commercial Broadcasting Stations in 1929 and Worrall was an active member all his professional life, serving as president in 1938 after he had successfully opposed ownership limits on radio proposed by the Federal government the year before. He was a member of the Advertising Club of Victoria and a regular personality at the club's annual revues where his sense of humour shone. In 1958 he stepped down as head of 3DB. For the next three years he chaired the station's board of management. He died on 12 April 1968 at East St Kilda and was cremated. His wife and their son survived him; a daughter had predeceased him.

R. R. Walker, *Dial 1179: The 3KZ Story* (Melb, 1984); C. Jones, *Something in the Air* (Syd, 1995); *Herald* (Melb), 14 June 1951; *Sun News-Pictorial*, 1 July 1961; *Age* (Melb), 13 Apr 1968; *Newspaper News and Advertising News*, 26 Apr 1968; Federation of Aust Radio Broadcasters archives (Syd).

JOHN SPIERINGS

WRIGHT, ERIC JOSEPH (1912-1979), medical practitioner, was born on 11 December 1912 at St Leonards, Sydney, second child of Joseph Clement Wright, carpenter, and his wife Violet May, née De Meur, both born in New South Wales. Educated at Lewisham Public School, Eric joined the Department of Public Health, Papua, as a medical assistant in 1930. He travelled throughout the Territory on foot, sometimes on patrols of up to 1500 miles (2400 km). During the 1939 influenza epidemic in the mountains behind Port Moresby, which killed one in eight of the population, he was compared to the 'bare foot healers' of China. In the following year he established at Divinukoiari (in the Northern Division) a school for medical assistants, believing that they should be trained in their own country.

Unable to join the armed forces because of poor health, Wright studied medicine (from 1942) at the University of Sydney (M.B., B.S., 1948). He also completed a diploma of tropical medicine (1951). Returning to the Territory of Papua and New Guinea as medical officer at Rabaul, he later set up a private practice among the town's Asian population. Shirley May Chan Wong, née Hee, a locally born Chinese nurse, worked for him as a receptionist. They were married on 18 July 1959 at the United Church, Boroko, Port Moresby.

Wright had rejoined the Department of Public Health in 1958 as assistant-director of medical training. One of his first achievements was to see to fruition plans for the establishment of a nursing school in Port Moresby, at which he did much of the teaching. Under his authority a second school of nursing was established at Rabaul in 1959. As a foundation member (1964) of the Nursing Council of Papua New Guinea, he insisted on a thoroughly professional training for the country's nurses.

In 1960 the Papuan Medical College, established to train indigenous doctors (previously educated in Suva), enrolled its first twenty students in temporary accommodation. Wright was appointed principal. Despite the lack of buildings and equipment, he was able to attract motivated and dedicated staff. He acquired the nearby Boroko newsagency and used some of the profits from the business to supplement government funds for the construction of the college's permanent buildings which were opened in 1964. Active in the Boy Scout movement in Sydney in his early life, he continued to participate in scouting in Papua New Guinea. In 1974 he was elected to the Port Moresby City Council.

A small man, Wright was 'a complex personality, at times brilliant in foresight and understanding, unorthodox, and frequently intolerant of others who did not see things in the same way he did'. In 1975 his deemed interference in the political affairs of the emerging nation and his close association with Josephine Abaijah's separatist Papua Besena movement led to his expulsion from the country. He left Port Moresby on 21 August and, in failing health, rejoined his family in Sydney. Suffering from cancer, he died of acute myocardial ischaemia on 21 December 1979 at Lewisham Hospital and was cremated; his wife, and their son and two daughters survived him.

E. Kettle, *That They Might Live* (Syd, 1979); I. Downs, *The Australian Trusteeship* (Canb, 1980); B. G. Burton-Bradley (ed), *A History of Medicine in Papua New Guinea* (Syd, 1990); *PIM*, Dec 1943, p 37; *SMH*, 28, 30 Aug 1973, 29 July 1975; information from Mrs S. Wright, Castle Hill, Syd; personal knowledge.   ALBERT SPEER

WRIGHT, PHILLIP ARUNDELL (1889-1970), grazier and benefactor, was born on 20 July 1889 at Wongwibinda, Armidale, sixth child and youngest son of native-born parents Albert Andrew Wright, grazier, and his wife Charlotte May, née Mackenzie, grand-daughter of George Wyndham [q.v.2]. Phillip's father died in 1890. His strong-willed mother quietly achieved much that her husband had tried to do. She purchased Wallamumbi in 1900 and Jeogla in 1901, creating a vast estate for her descendants whose name became associated with the 'Falls' country between the New England tableland and the Dorrigo plateau. Phillip's mother and sisters reared him on stories of the family's origins and his father's struggle to achieve a place on the land. Mostly educated at home by his eldest sister Weeta, in 1902 he had a few months at Bedford Grammar School during a visit to England with his mother. On his return, he attended Sydney Church of England Grammar School (Shore). From childhood he gained experience through hard work, riding, shooting and exploring the gorges of eastern New England.

In 1911 'P.A.', as Wright was known, visited Italy, France and Britain with a family party and returned through Canada. On 2 April 1913 he married with Anglican rites Ethel Mabel Bigg at All Saints Church, Thalgarrah. He was a member of Dumaresq Shire Council in 1917-20 and 1924-50. His family and properties, producing essential food supplies, were his first priority during World War I. In the 1917 transport strike, he volunteered to drive horse lorries in Sydney. Apart from Wallamumbi, which was always his headquarters, and Jeogla, he also owned, at different times Hernani, and in Queensland, Krui and Kindon. Ethel died in 1927 leaving three children. At All Saints Church of England,

Murwillumbah, he married Dora Isabella Temperley on 21 November 1928.

From 1927 to 1967, apart from two years, Wright served as a councillor (president 1946-48) of the Graziers' Association of New South Wales. He was president of the Graziers' Federal Council of Australia in 1949-50. Well known as a cattle-breeder, he was a committee-member (1926-65), president (1938-48) and treasurer (1955-61) of the Australian Hereford Society and president of the United Stud Beef Cattle Breeders' Association. He supported local enterprises: from 1928 he was a director of the New England North & North-West Producers Co. Ltd (which established wool auctions at Newcastle). Later he backed the establishment of D. M. Shand's [q.v.] East-West Airlines Ltd, and belonged to the Armidale Chamber of Commerce. He remained chairman of the family company, P. A. Wright & Sons Pty Ltd, until 1970.

Large in build and vision, Wright was a proud man. Perhaps his greatest love was for the natural beauty of the New England gorge country. Following his strong campaign, the New England National Park, 34 600 acres (14 002 ha) of State forest, was gazetted in 1934. He was foundation chairman (1933-59) of the trust that administered it. Wright had believed that a political party focussing on rural needs and development was required to counter the trend towards centralization. He was a member of the United Country Party's central council during World War II. From the 1920s he fought for a new State; in 1944-46 he was president of the New England New State Movement.

Although Wright had little formal education, he appreciated its value, particularly for young people isolated in rural areas. He was a board-member of The Armidale School. An original donor to New England University College, he was a foundation member (1938) and vice-chairman (1943-53) of its advisory council. When the college achieved independence in 1954, he was vice-chairman (deputy-chancellor from 1955) of the University of New England; in 1960 he succeeded Sir Earle Page [q.v.11] as chancellor. Wright donated Laureldale to the university as a farm for rural research, contributed to the school of natural resources and to Wright College, and gave a mace to the university, as well as prizes. In 1957 the university had conferred on him an honorary D.Sc.; he was appointed C.M.G. in 1962.

Wright belonged to the Australian Club, Sydney, and the Armidale Club, and enjoyed playing tennis. He died on 30 August 1970 at Wallamumbi and was cremated. His wife, and their son and daughter survived him, as did the daughter and two sons of his first marriage. His eldest child Judith Wright became a distinguished poet. Wright's memoirs, *Memories of a Bushwhacker* (1972), were published posthumously. Two portraits (1963 and 1971) of Wright by W. E. Pidgeon are held by the University of New England, Armidale.

J. Wright, *The Generations of Men* (Melb, 1959) and *Collected Poems, 1942-1970* (Syd, 1971) and *The Cry for the Dead* (Melb, 1981) and *Half a Lifetime* (Melb, 1999); O. Wright, *Wongwibinda* (Armidale, NSW, 1985); C. M. Wright, *Memories of Far Off Days* (Armidale, NSW, 1985); *Pastoral Review*, 17 Sept 1970, p 769; Armidale and District Hist Soc, *J and Procs*, no 25, 1982, p 1; Wright family papers (UNE Archives).
JILLIAN OPPENHEIMER

WRIGHT, SYDNEY EDWARD (1914-1966), pharmaceutical chemist, was born on 3 June 1914 at Waverley, Sydney, second child of Lancashire-born parents William Alfred Wright, carpenter, and his wife Emily Jane, née Hayes. After attending Sydney Boys' High School, he was apprenticed to a pharmacist with Washington H. Soul [q.v.6], Pattinson & Co. In 1934 Syd completed the required two years of part-time study at the University of Sydney, winning the gold medal of the Pharmaceutical Society of New South Wales. Too young to be registered as a pharmacist, he continued at university and in 1935 gained a diploma in pharmaceutical science. Once registered, he moved to Brisbane where he taught (1938-44) pharmacy at Central Technical College and studied science at the University of Queensland (B.Sc. Hons, 1942; M.Sc., 1944; D.Sc., 1963). He lectured in chemistry at the university in 1944-46. On 16 January 1943 at the Methodist Church, Clayfield, he had married Phyllis May Edwards, also a pharmacist.

In 1946 Wright was appointed principal of the New Zealand College of Pharmacy, Wellington. Convinced that pharmacists required an education soundly based on the chemical and biological sciences, he tried to persuade members of the Pharmaceutical Society of New Zealand and the government to replace the existing training system with a full-time university course. Unsuccessful, he returned to Australia in 1950 as senior lecturer in pharmacy at the University of Sydney (Ph.D., 1956) and was promoted to associate professor in 1956. He published his doctoral research results as *The Metabolism of Cardiac Glycosides* (Springfield, Illinois, 1960).

Prominent in the peace movement, Wright was a member of the executive committee of the Australian Convention on Peace and War which was held in Sydney in September 1953. In April next year he arranged an anti-war meeting at the Town Hall; speakers included (Sir) Marcus Oliphant, Canon (Bishop) E. J.

Davidson [q.v.13] and professors Alan Stout and Julius Stone. Wright was censured by the university's administration for hosting a reception in September for two peace activists, Josef Hromadka and Kathleen Lonsdale, on the premises of the Sydney University Union.

Wright pressed for a professional qualification for pharmacists in New South Wales, and for a research school to provide postgraduate degrees and diplomas. Due to his reputation as a left-winger, his first application for an entry visa to the United States of America had been refused, but in 1956 he was permitted to travel there; he also visited Europe to evaluate curricula and design a course suitable for Australians. The first students in a full-time, three-year degree course in pharmacy were enrolled at the University of Sydney in 1960; that year Wright became professor of pharmaceutical chemistry.

Although he continued to pursue his research interests—including the metabolism of food additives, especially dyes and antioxidants—Wright's main concern remained the promotion of professional pharmacy. In 1952-66 he was a member of the Pharmacy Board of New South Wales and the council of the Pharmaceutical Society of New South Wales. He helped to set up the New South Wales Pharmacy Research Trust in 1961 to provide research equipment, and stipends and conference expenses for postgraduate students. He sat on various panels: the State poisons advisory committee, the poisons schedule and food additives committees of the National Health and Medical Research Council, a group revising the British Pharmacopoeia, and the Commonwealth Department of Health's therapeutic substances standards committee. Revitalizing the pharmaceutical science section of the Australian and New Zealand Association for the Advancement of Science, he had served as president at the Melbourne meeting in 1955.

In 1962 Wright helped to organize 'ban the bomb' marches in Sydney. The minutes of the university's professorial board recorded in 1966 that 'Professor Wright had a strong sense of social responsibility, and he became associated with movements whose *bona fides* have been the subject of public debate; whatever may be the final verdict on such movements, Professor Wright's complete sincerity has never been in question'.

A quick thinker, Wright was strong minded, demanding, impatient, often impulsive, and intolerant of obfuscation. He was also kind, charming, generous, and occasionally stubborn. Although not an accomplished sportsman, he had the physique of a Rugby forward, and enjoyed surfing and bushwalking. Survived by his wife and their son, he died suddenly on 7 October 1966 while driving his car at Drummoyne, Sydney. He was cremated.

Later that year the Pharmaceutical Society's research trust was named after him.

G. Haines, *'The Grains and Threepenn'orths of Pharmacy'* (Kilmore, Vic, 1976) and *Pharmacy in Australia* (Syd, 1988); R. Combes, *Pharmacy in New Zealand* (Auckland, NZ, 1981); D. Branagan and G. Holland (eds), *Ever Reaping Something New* (Syd, 1985); *Aust J of Science*, 29, no 6, 1966, p 165; personal knowledge.   TOM WATSON

WRIGLEY, HUGH (1891-1980), army officer, was born on 1 December 1891 at Scarsdale, Victoria, sixth child of John Wrigley, a mine-engine driver from England, and his Scottish-born wife Isabella, née McGeachin. Educated at state schools and privately, Hugh joined the Department of Defence, Melbourne, as a military staff clerk in May 1911.

On 17 August 1914 Wrigley enlisted in the Australian Imperial Force as a staff sergeant and was allotted to 3rd Brigade headquarters. He served at Gallipoli from April 1915 and was made temporary warrant officer in October. Commissioned on 20 February 1916 in Egypt, he was posted to the 59th Battalion. In June he was promoted lieutenant and sent to France as adjutant of the 60th Battalion. For his 'gallant leadership' at the battle of Fromelles (19 July), during an attack on enemy trenches in which he was severely wounded, he was awarded the Military Cross. He spent two months in hospital in England and was promoted captain in November. Rejoining the 60th Battalion in January 1917, he resumed duty as adjutant in May.

Wrigley transferred to the Indian Army in July and joined the 6th Rajputana Rifles as a second lieutenant. He took part in campaigns in Afghanistan (1919), Iraq (1920-21) and Waziristan (1922) as a captain before returning to Australia in 1922. In partnership with several Indian Army friends, he bought a grazing property at Balmoral, Victoria. On 8 January 1926 at Gardiner Presbyterian Church, Melbourne, he married Alison Grove Wilson; they had a son before being divorced. After moving to a property at Urangeline, New South Wales, Wrigley worked (from 1930) as a representative of the Vacuum Oil Co. Pty Ltd, first at Hay and later at Sale, Victoria.

An active member of the Militia in 1933-36 and again from March 1939, Major Wrigley was appointed second-in-command of the 2nd/6th Battalion, A.I.F., on 13 October. He embarked with the unit for the Middle East in April 1940. In December he was promoted lieutenant colonel and given command of the 2nd/5th Battalion. At Bardia, Libya, he was wounded in the shoulder by shell-fire on 3 January 1941. After convalescing, he rejoined the 2nd/6th Battalion in March and led it in the Greek campaign in April. A 'respected commander', he was seen by his soldiers as a 'severe man' who wielded 'uncompromising authority' over his unit. Privately he was gentle, with a good sense of humour.

In January 1942 Wrigley was promoted colonel. Next month he took charge of the A.I.F. Reinforcement Depot in Palestine. Appointed temporary brigadier on 28 September, he commanded the 20th Brigade at the Battle of El Alamein, Egypt, where he displayed 'personal courage, power of command, and battle knowledge of a high order'. On 27 October he relinquished his acting rank and resumed his post at the reinforcement depot. He was mentioned in dispatches and appointed C.B.E. (1943).

Back in Australia in February 1943, Wrigley served as commandant of various training depots and bases, again as a temporary brigadier. He assumed control of the 1st Base Sub-Area in September 1944 and took it to Morotai, Netherlands East Indies, in March 1945. Following the Japanese surrender in August, he led the 3rd Australian Prisoner of War Reception Group in Manila. There he managed the recovery of over 12 000 British and 3000 Australian personnel from the Japanese. In November he was given command of the 33rd Brigade on Ambon, N.E.I. He returned to Australia in February 1946 and was transferred to the Reserve of Officers on 30 April.

Wrigley was appointed to the Department of Commerce and Agriculture in November 1946. Next year he joined a trade delegation sent to Japan to buy textiles, then stayed for two years as commercial counsellor at the Australian mission. Later he was trade commissioner in Hong Kong and the Philippines (1949-52), and at Bombay, India (1953-55), and Vancouver, Canada (1955-57). He was interested in art and antiques, and enjoyed golf and riding; in Hong Kong and India he had owned racehorses.

Retiring in Australia, Wrigley became a company director and bought property in New South Wales at Bringelly and Wagga Wagga, in partnership with his son. At the Presbyterian Church, Burleigh Heads, Queensland, on 18 September 1968 he married Jean Stewart, née Pirrit, a widow. Survived by his wife and the son of his first marriage, he died on 3 June 1980 at Caringbah, Sydney, and was cremated. H. W. Parry's portrait of Wrigley was submitted for the 1944 Archibald [q.v.3] prize.

C. E. W. Bean, *The A.I.F. in France, 1916* (Syd, 1929); G. Long, *To Benghazi* (Canb, 1952) and *Greece, Crete and Syria* (Canb, 1953); B. Maughan, *Tobruk and El Alamein* (Canb, 1966); H. Gullett, *Not as a Duty Only* (Melb, 1976); D. Hay, *Nothing Over Us* (Canb, 1984); S. Trigellis-Smith, *All the King's Enemies* (Vic, 1988); *Aust Women's Weekly*, 16 Apr 1949; *SMH*, 7 Nov 1946, 27 Mar 1947, 11 Oct 1952, 5 Sept 1953; A. R. Taysom, History of the Australian Trade Commissioner Service, 2 (ts, 1983, NL); information from Mr H. N. Wrigley, Wagga Wagga, NSW.
                                      C. D. COULTHARD-CLARK

WUNDERLY, SIR HARRY WYATT (1892-1971), medical practitioner and public-health administrator, was born on 30 May 1892 at Hawthorn, Melbourne, third son of Jacques Wunderly, an accountant born in Italy, and his wife Mary Jane, née Hawkeswood, who came from England. His father died of tuberculosis in 1897, leaving the family in straitened circumstances. Scholarships enabled Harry to attend Wesley College and the University of Melbourne (M.B., B.S., 1915; M.D., 1927) where he lived at Queen's College. He was obliged to take a year off from his studies when he himself developed tuberculosis. After graduating, he joined a general practice in the Adelaide Hills, South Australia. At Christ Church, Mount Barker, on 18 February 1919 he married with Anglican rites Alice Jean Bowman Barker; having no children she was to become his enthusiastic partner in every phase of his professional life.

In 1924 Wunderly began practising in Adelaide as a consultant physician specializing in tuberculosis. Appointed by the South Australian government to inquire into methods of treating the disease, he visited England, Switzerland and Austria in 1924-25. He later advocated a policy of tuberculosis control that included strict supervision of milk supplies, coupled with early diagnosis and notification. During the 1930s he carried out a tuberculin survey of young women in Adelaide. Those who reacted positively to the Mantoux test were given chest X-rays. He promoted the design and manufacture of radiographic machines suitable for mass surveys.

At the outbreak of World War II Wunderly helped to secure the routine screening of troops for tuberculosis. On 1 June 1942 he was appointed captain, Australian Army Medical Corps. Next month he was promoted temporary major. He served at the 116th Australian General Hospital, Charters Towers, Queensland, and at the 106th A.G.H., a sanatorium at Bonegilla, Victoria. Rising to temporary lieutenant colonel in May 1945, he transferred to the 115th Military Hospital, Heidelberg, Melbourne, in August 1946. His appointment terminated on 7 May 1947.

That year Wunderly became the first director of tuberculosis in the Commonwealth Department of Health, Canberra. Owing to the housing shortage, he lived with his wife for some five years in one room of the Hotel Canberra before moving to Forrest. Within two years he had persuaded the Federal and State governments to adopt a national tuberculosis control programme, encompassing case-finding in a network of chest clinics supplemented by mass X-ray surveys. Free medical, hospital and follow-up care was provided for those with active tuberculosis, together with a generous living allowance for breadwinners undergoing treatment. Preventive measures, including Bacillus Calmette-Guérin vaccination, were also part of the programme. He was helped by the development of the first effective anti-tuberculosis drugs—streptomycin and isoniazid.

Wunderly was a fellow of the Royal Australasian College of Physicians (1938), the Royal College of Physicians, London (1952), and the American College of Chest Physicians (1952). In 1947 he gave £18 000 to the R.A.C.P. to fund travelling scholarships in thoracic disease. Knighted in 1954, Sir Harry retired three years later, secure in the knowledge that the rate of tuberculosis in Australia was among the lowest in the world and still falling. He was president of the National Association for the Prevention of Tuberculosis in Australia in 1959-61. His latter years were spent as a consultant with the World Health Organization. Always gentle and unassuming, he enjoyed reading, gardening and travel. Six months after the death of his wife, he died on 14 April 1971 in Canberra and was cremated.

A. S. Walker, *Clinical Problems of War* (Canb, 1952); G. L. McDonald (ed), *Roll of the Royal Australasian College of Physicians*, 1, 1938-1975 (Syd, 1988); A. J. Proust (ed), *History of Tuberculosis in Australia, New Zealand and Papua New Guinea* (Canb, 1991); *MJA*, 28 Aug 1971, p 496; information from Dr M. de L. Faunce, Weetangera, Canb.

ANTHONY PROUST

WURTH, WALLACE CHARLES (1896-1960), public servant and university chancellor, was born on 14 January 1896 at Pipeclay Creek, Mudgee, New South Wales, second of five children of native-born parents William George Wurth, schoolteacher, and his wife Edith, née Webster. His drive, ambition and independence were in evidence even as a child. By the age of 11, 'very much his own man', Wally won a bursary to Sydney Boys' High School and boarded with an aunt at Lewisham.

Successful at the State public service competitive examination in May 1912, Wurth was appointed a junior clerk in the Department of Lands. Quickly deciding that this was a dead-end posting, he transferred to the Department of Attorney-General and Justice. His shorthand speed was 80 words per minute (a skill he had acquired when he decided that he did not want to miss a word of lessons—to the consternation of his teachers). He found his new duties of dealing with ministerial correspondence more congenial.

On 1 February 1916 Wurth enlisted in the Australian Imperial Force. He served on the Western Front as a stretcher-bearer with the 7th Field Ambulance and was wounded at Bullecourt, France. Later he recalled that war was 'a filthy, terrible business'. The 'sheer horror' of the front left him sympathetic to the problems of ex-servicemen and their families. Promoted sergeant in April 1919, he returned to Sydney where he was demobilized on 10 August. With four months leave on full public service pay, Wurth after two weeks was agitating to return to his position of clerk at the Public Service Board, to which he had been appointed in October 1915. Enforced idleness was to him a yoke, not a reward. On 10 January 1920 he married Phyllis Bertha Cavell at St Philip's Church of England, Sydney.

A protégé of James Williams, later chairman of the board, Wurth noted that a law degree had helped Williams's advancement and in 1920 enrolled as a part-time student in the faculty of law at the University of Sydney (LL.B., 1924). By 1928 he had risen to the position of inspector—not merely as a result of his friendship with Williams, but by ability and hard work. Wurth realized the importance of cultivating powerful patrons, which he did by exercising considerable charm and by completing inquiries and projects promptly and efficiently, not only for his administrative superiors but also for ministers and premiers. At the behest of (Sir) William McKell, then a minister in J. T. Lang's [q.v.9] government, he headed a small committee to investigate the fraudulent use of food and medical relief funds for the unemployed. McKell later wrote that the excellence of his work 'permanently established him as a public servant of courage and capacity with a very bright future'.

A colleague and friend of Wurth at the board, (Sir) Bertram Stevens [q.v.12], became premier in 1932; he secured Wurth's appointment as industrial registrar and assistant under-secretary of the Department of Labour and Industry that year, then as a member of the Public Service Board in 1936, and finally as chairman of the board in 1939. While many Labor supporters saw these appointments as strengthening the conservative grip on administration, Wurth's legal qualifications and industrial experience fitted him for the task of dealing with both employers and unions.

His return to the board marked its resurgence as the most powerful of the state's central agencies. (Sir) George Mason Allard's [q.v.7] 1917 report on the public service became 'Holy Writ' for Wurth; he kept a well-thumbed copy in the top drawer of his desk with the recommendations ticked as they were implemented—a return to the board's traditional basics of efficiency, economy and recruitment. Initially, however, Wurth's dealings with E. J. Payne, the somewhat ponderous chairman, were inauspicious. 'Virtually quarantined' without work, he warned Payne that unless papers appeared on his desk, he would remain at home. Papers duly appeared. With typical zeal he made himself useful to Payne. Following Payne's retirement, Wurth's succession as chairman, on 24 May 1939, was a formality. In 1941 he was appointed C.M.G.

Aided by an almost photographic memory, Wurth maintained a prodigious output. An impersonal martinet, he set impossibly short deadlines for staff. He could not bear to be idle, constantly fidgeted and took work home each evening (and without fail completed it), spending Sunday mornings at the local harbourside park with one eye on his two young sons playing at the water's edge and the other on his files. With rare exceptions his official relationships were marked by formality, yet with individuals and small groups he could be charming. On country trips he became a 'delightful' and sociable companion. Physically Wurth made an unprepossessing ogre—he was short, bespectacled and undistinguished-looking. Yet when he spoke, 'he delivered his words forcefully, rapidly and apparently without premeditation'. The meaning was 'clear and precise', but he was not an impressive public speaker. Nor was he comfortable with the press.

World War II resulted in interruptions for both Wurth and the public service as a whole. The 'ingenuous and generous' Alexander Mair [q.v.10], who succeeded Stevens as premier in July 1939, saw no reason to interfere in Wurth's administration of the service, while McKell, who swept to power in May 1941, did not share Lang's dislike of senior public servants. The future of the board was secure but the transformation of Australian society to a total-war footing saw almost 65 per cent of male public servants between the ages of 18 and 40 serving with the armed forces and another 4 per cent seconded to the Commonwealth Public Service.

Released from the board in July 1941, Wurth served as Federal director of manpower priorities and chairman of the Manpower Priorities Board. At first he investigated and advised but exercised little executive power. By virtue of 'the circumstances of the time and the personality of the board's chairman', a blueprint was drawn up for a directorate of manpower and the machinery to implement its policies. In January 1942 Wurth was designated director-general of manpower. As he wrote in his *Control of Manpower in Australia* (1944), the edifice rested on five pillars: reserved occupations, protected industries, control of labour engagements, and the direction and registration of labour. Wurth was acutely aware of the need to balance the demands of war mobilization against 'individual susceptibilities', which he saw as the central problem of a democracy at war. The directorate's offices spread throughout the country as it absorbed State public servants; between February 1942 and January 1944 the staff grew from 324 to 2556. With his headquarters in Sydney, Wurth did not relinquish his grip on the public service, working as chairman of the Public Service Board every Saturday.

Commonwealth wartime administration was characterized by powerful institutions headed by powerful individuals, with overlapping spheres of responsibilities. Wurth soon locked horns with his minister, the firebrand E. J. Ward [q.v.], over a scheme of national registration, stating that he would resign rather than carry out Ward's policy. Their 'cold formality degenerated into smouldering hatred'. J. B. Chifley [q.v.13], then treasurer, esteemed Wurth highly and persuaded his cabinet colleagues not to back Ward. Thereafter Wurth used Chifley as his conduit to government. A more formidable opponent in the administrative battle for control of manpower was the controversial E. G. Theodore [q.v.12], head of the Allied Works Council which oversaw all civil and military engineering and construction works in Australia. Equally aggressive was the redoubtable Essington Lewis [q.v.10], managing director of the Broken Hill Proprietary Co. Ltd, who as director-general of munitions was the 'industrial dictator' of the war effort. All the principals were conscious of their own responsibilities, and robust and acrimonious exchanges occurred before good sense prevailed and compromises were achieved. Wurth's position was strengthened with his appointment as chairman of the War Commitments Committee which had been formed in September 1942 and, in effect, became the War Cabinet's standing committee on manpower allocation and 'the principal protagonist for the indirect war effort', a counterweight to the strength of the defence structure. This 'balancing' of the war effort was due largely to Wurth's efforts—his 'persistence and stubborn refusal to be sidetracked, together with the high quality of the Manpower Directorate's submissions'.

Wurth himself made sacrifices for the war effort. He refused the use of an official car, travelling by bus each day to and from his home at Vaucluse. Already troubled by angina, he obtained a neighbour's permission to take a short cut through his property when climbing the hill to the bus stop. He refused a salary for the director-general's position, and later joked that he was the only bureaucrat who had ever sacked himself when, in September 1944, he handed over the manpower organization to his deputy William Funnell [q.v.14].

Forgoing opportunities to join the Commonwealth Public Service during postwar reconstruction, mainly because in Canberra he would have faced greater competition for control and domination of the bureaucracy, Wurth returned to the New South Wales Public Service Board. He set about refining its examination system, and although entry was still by the Intermediate and Leaving certificates, external accountancy, secretarial, technical and university qualifications could be substituted for the various 'grade' internal examinations. Ostensibly promotions were based on merit, with seniority subordinated to 'special fitness'. Both merit and 'special fitness' developed a Wurthian flavour. Disappointed with the managerial abilities of the 'decent fellows' in the Treasury and the Premier's Department during the war, McKell asked Wurth to scour the public service for the best men available to revitalize these two traditional rivals for control of the State's administrative machinery. Not surprisingly, it was Wurth's protégés who happened to be best fitted for the task, young men whom he had found to be intelligent, conscientious and, above all, loyal to him. After a period of understudy sufficient to avoid criticism, they were promoted to permanent head positions.

An earlier plan of having personnel officers in all departments could now be implemented and they, too, soon began keeping Wurth informed, encouraged by the prospects of promotion to the board and then to senior departmental positions. Wurth's record in industrial relations was one of union containment, with certain exceptions. The board's powers to control salaries, working conditions and discipline in both the public service and teaching service were modified only by the establishment of the Crown Employees Appeal Board in 1944. The New South Wales Teachers' Federation in particular campaigned strongly for their members to be freed from the yoke of the board and placed under a separate education commission. Although Wurth had deflected most of these and other attacks, he feared that the board could eventually lose its control over the teaching service. In 1954 he thus embraced a suggestion of (Sir) Harold Dickinson, the board's secretary, that its size be increased by the appointment of a teachers' representative, namely Harry Heath who had emerged as the 'moderate' federation president owing 'allegiance neither to Moscow nor to Rome'. Thereafter criticism became less strident.

The longstanding requirement that the board inspect departments to ensure efficiency and economy had since 1919 been delegated to inspectors, but Wurth's determination to lead by example was demonstrated in numerous anecdotes, many of which illustrated reduction of costs, rather than increases in effectiveness. The austerity of the war years (replacing corks in ink bottles between dipping the nib to prevent evaporation and encasing the stubs of pencils in metal holders) was maintained, and 'The Case of Lennie's Carpet' became part of the board's folklore. Leonard Verrills, an inspector, asked for the replacement of decrepit carpet which regularly tripped visitors to his office. Wurth's solution was to remove the carpet and, lest he be accused of victimizing Verrills, the carpets from the offices of all other inspectors. Air travel by public servants was prohibited, except in cases of urgency approved by the board, so that magistrates on country circuits were sometimes forced to wait two or three days for the next train to Sydney. Motorcars, too, were frowned on, although after petrol rationing ended Wurth travelled to and from the office in a car from the pool. This indulgence (not extended to departmental heads) may have resulted partly from his cardiac condition. His own principles were above reproach; he returned Christmas presents or sent a gift of equal value.

Wurth was remarkably successful in imposing these standards on the public service: 'corruption used to upset him more than anything else', especially theft or bribery. Present at every disciplinary hearing of the board, he ruthlessly held to the dictum of exemplary punishment. When a confidant remonstrated with him about his savage downgrading of a conscientious officer discovered by a random audit to have borrowed a trifling amount from petty cash the afternoon before pay day for his fare home, Wurth agreed that it was too harsh, but added that news of the decision would spread rapidly throughout the public service and in future 'no one will even *think* about borrowing money from petty cash'. In 1953 two Department of Education officers were accused of letting school building contracts to an individual with previous criminal convictions. The press thought that at last it had a *cause célèbre*. For the next eight months Wurth spent an average of two days per week on this inquiry to find that a number of witnesses had perjured themselves and that the two officials had acted imprudently rather than dishonestly.

Ever the centralist, Wurth extended his influence, if not control, over the State's statutory authorities. He bridled at the lack of uniformity in the 'terms and conditions of employment', and soon after his appointment as chairman was lecturing governments on the 'undesirability of creating independent bodies' outside the Public Service Act and the necessity for the board to be the final authority on personnel matters. Successive governments did exercise restraint; public service departments undertook most of the new or expanded functions of government between 1939 and 1960. A plant and equipment-pooling scheme was introduced in 1941. From 1950 Wurth chaired regular meetings with the heads of major authorities to co-ordinate policies on common issues such as scarce material, consistency in industrial relations and conditions of service, and competition for essential personnel.

By 1960 Wurth had re-established the board in conformity with the principles of the 1896 Act, as re-stated by Allard in 1919. He was the undisputed head of the public service. But he was much more. He achieved his dominance and independence from political interference by ensuring that he made himself indispensable. Six premiers, from both sides of politics, came to depend on him for shrewd counsel and advice. His standing with the Australian Labor Party was enhanced by the high regard in which he was held by Chifley. McKell considered him his chief adviser, even at premiers' conferences and the Loan Council. James McGirr and Joseph Cahill [qq.v.15, 13] were happy to continue these arrangements. (Sir) Robert Menzies [q.v.15] recalled these conferences and meetings with the comment: 'I have always regarded him [Wurth] as the most perfect public servant we have ever had in Australia. He used to listen ... make notes and not say a word. Yet, I'm sure he would go out after the meeting and tell Joe Cahill exactly what he should do'. Although Cahill and Wurth 'struck sparks' early in their dealings they were soon on the best of terms. Cahill had a direct telephone line connected to the chairman's office; Wurth spent much time sitting in on ministerial conferences. He kept ministers in line by his control over their personal staff appointments and office accommodation. In the ultimate negation of Westminster principles, at one stage he received all cabinet minutes for comment as well as preparing the premier's policy speeches for the elections of 1953, 1956 and 1959, delegating the actual writing to selected subordinates. As the Opposition 'couldn't wait to use him themselves when they got into office', no one objected to this practice. His political influence reached its apogee with R. J. Heffron [q.v.14]. Their relationship was of long standing; the Wurth and Heffron families had been friends since the 1940s.

Many ministers were in his debt; one stated publicly that he 'knows everything ... the minute one of us gets into a bit of trouble he's the first man we go to'. Nevertheless, Wurth did not always get his way. Senior appointments sometimes involved compromises: Clive Evatt, the left-wing minister who held various portfolios between 1941 and 1956,

was constantly at odds with Wurth over public service and personal staff appointments, sharing Lang's dislike of the board and calling for its abolition.

Wurth's intimacy with premiers and ministers enabled him to achieve a long-cherished goal: after the war he set about founding a technical university. His manpower experiences had highlighted the shortage of scientists and engineers and the importance of the technical professions to Australia. He had little time for the humanities, preferring practical subjects such as medicine, engineering, the sciences and, to a lesser extent, industrial psychology. The proposed institute of technology was approved by cabinet in July 1946. Wurth visited Britain to seek staff, but found little enthusiasm. On his return he used his position to secure administrative staff and the former Kensington racecourse as a suitable site for the New South Wales University of Technology (University of New South Wales from 1958). One quarter of its board were senior public servants—the president and director respectively were Wurth and Arthur Denning, director of technical education, while J. O. A. Bourke [qq.v.13], from the Public Service Board, occupied the powerful post of bursar. The image of 'Wurth's circus' was that of a government department. Inevitably there were clashes between the academic staff and the administration. In 1955 Wurth assumed the title of chancellor.

One indulgence he did allow himself was a whisky at 5.30 p.m. with the secretary of the board before leaving half an hour later with his files, but this small relaxation was not sufficient to compensate for his cardiac problems. His first heart attack occurred in October 1956, after which he visited Europe for three months with his elder son to recuperate. 'Recuperation' took the form of investigating the New South Wales government offices in London. On his return to the board Wurth ignored medical advice to limit his workload, despite a second attack in 1957. The prospect of retirement in January 1961 held no allure. No sportsman, he had, by 1960, become president of the board of trustees of the Australian Museum and of Nielsen-Vaucluse Park, a member of the Soldiers' Children Education Board, and a patron of a number of sporting bodies.

Nursing a 'lingering distrust' of Catholics, Wurth engineered the appointment (announced in August 1960) of John Goodsell, president of the Metropolitan Water, Sewerage and Drainage Board and a nominal Methodist, as his successor—although most of the cabinet ministers were Catholics. He died of myocardial infarction on 16 September 1960 at St Vincent's Hospital, Darlinghurst, and was cremated with Anglican rites. His wife and their two sons survived him.

As a person Wurth was enigmatic. An anti-intellectual, he established a major Australian university; an allegedly Liberal voter, he helped substantially in the electoral success of Labor governments by ensuring a virtually corruption-free public service and by providing wise counsel. A passionate defender of a public service free from political patronage, he ruled in a ruthless and pragmatic manner. He made decisions quickly, 'without agonizing'. He bequeathed little theory of administration, declaring that his philosophy was simple: 'Get things done!' His published writings were few and conveyed his no-nonsense approach to administration. The University of New South Wales remains Wurth's most enduring legacy. An equivalent achievement (although not yet fully acknowledged) was creating and managing the Directorate of Manpower during World War II. Although the Public Service Board no longer exists, for over two decades he worked to restore its position as the linchpin of New South Wales public administration. From it he achieved a degree of political influence rarely equalled by any public servant in Australia.

P. Hasluck, *The Government and the People 1939-1941* (Canb, 1952); S. J. Butlin, *War Economy 1939-1942* (Canb, 1955); S. J. Butlin and C. B. Shedvin, *War Economy 1942-1945* (Canb, 1977); P. O'Farrell, *UNSW, a Portrait* (Syd, 1999); *Public Administration* (Syd), 8, no 4, Dec 1949, p 149, 20, no 1, Mar 1961; *Observer* (Syd), 22 Aug 1959; *Bulletin*, 4 May 1960; B. N. Moore, Administrative Style: its Effect on the Functioning of an Organisation (Ph.D. thesis, Univ Syd, 1985); Public Service Board (NSW), *Annual Report*, 1920-60, and records, 13/12303-13/12330 (NSWA); Honours, A463, item 1959/6659 (NAA, Canb).   ROSS CURNOW

WYATT, ANNIE FORSYTH (1885-1961), conservationist, was born on 3 January 1885 at Redfern, Sydney, eldest of eight children of George Trotter Evans, an English-born railway superintendent, and his second wife Isabella Anne, daughter of Archibald Forsyth [q.v.4]. Annie also had two half-brothers and a half-sister. In 1891 the family moved to Rooty Hill, a fertile district where orchards and vineyards were encroaching on the bushland. After lessons at home Annie, aged 10, became a boarder at the Methodist Ladies' College, Burwood. She admired the headmaster Rev. C. J. Prescott [q.v.11], and tried to abide by his dictum, 'be concise'. At the Presbyterian Church, Manly, on 6 December 1913, she married Ivor Bertie Wyatt (d.1958), a salesman and later tea merchant.

In 1926 the family (with two children) moved to Gordon. Dismayed at the total clearing of bushland for home sites and the use of Gordon gully for waste, Annie invited neighbours to her home to share her indignation. This gathering, led by the mayor of Ku-ring-gai, W. Cresswell O'Reilly [q.v.11], established the Ku-ring-gai Tree Lovers' Civic League in 1927. The influence of the league was widespread. Wyatt was prominent in moves to create and gazette Balls Head reserve, on Sydney Harbour (1931), Dalrymple forest reserve, Pymble (1934), and the A. F. Wyatt reserve, overlooking Palm Beach (1938), named in her honour.

For twenty years Wyatt worked for the Prisoners' Aid Association of New South Wales and was president (1938-41) of the women's section. She regularly visited gaols, where such 'old lags' as Tilly Devine and Kate Leigh [qq.v.8,10] regarded her as trustworthy. On friendly terms with the comptroller of prisons, she succeeded in gaining less ugly clothes for the inmates. Horrified at seeing women dampen red-covered library books to colour their lips, she gained permission for them to receive presents of lipstick and face powder.

Annie Wyatt loved old Sydney and the County of Cumberland and spoke with knowledge and enthusiasm on their history. She deplored the ruinous state of two Georgian mansions, Graystanes, Prospect, and Bungaribee, Doonside. The demolition of Burdekin House, Macquarie Street, in 1934 and the Commissariat Stores at West Circular Quay in 1939 (which she described as 'official vandalism at its worst') galvanized her into action. Aware of the work of the National Trust in Britain, at a Tree Lovers' meeting on 11 April that year, she proposed setting up a similar organization in which buildings and landscapes could be permanently vested.

World War II intervened and Annie was occupied with the Prisoners' Aid Association and the Australian Red Cross Society (she was president of the Gordon branch). In 1941 she published a historical romance, *Doors that Slam*, and gave the proceeds to the Red Cross. Her friends included the historians C. H. Bertie and J. H. Watson, an early conservationist Minard Crommelin, and the commissioner for forestry E. H. Swain [qq.v.7, 12,8,12].

At the Australian Forest League's 'Save our Trees' conference in Sydney in November 1944, Wyatt spoke, to acclamation, for a national trust. In April 1945 the National Trust of Australia (New South Wales) was established; O'Reilly chaired the provisional committee (Annie believed that this was not a role for a woman, but she was secretary). She served on the trust's council from its official foundation on 5 November 1947 to her death and was vice-president in 1951-61. She was also vice-president (1947-53) of the Forestry Advisory Council of New South Wales. In 1960 she was appointed O.B.E.

The attitude of (Sir) William McKell's government to a national trust was unenthusiastic, not surprisingly, in view of its plans to demolish Hyde Park Barracks, the Mint and Parliament House to remodel Macquarie Street. The fledgling trust waged a campaign against the forces of government—and won. Public apathy towards the preservation of old buildings now turned to support, especially from the *Sydney Morning Herald*.

Known to her children as 'Mater', Mrs Wyatt was considered odd: a housewife who struggled to awaken public interest in conservation. She skilfully combined her work—in which her husband took great pride—with her marriage, and endured his camping holidays, concealing from him her lack of enthusiasm. Of medium plump build, with golden hair, blue eyes, and a serious demeanour, she had vision and determination. She died on 27 May 1961 at her home at St Ives and was cremated. Her daughter and son Ivor, who served (1969-73) as president of the National Trust, survived her.

I. F. Wyatt, *Ours in Trust* (Syd, 1987); H. Malcher (ed), *Women of Ku-ring-gai* (Syd, 1999); National Trust of Aust (NSW), *Bulletin*, no 2, 1961; *SMH*, 27 May 1938, 2 July 1946, 29 May 1961; *Sunday Sun* (Syd), 31 Mar 1946; *Sunday Telegraph* (Syd), 24 Mar 1947; Honours, A463, item 1959/4816 (NAA, Canb); information from Mr I. F. Wyatt, St Ives, Mrs C. Lee, Pymble, and Mr E. L. Sommerlad, Wollstonecraft, Syd.   CAROLINE SIMPSON

WYLDE, ARNOLD LOMAS (1880-1958), Anglican bishop, was born on 31 March 1880 at Horsforth, Yorkshire, England, son of James Lomas Wylde, woollen manufacturer, and his wife Sarah Jane, née Taylor. Arnold was educated at Wakefield Grammar School and University College, Oxford (B.A., 1903; M.A., 1906). After three years in the East End of London at Oxford House, he prepared for the Anglican ministry at Cuddesdon College and was made deacon by A. F. Winnington-Ingram, bishop of London, on 23 December 1906. Ordained priest on 22 December 1907, he went as curate to St Simon Zelotes, Bethnal Green, becoming vicar in 1912. The administrative work of the parish kept Wylde from the pastoral aspect of his ministry which he believed was his primary priestly commitment. On 31 March 1921 he resigned to volunteer for missionary service with the Brotherhood of the Good Shepherd in New South Wales.

Wylde's years with the Brotherhood were carefree: he wrote to his former London parish of his excitement at the adventure which the bush offered him. In 1923 George Merrick Long [q.v.10], bishop of Bathurst, appointed him principal of the Brotherhood.

Based at Gilgandra, where he was also rector, Wylde again accepted administrative responsibilities. His ministry with the Brotherhood was characterized by compassion. Understanding their isolation, he developed a special affinity with the people of the far west of the State, who found him 'full of fun'. He travelled countless miles to conduct services in small centres, and frequently gave lifts to swagmen in his battered T-model Ford. Both practical and spiritual in his approach, he was held in affection and esteem.

On 1 November 1927 Bishop Long consecrated Wylde coadjutor bishop of Bathurst in All Saints Cathedral; he remained principal of the Brotherhood until December 1928. When Long became bishop of Newcastle that year, Wylde served Bishop Crotty who resigned in 1936. After administering the diocese in the interregnum, Wylde was enthroned as bishop of Bathurst on 23 February 1937. During his episcopate the intellectual emphasis of Long and Crotty were oriented towards a greater pastoral focus. As bishop he immersed himself in every aspect of diocesan life and was highly regarded for his thoughtfulness and courtesy. At the same time, some parishioners objected to his High Church liturgical approach to worship.

In 1942 Wylde compiled and introduced a service book, *The Holy Eucharist*, which became known as the 'Red Book', because of its red cover. A legal suit (*Attorney-General v. Wylde*) was instituted in 1944 by a number of complainants in the diocese of Bathurst, assisted by elements within the diocese of Sydney led by Canon T. C. Hammond [q.v.14]. They alleged that Wylde had been guilty of heresy, that he had deviated from the Book of Common Prayer and that the mandatory use of the Sign of the Cross and the sanctus bell were 'in direct conflict with the doctrines of the Church of England'. Wylde, relying on the expert advice of Canon Farnham Maynard and Bishop Francis de Witt Batty [qq.v.15,7], maintained that a secular court had no jurisdiction to hear an ecclesiastical case, and claimed the right as bishop to authorize deviations from and additions to the Book of Common Prayer. The charge of heresy was withdrawn and the case proceeded on a charge of breach of trust. In 1948 the chief judge in Equity E. D. Roper [q.v.] granted injunctions against use of the 'Red Book'. The High Court of Australia dismissed Wylde's appeal but limited the judgement to twenty parishes and *The Holy Eucharist* continued to be used widely within the diocese. Bishop Batty believed that the 'Red Book Case' 'emphasised the need for the Church in Australia to obtain full power to enforce its own discipline and order its own law of worship'.

Wylde's style of worship, commitment to pastoral ministry and work among young people, his love of the outback and simplicity of manner were the standard in the diocese of Bathurst for nearly fifty years. The Archbishop of York in 1952 commented that 'Bishop and people knew and trusted each other'. In 1957 Wylde was appointed C.B.E. He did not marry. Wylde died on 7 June 1958 at Bishopscourt, Bathurst; his ashes were buried beneath the high altar in All Saints Cathedral.

T. C. Hammond (preface), *The Bathurst Ritual Case* (Syd, 1948); *Cwlth Law Reports*, 78, 1948-49, p 224; *J of Religious Hist*, 12, no 1, 1982, p 74; *Sun-Herald* (Syd), 22 June 1958; C. G. Whittall, 'My Land of Righteousness?' The Life and Times of Arnold Lomas Wylde (M.A. thesis, Univ Syd, 1986); D. Galbraith, Just Enough Religion to Make Us Hate: An Historico-legal Study of the Red Book Case (Ph.D. thesis, Univ NSW, 1998); Wylde papers (Anglican Diocese of Bathurst archives).

CHRISTOPHER WHITTALL

WYNTER, HENRY DOUGLAS (1886-1945), army officer, was born on 5 June 1886 at Walla, near Gin Gin, Queensland, sixth surviving child of Henry Philip Walter Wynter (d.1889), a sugar-cane farmer from New South Wales, and his Irish-born wife Maria Louisa, née Maunsell. Educated at Maryborough Grammar School, Douglas worked on his mother's farm and later in a butter factory at Bundaberg. Having served in the senior cadets, he was commissioned in the Wide Bay Infantry Regiment, Militia, in 1907. By 1909 he had attained the rank of captain.

On 1 February 1911 Wynter transferred to the Permanent Military Forces and was appointed probationary lieutenant on the Administrative and Instructional Staff, 1st Military District (Queensland). At St John's Church of England, Dalby, on 5 September that year he married Ethel May White, a nurse. Attached to the adjutant-general's department at Army Headquarters, Melbourne, from October 1912, he was appointed temporary director of personnel in November 1914 and made a brevet major in December 1915.

Seconded to the Australian Imperial Force as brigade major of the 11th Brigade on 27 April 1916, Wynter arrived in England in July. He became deputy assistant adjutant and quartermaster general at 4th Division headquarters in October before being sent to Lieutenant General Sir William (Baron) Birdwood's [q.v.7] I Anzac Corps headquarters in France in March 1917. There Wynter assisted Birdwood with his A.I.F. administrative duties. In July Wynter was promoted lieutenant colonel and appointed assistant adjutant-general on Birdwood's A.I.F. staff. He commanded the A.I.F. troops in France and Flanders in June-November 1919. For his service as a staff officer he was awarded the Distinguished Service Order (1918), appointed C.M.G. (1919) and mentioned in dispatches four times. His A.I.F. appointment terminated in Brisbane on 18 April 1920.

Posted as deputy assistant adjutant-general, 4th Military District (South Australia), Wynter transferred to the newly formed Staff Corps in October 1920. He attended the Staff College, Camberley, England, in 1921-22. Back in Melbourne, he joined the General Staff at A.H.Q. In February 1925 he became director of mobilization. His duties included compiling the Commonwealth War Book which detailed plans for the mobilization of the nation's military forces in the event of war. He completed the 1930 course at the Imperial Defence College, London. From July 1932 he was general staff officer, 1st grade, at 1st Division headquarters, Sydney. In April 1935 he returned to A.H.Q. to become director of military training. He was promoted temporary colonel in June.

In a lecture to the United Service Institution of Victoria in September 1926 (published in the British *Army Quarterly* in April 1927), Wynter had said that 'if war were to break out with a Pacific Power, it would be at some time when Great Britain was involved in war in Europe'. He argued that the security of Britain was the primary consideration of Imperial defence, and that Australia should provide a naval base in its own territory, apart from the base then under construction at Singapore which he regarded as vulnerable. The 'principal instruments of the local defence of Australia', however, were the army and the air force.

In 1935 Wynter gave a further lecture to the United Service institutions in Melbourne and Sydney on the defence of Australia. The minister for defence (Sir) Archdale Parkhill requested a copy, as did Senator C. H. Brand [qq.v.11,7], who distributed a synopsis of the paper to other parliamentarians. On 5 November 1936 John Curtin [q.v.13], the leader of the Opposition, used it as the basis of a speech attacking government policy, embarrassing Parkhill. Furthermore, Parkhill alleged that an article in the Sydney *Daily Telegraph*, written by Wynter's son Philip, contained information found in a secret defence document. By ministerial direction, Wynter was posted in March 1937 to the inferior position of G.S.O.1 of the 11th Mixed Brigade in Queensland. He also reverted to his substantive rank of lieutenant colonel, with a reduced salary. The minister refused Wynter a court martial to contest the accusation that he improperly disclosed classified information. It was generally believed in the army that Wynter was unjustly treated.

After Parkhill was defeated at a general election in October 1937, Wynter was promoted colonel (with effect from July 1937) and in July 1938 was appointed commandant and chief instructor of the newly created Command and Staff School, Sydney. Following the outbreak of World War II, in October 1939 he was given Northern Command, based in Queensland, with the local rank of major general. On 4 April 1940 he was seconded to the A.I.F. as a temporary brigadier and made deputy-adjutant and quartermaster general of I Corps.

Arriving in Britain in June 1940, Wynter was promoted major general and appointed commandant of the A.I.F. in the United Kingdom. He took command of the 9th Division in October and sailed for the Middle East next month to prepare for military operations. However, just as he was about to bring to fruition his long years of study, training and experience, his health failed. Declared temporarily medically unfit, he was forced to relinquish his command in February 1941 and return to Australia. His A.I.F. appointment terminated on 6 July and he became major general, General Staff, at headquarters, Eastern Command, Sydney. On 19 December he rose to temporary lieutenant general and took over Eastern Command. He was appointed C.B. (1942).

In April 1942 Wynter became lieutenant general-in-charge of administration at Land Headquarters, Melbourne. Responsible directly to the commander-in-chief General Sir Thomas Blamey [q.v.13], he supervised and co-ordinated the work of his principal subordinates, the adjutant-general, quartermaster general and master-general of the ordnance. Suffering from high blood pressure, he relinquished his position on 19 September 1944 and was placed on the Supernumerary List, pending retirement, the following day.

Wynter was 5 ft 9 ins (175 cm) tall, with fair hair, blue eyes and a physique that was lean but strong. He enjoyed playing tennis. An unassuming and modest man, he was a patient instructor and a clear and forceful public speaker. He was one of a small group of officers who, in the interwar period, had tried to stimulate military thought in and beyond the Australian army. The war historian Gavin Long [q.v.15] regarded him as 'perhaps the clearest and most profound thinker the Australian Army of his generation had produced'. Survived by his wife and their two sons, he died on 7 February 1945 in the 115th Military Hospital, Heidelberg, and was buried with military honours in Springvale cemetery. His portrait (1944) by (Sir) Ivor Hele is held by the Australian War Memorial, Canberra.

G. Long, *To Benghazi* (Canb, 1952); D. M. Horner, *High Command* (Canb, 1982); P. Dennis et al, *The Oxford Companion to Australian Military History* (Melb, 1995); B. Lodge, *Lavarack* (Syd, 1998); W. Perry, 'Lieutenant General Henry Douglas Wynter: An Officer of the Australian Staff Corps', *VHM*, 43, no 2, May 1972, p 837.

WARREN PERRY

Y

YALI (c.1912-1975), political and religious leader, was born about 1912 at Sor village, Madang district, German New Guinea, son of Singina and his wife Garang. Educated in the local tradition, he underwent male initiation rites. By 1928 he was an indentured labourer at Wau, working as a waiter in the hotel. He returned to Sor about 1931 and married. As village *tultul*, he accompanied Australian government patrols through the area.

After his wife died, Yali joined the Armed Native Constabulary in 1937 and was sent to Rabaul for training. While he was serving in Lae, the Japanese occupied the town in February 1942 and he helped to evacuate labourers to their homes. In June he was posted to Talasea, New Britain, for coast-watching service. His party was attacked by Japanese soldiers in November and withdrawn a month later. Yali's loyal service earned him the rank of sergeant of police and a transfer to Queensland for a six-month training course in jungle warfare. In 1943 he resigned from the police force and joined the Allied Intelligence Bureau.

About June Yali returned to New Guinea to take part in 'M' Special Unit operations, monitoring Japanese troop movements at Bongu and Finschhafen. Again ordered to Queensland, he spent five months training recruits for the A.I.B. and was promoted sergeant major, natives. In March 1944 he was one of a twelve-man party of coastwatchers sent ashore near Hollandia from an American submarine in advance of a planned landing in the following month. Two days later the party was ambushed and five of its members were killed. Separated from other survivors, Yali and another soldier set out for the allied lines, equipped with a carbine and a compass, but lacking food and matches. After an epic, three-month, 120-mile (193 km) journey, Yali reached Aitape alone.

When World War II ended, Yali drew on the knowledge of Western life gleaned from his three visits to Australia and embarked on propaganda tours in the Madang district to promote his vision for the future. He set up rules for village life, urged his compatriots to engage in the cash-crop economy, encouraged them to strive for education, and prophesied self-government and independence for the Territory of Papua-New Guinea. Yali also initiated a revitalization of traditional religion. In a short time he emerged as the powerful charismatic leader of a social movement in the Madang district.

Tall, well spoken and dignified, he gained the support of the district officer J. K. Mc-Carthy [q.v.15] who saw him as promoting the government's objectives. But by the end of the 1940s European observers, alarmed at his influence, denounced the movement as a 'cargo cult'. In 1950 Yali was sentenced to prison terms of six months for deprivation of liberty and six years for incitement to rape. After his release in 1955, embittered by this experience, he allowed the movement to be subverted by followers who ascribed super-human powers to him and engaged in ritual practices.

Ambitious to participate formally in regional and national politics, Yali served as president (1964-66) of the Rai Coast Council. In 1964 and 1968 he stood unsuccessfully as a candidate for the Rai Coast Open electorate in the House of Assembly elections. Of his numerous traditional marriages, the longest lasting were those with Sunggum and with Rebecca. He died on 26 September 1975 at Sor, having lived long enough to witness the declaration of his country's independence.

E. Feldt, *The Coast Watchers* (Melb, 1946); P. Lawrence, *Road Belong Cargo* (Melb, 1964); D. G. Bettison et al (eds), *The Papua-New Guinea Elections, 1964* (Canb, 1965); A. L. Epstein et al (eds), *The Politics of Dependence* (Canb, 1971); L. Morauta, *Beyond the Village* (Lond, 1974); E. Hermann, *Emotionen und Historizität* (Berlin, 1995).

ELFRIEDE HERMANN

YARNOLD, STEPHEN EDWIN (1903-1978), Presbyterian and Uniting Church minister, was born on 9 August 1903 at Ramsgate, Kent, England, son of Stephen George Hogbin, butcher, and his wife Mary Elizabeth, née Clapp. His father died when Stephen was young. After his mother remarried, he took his stepfather's name of Yarnold. The family moved to Rosyth, Scotland, where Yarnold senior was employed at the dockyard as chief rigger. Steve, as he was known then and in later life, worked as a dockyard boy until 1922 when he and his brother were declared redundant. From an early age he knew the insecurity of uncertain employment, and observed its effects on his peers. He later found a job as a stoker in a coastal steamship.

At Rosyth Yarnold joined the Church of Scotland and became a leader of the local Red Triangle club of the Young Men's Christian Association. In his mid-twenties he was recruited by the Presbyterian Church of Victoria as a candidate for the ministry and brought to Melbourne. Lacking the formal education necessary to enable him to enter the Theological Hall at Ormond [q.v.5] College, University of Melbourne, he attended (1928-30) St Andrew's Theological Training College, Carlton, to prepare himself intellectually for the exacting course awaiting him.

Concurrently, at the Napier Street Mission, Fitzroy, Yarnold became acquainted with some of the worst poverty in the city, an awareness that never left him. In 1931-33 he was a student at the Theological Hall where he undertook the full course in the major disciplines of theology. He was deeply affected by his study of Old Testament prophecy, and by the teaching of Professor Hector Maclean [q.v.15]. The implications of Israel's faith and the Church's message left him constantly uneasy in contemporary Australian society.

Ordained on 14 March 1934, Yarnold became chaplain of Scotch College in June 1935. The principal, Colin Gilray [q.v.14], appointed him on the recommendation of Maclean and later protected him against criticism by some members of the school's council. The influence of his independent mind on a number of the ablest boys was considerable. He developed an interest in religious films. Placed in charge of the Dramatic Society, he produced a variety of one-act and Shakespearian plays. His term at the school ended in 1945. By this time he was widely known, although not universally popular, as a commentator (to November 1943) on radio-station 3AW. In the early 1940s he had been a founder of the Common Wealth Christian Movement which advocated socialism and for which in 1944 he prepared a radio talk that a commercial station refused to broadcast.

On 5 June 1945 Yarnold was commissioned chaplain, fourth class, Australian Imperial Force. During his service, in Darwin and Rabaul, he contracted malaria. He was particularly concerned with preparing soldiers for their return to civilian life. His A.I.F. appointment terminated in Melbourne on 24 July 1946. At the Presbyterian manse, North Essendon, two days later, he married Winifred Atwood Jacobs, a kindergarten teacher.

In 1950-70 the Yarnolds exercised a far-reaching ministry from North Melbourne which, with Steve's chaplaincy (1963-70) at Pentridge gaol and his membership of the presbytery of Melbourne West, gave them a base from which to expand their interests in social and political questions and enjoy a rich cultural life. A prominent figure in the Presbyterian Church of Victoria, Yarnold was moderator of the assembly in 1963-64. His influence was strong among students for the ministry and in the direction of theological education.

Yarnold's diverse experiences left him enriched in personality for the benefit of others. He made many friends from Rosyth to North Melbourne and his companionable nature

complemented his interest in co-operative societies. His membership of the Australian Labor Party led to a warm and close relationship with Arthur Calwell [q.v.13]. Six feet (183 cm) tall, slim and with intense eyes, a deep voice and 'long-fingered expressive hands', Yarnold had presence. Without knowing that he was doing so, he exercised authority, whether chairing a meeting, leading worship or contributing to discussion. By nature a dignified man, he recognized dignity as a quality to be respected in others but knew that 'the worst thing you can do with your dignity is to stand on it'. He died on 25 September 1978 at his home at Silvan and was cremated. His wife survived him.

Herald (Melb), 23 Mar 1963; B. Johnston, 'I Remember Yarnold', ABC Radio broadcast, 1984 (ABC Archives, Syd); records of the Presbyterian Church of Vic and the Vic Synod of the Uniting Church in Aust (Uniting Church in Aust, Synod of Vic Archives, Elsternwick, Vic); Common Wealth Christian Movement papers (Uniting Church Archives, Melb); information from the late Mrs W. Yarnold.   DAVIS McCAUGHEY

YEO, SIR WILLIAM (1896-1972), farmer and State president of the Returned Servicemen's League, was born on 1 May 1896 at Alectown, near Condobolin, New South Wales, son of native-born parents Arthur Plane Yeo, schoolteacher, and his wife Louisa Mary, née Curry. Educated at Peak Hill Public School, then employed as a wheat-buyer, Bill enlisted in the Australian Imperial Force on 7 March 1915 and was posted to the 18th Battalion. He served at Gallipoli and in France and Belgium, and, suffering from shell-shock, was evacuated to England for three months in 1916. Rejoining his unit in November, he became battalion bandsman in 1917, and returned to Australia in March 1919. After his discharge from the A.I.F. on 26 July, Yeo purchased a farming and grazing property at Peak Hill, which he ran for many years. On 6 March 1925 he married Eileen Theresa Golding, a schoolteacher, at the registry office, Hurstville, Sydney.

The cause of returned soldiers became Yeo's passion. In 1919 he joined the Returned Sailors' and Soldiers' Imperial League of Australia (later R.S.S. and Airmen's I.L.A., then Returned Servicemen's League of Australia). Honorary secretary of the Peak Hill sub-branch, in 1928 he became a delegate to the league's annual State Congress and Soldier Settlers' Conference, a position he held for forty-four years. In 1936 he became State councillor for the Western Districts division. Despite his active involvement Yeo was regarded as the dark horse of the ten candidates when he was elected State president of the

R.S.L. in 1949. He was to remain president for twenty turbulent years. From 1949 he also served on the national executive. Increasingly his duties kept him in Sydney, where he resided at Elizabeth Bay and later at Maroubra.

When first elected Yeo pledged to heal the divisions within the league. The immediate postwar years were consumed with the alleged menace of communism in the ranks. Some members feared that they were becoming targets of a 'witch-hunt' because they supported the labour movement. Yeo declared that he would uphold the league policy on 'keeping communists out', but would do so in 'a sane and reasonable manner'. For him, it was essential to return to the roots of the R.S.L. as a servicemen's welfare organization committed to a non-party and non-sectarian position. He was immediately condemned by some as a communist sympathiser and forced to send a circular to all members repudiating the charge.

At a practical level Yeo supported the R.S.L. Youth Movement and, as deputy chairman, gave much time to the War Veterans' Home. Other commitments included the Lord Mayor's flood and bushfire relief appeal. He was appointed C.B.E. in 1954 and knighted in 1964. Although he insisted that the R.S.L. existed to obtain better entitlements for returned men and women, he lost few opportunities to involve the league in a broad range of political issues. Declaring himself a staunch nationalist, he was an outspoken defender of the White Australia policy, a stern critic of Japan, a fierce anti-communist and a strong campaigner for a greater war effort in Korea, Malaya and Vietnam.

By the late 1960s, however, Yeo's outspokenness was creating internal tensions. In 1968 he carried a motion at the R.S.L. National Congress to expel members guilty of conduct 'subversive' to the league. This caused alarm among federal colleagues who feared that members of the Australian Labor Party who opposed the Vietnam War would be expelled. Yeo advocated harsh police measures, such as fire hoses, against moratorium protesters. A few months later he condemned members of the British Commonwealth as a 'polyglot lot of wogs, bogs, logs and dogs'. The national press roundly condemned him as a 'sabre-rattling war monger', out of touch with contemporary Australian society. He still commanded support within the league, but leading members, notably the national president Sir Arthur Lee, sought to distance themselves and the league from Yeo's more extreme pronouncements.

Increasingly Yeo was seen as an embarrassing anachronism, the last remaining veteran of 'the Great War' on the R.S.L. executive and the butt of media jibes. His presidency was under threat. In 1969 he was defeated by F. S. Maher, former prisoner-of-war and suburban schoolteacher, a result greeted with loud cheers from some delegates.

A dark-haired, nuggety, bespectacled man, Yeo remained on the executive for a further year in the newly created position of past-president. He died on 9 December 1972 at the Repatriation General Hospital, Concord, and was cremated with Anglican rites. His wife survived him; they had no children. He was remembered, somewhat ambiguously, as a man who 'did what he solemnly believed to be in the interest of every ex-serviceman and woman'.

SMH, 19, 20, 25 May 1949, 29, 31 Oct, 2, 3 Nov 1968, 6 Aug 1969, 2 June 1970, 11 Dec 1972; *Sunday Herald*, 24 July 1949; *Sunday Telegraph* (Syd), 10 Dec 1972; *Australian*, 11 Dec 1972; Honours, A463, item 1962/2967 (NAA, Canb).

STEPHEN GARTON

YIP HO NUNG (HARRY HORNUNG) (1909-1979), café proprietor, was born on 18 October 1909 at Chien Mei village, Dongguan, Canton (Guangdong) Province, China, son of Yip Fong Siu and his number two wife Hun Tong Chew. The Chien Mei Yips could trace their ancestry back twenty-five generations. Harry came to Sydney in the 1920s with several of his siblings. He and a younger brother Dong Hoi (Don) lived with their half-brother Yip Tung Kwai, known in Sydney as Gilbert Quoy, and his wife Edith. Quoy was a prosperous wholesale fruit merchant and a conservative leader of the small Chinese community of Sydney.

Having attended Randwick Public and Boys' Intermediate High schools, Harry worked in the City Markets with other family members. In the late 1930s he became a partner in a new wholesale produce firm, Yep Lum & Co. At a time and date indicated as propitious by Chinese texts, he married with Catholic rites Beryl Agnes Yow at the Church of St Francis de Sales, Surry Hills, on 30 December 1935. The Australian-born daughter of a Chinese father and an Irish-Australian mother, Beryl was a practising Catholic and could speak no Chinese.

During World War II, Yip had to register as an alien; Beryl ran a fruit shop at Botany. By 1945, when they moved to Hay Street in Chinatown, Harry was a general merchant. Well known in the Chinese community, he helped applicants with documentation for naturalization, sponsored immigrants and paid the water and council rates for impoverished market gardeners. He acted as a 'go-between' for his community with immigration and customs officials and the police, and counted the police commissioner Norman Allan [q.v.13] among his friends.

In 1956 the Yips established the Green Jade café in Dixon Street. They were determined to attract a non-Chinese clientele and employed only waiters who could speak English. Beryl, who worked as the cashier, insisted on using tablecloths (unknown in Dixon Street). The Green Jade became a popular place of introduction to the local Chinese community for many Europeans and eventually it acquired 'celebrity' status (Danny Kaye once dined there). Bridging cultural divides was one of Yip's passions.

Following instruction given by Father (Cardinal) Freeman, Yip had converted to Catholicism in 1954. He was naturalized in 1957. For six years from about 1958 he served as president of the Chinese Chamber of Commerce, an informal group of Haymarket businessmen. At their home at Dover Heights, where they had settled in 1950, the Yips often entertained visiting dignitaries, politicians and performers. Outgoing and gregarious, Harry loved traditional Chinese opera, and often amused his children with his favourite excerpts.

In the 1970s Yip and other Chinese worked together on various schemes to encourage the revival of Chinese customs in Sydney and helped to organize the building of the Chinese Pavilion at Rookwood cemetery. He and his friend Father Pascal Chang, who ran the Asiana Centre at Ashfield, organized the first August Moon Festival in 1974. Yip also tried to involve the Chinese in the Waratah Festival.

Harry Yip stopped working at the Green Jade in 1977 after suffering a stroke. A diabetic for forty years, he died on 6 October 1979 at St Vincent's Hospital, Darlinghurst. He was buried in the Chinese section of Rookwood cemetery following a requiem Mass at St Theresa's, Dover Heights, and a traditional Chinese civil ceremony in Dixon Street. His wife, and their daughter and two sons survived him.

S. Fitzgerald, *Red Tape, Gold Scissors* (Syd, 1997); immigration file, SP11/2, item Chinese/Yip Harry Hornung (NAA, Syd); naturalization certificate, A1802/1, vol EM(1)30019 (NAA, Canb); information from Mr A. Yip, Strathfield, Fr P. Chang, Ashfield, Mr J. Wong, Killarney Heights, and Dr G. Yip, Canley Vale Heights, Syd.   SHIRLEY FITZGERALD

YIRAWALA (c.1897-1976), artist and Aboriginal elder, was a member of the Naborn clan of Gunwinggu language speakers whose traditional lands lie in the Marugulidban (also called Morgaleetbah) region straddling the Liverpool River, south-west of Maningrida, Northern Territory. He was born in his home country. The date of his birth is not known but in 1970 he gave his age as 73. His father was Nowaritj, a religious leader and keeper of his people's sacred symbols and cave galleries of rock paintings; Yirawala's mother's name is not recorded. He was raised in the customary manner, learning his father's designs, songs and stories. The dramatic rock art of western Arnhem Land influenced his artistic development.

For a time Yirawala lived at Oenpelli (Gunbalunya) with his first wife, who died after giving birth to three children. He then married with the rites of his people Mary Malilba with whom he had a daughter and two sons, and Margaret Monanggu with whom he had one son. Moving around Arnhem Land, he took a variety of labouring jobs. In the late 1950s he and his family settled on Croker Island. By this time he was an important and influential bark painter. He was also a leader in the ceremonial life of the Gunwinggu, a law-carrier and a 'clever man' (medicine man and healer).

In the early 1960s Yirawala formed a close association with Sandra Le Brun Holmes, a Darwin resident who helped Aborigines to preserve their religion and culture. She and her husband Cecil accompanied Yirawala and his family on a visit to Marugulidban in 1970. Yirawala wished to show the ancestral cave paintings to his sons and explain their meaning—'so we don't lose the old law'—and to confirm his people's ownership of the land at a time when mining companies were increasingly active in Arnhem Land. Cecil Holmes made a film of the journey, *Return to the Dreaming*. In June 1973 Yirawala represented the Gunwinggu at hearings of the Aboriginal Land Rights Commission held at Maningrida.

Sandra Holmes had assisted Yirawala to take a travelling exhibition of his bark paintings to Adelaide, Melbourne, Sydney, Orange and Port Moresby in 1971. That year he was appointed M.B.E. and was the recipient of the International Co-operation Art Award. He opposed the commercialization of his work. His genius as a bark painter is evident in the individual pieces and series that he produced addressing major ceremonial themes of the western Arnhem Land region: Mardayin (Maraian), Lorrkkon (Lorrgon) and Wubarr (Ubar). He creatively interpreted these themes by depicting the subjects and incorporating elements from the geometric body designs used in the ceremonies. One of his purposes was to inform a non-Aboriginal audience about the depth of Aboriginal culture.

Through his art and his struggle for land rights, Yirawala was part of the broader movement among Aboriginal people to gain self-determination. He impressed Holmes with his courage and integrity. She described 'his penetrating eyes' and 'his face, handsome and dignified with its lines of experience and wisdom'. He died on 17 April 1976 on Croker Island and was buried in Minjilang cemetery. Holmes's collection of his paintings was purchased by the National Gallery of Australia later that year. In 1982 one of the paintings was chosen for the Australian twenty-seven-cent stamp commemorating the gallery's official opening. Most Australian State galleries hold works by Yirawala, as do major collections overseas.

S. Holmes, *Yirawala: Artist and Man* (Brisb, 1972) and *Yirawala: Painter of the Dreaming* (Syd, 1992); D. Carment et al, *Northern Territory Dictionary of Biography*, 1 (Darwin, 1990); *Aboriginal News*, 3, no 1, Feb 1976.   LUKE TAYLOR

YOUNG, JOHN HENRY (1880-1946), gallery director, art dealer and collector, was born on 27 October 1880 at Petersham, Sydney, second child of English-born parents Enoch William Young, grocer, and his second wife Ann, née Gregson; John had three half-brothers. After leaving the local public school, he read widely, influenced by his lifelong friends Leslie Holdsworth and (Sir) Carleton Kemp Allen [qq.v.7]. Young worked for some years in his father's grocery shop then as a commercial traveller for Poole & Holmes, coffee and spice merchants. On 4 September 1909 he married Eva Clarice Miller at the Congregational Church, Petersham, with which he was closely associated.

An amateur collector of antiques, paintings and prints, Young opened a picture-framing and restoring business in Bond Street, Sydney, in 1916. Artists employed by (S. Ure) Smith [q.v.11] & Julius, including Roland Wakelin, Percy Leason [qq.v.12,10] and Lloyd Rees, gathered at the shop at lunchtime. Young provided space for Roy de Maistre [q.v.8] and Wakelin to experiment on their colour and music theories, and framed their works. He sold the business before visiting Europe in 1922-23, to educate himself and his family. On this tour (and during another in 1929-30) Young located neglected Australiana and prints in antique shops, for his own collection and later for sale. He also forged connexions with English galleries, dealers and artists.

Back in Sydney in 1923, Young re-established his business, this time in Phillip Street. With Basil Burdett [q.v.7], he opened the Macquarie Galleries at 19 Bligh Street in 1925; John Aeneas McDonnell was another partner (1929-36). The galleries consisted of three exhibition rooms elegantly appointed with antique furniture. The opening exhibition (of Wakelin's work) established an eclectic and busy programme of two-weekly shows of both conventional and modernist artists who benefited from the Macquarie Galleries' exhibitions of contemporary European art (mostly English prints).

In the 1930s Young also operated as an art dealer at 9 Bligh Street, managed exhibitions for such associations as the Society of Artists and the Contemporary Group, gave talks on art for the Australian Broadcasting Commission (1936-37) and wrote occasional pieces for *Art in Australia* (sometimes as 'J. Matthew Gregson') and the *Sydney Morning Herald*. He retired from the Macquarie Galleries in 1938 and moved his business as a restorer, valuer, art adviser and dealer to 3 Castlereagh Street. That year he was awarded the Society of Artists medal. A quiet man of medium height and slight build, Young had very white skin, a thick thatch of neatly brushed, long, dark hair, a slight stoop and broad brow, and wore glasses. Rees described him as a mystic, philosopher and skilled debater, and attributed his success as a gallery director to a combination of knowledge and intuition and his ability as a salesman. His main contribution to Australian art was his unstinting support, both financial and moral, for a wide range of artists, especially women.

Young was appointed acting-director of the National Art Gallery of New South Wales in June 1944. He was disillusioned and depressed by the court case later that year over the award of the Archibald [q.v.3] prize to (Sir) William Dobell [q.v.14] for his controversial portrait of Joshua Smith. Believing that the portrait was a caricature and that his testimony in favour of the plaintiffs would cause a conflict of interest with the gallery's trustees, he resigned in September. Young's health deteriorated, aggravating respiratory complaints from which he suffered all his life. He died of heart failure on 7 September 1946 at Royal North Shore Hospital and was cremated. His wife and their three daughters survived him. A bronze (1941) bust of Young by Daphne Mayo is held by the Art Gallery of New South Wales. Portraits in oils by Leason, Robert Campbell, Douglas Dundas and Wakelin are held in private collections.

J. R. Lawson [auctioneers], *Catalogue of Prints and Pictures. The Private Collection of Mr John Young* (Syd, 1922?) and *An Important Collection of Pictures Drawn from the Collections of Mr F. W. Allen and Mr John Young* (Syd, 1933) and *Catalogue of the John Young Collection* (Syd, 1940); J. Campbell, *Early Sydney Moderns* (Syd, 1988); H. Johnson, *The Sydney Art Patronage System 1890-1940* (Syd, 1997); *SMH*, 22 June, 16, 25 Oct, 9 Nov 1944; C. Thomas, Family Tree and History, ms, *and* J. Young file (Art Gallery of NSW Archives).   HEATHER JOHNSON

YOUNG, WILLIAM GORDON (1904-1974), physical educationist, was born on 15 June 1904 at Guelph, Ontario, Canada, son of David Young, principal, and later inspector of public schools, and his wife Mary, née Underhill.

Gordon attended the Central School and the Collegiate Institute at Guelph, then the International Young Men's Christian Association College, Springfield, Massachusetts, United States of America (B.P.E., 1927). Back in Canada, he studied arts part time at the University of Western Ontario, London (B.A., 1936), and taught physical education at that university and at the Y.M.C.A. He represented the university in football, swimming, ice hockey, gymnastics and wrestling. On 7 June 1930 he married Ellen Patricia Fletcher. During the 1930s he obtained a pilot's licence and competed in American air races. He was director of physical education at Montreal central Y.M.C.A. from 1936 and sometime president of the Canadian Physical Education Association.

In 1938 Young was appointed director of physical education within the Department of Education, New South Wales, and, next year, executive officer of the National Fitness Council of New South Wales. He found that, because of his dual role, he had to serve two masters, the Department of Education and its minister. The department lacked physical education teachers and training; facilities and equipment at schools were virtually non-existent. His promised annual budget of up to £500 000 was not forthcoming.

A man of abundant energy and enthusiasm, Young responded with a flurry of community consultation to promote a more professional concept of physical education, emphasizing fitness and health. He set up in-service courses for teachers during vacations, reformed the curriculum, organized better facilities and resources, and initiated a 'flying squad' of eight men and seven women to visit schools. Frustrated at many points because he was never given full control of his field, he failed to have physical education courses introduced at the University of Sydney in 1943; instructors were trained instead at Teachers' College, Sydney. Young himself graduated M.Ed. at the University of Sydney in 1962. He was president of the Australian Physical Education Association (1959-62) and of its successor the Australian Council for Health, Physical Education and Recreation (1972-74).

The Youngs lived at Neutral Bay. He enjoyed camping, golf and surfing, and belonged to the Royal Empire (Commonwealth) Society. His greatest success was developing community fitness programmes. As a member (vice-president 1960) of the Rotary Club of Sydney, he persuaded it to build nine huts to sleep 180 campers at the State's first national fitness camp, at Broken Bay. A jack of all trades, he led teams of volunteers at weekends, even driving the bulldozer himself, to clear the site. In 1969 there were ten national fitness camps in the State; over three decades, 700 000 children had had an outdoor experience in the bush. Equally popular were his vacation play and swimming centres, and his learn-to-play and community recreation programmes.

By the 1960s coaching and training camps were held at Narrabeen. Young hoped that the camp would become a national sports centre, but its potential was not realized because he preferred North American games such as softball and basketball, failing to appreciate the importance to Australians of cricket and their traditional football codes. He had introduced softball to schools in 1939 and next year was appointed commissioner for softball in Australia by the Amateur Softball Association of America. His interest was shared by his wife Pat, who was founding president of the New South Wales Women's Softball Association in 1947.

A charismatic and forceful man, Young attracted people to his cause 'with his humour, energy and drive', although he did have some detractors who saw him as ruthless and inflexible. Public servants regarded him with trepidation because of his unorthodox approach: Young never believed in saying 'no', sometimes promising support that he could not deliver or spending money that he did not have. His enthusiasm could lead to reckless behaviour. Dr Jack Cross recalled that, while excavating at Broken Bay, Young went 'wild with explosives—it was miraculous on occasions that he didn't blow himself away'.

For four decades Young was known affectionately as 'Mr Phys.Ed.' and 'Mr Fitness'. In 1969 he retired and was appointed M.B.E. He had suffered a severe heart attack after the 1960 Olympic Games in Rome, but rather than slowing down, he planned a rehabilitation centre for coronary victims. Gordon Young died of ischaemic heart disease on 6 September 1974 at Marrickville and was cremated. His wife survived him; they had no children.

W. Ewens, *Gordon Young* (Syd, 1994), and for bib; *Aust J of Physical Education*, no 66, Dec 1974, p 21; *SMH*, 24 Sept, 17 Dec 1938, 1 Jan 1969, 8 Sept 1974; I. Fischer, Years of Silent Control: the Influence of the Commonwealth in State Physical Education in Victoria and New South Wales (Ph.D. thesis, Univ Syd, 2000).   R. I. CASHMAN

YUEN, GUM (1875-1943), furniture manufacturer, was born in October 1875 at Chung Gwok village, Heungshan (Zhongshan), Kwangtung (Guangdong), China, second son of Gang Poy, a watchman (policeman), and his wife Young Fong. After leaving school Gum worked as a baker. He migrated to Australia in 1897 and was first employed in the Quong Hing furniture factory in Melbourne. In 1903 he moved to West Perth and worked as a cabinet-maker for Yen (Yuen) Hoy Poy, also from Chung Gwok, in the See Wah & Co. Ltd furniture factory. On 15 June 1910 at the Methodist Church, West Perth, he married Australian-born May Sam. Following a family visit in 1911-12 his wife and their child remained in China. A second son was born there after Yuen stayed with them in 1914-15.

By 1916, in partnership with two compatriots from his home village, Yen Hay Hoy and Mew Toy, Yuen owned and managed the J. W. Wing & Co. furniture factory in Newcastle Street, Perth. He returned to China in June 1923 and a year later brought his wife and sons to Australia; they arrived shortly before the birth of his third son. The family lived near the factory, which at first employed seven Chinese cabinet-makers and a polisher. In 1933 his partners retired and Yuen became the sole owner of the business. At that time he employed fourteen Chinese and four European workers. They manufactured bedroom, dining and kitchen suites and occasional furniture, using a variety of timbers, including jarrah, Tasmanian oak and pine. Dealing mainly with wholesale orders, the firm supplied a number of local stores, among them the Bairds Co. Ltd and W. Zimpel [qq.v.7,12] Ltd.

Yuen developed an interest in the restaurant business and in 1930, in partnership with Yuen Bow, a herbalist from Chung Gwok, he established the Nanking Café in Barrack Street, Perth. It catered for both Chinese and European customers, and provided work for Chinese. Acquiring a reputation for his fair and honest business dealings and his willingness to help anyone in need, Yuen became a highly respected businessman. He was a founding member (1910) of Perth's Chung Wah Association, serving as its secretary and treasurer for many years, and helping to arrange for the purchase of land and the construction of a hall in James Street. In 1921 he was an organizer of the local branch of the Kuomintang (Chinese Nationalist Party).

During World War II Yuen was treasurer of the Chinese Patriotic Society, which raised funds for the anti-Japanese forces in China. He also supported the Australian war effort. With his wife he assisted members of the Chinese community and helped billet refugees, especially from Malaya, Singapore and other parts of Asia. Survived by his wife, their two daughters and two of their three sons, he died of chronic emphysema on 15 May 1943 at his Newcastle Street home and was buried in the Chinese section of Karrakatta cemetery. J. W. Wing Ltd's factory closed in 1951.

P. Goh (ed), *75th Anniversary—Chung Wah Association* (Perth, 1985); A. Atkinson (comp), *Asian Immigrants to Western Australia, 1829-1901* (Perth, 1988), *and* Chinese Labour and Capital in Western Australia, 1847-1947 (Ph.D. thesis, Murdoch Univ, 1991); Chung Wah Assn (Perth), Minutes of meetings, 1909-25; Dept Immigration file, PP6/1, item 1947/H/1563 *and* Customs files, K1145, items 1911/80, 1914/82 and 1923/59 (NAA, Perth); Dept Labour, Factory register, 1912, 400/4 (WAA); information from the late Mrs R. Yuen and Mr W. Yuen.

ANNE ATKINSON

Z

ZEPPS, KATRINA (1918-1980), registered nurse, was born on 15 November 1918 at Glukhov, Ukraine, Russia, daughter of Alexander Chalders and his wife Praskovia, who were Latvian refugees from World War I. In 1922 the family returned to Latvia and Alexander became prison governor at Jelgava. There, Katie qualified (1943) in general nursing and midwifery at the Red Cross hospital. That year she married Adolfs Ozols, who was killed in action in 1944. She joined the staff of a military hospital and was evacuated ahead of the advancing Russians. Charge sister (1945-46) at the displaced persons' hospital at Lübeck, Germany, she entered the medical faculty for displaced persons at the Baltic University, Pinneburg. On 21 February 1947 at Lübeck she married Olegs ('Alec') Zepps, a Latvian electrical engineer; her marriage was childless.

Knowing almost no English, the couple reached Melbourne in the *General W. M. Black* on 27 April 1948. They settled in North Queensland and worked in the cane-fields. By 1950 Alec had his own business as an electrical contractor; Katie, having learned English, was a Queensland registered nurse (1951-60), mainly at Tully District Hospital. They were naturalized in 1955; she visited her sister in the United States of America in 1956-57. Moving to Sydney with her husband, Katie joined the staff at Royal Prince Alfred Hospital in January 1961. She gained a certificate in ward management (1963) and a diploma in nursing education (1964) from the New South Wales College of Nursing. At R.P.A.H. she was successively deputy-principal (nurse education) and tutor in charge of the preliminary training school.

In September 1966 Zepps was appointed education officer at the college of nursing. As deputy-principal from 1967, she helped the college to survive severe financial crises. In 1972, on a travelling scholarship, she investigated nursing education overseas. One year later Zepps became executive director of the college. After its teaching programmes had been transferred to the New South Wales College of Paramedical Studies, she was one of a small group who carved out a new and highly successful role for it by developing short courses and seminars for graduate nurses. Almost single-handed she fought to save the college library (later named after her). She retired from the college in 1976 but, elected to its council, served as president (1979-80) and senior vice-president (1980).

Katie Zepps inspired great affection through her warmth, passionate commitment and professionalism. Regarding herself as an Australian, she took pride in her hard work and encouraged others. She sought assistance and support for overseas students educated at the college under the Colombo Plan and helped migrant nurses and their families, especially those from the Baltic countries. From 1976 until her death she was executive-secretary of the New South Wales branch of the Royal Australian Nursing Federation. She was a fellow of the New South Wales College of Nursing and an honorary fellow of the College of Nursing, Australia. In 1977 she was appointed M.B.E. Survived by her husband, she died suddenly of a cerebral haemorrhage on 8 July 1980 at her Turramurra home and was cremated with Lutheran forms.

H. Creighton and F. Lopez, *A History of Nursing Education in New South Wales* (Syd, 1982); M. Dickenson, *An Unsentimental Union* (Syd, 1993); NSW College of Nursing, *Annual Report*, 1980; *Lamp*, Sept 1980, p 27; naturalization files, J25, items 1954/3791 and 1956/679 (NAA, Brisb); NSW College of Nursing Archives (Glebe, Syd); information from Mr A. Zepps, Riga, Latvia, Ms J. Cornell, Burwood, Ms C. Harte, Rockdale, Mr P. Manass, Campbelltown and Ms V. Wiles, Syd.   JUDITH GODDEN

ZERNER, WILHELM (WILLIAM) AUGUST (1882-1963), schoolteacher, was born on 21 September 1882 at Fassifern Scrub, Queensland, third of ten children of Prussian-born parents Wilhelm Zerner, farmer, and his wife Margaretha, née Duhs. The boy soon became known as William. Educated at Dugandan and Templin State schools, near Boonah, he was a pupil-teacher in 1896-1900 at the Templin school, which had been built on land donated from his father's 160-acre (65 ha) selection. He moved to Roma as head teacher in 1901. On 17 October that year at his residence at Roma he married with Methodist forms Ottillie Emilie Johanna Dittberner (d.1951), a dressmaker who had been born in Germany. He taught at Albany Creek (1902-09), Blenheim (1909-15), Yuleba (1915), Dutton Park (1916-20), Gatton (1920-22) and Rosewood (1922-27) State schools, and at Nambour Rural School (1928-38). In 1935 he was an acting-inspector of schools.

In August 1938 Zerner was promoted to supervisor of the Queensland Primary Correspondence School, with over one hundred staff and more than five thousand pupils. Next year he began a school magazine, *Mail Way*, to display children's work, and in 1940 established the Allen lending library (named after its benefactor, Mrs F. A. Allen, of Duchess). On 3 February 1941 he conducted the primary correspondence school's first radio session, 'My School Speaks', broadcast by the Australian Broadcasting Commission. Radio lessons soon became a regular part of the school's programme; tests in mental arithmetic and dictation were given, with the children returning their answers to the school. Enrolment increased during World War II, when families moved from 'danger zones' to areas considered safer, peaking in May 1942 at over seven thousand. Soldiers in the Northern Territory and Papua took lessons through the school, and pupils became involved in the war effort through a school branch of the Australian Junior Red Cross.

An advocate of personal and individual instruction, Zerner encouraged each pupil to proceed at his own pace. In 1948 in *Mail Way* he urged the children: 'Give to your job, whatever it may be, the best that is in you'. He did not favour coercion, detention or other forms of punishment, and discouraged homework, insisting that all lessons should be done in school hours. Regarding parents as equal partners in the educative process, he wrote in the magazine, also in 1948: 'Amongst the staff I feel I must include our thousands of Bush Mothers. These mothers are truly heroic'.

Zerner retired in June 1949, but within months was re-employed as officer-in-charge of the Special School for New Australians, Wacol East, Brisbane. He resigned in May 1952. On the council of the Queensland Bush Children's Health Scheme until 1962 and of the Australian-American Association, he was also a vice-president of the (Royal) Overseas League, Queensland branch. Survived by his son and two daughters, he died on 28 May 1963 in Brisbane and was cremated with Anglican rites.

B. Corvi et al (eds), *Seventy-five Years of Primary Distance Education in Queensland 1922-1997* (Brisb, 1997); *Courier-Mail*, 29 May 1963; D. O'Donnell, Schools of the Fassifern, 1867-1933: A Window to Queensland Education (Ph.D. thesis, Univ Qld, 1995); Qld School of Distance Education archives, West End, South Brisb; information about Templin State School, QSA EDU/Z2629 and QSA EDU/AB 657 (QA).   DAN O'DONNELL

ZIMIN, INNOKENTIY TEMOFEEVECH ('JIM') (1902-1974), peanut-farmer, was born on 26 November 1902 at Sretensk, Siberia, Russia, son of Tomefoy Nikolaevisch Zimin. A Cossack, he settled at Harbin, China, after the Russian Civil War (1918-20). He gained a chauffeur-mechanic's certificate from the Young Men's Christian Association in 1925.

Migrating to Australia in 1927, 'Jim' Zimin worked in various parts of Queensland before arriving in the Northern Territory. In 1929 he took up government land, at Adelaide River, made available for peanut growing. He was joined by five other Russians and they formed I. T. Zimin & Co. With little money and no machinery they were faced with the back-breaking task of clearing the trees, tilling the soil and planting the seed by hand. Harvesting was also done manually. Despite their sending 150 bags of peanuts to the markets in Darwin, the partnership was dissolved in 1930 and Zimin moved to Katherine.

In 1933 Zimin began to clear and cultivate a block of land on the Katherine River. Next year he was naturalized; he was then 5 ft 8¼ ins (173 cm) tall in his boots, with fair hair and blue eyes. Although he and two other Russians returned to Harbin in 1935 to seek wives, he was to remain single. Back at Katherine in 1936, Zimin purchased a new peanut-farm on the banks of the Katherine River. Within two years he was producing the best germination seed in the district. Experiencing difficulty in obtaining loans to buy machinery for his farm, he designed and built his own peanut digger, which was to receive (in 1949) the first agricultural patent awarded to a resident of the Northern Territory.

Continual problems, such as unreliable rainfall, disease, fluctuations in seasonal yields, and trouble with marketing and grading, eventually led to many peanut-farmers, including Zimin, seeking permission to grow other crops. In 1939 he began to experiment with cotton and millet. Only three Russians and one other farmer remained on their land by 1942. With tens of thousands of troops in the region after the bombing of Darwin in February, Zimin was contracted to supply tomatoes, cabbages, pumpkins and watermelons to the army. Aboriginal labourers assisted with the work. In 1942 the 121st (later 101st) Australian General Hospital was built on Zimin's land.

After World War II the farmers no longer had a market for their produce and many were forced from their land. Crown rot was affecting the peanut crop by 1951. Following the flood of 1957, Zimin took a job with the Commonwealth Scientific and Industrial Research Organization. In 1962 he sold 200 acres (81 ha) of his property to a meatworks and in 1971 gave up most of his remaining land. Remembered as a diligent farmer, he had continued with his neighbours to observe the customs and traditions of his native Russia. He died on 31 August 1974 on his small block and was buried in Katherine cemetery.

D. Carment et al (eds), *Northern Territory Dictionary of Biography*, 1 (Darwin, 1990); M. Canavan, *Russian Peanut Farming at Katherine 1929-1960* (Katherine, NT, 1991); W. S. Mollah, Agriculture at

Katherine, Northern Territory: Elusive or Illusory? (B.Litt. thesis, UNE, 1980); T. Shorter, taped interview with Erina Tokmakoff-Hill, 1990, NTRS 226, ts 595 *and* Primary Producers Board, correspondence files, F 114 (NT Archives, Darwin); naturalization file, A1, item 1933/8343 (NAA, Canb); Katherine Hist Soc Museum Archives, NT.   SUE HARLOW

ZINNBAUER, ALFRED FREUND- (1910-1978), Lutheran pastor, and HELGA JOSEPHINE FREUND- (1909-1980), librarian, were husband and wife. Alfred was born on 26 June 1910 in Vienna, only child of Bohemian-born Karl Freund, medical practitioner, and his Viennese wife Maria, née Zinnbauer. His father was Jewish and his mother Catholic. He was educated at the *Bundesrealgymnasium*. In 1931, attempting to counter discrimination, he added his mother's name to his surname and became known as Freund-Zinnbauer. Although raised as a Catholic, he trained as a Lutheran pastor in the Evangelical Church of the Augsburg Confession, having studied theology at the University of Vienna. Appointed curate in the village of Wallern (220 km west of Vienna) in 1934, he was ordained on 27 July 1936. He was dismissed from his post twelve months later when his Jewish background was discovered.

Helga was born on 24 February 1909 at Orsova, Austria-Hungary (Romania), daughter of Otto Alscher, journalist, and his wife Else Leopoldine, née Amon. The family moved several times because of political unrest; Helga was educated at a Catholic secondary school at Timisoara, and the University of Vienna (Ph.D., 1936) where she studied psychology. Fluent in six languages, she was accredited as a high school teacher. On 20 March 1938 she and Alfred married in the Gumpendorf Lutheran Church, Vienna.

After failing to obtain a post with the church in Europe or North America, Freund-Zinnbauer was accepted by the United Evangelical Lutheran Church in Australia. Under the auspices of the Bishop of Chichester's rescue mission for the victims of Nazi persecution, the couple travelled to England in May 1939. On 21 February next year they reached Adelaide in the *Orontes*. Four months later Alfred Freund-Zinnbauer was interned 'chiefly as a precautionary measure'; he spent four years at camps at Tatura, Victoria, and Loveday, South Australia. Released on 25 February 1944 he worked for over a year as a metalworker at Pope Products Ltd at Beverley, Adelaide. In April 1945 he was appointed Lutheran city missioner in Adelaide. His wife, meanwhile, had been employed from 1943 as a librarian at the Barr Smith [q.v.6] library at the University of Adelaide. Completing the qualifying certificate of the Australian Insti-

tute of Librarians in 1946, she was to remain there until she retired in 1974. Zinnbauer—as he now called himself—was naturalized on 21 February 1946.

As city missioner Zinnbauer provided pastoral care for Lutherans in institutions and directed 'unattached' members to established Adelaide congregations. He became well informed on the needs of the sick, aged and poor, and of prisoners and young people. His perception of the task varied from that of the committee set up to supervise his work: he believed that spiritual care could not be separated from practical assistance, and that he had a duty to help all people in need, irrespective of class, race, creed or religion. He received the full support of his wife and, as very little money was available from official sources, the pair financed a great deal of their work from their own salaries. Inspired by the Zinnbauers, church-members responded enthusiastically to their appeals for material and practical assistance.

So that they could care for the crews of Scandinavian ships calling at Adelaide, the Zinnbauers learnt Swedish; over four thousand seamen were entertained during 1949 alone. When Baltic migrants from the displaced persons camps in Germany began arriving in 1948, followed later by other European refugees, Zinnbauer was at the wharf or railway station to meet them and settle them into their new homes. He found housing and jobs for them, provided household equipment and clothing, organized schooling for children, and helped with personal problems. In 1951 he established a hostel at College Park. The Zinnbauers lived there for twenty-four years, accommodating thousands of people including seamen, people discharged from hospital or prison, and the homeless.

Zinnbauer held church services for migrants and, with the help of supporters, ran Sunday schools for their children. To preserve their cultural heritage, he encouraged them to establish choirs, theatre guilds and language schools. At the same time he urged them to learn English and to become loyal Australians. He helped 'old' Australians to understand and accept the newcomers. Although he lacked the organizational ability to carry all his ideas through to fruition, many of his proposals were taken up by the wider community, including legal aid for needy defendants, proper support systems for immigrants, flats for aged pensioners and help for patients in psychiatric hospitals. He also found the time to study at the University of Adelaide (B.A., 1958). In 1967 he was appointed M.B.E.; he was also awarded the officers' cross of the order of merit of the Federal Republic of Germany (1972) and a medal of merit of the Republic of Austria (1978).

After they retired in 1974, the Zinnbauers lived at Trinity Gardens. Childless, they had adopted a 14-year-old girl and permanently fostered two boys. Alfred Zinnbauer died of myocardial infarction on 9 November 1978 in Adelaide; Helga Zinnbauer died on 16 December 1980, also in Adelaide. Both were buried in Enfield cemetery.

M. Rilett, *And You Took Me In* (Adel, 1992); *Offset*, 30 Nov 1978; *Lutheran*, 4 Dec 1978, p 10; immigration and security files, D1915, item SA11087, D1976, item SB1940/25 (NAA, Adel); A367, item C61896 (NAA, Canb).   MARGARET RILETT*

ZIONS, NORMAN; *see* HAIRE